Blackstone's Statutes Series

Trusted by millions

For your **course**, your **exam**, your **success**

Cases & Materials on

Constitutional & Administrative Law

Twelfth Edition

Brian Thompson
LLB, MLitt

Michael Gordon
MA, PhD

OXFORD
UNIVERSITY PRESS

OXFORD
UNIVERSITY PRESS

Great Clarendon Street, Oxford, OX2 6DP,
United Kingdom

Oxford University Press is a department of the University of Oxford.
It furthers the University's objective of excellence in research, scholarship,
and education by publishing worldwide. Oxford is a registered trade mark of
Oxford University Press in the UK and in certain other countries

© B. Thompson and M. Gordon 2017

The moral rights of the authors have been asserted

Ninth edition 2008
Tenth edition 2011
Eleventh edition 2014

Impression: 1

Public sector information reproduced under Open Government Licence v3.0
(http://www.nationalarchives.gov.uk/doc/open-government-licence/
open-government-licence.htm)

Published in the United States of America by Oxford University Press
198 Madison Avenue, New York, NY 10016, United States of America

British Library Cataloguing in Publication Data
Data available

Library of Congress Control Number: 2017934730

ISBN 978–0–19–876773–2

Printed in Great Britain by
Bell & Bain Ltd., Glasgow

Links to third party websites are provided by Oxford in good faith and
for information only. Oxford disclaims any responsibility for the materials
contained in any third party website referenced in this work.

OUTLINE CONTENTS

1   Constitutional Law in the United Kingdom   1

2   The Legislative Sovereignty of Parliament   46

3   The Rule of Law   102

4   Judicial Independence   141

5   The Royal Prerogative and Constitutional Conventions   173

6   Parliament: Scrutiny of Policy and Administration   217

7   Parliament: Law-making   278

8   Devolution   342

9   Human Rights   396

10 Judicial Review: The Grounds   492

11 The Availability of Judicial Review   568

12 Ombudsmen   609

13 Statutory Tribunals   649

    Index   691

DETAILED CONTENTS

Preface   x
Acknowledgements   xii
Table of Cases   xv
Table of Legislation   xxv
Table of European Union Legislation   xxxix

1   Constitutional Law in the United Kingdom   1

SECTION 1:   Introduction   1
SECTION 2:   Legitimacy   10
SECTION 3:   Democracy   16
SECTION 4:   Legal and Political Constitutionalism   23
             A: Legal constitutionalism   24
             B: Political constitutionalism   26
SECTION 5:   Conditioning Power   29
             A: Separation of powers   29
             B: Responsible government   35
SECTION 6:   The State   39

2   The Legislative Sovereignty of Parliament   46

SECTION 1:   The Nature of the Legislative Sovereignty of Parliament   46
             A: Parliament—emergence of supreme law-making authority   47
             B: The unlimited legislative power of Parliament   50
             C: Ruling on the validity of Parliament's enactments   51
SECTION 2:   Can Parliament Limit the Powers of its Successors?   56
             A: Substantive limits   58
             B: Procedural conditions   65
SECTION 3:   Modern Challenges to the Sovereignty of Parliament   68
             A: Membership of the European Union   68
             B: Human rights   84
             C: *Jackson v Attorney General*   88
             D: European Union Act 2011   95

3   The Rule of Law   102

SECTION 1:   Introduction   102
SECTION 2:   Dicey and the Rule of Law   104
             A: The rule of law and discretionary powers   104
             B: The rule of law and equality   106
SECTION 3:   The Rule of Law—Formal or Substantive?   111
SECTION 4:   The Rule of Law as a Broad Political Doctrine   117
             A: Laws should be clear   118
             B: Laws should be prospective   120
             C: The independence of the judiciary must be guaranteed   123
SECTION 5:   Government According to the Law   124

| 4 | **Judicial Independence** | **141** |

SECTION 1:	Judicial Independence	141
	A: An expanded constitutional role for the courts?	141
	B: The Constitutional Reform Act 2005	142
	C: The Lord Chancellor	147
	D: The Supreme Court	150
	E: Judicial appointments	152
	F: Discipline	160
	G: Accountability of the judiciary to Parliament	161
	H: The judiciary, media, and the public	164
	I: Judicial independence and parliamentary privilege	168

| 5 | **The Royal Prerogative and Constitutional Conventions** | **173** |

SECTION 1:	Royal Prerogative	173
	A: What is the Royal Prerogative?	173
	B: Putting the prerogative on a statutory basis	177
	C: Codification of the prerogative	186
	D: The prerogative in the courts	191
SECTION 2:	Constitutional Conventions	196
	A: Sources of the constitution	196
	B: What are conventions?	198
	C: Laws, sanctions, and conventions	200
	D: Conventions in the courts	202
	E: Can conventions obtain legal force?	212
	F: Codification of conventions	213

| 6 | **Parliament: Scrutiny of Policy and Administration** | **217** |

SECTION 1:	The Role of Parliament	217
SECTION 2:	Policy and Administration	221
	A: Ministerial responsibility	221
	B: Select committees	240
	C: The floor of the House of Commons	245
	D: Correspondence	261
	E: Reviewing rebalancing reforms	269

| 7 | **Parliament: Law-making** | **278** |

SECTION 1:	Law-making	278
	A: Types of legislative measure	278
	B: Control	283

| 8 | **Devolution** | **342** |

SECTION 1:	Background to Devolution	342
SECTION 2:	The Asymmetrical Regimes	348
	A: Institutions	348
	B: Legislative competence	353
	C: Key specific examples of asymmetry	367

SECTION 3:   Devolution Issues in the UK Courts   370
             A: Interpretation of the Devolution Acts   370
             B: Judicial review of devolved legislation   377
             C: References to the Supreme Court   381

SECTION 4:   Devolution as a Dynamic Settlement   385
             A: The Scottish independence referendum and its aftermath   386
             B: Change to the model of devolution in Wales   389
             C: Devolution of police and justice powers to Northern Ireland   392

9   **Human Rights**   **396**

SECTION 1:   Introduction   396
SECTION 2:   The European Convention on Human Rights   399
SECTION 3:   Incorporation of the European Convention on Human Rights into
             UK Law   409
             A: The Human Rights Act 1998   409
             B: The implications of the Human Rights Act for human rights   424
             C: How does the Human Rights Act operate in practice?   426

10   **Judicial Review: The Grounds**   **492**

SECTION 1:   Introduction   492
             A: The role of judicial review in the constitution   492
             B: The distinction between review and appeal   495
             C: The use of judicial review   497

SECTION 2:   The Grounds for Judicial Review   497
             A: The prerogative orders   498
             B: Illegality   499
             C: Procedural impropriety   520
             D: Irrationality   540
             E: Substantive legitimate expectations   547
             F: Irrationality and/or proportionality   562

11   **The Availability of Judicial Review**   **568**

SECTION 1:   The Claim for Judicial Review   568
SECTION 2:   The Exclusivity Principle   581
SECTION 3:   Who May Apply for Judicial Review?   590
SECTION 4:   Against Whom, and in Respect of What Activities, may Judicial
             Review be Sought?   594
SECTION 5:   Justiciability   597
SECTION 6:   Judicial Review as a Discretionary Remedy   600
             A: The availability of alternative remedies   600
             B: Needs of good administration   604
SECTION 7:   Exclusion of Judicial Review   606

12   **Ombudsmen**   **609**

SECTION 1:   Introduction   609
SECTION 2:   Access to the Ombudsman   613

SECTION 3: Jurisdiction of the Ombudsman   617
    A: Overlap with alternative remedies   621
SECTION 4: Meaning of Injustice in Consequence of Maladministration   623
SECTION 5: Investigation, Resolution, and Improvement   627
    A: Investigation and resolution   627
    B: Improvement   630
SECTION 6: Outcome of Investigations and Remedies   638
    A: Compliance with ombudsmen's reports   641
    B: Findings and recommendations   645
SECTION 7: Arrangements for Dissatisfied Complainants   647

13   **Statutory Tribunals**   **649**

SECTION 1: Introduction: The Rationale for Tribunals   649
SECTION 2: The Structure and Organization of Tribunals   654
    A: The two-tier structure   654
    B: Judicial leadership and tribunal composition   657
    C: Appeals and judicial review   663
SECTION 3: Tribunals and Dispute Resolution   666
    A: Tribunal caseload statistics   666
    B: Tribunal characteristics   669
    C: Alternative dispute resolution   676
    D: Proportionate dispute resolution   680
    E: The transformation of justice reforms   684
SECTION 4: Reviewing the Administrative Justice System   687

    Index   691

PREFACE

The result of the June 2016 referendum on the United Kingdom's membership of the European Union will prompt a period of radical change to constitutional and administrative law. The decision to leave the EU arrives in an already significant era of change in public law, will take years to implement, and poses a range of challenges (perhaps unprecedented in scale) to the UK's legal and political system. At such a moment, constitutional and administrative law will have immense significance, and a clear understanding of its core ideas and principles will be of great value. We hope the revised and updated 12th edition of this book can provide such clarity and understanding.

Chapter 1, which explores the fundamental concepts of constitutional law in the UK, has been updated to include new extracts, including from the cases of *Keyu* v *Secretary of State for Foreign and Commonwealth Affairs* and *Carlile* v *Secretary of State for the Home Department*, alongside classic material.

In Chapter 2, on parliamentary sovereignty, analysis of the challenge posed by the supremacy of EU law has been retained, although refocused in anticipation of Brexit. Major new extracts in this area are included from *HS2* v *Secretary of State for Transport* and *Pham* v *Secretary of State for the Home Department*, with the broader relevance of the idea of judicially established 'constitutional statutes' or 'constitutional instruments' also considered. Aspects of *Moohan* v *Lord Advocate* and *Wheeler* v *Prime Minister* of significance for our understanding of parliamentary sovereignty are also discussed.

Chapter 3 includes significant new discussion of the case of *Evans* v *Attorney General* and its implications for the rule of law. The consideration of *Nicklinson* v *Ministry of Justice* and *Reilly* v *Secretary of State for Work and Pensions* has been updated and extended.

Discussion of judicial independence in Chapter 4 now includes new material on the role and office of the Lord Chancellor. Discussion of judicial disciplinary procedures has been streamlined, and renewed attention given to judicial diversity, considering various extrajudicial interventions in the debate from Justices of the Supreme Court, and the implementation of the 'equal merit tie-breaker provision' introduced by the Equality Act 2010.

Chapter 5 includes extracts from and detailed analysis of the high-profile case of *Miller* v *Secretary of State for Exiting the European Union*, dealing with the issues relating to the Royal Prerogative and constitutional conventions arising in the decision of the Supreme Court.

Chapter 6 has been broadly updated and streamlined. It includes new academic material considering the policy power and influence of the UK Parliament, and extended discussion of ministerial responsibility, drawing on a number of new examples and sources. The process and implications of Brexit inform a number of other issues discussed, including the future reform of the civil service. An extract from the debate on the second reading of the European Union (Referendum) Bill is used to highlight the functioning of Parliament. New material has also been included on departmental guidance for the handling of questions, backbench business, e-petitions, and parliamentary scrutiny of public appointments.

Chapter 7 on law-making has been updated to include the new procedure under the House of Commons Standing Orders regulating bills which refer only to England, or England and Wales. This is known as English Votes for English Laws and seeks to resolve the difficulties in our asymmetrical devolution arrangements and concern about the degree of influence of MPs representing constituencies outside England (and England and Wales) on legislation which would not affect their constituencies. The role of the

House of Lords in the making of delegated legislation is considered in the Government-commissioned Strathclyde review and the responses by a House of Commons and three House of Lords select committees, illustrating the tension between the executive and legislative branches.

Devolution has been an area of rapid constitutional change, and Chapter 8 has been significantly revised as a result. The effects of legislative change in the form of the Wales Act 2014 and the Scotland Act 2016 are considered in particular, along with (at time of writing) further proposed change to Welsh devolution in the Wales Bill 2016–17. New case law is discussed, including *Re Recovery of Medical Costs for Asbestos Diseases (Wales) Bill*. The constitutional implications of the adoption of English Votes for English Laws in the UK Parliament are analysed, along with developments within England, such as the 'Northern Powerhouse' and similar combined authority 'devolution' deals. There is extended discussion of the Sewel convention—including in light of the decision of the Supreme Court in *Miller*—and updated discussion of developments in Northern Ireland, including in relation to the Stormont Agreement on welfare reform, and the implications of the Renewable Heat Incentive scandal.

The material on human rights and the grounds of judicial review in Chapters 9 and 10 has been streamlined. There has been some significant new discussion on irrationality and proportionality, in *Pham* and *Keyu* and their place and interrelationship in common law and protection of rights. Particular attention is paid to *Pham*.

In the previous edition, consultation proposals for reform of judicial review were noted in Chapter 11 and now the changes which have been introduced are considered. In particular, the changed test for materiality used when the court is deciding if relief should be granted, if the court is of the view that the outcome would not have been substantially different if the conduct complained about had not occurred. The latest research on the impact of the regionalization of the Administrative Court is also considered.

The much-anticipated reform of the Ombudsmen operating in England and at the wider UK level moves closer with the December 2016 publication of the draft Public Service Ombudsman Bill. This was too late to be fully considered in Chapter 12, but the Gordon review which influenced its contents is considered, along with updated material on how those ombudsmen are operating under the current legislation.

Finally, in Chapter 13 there is consideration of the new step in the appeals process in social security where a mandatory reconsideration is held as a prerequisite for a tribunal hearing. This version of administrative review and two others are considered. Attention is also paid to the announcement of reform to courts and tribunals. We will have to wait for the proposals to be fleshed out and implemented but the consequences of digitizing the processes are intended to reduce the number of hearings with online lodging and case management and, where held, to allow them to be conducted online. It is planned to use social security as the pathfinder in tribunals, but it is acknowledged that such tribunals have a high proportion of users who are 'digitally excluded' and this will have to be taken into account.

For her help and support in preparing this new edition, and her ideas for refreshing the book, we would like to thank our editor at OUP, Carol Barber.

We would also like to thank all of our colleagues who teach on the Public Law modules at the University of Liverpool—we continue to be extremely grateful for your enthusiasm and dedication. We also thank successive cohorts of students on those modules for your engagement, hard work, and many thought-provoking questions.

Brian Thompson
Mike Gordon
February 2017

ACKNOWLEDGEMENTS

Grateful acknowledgement is made to all the authors and publishers of the copyright material that appears in this book, and in particular to the following for permission to reprint material from the sources indicated:

Parliamentary copyright material is reproduced with the permission of the Controller of Her Majesty's Stationery Office on behalf of Parliament. Crown copyright material is reproduced under Class Licence Number C2006010631 with the permission of the Controller of OPSI and the Queen's Printer for Scotland.

Extracts from the reports of the European Court of Justice and Court of First Instance (ECR) are taken from https://www.curia.europa.eu. These are unauthenticated reports and are reproduced free of charge. The definitive versions are published in *Reports of cases before the Court of Justice* or the *Official Journal of the European Union*.

Ashgate Publishing and the authors for a table from T. Buck, R. Kirkham and B. Thompson: *The Ombudsman Enterprise and Administrative Justice* (Ashgate Publishing, 2011).

Basic Books for US rights to an extract from *Comparative Government* by S.E. Finer (1970).

Cambridge Law Journal and the editors for extracts from *Cambridge Law Journal*: Ian Leigh and Laurence Lustgarten: 'Making Rights Real: the Courts, Remedies and the Human Rights Act' 58 (1999) and H. W. R. Wade: 'The Basis of Legal Sovereignty' 13 (1955).

Cambridge University Press and the editors for an extract from the Introduction to J. Elster and R. Slagstad (eds.): *Constitutionalism and Democracy* (Cambridge University Press, 1988), copyright © Cambridge University Press and Universitetsforlaget (Norwegian University Press) 1988, reproduced with permission.

Carswell (Thomson Reuters) for an extract from *Reference Re Amendment of the Constitution of Canada* (1982) 125 DLR (3d) 1. Reproduced by permission Canada Law Book, a division of Thomson Reuters Canada Limited.

Cornell University Press for an extract from Charles Howard McIlwain: *Constitutionalism Ancient and Modern.* Copyright © 1947 Cornell University; Renewed © 1975 by Charles Howard McIlwain. Used by permission of the publisher, Cornell University Press.

Hansard Society for extracts from *Making the Law* (1993).

Hart Publishing Limited for extracts from *Constitutional Reform in the United Kingdom: Practice and Principles* (1998): Peter Duffy QC: 'The European Convention on Human Rights, Issues Relating to its Interpretation in the Light of the Human Rights Bill' and G. Marshall: 'Patriating Rights—with Reservations: the Human Rights Bill 1998'. The Incorporated Council of Law Reporting for extracts from the *Appeal Cases Reports*; *Chancery Reports*; *Queen's Bench Reports*; and *Weekly Law Reports*.

Lexis Nexis for extracts from *Essays in Constitutional Law* (2nd edition, 1964) and from *Robinson v Secretary of State for Northern Ireland* [2002] UKHL 32; [2002] N.I. 390, House of Lords.

The Right Honourable the Lord Irvine of Lairg for extracts from The Tom Sargant Memorial Lecture, 'The Development of Human Rights in Britain under an Incorporated Convention on Human Rights', 16 December 1997; and Address to the Third Clifford Chance Conference on the Impact of a Bill of Rights on English Law, 28 November 1997.

MBA Literary Agents Ltd for an extract from R. Miliband: *The State in Capitalist Society* (Weidenfeld & Nicolson, 1969). Material from *The State in Capitalist Society* by Ralph Miliband is reproduced by kind permission of the author's estate.

Oxford University Press for extracts from R. Barker: *Political Legitimacy and the State* (OUP, 1990); Peter Cane: *Administrative Law* (5e, OUP, 2011); Hazel Genn: 'Tribunal Review of Administrative Decision Making' in Genevra Richardson and Hazel Genn: *Administrative Law and Government Action: The Courts and Alternative Mechanisms of Review* (OUP, 1994); B. Hadfield: 'Devolution: A National Conversation?' in Jeffrey Jowell and Dawn Oliver (eds.): *The Changing Constitution* (7e, OUP, 2011); C. B. Macpherson: *The Real World of Democracy* (OUP, 1966); Geoffrey Marshall: *Conventions: The Rules and Forms of Political Accountability* (OUP, 1984); C. R. Munro, Studies in Constitutional Law 2e (OUP, 1999); W. F. Murphy: 'Constitutions, Constitutionalism and Democracy' in D. Greenberg, S. N. Katz, M. B. Oliveiro, and S. C. Wheatley (eds.): *Constitutionalism and Democracy: Transitions in the Contemporary World* (OUP, 1993); A. Tomkins: *Public Law* (OUP, 2003); and C. Turpin: 'Ministerial Responsibility: Myth or Reality?' in Jeffrey Jowell and Dawn Oliver (eds.): *The Changing Constitution* (2e, OUP, 1989); Jeremy Waldron: *Law and Disagreement* (OUP, 1999); G. Marshall: *Constitutional Theory* (1971); and K. C. Wheare: *Modern Constitutions* (2e, OUP, 1966).

Oxford University Press Journals for extracts from *Parliamentary Affairs*: A. Abraham: 'The Ombudsman as Part of the UK Constitution: A Contested Role?' 61 (2008); F. F. Ridley: 'There is no British Constitution: A Dangerous Case of the Emperor's Clothes' 41 (1988); R. Rose: 'Law as a Resource of Public Policy' 39 (1986); Leslie Wolf-Phillips: 'A Long Look at the British Constitution' 37 (1984); and P. Leyland: 'The Multifaceted Constitutional Dynamics of UK Devolution' in 9 *International Journal of Constitutional Law* (2011).

Palgrave MacMillan for an extract from David Beetham: *The Legitimation of Power* (Palgrave MacMillan, 1991).

Parliamentary and Health Service Ombudsman for extracts from 'The Ombudsman's Annual Report and Accounts 2015–16 and HC 779 of 2016–17.

Pearson Education Inc, Upper Saddle River, NJ 07458, for an extract from Carl Friedrich: *Limited Government: A Comparison* (Prentice Hall, 1974), copyright © 1974.

Penguin for an extract from S. E. Finer: *Comparative Government* (Pelican, 1970).

Queen's Belfast for an extract from R. Brazier, 'How Near is a Written Constitution?' (2001) in *Northern Ireland Legal Quarterly*.

Sage Publications Ltd for extracts from David Beetham: 'Key Principles and Indices for a Democratic Audit' in David Beetham (ed.): *Defining and Measuring Democracy* (Sage, 1994), copyright © David Beetham 1994 and M. Flinders and A. Kelso 'Mind the Gap: Political Analysis, Public Expectations and the Parliamentary Decline Thesis' (2011) *British Journal of Politics and International Relations*.

Scottish Council of Law Reporting for an extract from *MacCormick v Lord Advocate* [1953] SC 396, *Reports of the Court of Sessions in Scotland* [SC].

Sweet & Maxwell Ltd for extracts from R. Blackburn and A. Kennon: *Griffith and Ryle on Parliament, Functions, Practices and Procedures* (Sweet & Maxwell, 2003); P. McAuslan and J. F. McEldowney: 'Legitimacy and the Constitution: The Dissonance between Theory and Practice' in *Law, Legitimacy and the Constitution: Essays Marking the Centenary of Dicey's 'Law of the Constitution'* (Sweet & Maxwell, 1985); K. H. Hendry: 'The Tasks of Tribunals: Some Thoughts' 1 *Civil Justice Quarterly* (1982); Lord Irvine of Lairg: 'Activism and Restraint: Human Rights and the Interpretative Process' *European Human Rights Law Review* (1999); M. Gordon and M. Dougan: 'The United Kingdom's European Union Act 2011: "Who Won the Bloody War Anyway"' *European Law Review* (2012); from *Law Quarterly Review*: J. Raz: 'The Rule of Law and its Virtue' 93 (1977) and H. W. R. Wade: 'Sovereignty—Revolution or Evolution?' 112 (1996); Murray Hunt: 'The Horizontal Effect of the Human Rights Act' (1998); Sir John Laws: 'Law and Democracy' (1995); A. Page: 'MPs and the Redress of Grievances' (1985); and case reports from *Scots Law Times*.

Taylor and Francis for an extract from Lord Bingham of Cornhill's 'The Courts and the Constitution' (1996/7), *King's College Law Journal*.

The Estate of Sir William Wade QC for Sir William Wade: 'The United Kingdom's Bill of Rights' in *Constitutional Reform in the United Kingdom: Practice and Principles* (Centre for Public Law, 1998).

Wiley-Blackwell Publishing Ltd for extracts from P. Norton *The Commons in Perspective* (Blackwell, 1981) and *Parliament in the 1980s* (Blackwell, 1985); M. Adler: 'Tribunal Reform: Proportionate Dispute Resolution and the Pursuit of Administrative Justice', 69 *Modern Law Review* (2006); H. F. Rawlings: 'Judicial Review and the Control of Government', 64 *Public Administration* (1986); C. Scott: 'Accountability in the Regulatory State', 27 *Journal of Law and Society* (2000); J. Webber: 'Supreme Courts, Independence and Democratic Agency', 24 *Legal Studies* (2004); M. Russell and P. Cowley: 'The Policy Power of the Westminster Parliament: "The Parliamentary State" and the Empirical Evidence' *Governance* (2016); and Report of the Committee on Minister's Powers CMD 4060 (1932).

Every effort has been made to trace and contact copyright holders prior to publication, but this has not been possible in every case. If notified, the publisher will undertake to rectify any errors or omissions at the earliest opportunity.

TABLE OF CASES

*References in **bold** indicate that the case is discussed significantly.*

United Kingdom

A v B plc [2002] EWCA Civ 337; [2003] QB 195 . . . 443

A v Scottish Ministers 2001 SLT 1331 (PC) . . . 482

A v Secretary of State for the Home Department [2004] UKHL 56; [2005] 2 AC 68 . . . 167, 486

A v Secretary of State for the Home Department (No. 2) [2005] UKHL 71; [2006] 2 AC 221 . . . 131

A v Treasury [2010] UKSC 2; [2010] 2 AC 534 (SC) . . . **131–4**

A and ors v Secretary of State for the Home Department [2004] UKHL 56 . . . 337

Abdi and Gawe v Secretary of State [1996] 1 WLR 298 . . . 517

Al Rawi v The Security Services [2011] UKSC 34; [2012] 1 AC 531 . . . 134

Al-Mehdawi v Secretary of State for the Home Department [1990] AC 876 . . . 537

Anisminic Ltd v Foreign Compensation Commission [1969] 2 AC 147 (HL) . . . 493, **500–2**, 503, **606–7**, 608

Aspinall, Pepper & Ors v Secretary of State for Work and Pensions [2014] EWHC 4143 . . . 520

Associated Provincial Picture Houses Ltd v Wednesbury Corporation [1947] 2 All ER 680; [1948] 1 KB 223 . . . 31, 136, 398–9, 464–5, 467, 473, 481, 499, 504, 514, 541–8, 550–1, 561–7, 587

Aston Cantlow [2003] UKHL 37; [2003] 3 WLR 283 (HL) . . . 427–8, 430

Attorney-General v De Keyser's Royal Hotel Ltd [1920] AC 508 (HL) . . . **191,** 326–7, 329–31

Attorney-General v Guardian Newspapers (No. 2) [1990] 1 AC 109 . . . 437

Attorney-General v Jonathan Cape Ltd [1976] QB 752 (HC) . . . **202–4,** 205, 212, 225

Attorney-General v National Assembly for Wales Commission [2012] UKSC 53; [2013] 1 AC 792 . . . **381–2**

Attorney-General v Times Newspapers Ltd [1992] 1 AC 191 . . . 442

Attorney-General v Wilts United Dairies Ltd (1921) 37 TLR 884 . . . 332

Attorney-General ex relator Tilley v Wandsworth LBC [1981] 1 WLR 854 . . . 514

Attorney-General for New South Wales v Trethowan and others [1932] AC 526 (PC) . . . **65–6,** 67

Attorney-General of Hong Kong v Ng Yuen Shiu [1983] 2 AC 629 . . . 539, 548, 559–60

AXA General Insurance Ltd v Lord Advocate [2011] UKSC 46; [2012] 1 AC 868 . . . 94–5, 101, **138, 377–80,** 381–3

Bank Mellat v Her Majesty's Treasury (No. 1) [2013] UKSC 38 . . . 134, 490

Bank Mellat v Her Majesty's Treasury (No. 2) [2013] UKSC 39 . . . 383

Belfast City Council v Miss Behavin' Ltd [2007] UKHL 19; [2007] 1 WLR 1420 . . . 477

Bellinger v Bellinger [2003] 2 AC 467; [2003] 2 WLR 1174 . . . 448–50

Blackburn v Attorney-General [1971] 1 WLR 1037 . . . **61,** 73

Blackpool Corporation v Locker [1948] 1 KB 349 . . . 122

Boddington v British Transport Police [1997] 2 AC 143 . . . 584

Boyce v The Queen [2005] 1 AC 400 . . . 373

Bracking v Secretary of State for Work and Pensions [2013] EWCA Civ 1345 . . . 520

Bradbury v London Borough of Enfield [1967] 3 All ER 434 . . . 521

Bribery Commissioner v Ranasinghe [1965] AC 172 . . . 67, 91

British Coal Corporation v The King [1935] AC 500 . . . 61

British Oxygen Co Ltd v Minister of Technology [1971] AC 610 (HL) . . . **512–13,** 549, 552

Brown v Stott (Procurator Fiscal, Dunfermline) and Another [2001] 2 WLR 817 (PC) . . . 444, **468–73**

Bugg v DPP [1993] QB 473 . . . 584

Burmah Oil Co Ltd v Lord Advocate [1965] AC 75 (HL); 1964 SC (HL) 117 . . . 51, 121, 327

Cadder v HM Advocate [2010] UKSC 43 . . . 349

Campbell v Mirror Group Newspapers [2004] UKHL 22; [2004] 2 WLR 1232 . . . 443

Canon Selwyn, ex parte (1872) 36 JP 54 . . . 52, 60

Carltona v Commissioners of Works [1943] 2 All ER 560 . . . 202

Case of Impositions (Bate's Case) (1606) 2 St Tr 371 . . . 48

Case of Proclamations (1611) 12 Co Rep 74; 77 ER 1352 . . . **47–8,** 174, 191, 326–7

Case of Shipmoney (R v Hampden) (1637) 3 St Tr 825 . . . 48

Ceylon University v Fernando [1960] 1 WLR 223 . . . 531

Chandler v Director of Public Prosecutions [1964] AC 763 (HL) . . . **42–3,** 598–9

Cheney v Conn [1968] 1 All ER 779 . . . 51

Chester v Bateson [1920] 1 KB 829 . . . 132, 333

Chesterfield Properties plc v Secretary of
State for the Environment [1998] JPL
568 . . . 127, 399

**Chief Constable of the North Wales Police v
Evans** [1982] 1 WLR 1155 (HL) . . . **496–7**

Christian Institute v Lord Advocate [2016]
UKSC 51; 2016 SLT 805 . . . **377**

CICB case *see* R v Criminal Injuries
Compensation Board, ex parte A [1999]

**Clarke v University of Lincolnshire
and Humberside** [2000] 1 WLR 1988
(CA) . . . **587–90**, 600

Cocks v Thanet District Council [1983] 2 AC
286 . . . 583, 585–6

Coco v A N Clark (Engineers) Ltd [1969]
RPC 41 . . . 437

Colman v Eastern Counties Railway Co (1846)
10 Beav 1 . . . 549

Coney v Choyce [1975] 1 All ER 979 . . . 521

Confederation of Passenger Transport UK v The
Humber Bridge Board and the Secretary of
State for Transport, Local Government and
the Regions [2003] EWCA Civ 842 . . . 341

Congreve v Home Office [1976] 1 QB
629 . . . 505

Cooper v Wandsworth Board of Works (1863)
14 CBNS 180 . . . 528

**Council of Civil Service Unions v Minister
for the Civil Service (GCHQ case)** [1984] 3
All ER 935; [1985] AC 374 (HL) . . . 15, **326–8**,
330, 426, 494–5, **499**, 520, **521**, **538–9**,
540–2, 551, 595–6, **598–9**

Countryside Alliance v Attorney General
[2007] UKHL 52; [2008] 1 AC 719 . . . 95

Crichel Down case . . . 226–8

Customs & Excise Commissioners v Cure &
Deely Ltd [1962] 1 QB 340 . . . 333

**D v National Society for the Prevention
of Cruelty to Children** [1978] AC 171
(HL) . . . **42**

Davies v Price [1958] 1 WLR 434 . . . 501

Davy v Spelthorne Borough Council [1984] AC
262 . . . 585–7

Daymond v Plymouth City Council [1976] AC
609 . . . 338–40

de Freitas v Permanent Secretary of Ministry
of Agriculture, Fisheries, Lands and Housing
[1999] 1 AC 69 (PC) . . . 476, 481, 546

Derbyshire County Council v Times
Newspapers Ltd [1993] AC 534 . . . 79, 446,
519

Dimes v Proprietors of Grand Junction Canal
(1852) 3 HL Cas 759 . . . 522–3

Doody v Secretary of State for the Home
Department [1993] 3 All ER 92 (HL) . . . 511

Douglas v Hello! Ltd [2001] IP & T 391; [2001]
2 WLR 992 . . . 437–41

DPP v Hutchinson [1990] 2 AC 783
(HL) . . . **338–41**

Dr Bonham's Case (1610) 8 Co Rep 114 . . . 51

Duchess of Argyll v Duke of Argyll [1967] Ch
302 . . . 203

Dunkley v Evans [1981] 1 WLR 1522 . . . 338–9

Duport Steels Ltd v Sirs [1980] 1 WLR 142
(HL) . . . **31–2**

**E v Secretary of State for the Home
Department** [2004] EWCA Civ 49; [2004] 2
WLR 1351 (CA) . . . **514–17**

Edinburgh and Dalkeith Railway Co v
Wauchope (1842) 8 Cl & F 710; 1 Bell
252 . . . 54–5, 81, 92

Edwards v A-G for Canada [1930] AC
124 . . . 470

Edwards v Bairstow [1956] AC 14
(HL) . . . 499, 516

Edwards v SOGAT [1971] Ch 354 . . . 538

**Ellen Street Estates Limited v Minister of
Health** [1934] 1 KB 590 (CA) . . . **52–3**, 67

Enderby Town Football Club Ltd v Football
Association Ltd [1971] Ch 591 . . . 537–8

Entick v Carrington (1765) 19 St Tr 1030
(Court of Common Pleas) . . . **124–5**, 127,
131–2, 398

Equitable Life case *see* R (Equitable Members
Action Group) v HM Treasury [2009] EWHC
2495 (Admin)

Evans v Information Commissioner [2012]
UKUT 313 (AAC), Upper Tribunal . . . **207–11**

F v London Borough of Lambeth (28 September
2001, unreported) . . . 455

Fairmount Investments v Secretary of State
[1976] 1 WLR 1255 . . . 517

Felixstowe Dock and Railway Co v
British Transport Docks Board [1976] 2
CMLR 655 . . . 73

Findlay, In re [1985] AC 318 . . . 548–9,
551, 560

Fitzpatrick v Sterling Housing Association Ltd
[2001] 1 AC 27 (HL) . . . 447

Fraser v HM Advocate [2011] UKSC 24 . . . 349

Gallagher v Lynn [1937] AC 863 . . . 375

GCHQ case *see* Council of Civil Service Unions
v Minister for the Civil Service

General Medical Council v Spackman [1943]
AC 627 . . . 531

Ghaidan v Godin-Mendoza [2004] UKHL 30;
[2004] 2 AC 557 (HL) . . . 133, **446–53**

Gibson v Lord Advocate 1975
SLT 134 . . . 60–1

Gillick v West Norfolk and Wisbech Area
Health Authority [1986] AC 112 . . . 595

Glynn v Keele University [1971] 1 WLR
487 . . . 606

Gouriet v Union of Post Office Workers [1978]
AC 435 . . . 593, 600

H v Lord Advocate [2012] UKSC 24, [2013] 1 AC
413 . . . 376

Hanks v Minister of Housing and Local
Government [1963] 1 QB 999 . . . 507

HK, Re [1967] 2 QB 617 . . . 521, 536

HM Advocate v R [2004] 1 AC 462 . . . 376, 380

HTV Ltd v Price Commission [1976] ICR
170 . . . 517

Huang v Secretary of State for the Home
Department and Kashmiri v Secretary
of State for the Home Department [2007]
UKHL 11; [2007] 2 AC 167 (HL) . . . **473–6**,
477–8, 485–6, 489–90
Hughes v Department of Health and Social
Security [1985] AC 766 . . . 552

IBA Health Ltd v Office of Fair Trading [2004]
EWCA Civ 142 . . . 563
**Imperial Tobacco Limited v The Lord
Advocate (Scotland)** [2012] CSIH 9; [2012]
UKSC 61 (SC) . . . **373–6**
Inco Europe Limited v First Choice Distribution
[2000] 1 WLR 586 . . . 341
**Inland Revenue Commissioners v National
Federation of Self-Employed and Small
Businesses Ltd** [1982] AC 617 (HL) . . . 583,
591–3, 627
Institute of Patent Agents v Lockwood [1894]
AC 347 . . . 337
Iveson's case, 7 Ves 251 . . . 442

Jackson v Attorney General [2006] *see* R
(Jackson) v Attorney General [2006]
John v Rees [1970] Ch 345 . . . 606
Jones v Wrotham Park Settled Estates [1980]
AC 74 . . . 341
Joyce v Director of Public Prosecutions [1946]
AC 347 . . . 64

Kay v Lambeth London Borough Council
[2006] UKHL 10; [2006] 2 AC 465 . . . 426,
475, 477
Kelly v British Broadcasting Corpn [2001] 2
WLR 253 . . . 438
Kennedy v The Charity Commission [2014]
UKSC 20 . . . 134, 563–4, 567
Keyu v Secretary of State for Foreign and
Commonwealth Affairs [2015] UKSC 69 . . . x,
xi, 566–7
Kruse v Johnson [1898] 2 QB 91 . . . 333

Laker Airways Ltd v Department of Trade [1977]
QB 643 . . . 136
Law v National Greyhound Racing Club [1983]
1 WLR 1302 . . . 597
Lee v Bude and Torrington Junction Railway
Co (1871) LR 6 CP 576 . . . 55, 81
Lee-Hirons v Secretary of State for Justice
[2016] UKSC 46 . . . 134
Leonard Cheshire [2002] EWCA Civ 366;
[2002] 2 All ER 936 . . . 428
Litster v Forth Dry Dock & Engineering Co Ltd
[1990] 1 AC 546 . . . 448–9
Liversidge v Anderson [1942] AC
206 . . . 202, 333
Lloyd v McMahon [1987] AC 625; [1987] 1 All
ER 1118 . . . 530, 533
Locabail (UK) Ltd v Bayfield Properties Ltd
[2000] QB 451 (CA) . . . **524–5**, 526
Locabail (UK) Ltd v Waldorf Investment
Corp . . . 525
Local Government Board v Arlidge [1915] AC
120 . . . 529, 535

London & Quadrant Housing Trust v Weaver
[2009] EWCA Civ 587 . . . **430–2**
London Borough of Wandsworth v Winder
(No. 2) (1987) 19 HLR 204; (1988) 20 HLR
400 . . . 584
London and Clydeside Estates Ltd v Aberdeen
DC [1979] 2 All ER 876 . . . 521
Lonrho plc v Secretary of State [1989] 2 All ER
609 . . . 511

M, In re [1993] 3 WLR 433
(HL) . . . **108–10**, 498
M v Home Office . . . 110
Macarthys v Smith [1979] ICR 785 . . . 73
McCawley v The King [1920] AC 691 . . . 91
McCord, Re [2016] NIQB 85 . . . 212
MacCormick v Lord Advocate [1953] SC 396
(COIH) . . . **59–60**, 61, 397
McEldowney v Forde [1971] AC 632
(HL) . . . **333–7**
McGowan v B [2011] 1 WLR 3121 . . . 376
McGuinness's Application, Re [1997] NI
359 . . . 169
McInnes v Onslow Fane [1978] 1 WLR
1520 . . . 521
Madzimbamuto v Lardner-Burke [1969] 1 AC
645 . . . **62**, 63
Malone v Metropolitan Police Commissioner
(No. 2) [1979] 1 Ch 344 . . . 466
Mandalia v Secretary of State for the Home
Department [2015] UKSC 59 . . . 560
Manuel v Attorney-General [1983] Ch 77
(Ch) . . . **52, 62–5**
Martin v Most 2010 SC (UKSC)
40 . . . 374 5
Maynard v Osmond [1977] QB 240 . . . 538
Medicaments and Related Classes of
Goods (No. 2), In Re [2001] 1
WLR 700 (CA). . . 526
**Merkur Island Shipping Corp. v
Laughton and Others** [1983] 2 AC 570
(CA) . . . **118–19**
Miller [2016] EWHC 2768 (Admin) . . . 376
Minister of Health v R, ex parte Yaffe [1931] AC
494 . . . 337
Moohan v Lord Advocate [2014] UKSC 67;
[2015] AC 901 . . . x, 94–5
Mortensen v Peters (1906) 14 SLT 227 (High
Court of Justiciary) . . . **50–1**
Moyna v Secretary of State for Work and
Pensions [2003] UKHL 44 . . . 515

**Nadarajah v Secretary of State for the
Home Department** [2005] EWCA Civ 1363
(CA) . . . **558–60**
Nakkuda Ali v Jayaratne [1951] AC 66 . . . 530
**Nottinghamshire CC v Secretary of State
for the Environment** [1986] 1 AC 240
(HL) . . . 333, **543–5**, 599

Occupational Pensions case *see* R (Bradley) v
Secretary of State for Work & Pensions
OGC v Information Commissioner
[2008] EWHC 774 (Admin); [2010]
QB 98 . . . 171

O'Reilly v Mackman [1983] 2 AC 237 (HL) . . . 503, 539, 568, **581–3**, 584–9, 594–5, 606

Osborn v The Parole Board [2013] UKSC 61 . . . 134, 521

Padfield v Minister for Agriculture, Fisheries and Food [1968] AC 997 (HL) . . . **508–10**, 511–12

Page v Hull University Visitor [1993] AC 682 . . . 588, 597

Paponette v Attorney General of Trinidad and Tobago [2010] UKPC 32 . . . 561

Pepper v Hart [1993] AC 593 (HL) . . . 79, 171, 493

Pham v Secretary of State for the Home Department [2015] UKSC 19; [2015] 1 WLR 1591 . . . x, xi, **83–4**, 563–7

Phillips v Eyre (1870) LR 6 QB 1, Exch . . . **120–1**

Pickin v British Railways Board [1974] AC 765 (HL) . . . **52–5**, 63, 81, 91–2, 94

Pickstone v Freemans plc [1989] AC 66 . . . 448–9

Pierson v Secretary of State [1998] AC 539 . . . 79, 106

Poplar Housing and Regeneration Community Association Ltd v Donoghue [2001] 3 WLR 183 . . . 455

Poplar Housing and Regeneration Community Association Ltd v Donoghue [2001] EWCA Civ 595; [2002] QB 48 . . . 428, 431, 446

Porter v Magill [2001] UKHL 67; [2002] 2 AC 357 (HL) . . . **525–6**

Practice Direction (2012) . . . 666

Practice Statement (Administrative Court: Listing and Urgent Cases) . . . 600, 603

Practice Statement (Judicial Precedent) [1966] 1 WLR 1234 . . . 33

Prohibitions del Roy (1608) 12 Co Rep 63; [1607] EWHC KB J23; 77 ER 1342 . . . **103**, **139**, 326

Pyx Granite Co Ltd v Ministry of Housing and Local Government [1960] AC 260 . . . 132, 586

R v A (No. 2) [2002] 1 AC 45 . . . 448, 451, 453, 456

R v Abdroikov, R v Green, R v Williamson [2007] UKHL 37; [2007] 1 WLR 2679 (HL) . . . **526–7**

R v Advertising Standards Authority Limited, ex parte The Insurance Service (1989) 133 SJ 1545 . . . 597

R v Army Board of the Defence Council, ex parte Anderson [1991] 3 WLR 42 (Div Ct) . . . **533–5**, 537

R v Attorney-General, ex parte ICI plc [1987] 1 CMLR 72 . . . 593

R v Barnsley Metropolitan Borough Council, ex parte Hook [1976] 1 WLR 1052 . . . 565

R v BBC, ex parte Lavelle [1983] 1 WLR 23 . . . 594, 597

R v BBC, ex parte Owen [1985] 2 All ER 522 . . . 510

R v (Begum) Headteacher and Governors of Denbigh High School [2006] UKHL 15; [2007] 1 AC 100 . . . 477

R v Board of Visitors of HM Prison, The Maze, ex parte Hone [1988] 2 WLR 177 . . . 537

R v Board of Visitors of Hull Prison *see* R v Hull Prison Board of Visitors

R v Bow Street Metropolitan Stipendiary Magistrate, ex parte Pinochet Ugarte (No. 2) [2000] 1 AC 119 (HL) . . . 150, **522–4**, 525

R v Bristol Betting and Gaming Licensing Committee, ex parte O'Callaghan . . . 525

R v Brixton Prison Governor, ex parte Soblen [1963] 2 QB 243 . . . 107

R v Burah (1878) 3 App Cas 889 . . . 91

R v Cambridge Health Authority, ex parte B [1995] 2 All ER 129 . . . 556

R v Central Independent Television plc [1994] 3 All ER 641; [1994] Fam 192 . . . 438–9, 441

R v Chaytor and others [2010] UKSC 52 (SC) . . . **168–70**, 171

R v Chief Constable of Merseyside Police, ex parte Calvely [1986] 2 WLR 144 . . . 603–4

R v Chief Constable of Sussex, ex parte International Trader's Ferry Ltd [1999] 2 AC 418 . . . 511, **562–3**

R v Civil Service Appeal Board, ex parte Cunningham [1991] 4 All ER 310 . . . 511

R v Code of Practice Committee of the Association of the British Pharmaceutical Industry, *The Times*, 7 November 1990 . . . 597

R v Commissioner for Racial Equality, ex parte Cottrell and Rothon [1980] 1 WLR 1580 (CA) . . . **532–3**, 536–7

R v Criminal Injuries Compensation Board, ex parte A [1999] 2 AC 330 . . . 515–17

R v Criminal Injuries Compensation Board, ex parte Lain [1967] 2 QB 864 . . . 327, 331, 549, 595–6

R v Dairy Produce Quota Tribunal, ex parte Caswell [1990] 2 AC 738 . . . 584

R v Deputy Industrial Injuries Commissioner, ex parte Moore [1965] 1 QB 456 . . . 521, 530–1

R v Devon CC, ex parte G [1988] 3 WLR 49 . . . 540

R v Disciplinary Committee of the Jockey Club, ex parte Aga Khan [1993] 1 WLR 909 . . . 560, 597

R v Dover Magistrates' Court, ex parte Pamment (1994) 15 Cr App R (S) 778 . . . 549

R v DPP, ex parte Kebilene [1999] 4 All ER 801; [2000] 2 AC 326 . . . 468, 472, 485

R v East Berkshire Health Authority, ex parte Walsh [1985] QB 152 (CA) . . . 597

R v East Sussex County Council, ex parte Tandy [1998] 2 All ER 769 (HL) . . . 510

R v Electricity Commissioners, ex parte London Electricity Joint Committee Co [1924] 1 KB 171 . . . 529

R v Epping and Harlow General Commissioners, ex parte Goldstraw [1983] 3 All ER 257 . . . 603

R v Essex Justices, ex parte Perkins [1927] 2 KB 475 . . . 525

R v Gaming Board of Great Britain, ex parte Benaim and Khaida [1970] 2 QB 417 . . . 530

R v Gloucestershire County Council, ex parte Barry [1997] AC 584 (HL) . . . 510

R v Gough [1993] AC 646 . . . 525–6

R v Governor of Brixton Prison, ex parte Armah [1968] AC 192 . . . 500

R v Greenwich London Borough Council, ex parte Lovelace [1991] 3 All ER 511 . . . 508

R v Grice (1977) 66 Cr App R 167 . . . 549

R v Halliday [1917] AC 260 . . . 132

R v Hallstrom, ex parte W [1985] 3 All ER 775, *sub nom* ex parte Waldron [1985] 3 WLR 1090 (CA) . . . 603

R v Higher Education Funding Council, ex parte Institute of Dental Surgery [1994] 1 All ER 651 . . . 511

R v Hillingdon London Borough Council, ex parte Puhlhofer [1986] AC 484 . . . 557

R v Hillingdon London Borough Council, ex parte Royco Homes Ltd [1974] QB 720 . . . 603

R v HM Inspector of Pollution, ex parte Greenpeace Ltd (No. 2) [1994] 4 All ER 329 . . . 593

R v Horncastle [2009] UKSC 14 . . . 444

R v Hull Prison Board of Visitors, ex parte St Germain [1979] 1 All ER 701; [1979] QB 425 . . . 533, 539

R v Hull Prison Board of Visitors, ex parte St Germain (No. 2) [1979] 1 WLR 1401 (Div Ct) . . . **531–2**, 536–7

R v Hull University Visitor, ex parte Page [1993] AC 682 . . . 551

R v Immigration Appeal Tribunal, ex parte Jones [1988] 1 WLR 477 . . . 535

R v Independent Television Commission, ex parte T.S.W. Broadcasting Ltd, *The Times*, 7 February 1992 . . . 551

R v Inland Revenue Commissioners, ex parte MFK Underwriting Agents Ltd [1990] 1 WLR 1545 . . . 551

R v Inland Revenue Commissioners, ex parte National Federation of Self-Employed and Small Businesses Ltd [1982] AC 617 . . . 550

R v Inland Revenue Commissioners, ex parte Preston [1985] AC 835 . . . 517, 550–1, 555, 603

R v Inland Revenue Commissioners, ex parte Rossminster Ltd [1980] AC 952 (CA) . . . **125–7**, 131

R v Inland Revenue Commissioners, ex parte Unilever plc [1996] STC 681 . . . 550–1, 555

R v Inner London Education Authority, ex parte Westminster City Council [1986] 1 WLR 28 (HC) . . . **506–8**, 510

R v Lambert [2001] 3 WLR 206; [2002] 2 AC 545 . . . 453, 455

R v Lambert, Ali and Jordan [2001] 1 All ER 1014 . . . **468**

R v Legislative Committee of the Church Assembly, ex parte Haynes-Smith [1928] 1 KB 411 . . . 529

R v Lewes Justices, ex parte Secretary of State for the Home Department [1973] AC 388 . . . 203

R v Lichfield DC, ex parte Lichfield Securities Ltd [2001] 3 LGLR 35 . . . 584

R v Liverpool Corporation, ex parte Liverpool Taxi Fleet Operators Association [1972] 2 QB 299 . . . 539

R v Local Commissioner for Administration for the North and East Area of England, ex parte Bradford Metropolitan City Council [1979] QB 287 . . . 625

R v Local Commissioner for Administration in North and North East England, ex parte Liverpool City Council [2001] All ER 462 . . . 623

R v Local Commissioner, ex parte Eastleigh Borough Council [1988] 3 WLR 116 (CA) . . . **624–6**

R v London Borough of Hammersmith and Fulham and Others, ex parte Burkett [2002] UKHL 23; [2002] 1 WLR 593 . . . 584

R v Lord Chancellor, ex parte Witham [1998] QB 575 . . . 79, 127, 333, 398

R v Lord Chancellor's Department, ex parte Nangle [1992] 1 All ER 897 . . . 597

R v Lord President of the Privy Council, ex parte Page [1993] AC 682 . . . 503

R v Lord Saville, ex parte A [1999] 4 All ER 860 . . . 127, 399

R v Ministry of Agriculture, Fisheries and Food, ex parte Hamble (Offshore) Fisheries Ltd [1995] 2 All ER 714 . . . 550, 552

R v Ministry of Defence, ex parte Murray [1998] COD 134 . . . 512

R v Ministry of Defence, ex parte Smith [1996] QB 517 (CA) . . . 398–9, 465, 467–8, 473, 476, 481, 519, 546–7

R v Monopolies and Mergers Commission, ex parte Argyll Group plc [1986] 1 WLR 763(CA) . . . **604–5**, 606

R v Monopolies and Mergers Commission, ex parte Matthew Brown plc [1987] 1 WLR 1235 . . . 535

R v National Joint Council for the Craft of Dental Technicians (Disputes Committee), ex parte Neate [1953] 1 QB 704 . . . 596

R v North and East Devon Health Authority, ex parte Coughlan [2000] 2 WLR 622 (CA) . . . **547–54**, 555, 557–60

R v Oakes [1986] 1 SCR 103 . . . 476

R v Paddington Valuation Officer, ex parte Peachey Property Corporation Ltd [1966] 1 QB 380 . . . 603

R v Panel on Take-overs and Mergers, ex parte Datafin plc [1987] QB 815 (CA) . . . 495, 549, **594–7**, 597–8, 605

R v Parliamentary Commissioner for Standards, ex parte Al Fayed [1998] 1 WLR 669 . . . 169

R v Port of London Authority, ex parte Kynoch [1919] 1 KB 176 . . . 513

R v Registrar of Companies, ex parte Central Bank of India [1986] QB 1114 . . . 608

R v Reilly [1982] QB 1208 . . . 549

R v Rochdale Metropolitan Borough Council, ex parte Cromer Ring Mill Ltd [1982] 3 All ER 761 . . . 584

R v Secretary of State for Education and Employment, ex parte Begbie [1999] EWCA Civ 2100; [2000] 1 WLR 1115 . . . 554–6, 559, 561

R v Secretary of State for Employment, ex parte Equal Opportunities Commission [1994] 2 WLR 409 . . . 75

R v Secretary of State for the Environment, ex parte Alconbury [2003] 2 AC 295; [2001] UKHL 23 . . . 516

R v Secretary of State for the Environment, ex parte Brent LBC [1982] QB 593 . . . 514

R v Secretary of State for the Environment, ex parte Hammersmith and Fulham LBC [1990] 3 All ER 589 (HL) . . . 545

R v Secretary of State for the Environment, ex parte Hammersmith and Fulham LBC [1991] 1 AC 521 . . . 563

R v Secretary of State for the Environment, ex parte Nottinghamshire County Council [1986] AC 240 . . . 551

R v Secretary of State for the Environment, ex parte Ostler [1977] QB 122 . . . 608

R v Secretary of State for the Environment, ex parte Rose Theatre Trust [1990] 1 QB 504 . . . 593

R v Secretary of State, ex parte Santillo [1981] QB 778 . . . 535

R v Secretary of State for Foreign Affairs, ex parte World Development Movement Ltd [1995] 1 WLR 386 . . . 593

R v Secretary of State for Foreign and Commonwealth Affairs, ex parte Everett [1989] 2 WLR 224 . . . 600

R v Secretary of State for Foreign and Commonwealth Affairs, ex parte Rees-Mogg [1994] QB 552 . . . 600

R v Secretary of State for Home Affairs, ex parte Hosenball [1977] 1 WLR 766 . . . 327

R v Secretary of State for the Home Department, ex parte Anderson [2002] UKHL 46 . . . **457–60**

R v Secretary of State for the Home Department, ex parte Asif Mahmood Khan [1984] 1 WLR 1337 . . . 551

R v Secretary of State for the Home Department, ex parte Bentley [1994] QB 349 . . . 600

R v Secretary of State for the Home Department, ex parte Benwell [1985] QB 152 . . . 597

R v Secretary of State for the Home Department, ex parte Brind [1991] 1 AC 696 . . . 426, 547, 562, 565

R v Secretary of State for the Home Department, ex parte Bugdaycay [1987] AC 514 . . . 565

R v Secretary of State for the Home Department, ex parte Daly [2001] UKHL 26 . . . 565

R v Secretary of State for the Home Department, ex parte Doody [1994] 1 AC 531 . . . 128–9, 458

R v Secretary of State for the Home Department, ex parte Fayed [1997] 1 All ER 228 . . . 512

R v Secretary of State for the Home Department, ex parte Fire Brigades Union [1995] 2 AC 513 (HL) . . . **141–2, 328–32**

R v Secretary of State for the Home Department, ex parte Hargreaves [1997] 1 WLR 906 . . . 548, 551, 560

R v Secretary of State for the Home Department, ex parte Isiko (unreported), 20 December 2000 (CA) . . . 546

R v Secretary of State for the Home Department, ex parte Leech [1994] QB 198 (CA) . . . 79, 518–19, 565

R v Secretary of State for the Home Department, ex parte Mughal [1974] QB 313 . . . 535

R v Secretary of State for the Home Department, ex parte Northumbria Police Authority [1989] QB 26, (CA) . . . 174

R v Secretary of State for the Home Department, ex parte Pierson [1998] AC 539 (HL) . . . 89, 121, **128–30**, 131, 133, **138**, 458, 478, 519

R v Secretary of State for the Home Department, ex parte Ruddock [1987] 1 WLR 1482 . . . 599

R v Secretary of State for the Home Department, ex parte Samaroo (unreported), 20 December 2000 (CA) . . . 546

R v Secretary of State for the Home Department, ex parte Simms [1999] QB 349 (CA); [1999] 3 WLR 328; [2000] 2 AC 115 (HL) . . . 79, 89, 130, 132, **133**, 380, 438, **445–6**, 479–80, 483–4, **518–20**

R v Secretary of State for the Home Department, ex parte Stafford [1998] 1 WLR 503 . . . 458

R v Secretary of State for the Home Department, ex parte Tarrant [1985] QB 251 . . . 533, 537

R v Secretary of State for the Home Department, ex parte Thakrar [1974] QB 684 . . . 51

R v Secretary of State for the Home Department, ex parte Venables [1997] 3 WLR 23 (HL) . . . 511

R v Secretary of State for the Home Department, ex parte Venables and Thompson [1998] AC 407 . . . 458

R v Secretary of State for Social Services, ex parte Association of Metropolitan Authorities [1986] 1 WLR 1 (QB) . . . **283–5**, 333, 337

R v Secretary of State for Transport, ex parte Factortame Ltd [1989] 3 CMLR 1 . . . 74

R v Secretary of State for Transport, ex parte Factortame Ltd and Others [1990] 2 AC 85 (HL) . . . **74**, 77–80

R v Secretary of State for Transport, ex parte Factortame Ltd (No. 2) [1991] 1 AC 603 (HL) . . . 34, **75**, 76–7, 79, 81–2, 93, 99, 498

R v Sefton Metropolitan Borough Council, ex parte Help the Aged [1997] 4 All ER 532 (CA) . . . 510

R v Shayler [2002] UKHL 11 (HL) . . . 478,
482–3

R v Sheer Metalcraft Ltd [1954] 1 QB 586
(Kingston-upon-Thames Assizes) . . . **290–2**

R v Sussex Justices, ex parte McCarthy [1924] 1
KB 256 . . . 523, 527

R v Turnbull [1977] QB 224 . . . 531

R v Wicks [1998] AC 92 . . . 584

R (Al-Jedda) v Secretary of State for Defence
[2008] 1 AC 332 . . . 131

R (Al-Skeini) v Secretary of State for Defence
[2007] UKHL 26; [2007] 3 WLR 33 . . . 426

R (Alconbury Developments Ltd) v Secretary
of State for the Environment, Transport and
the Regions [2001] UKHL 23; [2003] 2 AC
295 . . . 34, 136, 139, 444, 475

R (Anderson) v Secretary of State for the
Home Department [2002] 2 WLR 1143
(CA) . . . 458, 460

R (Anderson) v Secretary of State for the Home
Department [2003] 1 AC 837 . . . 449

R (Anufrijeva) v Secretary of State for the
Home Department [2004] 1 AC 604 . . . 132–
4, **380**

R (Bancoult) v Secretary of State for Foreign
and Commonwealth Affairs (No. 2) [2008]
UKHL 61; [2009] 1 AC 453 (HL) . . . **43–4**,
539, 560–1

R (Bancoult) v Secretary of State for Foreign
and Commonwealth Affairs (No. 2) [2016]
UKSC 35 . . . **44**

R (Bancoult) v Secretary of State for Foreign and
Commonwealth Affairs (No. 3) [2013] EWHC
1502 (Admin); [2014] EWCA Civ 708 . . . 43–4

R (Bhatt Murphy) v The Independent
Assessor [2008] EWCA Civ 755 . . . **285–6**,
560–1

R (Bibi) v Newham London Borough Council
[2001] EWCA Civ 607; [2002] 1 WLR 237
(CA) . . . 511, **554–8**, 560

R (Bradley) v Secretary of State for Work &
Pensions [2007] EWHC 242 (Admin) . . . 645

R (Bradley) v Secretary of State for Work &
Pensions [2008] EWCA Civ 36 . . . **645**, 646

R (British Broadcasting Corporation) v
Secretary of State for Justice [2012] EWHC
12 (Admin) (Divisional Court) . . . 478,
483–90

R (Cart) v Upper Tribunal [2011]
UKSC 28 . . . 666

R (Chester) v Secretary of State for Justice [2013]
UKSC 63; [2014] AC 271 . . . 85

R (Cindo) v Secretary of State [2002] EWHC
246 . . . 517

R (Corner House Research) v Director of
Serious Fraud Office [2008] UKHL 60;
[2009] 1 AC 756; [2008] EWHC 714 . . . 106,
135–6, 511

R (Countryside Alliance) v Attorney General
[2008] AC 719 . . . 379

R (Cowl) v Plymouth City Council (Practice
Note) [2001] EWCA Civ 1935; [2002] 1 WLR
803 (CA) . . . 600, **601–2**, 603

R (Daly) v Secretary of State for the
Home Department [2001] UKHL 26; [2001]

2 AC 532 (HL) . . . 473, 476, **478–82**, 520,
546–7

R (Edison First Power Limited) v Central
Valuation Officer [2003] UKHL 20; [2003] 4
All ER 209 . . . 89

R (Equitable Members Action Group) v HM
Treasury [2009] EWHC 2495 (Admin) . . . 646

R (Evans) v Attorney General [2015] UKSC 21;
[2015] AC 1787 (SC) . . . x, **137–9**, 211, 266

R (Ewing) v Office of the Deputy Prime
Minister [2005] EWCA Civ 1583 . . . 571

R (Farrakhan) v Secretary of State for the Home
Department [2002] EWCA Civ 606; [2002]
QB 1391 . . . 474

R (Greenpeace) v Secretary of State for
Trade and Industry [2007] EWHC 311
(Admin) . . . 285, 539

R (HS2 Action Alliance) v Secretary of State
for Transport [2014] UKSC 3; [2014] 1 WLR
324, Sup Ct . . . x, **80–2**, 84, 171, 376

R (Hurley & Moore) v Secretary of State for
Business, Innovation & Skills [2012] EWHC
201 (Admin) . . . **605**

R (Jackson) v Attorney General [2005] UKHL
56; [2006] 1 AC 262 (HL) . . . 46, 55, 68, 87,
88–91, 91, 93–5, 101, 378–9, 381

R (Keyu) v Secretary of State for Foreign and
Commonwealth Affairs [2015] UKSC 69;
[2016] AC 1355 . . . 31

R (Lord Carlile of Berriew) v Secretary of State
for the Home Department [2014] UKSC 60;
[2015] AC 945 . . . x, 34–5

R (Mahmood) v Secretary of State for the Home
Department [2001] 1 WLR 840 . . . 480,
482, 546–7

R (Mencap) v Parliamentary & Health Service
Ombudsman [2010] EWCA Civ 875 . . . 571

R (Miller) v Secretary of State for Exiting
the European Union [2016] EWHC 2768
(Admin) . . . 149–50, 166

R (Miller) v Secretary of State for Exiting the
European Union [2017] UKSC 5 . . . x, xi,
212–13, 166, 180, **192–4**, 194–5, 366, 370,
376

R (Morgan Grenfell & Co Ltd) v Special
Commissioner of Income Tax [2003] 1
AC 563 . . . 89

R (Nadarajah) v Secretary of State for the
Home Department [2005] EWCA Civ
1363 . . . 561

R (Nicklinson) v Ministry of Justice [2013]
EWCA Civ 961 (CA); [2014] UKSC 38; [2015]
AC 657 (SC) . . . x, **119–20**

R (P) and R (Q) v Secretary of State for the
Home Department [2001] EWCA Civ 1151;
[2001] 1 WLR 2002 (CA) . . . 514

R (Patel) v General Medical Council [2013]
EWCA Civ 327 . . . 561

R (Pro Life Alliance) v British
Broadcasting Corporation [2004] 1 AC
185 . . . 484–5, 488–90

R (Purdy) v DPP [2009] UKHL 45; [2010] 1 AC
345 . . . 119–20

R (Quintavalle) v Secretary of State for Health
[2003] 2 AC 687 . . . 374

R (Razgar) v Secretary of State for the Home
Department [2004] UKHL 27; [2004] 2 AC
368 . . . 476
**R (Reilly) v Secretary of State for Work and
Pensions** [2013] UKSC 38 (SC) . . . x, **121–3**
R (Reprotech (Pebsham) Ltd) v East Sussex CC
[2002] UKHL 8; [2003] 1 WLR 348 . . . 561
R (Ullah) v Special Adjudicator [2004] UKHL
26; [2004] 2 AC 323 . . . 475
R (Wheeler) v Office of the Prime Minister
[2008] EWHC 1409 (Admin) . . . 81
Racal Communications Ltd, Re [1981] AC
374 . . . 502–3
Raymond v Honey [1983] 1 AC 1, 10H . . . 128
**Recovery of Medical Costs for Asbestos
Diseases (Wales) Bill, Re** [2015] UKSC 3;
[2015] AC 1016 . . . xi, **382–4**, 385
Reilly (No. 2) v Secretary of State for Work and
Pensions [2014] EWHC 2182 (Admin) . . . x,
123
Reilly (No. 2) v Secretary of State for Work and
Pensions [2016] EWCA Civ 413 . . . 123, 171
Ridge v Baldwin [1964] AC 40 (HL) . . . 496,
502, **527–30**, 536
Roberts v Hopwood [1925] AC 578 . . . 136
Robinson v Secretary of State for Northern
Ireland [2002] N.I. 390 . . . 380
**Robinson v Secretary of State for Northern
Ireland** [2002] UKHL 32; [2002] N.I. 390
(HL) . . . **370–3**, 374, 376, 380, 390
Rossminster v IRC . . . 131
Rothwell v Chemical Insulating Co Ltd [2008]
AC 281 . . . 377
Rowland v Environment Agency [2003] EWCA
Civ 1885 . . . 561
Roy v Kensington and Chelsea FPC [1989] 1
Med LR 10 . . . 586
Roy v Kensington and Chelsea FPC [1992] 2
WLR 239 (HL) . . . **585–7**, 597
Russell v Duke of Norfolk [1949] 1 All ER
109 . . . 521

**S (Minors) (Care Order: Implementation of
Care Plan), In Re** [2002] UKHL 10 . . . 448,
453–6, **459-60**
Samaroo v Secretary of State for the Home
Department [2001] EWCA Civ 1139; [2002]
INLR 55 . . . 474
Schrager v Basil Dighton Ltd [1924] 1 KB
274 . . . 525
Secretary of State for Defence v Guardian
Newspapers Ltd [1985] AC 339 . . . 599
Secretary of State for Education and Science
v Tameside Metropolitan Borough Council
[1977] AC 1014 . . . 515, 517, 549
Secretary of State for the Home Department
v GG [2009] EWCA Civ 786; [2010] 2 WLR
731 . . . 134
Selvarajan v Race Relations Board [1975] 1 WLR
1686 . . . 535
Sheldrake v Director of Public Prosecutions
[2005] 1 AC 264 . . . 133
Simmonds v Newell [1953] 1 WLR 826 . . . 291
Somerville v Scottish Ministers (HM Advocate
General for Scotland intervening) [2007] 1
WLR 2734 . . . 378

Starrs v Ruxton 2000 SLT 42 . . . **144–5**
Stockdale v Hansard (1839) 9 Ad & E 1; 112 ER
1112 . . . 171
Stradling v Morgan (1560) 1 Plow 199 . . . 89

**Thoburn v Sunderland City
Council** [2002] EWHC 195 (Admin); [2003]
QB 151 . . . **78–9**, 80, 82–4, 99
**Thompson and Venables v News Group
Newspapers Ltd** [2001] 2 WLR 1038 (Family
Division) . . . **436–43**
Town Investments Ltd v Department of the
Environment [1978] AC 359 . . . 109
Trial of Earl Russell [1901] AC 446 . . . 63

United Kingdom Association of Fish Producer
Organisations v Secretary of State for
Environment, Food and Rural Affairs [2013]
EWHC 1959 (Admin) . . . 560

Waddington v Miah [1974] 2 All
ER 377 . . . 121
Wainwright v Home Office [2003] UKHL 53;
[2003] 3 WLR 1137 . . . 443
Waldron, ex parte [1985] 3 WLR 1090 see R v
Hallstrom, ex parte W 603
Wandsworth London Borough Council v
Michalak [2003] 1 WLR 617 . . . 34
Wandsworth London Borough Council v
Winder [1985] AC 461 (HL) . . . 584–7, 606
Westminster Corp v London and North Western
Rly Co [1905] AC 426 . . . 506, 508
Wheeler v Leicester City Council [1985] AC
1054 (HL) . . . **503–5, 540–2**
Wheeler v Office of the Prime Minister [2014]
EWHC 3815 (Admin) . . . x, 101
Williams v HM Inspector of Taxes . . . 525
Wilson v First County Trust Ltd (No. 2) [2003]
UKHL 40; [2004] 1 AC 816 . . . 34, 81

X (A Minor) (Wardship: Injunction), In Re
[1984] 1 WLR 1422 . . . 442
X (Mary Bell) and another v News Group
Newspapers and another [2003] EWHC QB
1101; [2003] EMLR 37 . . . 443

YL v Birmingham City Council [2007] UKHL
27; [2007] 3 WLR 112 . . . 429–31
Youssef v Secretary of State for Foreign
and Commonwealth Affairs [2016]
UKSC 3 . . . 567

Zamora, The [1916] 2 AC 77 . . . 598–9

Australia

Attorney General for New South Wales v
Trethowan (1931) 44 CLR 394 . . . 93
Clayton v Heffron (1960)
105 CLR 214 . . . 91
Rex v Commonwealth Court of Conciliation
and Arbitration, ex parte Whybrow & Co.
(1910) 11 CLR 1 . . . 339
Taylor v Attorney General of Queensland
(1917) 23 CLR 457 . . . 91
Vakauta v Kelly (1989) 167 CLR 568 . . . 525

Canada

Reference Re Amendment of the
Constitution of Canada (1982) 125
DLR (3d) 1 (Supreme Court of
Canada) . . . 205–6

Court of Justice of the European Union

Alphabetical order

**Amministrazione delle Finanze dello Stato
v Simmenthal SpA** (Case 106/77) [1978]
ECR 629 . . . 71

Commission of the European Communities v
French Republic (Case C–265/95) [1997] ECR
I–6959 . . . 563

Costa v ENEL (Case 6/64) [1964] ECR 585,
CJEU . . . 69

**Internationale Handelsgesellschaft mbH v
Einfuhr und Vorratsstelle für Getreide und
Futtermittel** (Case 11/70) . . . 70

Marleasing SA v La Comercial Internacional de
Alimentación SA (Case C–106/89) [1990] ECR
I–4135 . . . 447, 449

Nationality of Fishermen, Re: EC
Commission v UK (Case C–246/89) [1991] 3
CMLR 706 . . . 75

Nationality of Fishermen, Re: EC Commission
v UK (Case C–246/89R) [1989] 3
CMLR 601 . . . 75

R v Secretary of State for Transport, ex parte
Factortame Ltd (No. 3) (Case C–221/89)
[1991] 3 CMLR 589 . . . 75

Simmenthal SpA v Italian Minister of Finance
(Case 35/76) [1976] ECR 1871   71

Uniplex (Case C–406/08) [2010] ECR
I–817 . . . 584

Van Gend en Loos v Nederlandse Administratie
der Belastingen (Case 26/62) [1963]
ECR 1 . . . 69

Numerical order

Case 26/62, Van Gend en Loos v Nederlandse
Administratie der Belastingen [1963]
ECR 1 . . . 69

Case 6/64, **Costa v ENEL** [1964] ECR 585,
CJEU . . . 69

Case 11/70, **Internationale
Handelsgesellschaft mbH v Einfuhr
und Vorratsstelle für Getreide und
Futtermittel** . . . 70

Case 35/76, Simmenthal SpA v Italian Minister
of Finance [1976] ECR 1871 . . . 71

Case 106/77, **Amministrazione delle Finanze
dello Stato v Simmenthal SpA** [1978]
ECR 629 . . . 71

Case C–106/89, Marleasing SA v La Comercial
Internacional de Alimentación SA [1990] ECR
I–4135 . . . 447, 449

Case C–221/89, R v Secretary of State for
Transport, ex parte Factortame Ltd (No. 3)
[1991] 3 CMLR 589 . . . 75

Case C–246/89, Nationality of Fishermen,
Re: EC Commission v UK [1991] 3
CMLR 706 . . . 75

Case C–246/89R, Nationality of Fishermen,
Re: EC Commission v UK [1989] 3
CMLR 601 . . . 75

Case C–265/95, Commission of the European
Communities v French Republic, [1997] ECR
I–6959 . . . 563

Case C–406/08, Uniplex [2010] ECR
I–817 . . . 584

European Court of Human Rights

Al-Jedda v United Kingdom (Application No.
27021/08) (2011) 53 EHRR 23 . . . 131

Artico, judgment of 13 May 1980, Series A No.
37, p. 16, § 33 . . . 407

Bamber v United Kingdom (Application No.
33742/96, 11 September 1997, BAILII [1997]
ECHR 205) . . . 486

Belgian Linguistic (1968) 1 EHRR 252 . . . 467

Benjamin and Wilson v United Kingdom
(Application No. 28212/95, 26 September
2002) . . . 458

Bergens Tidende v Norway (2001) 31
EHRR 16 . . . 486

Bladet Tromso and Stensaas v Norway (2000)
29 EHRR 125 . . . 483

Bromfield v United Kingdom (Application No.
32003/96, 1 July 1998) . . . 457

Earl Spencer v United Kingdom (1998) 25 EHRR
CD 105 . . . 439

Eckle v Germany (1983) 5 EHRR 1 . . . 457

Engel v The Netherlands (No. 1) (1976) 1 EHRR
647 . . . 482

Glaser v United Kingdom [2000] 3 FCR
193 . . . 436–7

Handyside v UK, Series A, No. 24 (1976) 1 EHRR
737 . . . 407–8, 464, 485

Ireland v United Kingdom (1978) 2 EHRR
25 . . . 130, 407

Keegan v Ireland (1994) 18 EHRR 342 . . . 437

Kjeldsen, Busk Madsen and Pedersen, judgment
of 7 December 1976, Series A No. 23, p. 27, §
53 . . . 407

Loizidou v Turkey (1995) 20 EHRR 99 . . . 466

McGonnell v UK (2000) 30 EHRR 289 . . . 144

Malone v United Kingdom (1985) 7
EHRR 14 . . . 466

Murray v UK (1996) 22 EHRR 29 . . . 472

News Verlags GmbH and CoKG v Austria (2001)
31 EHRR 8 . . . 484

Niemietz v Germany, 16 EHRR 97 . . . 466

Nilsen v United Kingdom (Application No.
36882/05, 9 March 2010, BAILII [2010]
ECHR 470) . . . 487

Osman v United Kingdom (1998) 29 EHRR
245 . . . 437, 439, 442

Pullar v United Kingdom (1996) 22 EHRR
391 . . . 527

Ringeisen v Austria (No. 1) (1971) 1 EHRR
455 . . . 457

Saunders v UK (1997) 23 EHRR 313 . . . 471–2

Sheffield v UK (1998) 27 EHRR 163 . . . 470

Silver v United Kingdom (1980) 3 EHRR 475;
(1983) 5 EHRR 347 . . . 519–20

Smith and Grady v United Kingdom (1999) 29
EHRR 493 . . . 473, 480–1, 547

Socialist Party v Turkey (1998) 27
  EHRR 51 . . . 407
Soering v United Kingdom Series A No. 161,
  (1989) 11 EHRR 439 . . . 407
Sporrong v Sweden (1982) 5 EHRR 35 . . . 470
Stafford v United Kingdom (Application No.
  46295/99, May 28, 2002) . . . 458
Stretch v UK (2004) 38 EHRR 12 . . . 561
Sunday Times v United Kingdom (1979) 2
  EHRR 245 . . . 438, 482–3, 485–7
Tyrer v UK, Series A No. 26, (1978) 2
  EHRR 1 . . . 407
United Communist Party of Turkey v Turkey
  (1998) 26 EHRR 121 . . . 20, 407
V v United Kingdom (1999) 30 EHRR
  121 . . . 457–9
von Hannover v Germany 16 BHRC 545 . . . 443
Winterwerp v The Netherlands (1979) 2 EHRR
  387 . . . 482
X and Y v The Netherlands (1985) 8 EHRR
  235 . . . 437, 440

France

KFTCIC v Icori Estero SpA (Paris Court of
  Appeal, 28 June 1991) . . . 524

Germany

Federal Constitutional Court judgment of
  24 April 2013 on the Counter-Terrorism
  Database Act, 1 BvR 1215/07, para 91 . . . 82

Ireland

Deaton v Attorney-General and the Revenue
  Commissioners [1963] IR 170, Supreme Ct of
  Ireland . . . 457

New Zealand

Auckland Casino case [1995] 1 NZLR
  142 . . . 525

South Africa

Harris v Minister of the Interior 1952
  (2) SA 428 . . . 67
Minister of the Interior v Harris 1952
  (4) SA 769 . . . 91

United States of America

Abrams v United States (1919) 250 US
  616 . . . 438, 483–4
Marbury v Madison (1803) 1 Cranch
  137 . . . 31, 51
Mathews v Eldridge, 424 US 319
  (1976) . . . 686
Pell v Procunier (1974) 417 US 817 (Supreme
  Ct) . . . 518–19
Turner v Safley (1987) 482 US 78 (Supreme
  Ct) . . . 519
West Virginia State Board of
  Education v Barnette (1943) 319 US
  624 . . . 483

TABLE OF LEGISLATION

*Page references in **bold** indicate the text is reproduced in full.*

United Kingdom

Access to Justice Act 1999, s 55 . . . 666
Acquisition of Land Act 1981, ss 23–25 . . . 608
Acquisition of Land (Assessment of
    Compensation) Act 1919 . . . 52
    s 2 . . . 52
    s 7(1) . . . 52
Act of Settlement 1701 . . . 50, 60, 82, 146,
    160, 199
Act of Union with England 1707
    (Scotland) . . . 58–9, 61, 79–80, 82, 349
Act of Union with Scotland 1707
    (England) . . . 50, 58–9, 61, 79–80, 349, 397
Agricultural Marketing Act 1958 . . . 508–10
    s 19 . . . 509
    s 19(3) . . . 508
    s 19(3)(b) . . . 508
    s 19(6) . . . 509
    s 20 . . . 509
Air Force Act 1955 . . . 424
Anti-Terrorism, Crime and Security Act
    2001 . . . 167
    s 23 . . . 337
Appropriation Act 1994 . . . 328
Army Act 1955 . . . 424
    ss 92–103 . . . 534
    s 135 . . . 534
    s 137 . . . 534
    s 181 . . . 534–5
Articles of Union (Scotland) . . . 60
Asylum and Immigration (Treatment of
    Claimants) Act 2004 . . . 608

Bail, Judicial Appointments etc. (Scotland)
    Act 2000
    s 6 . . . 145
    s 7 . . . 145
Bill of Rights 1688 (England) . . . 397
Bill of Rights 1689 (England) . . . **48–9**,
    79–80, 191
    Art 9 . . . 81–2, 92, 123, 168–70, 212
Bills of Exchange Act 1882 . . . 118
British Nationality Act 1981
    s 40(2) . . . 564
    s 44(2) . . . 512
British North America Acts . . . 62–3
British Railways Act 1968 . . . 53–4
    s 18 . . . 53
Broadcasting Act 1990, s 6(1)(a) . . . 489

Canada Act 1982 . . . 62–5, 207
    s 2 . . . **62**
Childcare Payments Act 2014 . . . 363
Children Act 1989 . . . 432, 453–6
    Pt III . . . 453
    Pt IV . . . 453
    s 9(1) . . . 454

s 17 . . . 514
s 26 . . . 456
s 33 . . . 454
s 34 . . . 454
s 39 . . . 454
s 91(1) . . . 454
s 100(2)(c) . . . 454
s 100(2)(d) . . . 454
Children and Adoption Act 2002, s 118 . . . 456
Children and Families Act 2014 . . . 686
    s 51 . . . 686
    s 55 . . . 686
Children and Young People (Scotland) Act
    2014 . . . 377
    Pt 4 . . . 377
Chronically Sick and Disabled Persons Act
    1970, s 2(1) . . . 510
Cities and Local Government Devolution Act
    2016 . . . 5, 345
Civil Authorities (Special Powers) Act
    (Northern Ireland) 1922 . . . 130, 334
    s 1(1) . . . 333
    s 1(3) . . . 334, 336
    s 3(2) . . . 337
Claim of Rights Act 1689 (Scotland) . . . 82, 397
Colonial Laws Validity Act 1865, s 5 . . . 65–6
Constitution (Legislative Council) Amendment
    Act 1929 . . . 65
Constitutional Reform Act 2005 . . . 5, 34, 82,
    123, 134, 141–3, 145–8, 152–4, 158, 275, 355,
    362, 660
    Pt 4 . . . 158
    s 1 . . . 31, **104**
    s 3 . . . 149
    s 3(1) . . . **147**
    s 3(4) . . . **147**
    s 3(5) . . . **147**
    s 3(6) . . . **147**
    s 3(7) . . . **147**
    s 3(7A) . . . **658**
    s 3(7B) . . . **658**
    s 5 . . . 163
    s 26 . . . 153
    s 27(1) . . . **153**
    s 27(1A) . . . **153**
    s 27(1B) . . . **153**
    s 27(1C) . . . **153**
    s 27(1D) . . . **153**
    s 27(4) . . . **153**
    s 27(5) . . . **153**
    s 27(5A) . . . **153**
    s 27(6) . . . **153**
    s 27(7) . . . **153**
    s 27(8) . . . **153**, 158
    s 27(9) . . . **154**
    s 27(10) . . . **154**
    s 27(11) . . . **154**

s 27A . . . 154
ss 28–31 . . . 154
s 40(4)(b) . . . 349
s 59 . . . 568
s 63(1) . . . **157**
s 63(2) . . . 146, 156, **157**
s 63(3) . . . **157**
s 63(4) . . . **157**
s 64 . . . 156
s 64(1) . . . 146
s 86 . . . 154
s 94C . . . 154
s 108 . . . 160
s 108(1) . . . **160**
s 108(2) . . . **160**
s 108(3) . . . **160**
s 108(4) . . . **160**
s 108(5) . . . **160**
s 108(6) . . . 146, **160**
s 108(7) . . . **160**
s 108(8) . . . **160**
s 137A . . . **157**
Sch 2, Pt 1 . . . 664
Sch 11 . . . 568
Sch 12 . . . 275
   para 1 . . . **154**
   para 2(1) . . . **154**
   para 3A . . . **154**
   para 3B(1) . . . **154**
   para 3B(2) . . . **154**
   para 3B(3) . . . **155**
Sch 14 . . . 154
Constitutional Reform and Governance Act
2010 . . . 5, 177, 186, 211, 233
   Pt 1 . . . 177
   s 2 . . . 177
   ss 3–4 . . . 177
   s 5 . . . 177
   s 6 . . . 177
   s 8 . . . 177
   s 9 . . . 177
   ss 10–12 . . . 177
   s 11 . . . 177
   s 16 . . . 177
   s 20(1) . . . **178**
   s 20(2) . . . **178**
   s 20(3) . . . **178**
   s 20(4) . . . **178**
   s 20(5) . . . **178**
   s 20(6) . . . **178**
   s 20(7) . . . **178**
   s 20(8) . . . **178**
   s 20(9) . . . **178**
   s 21(1) . . . **178**
   s 21(2) . . . **178**
   s 21(3) . . . **178**
   s 21(4) . . . **178**
   s 21(5) . . . **178**
   s 22(1) . . . **178**
   s 22(2) . . . **178**
   s 22(3) . . . **178**
   s 23(1) . . . **179**
   s 23(2) . . . **179**
   s 23(2A) . . . **179**
   s 23(2B) . . . **179**
   s 23(3) . . . **179**
   s 23(4) . . . **179**
   s 24 . . . **179**
   s 25(1) . . . **179**
   s 25(2) . . . **179**
   s 25(3) . . . **179**
   s 25(4) . . . **179**
Contempt of Court Act 1981, s 10 . . . 432, 598
Continental Shelf Act 1964 . . . 63
Convention Rights (Compliance) (Scotland)
   Act 2001 . . . 459
Corporation Tax (Northern Ireland) Act
   2015 . . . 393
Crime and Courts Act 2013 . . . 146,
   153–4, 157–9
   s 20 . . . 146
   s 22 . . . 608
   s 31A(2) . . . 608
   Sch 13 . . . 146
Crime (Sentences) Act 1997
   s 28 . . . 459
   s 29 . . . 459
Criminal Appeal Act 1968, s 9 . . . 458
Criminal Damage Act 1971, s 6(1) . . . 125
Criminal Injuries Compensation Act 1995,
   s 5 . . . 658
Criminal Justice Act 1961, s 61 . . . 128
Criminal Justice Act 1987, s 2(4) . . . 125
Criminal Justice Act 1988 . . . 142, 328–30
   Pt VII . . . 331–2
   s 36 . . . 459
   ss 108–117 . . . 328
   s 117(1) . . . 330
   s 171(1) . . . 328–9, 331–2
   Sch 6 . . . 328
   Sch 7 . . . 328
Criminal Justice Act 2003 . . . 460, 527
Criminal Justice and Courts Act 2015,
   Pt 4 . . . 571
Criminal Justice (Northern Ireland) Act
   2013 . . . 393
Crown Proceedings Act 1947 . . . 109, 176, 423
   s 21 . . . 108, 498
Customs and Excise Management Act 1979,
   s 161 . . . 398

Damages (Asbestos-related Conditions)
   Scotland Act 2009 . . . 377, 380
Data Protection Act 1998 . . . 377, 665
Declarations of Indulgence 1687
   (Scotland) . . . 48
Declarations of Indulgence 1688
   (Scotland) . . . 48
Defence Act 1842 . . . 191
Defence of the Realm Acts . . . 281
Defence of the Realm Act 1914 . . . 105
Deregulation and Contracting Out Act
   1994 . . . 317

Education Acts . . . 406
Education Act 1993, s 298 . . . 510
Education Reform Act 1988 . . . 587
Emergency Powers Act 1920 . . . 281
Employment Act 1980 . . . 118
   s 17 . . . 118

s 17(6) . . . 118
Equal Pay Act 1970 . . . 73
  s 1(2) . . . 448
Equality Act 2006 . . . 415
Equality Act 2010 . . . x, 149
  Pt 5 . . . 153, 157
  s 149 . . . 520
  s 159 . . . 153, 157
Estate Agents Act 1979 . . . 532
European Communities Act 1972 . . . 50, 60,
  72–3, 75–84, 98–9, 192–5, 376, 412, 426,
  460, 494
  s 1(2) . . . 193
  s 2 . . . 192–3
  s 2(1) . . . **72**, 73–4, 98, 192–3
  s 2(2) . . . **72**, 73, 78, 192–3, 282
  s 2(4) . . . 34, **72**, 73–4, 76–7, **78**, 79–80, 84
  s 3(1) . . . **72**
  s 3(2) . . . **72**
  Sch 2 . . . 73
European Communities (Amendment) Act
  1986 . . . 282
European Union (Amendment) Act 2008,
  s 5 . . . 179
European Union Act 2011 . . . 46, 80, 95, 98,
  100–1, 195
  Pt 1 . . . 179
  s 2 . . . 98, 100
  s 2(1) . . . **96**
  s 2(2) . . . **96**
  s 2(3) . . . **96**
  s 3 . . . 98, 100
  s 3(1) . . . **96**
  s 3(2) . . . **96**
  s 3(3) . . . **96**
  s 3(4) . . . **96**
  s 4 . . . 98
  s 4(1) . . . **96–7**
  s 4(2) . . . **97**
  s 4(3) . . . **97**
  s 4(4) . . . **97**
  s 6 . . . 98, 100–1
  s 6(1) . . . **97**
  s 6(2) . . . **97**
  s 6(3) . . . **97**, 101
  s 6(4) . . . **97**
  s 6(5) . . . **97–8**
  s 6(5)(c) . . . 101
  s 6(5)(d) . . . 101
  s 6(6) . . . **98**
  s 18 . . . 98–9, **98**, 101, 194
European Union (Approval of Treaty
  Amendment Decision) Act 2012 . . . 100
European Union (Croatian Accession and Irish
  Protocol) Act 2013 . . . 100
European Union (Referendum) Act
  2015 . . . 252
Explosives Act (Northern Ireland) 1970,
  s 2 . . . 364
Extradition Act 2003 . . . 376, 491, 579
  Pt 1 . . . 174

Fair Trading Act 1973 . . . 605
Finance Act 1964 . . . 51
Finance Act 1972, s 40 . . . 650

Finance Act 1976 . . . 398
  s 57 . . . 127
Finance Act 2006, s 173 . . . 179
Finance Act 2011, Sch 19, para 66 . . . 179
Finance Act 2012, s 218(1) . . . 179
Financial Services and Markets Act
  2000 . . . 611
Firearms Act 1968, s 46 . . . 125
Fixed-term Parliaments Act 2011 . . . 5, 182–3,
  186–7, 223
  s 1(1) . . . **180**
  s 1(2) . . . **180**
  s 1(3) . . . **180**
  s 1(4) . . . **180**
  s 1(5) . . . **180**
  s 1(6) . . . **180**
  s 1(7) . . . **180**
  s 2(1) . . . **180**
  s 2(2) . . . **180**
  s 2(3) . . . **180**
  s 2(4) . . . **180**
  s 2(5) . . . **180**
  s 2(6) . . . **181**
  s 2(7) . . . **181**
  s 3(1) . . . **181**
  s 3(2) . . . **181**
  s 3(3) . . . **181**
  s 3(4) . . . **181**
  s 6(1) . . . **181**
  s 6(2) . . . **181**
  s 7(4) . . . **181**
  s 7(5) . . . **181**
  s 7(6) . . . **181**
Foreign Compensation Act 1950 . . . 493, 502
  s 4(4) . . . 606–7
Foreign Compensation Act 1969 . . . 607
  s 3 . . . 607
  s 3(9) . . . 607
Forgery and Counterfeiting Act 1981
  s 7 . . . 125
  s 24 . . . 125
Freedom of Information Act 2000 . . . 5, 137–8,
  207, 233, 243, 265–6, 268, 665
  s 21 . . . 266
  s 22 . . . 266
  s 23 . . . 266
  s 24 . . . 266
  s 26 . . . 266
  s 27 . . . 266
  s 28 . . . 266
  s 29 . . . 266
  s 30 . . . 266
  s 31 . . . 266
  s 32 . . . 266
  s 33 . . . 266
  s 34 . . . 266
  s 35 . . . 266
  s 36 . . . 266
  s 37 . . . 207, 211, 266
  s 38 . . . 266
  s 40(1)–(2) . . . 266
  s 41 . . . 208, 266
  s 42 . . . 266
  s 43 . . . 266
  s 44 . . . 266

s 53 . . . 137–9, 266
s 53(2) . . . 137–9, 211
s 53(4)(b) . . . 138
s 57 . . . 138
s 58 . . . 138

Government of Ireland Act 1920 . . . 351
Government of Wales Act 1998 . . . 79,
350, 358–9
Government of Wales Act 2006 . . . 343, 350,
358, 369, 385, 390
Pt 3 . . . 358
Pt 4 . . . 358
s 1(1) . . . **350**
s 1(2) . . . **350**
s 1(3) . . . **350**
s 1(4) . . . **350**
s 1(5) . . . **350**
s 2 . . . 383
s 14 . . . 384
s 45(1) . . . **350**
s 45(2) . . . **350**
ss 46–47 . . . 350
s 48 . . . 350
s 58 . . . 382, 385
s 78(1) . . . **368**
s 78(4) . . . **368**
s 78(5) . . . **368**
s 78(6) . . . **368**
s 78(7) . . . **368**
s 78(8) . . . **368**
s 78(9) . . . **368**
s 78(10) . . . **368**
ss 93–102 . . . 358
s 103 . . . 358
s 107(1) . . . **356**
s 107(2) . . . **356**
s 107(3) . . . **356**
s 107(4) . . . **356**
s 107(5) . . . **356**
s 108 . . . 382
s 108(1) . . . **356**
s 108(2) . . . **356**
s 108(3) . . . **357**
s 108(4) . . . **357**, 382–4
s 108(4A) . . . **357**
s 108(5) . . . **357**, 382–4
s 108(6) . . . **357**, 382
s 108(7) . . . **357**
s 109(1) . . . **357**
s 109(2) . . . **357**
s 109(3) . . . **357**
s 109(5) . . . **357**
s 110(1) . . . **357**
s 110(2) . . . **358**
s 110(3) . . . **358**
s 112(1) . . . **358**
s 112(2) . . . **358**
Sch 7 . . . 358, 381–2
Pt 1 . . . **359**
para 9 . . . 383–4
Greater London Authority Act 1999 . . . 345

Health and Social Care Act 2008,
s 145(1) . . . 430

Herring Fishery (Scotland) Act 1889 . . . 50
s 7 . . . 50
House of Commons Disqualification Act 1975
s 2 . . . 349
Sch 1 . . . 154
House of Lords Act 1999 . . . 5
House of Lords Reform Act 2014 . . . 5
Housing Acts . . . 451, 504
Housing Act 1925 . . . 52
s 46 . . . 52
s 46(1) . . . 52
s 46(2) . . . 52
Housing (Homeless Persons) Act
1977 . . . 554, 557
s 65(2) . . . 558
Human Rights Act 1998 . . . 5, 33–4, 79, 82,
84–5, 87, 93, 95, 116, 131, 133, 142, 144,
326, 337, 381, 396, 398–9, 409, 415–16, 424,
426–9, 432, 434–7, 442, 444–7, 455, 457, 463,
468, 474, 477–8, 480–1, 483, 486, 488, 494–5,
520–1, 546–7, 549, 562, 569, 630, 666
s 1 . . . 133
s 1(1) . . . **416**
s 1(2) . . . **416**
s 1(3) . . . **416**
s 1(4) . . . **416**
s 1(5) . . . **416**
s 1(6) . . . **416**
s 2 . . . 436, 475, 481, 546
s 2(1) . . . **416**, 444, 467
s 3 . . . 85, 116, 133–4, 439, 446–51,
454–6, 459
s 3(1) . . . 133, **416**, 434, 444, 447–9, 452–3,
455, 459–60
s 3(2) . . . **416**, 447
s 3(2)(b) . . . 455
s 4 . . . 85, 116, 448–50, 455, 459, 489
s 4(1) . . . **416**, 447
s 4(2) . . . **416**, 447, 457
s 4(3) . . . **417**, 457
s 4(4) . . . **417**
s 4(5) . . . **417**
s 4(6) . . . **417**, 460
s 5(1) . . . **417**
s 5(2) . . . **417**
s 5(3) . . . **417**
s 5(4) . . . **417**
s 6 . . . 34, 429–30, 432–4
s 6(1) . . . **417**, 434–6, 490
s 6(2) . . . **417**
s 6(3) . . . **417**, 430, 436
s 6(3)(a) . . . 427, 432
s 6(3)(b) . . . 427–30, 434
s 6(4) . . . **418**
s 6(5) . . . **418**, 427, 430, 434
s 6(6) . . . **418**
s 7(1) . . . **418**, 436
s 7(2) . . . **418**
s 7(3) . . . **418**
s 7(4) . . . **418**
s 7(5) . . . **418**
s 7(6) . . . **418**
s 7(7) . . . **418**
s 7(8) . . . **418**
s 8 . . . 436

s 8(1) . . . **418**
s 8(2) . . . **418**
s 8(3) . . . **418**
s 8(4) . . . **419**
s 8(6) . . . **419**
s 9(1) . . . **419**
s 9(2) . . . **419**
s 9(3) . . . **419**
s 9(4) . . . **419**
s 9(5) . . . **419**
s 10 . . . 460, 463
s 10(1) . . . **419**
s 10(2) . . . **419**
s 10(3) . . . **420**
s 10(4) . . . **420**
s 10(5) . . . **420**
s 10(6) . . . **420**
s 11 . . . **420**
s 12 . . . 438–9
s 12(1) . . . **420**, 438, 440
s 12(2) . . . **420**
s 12(3) . . . **420**
s 12(4) . . . **420**, 437–8, 440
s 12(5) . . . **420**
s 13(1) . . . **420**
s 13(2) . . . **420**
s 14(1) . . . **421**
s 14(2) . . . **421**
s 14(3) . . . **421**
s 14(4) . . . **421**
s 14(5) . . . 362, **421**
s 14(6) . . . **421**
s 15(1) . . . **421**
s 15(2) . . . **421**
s 15(3) . . . **421**
s 15(4) . . . **421**
s 15(5) . . . **421**
s 16(1) . . . **421**
s 16(2) . . . **421**
s 16(3) . . . **421**
s 16(4) . . . **421**
s 16(5) . . . **421**
s 16(6) . . . **421**
s 16(7) . . . **422**
s 17(1) . . . **422**
s 17(2) . . . **422**
s 17(3) . . . **422**
s 18(1) . . . **422**
s 18(2) . . . **422**
s 18(3) . . . **422**
s 19 . . . 362, 446
s 19(1) . . . **422**, 462
s 19(2) . . . **422**
s 20(1) . . . **422**
s 20(2) . . . **422**
s 20(3) . . . **422**
s 20(4) . . . **422**
s 20(5) . . . **423**
s 21(1) . . . **423**
s 22(1) . . . **424**
s 22(2) . . . **424**
s 22(3) . . . **424**
s 22(4) . . . **424**
s 22(5) . . . **424**
s 22(6) . . . **424**

s 22(7) . . . **424**
Sch . . . 406
Sch 2 . . . 460
Hunting Act 2004 . . . 88, 91–2, 95

Immigration Act 1971, s 12 . . . 651
Immigration Act 2014 . . . 683
Immigration and Asylum Act 1999
  s 65 . . . 473–4, 476
  Sch 4
    Pt III . . . 473
    para 21(1)(a) . . . 475
Income Tax Act 2007, s 11A . . . 367
Industrial Development Act 1966
  s 1 . . . 512
  s 1(1) . . . 512
Industrial Training Act 1982 . . . 617
Inheritance Tax Act 1984, s 158 . . . 179
Inquiries Act 2005 . . . 175
Ireland Act 1949, s 1(2) . . . 369
Irish Church Act 1869 . . . 52, 58, 60

Jobseekers Act 1995
  s 17A . . . 121
  s 17A(1) . . . 122
Jobseekers (Back to Work Schemes) Act
  2013 . . . 122–3
  s 1(2) . . . 122
  s 1(3) . . . 122
  s 1(4)–(8) . . . 122
  s 1(10)–(12) . . . 122
  s 1(14) . . . 122
Judicature (Northern Ireland) Act 1978,
  s 25A . . . 665
Judiciary and Courts (Scotland) Act
  2008 . . . 152
Justice Act (Northern Ireland) 2011 . . . 393
Justice (Northern Ireland) Act
  2002 . . . 153, 362
Justice (Northern Ireland) Act 2004 . . . 153
Justice and Security Act 2013 . . . 134

Legal Services Act 2007 . . . 611
Legislative and Regulatory Reform Act 2006
  s 1 . . . 319
Local Authority Social Services Act 1970
  s 7B . . . 601
Local Government Act 1972, s 142(2) . . . 506
Local Government Act 1974 . . . 611, 627,
  642, 646
  s 25(1) . . . **618**
  s 25(2) . . . **619**
  s 25(3) . . . **619**
  s 25(4) . . . **619**
  s 25(4A) . . . **619**
  s 25(4B) . . . **619**
  s 25(5) . . . **619**
  s 26 . . . **623**
  s 26(1) . . . 624, **625**
  s 26(5) . . . 614, 628
  s 26(6) . . . **619**
  s 26(7) . . . **619**, 627
  s 26(8) . . . **619**
  s 26(9) . . . **619**
  s 26(10) . . . **620**

s 26A(1) . . . **614**
s 26A(2) . . . **614**
s 26B(1) . . . **614**
s 26B(2) . . . **615**
s 26B(3) . . . **615**
s 26C(1) . . . **615**
s 26C(2) . . . **615**
s 26C(3) . . . **615**
s 26C(4) . . . **615**
s 26C(5) . . . **615**
s 26D(1) . . . **615**
s 26D(2) . . . **615**
s 26D(3) . . . **615**
ss 28–29 . . . 628
s 30(1) . . . **639**
s 30(1A) . . . **639**
s 30(1B) . . . **639**
s 30(1C) . . . **639**
s 30(1D) . . . **639**
s 31(2) . . . 642
s 31(2D)–(2H) . . . 642
s 31(2)–(2c) . . . 642
s 31A(1) . . . 642
s 31A(4) . . . 642
s 31A(5) . . . 642
s 34(3) . . . **624**
Local Government Finance Act 1988 . . . 545
Local Government and Housing Act 1989
    s 26 . . . 642
    s 28 . . . 642
Local Government Planning and Land Act
    1980 . . . 543
    s 59(11A) . . . 543
    s 60 . . . 543

Magna Carta . . . 79–80, 82
Marine Insurance Act 1906 . . . 118
Mental Health Act 1959, s 3 . . . 651
Merchant Shipping Act 1894 . . . 74
Merchant Shipping Act 1988 . . . 74–6, 80
    Pt II . . . 74, 78
    s 14 . . . 75
Military Lands Act 1892, s 14(1) . . . 338
Misuse of Drugs Act 1971, s 23(3) . . . 125
Municipal Corporations Act 1882 . . . 528–30
    s 191(4) . . . 527, 530
Murder (Abolition of Death Penalty) Act 1965,
    s 1(2) . . . 459

National Assistance Act 1948
    s 21 . . . 429
    s 21(1) . . . 510
National Health Service and Community Care
    Act 1990, s 50 . . . 601
National Health Service (Wales) Act
    2006 . . . 384
Nationality, Immigration and Asylum Act
    2002, s 103A . . . 657
Naval Discipline Act 1957 . . . 424
Northern Ireland Act 1998 . . . 351, 362, 369–
    71, 373, 380, 423
    s 1 . . . 370–1
    s 1(1) . . . **369**
    s 1(2) . . . **369**
    s 4(1) . . . 359

s 4(2) . . . 359
s 4(2A) . . . 392
s 4(3) . . . 360
s 4(4) . . . 360
s 4(5) . . . 351, 360
s 5(1) . . . 360
s 5(2) . . . 360
s 5(3) . . . 360
s 5(4) . . . 360
s 5(5) . . . 360
s 5(6) . . . 360
s 6(1) . . . 360
s 6(2) . . . 360
s 6(3) . . . 360–1
s 6(4) . . . 361
s 6(5) . . . 361
s 8 . . . 361
s 9(1) . . . 361
s 9(2) . . . 361
s 10(1) . . . 361
s 10(2) . . . 361
s 10(3) . . . 361
s 11 . . . 382
s 11(1) . . . 361
s 11(2) . . . 362
s 11(3) . . . 362
s 11(4) . . . **362**
s 16 . . . 373
s 16(1) . . . 372–3
s 16(8) . . . 370, 372–3
s 16A . . . 353
s 16A(1) . . . **351**
s 16A(2) . . . **351**
s 16A(3) . . . **351**
s 16A(4) . . . **351**
s 16A(5) . . . **352**
s 16A(6) . . . **352**
s 16A(7) . . . **352**
s 16A(8) . . . **352**
s 16A(9) . . . **352**
s 16A(12) . . . **352**
s 16C . . . 353
s 16C(3) . . . **352**
s 16C(4) . . . **352**
s 17 . . . 353
s 17(1) . . . **352**
s 17(2) . . . **352**
s 17(3) . . . **352**
s 17(4) . . . **352**
s 17(5) . . . **352**
s 18 . . . 353
s 20(1) . . . **353**
s 20(2) . . . **353**
s 20(4) . . . **353**
s 30 . . . 353
s 31 . . . 372
s 32 . . . 372–3
s 32(1) . . . 371
s 32(3) . . . 370–3
Sch 1
    para 1 . . . **369**
    para 2 . . . **369**
    para 3 . . . **369**
    para 4(1) . . . **369**
    para 4(2) . . . **369**

Sch 2 . . . **363**
Sch 3 . . . **364**
Sch 15 . . . 351
Northern Ireland Assembly Act 1973, s 1 . . . 423
Northern Ireland Constitution Act
1973 . . . 351, 363
s 1 . . . 369
s 36(1)(c) . . . 363
s 38(1)(a) . . . 423
Northern Ireland (Elections) Act 1998 . . . 351
s 1(1) . . . **351**
s 1(2) . . . **351**
s 1(3) . . . **351**
s 1(4) . . . **351**
s 1(5) . . . **351**
s 1(6) . . . **351**
Northern Ireland (Miscellaneous Provisions)
Act 2006 . . . 362, 392
Northern Ireland (Miscellaneous Provisions)
Act 2014 . . . 362
Northern Ireland (Monitoring Commission
etc.) Act 2003 . . . 353
Northern Ireland (St Andrews Agreement) Act
2006 . . . 353
Northern Ireland (Stormont Agreement and
Implementation Plan) Act 2016 . . . 353, 393
Northern Ireland (Welfare Reform) Act
2015 . . . 393

Obscene Publications Act 1959 . . . 408
s 3 . . . 125
Official Secrets Act 1911 . . . 16, 43
s 1 . . . 42
s 3 . . . 42
s 9 . . . 398
Official Secrets Acts 1911–1939 . . . 638
Open Spaces Act 1906 . . . 541
s 10 . . . 503
Overseas Development and Co-operation Act
1980 . . . 593

Parliament Acts *see* Parliament Acts 1911
and 1949
Parliament Act 1911 . . . 47, 50, 68, 88–91, 93,
116, 213–14, 322
Preamble . . . 89
s 1 . . . 89–90
s 1(1) . . . 88–9
s 1(2) . . . 90
s 2 . . . 89–90
s 2(1) . . . 88–90, 92
s 2(4) . . . 90
s 3 . . . 90
s 4(2) . . . 90
s 5 . . . 90
s 7 . . . 92
Parliament Act 1949 . . . 47, 50, 68, 88, 91–3,
116, 213–14
Parliamentary Commissioner Act 1967 . . . 611,
622, 646
s 4(1) . . . **617**
s 4(2) . . . **617**
s 4(3) . . . **617**
s 4(3A) . . . **617**
s 4(3B) . . . **617**
s 4(4) . . . **617**
s 4(5) . . . **617**
s 4(6) . . . **618**
s 4(7) . . . **618**
s 5(1) . . . **614**, 623
s 5(2) . . . **618**, 621
s 5(3) . . . **618**
s 5(4) . . . **618**
s 5(5) . . . **618**
s 5(5A) . . . **618**
s 5(5B) . . . **618**
s 5(6) . . . **618**
s 6(3) . . . 614
s 7(1) . . . **627**
s 7(2) . . . **628**
s 7(3) . . . **628**
s 7(4) . . . **628**
s 8(1) . . . **628**
s 8(2) . . . **628**
s 8(3) . . . **628**
s 8(4) . . . **628**
s 8(5) . . . **628**
s 9(1) . . . **628**
s 10(1) . . . **638**
s 10(2) . . . **638**
s 10(3) . . . **638**, **641**, 642–5
s 10(4) . . . **638**
s 11(2) . . . **638**
s 11(3) . . . **638**
s 12(3) . . . **623**
Sch 3 . . . 618
Parliamentary Oaths Act 1866 . . . 169
Parliamentary Voting System and
Constituencies Act 2011 . . . 5
Pension Schemes Act 2015 . . . 669
Petition of Right 1628 . . . 82, 103
Police Act 1997, ss 92–108 . . . 398
Police (Appeals) Act 1927 . . . 527
Police and Criminal Evidence Act 1984
s 8 . . . 125, 398
s 76 . . . 432
s 78 . . . 432
Police (Northern Ireland) Act 1998, s 51 . . . 611
Political Parties, Elections and Referendums
Act 2000 . . . 252, 363
Prison Act 1952 . . . 473
s 47 . . . 531
s 47(1) . . . 478, 480
Proceeds of Crime Act 2002 . . . 579
ss 47B–47R . . . 125
Protection from Harassment Act 1997 . . . 442
Protection of Trading Interests Act
1980 . . . 363
Public Bodies Act 2011 . . . 241, 320
ss 1–5 . . . 320
s 8 . . . 320
s 10 . . . 320
s 11 . . . 320
Schs 1–5 . . . 320
Public Health Acts . . . 504, 541
Public Health Act 1925, s 56 . . . 503
Public Health (Amendment) Act 1907,
s 76 . . . 503
Public Health (London) Act 1891 . . . 506
s 44 . . . 506

Public Processions (Northern Ireland) Act
 1998 . . . 364
Public Services Ombudsman Act (Northern
 Ireland) 2015, s 8 . . . 637
Public Services Ombudsman Act (Northern
 Ireland) 2016 . . . 610, 645
Public Services Ombudsman (Wales) Act
 2005 . . . 610, 617, 645
 s 3 . . . 629
 s 3(1) . . . **629**
 s 3(2) . . . **629**
 s 3(3) . . . **629**
 s 20 . . . 645

Race Relations Act 1976 . . . 398, 504–5, 532–3,
 535, 537, 540–1
 Pt III . . . 534, 540
 Pt X . . . 540
 s 4 . . . 534
 s 4(1)(c) . . . 534
 s 48 . . . 532
 s 54(1) . . . 534
 s 54(2) . . . 534
 s 58 . . . 532
 s 58(5) . . . 532
 s 71 . . . 504, 540–2
Recall of MPs Act 2015 . . . 5
Reform Acts . . . 79–80
Regulatory Enforcement and Sanctions Act
 2008 . . . 655
Regulatory Reform Act 2001 . . . 319
Rent Act 1977, Sch 1, para 2(2) . . . 447
Representation of the People Act 1983
 Sch 1
  r 1 . . . 180–1
  r 3 . . . 181
Road Traffic Act 1988
 s 5(1)(a) . . . 468
 s 172 . . . 470–1
 s 172(2) . . . **469**, 472–3
 s 172(2)(a) . . . 468
 s 172(2)(b) . . . 471
 s 172(3) . . . **469**
Royal Titles Act 1953 . . . 59

Sale of Goods Act 1893 . . . 118
Savings (Government Contributions) Act
 2017 . . . 363
School Standards and Framework Act 1998
 Pt III, Ch 1 . . . 619
 s 24 . . . 619
 Sch 18 . . . 619
 Sch 24 . . . 619
 Sch 25, para 3 . . . 619
Scotland Act 1998 . . . 79, 93, 163, 310, 349, 355,
 367, 373–81, 387, 445, 617–18
 Pt 4 . . . 377
 s 1(1) . . . **348**, **378**
 s 1(2) . . . **348**, 378
 s 1(3) . . . **348**, 378
 s 1(4) . . . **348**
 s 1(5) . . . **348**
 s 28 . . . 375, 382
 s 28(1) . . . **353**, 378
 s 28(2) . . . **353**, 378

s 28(3) . . . **353**
s 28(4) . . . **353**
s 28(5) . . . **353**, 378
s 28(6) . . . **353**, 445
s 28(7) . . . 212, **353**, 378
s 28(8) . . . 212, **353**, 366
s 29 . . . 94, 375, 377–8, 381–2
s 29(1) . . . **353**
s 29(2) . . . **354**, 379–80
s 29(2)(b) . . . 375
s 29(2)(d) . . . 366, 379
s 29(3) . . . **354**
s 29(4) . . . **354**
s 29(5) . . . **354**
s 30 . . . 374, 386
s 30(1) . . . **354**
s 30(2) . . . **354**
s 30(5) . . . **354**
s 30(6) . . . **354**
s 31(1) . . . **354**
s 31(2) . . . **354**
s 31(3) . . . **354**
s 33(1) . . . **354**
s 33(2) . . . **354**
s 44(1) . . . **349**
s 44(2) . . . **349**
s 44(3) . . . **349**
s 44(4) . . . **349**
s 45 . . . 349
s 46 . . . 349
s 47 . . . 349
s 53 . . . 382
s 57(2) . . . 376
s 63A . . . 213, 349, 355, 368
s 63A(1) . . . **389**
s 63A(2) . . . **389**
s 63A(3) . . . **389**
s 67A . . . 368
s 80B . . . 367
s 80C(1) . . . **367**
s 80C(2A) . . . **367**
s 80C(2B) . . . **367**
s 80C(2C) . . . **367**
s 80C(5) . . . **367**
s 80C(6) . . . **367**
s 80C(7) . . . **367**
s 80C(8) . . . **367**
s 80I . . . 367
s 80K . . . 367
s 80L . . . 368
s 93 . . . 618
Sch 4 . . . 374–5, 382
Sch 5 . . . 355, 374–5, 382, 386
 Pt I . . . **355**
 para 1(b) . . . 386
 Pt II . . . **355–6**
Scotland Act 2012 . . . 163, 355, 367–8,
 387, 389–90
 s 12(2) . . . 349
 s 12(2)(a) . . . 349
 ss 34–37 . . . 349
Scotland Act 2016 . . . xi, 356, 368, 388
 s 1 . . . 213, 349, 355, 366, 389
 s 13 . . . 367
 ss 22–31 . . . 368

s 28 . . . 368
s 39 . . . 655
Scottish Independence Referendum Act
  2013 . . . **386**
s 1 . . . **386**
s 1(1) . . . **386**
s 1(2) . . . **386**
s 1(3) . . . **386**
s 1(4) . . . **386**
s 1(5) . . . **386**
s 1(6) . . . **386**
s 1(7) . . . **386**
s 2 . . . **386**, 387
Scottish Independence Referendum (Franchise)
  Act 2013 . . . 94, 386–7
Scottish Public Services Ombudsman Act
  2002 . . . 610, 645
s 2(4) . . . **629**
s 2(5) . . . **629**
Security and Courts Act 2013 . . . 657
Security Services Act 1989, s 5(4) . . . 608
Senior Courts Act 1981 . . . 157–8, 160, 568,
  572, 591
s 9(1) . . . 158
s 31 . . . 571, 575
s 31(1) . . . **569**
s 31(2) . . . **569**
s 31(2A) . . . **569**, 571
s 31(2B) . . . **569**, 571
s 31(2C) . . . **569**
s 31(3) . . . **569**, 583
s 31(3A) . . . **569**
s 31(3A)–(3B) . . . 571
s 31(3B) . . . **569**
s 31(3)(b) . . . 571
s 31(3C) . . . **570**
s 31(3C)–(3F) . . . 571
s 31(3D) . . . **570**
s 31(3E) . . . **570**
s 31(3F) . . . **570**, 573
s 31(4) . . . **570**
s 31(5) . . . **570**
s 31(5A) . . . **570**
s 31(5B) . . . **570**
s 31(6) . . . **570**, 584
s 31(7) . . . **570**
s 31(8) . . . **570**
s 31A . . . 571, 665–6
s 89 . . . 155
see also Supreme Court Act 1981
Sex Discrimination Act 1975 . . . 73, 398
s 8 . . . 448
Sheriff Courts (Scotland) Act 1971, s 12 . . . 144
Small Charitable Donations Act 2012 . . . 363
Social Care Act 2014, s 73 . . . 430
Social Security Administration Act 1992,
  s 173(1)(a) . . . 283
Social Security and Housing Benefits Act
  1982 . . . 284
s 36(1) . . . 283
Southern Rhodesia Act 1965 . . . 62
Statute of Westminster 1931 . . . 62–4, 197
Preamble . . . 64–5, 198, 206, 365
s 4 . . . 61, 365
s 7 . . . 63

Statutory Instruments Act 1946 . . . 281,
  289–92, 316
s 1 . . . 291
s 1(1) . . . **290**
s 2 . . . 291
s 2(1) . . . **290**
s 3 . . . 291–2
s 3(1) . . . **290**, 291
s 3(2) . . . **290**, 291
s 3(3) . . . **290**
s 8(1) . . . **290**
Succession to the Crown Act 2013 . . . 5
Suicide Act 1961
s 2 . . . 119
s 2(1) . . . 119
Supreme Court Act 1981 . . . 568, 572
s 30 . . . 572
s 31 . . . 582
s 31(3) . . . 591
s 130 . . . 398
see also Senior Courts Act 1981

Tax Credits Act 2002 . . . 322
Taxation (International and Other Provisions)
  Act 2010, s 2 . . . 179
Taxes Management Act 1970 . . . 126
s 20C . . . 125–6, 398
Terrorism Act 2000 . . . 490
Sch 5 . . . 125
Terrorist Asset-Freezing (Temporary Provisions)
  Act 2010 . . . 134
Theft Act 1968 . . . 127
s 17(1)(b) . . . 168
s 26(1) . . . 125
Tobacco and Primary Medical Services
  (Scotland) Act 2010 . . . 373
s 1 . . . 373
s 9 . . . 373
Town and Country Planning Acts . . . 504
Trade Union and Labour Relations Act
  1974 . . . 32, 118
s 13(1) . . . 31–2
Trade Union and Labour Relations
  (Amendment) Act 1976 . . . 32, 118
s 13(1) . . . 32
Treasure Act 1996 . . . 175
Treaty of Union (with Ireland) 1800 . . . 58–9
Art I . . . 59
Art 5 . . . 60
Art 18 . . . 58–60
Art 19 . . . 59
Tribunals, Courts and Enforcement Act
  2007 . . . 657, 660–2, 687–8
s 1 . . . **658**
s 2(1) . . . **658**
s 2(2) . . . **658**
s 2(3) . . . **658**
s 2(4) . . . **658**
s 3(1) . . . **654**
s 3(2) . . . **654**
s 3(3) . . . **654**
s 3(4) . . . **654**
s 3(5) . . . **654**
s 4(3)(c) . . . 662
s 4(3)(d) . . . 662

s 5(2)(c) . . . 662
s 5(2)(d) . . . 662
s 7(1) . . . **654, 659**
s 7(2) . . . **655, 659**
s 7(3) . . . **655, 659**
s 7(4) . . . **655, 659**
s 7(5) . . . **655, 659**
s 7(6) . . . **655, 659**
s 7(7) . . . **655, 659**
s 7(8) . . . **655, 659**
s 7(9) . . . **655, 659**
s 8(1) . . . **659**
s 8(1A) . . . **659**
s 8(2) . . . **659**
s 8(3) . . . **659**
s 8(4) . . . **659**
s 8(5) . . . **659**
s 9 . . . 665
s 10 . . . 665
s 11 . . . 665
s 11(5) . . . 665–6
s 13 . . . 666
s 15 . . . 666
s 15(1) . . . 666
s 18(1) . . . **664**
s 18(2) . . . **664**
s 18(3) . . . **664**
s 18(4) . . . **664**
s 18(5) . . . **664**
s 18(6) . . . **664**
s 18(7) . . . **664**
s 18(8) . . . **664–5**
s 18(9) . . . **665**
s 18(10) . . . **665**
s 19 . . . 571, 666
s 19(1) . . . 666
s 19(2) . . . 666
s 19(3) . . . **665**
s 19(4) . . . **665**
s 19(5) . . . **665**
s 20 . . . 666
s 21 . . . 666
s 31(2) . . . 155
s 43 . . . 680
s 44 . . . 687
Sch 2
    para 1(1) . . . 155
    para 2(1) . . . 661
Sch 3, para 2(1) . . . 661
Sch 7, para 13(4) . . . 687
Tribunals and Inquiries
    Act 1958 . . . 649
s 11 . . . 607, 608
Tribunals and Inquiries Act
    1971 . . . 649, 652
Sch 1 . . . 652
Tribunals and Inquiries Act 1992 . . . 649
s 10 . . . 511
s 12(1) . . . 607

United Nations Act 1946 . . . 133
s 1 . . . 131–2
s 1(1) . . . 133
Universities (Scotland) Act 1853 . . . 58

Wales Act 2014 . . . xi, 359, 390
s 4 . . . 350
s 12 . . . 390
War Crimes Act 1991
s 1(1) . . . **121**
s 1(2) . . . **121**
s 35(2) . . . 128–30
War Damage Act 1965 . . . 51, 121
Weights and Measures Act 1985 . . . 78
Welsh Language (Wales) Measure 2011 . . . 369

Youth Justice and Criminal Evidence Act 1999
s 41 . . . 448
s 41(1) . . . 448
s 41(3)(c) . . . 448

Bills
Adoption and Children Bill (2001–02) . . . 304
Age-related Payments Bill (2003–04) . . . 323
Agricultural Sector (Wales) Bill . . . 382, 385
Armed Forces Bill . . . 302
Asylum and Immigration (Treatment of
    Claimants) Bill . . . 608
Banking No. 2 Bill (2008–09) . . . 324
    Pt 1 . . . 324
Charities Bill (draft) . . . 299, 306
Childcare Bill (2015–16) . . . 324
Civil Contingencies Bill . . . 299–300
Civil Partnerships Bill . . . 451–2
Communications Bill (draft) . . . 299
Company Law Reform Bill (2003) (later the
    Companies Bill) (2005–06) . . . 300, 324
Constitutional Reform Bill 2003 . . . 143, 146–7
Constitutional Reform and Governance Bill
    (2008–09) . . . 177
Coroners Bill (draft) . . . 301
Corporate Manslaughter Bill (draft) . . . 303
Corruption Bill (draft) . . . 300
Damages (Asbestos-related Conditions)
    (Northern Ireland) Bill . . . 382
Department of Justice Bill (Wales) . . . 392
Disability Discrimination Bill . . . 299
Energy Bill (2013–14) . . . 323
European Union (Notification of Withdrawal)
    Bill (2017) . . . 194
European Union (Referendum) Bill
    (2013–14) . . . x, 247–9, 251
Finance Bill . . . 303
Financial Services and Markets Bill
    (1998–99) . . . 298
Fixed-Term Parliaments (Repeal) Bill
    (2014–15) . . . 182
Higher Education and Research Bill . . . 255
Human Rights Bill (1997) . . . 409–12, 414–15,
    424, 426, 433–4, 447, 461–3, 466
Jobseekers Bill (1994–95) . . . 323, 447
Legal Services Bill (draft) . . . 301
Local Government Byelaws (Wales) Bill (2012),
    s 9 . . . 381
Local Government (Wales) Bill
    (1993–94) . . . 324
Parliament Acts (Amendment) Bill (2001) . . . 91
Pensions Bill (2013–14) . . . 324
Planning Bill (2007–08) . . . 323

Pt 11 . . . 323
Pollution Prevention and Control Bill
(1998–99) . . . 323
Public Service Ombudsman Bill 2016 . . . xi, 629
cl 7 . . . 623
Scotland Bill . . . 163, 365
Wales Bill (2016–17) . . . xi, 212, 359,
389–91, 637
cl 17 . . . 390

Statutory Instruments
Al-Qaida and Taliban (Asset-Freezing)
Regulations 2010 (SI 2010/1197) . . . 134
Al-Qaida and Taliban (United Nations
Measures) Order 2006 (SI 2006/2952) . . . 131
s 3(1)(b) . . . 134
British Indian Ocean Territory (Constitution)
Order 2004, s 9 . . . 43
Civil Authorities (Special Powers) Act
(Northern Ireland) Regulations 1922
(SI 1922/35), reg 24A . . . 334
Civil Procedure Rules 1998 (SI 1998/
3132) . . . 568, 572, 588–90, 601
Pt 1 . . . 588, 590
r 1.1(2)(d) . . . 589
r 1.3 . . . 589
r 1.4(1)(e) . . . 589
Pt 7 . . . 588
Pt 8 . . . 588
Pt 24 . . . 588–9
Pt 30 . . . 574
Pt 34 . . . 583
Pt 45
rr 45.41–45.44 . . . 577
Practice Direction 45   577
Pt 54 . . . 497, 578, 583–4, 590
r 54.1(1) . . . 572
r 54.1(2) . . . 572
r 54.2 . . . 572
r 54.3(1) . . . 594
r 54.4 . . . 572, 583
r 54.5 . . . 584
r 54.5(1) . . . 572, 575
r 54.5(1)(a) . . . 584
r 54.5(2) . . . 572
r 54.5(3) . . . 572
r 54.5(4) . . . 572
r 54.5(5) . . . 572
r 54.5(5)–(6) . . . 575
r 54.5(6) . . . 572
rr 54.6–54.9 . . . 575
r 54.7(A) . . . 575
r 54.10(1) . . . 573
r 54.10(2) . . . 573
r 54.11 . . . 573
r 54.11A(1) . . . 573
r 54.11A(2) . . . 573
r 54.11A(3) . . . 573
r 54.11A(4) . . . 573
r 54.11A(5) . . . 573
r 54.12(1) . . . 573
r 54.12(2) . . . 573
r 54.12(3) . . . 573
r 54.12(4) . . . 573

r 54.12(5) . . . 573
r 54.12(6) . . . 573
r 54.12(7) . . . 573
r 54.13 . . . 574
r 54.14 . . . 575
r 54.14(1) . . . 574
r 54.15 . . . 574
r 54.16(1) . . . 574
r 54.16(2) . . . 574
r 54.17(1) . . . 574
r 54.17(2) . . . 574
r 54.18 . . . 574
r 54.19(1) . . . 574
r 54.19(2) . . . 574
r 54.20 . . . 574
rr 54.21–54.24 . . . 575
Practice Direction 54D . . . 580
para 1.1 . . . 578
para 1.2 . . . 578
para 2.1(1) . . . 578
para 2.1(2) . . . 579
para 2.2 . . . 579
para 3.1(1) . . . 579
para 3.1(2) . . . 579
para 3.1(3) . . . 579
para 3.1(4) . . . 579
para 3.1(5) . . . 579
para 3.1(6) . . . 579
para 3.2 . . . 579
para 4.1 . . . 579
para 4.2 . . . 579
para 5.1 . . . 579
para 5.2(1) . . . 579
para 5.2(2) . . . 579
para 5.2(3) . . . 579
para 5.2(4) . . . 579
para 5.2(5) . . . 579
para 5.2(6) . . . 579
para 5.2(7) . . . 579–80
para 5.2(8) . . . 580
para 5.2(9) . . . 580
para 5.2(10) . . . 580
para 5.3(1) . . . 580
para 5.3(2) . . . 580
para 5.3(3) . . . 580
para 5.4 . . . 580
para 5.5 . . . 580
para 5.6 . . . 580
Practice Direction 54E . . . 575
Pre-action Protocol for Judicial
Review . . . 578
para 1 . . . 575
para 2 . . . 575
para 3 . . . 575
para 5 . . . 575
para 6 . . . 575
para 7 . . . 576
para 8 . . . 576
para 9 . . . 576
para 10 . . . 576
para 11 . . . 576
para 12 . . . 576
para 13 . . . 576–7
para 14 . . . 577

para 15 . . . **577**
para 16 . . . **577**
para 17 . . . **577**
para 18 . . . **577**
para 20 . . . **577**
para 21 . . . **577**
para 22 . . . **577**
para 23 . . . **577–8**
para 24 . . . **578**
Commissioner for Complaints Order (Northern Ireland) 1996
Art 16(5) . . . 645
Art 17 . . . 645
Commissioner for Complaints Order (Northern Ireland) 1996 (SI 1996/1297 (N.I.)),
Art 16(2) . . . 645
Copyright (Regulation of Relevant Licensing Bodies) Regulations 2014 . . . 669
Defence (General) Regulations 1939
reg 55AB . . . 291
reg 98 . . . 291
Employment Tribunals (Constitution and Rules of Procedure) Regulations 2004 (SI 2004/1861)
reg 6(1) . . . 155
reg 8(1) . . . 155
reg 8(3a) . . . 155
Environmental Information Regulations (EIR) 2004 (SI 2004/3391) . . . 268
Equal Pay (Amendment) Regulations 1983 (SI 1983/1794), reg 2 . . . 448
Firearms (Northern Ireland) Order 2004 (SI 2004/702 (N.I.3))
Art 45(1) . . . 364
Art 45(2) . . . 364
Art 45(10) . . . 364
Foreign Compensation (Egypt) (Determination and Registration of Claims) Order 1962 (SI 1962/2187) . . . 501
Art 4 . . . **500**
Art 4(1)(b)(ii) . . . 501
Housing Benefits Amendment (No. 4) Regulations 1984 (SI 1984/65) . . . 283, 285
Housing Benefits Regulations 1985 (SI 1985/677) . . . 285
Iron and Steel Prices Order 1951 (SI 1951/252) . . . 290
Jobseeker's Allowance (Employment, Skills and Enterprise Scheme) Regulations 2011 (SI 2011/917) . . . 121–3
reg 2 . . . 122
reg 3(2) . . . 122
reg 4 . . . 122
Jobseeker's Allowance (Schemes for Assisting Persons to Obtain Employment) Regulations 2013 (SI 2013/276) . . . 122–3
reg 3(2) . . . 122
Judicial Appointments Commission Regulations 2013 (SI 2013/2191) . . . **155**
reg 3 . . . **155**
reg 4(1) . . . **155**
reg 4(2) . . . **155**
reg 4(3) . . . **155**
reg 4(4) . . . **155**

reg 4(5) . . . **155**
reg 5 . . . 156
reg 11 . . . 156
reg 17 . . . 156
reg 23 . . . 156
Judicial Discipline (Prescribed Procedures) Regulations (SI 2006/676) . . . 660
Merchant Shipping Act (Amendment) Order 1989 (SI 1989/2006) . . . 75
Merchant Shipping (Registration of Fishing Vessels) Regulations 1988 (SI 1988/1926) . . . 74
Microchipping of Dogs (England) Regulations 2015 (SI 2015/108) . . . 669
National Health Service (General Medical and Pharmaceutical Services) Regulations 1974 (SI 1974/160) . . . 585
Northern Ireland Act 1998 (Amendment of Schedule 3) Order 2010 (SI 2010/977) . . . 393–4
Northern Ireland Act 1998 (Devolution of Policing and Justice Functions) Order 2010 (SI 2010/976) . . . 393–4
Police (Appeals) Rules 1977 (SI 1977/759) . . . 603
Police (Discipline) Regulations 1977 (SI 1997/580) . . . 603–4
reg 7 . . . 603–4
Prison Rules 1964 (SI 1964/388) . . . 531
r 5(2) . . . 581
r 49 . . . 531
Public Bodies (Abolition of Administrative Justice and Tribunals Council) Order 2013 (SI 2013/2042) . . . 687
Public Contracts Regulations 2006 (SI 2006/5) . . . 572
reg 47D(2) . . . 572
Public Services Ombudsman (Wales) Act 2005 (Commencement No. 1 and Transitional Provisions and Savings) Order 2005 (SI 2005/2800) . . . 645
RAF Greenham Common Bye-laws 1985 (SI 1985/485) . . . 338, 340
Bye-law 2 . . . **339**
Bye-law 2(b) . . . 338, 340
Regulation of Investigatory Powers (Monetary Penalty Notices and Consents for Interceptions) Regulations 2011 (SI 2011/1340) . . . 669
Regulatory Reform (Collaboration etc. Between Ombudsmen) Reform Order 2007 (SI 2007/1889) . . . 610, 628–9
Rules of the Supreme Court (SI 1977/1955) . . . 582
Order 53 . . . 496, 568, 581–3, 588–90, 592, 594, 596–7
r 1(2) . . . 594
r 3 . . . 592
r 3(5) . . . 591–2
r 4 . . . 584
r 5(2)(A) . . . 588
r 9(5) . . . 582
Order 115 . . . 579
Rules of the Supreme Court (Amendment No. 4) 1980 (SI 1980/2000) . . . 568

Scotland Act 1998 (Modification
of Schedule 5) Order 2013 (SI 2013/
242) . . . 386
Statutory Instruments Regulations 1947
(SI 1948/1)
reg 5 . . . 290
regs 5–8 . . . 290
reg 6 . . . 290
regs 6–8 . . . 290
reg 7 . . . 290–2
reg 8 . . . 290
Supreme Court Fees (Amendment) Order 1996
(SI 1996/3191), Art 3 . . . 398
Supreme Court (Judicial Appointments)
Regulations 2013
(SI 2013/2193) . . . 154
reg 5 . . . 155
reg 11 . . . 155
Terrorism (United Nations Measures) Order
2006 (SI 2006/2657) . . . 131–2, 134
Tobacco and Related Products Regulations 2016
(SI 2016/507) . . . 257
Transfer of Functions of the Asylum and
Immigration Tribunal Order 2010 (SI 2010/
21) . . . 657
Tribunal Procedure Rules . . . 665
Welsh Language (Wales) Measure 2011
(Consequential Provisions) Order (SI 2016/
409) . . . 369

Codes

City Code on Take-overs and
Mergers . . . 594–5, 597
Civil Service Code . . . 243, 594, 630
Code of Practice on Consultation . . . 285–6
Code of Practice for Ministerial Appointments
to Public Bodies . . . 274
Constitutional Reform and Governance Act
2010, Codes of Conduct . . . 177
Ministerial Code . . . 148, 233
Ministerial Code 2005 . . . 259
Ministerial Code 2010 . . . 150, 224
Ministerial Code 2015 . . . 150, 224
Ministerial Code 2016 . . . 150, 205, 225,
228–9, 266
PACE Codes of Practice . . . 282

Australia

Constitution Act 1902 (NSW)
s 7A . . . 65–6
s 7A(6) . . . 66
Parliamentary Privileges Act 1987,
s 16(3) . . . 171

Barbados

Constitution . . . 373

Canada

Bill of Rights . . . 58
Charter of Rights and Freedoms 1982 . . . 411
Constitution . . . 62, 205–6

Ceylon

Constitution . . . 67

France

Constitution, 3rd, 4th and 5th
Republics . . . 30

Germany

Basic Law . . . 70
Art 2(1) . . . 70
Art 14 . . . 70

Hong Kong

Bill of Rights Ordinance 1991 . . . 412

Ireland

Constitution . . . 9

Jamaica

Indemnity Act . . . 120

New Zealand

Bill of Rights Act 1990 . . . 411, 447
s 6 . . . 444

Rhodesia

Unilateral Declaration of Independence . . . 62

United States of America

Bill of Rights . . . 18
Constitution . . . 1, 8–9, 18, 29–30, 51, 371, 412
First Amendment . . . 484
Declaration of Independence . . . 18

International

Aarhus Convention . . . 577–8
Anglo-Irish Agreement 1985 . . . 224
European Convention for the Protection of
Human Rights and Fundamental Freedoms
(ECHR) . . . 5, 33–4, 68, 84–5, 93, 95, 116,
120, 133–4, 167, 326, 337, 349, 355, 362, 366,
371, 377, 379–81, 396, 399–400, 406–8, 410–
14, 416, 424–5, 431–5, 444–9, 451, 453, 457,
460, 462–5, 467–8, 470, 473–4, 478, 480–2,
484, 493–5, 521, 546–7, 563–4, 566
Art 1 . . . **401**
Art 2 . . . 439–41, 608
Art 2(1) . . . **401**, 472
Art 2(2) . . . **401**
Arts 2–4 . . . 464
Arts 2–12 . . . 133, 416
Art 3 . . . 130–1, **401**, 440–1, 469, 608
Art 4 . . . 469
Art 4(1) . . . **401**
Art 4(2) . . . **401**
Art 4(3) . . . **401**
Art 5 . . . 337, 433
Art 5(1) . . . **402**
Art 5(2) . . . **402**
Art 5(3) . . . **402**
Art 5(4) . . . **402**
Art 5(5) . . . **402**, 419
Art 6 . . . 123, 144–5, 349, 406, 436, 448–9,
451, 455, 459, 461, 469, 472–3, 494
Art 6(1) . . . **402**, 457–8, 468, 472, 482, 584,
608, 686

Art 6(2) . . . **402**, 472, 487
Art 6(3) . . . **402**
Art 7 . . . 121
Art 7(1) . . . **403**
Art 7(2) . . . **403**
Art 8 . . . 119, 210, 432–3, 436, 439–41, 443,
  455, 466, 469, 473–6, 481, 485, 547, 554,
  571, 608
Art 8(1) . . . **403**, 480
Art 8(2) . . . 119, **403**, 474–5, 514
Arts 8–11 . . . 407, 410, 425, 464
Arts 8–12 . . . 406
Art 9 . . . 466, 469, 477
Art 9(1) . . . **403**
Art 9(2) . . . **403**
Art 10 . . . 34, 408, 425, 433, 437–40, 466,
  469, 478, 483–6, 488–90
Art 10(1) . . . **403**, 438–9, 482–3
Art 10(2) . . . **403**, 408–9, 438–41, 464,
  482–4, 486
Art 11 . . . 466, 469
Art 11(1) . . . **403**
Art 11(2) . . . **403**
Art 12 . . . **403**
Art 13 . . . **403**, 462, 608
Art 14 . . . 133, 337, **404**, 416, 427, 608
Art 15(1) . . . **404**
Art 15(2) . . . **404**
Art 15(3) . . . **404**
Art 16 . . . **404**
Arts 16–18 . . . 416
Art 17 . . . **404**, 440
Art 18 . . . **404**
Art 26 . . . 408, 416
Art 27(2) . . . 416
Art 31 . . . 416
Art 34 . . . 418
Art 41 . . . 419
Art 46 . . . 416
Art 50 . . . 408
Protocol 1
  Art 1 . . . 383, **404**, 561
  Arts 1–3 . . . 133, 416

Art 2 . . . **404**, 406, 421
Art 3 . . . **404**
Protocol 4 . . . 406
  Art 1 . . . **405**
  Art 2(1) . . . **405**
  Art 2(2) . . . **405**
  Art 2(3) . . . **405**
  Art 2(4) . . . **405**
  Art 3(1) . . . **405**
  Art 3(2) . . . **405**
  Art 4 . . . **405**
Protocol 6
  Art 1 . . . **405**, 406
  Arts 1–2 . . . 416
  Art 2 . . . **405**, 406
  Art 3 . . . **405**
  Art 4 . . . **405**
Protocol 7 . . . 406
  Art 1(1) . . . **405**
  Art 1(2) . . . **406**
  Art 2(1) . . . **406**
  Art 2(2) . . . **406**
  Art 3 . . . **406**
  Art 4(1) . . . **406**
  Art 4(2) . . . **406**
  Art 4(3) . . . **406**
  Art 5 . . . **406**
Protocol 11 . . . 400
Protocol 13 . . . 406
  Art 1 . . . 133
Protocol 14 . . . 401
Geneva Convention . . . 51
United Nations Charter . . . 131–2
  Art 103 . . . 132
United Nations Convention Against
  Torture and Other Cruel Inhuman or
  Degrading Treatment or Punishment
  (1987) Art 15 . . . 131
Universal Declaration of Human Rights . . . 399

TABLE OF EUROPEAN UNION LEGISLATION

Page references in **bold** *indicate the text is reproduced in full.*

Treaties and Conventions

EC Treaty
  Art 34 . . . 562
  Art 36 . . . 562–3
  Art 177 . . . 563
EEC Treaty . . . 69, 75, 447
  Art 5(2) . . . 69
  Art 7 . . . 69, 75
  Art 12 . . . 71
  Art 30 . . . 71
  Art 37 . . . 69
  Art 52 . . . 75
  Art 53 . . . 69
  Art 86 . . . 73
  Art 93 . . . 69
  Art 102 . . . 69
  Art 169 . . . 75
  Art 177 . . . 69
  Art 189(3) . . . 448
  Art 221 . . . 75
Maastricht Treaty *see* Treaty on
  European Union
Schengen acquis, Protocol (No. 19) . . . 98
Single European Act 1986 . . . 248, 282
Treaty of Amsterdam . . . 248
Treaty on European Union
  (TEU) . . . 68–9, 96–7
  Social Chapter . . . 223, 248
  Art 3 . . . 96
  Art 19 . . . 282
  Art 31(2) . . . 97
  Art 31(3) . . . 97
  Art 37(2) . . . 69
  Art 42(2) . . . 97
  Art 48(7) . . . 97
  Art 50 . . . 149, 192, 194–5, 212–13
  Art 50(1) . . . 192
  Art 50(3) . . . 192
  Protocol (No. 21) on the position of the
    United Kingdom and Ireland in respect of
    the area of freedom, security and justice
    Art 4 . . . 97
Treaty on the Functioning of the European
  Union (TFEU) . . . 68–9, 96–7
  Art 10(2) . . . 69
  Art 30 . . . 71

Art 34 . . . 71
Art 35 . . . 562
Art 36 . . . 562–3
Art 37 . . . 69
Art 48 . . . 97
Art 48(6) . . . 96–7
Art 49 . . . 75
Art 55 . . . 75
Art 82(3) . . . 97
Art 83(3) . . . 97
Art 86(1) . . . 98
Art 86(4) . . . 98
Art 102 . . . 73
Art 108 . . . 69
Art 117 . . . 69
Art 119 . . . 73
Art 140(3) . . . 98
Art 153(2) . . . 98
Art 157 . . . 73
Art 192(2) . . . 98
Art 258 . . . 75
Art 263 . . . 282
Art 264 . . . 282
Art 267 . . . 69, 563
Art 288 . . . 282
Art 296 . . . 282
Art 297 . . . 282
Art 312(2) . . . 98
Art 333(1) . . . 98
Art 333(2) . . . 98
Protocol (No. 21) on the position of the
  United Kingdom and Ireland in respect of
  the area of freedom, security and justice
  Art 4 . . . 97
Treaty of Lisbon . . . 68, 248, 251
Treaty of Nice . . . 248
Treaty of Rome *see* EEC Treaty

Directives

Directive 85/337/EEC (Environmental Impact
  Assessment) . . . 81–2
  Art 1(4) . . . 81
Directive 95/46/EC . . . 377
Directive 2001/42/EC . . . 81
Directive 2003/88/EC (Working time) . . . 669
Directive 2011/92/EU . . . 81

1

Constitutional Law in the United Kingdom

OVERVIEW

In this chapter we begin by introducing the idea of a constitution and then examine the key concepts of legitimacy, democracy, legal and political constitutionalism, the conditioning of power (via the principles of the separation of powers and responsible government), and the state.

SECTION 1: INTRODUCTION

Constitutional law is the law relating to the constitution. To study constitutional law we need to discover what a constitution is. There are many competing definitions. While many clubs, organizations, and other groupings have constitutions, our concern is with the constitutions of nation-states and, in particular, the constitution of the United Kingdom. Initially, we must consider whether the United Kingdom can even be said to have a constitution *at all*.

T. Paine, *Rights of Man* in *The Complete Works of Thomas Paine*
(1791), pp. 302–3

A constitution is not the act of a government, but of a people constituting a government, and a government without a constitution is power without right. ... A constitution is a thing antecedent to a government; and a government is only the creature of a constitution.

It was Paine's belief that England lacked a constitution, as he stated at p. 370 that 'the continual use of the word "constitution" in the English parliament shows there is none and the whole is merely a form of government without a constitution, and constituting itself with what power it pleases'. Paine admired, by contrast, the recent American Constitution.

C. H. McIlwain, *Constitutionalism Ancient and Modern*
(1947), pp. 8–10

... [T]he analysis Paine made of the early American constitution was remarkably acute. The significant points in that analysis are these:

That there is a fundamental difference between a people's government and that people's constitution, whether the government happens to be entrusted to a king or to a representative assembly.

That this constitution is 'antecedent' to the government.

That it defines the authority which the people commits to its government, and in so doing thereby limits it.

That any exercise of authority beyond these limits by any government is an exercise of 'power without right.'

That in any state in which the distinction is not actually observed between the constitution and the governent there is in reality no constitution, because the will of the government has no check upon it, and that state is in fact a despotism.

One thing alone Paine fails to make fully clear. If a government exercises some 'power without right,' it seems to be necessarily implied that the people have a corresponding right to resist. But is this a legal or is it only a political right? Is such resistance a legalized rebellion or merely an extralegal revolution? Or, further, is it possible to incorporate in the framework of the state itself some provision or institution by which a governmental act or command *ultra vires* may be declared to be such, and subjects therefore exempted from its operation and released from any legal obligation to observe or obey it? In short, can government be limited legally and effectively by any method short of force? To these questions Paine gives no clear answer. It might be assumed that forcible resistance to power without right must itself be legal and not revolutionary; but in every case there seems no recourse except to force of some kind.

The one conspicuous element lacking in Paine's construction therefore seems to be the element of judicial review. Writing when he did, and as he did, to justify an actual rebellion, it is perhaps not strange that he was thinking primarily of politics rather than of law, that the 'rights' he had in mind were the rights of man rather than the rights of the citizen, or that the sanction for these rights should be extra legal action rather than any constitutional check. Paine, like many idealists in a hurry, was probably impatient of the slowness of legal remedies for existing abuses. But others, who were more constitutionally minded than he, had begun to feel that any such remedies, to be truly effective, must ultimately have the sanction of law. Years before, Lord Camden had insisted that the principles of the law of nature must be incorporated in the British Constitution if they were to be observed, and that they actually were so incorporated. The necessary inference from such a principle as his is that the interpreters of law should be the ones to define the rights of individuals and to trace the bounds of legitimate government over them. The protection of rights became for him, and for all who thought as he did, the enforcement of 'constitutional limitations.'

■ QUESTION

What did Paine mean by 'antecedent'? Did he mean that the constitution must exist *prior in time* to the Government or that the principles of the constitution should be *superior in character*, and binding in authority, to the actions of government? If the former is correct, does the United Kingdom have a constitution? (See the following discussion.) If the latter is correct, could the United Kingdom ever have constitutional government? (See Chapter 2 on the Legislative Sovereignty of Parliament.)

NOTE: Paine expressed a concept of constitutions which involved 'the conscious formulation by a people of its fundamental law' (see McIlwain, earlier in this section at p. 1). This would find expression in a written document or documents. The alternative view sees a constitution not as a conscious creation but rather as an evolutionary consequence made up of 'substantive principles to be deduced from a nation's actual institutions and their development' (see McIlwain, *ibid.*). This could include an unwritten or uncodified constitution. This view was expressed by Bolingbroke.

Lord Bolingbroke, *A Dissertation upon Parties (1733–34)* in *The Works of Lord Bolingbroke*
(1841), II, p. 88

By constitution we mean, whenever we speak with propriety and exactness, that assemblage of laws, institutions and customs, derived from certain fixed principles of reason, directed to certain fixed objects of public good, that compose the general system according to which the community hath agreed to be governed. ... We call this a good government, when ... the whole administration of public affairs is wisely pursued, and with a strict conformity to the principles and objects of the constitution.

NOTE: It can be argued that, according to Bolingbroke's definition, the United Kingdom has a constitution, as there are laws, institutions, and customs which combine to create a system of government to which the community agrees or, at least, from which it does not appear to dissent. This is the traditional view of most constitutional lawyers. Constitutional theorists have further refined their analysis of constitutions, creating other points of comparison. For example, K. C. Wheare, *Modern Constitutions* (1966), chap. 2, proposed six classifications of constitutions: (1) written and unwritten; (2) rigid and flexible; (3) supreme and subordinate; (4) federal and unitary; (5) separated powers and fused powers; (6) republican and monarchical. If Wheare's definitions are applied to the United Kingdom, it may be said that there is an unwritten constitution in the sense that it is uncodified. There is no supreme or fundamental constitutional law, and the processes for changing the constitution are flexible. The state is formally unitary (power has been devolved to three constituent nations but could in principle be reclaimed: see Chapter 8; perhaps the better term is union state which can accommodate the asymmetrical devolution in the United Kingdom), and monarchical where powers are fused, there being a parliamentary Executive as opposed to a presidential Executive.

While most writers on the constitution are satisfied that, by comparison with the various definitions, the United Kingdom does have a constitution, some writers insist that there is no constitution.

F. F. Ridley, 'There is no British Constitution: A Dangerous Case of the Emperor's Clothes'

(1988) 41 *Parliamentary Affairs* 340, 340–3, 359–60

Having a constitution seems to be a matter of self-respect: no state is properly dressed without. Every democracy except Britain, New Zealand and (with qualifications) Israel seems to have a written constitution, plainly labelled. Not to be left out of the world of constitutional democracies, British writers define constitution in a way which appears to give us one too, even though there is no document to prove it. The argument is that a constitution need not be embodied in a single document or, indeed, wholly written. We say instead that a country's constitution is a body of rules—some laws, some conventions—which regulate its system of government. Such a definition does not, however, bridge the gap between Britain and the rest of the world by providing us with a substitute for a documentary constitution: it simply shifts the ground, by using the word in an entirely different way ...

Though there is broad agreement on the contents of such books on constitutional law, in the last resort it depends on what academic lawyers consider relevant—and a quick survey of standard textbooks will show that at the margins there are significant variations in what is brought into the orbit of the British 'constitution'. In the absence of legal criteria that distinguish constitutional law from other laws, the definition becomes so broad that it defines nothing at all. In the context of the British legal system, the term constitutional law is thus literally meaningless. Borrowing from political science for their definition of the British constitution, however, academic lawyers hardly even really address the question whether in legal, or indeed logical, terms Britain has a constitution at all.

Such accounts of the British 'constitution' are only superficially the result of the absence of a constitutional document. Because we feel uneasy about our difference from other democracies which do have labelled constitutions, we turn to what is now a peculiarly British usage of the word to prove that we are not really different at all. One purpose of this article is to show that Britain *is* different, and different in ways that are important politically as well as in law. It is to show that Britain does not really have a constitution at all, merely a system of government, even if some parts of it are more important to our democratic order than others or are treated (perhaps: were treated until Mrs Thatcher's time) with greater veneration. It may be embarrassing to explain that, as in the nursery tale, the Emperor has no clothes after all, that the constitutional attire his courtiers claim to see is empty words, but that is the essential of this article. Unless we face up to that fact, moreover, any discussion of how we can safeguard certain democratic arrangements that we regarded as part of the British 'constitution' in the past (e.g. the independence of local government) or entrench others (e.g. a Bill of Rights) against an 'elective dictatorship' will run into the sand ...

… [T]he term British constitution is near meaningless even as used by British writers. It is impossible to isolate parts of the system of government to which the label may authoritatively be attached. There is no test to discriminate between constitutional and less than constitutional elements since labelling has no defined consequence, unlike countries where constitutions are a higher form of law. If used descriptively, as Wheare and others suggest, it is simply a fancy-dress way of saying the British system of government and at best redundant. More dangerous, those who talk of a British constitution may mislead themselves into thinking that there are parts of the system to which a special sanctity attaches. But in that normative sense the term is equally meaningless. When significant parts of the system are reformed, we have no test to tell us whether the outcome is an improper breach of the constitutional order, a proper amendment, or whether the reformed institutions were not part of the 'constitution' at all. I may be told that this is an academic quibble since our democratic politicians know what is of constitutional significance in our way of government, approach such matters differently from other reforms, and are politically if not legally constrained. That, however, is not the case. Our system of government is being changed, with increasing disregard for tradition, the only unwritten rules to which one might appeal as 'constitutional' principles.

There is cause for concern about the muddled way we think about the British 'constitution'; there is even greater cause for concern about the political consequences of its nature. It is sometimes said that our 'constitution' is now under stress as major changes occur far more rapidly than before in its written and unwritten parts. Is this due to changing ideas about how the British system of government should be organised, widely held, or is it simply that the government of the day is using its power to change the system in the pursuit of its own political goals? Is the constitutional order evolving or is it under attack? We have moved from consensus to conflict in politics: have we moved in that direction, too, as regards our constitutional order, taking that to mean the broad principles underlying the way government is organised and power exercised? Many old principles no longer command universal agreement and there are well-supported demands for new principles. We have had debates on the entrenchment of rights; on federalism or regional devolution as against the unitary state; on the case for consensus rather than majority as a basis for government, on the relative weight of national versus local mandates and the independence of local government; on the duty of civil servants; on electoral reform with all its implications for the operations of government; on who should define the national interest; on open government and official secrecy; on complementing representative democracy by referenda and other forms of participation—and much else. Political disagreement and disagreement on the proper constitutional order are linked. An ideologically-committed government, determined to implement its policies, will support different constitutional principles from those who want consensus policy-making; those concerned primarily with individual freedom and the rights of the public will support different principles from those who want strong government—and so on. Since opinion is now deeply divided on so many issues, one can probably no longer talk of the constitutional order as if it were a reflection of public opinion.

There are no grounds for complacency about British democracy.

NOTE: In the extract which follows, Brazier makes the important point that the British constitution is largely written but remains uncodified.

R. Brazier, 'How Near is a Written Constitution?'
(2001) 52 *Northern Ireland Legal Quarterly* 1, 3–5

As every schoolchild is supposed to know, the United Kingdom does not have a written constitution. A British citizen has to seek the rules of the constitution in a daunting number of places—legislation, judicial decisions, statements about constitutional conventions, the law and practice of Parliament, European Community law, and so on. It is hardly surprising that the interested citizen will normally leave those sources to one side and rely instead on books written by authoritative writers, and those who aspire to be authoritative. But just listing the primary materials which form the constitution demonstrates the extent to which the British constitution is largely a written one. Indeed, all the sources exist as official statements made by organs of the state, except for conventions, most of which have been reduced to writing only by the unofficial efforts of constitutional commentators. The British constitution is written, but it is not codified into a single official document, or limited number of such documents, setting out those legal rules which prescribe how the state is to be governed.

In implementing its range of reforms the Labour Government has caused Parliament to enact an additional and substantial corpus of statute law of a constitutional character. While, therefore, the United Kingdom still lacks a codified constitution, it has been given rather more of a written constitution by the addition of sixteen Acts of Parliament which, in whole or in part, add to the British constitution. Perhaps most importantly towards that end, the United Kingdom now has the kind of Bill of Rights which features prominently in so many national constitutions, supplied by the Human Rights Act 1998. The lacuna which had existed in the enforcement of civil rights has now been filled. The devolution statutes have answered—at least for the time being—many long-standing queries about the appropriate relationships between the various parts of Great Britain, and with luck of the United Kingdom, and have redefined the juridical balance between them; the composition of the national legislature has been radically altered by the House of Lords Act 1999; and so on. There has been an exponential growth in the body of constitutional statute law since 1997, and because statute overrides case law and convention in the constitutional order the new laws represent some of the ground work which would be required for the production of a codified constitution. When it was still in opposition the Labour Party recognized that its legislative programme would have that effect in the narrower sense of the phrase constitution-making. In what was then its main constitutional policy document, *A New Agenda for Democracy*, adopted four years before coming to power, the party claimed that its changes would be a significant step in the direction of a written constitution, and the paper stated that the party would leave open the question of whether at a later stage progress should be made towards formal codification. Now that statement needs to be put into context. On the one hand, it was the first move—however tentative—by either of the two big political parties towards the idea of constitutional codification. On the other hand the statement did not really take account of all the other areas of the constitution which Labour's proposed changes would not affect but which would have to be reassessed and considered for inclusion in any constitutional code. For even after Labour's current reform programme has been fully implemented it would leave vital matters untouched, such as the monarchy, prerogative powers enjoyed by ministers, the powers of the House of Commons, and the judicial system. Clearly, too, that statement in the policy paper was over-terse, in that it ignored other important matters which would be crucial in any codification exercise, such as how and by whom it would be undertaken. Nor did the comments about codification find any place in Labour's 1997 General Election manifesto.

NOTES

1. The list given by Brazier would now need to be supplemented. Statutes which might be added include the Freedom of Information Act 2000, the Constitutional Reform Act 2005, the Constitutional Reform and Governance Act 2010, the Parliamentary Voting System and Constituencies Act 2011, the Fixed-term Parliaments Act 2011, the Succession to the Crown Act 2013, the House of Lords Reform Act 2014, the Recall of MPs Act 2015, and the Cities and Local Government Devolution Act 2016.

2. This is clear evidence that the UK constitution is changing significantly, and at a rapid pace. In 'Our Constitutional Unsettlement' [2014] *Public Law* 529–48, Walker describes the UK as experiencing a constitutional unsettlement that may be 'here to stay for the unforeseeable future', p. 542:

> The idea of a constitutional unsettlement emerges from a sense that each of the alternatives for the British constitution—the settled constitution, the temporarily unsettled constitution, and the new Constitutional settlement, are either unavailable or increasingly remote in prospect.

In such circumstances, achieving agreement as to the core components of the UK constitution may become even more challenging. Yet as Walker notes, there may be virtue in the fluidity of constitutional unsettlement, and its ability to accommodate a diverse range of perspectives on the constitution openly and simultaneously.

3. The House of Lords Select Committee on the Constitution has the following terms of reference:

> To examine the constitutional implications of all public bills coming before the House; and to keep under review the operation of the constitution.

One of the first problems the Committee faced was to determine what the constitution was. It sought to address this question in its First Report.

Select Committee on the Constitution, *Reviewing the Constitution:*
Terms of Reference and Method of Working
HL 11 of 2001–02, paras 17–21

17. ... [T]he Committee could, if we so wished, look at any of a wide range of topics within our terms of reference. A glance at the contents page of any book on constitutional matters reveals the wide range of possible headings:

- Government
- the Royal Prerogative
- Parliament
- the Judiciary and judicial review
- the constitutional position of the Civil Service
- citizenship
- personal freedoms, liberties and free speech
- the EU
- devolution
- referendums
- electoral reform.

18. Many books have been written on, and many attempts have been made to consider, these and other topics which are thought to form the constitution of the United Kingdom. The constitution is said to be in flux, and the sense of what it is constantly evolving. The constitution is uncodified and although it is in part written there is no single, accepted and agreed list of statutes which form that part of the constitution which is indeed written down. While we would not wish, nor would we have the time, to write another such book ourselves, we nevertheless agreed that there was need to set for ourselves some kind of definition of what issues might fall within our remit. We do not see this as a dry academic exercise: our primary motive in doing so is as the first stage in determining which constitutional issues are in fact significant. There are many issues that are politically important both to individuals in the House and outside, and there are many issues which are matters of public debate. We would not wish to become a parliamentary magnet to which issues were attracted merely because the label 'constitutional' was attached to them by those who thought them important. A definitional exercise will, in our view, both help us to determine which issues are indeed of significance, and therefore form topics for our consideration, and assist us in working out the boundaries of our work in terms of overlap with that of other committees.

19. We accordingly asked all our witnesses what their definition was of the constitution. We are very grateful to those who responded and also to those who gave good reasons for not supplying a definition as such. We are very conscious that, given everything said in the preceding paragraphs, this was indeed something of a trick question. Lord Alexander of Weedon told us 'it is of the essence of our constitution that it is constitutional issues as they evolve. That seems to me largely to defy any attempt at a rigid definition' (Q 23). The Leader of the House, Baroness Jay of Paddington, said that it was 'quite difficult to formulate a specific definition' but that the Government understood what was meant by the specifics of constitutional reform and that they did constitute a constitutional package (Q 175). Lord Strathclyde, Leader of the Conservative Peers offered us 'anything that affects the way we are

governed, the balance between the different powers of Parliament and its associated repositories of powers. It is about the authorities under which we are governed' (Q 128). Lord Rodgers of Quarry Bank, Leader of the Liberal Democrat Peers, offered us 'the political and administrative structure, whether based on statute or convention, by which we are governed' (Q 63). Lord Craig of Radley, Convenor of the Cross Bench Peers, while not claiming to have any instant answer, referred to power, the exercise of power and the sharing of the exercising of power, a need for 'some form of checking balance' and 'a form of consensus or as near consensus as is reasonable to expect to be able to go ahead'. He referred to the balance between the various elements exercising authority and power (Q 154). Tony Wright MP, Chairman of the Commons Public Administration Committee, suggested that 'the constitution is ... whatever it is at any one time and we make it up as we go along ... it is something to do with the relationship between citizens and the state and between the different parts of the state' (QQ 89, 91).

20. Against the background of these very helpful comments, which serve not least to illustrate the difficulties of any attempt to define a constitution we offer as our own working definition: 'the set of laws, rules and practices that create the basic institutions of the state, and its component and related parts, and stipulate the powers of those institutions and the relationship between the different institutions and between those institutions and the individual.'

21. We offer the following as the five basic tenets of the United Kingdom Constitution (phrases in italics indicate subjects falling within the remit of other parliamentary committees ...):

- Sovereignty of the Crown in Parliament
- The Rule of Law, encompassing *the rights of the individual*
- Union State
- Representative Government
- Membership of the Commonwealth, *the European Union*, and other international organisations.

■ QUESTIONS

1. Does the provision of a list of tenets of the constitution amount to a definition of the constitution?
2. Is there any truth in the following statement by Sidney Low, in *The Governance of England* (1904), p. 12: 'British government is based upon a system of tacit understandings. But the understandings are not always understood'?
3. Colin Munro, *Studies in Constitutional Law* (1999), p. 3, states:

> The true distinction ... is between states where some of the more important constitutional rules have been put in a document, or a set of associated documents, given special recognition, and states where the constitution has many sources, none of which enjoys such recognition.

Is this an adequate explanation, or does the sanctity accorded to a constitution serve other purposes such as placing restraints on the exercise of power by government, or providing a statement of the rules of symbolic importance to citizens?
4. Is there any inherent virtue in a system of government derived from a constitution, which is lacking in a country which does not have such a codified constitution? Indeed, why are constitutions enacted? See Wheare, in the following extract.

K. C. Wheare, *Modern Constitutions*
(1966), pp. 4–8

[W]hat a Constitution says is one thing, and what actually happens in practice may be quite another. We must take account of this possible difference in considering the form and worth of Constitutions. What is more, we must be ready to admit that although almost all countries in the world have a Constitution, in many of them the Constitution is treated with neglect or contempt. Indeed in the middle of the twentieth century it can be said that the majority of the world's population lives under systems of government where the government itself and particularly the executive government are of more importance and are treated with more respect or fear than the Constitution. It is only in the states of Western Europe, in the countries of the British Commonwealth, in the United States of America, and in a few Latin-American states that government is carried on with due regard to the limitations imposed by a Constitution; it is only in these states that truly 'constitutional government' can be said to exist. ...

Since the Constitution of a country is only a part of that country's whole system of government, does it make any difference whether a country has a Constitution or not? The short answer is that in many countries the fact that there is a Constitution does make a difference. This brings to light a characteristic which most Constitutions exhibit. They are usually endowed with a higher status, in some degree, as a matter of law, than other legal rules in the system of government. At the least it is usually laid down that the amendment of the Constitution can take place only through a special process different from that by which the ordinary law is altered. ...

It is natural to ask ... why it is that countries have Constitutions, why most of them make the Constitution superior to the ordinary law, and, further, why Britain, at any rate, has no Constitution, in this sense, at all.

If we investigate the origins of modern Constitutions, we find that, practically without exception, they were drawn up and adopted because people wished to make a fresh start, so far as the statement of their system of government was concerned. The desire or need for a fresh start arose either because, as in the United States, some neighbouring communities wished to unite together under a new government; or because, as in Austria or Hungary or Czechoslovakia after 1918, communities had been released from an Empire as the result of a war and were now free to govern themselves; or because, as in France in 1789 or the U.S.S.R. in 1917, a revolution had made a break with the past and a new form of government on new principles was desired; or because, as in Germany after 1918 or in France in 1875 or in 1946, defeat in war had broken the continuity of government and a fresh start was needed after the war. The circumstances in which a break with the past and the need for a fresh start come about vary from country to country, but in almost every case in modern times, countries have a Constitution for the very simple and elementary reason that they wanted, for some reason, to begin again and so they put down in writing the main outline, at least, of their proposed system of government. This has been the practice certainly since 1787 when the American Constitution was drafted, and as the years passed no doubt imitation and the force of example have led all countries to think it necessary to have a Constitution.

This does not explain, however, why many countries think it necessary to give the Constitution a higher status in law than other rules of law. The short explanation of this phenomenon is that in many countries a Constitution is thought of as an instrument by which government can be controlled. Constitutions spring from a belief in limited government. Countries differ however in the extent to which they wish to impose limitations. Sometimes the Constitution limits the executive or subordinate local bodies; sometimes it limits the legislature also, but only so far as amendment of the Constitution itself is concerned; and sometimes it imposes restrictions upon the legislature which go far beyond this point and forbid it to make laws upon certain subjects or in a certain way or with certain effects. Whatever the nature and extent of the restrictions, however, they are based upon a common belief in limited government and in the use of a Constitution to impose these limitations.

The nature of the limitations to be imposed on a government, and therefore the degree to which a Constitution will be supreme over a government, depends upon the objects which the framers of the Constitution wish to safeguard. In the first place they may want to do no more than ensure that the Constitution is not altered casually or carelessly or by subterfuge or implication; they may want to secure that this important document is not lightly tampered with, but solemnly, with due notice and deliberation, consciously amended. In that case it is legitimate to require some special process of constitutional amendment—say that the legislature may amend the Constitution only by a two-thirds majority or after a general election or perhaps upon three months' notice.

The framers of Constitutions often have more than this in mind. They may feel that a certain kind of relationship between the legislature and the executive is important; or that the judicature should have a certain guaranteed degree of independence of the legislature and executive. They may feel that there are certain rights which citizens have and which the legislature or the executive must not invade or remove. They may feel that certain laws should not be made at all. …

In some countries only one of the considerations mentioned above may operate, in others some, and in some, all. Thus, in the Irish Constitution, the framers were anxious that amendment should be a deliberate process, that the rights of citizens should be safeguarded, and that certain types of laws should not be passed at all, and therefore they made the Constitution supreme and imposed restrictions upon the legislature to achieve these ends. The framers of the American Constitution also had these objects in mind, but on top of that they had to provide for the desire of the thirteen colonies to be united for some purposes only and to remain independent for others. This was an additional reason for giving supremacy to the Constitution and for introducing certain extra safeguards into it.

NOTE: As Wheare recognizes, the framers of a constitution may have particular aims in mind. Constitutions may serve different functions in different countries or even within the same country at different times and, as the following extract from Murphy demonstrates, constitutions may therefore play a role which is positive or negative (or both).

W. F. Murphy, 'Constitutions, Constitutionalism and Democracy' in D. Greenberg, S. N. Katz, M. B. Oliviero, and S. C. Wheatley (eds), *Constitutionalism and Democracy* (1993), pp. 8–10

What Are the Functions of a Constitution?

A Constitution as Sham, Cosmetic, or Reality. The principal function of a sham constitutional text is to deceive. Lest US citizens revel in righteousness, they might recall that Charles A. Beard charged the framers of the US text with hypocrisy, and the Conference of Critical Legal Studies still so accuses the entire American legal system. Whether Beard and the Critics have told the full story, they have reminded us that a constitutional document's representation of itself, its people, their values, and decisional processes is imperfect. Thus, even reasonably authoritative texts play a cosmetic role, allowing a nation to hide its failures behind idealistic rhetoric. But, insofar as a text is authoritative, its rhetoric also pushes a people to renew their better selves.

A Constitution as a Charter for Government. At minimum, an authoritative constitutional text must sketch the fundamental modes of legitimate governmental operations: who its officials are, how they are chosen, what their terms of office are, how authority is divided among them, what processes they must follow, and what rights, if any, are reserved to citizens. Such a text need not proclaim any substantive values, beyond obedience to itself; if it does proclaim values, they might be those of Naziism or Stalinism, anathema to constitutional democracy.

A Constitution as Guardian of Fundamental Rights. Thus the question immediately arises about the extent to which a constitutional text relies on or incorporates democratic and/or constitutional theories. Insofar as a text is authoritative and embodies democratic theory, it must protect rights to political participation. Insofar as it is authoritative and embodies constitutionalism, it must protect substantive rights by limiting the power of the people's freely chosen representatives.

The Constitution as Covenant, Symbol, and Aspiration. Insofar as a constitution is a covenant by which a group of people agree to (re)transform themselves into a nation, it may function for the founding generation like a marriage consummated through the pledging partners' positive, active consent to remain a nation for better or worse, through prosperity and poverty, in peace and war.

For later generations, a constitution may operate more as an arranged marriage in which consent is passive, for the degree of choice is then typically limited. Even where expatriation is a recognized right, exit from a society offers few citizens a viable alternative. Revolution becomes a legal right only if it succeeds and transforms revolutionaries into founders. And deeply reaching reform from within a constitutional framework tends to become progressively more difficult, for a system usually endures only by binding many groups to its terms.

The myth of a people's forming themselves into a nation presents a problem not unlike that between chicken and egg. To agree in their collective name to a political covenant, individuals must have already had some meaningful corporate identity *as a people*. Thus the notion of constitution as covenant must mean it formalizes or solidifies rather than invents an entity: it solemnizes a previous alliance into a more perfect union.

A constitution's formative force varies from country to country and time to time. The French, one can plausibly argue, have been the French under monarchies, military dictatorships, and assorted republics. It is also plausible, however, to contend that Germans have been a different people under the Kaiser, the Weimar Republic, the Third Reich, and the Federal Republic. In polyglotted societies such as Canada, India, and the United States or those riven by religious divisions and bleeding memories of civil war such as Ireland, 'there may be no other basis for uniting a nation of so many disparate groups.' A constitution may thus function as a uniting force, 'the only principle of order', for there may be 'no [other] shared moral or social vision that might bind together a nation.' [Sanford Levinson, *Constitutional Faith* (1988) p. 73.] It is difficult to imagine what has united the supposedly United States more than the political ideas of the Declaration of Independence and the text of 1787.

Reverence for the constitution may transform it into a holy symbol of the people themselves. The creature they created can become their own mythical creator. This symbolism might turn a constitutional text into a semisacred covenant, serving 'the unifying function of a civil religion.' [T. Grey, 'The Constitution as Scripture' (1984) 37 *Stanford Law Review* 1, 18.] In America, 'The Bible of verbal inspiration begat the constitution of unquestioned authority.'

Religious allusions remind us, however, that this symbolic role may also have a dark side. Long histories of bitter and often murderous struggles among Christians and among Muslims demonstrate that a sacred text may foster division rather than cohesion, conflict rather than harmony. The 'potential of a written constitution to serve as the source of fragmentation and disintegration' [Levinson] is nowhere more savagely illustrated than in the carnage of the US Civil War. For, ultimately, that fratricidal struggle was over two visions of one constitutional document. The result was a gory war that wiped out more than 600,000 lives. Complicating analysis is the fact that when the blood of battle dried, the document of 1787, duly amended, resumed its unifying role.

In a related fashion, a constitution may serve as a binding statement of a people's aspirations for themselves as a nation. A text may silhouette the sort of community its authors/subjects are or would like to become: not only their governmental structures, procedures, and basic rights, but also their goals, ideals, and the moral standards by which they want others, including their own posterity, to judge the community. In short, a constitutional text may guide as well as express a people's hopes for themselves as a society. The ideals the words enshrine, the processes they describe, and the actions they legitimize must either help to change the citizenry or at least reflect their current values. If a constitutional text is not 'congruent with' ideals that form or will reform its people and so express the political character they have or are willing to try to put on, it will quickly fade.

NOTE: The form that a constitution takes will not definitively determine whether it is a good or effective constitution. Both codified and uncodified constitutions may be problematic to varying extents. Perhaps more important, then, is whether a constitution can be said to be legitimate.

SECTION 2: LEGITIMACY

Why, following a revolution, does a government which has effective power backed up with military force, seek to make a constitution? Friedrich, in *Limited Government: A Comparison*, p. 118, states that such a response is 'motivated by the belief that such a constitution, if popularly approved, would give them the right to rule, over and above the mere power to do so'. If a government has the right to rule it is regarded as legitimate, and this, in turn, provides it with authority. Legitimacy, therefore, is a quality which is valuable to government.

S. E. Finer, *Comparative Government*
(1970), pp. 30–1

The stable and effective exercise of a government's power is that which derives from its authority. By this I mean that the commands to do or to abstain proceed from persons who—no matter whether this is logical or reasonable or justifiable by any objective criterion—are *believed* to be persons who have the moral right to issue them: so that, correlatively, those to whom the commands are addressed feel a moral *duty* to *obey* them. Authority represents a two-way process: a claim to be obeyed, and a recognition that this claim is morally right. No public recognition of a claim means no authority.

Where a population recognizes a moral duty to obey, there is no need for the government to reason with it, persuade it, bribe it or threaten it, though all these exercises of power may be necessary for the marginal recalcitrants. The mere recognition of a duty to obey achieves for the government what an overwhelming application of violence would not satisfactorily achieve. As Rousseau said: 'The strongest is never strong enough unless he succeeds in turning might into right and obedience into duty.' As human nature goes, fear is certainly the father of power, but authority is its mother. To inculcate the population with the belief that their rulers have the right to demand obedience and they the corresponding duty to give it is the principal art of government.

■ QUESTION

What, then, is legitimacy, and how is it acquired? There may be a number of different elements to this concept.

D. Beetham, *The Legitimation of Power*
(1991), pp. 11–12, 15–20, 25–7, and 34–6

The different dimensions of legitimacy

The key to understanding the concept of legitimacy lies in the recognition that it is multi-dimensional in character. It embodies three distinct elements or levels, which are qualitatively different from one another. Power can be said to be legitimate to the extent that:

(i) it conforms to established rules
(ii) the rules can be justified by reference to beliefs shared by both dominant and subordinate, and
(iii) there is evidence of consent by the subordinate to the particular power relation. ...

(i) The first and most basic level of legitimacy is that of rules ... Power can be said to be legitimate in the first instance if it is acquired and exercised in accordance with established rules. For convenience I shall call the rules governing the acquisition and exercise of power the 'rules of power'. These rules may be unwritten, as informal conventions, or they may be formalised in legal codes or judgments. ...

The opposite of legitimacy according to the rules is, simply, *illegitimacy*; power is illegitimate where it is either acquired in contravention of the rules (expropriation, usurpation, coup d'état), or exercised in a manner that contravenes or exceeds them. The illegal acquisition of power usually has more profound, because more all-pervasive, consequences for legitimacy than some breach or contravention in its exercise, though that depends upon the seriousness of the breach, and whether it is repeated. Where the rules of power are continually broken, we could speak of a condition of chronic illegitimacy.

(ii) On its own, legal validity is insufficient to secure legitimacy, since the rules through which power is acquired and exercised themselves stand in need of justification. This is the second level of legitimacy: power is legitimate to the extent that the rules of power can be justified in terms of beliefs shared by both dominant and subordinate. What kinds of justification and what kinds of belief are needed? To be justified, power has to be derived from a valid source of authority (this is particularly true of political power); the rules must provide that those who come to hold power have the qualities appropriate to its exercise; and the structure of power must be seen to serve a recognisably general interest, rather than simply the interests of the powerful. These justifications in turn depend upon beliefs current in a given society about what is the rightful source of authority; about what qualities are appropriate to the exercise of power and how individuals come to possess them; and some conception of a common interest, reciprocal benefit, or societal need that the system of power satisfies.

No society is characterised by a complete uniformity of beliefs. Indeed, one of the distinctive features of power relations is the difference of circumstances, opportunities and values between dominant and subordinate groups. Yet without a minimum of the appropriate beliefs defined above being shared between the dominant and the subordinate, and indeed among the subordinate themselves, there can be no basis on which justifications for the rules of power can find a purchase. Naturally what counts as an adequate or sufficient justification will be more open to dispute than what is legally valid, and there is no ultimate authority to settle such questions; nevertheless clear limits are set by logic and the beliefs of a given society to what justifications are plausible or credible within it.

This second level or dimension of legitimacy has its corresponding negative or opposite. Rules of power will lack legitimacy to the extent that they cannot be justified in terms of shared beliefs: either because no basis of shared belief exists in the first place (e.g. slavery, 'artificial' or divided communities); or because changes in belief have deprived the rules of their supporting basis (e.g. hereditary rule or male power, in face of a declining belief in the superior qualities supposedly ascribed by birth or sex); or because changing circumstances have made existing justifications for the rules implausible, despite beliefs remaining constant. [For example] it is argued that the British electoral system, with its first-past-the-post rules determining who shall be elected in each constituency, is losing its legitimacy, and to an extent therefore also weakening that of the governments elected under it. This is not because of any shift in people's beliefs, but because the rules have increasingly delivered results that diverge, both regionally and nationally, from the proportion of votes cast, and hence from accepted notions about the representative purpose of elections in a democracy. It is the increasingly unrepresentative character of the electoral system, and its consequent vulnerability to attack in a society that believes in representation, that is the basis for the weakening legitimacy of governments appointed under it. The vulnerability was there before it was exploited, and the weakening of legitimacy took place before people publicly acknowledged it. It may have taken the poll-tax legislation to bring the issue to the forefront of public attention. But the potential for doing so was already present in the growing discrepancy between the rules and the beliefs or values underpinning them. ...

These different situations clearly have widely differing significance, but they can all be described as examples, not so much of illegitimacy, as of *legitimacy deficit* or weakness.

(iii) The third level of legitimacy involves the demonstrable expression of consent on the part of the subordinate to the particular power relation in which they are involved, through actions which provide evidence of consent. ... [T]he importance of actions such as concluding agreements with a superior, swearing allegiance, or taking part in an election, is the contribution they make *to* legitimacy. They do this in two ways. The first is that they have a subjectively binding force for those who have taken part in them, regardless of the motives for which they have done so. Actions expressive of consent, even if undertaken purely out of self-interest, will introduce a moral component into a relationship, and create a normative commitment on the part of those engaging in them. Secondly, such actions have a publicly symbolic or declaratory force, in that they constitute an express acknowledgement on the part of the subordinate of the position of the powerful, which the latter are able to use as confirmation of their legitimacy to third parties not involved in the relationship, or those who have not taken part in any expressions of consent. They are thus often associated with impressive forms of ceremonial. ...

What is common to legitimate power everywhere ... is the need to 'bind in' ... the subordinate, through actions or ceremonies publicly expressive of consent, so as to establish or reinforce their obligation to a superior authority, and to demonstrate to a wider audience the legitimacy of the powerful.

It is in the sense of the public actions of the subordinate, expressive of consent, that we can properly talk about the 'legitimation' of power, not the propaganda or public relations campaigns, the 'legitimations' generated by the powerful themselves. And if the public expression of consent contributes to the legitimacy of the powerful, then the withdrawal or refusal of consent will by the same token detract from it. Actions ranging from non-cooperation and passive resistance to open disobedience and militant opposition on the part of those qualified to give consent will in different measure erode legitimacy, and the larger the numbers involved, the greater this erosion will be. At this level, the opposite or negative of legitimacy can be called *delegitimation*.

For power to be fully legitimate, then, three conditions are required: its conformity to established rules; the justifiability of the rules by reference to shared beliefs; the express consent of the subordinate, or of the most significant among them, to the particular relations of power. All three components contribute to legitimacy, though the extent to which they are realised in a given context will be a matter of degree. Legitimacy is not an all-or-nothing affair. … Every power relation knows its breaches of the rules or conventions; in any society there will be some people who do not accept the norms underpinning the rules of power, and some who refuse to express their consent, or who do so only under manifest duress. What matters is how widespread these deviations are, and how substantial in relation to the underlying norms and conventions that determine the legitimacy of power in a given context. Legitimacy may be eroded, contested or incomplete; and judgements about it are usually judgements of degree, rather than all-or-nothing.

Above all, the analysis I have given above demonstrates that legitimacy is not a single quality that systems of power possess or not, but a set of distinct criteria, or multiple dimensions, operating at different levels, each of which provides moral grounds for compliance or cooperation on the part of those subordinate to a given power relation. By the same token, power can be non-legitimate in very different ways, which I have signalled by the different terms: illegitimacy, legitimacy deficit and delegitimation. The erosion of justificatory norms, slavery, conquest, dictatorship, coup d'état, separatist agitation, revolutionary mobilisation—all are examples where power lacks some element of legitimacy, but does so in very different ways. The accompanying diagram summarises in tabular form the different dimensions of legitimate and non-legitimate power that I have distinguished, to reinforce the argument of the text.

Table 1.1 The three dimensions of legitimacy

Criteria of Legitimacy	Form of Non-legitimate Power
i conformity to rules (legal validity)	illegitimacy (breach of rules)
ii justifiability of rules in terms of shared beliefs	legitimacy deficit (discrepancy between rules and supporting beliefs, absence of shared beliefs)
iii legitimation through expressed consent	delegitimation (withdrawal of consent)

The significance of legitimacy

Legitimacy, as we have seen, comprises the moral or normative aspect of power relationships; or, more correctly, the sum of these aspects. …

To consider first the behaviour of those subordinate within a power relationship; its legitimacy provides them with moral grounds for cooperation and obedience. Legitimate power or authority has the right to expect obedience from subordinates, even where they may disagree with the content of a particular law or instruction; and subordinates have a corresponding obligation to obey. This obligation is not absolute—hence the dilemmas that occur when people are required by a legitimate superior to do things that are morally objectionable to them, as opposed to inconvenient or merely stupid. But it is the right that legitimacy gives those in authority to require obedience in principle, regardless of the content of any particular law or instruction, that makes it so important to the coordination of people's behaviour in all spheres of social life.

The legitimacy or rightfulness of power, then, provides an explanation for obedience through the obligation it imposes on people to obey, and through the *grounds or reasons* it gives for their obedience.

However, normative grounds or reasons are not the only reasons people have for obedience. ...

[P]ower relations are almost always constituted by a framework of incentives and sanctions, implicit if not always explicit, which align the behaviour of the subordinate with the wishes of the powerful. They do so by giving people good reasons of a different kind, those of self-interest or prudence, for not stepping out of line. Obedience is therefore to be explained by a complex of reasons, moral as well as prudential, normative as well as self-interested, that legitimate power provides for those who are subject to it. This complexity may make it difficult to determine the precise balance of reasons in any one situation; but it is important to distinguish them analytically, since each makes a very different kind of contribution to obedience.

■ QUESTION

If a government, using its majority in Parliament, passes appropriate laws empowering it to do specified acts, are its activities thereby rendered legitimate because they are done in accordance with the law, regardless of how oppressive or repugnant those laws might be? See Chapter 3 and also the following extract, drawing a distinction between the lawfulness and the legitimacy of official conduct.

P. McAuslan and J. F. McEldowney, 'Legitimacy and the Constitution: the Dissonance between Theory and Practice' in P. McAuslan and J. F. McEldowney (eds), *Law, Legitimacy and the Constitution*

(1985), pp. 11–14

Legitimacy ... does not deal so much with whether activities of government are lawful as whether they accord with what are generally perceived to be or what have for long been held up to be, the fundamental principles of the constitution according to which government is or ought to be conducted. Lawfulness is clearly an issue in so far as one of the fundamental principles of the British, no less than most other constitutions, is that government action should take place under the authority of, and in accordance with law—the narrow literal meaning of the rule of law—so that repeated unlawful actions or a perceived casualness towards the duty to comply with the law would in itself begin to raise doubts about the legitimacy of governmental action. The rule of law is generally thought to have a broader 'political' meaning which covers the same ground as, if it is not quite synonymous with, the concept of limited government. This meaning embraces such matters as fair and equitable administrative practices; recognition of the rights of political opposition and dissent; complying with constitutional conventions; adequate means of redress of grievances about governmental action affecting one. Thus a government which while adhering to the rule of law narrowly defined, flouted all or most of the practices generally thought to be covered by the rule of law broadly defined would also give rise to doubts about its legitimacy. One of the clearest and best examples of a government on the whole scrupulous to comply with the rule of law narrowly defined yet consistently flouting it, as to the majority of its citizens, when broadly defined is the government of the Republic of South Africa, in relation to its non-white citizens.

What makes the issue of the legitimacy of our constitutional arrangements so problematic is the general open-endedness of those arrangements; that is, the difficulty of knowing whether a practice or non-practice is or is not constitutional.

Even where practices may not differ over time, or place, there may be an inconsistency about them or a lack of knowledge about them, or a long-standing dispute about them, which could make it equally difficult to argue that following or not following a practice was or was not constitutional or legitimate. Probably the best example of this is the use of the royal prerogative, and the extent to which the courts may pass judgment on any particular use. Notwithstanding that the royal prerogative as a source of power for the government antedates Acts of Parliament, has been at the root of a civil war and a revolution in

England and has been litigated about on countless major occasions in respect of its use both at home and overseas, its scope is still unclear as is the role of the courts in relation thereto. The use by the Prime Minister of powers under the royal prerogative to ban trade unions at the Government Communication Headquarters at Cheltenham in 1983 was contested both for its lawfulness—that is whether such powers could be used and if so whether they were used correctly—and also for its legitimacy—that is whether, even if the constitutional power existed, this was a proper and fair use of the power. It can be seen that questions of lawfulness and legitimacy shade into one another here though the answers do not: the lawfulness of the action taken, confirmed by the House of Lords in 1984 (*Council of Civil Service Unions* v *Minister for the Civil Service* [1984] 3 All ER 935) did not and does not dispose of its legitimacy.

The G.C.H.Q. case is valuable for another point. We have pointed out that lawfulness is not to be confused with legitimacy. No more is constitutionality. What the Prime Minister did was not merely lawful; she exercised the constitutional powers of her office in the way in which those powers had always been exercised. That is, the use of the royal prerogative as the legal backing for the management of the public service, the principle that a civil servant is a servant of the Crown and holds office at the pleasure of the Crown is one of the best known principles of constitutional law, hallowed by usage and sanctioned by the courts. What is in issue from the perspective of legitimacy is whether the particular use made of that undoubted constitutional power, the manner of its use, and the justification both for the use and manner of use—that considerations of national security required both a banning of trade unions and no consultation with affected officers before the ban was announced—was a fair and reasonable use of power? Did it accord with legitimate expectations of fair and reasonable persons or was it a high-handed exercise of power of a kind more to be expected of an authoritarian government than one guided by and subscribing to principles of limited government?

In considering the issue of legitimacy in relation to our constitutional arrangements and the exercise of governmental power, what has to be done is to examine a range of practices, decisions, actions (and non-practices, -decisions and -actions) statements and policies which between them can amount to a portrait of power, so that we can form a judgment or an assessment of that power set against the principles of limited government outlined and discussed so far. It is not every failure to comply with law or every constitutional and non-constitutional short cut which adds up to an approach to powers which give rise to questions of legitimacy. If that were so, there would scarcely be a government in the last 100 years which could be regarded as legitimate, but it is those uses of power and law which seem to betray or which can only be reasonably explained by a contempt for or at least an impatience with the principles of limited government and a belief that the rightness of the policies to be executed excuse or justify the methods whereby they are executed. If, as we believe to be the case, powers are being so exercised, then the issue of constitutional legitimacy which arises is quite simple: what is the value or use of a constitution based on and designed to ensure the maintenance of a system of limited government if it can, quite lawfully and even constitutionally, be set on one side? Have we not in such circumstances arrived at that 'elective dictatorship' of which Lord Hailsham gave warning in 1977:

> It is only now that men and women are beginning to realize that representative institutions are not necessarily guardians of freedom but can themselves become engines of tyranny. They can be manipulated by minorities, taken over by extremists, motivated by the self-interest of organised millions.

Occasionally the people from whom legitimacy ultimately derives, pass judgment on government.

P. McAuslan and J. F. McEldowney, 'Legitimacy and the Constitution: the Dissonance between Theory and Practice' in P. McAuslan and J. F. McEldowney (eds), *Law, Legitimacy and the Constitution*
(1985), p. 1

Mr Clive Ponting's acquittal by a jury in February 1985, after he had admitted to passing official Government papers to a person not authorised to receive them, the very essence of section 2 of the

Official Secrets Act 1911, and despite the most explicit summing up by the trial judge that they should convict, raises the question of what motivated the jury. It would suggest that when faced with a choice between a case which rests on constitutional theories about limited government derived from a 'higher law' which controlled what government could legitimately do, and a case which rested on actual practices of government bolstered by actual law, the jury preferred the theory of what the constitution ought to be to the practice of what it is. Little wonder that, as one newspaper put it, ministers were aghast at the verdict. The *Concise Oxford Dictionary* defines 'aghast' as meaning terrified. This essay will seek to show ministers would indeed have good reason to be terrified if ordinary people began preferring constitutional theory to government practice and acted on their preferences in their judgment of politicians. More particularly the jury's verdict in the Ponting trial may be seen then as the response of ordinary people to trends in government practices which seem to them to be, in perhaps indefinable ways, wrong.

■ QUESTIONS

1. In this case it was a jury of 12 which, by its verdict, appeared to be commenting on the legitimacy of governmental action in attempting to mislead the Foreign Affairs Select Committee about the circumstances surrounding the sinking of the *General Belgrano*, an Argentinian warship, during the Falklands Campaign in 1982. These 12 jurors may, or may not, have been representative of the views of the public. Are there more representative ways in which public sentiments regarding governmental action may be expressed?
2. Is majority rule under a system of parliamentary democracy a sufficient guarantee of legitimacy? What does majority rule mean in the context of the United Kingdom?

SECTION 3: DEMOCRACY

In the opening sentences of *Le Contrat Social* (1762) Rousseau stated:

Man is born free and everywhere he is in chains. One thinks himself the master of others, and still remains the greater slave than they. How did this change come about? I do not know. What can make it legitimate? That question I think I can answer.

The answer he gave was that the only ground of legitimacy is to be found in the general will of the people, as only the people can say who has the right to rule them. Thus it is the people who give legitimacy to a constitution—sovereignty resides with the people and, in turn, where the constitution sets up a system of elected representative government, that government acquires its authority both from the constitution and the people who elect it.

Does the constitution in the United Kingdom have a democratic basis? Is the system of government democratic? A starting point is to examine what a liberal-democracy is.

C. B. Macpherson, *The Real World of Democracy*
(1966), pp. 4–11

[O]ur liberal-democracy, like any other system, is a system of power; that it is, indeed, again like any other, a double system of power. It is a system by which people can be *governed*, that is, made to do things they would not otherwise do, and made to refrain from doing things they otherwise might do. Democracy as a system of government is, then, a system by which power is exerted by the state over individuals and groups within it. But more than that, a democratic government, like any other, exists to uphold and enforce a certain kind of society, a certain set of relations between individuals, a certain set of rights and claims that people have on each other both directly, and indirectly through their rights to property. These relations themselves are relations of power—they give different people, in different capacities, power over others. …

[L]iberal-democracy and capitalism go together. Liberal-democracy is found only in countries whose economic system is wholly or predominantly that of capitalist enterprise. And, with few and mostly temporary exceptions, every capitalist country has a liberal-democratic political system. …

The claims of democracy would never have been admitted in the present liberal-democracies had those countries not got a solid basis of liberalism first. The liberal democracies that we know were liberal first and democratic later. To put this in another way, before democracy came in the Western world there came the society and the politics of choice, the society and politics of competition, the society and politics of the market. This was the liberal society and state. It will be obvious that I am using liberal here in a very broad sense. I use it in what I take to be its essential sense, to mean that both the society as a whole and the system of government were organized on a principle of freedom of choice. …

To make this society work, or to allow it to operate, a non-arbitrary, or responsible, system of government was needed. And this was provided, by revolutionary action in England in the seventeenth century, in America in the eighteenth, in France in the eighteenth and nineteenth, and by a variety of methods in most other Western countries sometime within those centuries. What was established was a system whereby the government was put in a sort of market situation. The government was treated as the supplier of certain political goods—not just the political good of law and order in general, but the specific political goods demanded by those who had the upper hand in running that particular kind of society. What was needed was the kind of laws and regulations, and tax structure, that would make the market society work, or allow it to work, and the kind of state services—defence, and even military expansion, education, sanitation, and various sorts of assistance to industry, such as tariffs and grants for railway development—that were thought necessary to make the system run efficiently and profitably. These were the kinds of political goods that were wanted. But how was the demand to call forth the supply? How to make government responsive to the choices of those it was expected to cater to? The way was of course to put governmental power into the hands of men who were made subject to periodic elections at which there was a choice of candidates and parties. The electorate did not need to be a democratic one, and as a general rule was not; all that was needed was an electorate consisting of the men of substance, so that the government would be responsive to their choices.

To make this political choice an effective one, there had to be certain other liberties. There had to be freedom of association—that is, freedom to form political parties, and freedom to form the kind of associations we now know as pressure groups, whose purpose is to bring to bear on parties and on governments the combined pressure of the interests they represent. And there had to be freedom of speech and publication, for without these the freedom of association is of no use. These freedoms could not very well be limited to men of the directing classes. They had to be demanded in principle for everybody. The risk that the others would use them to get a political voice was a risk that had to be taken.

So came what I am calling the liberal state. Its essence was the system of alternate or multiple parties whereby governments could be held responsible to different sections of the class or classes that had a political voice. There was nothing necessarily democratic about the responsible party system. In the country of its origin, England, it was well established, and working well, half a century or a century before the franchise became at all democratic. This is not surprising, for the job of the liberal state was to maintain and promote the liberal society, which was not essentially a democratic or an equal society. The job of the competitive party system was to uphold the competitive market society, by keeping the government responsive to the shifting majority interests of those who were running the market society.

However, the market society did produce, after a time, a pressure for democracy which became irresistible. …

So finally the democratic franchise was introduced into the liberal state. It did not come easily or quickly. In most of the present liberal-democratic countries it required many decades of agitation and organization, and in few countries was anything like it achieved until late in the nineteenth century. The female half of the population had to wait even longer for an equal political voice: not until substantial numbers of women had moved out from the shelter of the home to take an independent place in the labour market was women's claim to a voice in the political market allowed.

So democracy came as a late addition to the competitive market society and the liberal state. The point of recalling this is, of course, to emphasize that democracy came as an adjunct to the competitive liberal society and state. It is not simply that democracy came later. It is also that democracy in these societies, was demanded, and was admitted, on competitive liberal grounds. Democracy was demanded, and admitted, on the ground that it was unfair not to have it in a competitive society. It was something the competitive society logically needed. ...

What the addition of democracy to the liberal state did was simply to provide constitutional channels for popular pressures, pressures to which governments would have had to yield in about the same measure anyway, merely to maintain public order and avoid revolution. By admitting the mass of the people into the competitive party system, the liberal state did not abandon its fundamental nature; it simply opened the competitive political system to all the individuals who had been created by the competitive market society. The liberal state fulfilled its own logic. In so doing, it neither destroyed nor weakened itself; it strengthened both itself and the market society. It liberalized democracy while democratizing liberalism.

■ QUESTION

If this view is correct, did, or does, the constitution in the United Kingdom have a democratic basis? Was, or is, its legitimacy to be found in the general will of the people? See the Ridley extract following.

F. F. Ridley, 'There is no British Constitution: A Dangerous Case of the Emperor's Clothes'

(1988) 41 *Parliamentary Affairs* 340, 343–5

The first characteristic of a constitution ... is that it constitutes—or reconstitutes—a system of government. ... [I]n constitutional theory a governmental order derives its legitimacy from the constituent act which establishes it. ...

Democratic constitutions universally state the principle of popular sovereignty and their legitimacy now rests on popular enactment. This follows the American tradition: 'We the people of the United States ... do ordain and establish this constitution'. Similar words are found almost everywhere. Some may invoke a higher sanctity for parts of the constitution than the will of the people. Thus the American Bill of Rights is founded on the Declaration of Independence's self-evident truths that all men are endowed by their Creator with certain inalienable rights, but that does not alter the source of the constitution's authority. ...

The people are generally called on to elect a special constituent assembly mandated to draft a constitution, though this may not always be the case—as in General de Gaulle's constitution for the Fifth Republic. Although the American constitution was ratified by state legislatures, in more recent times the people are almost universally called on to ratify it in a referendum. ...

Britain never developed this idea of popular sovereignty in constitutional terms, even if we sometimes talk of the sovereignty of the electorate in political terms. Even if the latter were true, it would merely allow the people to choose their government: it does not base the governmental order, the British 'constitution', on their authority and thus only gives them only half their right. (Moreover, since a parliamentary majority can change that order, prolong its own life, alter the franchise or reform the electoral system, even the political rights of the electorate depend on Parliament.) What we have, instead, is the sovereignty of Parliament. Parliament determines—and alters—the country's system of government. If we ask where that power comes from, the answer is broadly that Parliament claimed it and the courts recognised it. The people never came into the picture. The liberal (middle-class) democracies established in Europe had, despite their generally limited franchise, to base their constitutions on the principle that ultimate authority was vested in the people. Britain seems to be the sole exception to this democratic path.

■ QUESTION

If, as Ridley argues, the constitution of the United Kingdom had no foundational democratic basis, is the system of government still nevertheless democratic? See the Finer extract following.

S. E. Finer, *Comparative Government*

(1970), pp. 63–6

(1) The primary meaning of democracy is government which is derived from public opinion and is accountable to it. As to *accountability;* this implies that it is not sufficient for a government to justify its existence because at some time in the past it was representative of popular opinion; for the two may have diverged since then. 'Accountability' entails that a government must continuously test its representativeness, that is to say whether its claim that it is 'derived from public opinion' is still valid.

(2) This public opinion, it must therefore be presumed, is overtly and freely expressed. For if it is not, how can anybody *know* that the government is still 'derived from public opinion', i.e. is still representative? But 'overtly and freely to express opinion' implies some opportunity and machinery for making that opinion known, and therefore implies some kind of a suffrage, some kind of a voice or vote. …

(3) In matters of contention between sections of public opinion it is the majority opinion that prevails. These three characteristics must, it seems, form part of any definition of democracy. …

Thus the first assumption of liberal-democracy is that it is a democracy in the sense expressed above. But liberal-democracy is a *qualified* democracy. In this type of government there are other presuppositions or assumptions beyond the one which we have already stated.

The first of these is that government is *limited*. This implies that the government is operating in a world of autonomous, spontaneously self-creating, voluntary associations. In such conditions the government operates only at the margin of social activity. That it ought to interfere and regulate or even suppress these autonomous, self-creating, voluntary associations is a matter for it to prove: it is not assumed. … The authority of government therefore is limited; and this can be expressed by saying that certain rights of the individual and of the private association are safeguarded. A kind of ring fence is drawn around them and the onus lies on the government to show whether, why and to what extent this ought to be breached.

The second qualification to democracy in this particular 'liberal' form is that society is recognized as being *pluralistic*. … To recognize society as being pluralistic, therefore, carries the additional assumption that the government sets out to rule, not in the interest of any one group or alliance of groups, but in the common interest of all. …

This highlights the third qualification: the liberal-democratic type of government is one in which *it is denied that there is any objective science of society or of morals*. On the contrary, it is assumed that in the last resort truth is a matter of individual consciences where all consciences are held, by an act of faith, to be equal either in the sight of God or in the sight of man. Two working conclusions follow from this, namely, toleration and the qualification of majority rule.

Why toleration? Because if there is no objective science of society and morals, then clearly no group, not even the government, has any moral justification for imposing any creed, philosophy, religion or ideology upon the rest of society. Again, since it is assumed by this act of faith that all individuals are equal in the sight of God, man or both, then dissent must be tolerated and each has the right to put his own point of view. Again, since truth is held to be individual and also fallible, rulership will be both conditional and also temporary; because clearly the views as to what is true and therefore proper for government to act upon will change from time to time as opinion fluctuates amongst the body of the people. So, this qualified form of democracy entails that the government is representative of and responsive to public opinion; and that where this opinion is not unanimous it is representative of and responsive to the majority. But these majorities will usually be constantly changing. …

But even majority rule is seriously qualified in the liberal-democracy. … But being a liberal-democracy also implies that the minorities must be given a chance to become a majority; and that means, therefore, that they must be given a chance status and a means to convert the majority. In order to make this possible, certain guarantees and machinery would have to be established.

NOTES

1. The ideas in the last paragraph of the extract from Finer are taken further by Sir Stephen Sedley, 'The Common Law and the Constitution' in Lord Nolan and Sir Stephen Sedley, *The Making and Remaking of the British Constitution* (London, 1997), p. 5 where he states:

> A democracy is more than a state in which power resides in the hands of a majority of elected representatives: it is a state in which individuals and minorities have an assurance of certain basic protections from the majoritarian interest, and in which independent courts of law hold the responsibility for interpreting, applying and—importantly—supplementing the law laid down by Parliament in the interests of every individual, not merely the represented majority.

   (See further Chapter 9).

2. See further *United Communist Party of Turkey* v *Turkey* (1998) 26 EHRR 121 in Chapter 9, Section 2 at p. 407.

3. Where there is a permanent majority, however, representative democracy may fail to provide legitimation either of a government or of the system of government. See the Barker extract following.

R. Barker, *Political Legitimacy and the State*

(1990), pp. 141–3

It is difficult to determine in any precise way the contribution of elections to the maintenance of legitimacy. By comparing the history of Northern Ireland with that of the rest of the United Kingdom it is clear that the mere fact of elections is not sufficient. If the result is never in any doubt, so that it is not 'the people' but always and only a section and that the same section of them which confers consent on government, then those who feel themselves permanently excluded will also feel no great obligations to the regime. No legitimacy without representation. ...

On the other hand, so long as the electoral system appears to give due weight to most parties, the fact that individual votes may often have little effect does not deter them from being cast. Voters turn out in large numbers in safe seats where their individual support or opposition to the sitting candidate can make no difference whatsoever to the result. Voting has a ritual aspect, whereby citizens formally and publicly show their preferences for one party over others, and hence their willingness to accept the result of the contest, and their legitimation of that result. It enables people to identify with those who lead or govern them, to see politicians and rulers as both special and, at the same time, exemplifying the character of their followers. ...

Thus two broad sanctioning functions can be identified in voting. First of the policies of particular governments, second of the governing system in general, of the state. These may of course in practice be confused or entangled with each other, as they are in Northern Ireland, or as they are in any state where the elections are largely or wholly a political ritual or a way of mobilizing mass support or approval for a regime in which party and state are indistinguishable, and electoral choice between contestants for office non-existent. Once this occurs the democratic process can have an important function in *failing* to legitimize the state, and in providing justification for a rejection by groups of subjects not only of particular governments, but of more general constitutional arrangements. The predictable ineffectiveness of the nationalist vote in Northern Ireland can be used to justify rejection not just of a particular government but of the whole constitutional structure which maintains the inclusion of Northern Ireland in the United Kingdom rather than in a new all-Ireland state. In a smaller way after 1987 the emergence of a Scottish electorate overwhelmingly hostile to a Conservative government in power on the basis of English electoral success can sustain nationalist arguments for the general illegitimacy of the constitutional arrangements of the United Kingdom.

NOTE: Legitimate government may, therefore, be understood to demand more than simple majority rule. It is important to examine how the system of government in the United Kingdom has supplemented this idea of majority rule. This involves an examination of how elections operate, how governments acquire power, and how they use that power. Do they claim authority simply on the basis of electoral victory to do as they please, including changing the constitutional framework, or do they find themselves restrained from so acting by certain fundamental principles?

Endeavouring to answer such questions involves value judgments. Political scientists have attempted to develop indices to assist in informing such judgments. The Beetham extract which follows outlines some of the issues involved.

D. Beetham, 'Key Principles and Indices for a Democratic Audit' in D. Beetham (ed.), *Defining and Measuring Democracy*
(1994), pp. 25–30

First, it is necessary to explain the idea of a 'democratic audit' itself. This is the simple but ambitious project of assessing the state of democracy in a single country. Like other Western countries, the UK calls itself a democracy, and claims to provide a model for others to follow. Yet how democratic is it actually? And how does it measure up to the standards that it uses to assess others, including the countries of the Third World? Such questions are not accidental, but are provoked by a widespread sense of disquiet within the UK at the state of its political institutions—a disquiet which runs deeper than the mere fact that a single party has been in power for so long ...

The project of a democratic audit, then, not only requires a clear specification of what exactly is to be audited. It also requires a robust and defensible conception of democracy, from which can be derived specific criteria and standards of assessment. An account of this conception and these criteria is provided in the following section.

Principles and indices of democracy

... Democracy is a *political* concept, concerning the collectively binding decisions about the rules and policies of a group, association or society. It claims that such decision-making should be, and it is realized to the extent that such decision-making actually is, subject to the control of all members of the collectivity considered as equals. That is to say, democracy embraces the related principles of *popular control* and *political equality*. In small-scale and simple associations, people can control collective decision-making directly, through equal rights to vote on law and policy in person. In large and complex associations, they typically do so indirectly, for example through appointing representatives to act for them. Here popular control usually takes the form of control over decision-*makers*, rather than over decision-making itself; and typically it requires a complex set of institutions and practices to make the principle effective. Similarly political equality, rather than being realized in an equal say in decision-making directly, is realized to the extent that there exists an equality of votes between electors, an equal right to stand for public office, an equality in the conditions for making one's voice heard and in treatment at the hands of legislators, and so on.

These two principles, of popular control and political equality, form the guiding thread of a democratic audit. They are the principles which inform those institutions and practices of Western countries that are characteristically democratic; and they also provide a standard against which their level of democracy can be assessed. As they stand, however, they are too general. Like the indices developed by other political scientists, they need to be broken down into specific, and where possible, measurable, criteria for the purpose of assessment or audit.

To do this we have separated the process of popular control over government into four distinct, albeit overlapping, dimensions. First and most basic is the popular election of the parliament or legislature and the head of government. The degree or extent of popular control is here to be assessed by such criteria as: the *reach* of the electoral process (that is, which public offices are open to election, and what powers they have over non-elected officials); its *inclusiveness* (what exclusions apply, both formally and informally, to parties, candidates and voters, whether in respect of registration or voting itself); its *fairness* as between parties, candidates and voters, and the range of effective choice it offers the latter; its *independence* from the government of the day; and so on. These criteria can be summed up in the familiar phrase 'free and fair elections', though this phrase does not fully capture all the aspects needed for effective popular control.

The second dimension for analysis concerns what is known as 'open and accountable government'. Popular control requires, besides elections, the continuous accountability of government: directly, to the electorate, through the public justification for its policies; indirectly, to agents acting on the people's behalf. In respect of the latter, we can distinguish between the *political accountability* of government to the legislature or parliament for the content and execution of its policies; its *legal* accountability to the courts for ensuring that all state personnel, elected and non-elected, act within the laws and powers approved by the legislature; its *financial* accountability to both the legislature and the courts. Accountability in turn depends upon public knowledge of what government is up to, from sources that are independent of its own public relations machine. In all these aspects, a democratic audit will need to assess the respective powers and independence, both legal and actual, of different bodies: of the legislature and judiciary in relation to the executive; of the investigative capacity of the media; of an independent public statistical service; of the powers of individual citizens to seek redress in the event of maladministration or injustice.

Underpinning both the first two dimensions of popular control over government is a third: guaranteed civil and political rights or liberties. The freedoms of speech, association, assembly and movement, the right to due legal process, and so on, are not something specific to a particular *form* of democracy called 'liberal democracy'; they are essential to democracy as such, since without them no effective popular control over government is possible. … These rights or liberties are necessary if citizens are to communicate and associate with one another independently of government; if they are to express dissent from government or to influence it on an ongoing basis; if electoral choice and accountability is to be at all meaningful. A democratic audit will need to assess not only the legally prescribed content of these citizens' rights, but also the effectiveness of the institutions and procedures whereby they are guaranteed in practice.

A fourth dimension of popular control concerns the arena of what is called 'civil society': the nexus of associations through which people organize independently to manage their own affairs, and which can also act as a channel of influence upon government and a check on its powers. This is a more contestable dimension of democracy, not only because the criteria for its assessment are much less well formed than for the other three areas, but also because there is room for disagreement as to whether it should be seen as a necessary *condition for* democracy, or as an essential *part of* it. Our view is that a democratic society is a part of democracy, and goes beyond the concept of 'civil society', with its stress on the *independence* of societal self-organization, to include such features as: the representativeness of the media and their accessibility to different social groups and points of view; the public accountability and internal democracy of powerful private corporations; the degree of political awareness of the citizen body and the extent of its public participation; the democratic character of the political culture and of the education system.

The criteria or indices of popular control can thus be divided into four interrelated segments, which go to make up the major dimensions of democracy for contemporary societies. … A complete democratic audit should examine each segment in turn, to assess not only the effectiveness of popular control in practice, but also the degree of political equality in each area: under free and fair elections, how far each vote is of equal value, and how far there is equality of opportunity to stand for public office, regardless of which section of society a person comes from; under open and accountable government, whether any individuals or groups are systematically excluded from access to, or influence upon, government, or redress from it; under civil and political rights or liberties, whether these are effectively guaranteed to all sections of society; under democratic society, the degree of equal opportunity for self-organization, access to the media, redress from powerful corporations, and so on.

NOTE: A comprehensive analysis of the extent to which a state such as the United Kingdom is 'democratic' must, therefore, be based on a broad range of factors. For the most recent 'audit' of UK democracy, completed in 2016, see http://www.democraticaudit.com/our-work/the-2016-audit-of-uk-democracy/.

Yet while democracy is certainly about *more* than majoritarian decision-making, it can also be argued that it should not be about *less* than majoritarian decision-making. A key concern, outlined in the following Waldron extract, is whether empowering courts to protect fundamental constitutional rights and liberties is undemocratic, in so far as it limits the ability of 'the people' to make certain policy decisions.

J. Waldron, *Law and Disagreement*
(1999), pp. 15–16

When citizens or their representatives disagree about what rights we have or what those rights entail, it seems something of an insult to say that this is not something they are to be permitted to sort out by majoritarian processes, but that the issue is to be assigned instead for final determination to a small group of judges. It is particularly insulting when they discover that the judges disagree among themselves along exactly the same lines as the citizens and representatives do, and that the judges make their decisions, too, in the courtroom by majority-voting. The citizens may well feel that if disagreements on these matters are to be settled by counting heads, then it is their heads or those of their accountable representatives that should be counted.

Disagreement on matters of principle is, as I have emphasized, not the exception but the rule in politics. It follows that those who value popular participation in politics should not value it in a spirit that stops short at the threshold of disagreements about rights. Such curtailment, I believe, betrays the spirit of those who struggled for democracy and universal suffrage. The workers who braved cavalry charges at Peterloo in 1819, the women who chained themselves to the White House railings or threw themselves under the hooves of the King's horse at Epsom in turn-of-the-century suffrage campaigns, the African-Americans who faced batons, police-dogs, fire hoses, and worse in the Civil Rights movement in the 1950s and '60s, did these things to secure a voice on the matters of political principle that confronted their community. They did not do them simply for the sake of a vote on interstitial issues of policy that had no compelling moral dimension. They fought for the franchise because they believed that controversies about the fundamental ordering of their society – factory and hours legislation, property rights, free speech, police powers, temperance, campaign reform – were controversies for them to sort out, respectfully and on a basis of equality, because *they* were the people who would be affected by the outcome. Moreover, they did not fight for the vote on the assumption that they would then all *agree* about the issues that they wanted the right to vote on. Every individual involved in these movements was well aware that there were others standing alongside him who believed that his political views on matters of substance were mistaken. But they fought for the vote anyway on the ground that the existence of such principled disagreements was the essence of politics, not that it should be regarded as a signal to transfer the important issues that they disagreed about to some other forum altogether, which would privilege the opinions and purses of a few.

■ QUESTIONS

1. Is it democratic for the decisions of representative institutions to be overturned by courts to protect fundamental rights?
2. Can democratic decisions which interfere with basic rights be described as legitimate? Are judicial decisions which undermine basic rights any more or less legitimate?

SECTION 4: LEGAL AND POLITICAL CONSTITUTIONALISM

Whether certain constitutional arrangements or practices are, or are not, democratically legitimate can be the subject of much debate. Recent debate in the United Kingdom (and elsewhere) about democratic legitimacy in constitutional law has often focused on two competing ideas: legal constitutionalism and political constitutionalism. These two contrasting constitutional philosophies offer alternative answers to a question central to the study of constitutional law: how should those who wield public power be limited and/or held to account?

A: Legal constitutionalism

The principle of constitutionalism rests on the idea of restraining the government in its exercise of power, and is closely associated with theories as to the importance of limited government.

M. J. C. Vile, *Constitutionalism and the Separation of Powers*
(1967), p. 1

Western institutional theorists have concerned themselves with the problem of ensuring that the exercise of governmental power, which is essential to the realization of the values of their societies, should be controlled in order that it should not itself be destructive of the values it was intended to promote. The great theme of the advocates of constitutionalism, in contrast either to the theorists of utopianism, or of absolutism, of the right or of the left, has been the frank acknowledgment of the role of government in society, linked with the determination to bring that government under control and to place limits on the exercise of its power.

C. J. Friedrich, *Limited Government: A Comparison*
(1974), pp. 13–14

Constitutionalism by dividing power provides a system of effective restraints upon governmental action. In studying it, one has to explore the methods and techniques by which such restraints are established and maintained. Putting it another, more familiar, but less exact way, it is a body of rules ensuring fair play, thus rendering the government 'responsible.' There exist a considerable number of such techniques or methods.

The question confronts us: how did the idea of restraints arise? And who provided the support that made the idea victorious in many countries? There are two important roots to the idea of restraints. One is the medieval heritage of natural-law doctrine. For while the royal bureaucrats gained the upper hand in fact, the other classes in the community who had upheld the medieval constitutionalism—the barons and the free towns, and above all the church—developed secularized versions of natural law. At the same time, they clung to residual institutions, such as the *parlements* in France. After the task of unification had been accomplished, and the despotic methods of absolutism could no longer be justified, these elements came forward with the idea of a separation of power. Both the English and the French revolutions served to dramatize these events.

The other root of the idea of restraints is shared by medieval and modern constitutionalism and is peculiar to some extent to Western culture. It is Christianity, and more specifically the Christian doctrine of personality. The insistence upon the individual as the final value, the emphasis upon the transcendental importance of each man's soul, creates an insoluble conflict with any sort of absolutism. Here lies the core of the objection to all political conceptions derived from Aristotelian and other Greek sources. Since there exists a vital need for government just the same, this faith in the worth of each human being is bound to seek a balance of the two needs in some system of restraints which protects the individual, or at least minorities, against any despotic exercise of political authority. It is quite in keeping with this conflict that the apologists of unrestrained power have, in all ages of Western civilization, felt the necessity of *justifying* the exercise of such power, a necessity which was not felt elsewhere.

Nor was it felt by all in the West. Bacon and Hobbes, Bodin and Spinoza, and even Machiavelli insisted that some sort of inanimate force, such as reason, natural law, or enlightened self-interest would bring about a self-restraint. But a deep-seated distrust of power was part of the tradition that taught that 'my Kingdom is not of this world,' and that states are usually just 'great robber bands,' since they lack justice. Hence self-restraint of the ruler must be reinforced by effective institutions: restraints upon the arbitrary exercise of governmental power.

Modern constitutionalism then has always been linked with the problem of power, in theory as well as in practice. Historically, it constitutes a reaction against the concentration of power that accompanied the consolidation of modern states, dynastic and national. Its theorists have insisted on the importance of limiting and defining the power acquired by monarchs. Whilst Hobbes described the rational structure of such a concentration of power and developed it into a veritable philosophy of power, Locke, taking up the challenge, demanded that the exercise of this power, although it was derived from the ultimate and unified source of all power—the people—remain divided by virtue of a fundamental decision.

NOTE: If the goal of constitutionalism is to prevent the exercise of arbitrary power, for the legal constitutionalist, law will have a vital role to play in constraining governments. But is the notion of constraining the power of the state by law problematic? How legal constitutionalism might be justified, and its implications, are considered in the following extracts from Elster and Loughlin.

J. Elster, 'Introduction' in J. Elster and R. Slagstad (eds), *Constitutionalism and Democracy*

(1988), pp. 8–9

Why would a political assembly want to abdicate from the full sovereignty which in principle it possesses, and set limits on its own future actions? In an intergenerational perspective, the question is what right one generation has to limit the freedom of action of its successors, and why the latter should feel bound by constraints laid down by their ancestors. A natural (although possibly misleading) point of departure is to consider individual analogies. Why, for instance, would two individuals want to form a legal marriage instead of simply cohabiting? What possible advantages could they derive from limiting their future freedom of action and by making it more difficult to separate should they form the wish to do so? One obvious answer is that they want to protect themselves against their own tendency to act rashly, in the heat of passion. By raising the costs of separation and imposing legal delays, marriage makes it less likely that the spouses will give way to strong but temporary impulses to separate. By increasing the expected duration of the relationship, legal marriage also enhances the incentive to have children, to invest in housing and make other long-term decisions. These decisions, in turn create bonds between the spouses and reinforce the marriage.

These answers have partial analogues in the constitutional domain. It is a truism that constitutional constraints make it more difficult for the assembly or the society to change its mind on important questions. Groups no less than individuals (although not in quite the same sense as individuals) are subject to fits of passion, self-deception and hysteria which may create a temporary majority for decisions which will later be regretted. But then, one may ask, why could the members of the assembly not simply undo the decisions if and when they come to regret them? The presumption must be, after all, that the assembly knows what it is doing, not that it needs to be protected against itself.

Part of the answer to this question is suggested by the marriage analogy. The expected stability and duration of political institutions is an important value in itself, since they allow for long-term planning. Conversely, if all institutions are up for grabs all the time, individuals in power will be tempted to milk their positions for private purposes, and those outside power will hesitate to form projects which take time to bear fruit. Moreover, if nothing could ever be taken for granted, there would be large deadweight losses arising from bargaining and factionalism.

Another part of the answer is that not all unwise decisions can be undone. Imagine that a majority untrammelled by constitutional constraints decides that an external or internal threat justifies a suspension of civil liberties, or that retroactive legislation should be enacted against 'enemies of the people.' In the first place, such measures have victims whom one cannot always compensate at later times. Examples abound: the internment of the American Japanese during the Second World War, the excesses during the Chinese Cultural Revolution, the *Berufsverbot* against Communists in several countries. When society again comes to its senses, the victims may be dead or their lives destroyed. In the second place, the temporary suspension of rights easily leads to the permanent abolition of majority rule itself and to its replacement by dictatorship. It suffices to cite the years 1794 and 1933. This is possibly the central argument for constitutional constraints on democracy: without such constraints democracy itself becomes weaker, not stronger.

M. Loughlin, *Sword and Scales*
(2000), pp. 232–3

In modern times, politics and law have become more formally differentiated and, most recently, law has come to be viewed as establishing a cordon within which politics is conducted. But this development remains politically contentious. The project of establishing law as an objective framework of rational principles, whether treated as an exercise in philosophy or in jurisprudence, has not been successful. With the ascendancy of law as right we do not therefore reach the end of history, or an escape from politics. Instead, this legalization of politics has led primarily to a politicization of law.

The age-old controversies over the meaning of liberty, equality, democracy and the like are now taking place within a more explicit legal-constitutionalist framework. This means that the institution of courts will now play a more important role in giving precise meaning to the core values of society. Whether the judiciary is adequately equipped to undertake this task and whether the formal and adversarial procedures of courts are appropriate for determining these issues must remain matters of debate. But no one should be in any doubt about the political character of the exercise. In the United States, where the jurisprudence of rights is most highly developed, powerful arguments have recently been presented for claims of fundamental rights rooted in a variety of irreconcilable positions, including the maintenance of property, the promotion of the right to equal concern and respect, the protection of rights of access to the political process, the defence of the rights of disadvantaged groups, and the realization of the conditions of 'deliberative democracy'. Each of these claims can be justified by reference to some notion of equality, and each finds evidential support in constitutional texts. But since none can be shown to provide an objective rendering of constitutional requirements, this type of engagement must be acknowledged to be simply a more explicitly rationalized form of political discourse.

NOTE: For an influential modern statement of a legal constitutionalist position, see also the extract from Sir John Laws discussed in Chapter 2, Section 3B at pp. 85–7.

B: Political constitutionalism

While legal constitutionalism emphasizes the importance of the limitation of government by law, political constitutionalism is focused on mechanisms of political accountability. Such an approach has been historically associated with the United Kingdom constitution, lacking as it does a higher-order codified constitutional instrument or text which could operate so as to constrain absolutely public power.

J. A. G. Griffith, 'The Political Constitution'
(1979) 42 *Modern Law Review* 16, 19

The fundamental political objection is this: that law is not and cannot be a substitute for politics. This is a hard truth, perhaps an unpleasant truth. For centuries political philosophers have sought that society in which government is by laws and not by men. It is an unattainable ideal. Written constitutions do not achieve it. Nor do Bills of Rights or any other devices. They merely pass political decisions out of the hands of politicians and into the hands of judges or other persons. To require a supreme court to make certain kinds of political decisions does not make those decisions any less political.

I believe firmly that political decisions should be taken by politicians. In a society like ours this means by people who are removable. It is an obvious corollary of this that the responsibility and account-ability of our rulers should be real and not fictitious. And of course our existing institutions, especially the House of Commons, need strengthening. And we need to force governments out of secrecy and into the open. So also the freedom of the Press should be enlarged by the amendment of laws which restrict discussion. Governments are too easily able to act in an authoritarian manner. But the remedies are political. It is not by attempting to restrict the legal powers of government that we shall defeat authoritarianism. It is by insisting on open government. …

Only political control, politically exercised, can supply the remedy….

I am arguing then for a highly positivist view of the constitution; of recognising that Ministers and others in high positions of authority are men and women who happen to exercise political power but without any such right to that power which could give them a superior moral position; that laws made by those in authority derive validity from no other fact or principle, and so impose no moral obligation of obedience on others; that so-called individual rights are no more and no less than political claims made by individuals on those in authority; that society is endemically in a state of conflict between warring interest groups, having no consensus or unifying principles sufficiently precise to be the basis of a theory of legislation.

NOTE: The clash between legal and political constitutionalism may therefore go to the very heart of debates about the purpose of government. How might the advantages and disadvantages of politi-cal constitutionalism—and by contrast, legal constitutionalism—be assessed?

A. Tomkins, *Public Law*

(2003), pp. 18–21

A constitutional distinction which is of rather more significance than the familiar distinction between written and unwritten constitutions is that between political and legal constitutions. It is a central theme of this book that public law does two things: it provides for the institutions which exercise public power, and it seeks to hold those institutions to some form of account. Thus, public law regulates the enterprise of government. One way of putting this is to say that the purpose of a constitution is to find ways of allowing the government to get away with less. Now, there are essentially two ways in which this may be achieved: politically, or legally. A political constitution is one in which those who exercise political power (let us say the government) are held to constitutional account through political means, and through political institutions (for example, Parliament). Thus, government ministers and senior civil servants might be subjected to regular scrutiny in Parliament. The scrutiny may consist of taking part in debates, answering questions, participating in and responding to the investigations of committees of inquiry, and so forth. A legal constitution, on the other hand, is one which imagines that the principal means, and the principal institution, through which the government is held to account is the law and the court-room. If you dislike something which the government has done or is proposing to do, instead of lobbying for parliamentary scrutiny, you simply sue the government in court or seek some form of judicial review.

How may we evaluate the respective merits and limitations of each of these basic models? Two methods suggest themselves: one would be to examine their effectiveness, and the other would be to consider the values which they represent – which is the more democratic, or open, or accessible? Let us briefly consider each of these methods. To be effective a political constitution would clearly require strong and vibrant politics; it would require those performing the scrutiny function to take that func-tion seriously, and to have a relatively high degree of independence from the government of the day.

If these conditions were met, it can readily be seen that the model promises much. Governments in a democracy are entirely dependent on politics – it is through the political act of election that they attain much of their legitimacy (as well as their power) and democratic governments continue to possess such power for only as long as they continue to enjoy the support of the majority. This is an exceptionally difficult task for governments to achieve: governments are subject to endless press and media scrutiny, as well as to political opposition from opponent political parties. Thus, politics looks at first sight to be potentially an extraordinarily potent source of accountability: governments will not do things which they cannot politically get away with, as they will lose power. Therefore, imposing on governments systems which allow them politically to get away with less seems to make good constitutional sense.

For a legal constitution to be effective the same initial criteria of seriousness and independence are equally as important as in the political constitution model. Legal systems, courts, and judges will require independence from the government of the day, and will be required to take seriously the idea that law can and ought to be used as a technique of holding the government to account. This may seem axiomatic, but it cannot be taken for granted, as we shall see. Even if these ingredients can be secured, the potential effectiveness of the legal constitution does not seem as obvious as it does for the political constitution. Suing is notoriously expensive, and access to the courts is limited to the well-resourced. Once over that hurdle, suppose a court does find that a government Minister has acted unlawfully. What then? What is there to ensure that in implementing the judgment of the court the government does as the court wishes? ...

What of the values which the two models embody? The political constitution relies on the rigour and the vigour of the political process. The more open, transparent, participatory, representative and deliberative politics is, the better the model will work in practice. These are commendable values, but there are two problems with them: first, these values are far easier to articulate than they are to follow in practice, and most, if not all, political systems fail to live up to them. Secondly, there is the inescapable problem of what a democracy (based on majority rule) does with its minorities. This is the strength, perhaps, of the legal model of constitutionalism. Suing may be expensive, but it is at least equally expensive whether you form part of the political majority or not – unlike the political constitution model, there is no inherent discrimination in favour of the majority. The downside, however, is that, unlike those who in a democracy hold political office, judges are neither democratically elected, accountable or representative. In England they remain overwhelmingly male, white, old, upper-middle class lawyers. The greater their constitutional and political role, the more this matters.

NOTE: A critical question in contemporary constitutional law in the United Kingdom is the extent to which the political constitution has been replaced by a legal constitution. For some, however, this is a false dichotomy. Loughlin argues that '[t]he basic question for constitutional lawyers is not whether we have a legal or political constitution: it is how the idea of law within the political constitution (i.e. the constitution of the polity) might best be conceptualized'; 'Towards A Republican Revival?' (2006) *Oxford Journal of Legal Studies* 425–37, 435–6. Perhaps this can be understood as a useful reminder that when we speak of 'legal' and 'political' constitutions we are making claims about the *relationship* between law and politics within a constitution, and not whether one or the other should be excluded. In other words, and in very crude terms, what we are asking is should a constitution be structured on the premise that law should take priority over politics, or on the premise that politics should take priority over law? The constitutions that result could vary significantly depending on our answer.

■ QUESTIONS

1. Is the difference between legal and political constitutionalism significant? Which presents the more appealing model of constitutionalism?

2. To what extent does the distinction between legal and political constitutionalism help us understand the changes which have recently occurred to the United Kingdom constitution?

SECTION 5: CONDITIONING POWER

As we have seen, legal and political constitutionalism (if accepted as distinct constitutional philosophies) take contrasting approaches to conditioning the exercise of public power. In this section, we will look at two crucial constitutional principles which can be invoked to structure the power of institutions of government. These two principles are the separation of powers and responsible government. The significance of the (legal) doctrine of the separation of powers is more likely to be emphasized by legal constitutionalists, whereas the significance of (politically) responsible government is more likely to be emphasized by political constitutionalists. Nevertheless, these principles do not need to be understood as competing alternatives; a constitution may exploit both to varying degrees to condition the exercise of the power it creates or recognizes.

A: Separation of powers

At the outset it must be recognized that in principle there are three institutions of government, each with specific functions. The legislature has the function of making new law or amending or repealing existing law. The executive has the administrative function of conducting government in accordance with the law. The judiciary has the function of interpreting the law and applying it to specific cases. In 1690 John Locke identified a danger arising from the possession of more than one power. In his *Second Treatise of Civil Government*, chap. XII, para. 143, Locke stated:

> It may be too great a temptation to human frailty, apt to grasp at power, for the same persons who have the power of making laws, to have also in their hands the power to execute them, whereby they may exempt themselves from obedience to the laws they make, and suit the law, both in its making and execution, to their own private advantage.

This idea was developed further by Montesquieu, the French philosopher, who expressed the view that it was the separation of powers of government which ensured the liberty of the English. He expressed the doctrine in *L'Esprit des Lois*, Book XI, chap. VI (2nd edn, vol. 1, p. 220) as follows:

> When the Legislative Power is united with the Executive Power in the same person or body of magistrates, there is no liberty because it is to be feared that the same Monarch or the same Senate will make tyrannical laws in order to execute them tyrannically. There is no liberty if the Judicial Power is not separated from the Legislative Power and from the Executive Power. If it were joined with the Legislative Power, the power over the life and liberty of citizens would be arbitrary, because the Judge would be Legislator. If it were joined to the Executive Power, the Judge would have the strength of an oppressor. All would be lost if the same man, or the same body of chief citizens, or the nobility, or the people, exercised these three powers, that of making laws, that of executing public decisions, and that of judging the crimes or the disputes of private persons.

This was a somewhat idealized view which did not truly reflect the political reality in England at the time. Montesquieu's views, however, were particularly influential in the eighteenth century as a reading of the Constitution of the United States of America reveals.

C. F. Strong, *Modern Political Constitutions*
(1972), pp. 211–12

> Now, in no constitutional state is it true that the legislative and executive functions are in precisely the same hands, for ... the executive must always be a smaller body than the legislature. But it is not to this

distinction that the theory of the separation of powers points. The application of the theory means not only that the executive shall not be the same body as the legislature but that these two bodies shall be isolated from each other, so that the one shall not control the other. Any state which has adopted and maintained this doctrine in practice in its full force has an executive beyond the control of the legislature. Such an executive we call non-parliamentary or fixed. This type of executive still exists in the United States, whose Constitution has not been altered in this particular since its inception. But France, which, as we have said, applied the doctrine in its first constitutions born of the Revolution, later adopted the British executive system, and this feature appeared in the Constitutions of the Third and Fourth Republics, and again, though greatly modified, in that of the Fifth Republic. The system is one in which a cabinet of ministers is dependent for its existence on the legislature of which it is a part, the members of the executive being also members of the legislature.

This system, generally known as the Cabinet system, has been, in its broad features, adopted by most European constitutional states, and it matters not at all whether they are called monarchies or republics. It is also characteristic of the governments of British Commonwealth countries, old and new. The non-parliamentary system, on the other hand, is peculiar to the United States and those Latin American Republics which have founded their constitutions upon that of their great neighbour.

Lord Bingham of Cornhill, 'The Courts and the Constitution'
(1996/97) 7 *King's College Law Journal* 15–16

Every fourth-former knows that powers exercised on behalf of the state fall under three broad heads, the legislative, the executive and the judicial. The legislature makes the law, the executive carries it out and the judiciary, in case of doubt or dispute, interprets and applies it. Life in the fourth form is pleasantly simple.

But of course it is not quite as simple as that. True, Parliament does enact new laws—3,233 pages of it in 1985—but it also has important functions in debating policy, holding ministers to account and providing a forum for the redress of grievances. True, the executive does implement the laws made by Parliament, but it also plays a crucial role in initiating almost all new legislation; ministers exercise many powers which are not conferred by Parliament and ministers also, acting under legislative authority and usually subject to parliamentary control, make laws in the form of subordinate legislation—6,518 pages of it in 1985. True again, the judges interpret and apply the laws made by Parliament. But the cases which reach the courts are not usually cases in which Parliament has made its intention clear. In such cases there is nothing to litigate about. It is when the intention of parliament is unclear, or where Parliament has failed to provide for a particular eventuality at all, that litigation ensues. The essential function of the court is then to declare the law which it infers that Parliament intended to make, or would have made if it had addressed the point at all. This is not a legislative role, but nor is it a purely interpretative role, since the court may have to do a good deal more than elicit the meaning of what Parliament has enacted. In the great expanses of English law which are largely untouched by statute, the function of the courts is, I would suggest, even less interpretative, since the legal issues which fall to be decided rarely fall squarely within the ratio of an earlier decision, unless it is sought to challenge that decision. More often cases arise on the border between one decision and another, or at the confluence of two or more competing principles or in an area where there is virtually no relevant authority. The courts have then to decide, in the light of legal principle and such authority as there is, and having regard to the apprehended practical consequences of one decision as opposed to another, what the law should be. The courts also have a role in providing a forum for the redress of grievances and in holding the executive to account, if in either case (but only if) a breach of the law is shown. So the functions of legislature, executive and judiciary are not quite as distinct as one might suppose.

Nor, in contrast with many constitutions, notably the American, does our constitution provide for any rigid separation of powers. The fact that the cabinet, as the engine of the executive, and all other ministers, are necessarily members of one or other House of the legislature is indeed the clearest possible negation of the doctrine. But between the legislature and the executive on the one hand and the judiciary on the other the separation is all but total. ...

G. Marshall, *Constitutional Theory*
(1971), pp. 103–4

A separation between the judicial and the legislative and executive branches obviously exists in both Britain and the United States in the sense that in practice the judges are secure in their offices and have an independent status. But whether the separation of powers doctrine implies the existence of that degree of checking or controlling which has come to be known as judicial review in the American sense is not easy to decide. The right to invalidate legislation obviously in one sense invades the principle that each department has an independent sphere of action and a right to take its own view on matters of constitutionality. On the other hand, the controlling or checking functions of the judicial branch can only consist in impartial application of the law, and where constitutional law places restrictions on legislative power, a duty to declare the law seems to imply a duty to declare when such restrictions have been violated, whether by the legislature or by anyone else.

NOTE: In the United States the Supreme Court in *Marbury* v *Madison* (1803) 1 Cranch 137, decided that it had the power to declare both the acts of Congress and of the President to be unconstitutional. In the United Kingdom courts have refused to adjudicate upon the validity of Acts of Parliament, but they have developed the doctrine of judicial review by which the exercise of power by other authorities may be reviewed in the courts.

R (Keyu) v *Secretary of State for Foreign and Commonwealth Affairs*
[2015] UKSC 69, [2016] AC 1355, Supreme Court

LORD NEUBERGER:

[127] There is no more fundamental aspect of the rule of law than that of judicial review of executive decisions or actions. Where a member of the executive, such as the respondents in this case, is given a statutory discretion to take a particular course or action, such as ordering an inquiry under section 1 of the 2005 Act, the court has jurisdiction to overrule or quash the exercise of that discretion. However, the exercise of that jurisdiction is circumscribed by very well established principles, which are based on the self-evident propositions that the member of the executive is the primary decision-maker, and that he or she will often be more fully informed and advised than a judge. The area covered by judicial review is so great that it is impossible to be exhaustive, but the normal principle is that an executive decision can only be overruled by a court if (i) it was made in excess of jurisdiction, (ii) it was effected for an improper motive, (iii) it was an irrational decision, or, as it is sometimes put, a decision which no rational person in the position of the decision-maker could have taken, or (iv) the decision-maker took into account irrelevant matters or failed to take into account relevant matters. An attack on an executive decision based on such grounds is often known as a Wednesbury challenge (see *Associated Provincial Picture Houses Ltd v Wednesbury Corpn* [1948] 1 KB 223). If one or more of these grounds (which often overlap to some extent) is or are satisfied, the court may (but need not in every case) quash the decision. If none of these grounds is satisfied, then the decision will almost always stand.

The role of the courts in the constitution was further elucidated in the following case, drawing on the concept of the separation of powers to explain the limits of judicial power when considering legal challenges to controversial political decisions.

Duport Steels Ltd v *Sirs*
[1980] 1 WLR 142, House of Lords

Private steel companies sought injunctions against the Iron and Steel Trades Confederation who were calling on workers in the private sector of the steel industry to come out on strike to support workers in the public sector who were striking over pay. The correct interpretation of s. 13(1) of the Trade Union and Labour

Relations Act 1974 (as amended in 1976) was central to the case. Section 13(1) conferred immunity from liability in tort for an act done by a person 'in contemplation or furtherance of a trade dispute'. The Court of Appeal reversed the judge's decision to refuse the injunctions sought; the decision was appealed to the House of Lords.

LORD DIPLOCK: ... My Lords, at a time when more and more cases involve the application of legislation which gives effect to policies that are the subject of bitter public and parliamentary controversy, it cannot be too strongly emphasised that the British constitution, though largely unwritten, is firmly based upon the separation of powers; Parliament makes the laws, the judiciary interpret them. When Parliament legislates to remedy what the majority of its members at the time perceive to be a defect or a lacuna in the existing law (whether it be the written law enacted by existing statutes or the unwritten common law as it has been expounded by the judges in decided cases), the role of the judiciary is confined to ascertaining from the words that Parliament has approved as expressing its intention what that intention was, and to giving effect to it. Where the meaning of the statutory words is plain and unambiguous it is not for the judges to invent fancied ambiguities as an excuse for failing to give effect to its plain meaning because they themselves consider that the consequences of doing so would be inexpedient, or even unjust or immoral. In controversial matters such as are involved in industrial relations there is room for difference of opinion as to what is expedient, what is just and what is morally justifiable. Under our constitution it is Parliament's opinion on these matters that is paramount.

A statute passed to remedy what is perceived by Parliament to be a defect in the existing law may in actual operation turn out to have injurious consequences that Parliament did not anticipate at the time the statute was passed; if it had, it would have made some provision in the Act in order to prevent them. It is at least possible that Parliament when the Acts of 1974 and 1976 were passed did not anticipate that so widespread and crippling use as has in fact occurred would be made of sympathetic withdrawals of labour and of secondary blacking and picketing in support of sectional interests able to exercise 'industrial muscle.' But if this be the case it is for Parliament, not for the judiciary, to decide whether any changes should be made to the law as stated in the Acts, and, if so, what are the precise limits that ought to be imposed upon the immunity from liability for torts committed in the course of taking industrial action. These are matters on which there is a wide legislative choice the exercise of which is likely to be influenced by the political complexion of the government and the state of public opinion at the time amending legislation is under consideration.

It endangers continued public confidence in the political impartiality of the judiciary, which is essential to the continuance of the rule of law, if judges, under the guise of interpretation, provide their own preferred amendments to statutes which experience of their operation has shown to have had consequences that members of the court before whom the matter comes consider to be injurious to the public interest. The frequency with which controversial legislation is amended by Parliament itself (as witness the Act of 1974 which was amended in 1975 as well as in 1976) indicates that legislation, after it has come into operation, may fail to have the beneficial effects which Parliament expected or may produce injurious results that Parliament did not anticipate. But, except by private or hybrid Bills, Parliament does not legislate for individual cases. Public Acts of Parliament are general in their application; they govern all cases falling within categories of which the definitions are to be found in the wording of the statute. So in relation to section 13(1) of the Acts of 1974 and 1976, for a judge (who is always dealing with an individual case) to pose himself the question: 'Can Parliament really have intended that the acts that were done in this particular case should have the benefit of the immunity?' is to risk straying beyond his constitutional role as interpreter of the enacted law and assuming a power to decide at his own discretion whether or not to apply the general law to a particular case. The legitimate questions for a judge in his role as interpreter of the enacted law are: 'How has Parliament, by the words that it has used in the statute to express its intentions, defined the category of acts that are entitled to the immunity? Do the acts done in this particular case fall within that description?'

LORD SCARMAN: … My basic criticism of all three judgments in the Court of Appeal is that in their desire to do justice the court failed to do justice according to law. When one is considering law in the hands of the judges, law means the body of rules and guidelines within which society requires its judges to administer justice….

[I]n the field of statute law the judge must be obedient to the will of Parliament as expressed in its enactments. In this field Parliament makes, and un-makes, the law: the judge's duty is to interpret and to apply the law, not to change it to meet the judge's idea of what justice requires. Interpretation does, of course, imply in the interpreter a power of choice where differing constructions are possible. But our law requires the judge to choose the construction which in his judgment best meets the legislative purpose of the enactment. If the result be unjust but inevitable, the judge may say so and invite Parliament to reconsider its provision. But he must not deny the statute. Unpalatable statute law may not be disregarded or rejected, merely because it is unpalatable. Only if a just result can be achieved without violating the legislative purpose of the statute may the judge select the construction which best suits his idea of what justice requires. Further, in our system the rule 'stare decisis' applies as firmly to statute law as it does to the formulation of common law and equitable principles. And the keystone of 'stare decisis' is loyalty throughout the system to the decisions of the Court of Appeal and this House. The Court of Appeal may not overrule a House of Lords decision: and only in the exceptional circumstances set out in the Practice Statement of July 1, 1966 (*Practice Statement (Judicial Precedent)* [1966] 1 WLR 1234), will this House refuse to follow its own previous decisions.

Within these limits, which cannot be said in a free society possessing elective legislative institutions to be narrow or constrained, judges, as the remarkable judicial career of Lord Denning himself shows, have a genuine creative role. Great judges are in their different ways judicial activists. But the constitution's separation of powers, or more accurately functions, must be observed if judicial independence is not to be put at risk. For, if people and Parliament come to think that the judicial power is to be confined by nothing other than the judge's sense of what is right (or, as Selden put it, by the length of the Chancellor's foot), confidence in the judicial system will be replaced by fear of it becoming uncertain and arbitrary in its application. Society will then be ready for Parliament to cut the power of the judges. Their power to do justice will become more restricted by law than it need be, or is today.

Appeal allowed.

NOTE: In the long-running debate preceding the enactment of the Human Rights Act 1998 (see Chapter 9), the issue of separation of powers, particularly the relationship between Parliament and the courts, was a recurrent theme. The respective roles of Parliament and the courts following the Act coming into force in October 2000 have been considered by Lord Irvine of Lairg, a former Lord Chancellor, and in the courts.

Lord Irvine of Lairg LC, 'Constitutional Reform and a Bill of Rights'
[1997] *European Human Rights Law Review* 483

The British Constitution is firmly based on the separation of powers. It is essential that incorporation is achieved in a way which does nothing to disturb that balance. It is for Parliament to pass laws, not the judges. It is for the judges to interpret these laws and to develop the common law, not for Parliament or the executive. It is also for the courts to ensure that the powers conferred by Parliament on the executive and other bodies are neither exceeded nor abused but exercised lawfully. That will continue to be so after the European Convention becomes part of our domestic law.

Incorporation will enhance the judges' powers to protect the individual against the abuse of power by the State. We have a high quality of judicial review in this country. It has often rightly held the executive to account and improved the quality of administrative decision making. So the concept of judges protecting the citizen and holding the executive to account is nothing new. What is new is that the judges will be given a framework by Parliament within which to interpret the law.

Incorporating basic human rights into our domestic law will be a major new departure. It will offer new challenges. What is critical is that the form of incorporation sits comfortably with our United Kingdom institutions. It must not disturb the supremacy of Parliament. It should not put the judges in a position where they are seen as at odds with Parliament. That would be a recipe for conflict and mutual recrimination. It is vital that the courts should not become involved in a process of policy evaluation which goes far beyond its allotted constitutional role. In a democratic society, compromises between competing interests must be resolved by Parliament—or if Parliament so decides, by Ministers.

R (Lord Carlile of Berriew) v *Secretary of State for the Home Department*
[2014] UKSC 60, [2015] AC 945, Supreme Court

The case concerned a challenge to the decision of the Home Secretary to exclude a dissident Iranian politician from entering the UK at the invitation of a number of parliamentarians. The argument of the parliamentarians that their right to freedom of expression, contained in Art. 10 of the ECHR, had been violated was rejected in the Court of Appeal. In the Supreme Court, there was consideration of whether sensitive decisions allocated to the executive, including those concerning national security and international relations, must be respected by the courts.

LORD SUMPTION:

[28] The first possibility is that it is being invited to respect the separation of powers and the special constitutional function of the executive. The Human Rights Act 1998 did not abrogate the constitutional distribution of powers between the organs of the state which the courts had recognised for many years before it was passed. The case law of the Strasbourg court is not insensitive to questions of democratic accountability, even though their significance will vary from case to case. Even in the context of Convention rights, there remain areas which although not immune from scrutiny require a qualified respect for the constitutional functions of decision-makers who are democratically accountable. Examples are decisions involving policy choices (*R (Alconbury Developments Ltd) v Secretary of State for the Environment, Transport and the Regions* [2003] 2 AC 295, paras 75-76); broad questions of economic and social policy (*Wilson v First County Trust Ltd (No. 2)* [2004] 1 AC 816, para 70); or issues involving the allocation of finite resources: *Wandsworth London Borough Council v Michalak* [2003] 1 WLR 617, para 41 (Brooke LJ).

[29] However, traditional notions of the constitutional distribution of powers have unquestionably been modified by the Human Rights Act 1998. In the first place, any arguable allegation that a person's Convention rights have been infringed is necessarily justiciable. Section 6 of the Act requires public authorities, including the courts, to give effect to those rights. Secondly, the jurisprudence of the European Court of Human Rights calls for a standard of review of the proportionality of the decisions of public authorities which is not only formal and procedural but to some extent substantive.

Appeal dismissed (Lord Kerr dissenting).

NOTES

1. The form of incorporation which has been adopted will not permit the courts to strike down or disapply legislation which is incompatible with the European Convention on Human Rights. This contrasts with the position arising during UK membership of the European Union. As a result of s. 2(4) of the European Communities Act 1972, domestic courts acquired the power to disapply legislation which is inconsistent with EU law (see *R v Secretary of State for Transport, ex parte Factortame Ltd (No. 2)* [1991] 1 AC 603, in Chapter 2, Section 3A(b) at pp. 74–5).
2. The impact of the Human Rights Act 1998 on the separation of powers cannot not be considered in isolation. The more formal recognition of judicial independence resulting from the changes made by the Constitutional Reform Act 2005 (discussed in Chapter 4) may also be understood to

reinforce this concept in the UK; see Roger Masterman, *The Separation of Powers in the Contemporary Constitution: Judicial Competence and Independence in the United Kingdom* (2010).

3. The case of *Carlile* demonstrates that a reinvigorated understanding of the separation of powers (if that is what now exists in the UK) may not have a straightforward impact on the powers of the courts. As Masterman notes at p. 248:

> while separation of powers is increasingly used as a tool of judicial reasoning which lends weight to the checking and balancing role of the courts, it is also invoked as justification for deference and in order to effect the legitimate policy role of the executive. The contemporary separation of powers both empowers and restrains the courts ...

■ QUESTIONS

1. Can we be confident that the United Kingdom's constitution is 'firmly based on the separation of powers', as both Lord Diplock and Lord Irvine assert, when, in practice, the government of the day wields significant control over both executive and legislative power?

2. Given that the doctrine of the separation of powers can be cited both in support of, and in opposition to, judicial interference with acts of the legislature, is the principle of any real value? Marshall concludes his essay on the subject in *Constitutional Theory* (1971), p. 124:

> In short, the principle is infected with so much imprecision and inconsistency that it may be counted little more than a jumbled portmanteau of arguments for policies which ought to be supported or rejected on other grounds.

Is this correct? And if so, would anything be lost if the principle was removed from our constitutional discourse?

B: Responsible government

The institutions of government must all act lawfully, within the scope of their respective constitutional roles. But in addition, it is also important that government acts responsibly, within the scope of its lawful powers. This means government must be changeable, open to challenge, and held to account.

J. Lively, *Democracy*
(1975), pp. 43–4

What then are the conditions necessary for the existence of responsible government? What is needed to ensure that some popular control can be exerted over political leadership, some governmental accountability can be enforced? Two main conditions can be suggested, that governments should be removable by electoral decisions and that some alternative can be substituted by electoral decision. The alternative, it should be stressed, must be more than an alternative governing group. It must comprehend alternatives in policy, since it is only if an electoral decision can alter the actions of government that popular control can be said to be established. ... To borrow the economic analogy, competition is meaningless, or at any rate cannot create consumer sovereignty, unless there is some product differentiation.

In detail there might be a great deal of discussion about the institutional arrangements necessary to responsible government, but in general some are obvious. There must be free elections, in which neither the incumbent government nor any other group can determine the electoral result by means other than indications of how they will act if returned to power. Fraud, intimidation and bribery are thus incompatible with responsible government. ... Another part of the institutional frame necessary to responsible government is freedom of association. Unless groups wishing to compete for leadership have the freedom to organize and formulate alternative programmes, the presentation of alternatives would be impossible.

Lastly, freedom of speech is necessary since silent alternatives can never be effective alternatives. In considering such arrangements, we cannot stick at simple legal considerations; we must move from questions of 'freedom from' to questions of 'ability to'. The absence of any legal bar to association will not, for example, create the ability to associate if there are heavy costs involved which only some groups can bear. Nor will the legal guarantee of freedom of speech be of much use if access to the mass media is severely restricted.

This could be summed up by saying that responsible government depends largely upon the existence of, and free competition between, political parties.

Whether the British system of government creates the conditions for responsible government is doubted in some quarters. Lord Hailsham spoke of 'elective dictatorship' in the following extract.

Lord Hailsham, *The Dilemma of Democracy*
(1978), pp. 21–2

The old party structure, which for so long guaranteed the evolutionary character of our society, seems to me to have broken down. ...

[I]t seems to me that we are moving more and more in the direction of an elective dictatorship, not the less objectionable in principle because it is inefficient in practice, and not the less tyrannical in its nature because the opposed parties, becoming more and more polarized in their attitudes, seek with some prospects of success to seize the new levers of power and use them alternately to reverse the direction taken by their immediate predecessors. All the more unfortunate does this become in the presence of narrow majorities, each representing a minority of the electorate, sometimes a small minority, and when at least one of the parties believes that the prerogatives and rights conferred by electoral victory, however narrow, not merely entitle but compel it to impose on the helpless but unorganized majority irreversible changes for which it never consciously voted and to which most of its members are opposed.

It seems to me that this is a situation the reverse of liberal and even the reverse of democratic, in the sense in which the word has hitherto been understood. Fundamental and irreversible changes ought only to be imposed, if at all, in the light of an unmistakable national consensus. It follows that, if I am right, the overriding need of the moment is to pursue policies and enact legislation to ensure that a like situation to the present is never allowed to recur. It is true that the present nature of the threat can be seen to come from the left. But this need not necessarily be so, and almost certainly it will not always be so. ...

My thesis is that our institutions must be so structurally altered that, so far as regards permanent legislation, the will of the majority will always prevail against that of the party composing the executive for the time being, and that, whoever may form the government of the day will be compelled to follow procedures and policies compatible with the nature of Parliamentary democracy and the rule of freedom under law.

■ QUESTIONS

1. Lord Hailsham wrote in 1978; has anything changed since then to contradict his thesis, or have subsequent events confirmed his worst fears? See also Leslie Wolf-Phillips in the following extract.

2. N. Johnson, 'Constitutional Reform: Some Dilemmas for a Conservative Philosophy' in *Conservative Party Politics* (Layton-Henry, ed., 1980), p. 139, stated:

> A relative majority in the House of Commons may rest on a minority position in the country. Government on these terms is tolerable if the party in power recognises that there are limits to what it is entitled to do.

Is there evidence that such limits have been recognized—and shaped the actions of governments—in the last 40 years?

L. Wolf-Phillips, 'A Long Look at the British Constitution'
(1984) 37 *Parliamentary Affairs* 385, 398–401

The idealised view of the British system is that, under a head of State insulated from politics, generally admired, and with long and varied experience, the government of the day is led by a Prime Minister whose party has been given a parliamentary majority by a mature electorate which has participated in free and open elections. Parliament debates the great issues of the day, controls national expenditure and taxation, criticises government policy as an aid to its improvement, scrutinises the work of the central administration, and ensures the redress of collective and individual grievances. The Prime Minister heads a government composed of a Cabinet of her senior ministers and about eighty non-Cabinet ministers all bound to a policy implicitly approved by the electorate; the Prime Minister and all her colleagues must justify their actions and their policies before parliament, and if parliament withdraws its confidence, they must resign and face the stern judgment of the electorate upon their stewardship. Each minister has departmental responsibility and can be called to account for the working of his department before parliament; if incompetence or maladministration be proved then the minister will be called upon to resign either by the Prime Minister or by the direct action of parliament. The Queen as Head of State gives overall stability to the political system and the Prime Minister as Head of Government is one who has served a long apprenticeship in parliament in high office of state and who is the elected leader of a party which has the confidence of the nation. The 'Unwritten Constitution' has the virtue of flexibility and permits the wide use of constitutional conventions, both permitting and facilitating evolutionary consensual change. Finally, the House of Lords provides a forum removed from party ties and considerations, where the experienced and distinguished perform functions of assistance, advice, continuity and, when needed, a measure of restraint on the popularly-elected transient majority in the House of Commons.

What is the reality? The extension of the franchise, the growth of national mass parties and the development of the mass media have changed the nature of general elections, which have become largely personalised into a contest between party leaders. The majority of the electorate are only marginally politically conscious, and the personalisation of political issues and allegiances reflect this marginality. The voting pattern for the parties is so uniform throughout the country that the influence on a constituency of a particular candidate is insignificant; candidates without the support of a major party can expect to fail and minor or ad hoc or single-interest parties can expect to be swept aside. … Elections cannot be, and should not be regarded as, a means for approving the details of comprehensive manifestoes and the electors often seem to vote against a party rather than for the winning party. …

The only mandate that most electors consider they have given to newly-elected Members of Parliament is to support the party and its leader; certainly, the Prime Minister expects, and usually gets, the support of the mass of the parliamentary majority party and the entire hundred or so members of the Government that is formed.

In brief, the actual Westminster model is that of authoritarian single-party governments in a House of Commons dominated by the Prime Minister and composed largely of disciplined parties with most votes in the House of Commons being highly predictable; every three or four years there is a general election held under a crude simple majority electoral system with minimal participation by the electorate in the choice of who shall be their candidate, though they do have the choice between the candidates who are selected by the party activists; between 20% and 30% of the electorate do not vote at all. Governments rarely fall as a result of a vote in the House of Commons and resignations under ministerial responsibility are almost as rare. The vast majority of legislation proposed by the government of the day is passed; it is rare, indeed it is well-nigh impossible, for legislation to be passed of which the government does not approve. Orthodox constitutional theory bestows on individual members the right of independent action and does not regard them as the representative of the party without which they would not have been elected; over-solicitude for the wishes of their constituents would probably lead them into conflict with the party in parliament. The parties at large are not seen as the formers of policy for the government; that is a task reserved for the parliamentary members of the governing party.

■ **QUESTIONS**

1. To what extent are such objections a result of the acceptance of a legal constitutionalist outlook? If the flaws of the United Kingdom's constitutional system are as described, what is the solution? Should faith in the political constitution be abandoned, and a codified constitution enacted?

2. Do such objections underestimate the effectiveness of political accountability mechanisms? See the extract which follows from Flinders and Kelso, which assesses critically the 'Parliamentary Decline Thesis'—the position that there has been a modern decline in the power of parliaments to control governmental activity.

M. Flinders and A. Kelso, 'Mind the Gap: Political Analysis, Public Expectations and the Parliamentary Decline Thesis'

(2011) *British Journal of Politics and International Relations* 251, 257–8

We are not arguing that the balance of power has not shifted from legislatures to executives in many parliamentary democracies around the world. Certainly in the post-war era, executives have dramatically expanded both their public policy universes and their capacity to operate within them, while legislatures have not benefited from increases in institutional resources and capacity of a commensurate magnitude. To this extent the PDT [Parliamentary Decline Thesis] is correct. Our argument, rather, is more subtle. The PDT has *over-stated* the extent of this shift in the constitutional balance of power, it has failed to acknowledge that parliamentary democracy was founded on the principle of 'strong government' and did not therefore include a proactive or assertive role for the legislature, and it has largely overlooked the existence of informal, but no less important, executive control mechanisms. Scholars may have inadvertently played a key role in widening the 'expectations gap' and therefore contributed to the erosion of political support. ...

It is this failure by contemporary commentators ... to take account of the real complexities of parliament that is so problematic in terms of understanding the impact of the PDT. There are at least four sources of detailed empirical evidence that contradict, or at the very least challenge, the PDT. First, there is the work of scholars like Lord Norton (1983) and Philip Cowley (2002) which has clearly demonstrated that Commons voting behaviour has become far more complex, and that back-bench MPs have become more likely to vote against their parties. The notion of MPs as little more than 'lobby fodder' is highly dubious. Second, since the influential work of Anthony King on 'modes of executive–legislative relations' in 1976 a number of scholars have examined and emphasised the role of intra-party machinery and processes as critical but generally unobserved control mechanisms. ... Third, research on voting behaviour in the House of Lords by Meg Russell and Maria Sciara (2007) has shown that a vastly more complicated picture now exists in terms of how peers vote on government legislation, and that the second chamber now has a reasonably substantial impact on government legislation. Finally, possibly the most important challenge to the PDT lies not in scholarly work but in the diaries and memoirs of former politicians. This paints a consistent picture of an executive–legislative relationship that is more balanced, or at the very least respectful, than many academic and journalistic accounts would entertain (for a review see Flinders 2000). Two contemporary examples support this point: David Richards and Helen Mathers' (2010) analysis of David Blunkett's taped memoirs provide a full and frank account of the formal and informal relationships between ministers and parliament; while Chris Mullin's (2010) *View from the Foothills* provides a similarly detailed account of the role of intra-party channels (notably the Parliamentary Committee and the Parliamentary Labour Party) in moderating relationships. ...

In arguing that parliament has been relieved of its powers and that this is to be regretted, the PDT makes fundamentally misguided assumptions about the role of parliament in modern British politics. ... We are not arguing that a shift in the balance of power between the executive and parliament has not occurred; we are arguing that a misunderstanding of constitutional development has led to the overinflation of that shift. This overinflation has created an expectations gap between what the public expects parliament to do and what its role actually is within the political system. Put simply, the PDT would not be so critical, and public confidence in the efficacy of parliament might not be so low, if the expectations of parliament were more realistic.

See also discussion of the constitutional responsibilities of government ministers, and the scrutiny functions of Parliament, in Chapter 6.

SECTION 6: THE STATE

The final idea to consider in this chapter is the state. Bradley and Ewing in *Constitutional and Administrative Law* (2011), p. 3, state that:

... constitutional law concerns the relationship between the individual and the state, seen from a particular viewpoint, namely the notion of law. ... Law is not merely a matter of the rules which govern relations between private individuals. ... Law also concerns the structure and powers of the state.

If we are to examine the ambit of constitutional law in the United Kingdom, we need to have some notion of what the state is.

C. F. Strong, *Modern Political Constitutions*
(1972), pp. 4–5

[T]he state is something more than a mere collection of families, or an agglomeration of occupational organisation, or a referee holding the ring between the conflicting interests of the voluntary associations which it permits to exist. In a properly organized political community the state exists for society and not society for the state; yet, however socially advanced a people may be, the society which it constitutes—made up of families, clubs, churches, trade unions, etc.—is not to be trusted to maintain itself without the ultimate arbitrament of force.

All associations make rules and regulations for their conduct, and when men are associated politically these rules and regulations are called laws, the power to make these being the prerogative of the state and of no other association. Thus, in the words of R M MacIver, a 'state is the fundamental association for the maintenance and development of social order, and to this end its central institution is endowed with the united power of the community.' But this definition might conceivably cover a pastoral or nomadic society which, indeed, found a bond of union in the patriarch or head of the family who, in some sort, discharged the powers of government. Such a society, however, lacks territoriality, an indispensable condition of true political organization, a condition emphasized by H J W Hetherington when he says: 'The state is the institution or set of institutions which, in order to secure certain elementary common purposes and conditions of life, unites under a single authority the inhabitants of a clearly-marked territorial area.' But what is this 'united power of the community' in the first, this 'single authority' in the second definition? It is the power or authority to make law. So we come to the definition given by Woodrow Wilson: 'A state is a people organized for law within a definite territory.'

S. E. Finer, *Comparative Government*
(1970), p. 24

The defining characteristics of a state ... are: (1) It is a territorially defined association. (2) It embraces, compulsorily, all the persons in that territory. (3) It possesses the monopoly of violence throughout this area, by virtue of which it has the capacity, even if not the moral authority, to guarantee the finality of its decision in political disputes arising from the conflict of individuals or groups within its territory. (4) As a necessary accompaniment of all this, it has a body of persons who exercise this monopoly of violence in its name, namely, the common government.

We must also consider critical perspectives on the state, and the roles of the branches of government within it. In a broad sense, different constitutional institutions and officials may be seen as operating in a way which is mutually reinforcing of state power.

R. Miliband, *The State in Capitalist Society*
(1969), pp. 49–54

There is one preliminary problem about the state which is very seldom considered, yet which requires attention if the discussion of its nature and role is to be properly focused. This is the fact that 'the state' is not a thing, that it does not, as such, exist. What 'the state' stands for is a number of particular institutions which, together, constitute its reality, and which interact as parts of what may be called the state system.

The point is by no means academic. For the treatment of one part of the state—usually the government—as the state itself introduces a major element of confusion in the discussion of the nature and incidence of state *power*; and that confusion can have large political consequences. Thus, if it is believed that the government is in fact the state, it may also be believed that the assumption of governmental power is equivalent to the acquisition of state power. Such a belief, resting as it does on vast assumptions about the nature of state power, is fraught with great risks and disappointments. To understand the nature of state power, it is necessary first of all to distinguish, and then to relate, the various elements which make up the state system.

It is not very surprising that government and state should often appear as synonymous for it is the government which speaks on the state's behalf. It was the state to which Weber was referring when he said, in a famous phrase, that, in order to be, it must 'successfully claim the monopoly of the legitimate use of physical force within a given territory'. But 'the state' cannot claim anything: only the government of the day, or its duly empowered agents, can. Men, it is often said, give their allegiance not to the government of the day but to the state. But the state, from this point of view, is a nebulous entity; and while men may choose to give their allegiance to it, it is to the government that they are required to give their obedience. A defiance of its orders is a defiance of the state, in whose name the government alone may speak and for whose actions it must assume ultimate responsibility. …

A second element of the state system which requires investigation is the administrative one, which now extends far beyond the traditional bureaucracy of the state, and which encompasses a large variety of bodies, often related to particular ministerial departments, or enjoying a greater or lesser degree of autonomy—public corporations, central banks, regulatory commissions, etc.—and concerned with the management of the economic, social, cultural and other activities in which the state is now directly or indirectly involved. The extraordinary growth of this administrative and bureaucratic element in all societies, including advanced capitalist ones, is of course one of the most obvious features of contemporary life; and the relation of its leading members to the government and to society is also crucial to the determination of the role of the state.

Formally, officialdom is at the service of the political executive, its obedient instrument, the tool of its will. In actual fact it is nothing of the kind. Everywhere and inevitably the administrative process is also part of the political process; administration is always political as well as executive, at least at the levels where policy-making is relevant, that is to say in the upper layers of administrative life. … Officials and administrators cannot divest themselves of all ideological clothing in the advice which they tender to their political masters, or in the independent decisions which they are in a position to take. The power which top civil servants and other state administrators possess no doubt varies from country to country, from department to department, and from individual to individual. But nowhere do these men *not* contribute directly and appreciably to the exercise of state power. …

Some of these considerations apply to all other elements of the state system. They apply for instance to a third such element, namely the military, to which may, for present purposes, be added the paramilitary, security and police forces of the state, and which together form that branch of it mainly concerned with the 'management of violence'.

In most capitalist countries, this coercive apparatus constitutes a vast, sprawling and resourceful establishment, whose professional leaders are men of high status and great influence, inside the state system and in society. …

Whatever may be the case in practice, the formal constitutional position of the administrative and coercive elements is to serve the state by serving the government of the day. In contrast, it is not at all the formal constitutional duty of judges, at least in Western-type political systems, to serve the purposes of their governments. They are constitutionally independent of the political executive and protected from it by security of tenure and other guarantees. Indeed, the concept of judicial independence is deemed to entail not merely the freedom of judges from responsibility to the political executive, but their active duty to protect the citizen *against* the political executive or its agents, and to act, in the state's encounter with members of society, as the defenders of the latter's rights and liberties. … But in any case, the judiciary is an integral part of the state system, which affects, often profoundly, the exercise of state power.

So too, to a greater or lesser degree, does a fifth element of the state system, namely the various units of sub-central government. In one of its aspects, sub-central government constitutes an extension of central government and administration, the latter's antennae or tentacles. In some political systems it has indeed practically no other function. In the countries of advanced capitalism, on the other hand, sub-central government is rather more than an administrative device. In addition to being agents of the state these units of government have also traditionally performed another function. They have not only been the channels of communication and administration from the centre to the periphery, but also the voice of the periphery, or of particular interests at the periphery; they have been a means of overcoming local particularities, but also platforms for their expression, instruments of central control and obstacles to it. For all the centralisation of power, which is a major feature of government in these countries, sub-central organs of government … have remained power structures in their own right, and therefore able to affect very markedly the lives of the populations they have governed.

Much the same point may be made about the representative assemblies of advanced capitalism. Now more than ever their life revolves around the government; and even where, as in the United States, they are formally independent organs of constitutional and political power, their relationship with the political executive cannot be a purely critical or obstructive one. That relationship is one of conflict *and* cooperation.

Nor is this a matter of division between a pro-government side and an anti-government one. *Both* sides reflect this duality. For opposition parties cannot be wholly uncooperative. Merely by taking part in the work of the legislature, they help the government's business.

As for government parties, they are seldom if ever single-minded in their support of the political executive and altogether subservient to it. They include people who, by virtue of their position and influence must be persuaded, cajoled, threatened or bought off.

It is in the constitutionally-sanctioned performance of this cooperative and critical function that legislative assemblies have a share in the exercise of state power. That share is rather less extensive and exalted than is often claimed for these bodies. But … it is not, even in an epoch of executive dominance, an unimportant one.

■ QUESTIONS

1. What difficulties does this view of the State pose for legal and political constitutionalists? Can legal limits enforced by the judiciary be an effective restraint on State action? Can mechanisms of political accountability be effective when representative assemblies and opposition parties must to some extent cooperate with the Government?

2. How has the concept of the State been used in constitutional practice in the United Kingdom? Is the Government the State, or is it an institution or servant of the State? See the cases which follow.

D v National Society for the Prevention of Cruelty to Children
[1978] AC 171, House of Lords

The mother of a child (alleged by an informant to be the victim of ill-treatment) brought an action against the NSPCC for damages for nervous shock alleged to be the result of the society's investigation pursuant to the informant's complaint. The mother sought discovery of the identity of the informant. The NSPCC, an independent body incorporated by royal charter, claimed 'public interest immunity' as justifying its refusal to disclose the identity of its informants. The mother argued unsuccessfully that the society could not rely on this defence as it was not part of the State.

LORD SIMON OF GLAISDALE: ... '[T]he state' cannot on any sensible political theory be restricted to the Crown and the departments of central government (which are, indeed, part of the Crown in constitutional law). The state is the whole organisation of the body politic for supreme civil rule and government—the whole political organisation which is the basis of civil government. As such it certainly extends to local—and, as I think, also statutory—bodies in so far as they are exercising autonomous rule.

Chandler v Director of Public Prosecutions
[1964] AC 763, House of Lords

The appellants, in seeking to further the aims of the Campaign for Nuclear Disarmament, entered and sought to immobilize an airfield. The airfield was a 'prohibited place' under s. 3 of the Official Secrets Act 1911. The appellants were charged with conspiracy to commit a breach of s. 1 of the Act, whereby it is an offence to enter any prohibited place 'for any purpose prejudicial to the safety or interests of the State'. The appellants argued that their actions were not prejudicial to the safety or interests of the State, but rather it was their belief that their actions would be beneficial to the State. They further argued that 'State' means the numerical collection of inhabitants in the geographical area and not the Government or organs of government through which the State expresses its intentions.

LORD REID: ... Next comes the question of what is meant by the safety or interests of the State. 'State' is not an easy word. It does not mean the Government or the Executive. 'L'Etat c'est moi' was a shrewd remark, but can hardly have been intended as a definition even in the France of the time. And I do not think that it means, as counsel argued, the individuals who inhabit these islands. The statute cannot be referring to the interests of all those individuals because they may differ and the interests of the majority are not necessarily the same as the interests of the State. Again we have seen only too clearly in some other countries what can happen if you personify and almost deify the State. Perhaps the country or the realm are as good synonyms as one can find and I would be prepared to accept the organised community as coming as near to a definition as one can get.

LORD DEVLIN: ... What is meant by 'the State'? Is it the same thing as what I have just called 'the country'? Mr Foster, for the appellants, submits that it means the inhabitants of a particular geographical area. I doubt if it ever has as wide a meaning as that. I agree that in an appropriate context the safety and interests of the State might mean simply the public or national safety and interests. But the more precise use of the word 'State,' the use to be expected in a legal context, and the one which I am quite satisfied ... was intended in this statute, is to denote the organs of government of a national community. In the United Kingdom, in relation at any rate to the armed forces and to the defence of the realm, that organ is the Crown. So long as the Crown maintains armed forces for the defence of the realm, it cannot be in its interest that any part of them should be immobilised.

LORD PEARCE: ... I cannot accept the argument that the words 'the interests of the State' in this context mean the interests of the amorphous populace, without regard to the guiding policies of those in authority, and that proof of possible ultimate benefit to the populace may for the purposes of the Act justify an act of spying or sabotage. The protection covers certain specified places which are obviously vital to defence and other places to which the Secretary of State sees fit to extend the protection. ... Parliament clearly intended to give stringent protection to such places. It is hard to believe that it intended to withhold that protection in all cases where a jury might think that the place in question was not necessary or desirable or where the authorities could not by evidence justify their policies to a jury's satisfaction. Questions of defence policy are vast, complicated, confidential, and wholly unsuited for ventilation before a jury. In such a context the interests of the State must in my judgment mean the interests of the State according to the policies laid down for it by its recognised organs of government and authority, the policies of the State as they are, not as they ought, in the opinion of a jury, to be. Anything which prejudices those policies is within the meaning of the Act 'prejudicial to the interests of the State.'

■ QUESTION

If the Government determines the interests of the State, does this harbour any threat to individual liberty? Can the interests of the State, understood broadly, justify a limitation of the rights of a particular group of individuals? See the following case.

Regina (Bancoult) v Secretary of State for Foreign and Commonwealth Affairs (No. 2)
[2008] UKHL 61, [2009] 1 AC 453, House of Lords

The inhabitants of the Chagos Islands, a part of the British Indian Ocean Territory, had their right of abode on the islands removed by s. 9 of the British Indian Ocean Territory (Constitution) Order 2004. This constitution, made by prerogative Order in Council, reintroduced a historic ban on settlement on the Chagos Islands which had previously been held to be unlawful in the United Kingdom courts. The original ban, implemented in 1971, served to allow the establishment by the United States of America of a military base on the island of Diego Garcia. A report into the economic feasibility of returning the Chagossians to the islands having been conducted, the Government determined that it could not support resettlement, and legislated to prevent it. Before the House of Lords, the question of whether the power of Her Majesty in Council to legislate for the British Indian Ocean Territory had to be exercised in the interests of the Chagossians, or in the broader interests of the United Kingdom, was considered.

LORD RODGER: ... 114. Of course, the decision was adverse to the claim of the Chagossians to return to settle on the outer islands. But that does not mean that their interests had been ignored: a realistic assessment of the long-term position of any potential Chagossian settlers on the outer islands was central to the expert report on which the Government relied. In addition, the Government considered the overall interests of the United Kingdom. It was entitled to do so. There is no support whatever for a proposition that, as a matter of English law, in legislating for a colony, either Parliament or Her Majesty in Council must have regard only, or even predominantly, to the immediate interests of the population of the colony. On the contrary, the authority of Parliament and the Crown could always be exercised on 'trade, shipping, or matters of law and policy affecting the whole empire': *Jenkyns, British Rule and Jurisdiction beyond the Seas*, p 22. Since most colonies had legislatures, these wider interests were usually given effect by making an Order in Council disallowing offending statutes rather than by enacting legislation. But, in crucial areas, such as the abolition of slavery, or the regulation of merchant shipping, Parliament would enact legislation for Her Majesty's possessions as a whole. The underlying assumption was, of course, that the policies in question were for the ultimate benefit of all those pos-sessions. Similarly, assuming, of course, that the Government had to take account of the interests of the islanders, it was nevertheless entitled to give appropriate weight to the wider, economic, foreign affairs and defence interests of the United Kingdom when it decided whether to enact the Orders in Council. In the absence of any relevant legal criteria, judges are not well placed to second-guess the balance struck by ministers on such a matter.

LORD MANCE (dissenting): ... 157. [The Government's] submission treats BIOT and the prerogative power to make constitutional or other laws relating to BIOT as if they related to nothing more than the bare land, and as if the people inhabiting BIOT were an insignificant inconvenience (a phrase which reflects the flavour of some of the Government's internal memoranda in the 1960s), liable to be dis-possessed at will for any reason that might seem good to the executive in the interests of the United Kingdom. Sir Sydney accepts that in administering BIOT the Crown in Council was entitled to have regard to the interests of the United Kingdom and its territories generally, and was not confined to con-sideration of the benefits to BIOT alone. He also accepts that the United Kingdom could, in the defence interests of itself and its ally, require Chagossians resident in one part of the territory (Diego Garcia) to move to another part, and that there might be extreme circumstances of necessity (eg where a whole territory became unsafe for inhabitation, due to volcanic eruption or imminent threat of inundation) where the United Kingdom could by Order in Council require its evacuation. But enacting a constitu-tion for a conquered or ceded colony which has the aim of depopulating the whole of a habitable terri-tory in the interests of the United Kingdom or its allies is another matter. A colony, whether conquered, ceded or settled, consists, first and foremost, of people living in a territory, with links to a parent state. The Crown's 'constituent' power to introduce a constitution for a ceded territory is a power intended to enable the proper governance of the territory, at least among other things for the benefit of the people inhabiting it. A constitution which exiles a territory's inhabitants is a contradiction in terms. The absence of any precedent for the exercise of the royal prerogative to exclude the inhabitants of a colony from the colony is significant, although to my mind entirely unsurprising. Until the present case, no-one can have conceived of its exercise for such a purpose. Territories, such as Gibraltar or Malta, have been conquered or ceded with military purposes in mind, but never, so far as appears, has there been either an original purpose or a subsequent attempt compulsorily to exclude their natural inhabitants. It may not have been necessary in the present case to use force to empty BIOT, but the logic of the Government's position is that this too would have been permissible.

Appeal allowed (Lords Bingham and Mance dissenting).

NOTES

1. In the aftermath of this case, following a public consultation, the Government created a 'marine protection area' (MPA) to prevent fishing around the Chagos Islands. Judicial review of this deci-sion was sought on the grounds that the Government had an improper motive for the creation of the MPA (to prevent resettlement of the Chagos Islands definitively), but this claim was dismissed in the Administrative Court (see *R (Bancoult) v Secretary of State for Foreign and Commonwealth Affairs (No. 3)* [2013] EWHC 1502 (Admin), upheld in the Court of Appeal [2014] EWCA Civ 708).
2. In the Supreme Court [2016] UKSC 35, the 2008 judgment of the House of Lords in *Bancoult (No. 2)* was subsequently challenged on the basis that the Secretary of State had failed in his pub-lic law duty of candour, by not disclosing relevant documents (which had later emerged, raising doubts about the initial resettlement feasibility study from 2002) which would have changed the original decision reached in the courts. The application for the 2008 decision to be set aside was rejected (again on a 3–2 majority, Lord Kerr and Lady Hale dissenting), on the basis that the new evidence did not undermine the original conclusions as to the legal rationality of the removal of the Chagossians' rights of abode. The majority also noted, however, that: (i) a new feasibility study carried out between 2014 and 2015 had reopened the possibility of supported resettlement of the Chagos Islands, and that challenge to the 2004 constitutional ban in light of this new report might be the appropriate way to proceed; and (ii) that the Government accepted during the most recent proceedings that the MPA (under challenge in *Bancoult (No. 3)*) was not in itself a bar to resettlement, [72]–[75], [77]–[80].

■ QUESTIONS

The issues considered in this chapter have been, to a certain extent, theoretical. They are, however, issues of continuing relevance to any study of the constitution of the United Kingdom. Questions which it is worth keeping in mind when reading the remaining chapters in this book would be the following:

1. Is it significant that the United Kingdom constitution is uncodified? Should it remain so?
2. To what extent does the principle of legitimacy inform constitutional debate?
3. To what extent is government made accountable by (i) Parliament, (ii) the electorate, and (iii) the courts?
4. To what extent are legal constitutionalist and political constitutionalist approaches to government reflected in the UK constitution?
5. Should the rights of individuals be limited by reference to the interests of the state (so far as the concept is recognized in United Kingdom constitutional law)? Is the protection of individual rights in the United Kingdom adequate?

2

The Legislative Sovereignty of Parliament

OVERVIEW

In this chapter we deal with parliamentary sovereignty, one of the key doctrines of constitutional law in the United Kingdom. First we consider the nature of the legislative sovereignty of Parliament. We then consider whether Parliament can limit the power of its successors, either substantively or as to the future legislative procedure which must be adhered to. We finally assess a range of modern challenges to the doctrine: those posed by membership of the European Union, human rights, the decision of the House of Lords in *Jackson*, and the enactment of the European Union Act 2011.

NOTE: The doctrine of 'the legislative sovereignty of Parliament' is sometimes referred to as parliamentary or legislative 'supremacy'. 'Sovereignty' is a word open to misunderstanding and one that is used in the sphere of international law (for example, the dispute with Argentina over the sovereignty of the Falkland Islands), and also in the political arena (for example, there has been considerable rhetoric on sovereignty in the debates on the United Kingdom's membership of the European Union, culminating in the June 2016 referendum vote to leave the EU). Yet the terminology of 'sovereignty' will in general be preferred to that of 'supremacy' in this chapter, because the notion of sovereignty tells us something about the legislative power of Parliament that the notion of supremacy does not: on the orthodox understanding of the doctrine, Parliament is not just the supreme or ultimate law-maker, but a legally unlimited law-maker. Nevertheless, in the extracts from cases and other materials which follow, the terms 'sovereignty' and 'supremacy' may be generally understood to be used interchangeably.

SECTION 1: THE NATURE OF THE LEGISLATIVE SOVEREIGNTY OF PARLIAMENT

What do we mean by the 'legislative sovereignty of Parliament'? This is a doctrine at the heart of UK constitutional law, about which there is much contemporary debate. Before exploring the modern challenges to the notion of parliamentary sovereignty, we must establish the nature of the doctrine as traditionally understood. And for the key definition of the orthodox approach, we must turn to one of the most famous UK constitutional lawyers, A. V. Dicey.

A. V. Dicey, *An Introduction to the Study of the Law of the Constitution*
(10th edn, 1985), pp. 39–40

The principle of Parliamentary sovereignty means neither more nor less than this, namely, that Parliament thus defined has, under the English constitution, the right to make or unmake any law whatever; and, further, that no person or body is recognised by the law of England as having a right to override or set aside the legislation of Parliament.

A law may, for our present purpose, be defined as 'any rule which will be enforced by the courts.' The principle then of Parliamentary sovereignty may, looked at from its positive side, be thus described: Any Act of Parliament, or any part of an Act of Parliament, which makes a new law, or repeals or modifies an existing law, will be obeyed by the courts. The same principle, looked at from its negative side, may be thus stated: There is no person or body of persons who can, under the English constitution, make rules which override or derogate from an Act of Parliament, or which (to express the same thing in other words) will be enforced by the courts in contravention of an Act of Parliament.

NOTES

1. Parliament is the supreme law-maker, but what is Parliament? The words of enactment at the beginning of every statute are as follows:

> Be it enacted by the Queen's most Excellent Majesty, by and with the advice and consent of the Lords Spiritual and Temporal, and Commons, in this present Parliament assembled, and by the authority of the same, as follows:—

Thus it is 'the Queen in Parliament' which enacts legislation. A measure having received the approval of a majority in both Houses and the Royal Assent is recognized as an Act of Parliament. This position has been modified, however, by the Parliament Acts of 1911 and 1949, under which a Bill may be presented for the Royal Assent provided it has been passed by the House of Commons and other procedural requirements complied with, although it has not been passed by the House of Lords. If a Bill does not obtain the approval of a majority in each House, or if the Parliament Acts are not complied with, or if the Royal Assent is withheld, the product should not be regarded as an authentic Act of Parliament. The courts, therefore, recognize as law and accord primacy to those measures which Parliament passes as Acts.

2. Dicey's nineteenth-century statement of the nature of parliamentary sovereignty still provides a basis for contemporary understanding of the doctrine. Two key propositions can be discerned from Dicey's formulation, which will be examined in more detail later in this section. (i) the legislative power of Parliament is unlimited; and (ii) no other body has authority to rule on the validity of its enactments. Initially, however, we must look at how the legislative sovereignty of Parliament emerged as a fundamental doctrine of UK constitutional law.

A: Parliament—emergence of supreme law-making authority

In the fourteenth century Parliament emerged as an effective, if not supreme, law-making body. In the seventeenth century James I, by insisting on his right to rule by prerogative, created the conditions in which the battle between the Monarch and Parliament for supremacy was fought in the courts.

The Case of Proclamations
(1611) 12 Co Rep 74, 77 ER 1352

The King sought to check the overgrowth of the capital by issuing a proclamation to prohibit the building of new homes in London. He also sought to preserve wheat for human consumption and issued a proclamation prohibiting the manufacture of starch from wheat. The Commons complained that this was an abuse of proclamations, and the King sought the opinion of Chief Justice Coke who consulted with his fellow judges.

In the same term it was resolved by the two Chief Justices, Chief Baron, and Baron Altham, upon conference betwixt the Lords of the Privy Council and them, that the King by his proclamation cannot create any offence which was not an offence before, for then he may alter the law of the land by his proclamation in a high point; for if he may create an offence where none is, upon that ensues fine and imprisonment: also the law of England is divided into three parts, common law, statute law, and custom; but the King's proclamation is none of them: also *malum aut est malum in se, aut prohibitum*, that which is against common law is *malum in se, malum prohibitum* is such an offence as is prohibited by Act of Parliament, and not by proclamation.

Also, it was resolved, that the King hath no prerogative, but that which the law of the land allows him.

But the King for prevention of offences may by proclamation admonish his subjects that they keep the laws, and do not offend them; upon punishment to be inflicted by the law, &c.

Lastly, if the offence be not punishable in the Star-Chamber, the prohibition of it by proclamation cannot make it punishable there: and after this resolution, no proclamation imposing fine and imprisonment was afterwards made, &c.

NOTE: The Stuart kings also claimed to have other prerogative powers of considerable importance, namely a *suspending* power, which could be used to postpone the operation of a statute for an indefinite period, and a *dispensing* power, which could be used to relieve offenders from the statutory penalties they had incurred. It was James II's use of the suspending power in respect of penal laws relating to religion in the Declarations of Indulgence 1687 and 1688 which led to the revolution of 1688.

In the area of taxation it had been established by the time of Edward I that direct taxes could only be levied with the consent of Parliament. However, the Stuarts claimed they could raise money by means of the prerogative. First, the prerogative relating to foreign affairs was used to regulate trade by the imposition of duties (see *The Case of Impositions (Bate's Case)* (1606) 2 St Tr 371). Secondly, the prerogative power to defend the realm in face of an emergency was used to raise money for the navy. The King was found to be the sole judge of whether an emergency existed (see *The Case of Shipmoney (R v Hampden)* (1637) 3 St Tr 825).

The claims by the Stuart kings to rule by prerogative were resolved by the Bill of Rights 1689.

Bill of Rights 1689
I Will & Mary Sess 2 ch 2

Whereas the late King James the second, by the Assistance of divers Evil Counsellors, Judges, and Ministers, imployed by him did endeavour to Subvert and extirpate the Protestant Religion, and the Lawes and Liberties of this Kingdome ....

And whereas the said late King James the second having abdicated the Government and the throne being thereby vacant.

His Highnesse the Prince of Orange (whom it hath pleased Almighty God to make the glorious Instrument of delivering this Kingdom from Popery and Arbitrary Power) Did (by the advice of the Lords Spirituall and Temporall and divers principall persons of the Commons) Cause Letters to be written to the Lords Spirituall and Temporall being Protestants and other Letters to the several Countyes Citties Universities Burroughs and Cinqe Ports for the chuseing of such persons to represent them as were of right to be sent to Parliament to meet and sitt at Westminster upon the two and twentieth day of January in this Year 1688 in order to such an establishment as that their Religion Lawes and Libertyes might not againe be in danger of being subverted.

Upon which Letters Elections haveing been accordingly made.

And thereupon the said Lords Spirituall and Temporall and Commons pursuant to their respective letters and Elections being now assembled in a full and free representative of this nation taking into their most serious consideration the best meanes for atteyneing the ends aforesaid Doe in the first place (as their Ancestors in like Case have usually done) for the vindicating and asserting their antient rights and Liberties, Declare.

[1.] That the pretended power of suspending of Lawes or the execution of Lawes by Regall Authority without Consent of Parliament is illegall.

[2.] That the pretended power of dispensing with lawes or the Execution of lawes by regall authority as it has been assumed and exercised of late is illegall.

[3.] That the Commission for erecting the late Courte of Commissioners for Ecclesiasticall Causes and all other Commissions and Courts of like nature are illegall and pernicious.

[4.] That levying of money for or to the use of the Crowne by pretence of Prerogative without Grant of Parliament for longer time or in other manner, than the same is or shall be granted is illegall.

[5.] That it is the right of the Subjects to petition the King and all Committments and prosecutions for such petitioning are illegall.

[6.] That the raiseing or keeping a Standing Army within the Kingdom in time of Peace unlesse it be with consent of Parliament is against Law.

[7.] That the Subjects which are Protestants may have Armes for their defence Suitable to their Condition and as allowed by Law.

[8.] That Elections of Members of Parliament ought to be free.

[9.] That the freedome of Speech and debates or proceedings in Parliament ought not to be impeached or questioned in any Courte or place out of Parliament.

[10.] That excessive Bayle ought not to be required nor excessive fynes imposed nor cruel and unusuall Punishments inflicted.

[11.] That Jurors ought to be duely impannelled and returned and Jurors which passe upon men in tryalls for high Treason ought to be freeholders.

[12.] That all Grants and promises of fynes and forfeitures of particular persons before conviction are illegall and void.

[13.] And that for redress of all greivances and for the amending, strengthening and preserving of the Lawes, Parliaments ought to be held frequently.

D. Judge, *The Parliamentary State*
(1993), p. 20

The Constitutional Settlement of 1689 and the Rise of the Liberal State

The potency of the Constitutional Settlement of 1689 stems from its implicit principle of the supremacy of parliament in law. The acceptance by William and Mary of the gift of the crown was conditional upon the terms set by parliament. Henceforth, monarchical power was dependent upon parliament rather than *vice versa*. After 1689, as Munro points out:

> Parliament was to be its own master and free from interference … Parliaments were to be held frequently, and the election of their members was to be free. The Crown's power to levy taxes was made subject to parliamentary consent, its power to keep a standing army made subject to statute, and powers of suspending or dispensing with laws … were declared illegal. (1987: 80)

In other words, what was asserted and accepted in 1689 was the principle of *parliamentary sovereignty*, whereby parliament secured legal supremacy amongst the institutions of the state. Thus, not only was the monarchy subordinated to parliament, but, also, the last vestiges of the claim of the courts that parliament could not legislate in derogation of the principles of the common law were removed. Constitutional theory was at last reconciled to the legal practice that had been developing for nearly a century.

Above all, therefore, the Bill of Rights was a restraint upon arbitrary behaviour. Its passage confirmed the distinctiveness of English state development from its continental European counterparts. The concentration of power in the hands of the monarch and the exclusion of parliament from policy making—the political hallmarks of absolutism—were outlawed in England in 1689. The authority of statute was conferred upon the pre-existing principles—of consent and representation—so confirming the differences between the state-form in England and those in the absolutist regimes in France and Prussia for example ….

NOTE: For detailed consideration of the emergence of the doctrine of parliamentary sovereignty, see J. Goldsworthy, *The Sovereignty of Parliament: History and Philosophy* (1999).

B: The unlimited legislative power of Parliament

There are two ways in which this proposition may be assessed. On one hand, we can look at the vast changes which have been made to the constitution by a simple Act of Parliament: changing the line of succession to the Crown (e.g. Act of Settlement 1701), altering the very structure of the United Kingdom (e.g. Act of Union 1707), limiting the power of one of Parliament's constituent Houses (e.g. Parliament Acts 1911 and 1949), and providing for accession to a supranational union of sovereign states (e.g. European Communities Act 1972). On the other hand, several cases have arisen where this idea has been tested.

There is a presumption used by the courts when construing statutes that Parliament does not intend to legislate contrary to the principles of international law, and, as far as possible, a statute will be interpreted in a way which avoids conflict. What do the courts do, however, when there is a clear conflict between a statute of the United Kingdom Parliament and the principles of international law? The answer is given in the following case.

Mortensen v Peters

(1906) 14 SLT 227, High Court of Justiciary

Mortensen was the captain of a Norwegian trawler charged with illegal trawl fishing in waters within the Moray Firth contrary to a bye-law made by the Fishery Board for Scotland under s. 7 of the Herring Fishery (Scotland) Act 1889. The Act defined the area for which bye-laws could be made, that is, all of the Moray Firth, although much of it comprised international waters. The trawler had been fishing five miles off the coast in international waters but within the prohibited area. Mortensen was convicted by the Sheriff's Court and appealed.

THE LORD JUSTICE GENERAL: My Lords, I apprehend that the question is one of construction and of construction only. In this Court we have nothing to do with the question of whether the legislature has or has not done what foreign powers may consider a usurpation in a question with them. Neither are we a tribunal sitting to decide whether an act of the legislature is *ultra vires* as in contravention of generally acknowledged principles of international law. For us an Act of Parliament duly passed by Lords and Commons and assented to by the King, is supreme, and we are bound to give effect to its terms ....

It is said by the appellant ... that International Law has firmly fixed that a locus such as this is beyond the limits of territorial sovereignty; and that consequently it is not to be thought that in such a place the legislature could seek to affect any but the King's subjects.

It is a trite observation that there is no such thing as a standard of International Law, extraneous to the domestic law of a kingdom, to which appeal may be made. International Law, so far as this Court is concerned, is the body of doctrine regarding the international rights and duties of States which has been adopted and made part of the Law of Scotland. Now can it be said to be clear by the law of Scotland that the locus here is beyond what the legislature may assert right to affect by legislation against all whomsoever for the purpose of regulating methods of fishing? ...

It seems to me therefore, without laying down the proposition that the Moray Firth is for every purpose within the territorial sovereignty, it can at least be clearly said that the appellant cannot make out his proposition that it is inconceivable that the British legislature should attempt for fishery regulation to legislate against all and sundry in such a place. And if that is so, then I revert to the considerations already stated which as a matter of construction make me think that it did so legislate.

LORD KYLLACHY: … A legislature may quite conceivably, by oversight or even design, exceed what an international tribunal (if such existed) might hold to be its international rights. Still, there is always a presumption against its intending to do so. I think that is acknowledged. But then it is only a presumption; and, as such, it must always give way to the language used if it is clear, and also to all counter presumptions which may legitimately be had in view in determining, on ordinary principles, the true meaning and intent of the legislation. Express words will, of course, be conclusive; and so also will plain implication.

Now it must, I think, be conceded that the language of the enactment here in question is fairly express—express, that is to say, to the effect of making an unlimited and unqualified prohibition, applying to the whole area specified, and affecting everybody—whether British subjects or foreigners.

Appeal dismissed.

NOTE: In *Cheney* v *Conn* [1968] 1 All ER 779, a taxpayer challenged an assessment of income tax made under the Finance Act 1964 on the ground that part of the money raised would be used for the manufacture of nuclear weapons contrary to a treaty, the Geneva Convention, to which the United Kingdom was party. Ungoed-Thomas J stated:

What the statute itself enacts cannot be unlawful, because what the statute says and provides is itself the law, and the highest form of law that is known to this country. It is the law which prevails over every other form of law, and it is not for the court to say that a parliamentary enactment, the highest law in this country, is illegal.

See also *R* v *Secretary of State for the Home Department, ex parte Thakrar* [1974] QB 684.

If international law can place no limitation on Parliament's powers, can time do so?

In *Burmah Oil Co* v *Lord Advocate* [1965] AC 75, HL, the company was successful in its claim for compensation against the Crown for the destruction of its installations in Burma during the Second World War, the destruction having been ordered by the commander of British forces to prevent the installations falling into the hands of the advancing Japanese forces. In response to this decision Parliament hastily passed the War Damage Act 1965 with retrospective effect to deny entitlement to compensation, at least as a matter of common law, for damage for acts lawfully done by the Crown during a war.

C: Ruling on the validity of Parliament's enactments

The extract from Dicey (see earlier in this chapter in Section 1 at pp. 46–7) also suggests that no person or body has authority to rule on the validity of Parliament's enactments. Is it possible to challenge the validity of an Act of Parliament in the courts? In countries with a written constitution the ordinary courts or a constitutional court will often have jurisdiction to determine whether the acts of the legislature are constitutional. In the United States the Supreme Court, in *Marbury* v *Madison* (1803) 1 Cranch 137, declared that it had power to decide whether or not the Acts of Congress conformed with the Constitution. In the United Kingdom the doctrine of legislative sovereignty dictates that Parliament has power to legislate on constitutional matters. Thus Parliament may change the constitution by Act of Parliament. This being so, is it possible to challenge an Act on the ground that it is unconstitutional? Chief Justice Coke was of the opinion that the courts could intervene if Parliament enacted outrageous legislation. He stated in *Dr Bonham's Case* (1610) 8 Co Rep 114, at p. 118:

In many cases, the common law will control Acts of Parliament, and sometimes adjudge them to be utterly void: for when an Act of Parliament is against common right and reason, or repugnant, or impossible to be performed, the common law will control it, and adjudge such an Act to be void.

However, this statement precedes the Glorious Revolution of 1688, after which the doctrine of the sovereignty of Parliament developed its modern meaning. In *Ex p Canon Selwyn* (1872) 36 JP 54 a question arose regarding the validity of the Irish Church Act 1869. Cockburn CJ stated:

> [T]here is no judicial body in the country by which the validity of an act of parliament could be questioned. An act of the legislature is superior in authority to any court of law. We have only to administer the law as we find it, and no court could pronounce a judgment as to the validity of an act of Parliament.

In *Pickin* v *British Railways Board* [1974] AC 765, Lord Reid stated:

> In earlier times many learned lawyers seem to have believed that an Act of Parliament could be disregarded in so far as it was contrary to the law of God or the law of nature or natural justice, but since the supremacy of Parliament was finally demonstrated by the Revolution of 1688 any such idea has become obsolete.

In *Manuel* v *Attorney-General* [1983] Ch 77, Sir Robert Megarry V-C stated, at p. 86:

> [T]he duty of the court is to obey and apply every Act of Parliament, and ... the court cannot hold any such Act to be *ultra vires*. Of course there may be questions about what the Act means, and of course there is power to hold statutory instruments and other subordinate legislation *ultra vires*. But once an instrument is recognised as being an Act of Parliament, no English court can refuse to obey it or question its validity.

But what happens if there are two Acts on the statute books which conflict with one another? See the case which follows.

Ellen Street Estates Limited v *Minister of Health*
[1934] 1 KB 590, Court of Appeal

The Acquisition of Land (Assessment of Compensation) Act 1919 provided by s. 2 for the assessment of compensation in respect of land acquired compulsorily for public purposes according to certain rules. Section 7(1) stated 'The provisions of the Act or order by which the land is authorised to be acquired, or of any Act incorporated therewith, shall in relation to the matters dealt with in this Act, have effect subject to this Act, and so far as inconsistent with this Act those provisions shall cease to have or shall not have effect ... '. The Housing Act 1925, s. 46 provided for the assessment of compensation for land acquired compulsorily under an improvement or reconstruction scheme made under that Act in a manner differing in certain respects from that prescribed by the Act of 1919. Section 7(1) could be construed as applying to previous enactments, but it was argued that it applied also to subsequent enactments. If this was so, inconsistent provisions in the 1925 Act would be of no effect.

> SCRUTTON LJ: ... Such a contention involves this proposition, that no subsequent Parliament by enacting a provision inconsistent with the Act of 1919 can give any effect to the words it uses. Sect. 46, sub-s. 1, of the Housing Act, 1925, says this: 'Where land included in any improvement or reconstruction scheme ... is acquired compulsorily,' certain provisions as to compensation shall apply. These are inconsistent with those contained in the Acquisition of Land (Assessment of Compensation) Act, 1919, and then s. 46, sub-s. 2, of the Act of 1925 provides: 'Subject as aforesaid, the compensation to be paid for such land shall be assessed in accordance with the Acquisition of Land (Assessment of Compensation) Act, 1919.' I asked Mr Hill [for the appellants] what these last quoted words mean, and he replied they

mean nothing. That is absolutely contrary to the constitutional position that Parliament can alter an Act previously passed, and it can do so by repealing in terms the previous Act—Mr Hill agrees that it may do so—and it can do it also in another way—namely, by enacting a provision which is clearly inconsistent with the previous Act.

MAUGHAM LJ: ... The Legislature cannot, according to our constitution, bind itself as to the form of subsequent legislation, and it is impossible for Parliament to enact that in a subsequent statute dealing with the same subject-matter there can be no implied repeal. If in a subsequent Act Parliament chooses to make it plain that the earlier statute is being to some extent repealed, effect must be given to that intention just because it is the will of the Legislature.

Appeal dismissed.

■ QUESTIONS

1. Was this case concerned with the *content* of the legislation or the *form* of the legislation?
2. When Maugham LJ stated that Parliament cannot bind itself as to the *form* of subsequent legislation, was this obiter or ratio?

NOTE: The doctrine of implied repeal is seemingly a consequence of the traditional Diceyan view of sovereignty: to ensure that Parliament is able to make or unmake any law whatever, new legislation which is incompatible with a previous Act necessarily must be taken to have repealed the incompatible earlier provision. Yet paradoxically, if there are things the legislature cannot do, this may also constitute a limit on Parliament's power to legislate.

■ QUESTIONS

1. Could the decision in *Ellen Street Estates* misstate the traditional doctrine of parliamentary sovereignty? When a court applies the doctrine of implied repeal in respect of an earlier statutory provision which is incompatible with a later Act of Parliament, is it respecting the will of Parliament or is it setting itself above Parliament and adjudicating on the validity of legislation? Could Parliament legislate to limit the effect of the doctrine of implied repeal in specified circumstances, or would the courts be justified in rejecting such an attempt?
2. While there may be reluctance on the part of the courts to rule on the validity of Acts of Parliament, a related issue which has arisen is whether they may adjudicate upon the question of whether something purporting to be an Act of Parliament actually is such. It is the Queen in Parliament which enacts legislation. Under the common law, for a Bill to become law it must be approved by the Lords and Commons and receive the Royal Assent. If an Act is challenged on the basis that there have been procedural defects during its passage through Parliament, will the courts look behind the formal words of enactment and inquire whether the requirements of the common law have been satisfied? See the following case.

Pickin **v** *British Railways Board*
[1974] AC 765, House of Lords

Pickin was a railway enthusiast who, in 1969, purchased from the owner of a piece of land adjoining a disused railway line, all his estate and interest in the railway land and track. By s. 259 of a private Act of Parliament of 1836 setting up the railway line, it was provided that, if a line should be abandoned, the lands acquired for the track should vest in the owners for the time being of the adjoining lands. Pickin brought an action against the Board, claiming that by virtue of s. 259 he was the owner of that land to mid-track. The Board claimed that it owned the land by virtue of a private Act of Parliament, the British Railways Act 1968. Pickin claimed that the relevant provision (s. 18) of the 1968 Act was invalid and ineffective to deprive him of his title, as Parliament had been misled by the Board to obtain the passage of the Act. In particular the Bill was presented as being unopposed, but notice had not been given to affected landowners as required by Standing Orders. In addition, the preamble to the Bill contained a false recital that plans of the lands and a book of reference to such plans containing the names of the owners, lessees, and occupiers of the said land were duly deposited with the clerk of the county council. The Board sought to have these claims struck out as frivolous, vexatious, and an abuse of the process of the court.

LORD REID: ... The idea that a court is entitled to disregard a provision in an Act of Parliament on any ground must seem strange and startling to anyone with any knowledge of the history and law of our constitution, but a detailed argument has been submitted to your Lordships and I must deal with it.

I must make it plain that there has been no attempt to question the general supremacy of Parliament. In earlier times many learned lawyers seem to have believed that an Act of Parliament could be disregarded in so far as it was contrary to the law of God or the law of nature or natural justice, but since the supremacy of Parliament was finally demonstrated by the Revolution of 1688 any such idea has become obsolete.

The respondent's contention is that there is a difference between a public and a private Act. There are of course great differences between the methods and procedures followed in dealing with public and private Bills, and there may be some differences in the methods of construing their provisions. But the respondent argues for a much more fundamental difference. There is little in modern authority that he can rely on. ...

In my judgment the law is correctly stated by Lord Campbell in *Edinburgh and Dalkeith Railway Co.* v *Wauchope* (1842) 8 Cl & F 710, 1 Bell 252. Mr Wauchope claimed certain wayleaves. The matter was dealt with in a private Act. He appears to have maintained in the Court of Session that the provisions of that Act should not be applied because it had been passed without his having had notice as required by Standing Orders . . . . Lord Campbell [stated]:

> I must express some surprise that such a notion should have prevailed. It seems to me there is no foundation for it whatever; all that a court of justice can look to is the parliamentary roll; they see that an Act has passed both Houses of Parliament, and that it has received the royal assent, and no court of justice can inquire into the manner in which it was introduced into Parliament, what was done previously to its being introduced, or what passed in Parliament during the various stages of its progress through both Houses of Parliament. I therefore trust that no such inquiry will hereafter be entered into in Scotland, and that due effect will be given to every Act of Parliament, both private as well as public, upon the just construction which appears to arise upon it.

No doubt this was obiter but, so far as I am aware, no one since 1842 has doubted that it is a correct statement of the constitutional position.

The function of the court is to construe and apply the enactments of Parliament. The court has no concern with the manner in which Parliament or its officers carrying out its Standing Orders perform these functions. Any attempt to prove that they were misled by fraud or otherwise would necessarily involve an inquiry into the manner in which they had performed their functions in dealing with the Bill which became the British Railways Act 1968.

In whatever form the respondent's case is pleaded he must prove not only that the appellants acted fraudulently but also that their fraud caused damage to him by causing the enactment of section 18. He could not prove that without an examination of the manner in which the officers of Parliament dealt with the matter. So the court would, or at least might, have to adjudicate upon that.

For a century or more both Parliament and the courts have been careful not to act so as to cause conflict between them. Any such investigations as the respondent seeks could easily lead to such a conflict, and I would only support it if compelled to do so by clear authority. But it appears to me that the whole trend of authority for over a century is clearly against permitting any such investigation.

The respondent is entitled to argue that section 18 should be construed in a way favourable to him and for that reason I have refrained from pronouncing on that matter. But he is not entitled to go behind the Act to show that section 18 should not be enforced. Nor is he entitled to examine proceedings in Parliament in order to show that the appellants by fraudulently misleading Parliament caused him loss. I am therefore clearly of opinion that this appeal should be allowed ....

LORD MORRIS OF BORTH-Y-GEST: ... The question of fundamental importance which arises is whether the court should entertain the proposition that an Act of Parliament can so be assailed in the courts that matters should proceed as though the Act or some part of it had never been passed. I consider that such doctrine would be dangerous and impermissible. It is the function of the courts to administer the laws which Parliament has enacted. In the processes of Parliament there will be much consideration whether a Bill should or should not in one form or another become an enactment. When an enactment is passed there is finality unless and until it is amended or repealed by Parliament. In the courts there may be argument as to the correct interpretation of the enactment: there must be none as to whether it should be on the Statute Book at all....

The conclusion which I have reached results, in my view, not only from a settled and sustained line of authority which I see no reason to question and which I think should be endorsed but also from the view that any other conclusion would be constitutionally undesirable and impracticable. It must surely be for Parliament to lay down the procedures which are to be followed before a Bill can become an Act. It must be for Parliament to decide whether its decreed procedures have in fact been followed. It must be for Parliament to lay down and to construe its Standing Orders and further to decide whether they have been obeyed: it must be for Parliament to decide whether in any particular case to dispense with compliance with such orders. It must be for Parliament to decide whether it is satisfied that an Act should be passed in the form and with the wording set out in the Act. It must be for Parliament to decide what documentary material or testimony it requires and the extent to which Parliamentary privilege should attach. It would be impracticable and undesirable for the High Court of Justice to embark upon an inquiry concerning the effect or the effectiveness of the internal procedures in the High Court of Parliament or an inquiry whether in any particular case those procedures were effectively followed.

[His Lordship referred to *Edinburgh and Dalkeith Railway Co.* v *Wauchope* and several other cases and continued.]

Of equal clarity was the passage in the judgment of Willes J in 1871 when in *Lee* v *Bude and Torrington Junction Railway Co.* (1871) LR 6 CP 576 (in which case it was alleged that Parliament had been induced to pass an Act by fraudulent recitals) he said, at p. 582:

'Are we to act as regents over what is done by Parliament with the consent of the Queen, Lords, and Commons? I deny that any such authority exists. If an Act of Parliament has been obtained improperly, it is for the legislature to correct it by repealing it: but, so long as it exists as law, the courts are bound to obey it. The proceedings here are judicial, not autocratic, which they would be if we could make laws instead of administering them.'

... In the result I have not been persuaded that any doubt has been cast upon principles which are soundly directed as being both desirable and reasonable and which furthermore have for long been firmly established by authority.

I would allow the appeal.

Appeal allowed.

NOTES

1. See also *Jackson* v *Attorney General* [2005] UKHL 56, [2006] 1 AC 262 later in this chapter in Section 3C at pp. 88–95 on courts considering legislation.
2. For a challenge to the traditional reading of *Pickin*, see Tucker, 'Uncertainty in the Rule of Recognition and in the Doctrine of Parliamentary Sovereignty' (2011) *Oxford Journal of Legal Studies*, 61–88, arguing that the rules of the UK constitution are:

in fact indeterminate at the boundaries of parliamentary power, a point overlooked in the orthodoxy's dogmatic insistence on the simplistic no-limits thesis. This indeterminacy falsifies the insistence that there are no limits to Parliament's law-making power.

■ QUESTION

When Lord Morris stated 'It must surely be for Parliament to lay down the procedures which are to be followed before a Bill can become an Act. It must be for Parliament to decide whether its decreed procedures have in fact been followed', was he referring to procedures laid down in Standing Orders or in Acts of Parliament? Can such procedures be subject to judicial challenge in either circumstance?

SECTION 2: CAN PARLIAMENT LIMIT THE POWERS OF ITS SUCCESSORS?

If Parliament has, under the UK constitution, legislative sovereignty, can it use this unlimited law-making power to enact legislation which limits the power of its successors? There are differing answers to this question, which reflect disagreement about the nature of parliamentary sovereignty. H.L.A. Hart identified two alternate approaches: 'continuing sovereignty'—according to which Parliament could not legislate to limit the power of its successors—and 'self-embracing sovereignty'—according to which Parliament could legislate to limit the power of its successors (*The Concept of Law*, 1961, pp. 145–6). The following extracts from Wade, Jennings, Heuston, and Marshall represent the competing answers which have been developed to this problem, while also suggesting that Hart's classic distinction may not the best available.

H. W. R. Wade, 'The Basis of Legal Sovereignty'

(1955) *Cambridge Law Journal* 172, 186–9

At the heart of the matter lies the question whether the rule of common law which says that the courts will enforce statutes can itself be altered by a statute. Adherents of the traditional theory, who hold that future Parliaments cannot be bound, are here compelled to answer "no." For it they answer "yes," they must yield to Jennings' reasoning. But to deny that Parliament can alter this particular rule of law is not so daring as it may seem at first sight; for the sacrosanctity of the rule is an inexorable corollary of Parliament's continuing sovereignty. If the one proposition is asserted, the other must be conceded. Nevertheless some further justification is called for, since there must be something peculiar about a rule of common law which can stand against a statute.

The peculiarity lies in this, that the rule enjoining judicial obedience to statutes is one of the fundamental rules upon which the legal system depends....

Once this truth is grasped, the dilemma is solved. For if no statute can establish the rule that the courts obey Acts of Parliament, similarly no statute can alter or abolish that rule. The rule is above and beyond the reach of statute, as Salmond so well explains, because it is itself the source of the authority of statute. This puts it into a class by itself among rules of common law, and the apparent paradox that it is unalterable by Parliament turns out to be a truism. The rule of judicial obedience is in one sense a rule of common law, but in another sense – which applies to no other rule of common law – it is the ultimate *political* fact upon which the whole system of legislation hangs. Legislation owes its authority to the rule: the rule does not owe its authority to legislation. To say that Parliament can change the rule, merely because it can change any other rule, is to put the cart before the horse....

What Salmond calls the "ultimate legal principle" is therefore a rule which is unique in being unchangeable by Parliament – it is changed by revolution, not by legislation; it lies in the keeping of the courts, and no Act of Parliament can take it from them. This is only another way of saying that it is always for the courts, in the last resort, to say what is a valid Act of Parliament; and that the decision of this question is not determined by any rule of law which can be laid down or altered by any authority outside the courts. It is simply a political fact. If this is accepted, there is a fallacy in Jennings' argument that the law requires the courts to obey any rule enacted by the legislature, *including a rule which alters this law itself.* For this law itself is ultimate and unalterable by any *legal* authority.

NOTE: Dicey was also a proponent of the 'continuing' theory of parliamentary supremacy, often referred to as the 'traditional' theory. The following extracts, in contrast, develop what has been described as a 'manner and form' understanding of parliamentary sovereignty, or the 'new view'.

W. I. Jennings, *The Law and the Constitution*
(2nd edn, 1938), pp. 139–40, 143

...[L]egal sovereignty is not sovereignty at all. It is not supreme power. It is a legal concept, a form of expression which lawyers use to express the relations between Parliament and the courts. It means that the courts will always recognise as law the rules which Parliament makes by legislation; that is, rules made in the customary manner and expressed in the customary form....

The difference is this. In the one case there is sovereignty. In the other, the courts have no concern with sovereignty, but only with the established law. "Legal sovereignty" is merely a name indicating that the legislature has for the time being power to make laws of any kind in the manner required by the law. That is, a rule expressed to be made by the King, "with the advice and consent of the Lords spiritual and temporal, and Commons in this present Parliament assembled, and by authority of the same," will be recognised by the courts, *including a rule which alters this law itself.* If this is so, the "legal sovereign" may impose legal limitations upon itself, because its power to change the law includes the power to change the law affecting itself.

R. F. V. Heuston, *Essays in Constitutional Law*
(2nd edn, 1964), Ch. 1, pp. 6–8

Summary of New View

It is suggested that the new view can be summarised thus:

(1) Sovereignty is a legal concept: the rules which identify the sovereign and prescribe its composition and functions are logically prior to it.
(2) There is a distinction between rules which govern, on the one hand, (a) the composition, and (b) the procedure, and, on the other hand, (c) the area of power, of a sovereign legislature.
(3) The courts have jurisdiction to question the validity of an alleged Act of Parliament on grounds 2 (a) and 2 (b), but not on ground 2 (c).
(4) This jurisdiction is exercisable either before or after the Royal Assent has been signified—in the former case by way of injunction, in the latter by way of declaratory judgment.

G. Marshall, *Constitutional Theory*
(1971), pp. 42–3

Dicey simply implied, without examining, the proposition that authority in a 'sovereign' Parliament must be exercised at all times by a simple majority of legislators, who, since they are unrestricted in their powers, can always repeal any constitutional protections or restrictions on power enacted into law by their predecessors. To do Dicey justice, the Sovereign described in the *Law of the Constitution* is the British Parliament (though he did sometimes speak in terms of sovereigns in general). But even in relation to the British Parliament he did not fully examine the possibility that Parliament as at present constituted might conceivably bind the future or circumscribe the freedom of future legislators, not by laying down blanket prohibitions or attempting to enact a fundamental Bill of Rights, but by using their authority to provide different forms and procedures for legislation. A referendum or a joint sitting, for example, might be prescribed before certain things could be done. Or a two-thirds majority. Or a seventy-five per cent or eighty per cent majority. If it is also provided that any repeal of such provisions should not be by simple majority, the courts may be able to protect the arrangements laid down by declaring in suitable proceedings that any purported repeal by simple majority of a protected provision is *ultra vires* as being not, in the sense required by law, an 'Act of Parliament'. In this finding they would not be in any way derogating from parliamentary sovereignty but protecting Parliament's authority from usurpation by those not entitled for the purpose in hand to exercise it. Thus, for the English lawyer or political theorist, sovereignty may be purged of its dangerous absolutism. He can believe both in an ultimate Sovereign and in the possibility of restraint imposed by law upon the way in which legal power is used. He can believe in the possibility even of a modified Bill of Fundamental Rights grafted into the British constitution—or, to be more accurate, in a relatively fundamental set of provisions in which selected civil liberties are protected from attack in the future by, so to speak, taking out legislative insurance in the present, in the shape of requirements of special procedures or majorities. This would be to do rather more than is done in Canada's Bill of Rights, which declares certain rights and freedoms to be fundamental, but leaves them open to attack by any future legislation which specifically declares itself to apply, notwithstanding the Bill of Rights.

NOTES

1. To view these alternative answers to the question 'can Parliament bind its successors?' as being based on a difference of opinion as to whether sovereignty must be 'continuing' or 'self-embracing' leads to an irresolvable logical conundrum. It also misrepresents the nature of the argument advanced by Jennings, and other 'manner and form' theorists, who accept with Dicey and Wade that absolute *substantive* limits could not be lawfully created by legislation, but contend that *procedural* conditions may be validly enacted in an Act of Parliament. This is not a self-embracing theory which is designed to limit legislative power, but one which gives Parliament the authority to alter the way in which that power is to be used; see M. Gordon, 'The Conceptual Foundations of Parliamentary Sovereignty: Reconsidering Jennings and Wade' [2009] *Public Law* 519–43, 525–31.
2. We therefore have multiple answers to our original question. How can we determine which is 'correct' as a matter of UK constitutional law? The following extracts indicate how some substantive and procedural limits on the sovereignty of Parliament have been treated in the UK and comparable jurisdictions but, as we shall subsequently see, this matter may have been re-opened by some of the modern challenges to the doctrine.

A: Substantive limits

(a) The Acts of Union

So far it has been assumed that Parliament is not subject to any constituent instrument. However, in 1707 the Parliaments of England and Scotland passed Acts of Union ratifying the Treaty of Union and creating the new Parliament of Great Britain. In 1800 a similar union took place between Great Britain and Ireland, creating the United Kingdom of Great Britain and Ireland. As these Acts of Union were antecedent to the new Parliaments they created, it is arguable that they were constituent Acts bringing into being a new state and a new Parliament (see Mitchell, *Constitutional Law* (2nd edn, 1968), pp. 69–74; Calvert, *Constitutional Law in Northern Ireland* (1968), chap. 1; for a contrary view see Munro, *Studies in Constitutional Law* (1999), chap. 5).

Certain provisions of the Treaties were declared to be fundamental and unalterable. The subsequent history reveals, however, that such provisions have been amended or repealed (see, e.g. the Universities (Scotland) Act 1853 and the Irish Church Act 1869); indeed, the Union with Ireland was dissolved in 1922 when most of Ireland obtained independence, with only Northern Ireland remaining in the United Kingdom. The issue presented by the Acts of Union has been considered in several Scottish cases but not finally adjudicated upon.

MacCormick v Lord Advocate
[1953] SC 396, Court of Session, Inner House

Two members of the Scottish public petitioned the Court of Session for a declaration that a proclamation describing the Queen as 'Elizabeth the Second of the United Kingdom of Great Britain' was illegal, as being contrary to Article I of the Treaty and Acts of Union. The Lord Advocate argued that there was no conflict with Article I and that the number 'II' was authorized by the Royal Titles Act 1953.

Held: The petition was dismissed on the grounds that there was nothing in Article I which forbade the use of the numeral, the petitioners had no title to sue, and the Royal Titles Act 1953 was irrelevant as it was enacted after the designation 'Elizabeth the Second' had been adopted and used. The President then went on to express his opinion on the Union legislation.

THE LORD PRESIDENT (COOPER): ... The principle of the unlimited sovereignty of Parliament is a distinctively English principle which has no counterpart in Scottish constitutional law.... Considering that the Union legislation extinguished the Parliaments of Scotland and England and replaced them by a new Parliament, I have difficulty in seeing why it should have been supposed that the new Parliament of Great Britain must inherit all the peculiar characteristics of the English Parliament but none of the Scottish Parliament, as if all that happened in 1707 was that Scottish representatives were admitted to the Parliament of England. That is not what was done. Further, the Treaty and the associated legislation, by which the Parliament of Great Britain was brought into being as the successor of the separate Parliaments of Scotland and England, contain some clauses which expressly reserve to the Parliament of Great Britain powers of subsequent modification, and other clauses which either contain no such power or emphatically exclude subsequent alteration by declarations that the provision shall be fundamental and unalterable in all time coming, or declarations of a like effect. I have never been able to understand how it is possible to reconcile with elementary canons of construction the adoption by the English constitutional theorists of the same attitude to these markedly different types of provisions.

The Lord Advocate conceded this point by admitting that the Parliament of Great Britain 'could not' repeal or alter such 'fundamental and essential' conditions.... I have not found in the Union legislation any provision that the Parliament of Great Britain should be 'absolutely sovereign' in the sense that that Parliament should be free to alter the Treaty at will....

But the petitioners have still a grave difficulty to overcome on this branch of their argument. Accepting that there are provisions in the Treaty of Union and associated legislation which are 'fundamental law,' and assuming for the moment that something is alleged to have been done—it matters not whether with legislative authority or not—in breach of that fundamental law, the question remains whether such a question is determinable as a justiciable issue in the Courts of either Scotland or England, in the same fashion as an issue of constitutional *vires* would be cognisable by the Supreme Courts of the United States, or of South Africa or Australia. I reserve my opinion with regard to the provisions relating expressly to this Court and to the laws 'which concern private right' which are administered here. This is not such a question, but a matter of 'public right' (articles 18 and 19). To put the matter in another way, it is of little avail to ask whether the Parliament of Great Britain 'can' do this thing or that, without going on to inquire who can stop them if they do. Any person 'can' repudiate his solemn engagement but he cannot normally do so with impunity. Only two answers have been suggested to this corollary to the main question. The first is the exceedingly cynical answer implied by Dicey (*Law of the Constitution*, (9th ed.) p. 82) in the statement that 'it would be rash of the Imperial Parliament to abolish the Scotch law courts, and assimilate the Law of Scotland to that of England. But no one can feel sure at what point Scottish resistance to such a change would become serious.' The other answer was that nowadays there may be room for the invocation of an 'advisory opinion' from the International Court of Justice. On these matters I express no view. This at least is plain, that there is neither precedent nor authority of any kind for the view that the domestic Courts of either Scotland or England have jurisdiction to determine whether a governmental act of the type here in controversy is or is not conform to the provisions of a Treaty, least of all when that Treaty is one under which both Scotland and England ceased to be independent states and merged their identity in an incorporating union. From the standpoint both of constitutional law and of international law the position appears to me to be unique, and I am constrained to hold that the action as laid is incompetent in respect that it has not been shown that the Court of Session has authority to entertain the issue sought to be raised....

NOTE: In *Gibson* v *Lord Advocate* 1975 SLT 134, a Scottish fisherman challenged an EU Regulation which had become law by virtue of the European Communities Act 1972. The Regulation gave Member States equal access to fishing grounds. Gibson argued that this was invalid, being in breach of Art. XVIII which forbade 'alteration ... in the laws which concern private right except for the evident utility of the subjects within Scotland'. Lord Keith held that the control of fishing in territorial waters was not a matter of private right but of public law, and thus was not protected by Art. XVIII. However, he went on to state obiter:

> Like Lord President Cooper, I prefer to reserve my opinion on what the question would be if the United Kingdom Parliament passed an Act purporting to abolish the Court of Session or the Church of Scotland or to substitute English law for the whole body of Scots private law. I am, however, of opinion that the question whether a particular Act of the United Kingdom Parliament altering a particular aspect of Scots private law is or is not 'for the evident utility' of the subjects within Scotland is not a justiciable issue in this court. The making of decisions upon what must essentially be a political matter is no part of the function of the court, and it is highly undesirable that it should be.

The question of the constitutional effect of the Scots Articles of Union continues to remain unresolved, although doubt has been cast on Lord Cooper's claim that the doctrine of parliamentary sovereignty was no part of Scottish constitutional law; see J.D. Ford, 'The Legal Provisions in the Acts of Union' (2007) *Cambridge Law Journal* 106, 137–9.

In *Ex p Canon Selwyn* (1872) 36 JP 54, the issue of the validity of the Irish Church Act 1869 was raised. This Act disestablished and disendowed the Episcopal Church in Ireland which Art. 5 of the Treaty of Union had established forever. Mandamus was sought against the Lord President of the Council, commanding him to present to the Queen a petition asking her to refer for adjudication the question whether her assent to the Irish Church Act 1869 was contrary to the Coronation Oath and the Act of Settlement 1700. The application was refused by Cockburn CJ on the ground that 'there is no judicial body in the country by which the validity of an act of parliament could be questioned. An act of the legislature is superior in authority to any court of law'. Calvert takes issue with Cockburn CJ in the following extract.

H. Calvert, *Constitutional Law in Northern Ireland*
(1968), p. 21

These are strong words. But whilst the Coronation Oath did contain a solemn pledge to maintain the unified and established Church of England and Ireland, it is not here suggested that an Act can be challenged on this ground, or on grounds of contravention of the Act of Settlement. What it is suggested could have been, and what, surprisingly, was not argued in *Ex parte Canon Selwyn*, is that the severance and disestablishment of the Church of Ireland was a legal act power to effect which was withheld from the Parliament of the United Kingdom by its constituent Acts. It is all very well to speak of applying 'the law as we find it.' That begs the question of what we find. A judge appointed before 1800 and continuing in office after 1800 would find himself in a considerable dilemma. Sworn to uphold the laws of parliament, he would find two conflicting laws of two different parliaments, one purporting to disestablish the Irish Church and the other, which constituted the parliament enacting the first, having imposed upon it a statutory prohibition from disestablishing. It is, again, all very well to speak of 'an act of the legislature' being 'superior in authority to any court of law.' No doubt it is—but that is not the question.

The question may be viewed as being whether 'an act of the legislature' is 'superior in authority' to a prior constituent Act of a predecessor parliament. There is a difference, which has been overlooked but which may well be crucial, between a parliament repealing its own Acts, and a parliament purporting to repeal the Acts of its constituent predecessor. English courts have never been faced, four square, with this question and English law has therefore never finally made up its mind—*a fortiori* Irish law.

■ QUESTIONS

1. Is Cockburn CJ's dictum reconcilable with the obiter dicta in *MacCormick* and *Gibson*?
2. Middleton, in 'New Thoughts on the Union' [1954] JR 37, at p. 49, states that 'the fact that Parliament has done something cannot prove that it was entitled to do it'. Do the amendments to, and breaches and repeals of, provisions of the Acts of Union reveal that Parliament is sovereign and unconstrained in its powers, or is it the case that Parliament is limited but there is no authority competent to rule on the validity of its Acts; that is, the amendments and repeals are invalid in legal theory but in political reality they exist and are acted upon? Does such a distinction matter?
3. Jennings, in *The Law and the Constitution* (5th edn, 1959), p. 170, argues that as the Acts of Union were passed to ratify two treaties, the amendments to these treaties were carried out in accordance with the maxim *nebus sic stantibus*—this means that it is a tacit condition attaching to all treaties that they shall cease to be obligatory so soon as the state of facts and conditions upon which they were founded has substantially changed. Is this a satisfactory explanation for the subsequent amendments to these treaties? If the conditions have not substantially changed in respect of a particular provision, would legislation purporting to alter it be illegal? If so, could or would any court declare it invalid?

(b) Independence

One of the challenges with which constitutional lawyers have had to deal is the granting of independence to many Commonwealth countries. This usually followed a two-stage process, with the colony first being granted Dominion status and subsequently being granted full independence. Section 4 of the Statute of Westminster provides:

No Act of Parliament of the United Kingdom passed after the commencement of this Act shall extend, or be deemed to extend, to a Dominion as part of the law of that Dominion unless it is expressly declared in that Act that that Dominion has requested and consented to, the enactment thereof.

This gives rise to the question whether Parliament could ignore this provision and legislate directly for a Dominion without its request or consent? In *British Coal Corporation* v *The King* [1935] AC 500, at p. 520, Lord Sankey stated, regarding the application of s. 4 to Canada:

It is doubtless true that the power of the Imperial Parliament to pass on its own initiative any legislation that it thought fit extending to Canada remains in theory unimpaired: indeed, the Imperial Parliament could, as a matter of abstract law, repeal or disregard s. 4 of the Statute…. But that is theory and has no relation to realities.

In *Blackburn* v *Attorney-General* [1971] 1 WLR 1037, at p. 1040, Lord Denning stated:

We have all been brought up to believe that, in legal theory, one Parliament cannot bind another and that no Act is irreversible. But legal theory does not always march alongside political reality. Take the Statute of Westminster 1931, which takes away the power of Parliament to legislate for the Dominions. Can anyone imagine that Parliament could or would reverse that Statute? Take the Acts which have granted independence to the Dominions and territories overseas. Can anyone imagine that Parliament could or would reverse those laws and take away their independence? Most clearly not. Freedom once given cannot be taken away. Legal theory must give way to practical politics.

However, legal theory still dominates judicial reasoning. In 1965 when Rhodesia made a Unilateral Declaration of Independence, the Southern Rhodesia Act 1965 was rushed through Parliament. In terms of practical politics the Act had no effect in Rhodesia, where it was ignored. However, in *Madzimbamuto* v *Lardner-Burke* [1969] 1 AC 645, Lord Reid recited legal theory:

It is often said that it would be unconstitutional for the United Kingdom Parliament to do certain things, meaning that the moral, political and other reasons against doing them are so strong that most people would regard it as highly improper if Parliament did these things. But that does not mean that it is beyond the power of Parliament to do these things. If Parliament chose to do any of them, the courts could not hold the Act of Parliament invalid.

Is it therefore impossible for Parliament to divest itself of the legal power to legislate for independent territories? Dicey's solution to the problem was the idea of abdication. He stated in *The Law of the Constitution* (1965), at p. 68:

The impossibility of placing a limit on the exercise of sovereignty does not in any way prohibit either logically, or in matter of fact, the abdication of sovereignty. This is worth observation, because a strange dogma is sometimes put forward that a sovereign power, such as the Parliament of the United Kingdom, can never by its own act divest itself of sovereignty. This position is, however, clearly untenable.

■ **QUESTION**

In 1982 the United Kingdom Parliament enacted a new constitution for Canada by the Canada Act, and terminated its own legislative competence for Canada. Section 2 provides:

> No Act of the Parliament of the United Kingdom passed after the Constitution Act 1982 comes into force shall extend to Canada as part of its law.

If Parliament subsequently legislated for Canada would this legislation be *ultra vires*? Would a United Kingdom court be acting unconstitutionally in light of Dicey's doctrine of abdication, if it did not declare the offending statute invalid?

NOTE: The difficulties which exist in this area are evident in the following case.

Manuel v *Attorney-General*
[1983] Ch 77, Chancery Division

The Canada Act 1982 was enacted following the request of the Senate and House of Commons of Canada, and with the agreement of nine of the ten provincial governments. The claimants were Aboriginal Chiefs and sought declarations to the effect that the United Kingdom parliament had no power to amend the constitution of Canada so as to prejudice the Aboriginal nations without their consent, and that the Canada Act 1982 was *ultra vires*. The basis of their claim was that the enactment of the Canada Act 1982 was inconsistent with and a derogation from the constitutional safeguards provided for the Aboriginal peoples by the Statute of Westminster 1931 and the British North America Acts. The claimants' contention was that the consent of all the provincial legislatures, the Aboriginal nations of Canada and the federal Parliament were necessary before amendments to the Canadian Constitution (contained in the British North America Acts) could be enacted. The Attorney-General moved that the statement of claim be struck out as showing no reasonable cause of action.

MEGARRY V-C: ... On the face of it, a contention that an Act of Parliament is *ultra vires* is bold in the extreme. It is contrary to one of the fundamentals of the British Constitution....

As was said by Lord Morris of Borth-y-Gest, at p. 789, it is not for the courts to proceed 'as though the Act or some part of it had never been passed'; there may be argument on the interpretation of the Act, but 'there must be none as to whether it should be on the Statute Book at all.' Any complaint on such matters is for Parliament to deal with and not the courts....

Mr Macdonald [counsel for the claimants] was, of course, concerned to restrict the ambit of the decision in *Pickin* v *British Railways Board*. He accepted that it was a binding decision for domestic legislation, but he said that it did not apply in relation to the Statute of Westminster 1931 or to the other countries of the Commonwealth. He also contended that it decided no more than that the courts would not inquire into what occurred in the course of the passage of a bill through Parliament, relying on what Lord Reid said at p. 787. This latter point is, I think, plainly wrong, since it ignores the words 'what was done previously to its being introduced' which Lord Reid cited with approval on that page. The wider point, however, is founded upon the theory that Parliament may surrender its sovereign power over some territory or area of land to another person or body.... After such a surrender, any legislation which Parliament purports to enact for that territory is not merely ineffective there, but is totally void, in this country as elsewhere, since Parliament has surrendered the power to legislate; and the English courts have jurisdiction to declare such legislation *ultra vires* and void....

The claimants argued that the United Kingdom Parliament had, by the Statute of Westminster 1931, transferred sovereignty to Canada and had deprived itself of all power to legislate for Canada subject only to s. 7 of that Act. Section 7 reserved to Parliament the power to repeal, amend, or alter the British North America Acts. The claimants further argued that the true meaning of s. 1 of the 1931 Act dictated that these residuary legislative powers could only be exercised pursuant to the actual request and consent of the Dominion. For these purposes 'Dominion' meant not merely the Parliament of Canada but all the constituent constitutional factions of the Dominion, namely, Parliament, the provincial legislatures, and the Aboriginal nations. As no such general consent had been given it was argued that the United Kingdom Parliament could not legislate for Canada. Megarry V-C continued:

I am bound to say that from first to last I have heard nothing in this case to make me doubt the simple rule that the duty of the court is to obey and apply every Act of Parliament, and that the court cannot hold any such Act to be *ultra vires*. Of course there may be questions about what the Act means, and of course there is power to hold statutory instruments and other subordinate legislation *ultra vires*. But once an instrument is recognised as being an Act of Parliament, no English court can refuse to obey it or question its validity.

In the present case I have before me a copy of the Canada Act 1982 purporting to be published by Her Majesty's Stationery Office. After reciting the request and consent of Canada and the submission of an address to Her Majesty by the Senate and House of Commons of Canada, there are the words of enactment:

'Be it therefore enacted by the Queen's Most Excellent Majesty, by and with the advice and consent of the Lords Spiritual and Temporal, and Commons, in this present Parliament assembled, and by the authority of the same, as follows: ... '

There has been no suggestion that the copy before me is not a true copy of the Act itself, or that it was not passed by the House of Commons and the House of Lords, or did not receive the Royal Assent.... The Canada Act 1982 is an Act of Parliament, and sitting as a judge in an English court I owe full and dutiful obedience to that Act.

I do not think that, as a matter of law, it makes any difference if the Act in question purports to apply outside the United Kingdom. I speak not merely of statutes such as the Continental Shelf Act 1964 but also of statutes purporting to apply to other countries. If that other country is a colony, the English courts will apply the Act even if the colony is in a state of revolt against the Crown and direct enforcement of the decision may be impossible: see *Madzimbamuto* v *Lardner-Burke* [1969] 1 AC 645. It matters not if a convention had grown up that the United Kingdom Parliament would not legislate for that colony without the consent of the colony. Such a convention would not limit the powers of Parliament, and if Parliament legislated in breach of the convention, 'the courts could not hold the Act of Parliament invalid': see p. 723. Similarly if the other country is a foreign state which has never been British, I do not think that any English court would or could declare the Act *ultra vires* and void. No doubt the Act would normally be ignored by the foreign state and would not be enforced by it, but that would not invalidate the Act in this country. Those who infringed it could not claim that it was void if proceedings within the jurisdiction were taken against them. Legal validity is one thing, enforceability is another. Thus a marriage in Nevada may constitute statutory bigamy punishable in England (*Trial of Earl Russell* [1901] AC 446), just as acts in Germany may be punishable here as statutory treason: *Joyce* v *Director of Public Prosecutions* [1946] AC 347. Parliament in fact legislates only for British subjects in this way; but if it also legislated for others, I do not see how the English courts could hold the statute void, however impossible it was to enforce it, and no matter how strong the diplomatic protests.

I do not think that countries which were once colonies but have since been granted independence are in any different position. Plainly once statute has granted independence to a country, the repeal of the statute will not make the country dependent once more; what is done is done, and is not undone by revoking the authority do to it. Heligoland did not in 1953 again become British. But if Parliament then passes an Act applying to such a country, I cannot see why that Act should not be in the same position as an Act applying to what has always been a foreign country, namely, an Act which the English courts will recognise and apply but one which the other country will in all probability ignore....

For the reasons that I have given, I have come to the conclusion that the statement of claim in the Manuel action discloses no reasonable cause of action, and that, despite the persuasions of Mr Macdonald, this is plain and obvious enough to justify striking out the statement of claim....

Perhaps I may add this. I have grave doubts about the theory of the transfer of sovereignty as affecting the competence of Parliament. In my view, it is a fundamental of the English constitution that Parliament is supreme. As a matter of law the courts of England recognise Parliament as being omnipotent in all save the power to destroy its own omnipotence. Under the authority of Parliament the courts of a territory may be released from their legal duty to obey Parliament, but that does not trench on the acceptance by the English courts of all that Parliament does. Nor must validity in law be confused with practical enforceability.

The claimants appealed.

In the Court of Appeal, in contrast, while the court emphasized that it was not necessarily endorsing this position or deciding the point, argument proceeded on the basis that 'that Parliament can effectively tie the hands of its successors, if it passes a statute which provides that any future legislation on a specified subject shall be enacted only with certain specified consents'. The judgment therefore focused on the question of whether consent had indeed been given, as necessary to satisfy s. 4 of the Statute of Westminster.

SLADE LJ:

Mr Macdonald submitted in the alternative that ... the actual request and consent of the Dominion is necessary before a law made by the United Kingdom Parliament can extend to that Dominion as part of its law. Whether or not an argument on these lines might find favour in the courts of a Dominion, it is in our opinion quite unsustainable in the courts of this country. The sole condition precedent which has to be satisfied if a law made by the United Kingdom Parliament is to extend to a Dominion as part of its law is to be found stated in the body of the Statute of 1931 itself (section 4). This court would run counter to all principles of statutory interpretation if it were to purport to vary or supplement the terms of this stated condition precedent by reference to some supposed convention, which, though referred to in the preamble, is not incorporated in the body of the Statute.

In the present instance, therefore, the only remaining question is whether it is arguable that the condition precedent specified in section 4 of the Statute of 1931 has not been complied with in relation to the Canada Act 1982. Is it arguable that it has not been 'expressly declared in that Act that that Dominion has requested, and consented to, the enactment thereof'? In our judgment this proposition is not arguable, inasmuch as the preamble to the Canada Act 1982 begins with the words 'Whereas Canada has requested and consented to the enactment of an Act of the Parliament of the United Kingdom to give effect to the provisions hereinafter set forth ... '.

... [W]e conclude that, if and so far as the conditions of section 4 of the Statute of 1931 had to be complied with in relation to the Canada Act 1982, they were duly complied with by the declaration contained in the preamble to that Act.

Appeal dismissed.

■ QUESTIONS

1. Which approach to the issues raised in this case is preferable: that of Megarry V-C, focused on the fact that an Act of Parliament cannot be held *ultra vires*, or that of the Court of Appeal, focused on whether the consent requirement had been satisfied? Was the Court of Appeal right to accept, for the purposes of argument, that Parliament may effectively tie the hands of its successors in such circumstances? Would the Court have been free to decide this point, had it so wished?

2. Does a grant of independence to a former Dominion create a substantive limit on Parliament's power? Is this compatible with the doctrine of parliamentary sovereignty?

NOTE: For further discussion of the legal problems associated with achieving independence, see P. Oliver, *The Constitution of Independence* (2005).

B: Procedural conditions

The 'manner and form' theory, defended by Jennings and others, allows Parliament to change the process by which legislation is enacted. This can be done by inserting procedural conditions into the existing legislative process by Act of Parliament, for example a requirement that a majority of voters vote in a referendum in favour of the proposed legislation, or a requirement of an enhanced majority in the Commons, such as two-thirds instead of a simple majority. This issue has arisen in several Commonwealth cases.

Attorney-General for New South Wales v *Trethowan and others*
[1932] AC 526, Privy Council

Under s. 5 of the Colonial Laws Validity Act 1865, the legislature of New South Wales had full power to legislate for its own constitution, powers, and procedure, provided that these laws were passed in 'the manner and form' required by the law in force at the time, whether it be imperial or colonial. In 1929 the Constitution (Legislative Council) Amendment Act was passed, which inserted a new s. 7A in the Constitution Act 1902, providing that no Bill for abolishing the Legislative Council should be presented to the Governor for His Majesty's assent until it had been approved by a majority of electors voting in a referendum and, further, that any Bill to repeal this referendum requirement must also be approved at a referendum. In 1930, following a change in government, both houses of the legislature passed two Bills, one to repeal s. 7A and the other to abolish the Legislative Council, both of which the Government intended to present for the Royal Assent without referenda being held. The plaintiffs were members of the Legislative Council and sought a declaration that the two Bills could not be presented for Royal Assent until approved by the electors in accordance with s. 7A, and injunctions restraining the presentation of the Bills.

LORD SANKEY LC: ... [T]he point involved in the case, ... is really a short one—namely, whether the legislature of the State of New South Wales has power to abolish the Legislative Council of the said State, or to repeal s. 7A of the Constitution Act, 1902, except in the manner provided by the said s. 7A. It will be sufficient for this Board to decide any other question if, and when, it arises.

... In their Lordships' opinion the legislature of New South Wales had power under s. 5 of the Act of 1865 to enact the Constitution (Legislative Council) Amendment Act, 1929, and thereby to introduce s. 7A into the Constitution Act, 1902. In other words, the legislature had power to alter the constitution of New South Wales by enacting that Bills relating to specified kind or kinds of legislation (e.g., abolishing the Legislative Council or altering its constitution or powers, or repealing or amending that enactment) should not be presented for the Royal assent until approved by the electors in a prescribed manner. There is here no question of repugnancy. The enactment of the Act of 1929 was simply an exercise by the legislature of New South Wales of its power (adopting the words of s. 5 of the Act of 1865) to make laws respecting the constitution, powers and procedure of the authority competent to make the laws for New South Wales.

The whole of s. 7A was competently enacted. It was intra vires s. 5 of the Act of 1865, and was (again adopting the words of s. 5) a colonial law for the time being in force when the Bill to repeal s. 7A was introduced in the Legislative Council.

The question then arises, could *that* Bill, a repealing Bill, after its passage through both chambers, be lawfully presented for the Royal assent without having first received the approval of the electors in the prescribed manner? In their Lordships' opinion, the Bill could not lawfully be so presented. The proviso in the second sentence of s. 5 of the Act of 1865 states a condition which must be fulfilled before the legislature can validly exercise its power to make the kind of laws which are referred to in that sentence. In order that s. 7A may be repealed (in other words, in order that *that* particular law 'respecting the constitution, powers and procedure' of the legislature may be validly made) the law for that purpose must have been passed in the manner required by s. 7A, a colonial law for the time being in force in New South Wales. An attempt was made to draw some distinction between a Bill to repeal a statute and a Bill for other purposes and between 'making' laws and the word in the proviso, 'passed.' Their Lordships feel unable to draw any such distinctions. As to the proviso they agree with the views expressed by Rich J [in the High Court of Australia] in the following words: 'I take the word "passed" to be equivalent to "enacted." The proviso is not dealing with narrow questions of parliamentary procedure'; and later in his judgment: 'In my opinion the proviso to s. 5 relates to the entire process of turning a proposed law into a legislative enactment, and was intended to enjoin fulfilment of every condition and compliance with every requirement which existing legislation imposed upon the process of law making.'

Again, no question of repugnancy here arises. It is only a question whether the proposed enactment is intra vires or *ultra vires* s. 5. A Bill, within the scope of sub-s. 6 of s. 7A, which received the Royal assent without having been approved by the electors in accordance with that section, would not be a valid Act of the legislature. It would be *ultra vires* s. 5 of the Act of 1865. Indeed, the presentation of the Bill to the Governor without such approval would be the commission of an unlawful act.

In the result, their Lordships are of opinion that s. 7A of the Constitution Act, 1902, was valid and was in force when the two Bills under consideration were passed through the Legislative Council and the Legislative Assembly. Therefore these Bills could not be presented to the Governor for His Majesty's assent unless and until a majority of the electors voting had approved them.

For these reasons, their Lordships are of opinion that the judgment of the High Court dismissing the appeal from the decree of the Supreme Court of New South Wales was right....

Appeal dismissed.

■ QUESTION

If the United Kingdom Parliament enacted a provision to the same effect as s. 7A, designed to protect the position of the House of Lords, would a subsequent Bill abolishing this provision and the House of Lords become an Act on receiving the Royal Assent, or would the referendum requirements be regarded by the courts as necessary prerequisites to the Bill becoming an Act?

NOTE: There is a division of views among constitutional theorists as to the relevance of the *Trethowan* case to the United Kingdom. Those who adhere to the traditional theory of supremacy argue that the decision is of no relevance as the New South Wales legislature was a subordinate legislature (see, e.g. Wade, 'The Basis of Legal Sovereignty' [1955] CLJ 172). The proponents of this view rely on *Ellen St Estates Ltd* v *Minister of Health* and the idea that a new Act of Parliament will repeal an earlier inconsistent statute by implication (see earlier in this chapter in Section 1C at pp. 52–3). Opponents of this view argue that the decision is applicable on the basis that at common law there is a rule that legislation may be enacted only in such manner and form as is prescribed by the law (see, e.g. Heuston, *Essays in Constitutional Law*, chap. 1). If an Act lays down a specific procedure to be followed before it may be repealed, this is the law; a measure passed in the normal way ignoring this procedure has not been passed in the manner and form prescribed by the law, and is not therefore an Act of Parliament. Support for this view is found in *Harris* v *Minister of the Interior* 1952 (2) SA 428, and *Bribery Commissioner* v *Ranasinghe* [1965] AC 172. In the latter case, the Privy Council held that a procedural requirement of the constitution of Ceylon, which imposed a two-thirds majority threshold for legislation concerning judicial appointments, was binding on the sovereign Parliament of Ceylon, which could not, therefore, set up the Bribery Commission by an ordinary Act of Parliament. The Privy Council held that the official copy of the statute was not conclusive of its validity if the correct procedures had not been followed. Lord Pearce stated, at p. 197:

> [A] legislature has no power to ignore the conditions of law-making that are imposed by the instrument which itself regulates its power to make law. This restriction exists independently of the question whether the legislature is sovereign....

This statement would appear to lend support to the manner and form theorists. However, the traditional theorists argue that *Harris* and *Ranasinghe* are not relevant to the United Kingdom because the legislatures of South Africa and Ceylon were subject to constituent instruments, whereas the United Kingdom has no written constitution. Latham in *The Law and the Commonwealth* (1949), p. 523, states:

> When the purported sovereign is anyone but a single actual person, the designation of him must include the statement of the rules for ascertainment of his will, and these rules, since their observance is a condition of the validity of his legislation are Rules of Law logically prior to him.

Is it crucial that these rules should be contained in a formal written constitution? Heuston believes not; he states (Heuston, *Essays in Constitutional Law*, p. 26):

> It cannot make any difference whether the rules which identify the sovereign come entirely from the common law (as they did before 1911 in the United Kingdom) or entirely from statute (as they do in Ireland, New South Wales and South Africa) or partly from the common law and partly from statute (as they do in the United Kingdom since 1911). It is hard to see why those who argue thus should attach so much importance to the formal source of the complex set of rules identifying the location and composition of the sovereign.... The point here is the simple one that until these rules (whatever their source) have been changed in accordance with the manner which they themselves prescribe they must be obeyed.

For further discussion of the manner and form theory and its potential relevance to the UK constitution, see Gordon, *Parliamentary Sovereignty in the UK Constitution: Process, Politics and Democracy* (2015), chs 2, 7, and 8.

■ QUESTIONS

1. Is it a necessary concomitant of supremacy that Parliament's powers to legislate be not subject to any procedural restraint? Marshall, 'Parliamentary sovereignty: the new horizons' [1997] *Public Law* 1, at p. 4, states:

> ... May a sovereign legislative body that acts by simple majority protect particularly important statutes of its own making ... by providing for its repeal or amendment to require a specific majority, or possibly the backing of a referendum? ... No UK enactment has ever attempted such a thing and in 1978 the House of Lords Select Committee on a Bill of Rights was advised that it was not possible. But of course it is possible if the courts believe that the power to change the law extends to a power to change the law about the way law is made. There is nothing in Dicey's concept of parliamentary sovereignty that is incompatible with this possibility. Procedurally and tactically it would be prudent for a special majority requirement to be applied not to an enacted Bill at the stage of a royal assent, but so as to prevent the further progress of any Bill of the prescribed kind that has not been carried by the required special

> majority at its second reading. Caution would suggest that an entrenching Act should also provide a judicial remedy to secure its enforcement, expressed to operate notwithstanding any existing rules as to standing or parliamentary privilege. If the remedy is effective, there would not then, on any view, be a later alleged Act of Parliament to rival the authority of the entrenchment statute or to threaten it with implicit repeal.

2. The examples considered above all relate to a Parliament enacting procedural conditions in a statute which make it *harder* to legislate in future about a particular topic. Adopting Jennings' manner and form understanding of parliamentary sovereignty, could Parliament also legislate to make it *easier* to legislate? As we shall see, this issue has now been argued before the UK courts, in the important case of *Jackson* v *Attorney General* [2005] UHL 56, [2006] 1 AC 262, which relates to the legal status of the Parliament Acts 1911 and 1949. The decision in *Jackson* is one of the modern challenges to parliamentary sovereignty we will now consider.

SECTION 3: MODERN CHALLENGES TO THE SOVEREIGNTY OF PARLIAMENT

In this section we consider the implications for parliamentary sovereignty as a result of some of the major constitutional developments of the last quarter of the twentieth century, and the early part of the twenty-first century. A further challenge to parliamentary sovereignty may be posed by the UK's devolution settlement, but this will be considered separately in Chapter 8. The partial incorporation of the European Convention on Human Rights into UK law is considered here, and in more detail in Chapter 9.

A: Membership of the European Union

The greatest, and most controversial, challenge to the legislative sovereignty of Parliament has been that posed by the United Kingdom's membership of the European Union. To become a member of the EU is to accept the supremacy of EU rules over national legislation. Yet at a referendum in June 2016, a majority of the UK electorate voted, by 51.7 per cent to 48.3 per cent, to leave the EU. The government has committed to deliver this result, yet 'Brexit' will take time to negotiate and implement (for initial analysis see Craig, 'Brexit: A Drama in Six Acts' (2016) *European Law Review* 447–68; Gordon, 'Brexit: A Challenge *of* the UK Constitution, *for* the UK Constitution?' (2016) *European Constitutional Law Review* 409–44).

There are at least two reasons why we must still consider the implications of EU membership for parliamentary sovereignty. First, until the UK's withdrawal comes into effect, the constitutional position is unchanged, and EU law continues to apply in the domestic legal system. Second, the impact of EU membership on the UK constitution has been profound, and even after exit—and regardless of what future relationship with the EU the UK may eventually agree—the legacy of that membership is likely to continue to shape the way we now think about the idea of parliamentary sovereignty. So, we must consider whether the supremacy of EU law has meant that the UK Parliament's power to 'make or unmake any law' is limited.

(a) Supremacy of Union law

The United Kingdom joined the European Union in 1973. The European Union currently has 28 Member States whose relations with each other in a special legal order are founded on two treaties, the Treaty on European Union (TEU) and the Treaty on the Functioning of the European Union (TFEU) as amended by the Treaty of Lisbon, which came in to effect on 1 December 2009. The EU has competence to make law applicable to its Member States in a range of policy areas, primarily to establish a single market in which there are (a) no barriers to trade amongst the Member States, and (b) freedom of movement of capital and of people, both as workers and as providers of services.

One of the most important doctrines of EU law developed by the Court of Justice of the European Union (CJEU) is that of its supremacy over inconsistent national law. If a European single market is to be created and operate effectively, Member States must not be permitted to deviate from EU rules common to all. In *Van Gend en Loos* v *Nederlandse Administratie der Belastingen* (Case 26/62) [1963] ECR 1 the CJEU concluded that a new legal order had been created by the Treaties, and that the CJEU was to be the final authority on the interpretation of the Treaties and EU law. The nature of this new legal order was further developed in the following case.

Costa v *ENEL* (Case 6/64)
[1964] ECR 585, CJEU

Mr Costa refused to pay an electricity bill. He was opposed to the nationalization of the Italian electricity industry which had occurred after the EEC Treaty had come into force. In defending his non-payment Mr Costa argued that the nationalization legislation breached Arts 102, 93, 53, and 37 of the EEC Treaty (now Arts 117, 108, and 37 of the TFEU). The magistrate, the *Giudice Conciliatore*, sought a preliminary ruling from the CJEU.

On the submission that the court was obliged to apply the national law

The Italian Government submits that the request of the Giudice Conciliatore is 'absolutely inadmissible', inasmuch as a national court which is obliged to apply a national law cannot avail itself of Article 177 [now 267].

By contrast with ordinary international treaties, the EEC Treaty has created its own legal system which, on the entry into force of the Treaty, became an integral part of the legal systems of the Member States and which their courts are bound to apply.

By creating a Community of unlimited duration, having its own institutions, its own personality, its own legal capacity and capacity of representation on the international plane and, more particularly, real powers stemming from a limitation of sovereignty or a transfer of powers from the States to the Community, the Member States have limited their sovereign rights, albeit within limited fields, and have thus created a body of law which binds both their nationals and themselves.

The integration into the laws of each Member State of provisions which derive from the Community, and more generally the terms and the spirit of the Treaty, make it impossible for the States, as a corollary, to accord precedence to a unilateral and subsequent measure over a legal system accepted by them on a basis of reciprocity. Such a measure cannot therefore be inconsistent with that legal system. The executive force of Community law cannot vary from one State to another in deference to subsequent domestic laws, without jeopardizing the attainment of the objectives of the Treaty set out in Article 5(2) [now 10(2)] and giving rise to the discrimination prohibited by Article 7 [now repealed]. . . .

The transfer by the States from their domestic legal system to the Community legal system of the rights and obligations arising under the Treaty carries with it a permanent limitation of their sovereign rights, against which a subsequent unilateral act incompatible with the concept of the Community cannot prevail. Consequently Article 177 [now 267] is to be applied regardless of any domestic law, whenever questions relating to the interpretation of the Treaty arise.

The CJEU ruled that subsequent national measures cannot take precedence over EC law and that, whilst Articles 53 and 37(2) produced direct effects creating rights for individuals which national courts must protect, this was not so for Articles 102 and 93.

NOTE: The decision of the CJEU showed that EU provisions which do not specifically mention individuals may still create rights for them. The CJEU also developed its views about the new legal order, and stated that the logic of EU law gives it supremacy over the municipal law of the Member States.

The full extent of this supremacy of EU law is revealed in the following case.

Internationale Handelsgesellschaft mbH v Einfuhr und Vorratsstelle für Getreide und Futtermittel (Case 11/70)

[1970] ECR 1125, CJEU

The claimant (then called the 'plaintiff'), a German company, had to obtain a licence to export corn flour. The EU provisions required a performance deposit, that is, if a licensee failed to export the full amount permitted in the licence then the deposit would be forfeit. The claimant failed to export the full amount specified in the licence and so forfeited the deposit. The claimant challenged this in the administrative court, the *Verwaltungsgericht*. The German court sought a preliminary ruling on the EU provisions, as the court thought that they were in conflict with the basic rights guaranteed in the West German constitution.

[2] ... It appears from the grounds of the order referring the matter that the Verwaltungsgericht has until now refused to accept the validity of the provisions in question and that for this reason it considers it to be essential to put an end to the existing legal uncertainty. According to the evaluation of the Verwaltungsgericht, the system of deposits is contrary to certain structural principles of national constitutional law which must be protected within the framework of Community law, with the result that the primacy of supranational law must yield before the principles of the German Basic Law. More particularly, the system of deposits runs counter to the principles of freedom of action and of disposition, of economic liberty and of proportionality arising in particular from Articles 2 (1) and 14 of the Basic Law. The obligation to import or export resulting from the issue of the licences, together with the deposit attaching thereto, constitutes an excessive intervention in the freedom of disposition in trade, as the objective of the regulations could have been attained by methods of intervention having less serious consequences.

The protection of fundamental rights in the Community legal system

[3] Recourse to the legal rules or concepts of national law in order to judge the validity of measures adopted by the institutions of the Community would have an adverse effect on the uniformity and efficacy of Community law. The validity of such measures can only be judged in the light of Community law. In fact, the law stemming from the Treaty, an independent source of law, cannot because of its very nature be overridden by rules of national law, however framed, without being deprived of its character as Community law and without the legal basis of the Community itself being called in question. Therefore the validity of a Community measure or its effect within a Member State cannot be affected by allegations that it runs counter to either fundamental rights as formulated by the constitution of the State or the principles of a national constitutional structure.

[4] However, an examination should be made as to whether or not any analogous guarantee inherent in Community law has been disregarded. In fact, respect for fundamental rights forms an integral part of the general principles of law protected by the Court of Justice. The protection of such rights, whilst inspired by the constitutional traditions common to the Member States, must be ensured within the framework of the structure and objectives of the Community. It must therefore be ascertained, in the light of the doubts expressed by the Verwaltungsgericht, whether the system of deposits has infringed rights of a fundamental nature, respect for which must be ensured in the Community legal system.

The CJEU upheld the provisions creating the system of performance deposits.

NOTE: So far we have looked at conflicts between the municipal law of Member States and EU law where the CJEU, in its rulings, has affirmed the supremacy of the latter. The CJEU has even declared that EU law prevails over any conflicting provisions of Bills of Rights in Member States' constitutions. The declaration of the supremacy of EU law by the CJEU creates a problem for national courts: they are supposed to protect the rights conferred by EU law even where they conflict with the law of Member States. How can this be done if a national court cannot strike down a municipal statute, as where, for example, only the Member State's Constitutional Court can carry out such action? Advice was offered in the following case.

Amministrazione delle Finanze dello Stato v *Simmenthal SpA* (Case 106/77)
[1978] ECR 629, CJEU

Simmenthal imported beef into Italy. In an earlier case, *Simmenthal SpA* v *Italian Minister of Finance* (Case 35/76) [1976] ECR 1871, the ECJ had ruled that the Italian law requiring importers to pay for public health and veterinary checks at the border was contrary to Arts 30 and 12 of the EEC Treaty (now Arts 34 and 30 of the TFEU). The Italian court ordered the refund of these fees paid by Simmenthal, and the Ministry argued that until the Constitutional Court set aside the legislation it had a good defence. The Italian court sought a preliminary ruling.

[13] The main purpose of the first question is to ascertain what consequences flow from the direct applicability of a provision of Community law in the event of incompatibility with a subsequent legislative provision of a Member State.

[14] Direct applicability in such circumstances means that rules of Community law must be fully and uniformly applied in all the Member States from the date of their entry into force and for so long as they continue in force.

[15] These provisions are therefore a direct source of rights and duties for all those affected thereby, whether Member States or individuals, who are parties to legal relationships under Community law.

[16] This consequence also concerns any national court whose task it is as an organ of a Member State to protect, in a case within its jurisdiction, the rights conferred upon individuals by Community law. . . .

[21] It follows from the foregoing that every national court must, in a case within its jurisdiction, apply Community law in its entirety and protect rights which the latter confers on individuals and must accordingly set aside any provision of national law which may conflict with it, whether prior or subsequent to the Community rule.

[22] Accordingly any provision of a national legal system and any legislative, administrative, or judicial practice which might impair the effectiveness of Community law by withholding from the national court having jurisdiction to apply such law the power to do everything necessary at the moment of its application to set aside national legislative provisions which might prevent Community rules from having full force and effect are incompatible with those requirements which are the very essence of Community law. . . .

The CJEU ruled:

'A national court which is called upon, within the limits of its jurisdiction, to apply provisions of Community law is under a duty to give full effect to those provisions, if necessary refusing of its own motion to apply any conflicting provisions of national legislation, even if adopted subsequently, and it is not necessary for the court to request or await the prior setting aside of such provisions by legislation or other constitutional means.'

NOTE: While the CJEU states that any national court may set aside municipal legislation, this does not mean that such legislation is entirely void. It is only of no effect where there is a conflict between it and EU law.

(b) EU supremacy in the United Kingdom courts

The traditional view of the legislative sovereignty of Parliament would appear to conflict with the CJEU's rulings on the supremacy of Union law. For Parliament's legislation would seem to take effect subject to EU rules, with any domestic court required to reject the provisions of an Act of Parliament which violated EU law. We must now consider how the UK courts have responded to this challenge.

In order for EU law (known at the time of the UK's accession as European Community, or EC, law) to become part of the United Kingdom's domestic law, it had to be incorporated by legislation. This was done by the following provisions.

European Communities Act 1972

2. —(1) All such rights, powers, liabilities, obligations and restrictions from time to time created or arising by or under the Treaties, and all such remedies and procedures from time to time provided for by or under the Treaties, as in accordance with the Treaties are without further enactment to be given legal effect or used in the United Kingdom shall be recognised and available in law, and be enforced, allowed and followed accordingly; and the expression 'enforceable Community right' and similar expressions shall be read as referring to one to which this subsection applies.

(2) Subject to Schedule 2 of this Act, at any time after its passing Her Majesty may by Order in Council, and any designated Minister or department may by regulations, make provision—

   (a) for the purpose of implementing any Community obligation of the United Kingdom, or enabling any such obligation to be implemented, or of enabling any rights enjoyed or to be enjoyed by the United Kingdom under or by virtue of the Treaties to be exercised; or
   (b) for the purpose of dealing with matters arising out of or related to any such obligation or rights or the coming into force, or the operation from time to time, of subsection (1) above;

and in the exercise of any statutory power or duty, including any power to give directions or to legislate by means of orders, rules, regulations or other subordinate instrument, the person entrusted with the power or duty may have regard to the objects of the Communities and to any such obligation or rights as aforesaid. In this subsection 'designated Minister or department' means such Minister of the Crown or government department as may from time to time be designated by Order in Council in relation to any matter or for any purpose, but subject to such restrictions or conditions (if any) as may be specified by the Order in Council....

(4) The provision that may be made under subsection (2) above includes, subject to Schedule 2 to this Act, any such provision (of any such extent) as might be made by Act of Parliament, and any enactment passed or to be passed, other than one contained in this Part of this Act, shall be construed and have effect subject to the foregoing provisions of this section; but, except as may be provided by any Act passed after this Act, Schedule 2 shall have effect in connection with the powers conferred by this and the following sections of this Act to make Orders in Council and regulations.

3. —(1) For the purposes of all legal proceedings any question as to the meaning or effect of any of the Treaties, or as to the validity, meaning or effect of any Community instrument, shall be treated as a question of law (and, if not referred to the European Court, be for determination as such in accordance with the principles laid down by and any relevant decision of the European Court).

(2) Judicial notice shall be taken of the Treaties, of the Official Journal of the Communities and of any decision of, or expression of opinion by, the European Court on any such question as aforesaid; and the Official Journal shall be admissible as evidence of any instrument or other act thereby communicated of any of the Communities or of any Community institution.

NOTES

1. Section 2(1) incorporated *some* EU law into United Kingdom law. This EU law has been known as directly applicable EU law. Such law came into effect in the UK without any further legislative action being taken by Parliament.

Section 2(2) provided for the making of delegated legislation in order to implement EU obligations. Schedule 2 specified the limitations upon such legislative action, and some of these included the inability to increase taxation, to introduce retrospective measures, or to create new criminal offences.

Section 2(4) provided that subsequent legislation was to be construed and to have effect subject to s. 2(1) and (2). This has been the main source of the potential problem for the doctrine of parliamentary sovereignty: in effect, s. 2(4) seemed to indicate that *future* legislation enacted by Parliament could not contravene EU law. It could therefore be understood to place a substantive limit on the legislative power of subsequent Parliaments.

2. In October 2016, in response to the June referendum vote to leave the EU, the government of Prime Minister Theresa May announced that it would bring forward legislation to repeal the European Communities Act 1972. It was proposed that this 'Great Repeal Bill' would initially incorporate substantive EU rules into the UK legal system, allowing Parliament subsequently to amend this very considerable body of law covering a range of topics over a longer period of time, as the nature of any future relationship with the EU is established (see 'Legislating for Brexit: the Great Repeal Bill', *House of Commons Library Briefing Paper 7793*, November 2016). Until that point, the 1972 Act will remain in force in the UK.

3. There have been a variety of approaches taken by UK courts to the issue of the supremacy of EU law. One approach focused on implied repeal, as illustrated by a dictum from Lord Denning MR in *Felixstowe Dock and Railway Co* v *British Transport Docks Board* [1976] 2 CMLR 655. In this case the British Transport Docks Board (the Board) wished to take over the Felixstowe Dock and Railway Company (the Company). Terms were agreed between the parties but the Board, as a statutory body with limited powers, needed parliamentary approval for this action. In an unsuccessful challenge to the agreement by the Company, the ownership of which had changed, it was argued, *inter alia*, that the agreement was contrary to EU competition law and Art. 86 of the EEC Treaty (now Art. 102 of the TFEU) in particular. Lord Denning MR said, at pp. 644–5:

> It seems to me that once the Bill is passed by Parliament and becomes a Statute that will dispose of all discussion about the Treaty. These courts will have to abide by the Statute without regard to the Treaty at all.

Another approach was to afford priority to Union law over inconsistent United Kingdom law, unless the domestic legislation expressly repudiated Community obligations. This approach can also be illustrated by dicta from Lord Denning MR, on this occasion from *Macarthys* v *Smith* [1979] ICR 785. This case involved a claim of unlawful discrimination on grounds of sex in relation to equal pay. Smith's contract of employment contained some minor differences from the contract of her male predecessor in the post. She received a smaller weekly wage than her male predecessor. The company's defence was that provisions of the Equal Pay Act 1970, as amended by the Sex Discrimination Act 1975, meant that Smith was only entitled to compare her pay with that of a male employee engaged in 'like work' at the same time as her. Smith argued that Art. 119 of the EEC Treaty (now Art. 157 of the TFEU) permitted her to base a claim on a comparison with her male predecessor. In the Court of Appeal Lord Denning MR said, at p. 789:

> In construing our statute, we are entitled to look to the Treaty as an aid to its construction, and even more, not only as an aid but as an overriding force. If on close investigation it should appear that our legislation is deficient—or is inconsistent with Community law—by some oversight of our draftsmen—then it is our bounden duty to give priority to Community law. Such is the result of section 2(1) and (4) of the European Communities Act 1972.
>
> I pause here, however, to make one observation on a constitutional point. Thus far I have assumed that our Parliament, whenever it passes legislation, intends to fulfil its obligations under the Treaty. If the time should come when our Parliament deliberately passes an Act—with the intention of repudiating the Treaty or any provision in it—or intentionally of acting inconsistently with it—and says so in express terms—then I should have thought that it would be the duty of our courts to follow the statute of our Parliament. I do not however envisage any such situation. As I said in *Blackburn* v *Attorney-General* [1971] WLR 1037, 1040: 'But, if Parliament should do so, then I say we will consider that event when it happens.' Unless there is such an intentional and express repudiation of the Treaty, it is our duty to give priority to the Treaty. In the present case I assume that the United Kingdom intended to fulfil its obligations under article 119.

Yet finally, the House of Lords was confronted with a case that required the implications of the supremacy of EU law for the legislative sovereignty of Parliament to be addressed.

R v Secretary of State for Transport, ex parte Factortame Ltd and Others
[1990] 2 AC 85, House of Lords

The applicants were companies which owned fishing vessels, the majority of which had first been registered as Spanish before being re-registered as British vessels. The United Kingdom Government was concerned that the operation of quotas under the Common Fisheries Policy would adversely affect the British fishing industry by the inclusion in the United Kingdom quotas of vessels fishing for the Spanish market. Parliament passed the Merchant Shipping Act 1988 and the Merchant Shipping (Registration of Fishing Vessels) Regulations 1988 (S.I. 1988 No. 1926) which would have the effect of ending the applicants' registration under the Merchant Shipping Act 1894 and precluding them from registration under the new regulations. The applicants claimed that the legislation was contrary to those provisions of EU law which (i) prohibited discrimination on grounds of nationality between Member States, (ii) prohibited restrictions on exports between Member States, (iii) created a common market in agricultural products, (iv) provided for the freedom of movement of workers and the freedom of establishment of companies, and (v) required that nationals of Member States are to be treated equally with respect to participation in the capital of companies established in the EU. The Divisional Court decided to seek a preliminary ruling from the CJEU and ordered as interim relief that, pending the CJEU's preliminary ruling on the compatibility of the United Kingdom law with EU law, Part II of the 1988 Act and the 1988 regulations be disapplied, and that the Secretary of State be restrained from applying them in respect of the applicants so as to enable the applicants' vessels to continue to be registered as British. On appeal the Court of Appeal reversed the decision on the granting of interim relief, which involved the overriding of the United Kingdom legislation. This was appealed to the House of Lords. The relationship between domestic law and Community law was explained in a preliminary passage before dealing with the point about interim relief.

LORD BRIDGE: ... By virtue of section 2(4) of the Act of 1972 Part II of the Act of 1988 is to be construed and take effect subject to directly enforceable Community rights and those rights are, by section 2(1) of the Act of 1972, to be 'recognised and available in law, and ... enforced, allowed and followed accordingly; ... ' This has precisely the same effect as if a section were incorporated in Part II of the Act of 1988 which in terms enacted that the provisions with respect to registration of British fishing vessels were to be without prejudice to the directly enforceable Community rights of nationals of any member state of the EEC. Thus it is common ground that, in so far as the applicants succeed before the ECJ in obtaining a ruling in support of the Community rights which they claim, those rights will prevail over the restrictions imposed on registration of British fishing vessels by Part II of the Act of 1988 and the Divisional Court will, in the final determination of the application for judicial review, be obliged to make appropriate declarations to give effect to those rights.

NOTE: Both the Court of Appeal and the House of Lords were of the view that domestic law did not allow, as interim relief, the disapplication of a statute where it had not been established that the statute was in breach of Union law. The House of Lords sought a preliminary ruling on this point from the CJEU which ruled that 'a national court which in a case before it concerning Union law considers itself that the sole obstacle which precludes it from granting interim relief is a rule of national law must set aside that rule' (*R v Secretary of State for Transport, ex parte Factortame Ltd* [1989] 3 CMLR 1). Subsequently the House of Lords considered the application for interim relief and decided to grant it. Lord Bridge commented on the impact of this decision on the legislative sovereignty of Parliament.

R v *Secretary of State for Transport, ex parte Factortame Ltd (No. 2)*
[1991] 1 AC 603, House of Lords

LORD BRIDGE: ... Some public comments on the decision of the Court of Justice, affirming the jurisdiction of the courts of the member states to override national legislation if necessary to enable interim relief to be granted in protection of rights under Community law, have suggested that this was a novel and dangerous invasion by a Community institution of the sovereignty of the United Kingdom Parliament. But such comments are based on a misconception. If the supremacy within the European Community of Community law over the national law of member states was not always inherent in the EEC Treaty it was certainly well established in the jurisprudence of the Court of Justice long before the United Kingdom joined the Community. Thus, whatever limitation of its sovereignty Parliament accepted when it enacted the European Communities Act 1972 was entirely voluntary. Under the terms of the 1972 Act it has always been clear that it was the duty of a United Kingdom court, when delivering final judgment, to override any rule of national law found to be in conflict with any directly enforceable rule of Community law. Similarly, when decisions of the Court of Justice have exposed areas of United Kingdom statute law which failed to implement Council directives, Parliament has always loyally accepted the obligation to make appropriate and prompt amendments. Thus there is nothing in any way novel in according supremacy to rules of Community law in areas to which they apply and to insist that, in the protection of rights under Community law, national courts must not be prohibited by rules of national law from granting interim relief in appropriate cases is no more than a logical recognition of that supremacy.

NOTES

1. The CJEU subsequently ruled on the Divisional Court's questions about the compatibility of the Merchant Shipping Act 1988 with Union law and ruled that Art. 52 of the EEC Treaty (now Art. 49 of the TFEU) had been infringed because of the local national and residence requirements for registration of owners of fishing vessels (*R* v *Secretary of State for Transport, ex parte Factortame Ltd (No. 3)* (Case C–221/89) [1991] 3 CMLR 589).

   Before the CJEU gave its rulings on the questions referred to it by the High Court and House of Lords, the European Commission brought a successful action for interim relief in an action under Art. 169 of the EEC Treaty (now Art. 258 of the TFEU) against the United Kingdom, requiring that the nationality requirement of s. 14 of the Merchant Shipping Act 1988 be suspended (*Re Nationality of Fishermen: EC Commission* v *UK* (Case C–246/89R) [1989] 3 CMLR 601). This was implemented by the Merchant Shipping Act (Amendment) Order 1989 (S.I. 1989 No. 2006). Finally the CJEU upheld the Commission's challenge under Art. 169 of the EEC Treaty (now Art. 258 of the TFEU) that the nationality requirements breached Arts 7, 52, and 221 of the EEC Treaty (now repealed by Arts 49 and 55 of the TFEU) (*Re Nationality of Fishermen: EC Commission* v *UK* (Case C–246/89) [1991] 3 CMLR 706).

2. That the United Kingdom courts were obliged to 'disapply' domestic legislation which violated EU law was further confirmed in *R* v *Secretary of State for Employment, ex parte Equal Opportunities Commission* [1994] 2 WLR 409.

3. Lord Bridge accepted that EU law has priority over domestic legislation, and that conflicting national law can be overridden by the courts. This seems far removed from Dicey's orthodox understanding of Parliament's power. Yet Lord Bridge also refused to accept that this was 'in any way novel', and attributed responsibility for the domestic supremacy of EU law to Parliament, through its enactment of the European Communities Act 1972. In this way, Lord Bridge avoided explicitly answering the question of whether the sovereignty of Parliament had been displaced, altered or remained unaffected, while seeming to suggest that EU supremacy and parliamentary sovereignty could co-exist. A number of explanations of the decision in *Factortame (No. 2)*, and the relationship between EU supremacy and parliamentary sovereignty it established, have been advanced, as the following extracts show.

■ QUESTION

What was the impact of the decision in *Factortame (No. 2)* on the legislative sovereignty of Parliament?

H. W. R. Wade, 'Sovereignty – Revolution or Evolution?'

(1996) 112 *Law Quarterly Review* 568, 568–9, 572–3, 574–5

When in the second *Factortame* case the House of Lords granted an injunction to forbid a minister from obeying an Act of Parliament, and the novel term "disapplied" had to be invented to describe the fate of the Act, it was natural to suppose that something drastic had happened to the traditional doctrine of Parliamentary sovereignty. The established rule about conflicting Acts of Parliament, namely that the later Act must prevail, was evidently violated, since the later Act in this case was the Merchant Shipping Act 1988, yet it was disapplied under the European Communities Act 1972. The Act of 1972 had provided for the subordination of English law to European Community law by section 2(4), enacting that European Community law was to prevail over Acts of Parliament "passed or to be passed". When that Act was nevertheless held to prevail it seemed to be fair comment to characterise this, at least in a technical sense, as a constitutional revolution. The Parliament of 1972 had succeeded in binding the Parliament of 1988 and restricting its sovereignty, something that was supposed to be constitutionally impossible. It is obvious that sovereignty belongs to the Parliament of the day and that, if it could be fettered by earlier legislation, the Parliament of the day would cease to be sovereign.

There is however a rival and less revolutionary view which holds that the disapplication of the Act of 1988 was achieved merely by way of statutory construction under ordinary principles. This might be called the "construction" view as opposed to the "revolution" view. The two views are compared and contrasted very fairly by Paul Craig in a lucid article [P.P. Craig, 'Sovereignty of the United Kingdom Parliament after Factortame' (1991) 11 Y.B.E.L. 221] in which he summarises the construction view as

"a rule of interpretation to the effect that Parliament is presumed not to intend statutes to override EEC law. On this view inconsistencies between United Kingdom statutes and EEC law would be resolved in favour of the latter unless 'Parliament clearly and expressly states in a future Act that it is to override Community law' … The longer that we remain in the EEC the more likely it is that the courts will adopt this rule of construction which serves to preserve the formal veneer of Diceyan orthodoxy while undermining its substance."

Craig then concludes, to paraphrase him concisely, that the construction view is more likely to commend itself to judges because it is based upon the will of Parliament, both expressed and implied, and does not require them to accept and enforce some novel limitation of Parliament's sovereignty. It is the easy way out. But is it the right way out? And is it, as Craig also suggests, more consistent than the revolution view with the reasoning of the House of Lords? …

The essence of [Lord Bridge's] important passage [in *Factortame (No. 2)*], for present purposes, is that by passing the Act of 1972 Parliament voluntarily accepted a limitation of its sovereignty, making it clear that Community law must in future prevail; and that "there was nothing in any way novel" in this situation, since the obligation was known from the outset. Nothing in Lord Bridge's language suggests that he regarded the issue as one of statutory construction. He takes it for granted that Parliament can "accept" a limitation of its sovereignty which will be effective both for the present and for the future. It is a statement which could hardly be clearer: Parliament can bind its successors. If that is not revolutionary, constitutional lawyers are Dutchmen. Craig seems to be putting it mildly when he says "the reasoning of Lord Bridge does not therefore fit well with that articulated by the traditional theory".

But neither does Lord Bridge's reasoning fit well with any theory based upon statutory construction, such as the theory that every post-1972 statute is to be construed as impliedly subject to Community law, subject only to express provision to the contrary. Nothing of that kind is suggested by Lord Bridge's doctrine of "voluntary acceptance" by Parliament of Community law as a "limitation of its sovereignty". The truth is, apparently, that so far from containing "nothing in any way novel", the new doctrine makes sovereignty a freely adjustable commodity whenever Parliament chooses to accept some limitation. The effect may be similar to implying limitations into future statutes, as Lord Bridge himself explains. But "voluntary acceptance" goes much deeper into the foundations of the constitution, suggesting by its very novelty that the courts are reformulating the fundamental rules about the effectiveness of Acts of Parliament....

In the House of Lords' *Factortame* decisions it was only in the speeches of Lord Bridge that any constitutional aspect was discussed. Since Lord Bridge held that the situation was "in no way novel", and since he did not appear to recognise that there was any problem of a constitutional kind, it is hazardous to draw conclusions. At least it is clear that Lord Bridge is not invoking any doctrine of construction. Although Craig may well be right in suggesting that the construction view may nevertheless find favour as a plausible escape from the constitutional dilemma, in reality it can only be camouflage for the fundamental change which has evidently occurred.

To predict just what that change may entail can only be guesswork. Is it now to be possible at any time, and to any extent, for Parliament to signify its "voluntary acceptance" of limitations on its successors' sovereignty in the manner stated by Lord Bridge? Or, at the other extreme, was accession to the Community a unique legal event, demanding concessions of sovereignty for obvious political reasons, but otherwise setting no precedent of any kind? Or might there be intermediate positions, for example allowing entrenchment where a safeguard is needed to ensure observance of a treaty, or where a treaty has been approved in a national referendum, as in 1975?... [T]he prudential course may be to follow the example of the House of Lords and turn a blind eye to constitutional theory altogether. Unsatisfying as that may be to the academic mind, it at least provides a further example of the constitution bending before the winds of change, as in the last resort it will always succeed in doing.

NOTE: Wade thus rejected the 'construction' view, placing more emphasis on Lord Bridge's speech in *Factortame (No. 2)* than his less definitive observations in *Factortame (No. 1)*. Yet his view that the *Factortame* cases provide evidence that a 'revolution'—whether technical or otherwise—has occurred can also be challenged. With reference to debates between Dicey and Wade on one hand, and the manner and form theorists on the other, this has been questioned by John Eekelaar ('The Death of Parliamentary Sovereignty – a Comment' (1997) *Law Quarterly Review* 185–7, 185):

Yet, is it revolutionary; or if so, in what sense? It does not seem that the abandonment of one theory of sovereignty in favour of another long held by other constitutional lawyers can be so described.... Ignoring variations of detail between authors, [the manner and form theory's] essential thesis is that inherent in the doctrine of parliamentary sovereignty is the acceptance by the courts of antecedent rules of law which allocate exclusive legislative competence for the time being to the Commons, Lords and Monarch; it follows that if that body changes the allocation of that competence, the courts must follow the new allocation until that is changed in a manner stipulated in the new allocation. On this view, then, legal acceptance of the re-allocation of legislative competence by section 2(4) of the European Communities Act 1972 for as long as the provision remains in force is implicit in existing constitutional theory, not a departure from it.

■ QUESTIONS

1. If the supremacy of EU law and UK parliamentary sovereignty were able to coexist in constitutional practice, was it right for the House of Lords in *Factortame (No.2)* to overlook the theoretical problems that may have been seen to result? Is it necessary that all difficult questions of constitutional principle be resolved neatly by courts? Or, for that matter, by Parliament, or the government, or academic theorists?

2. Was Parliament still sovereign despite the United Kingdom's membership of the EU? If the answer to this question is based on the fact that Parliament retained the power to repeal the European Communities Act 1972, and exit the EU—which the 2016 referendum result will now make a reality—could the sovereignty of Parliament nevertheless have changed from the understanding advanced by Dicey? Barber argues that the post-1991 (i.e. post-*Factortame*) understanding of parliamentary sovereignty is 'subtly different' from the pre-1991 understanding of the doctrine: 'Even if the 1972 act were repealed, this would not resurrect the old rule of Parliamentary sovereignty' (Barber, 'The Afterlife of Parliamentary Sovereignty' (2011) *International Journal of Constitutional Law* 144–54, 152). Do you agree? If Parliament retains legally unlimited legislative power, does this matter?

Whether or not parliamentary sovereignty has changed as a result of membership of the EU will be an important question as UK withdrawal is implemented. On the one hand, a prominent argument in the referendum campaign was that leaving the EU would allow sovereignty to be restored in the UK, with Parliament regaining full power to legislate on all policy matters previously covered by EU law (such as competition, the environment, labour rights, and consumer protection). On the other hand, the domestic constitution may have changed substantially during, and as a result of, the UK's membership of the EU. One issue of particular importance which has arisen in the relation to the status of the European Communities Act 1972, is whether the UK constitution now recognizes a special category of 'constitutional statutes', as was considered in the following case.

Thoburn v Sunderland City Council
[2002] EWHC (Admin) 195, [2003] QB 151, Divisional Court

A challenge to prosecutions for using imperial measurement units rather than metric units claimed that the regulations implementing directives, and based on European Communities Act 1972 (ECA) s. 2(2), were invalid as the ECA provisions had been impliedly repealed by the Weights and Measures Act 1985. This argument was rejected. The court considered implied repeal more generally.

LAWS LJ: ... 60. The common law has in recent years allowed, or rather created, exceptions to the doctrine of implied repeal: a doctrine which was always the common law's own creature. There are now classes or types of legislative provision which cannot be repealed by mere implication. These instances are given, and can only be given, by our own courts, to which the scope and nature of Parliamentary sovereignty are ultimately confided. The courts may say—have said—that there are certain circumstances in which the legislature may only enact what it desires to enact if it does so by express, or at any rate specific, provision. The courts have in effect so held in the field of European law itself, in the *Factortame* case, and this is critical for the present discussion. By this means, as I shall seek to explain, the courts have found their way through the *impasse* seemingly created by two supremacies, the supremacy of European law and the supremacy of Parliament.

61. The present state of our domestic law is such that substantive Community rights prevail over the express terms of any domestic law, including primary legislation, made or passed after the coming into force of the ECA, even in the face of plain inconsistency between the two. This is the effect of *Factortame (No 1)* [1990] 2 AC 85. To understand the critical passage in Lord Bridge's speech it is first convenient to repeat part of ECA s.2(4):

'The provision that may be made under subsection (2) above includes ... any such provision (of any such extent) as might be made by Act of Parliament, and any enactment passed or to be passed, other than one contained in this Part of this Act, shall be construed and have effect subject to the foregoing provisions of the section.'

In *Factortame (No 1)* Lord Bridge said this at 140:

'By virtue of section 2(4) of the Act of 1972 Part II of the [Merchant Shipping] Act of 1988 is to be construed and take effect subject to directly enforceable Community rights ... This has precisely the same effect as if a section were incorporated in Part II of the Act of 1988 which in terms enacted that the provisions with respect to registration of British fishing vessels were to be without prejudice to the directly enforceable Community rights of nationals of any member state of the EEC.'

So there was no question of an implied *pro tanto* repeal of the ECA of 1972 by the later Act of 1988; on the contrary the Act of 1988 took effect subject to Community rights incorporated into our law by the ECA. In *Factortame* no argument was advanced by the Crown in their Lordships' House to suggest that such an implied repeal might have been effected. It is easy to see what the argument might have been: Parliament in 1972 could not bind Parliament in 1988, and s. 2(4) was therefore ineffective to do so. It seems to me that there is no doubt but that in *Factortame (No 1)* the House of Lords effectively accepted that s. 2(4) could not be impliedly repealed, albeit the point was not argued.

62. Where does this leave the constitutional position which I have stated? Mr Shrimpton would say that *Factortame (No 1)* was wrongly decided; and since the point was not argued, there is scope, within the limits of our law of precedent, to depart from it and to hold that implied repeal may bite on the ECA as readily as upon any other statute. I think that would be a wrong turning. My reasons are these. In the present state of its maturity the common law has come to recognise that there exist rights which should properly be classified as constitutional or fundamental: see for example such cases as *Simms* [2000] 2 AC 115 *per* Lord Hoffmann at 131, *Pierson* v *Secretary of State* [1998] AC 539, *Leech* [1994] QB 198, *Derbyshire County Council* v *Times Newspapers Ltd.* [1993] AC 534, and *Witham* [1998] QB 575. And from this a further insight follows. We should recognise a hierarchy of Acts of Parliament: as it were 'ordinary' statutes and 'constitutional' statutes. The two categories must be distinguished on a principled basis. In my opinion a constitutional statute is one which (a) conditions the legal relationship between citizen and State in some general, overarching manner, or (b) enlarges or diminishes the scope of what we would now regard as fundamental constitutional rights. (a) and (b) are of necessity closely related: it is difficult to think of an instance of (a) that is not also an instance of (b). The special status of constitutional statutes follows the special status of constitutional rights. Examples are the Magna Carta, the Bill of Rights 1689, the Act of Union, the Reform Acts which distributed and enlarged the franchise, the HRA, the Scotland Act 1998 and the Government of Wales Act 1998. The ECA clearly belongs in this family. It incorporated the whole corpus of substantive Community rights and obligations, and gave overriding domestic effect to the judicial and administrative machinery of Community law. It may be there has never been a statute having such profound effects on so many dimensions of our daily lives. The ECA is, by force of the common law, a constitutional statute.

63. Ordinary statutes may be impliedly repealed. Constitutional statutes may not. For the repeal of a constitutional Act or the abrogation of a fundamental right to be effected by statute, the court would apply this test: is it shown that the legislature's *actual*—not imputed, constructive or presumed intention was to effect the repeal or abrogation? I think the test could only be met by express words in the later statute, or by words so specific that the inference of an actual determination to effect the result contended for was irresistible. The ordinary rule of implied repeal does not satisfy this test. Accordingly, it has no application to constitutional statutes. I should add that in my judgment general words could not be supplemented, so as to effect a repeal or significant amendment to a constitutional statute, by reference to what was said in Parliament by the minister promoting the Bill pursuant to *Pepper* v *Hart* [1993] AC 593. A constitutional statute can only be repealed, or amended in a way which significantly affects its provisions touching fundamental rights or otherwise the relation between citizen and State, by unambiguous words on the face of the later statute.

64. This development of the common law regarding constitutional rights, and as I would say constitutional statutes, is highly beneficial. It gives us most of the benefits of a written constitution, in which fundamental rights are accorded special respect. But it preserves the sovereignty of the legislature and the flexibility of our uncodified constitution. It accepts the relation between legislative supremacy and fundamental rights is not fixed or brittle: rather the courts (in interpreting statutes, and now, applying the HRA) will pay more or less deference to the legislature, or other public decision-maker, according to the subject in hand. Nothing is plainer than that this benign development involves, as I have said, the recognition of the ECA as a constitutional statute.

Appeals dismissed.

NOTE: Laws LJ's controversial attempt to explain the status of the European Communities Act 1972 and the decision in *Factortame (No. 2)* was obiter dictum. The notion that the common law could recognize a new category of constitutional statutes, and protect them from some kinds of repeal, may in itself (aside from the challenge presented by EU membership) pose problems for the sovereignty of Parliament, according to which no such form of legislation exists. For an alternative view on Laws LJ's distinction between ordinary and constitutional statutes, see the following extract from Tomkins.

A. Tomkins, *Public Law*
(2003) pp. 123–4

What is of interest in the [*Thoburn*] case is not so much the outcome as the reasoning employed by Laws LJ. He offered a number of reasons why the implied repeal argument failed. His main reason was (correctly) that there was no inconsistency between the provisions of the 1972 Act and those of the 1985 Act. If he had stopped there, all would be well, but he continued to opine that even if there had been an irreducible inconsistency between the provisions of the ECA and those of a later Act there could in any event be no implied repeal of the ECA because it was 'by force of the common law, a constitutional statute' [para. 62]. While 'ordinary' statutes may be impliedly repealed, 'constitutional' statutes may not, according to Laws LJ. This previously unheard of category of constitutional statutes would include, in his opinion, Magna Carta, the Bill of Rights 1689, the Acts of Union, the Reform Acts (concerning the franchise), the Human Rights Act, and the devolution legislation of 1998, as well as the ECA.

The only authority Laws LJ cited in support of these—wholly novel—propositions was *Factortame I*, of which he stated that 'in *Factortame I* the House of Lords effectively accepted that section 2(4) [of the ECA] could not be impliedly repealed, albeit that the point was not argued' [para. 61]. Not only is it extremely unlikely that the House of Lords would ever accept a novel and controversial point that had not even been argued before it, but, as we have seen, this is emphatically not what the House of Lords held in *Factortame*. There was no issue of implied repeal in *Factortame*, as the two statutes (the ECA and the Merchant Shipping Act) each dealt with an entirely different subject-matter, such that there was no way the one could be held impliedly to have repealed the other. Only a statute that dealt with the same subject-matter as the ECA could impliedly repeal it. If Parliament were to re-legislate on the subject of the relationship between domestic and European Community law, and were to do so in a way that was inconsistent with the terms of the ECA 1972 without expressly repealing the 1972 provisions, then there is no reason why the courts would not hold that the later Act must be construed as having impliedly repealed the 1972 Act. All of this is very unlikely, of course. If Parliament were to re-legislate on the subject-matter of the ECA it would be absurd for it to do so without making express reference to the 1972 Act. Such a move would be exceptionally foolish, and extremely unlikely.

Acts can be impliedly repealed only by subsequent Acts that deal with the same subject-matter. Thus, Acts that deal with constitutional subjects can be impliedly repealed only by subsequent Acts that deal with the same, constitutional, subjects. An Act that concerns fishing, or weights and measures, cannot impliedly repeal statutes that concern constitutional law. But this is not to create a new and special category of constitutional statute that is different from ordinary statute. This is merely to restate the law of implied repeal, which has clearly been much misunderstood in recent years.

NOTES

1. Tomkins points out that Laws LJ's assumption that the Acts of Union have not been substantially amended is incorrect, citing C. Munro, *Studies in Constitutional Law* (1987), pp. 66–71. The first edition gives greater detail on this point than the second edition (1999), at pp. 132–42.
2. The recent enactment of the European Union Act 2011 poses new questions for parliamentary sovereignty in the context of the United Kingdom's changing membership of the EU. These new developments will be considered later (see later in this chapter in Section 3D at pp. 95–101).
3. The debate concerning the existence of 'constitutional statutes' in the UK—and most importantly, whether any special legal status attaches to Acts of Parliament designated as 'constitutional' in this way—has continued and evolved. It has developed in the context of the interpretation of the devolution Acts (discussed in Chapter 8, Section 3A at pp. 370–6). The existence of 'constitutional' statutes and principles has also been explored by the courts in relation to the question of whether there could have been limits on the domestic supremacy afforded to EU law by the European Communities Act 1972 itself, as seen in the following case.

R (HS2 Action Alliance) v Secretary of State for Transport
[2014] UKSC 3, [2014] 1 WLR 324, Supreme Court

The case concerned a challenge to the government's decision to promote a high-speed rail link ('HS2') from London to cities in the north of England. The appellants argued first that the government command paper used to announce the project should have been subject to a strategic environmental assessment, in accordance with EU law (Directive 2001/42/EC). And second, that the hybrid Act of Parliament which would be used to authorize the decision would need to comply with certain procedural requirements, also as a matter of EU law (Directive 2011/92/EU). Both arguments were rejected in the Court of Appeal, with the second in particular posing a problem of domestic constitutional law: the idea that the courts might be required, as a matter of EU law, to evaluate the adequacy of parliamentary procedure when enacting a statute, would appear to violate parliamentary privilege, and the ban on courts questioning proceedings in Parliament, contained in Art. 9 of the Bill of Rights 1689. The case was appealed to the Supreme Court.

LORD REED:

Constitutional issues

[78] The argument presented on behalf of the appellants as to the implications of the EIA Directive, if well founded, impinges upon long-established constitutional principles governing the relationship between Parliament and the courts, as reflected for example in article 9 of the Bill of Rights 1689, in authorities concerned with judicial scrutiny of Parliamentary procedure, such as *Edinburgh and Dalkeith Railway Co v Wauchope* (1842) 8 Cl & F 710; 1 Bell 252, Lee v Bude and Torrington Junction Railway Co (1871) LR 6 CP 576, *Pickin v British Railways Board* [1974] AC 765 and *Wilson v First County Trust Ltd (No. 2)* [2003] UKHL 40; [2004] 1 AC 816, and in other cases concerned with judicial scrutiny of decisions whether to introduce a bill in Parliament, such as *R (Wheeler) v Office of the Prime Minister* [2008] EWHC 1409 (Admin). Neither the Bill of Rights nor any of the authorities I have mentioned was however referred to in the parties' printed cases; nor was this issue mentioned before us until it was raised by the court. Nevertheless, it follows that the appellants' contentions potentially raise a question as to the extent, if any, to which these principles may have been implicitly qualified or abrogated by the European Communities Act 1972.

[79] Contrary to the submission made on behalf of the appellants, that question cannot be resolved simply by applying the doctrine developed by the Court of Justice of the supremacy of EU law, since the application of that doctrine in our law itself depends upon the 1972 Act. If there is a conflict between a constitutional principle, such as that embodied in article 9 of the Bill of Rights, and EU law, that conflict has to be resolved by our courts as an issue arising under the constitutional law of the United Kingdom. Nor can the issue be resolved, as was also suggested, by following the decision in *R v Secretary of State for Transport, Ex p Factortame Ltd (No 2)* [1991] 1 AC 603, since that case was not concerned with the compatibility with EU law of the process by which legislation is enacted in Parliament. In the event, for reasons which I shall explain, it is possible to determine the appeal without requiring to address these matters. ...

[109] The contention that the procedure currently envisaged by the Government will not permit an adequate examination of the environmental information to take place appears to me to be equally unpersuasive. I observe in the first place that there is nothing either in the text of article 1(4) of the EIA Directive, or in the exegesis of that text by the Court of Justice, to suggest that national courts are required not only to confirm that there has been a substantive legislative process and that the appropriate information was made available to the members of the legislature, but must in addition review the adequacy of the legislature's consideration of that information, for example by assessing the quality of the debate and examining the extent to which members participated in it. These are not matters which are apt for judicial supervision. Nor is there anything to suggest the inevitable corollary: that national courts should strike down legislation if they conclude that the legislature's consideration of the information was inadequate.

[110] There is a further difficulty with the contention that EU law requires the internal proceedings of national legislatures to be subject to judicial oversight of this nature. The separation of powers is a fundamental aspect of most if not all of the constitutions of the member states. The precise form in which the separation of powers finds expression in their constitutions varies; but the appellants' contentions might pose a difficulty in any member state in which it would be considered inappropriate for

the courts to supervise the internal proceedings of the national legislature, at least in the absence of the breach of a constitutional guarantee.

[111] Against this background, it appears unlikely that the Court of Justice intended to require national courts to exercise a supervisory jurisdiction over the internal proceedings of national legislatures of the nature for which the appellants contend. There is in addition much to be said for the view, advanced by the German Federal Constitutional Court in its judgment of 24 April 2013 on the Counter-Terrorism Database Act, 1 BvR 1215/07, para 91, that as part of a co-operative relationship, a decision of the Court of Justice should not be read by a national court in a way that places in question the identity of the national constitutional order. . . .

[116] Without therefore considering the fundamental constitutional objection to this line of argument – that the court would be presuming to evaluate the quality of Parliament's consideration of the relevant issues, during the legislative process leading up to the enactment of a statute – I conclude that the argument is based on an incorrect interpretation of the EIA Directive, and is in addition unsupported by the evidence as to the procedure which might be followed.

LORDS NEUBERGER AND MANCE:

[206] Under the European Communities Act 1972, United Kingdom courts have also acknowledged that European law requires them to treat domestic statutes, whether passed before or after the 1972 Act, as invalid if and to the extent that they cannot be interpreted consistently with European law: *R v Secretary of State, Ex p Factortame Ltd (No 2)* [1991] 1 AC 603. That was a significant development, recognising the special status of the 1972 Act and of European law and the importance attaching to the United Kingdom and its courts fulfilling the commitment to give loyal effect to European law. But it is difficult to see how an English court could fully comply with the approach suggested by the two Advocates General without addressing its apparent conflict with other principles hitherto also regarded as fundamental and enshrined in the Bill of Rights. Scrutiny of the workings of Parliament and whether they satisfy externally imposed criteria clearly involves questioning and potentially impeaching (i.e. condemning) Parliament's internal proceedings, and would go a considerable step further than any United Kingdom court has ever gone.

[207] The United Kingdom has no written constitution, but we have a number of constitutional instruments. They include Magna Carta, the Petition of Right 1628, the Bill of Rights and (in Scotland) the Claim of Rights Act 1689, the Act of Settlement 1701 and the Act of Union 1707. The European Communities Act 1972, the Human Rights Act 1998 and the Constitutional Reform Act 2005 may now be added to this list. The common law itself also recognises certain principles as fundamental to the rule of law. It is, putting the point at its lowest, certainly arguable (and it is for United Kingdom law and courts to determine) that there may be fundamental principles, whether contained in other constitutional instruments or recognised at common law, of which Parliament when it enacted the European Communities Act 1972 did not either contemplate or authorise the abrogation.

[208] We are not expressing any view on whether or how far article 9 of the Bill of Rights would count among these, but the point is too important to pass without mention. We would wish to hear full argument upon it before expressing any concluded view. It is not a point upon which the parties before us proposed to make any submissions until it was raised by the Court. We were then told that the attention of the Parliamentary authorities (and we deliberately use a vague expression) had been drawn to this appeal, and they elected not to be represented. If and when the point does fall to be considered, the Parliamentary authorities may wish to reconsider whether they should be represented, and, particularly if they still regard that course as inappropriate, it may well be the sort of point on which the Attorney General should appear or be represented. Important insights into potential issues in this area are to be found in their penetrating discussion by Laws LJ in the Divisional Court in *Thoburn v Sunderland City Council* [2002] EWHC 195 (Admin), [2003] QB 151 (The Metric Martyrs case), especially paras 58–70, although the focus there was the possibility of conflict between an earlier "constitutional" and later "ordinary" statute, rather than, as here, between two constitutional instruments, which raises yet further considerations.

Appeal dismissed.

NOTES

1. The Supreme Court determined that the question of whether the European Communities Act 1972 had afforded absolute domestic supremacy to EU law, or a supremacy potentially subject to constitutional limits, did not require resolution on the facts of this case. Yet there is clear sympathy for this position in the judgments above. This raises the question: did Parliament ever intend for such limits to operate on the supremacy which it afforded to EU law in the 1972 Act? Or would the courts be imposing limits artificially on the domestic supremacy of EU law, after the fact and aside from the literal terms of the 1972 Act? That might be understood to represent a *challenge* to the sovereignty of Parliament, under the guise of a challenge to EU law.

2. The discussion of constitutional instruments and principles in the judgment of Lords Neuberger and Mance seems to develop further the lines of discussion of Laws LJ in *Thoburn*, although the joint judgment stops short of explicitly endorsing this analysis. Again, we see judicial attempts to establish a more explicit legal 'constitutional' framework for the UK, by defining it in opposition to EU law. Yet the authority of such statements—which surely remain obiter dicta—would extend beyond this particular context, and presumably retain potential force (if subsequently endorsed) even after the UK has withdrawn from the EU. For critical discussion, see Gordon, *Parliamentary Sovereignty in the UK Constitution: Process, Politics and Democracy* (2015), pp. 185–91.

3. Similar issues were considered by the Supreme Court in the following case.

Pham v *Secretary of State for the Home Department*
[2015] UKSC 19; [2015] 1 WLR 1591

The case concerned the withdrawal of UK citizenship of a suspected terrorist, and whether the withdrawal of EU citizenship which this would necessarily effect was subject to challenge on (potentially more demanding) EU law grounds of review. Although the point was not definitively decided (the case being remitted for reconsideration by the court below, which had not considered EU law arguments), suggestions in CJEU case law that this might be possible were received with scepticism by the justices. Lord Mance endorsed the sovereignty of Parliament as the fundamental principle of the UK constitution, before considering whether there could be domestically enforceable limits on the power of the CJEU to determine the requirements of EU law:

[80] For a domestic court, the starting point is, in any event, to identify the ultimate legislative authority in its jurisdiction according to the relevant rule of recognition. The search is simple in a country like the United Kingdom with an explicitly dualist approach to obligations undertaken at a supranational level. European law is certainly special and represents a remarkable development in the world's legal history. But, unless and until the rule of recognition by which we shape our decisions is altered, we must view the United Kingdom as independent, Parliament as sovereign and European law as part of domestic law because Parliament has so willed. The question how far Parliament has so willed is thus determined by construing the 1972 Act....

[90] A domestic court faces a particular dilemma if, in the face of the clear language of a treaty and of associated declarations and decisions, such as those mentioned in paras 86–89, the Court of Justice reaches a decision which oversteps jurisdictional limits which member states have clearly set at the European Treaty level and which are reflected domestically in their constitutional arrangements. But, unless the Court of Justice has had conferred on it under domestic law unlimited as well as unappealable power to determine and expand the scope of European law, irrespective of what the member states clearly agreed, a domestic court must ultimately decide for itself what is consistent with its own domestic constitutional arrangements, including in the case of the 1972 Act what jurisdictional limits exist under the European Treaties and on the competence conferred on European institutions including the Court of Justice.

[91] It will be a very rare case indeed where any problem arises in this connection, and the recipe for avoiding any problem is that all concerned should act with mutual respect and with caution in

areas where member states' constitutional identity is or may be engaged—particularly so where, as in the present context, great care has been taken to emphasise this by declarations accompanying the relevant treaty commitments. That reflects the spirit of co-operation of which both the Bundesverfassungsgericht [the German Constitutional Court] and this court have previously spoken.

NOTES

1. For similar critical discussion see Lord Carnwath at [54]–[55], [58].
2. UK withdrawal from the EU may make irrelevant the substantive point as to the implied constitutional limitations (if any) applicable to EU law by virtue of the European Communities Act 1972. Yet this issue has provided a vehicle for the courts to consider more explicitly the nature of the UK's constitutional framework, and the legal force of domestic constitutional sources within it. Whether this judicial framework functions to preserve parliamentary sovereignty, or could develop to impose constitutional limits on the legislative power of Parliament, remains an important question of domestic constitutional law.

■ QUESTIONS

1. Do you see evidence that Parliament, when enacting the European Communities Act 1972, intended to make the domestic supremacy afforded to EU law subject to constitutional limits? Consider in particular s. 2(4), in this chapter at p. 72.
2. What is the authority for judicial attempts to establish a more explicit constitutional framework for the UK? Are attempts to identify constitutional statutes, instruments, and principles simply the recognition of what exists as a matter of practice, or are the courts crafting new constitutional ideas? Is such a process of constitutional change legitimate?
3. Are the constitutional concepts discussed in *Thoburn*, *HS2*, and *Pham* satisfactory? Do they capture the key aspects of the UK constitution when defining what is 'constitutional'?
4. If there are fundamental principles of the UK constitution, what is justification for Parliament possessing the power to violate them? Could similar considerations apply to constitutional rights? This issue is considered in the next section.

B: Human rights

The Human Rights Act 1998 seeks to reconcile protecting human rights with preserving legislative sovereignty by requiring courts to interpret legislation so far as it is possible to do so in conformity with convention rights (see Chapter 9, Section 3 at pp. 444–5 and the dicta on what this requires the judges to do at pp. 446–56) or to make a declaration of incompatibility if such an interpretation cannot be achieved (see Chapter 9, Section 3 at pp. 456–63). Issuing such a declaration puts the ball in Parliament's court; it can use a fast-track procedure to legislate so as to bring the law into conformity with Convention rights (see Chapter 9, Section 3 at p. 460).

Tomkins says, in *Public Law* (2003) p. 122:

... if Parliament decides not to amend or repeal a provision that has been declared by a court to be incompatible with a Convention right, so be it. Parliament continues to have the supreme legislative authority to legislate in contravention of convention rights if it so wishes, and no domestic court or tribunal may overturn or set aside such legislation notwithstanding the incomparability.

Whereas Ewing has remarked at (1999) 62 *Modern Law Review* 79, 92:

As a matter of constitutional legality, Parliament may well be sovereign, but as a matter of constitutional practice it has transferred significant power to the judiciary.

For Kavanagh, in *Constitutional Review under the UK Human Rights Act* (2009), pp. 325, 336, parliamentary sovereignty has been 'compromised':

the HRA only preserves the doctrine of parliamentary sovereignty in formal terms, but limits the legislative power of Parliament in substance.

So far declarations of incompatibility have not been ignored, with the exception of that made in relation to the statutory prohibition on voting by convicted prisoners, considered by the Supreme Court in *R (Chester)* v *Secretary of State for Justice* [2013] UKSC 63; [2014] AC 271 (see Chapter 9, Section 3 at p. 463).

Some senior judges have characterized the powers of the courts under the Human Rights Act 1998 in strikingly bold terms. In his FA Mann lecture ' "Judge not, that ye be not judged": Judging Judicial Decision-Making' in January 2015, Lord Neuberger, the President of the Supreme Court, suggested:

[47] The revolutionary effect of the 1998 Act is, in summary terms, threefold. First, Judges are now called upon more frequently to rule on moral and political issues, given that is what human rights involve. This means that we have to engage on a review of the merits of any decision or action which impinges on an individual's fundamental rights. Before the 1998 Act, our role in relation to government acts was more circumscribed. Secondly, Judges must perform a quasi-statute-writing function as section 3 of the 1998 Act requires Judges to read and give effect to legislation "[s]o far as it is possible to do so ... in a way which is compatible with the Convention rights". If legislation does not appear to comply, we must, if we can, recast it so that it does comply. Thirdly, under section 4 of that Act, Judges must tell Parliament when legislation cannot be made to comply and, with one exception (prisoners' votes), it has done so.

■ QUESTION

Even if the Human Rights Act 1998 has formally preserved parliamentary sovereignty, has it challenged the power of Parliament in practice? Or is this an example of the flexibility of parliamentary sovereignty, which can be reconciled with the statutory protection of human rights?

Looking beyond the statutory protection offered by the Human Rights Act 1998, does the common law provide any protection for fundamental rights? In principle, it might be possible for such common law rights to exist without challenging the sovereignty of Parliament (as will be considered in Chapter 3 on the rule of law). Yet it is also possible that, if recognized by the courts as being of fundamental importance, such rights might ultimately be used to challenge the notion of legislative sovereignty itself, placing substantive limits on what can lawfully be done by Act of Parliament. This matter has been considered in the extra-judicial writings of some senior judges.

Sir J. Laws, 'Law and Democracy'

[1995] *Public Law* 72, 81–5, 87–8, 92–3

As a matter of fundamental principle, it is my opinion that the survival and flourishing of a democracy in which basic rights (of which freedom of expression may be taken as a paradigm) are not only respected but enshrined requires that those who exercise democratic, political power must have limits set to what they may do: limits which they are not allowed to overstep. If this is right, it is a function of democratic power itself that it be not absolute....

The imperative of higher-order law

Now it is only by means of compulsory law that effective rights can be accorded, so that the medium of rights is not persuasion, but the power of rule: the very power which, if misused, could be deployed to subvert rights. We therefore arrive at this position: the constitution must guarantee by positive law such rights as that of freedom of expression, since otherwise its credentials as a medium of honest rule are fatally undermined. But this requires for its achievement what I may call a higher-order law: a law which cannot be abrogated as other laws can, by the passage of a statute promoted by a government with the necessary majority in Parliament. Otherwise the right is not in the keeping of the constitution at all; it is not a guaranteed right; it exists, in point of law at least, only because the government chooses to let it exist, whereas in truth no such choice should be open to any government.

The democratic credentials of an elected government cannot justify its enjoyment of a right to abolish fundamental freedoms. If its power in the state is in the last resort absolute, such fundamental rights as free expression are only privileges; no less so if the absolute power rests in an elected body. The byword of every tyrant is 'My word is law'; a democratic assembly having sovereign power beyond the reach of curtailment or review may make just such an assertion, and its elective base cannot immunise it from playing the tyrant's role....

Since in the last resort the government rules by consent, the source of public power is not the strong arm of the ruler, but the people themselves.

Even so, the fundamental sinews of the constitution, the cornerstones of democracy and of inalienable rights, ought not by law to be in the keeping of the government, because the only means by which these principles may be enshrined in the state is by their possessing a status which no government has the right to destroy. I have already argued this position in relation to fundamental individual rights; now I assert it also as regards democracy itself. It is a condition of democracy's preservation that the power of a democratically elected government—or Parliament—be not absolute. The institution of free and regular elections, like fundamental individual rights, has to be vindicated by a higher-order law: very obviously, no government can tamper with it, if it is to avoid the mantle of tyranny; no government, therefore, must be allowed to do so....

The thrust of this reasoning is that the doctrine of Parliamentary sovereignty cannot be vouched by Parliamentary legislation; a higher-order law confers it, and must of necessity limit it. Thus it is not, and cannot be, established by the measures which set in place the constitutional reforms of the late seventeenth century; nor by any legislation....

Conclusion

We may now come full circle, and after this long discussion I can identify what seems to me to be the essence of the difference between judicial and elective power. The latter consists in the authority to make decisions of policy within the remit given by the electorate; this is a great power, with which neither the judges nor anyone else have any business to interfere. This is the place held by democracy in our constitution. It is the place of government. Within it, Parliament, even given its present unsatisfactory relationship with the Executive, is truly and totally supreme. It possesses what we may indeed call a political sovereignty. It is a sovereignty which cannot be objected to, save at the price of assaulting democracy itself. But it is not a constitutional sovereignty; it does not have the status of what earlier I called a sovereign text, of the kind found in states with written constitutions. Ultimate sovereignty rests, in every civilised constitution, not with those who wield governmental power, but in the conditions under which they are permitted to do so. The constitution, not the Parliament, is in this sense sovereign. In Britain these conditions should now be recognised as consisting in a framework of fundamental principles which include the imperative of democracy itself and those other rights, prime among them freedom of thought and expression, which cannot be denied save by a plea of guilty to totalitarianism.

For its part judicial power in the last resort rests in the guarantee that this framework will be vindicated. It consists in the assurance that, however great the democratic margin of appreciation (to use Strasbourg's language) that must be accorded to the elected arm of the state, the bedrock of pluralism will be maintained. We have no other choice. The dynamic settlement between the powers of the state requires, in the absence of a constitutional scripture, just such a distribution of authority. The judges are rightly and necessarily constrained not only by a prohibition against intrusion into what is Parliament's proper sphere, but by the requirement, and the truth, that they have in their duty no party political bias. Their interest and obligation in the context of this discussion is to protect values which no democratic politician could honestly contest: values which, therefore, may be described as apolitical, since they stand together above the rancorous but vital dissensions of party politicians. The judges are constrained also, and rightly, by the fact that their role is reactive; they cannot initiate; all they can do is to apply principle to what is brought before them by others. Nothing could be more distinct from the duty of political creativity owed to us by Members of Parliament.

Though our constitution is unwritten, it can and must be articulated. Though it changes, the principles by which it goes can and must be elaborated. They are not silent; they represent the aspirations of a free people. They must be spoken and explained and, indeed, argued over. Politicians, lawyers, scholars, and many others have to do this. Constitutional theory has, perhaps, occupied too modest a place here in Britain, so that the colour and reach of public power has not been exposed to a glare that is fierce enough. But the importance of these matters is so great that, whatever the merits or demerits of what I have had to say, we cannot turn our backs on the arguments. We cannot risk the future growth without challenge of new, perhaps darker, philosophies. We cannot fail to give principled answers to those who ask of the nature of state power by what legal alchemy, in any situation critical to the protection of our freedoms, the constitution measures the claims of the ruler and the ruled. The imperatives of democracy and fundamental rights do not only demand acceptance; they demand a vindication that survives any test of intellectual rigour.

NOTES

1. Sir John Laws understands individual rights to be fundamental, and inherently due to be protected by law. This argument therefore poses a direct challenge to the doctrine of parliamentary sovereignty, in so far as Laws is suggesting that there are some rights which Parliament should not be free to legislate about because they form part of a higher order law. This may seem both controversial and to deviate from established constitutional practice in the United Kingdom, yet in a recent decision of the House of Lords, similar views were advanced by a number of judges (albeit a minority, and only then in obiter dicta). This decision—*Jackson* v *Attorney General* [2005] UKHL 56, [206] 1 AC 262—will be considered later in this chapter in Section 3C at pp. 88–95.

2. The arguments advanced by Laws have been criticised by John Griffith ('The Brave New World of Sir John Laws' (2000) 63 *Modern Law Review* 159, 165):

> The trouble with the higher-order law is that it must be given substance, be interpreted, and be applied. It claims superiority over democratically elected institutions; it prefers philosopher-kings to human politicians; it puts its faith in judges whom I would trust no more than I trust princes. And it will not even make the trains run on time. If we are to create a more just and a more free society, we must do it the hard way – without Moses. And our vigilance must be extended to judges, no less than to others in authority.

The disagreement between Laws and Griffith as to the existence and desirability of judicially enforced limits on the power of Parliament can be seen to reflect the disagreement between legal and political constitutionalists, encountered in Chapter 1, Section 4 at pp. 23–8. That judges are willing to question the continuing relevance of the sovereignty of Parliament in the United Kingdom could be interpreted as a shift towards legal constitutionalism. Yet as we shall see, while some judges argue that Parliament *should* be limited, it is far from established that Parliament *is* limited.

■ QUESTIONS

1. Should—as Laws argues—the courts be free to recognize fundamental rights at common law, and prevent Parliament from enacting legislation which violates them? Or should—as Griffith argues—decisions about the scope of individual rights be left to Parliament, on the basis that people who are democratically elected, representative, and accountable should make them?

2. Should the fact that Parliament has enacted legislation instructing courts to protect human rights—the Human Rights Act 1998—but in a way which preserves the sovereignty of Parliament be understood to limit the jurisdiction of the courts to develop greater protection for individual rights at common law?

C: *Jackson* v *Attorney General*

The next challenge to the sovereignty of Parliament is presented by the *Jackson* case. It is perhaps better, however, to think about the *Jackson* case as presenting a *range* of challenges to the orthodox Diceyan understanding of the doctrine of parliamentary sovereignty. In particular, we will consider: (i) the jurisdiction of the court to hear this case; (ii) the decision of the court as to the status of the Parliament Act 1949, and the implications of this decision; and (iii) the controversial obiter dicta of three of the Law Lords.

Jackson v *Attorney General*
[2005] UKHL 56, [2006] 1 AC 262, House of Lords

The Parliament Act 1911 removed the power of the House of Lords to veto legislation, replacing it with a two-year delaying power. This was enacted in accordance with the then existing law which required majorities in both Houses approving the Bill before it received the Royal Assent. The delaying power was reduced to one year by the Parliament Act 1949 which was itself passed without Lords' consent using the 1911 Act. The Hunting Act 2004 was enacted after one year using the Parliament Acts 1911 and 1949 and its legality was unsuccessfully challenged in the High Court. The Court of Appeal dismissed the appeal. The appeal to the House of Lords was heard by a panel of nine of their Lordships.

LORD BINGHAM OF CORNHILL: ... 7. Sir Sydney helpfully encapsulated the appellants' submissions in a series of key propositions, which he elaborated in written and oral argument. The propositions are these:

(1) Legislation made under the 1911 Act is delegated or subordinate, not primary.

(2) The legislative power conferred by section 2(1) of the 1911 Act is not unlimited in scope and must be read according to established principles of statutory interpretation.

(3) Among these is the principle that powers conferred on a body by an enabling Act may not be enlarged or modified by that body unless there are express words authorising such enlargement or modification.

(4) Accordingly, section 2(1) of the 1911 Act does not authorise the Commons to remove, attenuate or modify in any respect any of the conditions on which its law-making power is granted.

(5) Even if, contrary to the appellants' case, the Court of Appeal was right to regard section 2(1) of the 1911 Act as wide enough to authorise "modest" amendments of the Commons' law-making powers, the amendments in the 1949 Act were not "modest", but substantial and significant.

...

22. Sir Sydney submits that whereas legislation duly enacted by the Crown in Parliament commands general obedience and recognition as such, and is the ultimate political fact upon which the whole system of legislation hangs, legislation made under the 1911 Act is required to state on its face that it is made by the authority of the 1911 Act. Such legislation is not primary because it depends for its validity on a prior enactment, and legislation is not primary where that is so. Legislation under the 1911 Act is not similar to other delegated or subordinate legislation, such as statutory instruments and bylaws made under the authority of statute, but it is delegated or subordinate or derivative in the sense that its validity is open to investigation in the courts, which would not be permissible in the case of primary legislation.

...

24. Despite the skill with which the argument is advanced and the respect properly due to the authorities relied on, I am of opinion that the Divisional Court was right to reject it, for two main reasons. First, sections 1(1) and 2(1) of the 1911 Act provide that legislation made in accordance with

those provisions respectively shall "become an Act of Parliament on the Royal Assent being signified". The meaning of the expression "Act of Parliament" is not doubtful, ambiguous or obscure. It is as clear and well understood as any expression in the lexicon of the law. It is used, and used only, to denote primary legislation. If there were room for doubt, which to my mind there is not, it would be resolved by comparing the language of the second resolution, quoted in para. 15 above, with the language of section 2(1) as enacted. The resolution provided that a measure meeting the specified conditions "shall become Law without the consent of the House of Lords on the Royal Assent being declared". Section 2(1), as just noted, provides that a measure shall become an Act of Parliament. The change can only have been made to preclude just such an argument as the appellants are advancing. The 1911 Act did, of course, effect an important constitutional change, but the change lay not in authorising a new form of sub-primary parliamentary legislation but in creating a new way of enacting primary legislation.

25. I cannot, secondly, accept that the 1911 Act can be understood as a delegation of legislative power or authority by the House of Lords, or by Parliament, to the House of Commons ... Section 1 of the 1911 Act involved no delegation of legislative power and authority to the Commons but a statutory recognition of where such power and authority in relation to supply had long been understood to lie. It would be hard to read the very similar language in section 2 as involving a delegation either, since the overall object of the Act was not to enlarge the powers of the Commons but to restrict those of the Lords. This is, in my opinion, clear from the historical context and from the Act itself. The first resolution (see para. 15 above) was that "it is expedient that the House of Lords be disabled by Law from" ... The second resolution (para. 15 above) was that "it is expedient that the powers of the House of Lords, as respects Bills other than Money Bills, be restricted by Law" ... The effect of section 1 of the 1911 Act is to restrict the power of the Lords to amend or reject money bills. The effect of section 2(1) is, despite the different conditions, the same, and is aptly summarised in the sidenote: "Restriction of the powers of the House of Lords as to Bills other than Money Bills". The certification of a money bill by the Speaker under section 1 and of a bill other than a money bill under section 2 is mandatory, and the presentation of a bill to the monarch for the royal assent to be signified under sections 1(1) and 2(1) is automatic, "unless the House of Commons direct to the contrary". If it be permissible to resort to the preamble of the 1911 Act, one finds reference to the expediency of making "such provision as in this Act appears for restricting the existing powers of the House of Lords". The overall object of the 1911 Act was not to delegate power: it was to restrict, subject to compliance with the specified statutory conditions, the power of the Lords to defeat measures supported by a majority of the Commons, and thereby obviate the need for the monarch to create (or for any threat to be made that the monarch would create) peers to carry the government's programme in the Lords.

...

(2) The scope of section 2(1)

28. Sir Sydney submits that, in accordance with long-established principles of statutory interpretation, the courts will often imply qualifications into the literal meaning of wide and general words in order to prevent them having some unreasonable consequence which Parliament could not have intended. He cites such compelling authority as *Stradling v Morgan* (1560) 1 Plow 199; *R (Edison First Power Limited) v Central Valuation Officer* [2003] UKHL 20, [2003] 4 All ER 209, para. 25; *R v Secretary of State for the Home Department, Ex p Pierson* [1998] AC 539, 573–575, 588; *R v Secretary of State for the Home Department, Ex p Simms* [2000] 2 AC 115, 131; and *R (Morgan Grenfell & Co Ltd) v Special Commissioner of Income Tax* [2003] 1 AC 563, paras 8, 44–45. He relies on these authorities as establishing (as it is put in the appellants' printed case)

> that general words such as section 2(1) should not be read as authorising the doing of acts which adversely affect the basic principles on which the law of the United Kingdom is based in the absence of clear words authorising such acts. There is no more fundamental principle of law in the UK than the identity of the sovereign body. Section 2(1) should not be read as modifying the identity of the sovereign body unless its language admits of no other interpretation.

The Divisional Court did not accept that the 1911 Act, properly construed, precluded use of the procedure laid down in that Act to amend the conditions specified in section 2: see Maurice Kay LJ in paras 17–19 of his judgment, and Collins J in paras 41–44 of his. The Court of Appeal took a different view (paras 40–41); it concluded that section 2(1) conferred powers which could be used for some purposes but not others (paras 42–45).

29. The Attorney General does not, I think, take issue with the general principles relied on by the appellants, which are indeed familiar and well-established. But he invites the House to focus on the language of the 1911 Act, and in this he is right, since a careful study of the statutory language, read in its statutory and historical context and with the benefit of permissible aids to interpretation, is the essential first step in any exercise of statutory interpretation. Here, section 2(1) makes provision, subject to three exceptions, for any public bill which satisfies the specified conditions to become an Act of Parliament without the consent of the Lords. The first exception relates to money bills, which are the subject of section 1 and to which different conditions apply. The second relates to bills containing any provision to extend the maximum duration of Parliament beyond five years. I consider this exception in detail below. The third relates to bills for confirming a provisional order, which do not fall within the expression "public bill" by virtue of section 5. Subject to these exceptions, section 2(1) applies to "any" public bill. I cannot think of any broader expression the draftsman could have used. Nor can I see any reason to infer that "any" is used in a sense other than its colloquial, and also its dictionary, sense of "no matter which, or what". The expression is repeatedly used in this sense in the 1911 Act, and it would be surprising if it were used in any other sense: see section 1(2) ("any of the following subjects", "any such charges", "any loan", "those subjects or any of them", "any taxation, money, or loan"); section 2(4) ("any amendments", "any further amendments", "any such suggested amendments"); section 3 ("Any certificate", "any court of law"); section 4(2) ("Any alteration"); section5 ("any Bill"). "Any" is an expression used to indicate that the user does not intend to discriminate, or does not intend to discriminate save to such extent as is indicated.

30. Sir Sydney is of course correct in submitting that the literal meaning of even a very familiar expression may have to be rejected if it leads to an interpretation or consequence which Parliament could not have intended. But in this case it is clear from the historical background that Parliament did intend the word "any", subject to the noted exceptions, to mean exactly what it said. Sir Henry Campbell-Bannerman's resolution of June 1907, adopted by the Commons before rejection of the 1909 Finance Bill, referred quite generally to "Bills passed by this House" … The second of the resolutions adopted on 14 April 1910 … referred to "Bills other than Money Bills". Attempts to amend the resolution so as to enlarge the classes of bill to which the new procedure would not apply were all rejected (para. 15 above). During the constitutional Conference which followed the death of the King there was provisional agreement to exclude "the Act which is to embody this agreement" from application of the new procedure, but such a provision was never included in the Bill … During the passage of the Bill through Parliament, there were again repeated attempts to enlarge the classes of bill to which the new procedure would not apply, but save for the amendment related to bills extending the maximum duration of Parliament they were uniformly rejected … The suggestion that Parliament intended the conditions laid down in section 2(1) to be incapable of amendment by use of the Act is in my opinion contradicted both by the language of the section and by the historical record. This was certainly the understanding of Dicey, who was no friend of the 1911 Act. In the first edition of his *Introduction* after 1911 (the 8th edition, 1915), he wrote at p xxiii:

> "The simple truth is that the Parliament Act has given to the House of Commons, or, in plain language, to the majority thereof, the power of passing any Bill whatever, provided always that the conditions of the Parliament Act, section 2, are complied with."

31. The Court of Appeal concluded (in paras 98–100 of its judgment) that there was power under the 1911 Act to make a "relatively modest and straightforward amendment" of the Act, including the amendment made by the 1949 Act, but not to making "changes of a fundamentally different nature to the relationship between the House of Lords and the Commons from those which the 1911 Act had

made". This was not, as I understand, a solution which any party advocated in the Court of Appeal, and none supported it in the House. I do not think, with respect, that it can be supported in principle. The known object of the Parliament Bill, strongly resisted by the Conservative party and the source of the bitterness and intransigence which characterised the struggle over the Bill, was to secure the grant of Home Rule to Ireland. This was, by any standards, a fundamental constitutional change. So was the disestablishment of the Anglican Church in Wales, also well known to be an objective of the government. Attempts to ensure that the 1911 Act could not be used to achieve these objects were repeatedly made and repeatedly defeated … Whatever its practical merits, the Court of Appeal solution finds no support in the language of the Act, in principle or in the historical record. Had the government been willing to exclude changes of major constitutional significance from the operation of the new legislative scheme, it may very well be that the constitutional Conference of 1910 would not have broken down and the 1911 Act would never have been enacted.

(3) Enlargement of powers

33. Sir Sydney relies on what Hood Phillips and Jackson describe as the general principle of logic and law that delegates (the Queen and Commons) cannot enlarge the authority delegated to them: *Constitutional and Administrative Law*, 8th edn (2001), p 80. He also prays in aid the observations of Lord Donaldson of Lymington speaking extra-judicially in support of his Parliament Acts (Amendment) Bill (HL Hansard, 19 January 2001, cols 1308–1309): "As your Lordships well know, it is a fundamental tenet of constitutional law that, *prima facie*, where the sovereign Parliament—that is to say, the Monarch acting on the advice and with the consent of both Houses of Parliament—delegates power to legislate, whether to one House unilaterally, to the King or Queen in Council, to a Minister or to whomsoever, the delegate cannot use that power to enlarge or vary the powers delegated to him. The only exception is where the primary legislation, in this case the 1911 Act, expressly authorises the delegate to do so. In other words there has to be a Henry VIII clause." To support his argument Sir Sydney cites a number of cases relating to colonial and Dominion legislatures, the most significant of these cases perhaps being *R v Burah* (1878) 3 App Cas 889, 904–905; *Taylor v Attorney General of Queensland* (1917) 23 CLR 457; *McCawley v The King* [1920] AC 691, 703–704, 710–711; *Minister of the Interior v Harris* 1952 (4) SA 769, 790; *Clayton v Heffron* (1960) 105 CLR 214 and *Bribery Commissioner v Ranasinghe* [1965] AC 172, 196–198. In written submissions in reply this argument was elaborated and the authorities further analysed.

…

36. I cannot accept the appellants' submissions on this issue, for three main reasons. First, for reasons given in para. 25 above, the 1911 Act did not involve a delegation of power and the Commons, when invoking the 1911 Act, cannot be regarded as in any sense a subordinate body. Secondly, the historical context of the 1911 Act was unique. The situation was factually and constitutionally so remote from the grant of legislative authority to a colonial or Dominion legislature as to render analogies drawn from the latter situation of little if any value when considering the former. Thirdly, the Court of Appeal distilled from the authorities what is in my judgment the correct principle. The question is one of construction. There was nothing in the 1911 Act to preclude use of the procedure laid down by the Act to amend the Act. As explained in paras 29–32 above, the language of the Act was wide enough, as the Divisional Court and the Court of Appeal held, to permit the amendment made by the 1949 Act, and also (in my opinion) to make much more far reaching changes. For the past half century it has been generally, even if not universally, believed that the 1949 Act had been validly enacted, as evidenced by the use made of it by governments of different political persuasions. In my opinion that belief was well-founded.

Appeal dismissed.

NOTES

1. *Jurisdiction*. Their Lordships held that despite the authority of *Pickin* it could entertain this challenge to the Hunting Act 2004, a matter which the Attorney General did not contest. Lord Bingham said at [27]:

> I am, however, persuaded that the present proceedings are legitimate, for two reasons. First, in *Pickin*, unlike the present case, it was sought to investigate the internal workings and procedures of Parliament to demonstrate that it had been misled and so had proceeded on a false basis. This was held to be illegitimate [His Lordship quoted the passage by Lord Campbell in *Wauchope* (see *Pickin*, earlier in this chapter in Section 1C at p. 54)] ... Here, the court looks to the parliamentary roll and sees bills (the 1949 Act, and then the 2004 Act) which have not passed both Houses. The issue concerns no question of parliamentary procedure such as would, and could only, be the subject of parliamentary inquiry, but a question whether, in Lord Simon's language, these Acts are "enacted law". My second reason is more practical. The appellants have raised a question of law which cannot, as such, be resolved by Parliament. But it would not be satisfactory, or consistent with the rule of law, if it could not be resolved at all. So it seems to me necessary that the courts should resolve it, and that to do so involves no breach of constitutional propriety.

Lord Nichols said at [49] that it was clear following *Pickin* and art. 9 of the Bill of Rights (see earlier in this chapter in Section 1C at pp. 53–6) that it was for each House of Parliament to judge the lawfulness of its own proceedings (see further discussion of judicial independence and parliamentary privilege in Chapter 4, Section 1I at pp. 168–72). He continued at [51]:

> Their challenge to the lawfulness of the 1949 Act is founded on a different and prior ground: the proper interpretation of section 2(1) of the 1911 Act. On this issue the court's jurisdiction cannot be doubted. This question of statutory interpretation is properly cognisable by a court of law even though it relates to the legislative process. Statutes create law. The proper interpretation of a statute is a matter for the courts, not Parliament. This principle is as fundamental in this country's constitution as the principle that Parliament has exclusive cognisance (jurisdiction) over its own affairs.

2. *Decision as to the status of the Parliament Act 1949.* All of their Lordships rejected the delegated legislation argument and (most) accepted that Parliament had, in enacting the Parliament Acts, created an alternative process by which primary legislation could be produced. All of the judges also agreed that, due to the explicit limitation set out in s. 2(1), the Parliament Acts procedure could not be used to extend the duration of a Parliament beyond five years. The court did not, however, find that there were additional broad *implied* exceptions as to what legislation could be made using the Parliament Acts, and rejected the view of the Court of Appeal that fundamental constitutional change could not be effected using this process. The judges disagreed, however, on the interesting, but obiter, point as to whether the s. 2(1) limit on extending the life of Parliament could be removed using the Parliament Acts. Only Lord Bingham, at [32], thought that extending the duration of a parliament could be achieved without the Lords' consent if it was done in two steps; the first step would be to remove the exception from s. 2(1) and the second would be to pass legislation extending the duration. A majority of their Lordships, Lords Nicholls, Steyn, Hope, and Carswell, and Baroness Hale, did not think that these two steps would be lawful, whereas Lords Rodger and Brown reserved their position, and Lord Walker did not consider the point. For Lord Nicholls at [59]:

> That express exclusion carries with it, by necessary implication, a like exclusion in respect of legislation aimed at achieving the same result by two steps rather than one. If this were not so the express legislative intention could readily be defeated.

Lord Carswell agreed with Lord Nicholl's reasoning at [175]. Lord Steyn said at [79]:

> In the context of a Parliamentary democracy the language of section 2(1) and section 7 supports the former interpretation. I would so rule.

Section 7 of the 1911 Act reduced the duration of a parliament from seven to five years. Lord Hope said at [122]:

> ... there is an implied prohibition against the use of the section 2(1) procedure in such circumstances.

3. *Implications of the decision.* For Baroness Hale, the Parliament Acts had the effect of redefining Parliament for certain legislative purposes, so as to include only the House of Commons and the sovereign. Whether it is helpful to think of the Parliament Acts as 'redefining' Parliament, as opposed to creating an alternative process by which primary legislation can be enacted, is unimportant for present purposes. Most interesting is what Baroness Hale understood the potential implications of this to be at [163]:

> If the sovereign Parliament can redefine itself downwards, to remove or modify the requirement for the consent of the Upper House, it may very well be that it can also redefine itself upwards, to require a particular Parliamentary majority or a popular referendum for particular types of measure. In each case, the courts would be respecting the will of the sovereign Parliament as constituted when that will had been expressed. But that is for another day.

Lord Steyn was more certain than Baroness Hale saying at [81]:

> The word Parliament involves both static and dynamic concepts. The static concept refers to the constituent elements which make up Parliament: the House of Commons, the House of Lords, and the Monarch. The dynamic concept involves the constituent elements functioning together as a law making body. The inquiry is: has Parliament spoken? The law and custom of Parliament regulates what the constituent elements must do to legislate: all three must signify consent to the measure. But, apart from the traditional method of law making, Parliament acting as ordinarily constituted may functionally redistribute legislative power in different ways. For example, Parliament could for specific purposes provide for a two-thirds majority in the House of Commons and the House of Lords. This would involve a redefinition of Parliament for a specific purpose. Such redefinition could not be disregarded. Owen Dixon neatly summarised this idea in 1935:
>
> " ... The very power of constitutional alteration cannot be exercised except in the form and manner which the law for the time being prescribes. Unless the Legislature observes that manner and form, its attempt to alter its constitution is void. It may amend or abrogate for the future the law which prescribes that form or that manner. But, in doing so, it must comply with its very requirements."

See: 'The Law and the Constitution', 51 *Law Quarterly Review* 590, 601. This formulation can be traced to the majority judgment in *Attorney General for New South Wales* v *Trethowan* (1931) 44 CLR 394, and in particular to the judgment of Dixon J at 424.

Lord Hope was the only other Law Lord to comment on this point and he stated the traditional view at [113]:

> Nor does it seem to me to be helpful ... to describe the 1911 Act as having remodelled or re-defined Parliament. The concept is not an easy one to grasp, because it is a fundamental aspect of the rule of sovereignty that no Parliament can bind its successors. There are no means by whereby, even with the assistance of the most skilful draftsman, it can entrench an Act of Parliament. It is impossible for Parliament to enact something which a subsequent statute dealing with the same subject matter cannot repeal. But there is no doubt that, in practice and as a matter of political reality, the 1911 Act did have that effect ... It did what it was designed to do. It has limited the power of the House of Lords to legislate. In practice it has altered the balance of power between the two Houses.

4. *Obiter dicta overtly questioning the sovereignty of Parliament.* Perhaps most controversially of all in *Jackson*, three of the Law Lords offered some obiter general observations on the limits of Parliament's legislative sovereignty. Lord Steyn contended at [102]:

> ... If the Attorney General is right the 1949 Act could also be used to introduce oppressive and wholly undemocratic legislation. For example, it could theoretically be used to abolish judicial review of flagrant abuse of power by a government or even the role of the ordinary courts in standing between the executive and citizens. This is where we may have to come back to the point about the supremacy of Parliament. We do not in the United Kingdom have an uncontrolled constitution as the Attorney General implausibly asserts. In the European context the second Factortame decision [1991] 1 AC 603 made that clear. The settlement contained in the Scotland Act 1998 also point to a divided sovereignty. Moreover, the European Convention on Human Rights as incorporated into our law by the Human Rights Act 1998, created a new legal order. One must not assimilate the European Convention on Human Rights with multilateral treaties of the traditional type. Instead it is a legal order in which the United Kingdom assumes obligations to protect fundamental rights, not in relation to other states, but towards all individuals within its jurisdiction. The classic account given by Dicey of the doctrine of the supremacy of Parliament, pure and absolute as it was, can now be seen to be out of place in the modern United Kingdom. Nevertheless, the supremacy of Parliament is still the *general* principle of our constitution. It is a construct of the common law. The judges created this principle. If that is so, it is not unthinkable that circumstances could arise where the courts may have to qualify a principle established on a different hypothesis of constitutionalism. In exceptional circumstances involving an attempt to abolish judicial review or the ordinary role of the courts, the Appellate Committee of the House of Lords or a new Supreme Court may have to consider whether this is constitutional fundamental which even a sovereign Parliament acting at the behest of a complaisant House of Commons cannot abolish. It is not necessary to explore the ramifications of this question in this opinion. No such issues arise on the present appeal.

Lord Hope said that 'parliamentary sovereignty is no longer, if it ever was, absolute', but increasingly 'qualified' at [104]. Further, according to Lord Hope at [107]:

> ... the rule of law enforced by the courts is the ultimate controlling factor on which our constitution is based.

He stated that there are limits to the power to legislate as people must be prepared to recognize legislation as law and this 'depends upon the legislature maintaining the trust of the electorate' and that at [126]:

> The principle of parliamentary sovereignty which, in the absence of higher authority, has been created by the common law is built upon the assumption that Parliament represents the people whom it exists to serve.

Baroness Hale did not go as far as Lord Steyn or Lord Hope, but did comment that at [159]:

> The courts will treat with particular suspicion (and might even reject) any attempt to subvert the rule of law by removing governmental action affecting the rights of the individual from all judicial scrutiny.

5. *Aftermath of* Jackson. In a more recent case concerning the legislative power of the Scottish Parliament—*Axa General Insurance Ltd* v *Lord Advocate* [2011] UKSC 46; [2012] 1 AC 868 (considered in more detail in Chapter 8, Section 3B at pp. 377–81)—Lord Hope briefly returned, at [50], to the question of whether the UK Parliament remained sovereign:

> The question whether the principle of the sovereignty of the United Kingdom Parliament is absolute or may be subject to limitation in exceptional circumstances is still under discussion. For Lord Bingham, writing extrajudicially, the principle is fundamental and in his opinion, as the judges did not by themselves establish the principle, it was not open to them to change it: *The Rule of Law* (2010), p 167. Lord Neuberger of Abbotsbury, in his Lord Alexander of Weedon lecture, "Who are the masters Now?" (6 April 2011), said at para 73 that, although the judges had a vital role to play in protecting individuals against the abuses and excess of an increasingly powerful executive, the judges could not go against the will of Parliament as expressed through a statute. Lord Steyn on the other hand recalled at the outset of his speech in Jackson, para 71, the warning that Lord Hailsham of St Marylebone gave in *The Dilemma of Democracy* (1978), p 126 about the dominance of a government elected with a large majority over Parliament. This process, he said, had continued and strengthened inexorably since Lord Hailsham warned of its dangers. This was the context in which he said in para 102 that the Supreme Court might have to consider whether judicial review or the ordinary role of the courts was a constitutional fundamental which even a sovereign Parliament acting at the behest of a complaisant House of Commons could not abolish.

The matter of whether legislation of the Parliament of the United Kingdom could be challenged at common law in extreme or exceptional circumstances did not need to be disposed of in *Axa*, although the Supreme Court held (arguably obiter) that legislation of the Scottish Parliament could be so reviewed, as a supplement to the statutory review of legislation explicitly authorised by s. 29 of the Scotland Act 1998. Yet the rationale advanced by Lord Hope at [51] to justify his view that Acts of the Scottish Parliament could be subject to common law review in exceptional circumstances could, in principle, equally be applied to the sovereign UK Parliament:

> We now have in Scotland a government which enjoys a large majority in the Scottish Parliament. Its party dominates the only chamber in that Parliament and the committees by which bills that are in progress are scrutinised. It is not entirely unthinkable that a government which has that power may seek to use it to abolish judicial review or to diminish the role of the courts in protecting the interests of the individual. Whether this is likely to happen is not the point. It is enough that it might conceivably do so. The rule of law requires that the judges must retain the power to insist that legislation of that extreme kind is not law which the courts will recognise.

For some judges, comments of this kind now provide evidence that there is an active debate about the potential limits on the UK Parliament's legislative power. In *Moohan* v *Lord Advocate* [2014] UKSC 67; [2015] AC 901, the Supreme Court rejected a challenge to the Scottish Independence Referendum (Franchise) Act 2013, which excluded convicted prisoners from voting in the 2014 independence referendum. After rejecting an argument on common law grounds, Lord Hodge, giving the leading judgment with which a majority agreed, observed:

> [35] While the common law cannot extend the franchise beyond that provided by parliamentary legislation, I do not exclude the possibility that in the very unlikely event that a parliamentary majority abusively sought to entrench its power by a curtailment of the franchise or similar

device, the common law, informed by principles of democracy and the rule of law and international norms, would be able to declare such legislation unlawful. The existence and extent of such a power is a matter of debate, at least in the context of the doctrine of the sovereignty of the United Kingdom Parliament: see *AXA General Insurance Ltd v HM Advocate* [2012] 1 AC 868, Lord Hope of Craighead DPSC (paras 49–51) and in relation to the Scottish Parliament Lord Reed JSC: paras 153–154. But such a circumstance is very far removed from the present case, and there is no need to express any view on that question.

■ QUESTIONS

1. Has the House of Lords in *Jackson* rejected the authority of *Pickin* and held that they can review legislation? Is it relevant that the House of Lords was not hearing a challenge to the *substance* of the Hunting Act 2004, but a *procedural* challenge to the process by which it was enacted? A substantive challenge to the Hunting Act 2004 was subsequently brought both under the Human Rights Act 1998 and EU law in *Countryside Alliance* v *Attorney General* [2007] UKHL 52, [2008] 1 AC 719. Both arguments were rejected by the House of Lords, but does the fact that a substantive challenge had to be pursued separately, and only then in relation to the ECHR and EU law, indicate that Parliament's sovereign power to make or unmake any law is undiminished by *Jackson*?

2. Do the comments of Baroness Hale in particular indicate that the decision in *Jackson* provides support to the manner and form theorists' understanding of legislative sovereignty? Baroness Hale stated that the matter of whether Parliament could lawfully introduce a referendum requirement into the legislative process for some types of measure was for 'another day'. Yet as we shall see, the enactment of the European Union Act 2011 may raise exactly these questions.

3. Are the obiter dicta of Lord Steyn, Lord Hope, and Baroness Hale persuasive, given they were offered only by a minority of judges? Lord Bingham—who in *Jackson* described the sovereignty of Parliament as the 'bedrock' of the constitution, at [9]—subsequently rejected the comments made by his fellow judges as 'related to no issue raised and no argument advanced in the case, they were based on no authority and were supported by no reasoning' ('Publication Review: The New British Constitution' (2010) 126 *Law Quarterly Review* 131–5, 134). Is this correct? In particular, are claims that the sovereignty of Parliament is a construct of the common law compatible with the idea that the doctrine emerged in the aftermath of the English Civil War and Revolution of 1688?

4. Is the possibility of a common law limit on Parliament's legislative power in exceptional circumstances 'a matter for debate' as claimed in *Moohan*? Has any such debate been manufactured by the judicial speculation beginning in *Jackson* and continuing in *Axa*? Does the very cultivation of debate about possible limits on legislative authority in the most extreme (and therefore unlikely) circumstances have the potential to diminish parliamentary sovereignty, even if such limits never materialize? Or is a legitimate way for the judges to suggest that if Parliament were to abuse its power substantially, old constitutional principles could be abandoned?

D: European Union Act 2011

The final modern challenge to the sovereignty of Parliament to be considered in this chapter is that posed by a recently enacted statute: the European Union Act 2011. In one sense this statute might be regarded as a contradiction in terms; it has two main innovations, both of which engage with the doctrine of parliamentary sovereignty in quite different ways. First, the European Union Act 2011 sought, in an unprecedented constitutional experiment, to introduce a wide range of referendum locks into the United Kingdom constitution. Secondly, the Act purported to reaffirm explicitly the continuing authority of the doctrine of parliamentary sovereignty in a statute. The decision to withdraw from the EU will prompt the repeal of the 2011 Act. Yet it is still important to try to understand the possible implications of this legislation, for it may provide us with significant insights into how Parliament understands the scope of its own sovereignty.

European Union Act 2011

2. Treaties amending or replacing TEU or TFEU

(1) A treaty which amends or replaces TEU or TFEU is not to be ratified unless—

    (a) a statement relating to the treaty was laid before Parliament in accordance with section 5,

    (b) the treaty is approved by Act of Parliament, and

    (c) the referendum condition or the exemption condition is met.

(2) The referendum condition is that—

    (a) the Act providing for the approval of the treaty provides that the provision approving the treaty is not to come into force until a referendum about whether the treaty should be ratified has been held throughout the United Kingdom or, where the treaty also affects Gibraltar, throughout the United Kingdom and Gibraltar,

    (b) the referendum has been held, and

    (c) the majority of those voting in the referendum are in favour of the ratification of the treaty.

(3) The exemption condition is that the Act providing for the approval of the treaty states that the treaty does not fall within section 4.

3. Amendment of TFEU under simplified revision procedure

(1) Where the European Council has adopted an Article 48(6) decision subject to its approval by the member States, a Minister of the Crown may not confirm the approval of the decision by the United Kingdom unless—

    (a) a statement relating to the decision was laid before Parliament in accordance with section 5,

    (b) the decision is approved by Act of Parliament, and

    (c) the referendum condition, the exemption condition or the significance condition is met.

(2) The referendum condition is that—

    (a) the Act providing for the approval of the decision provides that the provision approving the decision is not to come into force until a referendum about whether the decision should be approved has been held throughout the United Kingdom or, where the decision also affects Gibraltar, throughout the United Kingdom and Gibraltar,

    (b) the referendum has been held, and

    (c) the majority of those voting in the referendum are in favour of the approval of the decision.

(3) The exemption condition is that the Act providing for the approval of the decision states that the decision does not fall within section 4.

(4) The significance condition is that the Act providing for the approval of the decision states that—

    (a) the decision falls within section 4 only because of provision of the kind mentioned in subsection (1)(i) or (j) of that section, and

    (b) the effect of that provision in relation to the United Kingdom is not significant.

4. Cases where treaty or Article 48(6) decision attracts a referendum

(1) Subject to subsection (4), a treaty or an Article 48(6) decision falls within this section if it involves one or more of the following—

    (a) the extension of the objectives of the EU as set out in Article 3 of TEU;

    (b) the conferring on the EU of a new exclusive competence;

    (c) the extension of an exclusive competence of the EU;

    (d) the conferring on the EU of a new competence shared with the member States;

    (e) the extension of any competence of the EU that is shared with the member States;

    (f) the extension of the competence of the EU in relation to—

        (i) the co-ordination of economic and employment policies, or

        (ii) common foreign and security policy;

    (g) the conferring on the EU of a new competence to carry out actions to support, co-ordinate or supplement the actions of member States;

(h) the extension of a supporting, co-ordinating or supplementing competence of the EU;

(i) the conferring on an EU institution or body of power to impose a requirement or obligation on the United Kingdom, or the removal of any limitation on any such power of an EU institution or body;

(j) the conferring on an EU institution or body of new or extended power to impose sanctions on the United Kingdom;

(k) any amendment of a provision listed in Schedule 1 that removes a requirement that anything should be done unanimously, by consensus or by common accord;

(l) any amendment of Article 31(2) of TEU (decisions relating to common foreign and security policy to which qualified majority voting applies) that removes or amends the provision enabling a member of the Council to oppose the adoption of a decision to be taken by qualified majority voting;

(m) any amendment of any of the provisions specified in subsection (3) that removes or amends the provision enabling a member of the Council, in relation to a draft legislative act, to ensure the suspension of the ordinary legislative procedure.

(2) Any reference in subsection (1) to the extension of a competence includes a reference to the removal of a limitation on a competence.

(3) The provisions referred to in subsection (1)(m) are—

(a) Article 48 of TFEU (social security),

(b) Article 82(3) of TFEU (judicial co-operation in criminal matters), and

(c) Article 83(3) of TFEU (particularly serious crime with a cross-border dimension).

(4) A treaty or Article 48(6) decision does not fall within this section merely because it involves one or more of the following—

(a) the codification of practice under TEU or TFEU in relation to the previous exercise of an existing competence;

(b) the making of any provision that applies only to member States other than the United Kingdom;

(c) in the case of a treaty, the accession of a new member State.

....

6. Decisions requiring approval by Act and by referendum

(1) A Minister of the Crown may not vote in favour of or otherwise support a decision to which this subsection applies unless—

(a) the draft decision is approved by Act of Parliament, and

(b) the referendum condition is met.

(2) Where the European Council has recommended to the member States the adoption of a decision under Article 42(2) of TEU in relation to a common EU defence, a Minister of the Crown may not notify the European Council that the decision is adopted by the United Kingdom unless—

(a) the decision is approved by Act of Parliament, and

(b) the referendum condition is met.

(3) A Minister of the Crown may not give a notification under Article 4 of Protocol (No. 21) on the position of the United Kingdom and Ireland in respect of the area of freedom, security and justice annexed to TEU and TFEU which relates to participation by the United Kingdom in a European Public Prosecutor's Office or an extension of the powers of that Office unless—

(a) the notification has been approved by Act of Parliament, and

(b) the referendum condition is met.

(4) The referendum condition is that set out in section 3(2), with references to a decision being read for the purposes of subsection (1) as references to a draft decision and for the purposes of subsection (3) as references to a notification.

(5) The decisions to which subsection (1) applies are—

(a) a decision under the provision of Article 31(3) of TEU that permits the adoption of qualified majority voting;

(b) a decision under Article 48(7) of TEU which in relation to any provision listed in Schedule 1—

(i)   adopts qualified majority voting, or

(ii) applies the ordinary legislative procedure in place of a special legislative procedure requiring the Council to act unanimously;

(c) a decision under Article 86(1) of TFEU involving participation by the United Kingdom in a European Public Prosecutor's Office;

(d) where the United Kingdom has become a participant in a European Public Prosecutor's Office, a decision under Article 86(4) of TFEU to extend the powers of that Office;

(e) a decision under Article 140(3) of TFEU which would make the euro the currency of the United Kingdom;

(f) a decision under the provision of Article 153(2) of TFEU (social policy) that permits the application of the ordinary legislative procedure in place of a special legislative procedure;

(g) a decision under the provision of Article 192(2) of TFEU (environment) that permits the application of the ordinary legislative procedure in place of a special legislative procedure;

(h) a decision under the provision of Article 312(2) of TFEU (EU finance) that permits the adoption of qualified majority voting;

(i) a decision under the provision of Article 333(1) of TFEU (enhanced co-operation) that permits the adoption of qualified majority voting, where the decision relates to a provision listed in Schedule 1 and the United Kingdom is a participant in the enhanced co-operation to which the decision relates;

(j) a decision under the provision of Article 333(2) of TFEU (enhanced co-operation) that permits the adoption of the ordinary legislative procedure in place of a special legislative procedure, where—

(i) the decision relates to a provision listed in Schedule 1,

(ii) the special legislative procedure requires the Council to act unanimously, and

(iii) the United Kingdom is a participant in the enhanced co-operation to which the decision relates;

(k) a decision under Article 4 of the Schengen Protocol that removes any border control of the United Kingdom.

(6) In subsection (5)(k) "*the Schengen Protocol*" means the Protocol (No. 19) on the Schengen *acquis* integrated into the framework of the European Union, annexed to TEU and TFEU....

18. Status of EU law dependent on continuing statutory basis

Directly applicable or directly effective EU law (that is, the rights, powers, liabilities, obligations, restrictions, remedies and procedures referred to in section 2(1) of the European Communities Act 1972) falls to be recognised and available in law in the United Kingdom only by virtue of that Act or where it is required to be recognised and available in law by virtue of any other Act.

NOTES

1. The referendum locks contained in ss 2, 3, and 6 of the European Union Act 2011 purported to make future transfers of power or competence to the EU, whether via a change to the EU Treaties or by some other specified decision, lawful only if approved by a referendum. An Act of Parliament which sought to authorize the approval of such action by the government would not lawfully do so unless it provided that either the 'referendum condition' or the 'exemption condition' had been met (or in the case of a decision under s. 3 of the EU Act only, the 'significance condition'). In enacting this legislation, the Parliament of 2011 appeared to be attempting to bind successor Parliaments as to the 'manner and form' of future legislation, or in other words, impose procedural conditions on the exercise of legislative power.

2. Section 18, in contrast, is more straightforward. It sought simply to confirm that the EU law was dependent on a domestic statute—the European Communities Act 1972—for its status in the United Kingdom legal system. The following extract seeks to analyse the effect and implications of both aspects of the European Union Act 2011.

M. Gordon and M. Dougan 'The United Kingdom's European Union Act 2011: "Who Won the Bloody War Anyway?"'

(2012) *European Law Review* 1, 6–9, 23–4

Section 18: the "sovereignty clause"

....

The provision is therefore declaratory, affirming that EU legal norms are effective in the United Kingdom because, and only because, Parliament has specifically legislated to make it so. It is intended to neuter the potential argument that a shift in the United Kingdom's constitutional paradigm has occurred, and that the supremacy of EU law throughout the Union derives from a European grund-norm, which is not susceptible to domestic alteration or renunciation. Such an argument is, however, essentially political, and most closely associated with a Eurosceptic rhetoric lacking a persuasive evidential foundation. It is well established as a matter of UK constitutional law that the domestic supremacy of EU law stems from Parliament's enactment of the ECA. In the seminal case of *R. v Secretary of State for Transport Ex p. Factortame (No.2)*, the House of Lords held as much…. EU law was therefore supreme in the United Kingdom because Parliament had chosen to afford it this status, with the courts bound to give effect to this choice.

Fundamentally, s.18 of the EUA takes us no further than this. The provision leaves any detail as to the precise status and effect of the ECA to be inferred from an underdeveloped premise, with UK constitutional lawyers in an almost identical position as before, when left to conjure arguments about the ultimate domestic scope of EU law from Lord Bridge's truncated analysis in *Factortame (No.2)*. We may know beyond all doubt that the supremacy of EU law depends on the ECA. Yet whether Parliament could repeal the ECA, extinguishing the applicability and effectiveness of EU law, is not overtly confirmed, and is still left to implication. If it is accepted that Parliament remains sovereign, it seems clear that the ECA could be repealed. But the fact of this stems from an understanding of the nature of Parliament's legally unlimited legislative authority, not from s.18 of the EUA. Furthermore, the form that such a repeal would need to take to be effective has not been clarified in any way by s.18, which is silent on the matter. This point may be immaterial in relation to an Act of Parliament seeking to effect a complete withdrawal from the European Union, but it could be crucial with respect to a legislative attempt to contravene specific EU norms while the United Kingdom remained a Member State. Would it be possible for Parliament to evince a clear intention to take the latter course of action, and if so, what form of words would be required to give the courts such an instruction? Of course, the Government may have considered it politically inadvisable to clarify such a matter in statute, not wishing to suggest a lack of commitment to the European project. Nevertheless, if such *realpolitik* has led the Government to retreat from its bombastic talk of a sovereignty clause and left us with a skeletal declaratory provision, it is difficult to see what the enactment of s.18 has accomplished.

It may be that, some two decades after the decision of the House of Lords in *Factortame (No.2)*, there is some virtue in s.18 reminding us that the domestic supremacy of EU law rests alone on its continuing statutory basis. It certainly seems to provide further evidence that while Laws L.J. was correct to assert in *Thoburn v Sunderland City Council* that the domestic supremacy of EU law did not stem from EU law itself, he was wrong to argue that it was achieved as a result of the common law affording the ECA a special "constitutional" status, thus rendering it immune from implied repeal. Instead, the applicability and effectiveness of EU law within the United Kingdom is exclusively traced by s.18 to the legislation itself, with no mention of an intervention by the common law. This point is, however, principally a matter of domestic interest, relating in particular to the clash between common law constitutionalism and parliamentary sovereignty, and has only an incidental impact on the relationship between domestic and European law, in so far as it might establish which constitutional agent, the courts or Parliament, is entitled to determine the extent to which these two legal orders can coexist. Nonetheless, the mismatch between the Government's original vision for s.18 and its eventual substance is palpable. The provision is patently not a sovereignty clause, and offers no guidance as to how the reconciliation between EU supremacy and parliamentary sovereignty has been achieved, and no clarity about what the limits of this reconciliation might be….

The enforceability of the Act's referendum requirements

Whether the UK Parliament possesses the legislative authority to create binding "referendum locks", to which future governments will be bound to adhere, critically depends on our understanding of the doctrine of parliamentary sovereignty…. In accordance with the orthodox conception of parliamentary sovereignty, as influentially explicated by A.V. Dicey, Parliament's authority "to make or unmake any law whatever" serves to preclude the legislature from binding its successors, either absolutely as to the substantive scope of its future lawmaking power, or as to the procedure by which this power is to be exercised. If this classical analysis of the sovereignty of Parliament remains applicable today, the referendum locks contained in ss. 2, 3 and 6 of the EUA will be legally unenforceable, and could be entirely disregarded by a future government which sought to enact legislation securing an extension of the power or competence of the European Union.

The Diceyan orthodoxy has not, however, gone unchallenged. Of particular relevance to the present inquiry is the "manner and form" conception of the sovereignty of Parliament, which derives from the work of Sir Ivor Jennings. The manner and form theory is a reconfiguration of the notion of parliamentary sovereignty which postulates that Parliament's power to make or unmake any law whatever must include the power to legislate so as to modify the future lawmaking process. Parliament thus remains unable to bind its successors absolutely as to the substance of future legislation, but it is understood to be constitutionally capable of legislating to ensure that future statutes must be created in a particular way, in accordance with a specified "manner" and/or "form". As such, if the reinterpretation of the doctrine of parliamentary sovereignty offered by the manner and form theory is accepted, the referendum locks contained in the EUA could be viewed as legally valid alterations of the legislative process with which future parliaments would be bound to comply in order to enact legislation extending the power or competence of the European Union….

[T]he EUA, while still an unprecedented constitutional experiment, can perhaps be seen to fit with the emerging recognition that the manner and form theory provides the best account of Parliament's contemporary legislative power. For in promulgating the EUA, the coalition government seems implicitly to have embraced the logic of the manner and form understanding of parliamentary sovereignty. And in enacting a statute which purports to modify the future legislative process, it seems that Parliament has accepted an interpretation of its sovereign authority which permits it to make statutory alterations to the manner and form which must be followed for the creation of valid legislation…. Yet even if the contentious argument that Parliament possesses the legislative power to make procedural modifications to the future lawmaking process which will bind its successors is not accepted in and of itself, it will be argued that a manner and form analysis of the EUA ought still to be adopted. For whether the creation of referendum locks is within or without Parliament's legislative power will have significant consequences for the way in which the legislation might, if ever, be repealed;… it will effectively determine whether an implied repeal would be sufficient to avoid the EUA's referendum requirements, or whether the locks would need to be repealed in express terms. On this basis, if a future government is confronted by the practical problem of how to circumvent the effects of the s. 2, s. 3 or s. 6 referendum locks, we argue that the manner and form interpretation of the EUA—according to which the referendum requirements contained within are legally enforceable but, crucially, ultimately avoidable—offers the clearest way forward.

NOTES

1. Since the enactment of the 2011 Act, it has not been necessary for Parliament to satisfy a referendum condition set out in s. 2, 3, or 6. Yet it has complied with other conditions set out in this legislative scheme, including legislating explicitly to satisfy the exemption condition in s. 2—in the European Union (Croatian Accession and Irish Protocol) Act 2013—and the exemption condition in s. 3—European Union (Approval of Treaty Amendment Decision) Act 2012. This evidence suggests that Parliament has felt obliged to comply with the procedural conditions set out in the European Union Act 2011, where applicable and while in force.

2. The applicability of the referendum conditions set out in the 2011 Act was considered in principle by the Administrative Court in *Wheeler* v *Office of the Prime Minister* [2014] EWHC 3815 (Admin). The Court rejected the argument that a referendum was required to authorize the government's decision to participate in the European Arrest Warrant framework, as falling outside the explicit terms of s. 6 of the 2011 Act. Yet the judgment of the Court was premised on the notion that a referendum condition would be enforceable if applicable:

> [29] Mr Fisher's second formulation of this first ground was that it is the clear and settled intention of Parliament, following the enactment of the 2011 Act, that no aspect of sovereignty should be transferred to an organ of the EU in the absence of a referendum. Mr Fisher refers to the preamble and to the Explanatory Notes. However, both of these must also be read in context, particularly the context of what the 2011 Act expressly provides. In our judgment, it provides, by section 6, for a detailed series of circumstances which, on the occurrence of any of them, the requirement for both primary legislation and the fulfilment of the referendum condition will be triggered. If the case falls outside the circumstances expressly specified, it cannot be accommodated within the statutory scheme by invoking some vague and generalised principle of 'Parliamentary intent'. There is no recognised principle of statutory construction which vouches such an approach: it is simply wrong.
>
> [30] Mr Fisher's third argument was that the section 6 trigger applies because the decision involves a transfer of sovereignty to the [European Public Prosecutor's Office] and the Court of Justice of the European Union in connection with a criminal cause of matter. This argument was not expressly addressed in Mr Eadie's written submissions, but it can be dealt with very briefly. The issue is not whether a 'transfer of sovereignty' is involved in some imprecise and general sense; rather, the issue is whether what is proposed falls within section 6(3), section 6(5)(c) or section 6(5)(d) of the 2011 Act. If it does, the referendum condition must be fulfilled; if it does not, there is no requirement under this statute to hold a referendum. I have already addressed section 6(5)(c), in relation to Mr Fisher's first formulation, and, subject to what follows, I see no basis on which these other provisions could apply. It follows that this submission must fail.

3. The innovations in the 2011 Act may represent the start of a new trend; see further, in the context of devolution, Parliament's enactment of provisions recognizing the permanence of the Scottish Parliament and Government, subject to a referendum lock, and statutory recognition of the Sewel convention, by which the consent of the devolved institutions will 'normally' be sought where the sovereign UK Parliament legislates in relation to devolved topics (see Chapter 8, Section 2B, at pp. 364–6, and Section 4A, at p. 389).

■ QUESTIONS

1. Does the European Union Act 2011 provide evidence that the manner and form theory offers the better understanding of the implications of the legislative sovereignty of Parliament? Or has Parliament enacted legislation which binds its successors, and which would therefore be unlawful and invalid (and crucially, would not need to have been repealed expressly to be avoided)?

2. Is s. 18 of the European Union Act a 'sovereignty clause'? If so, does it provide a general reaffirmation of the sovereignty of Parliament *by Parliament itself*, and demonstrate that the doctrine remains of relevance in the UK constitution? Or is it applicable specifically to the challenge which has been posed by membership of the European Union? Could it have implications for any other challenges to the sovereignty of Parliament, such as the judicial speculation in *Jackson* and *Axa* about the possibility of developing a common law power to challenge the validity of Acts of Parliament in exceptional circumstances?

3. What is the overall effect of the challenges to parliamentary sovereignty considered in this section? Do you think the doctrine is still a fundamental part of the UK constitution? Has it been altered by modern developments? If so, how?

3

The Rule of Law

OVERVIEW

In this chapter we consider another fundamental constitutional principle, the rule of law. First the rule of law is introduced, and then we focus on Dicey's conception of it, and criticism of this. We next consider the difference between formal and substantive understandings of the rule of law, the rule of law as a broad political doctrine, and finally what is meant by the idea of government according to law in the UK.

SECTION 1: INTRODUCTION

The rule of law is considered to be one of the fundamental doctrines of the constitution of the United Kingdom. The constitution is said to be founded on the idea of the rule of law, and this is a concept favoured by politicians and lawyers, being imported into many debates. Despite its currency in political and constitutional discussion its meaning is far from precise, and it may mean different things to different people at different times.

Governments wield considerable power. Constitutions are concerned with the allocation of power and the control of its exercise. The doctrine of the rule of law is concerned with the latter. Aristotle stated that 'the rule of law is preferable to the rule of any individual'. This sentiment was echoed centuries later by English jurists.

Report of the Committee on Ministers' Powers
Cmd 4060, 1932, pp. 71–2

The supremacy or rule of law—Its history and meaning

1. The supremacy or rule of the law of the Land is a recognised principle of the English Constitution. The origin of the principle must be sought in the theory, universally held in the Middle Ages, that law of some kind—the law either of God or man—ought to rule the world. Bracton, in his famous book on English law, which was written in the first half of the thirteenth century, held this theory, and deduced from it the proposition that the king and other rulers were subject to law. He laid it down that the law bound all members of the state, whether rulers or subjects; and that justice according to law was due both to ruler and subject. This view was accepted by the common lawyers of the fourteenth and fifteenth centuries and is stated in the Year Books. In 1441, in the Year Book 19 Henry VI Pasch. pl. 1, it is said: 'the law is the highest inheritance which the king has; for by the law he and all his subjects are ruled, and if there was no law there would be no king and no inheritance.'

The rise of the power of Parliament in the fourteenth and fifteenth centuries both emphasized and modified this theory of the supremacy of the law. That the rise of the power of Parliament emphasized the theory is shown by the practical application given to it by Chief Justice Fortescue in Henry VI's reign. He used it as the premise, by means of which he justified the control which Parliament had gained over legislation and taxation. That the rise of the power of Parliament modified the theory is shown by the manner in which the theory of the supremacy of the law was combined with the doctrine of the supremacy of Parliament. The law was supreme, but Parliament could change and modify it …

The only period when this conception of the rule of law was seriously questioned was in the Stuart period. The Stuart Kings considered that the Royal prerogative was the sovereign power in the State, and so could override the law whenever they saw fit. Chief Justice Coke was dismissed from the bench because he asserted the supremacy of the law. But his views as to the supremacy of the law were accepted by Parliament when it passed the Petition of Right in 1628, and when it abolished the Court of the Star Chamber and the jurisdiction of the Privy Council in England in 1641. Those views finally triumphed as the result of the Great Rebellion, and the Revolution of 1688. In this, as in other matters, Coke's writings passed on the views of the medieval English lawyers into modern English law. But these views were passed on with one important addition, which was the result of the rise, in the sixteenth century, of the modern territorial state. The law which was thus supreme was the law of England; and this included the law, written and unwritten, administered by the Courts of Common Law, by the Courts of Equity, by the Court of Admiralty, and by the Ecclesiastical Courts. Thus the modern doctrine of the rule of law has come, as the result of this long historical development, to mean the supremacy of all parts of the law of England, both enacted and unenacted.

NOTE: Chief Justice Coke's assertion of the supremacy of law was stated clearly in the case which follows.

Prohibitions del Roy
(1607) 12 Co Rep 63, 77 ER 1342

Note, upon Sunday the 10th of November in this same term, the King, upon complaint made to him by Bancroft, Archbishop of Canterbury, concerning prohibitions, the King was informed, that when the question was made of what matters the Ecclesiastical judges have cognizance, either upon the exposition of the statutes concerning tithes, or any other thing ecclesiastical, or upon the statute 1 El. concerning the high commission or in any other case in which there is not express authority in law, the King himself may decide it in his Royal person; and that the Judges are but the delegates of the King, and that the King may take what causes he shall please to determine, from the determination of the Judges, and may determine them himself. And the Archbishop said, that this was clear in divinity, that such authority belongs to the King by the word of God in the Scripture. To which it was answered by me, in the presence, and with the clear consent of all the Judges of England, and Barons of the Exchequer, that the King in his own person cannot adjudge any case, either criminal, as treason, felony, &c. or betwixt party and party, concerning his inheritance, chattels, or goods, &c. but this ought to be determined and adjudged in some Court of Justice.… And the Judges informed the King, that no King after the Conquest assumed to himself to give any judgment in any cause whatsoever, which concerned the administration of justice within this realm, but these were solely determined in the Courts of Justice.

… [T]hen the King said, that he thought the law was founded upon reason, and that he and others had reason, as well as the Judges: to which it was answered by me, that true it was, that God had endowed His Majesty with excellent science, and great endowments of nature; but His Majesty was not learned in the laws of his realm of England, and causes which concern the life, or inheritance, or goods, or fortunes of his subjects, are not to be decided by natural reason but by the artificial reason and judgment of law, which law is an act which requires long study and experience, before that a man can attain to the cognizance of it: that the law was the golden met-wand and measure to try the causes of the subjects; and which protected His Majesty in safety and peace: with which the King was greatly offended, and said, that then he should be under the law, which was treason to affirm, as he said; to which I said, that Bractonsaith, *quod Rex non debet esse sub homine, sed sub Deo et lege.*

NOTE: The law to which the Crown was subject was the common law as changed from time to time by Parliament. It is worth noting that at this time Parliament was not as active in legislating as it is now; the common law was the main source of law and legislation was very much a subsidiary source. The continuing existence and, implicitly, the importance of the principle of the rule of law has now been recognized in statute.

Constitutional Reform Act 2005

1. The rule of law

This Act does not adversely affect–

    (a) the existing constitutional principle of the rule of law, or

    (b) the Lord Chancellor's existing constitutional role in relation to that principle.

Lord Bingham commented on this provision in 'The Rule of Law' (2007) *CLJ* 67, p. 69:

[T]he statutory affirmation of the rule of law as an existing constitutional principle and of the Lord Chancellor's existing role in relation to it does have an important consequence: that the judges, in their role as journeymen and judgment-makers, are not free to dismiss the rule of law as meaningless verbiage, the jurisprudential equivalent of motherhood and apple pie, even if they were inclined to do so. They would be bound to construe a statute so that it did not infringe an existing constitutional principle, if it were reasonably possible to do so. And the Lord Chancellor's conduct in relation to that principle would no doubt be susceptible, in principle, to judicial review.

SECTION 2: DICEY AND THE RULE OF LAW

Dicey's views on the rule of law cannot be ignored because of the lasting influence he has had. His influence is all the more remarkable in light of the widespread criticisms which have been levelled against his views. In *An Introduction to the Study of the Law of the Constitution*, Dicey devoted a large part of the book to his exposition of the rule of law, to which he attributed three meanings (but we will not consider the third, about individual rights). The views of Dicey's critics will be stated after each.

A: The rule of law and discretionary powers

A. V. Dicey, *An Introduction to the Study of the Law of the Constitution*
(10th edn, 1985), pp. 188 and 202

We mean, in the first place, that no man is punishable or can be lawfully made to suffer in body or goods except for a distinct breach of law established in the ordinary legal manner before the ordinary courts of the land. In this sense the rule of law is contrasted with every system of government based on the exercise by persons in authority of wide, arbitrary, or discretionary powers of constraint.... It means ... The absolute supremacy or predominance of regular law as opposed to the influence of arbitrary power, and excludes the existence of arbitrariness, of prerogative, or even of wide discretionary authority on the part of the government. Englishmen are ruled by the law, and by the law alone; a man may with us be punished for a breach of the law, but he can be punished for nothing else.

Sir I. Jennings, *The Law and the Constitution*
(5th edn, 1959), pp. 54–8

Dicey and the Rule of Law

The particular principle of the individualist or *laissez-faire* school was that any substantial discretionary power was a danger to liberty. The fact that he held such a principle was not explicitly avowed by Dicey, because he assumed that he was analysing not his own subjective notions (shared, of course, by many of his contemporaries), but the firm and unalterable principles of English constitutional law…. We need only contest the idea that the rule of law and discretionary powers are contradictory.

If we look around us we cannot fail to be aware that public authorities do in fact possess wide discretionary powers. Many of them formed part of the law even when Dicey wrote in 1885. Any court can punish me for contempt of court by imprisoning me for an indefinite period. If I am convicted of manslaughter, I may be released at once or imprisoned for life. If I am an alien, my naturalisation is entirely within the discretion of the Home Secretary. If the Queen declares war against the rest of the world, I am prohibited from having dealings abroad. If the country is in danger, my property can be taken, perhaps without compensation. If a public health authority wants to flood my land in order to build a reservoir, it can take it from me compulsorily. I can be compelled to leave my work for a month or more, in order to serve on a jury. All these powers, and many more, were possessed by public authorities in 1885, and can still be exercised.

Dicey did not mention all these, because nowhere in his book did he consider the *powers* of authorities. He seemed to think that the British Constitution was concerned almost entirely with the *rights of individuals*. He was imagining a constitution dominated by the doctrine of *laissez-faire*. The function of government, as he unconsciously assumed, was to protect the individual against internal and external aggression. Given such protection, each individual was allowed to live his life almost as he pleased, so long as he did not interfere with the similar liberty of others. He regarded this as desirable, and therefore tended to minimise the extent to which public authorities could interfere with private action….

Nevertheless, the argument need not be placed entirely on this narrow ground. For the main discretionary power is placed in England not in the executive but in Parliament. Parliament, as has already been emphasised, can pass what legislation it pleases. It is not limited by any written constitution. Its powers are not only wide, but unlimited. In most countries, not only the administrative authorities but also the legislature have powers limited by the constitution. This, one would think, is the most effective rule of law. In England, the administration has powers limited by legislation, but the powers of the legislature are not limited at all. There is still, it may be argued, a rule of law, but the law is that the law may at any moment be changed.

Dicey attempts to meet this argument in two ways. 'The commands of Parliament,' he said, 'can be uttered only through the combined action of its three constituent parts, and must, therefore, always take the shape of formal and deliberate legislation.' Formal it may be; it may not be deliberate. We saw—Dicey saw before he died in 1922—how the Defence of the Realm Act was passed in 1914. The Cabinet decided that it wanted drastic powers. The majority which it commanded in the House of Commons supported its motion to suspend the Standing Orders. The Bill was passed through at one sitting. The House of Lords did the same. Thus at one stroke, without any long deliberation, the Cabinet acquired the powers it needed. The 'gold standard' was similarly swept away in 1931. The Cabinet ordered the Bank of England not to exchange notes into gold. The next day Parliament met and the necessary legislation was passed through not only to make paper currency inconvertible, but also to ratify the illegal acts of the Cabinet and of the Bank before the Act was passed. Here was arbitrary power indeed, but it was by no means as arbitrary as the powers exercised by Parliament in 1939 and 1940.

K. Culp Davis, *Discretionary Justice*
(1971), pp. 17 and 42

Even when rules can be written, discretion is often better. Rules without discretion cannot fully take into account the need for tailoring results to unique facts and circumstances of particular cases. The justification for discretion is often the need for individualized justice. This is so in the judicial process as well as in the administrative process.

Every governmental and legal system in world history has involved both rules and discretion. No government has ever been a government of laws and not of men in the sense of eliminating all discretionary power. Every government has always been *a government of laws and of men*. A close look at the meaning of Aristotle, the first user of the phrase 'government of laws and not of men,' shows quite clearly that he did not mean that governments could exist without discretionary power....

Elimination of all discretionary power is both impossible and undesirable. The sensible goal is development of a proper balance between rule and discretion. Some circumstances call for rules, some for discretion, some for mixtures of one proportion, and some for mixtures of another proportion. In today's American legal system, the special need is to eliminate *unnecessary* discretionary power, and to discover more successful ways to confine, to structure, and to check necessary discretionary power.

NOTE: The relationship between the rule of law and discretionary power remains at the core of debates about the principle. When the executive is given broad power by a statute created by Parliament, to what extent can that power be understood to be limited by implication? See the 'principle of legality' outlined in the case of *Pierson*, and the case of *Corner House Research*, considered later in this chapter in Section 5 at pp. 128–30 and 135–7.

B: The rule of law and equality

A. V. Dicey, *An Introduction to the Study of the Law of the Constitution*
(10th edn, 1985), pp. 202–3

It means ... equality before the law, or the equal subjection of all classes to the ordinary law of the land administered by the ordinary law courts; the 'rule of law' in this sense excludes the idea of any exemption of officials or others from the duty of obedience to the law which governs other citizens or from the jurisdiction of the ordinary tribunals; there can be with us nothing really corresponding to the 'administrative law' (*droit administratif*) or the 'administrative tribunals' (*tribunaux administratifs*) of France. The notion which lies at the bottom of the 'administrative law' known to foreign countries is, that affairs or disputes in which the government or its servants are concerned are beyond the sphere of the civil courts and must be dealt with by special and more or less official bodies. This idea is utterly unknown to the law of England, and indeed is fundamentally inconsistent with our traditions and customs.

R. F. V. Heuston, 'The Rule of Law' in *Essays in Constitutional Law*
(2nd edn, 1964), pp. 44–8

This exposition is still perfectly true in the sense that the social or political or economic status of an individual is by itself no answer to legal proceedings, civil or criminal. Everyone, whatever his position, must be ready to justify his actions by reference to some specific legal rule and be ready so to justify them in the ordinary courts ...

This aspect of Dicey's doctrine has been criticised by Sir Ivor Jennings on the ground that it seems to suggest that officials have the same rights and duties as citizens. If Dicey did indeed mean that, then he was obviously wrong, for modern statutes have conferred wide powers on officials which the ordinary citizen has not got. Gas Board officials may enter my premises to collect the money from the meter, but my neighbours cannot. Officials of the Ministry of Supply can enter my rooms to see if I am conducting researches into nuclear fission, but the college porter cannot. Conversely, the Oxford City Council, as the local education authority, is under a duty to educate my children free although my employers, the University of Oxford and Pembroke College, are not. Many other examples could be produced. There is something in this criticism. We have already seen that Dicey was perhaps a little reluctant to read the Statute Book, and that if he had done so more regularly he might perhaps have altered some of his phrases. Nevertheless, I do not think that Sir Ivor Jennings' criticism touches the heart of the matter. This has been very well put by Lord Wright: 'all are equally subject to the law, though the law as to which some are subject may be different from the law to which others are subject.' In other words, however great the powers or the duties conferred upon the executive, all are equally responsible before the ordinary courts for the exercise of their powers, rights and duties. As was said in *R* v *Brixton Prison Governor, ex parte Soblen* [1963] 2 QB 243 at p. 273, *per* Stephenson J:

> I have no doubt that one of the court's most important duties is to see so far as possible that the great officers of State and those who act under their orders, no less than public bodies and private individuals, act lawfully in the exercise of their powers; and the greater the power which is exercised, and the higher the authority exercising it, the more important is the discharge by the court of this duty, and the more difficult.

A second criticism is much more serious. It arises from Dicey's assertion that the Rule of Law precludes anything corresponding to the administrative law (*droit administratif*) of France. This belief dominated English thinking for so long that not many years ago a Lord Chief Justice could refer to the phrase 'administrative law' as 'Continental jargon.' It is only within the last decade that it has become a respectable phrase. It is clear to us today that Dicey misunderstood the nature and functions of French administrative law, and especially the function of the *conseil d'état*, the chief court in the administrative hierarchy. This is not the time to go into detail; it is enough to say here that although the *conseil d'état* is not composed of professional judges, there are no grounds for supposing that it is in any way biased in favour of the administration. Indeed, there seems to be good reason to think that the liberties of the citizen are in many ways better protected by the *conseil d'état* than by the High Court of Justice. The mere fact that French officials are exempt from process in the ordinary civil courts does not necessarily mean that they are legally irresponsible. To Dicey, however, who had to the full the common lawyer's belief that it is the duty of the Queen's courts to control and supervise the activities of all other tribunals and persons within the realm, the notion that officials might be subject to a special system of rules administered in a special system of courts, was necessarily a very curious one.

NOTE: While it is accepted that, if the rule of law is to be adhered to, it is necessary that citizens be given legal protection against unlawful conduct on the part of officials, Dicey regarded it as necessary that such protection be afforded by the ordinary courts. He did not consider it possible to maintain the rule of law if there was a separate system of public law administered by separate courts, as occurred in France and many other continental countries. Dicey believed that this system was biased in favour of officials and that English law provided better protection. Dicey's influence was such that this view affected the development of administrative law for many years. It is only within the last 40 to 50 years that administrative law has come to be recognized as a separate branch of law, and the United Kingdom has since 2000 had an 'Administrative Court', as part of the Queen's Bench Division of the High Court, which has taken jurisdiction over, among other matters, claims of judicial review against administrative action. There are also many tribunals dealing with administrative matters. In whatever way it is to be administered, the essential issue, if the rule of law is to be respected, is simply whether officials are subject to, and controlled by, the law.

Equality before the law should mean that no one is above the law. As with all rules, however, there are exceptions: for example, foreign sovereigns and diplomats, their staffs and families are immune from criminal prosecution or civil action; members of Parliament enjoy certain privileges; and judges enjoy the privilege of being immune from civil liability for anything said or done in the course of their office. These exceptions are limited and, in the case of judges and MPs, are designed to further the rule of law by giving protection to the institutions upon which a liberal democracy is founded, namely, an independent judiciary and an elected legislature.

In explaining his second proposition, Dicey stated that 'every man, whatever be his rank or condition, is subject to the ordinary law of the realm and amenable to the jurisdiction of the ordinary tribunals' (at p. 193). The accuracy of this statement, as to the equal applicability of the law to officials and non-officials alike, came under challenge in the following case.

In re M
[1993] 3 WLR 433, House of Lords

M, a citizen of Zaire, arrived in the United Kingdom seeking political asylum. The Home Office rejected his application and ordered his removal from the United Kingdom. After the Court of Appeal had refused an application for leave to apply for judicial review of the decision, a fresh last-minute application for judicial review, alleging new grounds, was made to Garland J, who indicated that M's departure was be postponed pending consideration of the application. Due to bungling and breakdown in lines of communication, M's departure was not prevented, nor was he removed from the onward flight to Zaire during a stopover at Paris. Garland J, being informed of M's removal from the jurisdiction, ordered the Home Secretary to procure the return of M to the jurisdiction. Proceedings were brought on behalf of M against the Home Office and the Home Secretary alleging contempt of court in respect of the breach of the undertaking and the order requiring M's return. Simon Brown J dismissed this motion on the basis that since the Crown's immunity from injunction was preserved by s. 21 of the Crown Proceedings Act 1947, neither it nor its departments, ministers, and officials acting in the course of their duties could be impleaded for contempt of court. The applicant appealed.

The Court of Appeal held that the original order by Garland J should not have been made, as injunctions could not be issued against the Crown. However, as the order was binding until set aside, failure to comply with it was a contempt.

The Secretary of State appealed and the applicant cross-appealed in respect of his original application against the Home Office. The House of Lords considered two issues of constitutional import: first, could injunctions be issued against a government minister or department, and, secondly, could a government minister or department be found to be in contempt of court for failure to comply with an order of the court.

LORD TEMPLEMAN: My Lords, Parliament makes the law, the executive carry the law into effect and the judiciary enforce the law. The expression 'the Crown' has two meanings; namely the monarch and the executive. In the 17th century Parliament established its supremacy over the Crown as monarch, over the executive and over the judiciary. Parliamentary supremacy over the Crown as monarch stems from the fact that the monarch must accept the advice of a Prime Minister who is supported by a majority of Parliament. Parliamentary supremacy over the Crown as executive stems from the fact that Parliament maintains in office the Prime Minister who appoints the ministers in charge of the executive. Parliamentary supremacy over the judiciary is only exercisable by statute. The judiciary enforce the law against individuals, against institutions and against the executive. The judges cannot enforce the law against the Crown as monarch because the Crown as monarch can do no wrong but judges enforce the law against the Crown as executive and against the individuals who from time to time represent the Crown. A litigant complaining of a breach of the law by the executive can sue the Crown as executive bringing his action against the minister who is responsible for the department of state involved, in the present case the Secretary of State for Home Affairs. To enforce the law the courts have power to grant remedies including injunctions against a minister in his official capacity. If the minister has personally broken the law, the litigant can sue the minister, in this case Mr Kenneth Baker, in his personal capacity. For the purpose of enforcing the law against all persons and institutions, including ministers in their official capacity and in their personal capacity, the courts are armed with coercive powers exercisable in proceedings for contempt of court.

In the present case, counsel for the Secretary of State argued that the judge could not enforce the law by injunction or contempt proceedings against the minister in his official capacity. Counsel also argued that in his personal capacity Mr Kenneth Baker the Secretary of State for Home Affairs had not been guilty of contempt.

My Lords, the argument that there is no power to enforce the law by injunction or contempt proceedings against a minister in his official capacity would, if upheld, establish the proposition that the executive obey the law as a matter of grace and not as a matter of necessity, a proposition which would reverse the result of the Civil War. For the reasons given by my noble and learned friend, Lord Woolf, and on principle, I am satisfied that injunctions and contempt proceedings may be brought against the minister in his official capacity and that in the present case the Home Office for which the Secretary of State was responsible was in contempt. I am also satisfied that Mr Baker was throughout acting in his official capacity, on advice which he was entitled to accept and under a mistaken view as to the law. In these circumstances I do not consider that Mr Baker personally was guilty of contempt. I would therefore dismiss this appeal substituting the Secretary of State for Home Affairs as being the person against whom the finding of contempt was made.

LORD WOOLF:

The fact that these issues have only now arisen for decision by the courts is confirmation that in ordinary circumstances ministers of the Crown and government departments invariably scrupulously observe decisions of the courts. Because of this, it is normally unnecessary for the courts to make an executory order against a minister or a government department since they will comply with any declaratory judgment made by the courts and pending the decision of the courts will not take any precipitous action.

Jurisdiction to make a finding of contempt
The Court of Appeal were of the opinion that a finding of contempt could not be made against the Crown, a government department or a minister of the Crown in his official capacity. Although it is to be expected that it will be rare indeed that the circumstances will exist in which such a finding would be justified, I do not believe there is any impediment to a court making such a finding, when it is appropriate to do so, not against the Crown directly, but against a government department or a minister of the Crown in his official capacity. Lord Donaldson of Lymington MR considered that a problem was created in making a finding of contempt because the Crown lacked a legal personality. However, at least for some purposes, the Crown has a legal personality. It can be appropriately described as a corporation sole or a corporation aggregate: *per* Lord Diplock and Lord Simon of Glaisdale respectively in *Town Investments Ltd* v *Department of the Environment* [1978] AC 359. The Crown can hold property and enter into contracts. On the other hand, even after the Act of 1947, it cannot conduct litigation except in the name of an authorised government department or, in the case of judicial review, in the name of a minister. In any event it is not in relation to the Crown that I differ from the Master of the Rolls, but as to a government department or a minister.

Nolan LJ, at p. 311, considered that the fact that proceedings for contempt are 'essentially personal and punitive' meant that it was not open to a court, as a matter of law, to make a finding of contempt against the Home Office or the Home Secretary. While contempt proceedings usually have these characteristics and contempt proceedings against a government department or a minister in an official capacity would not be either personal or punitive (it would clearly not be appropriate to fine or sequest the assets of the Crown or a government department or an officer of the Crown acting in his official capacity), this does not mean that a finding of contempt against a government department or minister would be pointless. The very fact of making such a finding would vindicate the requirements of justice. In addition an order for costs could be made to underline the significance of a contempt. A purpose of the courts' powers to make findings of contempt is to ensure that the orders of the court are obeyed. This jurisdiction is required to be coextensive with the courts' jurisdiction to make the orders which need the protection which the jurisdiction to make findings of contempt provides. In civil proceedings the court can now make orders (other than injunctions or for specific performance) against authorised government departments or the Attorney-General. On applications for judicial review orders can be made against ministers. In consequence of the developments identified already such orders must be taken not to offend the theory that the Crown can supposedly do no wrong. Equally, if such orders are made and not obeyed, the body against whom the orders were made can be found guilty of contempt without offending that theory, which would be the only justifiable impediment against making a finding of contempt....

It is for these reasons that I would dismiss this appeal and cross-appeal save for substituting the Secretary of State for Home Affairs as being the person against whom the finding of contempt was made. This was the alternative decision which was the subject of the cross-appeal, except that there the order was sought against the Home Office rather than the Home Secretary.

Order of Court of Appeal affirmed save for substitution of designation 'Secretary of State for Home Affairs' as proper object of finding of contempt.

Appeal and cross-appeal dismissed with costs.

■ QUESTIONS

1. Does this decision give effect to Dicey's second proposition regarding the rule of law? Might it be argued that what is most remarkable about the decision in *M v Home Office* is that it was not until 1993 that the courts were able to confirm that injunctions and contempt proceedings could be brought against government ministers when acting in an official capacity?

2. Is it desirable that courts should seek to compel the Government to comply with their orders rather than leaving it to the electorate to condemn them in a future election for their failure to comply?

3. Bagehot in *The English Constitution* (1867) drew a distinction between what he referred to as the 'dignified' parts of the constitution and the 'efficient' parts. The former he claimed 'excite and preserve the reverence of the population'. One of the dignified institutions is the monarchy, i.e. the Crown, to whom loyalty is felt or allegiance is owed. The institutions of government are the efficient parts of the constitution wherein real power is vested. In the United Kingdom Government is conducted in the name of the Crown; thus it is referred to as Her Majesty's Government. When Lords Templeman and Woolf distinguished between the Crown as Monarch and the Crown as Executive, were they thereby adopting this distinction drawn by Bagehot? Does the fact that the Crown as Monarch can do no wrong as a matter of law—which is not disturbed by the decision in *M v Home Office*—offend against the principle of the rule of law?

NOTE: A contemporary account of the rule of law which appears as if it could be as influential as that set out by Dicey has recently been developed by Tom Bingham (formerly the Senior Law Lord). In *The Rule of Law* (2010), Bingham identifies the following eight principles which together comprise his account of the rule of law, and some overlap with, or develop, the notions identified by Dicey (pp. 37, 48, 55, 60, 66, 85, 90, and 110):

1. The law must be accessible and so far as possible intelligible, clear and predictable
2. Questions of legal right and liability should ordinarily be resolved by application of the law and not the exercise of discretion
3. The laws of the land should apply equally to all, save to the extent that objective differences justify differentiation

4. Ministers and public officers at all levels must exercise the powers conferred on them in good faith, fairly, for the purpose for which the powers were conferred, without exceeding the limits of such powers and not unreasonably
5. The law must afford adequate protection of fundamental human rights
6. Means must be provided for resolving, without prohibitive cost or inordinate delay, bona fide civil disputes which the parties themselves are unable to resolve
7. Adjudicative procedures provided by the state should be fair
8. The rule of law requires compliance by the state with its obligations in international law as in national law

Many of these principles may attract broad acceptance. Yet others may be the subject of debate—principles 6 and 8 perhaps constituting the best examples. This is not necessarily to argue that they are not desirable principles, but whether adherence to them is required to satisfy the rule of law. To be able to assess such accounts of the rule of law adequately, it may be helpful to draw a distinction between two ways of thinking about the concept: formal and substantive approaches to the rule of law. Drawing this distinction, as we do in Section 3, should assist us in determining whether some, most or all of the practical principles set out by Bingham provide the essence of the rule of law.

SECTION 3: THE RULE OF LAW—FORMAL OR SUBSTANTIVE?

The meaning of the rule of law, and what it requires to be satisfied, is clearly contested by writers on the subject. One way in which we may seek to understand the modern versions of these debates is to distinguish between 'formal' and 'substantive' approaches to the rule of law. While these categories are not absolute, and may indeed be better understood as representing opposite ends of a spectrum rather than entirely distinct conceptions, the terms may help us to appreciate what different writers take to be the purpose (or as Raz would say, 'virtue') of the rule of law. The following extracts set out the essential differences between a formal and a substantive approach to the rule of law.

J. Raz, 'The Rule of Law and its Virtue'
(1977) 93 *Law Quarterly Review* 195–202

The rule of law is a political ideal which a legal system may lack or may possess to a greater or lesser degree. That much is common ground. It is also to be insisted that the rule of law is just one of the virtues which a legal system may possess and by which it is to be judged. It is not to be confused with democracy, justice, equality (before the law or otherwise), human rights of any kind or respect for persons or for the dignity of man. A non-democratic legal system, based on the denial of human rights, on extensive poverty, on racial segregation, sexual inequalities and religious persecution may, in principle, conform to the requirements of the rule of law better than any of the legal systems of the more enlightened western democracies. This does not mean that it will be better than those western democracies. It will be an immeasurably worse legal system, but it will excel in one respect: in its conformity to the rule of law.

...

1. The Basic Idea
'The rule of law' means literally what it says: The rule of the law. Taken in its broadest sense this means that people should obey the law and be ruled by it. But in political and legal theory it has come to be read in a narrower sense, that the government shall be ruled by the law and subject to it. The ideal of

the rule of law in this sense is often expressed by the phrase 'government by law and not by men.' No sooner does one use these formulae than their obscurity becomes evident. Surely government must be both by law and by men. It is said that the rule of law means that all government action must have foundation in law, must be authorised by law. But is not that a tautology? Actions not authorised by law cannot be the actions of the government as a government. They would be without legal effect and often unlawful.... There is more to the rule of law than the law and order interpretation allows. It means more even than law and order applied to the government. I shall proceed on the assumption that we are concerned with government in the legal sense and with the conception of the rule of law which applies to government and to law and is no mere application of the law and order conception.

The problem is that now we are back with our initial puzzle. If the government is, by definition, government authorised by law the rule of law seems to amount to an empty tautology, not a political ideal....

Let us, therefore, return to the literal sense of the 'rule of law.' It has two aspects: (1) that people should be ruled by the law and obey it, and (2) that the law should be such that people will be able to be guided by it. As was noted above, it is with the second aspect that we are concerned: the law must be capable of being obeyed. A person conforms with the law to the extent that he does not break the law. But he obeys the law only if part of his reason for conforming is his knowledge of the law. Therefore, if the law is to be obeyed it *must be capable of guiding the behaviour* of its subjects. It must be such that they can find out what it is and act on it.

This is the basic intuition from which the doctrine of the rule of law derives: the law must be capable of guiding the behaviour of its subjects. It is evident that this conception of the rule of law is a formal one. It says nothing about how the law is to be made: by tyrants, democratic majorities or any other way. It says nothing about fundamental rights, about equality or justice. It may even be thought that this version of the doctrine is formal to the extent that it is almost devoid of content. This is far from the truth. Most of the requirements which were associated with the rule of law before it came to signify all the virtues of the state can be derived from this one basic idea.

2. Some Principles

Many of the principles which can be derived from the basic idea of the rule of law depend for their validity or importance on the particular circumstances of different societies. There is little point in trying to enumerate them all, but some of the more important ones might be mentioned:

(1) *All laws should be prospective, open and clear.* One cannot be guided by a retroactive law. It does not exist at the time of action. Sometimes it is then known for certain that a retroactive law will be enacted. When this happens retroactivity does not conflict with the rule of law (though it may be objected to on other grounds). The law must be open and adequately publicised. If it is to guide people they must be able to find out what it is. For the same reason its meaning must be clear. An ambiguous, vague, obscure or imprecise law is likely to mislead or confuse at least some of those who desire to be guided by it.

(2) *Laws should be relatively stable.* They should not be changed too often. If they are frequently changed people will find it difficult to find out what the law is at any given moment and will be constantly in fear that the law has been changed since they last learnt what it is. But more important still is the fact that people need to know the law not only for short-term decisions (where to park one's car, how much alcohol is allowed in duty free, etc.) but also for long-term planning. Knowledge of at least the general outlines and sometimes even of details of tax law and company law are often important for business plans which will bear fruit only years later. Stability is essential if people are to be guided by law in their long-term decisions....

(3) *The making of particular laws (particular legal orders) should be guided by open, stable, clear and general rules.* It is sometimes assumed that the requirement of generality is of the essence of the rule of law. This notion derives (as noted above) from the literal interpretation of 'the rule of law' when 'law' is read in its lay connotations as being restricted to general, stable and open law. It is

also reinforced by a belief that the rule of law is particularly relevant to the protection of equality and that equality is related to the generality of law. The last belief is, as has been often noted before, mistaken. Racial, religious and all manner of discrimination is not only compatible but often institutionalised by general rules.

The formal conception of the rule of law which I am defending does not object to particular legal orders as long as they are stable, clear, etc. But of course particular legal orders are mostly used by government agencies to introduce flexibility into the law. A police constable regulating traffic, a licensing authority granting a licence under certain conditions, all these and their like are among the more ephemeral parts of the law. As such they run counter to the basic idea of the rule of law. They make it difficult for people to plan ahead on the basis of their knowledge of the law. This difficulty is overcome to a large extent if particular laws of an ephemeral status are enacted only within a framework set by general laws which are more durable and which impose limits on the unpredictability introduced by the particular orders.

(4) *The independence of the judiciary must be guaranteed.* It is of the essence of municipal legal systems that they institute judicial bodies charged, among other things, with the duty of applying the law to cases brought before them and whose judgments and conclusions as to the legal merits of those cases are final. Since just about any matter arising under any law can be subject to a conclusive court judgment it is obvious that it is futile to guide one's action on the basis of the law if when the matter comes to adjudication the courts will not apply the law and will act for some other reasons.

(5) *The principles of natural justice must be observed.* Open and fair hearing, absence of bias and the like are obviously essential for the correct application of the law and thus, through the very same considerations mentioned above, to its ability to guide action.

(6) *The courts should have review powers over the implementation of the other principles.* This includes review of both subordinate and parliamentary legislation and of administrative action, but in itself it is a very limited review—merely to ensure conformity to the rule of law.

(7) *The courts should be easily accessible.* Given the central position of the courts in ensuring the rule of law (see principles 4 and 6) it is obvious that their accessibility is of paramount importance. Long delays, excessive costs, etc., may effectively turn the most enlightened law to a dead letter and frustrate one's ability effectively to guide oneself by the law.

(8) *The discretion of the crime preventing agencies should not be allowed to pervert the law.* Not only the courts but also the actions of the police and the prosecuting authorities can subvert the law. The prosecution should not be allowed, e.g. to decide not to prosecute for commission of certain crimes, or for crimes committed by certain classes of offenders. The police should not be allowed to allocate its resources so as to avoid all effort to prevent and detect certain crimes or prosecute certain classes of criminals.

The eight principles listed fall into two groups. Principles 1 to 3 require that the law should conform to standards designed to enable it effectively to guide action. Principles 4 to 8 are designed to ensure that the legal machinery of enforcing the law should not deprive it of its ability to guide through distorted enforcement and that it shall be capable of supervising conformity to the rule of law and provide effective remedies in cases of deviation from it. All the principles directly concern the system and method of government in matters directly relevant to the rule of law. Needless to say many other aspects in the life of a community may, in more indirect ways, either strengthen or weaken the rule of law. A free press run by people anxious to defend the rule of law is of great assistance in preserving it, just as a gagged press or one run by people wishing to undermine the rule of law is a threat to it. But we need not be concerned here with these more indirect influences.

NOTE: See also Lon L. Fuller, *The Morality of Law* (2nd edn, 1969).

P. Craig, The Rule of Law, Select Committee on the Constitution, *Relations between the executive, the judiciary and Parliament*

HL 151 of 2006–07, pp. 97, 100–6

The rule of law as presented thus far is not concerned with the actual content of the law, in the sense of whether the law is just or unjust, provided that the formal precepts of the rule of law are themselves met. To put the same point in another way, it is necessary on this view to consider the content of the law in order to decide whether it complies with the precepts of the rule of law concerning clarity, generality, non-retrospectivity etc, but provided that it does so comply then that is the end of the inquiry.

The rationale for restricting the rule of law in this manner is as follows. [J. Raz (1977) 93 *Law Quarterly Review* 195.] We may all agree that laws should be just, that their content should be morally sound and that rights should be protected within society. The problem is that if the rule of law is taken to encompass the necessity for 'good laws' in this sense then the concept ceases to have an independent function. There is a wealth of literature which should subsist therein, and the appropriate boundaries of governmental action. Political theory has tackled questions such as these from time immemorial. To bring these issues within the rubric of the rule of law would therefore rob this concept of an independent function. Laws would be condemned or upheld as being in conformity with, or contrary to, the rule of law when the condemnation or praise would simply be reflective of attachment to a particular conception of rights, democracy or the just society. The message is therefore that if you wish to argue about the justness of society do so by all means. If you wish to defend a particular type of individual right then present your argument. Draw upon the wealth of literature which addresses these matters directly. It is however on this view not necessary or desirable to cloak the conclusion in the mantle of the rule of law, since this will merely reflect the conclusion which has already been arrived at through reliance on a particular theory of rights or the just society.

(c) The Rule of Law, Justice and Accountable Government

The view presented above has however been challenged. Those who support the opposing view accept that the rule of law has the attributes mentioned in the previous section, but they argue that the concept has more far-reaching implications. Certain rights are said to be based on, or derived from, the rule of law. The concept is used as the foundation for these rights, which are then used to evaluate the quality of the laws produced by the legislature and courts.

It has also been argued that the rule of law provides the foundation for the controls exercised by the courts over governmental action through judicial review. In this sense the rule of law is expressive of how the state ought to behave towards individuals in society. The rule of law is said to demand that governmental action conforms to precepts of good administration developed through the courts, this being an essential facet of accountable government in a democratic society. The constraints imposed on government through judicial review are in part procedural and in part substantive. The range of these principles varies, but normally includes ideas such as: legality, procedural propriety, participation, fundamental rights, openness, rationality, relevancy, propriety of purpose, reasonableness, equality, legitimate expectations, legal certainty and proportionality. There has been a vibrant academic debate as to whether such principles must be legitimated by reference to legislative intent. There is nonetheless general agreement that it is the courts that have developed the principles of judicial review over the past 350 years.

This general view has been advanced by a number of writers and judges, although the precise detail of their analyses differ.

Thus Dworkin has argued forcefully that subject to questions of 'fit', the courts should decide legal questions according to the best theory of justice, which is central to the resolution of what rights people currently possess. [R. Dworkin, *Law's Empire* (1986)] According to this theory, 'propositions of law are true if they figure in or follow from the principles of justice, fairness and procedural due process that provide the best constructive interpretation of the community's legal practice'. It is integral to the Dworkinian approach that, subject to questions of fit, the court should choose between 'eligible interpretations by asking which shows the community's structure of institutions as a whole in a better light from the stand-point of political is forthcoming from the application of the above test.

Dworkin accepts the formal idea of the rule of law set out above, labelling this the 'rule book' conception. This requires that the government should never exercise power against individuals except in accordance with rules which have been set out in advance and made available to all. [R. Dworkin, *A Matter of Principle* (1985)] Such values feature in any serious theory of justice. However as Dworkin notes, this says little if anything about the content of the laws which exist within a legal system. Those who restrict the rule of law in this manner care about the content of the law, but regard this as a matter of substantive justice, which is 'an independent ideal, in no sense part of the ideal of the rule of law'.

Dworkin argues that we should however also recognise a rights-based conception of the rule of law. On this view citizens have moral rights and duties with respect to one another, and political rights against the state. These moral and political rights should be recognised in positive law, so that they can be enforced by citizens through the courts. The rule of law on this conception is the ideal of rule by an accurate public conception of individual rights. In the words of Dworkin, this view of the rule of law 'does not distinguish, as the rule book conception does, between the rule of law and substantive justice; on the contrary it requires, as part of the ideal of law, that the rules in the book capture and enforce moral rights'. It does not mean that this conception of the rule of law is consistent with only one theory of justice or freedom. There is no such argument. It does mean that it is not independent of the particular theory of justice, or vision of freedom, which constitutes its content at any point in time.

Allan's interpretation of the rule of law also contains an admixture of formal and substantive elements. [T. R. S. Allan, *Constitutional Justice: A Liberal Theory of the Rule of Law* (2001)] He argues that we should go beyond the formal conception of the rule of law, but that we should stop short of regarding the rule of law as the expression of any particular theory of substantive justice. The rule of law on this view does not entail commitment to any particular vision of the public good or any specific conception of social justice, but does require that all legal obligations be justified by appeal to some such vision. The rule of law should embrace, in addition to its formal attributes, ideals of equality and rationality, proportionality and fairness, and certain substantive rights. These are said to constitute central components of any recognisably liberal theory of justice, while leaving the scope and content of the rights and duties which citizens should possess largely as a matter for independent debate and analysis. Formal equality is to be supplemented by a more substantive equality, which requires that relevant distinctions must be capable of reasoned justification in terms of some conception of the common good. Allan's theory also embraces certain substantive rights, namely freedoms of speech, conscience, association, and access to information. It is recognised that there will be other rights within a liberal polity, which should be faithfully applied, but these are not regarded as a constituent part of the rule of law.

It should be recognised that any approach of the kind under examination will require some choice as to what are to count as fundamental rights, and the more particular meaning ascribed to such rights. This choice will reflect assumptions as to the importance of differing interests in society. This is unavoidable. It is of course true that any democracy to be worthy of the name will have some attachment to particular liberty and equality interests. If, however, we delve beneath the surface of phrases such as liberty and equality then significant differences of view become apparent even amongst those who subscribe to one version or another of liberal belief. This leaves entirely out of account the issue as to how far social and economic interests ought to be protected. It also fails to take account of other visions of democracy, of a communitarian rather than liberal nature, which might well interpret the civil/political rights and the social/economic rights differently. It is therefore neither fortuitous, nor surprising, that in other common law systems which possess constitutionally enshrined rights, such as the United States and Canada, there is considerable diversity of opinion even amongst those who support a rights-based approach, as to whether this should be taken to mean some version of liberalism, a pluralist model, or a modified notion of republicanism.

This point is equally true of ideas such as legality, rationality, participation, openness, proportionality, procedural fairness and the like, which can be given interpreted differently depending upon the more general scheme into which they are to fit.

The consequences of breach of the rule of law in the sense considered within this section should also be addressed. It is important, as when discussing other versions of the concept, to distinguish between the consequences of breach of the rule of law in relation to primary statute and in relation to other measures.

The short answer in relation to a primary statute that violates the rule of law is as follows. The fact that a statute does not conform to this conception of the rule of law does not in itself lead to its invalidation. The UK courts have not traditionally exercised the power of constitutional review to annul primary statutes for failure to conform to fundamental rights, or other precepts of the rule of law that constitute the principles of judicial review. This proposition must nonetheless be qualified in three ways.

First, there are statements by judges countenancing the possibility that the courts might refuse to apply an Act of Parliament in certain extreme circumstances. The examples tend to be of (hypothetical) legislation that is morally repugnant, or of legislation through which Parliament seeks to re-order the constitutional structure by abolishing judicial review, by making illegitimate use of the Parliament Acts or by extending very considerably the life of a current Parliament. It should moreover be recognised that the case law authority for the traditional proposition that courts will not invalidate or refuse to apply statute is actually rather thin. There are to be sure many judicial statements extolling the sovereignty of Parliament, but they are principally just that, judicial statements rather than formal decisions. Insofar as there are formal decisions that could be said to be based on the traditional proposition, the facts of such cases were generally relatively innocuous. They were a very long way from the types of case where courts might consider it to be justified to refuse to apply a statute, which also means that such cases could be readily distinguished should a court feel minded to do so.

Secondly, one who subscribes to the version of the rule of law discussed in this section might well argue that courts should generally exercise the ultimate power to invalidate statute for failure to comply with constitutionally enshrined rights, or with rights that are regarded as fundamental or foundational even where they are not formally enshrined in a written constitution. Dworkin is a prominent exponent of this view. The literature on this topic is vast, with the debate for and against such judicial power being replayed in successive academic generations.

Thirdly, courts or judges who subscribe to the conception of the rule of law discussed in this section have in any event powerful interpretive tools at their disposal through which to read legislation so that it does not violate fundamental rights or other facets of the rule of law. Thus even prior to the Human Rights Act 1998, the courts made it clear through the principle of legality that statutes would be read so as to conform to such rights. If Parliament intended to infringe or limit fundamental rights then this would have to be stated expressly in the legislation, or be the only plausible reading of the statutory language. Legislation was therefore read subject to a principle of legality, which meant that fundamental rights could not be overridden by general or ambiguous words. This was, said Lord Hoffmann, because there was too great a risk that the full implications of their unqualified meaning might have passed unnoticed in the democratic process. In the absence of express language or necessary implication to the contrary, the courts would therefore presume that even the most general words were intended to be subject to the basic rights of the individual. Parliament had, therefore, to squarely confront what it was doing and accept the political cost. An interpretive approach is clearly evident once again in the Human Rights Act 1998, section 3, which provides that 'so far as it is possible to do so, primary legislation and subordinate legislation must be read and given effect in a way which is compatible with the Convention rights'. Section 3 does not, however, affect the validity, continuing operation or enforcement of any incompatible primary legislation. Where a court is satisfied that primary legislation is incompatible with a Convention right then it can, pursuant to section 4 of the HRA, make a declaration of that incompatibility.

The consequence of breach of the rule of law in relation to measures other than primary statute is more straightforward. Insofar as the rule of law is regarded as the foundation of the principles of judicial review then it follows that breach of the rule of law, manifested through breach of one of the more particular principles of judicial review, can lead to annulment of the measure. This says nothing about whether the judicial decision will be controversial or not. The great many judicial review decisions generate no political controversy, but there will inevitably be instances where Parliament, or more usually the relevant minister, feels that the court's judgment was 'wrong' in some way. There will more generally be wide ranging academic debate about the principles of judicial review and the way in which they are applied in particular cases.

NOTES

1. As this extract demonstrates, a substantive approach to the rule of law will generally also accept many aspects of the formal account defended by Raz. Consequently, when we talk about formal *versus* substantive understandings of the rule of law, what we mean is: should the formal aspects of the rule of law (about which there is much consensus) be supplemented with substantive requirements? An alternative way of describing these different approaches to the rule of law is that a theory of what the principle requires can be either 'thicker' or 'thinner'; see B. Tamanaha, *On the Rule of Law: History, Politics, Theory* (2004). Is the rule of law concerned with the narrower task of establishing a legal system which is comprised of rules which it is possible for citizens to follow—meaning that its requirements will be relatively thin? Or is the rule of law concerned with the broader task of ensuring that the law of a legal system is *good* law—meaning that its requirements will be much thicker?

2. Argument about whether a formal or substantive understanding of the rule of law is to be preferred may map onto the debates encountered in Chapter 1, Section 4 at pp. 23–8 between legal and political constitutionalism. The disagreement is not about whether we want our law to be good, as all would agree with this objective. Instead, it concerns how this goal can be achieved. Those who defend a formal account of the rule of law may, in common with political constitutionalism, believe that what 'good' law is must be settled politically, and law is simply the tool with which to implement such decisions. Those who defend a substantive account of the rule of law may, in common with legal constitutionalism, believe that the law should inherently protect certain values against political interference. Perhaps the key problem for the former is that the rule of law may ultimately be understood to require the enforcement of 'bad' law. Perhaps the key problem for the latter is that in practice it may be very difficult to determine or agree about what is 'good' or 'bad' law, and the appropriateness of allocating such decisions to the courts is questionable.

3. As Craig's extract shows, it is one thing to advance a more substantive understanding of the rule of law in the abstract, but another thing to see what the consequences of breaching that account of the rule of law will be. In the United Kingdom, the principle of the rule of law operates subject to the doctrine of parliamentary sovereignty, considered in Chapter 2. Parliament can make or unmake any law, even one which violates the rule of law, and the courts cannot invalidate such legislation (although as Craig notes, some writers question this orthodoxy and, even if true, the courts have other tools which might be used to try to ensure that statutes do not violate the rule of law). But this does not mean the rule of law is unimportant in the UK constitution; instead, we must look carefully to see how this principle has been employed in the United Kingdom. As will be seen in this chapter in Section 4 at pp. 117–23, the rule of law is not just a principle the violation of which has legal consequences.

SECTION 4: THE RULE OF LAW AS A BROAD POLITICAL DOCTRINE

While it is concerned with the law, the rule of law is not simply a legal principle.

A. W. Bradley, K. D. Ewing, and C. J. S. Knight, *Constitutional and Administrative Law*
(16th edn, 2015), p. 84

If the law is not to be merely a means of achieving whatever ends a particular government may favour, the rule of law must go beyond the principle of legality. The experience and values of the legal system are relevant not only to the question, 'What legal authority *does* the government have for its acts?' but also to the question, 'What legal powers *ought* the government to have?'

We will look at the notion of government according to law later in this chapter in Section 5 at p. 124. In this section, however, we will consider some of the minimum standards which laws should attain. Here, the rule of law can be understood to operate as a prescriptive political doctrine, indicating how a legal system should be constituted, and how the governmental power it creates should be exercised. A number of the principles identified in the formal account of the rule of law developed by Raz are of particular importance, and have been recognized in UK constitutional law.

A: Laws should be clear

Merkur Island Shipping Corp. v Laughton and Others
[1983] 2 AC 570, Court of Appeal

In an action arising from a trade dispute between the owners and crew of a ship, members of the International Transport Workers' Federation were sued for damages for losses arising from secondary industrial action in which they had been involved. In deciding whether a trade union was immune from tortious liability, the court had to construe three statutes: the Trade Union and Labour Relations Act 1974, the Trade Union and Labour Relations (Amendment) Act 1976, and the Employment Act 1980.

LORD DONALDSON MR: ... At the beginning of this judgment I said that whilst I had reached the conclusion that the law was tolerably clear, the same could not be said of the way in which it was expressed. The efficacy and maintenance of the rule of law, which is the foundation of any parliamentary democracy, has at least two pre-requisites. First, people must understand that it is in their interests, as well as in that of the community as a whole, that they should live their lives in accordance with the rules and all the rules. Second, they must know what those rules are. Both are equally important and it is the second aspect of the rule of law which has caused me concern in the present case, the ITF having disavowed any intention to break the law.

In industrial relations it is of vital importance that the worker on the shop floor, the shop steward, the local union official, the district officer and the equivalent levels in management should know what is and what is not 'offside.' And they must be able to find this out for themselves by reading plain and simple words of guidance. The judges of this court are all skilled lawyers of very considerable experience, yet it has taken us hours to ascertain what is and what is not 'offside,' even with the assistance of highly experienced counsel. This cannot be right.

We have had to look at three Acts of Parliament, none intelligible without the other. We have had to consider section 17 of the Act of 1980, which adopts the 'flow' method of Parliamentary draftsmanship, without the benefit of a flow diagram. We have furthermore been faced with the additional complication that subsection (6) of section 17 contains definitions which distort the natural meaning of the words in the operative subsections. It was not always like this. If you doubt me, look at the comparative simplicity and clarity of Sir Mackenzie Chalmers's Sale of Goods Act 1893, his Bills of Exchange Act 1882, and his Marine Insurance Act 1906. But I do not criticise the draftsman. His instructions may well have left him no option. My plea is that Parliament, when legislating in respect of circumstances which directly affect the 'man or woman in the street' or the 'man or woman on the shop floor' should give as high a priority to clarity and simplicity of expression as to refinements of policy. Where possible, statutes, or complete parts of statutes, should not be amended but re-enacted in an amended form so that those concerned can read the rules in a single document. When formulating policy, ministers, of whatever political persuasion, should at all times be asking themselves and asking parliamentary counsel: 'Is this concept too refined to be capable of expression in basic English? If so, is there some way in which we can modify the policy so that it can be so expressed?' Having to ask such questions would no doubt be frustrating for ministers and the legislature generally, but in my judgment this is part of the price which has to be paid if the rule of law is to be maintained.

These sentiments were echoed by Lord Diplock in the House of Lords, at p. 612:

LORD DIPLOCK: ... Absence of clarity is destructive of the rule of law; it is unfair to those who wish to preserve the rule of law; it encourages those who wish to undermine it. The statutory provisions which it became necessary to piece together into a coherent whole in order to decide the stage 3 point are drafted in a manner which, having regard to their subject matter and the persons who will be called upon to apply them, can, in my view, only be characterised as most regrettably lacking in the requisite degree of clarity.

R (Nicklinson) v Ministry of Justice
[2013] EWCA Civ 961, Court of Appeal; [2014] UKSC 38, [2015] AC 657, Supreme Court

In the earlier case of *R (Purdy)* v *DPP* [2009] UKHL 45, [2010] 1 AC 345, the House of Lords held that the Director of Public Prosecutions was to publish guidance as to the factors which would be taken into account as part of a decision to prosecute (or not to prosecute) a person charged with assisting the suicide of another, made pursuant to s. 2 of the Suicide Act 1961 (as amended). A range of further challenges to the law on assisted suicide were brought by appellants who wished to end their own lives, but were physically unable to do so alone. One challenge concerned the precision with which the Director of Public Prosecutions had formulated the prosecution guidance he was obliged to publish following the decision in *Purdy*. It was argued that the published policy was an unjustified interference with the appellants right to respect for private and family life, protected by Art. 8 of the European Convention on Human Rights, because it was too uncertain to be 'in accordance with the law' as required by Art. 8(2), in relation to the guidance applicable to healthcare professionals, as opposed to the friends or family of a person who wishes to end their life. A majority of the Court of Appeal upheld this challenge.

LORD DYSON, M.R. AND ELIAS LJ: ...
[138] Despite the wording of the order made in Purdy, we consider that it is not sufficient for the Policy merely to list the factors that the DPP will take into account in deciding whether to consent to a prosecution under section 2(1). A list of factors which contains no clue as to how the discretion to grant or withhold consent will be exercised is not sufficient to meet the requirements of Article 8(2). Lord Hope clearly recognised this at para 41 of his opinion in Purdy. He said that the requirement of foreseeability will be satisfied where the person concerned "is able to foresee ... the *consequences* which a given action may entail" (emphasis added). This formulation was derived from the *Sunday Times* case at para 49. If a list of relevant factors does not enable the person concerned to foresee, to a degree that is reasonable and adequate in the circumstances, the *consequences* of his action, then the Article 8(2) requirement is not satisfied....
[140] In our judgment, the Policy is in certain respects not sufficiently clear to satisfy the requirements of Article 8(2) in relation to healthcare professionals.... In our view, the Policy should give some indication of the weight that the DPP accords to the fact that the helper was acting in his or her capacity as a healthcare professional and the victim was in his or her care. In short, we accept the submission of Mr Havers that the Policy does not provide medical doctors and other professionals with the kind of steer... that it provides to relatives and close friends acting out of compassion...

On appeal to the Supreme Court:

LORD NEUBERGER:

[141] Accordingly, we are here concerned with a very unusual crime which is the subject of a specific policy. However, that does not undermine the force of the constitutional argument that it is one thing for the court to decide that the DPP must publish a policy, and quite another for the court to dictate what should be in that policy. The purpose of the DPP publishing a code or policy is not to enable those who wish to commit a crime to know in advance whether they will get away with it. It is to ensure that, as far as is possible in practice and appropriate in principle, the DPP's policy is publicly available so that everyone knows what it is, and can see whether it is being applied consistently. While many may regret the fact that the DPP's policy is not clearer than it is in relation to assistance given by people who are neither family members nor close friends of the victim, and while many may believe that the policy should be the same for some categories of people who are not family members or close friends as for those who are, it would not be right for a court in effect to dictate to the DPP what her policy should be.

LORD SUMPTON:

[249] Ultimately, the question of legal principle posed by the reasoning of the House of Lords in *Purdy* is whether the uncertainty about the position of professionals allows the arbitrary and inconsistent exercise of executive discretion. In my opinion it does not. Any lack of clarity or precision does not arise from the terms of the Director's published policy. It arises from the discretionary character of the Director's decision, the variety of relevant factors, and the need to vary the weight to be attached to them according to the circumstances of each individual case. All of these are proper and constitutionally necessary features of the system of prosecutorial discretion. The terms of the published policy reflect them. The document sets out the principal relevant factors for and against. It treats the professional character of an assister's involvement as a factor tending in favour of prosecution. It is at least as clear as any sentencing guidelines for this offence could be.

Appeal allowed on this point.

NOTE: The competing approaches of the majority in the Court of Appeal and the Supreme Court in *Nicklinson* shows the difficulty that may arise when courts seek to determine whether there is sufficient certainty for the rule of law to be satisfied. This is especially the case when in relation to rules intended to structure the discretion lawfully to be exercised by public officials. Indeed, John Finnis has argued that the original decision in *Purdy*, the implementation of which was at issue in *Nicklinson*, was itself damaging to the rule of law (J. Finnis, 'Invoking the Principle of Legality against the Rule of Law' [2010] *New Zealand Law Review* 601–16, 613):

> … it undermines the legal certainty that Parliament has repeatedly insisted upon, and the ECHR has approved: the certainty – sought for the sake of protecting the lives of the vulnerable – that any assisting or encouraging of suicide will *be an offence, liable* to prosecution.

Even the more uncontroversial elements of the rule of law may therefore be the subject of significant disagreement when applied in a particular practical context.

B: Laws should be prospective

Phillips v Eyre
(1870) LR 6 QB 1, Exchequer Chamber

The legislature of Jamaica had passed an Indemnity Act following the suppression of a rebellion in the colony. If the Act was valid it would prevent the claimant suing for assault and false imprisonment.

WILLES J: … Retrospective laws are, no doubt, prima facie of questionable policy, and contrary to the general principle that legislation by which the conduct of mankind is to be regulated ought, when introduced for the first time, to deal with future acts, and ought not to change the character of past transactions carried on upon the faith of the then existing law.... Accordingly, the Court will not ascribe retrospective force to new laws affecting rights, unless by express words or necessary implication it appears that such was the intention of the legislature....

In fine, allowing the general inexpediency of retrospective legislation, it cannot be pronounced naturally or necessarily unjust. There may be occasions and circumstances involving the safety of the state, or even the conduct of individual subjects, the justice of which, prospective laws made for ordinary occasions and the usual exigencies of society for want of prevision fails to meet, and in which the execution of the law as it stood at the time may involve practical public inconvenience and wrong, summum jus summa injuria. Whether the circumstances of the particular case are such as to call for special and exceptional remedy is a question which must in each case involve matter of policy and discretion fit for debate and decision in the parliament which would have had jurisdiction to deal with the subject-matter by preliminary legislation, and as to which a court of ordinary municipal law is not commissioned to inquire or adjudicate.

NOTE: See also *R* v *Secretary of State for the Home Department, ex parte Pierson* [1998] AC 539, later in this chapter in Section 5 at pp. 128–30.

■ QUESTIONS

1. Can the doctrine of the rule of law prevent Parliament enacting retrospective laws? (See War Damage Act 1965, enacted pursuant to *Burmah Oil Co* v *Lord Advocate* [1965] AC 75, see Chapter 2, Section 1B at p. 51.)

2. Is Lord Reid's confidence misplaced when he states in *Waddington* v *Miah* [1974] 2 All ER 377, at p. 379, that 'it is hardly credible that any government department would promote or that Parliament would pass retrospective criminal legislation'?

   See s. 1 of the War Crimes Act 1991, which provides:

   1. Jurisdiction over certain war crimes

      (1) Subject to the provisions of this section, proceedings for murder, manslaughter or culpable homicide may be brought against a person in the United Kingdom irrespective of his nationality at the time of the alleged offence if that offence—

         (a) was committed during the period beginning with 1st September 1939 and ending with 5th June 1945 in a place which at the time was part of Germany or under German occupation; and

         (b) constituted a violation of the laws and customs of war.

      (2) No proceedings shall by virtue of this section be brought against any person unless he was on 8th March 1990, or has subsequently become, a British citizen or resident in the United Kingdom, the Isle of Man or any of the Channel Islands.

   Retrospective penal legislation contravenes Art. 7 of the ECHR ('no punishment without law'). Can such retrospective legislation be justified by the exceptional circumstances to which it applies? What if retrospective legislation is enacted to protect the government from financial liabilities, as in the following case?

R (Reilly) v *Secretary of State for Work and Pensions*
[2013] UKSC 38, Supreme Court

The Secretary of State for Work and Pensions appealed against a decision of the Court of Appeal that the Jobseeker's Allowance (Employment, Skills and Enterprise Scheme) Regulations 2011 had not been lawfully enacted pursuant to s.17A of the Jobseekers Act 1995. In particular, the 2011 Regulations were quashed because they failed to provide a 'prescribed description', as required by s.17A of the 1995 Act, of the 'work for benefit' scheme(s) they purported to introduce. Following the decision of the Court of Appeal, the Government introduced legislation in Parliament to validate retrospectively the legality of the 2011 Regulations. The Jobseekers (Back to Work Schemes) Act 2013 was subsequently enacted, ensuring in part that the Government would not be liable to re-pay jobseeker's allowance that had been withheld from claimants as a sanction for failing to participate in one of the 'work for benefit' schemes held to have been unlawful in the Court of Appeal.

LORD NEUBERGER AND LORD TOULSON (WITH WHOM LORD MANCE, LORD CLARKE AND LORD SUMPTION AGREED): ... 36. On 26 March 2013 (the same day as the Secretary of State sought permission to appeal the decision of the Court of Appeal), the 2013 Act came into force after having been fast-tracked through Parliament. The 2013 Act was plainly intended to "undo" the decision of the Court of Appeal, in that, pursuant to subsections (2), (3), (4)-(8), and (10)-(12) of section 1, it retrospectively validates (i) the 2011 Regulations, (ii) the programmes listed in regulation 3(2) of the 2013 Regulations, (iii) notices issued under regulation 4 of the 2011 Regulations, and (iv) the benefit sanctions imposed under those regulations in relation to the schemes. Subsection (14) of section 1 provides that "the 2011 Regulations are to be treated as having been revoked by the 2013 Regulations on the coming into force of the 2013 Regulations".

...

38. The substantive issues before us are the same as those before Foskett J and the Court of Appeal; they are set out in para 27 above, and the Court of Appeal's conclusion on each issue is as summarised in para 31 above. It is convenient to take each of the four points in turn.

39. However, before doing so, it is necessary to address the effect of the 2013 Regulations and the 2013 Act on this appeal and cross-appeal. On behalf of Miss Reilly and Mr Wilson, Ms Lieven QC submits that we should not consider the Secretary of State's appeal on issue (a), as that issue is now academic, because, even if the Court of Appeal was right to hold that, prior to the 2013 Act coming into force, the 2011 Regulations were ultra vires, Parliament has now validated those regulations through the 2013 Act.

40. The submission has obvious force as a matter of principle. This court, like other courts, is normally concerned with stating the law as it is, not as it was. Further, it is rather unattractive for the executive to be taking up court time and public money to establish that a regulation is valid, when it has already taken up Parliamentary time to enact legislation which retrospectively validates the regulation. That very point was made on behalf of Miss Reilly and Mr Wilson in order to oppose the Secretary of State's application for permission to appeal to this court, and, at least viewed from our present perspective, we consider that there was considerable force in the point.

41. However, permission to appeal has been given to the Secretary of State, the issue concerned is not the only point at stake in the appeal, the issue may be of some significance to the drafting of regulations generally, and the retrospectively validating legislation is under attack. Bearing in mind those factors, we are of the view that issue (a) should be considered, although the precise formulation of any order that is made will have to be carefully considered, bearing in mind the effect of the 2013 Act.

...

47. ... it appears clear to us that regulation 2 does not satisfy the requirements of section 17A(1). The courts have no more important function than to ensure that the executive complies with the requirements of Parliament as expressed in a statute. Further, particularly where the statute concerned envisages regulations which will have a significant impact on the lives and livelihoods of many people, the importance of legal certainty and the impermissibility of sub-delegation are of crucial importance. The observations of Scott LJ in *Blackpool Corporation v Locker* [1948] 1 KB 349, 362 are in point: "John Citizen" should not be "in complete ignorance of what rights over him and his property have been secretly conferred by the minister", as otherwise "[f]or practical purposes, the rule of law ... breaks down because the aggrieved subject's legal remedy is gravely impaired".

92. Accordingly, were it not for the 2013 Act and the 2013 Regulations, we would have affirmed the order of the Court of Appeal.

93. In the light of the 2013 Act and the 2013 Regulations, however, a more subtly expressed form of order will be required, and we would invite counsel to try and agree the appropriate wording.

NOTE: The retrospective 2013 Act was subsequently challenged on the grounds that it was incompatible with the right to a fair trial, protected by Art. 6 ECHR. In the Administrative Court, Lang J held in *Reilly (No. 2)* that the 2013 Act was an unjustified interference with the rights of those claimants who had already appealed against the (then unlawful) imposition of sanctions, in so far as the Act had determined unilaterally the outcome of an ongoing judicial process. A declaration of incompatibility in relation to the Act—as applicable to the small number of JSA claimants who had already instigated an appeal against the sanctions prior to the Act of 2013, and members of that group only (approximately 1 per cent of the total number of sanctioned jobseekers)—was granted; [2014] EWHC 2182 (Admin). This decision was upheld in the Court of Appeal, where it was also accepted that the approach of Lang J had been in part constitutionally controversial, in so far as 'in places in her judgment the judge does appear to have transgressed' the rule in art. 9 of the Bill of Rights that 'proceedings in Parliament ought not to be impeached or questioned in any court', when criticizing ministerial statements in the legislature as to the compatibility of the 2013 Act with the ECHR; [2016] EWCA Civ 413, [108]. The Government is considering its response to the declaration of incompatibility, which does not affect the legal validity or force of the 2013 Act (*Responding to Human Rights Judgments*, Cm 9360, November 2016, p. 60).

■ QUESTIONS

1. It may be argued that the logic of the Supreme Court's decision is that the failure of the 2011 Regulations to describe the 'work for benefit' schemes led to a lack of clarity, which violated the rule of law. If this is so, has the Government (and the opposition, who accepted that the 2013 Act could be 'fast-tracked' through Parliament) compounded one violation of the rule of law with another, in obtaining retrospective legislation to validate its earlier breach? Does this show the practical limits of the rule of law as a principle which conditions the exercise of public power?

2. How could the Government respond to the declaration of incompatibility issued in relation to the retrospective legislation in *Reilly (No. 2)*? If the rule of law requires the repayment of jobseeker's allowance only to the 1 per cent of claimants who had appealed their sanction at the time the 2013 Act was enacted—an estimated 2,500 out of 250,000 people—does this suggest the idea of the rule of law is not intrinsically connected with the idea of equality?

C: The independence of the judiciary must be guaranteed

The maintenance of the independence of the judiciary is essential if the rule of law is to be respected. In his presidential address to the Holdsworth Club in 1950, Lord Justice Denning, as he then was, stated:

No member of the Government, no Member of Parliament and no official of any government department has any right whatever to direct or influence or to interfere with the decisions of any of the judges. It is the sure knowledge of this that gives the people their confidence in judges.... The critical test which they must pass if they are to receive the confidence of the people is that they must be independent of the executive.

NOTE: This topic is covered in more detail in Chapter 4 which considers the provisions of the Constitutional Reform Act 2005 which declared a continued guarantee of judicial independence (s. 3); has changed the arrangements for the appointment and discipline of the judiciary; and established, after 2009, a new Supreme Court of the United Kingdom, separating the final court of appeal and its judges from the legislature.

SECTION 5: GOVERNMENT ACCORDING TO THE LAW

Government according to the law means that the Executive or any civil authority or government official cannot exercise public power unless such exercise of it is authorized by some specific rule of law.

Entick v Carrington
(1765) 19 St Tr 1030, Court of Common Pleas

Two King's messengers, under the authority of a warrant issued by the Secretary of State, broke and entered Entick's house and took away his papers. Entick was alleged to be the author of seditious writings. When the messengers were sued by Entick for trespass to his house and goods, it was argued that the warrant was legal, as the power to issue such warrants was essential to government as 'the only means of quieting clamours and sedition'.

LORD CAMDEN CJ: ... This power, so claimed by the Secretary of State, is not supported by one single citation from any law book extant. It is claimed by no other magistrate in this kingdom but himself....

Before I state the question, it will be necessary to describe the power claimed by this warrant in its full extent. If honestly exerted, it is a power to seize that man's papers, who is charged upon oath to be the author or publisher of a seditious libel; if oppressively, it acts against every man, who is so described in the warrant, though he be innocent....

Such is the power, and therefore one should naturally expect that the law to warrant it should be clear in proportion as the power is exorbitant.

If it is law, it will be found in our books. If it is not to be found there, it is not law.

The great end, for which men entered into society, was to secure their property. That right is preserved sacred and incommunicable in all instances, where it has not been taken away or abridged by some public law for the good of the whole. The cases where this right of property is set aside by positive law, are various. Distresses, executions, forfeitures, taxes, etc. are all of this description; wherein every man by common consent gives up that right, for the sake of justice and the general good.

By the laws of England, every invasion of private property, be it ever so minute, is a trespass. No man can set his foot upon my ground without my licence, but he is liable to an action, though the damage be nothing.... If he admits the fact, he is bound to shew by way of justification, that some positive law has empowered or excused him. The justification is submitted to the judges, who are to look into the books; and see if such a justification can be maintained by the text of the statute law, or by the principles of common law. If no such excuse can be found or produced, the silence of the books is an authority against the defendant, and the plaintiff must have judgment.

According to this reasoning, it is now incumbent upon the defendants to shew the law, by which this seizure is warranted. If that cannot be done, it is a trespass.

Papers are the owner's goods and chattels: they are his dearest property; and are so far from enduring a seizure that they will hardly bear an inspection; and though the eye cannot by the laws of England be guilty of a trespass, yet where private papers are removed and carried away, the secret nature of those goods will be an aggravation of the trespass, and demand more considerable damages in that respect. Where is the written law that gives any magistrate such a power? I can safely answer, there is none, and therefore it is too much for us without such authority to pronounce a practice legal, which would be subversive of all the comforts of society....

I come now to the practice since the Revolution, which has been strongly urged, with this emphatical addition, that an usage tolerated from the area of liberty, and continued downwards to this time through the best ages of the constitution, must necessarily have a legal commencement. Now, though that pretence can have no place in the question made by this plea, because no such practice is there alleged; yet I will permit the defendant for the present to borrow a fact from the special verdict, for the sake of giving it an answer.

If the practice began then, it began too late to be law now. If it was more ancient, the Revolution is not to answer for it; and I could have wished, that upon this occasion the Revolution had not been considered as the only basis of our liberty. . . .

With respect to the practice itself, if it goes no higher, every lawyer will tell you, it is much too modern to be evidence of the common law. . . .

This is the first instance I have met with, where the ancient immemorable law of the land, in a public matter, was attempted to be proved by the practice of a private office. The names and rights of public magistrates, their power and forms of proceeding as they are settled by law, have been long since written, and are to be found in books and records. Private customs indeed are still to be sought from private tradition. But who ever conceived a notion, that any part of the public law could be buried in the obscure practice of a particular person?

To search, seize, and carry away all the papers of the subject upon the first warrant: that such a right should have existed from the time whereof the memory of man runneth not to the contrary, and never yet have found a place in any book of law; is incredible. But if so strange a thing could be supposed, I do not see, how we could declare the law upon such evidence. . . .

I have now taken notice of everything that has been urged upon the present point; and upon the whole we are all of opinion, that the warrant to seize and carry away the party's papers in the case of a seditious libel, is illegal and void.

■ QUESTION

Lord Camden CJ stated that 'by the laws of England every invasion of private property, be it ever so minute, is a trespass'. Is this still true? (See, e.g. wide powers of search established in s. 8 of the Police and Criminal Evidence Act 1984; s. 26(1) of the Theft Act 1968; s. 6(1) of the Criminal Damage Act 1971; ss 7 and 24 of the Forgery and Counterfeiting Act 1981; s. 46 of the Firearms Act 1968; s. 23(3) of the Misuse of Drugs Act 1971; s. 3 of the Obscene Publications Act 1959; s. 47B–R of the Proceeds of Crime Act 2002; s. 2(4) of the Criminal Justice Act 1987; and Sch. 5 to the Terrorism Act 2000.)

NOTE: Views on the legality of official action, however, may differ. Lord Camden revealed an enthusiasm for liberty—and in particular, the liberty to own private property—in a sweeping declaration when he stated:

> The great end for which men entered into society, was to secure their property. That right is preserved sacred and incommunicable in all instances, where it has not been taken away or abridged by some public law for the good of the whole.

In the extracts from the case which follows, echoes of Lord Camden's approach may be discerned in the judgment of Lord Denning in the Court of Appeal; whereas an alternative approach was adopted in the House of Lords, with related consequences for the rights of the citizen, the power of government, and our understanding of the rule of law.

R v Inland Revenue Commissioners, ex parte Rossminster Ltd
[1980] AC 952, Court of Appeal

Section 20C of the Taxes Management Act 1970, as amended, provided for the issuing of a warrant authorizing the seizure and removal of 'any things whatsoever', found on the relevant premises, which there is 'reasonable cause to believe may be required as evidence' with respect to 'an offence involving any form of fraud in connection with, or in relation to, tax'. Suspecting that some unspecified tax fraud had been committed by Rossminster Ltd, officers of the Inland Revenue obtained warrants to search Rossminster's premises. The officers seized anything which they believed might be required as evidence of a tax fraud, but they did not inform Rossminster Ltd of the offences suspected or of the persons suspected of having committed them. The warrants simply followed the wording in s. 20C without specifying what particular offences were suspected. The Court of Appeal, reversing the decision of the Divisional Court, granted, *inter alia*, an order of certiorari to quash the warrants.

LORD DENNING: … Beyond all doubt this search and seizure was unlawful unless it was authorised by Parliament…. The trouble is that the legislation is drawn so widely that in some hands it might be an instrument of oppression. It may be said that 'honest people need not fear: that it will never be used against them: that tax inspectors can be trusted, only to use it in the case of the big, bad frauds.' This is an attractive argument, but I would reject it. Once great power is granted, there is a danger of it being abused. Rather than risk such abuse, it is, as I see it, the duty of the courts so to construe the statute as to see that it encroaches as little as possible upon the liberties of the people of England….

The warrant is challenged on the ground that it does not specify any particular offence…. The justification is: 'We do not wish to tell more to those we suspect because we do not want them to know too much about what we intend to do. Otherwise they will be on their guard.'

Is this a just excuse? The words 'an offence involving any form of fraud in connection with, or in relation to, tax' are very wide words. We were taken by Mr Davenport through a number of offences which might be comprised in them. There is no specific section in the Act itself. But there are a number of other offences which involve fraud…. It seems to me that these words 'fraud … in relation to … tax' are so vague and so general that it must be exceedingly difficult for the officers of the Inland Revenue themselves to know what papers they can take or what they cannot take…. The vice of a general warrant of this kind—which does not specify any particular offence—is two-fold. It gives no help to the officers when they have to exercise it. It means also that they can roam wide and large, seizing and taking pretty well all a man's documents and papers….

So here. When the officers of the Inland Revenue come armed with a warrant to search a man's home or his office, it seems to me that he is entitled to say: 'Of what offence do you suspect me? You are claiming to enter my house and to seize my papers.' And when they look at the papers and seize them, he should be able to say: 'Why are you seizing these papers? Of what offence do you suspect me? What have these to do with your case?' Unless he knows the particular offence charged, he cannot take steps to secure himself or his property. So it seems to me, as a matter of construction of the statute and therefore of the warrant—in pursuance of our traditional role to protect the liberty of the individual—it is our duty to say that the warrant must particularise the specific offence which is charged as being fraud on the revenue.

If this be right, it follows necessarily that this warrant is bad. It should have specified the particular offence of which the man is suspected. On this ground I would hold that certiorari should go to quash the warrant.

House of Lords

LORD WILBERFORCE: … The integrity and privacy of a man's home, and of his place of business, an important human right has, since the second world war, been eroded by a number of statutes passed by Parliament in the belief, presumably, that his right of privacy ought in some cases to be over-ridden by the interest which the public has in preventing evasions of the law. Some of these powers of search are reflections of dirigisme and of heavy taxation, others of changes in mores…. A formidable number of officials now have powers to enter people's premises, and to take property away, and these powers are frequently exercised, sometimes on a large scale. Many people, as well as the respondents, think that this process has gone too far; that is an issue to be debated in Parliament and in the press.

The courts have the duty to supervise, I would say critically, even jealously, the legality of any purported exercise of these powers. They are the guardians of the citizens' right to privacy. But they must do this in the context of the times, i.e. of increasing Parliamentary intervention, and of the modern power of judicial review. In my respectful opinion appeals to 18th century precedents of arbitrary action by Secretaries of State and references to general warrants do nothing to throw light on the issue. Furthermore, while the courts may look critically at legislation which impairs the rights of citizens and should resolve any doubt in interpretation in their favour, it is no part of their duty, or power, to restrict or impede the working of legislation, even of unpopular legislation; to do so would be to weaken rather than to advance the democratic process....

The Court of Appeal took the view that the warrants were invalid because they did not sufficiently particularise the alleged offence(s). The court did not make clear exactly what particulars should have been given—and indeed I think that this cannot be done. The warrant followed the wording of the statute 'fraud in connection with or in relation to tax': a portmanteau description which covers a number of common law (cheating) and statutory offences (under the Theft Act 1968 et al.). To require specification at this investigatory stage would be impracticable given the complexity of 'tax frauds' and the different persons who may be involved (companies, officers of companies, accountants, tax consultants, taxpayers, wives of taxpayers etc.). Moreover, particularisation, if required, would no doubt take the form of a listing of one offence and/or another or others and so would be of little help to those concerned. Finally, there would clearly be power, on principles well accepted in the common law, after entry had been made in connection with one particular offence, to seize material bearing upon other offences within the portmanteau. So, particularisation, even if practicable, would not help the occupier.

I am unable, therefore, to escape the conclusion, that adherence to the statutory formula is sufficient.

LORD SCARMAN: ... My Lords, I agree that these appeals should be allowed and add some observations only because of the importance of the issues raised, and because I share the anxieties felt by the Court of Appeal. If power exists for officers of the Board of Inland Revenue to enter premises, if necessary by force, at any time of the day or night and then seize and remove any things whatsoever found there which they have reasonable cause to believe may be required as evidence for the purposes of proceedings in respect of any offence or offences involving any form of fraud in connection with, or in relation to, tax, it is the duty of the courts to see that it is not abused: for it is a breath-taking inroad upon the individual's right of privacy and right of property. Important as is the public interest in the detection and punishment of tax frauds, it is not to be compared with the public interest in the right of men and women to be secure in the privacy of their homes, their offices, and their papers. Yet if the law is that no particulars of the offence or offences suspected, other than that they are offences of tax fraud, need be given, how can the householder, or occupier of premises, hope to obtain an effective judicial review of the entry, search and seizure at the time of the events or shortly thereafter? And telling the victim that long after the event he may go to law and recover damages if he can prove the revenue acted unlawfully is cold comfort—even if he can afford it.

It is therefore with regret that I have to accept that, if the requirements of section 20C of the Taxes Management Act 1970, a section which entered the law as an amendment introduced by section 57 of the Finance Act 1976, are met, the power exists to enter, and search premises, and seize and remove things there found and that the prospect of an immediate judicial review of the exercise of the power is dim. Nevertheless, what Lord Camden CJ said in *Entick* v *Carrington* (1765) 19 State Tr 1029, 1066, remains good law today:

'No man can set his foot upon my ground without my licence, but he is liable to an action, though the damage be nothing ... If he admits the fact, he is bound to show by way of justification, that some positive law has empowered or excused him.'

The positive law relied on in this case is the statute. If the requirements of the statute have been met, there is justification: but, if they have not, there is none ...

Appeals allowed.

NOTE: But where courts are asked to determine the legality of the exercise of a discretionary power conferred by a statute they have shown a readiness to impose limits derived from common law principles as the following case discloses. (See further, *R* v *Lord Chancellor, ex parte Witham* [1998] QB 575; *Chesterfield Properties plc* v *Secretary of State for the Environment* [1998] JPL 568; *R* v *Lord Saville, ex parte A* [1999] 4 All ER 860, in Chapter 9, Section 2 at pp. 398–9.)

R v Secretary of State for the Home Department, ex parte Pierson

[1998] AC 539, House of Lords

In 1985, P was convicted of the murder of his parents and received two mandatory life sentences to be served concurrently. Under the system then in operation in 1988 (Criminal Justice Act 1961, s. 61) the Home Secretary, on the basis
that P had committed a double premeditated murder, fixed the penal element
of the sentence (or 'tariff' which represents the minimum period to be served
to satisfy the requirements of retribution and deterrence, before any potential
release on licence) at 20 years. The trial judge and Lord Chief Justice had recommended a tariff of 15 years. In accordance with the then practice the judicial
recommendations on tariff, and reasons for the Home Secretary's departure
from them, were not communicated to P, neither was he asked to make representations thereon.

In June 1993 the House of Lords ruled in *R v Secretary of State for the Home
Department, ex parte Doody and Others* [1994] 1 AC 531 (P being one of the 'others') that before fixing the 'tariff' the Home Secretary was required to disclose
to a prisoner the recommendations of the judiciary and provide an opportunity for the prisoner to make written representations. In July 1993 the then
Home Secretary announced that the tariff period would be reviewed before
any mandatory life sentence prisoner would be considered for release, and in
exceptional cases it might be increased. In August 1993, P was informed of the
judicial recommendations in his case and the Home Secretary's reason for recommending 20 years, namely that 15 years would have been appropriate for a
single premeditated murder but that this was a double murder. In response P's
solicitors indicated that the murders were part of a single incident and were
unpremeditated. The Home Secretary responded in May 1994, accepting that
the murders were part of a single incident and unpremeditated, but indicating
that he considered 20 years the appropriate tariff. P applied by way of judicial
review for an order to quash the Home Secretary's decision on the grounds that
it was irrational, representing, in effect, an increase in the period, because it
had now been accepted that the aggravating factors justifying an increase from
a 15-year to 20-year tariff did not exist.

The House of Lords (by a majority of three to two) quashed the Home Secretary's
decision.

LORD STEYN: ... It is a general principle of the common law that a lawful sentence pronounced by a
judge may not retrospectively be increased. In 1971 that principle was put on a statutory basis.... The
general principle of our law is therefore that a convicted criminal is entitled to know where he stands so
far as his punishment is concerned. He is entitled to legal certainty about his punishment. His rights will
be enforced by the courts. Under English law a convicted prisoner, in spite of his imprisonment, retains
all civil rights which are not taken away expressly or by necessary implication: *Raymond v Honey* [1983]
1 AC 1, 10H. The question must now be considered whether the Home Secretary, in making a decision on
punishment, is free from the normal constraint applicable to a sentencing power. It is at this stage of the
examination of the problem that it becomes necessary to consider where in the structure of public law
it fits in. Parliament has not expressly authorised the Home Secretary to increase tariffs retrospectively. If
Parliament had done so that would have been the end of the matter. Instead Parliament has by section
35(2) of the Act of 1991 entrusted the power to take decisions about the release of mandatory life sentence prisoners to the Home Secretary. The statutory power is wide enough to authorise the fixing of a

tariff. But it does not follow that it is wide enough to permit a power retrospectively to increase the level of punishment.

The wording of section 35(2) of the Act of 1991 is wide and general. It provides that 'the Secretary of State may … release on licence a life prisoner who is not a discretionary life prisoner.' There is no ambiguity in the statutory language. The presumption that in the event of ambiguity legislation is presumed not to invade common law rights is inapplicable. A broader principle applies. Parliament does not legislate in a vacuum. Parliament legislates for a European liberal democracy founded on the principles and traditions of the common law. And the courts may approach legislation on this initial assumption. But this assumption only has prima facie force. It can be displaced by a clear and specific provision to the contrary.…

In his *Law of the Constitution*, 10th ed. (1959), Dicey explained the context in which Parliament legislates, at p. 414:

> 'By every path we come round to the same conclusion, that Parliamentary sovereignty has favoured the rule of law, and that the supremacy of the law of the land both calls forth the exertion of Parliamentary sovereignty, and leads to its being exercised in a spirit of legality.'

…

The operation of the principle of legality can further be illustrated by reference to the decision of the House of Lords in *Reg.* v *Secretary of State for the Home Department, Ex parte Doody* [1994] 1 AC 531.

In that case the House of Lords held that the common law principles of procedural fairness required disclosure to a prisoner of the advice to the Home Secretary of the trial judge and of the Lord Chief Justice in order to enable the prisoner to make effective representations before the Home Secretary fixed the tariff. The premise was that Parliament must be presumed to have intended that the Home Secretary would act in conformity with the common law principle of procedural fairness. And our public law is, of course, replete with other instances of the common law so supplementing statutes on the basis of the principle of legality.…

Turning back to the circumstances of the present case, it was easy to conclude that the legislation authorises the policy of fixing a tariff. The wide statutory discretion of the Home Secretary justified that conclusion. But a general power to increase tariffs lawfully fixed is qualitatively in a different category. It contemplates a power unheard of in our criminal justice system until the 1993 policy statement of the Home Secretary (Mr Michael Howard) (Hansard (HC Debates), 27 July 1993, cols. 861–864: written answer). Such a power is not essential to the efficient working of the system: without a power to increase tariffs the system worked satisfactorily between 1983 and 1993. But I do not rest my judgment on this point. The critical factor is that a general power to increase tariffs duly fixed is in disharmony with the deep rooted principle of not retrospectively increasing lawfully pronounced sentences. In the absence of contrary indications it must be presumed that Parliament entrusted the wide power to make decisions on the release of mandatory life sentence prisoners on the supposition that the Home Secretary would not act contrary to such a fundamental principle of our law. There are no contrary indications. Certainly, there is not a shred of evidence that Parliament would have been prepared to vest a general power in the Home Secretary to increase retrospectively tariffs duly fixed. The evidence is to the contrary. When Parliament enacted section 35(2) of the Act of 1991—the foundation of the Home Secretary's present power—Parliament knew that since 1983 successive Home Secretaries had adopted a policy of fixing in each case a tariff period, following which risk is considered. Parliament also knew that it was the practice that a tariff, once fixed, would not be increased. That was clear from the assurance in the 1983 policy statement (Mr Leon Brittan (Hansard (HC Debates), 30 November 1983, cols. 505–507: written answer) that 'except where a prisoner has committed an offence for which he has received a further custodial sentence, the formal review date will not be put back.' What Parliament did not know in 1991 was that in 1993 a new Home Secretary would assert a general power to increase the punishment of prisoners convicted of murder whenever he considered it right to do so. It would be wrong to assume that Parliament would have been prepared to give to the Home Secretary such an unprecedented power, alien to the principles of our law.…

The correct analysis of this case is in terms of the rule of law. The rule of law in its wider sense has procedural and substantive effect.... Unless there is the clearest provision to the contrary, Parliament must be presumed not to legislate contrary to the rule of law. And the rule of law enforces minimum standards of fairness, both substantive and procedural. I therefore approach the problem in the present case on this basis.

It is true that the principle of legality only has prima facie force. But in enacting section 35(2) of the Act of 1991, with its very wide power to release prisoners, Parliament left untouched the fundamental principle that a sentence lawfully passed should not retrospectively be increased. Parliament must therefore be presumed to have enacted legislation wide enough to enable the Home Secretary to make decisions on punishment on the basis that he would observe the normal constraint governing that function. Instead the Home Secretary has asserted a general power to increase tariffs duly fixed. Parliament did not confer such a power on the Home Secretary.

It follows that the Home Secretary did not have the power to increase a tariff lawfully fixed....

It was agreed before your Lordships' House that the Home Secretary's decision letter of 6 May 1994 did communicate a decision to Mr Pierson to increase the tariff in his case. That decision was in my judgment unlawful and ought to be quashed. My conclusion is based on the proposition that the Home Secretary has no general power to increase a tariff fixed and communicated.

NOTES

1. The 'principle of legality' identified in *ex parte Pierson* requires Parliament to legislate in express terms if it intends to give the government power to violate the rule of law, and the 'minimum standards' the courts understand this principle to protect. This is to ensure that there can be adequate political awareness and scrutiny of what is being done; see further *R v Secretary of State for the Home Department, ex parte Simms* [2000] 2 AC 115 (discussed later in this section at p. 133). Yet it could also be argued that there are circumstances in which utilitarian concerns of dealing with, for example, terrorist threats, might justify increasing the scope of action afforded to the State and its agents in taking protective action. This has been particularly acute in the UK in countering terrorism, first in relation to Ireland and the IRA and currently Al-Qaeda and other Islamist extremists.

2. In Northern Ireland in 1971, powers granted under the Civil Authorities (Special Powers) Act (NI) 1922 were exercised by the Northern Ireland Government to intern persons suspected of having acted or being about to act in a manner prejudicial to the preservation of peace or the maintenance of order. Some of those interned were interrogated by the security forces. The Crompton Report (Cmnd 4823, 1971) detailed the interrogation procedures as including keeping the detainees' heads covered with hoods; subjecting them to continuous monotonous noise; deprivation of sleep; deprivation of food and water, apart from meagre rations of bread and water at six-hourly intervals; and making the detainees stand facing a wall with legs apart and hands raised. Three Privy Councillors (Lord Parker of Waddington, a former Lord Chief Justice, J. A. Carpenter, a former Cabinet Minister, and Lord Gardiner, a former Lord Chancellor) were given the task of examining these procedures. They failed to agree and produced two conflicting reports. The majority, in 'Report of the Committee of Privy Councillors Appointed to Consider Authorised Procedures or the Interrogation of Persons Suspected of Terrorism' (Cmnd 4901, 1972), recommended that the interrogation techniques were acceptable in the light of the prevailing conditions and subject to safeguards which would limit the number of incidences of use and the degree to which they can be applied. The authority of a UK Government minister would be required to use them, and a doctor with psychiatric training should be present to observe and warn if the interrogation was being pressed too far, and there should be a procedure for the investigation of complaints. Lord Gardiner in his minority report found that the techniques were unlawful, morally repugnant, and contrary to international developments in the protection of human rights. The Government eventually accepted Lord Gardiner's view, and the interrogation techniques were discontinued. The issue of interrogation of internees was taken in an inter-State application to the European Court of Human Rights. In *Ireland v United Kingdom* (1978) 2 EHRR 25, it was alleged that the techniques breached Art. 3 of the ECHR. The Court held that they amounted to inhuman and degrading treatment contrary to Art. 3 but did not constitute torture.

3. More recently the House of Lords has ruled on the issue of whether evidence is admissible if it was produced by third parties not under the control of the British Government using torture (*A v Secretary of State for the Home Department (No. 2)* [2005] UKHL 71, [2006] 2 AC 221). Their Lordships ruled that such evidence was inadmissible but differed on the test to be used to decide admissibility where it was argued that torture had been used. The majority—Lords Hope, Carswell, Rodger, and Brown of Eaton-Under-Heywood—followed the approach in the United Nations Convention Against Torture and Other Cruel Inhuman or Degrading Treatment or Punishment (1987), Art. 15. The test for admissibility is, according to Lord Rodger at [121]:

> Is it *established*, by means of such diligent inquiries into the sources that it is practicable to carry out and on a balance of probabilities, that the information relied on by the Secretary of State *was* obtained under torture?

For the minority of Lords—Bingham, Nicholls, and Hoffmann—the more demanding test expressed by Lord Bingham at [56] is that if after considering the particular facts and circumstances it:

> ... is unable to conclude that there is not a real risk that the evidence has been obtained by torture, it should refuse to admit the evidence. Otherwise it should admit it.

4. As will be seen in Chapter 9, Section 3A at pp. 409–24, the United Kingdom has, through the Human Rights Act 1998, incorporated into domestic law many of the rights in the ECHR which includes, in Art. 3, a prohibition on torture, inhuman, and degrading treatment or punishment. There can be overlap between the statutory protection of rights under the Human Rights Act 1998, and the protection of fundamental rights offered by the common law principle of legality. In the context of counter-terrorism, this can be seen in the case of *A v Treasury* that follows.

■ QUESTION

Do the decisions in *Entick v Carrington*, *Rossminster v IRC*, and *ex parte Pierson* show a shift in judicial thinking and practice, away from a formal approach to the rule of law, and towards a more substantive understanding of the principle?

A v Treasury

[2010] UKSC 2, [2010] 2 AC 534, Supreme Court

The United Nations Act 1946 provided, by s. 1, for the making of Orders in Council to implement decisions of the United Nations Security Council. Acting under this power, Orders in Council were made authorizing the freezing of the financial assets of people designated as suspected of terrorism, or of facilitating terrorism. The applicants were subject to such freezing orders made under the Terrorism (United Nations Measures) Order 2006 and the Al-Qaida and Taliban (United Nations Measures) Order 2006. It was held that the Human Rights Act 1998 could not found a claim for the applicants, due to the decision of the House of Lords in *R (Al-Jedda) v Secretary of State for Defence* [2008] 1 AC 332, which had accepted that UN Charter obligations would prevail over obligations contained in another international treaty, such as the ECHR (a conclusion later rejected by the European Court of Human Rights, Application No. 27021/08). The applicants argued that the Orders were *ultra vires* at common law, in so far as they could not lawfully be enacted using the broad power granted by s. 1 of the United Nations Act 1946.

LORD HOPE: ... 44. [Section 1 of the UN Act 1946] leaves the question whether any given measure is "necessary" or "expedient" to the judgment of the executive without subjecting it, or any of the terms and conditions which apply to it, to the scrutiny of Parliament. In the context of what was envisaged when the Bill was debated in 1946, which was the use of non-military, diplomatic and economic sanctions as a means of deterring aggression between states, the surrender of power to the executive to ensure the taking of immediate and effective action in the international sphere is unsurprising use of the power as a means of imposing restraints or the taking of coercive measures targeted against individuals in domestic law is an entirely different matter. A distinction must be drawn in this respect between provisions made "for the apprehension, trial and punishment of persons offending against the Order" (see the concluding words of section 1(1)) and those against whom the Order is primarily directed. So long as the primary purpose of the Order is within the powers conferred by the section, ancillary measures which are carefully designed to ensure their efficacy will be also. The crucial question is whether the section confers power on the executive, without any Parliamentary scrutiny, to give effect in this country to decisions of the Security Council which are targeted against individuals.

45. It cannot be suggested, in view of the word "any", that the power is available only for use where the Security Council has called for non-military, diplomatic and economic sanctions to deter aggression between states. But the phrase "necessary or expedient for enabling those measures to be effectively applied" does require further examination. The closer those measures come to affecting what, in *R v Secretary of State for the Home Department, Ex p Simms* [2000] 2 AC 115, 131, Lord Hoffmann described as the basic rights of the individual, the more exacting this scrutiny must become. If the rule of law is to mean anything, decisions as to what is necessary or expedient in this context cannot be left to the uncontrolled judgment of the executive. In *Chester v Bateson* [1920] 1 KB 829, 837, Avory J referred to Lord Shaw of Dunfermline's warning in *R v Halliday* [1917] AC 260, 287 against the risk of arbitrary government if the judiciary were to approach actions of government in excess of its mandate in a spirit of compliance rather than that of independent scrutiny. The undoubted fact that section 1 of the 1946 Act was designed to enable the United Kingdom to fulfil its obligations under the Charter to implement Security Council resolutions does not diminish this essential principle. As Lord Brown of Eaton-under-Heywood JSC says in para 194, the full honouring of these obligations is an imperative. But these resolutions are the product of a body of which the executive is a member as the United Kingdom's representative. Conferring an unlimited discretion on the executive as to how those resolutions, which it has a hand in making, are to be implemented seems to me to be wholly unacceptable. It conflicts with the basic rules that lie at the heart of our democracy.

...

47. I would approach the language of section 1 of the 1946 Act, therefore, on the basis that Parliament did not surrender its legislative powers to the executive any more than must necessarily follow from the words used by it. The words "necessary" and "expedient" both call for the exercise of judgment. But this does not mean that its exercise is unlimited. The wording of the Order must be tested precisely against the words used by the Security Council's resolution and in the light of the obligation to give effect to it that article 25 lays down. A provision in the Order which affects the basic rights of the individual but was unavoidable if effect was to be given to the resolution according to its terms may be taken to have been authorised because it was "necessary". A provision may be included which is "expedient" but not "necessary". This enables provisions to be included in the Order which differ from those used by the resolution or are unavoidably required by it. But it does not permit interference with the basic rights of the individual any more that is necessary and unavoidable to give effect to the SCR and is consistent with the principle of legality.

...

75. .... Two fundamental rights were in issue in G's case, and as they were to be found in domestic law his right to invoke them was not affected by article 103 of the UN Charter. One was the right to peaceful enjoyment of his property, which could only be interfered with by clear legislative words: *Entick v Carrington* (1765) 19 State Tr 1029, 1066, per Lord Camden CJ. The other was his right of unimpeded access to a court: *R (Anufrijeva) v Secretary of State for the Home Department* [2004] 1 AC 604, para 26, per Lord Steyn. As it was put by Viscount Simonds in *Pyx Granite Co Ltd v Ministry of Housing and Local Government* [1960] AC 260, 286, the subject's right of access to Her Majesty's courts for the determination of his rights is not to be excluded except by clear words. As Mr Singh pointed out, both of these rights are embraced by the principle of legality, which lies at the heart of the relationship between Parliament and the citizen. Fundamental rights may not be overridden by general words. This can only be done by express language or by necessary implication. So it was not open to the Treasury to use

its powers under the general wording of section 1(1) of the 1946 Act to subject individuals to a regime which had these effects.

...

LORD PHILLIPS: ... The principle of legality

111. The appellants have put this principle at the forefront of their argument on the interpretation of the 1946 Act. Under this principle the court must, where possible, interpret a statute in such a way as to avoid encroachment on fundamental rights, sometimes described as constitutional rights. Lord Hope at para 46 has cited the passages in the speech of Lord Browne-Wilkinson in *Ex p Pierson* [1998] AC 539 in which he described this principle. Equally pertinent is the oft cited passage in the speech of Lord Hoffmann in *Ex p Simms* [2000] 2 AC 115, 131:

> "Parliamentary sovereignty means that Parliament can, if it chooses, legislate contrary to funda-mental principles of human rights. The Human Rights Act 1998 will not detract from this power. The constraints upon its exercise by Parliament are ultimately political, not legal. But the principle of legality means that Parliament must squarely confront what it is doing and accept the political cost. Fundamental rights cannot be overridden by general or ambiguous words. This is because there is too great a risk that the full implications of their unqualified meaning may have passed unnoticed in the democratic process. In the absence of express language or necessary implication to the contrary, the courts therefore presume that even the most general words were intended to be subject to the basic rights of the individual. In this way the courts of the United Kingdom, though acknowledging the sovereignty of Parliament, apply principles of constitutionality little different from those which exist in countries where the power of the legislature is expressly limited by a constitutional document."

112. Lord Hoffmann went on to say that the principle of legality applied as much to subordinate legislation as to Acts of Parliament. Lord Hoffmann made it plain that the principle of legality was one that applied to the interpretation of general or ambiguous words in the absence of express language or necessary implication to the contrary. At the time of his judgment the Human Rights Act 1998 had not yet come into effect and Lord Hoffmann commented that the principle of legal-ity had been expressly enacted as a rule of construction in section 3 of the Act. I believe that the House of Lords has extended the reach of section 3 of the HRA beyond that of the principle of legality.

113. Section 3(1) provides: "So far as it is possible to do so, primary legislation and subordinate legisla-tion must be read and given effect in a way which is compatible with the Convention rights."

114. The Convention rights are defined in section 1 to mean the rights and fundamental freedoms set out in articles 2 to 12 and 14 of the Convention, articles 1 to 3 of the First Protocol and article 1 of the Thirteenth Protocol.

115. The effect of section 3 has been the subject of extensive academic discussion: see the literature referred to in footnote 27 to para 4.08 in *Clayton and Tomlinson, The Law of Human Rights*, 2nd ed (2009). It has also been the subject of judicial consideration on a number of occasions in the House of Lords. It is not necessary to refer in detail to this body of authority. It suffices to note that it accords to section 3 a role of constitutional significance. By enacting section 3, Parliament has been held to direct the courts to interpret legislation in a way which is compatible with Convention rights, even where such interpretation involves departing from the "unambiguous meaning the legislation would otherwise bear", or the "legislative intention ... of the Parliament": see *Ghaidan v Godin-Mendoza* [2004] 2 AC 557, para 30, per Lord Nicholls of Birkenhead and *Sheldrake v Director of Public Prosecutions* [2005] 1 AC 264, para 24, per Lord Bingham. Such an interpretation must, however, be one that is "possible" having regard to the underlying thrust or intention of the legislation.

116. *Bennion on Statutory Interpretation*, 5th ed (2008), section 270, p 823, comments that the term "principle of legality" is likely to lead to confusion but goes on to suggest that the "so-called principle of legality" was widened by a majority of the House of Lords in *R (Anufrijeva) v Secretary of State for the*

Home Department [2004] 1 AC 604 so as to contradict what Lord Bingham (who dissented) called "a clear and unambiguous legislative provision" (para 20), the provision in question being contained in delegated legislation.

117. The other members of the House did not, however, purport to depart from wording that was clear and unambiguous: see Lord Steyn at para 31, Lord Hoffmann at para 37, Lord Millett, at para 43 and Lord Scott of Foscate, at para 58. I do not consider that the principle of legality permits a court to disregard an unambiguous expression of Parliament's intention. To this extent its reach is less than that of section 3 of the HRA.

Appeals allowed.

NOTES

1. Following the decision of the Supreme Court to quash the Terrorism Order and s. 3(1)(b) of the Al-Qaida and Taliban Order, the Government introduced emergency primary and subordinate legislation effectively to reinstate the asset freezing regime for suspected terrorists; see Terrorist Asset-Freezing (Temporary Provisions) Act 2010 and Al-Qaida and Taliban (Asset-Freezing) Regulations 2010/1197. The aftermath of this case provides further evidence that the rule of law takes effect subject to the sovereignty of Parliament in the UK, and that the interpretive presumption at the heart of the principle of legality can be displaced by express words to the contrary.

2. Lord Phillips' discussion of the relationship between the interpretive duty imposed on courts by s. 3 of the Human Rights Act 1998 and that reflected in the principle of legality suggests that the latter permits a less expansive approach to statutory interpretation. Yet it may still be sufficient to ensure that resort to arguments grounded in Convention Rights are not necessary; for an example of this, see *Secretary of State for the Home Department* v *GG* [2009] EWCA Civ 786; [2010] 2 WLR 731. On the relationship between ECHR rights and common law grounds of judicial review, see *Osborn* v *The Parole Board* [2013] UKSC 61, *Kennedy* v *The Charity Commissioner* [2014] UKSC 20, and *Lee-Hirons* v *Secretary of State for Justice* [2016] UKSC 46.

3. The principle of legality has also been considered in the context of the availability of 'closed material procedures' when cases are heard before UK courts. By such procedures sensitive evidence is heard in closed session (usually on the grounds of national security), even being concealed from those to whom it relates, who will be represented by special advocates with whom they will have no contact. In *Al Rawi* v *The Security Services* [2011] UKSC 34, [2012] 1 AC 531 the Supreme Court held that they had no inherent power at common law to authorize the use of such proceedings in a civil case; instead closed material procedures were only available in the circumstances specified by statute because they interfere with the fundamental common law principles of open justice and natural justice (the *Al-Rawi* decision has now, in effect, been overturned by the enactment of the Justice and Security Act 2013, which makes general provision for the availability of closed material procedures).

   In a subsequent case, *Bank Mellat* v *Her Majesty's Treasury (No. 1)* [2013] UKSC 38, the Supreme Court considered whether closed material procedures were available by implication, with reference to the general jurisdiction of the Court established in the Constitutional Reform Act 2005. In *Bank Mellat* arguments as to the relevance of the principle of legality were accepted only by a minority of Supreme Court Justices—Lords Hope, Kerr, and Reed argued that such procedures could only be made available by express statutory provision. The majority—Baroness Hale and Lords Neuberger, Dyson, Clarke, Sumption, and Carnwath—held, in contrast, that the use of closed material procedures could be authorized implicitly by a statute, although did not believe that this decision was a departure from the position established in *Al-Rawi*. See further C. Forsyth, 'Principle or Pragmatism: Closed Material Procedure in the Supreme Court' *UK Constitutional Law Association Blog* (29 July 2013) (available at http://ukconstitutionallaw.org).

4. The extent to which the rule of law requires, and is capable of providing, protection of the fundamental rights of individuals is an increasingly prominent issue. Yet concerns about individual rights are not always the trigger for calls for legal oversight of government action taken in the context of national security, as the following case, which also concerns the exercise of a broad statutory power, demonstrates.

R (Corner House Research) v Director of Serious Fraud Office
[2008] UKHL 60, [2009] 1 AC 756, House of Lords

A challenge was brought by public interest organizations to the legality of the decision by the Director of the Serious Fraud Office to discontinue an investigation into allegations of bribery by BAE Systems plc (BAE) in relation to the Al-Yamamah military aircraft contracts with the Kingdom of Saudi Arabia. Ministers had been informed by Saudi representatives that if the investigation did not stop, then there would be consequences which included ceasing Saudi cooperation with the United Kingdom over intelligence. The assessment of this threat recorded in a minute from the Prime Minister to the Attorney General and the Director was that it:

… risks endangering UK national security, both directly in protecting citizens and service people, and indirectly through impeding our search for peace and stability in this critical part of the world.

The Director decided that it not in the public interest to continue the investigation. This was successfully challenged in the Divisional Court [2008] EWHC 714 (Admin):

MOSES LJ: … 64. The rule of law is nothing if it fails to constrain overweening power. Spigelman CJ of New South Wales has described judges and lawyers as "boundary riders maintaining the integrity of the fences that divide legal constraint from the sphere of freedom of action": Address on Judicial Independence to the Seventh Worldwide Common Law Judicial Conference, April 2007. So too must the courts patrol the boundary between the territory which they safeguard and that for which the executive is responsible.

…

169. The claimants succeed on the ground that the Director and Government failed to recognise that the rule of law required the decision to discontinue to be reached as an exercise of independent judgment, in pursuance of the power conferred by statute. To preserve the integrity and independence of that judgment demanded resistance to the pressure exerted by means of a specific threat. That threat was intended to prevent the Director from pursuing the course of investigation he had chosen to adopt. It achieved its purpose.

170. The court has a responsibility to secure the rule of law. The Director was required to satisfy the court that all that could reasonably be done had been done to resist the threat. He has failed to do so. He submitted too readily because he, like the executive, concentrated on the effects which were feared should the threat be carried out and not on how the threat might be resisted. No-one, whether within this country or outside is entitled to interfere with the course of our justice. It is the failure of Government and the defendant to bear that essential principle in mind that justifies the intervention of this court. We shall hear further argument as to the nature of such intervention. But we intervene in fulfilment of our responsibility to protect the independence of the Director and of our criminal justice system from threat. On 11 December 2006, the Prime Minister said that this was the clearest case for intervention in the public interest he had seen. We agree.

The Director appealed to the House of Lords:

LORD BINGHAM: … 38. The Divisional Court held, ante p 782, para 67, that "No revolutionary principle needs to be created … we can deploy well settled principles of public law". But the court did, at para 98, lay down a principle which, if not revolutionary, was novel and unsupported by authority: "The principle we have identified is that submission to a threat is lawful only when it is demonstrated to a court that there was no alternative course open to the decision-maker." The virtues which the court saw in that principle have been summarised in para 27 above, but the second of those (that, as this case was said to demonstrate, "too ready a submission may give rise to the suspicion that the threat was not the real ground of the decision at all", rather it was a useful pretext) should not be understood as reflecting on the good faith of the Director or the Attorney General which has never been in issue. The objection to the principle formulated by the Divisional Court is that it distracts attention from what, applying well-settled principles of public law, was the right question: whether, in deciding that the public interest in pursuing an important investigation into alleged bribery was outweighed by the public interest in protecting the lives of British citizens, the Director made a decision outside the lawful bounds of the discretion entrusted to him by Parliament.

…

41. The Director was confronted by an ugly and obviously unwelcome threat. He had to decide what, if anything, he should do. He did not surrender his discretionary power of decision to any third party, although he did consult the most expert source available to him in the person of the Ambassador and he did, as he was entitled if not bound to do, consult the Attorney General who, however, properly left the decision to him. The issue in these proceedings is not whether his decision was right or wrong, nor whether the Divisional Court or the House agrees with it, but whether it was a decision which the Director was lawfully entitled to make. Such an approach involves no affront to the rule of law, to which the principles of judicial review give effect (see *R (Alconbury Developments Ltd) v Secretary of State for the Environment, Transport and the Regions* [2001] UKHL 23, [2003] 2 AC 295, para. 73, per Lord Hoffmann).

42. In the opinion of the House the Director's decision was one he was lawfully entitled to make. It may indeed be doubted whether a responsible decision-maker could, on the facts before the Director, have decided otherwise.

Appeal allowed.

NOTES

1. The press statement released announcing the Director's decision to cease the investigation said '[i]t has been necessary to balance the need to maintain the rule of law against the wider public interest'. The Divisional Court seems in places to regard such balancing as illegitimate, adopting a near absolutist approach to the rule of law, with the principle cited frequently, and discussed at significant length, in the judgment of the lower court. The Law Lords, in contrast, gave much less attention to the rule of law, regarding the issue raised as more straightforward—has a discretionary power been exercised lawfully?—and endorsing the argument that the rule of law was one factor among a number which the Director was entitled to consider when making his decision. Yet the House of Lords' judgment is still based on the rule of law, in so far as they are leaving to the Director a decision which Parliament has empowered him by law to make, rather than displacing it with their own view of what would be right in these circumstances. Whether the Divisional Court and House of Lords disagree about the meaning of the rule of law is unclear, but this case demonstrates that even if there is no disagreement about the principle (such as between the formal and substantive conceptions encountered in this chapter in Section 3 at pp. 111–17), there still may not be consensus as to how the rule of law is applied in particular circumstances, and what conduct it requires of officials and courts.

2. The judgment of Lord Bingham in *Corner House Research* makes reference to the relationship between the rule of law and judicial review, with the latter said at [41] to be designed to give effect to the former. The idea of government according to law has been illustrated in a range of decisions by the courts developing the principles of *ultra vires* (see Chapter 10) and natural justice (see Chapter 10) which are the central doctrines of administrative law. By development of these doctrines the courts have sought to control the ways in which authorities exercise their powers and the procedures they adopt. Thus the exercise of a power by an authority will be struck down as *ultra vires* where the authority acts in excess of the power (see, e.g. *Laker Airways Ltd v Department of Trade* [1977] QB 643), or it abuses the power by exercising it ignoring relevant considerations or taking irrelevant considerations into account (see, e.g. *Associated Provincial Picture Houses Ltd v Wednesbury Corporation* [1948] 1 KB 223), or where it exercises the power for an improper purpose (see, e.g. *Roberts v Hopwood* [1925] AC 578), or it exercises the power unreasonably (see *Associated Provincial Picture Houses Ltd v Wednesbury Corporation* [1948] 1 KB 223). Where powers are exercised courts may also impose procedural requirements upon the authority exercising the power to ensure that the decision to exercise the power was taken in accordance with the rules of natural justice or, more recently, that the decision respected the requirements of fairness. Thus the

decision-maker should be unbiased and the subject of the decision should have had a fair hearing. What is fair may vary with the circumstances, but matters which will be taken into account are whether the subject received adequate notice of the hearing and the charges, was allowed to present his case in a written or oral form and call witnesses, and whether he was allowed legal representation.

3. There is often debate about whether the courts, in an effort to uphold rule of law values through judicial review of official action, can exceed their own powers, and interfere too significantly with the decision-making authority allocated to the Government by Parliament. This controversy was acutely demonstrated in the following case.

R (Evans) v Attorney General
[2015] UKSC 21; [2015] AC 1787, Supreme Court

Evans sought judicial review of the Attorney General's decision to veto disclosure of letters written by Prince Charles, the heir to the throne, advocating certain policy positions to a number of government ministers. The disclosure of these letters had been ordered by the Upper Tribunal under the Freedom of Information Act 2000 (this aspect of the case, which has implications for our understanding of constitutional conventions, is considered in Chapter 5, Section 2D at pp. 207–11). Acting on behalf of the Government, the Attorney General used the power of veto contained in s. 53 of the Freedom of Information Act 2000, issuing a certificate explaining that he did not believe disclosure was in the public interest, because (among other reasons) it could potentially damage the Prince of Wales's political neutrality, and thus seriously undermine the Prince's ability to fulfil his duties when he becomes King. Evans argued that it was unreasonable to use the veto power simply because the Government disagreed with the conclusions of the Upper Tribunal, and that the decision was unlawful. This argument was rejected in the Divisional Court, but upheld in the Court of Appeal. The case was appealed to the Supreme Court.

LORD NEUBERGER:

[51] When one considers the implications of section 53(2) in the context of a situation where a court, or indeed any judicial tribunal, has determined that information should be released, it is at once apparent that [the argument that there has to be something more than simply a different assessment on the part of the Attorney General for a veto to be reasonable] has considerable force. A statutory provision which entitles a member of the executive (whether a Government Minister or the Attorney General) to overrule a decision of the judiciary merely because he does not agree with it would not merely be unique in the laws of the United Kingdom. It would cut across two constitutional principles which are also fundamental components of the rule of law.

[52] First, subject to being overruled by a higher court or (given Parliamentary supremacy) a statute, it is a basic principle that a decision of a court is binding as between the parties, and cannot be ignored or set aside by anyone, including (indeed it may fairly be said, least of all) the executive. Secondly, it is also fundamental to the rule of law that decisions and actions of the executive are, subject to necessary well established exceptions (such as declarations of war), and jealously scrutinised statutory exceptions, reviewable by the court at the suit of an interested citizen. Section 53, as interpreted by the Attorney General's argument in this case, flouts the first principle and stands the second principle on its head. It involves saying that a final decision of a court can be set aside by a member of the executive (normally the minister in charge of the very department against whom the decision has been given) because he does not agree with it. And the fact that the member of the executive can put forward cogent and/or strongly held reasons for disagreeing with the court is, in this context, nothing to the point: many court decisions are on points of controversy where opinions (even individual judicial opinions) may reasonably differ, but that does not affect the applicability of these principles....

[57] At least equally in point is the proposition set out by Lord Reed in *AXA General Insurance Ltd v HM Advocate* [2011] UKSC 46, [2012] 1 AC 868, para 152, that:

"The principle of legality means not only that Parliament cannot itself override fundamental rights or the rule of law by general or ambiguous words, but also that it cannot confer on another body, by general or ambiguous words, the power to do so."

In support of this proposition, Lord Reed cited two passages from the decision of the *House of Lords in R v Secretary of State for the Home Department, Ex p Pierson* [1998] AC 539. At p 575, Lord Browne-Wilkinson said that

"A power conferred by Parliament in general terms is not to be taken to authorise the doing of acts by the donee of the power which adversely affect the legal rights of the citizen or the basic principles on which the law of the United Kingdom is based unless the statute conferring the power makes it clear that such was the intention of Parliament."

To much the same effect, Lord Steyn said at p 591 that "[u]nless there is the clearest provision to the contrary, Parliament must be presumed not to legislate contrary to the rule of law".

[58] Accordingly, if section 53 is to have the remarkable effect argued for by Mr Eadie QC for the Attorney General, it must be "crystal clear" from the wording of the FOIA 2000, and cannot be justified merely by "general or ambiguous words". In my view, section 53 falls far short of being "crystal clear" in saying that a member of the executive can override the decision of a court because he disagrees with it. The only reference to a court or tribunal in the section is in subsection (4)(b) which provides that the time for issuing a certificate is to be effectively extended where an appeal is brought under section 57. It is accepted in these proceedings that that provision, coupled with the way that the tribunal's powers are expressed in sections 57 and 58, has the effect of extending the power to issue a section 53 certificate to a decision notice issued or confirmed by a tribunal or confirmed by an appellate court or tribunal. But that is a very long way away indeed from making it "crystal clear" that that power can be implemented so as to enable a member of the executive effectively to reverse, or overrule, a decision of a court or a judicial tribunal, simply because he does not agree with it.

[59] All this militates very strongly in favour of the view that where, as here, a court has conducted a full open hearing into the question of whether, in the light of certain facts and competing arguments, the public interest favours disclosure of certain information and has concluded for reasons given in a judgment that it does, section 53 cannot be invoked effectively to overrule that judgment merely because a member of the executive, considering the same facts and arguments, takes a different view.

LORD HUGHES (dissenting):
[154] The rule of law is of the first importance. But it is an integral part of the rule of law that courts give effect to Parliamentary intention. The rule of law is not the same as a rule that courts must always prevail, no matter what the statute says. I agree of course that in general the acts of the executive are, with limited exceptions, reviewable by courts, rather than vice versa. I agree that Parliament will not be taken to have empowered a member of the executive to override a decision of a court unless it has made such an intention explicit. I agree that courts are entitled to act on the basis that only the clearest language will do this. In my view, however, Parliament has plainly shown such an intention in the present instance.

[155] In the end this issue does not admit of much elaboration; it seems to me to be a matter of the plain words of the statute. The alternative postulated is simply too highly strained a construction of the section. Section 53(2) could, no doubt, have said that a certificate could be issued only if fresh material came to light after the decision of the Commissioner or the First-tier Tribunal, but it did not. Likewise, it could have said that a certificate could be issued if the decision of the Commissioner or court could be shown to be demonstrably flawed in law or fact, but it did not. If Parliament had wished to limit the power to issue a certificate to these two situations that is undoubtedly what the subsection would have said. If anyone had suggested at the time of the passage of the bill which became the Act that either of these things was what was meant, it seems to me that that suggestion would have received a decisive and negative response. The second possibility is, moreover, one which would afford clear grounds for

appeal, so that a certificate would not be necessary. Even if it were a second appeal, a demonstrably flawed decision upon a topic of public significance would be one for which there would nearly always be a compelling reason for leave to appeal to be given.

[156] In the end, the very fact that it is necessary to postulate so vestigial an extent for a generally expressed power if it is to be given any content at all is a potent demonstration that it does indeed mean what it says. The reality is that the section 53(2) provision for exceptional executive override was the Parliamentary price of moving from an advisory power for the Commissioner (and thus for the court on appeal) to an enforceable decision....

[160] It follows that the Attorney General was entitled to differ from the Upper Tribunal on where the balance of public interest lay. This was the principal purpose of section 53(2). His decision must be rational, but in this case it is not seriously suggested that it was not, and it is to be noted that it was shared by the Commissioner. Indeed, the law has now been changed so as to provide unqualified exemption from disclosure for communications with the monarch, the heir or the second in line to the throne, but not for those with other members of the Royal Family.

LORD WILSON (dissenting):
[168] I would have allowed the appeal. How tempting it must have been for the Court of Appeal (indeed how tempting it has proved even for the majority in this court) to seek to maintain the supremacy of the astonishingly detailed, and inevitably unappealed, decision of the Upper Tribunal in favour of disclosure of the Prince's correspondence! But the Court of Appeal ought (as, with respect, ought this court) to have resisted the temptation. For, in reaching its decision, the Court of Appeal did not in my view interpret section 53 of FOIA. It re-wrote it. It invoked precious constitutional principles but among the most precious is that of parliamentary sovereignty, emblematic of our democracy, ...

[171] A power of executive override of determinations of the Commissioner, or of tribunals or courts in ensuing appeals, on issues of *law* would have been an unlawful encroachment upon the principle of separation of powers: see the classic judgment of Sir Edward Coke, Chief Justice, in *Prohibitions del Roy* [1607] EWHC KB J23, 77 ER 1342, upon the claim of King James I to determine issues of law. But issues relating to the *evaluation of public interests* are entirely different. In the words of Lord Hoffmann in *R (Alconbury Developments Ltd) v Secretary of State for the Environment, Transport and the Regions* [2001] UKHL 23, [2003] 2 AC 295, at para 69, the principle is that "in a democratic country, decisions as to what the general interest requires are made by democratically elected bodies or persons accountable to them". This was the principle reflected in the first version of the Bill. In the later version Parliament sanctioned departure from it but, in enacting section 53, it no doubt continued to have in mind that the evaluation of public interests was not an exercise in relation to which the Commissioner, the tribunals and the courts, could claim any monopoly of expertise....

[177] [The effect of the majority's analysis] is that, for all practical purposes, no certificate can be given under section 53 by way of override of a decision notice upheld or substituted by the Upper Tribunal or, probably, by the First-tier Tribunal. In other words, namely in those of Ms Rose, it will "almost never" be reasonable for an accountable person to disagree with the decision of a court in favour of disclosure. The trouble is that, as is agreed, Parliament made clear, by subsection (4)(b), that such a certificate could be given in such circumstances.

Appeal dismissed.

NOTES:

1. The decision in *Evans* was reached by a 5–2 majority: Lords Kerr and Reed agreed with the judgment of Lord Neuberger, and Lord Mance gave a separate judgment with which Lady Hale agreed, concurring that the use of the veto was irrational, but on the different grounds. For them, the use of the veto could have been reasonable in principle, despite reaching a different conclusion to the judgment of the Upper Tribunal, but the certificate was irrational in these circumstances because

the Attorney General's certificate made assertions about the factual position and the scope of applicable constitutional conventions which deviated significantly from those accepted in the tribunal (including that the confidentiality of the correspondence was covered by the 'preparation for kingship' convention) 'without any substantial or sustainable basis being given for the disagreement'. The certificate had therefore 'not been justified on reasonable grounds', [145].

2. The disagreement in *Evans* exhibits a clash of constitutional principles: different approaches to the rule of law are taken by Lord Neuberger and Lord Hughes. Lord Neuberger focuses on substantive principles which he argues are central to the effectiveness rule of law, and, when summarizing the factors justifying the limited scope of the veto, makes an (unflattering) comparison between legal and political modes of decision-making:

> [69] [The limited scope of the veto was justified by] (i) the fact that the earlier conclusion was reached by a tribunal (a) whose decision could be appealed by the departments, (b) which had particular relevant expertise and experience, (c) which conducted a full hearing with witnesses who could be cross-examined, (d) which sat in public, and had full adversarial argument, and (e) whose members produced a closely reasoned decision, coupled with (ii) the fact that the later conclusion was reached by an individual who, while personally and ex officio deserving of the highest respect, (a) consulted people who had been involved on at least one side of the correspondence whose disclosure was sought, (b) received no argument on behalf of the person seeking disclosure, (c) received no fresh facts or evidence, and (d) simply took a different view from the tribunal.

This may present an idealized view of legal decision-making, and an unduly negative view of political decision-making. It may also overlook questions of accountability and representativeness when decisions are made about what is in the public interest (especially in controversial circumstances where there is scope for disagreement). Lord Hughes, in contrast, also relies on the rule of law to justify his decision, but focuses instead on giving full effect to the legal rules in the statute enacted by Parliament. This may be seen as a formal approach to the rule of law, which, it is implicitly suggested, the more substantive approach of Lord Neuberger may violate.

3. There is a second clash of constitutional principles: between the rule of law, as understood by Lord Neuberger, and the doctrine of parliamentary sovereignty, which is invoked by Lord Wilson. Whether the rule of law and parliamentary sovereignty are compatible principles will therefore depend on the understanding of the rule of law adopted: the formal approach to the rule of law, which suggests that the law must be clear, certain, and applied, is consistent with the idea that Parliament has a law-making power unlimited by law. A substantive approach to the rule of law, which attaches value to fundamental rights or (as in *Evans*) an unassailable supremacy to legal decision-making, offers greater potential for the sovereignty of Parliament to come under challenge.

4. See also M. Elliott, 'A Tangled Constitutional Web: the Black-Spider Memos and the British Constitution's Relational Architecture' [2015] *Public Law* 539–50.

■ QUESTIONS

1. How important is the rule of law in ensuring that the exercise of public power is controlled? Have the courts in the United Kingdom: (i) developed an adequate understanding of the rule of law; and (ii) applied it appropriately to the facts of the cases before them?

2. Does the formal or substantive understanding of the rule of law better reflect the way the principle operates in the United Kingdom? Does ongoing debate about the 'true' nature of the rule of law create a degree of uncertainty about the scope of the principle which limits its utility to those seeking to challenge the legality of official action?

3. How could the rule of law be better protected in the United Kingdom? Does it require action from courts, Parliament, officials, the Government, or some combination of these constitutional actors?

4. Is ensuring that public power is exercised lawfully sufficient to achieve good government? Or are political mechanisms and understandings also important, to ensure that power is used lawfully *and* responsibly?

4

Judicial Independence

OVERVIEW

In this chapter we look at the aspect of separation of powers theory which is most prominent in UK constitutional law and practice. We focus on the enhancement of judicial independence by the clearer separation between the judiciary and the other organs of government brought about by the Constitutional Reform Act 2005 and its changes to the office of Lord Chancellor and the arrangements for judicial appointment and discipline. We then examine the judiciary's accountability to Parliament and the public before finally looking at the position of the courts in relation to parliamentary privilege.

SECTION 1: JUDICIAL INDEPENDENCE

A: An expanded constitutional role for the courts?

Before we examine how judicial independence has been enhanced, we consider first a case in which one senior judge is raising the question as to whether it is appropriate that we move to a conception of the separation of the powers where the courts are playing more of a checking role on the executive and legislature.

R v Secretary of State for the Home Department, ex parte Fire Brigades Union
[1995] 2 AC 513, House of Lords

LORD MUSTILL: ... This prompts one final observation. It is a feature of the peculiarly British conception of the separation of powers that Parliament, the executive and the courts each have their distinct and largely exclusive domain. Parliament has a legally unchallengeable right to make whatever laws it thinks right. The executive carries on the administration of the country in accordance with the powers conferred on it by law. The courts interpret the laws, and see that they are obeyed. This requires the courts on occasion to step into the territory which belongs to the executive, not only to verify that the powers asserted accord with the substantive law created by Parliament, but also, that the manner in which they are exercised conforms with the standards of fairness which Parliament must have intended. Concurrently with this judicial function Parliament has its own special means of ensuring that the executive, in the exercise of delegated functions, performs in a way which Parliament finds appropriate. Ideally, it is these latter methods which should be used to check executive errors and excesses; for it is the task of Parliament and the executive in tandem, not of the courts, to govern the country. In recent years, however, the employment in practice of these specifically Parliamentary remedies has on occasion been perceived as falling short, and sometimes well short, of what was needed to bring the performance of the executive into line with the law, and with the minimum standards of fairness implicit in every Parliamentary delegation of a decision-making function. To avoid a vacuum in which the citizen would be left without protection against a misuse of executive powers the courts have had no option but to occupy the dead ground in a manner, and in areas of public life, which could not have been foreseen thirty years ago. For myself, I am quite satisfied that this unprecedented judicial role has been greatly to the public benefit. Nevertheless, it has its risks, of which the courts are well aware. As the judges themselves constantly remark, it is not they who are appointed to administer the country. Absent a written constitution much sensitivity is required of the parliamentarian, administrator and judge if the delicate balance of the unwritten rules evolved (I believe successfully) in recent years is not to be disturbed, and all the recent advances undone. I do not for a moment suggest that the judges of the Court of Appeal in the present case overlooked this need. The judgments show clearly that they did not. Nevertheless some of the arguments addressed would have the court push to the very boundaries of the distinction between court and Parliament established in, and recognised ever since, the Bill of Rights 1688. Three hundred years have passed since then, and the political and social landscape has changed beyond recognition. But the boundaries remain; they are of crucial significance to our private and public lives; and the courts should I believe make sure that they are not overstepped.

NOTES

1. The dispute in the case concerned the action of the Home Secretary in using the royal prerogative to create a replacement for a criminal injuries scheme also established under the prerogative, instead of implementing a statutory scheme authorized by the Criminal Justice Act 1988 (see Chapter 7, Section 1 at pp. 328–32).
2. Tomkins in *Public Law* (2003), pp. 24–30 and Barendt in 'Constitutional Law and the Criminal Injuries Compensation Act' [2005] *Public Law* 357 make a similar point about the approach taken by Lord Mustill in contrast to the majority. Barendt argues that Lord Mustill adopted a constitutional law approach and the majority an administrative law approach. For Tomkins, Lord Mustill is adopting more of a political constitutional approach compared to the majority who are legal constitutionalists carrying out statutory interpretation. Lord Mustill wonders if the increasing resort to the courts and the expansion of their reach, which in this case enlarged the judicial control of the royal prerogative, is appropriate, although he does not doubt that in relation to the judiciary, the concept of separation of powers means that they must be guaranteed independence from the other two organs of government.

■ QUESTION

As you read the reasons underlying the desirability for the changes made by the Constitutional Reform Act 2005, are they driven by principle, by trying to keep in line with other countries, or by a pragmatic approach to resolving problems in seeking to redress people's grievances?

B: The Constitutional Reform Act 2005

K. Malleson, 'The Effect of the Constitutional Reform Act 2005 on the Relationship Between the Judiciary, the Executive and Parliament', Select Committee on the Constitution, *Relations between the executive, the judiciary and Parliament*
HL 151 of 2006–07, pp. 60–1

The Background to the Constitutional Reform Act 2005

The origins of the Constitutional Reform Act lie in the expanding role played by the higher courts in the UK over the last thirty years. The combined effect of the growth of judicial review, the development of the EU and, most recently, the Human Rights Act and devolution has been to give the courts a more central place in the British constitution. The senior judges are now required to police constitutional boundaries and determine sensitive human rights issues in a way which would have been unthinkable forty years ago. This new judicial role is still developing, but it is clear that the effect of this trend will be to reshape the relationship between the judiciary and the other branches of government. In the light of these changes, the main provisions of the Constitutional Reform Act—reforming the office of Lord Chancellor, establishing a new Supreme Court and restructuring the judicial appointments process— were designed to bring the institutional relationships between the judiciary and the other branches of government into line with the changing substantive role of the courts. In particular, the reforms were intended to secure the independence of the judiciary by 'redrawing the relationship between the judiciary and the other branches of government' and putting it on a 'modern footing'.

Although the timing of the introduction of the Constitutional Reform Bill in 2003 took many by surprise, its content did not. Concerns about the relationship between the judiciary and the other branches of government had been building up over a number of years. Where once there had been a general consensus that the Lord Chancellor's three roles as member of cabinet, head of the judiciary and speaker of the House of Lords enhanced the functioning of the political system and strengthened judicial independence, they increasingly came to be regarded as a potential source of abuse of executive power. In particular, the Lord Chancellor's responsibility for appointing the judges became a source of growing concern as the senior judges' role in scrutinising government decision-making increased. Likewise, the presence of the top appellate court in Parliament had once been widely regarded as an effective means of drawing on the legal expertise of the top judges during the law-making process so enhancing the quality of legislation. By the 1990s, however, many Law Lords themselves had come to regard the lack of separation between the two as problematic as the same senior judges who participated in passing the laws were increasingly asked to decide on the conformity of those acts with basic human rights.

By the late 1990s, far fewer voices were heard in support of the argument that these overlaps between the branches of government were a source of its stability. Increasingly, the interconnection was seen as endangering judicial independence, breaching basic constitutional principles and out of step with the rest of Europe. By the start of the second term of the Labour Government in 2001, the long debate about these issues had slowly generated broad support across the political spectrum for a 'clearer and deeper' separation of the functions and powers of the judiciary from the other branches of government. The decision to embark upon extensive institutional reform was therefore anticipated, but the provisions set out in the Constitutional Reform Act were unusual in a number of respects. First, they ran counter to the trend of recent political developments in that they represented a conscious shift of power away from the executive. Second, they were forward looking, seeking to construct a new constitutional model which anticipated future needs rather than responding to an immediate perceived problem. In introducing the reforms the Government made clear that there was no suggestion that the overlapping constitutional roles of the Lord Chancellor or the presence of the Law Lords in the House of Lords had, in practice, undermined judicial independence but rather that the present system held inherent structural weaknesses which might give rise to such abuse in the future. The third surprising feature of the reforms is that they explicitly sought to promote constitutional principle above pragmatism. Whilst accepting that the previous arrangements had worked effectively, the changes were designed to restructure the relationship between the judiciary and the other branches of government so that it would conform more closely to the concept of the separation of powers. This elevation of principle above pragmatism is surprising given the traditional value ascribed to 'what works' in the British constitution.

NOTE: Various groups had been canvassing the creation of a judicial appointments commission and separating the Law Lords from Parliament and a restructuring to create a Ministry of Justice (see *Constitutional Innovation: the Creation of a Supreme Court for the United Kingdom; Domestic, Comparative and International Reflection* the special issue (2004) 24 *Legal Studies* 1–293). The Lord Chancellor, Lord Irvine of Lairg, was not in favour of reducing the roles and functions of the Lord Chancellor, and did not want to relinquish sitting as a judge, although he sat less frequently than many of his predecessors. When he left office unexpectedly in 2003, announcements were made about various reforms including the abolition of the post of Lord Chancellor and the renaming of the Lord

Chancellor's Department as the Department for Constitutional Affairs. The abolition of the post of Lord Chancellor did not happen as it was realized that the reallocation of the Lord Chancellor's responsibilities was complicated and would require primary legislation. Consultation papers on Judicial Appointments and the creation of a Supreme Court followed a month later.

The new Lord Chancellor, Lord Falconer, said that he would not sit as a judge. It is thought that this and the proposal to create a separate Supreme Court were partially attributable to the finding of a breach of Art. 6 of the European Convention in *McGonnell* v *UK* (2000) 30 EHRR 289. In this case the Bailiff of Guernsey determined a planning appeal having previously presided over proceedings in the legislature during which a development plan at issue in the planning appeal was adopted. The European Court of Human Rights ruled:

1. The Court can agree with the [UK] Government that neither Article 6 nor any other provision of the Convention requires States to comply with any theoretical constitutional concepts as such. The question is always whether, in a given case, the requirements of the Convention are met. The present case does not, therefore, require the application of any particular doctrine of constitutional law to the position in Guernsey: the Court is faced solely with the question whether the Bailiff had the required "appearance" of independence, or the required "objective" impartiality ...

2. The Court thus considers that the mere fact that the Deputy Bailiff presided over the States of Deliberation when DDP6 was adopted in 1990 is capable of casting doubt on his impartiality when he subsequently determined, as the sole judge of the law in the case, the applicant's planning appeal. The applicant therefore had legitimate grounds for fearing that the Bailiff may have been influenced by his prior participation in the adoption of DDP6. That doubt in itself, however slight its justification, is sufficient to vitiate the impartiality of the Royal Court, and it is therefore unnecessary for the Court to look into the other aspects of the complaint.

Following the judgment Lord Irvine stated that he would 'never sit in any case concerning legislation in the passage of which he had been directly involved nor in any case where the interests of the executive were directly engaged' (HL Debs. Vol. 610, 23 February 2000, WA33). Contrast that reaction with a Scottish case about temporary sheriffs (judges) decided under the Human Rights Act 1998 which entered into force earlier in Scotland than England, which did lead to action to restore compatibility with convention rights on both sides of the border, and adjust the constitutional climate to a greater awareness of (potential) threats to judicial independence.

Starrs v *Ruxton* 2000 SLT 42

LORD REED: ... In my opinion, the most important of the three factors relied upon by the appellants is the absence of security of tenure. It was common ground before us that, as a matter of law, a temporary sheriff can be removed from office at any time for any reason. It was also common ground that a temporary sheriff can be appointed on an annual basis and that his allocation to courts, and the renewal of his appointment, are thereafter within the unfettered discretion of the Executive. ... I am prepared to proceed on the basis that a temporary sheriff does not, as a matter of law, enjoy anything which constitutes security of tenure in the normally accepted sense of that term.

...

It is apparent that the system as operated depends on an assessment by the Scottish Executive, or in practice an assessment by the Lord Advocate, of what should be regarded as grounds for removal from office (or as grounds for not renewing the appointment or for deciding not to allocate work to a particular temporary sheriff, which are in substance equivalent to removal from office), and of what general policies should be followed (e.g. as to retiral age). The practice may alter from time to time, as in fact happened when the age limit of 65 was introduced. I do not doubt that the system has been operated by successive Lords Advocate with integrity and sound judgment, free from political considerations, and with a careful regard to the need to respect judicial independence. That is no doubt why it has operated for so long without occasioning any widespread expression of public concern, although disquiet has on occasion been expressed by members of the judiciary and others in Parliament and in academic or professional contexts. There is however no objective guarantee of security of tenure, such as can be found in section 12 of the 1971 Act; and I regard the absence of such a guarantee as fatal to the compatibility of the present system with Article 6.

The Solicitor General emphasised that it is inconceivable that the Lord Advocate would interfere with the performance of judicial functions. I readily accept that; but that is not the point. Judicial independence can be threatened not only by interference by the Executive, but also by a judge's being influenced, consciously or unconsciously, by his hopes and fears as to his possible treatment by the Executive. It is for that reason that a judge must not be dependent on the Executive, however well the Executive may behave: 'independence' connotes the absence of dependence. It also has to be borne in mind that judicial independence exists to protect the integrity of the judiciary and confidence in the administration of justice, and thus society as a whole, in bad times as well as good. The adequacy of judicial independence cannot appropriately be tested on the assumption that the Executive will always behave with appropriate restraint: as the European Court of Human Rights has emphasised in its interpretation of Article 6, it is important that there be 'guarantees' against outside pressures. In short, for the judiciary to be dependent on the Executive flies in the face of the principle of the separation of powers which is central to the requirement of judicial independence in Article 6 …

Appeals allowed. Bills of Advocation passed.

NOTE: This decision led to no new business being allocated to temporary sheriffs. In the Bail, Judicial Appointments etc. (Scotland) Act 2000, s. 6 abolished the position of temporary sheriff and s. 7 created the new position of part-time sheriff to address the concerns about security of tenure raised in the High Court.

The Lord Chancellor carried out a review of the terms of service of part-time judicial office-holders in England and Wales, and Northern Ireland. On 12 April 2000 he announced that all Assistant Recorders would be appointed Recorders and that new arrangements to ensure independence would be brought in for part-time judicial appointments and certain part-time Tribunals appointments. Part-time appointments would be for a period of not less than five years.

A. Bradley, 'The New Constitutional Relationship Between the Judiciary, Government and Parliament', Select Committee on the Constitution, *Relations between the executive, the judiciary and Parliament*

HL 151 of 2006–7, pp. 73–4

B The Constitutional Reform Act 2005

10. The principal structural changes made by the CRA may be very briefly summarised. They have provided for greater formal separation between government and judiciary (and, as regards the new Supreme Court, between Parliament and judiciary) and for a new statutory interface in England and Wales between government, in the person of the Lord Chancellor, and the judiciary, represented by the Lord Chief Justice.

(A) Contrary to the original intention of the Government, the Lord Chancellor remains in being, but he has lost his status as head of the judiciary in England and Wales and may not now sit as a judge. This greater separation between executive and judiciary made it essential for many functions of the Lord Chancellor to be reassigned, some being transferred to the Lord Chief Justice, others being exercisable jointly by the Lord Chancellor and the Lord Chief Justice. The Lord Chancellor retains many important executive functions relating to the judiciary (including funding the system of justice, making judicial appointments in accordance with new statutory rules, and approving procedural rules for the courts). Many of these functions are ring-fenced, to ensure that they are not transferred to another Minister by the Prime Minister without further primary legislation. Under the CRA, the Lord Chancellor is not required to have had a legal career, nor to be a member of the House of Lords.

(B) The Lord Chief Justice is now President of the Courts and Head of the Judiciary of England and Wales. He is responsible:

(i) for representing the views of the judiciary to Parliament, to the Lord Chancellor and to other Ministers;

(ii) for maintaining appropriate arrangements for the welfare, training and guidance of the judiciary within resources made available by the Lord Chancellor; and

(iii) for maintaining appropriate arrangements for the deployment of the judiciary and the allocation of work within courts.

These broad duties are accompanied by many specific responsibilities, some of which are exercisable jointly with the Lord Chancellor, or with the concurrence of the Lord Chancellor.

(C) There will be a new Supreme Court for the United Kingdom, to take over the appellate functions now performed by the Appellate Committees of the House of Lords, together with the power to decide devolution issues transferred from the Judicial Committee of the Privy Council. This separation between the 'Law Lords' and the House does not mean any change in the extent of appellate jurisdiction. New provision has been made for funding and administering the Supreme Court. The CRA sets out in detail the procedure for the selection and appointment of judges to the Supreme Court, in place of the present practice by which the Prime Minister nominates to the Queen persons for appointment as Lords of Appeal in Ordinary.

(D) Judicial appointments in general are entrusted to the Judicial Appointments Commission, and are no longer a matter primarily for decision by Ministers. Within the framework of the CRA, it will be for the Commission to give substance to the statutory rule that selection must be solely on merit (section 63(2)); and the Commission must have regard to the need to encourage diversity in the range of persons available for selection (section 64(1)).

(E) A new post of Judicial Appointments and Conduct Ombudsman is created to deal with two rather different classes of complaint: (a) in relation to the observance of proper procedure in judicial appointments, and (b) in respect of the conduct of judges.

(F) While the historic tenure of senior judges derived from the Act of Settlement continues (subject to a new power to suspend a judge while parliamentary proceedings for removal are pending: section 108(6)), the removal of other judges by the Lord Chancellor is now subject to statutory procedures; in general, disciplinary powers in respect of the judiciary (including power to suspend) may be exercised by the Lord Chief Justice, acting with the agreement of the Lord Chancellor.

11. The cumulative effect of the changes made by the CRA is very extensive. Alongside the statutory provisions has to be read a document known as the Concordat, entitled *Constitutional Reform: the Lord Chancellor's judiciary-related functions*, prepared in January 2004 while the Constitutional Reform Bill was before the House of Lords, at a time when the Government was proposing to abolish the office of Lord Chancellor and it was not known what the attitude of the judiciary would be to the proposals. The Concordat represented an agreement between the Lord Chancellor and the Lord Chief Justice (then Lord Woolf) regarding the future exercise of the Lord Chancellor's judiciary-related functions, and as such it facilitated the passage of the Constitutional Reform Bill through Parliament.

NOTE: The Constitutional Reform Act 2005 (CRA) has now been amended in part by the Crime and Courts Act 2013. A Consultation Paper, *Appointments and Diversity: A Judiciary for the 21st Century* was published by the Government on 21 November 2011, with the 2013 Act the eventual result of this process. In his foreword to the Government's response to the consultation exercise, published on 11 May 2012, the then Lord Chancellor and Secretary of State for Justice, Ken Clarke, summarized the aims of this further reform:

The overall effect of these changes will be to achieve **the proper balance** between executive, judicial and independent responsibilities; improve **clarity, transparency and openness**; create a more **diverse judiciary** that is reflective of society; and deliver **speed and quality of service** to applicants, the courts and tribunals and value for money to the taxpayer, ensuring that our judiciary, which is already a byword for integrity, independence and excellence, evolves into a modern, outward-facing institution that is fit for the 21st century and beyond.

The extracts from the CRA contained in the rest of this chapter are as amended, where appropriate, by s. 20 and Sch. 13 of the Crime and Courts Act 2013.

C: The Lord Chancellor

The Constitutional Reform Act did not, as the government had originally intended, abolish the office of Lord Chancellor, rather it made it possible for future holders of the office to be MPs and not to be legally qualified. Jack Straw MP was the first MP to hold the office, although he did qualify as a barrister as did his successor Ken Clarke QC, MP. Chris Grayling, who became Lord Chancellor in September 2012, was the first non-lawyer to be appointed to the post in the modern era. Two more non-lawyers have succeeded Grayling: Michael Gove held the office from May 2015 to July 2016, with Liz Truss taking over subsequently (the first woman to hold the historic office which can be traced back to the medieval period). There had been substantial opposition to these changes, not least amongst the judges who felt that the Lord Chancellor was both a link and a protecting barrier between the executive and the judiciary. The CRA provides:

3 Guarantee of continued judicial independence

(1) The Lord Chancellor, other Ministers of the Crown and all with responsibility for matters relating to the judiciary or otherwise to the administration of justice must uphold the continued independence of the judiciary ...

(4) The following particular duties are imposed for the purpose of upholding that independence.

(5) The Lord Chancellor and other Ministers of the Crown must not seek to influence particular judicial decisions through any special access to the judiciary.

(6) The Lord Chancellor must have regard to—

(a) the need to defend that independence;

(b) the need for the judiciary to have the support necessary to enable them to exercise their functions;

(c) the need for the public interest in regard to matters relating to the judiciary or otherwise to the administration of justice to be properly represented in decisions affecting those matters.

(7) In this section "the judiciary" includes the judiciary of any of the following—

(a) the Supreme Court;

(b) any other court established under the law of any part of the United Kingdom;

(c) any international court. ...

Thus all Ministers and those with administration of justice responsibilities must uphold judicial independence. During the passage of the bill some wanted the provision to be strengthened so as to be capable of enforcement and to be protected against implied repeal. In evidence to the House of Lords Select Committee which examined the Constitutional Reform Bill, Lord Woolf compared it to declaratory provisions that had been included in education and National Health Service legislation, and told the Committee that it was not intended that such declaratory provisions should be enforceable in the courts and that a minister failing to fulfil the responsibilities set out in the Clause 'would be answerable to Parliament and the public for the failure to do so' (HL 125 of 2003–4, para. 76).

The fears of those who were concerned about Ministers not upholding judicial independence appear to have been realized to some extent.

Select Committee on the Constitution, *Relations between the executive, the judiciary and Parliament*

HL 151 of 2006–07, paras 42–3, 45–9, 51

42. It seems there is widespread agreement on the limits of what ministers should and should not say about individual cases, but this does not mean that ministers will always behave accordingly. The Lord

Chancellor's duty, as the defender of judicial independence in the Cabinet, is both to ensure that ministers are aware of the need to avoid attacking individual judges and to reprimand them if they breach this principle. As Lord Falconer told us, "the effect of the Constitutional Reform Act is that I have got an obligation to speak out both privately and, if necessary, publicly to defend the independence of the judges". As to whether his performance of this role had been adversely affected by the fact that he was no longer a judge or head of the judiciary, he insisted "emphatically not".

43. The Lord Chief Justice has emphasised that this kind of intervention by the Lord Chancellor is "a most valuable constitutional protection of judicial independence", because the only alternative would be for the Lord Chief Justice himself to intervene publicly, which would risk a high-profile dispute that would not be "in the interests of the administration of justice". Lord Mackay of Clashfern added that "the sooner a response is made [by the Lord Chancellor] the better" …

45. There has moreover been one case since the CRA was enacted where the then Lord Chancellor, Lord Falconer, was forced to speak out publicly. The case concerned the convicted paedophile Craig Sweeney, who was given a life sentence with a minimum tariff of five years and 108 days. When passing sentence in the Crown Court at Cardiff in June 2003, Judge Griffith Williams, the Recorder of Cardiff, explained very clearly how he reached this tariff and emphasised that Sweeney would only be released "when and if there is no risk of you re-offending". Nonetheless, the then Home Secretary (John Reid MP) attacked the sentence as "unduly lenient" and asked the then Attorney General (Lord Goldsmith) to examine the case as the tariff "does not reflect the seriousness of the crime", thereby inappropriately casting aspersions on the competence of Judge Williams. Lord Goldsmith's spokesman responded sharply to Dr Reid's comments, pledging that "the Attorney will make a decision [on whether to appeal] purely on the merits of the case and not in response to political or public pressure".

46 … In short, Lord Falconer did not publicly defend Judge Williams until appearing on the BBC's *Question Time* programme three days after the sentence was handed down. Even then, he defended Dr Reid's intervention. Lord Falconer subsequently had to rebuke and extract an apology from his junior minister, Vera Baird MP, for directly criticising the judge when appearing on a radio programme. The Lord Chief Justice later labelled the attacks "intemperate, offensive and unfair", whilst the Secretary of the Council of Circuit Judges, Judge Keith Cutler, told the BBC that "some of the judges felt that there was quite a silence, and there was no-one actually speaking on behalf of the judges … We are thinking that we must perhaps change that". Ultimately, Judge Williams was vindicated when Lord Goldsmith decided not to appeal.

47. When we asked the panel of legal editors about this case, they were highly critical of the then Lord Chancellor. Frances Gibb, Legal Editor of *The Times*, told us that "the Lord Chancellor should have stepped in much more quickly to defend judges in the face of some of his colleagues' comments", and Joshua Rozenberg, Legal Editor of *The Daily Telegraph*, said that the Lord Chancellor had left the judges "to swing in the wind". Astonishingly, Mr Rozenberg had been told by a DCA press officer that it was for the Lord Chief Justice rather than the Lord Chancellor to speak out on these matters.

48. Although the Lord Chief Justice could have publicly criticised Dr Reid, this would probably have exacerbated tensions between the executive and the judiciary at a sensitive time. In fact, the Lord Chief Justice was in Poland at the time and the responsibility for dealing with the controversy fell to Sir Igor Judge. He did not speak to Lord Falconer until two days after the sentence was handed down, and in retrospect admitted that he should have contacted him "more quickly". The Lord Chief Justice should also have been more proactive in ensuring that the matter was being dealt with promptly.

49. The Sweeney case was the first big test of whether the new relationship between the Lord Chancellor and the judiciary was working properly, and it is clear that there was a systemic failure. Ensuring that ministers do not impugn individual judges, and restraining and reprimanding those who do, is one of the most important duties of the Lord Chancellor. In this case, Lord Falconer did not fulfil this duty in a satisfactory manner. The senior judiciary could also have acted more quickly to head off the inflammatory and unfair press coverage which followed the sentencing decision …

51. The key to harmonious relations between the judiciary and the executive is ensuring that ministers do not violate the independence of the judiciary in the first place. To this end, we recommend that when the Ministerial Code is next revised the Prime Minister should insert strongly worded guidelines setting out the principles governing public comment by ministers on individual judges.

NOTES:

1. The House of Lords Select Committee on the Constitution inquiry *The Office of the Lord Chancellor* (HL 75 of 2014–15) concluded (p. 4):

> It has become more difficult for post-reform Lord Chancellors with their wider policy responsibilities, more overtly political positions as Secretaries of State for Justice and their reduced role in relation to the judiciary to carry out this duty in relation to the rule of law. The effectiveness of Lord Chancellors in this regard is more directly dependent on the personal authority and effectiveness of the individual holding the office.
>
> Other guardians of the rule of law have become more significant as a result. In particular, the importance of the Law Officers has increased. As such, we recommend that they should receive the resources necessary to carry out this duty and that the Attorney General should continue to attend all Cabinet meetings. The Government should make clear the respective responsibilities of those charged with upholding the rule of law within Government and ensure that they receive the support necessary to fulfil those duties. In addition, Parliament must be aware of its importance as a guardian of the rule of law and scrutinise the actions and policies of Government to ensure it governs in accordance with the rule of law.
>
> We recognise concerns raised about the combination of the office of Lord Chancellor with that of the Secretary of State for Justice. However, the combination of the office of Lord Chancellor with a major department of state confers additional authority which assists the Lord Chancellor in his or her vital duties in relation to the rule of law.
>
> The Lord Chancellor has traditionally performed an important oversight role in relation to the United Kingdom constitution as a whole. Whilst responsibility for constitutional change passed to the Deputy Prime Minister in 2010, we have heard no evidence that he, or any other minister, currently takes responsibility for the state of the constitution as a whole. A senior Cabinet minister should be tasked with this responsibility; in our view most appropriately the Lord Chancellor.
>
> We conclude that, despite significant changes to the office of Lord Chancellor, it still retains important constitutional duties and responsibilities that go beyond those of other ministers. We recommend that the office and its associated responsibilities be retained and strengthened with an amended oath. The Lord Chancellor should be a politician with significant ministerial or other experience to ensure that they have sufficient authority and seniority to uphold the rule of law in Cabinet, and in dealings with ministerial colleagues.

The Government response (26 February 2015) did not propose any change in light of the Committee's recommendations.

2. A controversy over the conduct of the Lord Chancellor in fulfilling her statutory duty to protect the independence of the judiciary was provoked in the aftermath of the High Court decision regarding the domestic constitutional requirements for triggering Brexit negotiations under Art. 50 TFU, in *R (Miller)* v *Secretary of State for Exiting the European Union* [2016] EWHC 2768 (Admin) (discussed further in Chapter 5, Section 1D at pp. 192–5). A number of newspapers who had campaigned to leave the EU produced headlines attacking the judges involved in the case; most notably, the *Daily Mail* described the judges as 'Enemies of the People' on its front page on 3 November 2016, continuing 'Fury over "out of touch" judges who have "declared war on democracy" by defying 17.4m Brexit voters and who could trigger constitutional crisis'. The Lord Chancellor, Liz Truss, was criticized by MPs and the Bar Council for responding slowly, and then inadequately. On 5 November 2016, she released a statement in extremely general terms, which did not challenge the press headlines:

> The independence of the judiciary is the foundation upon which our rule of law is built and our judiciary is rightly respected the world over for its independence and impartiality. In relation to the case heard in the High Court, the government has made it clear it will appeal to the Supreme Court. Legal process must be followed.

The Prime Minister, Theresa May, was similarly criticized when on 6 November 2016 she commented:

> I believe in and value the independence of our judiciary. I also value the freedom of our press. I think these both underpin our democracy and they are important. Of course the judges will look at the legal arguments. We think we have strong legal arguments and we will be taking those arguments to the Supreme Court.

■ QUESTIONS

1. If the Lord Chancellor is a junior member of the Cabinet, might that play a part in the speed and robustness of action under the s. 3 duty taken against a more senior cabinet colleague? Is the lack of legal training of recent Lord Chancellors a cause for concern, or recognition that this is primarily a political office in government?

2. The most recent version of the Ministerial Code, published by the new Prime Minister Theresa May upon taking office in 2016, does not explicitly set out guidelines relating to public comments on individual judges by Ministers (and nor did the 2010 or 2015 Codes issued by David Cameron). The *Cabinet Manual* (which will be discussed in Chapter 5, Section 1C at pp. 187–91) includes the following, at para. 6.38:

> ... There is also a duty not to seek to influence judicial decision-making through special access; for example, individual cases should not be discussed between ministers and judges.

Is this adequate, or should Ministers be provided with more detailed guidance as to what public comments they are entitled to make about particular judges or judicial decisions? Might this, for example, have altered the reaction of Ministers to criticism of the High Court decision in *Miller*?

D: The Supreme Court

The point made by Malleson (see earlier in this chapter in Section 1B at p. 142) is that the creation of a Supreme Court was seemingly, and unusually in the UK, more driven by principle than pragmatism. The Government's case for the creation of a Supreme Court was that 'The Government believes that in so doing they will reflect and enhance the independence of the Judiciary from both the legislature and the executive'. How real were the threats to judicial independence by having judges who were also members of the legislature? Judicial independence assists the impartiality of the judges.

J. Webber, 'Supreme Courts, Independence and Democratic Agency'
(2004) 24 *Legal Studies* 55, 63, 67–8

... the law of bias has always required definite indication of extraneous influence or predetermination. Cases of bias tend to fall into one of three categories: 1) where the decision-maker has declared his or her opinion on the specific case in issue—where he or she has literally prejudged the issue on these facts; 2) where the judge has a strong antipathy or a close connection to a party—a connection that goes beyond mere sympathy, so that the judge might be seen to have an extraneous interest in the outcome (for example, the existence of family relationship, business association, professional partnership, or close friendship between the judge and a party); or 3) where the judge may obtain a direct personal benefit from the outcome. The disqualification of Lord Hoffmann in the Pinochet extradition case met this higher test: Lord Hoffmann was at the time a director of a charity that was closely aligned to Amnesty International and that shared Amnesty's objects; Amnesty itself had become a party to the Pinochet case precisely in order to argue for a particular outcome ... All that is left, in the great run of cases, is whether simple membership in the House of Lords is sufficient to generate bias in the same way that being an officer of a company might do so in a private dispute. Might the position of the Law Lords, when viewed in this light, be analogous to that of Lord Hoffmann? The arguments have not generally been posed in this form. They have focused instead on the possibility of bias on a specific issue, for good reason. The Parliament of the United Kingdom is not characterised by a unified commitment to a set of objects. It is a deliberative body in which individuals representing a wide range of interests come together to debate matters for society as a whole. It does not make sense, then, to presume bias on the basis of mere membership, but rather to focus on the specific impairment of decision-making ...

The constraints that the Law Lords have voluntarily assumed deal effectively, in substance, with both impartiality and judicial independence. The remaining concerns seem highly abstract and formal. Of course, problems of impartiality and substantive independence may still arise in particular cases—they arise even in courts that enjoy full institutional separation—but those can be addressed by the individual judges withdrawing from those cases. In fact, this remedy is more easily available in the Appellate

Committee than it is in most supreme courts. Most such courts have a set membership, combined with a strong ethic that each case should be heard by the full bench. In contrast, less than half the full-time membership of the Appellate Committee sits on any given case, and there remain a number of additional judges who may be called upon if necessary. There is therefore much greater scope for avoiding situations of conflict.

It is true that the Appellate Committee's independence and impartiality depends on the Law Lords' own good sense—on their judgment in restricting their activities in the legislative business of the House, on maintaining their relative freedom from party entanglements, and on recusing themselves when their engagements have compromised their ability to judge, in fact or in appearance. The current structure does not provide the peremptory barriers to legislative entanglement that institutional separation would create. There might be some reason to remove the judges from the House in order to erect such barriers, if the presence of the Law Lords offered no substantial benefits (although it is important to realise that barriers could supplement but not replace the role of a strong judicial ethic; in matters like this, structure can never do all the work). In weighing that balance, one would want to assess carefully the contributions made by the Law Lords to the legislative business of the House—a task I leave to others. But one would also want to weigh the symbolic implications of the change, implications that (I believe) speak to the important subtext that runs throughout the present debate.

NOTES

1. The argument was put that it was useful for the Law Lords to participate in the legislative proceedings of the House of Lords as they could contribute legal expertise but also they would gain knowledge and understanding from their involvement. The Royal Commission on Reform of the House of Lords in its 2000 report *A House for the Future* (Cm 4183) thought the Law Lords should be retained for their expertise and recommended that they issue a statement on the principles which would regulate their involvement in the legislature (para. 9.10). Lord Bingham as Senior Law Lord made a statement on behalf of the Law Lords (HL Debs. Vol. 610, col 419, 22 June 2000):

   > ... first, the Lords of Appeal in Ordinary do not think it appropriate to engage in matters where there is a strong element of party political controversy; and secondly the Lords of Appeal in Ordinary bear in mind that they might render themselves ineligible to sit judicially if they were to express an opinion on a matter which might later be relevant to an appeal to the House.

   The consequence of this was that only four Law Lords subsequently intervened in proceedings, Lords Nicholls and Hoffmann on one occasion each, Lord Hope on five occasions, and Lord Scott on 11 occasions (seven of which were debates on reports of the Lord's European Affairs Select Committee and he was the chairman of its sub-committee on Law and Institutions (Appendix 8, HL 124 of 2003–04)).

   A majority of the Law Lords in their response to the Government's consultation paper on the Supreme Court took the view that, 'on pragmatic grounds, the proposed change is unnecessary and will be harmful' (Lords Nicholls of Birkenhead, Hoffmann, Hope of Craighead, Hutton, Millett, Rodger of Earlsferry) and a minority 'regard the functional separation of the judiciary at all levels from the legislature and the executive as a cardinal feature of a modern, liberal, democratic state governed by the rule of law' (Lords Bingham of Cornhill, Steyn, Saville of Newdigate, Walker of Gestingthorpe). Lord Neuberger, President of the Supreme Court from 2012 to 2017, was also initially critical of the creation of the court he would go on to head, describing it in a BBC interview in 2009 as 'what appears to have been a last-minute decision over a glass of whisky', that the 'danger is that you muck around with a constitution like the British Constitution at your peril because you do not know what the consequences of any change will be', and that there was a real risk of 'judges arrogating to themselves greater power than they have at the moment'.

2. Another area of concern about Law Lords (and other judges too) is their chairing of inquiries which are politically controversial. The arguments for and against the involvement of judges were considered by the House of Commons Public Administration Select Committee report on the proposed legislation on inquiries. The committee endorsed Lord Woolf's wish that the legislation should not only require consultation by Ministers with the relevant Chief Justice or Senior Law Lord (now President of the Supreme Court) when proposing to appoint a judge but that the decision should be taken co-equally. The Government resisted this and when the Lords amended

the bill to give, in effect, the Chief Justice a veto, they were overturned in the Commons and the Lords did not press the matter. Mr Leslie MP, the Minister who moved the amendment to restore consultation said:

> It is important to emphasise that we are talking about inviting a judge to chair an inquiry, not forcing them. The sense that Ministers are somehow able to undermine the independence of a judge is slightly peculiar, to say the least. All our judges are of the highest standing and repute and would not take on inquiries if they felt that they were being used, as some would suggest. Judges will be able to decide for themselves whether to chair inquiries and neither the Lord Chief Justice nor the Minister should be able to force a judge to do so or have a veto on a judge's involvement (Standing Committee B 22 March col 67).

Earlier (at col. 62) he had said:

> The matter reaches further than consideration of just the impact on the judiciary and the admin-istration of justice because, when appointing an inquiry panel, Ministers should be able to weigh up what is in the wider public interest. That depends on many factors, including the nature of the problem and the level of public concern. To be blunt, public inquiries can be more important than the judicial business demands that apply from time to time in the courts. For instance, the appointment of Lord Phillips as chairman of the BSE inquiry is an example of a case in which the wider public interest of investigating that crisis outweighed the loss of the Lord to the courts.

See the Public Administration Committee Report HC 51 of 2005–06 and Sir J. Beatson 'Should Judges Conduct Public Inquiries?' (2005) 121 *Law Quarterly Review* 221.

Continuing enthusiasm for judges to serve as the chairs of public inquiries can be seen in the decision to invite Leveson LJ to chair, from 2011–12, an extremely prominent inquiry into the *Culture, Practice and Ethics of the Press* in the light of the phone-hacking scandal (available at http://www.levesoninquiry.org.uk).

■ QUESTIONS

1. Has the creation of the Supreme Court had a positive or negative impact on judicial inde-pendence? Have the initial concerns of senior members of the judiciary failed to transpire, or have the judges become comfortable with the greater authority that might be provided by their location in a Supreme Court?

2. If the principle of judicial independence requires the separation of senior judges from the legislature, does it not apply with as much, or even more force to Government invitations to conduct inquiries? Why do you think the Government continues to invite judges to chair public inquiries?

E: Judicial appointments

The judicial appointments process established under the CRA is somewhat complex with variations for different judges in (a) the Supreme Court, (b) for the Court of Appeal and for Heads of Division and the Lord Chief Justice, and (c) the High Court and below. In the consultation paper there were three models of judicial appointments commis-sion suggested: the appointing, the recommending and the hybrid. The Government's preference was for a recommending commission with a single candidate being put for-ward which the Minister could select for appointment by the Sovereign.

The first justices of the Supreme Court were the then Law Lords but future appoint-ments involved a Commission which is different from that used for High Court judges. In part this can be justified by the fact that the Supreme Court is a United Kingdom body and that there are judicial appointments bodies throughout the three jurisdictions. In Scotland a statutory Judicial Appointments Board (four judicial, two legal, and six lay members, chaired by a lay member) has functioned since June 2009, under the Judiciary and Courts (Scotland) Act 2008, replacing an administrative board in place since 2002. In Northern Ireland, the Northern Ireland Judicial Appointments Commission (chaired by the Lord Chief Justice with five other judicial members, five lay members, and a practising solicitor and barrister) operates under the Justice (Northern Ireland) Acts 2002 and 2004. And in England and Wales, there exists the Judicial Appointments Commission (JAC, see its composition later in this chapter in Section 1E at pp. 154–6).

Initially, under the 2005 Act, the members of the selection commission for the Supreme Court were the Supreme Court President and Deputy President, with one member each from the three judicial appointments bodies nominated by the Lord Chancellor on the recommendation of those bodies, one of whom was not to be legally qualified. This process has been amended by the Crime and Courts Act 2013, which prohibits the President or Deputy President of the Supreme Court from being a member of the commission which will select their successor. A commission which selects a future President must be chaired by a non-legally qualified member. Under s. 26, it will be the Prime Minister who nominates to the Sovereign the candidate for appointment to the Supreme Court. The process which notifies that nomination is as follows.

Constitutional Reform Act 2005

27. Selection process

(1) The commission must–

    (a) determine the selection process to be applied by it,

    (b) apply the selection process, and

    (c) make a selection accordingly.

(1A) The commission must have an odd number of members not less than five.

(1B) The members of the commission must include–

    (a) at least one who is non-legally-qualified,

    (b) at least one judge of the Court,

    (c) at least one member of the Judicial Appointments Commission,

    (d) at least one member of the Judicial Appointments Board for Scotland, and

    (e) at least one member of the Northern Ireland Judicial Appointments Commission,

    and more than one of the requirements may be met by the same person's membership of the commission.

(1C) If the commission is convened for the selection of a person to be recommended for appointment as President of the Court—

    (a) its members may not include the President of the Court, and

    (b) it is to be chaired by one of its non-legally-qualified members.

(1D) If the commission is convened for the selection of a person to be recommended for appointment as Deputy President of the Court, its members may not include the Deputy President of the Court.

(4) Subsections (5) to (10) apply to any selection under this section or regulations under section 27A.

(5) Selection must be on merit.

(5A) Where two persons are of equal merit—

    (a) section 159 of the Equality Act 2010 (positive action: recruitment etc) does not apply in relation to choosing between them, but

    (b) Part 5 of that Act (public appointments etc) does not prevent the commission from preferring one of them over the other for the purpose of increasing diversity within the group of persons who are the judges of the Court.

(6) A person may be selected only if he meets the requirements of section 25.

(7) A person may not be selected if he is a member of the commission.

(8) In making selections for the appointment of judges of the Court the commission must ensure that between them the judges will have knowledge of, and experience of practice in, the law of each part of the United Kingdom.

(9) The commission must have regard to any guidance given by the Lord Chancellor as to matters to be taken into account (subject to any other provision of this Act) in making a selection.

(10) Any selection must be of one person only.

(11) For the purposes of this section a person is non-legally-qualified if the person—

(a) does not hold, and has never held, any of the offices listed in Schedule 1 to the House of Commons Disqualification Act 1975 (judicial offices disqualifying for membership of the House of Commons), and

(b) is not practising or employed as a lawyer, and never has practised or been employed as a lawyer.

NOTES

1. This provision is as amended by the Crime and Courts Act 2013, which also repealed ss 28–31 of the 2005 Act. The principles with which the selection process in general must accord remain broadly unchanged, but the detailed rules will now be contained in secondary legislation, by s. 27A of the amended 2005 Act. In particular, the amended primary legislation confirms that the Lord Chancellor may retain in the regulations the power to reject, or require a commission to reconsider, a recommendation; that the regulations must be made in agreement with the senior judge of the Supreme Court; and that consultation must take place with specified judicial office-holders and those in devolved administrations. The Supreme Court (Judicial Appointments) Regulations 2013 have been enacted under the power in s. 27(A).

2. A similar restructuring of the rules originally contained in the 2005 Act relating to appointment to other judicial offices has also occurred—the detailed rules on selection are now contained in secondary legislation rather than in the Constitutional Reform Act itself. For appointments in England and Wales below the High Court, the JAC will conduct the selection exercise. Powers of acceptance, rejection, or reconsideration previously possessed by the Lord Chancellor have been transferred to the Lord Chief Justice or, for tribunal appointments, to the Senior President of Tribunals (s. 86, Sch. 14 of the 2005 Act). The Lord Chancellor retains the powers of acceptance, rejection, or reconsideration in relation to the appointment of senior judges, at the level of the High Court and above (the Judicial Appointments Regulations 2013, made under the power contained in s. 94C of the 2005 Act, and by agreement with the Lord Chief Justice).

Constitutional Reform Act 2005

Schedule 12

1 The Commission consists of–

(a) a chairman, and

(b) such number of other Commissioners as the Lord Chancellor may specify by regulations made with the agreement of the Lord Chief Justice,

appointed by Her Majesty on the recommendation of the Lord Chancellor.

2(1) The chairman must be a lay member.

3 A person must not be appointed as a Commissioner if he is employed in the civil service of the State.

3A The number of Commissioners who are holders of judicial office must be less than the number of Commissioners (including the chairman) who are not holders of judicial office.

3B (1) The Lord Chancellor may, by regulations made with the agreement of the Lord Chief Justice, make provision about the composition of the Commission.

(2) The power to make regulations under this paragraph is to be exercised so as to ensure that the Commission's members include—

(a) holders of judicial office,

(b) persons practising or employed as lawyers, and

(c) lay members.

(3) Regulations under this paragraph may (in particular)—

    (a) make provision about the number, maximum number or minimum number of Commissioners of a particular description;

    (b) make provision about eligibility for appointment as a Commissioner, eligibility for appointment as the chairman or eligibility for appointment as a Commissioner of a particular description.

The Judicial Appointments Commission Regulations 2013

Number of Commissioners

3. There are 15 Commissioners including the chairman.

Composition of the Commission

4. —(1) Of the 14 other Commissioners—

    (a) 7 must be holders of judicial office,

    (b) 5 must be lay members, and

    (c) 2 must be persons practising or employed as lawyers.

(2) Of the 7 Commissioners who are appointed as holders of judicial office—

    (a) 1 must be a Lord Justice of Appeal;

    (b) 1 must be a puisne judge of the High Court;

    (c) 1 must be a senior tribunal office-holder member;

    (d) 1 must be a circuit judge;

    (e) 1 must be a district judge of a county court, a District Judge (Magistrates' Courts) or a person appointed to an office under section 89 of the Senior Courts Act 1981;

    (f) 1 must be a holder of an office listed in paragraph (3);

    (g) 1 must be a non-legally qualified judicial member.

(3) The offices referred to in paragraph (2)(f) are—

    (a) judge of the First-tier Tribunal appointed under paragraph 1(1) of Schedule 2 to the Tribunals, Courts and Enforcement Act 2007;

    (b) transferred-in judge of the First-tier Tribunal (see section 31(2) of that Act);

    (c) Regional Employment Judge appointed under regulation 6(1) of the Employment Tribunals (Constitution and Rules of Procedure) Regulations 2004;

    (d) Employment Judge (England and Wales) appointed under regulation 8(1) and (3)(a) of those Regulations.

(4) Of the 2 Commissioners appointed who are persons practising or employed as lawyers—

    (a) each person must hold a qualification listed in paragraph (5),

    (b) but they must not hold the same qualification as each other.

(5) The qualifications referred to in paragraph (4) are—

    (a) barrister in England and Wales;

    (b) solicitor of the Senior Courts of England and Wales;

    (c) fellow of the Chartered Institute of Legal Executives.

NOTES

1. There are too many appointments for the Commissioners to be involved in all of them so the JAC appoints people to the panels. Commissioners, however, will be members of panels in the selection exercises for senior appointments. For the appointment of Supreme Court Justices, there will be one member of the JAC on a five-member panel (regs 5 and 11 of the Supreme Court (Judicial Appointments) Regulations 2013). For appointment of Lords and Lady Justices of Appeal, Senior

Presidents of Tribunals, Heads of Division, and the Lord Chief Justice, of the five people who will sit on such panels, either two or three will be members of the Commission, and at least one of them will be a lay member of the Commission (regs 5, 11, 17, and 23 of the Judicial Appointments Regulations 2013).

2. The JAC in 2015–16 ran 22 selection exercises for posts at High Court level and below for which there were 2,588 applications and 340 recommendations made. At the more senior level, panels supported the selection of four new Lords and Lady Justices of Appeal, and the new Senior President of Tribunals. The JAC was also asked to assist in the selection of a UK Judge for the European Court of Human Rights.

3. By s. 63(2) of the Constitutional Reform Act 2005, the JAC must make selections 'solely on merit'. The JAC also has a duty 'to have regard to the need to encourage diversity in the range of persons available for selection for appointments' (s. 64), although this is subject to the merit criterion. The Advisory Panel on Judicial Diversity reported in February 2010. Its analysis and recommendations included:

> 1. There is a strong case for a more diverse judiciary. Not only should there be equality of opportunity for those eligible to apply, but in a democratic society the judiciary should reflect the diversity of society and the legal profession as a whole. Judges drawn from a wide range of backgrounds and life experiences will bring varying perspectives to bear on critical legal issues. A judiciary which is visibly more reflective of society will enhance public confidence.
> 2. We have concluded that there is no quick fix to moving towards a more diverse judiciary. This will come as no surprise to those who have worked to promote diversity over recent years. . . .
> 4. The message from our research and consultations is consistent with research and experience in other jurisdictions: we will achieve significant transformation if, and only if, diversity is addressed systematically—not only within the appointments process, but throughout a legal and judicial career, from first consideration of the possibility of joining the judiciary to promotion at the most senior level. . .
> 5. Delivering a more diverse judiciary is not just about recruiting talent wherever it may be found, important though that is, but about retaining talent and enabling capable individuals to reach the top. . . .
> 7. Sustained progress on judicial diversity requires a fundamental shift in approach from a focus on selection processes towards a judicial career that addresses diversity at every stage.

The House of Lords Constitution Committee has also considered the question of judicial diversity.

Select Committee on the Constitution, *Judicial Appointments*
HL 272 of 2010–12, pp. 5–6

> We support the current appointments model and believe that no fundamental changes should be made. We therefore conclude that: ...
>
> • Merit must continue to remain the sole criterion for appointment. However, we do not consider merit to be a narrow concept based solely on intellectual capacity or high quality advocacy. We refute any notion that those from under-represented groups make less worthy candidates or that a more diverse judiciary would undermine the quality of our judges. ...
>
> In order to increase public trust and confidence in the judiciary, there is a need to increase judicial diversity. We do not consider that sufficient steps have yet been taken. Accordingly, we recommend that:
>
> • The recommendations of the Advisory Panel on Judicial Diversity should be implemented more rapidly.
> • Appointments panels must include lay persons who can bring a different perspective to the assessment of candidates' abilities. Lay membership of selection panels is also the key to avoiding the problem of self-replication within the judiciary.
> • All selection panels should themselves be gender and, wherever possible, ethnically diverse.
> • All those involved in the appointments process must be required to undertake diversity training.
> • The duty on the JAC, contained in s 64 of the CRA, to encourage diversity in the range of persons available for selection for appointments should be extended to the Lord Chancellor and the Lord Chief Justice.

- The "tipping provision" contained in s 159 of the Equality Act 2010 should be used as part of the appointments process.
- If there has been no significant increase in the numbers of women and BAME judicial appointments in five years' time, the Government should consider setting non-mandatory targets for the JAC to follow.
- There needs to be an increased commitment to flexible working and the taking of career breaks within the judiciary. The Senior Courts Act 1981 should be amended to allow part-time appointments to be made at High Court level and above.
- There needs to be a greater commitment on the part of the Government, the judiciary and the legal professions to encourage applications for judicial posts from lawyers other than barristers. Being a good barrister is not necessarily the same thing as being a good judge.

These recommendations constitute necessary first steps towards improving the diversity of the judiciary. We hope that they will prove sufficient, but goodwill and leadership will be required to bring about significant change. We regret that, to date, there has not been sufficient commitment to removing barriers to applications from under-represented groups.

The conclusions and recommendations which we reach in this report are based on our affirmation of the principles which we believe should continue to underpin the judicial appointments process: judicial independence, appointment on merit, accountability and the promotion of diversity. The achievement of the correct balance between these principles is vital in maintaining public confidence in the judiciary and the legal system as a whole.

NOTES

1. Many of these recommendations have been implemented by the Crime and Courts Act 2013. In particular, the duty to encourage diversity has been extended to the Lord Chancellor and Lord Chief Justice in the amended Constitutional Reform Act 2005:

> **137A. Encouragement of diversity**
>
> Each of the Lord Chancellor and the Lord Chief Justice of England and Wales must take such steps as that office-holder considers appropriate for the purpose of encouraging judicial diversity.

More significant is the amendment of the 2005 Act to permit the need to enhance the diversity of the judiciary as a 'tie-breaker' between candidates, reflecting the provision made in s. 159 of the Equality Act 2010:

> **63. Merit and good character**
>
> (1) Subsections (2) to (4) apply to any selection under this Part by the Commission or a selection panel ("the selecting body").
> (2) Selection must be solely on merit.
> (3) A person must not be selected unless the selecting body is satisfied that he is of good character.
> (4) Neither "solely" in subsection (2), nor Part 5 of the Equality Act 2010 (public appointments etc), prevents the selecting body, where two persons are of equal merit, from preferring one of them over the other for the purpose of increasing diversity within—
>   (a) the group of persons who hold offices for which there is selection under this Part, or
>   (b) a sub-group of that group.

It is not clear how dramatic the impact of this provision will be. In 2015–16, the first full year of the operation of the provision, the JAC reported that 14 recommendations (out of 340 in the year overall) were made following the application of its Equal Merit Provision Policy, designed to implement s. 63(4). That policy (published April 2014) indicates that:

> 3. Where the Commission considers two or more candidates are of equal merit when assessed against the published criteria for the post, it may use the provision to make the final selection decisions.
> 4. The provision will only be used when two or more candidates are assessed as having the skills, experience and expertise that result in them being considered equal in the assessment of the Commission. This decision, to be made by the Commission sitting as the Selection and Character Committee, will be based on all the evidence gathered throughout the selection process.
> 5. The provision will only be considered where under-representation of diversity characteristics within the judiciary can be demonstrated. Published data showing the diversity of the judiciary at a particular level, along with the 2011 Census, Detailed Characteristics, Office of National Statistics 2012 (or the latest updated population estimates), will be used.

6. The Commission has agreed to consider race and gender only at this stage. When applying the provision to the characteristic of race, the Commission will limit the definition to the two categories of white and BAME. This approach is supported by the published data.

7. Where two or more candidates are judged to be of equal merit and the provision is to be used, priority may be given to the candidate(s) with declared protected characteristics which are least well represented in the office (group) to which they are being recommended for appointment....

9. The provision will apply to all selections for judicial appointments under Part 4 of the CRA, whether recommended for appointment by the Commission "or by a selection panel" for senior appointments (above High Court) as such panels are committees of the Commission. The provision will also apply to the selection of persons for membership of a pool for requests under section 9(1) of the Senior Courts Act 1981 to act as deputy High Court judges.

Further changes made in the Crime and Courts Act 2013 to enhance judicial diversity include amending the Constitutional Reform Act 2005 and Senior Courts Act 1981 so that the maximum numbers of judges are to be calculated by reference to full-time equivalent numbers, opening up the possibility of part-time working throughout the court system.

2. The most radical of the Constitution Committee's suggestions—that the Government should, if judicial diversity has not improved in five years, set non-mandatory targets for the JAC to follow—has not been accepted. The response of the Government, published in May 2012 (Cm 8358), was:

15) The Government considers that mandatory quotas would undermine the principle of merit and should not be introduced. As the 2010 report from the Advisory panel on Judicial Diversity indicated, quotas were firmly rejected as a possible solution, by all that they spoke to in particular by those from under-represented groups.

A report prepared for the Labour Party by Geoffrey Bindman QC and Karon Monaghan QC in November 2014, at the request of the then Shadow Secretary of State for Justice, Sadiq Khan, concluded that quotas were necessary:

We have also concluded that the time has now come for quotas. Progress towards a diverse judiciary has been too slow. Without a requirement to appoint qualified women and ethnic minorities, we believe that the pace of change will remain intolerably slow.

The arguments considered in favour of judicial appointments quotas included their acceptance in other areas of public life, such as the use of all-woman shortlists for the selection of parliamentary candidates, and the de facto quota system already in place in practice in the Supreme Court, by which there will be two Justices from Scotland, and one from Northern Ireland (ensuring the court has knowledge and experience of the law of each part of the UK, as s. 27(8) of the CRA 2005 requires). The Labour Party was not elected to implement this recommendation after the 2015 general election.

3. Judicial diversity (or the lack thereof) is a topic discussed with some frequency by members of the senior judiciary, generating considerable controversy. In a newspaper interview in 2015, Lord Sumption said:

These things simply can't be transformed overnight, not without appalling consequence in other directions...

One has to look at the totality of these problems and not simply at one of them. The lack of diversity is a significant problem, but it isn't the only one. It takes time. You've got to be patient. The change in the status and achievements of women in our society, not just in the law but generally, is an enormous cultural change that has happened over the last 50 years or so. It has to happen naturally. It will happen naturally. But in the history of a society like ours, 50 years is a very short time.

[British justice] is a terribly delicate organism. We have got to be very careful not to do things at a speed which will make male candidates feel that the cards are stacked against them. If we do that we will find that male candidates don't apply in the right numbers. Eighty-five per cent of newly appointed judges in France are women because the men stay away. Eighty-five per cent women is just as bad as 85% men.

In contrast with Lord Sumption's rejection of positive discrimination (see also Lord Sumption's Bar Council Law Reform Lecture 'Home Truths About Judicial Diversity', 15 November 2012), Lady Hale has expressed support for intervention (Conference to mark the tenth anniversary of the Judicial Appointments Commission, University of Birmingham, 'Appointments to the Supreme Court', 6 November 2015):

So how are we doing with appointments to our own Supreme Court? I was sworn in as a 'Lord of Appeal in Ordinary' on 12 January 2004. 15 people have been sworn in as Lords of Appeal in Ordinary or Justices of the Supreme Court of the United Kingdom since then. Even if we leave out the two who were sworn in the day after me, the Court has more than replaced itself since then. One might have hoped that the opportunity would have been taken to achieve a more diverse collegium. It has not happened.

All of those 13 appointments were men. All were white. All but two went to independent fee-paying schools. All but three went to boys' boarding schools. All but two went to Oxford or Cambridge. All were successful QCs in private practice, although one was a solicitor rather than a barrister. All but two had specialised in commercial, property or planning law. None had spent much, if any, time as an employee. I share with them the experience of being white and having been to Cambridge. In every other of those respects I am different: I went to a state day school, my profession was University teacher and then Law Commissioner, my specialism was family and social welfare law. How is it that, despite their very different characters and outlooks, they remain such a homogenous group? ...

I believe that anyone who is appointing the Justices of the Supreme Court should be able to look at the body of Justices as a whole and ask how they can collectively best serve the needs of the UK justice system. Excellence is important (though I am embarrassed to claim it). But so is diversity of expertise. And so is diversity of background and experience. It really bothers me that there are women, who know or ought to know that they are as good as the men around them, but who won't apply for fear of being thought to be appointed just because they are a woman. We early women believed that we were as good as the men and would certainly not be put off in this way. I may well have been appointed because the powers that be realised the need for a woman. I am completely unembarrassed about that, because they were right, and I hope that I have justified their confidence in me. I don't think that all the talk about the best women being deterred is a plot to put them off, but I am sure that they should not be deterred by talk such as this. We owe it to our sex, but also to the future of the law and the legal system, to step up to the plate.

Baroness Hale also criticized the JAC Equal Merit Provision Policy, suggesting that it could be applied at the start of the selection process, rather than only informing the final decision at the end.

There will be six appointments to the Supreme Court made between 2017 and 2018. The outgoing President, Lord Neuberger, announced in November 2016 that there would be a composite round of three appointments in both 2017 and 2018, which 'improves the prospect of a more diverse and more coherent recruitment to the court'. The current Lord Chancellor, Liz Truss, also supported change to improve judicial diversity in 2016, including recognizing that an assessment of merit should include an assessment of potential, and opening up greater scope for direct-entry to the higher judiciary for talented individuals without existing judicial experience.

■ QUESTIONS

1. Have the changes made by the Crime and Courts Act 2013 improved the system of judicial appointments? Do you think it is right that judges are still very much involved in the appointment of other judges? Could it be argued that the JAC should have an even greater role in the appointment of the most senior judges?

2. The Lord Chancellor's powers of rejection or reconsideration have been very rarely used (in 2010, one request for reconsideration was made of a Head of Division position, the recommendation confirmed, and subsequently accepted by the Lord Chancellor; in 2011, two part-time medical tribunal appointments were rejected by a subsequent Lord Chancellor). What does this tell you about the work of the JAC, and the independence of the judicial appointments process?

3. As of 1 April 2016, there was one female Supreme Court Justice out of 12, no female Heads of Division out of five, eight female Justices of Appeal out of 39, and 22 female High Court Judges out of 106. None of the Supreme Court Justices, Heads of Division, or Lord and Lady Justices of Appeal were black or from minority ethnic groups. There were five black or minority ethnic (BME) High Court Judges out of 106 in total. Given these figures, is it arguable that more radical solutions are needed to the problem of the limited diversity of the senior judiciary in the UK? Do such statistics threaten to undermine the authority of the UK court system?

F: Discipline

The position in relation to judges in the High Court and above is that under the Act of Settlement 1701 and the Senior Courts Act 1981, they hold office 'during good behaviour' and may only be removed following an address to the Sovereign by both Houses of Parliament. The last (and, indeed, seemingly only) time this power was used was in 1830 in relation to Sir Jonah Barrington, a High Court Judge. Circuit and District Judges can be removed by the Lord Chancellor, with the agreement of the Lord Chief Justice. This has happened twice—in 1983 and 2009.

Where previously the Lord Chancellor as Head of the Judiciary would have exercised other disciplinary powers they are now, under s. 108 of the Constitutional Reform Act 2005, exercised concurrently with the Lord Chief Justice.

Constitutional Reform Act 2005

108 Disciplinary powers

(1) Any power of the Lord Chancellor to remove a person from an office listed in Schedule 14 is exercisable only after the Lord Chancellor has complied with prescribed procedures (as well as any other requirements to which the power is subject).

(2) The Lord Chief Justice may exercise any of the following powers but only with the agreement of the Lord Chancellor and only after complying with prescribed procedures.

(3) The Lord Chief Justice may give a judicial office holder formal advice, or a formal warning or reprimand, for disciplinary purposes (but this section does not restrict what he may do informally or for other purposes or where any advice or warning is not addressed to a particular office holder).

(4) He may suspend a person from a judicial office for any period during which any of the following applies—

   (a) the person is subject to criminal proceedings;

   (b) the person is serving a sentence imposed in criminal proceedings;

   (c) the person has been convicted of an offence and is subject to prescribed procedures in relation to the conduct constituting the offence.

(5) He may suspend a person from a judicial office for any period if—

   (a) the person has been convicted of a criminal offence,

   (b) it has been determined under prescribed procedures that the person should not be removed from office, and

   (c) it appears to the Lord Chief Justice with the agreement of the Lord Chancellor that the suspension is necessary for maintaining confidence in the judiciary.

(6) He may suspend a person from office as a senior judge for any period during which the person is subject to proceedings for an Address.

(7) He may suspend the holder of an office listed in Schedule 14 for any period during which the person—

   (a) is under investigation for an offence, or

   (b) is subject to prescribed procedures.

(8) While a person is suspended under this section from any office he may not perform any of the functions of the office (but his other rights as holder of the office are not affected).

NOTES

1. Complaints about the conduct of judges, tribunal judges and members, and lay magistrates are investigated by the Judicial Conduct Investigations Office (JCIO). The JCIO's Annual Report for 2015–16, shows that of 2,661 complaints received in the period, 1,615 were rejected as ineligible or out of time (60.7 per cent), 1,003 were dismissed (37.7 per cent), and 43 were upheld (1.6 per

cent). The work of the JCIO is subject to the overview of the Judicial Appointments and Conduct Ombudsman. In the 2015–16 period, the Ombudsman determined 161 complaints about JCIO investigations, and upheld complaints in six cases.

2. Recent high-profile examples of investigations into judicial conduct include:

- A complaint against Judge Patricia Lynch QC for swearing at a man she was sentencing, in retaliation after he had sworn at her. She was cleared of misconduct after apologizing for the inappropriate comments, with the investigation concluding the matter could be dealt with by informal advice.

- An investigation into the conduct of Peter Smith J, who following a newspaper column written by Lord Pannick QC (which criticized the High Court judge, who had to step aside in a case involving British Airways after he had complained during the hearing about the airline losing his luggage) wrote to the head of Pannick's chambers suggesting he would withdraw support from its members applying to become QCs. After the letter became public, the Court of Appeal overturned Peter Smith J's decision in a case involving barristers from Pannick's chambers on the grounds that there was a risk of the appearance of bias. Peter Smith J voluntarily agreed to refrain from sitting while the complaint was under consideration, the outcome of which was still pending as of January 2017.

■ QUESTION

Why should judges in the High Court and above have greater security of tenure than circuit judges? Given such senior judges are in practice never dismissed from office, does this mean judicial complaints procedures must be particularly robust?

G: Accountability of the judiciary to Parliament

The House of Lords Select Committee on the Constitution in its report on 'Relations Between the Executive, the Judiciary and Parliament' stated that it was an interesting argument put forward by Professor Bogdanor that:

> ... judges should not be "answerable" to Parliament in terms of justifying their decisions, but should "answer" to Parliament through committee appearances—in other words, they should be accountable to Parliament not in the "sacrificial" sense, but in the "explanatory" sense (HL 151 of 2006–7, para. 122).

As the Lord Chancellor could no longer answer on behalf of the judiciary, the report considered other ways in which Parliament could hold the judiciary accountable.

The Question of Accountability

The Role of Select Committees

186. We believe that select committees can play a central part in enabling the role and proper concerns of the judiciary to be better understood by the public at large, and in helping the judiciary to remain accountable to the people via their representatives in Parliament. Not only should senior judges be questioned on the administration of the justice system, they might also be encouraged to discuss their views on key legal issues in the cause of transparency and better understanding of such issues amongst both parliamentarians and the public. However, under no circumstances must committees ask judges to comment on the pros and cons of individual judgments. ...

A Parliamentary Committee on the Judiciary

187. We are not currently convinced of the need for a joint committee on the judiciary, but we shall keep the situation under review, not least in evaluating our Committee's effectiveness in providing the necessary oversight and contact. The Constitutional Affairs Select Committee in the House of Commons also has an important role to play ...

Response from the Judiciary to the House of Lords Select Committee on the Constitution report on relations between the executive, the judiciary and Parliament, Select Committee on the Constitution, *Relations between the executive, the judiciary and Parliament: Follow-up Report*

HL 177 of 2007–08, pp. 24–5

... 'sacrificial' ... accountability would be incompatible with the principle of the independence of the judiciary. It is right, however, that if the judiciary is to have the input we would like into all aspects of the administration of justice, then we should account for the way in which we have discharged our administrative responsibilities. The question is how to do this in a way which is not incompatible with the judiciary's core responsibility as the branch of the State responsible for providing the fair and impartial resolution of disputes between citizens and the State, in accordance with the prevailing rules of law.

Your Report suggests that Select Committees "can play an important role in holding the judiciary to account by questioning in public" ... we see merit in the suggestion that Select Committees can represent an appropriate and helpful forum for the Lord Chief Justice, after publication of his annual report, to explain his views on aspects of the administration of justice that are of general interest or concern and upon which it is appropriate for the judiciary to comment. There may, of course, be other circumstances in which the judiciary consider it appropriate to express views to Parliament on other issues ... we are cautious about your suggestion that this should include their views on "key legal issues". There are difficulties in judges giving views on new legislative proposals or the operation of the law. Although, as our guidance recognises, it is appropriate for a judge to comment on the operation and procedures of his or her jurisdiction and the implications of any Bill or Act in these respects we need to be particularly aware of the fact that a senior judge might, at some stage in the future, be asked to adjudicate on an issue they had commented on in the past. An awareness and appreciation of the guidelines, from both the judiciary and the Committee, should ensure that we avoid any such pitfalls.

We are concerned, however, that the appearance of judges and magistrates before Select Committees should not become routine for fear of stepping beyond the proper boundary between the judiciary and Parliament. We have already seen an increase in the number of invitations to appear in the 18 months since the implementation of the constitutional reforms. Therefore, while we welcome the indication that Committees would be open to additional appearances from the judiciary, such appearances need, we believe, to be truly necessary and appropriate.

Guidance to Judges on Appearances Before Select Committees

The Judicial Executive Board, October 2012

Judicial comment – the conventions

1. For the most part parliamentary business, including the business of select committees, is conducted without the involvement of the judiciary, and without the appearances of judges before them. Such appearances should be regarded as exceptional. Indeed, until the last quarter of the twentieth century there were virtually no appearances by judges before parliamentary committees.

2. If a judge is asked to appear before a select committee, the request will be administered by the Private Office of the Lord Chief Justice. ...

3. On being asked to give evidence to a parliamentary committee, longstanding constitutional conventions (and, in the case of IV, desirable practice) are likely to prevent judges from commenting on the following matters:

I.   The merits of individual cases, whether or not the judge giving evidence has adjudicated on that case, and whether these are pending, ongoing, or have concluded...

II. The personalities or merits of serving judges, politicians, or other public figures, or more generally on the quality of appointments;

III. The merits, meaning or likely effect of provisions in any Bill or other prospective legislation and the merits of government policy... ;

IV. Issues which are subject to government consultation on which the judiciary intend to make a formal institutional response, but have not yet done so.

NOTE: Section 5 of the Constitutional Reform Act 2005 allows the chief justice of any part of the UK to lay written representations before Parliament 'on matters that appear to him to be matters of importance relating to the judiciary, or otherwise to the administration of justice, in that part of the United Kingdom'. There is no equivalent power for the President of the Supreme Court.

This has been regarded as being exceptional and the Lords Select Committee on the Constitution suggested at para. 119 that if such representations are laid that they:

> ... should be published in Hansard; that the business managers should find time for the issue to be debated in the House at the earliest possible opportunity; and that the Government should respond to such representations in good time before either House has finished considering the bill or initiative in question. Further, this Committee will endeavour to scrutinise any such representations in time to inform deliberations in the House.

The judiciary's response to this was that:

> We welcome the proposed handling arrangements for any such representations made by the Lord Chief Justice; the opportunity for an early debate and a timely response from the Government will be essential to ensure that there can be full and proper consideration of issues that are raised.

The Lord Chief Justice had told the Constitutional Affairs Select Committee that he had considered if he should lay written representations on the issue of the creation of the Ministry of Justice, in respect of negotiations concerning a possible conflict between the Lord Chancellor's responsibilities to fund the court system and to resource the prisons which had been transferred from the Home Office.

The power under section 5 to lay written representations before Parliament has been exercised in relation to Scotland by the Lord President of the Court of Session. On 16 January 2012, as the legislation which would become the Scotland Act 2012 was before Parliament, the Lord President made two representations:

> I urge Parliament to provide in the Scotland Bill an amendment to the Scotland Act 1998 so as (1) to extend the jurisdiction of the Supreme Court in Scottish criminal appeals and references to the remedying of infringements of the European Convention by the courts below as well as by the prosecutor but (2) to restrict those cases in which leave may be granted to appeal to the Supreme Court from the High Court of Justiciary to cases in which the High Court has certified that a point of law of general public importance is involved in the decision.

The problem to which these representations were a response is discussed in Chapter 8, Section 2A at p. 349.

The former Lord Chief Justice of England and Wales, Lord Judge, recently indicated to the Constitution Committee of the House of Lords that he considered the use of the s. 5 power to lay representations before Parliament to be a 'nuclear option' (House of Lords Constitution Committee, Sessional Report 2012–13 (HL Paper 7, 20 May 2013) para. 24). There is nevertheless a tension between this characterization of the power, and its use for the more mundane purpose of laying an annual report from the Lord Chief Justice before Parliament, as was explicitly referenced in both the 2015 and 2016 reports (see also Gee, 'The Lord Chief Justice and Section 5 of the Constitutional Reform Act', *UK Constitutional Law Association Blog* (14 April 2014)). The 2016 report notes, p. 29:

> It is now a well-established convention that the Lord Chief Justice will appear annually before Select Committees of both Houses of Parliament to discuss his Annual Report. In addition, other judges have given evidence to Parliamentary Committees on matters ranging from courts and tribunals fees to the role of the magistracy. Adherence to Judicial Executive Board Guidance on such appearances, which relies on close and collaborative working between Select Committee clerks and Judicial Office staff, continues to ensure that judicial evidence is relevant, useful, and within the constitutional boundaries.

H: The judiciary, media, and the public

Sixth Report from the House of Lords Select Committee on the Constitution
HL 151 of 2006–07, paras 191–4

Public Perceptions

191. We believe that the media, especially the popular tabloid press, all too often indulge in distorted and irresponsible coverage of the judiciary, treating judges as 'fair game'. A responsible press should show greater restraint and desist from blaming judges for their interpretation of legislation which has been promulgated by politicians. If the media object to a judgment or sentencing decision, we suggest they focus their efforts on persuading the Government to rectify the legal and policy framework. In order to ensure more responsible reporting, we recommend that the Editors' Code of Practice, which is enforced by the Press Complaints Commission, be regularly updated to reflect these principles ...

The Role of Individual Judges

192. Whilst judges should never be asked to justify their decisions outside the courtroom, it is desirable for them to communicate with the public and the media on appropriate issues. We therefore strongly encourage the occasional use of media releases alongside judgments, as for example in the Charlotte Wyatt case. Further, we cannot see any reason why judges should not co-operate with the media on features about their activities outside the courtroom, if they so wish. However, we are strongly of the opinion that whatever the media pressure, judges should not give off-the-record briefings ...

The Role of the Lord Chief Justice

193. It is wholly within the discretion of the Lord Chief Justice to determine how he can most effec-tively communicate with the media and the public. However, we suggest that he may from time to time need to re-appraise his strategy in light of the new constitutional relationship between the judiciary, the executive and Parliament. We believe that, in these days of greater separation of powers, it is highly desirable for him to ensure that the views of the judiciary are effectively conveyed to the public ...

The Role of the Judicial Communications Office

194. We conclude that the judges should consider making the Judicial Communications Office more active and assertive in its dealings with the media in order to represent the judiciary effectively. We sug-gest that consideration be given to appointing one or more spokesmen with appropriate qualifications and legal experience who would be permitted to speak to the media with the aim of securing cover-age which accurately reflects the judgment or sentencing decision. However, under no circumstances should such spokesmen seek to justify decisions as opposed to explaining them.

Response from the Judiciary to the House of Lords Select Committee on the Constitution report on relations between the executive, the judiciary and Parliament
The Judiciary of England and Wales, October 2007 (available at http://www.judiciary.gov.uk/Resources/JCO/Documents/Consultations/const_committee_response.pdf)

We agree. Judges have their own part to play in maintaining public confidence in the judiciary and the justice system.

Public perceptions

We agree with the Committee's view on the public position Government Ministers should take in rela-tion to judicial decisions.

Role of individual judges

It is a cardinal principle that a judge should give his decision and the reasons for it in public. It has, for some time, been the practice that where a judgment is long and complex a judge will, where practi-cable, incorporate into his judgment a short summary to assist public understanding. When making sentencing remarks in shorter judgments a judge will always endeavour to explain the reasons for his decisions in a way that can be understood by the public who may not be familiar with the details of the case. Where reasons are given orally, as is almost always the case when sentencing, judges are encouraged to consider preparing a written note of their sentencing remarks to be given by hand to reporters in court. It is inappropriate for a judge outside of his decision to seek to amplify or explain his decision—his public judgment speaks for itself. It follows from this principle and the nature of judicial office that we endorse the Committee's views that judges should not give media briefings.

The Role of the Lord Chief Justice

The Lord Chief Justice has been Head of the Judiciary for 18 months. As the Committee acknowledges, there will always be a gap between the level of activity the media would like to see from the Lord Chief Justice and what is wise or even appropriate for the Lord Chief Justice to undertake. In fact, as the Committee advocates, this is kept under constant review, not least as interview bids and other requests arrive for him on a daily basis.

It is important to bear in mind that the Lord Chief Justice has now a direct means of communication with the public through the judicial website (www.judiciary.gov.uk): an illustration of this is the publication on the website of his two interviews with Marcel Berlins (there have been 8840 downloads since April 2006), as well as the publication of speeches and statements by him and other senior judges.

The Role of the Judicial Communications Office

The JCO is, in government terms, a small and relatively new unit responsible for providing communications support to more than 40,000 judicial office-holders. It provides support to the judiciary and to the media when questions arise about judicial issues and keeps up to date the judicial website which, as we have said, is an important means of external communication.

It is accepted there may be occasions, such as the media's reporting following the Sweeney judgment in June 2006, when the timely use of a judicial spokesperson, rather than a JCO press officer, to explain sentencing *process* might help provide a balance in the reportage. The Judges' Council is, therefore, considering the best means of developing a proposal, that whilst ensuring adherence to the principle that judicial decisions must speak for themselves, to provide in certain circumstances information through certain serving judges that will assist public understanding and debate.

Along with the judicial website, the JCO is actively involved in producing educational material for schools and the public generally about the work of judges within the operation of the justice system.

NOTES

1. A mapping exercise of different types of judicial accountability can aid an analysis of the select committee's and the judiciary's views.

A. Le Sueur, 'Developing Mechanisms for Judicial Accountability in the UK'

(2004) *Legal Studies* 74, 79–81

Individual (personal) accountability—examples	Institutional (court) accountability—examples
• discipline for personal misconduct (in serious + resulting in dismissal/an expectation of resignation); • writing individual reasoned judgments in a multi-judge court; • explanations of personal views on law and the constitution delivered in public lectures, interviews with the press or scholarly academic publications.	• publication of annual reports about the work of a court; • consultation over proposed changes to court rules and practice; • financial audit requirements; • the requirement for a court to sit in public; • the existence of rights of appeal to a higher court; • for courts of EU members states/Council of Europe, responding to judgments of the ECJ and ECtHR; • parliamentary debates on the judicial function (e.g. HL Debs., Vol. 648, col. 876, 21 May 2003).

Accountability via formal processes—examples	Accountability via civil society—examples
• publishing written reasons for a court's decisions; • rights of appeal to higher courts against alleged errors; publication of annual reports by a court; • scrutiny of individual judicial appointments and the appointments process generally.	• robust and accurate reporting on judgments in the news media; • academic commentary on particular judgments and the conduct of courts generally; • public education by the Bar and other legal professional organisations.

Content accountability—examples	Process accountability—examples	Performance accountability	Probity accountability—examples
Written, reasoned judgments	Methods for selecting which cases to hear	Explanations for time taken to determine cases	Basic financial audit of court's annual expenditure
Contributions of individual judges to law reviews and public speeches	Selection of panels of judges (in courts which do not sit en banc)		Systems for judges registering or disclosing pecuniary and other interests

2. The first two sets of tables showing individual and institutional aspects, and the formal and via civil society processes are more self-explanatory than the final table. It seems that the judiciary accept a linkage between the first two tables that they should engage with the media through the JCO to reach the public. Le Sueur suggested that more might be done with the format of law reports which would make them easier to understand, and he referred to the practice of the Supreme Court of the US which issues a 'prefatory syllabus', a summary of multiple judgments prepared by the court reporter but officially sanctioned. Would it not be possible for the format of judgments to include explanatory material? Surely that is just as important as the neutral citation system and numbered paragraphs which belatedly accommodated electronic publication and retrieval of law reports? A press summary is now commonly provided to accompany judgments of the Supreme Court; such summaries are 'provided to assist in understanding the Court's decision' but 'does not form part of the reasons for the decision'. In late 2016, in light of the unprecedented media and public interest in the *Miller* case, which concerned the constitutional requirements to commence UK exit from the EU, daily transcripts of the hearings in the High Court and Supreme Court were for the first time made available on the respective official websites as the case was argued, along with a range of other materials, including the parties' written submissions, and a timetable for the hearings.

3. Process accountability, it is suggested, encompasses the explanation and justification of the decision-making process a body uses for its job. Le Sueur points out that it was not until 2003 that the Appellate Committee of the House of Lords began to give reasons where they had refused permission to appeal. He suggests that explaining how panels will be composed to hear appeals in the House of Lords and Supreme Court is important. He referred to a point made by Lord Lester that political concern could arise in Edinburgh, Cardiff or Belfast in devolution cases previously before the Judicial Committee of the Privy Council if criteria on panel composition were not published. The Senior President of Tribunals will be under a duty to publish a policy on how judges and members will be assigned to chambers in the First-tier and Upper Tribunals (see Chapter 13, Section 2 at pp. 660–3). The Supreme Court's published Rules of Court now set out the criteria to be used when considering whether more than five judges should sit on a panel:

   - If the Court is being asked to depart, or may decide to depart from a previous decision.
   - A case of high constitutional importance.
   - A case of great public importance.
   - A case where a conflict between decisions in the House of Lords, Judicial Committee of the Privy Council, and/or the Supreme Court has to be reconciled.
   - A case raising an important point in relation to the European Convention on Human Rights.

4. The issue with content accountability is the extent to which judges may render an account of the legal and constitutional values which their judgments promote, beyond lectures and articles, at the request of Parliament. The judiciary accept this, with limitations on what they say and a concern about the frequency upon which they may be asked to do it. One problematic aspect of the tension between accountability and judicial independence was raised by Mr Charles Clarke MP, a former Home Secretary. He was concerned that after delivering their declaration of incompatibility with the European Convention on Human Rights and the Anti-Terrorism Crime and Security Act 2001 provisions on detention without trial provisions in *A* v *Secretary of State for the Home Department* [2004] UKHL 56, [2005] 2 AC 68, he was left with little guidance on what measures would be Convention compatible and also meet the security threat to the nation. He would have liked a meeting with the Law Lords to discuss what might be and what might not be lawful in devising the control orders. He thought that 'the idea that their independence would be corrupted by such discussions is risible' (HL 151 of 2006–07, paras 93–5). The Lords select committee did have sympathy with the difficulties outlined by Mr Clarke but accepted the views of Lord Bingham, the Senior Law Lord, and Lord Woolf, the former Lord Chief Justice and then a member of the committee, who pointed out respectively, that the Law Lords cannot appear to collude with the executive when they may have to determine challenges to actions taken by the executive, and that the Law Lords are 'the final arbiters of law on particular facts' (paras 96–7).

5. In the 2007 Green Paper *The Governance of Britain* (Cm 7170) the Government indicated it would review the arrangements for judicial appointments with the possibility of involving Parliament. The response to the consultation proposals indicated that while some felt that there may be a role for Parliament in overseeing the JAC and the appointments process, there was very limited support for Parliament holding judicial confirmation hearings. The role of Parliament in judicial appointments was recently discussed in the report of the House of Lords Constitution Committee on this topic which was considered earlier in this chapter in Section 1E at pp. 156–7.

Constitution Committee, *Judicial Appointments*
HL 272 of 2010–12, paras 46, 48, 52, 56

Pre- or post-appointment hearings

46. We are against any proposal to introduce pre-appointment hearings for senior members of the judiciary. However limited the questioning, such hearings could not have any meaningful impact without undermining the independence of those subsequently appointed or appearing to pre-judge their future decisions. In the United Kingdom, judges' legitimacy depends on their independent status and appointment on merit, not on any democratic mandate. ...

48. We agree that post-appointment hearings of senior judges would serve no useful purpose. There may be an exception in the case of the Lord Chief Justice and the President of the Supreme Court who undertake leadership roles for which they can properly be held to account. ...

Parliamentary participation in selection panels

52. Parliamentarians, acting in that capacity, should not sit on selection panels for judicial appointments. There is no useful role that parliamentarians could play that could not be played by lay members on selection panels. It would not be possible to choose one or two parliamentarians without recourse to political considerations and in so doing it would be difficult to maintain the appearance of an independent judicial appointments process. ...

Parliamentary oversight of the judicial appointments process

56. We welcome the willingness of judges, once appointed, to give evidence to parliamentary committees on the judicial appointments process and other matters relating to the administration of justice. We recognise that the majority of judges speak on an individual basis and not on behalf of their fellow judges: indeed, Parliament benefits from the diverse range of views thus offered. We believe that this dialogue is of mutual benefit to both the judiciary and Parliament as it enables both to explore areas of common interest and concern. We encourage its continuation in the future.

■ QUESTIONS

1. Do you agree that Parliament should play no role in judicial appointments? Is it arguable that in an era in which the courts have to make decisions about the meaning and scope of human rights, the political views of the judges should be known in advance of their appointment, even if they will be seeking to be objective when actually deciding the cases before them?

2. If the risk of politicization is too great to permit parliamentary involvement in appointments, is there a case for parliamentary involvement in appointment of judges as judicial managers, the Lord Chief Justice and Heads of Division, and, if so, what would be the appropriate types of question which parliamentarians could pose?

3. Do you think the judges are sufficiently accountable—in the range of ways considered above—in the contemporary UK constitution? Can you think of other ways increased judicial accountability could reinforce judicial independence and legitimacy?

I: Judicial independence and parliamentary privilege

As explained earlier in this chapter, it is important that the independence of the judiciary is maintained. Accepting this, are there corollary duties on the courts not to interfere unduly in the legitimate activities of Parliament? One way in which this might be evident is in the judicial acceptance of the legislation of the sovereign UK Parliament (discussed in Chapter 2, Section 1 at pp. 46–56). Another important issue is the extent to which the courts respect parliamentary privilege. Parliamentary privilege broadly covers two matters: (i) the right of each House of Parliament to control its own proceedings and precincts; and (ii) the prohibition on what is said in proceedings in Parliament being questioned in a court of law (established by Art. 9 of the Bill of Rights 1689). The nature and extent of parliamentary privilege arose in the aftermath of the 2009 MPs expenses crisis.

R v Chaytor and others
[2010] UKSC 52, Supreme Court

Three MPs and one peer were charged with false accounting under s. 17(1)(b) of the Theft Act 1968 in relation to their claims for allowances. Their defence was that the claims for allowances were submitted as part of proceedings in Parliament, which in accordance with parliamentary privilege, could not be questioned in court. Only the three MPs appealed to the Supreme Court, the peer was permitted to be an intervenor.

LORD PHILLIPS:

15. It is now accepted in Parliament that the courts are not bound by any views expressed by parliamentary committees, by the Speaker or by the House of Commons itself as to the scope of parliamentary privilege. On 4 March 2010 the Clerk of the Parliaments wrote to the solicitor acting for Lord Hanningfield a letter that had received the approval of the Committee for Privileges. This stated:

"Article 9 limits the application of parliamentary privilege to 'proceedings in Parliament.' The decision as to what constitutes a 'proceeding in Parliament', and therefore what is or is not admissible as evidence, is ultimately a matter for the court, not the House."

This statement was correct. It applies as much to the House of Commons as to the House of Lords, and to an issue as to the scope of the exclusive cognisance of Parliament as it does to an issue as to the application of article 9.

16. Although the extent of parliamentary privilege is ultimately a matter for the court, it is one on which the court will pay careful regard to any views expressed in Parliament by either House or by bodies or individuals in a position to speak on the matter with authority …

47. The jurisprudence to which I have referred is sparse and does not bear directly on the facts of these appeals. It supports the proposition, however, that the principal matter to which article 9 is directed is freedom of speech and debate in the Houses of Parliament and in parliamentary committees. This is where the core or essential business of Parliament takes place. In considering whether actions outside the Houses and committees fall within parliamentary proceedings because of their connection to them, it is necessary to consider the nature of that connection and whether, if such actions do not enjoy privilege, this is likely to impact adversely on the core or essential business of Parliament.

48. If this approach is adopted, the submission of claim forms for allowances and expenses does not qualify for the protection of privilege. Scrutiny of claims by the courts will have no adverse impact on the core or essential business of Parliament, it will not inhibit debate or freedom of speech. Indeed it will not inhibit any of the varied activities in which Members of Parliament indulge that bear in one way or another on their parliamentary duties. The only thing that it will inhibit is the making of dishonest claims …

61. There are good reasons of policy for giving article 9 a narrow ambit that restricts it to the important purpose for which it was enacted—freedom for Parliament to conduct its legislative and deliberative business without interference from the Crown or the Crown's judges. The protection of article 9 is absolute. It is capable of variation by primary legislation, but not capable of waiver, even by Parliamentary resolution. Its effect where it applies is to prevent those injured by civil wrongdoing from obtaining redress and to prevent the prosecution of Members for conduct which is criminal….

62. Thus precedent, the views of Parliament and policy all point in the same direction. Submitting claims for allowances and expenses does not form part of, nor is it incidental to, the core or essential business of Parliament, which consists of collective deliberation and decision making. The submission of claims is an activity which is an incident of the administration of Parliament; it is not part of the proceedings in Parliament. I am satisfied that Saunders J and the Court of Appeal were right to reject the defendants' reliance on article 9.

76 . …. The courts will respect the right of each House to reach its own decision in relation to the conduct of its affairs. Two examples will illustrate this. In *Re McGuinness's Application* [1997] NI 359 the applicant sought to challenge by judicial review the decision of the Speaker that those who had not complied with the requirements of the Parliamentary Oaths Act 1866 would be denied certain of the facilities of the House. Kerr J dismissed his application. He held at p 6:

> "I am quite satisfied that, whether it qualifies as a proceeding in Parliament or not, the Speaker's action lies squarely within the realm of internal arrangements of the House of Commons and is not amenable to judicial review."

77. In *R v Parliamentary Commissioner for Standards, Ex p Al Fayed* [1998] 1 WLR 669 the Parliamentary Commissioner for Standards had published a report relating to a complaint by the applicant against a Member of Parliament. The applicant sought permission to challenge this by judicial review. The application was refused by Sedley J and renewed before the Court of Appeal. Lord Woolf MR gave a judgment with which the other members of the court agreed dismissing the application. He said, at p 673:

> "The focus of the Parliamentary Commissioner for Standards is on the propriety of the workings and the activities of those engaged within Parliament. He is one of the means by which the select committee set up by the House carries out its functions, which are accepted to be part of the proceedings of the House. This being the role of the Parliamentary Commissioner for Standards, it would be inappropriate for this court to use its supervisory powers to control what the Parliamentary Commissioner for Standards does in relation to an investigation of this

sort. The responsibility for supervising the Parliamentary Commissioner for Standards is placed by Parliament, through its standing orders, on the Committee of Standards and Privileges of the House, and it is for that body to perform that role and not the courts." ...

92. Even if the House were not co-operating with the prosecuting authorities in these cases, I do not consider that the court would be prevented from exercising jurisdiction on the ground that they relate to matters within the exclusive cognisance of Parliament. If an applicant sought to attack by judicial review the scheme under which allowances and expenses are paid the court would no doubt refuse the application on the ground that this was a matter for the House. Examination of the manner in which the scheme is being implemented is not, however, a matter exclusively for Parliament. It was not suggested that Members have a contractual entitlement to allowances and expenses, but if they were to have such contractual rights, I see no reason why they should not sue for them. If a question were raised as to whether allowances and expenses were taxable, the court would be entitled to examine the circumstances in which they were paid. Equally there is no bar in principle to the Crown Court considering whether the claims made by the defendants were fraudulent. This is not to exclude the possibility that, in the course of a criminal prosecution, issues might arise involving areas of inquiry precluded by parliamentary privilege, although that seems unlikely having regard to the particulars of the charges in the cases before us.

93. For these reasons I am satisfied that neither article 9 nor the exclusive cognisance of the House of Commons poses any bar to the jurisdiction of the Crown Court to try these defendants. That is why I decided that each appeal should be dismissed.

Appeal dismissed.

NOTE: In light of this case a commitment was made by the coalition government to consider legislating to reform and clarify the scope of parliamentary privilege. A Green Paper was published on 26 April 2012 (Cm 8318), and a parliamentary Joint Committee on Parliamentary Privilege was constituted, and reported in July 2013.

Joint Committee on Parliamentary Privilege, *Parliamentary Privilege*
HL 30/HC 100 of 2013–14, paras 29–31, 135–6

The role of the courts

29. In the absence of an exhaustive definition of "proceedings in Parliament", certain matters are generally accepted as falling within the terms of Article 9, and in such cases Parliament's sole jurisdiction may be said, in the terms used in the *Vaid* judgment, to have been "authoritatively established". These matters include:

- the procedures adopted by the two Houses: the courts may not challenge the means by which legislation was passed or decisions reached;
- proceedings in Parliament: words spoken in the course of debate, votes cast, or decisions taken by either House;
- actions of Members, office-holders or officials which are necessarily linked to proceedings.

30. Although cases relating to such matters could in theory come before a court, our expectation is that where the existence of a privilege is authoritatively established (either by statute or, in some cases, by case law), the court will immediately decline jurisdiction, without enquiring further into the nature or origins of the privilege.

31. Yet even here there may be uncertainty, not over the existence of a privilege, but over its precise extent. For instance there may be uncertainty over the extent to which the protection afforded by Article 9 extends beyond words spoken in the course of debate to briefing or correspondence that

is preparatory to that debate. In such cases of uncertainty, the decision as to whether a matter falls within Parliament's sole jurisdiction rests, paradoxically, with the courts. This has been accepted at least since the case of *Stockdale v. Hansard* in the 1830s, in which the Lord Chief Justice, Lord Denham, while accepting in terms that "whatever be done within the walls of either [House] must pass without question in any other place", rejected the proposition that the House of Commons, in its guise as a court, had sole jurisdiction over the *extent* of its own privileges:

> "Where the subject matter falls within their jurisdiction, no doubt we cannot question their judgment; but we are now enquiring whether the subject matter does fall within the jurisdiction of the House of Commons. It is contended that they can bring it within their jurisdiction by declaring it so. To this claim, as arising from their privileges, I have already stated my answer: it is perfectly clear that none of these Courts could give themselves jurisdiction by adjudging that they enjoy it".

This approach was endorsed and re-stated by Lord Phillips of Worth Matravers in *R v. Chaytor*: "the extent of parliamentary privilege is ultimately a matter for the court".

Judicial questioning of proceedings in Parliament…

135. We are grateful for the Lord Chief Justice's assurance that recent instances of judicial questioning of proceedings in Parliament are best "treated as … mistakes", rather than a challenge to Parliament. We emphasise that such mistakes may have serious consequences: even if they are acknowledged to be mistakes, and do not establish a precedent, their frequency in judicial review cases risks having a chilling effect upon parliamentary free speech.

136. In conclusion:

- We welcome the clarification by the Lord Chief Justice as to the extent of the *Pepper v. Hart* principle, namely, that those instances in which proceedings, including Committee reports, are questioned, are best "treated as … mistakes".
- We consider that the comments of Mr Justice Stanley Burnton, in *OGC v. Information Commissioner* [[2008] EWHC 774 (Admin); [2010] QB 98], represent an accurate statement of the legal limitations upon the admissibility of Select Committee reports in court proceedings, including judicial review cases. Such reliance by the courts upon Select Committee reports is not only constitutionally inappropriate, but risks having a chilling effect upon parliamentary debate.
- We do not at this stage believe that the problem of judicial questioning is sufficiently acute to justify either legislation prohibiting use of privileged material by the courts, along the lines of section 16(3) of the Australian Parliamentary Privileges Act 1987, or the introduction of a formal and binding system of notification when reference to privileged material is contemplated.
- We trust that less formal means than those above, building on the current good relations between the judiciary and the parliamentary authorities, will address recent problems. But in this matter, as in others covered in our Report, Parliament should be prepared to legislate if it becomes necessary to do so in order to protect freedom of speech in Parliament from judicial questioning.

NOTE: Questions of parliamentary privilege have also been raised in cases considered elsewhere: first, in *Reilly (No. 2)*, where the judgment of Lang J in the Administrative Court was accepted in the Court of Appeal as having 'transgressed' rules concerning parliamentary privilege, in criticizing ministerial statements as to the human rights implications of legislation being introduced in Parliament (see Chapter 3, Section 4B at pp. 121–3). Second, in *HS2*, where the Supreme Court was eager to interpret EU law to avoid any requirement that the Court should assess the adequacy of legislative processes in relation to their engagement with the environmental implications of a major rail development (see Chapter 2, Section 3A at pp. 80–3).

■ QUESTIONS

1. Is the relationship between the courts and Parliament adequately structured at present by the principles of judicial independence and parliamentary privilege?

2. Do you agree with the Joint Committee that general legislation to clarify the present position is unnecessary?

3. How important are the less formal relations between judges, parliamentarians, and ministers in ensuring that all branches of government can carry out their functions effectively? Or should a far more formal separation of powers be established in the UK constitution, perhaps through enactment of a codified constitution?

5

The Royal Prerogative and
Constitutional Conventions

OVERVIEW

In this chapter we first consider the royal prerogative, a particular source of legislative and executive power in the UK constitution. We identify the various types of prerogative power, and consider recent reform which includes putting three prerogatives on a statutory basis, alongside an attempt to codify constitutional practice including the monarch's personal prerogative of appointment of the Prime Minister. We also consider the interaction between the prerogative and statute in the courts. In the second section of this chapter, we consider constitutional conventions as a source of the constitution, their relationship with law, and their nature as rules of political behaviour. We consider generally the treatment of conventions in the courts, whether they can obtain legal force, and conclude by assessing the feasibility and desirability of codifying conventions. We consider important interactions between the royal prerogative and constitutional conventions at various points throughout the chapter.

SECTION 1: ROYAL PREROGATIVE

A: What is the Royal Prerogative?

The royal prerogative provides legal authority for a fixed range of specific governmental activities. The prerogative is a special source of UK constitutional authority, as a relic of the historic legal powers attributed to the Crown. The majority of the prerogative powers are now exercised by the Government, although there remain some personal prerogatives exercised by the monarch, which are regulated by non-legal constitutional conventions (discussed in the second part of this chapter).

The Governance of Britain, Review of the Executive Royal Prerogative Powers: Final Report
(2009), pp. 7, 31–4

25. Originally the prerogative would have been exercised by the reigning Monarch. However, over time a distinction was drawn between the Monarch acting in his or her individual capacity and the powers possessed by the Monarch as an embodiment of the State. As the governance of the realm became more complex, power was devolved from the Monarch and exercised by his or her advisers. In modern times Government Ministers exercise the bulk of the prerogative powers, either in their own right or through the advice they provide to The Queen which she is constitutionally bound to follow.

26. A V Dicey defines the Royal prerogative as 'The residue of discretionary or arbitrary authority, which at any given time is legally left in the hands of the Crown' [*Introduction to the Study of the Law of the Constitution,* 10th edn, 1959, p. 424]. William Blackstone however describes the prerogative more tightly, as those powers that 'the King enjoys alone, in contradistinction to others, and not to those he enjoys in common with any of his subjects' [*Commentaries on the Laws of England, a facsimile of the first edition of 1765–1769* (University of Chicago Press, 1979, p 111)]. . . .

27. The scope of the Royal prerogative power is notoriously difficult to determine. It is clear that the existence and extent of the power is a matter of common law, making the courts the final arbiter of whether or not a particular type of prerogative power exists ["The King hath no prerogative, but that which the law of the land allows him"; see the *Proclamations Case* (1610) 12 Co Rep 74, 76]. The difficulty is that there are many prerogative powers for which there is no recent judicial authority and sometimes no judicial authority at all. In such circumstances, the Government, Parliament and the wider public are left relying on statements of previous Government practice and legal textbooks, the most comprehensive of which is now nearly 200 years old [Joseph Chitty, *A Treatise on the Law of the Prerogatives of the Crown* (1820)].

28. This uncertainty has been criticised. Professor Rodney Brazier has written '. . . . the demand for a statement of what may be done by virtue of [the Royal prerogative] is of practical importance' ['Constitutional Reform and the Crown' in M. Sunkin and S. Payne (eds), *The Nature of the Crown* (Oxford, OUP, 1999), p 339]. Yet it has been said judicially that such a statement cannot be arrived at, because only through a process of piecemeal judicial decisions over the centuries have particular powers been seen to exist, or not to exist, as the case may be [*R v Secretary of State for the Home Department, ex parte Northumbria Police Authority* [1989] QB 26, (CA) p 56 (Nourse LJ)]. . . .

The *Review* went on to try to capture many of the executive prerogative powers then thought to be in existence. This list that follows gives some insight into the range, extent, and, indeed, peculiarity of many of the prerogative powers still in operation in the UK constitution.

MINISTERIAL PREROGATIVE POWERS

(a) Government and the Civil Service
- Powers concerning the machinery of Government including the power to set up a department or a non-departmental public body
- Powers concerning the civil service, including the power to appoint and regulate most civil servants
- Power to prohibit civil servants and certain other crown servants from issuing election addresses or announcing themselves, or being announced as, a Parliamentary candidate or a Prospective Parliamentary candidate
- Power to set nationality rules for 'non-aliens'—British, Irish and Commonwealth citizens— concerning eligibility for employment in the civil service
- Power to require security vetting of contractors working alongside civil servants on sensitive projects
- Powers concerning the Office of the Civil Service Commissioners, the Security Vetting Appeals Panel, the Office of the Commissioner for Public Appointments, the Advisory Committee on Business, the Civil Service Appeal Board and the House of Lords Appointments Commission, including the power to establish those bodies, to appoint members of those bodies and the powers of those bodies

(b) Justice system and law and order
- Powers to appoint Queen's Counsel
- Power to make provisional and full order extradition requests to countries not covered by Part 1 of the Extradition Act 2003
- Prerogative of mercy
- Power to keep the peace

(c) Powers relating to foreign affairs

- Power to send ambassadors abroad and receive and accredit ambassadors from foreign states
- Recognition of states
- Governance of British Overseas Territories
- Power to make and ratify treaties
- Power to conduct diplomacy
- Power to acquire and cede territory
- Power to issue, refuse or withdraw passport facilities
- Responsibility for the Channel Islands and Isle of Man
- Granting diplomatic protection to British citizens abroad

(d) Powers relating to armed forces, war and times of emergency

- Right to make war or peace or institute hostilities falling short of war
- Deployment and use of armed forces overseas
- Maintenance of the Royal Navy
- Use of the armed forces within the United Kingdom to maintain the peace in support of the police or otherwise in support of civilian authorities (e.g. to maintain essential services during a strike)
- The government and command of the armed forces is vested in Her Majesty
- Control, organisation and disposition of armed forces
- Requisition of British ships in times of urgent national necessity
- Commissioning of officers in all three armed forces…
- Crown's right to claim Prize (enemy ships or goods captured at sea)
- Regulation of trade with the enemy
- Crown's right of angary, in time of war, to appropriate the property of a neutral which is within the realm, where necessity requires
- Powers in the event of a grave national emergency, including those to enter upon, take and destroy private property

(e) Miscellaneous

- Power to establish corporations by Royal Charter and to amend existing Charters (for example that of the British Broadcasting Corporation, last amended in July 2006)
- The right of the Crown to ownership of treasure trove (replaced for finds made on or after 24 September 1997 by a statutory scheme for treasure under the Treasure Act 1996)
- Power to hold public inquiries (where not covered by the Inquiries Act)
- Controller of Her Majesty's Stationery Office as Queen's Printer:
- Power to appoint the Controller
- Power to hold and exercise all rights and privileges in connection with prerogative copyright
- Sole right of printing or licensing the printing of the Authorised Version of the Bible, the Book of Common Prayer, state papers and Acts of Parliament…
- Powers connected with prepaid postage stamps…

OTHER PREROGATIVE POWERS

In the Governance of Britain Green Paper, the Government confirmed that no changes would be proposed to the majority of either the legal prerogatives of the Crown or the Monarch's constitutional or personal prerogatives. In some areas the Government proposes to change the mechanism by which Ministers arrive at their recommendations for the Monarch's exercise of the power. These prerogatives are listed below. Also listed are certain prerogatives of a largely historical nature.

Constitutional/personal prerogatives

Powers within the constitutional/personal prerogative category of powers include:

- Appointment and removal of Ministers
- Appointment of Prime Minister
- Power to dismiss government
- Power to summon, prorogue and dissolve Parliament
- Assent to legislation
- The appointment of privy counsellors
- Granting of honours, decorations, arms and regulating matters of precedence.
- Queen's honours—Order of the Garter, Order of the Thistle, Royal Victorian Order and the Order of Merit
- A power to appoint judges in a residual category of posts which are not statutory and other holders of public office where that office is non-statutory
- A power to legislate under the prerogative by Order in Council or by letters patent in a few residual areas, such as Orders in Council for British Overseas Territories
- Grant of special leave to appeal from certain non-UK courts to the Privy Council
- May require the personal services of subjects in case of imminent danger
- Grant of civic honours and civic dignities
- Grant of approval for certain uses of Royal names and titles

Archaic prerogative powers

The nature of the prerogative has changed overtime. Historically the Royal prerogative has been described as residual powers of the Crown. In particular there are some powers which can be described as residual powers relating to small, specific issues or which are a legacy of a time before legislation was enacted in that area. It is unclear whether some of these prerogative powers continue to exist.

- Guardianship of infants and those suffering certain mental disorders
- Right to *bona vacantia*
- Right to sturgeon, (wild and unmarked) swans and whales as casual revenue
- Right to wreck as casual revenue
- Right to construct and supervise harbours
- By prerogative right the Crown is *prima facie* the owner of all land covered by the narrow seas adjoining the coast, or by arms of the sea or public navigable rivers, and also of the foreshore, or land between high and low water mark
- Right to waifs & strays
- Right to impress men into the Royal Navy
- Right to mint coinage
- Right to mine precious metals (Royal Mines); also to dig for saltpetre
- Grant of franchises, e.g. for markets, ferries and fisheries; pontage & murage
- Restraining a person from leaving the realm when the interests of state demand it by means of the writ *ne exea tregno*
- The power of the Crown in time of war to intern, expel or otherwise control an enemy alien

Legal Prerogatives of the Crown

The legal prerogatives of the Crown are powers that the Monarch possesses as an embodiment of the Crown. Sometimes described as Crown "privileges or immunities", these prerogatives have been significantly affected by statute—in particular, the Crown Proceedings Act 1947.

- Crown is not bound by statute save by express words or necessary implication
- Crown immunities in litigation, including that the Crown is not directly subject to the contempt jurisdiction and the Sovereign has personal immunity from prosecution or being sued for a wrongful act
- Tax not payable on income received by the Sovereign
- Crown is a preferred creditor in a debtors insolvency
- Time does not run against the Crown (ie no prescriptive rights run)
- Priority of property rights of the Crown in certain circumstances

B: Putting the prerogative on a statutory basis

NOTES

1. The *Review of the Executive Royal Prerogative Powers* followed on from a programme of work on the prerogative announced in the 2007 Green Paper *The Governance of Britain* (Cm 7170, 2007) paras 15, 24:

> 15. The flow of power from the people to government should be balanced by the ability of Parliament to hold government to account. However, then the executive relies on the powers of the royal prerogative ... it is difficult for Parliament to scrutinise and challenge government's actions. If voters do not believe that government wields power appropriately or that it is properly accountable then public confidence in the accountability of decision-making risks being lost...
>
> 24. The Government believes that in general the prerogative powers should be put onto a statutory basis and brought under stronger parliamentary scrutiny and control. This will ensure that government is more clearly subject to the mandate of the people's representatives. Proposals in relation to certain specific powers are set out below and these can be addressed now. The Government also intends to undertake a wider review of the remaining prerogative powers and will consider whether in the longer term, all these powers should be codified or put on a statutory basis.
>
> [In a footnote it was made clear that]
>
> 'No changes are proposed to either the legal prerogatives of the Crown on the Monarch's constitutional or personal prerogatives, although in some areas the Government proposes to change the mechanism by which Ministers arrive at their recommendations on the Monarch's exercise of those powers.'

2. Subsequently Consultation Papers were published on the Role of the Attorney-General (Cm 7192, 2007), Judicial Appointments (Cm 7210, 2007), and War Powers and Treaties (Cm 7239, 2007). A White Paper, *The Governance of Britain—Constitutional Renewal* (Cm 7342, 2008) and draft Constitutional Renewal Bill were produced in 2008 and these were considered by select committees. A major new area was placing the civil service on a statutory basis.

3. The Constitutional Reform and Governance Bill was introduced in the 2008–09 session and carried over into the 2009–10 session. It was passed but a large part of the Bill was lost in the negotiations to deal with legislation in the 'wash-up', the period between the calling of a general election and the dissolution of Parliament. Two prerogatives were thereby placed on a statutory footing, the management of the civil service and the ratification of treaties.

   The first prerogative, regarding the management of the civil service, was replaced by Part 1 of the 2010 Act. It provided general statutory powers for the management of the Civil Service by the Secretary of State (ss 3–4), made provision for the creation of various Codes of Conduct applicable to civil servants (s. 5), those in diplomatic service (s. 6), and also special advisers (appointed to provide political support to a particular Minister while they hold office, contrasting with the permanence and neutrality of the rest of the civil service) (s. 8). The Act also made provision for the appointment of civil servants—including recognizing that 'selection must be on merit on the basis of fair and open competition' (ss 10–12). A Civil Service Commission was also established (s. 2), to exercise certain functions relevant to the recruitment process, including the development of the principles against which appointments would be made (s. 11), and to receive, consider, and investigate complaints made by civil servants about potential violations of a Code of Conduct (s. 9). The requirement for the Government to produce an Annual Report on the potentially controversial issue of the number and cost of special advisers, to be laid before Parliament, was also established in the statute (s. 16).

   The second prerogative placed on statutory footing by the Act—treaty ratification powers—can be seen in the following extract.

Constitutional Reform and Governance Act 2010

Ratification of treaties

20 Treaties to be laid before Parliament before ratification

(1) Subject to what follows, a treaty is not to be ratified unless—

    (a) a Minister of the Crown has laid before Parliament a copy of the treaty,

    (b) the treaty has been published in a way that a Minister of the Crown thinks appropriate, and

    (c) period A has expired without either House having resolved, within period A, that the treaty should not be ratified.

(2) Period A is the period of 21 sitting days beginning with the first sitting day after the date on which the requirement in subsection (1)(a) is met.

(3) Subsections (4) to (6) apply if the House of Commons resolved as mentioned in subsection (1)(c) (whether or not the House of Lords also did so).

(4) The treaty may be ratified if—

    (a) a Minister of the Crown has laid before Parliament a statement indicating that the Minister is of the opinion that the treaty should nevertheless be ratified and explaining why, and

    (b) period B has expired without the House of Commons having resolved, within period B, that the treaty should not be ratified.

(5) Period B is the period of 21 sitting days beginning with the first sitting day after the date on which the requirement in subsection (4)(a) is met.

(6) A statement may be laid under subsection (4)(a) in relation to the treaty on more than one occasion.

(7) Subsection (8) applies if—

    (a) the House of Lords resolved as mentioned in subsection (1)(c), but

    (b) the House of Commons did not.

(8) The treaty may be ratified if a Minister of the Crown has laid before Parliament a statement indicating that the Minister is of the opinion that the treaty should nevertheless be ratified and explaining why.

(9) "Sitting day" means a day on which both Houses of Parliament sit.

21 Extension of 21 sitting day period

(1) A Minister of the Crown may, in relation to a treaty, extend the period mentioned in section 20(1)(c) by 21 sitting days or less.

(2) The Minister does that by laying before Parliament a statement—

    (a) indicating that the period is to be extended, and

    (b) setting out the length of the extension.

(3) The statement must be laid before the period would have expired without the extension.

(4) The Minister must publish the statement in a way the Minister thinks appropriate.

(5) The period may be extended more than once.

22 Section 20 not to apply in exceptional cases

(1) Section 20 does not apply to a treaty if a Minister of the Crown is of the opinion that, exceptionally, the treaty should be ratified without the requirements of that section having been met.

(2) But a treaty may not be ratified by virtue of subsection (1) after either House has resolved, as mentioned in section 20(1)(c), that the treaty should not be ratified.

(3) If a Minister determines that a treaty is to be ratified by virtue of subsection (1), the Minister must, either before or as soon as practicable after the treaty is ratified—

    (a) lay before Parliament a copy of the treaty,

    (b) arrange for the treaty to be published in a way that the Minister thinks appropriate, and

    (c) lay before Parliament a statement indicating that the Minister is of the opinion mentioned in subsection (1) and explaining why.

23 Section 20 not to apply to certain descriptions of treaties

(1) Section 20 does not apply to—…

    (b) a treaty covered by section 5 of the European Union (Amendment) Act 2008 (treaty amending Treaty establishing European Atomic Energy Community not to be ratified unless approved by Act of Parliament).

    (c) a treaty that is subject to a requirement imposed by Part 1 of the European Union Act 2011 (restrictions on treaties and decisions relating to EU).

(2) Section 20 does not apply to a treaty in relation to which an Order in Council may be made under one or more of the following—

    (a) section 158 of the Inheritance Tax Act 1984 (double taxation conventions);

    (b) section 2 of the Taxation (International and Other Provisions) Act 2010 (double taxation arrangements);

    (c) section 173 of the Finance Act 2006 (international tax enforcement arrangements).

(2A) Section 20 does not apply to a treaty in relation to which an order may be made under paragraph 66 of Schedule 19 to the Finance Act 2011 (bank levy: arrangements affording double taxation relief).

(2B) Section 20 does not apply to any treaty referred to in section 218(1) of the Finance Act 2012.

(3) Section 20 does not apply to a treaty concluded (under authority given by the government of the United Kingdom) by the government of a British overseas territory, of any of the Channel Islands or of the Isle of Man.

(4) Section 20 does not apply to a treaty a copy of which is presented to Parliament by command of Her Majesty before that section comes into force.

24 Explanatory memoranda

In laying a treaty before Parliament under this Part, a Minister shall accompany the treaty with an explanatory memorandum explaining the provisions of the treaty, the reasons for Her Majesty's Government seeking ratification of the treaty, and such other matters as the Minister considers appropriate.

25 Meaning of "treaty" and "ratification"

(1) In this Part "treaty" means a written agreement—

    (a) between States or between States and international organisations, and

    (b) binding under international law.

(2) But "treaty" does not include a regulation, rule, measure, decision or similar instrument made under a treaty (other than one that amends or replaces the treaty (in whole or in part)).

(3) In this Part a reference to ratification of a treaty is a reference to an act of a kind specified in subsection (4) which establishes as a matter of international law the United Kingdom's consent to be bound by the treaty.

(4) The acts are—

    (a) deposit or delivery of an instrument of ratification, accession, approval or acceptance;

    (b) deposit or delivery of a notification of completion of domestic procedures.

NOTE: These provisions present, more or less, in statutory form the pre-existing situation. Thus the existing Civil Service Commissioners were to become members of the new statutory Civil Service Commission and so continued to have responsibility for ensuring that appointments were made on merit on the basis of fair and open competition. In relation to ratification of treaties, the House of Commons could resolve against ratification and thus make it unlawful for the Government, without further engagement, to ratify a treaty. The House of Lords would not be able to prevent the

Government from ratifying a treaty, but if it resolved against ratification the Government would have to produce a further explanatory statement explaining its belief that the agreement should be endorsed. These provisions concern scrutiny of the ratification of agreements entered into by the Government under international law, reflecting the prior position as a matter of constitutional convention under the 'Ponsonby Rule'. They do not change the established position that an Act of Parliament is required to give effect in domestic law to matters embodied in such an agreement (the potentially challenging consequences of this interaction between the positions as a matter of international law and domestic law are, however, demonstrated in the *Miller* case, discussed later).

A more recent example of the statutory replacement of a prerogative power provides an interesting contrast, in so far as it *did* change significantly the prior position. This example relates to the prerogative power of the Queen to dissolve Parliament so that new elections to the House of Commons may be held.

Fixed-term Parliaments Act 2011

1 Polling days for parliamentary general elections

(1) This section applies for the purposes of the Timetable in rule 1 in Schedule 1 to the Representation of the People Act 1983 and is subject to section 2.

(2) The polling day for the next parliamentary general election after the passing of this Act is to be 7 May 2015.

(3) The polling day for each subsequent parliamentary general election is to be the first Thursday in May in the fifth calendar year following that in which the polling day for the previous parliamentary general election fell.

(4) But, if the polling day for the previous parliamentary general election—

(a) was appointed under section 2(7), and
(b) in the calendar year in which it fell, fell before the first Thursday in May,
subsection (3) has effect as if for "fifth" there were substituted "fourth".

(5) The Prime Minister may by order made by statutory instrument provide that the polling day for a parliamentary general election in a specified calendar year is to be later than the day determined under subsection (2) or (3), but not more than two months later.

(6) A statutory instrument containing an order under subsection (5) may not be made unless a draft has been laid before and approved by a resolution of each House of Parliament.

(7) The draft laid before Parliament must be accompanied by a statement setting out the Prime Minister's reasons for proposing the change in the polling day.

2 Early parliamentary general elections

(1) An early parliamentary general election is to take place if—

(a) the House of Commons passes a motion in the form set out in subsection (2), and
(b) if the motion is passed on a division, the number of members who vote in favour of the motion is a number equal to or greater than two thirds of the number of seats in the House (including vacant seats).

(2) The form of motion for the purposes of subsection (1)(a) is—"That there shall be an early parliamentary general election."

(3) An early parliamentary general election is also to take place if—

(a) the House of Commons passes a motion in the form set out in subsection (4), and
(b) the period of 14 days after the day on which that motion is passed ends without the House passing a motion in the form set out in subsection(5).

(4) The form of motion for the purposes of subsection (3)(a) is—
"That this House has no confidence in Her Majesty's Government."

(5) The form of motion for the purposes of subsection (3)(b) is—
"That this House has confidence in Her Majesty's Government."

(6) Subsection (7) applies for the purposes of the Timetable in rule 1 in Schedule 1 to the Representation of the People Act 1983.

(7) If a parliamentary general election is to take place as provided for by subsection (1) or (3), the polling day for the election is to be the day appointed by Her Majesty by proclamation on the recommendation of the Prime Minister (and, accordingly, the appointed day replaces the day which would otherwise have been the polling day for the next election determined under section 1).

3 Dissolution of Parliament

(1) The Parliament then in existence dissolves at the beginning of the 17th working day before the polling day for the next parliamentary general election as determined under section 1 or appointed under section 2(7).

(2) Parliament cannot otherwise be dissolved.

(3) Once Parliament dissolves, the Lord Chancellor and, in relation to Northern Ireland, the Secretary of State have the authority to have the writs for the election sealed and issued (see rule 3 in Schedule 1 to the Representation of the People Act 1983).

(4) Once Parliament dissolves, Her Majesty may issue the proclamation summoning the new Parliament which may—

(a) appoint the day for the first meeting of the new Parliament;

(b) deal with any other matter which was normally dealt with before the passing of this Act by proclamations summoning new Parliaments (except a matter dealt with by subsection (1) or (3)).

…

6 Supplementary provisions

(1) This Act does not affect Her Majesty's power to prorogue Parliament.

(2) This Act does not affect the way in which the sealing of a proclamation summoning a new Parliament may be authorised; and the sealing of a proclamation to be issued under section 2(7) may be authorised in the same way. …

7 Final provisions

…

(4) The Prime Minister must make arrangements—

(a) for a committee to carry out a review of the operation of this Act and, if appropriate in consequence of its findings, to make recommendations for the repeal or amendment of this Act, and

(b) for the publication of the committee's findings and recommendations (if any).

(5) A majority of the members of the committee are to be members of the House of Commons.

(6) Arrangements under subsection (4)(a) are to be made no earlier than 1 June 2020 and no later than 30 November 2020.

NOTES

1. The prerogative power of dissolution has been replaced by legislation which prescribes a five-year term for each Parliament, with general election dates fixed in advance. Early general elections may be held in two situations: (i) where a two-thirds majority in the House of Commons votes in favour of such a motion; or (ii) where a government loses a vote of confidence in the House of Commons (which would be on a simple majority basis as at present, and not subject to a two-thirds majority requirement) and a government does not obtain a motion of confidence from the Commons within the next 14 days. In relation to the second of these options, it is not clear if the existing government would be entitled to use the 14-day period to attempt to regain the confidence of the Commons, or whether it would be expected to resign immediately allowing an alternative government to attempt to gain the confidence of the House. Previously, by constitutional convention, a government would either resign *or* seek dissolution of Parliament upon losing the confidence of the House (see Chapter 5, Section 1C at pp. 188–9). Given the latter is no

longer an option to a defeated government, is resignation now obligatory, or could a defeated government remain in office during the 14-day period and either (i) force dissolution by frustrating the possibility of an alternative administration being formed; or (ii) attempt in good faith to regain the confidence of the House (for example, by making concessions which would attract sufficient support to reacquire a majority)? If so, the Fixed-term Parliaments Act may have added to the options available to a defeated government.

2. The Bill that would become the 2011 Act was criticized by the House of Lords Constitution Committee (*Fixed-term Parliaments Bill*, Eighth Report of the House of Lords Constitution Committee Session of 2010–11, HL Bill 69 of 2010–11):

> 183. We take the view that the origins and content of this Bill owe more to short-term considerations than to a mature assessment of enduring constitutional principles or sustained public demand. We acknowledge the political imperative behind the coalition Government's wish to state in advance its intent to govern for the full five year term, but this could have been achieved under the current constitutional conventions. (Paragraph 20)

The Government's response rejected the claim that the legislation was designed to guarantee that the coalition would last for a full parliamentary term (*Government response to the report of the House of Lords Constitution Committee on the Fixed-term Parliaments Bill* (Cm 8011, 2011):

> 2. The Government does not accept this description of its proposals. The Government's proposals are concerned with establishing the principle that, save in exceptional circumstances, this and future Parliaments will last for a five-year term. As the Government has pointed out, this would engender a more long-term policy-making approach and lead to a more stable and predictable political cycle.

Initial evidence taken from government departments by the Political and Constitutional Reform Select Committee provided an indication that greater stability had been achieved, whether this was the primary purpose of the legislation or not (*The role and powers of the Prime Minister: The impact of the Fixed-term Parliaments Act 2011 on Government*, the Political and Constitutional Reform Select Committee, HC 440 of 2013–14):

> Emerging Benefits
>
> 8. Overwhelmingly, the written evidence we received from Departments welcomed the move to fixed terms: many responses cited the fact that a fixed term provided a platform of greater certainty for legislative, strategic and financial planning. The most commonly cited advantages of fixed terms were:
>
> - the potential to reduce uncertainty and instability;
> - a clear timetable for the next general election;
> - more effective forecasting;
> - ability to prioritise more effectively;
> - ability to allocate key staff in accordance with the policy priorities;
> - a sense of direction from the outset;
> - greater consistency and clarity of strategy.

3. The Government response to the House of Lords Constitution Committee also noted that the legislation would prevent 'the manipulation of election dates for political advantage'. The power of dissolution was previously exercised by the Queen on the advice of the Prime Minister, giving the incumbent of that office the chance to call a general election at a time which was politically advantageous to his or her party, while placing opposition parties at a disadvantage, with limited notice of when an election campaign was to commence. Professor Robert Hazell, in evidence to the Political and Constitutional Reform Committee's inquiry on the role and powers of the Prime Minister, described the Act as 'a very significant surrender of prime ministerial power', para [1].

4. The Act has remained controversial. There has been a backbench debate (unsuccessfully) considering its repeal (HC Deb, 23 October 2014, Vol. 586, col. 1069–1113), as well as Private Members' Bills introduced to that end (Fixed-Term Parliaments (Repeal) Bill 2014–15). Criticisms include that, in making the dissolution of Parliament more difficult, the Act takes

power from the electorate, and gives greater scope for unpopular governments to be sustained in office, or political coalitions to be formed at some point far removed from a general election. There is also an issue in relation to the status of the prerogative power of dissolution in the event the 2011 Act were repealed—has the prerogative power been destroyed by the legislation, and so requiring explicit replacement in any subsequent Act, or simply placed in abeyance, and therefore immediately revived on the removal of the statutory rules? See Horne and Kelly, 'Prerogative Powers and the Fixed-term Parliaments Act', *UK Constitutional Law Association Blog* (19 November 2014).

5. There has been consideration of replacing (or constraining) further significant prerogative powers with statutory rules. The final example considered in this section will be the power to use military force in or against other states.

The Governance of Britain—War Powers and Treaties: Limiting Executive Powers
Cm 7239, 2007, paras 1, 3–4, 6–8

1. The power to commit the country to international obligations through the conclusion of treaties, and the power to send armed forces into conflict situations, are two of the most important powers a government can wield. But there is presently no legal requirement for the people's representatives in the House of Commons in Parliament, which sustains the Government and which is the supreme body in our constitution, to have any particular role in either decision. In practice, no government these days would seek to commit troops to a substantial overseas deployment without giving Parliament the opportunity to debate it. But the terms of that debate are very much set by the Government. In particular, it has been rare in the past for Parliament to have a substantive vote on a proposed deployment before the troops are committed.

…

War powers

3. In his statement to the House of Commons on 3 July 2007, the Prime Minister gave a clear commitment that "the Government will now consult on a resolution to guarantee that on the grave issue of peace and war it is ultimately this House of Commons that will make the decision." In seeking to give Parliament the final say in decisions to commit UK troops to armed conflict overseas, it is nevertheless essential that we do not undermine the ability of the executive to carry out its proper functions. The responsibility to execute such operations with minimum loss of British lives has to remain with the executive.

4. There are a number of important issues which need to be taken into account in determining what will be the best way to enhance Parliament's role. Key considerations are:

- The need to ensure that the UK can continue to be able to fulfil its international obligations;
- The need to ensure that we do not undermine our reputation as a helpful and willing participant in multinational operations;
- The need to respect the views and information of any coalition partners;
- The need to ensure that any mechanism does not undermine the operational flexibility and freedom of the commanders in the field. The mechanism must provide sufficient flexibility for deployments which need to be made without prior Parliamentary approval for reasons of urgency or secrecy. Commanders should not be fearful that Parliament was trying to 'second guess' their decisions;
- The need not to impact on the morale of the armed forces. One objective of a more structured role for Parliament is to show the troops that Parliament, and through them the nation, is fully behind them and supports them in the difficult and dangerous task they are undertaking. The procedures put into place must not undermine that objective;

• The need to ensure that if, for whatever reason, the Government is not able (or indeed, in an exceptional case, willing) to respect the mechanism that is put into place, there are no consequences for individual soldiers, for example finding themselves accused of having acted illegally through taking part in a deployment which Parliament has not approved.

…

6. The final question asked in the consultation is whether any mechanism for obtaining Parliamentary approval should take the form of a Parliamentary convention, perhaps embodied in a resolution of the House of Commons, or whether it should be made statutory.

7. A Parliamentary convention in the form of a resolution has the advantages of being more flexible and adaptable. The interpretation of the resolution would lie clearly in the hands of Parliament rather than the courts. It could be framed in more general terms than is possible with statute. It is therefore less likely to interfere with the operational freedoms and responsibilities of commanders in the field.

8. Legislation might be seen as providing a stronger incentive for the government of the day to comply with an approval requirement as the need to obtain approval could only be resolved by further primary legislation. Legislation would also allow Parliament to make clear that failure to comply with the procedure was not intended to make the conflict unlawful nor expose any individuals to civil or criminal liability. It might be possible to combine the respective advantages of convention and legislation in a "hybrid" approach in the form of a short Act which requires the approval of Parliament or the House of Commons to deploying armed forces into armed conflict abroad, and provides very clear legal protection for individuals, while leaving the detailed Resolution arrangements to procedures that would be determined later.

NOTE: The consultation period ran from October 2007 to January 2008 but no proposed legislation was produced. The matter has been recently reconsidered by the House of Lords Constitution Committee.

Constitution Committee, *Constitutional Arrangements for the Use of Armed Force*
HL 46 of 2013–14, paras 61–4

Conclusion on formalisation

61. Our view is that formalising the Parliament's role in approving the deployment of Her Majesty's armed forces overseas would face a number of significant practical and definitional difficulties. The adoption of a formal resolution would potentially limit the options available to Parliament by removing flexibility; in addition, any such resolution might need to be regularly amended to reflect the changing nature of warfare and deployments. We consider that the risks and difficulties associated with formalisation outweigh any benefits which it might bring. **Neither primary legislation nor a resolution should be introduced as a means of formalising the role of Parliament in approving deployment decisions.**

A constitutional convention

62. The current arrangements for allowing parliamentary approval of deployment decisions seem to be working well. The Government have recognised that the need for Commons approval of deployment decisions is now a constitutional convention, and therefore politically binding on them. Parliamentary approval was sought and obtained for enforcing the no-fly zone over Libya. Recent debates in the House of Commons on Syria have shown that the existing convention is capable of adapting to reflect new circumstances. The House of Commons has secured a commitment from the Government that any decision to arm the Syrian National Coalition should be taken only after the Commons has voted on the matter. Provision of arms to a conflict such as that in Syria was not a scenario envisaged by previous proposals for formalising Parliament's role, yet a process has been crafted by which the House of Commons will have its say. This demonstrates the benefits of flexibility.

63. The current arrangements are such that it is inconceivable that the Prime Minister would either refuse to allow a Commons debate and vote on a deployment decision, or would refuse to follow the view of the Commons as expressed by a vote. **It seems that much of the impetus for formalising Parliament's role is to make a political statement about where decisions should be taken, rather than to correct deficiencies in the legal or military process.**

64. **We conclude that the existing convention—that, save in exceptional circumstances, the House of Commons is given the opportunity to debate and vote on the deployment of armed force overseas—provides the best framework for the House of Commons to exercise political control over, and confer legitimacy upon, such decisions. It is flexible, effective and consistent with the existing structure of parliamentary scrutiny of the executive. Parliamentary control over the Government in this area should remain a matter of constitutional convention.**

NOTES

1. Following publication of the Constitution Committee's report, on 29 August 2013 the Government held, and was defeated in, a vote in the House of Commons to authorize the use of military force against Syria to enforce a ban on the use of chemical weapons. In an exchange after the Government's defeat, the Leader of the Opposition sought an assurance from the Prime Minister.

House of Commons, HC Deb

Vol. 566, cols 1555–6, 29 August 2013

Edward Miliband: On a point of order, Mr Speaker. There having been no motion passed by this House tonight, will the Prime Minister confirm to the House that, given the will of the House that has been expressed tonight, he will not use the royal prerogative to order the UK to be part of military action before there has been another vote in the House of Commons?

Mr Speaker: That is of course not a matter for the Chair, but the Prime Minister has heard the right hon. Gentleman's point of order, and he is welcome to respond.

The Prime Minister: Further to that point of order, Mr Speaker. I can give that assurance. Let me say that the House has not voted for either motion tonight. I strongly believe in the need for a tough response to the use of chemical weapons, but I also believe in respecting the will of this House of Commons. It is very clear tonight that, while the House has not passed a motion,

29 Aug 2013: Column 1556

The British Parliament, reflecting the views of the British people, does not want to see British military action. I get that, and the Government will act accordingly.

The acceptance of this decision by the Prime Minister provides further evidence that the consultation convention identified by the Constitution Committee exists, and potentially binds the government to use the prerogative power to take military action only where approved by a vote in the House of Commons, where such approval can reasonably be sought in advance.

2. The Political and Constitutional Reform Committee of the House of Commons reached a different conclusion to that of the Lords Constitution Committee. In *Parliament's Role in Conflict Decisions: A Way Forward* (HC 892 of 2014–15) the committee argued for the adoption of a parliamentary resolution as a temporary solution, p. 3:

We ultimately favour Parliament's role being enshrined in law, but believe that agreeing a parliamentary resolution on this subject would serve as a useful interim step by embedding the current convention and clarifying some of the ambiguities that exist under current arrangements.

3. In a response to the Constitution Committee's report (published on 25 October 2013), the Government confirmed its 'commitment to respect the existing Parliamentary convention: that,

before UK troops are committed to conflict, the House of Commons should have the opportunity to debate the matter, except where there was an emergency and such action would not be appropriate'. The Government indicated that it was still considering whether to proceed with formalization of this convention, whether by primary legislation or a resolution of the House of Commons, given the challenge of doing so in a way which was 'strong and meaningful but none the less flexible enough to deal with what are, by definition, unpredictable circumstances'. This position did not change after the publication of the Political and Constitutional Reform Committee's report.

■ QUESTIONS

1. Should the royal prerogative continue to play a role in the modern UK constitution? In addition to being archaic, does it offer too much power to the government, which exercises nearly all of these powers in practice?

2. Has the replacement (or constraint) of the prerogative by statute in the three areas considered earlier in this section been a positive development? When placing particular prerogative powers on a statutory basis should the substance of these powers be reformed (as in the Fixed-term Parliaments Act 2011) or largely left to reflect the existing position (as in the Constitutional Reform and Governance Act 2010)?

3. Should prerogative war powers also be given a statutory basis, or are these powers suitably different from the management of the Civil Service, the ratification of treaties, and the dissolution of Parliament so as to justify alternative treatment? Is the existing convention an appropriate way to ensure parliamentary oversight of the Government's power in this area? How would you have advised the Government to respond to the recommendations of the House of Lords Constitution Committee and the House of Commons Political and Constitutional Reform Committee?

C: Codification of the prerogative

The archaic nature of the prerogative makes it a prime target for constitutional reform. In addition to the replacement (or constraint) of the prerogative by statute (considered in this chapter in Section 1B at pp. 177–86), the codification of certain powers (and accompanying constraints) in official and authoritative, but not legally binding, constitutional documents has been recently considered. We focus in particular here on the personal prerogative powers which are still vested in, and exercised by, the monarch. As in the example of constraining war powers already discussed, the close interaction between *legal* prerogative powers and *non-legal* constitutional conventions, which often develop to control or condition the use of the royal prerogative, is evident in this area.

House of Commons Library, *The Royal Prerogative*
Standard Note SN/PC/03862 (2009), p. 5

The Crown's personal prerogative powers

There are three main prerogative powers recognised under the common law which still reside in the jurisdiction of the Crown.

Firstly, the appointment of a Prime Minister; the sovereign must appoint that person who is in the best position to receive the support of the majority in the House of Commons. However, this does not involve the sovereign in making a personal assessment of leading politicians since no major party could fight a general election without a recognised leader.

However, if after an election no one party has an absolute majority in the House (as in 1923, 1929 and February 1974) then the Queen will send for the leader of the party with the largest number of seats (as in 1929 and 1974) or with the next largest number of seats (as in January 1924). Alternatively, the sovereign would have to initiate discussions with and between the parties to discover, for example, whether a government could be formed by a politician who was not a party leader or whether a coalition government could be formed.

Secondly, the dissolution of Parliament, in the absence of a regular term for the life of Parliament fixed by statute, the Sovereign may by the prerogative dissolve Parliament and cause a general election to be held. The sovereign normally accepts the advice of the Prime Minister and grants dissolution when it is requested; a refusal would probably be treated by the Prime Minister as tantamount to a dismissal. These areas of the prerogative are the subject of continuing academic debate.

Thirdly, the giving of royal assent to legislation, in 1708 Queen Anne was the last sovereign to refuse royal assent to a bill passed by Parliament. Additionally, no monarchs since the sixteenth century have signed Bills themselves and Queen Victoria was the last to give the Royal Assent in person in 1854.

NOTES

1. Of these three main personal prerogative powers, the power to dissolve Parliament has been replaced by the statutory rules contained in the Fixed-term Parliaments Act 2011, as considered earlier in this chapter in Section 1C at pp. 180–3. The granting of royal assent is in practice a formality, given not by the Queen personally, but by Lords Commissioners acting on the authority of the monarch in the House of Lords. This is done by the pronouncement in Norman French of 'La Reyne le veult' ('The Queen wills it') for public and private bills (the formulation varies slightly for supply and personal bills).

2. With respect to the appointment of a Prime Minister, the position with respect to one area of uncertainty has recently been clarified through codification of the relevant rules in a significant new official document, the 'Cabinet Manual', which aimed to provide guidance as to the operation of government. A key area of interest concerned government formation following the election of a 'hung Parliament' (one in which no party has an absolute majority of seats in the House of Commons). The Cabinet Secretary had been engaged in compiling a Cabinet Manual, the final version of which was published in October 2011 following a consultation exercise. The first public unveiling of a part of an earlier draft of the Cabinet Manual was chapter 2 ('Elections and Government Formation') when it was considered by the House of Commons Justice Select Committee and was reproduced in the report, Constitutional Processes Following a General Election, Fifth Report from the House of Commons Justice Committee, HC 396 of 2009–10. This chapter was of particular interest due to the fact that in the run-up to the general election in May 2010, the opinion polls were indicating that a 'hung' Parliament was a possibility. The extracts which follow deal with the purpose of the Cabinet Manual and, in particular, chapter 2.

Cabinet Office, *The Cabinet Manual: A Guide to Laws, Conventions, and Rules on the Operation of Government*

October 2011, pp. iv–v, 14–15

Preface by the Cabinet Secretary

Before the last general election, the previous Prime Minister, the Rt Hon Gordon Brown MP, asked that I lead work to produce a Cabinet Manual to provide a source of information on the laws, conventions and rules that affect the operation and procedures of the Government. With the endorsement of the current Prime Minister and Deputy Prime Minister, I published a draft in December 2010….

This updated text—the first edition of the Cabinet Manual – remains true to its original purpose. It is primarily a guide for those working in government, recording the current position rather than driving change. It is not intended to be legally binding or to set issues in stone. The Cabinet Manual records rules and practices, but is not intended to be the source of any rule.

While the document primarily provides a guide to the operation of the Government itself, it also sets out—from the view of the Executive—the Government's place in the UK's Parliamentary democracy. It therefore includes chapters on how the Government relates to the Sovereign, Parliament and the independent judiciary, as well as the other democratic institutions within the UK and key international bodies.

The content of the Cabinet Manual is not static, and the passage of new legislation, the evolution of conventions or changes to the internal procedures of government will mean that the practices and processes it describes will evolve over time. If the Cabinet Manual is to continue to play a useful role as a guide to the operations and procedures of government, it will need to be updated periodically to reflect such developments.

While some other administrations, most notably New Zealand, have developed their equivalent documents over a number of decades, this first edition of the Cabinet Manual has been produced in less than two years. This has been an intensive process and I am grateful to all those who have contributed to this achievement.

I am confident that the Cabinet Manual will come to be seen as an essential guide to our system of government and I hope that everyone working in, or with, the Government will use it as a key work of reference.

The crucial provisions of the Cabinet Manual regarding the formation of a government—including in circumstances where Parliament is 'hung' after a general election—are as follows.

The principles of government formation

2.7 The ability of a government to command the confidence of the elected House of Commons is central to its authority to govern. It is tested by votes on motions of confidence, or no confidence.... Commanding the confidence of the House of Commons is not the same as having a majority or winning every vote.

2.8 Prime Ministers hold office unless and until they resign. If the Prime Minister resigns on behalf of the Government, the Sovereign will invite the person who appears most likely to be able to command the confidence of the House to serve as Prime Minister and to form a government.

2.9 Historically, the Sovereign has made use of reserve powers to dismiss a Prime Minister or to make a personal choice of successor, although this was last used in 1834 and was regarded as having undermined the Sovereign. In modern times the convention has been that the Sovereign should not be drawn into party politics, and if there is doubt it is the responsibility of those involved in the political process, and in particular the parties represented in Parliament, to seek to determine and communicate clearly to the Sovereign who is best placed to be able to command the confidence of the House of Commons. As the Crown's principal adviser this responsibility falls especially on the incumbent Prime Minister, who at the time of his or her resignation may also be asked by the Sovereign for a recommendation on who can best command the confidence of the House of Commons in his or her place.

2.10 The application of these principles depends on the specific circumstances and it remains a matter for the Prime Minister, as the Sovereign's principal adviser, to judge the appropriate time at which to resign, either from their individual position as Prime Minister or on behalf of the government. Recent examples suggest that previous Prime Ministers have not offered their resignations until there was a situation in which clear advice could be given to the Sovereign on who should be asked to form a government. It remains to be seen whether or not these examples will be regarded in future as having established a constitutional convention.

Parliaments with an overall majority in the House of Commons

2.11 After an election, if an incumbent government retains an overall majority – that is, where the number of seats won by the largest party in an election exceeds the combined number of seats for all the other parties in the new Parliament – it will normally continue in office and resume normal business. There is no need for the Sovereign to ask the Prime Minister to continue. If the election results in an overall majority for a different party, the incumbent Prime Minister and government will immediately resign and the Sovereign will invite the leader of the party that has won the election to form a government....

Parliaments with no overall majority in the House of Commons

2.12 Where an election does not result in an overall majority for a single party, the incumbent government remains in office unless and until the Prime Minister tenders his or her resignation and the Government's resignation to the Sovereign. An incumbent government is entitled to wait until the new Parliament has met to see if it can command the confidence of the House of Commons, but is expected to resign if it becomes clear that it is unlikely to be able to command that confidence and there is a clear alternative.

2.13 Where a range of different administrations could potentially be formed, political parties may wish to hold discussions to establish who is best able to command the confidence of the House of Commons and should form the next government. The Sovereign would not expect to become involved in any negotiations, although there are responsibilities on those involved in the process to keep the Palace informed. This could be done by political parties or the Cabinet Secretary. The Principal Private Secretary to the Prime Minister may also have a role, for example, in communicating with the Palace.

2.14 If the leaders of the political parties involved in any negotiations seek the support of the Civil Service, this support may only be organised by the Cabinet Secretary with the authorisation of the Prime Minister. If the Prime Minister authorises any support it would be focused and provided on an equal basis to all the parties involved, including the party that was currently in government. The Civil Service would continue to advise the incumbent government in the usual way.

2.15 Following the election in May 2010, the Prime Minister authorised the Civil Service to provide such support to negotiations between political parties.

2.16 As long as there is significant doubt following an election over the Government's ability to command the confidence of the House of Commons, certain restrictions on government activity apply; see paragraphs 2.27–2.34.

2.17 The nature of the government formed will be dependent on discussions between political parties and any resulting agreement. Where there is no overall majority, there are essentially three broad types of government that could be formed:

- single-party, minority government, where the party may (although not necessarily) be supported by a series of ad hoc agreements based on common interests;
- formal inter-party agreement, for example the Liberal–Labour pact from 1977 to 1978; or
- formal coalition government, which generally consists of ministers from more than one political party, and typically commands a majority in the House of Commons.

NOTE: The constitutional implications of *The Cabinet Manual* are not yet clear. Inquiries carried out by two parliamentary committees reached somewhat different conclusions.

Constitution Committee, *The Cabinet Manual*
HL 107 of 2010–12, paras 95–6

95. In our view the Cabinet Manual has limited value and relevance. We acknowledge that it provides greater transparency on certain aspects of the operation of government and it is to be welcomed in that context. However, this value has been given undue prominence by the helpful publication of Chapter Two in draft prior to the May 2010 general election; the benefits of the publication of that chapter do not, on the whole, extend to the rest of the Manual.

96. In summary we conclude that the Cabinet Manual is not the first step towards a written constitution; it should be renamed the Cabinet Office Manual and its greater relevance to officials than to politicians emphasised; it should only seek to describe existing rules and practices; it should not be endorsed by the Cabinet nor formally approved by Parliament; and it must be entirely accurate and properly sourced and referenced.

Political and Constitutional Reform Committee, *Constitutional Implications of the*
Cabinet Manual
HC 734 of 2010–12, paras 2, 54, 92–3

2. We regard the Cabinet Manual as a highly significant document. As one of the first attempts to codify some of the practices in British Governance and politics it can be no other. As such its creation and publication are most welcome signs of openness and transparency. Any deficiencies that have been identified in the document are far outweighed by the benefit of publication itself.

…

54. The Cabinet Manual is not a written constitution. It has, however, considerable overlap in content with what might be expected of a constitution. The Cabinet Secretary has suggested to us that it would be likely to be a starting point for any attempt to produce such a constitution. By bringing together and publishing the Government's interpretation of existing constitutional rules and conventions, the Government has already begun to spark debate about both the nature of these rules and conventions, and if and how they should be written down. This is a debate in which Parliament needs to play a full part.

…

92. Our inquiry has revealed a fair measure of doubt and disagreement about the purpose and content of the draft Cabinet Manual. The next version of the Manual should be considerably improved as a result of the consultation that has been undertaken, and as a result of parliamentary scrutiny. It need not be perfect, however, provided that there are future opportunities to refine it, as it has been refined in New Zealand over the years.

93. We welcome the Cabinet Manual and the transparency it brings to the workings of government, and we look forward to future involvement in its development.

NOTES

1. A particular controversy over the content of chapter 2 of the (then draft) *Cabinet Manual* related to the inclusion in a footnote of the following statement:

> In 2010, the Leader of the Liberal Democrat Party expressed a view that "whichever party has won the most votes and the most seats, if not an absolute majority, has the first right to seek to govern, either on its own or by reaching out to other parties".

Both committees agreed that this statement should be removed from the *Manual*, with the Political and Constitutional Reform Committee noting:

> 79. There appears to be widespread agreement that the footnote to paragraph 49 represents a political negotiating position adopted in 2010 rather than a statement of an existing constitutional convention or practice. It should be deleted from the Manual.

The footnote was subsequently removed from what became para. 2.13 in the final version.

2. The *Cabinet Manual* demonstrates very clearly the inter-relationship between the royal prerogative and constitutional conventions in the UK constitution, with the prerogative power to appoint a Prime Minister following a General Election crucially conditioned by a range of non-legal rules and understandings (including, but certainly not limited to, those discussed earlier relating to government formation in a hung Parliament). Section 2 of this chapter, which follows, focuses on constitutional conventions. In reading it, notice the similarities in some aspects of the royal prerogative and convention: their nature, as well as the possibility of their codification; and the differences, with respect to the status of the prerogative as law, and the possibility of its conversion into statute without losing its essential (legal) character. Prior to this, we finally consider the status of the royal prerogative in the courts.

■ QUESTION

Is the *Cabinet Manual* 'of limited value and relevance' or 'a highly significant document'? Could it be the first step towards a written or codified constitution for the UK?

D: The prerogative in the courts

According to Blackstone, the Royal Prerogative was 'singular and eccentrical', because it encompassed rights and capacities only enjoyed by the Monarch. The *Case of Proclamations* (1611) 12 Co Rep 74 and the Bill of Rights 1689 (see Chapter 2, Section 1A at pp. 47–8) established that the prerogative could not be used as a means to bypass Parliament in order to change the general law of the land. There is, however, a further question as to the interaction of the royal prerogative with statute: what is the status of a prerogative power where legislation has been passed which covers an issue within its scope?

Attorney-General v *De Keyser's Royal Hotel Ltd*

[1920] AC 508, House of Lords

During the First World War the Crown took possession of the respondents' hotel in order to house staff of the Royal Flying Corps. The Crown purported to do this under the authority of the Defence of the Realm Regulations. The Crown contended that compensation was not payable to the respondents because there still existed a residue of the prerogative which permitted temporary occupation of a subject's property in time of war. This residue of the prerogative was exercised under the regulations. The respondents contended that the Defence Act 1842 required that compensation should be paid.

LORD ATKINSON: … It is quite obvious that it would be useless and meaningless for the Legislature to impose restrictions and limitations upon, and to attach conditions to, the exercise by the Crown of the powers conferred by a statute, if the Crown were free at its pleasure to disregard these provisions, and by virtue of its prerogative do the very thing the statutes empowered it to do. One cannot in the construction of a statute attribute to the Legislature (in the absence of compelling words) an intention so absurd. It was suggested that when a statute is passed empowering the Crown to do a certain thing which it might theretofore have done by virtue of its prerogative, the prerogative is merged in the statute. I confess I do not think the word 'merged' is happily chosen. I should prefer to say that when such a statute, expressing the will and intention of the King and of the three estates of the realm, is passed, it abridges the Royal Prerogative while it is in force to this extent: that the Crown can only do the particular thing under and in accordance with the statutory provisions, and that its prerogative power to do that thing is in abeyance. Whichever mode of expression be used, the result intended to be indicated is, I think, the same—namely, that after the statute has been passed, and while it is in force, the thing it empowers the Crown to do can thenceforth only be done by and under the statute, and subject to all the limitations, restrictions and conditions by it imposed, however unrestricted the Royal Prerogative may theretofore have been.

[Lord Atkinson found that the proper construction of the regulations meant that the 1842 statute governed the occupation and that compensation under that statute was payable. Lords Dunedin, Moulton, Sumner, and Parmoor delivered concurring speeches.]

Appeal dismissed.

Following the majority vote to leave the EU at the UK referendum on continuing membership held in 2016, the scope of the Government's prerogative power to act on the international level was considered in one of the most high-profile constitutional cases for decades.

R (Miller) v Secretary of State for Exiting the European Union
[2017] UKSC 5, Supreme Court

The case concerned the domestic constitutional requirements for giving notice of an intention to withdraw from the EU, in accordance with Art. 50(1) of the Treaty on European Union, so as to begin the process of negotiating the UK's withdrawal. Article 50(3) provided that the EU Treaties would cease to apply to a departing Member State either on the entry into force of a withdrawal agreement, or (unless the negotiation period was extended by unanimous vote of the European Council) two years after notification had been given. In implementation of the referendum decision to leave the EU, the Government indicated it would use its general powers to conduct international affairs and ratify treaties under the royal prerogative to give notice to the European Council by the end of March 2017. Miller challenged this, arguing that an Act of Parliament was required to authorize the giving of notice under Art. 50, because once triggered, the process of negotiation could inevitably lead to the removal of domestic rights conferred by the European Communities Act 1972 (the legislation making provision for the applicability of EU law within the UK) if the period of two years elapsed without a withdrawal agreement being concluded, or the period being extended. It would therefore be unlawful to use the royal prerogative in a way which could remove domestic rights conferred by statute. The Government argued that giving notice under the royal prerogative would have no direct impact on domestic law, because the 1972 Act would remain legally valid and effective unless repealed by Parliament, and it proposed that it would introduce legislation to achieve this end (a 'Great Repeal Bill') during the process of negotiating withdrawal. It further argued that the 1972 Act was intended by Parliament to be a conduit through which a supranational body of legal rules was given contingent domestic effect, and the possibility of those rights varying from time to time as EU law evolved was a fundamental feature of the design of the statute. Government action on the international level to change, or even remove, the legal rights applicable to the UK by virtue of the Treaties was compatible with, rather than contrary to, the scheme of the 1972 Act. The Divisional Court ruled in favour of Miller; the Secretary of State appealed to the Supreme Court.

LORD NEUBERGER (with whom LADY HALE, LORD MANCE, LORD KERR, LORD CLARKE, LORD WILSON, LORD SUMPTION and LORD HODGE agree):

76. We accept the proposition that the ambit of the rights and remedies etc which are incorporated into domestic law through section 2 of the 1972 Act varies with the United Kingdom's obligations from time to time under the EU Treaties. This proposition is reflected in the language of subsections (1) and (2) of section 2 .... However, this proposition is also limited in nature. Thus, the provisions of new EU Treaties are not automatically brought into domestic law through section 2: only once they have been statutorily added to "the Treaties" and "the EU Treaties" in section 1(2) can section 2 give effect to new EU Treaties. And section 2 can only apply to those rights and remedies which are capable of being "given legal effect or used" or "enjoyed" in the United Kingdom.

77. We also accept that Parliament cannot have intended that section 2 should continue to import the variable content of EU law into domestic law, or that the other consequences of the 1972 Act described in paras 62 to 64 above should continue to apply, after the United Kingdom had ceased to be bound by the EU Treaties. However, while acknowledging the force of Lord Reed's powerful judgment, we do not accept that it follows from this that the 1972 Act either contemplates or accommodates the abrogation of EU law upon the United Kingdom's withdrawal from the EU Treaties by prerogative act without prior Parliamentary authorisation. On the contrary: we consider that, by the 1972 Act, Parliament endorsed and gave effect to the United Kingdom's membership of what is now the European Union under the EU Treaties in a way which is inconsistent with the future exercise by ministers of any prerogative power to withdraw from such Treaties.

78. In short, the fact that EU law will no longer be part of UK domestic law if the United Kingdom withdraws from the EU Treaties does not mean that Parliament contemplated or intended that ministers could cause the United Kingdom to withdraw from the EU Treaties without prior Parliamentary approval. There is a vital difference between changes in domestic law resulting from variations in the content of EU law arising from new EU legislation, and changes in domestic law resulting from withdrawal by the United Kingdom from the European Union. The former involves changes in EU law, which are then brought into domestic law through section 2 of the 1972 Act. The latter involves a unilateral action by the relevant constitutional bodies which effects a fundamental change in the constitutional arrangements of the United Kingdom.

79. So far as the interpretation of subsections (1) and (2) of section 2 of the 1972 Act are concerned, any right available under EU law to the United Kingdom to withdraw from the EU Treaties does not, as Mr Eadie rightly accepted, fall within the subsection, as it is not one which would be given "legal effect or used in", or which would be "enjoyed by the United Kingdom". Further, the fact that section 2(1) envisages EU law rights and procedures applying "as in accordance with the Treaties" "from time to time" and "without further enactment" takes matters no further. Subsection 2(1) and (2) are concerned to ensure that the variable content of EU law as it stands from time to time, is given effect in domestic law, and there was no practical alternative to such an arrangement in a dualist system. However, it does not follow from this that prerogative powers may be used to withdraw from the Treaties and so cut off the source of EU law entirely.

80. One of the most fundamental functions of the constitution of any state is to identify the sources of its law. And, as explained in paras 61 to 66 above, the 1972 Act effectively constitutes EU law as an entirely new, independent and overriding source of domestic law, and the Court of Justice as a source of binding judicial decisions about its meaning. This proposition is indeed inherent in the Secretary of State's metaphor of the 1972 Act as a conduit pipe by which EU law is brought into the domestic UK law. Upon the United Kingdom's withdrawal from the European Union, EU law will cease to be a source of domestic law for the future (even if the Great Repeal Bill provides that some legal rules derived from it should remain in force or continue to apply to accrued rights and liabilities), decisions of the Court of Justice will (again depending on the precise terms of the Great Repeal Bill) be of no more than persuasive authority, and there will be no further references to that court from UK courts. Even those legal rules derived from EU law and transposed into UK law by domestic legislation will have a different status. They will no longer be paramount, but will be open to domestic repeal or amendment in ways that may be inconsistent with EU law.

81. Accordingly, the main difficulty with the Secretary of State's argument is that it does not answer the objection based on the constitutional implications of withdrawal from the EU. As we have said, withdrawal is fundamentally different from variations in the content of EU law arising from further EU Treaties or legislation. A complete withdrawal represents a change which is different not just in degree but in kind from the abrogation of particular rights, duties or rules derived from EU law. It will constitute as significant a constitutional change as that which occurred when EU law was first incorporated in domestic law by the 1972 Act. And, if Notice is given, this change will occur irrespective of whether Parliament repeals the 1972 Act. It would be inconsistent with long-standing and fundamental principle for such a far-reaching change to the UK constitutional arrangements to be brought about by ministerial decision or ministerial action alone. All the more so when the source in question was brought into existence by Parliament through primary legislation, which gave that source an overriding supremacy in the hierarchy of domestic law sources.

LORD REED (dissenting):

187 .... Parliament has recognised that rights given effect under the 1972 Act may be added to, altered or revoked without the necessity of a further Act of Parliament .... In response to this point, the majority of the court draw a distinction, described as "a vital difference", between changes in domestic law resulting from variations in the content of EU law arising from new EU legislation, and changes resulting from withdrawal by the UK from the European Union. There is no basis in the language of the 1972 Act

for drawing any such distinction. Under the arrangements established by the Act, alterations in the UK's obligations under the Treaties are automatically reflected in alterations in domestic law. That is equally the position whether the alterations in the UK's obligations under the Treaties result from the Treaties' ceasing to apply to the UK, in accordance with article 50, or from changes to the Treaties or to legislation made under the Treaties. The Act simply creates a scheme under which the effect given to EU law in domestic law reflects the UK's international obligations under the Treaties, whatever they may be. There is nothing in the Act to suggest that Parliament's intention to ensure an exact match depends on the reason why they might not match . . . .

219. More fundamentally, however, the argument that withdrawal from the EU would alter domestic law and destroy statutory rights, and therefore cannot be undertaken without a further Act of Parliament, has to be rejected even if one accepts that the 1972 Act creates statutory rights and that withdrawal will alter the law of the land. It has to be rejected because it ignores the conditional basis on which the 1972 Act gives effect to EU law. If Parliament grants rights on the basis, express or implied, that they will expire in certain circumstances, then no further legislation is needed if those circumstances occur. If those circumstances comprise the UK's withdrawal from a treaty, the rights are not revoked by the Crown's exercise of prerogative powers: they are revoked by the operation of the Act of Parliament itself . . . .

225 . . . . As a source of law, EU law, like legislation enacted by the devolved legislatures, or delegated legislation made by Ministers, is entirely dependent on statute (which is not, of course, to say that EU law has the same effects, as devolved or delegated legislation). It derives its legal authority from a statute, which itself derives its authority from the rule of recognition identifying Parliamentary legislation as a source of law. The recognition of its validity does not alter any fundamental principle of our constitution . . . .

227. Parliament has itself made it clear that EU law has not altered the UK's rule of recognition [in Section 18 of the European Union 2011 Act] . . . . Since EU law has no status in UK law independent of statute, it follows that the only relevant source of law has at all times been statute.

Appeal dismissed (Lord Carnwath and Lord Hughes also dissenting).

NOTES

1. The second main argument addressed by the Supreme Court in this case, on appeal from the High Court of Northern Ireland, was whether the Sewel convention functioned in such a way as to require the consent of the devolved legislatures to a bill to trigger Art. 50. The Court rejected this argument, which is considered in this chapter in Section 2E at pp. 212–13.
2. Public interest in this case was extraordinary: a live stream of the first day hearing was watched online by some 320,000 people. The immense constitutional significance of the issues under consideration in *Miller* was reflected in the fact that it was heard by an unprecedented panel of all 11 active Justices of the Supreme Court (Lord Toulson having retired, but not been replaced, at the time of the hearings).
3. The judgment of the majority had the effect that legislation was required to authorize notice under Art. 50. The majority did not impose any conditions on the form the Act of Parliament could take, noting at [122]:

   > There is no equivalence between the constitutional importance of a statute, or any other document, and its length or complexity. A notice under article 50(2) could no doubt be very short indeed, but that would not undermine its momentous significance.

   In response, the Government introduced the European Union (Notification of Withdrawal) Bill in the House of Commons two days after the judgment was delivered with a view to a short statute being enacted in accordance with the end-of-March timetable for the start of negotiation.
4. The majority concluded that EU law is an independent source of the domestic law, by virtue of its unique incorporation through statute, which could not be cut off by exercise of the royal prerogative. The scale of the change to UK constitutional arrangements, and the

inappropriateness of this being (potentially) effected by ministerial action alone, also appears to be a crucial consideration for the majority. This may raise questions about the extent to which *Miller* establishes a precedent of broad application, or whether it is a specific decision in extraordinary circumstances, which is essentially limited to its facts. This also seems based on a broader reading of the implicit purpose and effects of the 1972 Act than the approach of Lord Reed in the minority, for whom the absence of express displacement of the prerogative power to give Art. 50 notice was crucial—especially when read in the light of the broader statutory scheme, in which Parliament has demonstrated, in legislation such as the European Union Act 2011 (see Chapter 2, Section 3D at pp. 95–101), that it was 'perfectly capable of making clear its intention to restrict the exercise of the prerogative when it wishes to do so' [205]. The majority, in contrast, relied on the principle of legality (see Chapter 3, Section 5 at pp. 128–34) in suggesting that, [87]:

> it would have been open to Parliament to provide expressly that the constitutional arrangements and the EU rights introduced by the 1972 Act should themselves only prevail from time to time and for so long as the UK government did not decide otherwise.... But we must take the legislation as it is, and we cannot accept that, in Part I of the 1972 Act, Parliament "squarely confront[ed]" the notion that it was clothing ministers with the far-reaching and anomalous right to use a treaty-making power to remove an important source of domestic law and important domestic rights.

The dispute between the majority and the minority is therefore rooted in fundamental disagreement about the manner in which Parliament must exercise its sovereign legislative power, and the extent to which the rule of law permits the courts to read implied limitations into a statute.

6. The role and independence of the judiciary when engaging with delicate political questions, which had already been the subject of a divisive referendum decision, was also in issue in *Miller* (not least after the three judges who ruled against the Government in the Divisional Court were described in the tabloid press as 'Enemies of the People'; see Chapter 4, Section 1C at p. 149). The majority emphasized that the case had nothing to do with 'the wisdom of the decision to withdraw from the European Union', which was a political matter and not appropriate for resolution by judges, 'whose duty is to decide issues of law' legitimately brought before them in a democratic society [3]. The minority raised questions about the dangers of 'the legalisation of political issues', which 'is not always constitutionally appropriate, and may be fraught with risk, not least for the judiciary' (Lord Reed [240]). Similarly, Lord Carnwath noted that the 'principle of Parliamentary accountability' was 'fundamental to our constitution', that the 'Executive is accountable to Parliament for its exercise of the prerogative, including its actions in international law', and that the 'courts may not inquire into the methods by which Parliament exercises control over the Executive, nor their adequacy' [249]. For Lord Carnwath, in light of the division of power in operation in the UK constitution (see Chapter 1, Section 5A at pp. 29–35), [274]:

> The article 50 process must and will involve a partnership between Parliament and the Executive. But that does not mean that legislation is required simply to initiate it. Legislation will undoubtedly be required to implement withdrawal, but the process, including the form and timing of any legislation, can and should be determined by Parliament not by the courts.

■ QUESTIONS

1. Do you prefer the majority's analysis, that the prerogative would here have been used to undermine an independent source of law in the UK constitution, or the minority view, that Parliament had not legislated in such a way as to displace the well-established executive power to carry out activities at the international level?

2. What could be the long-term impact of the *Miller* case on the scope of the royal prerogative? Is it a welcome limitation of the archaic royal prerogative, or a potential barrier to the effective exercise of executive power in relation to treaties?

3. Given a short implementing Act of Parliament was all that was legally required to provide the necessary authority to provide notice under Art. 50, could this case ultimately be seen as 'an exercise in pure legal formalism' (Lord Carnwath [273])?

SECTION 2: CONSTITUTIONAL CONVENTIONS

A: Sources of the constitution

As the United Kingdom does not have a written constitution, the sources of our constitutional arrangements must be sought elsewhere. Most textbooks contain sections outlining the sources of the constitution. In these sections they highlight legislation, judicial precedent and the royal prerogative as the sources of the legal rules of the constitution. Constitutional conventions are the primary source of non-legal constitutional rules.

A. V. Dicey, *An Introduction to the Study of The Law of the Constitution*
(10th edn, 1985), pp. 23–4

[T]he rules which make up constitutional law, as the term is used in England, include two sets of principles or maxims of a totally distinct character.

The one set of rules are in the strictest sense 'laws,' since they are rules which (whether written or unwritten, whether enacted by statute or derived from the mass of custom, tradition, or judge-made maxims known as the common law) are enforced by the courts; these rules constitute 'constitutional law' in the proper sense of that term, and may for the sake of distinction be called collectively 'the law of the constitution.'

The other set of rules consist of conventions, understandings, habits, or practices which, though they may regulate the conduct of the several members of the sovereign power, of the Ministry, or of other officials, are not in reality laws at all since they are not enforced by the courts. This portion of constitutional law may, for the sake of distinction, be termed the 'conventions of the constitution,' or constitutional morality.

To put the same thing in a somewhat different shape, 'constitutional law,' as the expression is used in England, both by the public and by authoritative writers, consists of two elements. The one element, here called the 'law of the constitution,' is a body of undoubted law; the other element, here called the 'conventions of the constitution,' consists of maxims or practices which, though they regulate the ordinary conduct of the Crown, of Ministers, and of other persons under the constitution, are not in strictness laws at all.

E. C. S. Wade, 'Introduction' in A. V. Dicey, *An Introduction to the Study of The Law of the Constitution*
(10th edn, 1985), pp. cli–clvii

The Widened Sphere of Constitutional Conventions.—It is largely through the influence of Dicey that the term, convention, has been accepted to describe a constitutional obligation, obedience to which is secured despite the absence of the ordinary means of enforcing the obligation in a court of law. Dicey defined conventions as 'rules for determining the mode in which the discretionary powers of the Crown (or of the Ministers as servants of the Crown) ought to be exercised.' He was concerned to establish that conventions were 'intended to secure the ultimate supremacy of the electorate as the true political sovereign of the State.'

In discussing conventions as a source of constitutional law it must be noted that the obligation does not necessarily, or indeed usually, derive from express agreement. It is more likely to take its origin from custom or from practice arising out of sheer expediency. . . .

Dicey discusses mainly the rules governing the exercise of the royal prerogative by Ministers of the Crown and that part of the 'law and custom' of Parliament which rests upon custom alone. In both these cases the rules are based on custom or expediency rather than as a result of formal agreement.

Conventions, however, have a wider application and have, during the present century, played an important part in building up the political relationship between the various member States of the British Commonwealth. Some of these conventions, in particular the rules governing the full competence of Commonwealth Parliaments to legislate, were made statutory by the Statute of Westminster, 1931, and later enactments. But much of the relationship is still conventional and has been based on agreement reached by Prime Ministers at Imperial Conferences. Constitutional matters no longer figure prominently on the agenda of the periodic meetings of Prime Ministers or other Ministers of Commonwealth Governments which are less formal than the earlier Imperial Conferences. But this is because constitutional issues have now been settled and in no way minimises the important part which conventions have in the past played in this sphere of constitutional development.

Dicey concentrated attention upon the conventional rules which precedent showed were fundamental to the working of the Cabinet. . . .

It is the prerogative of the Sovereign to appoint the Prime Minister. Convention limits the range of choice to that of a party leader who can command a majority in the House of Commons. This convention to some extent lacks the binding force which conventions in other fields possess. This does not mean that the rules can normally be disregarded, but that unforeseen circumstances may deprive them of their force on a particular occasion; any departure from the normal would have to conform to recognising the supremacy of the electorate and not to serve autocratic ends. Some writers would not include a practice or usage which is not regarded as obligatory, though none the less usually followed, in the category of constitutional conventions. It is, however, very difficult to draw the line between an obligatory and a non-obligatory practice. The characteristic of conventions, namely, that they supplement the laws which are enforced by the courts, would seem to preclude their precise definition. On the whole it seems preferable to regard the political practices of Sovereigns in choice of Prime Ministers as within the category of conventional rules, even though those rules are still somewhat inconclusive and therefore sufficiently flexible to meet unforeseen circumstances. For they are clearly rules of conduct referable to the requirements of constitutional government and are aimed at reflecting the supremacy of the electorate. The same is true of the practices and precepts which surround the prerogative of dissolution of Parliament. But in this case there is the fundamental understanding that the power may only be exercised on the advice of Ministers. That advice may not be available to the Sovereign in the choice of a Prime Minister, where his predecessor has been removed by death or his own resignation.

Perhaps the relationship between law and convention is best illustrated by contrasting the legal and conventional position of Ministers. They, like civil servants and members of the armed forces, are in law the servants of the Crown. By convention they, unlike all other servants of the Crown, are responsible directly to Parliament both for their own activities and those of civil servants, their subordinates, who by custom are never referred to by name in Parliament. This responsibility of Ministers is designed to make them answerable through Parliament to the electorate. To rely solely on their legal responsibility to their master, the Sovereign, would entirely fail to secure their responsibility to the public in general and indeed might make them the agents of a Sovereign who disregarded the public will, as in the days before the prerogative powers were restricted by Parliament.

Conventions relating to internal government go much further than the examples which were chosen by Dicey from the exercise of the royal prerogative and the relationship between the two Houses of Parliament. They nowadays provide for the working of the whole complicated governmental machine. A Cabinet in deciding upon policy will require to know whether it already has the power in law to take the action which it proposes. It is certainly not limited to exercising those prerogative powers of the Sovereign which are entrusted to it by convention. Through its command of a majority in the House of Commons it is normally in a position to take legal powers if they do not already exist. Moreover it is the responsibility of the Cabinet to ensure unity in the constitutional system and in particular to avoid or, if need be, to settle conflicts of policy and of action by the various departments. In all these activities rules and practices develop in order to secure the desired end. The growth of the committee system within the Cabinet organisation is an extra-legal development which has introduced important changes in Cabinet government since Dicey formulated his views on the place of conventions in the working of the constitution. One can properly describe this development as conventional. It is in no sense an obligation imposed by law upon Ministers that they should consult an elaborate system of committees. Yet no one supposes that a modern government could be conducted without some such machinery. So we have the position that the Cabinet itself is to all intents and purposes the creation of convention designed to secure political harmony between the Crown and its subjects. From this conventional institution there have grown up in the present century such devices as formal committees, like the Defence Committee, and *ad hoc* committees, appointed for a particular purpose but often remaining in being after their original purpose has been fulfilled. ... In addition there are royal commissions, select committees of either House of Parliament, committees appointed by departmental Ministers, all of which play an important part in the formulation of policy. For none of these is there any legal requirement. But no appreciation of the working of the governmental machine would be complete without their inclusion. And since their purpose is to focus public opinion on a particular problem, they are designed to secure that harmony between the Ministers of the Crown and the public which is the principal justification for supplementing the law of the constitution with conventions.

■ QUESTION

What are the various ways in which conventions may arise?

B: What are conventions?

Conventions represent important rules of political behaviour which are necessary for the smooth running of the constitution. It is not only in the constitutional arrangements of the United Kingdom that conventions are important; K. C. Wheare, in *Modern Constitutions* (1966), p. 122, states that 'in all countries usage and convention are important and ... in many countries which have Constitutions usage and convention play as important a part as they do in England'. Conventions can facilitate evolution and change within a constitution while its legal form remains unchanged.

G. Marshall and G. C. Moodie, *Some Problems of the Constitution*
(5th edn, 1971), pp. 23–5

What then are the conventions of the British Constitution? One way of answering the question is to point to particular examples. Thus, among them are such rules as that the Monarch should normally on the resignation of a government, ask the Leader of the Opposition to form the new one; or (before 1911) that the House of Lords should not oppose a money bill duly passed by the House of Commons; or (to quote from the Preamble to the Statute of Westminster of 1931) 'that any alteration in the law touching the Succession to the Throne or the Royal Style and Titles shall hereafter require the assent as well of the Parliaments of all the Dominions as of the Parliament of the United Kingdom'. An alternative approach is to put forward a formal definition. By the conventions of the Constitution, then, we mean certain rules of constitutional behaviour which are considered to be binding by and upon those who operate the Constitution, but which are not enforced by the law courts (although the courts may recognise their existence), nor by the presiding officers in the Houses of Parliament. Not all writers would agree to the inclusion of this last phrase. But it seems best to exclude from the category of convention 'the law and custom of Parliament' which define much of its procedure, and which are applied and interpreted by, for example, the Speaker of the House of Commons. On the other hand, certain important rules of procedure—for example, resort to the usual channels through which, among other things, important decisions about the agenda of the House of Commons are reached—are 'unknown' both to the courts and to the Speaker and must clearly be counted as conventions.

Such conventions are to be found in all established constitutions, and soon develop even in the newest. One reason for this is that no general rule of law is self-applying, but must be applied according to the terms of additional rules. These additional rules may be concerned with the interpretation of the general rule, or with the exact circumstances in which it should apply, about either of which uncertainty may exist, and the greater the generality the greater will the uncertainty tend to be. Many constitutions include a large number of additional legal rules to clarify the meaning and application of their main provisions, but in a changing world it is rarely possible to eradicate or prevent all doubts on these points by enactment or even by adjudication. The result often is to leave a significant degree of discretion to those exercising the rights or wielding the powers legally conferred, defined, or permitted. As Dicey pointed out, it is to regulate the use of such discretionary power that conventions develop. Thus the rules prescribing the procedure to be followed by the Monarch in the selection of a Prime Minister regulate the way in which she should exercise her prerogative power to appoint advisers. The legal prerogative remains intact, and appointments to the office of Prime Minister (itself a conventional position) can still be made only by the Monarch. Similarly, it remains true that no bill can become a statute until it receives the Royal Assent; but the Monarch's discretion in deciding whether or not to assent is governed by a rule that she should always assent to a bill which has duly passed both Houses. In this case the royal discretion is so limited as virtually to have been abolished. But the legal position remains untouched and thus, it is sometimes argued, may still be exercised under certain circumstances.

The definition of 'conventions' may thus be amplified by saying that their purpose is to define the use of constitutional discretion. To put this in slightly different words, it may be said that conventions are non-legal rules regulating the way in which legal rules shall be applied. Sometimes, of course, they do so only indirectly, in that they relate primarily to already existing conventions. Not all discretionary powers are so limited, but the most important ones usually are in some degree. In Britain it has been the growth of conventional limitations of the royal prerogative, in conjunction with changes in the legal rules contained in such statutes as the Act of Settlement and the various Acts extending the suffrage (as well as those changes brought about by judicial interpretation), which has largely created our modern system of government. As Sir Kenneth Wheare has said, it is 'the association of law with convention within the constitutional structure which is the essential characteristic'. This is why it is impossible to settle constitutional disputes merely by reference to the state of the law.

G. Wilson, 'Postscript: The Courts, Law and Convention' in Lord Nolan and S. Sedley,
The Making and Remaking of the British Constitution
(1997), pp. 97–8

In spite of the use of the law for some of the changes it still remains the case that important parts of the constitution are regulated not by law but by convention, and this remains one of its major distinguishing features. There are, it is said, legal rules and there are conventional rules, each with the same binding force but with many of the conventions not supported by legal rule and therefore not falling within the jurisdiction of the courts. What might be called the grand conventions still lie at the heart of the constitution. They underpinned the gradual transfer of powers from the monarch to her ministers, the limitation of her freedom to choose who should be her ministers, in particular the prime minister, the person who was entitled to form a government, and to dismiss ministers or dissolve Parliament, and the virtual extinction of her power to refuse assent to legislation. But it does not stop there. Conventions reach into every part of the constitution. The rules of procedure and practice of the House of Commons, which help to shape the ground rules of political debate and include provisions as regards the legislative process, the curtailment of debate, the rights of the opposition to choose the subject matter of debate, and which strike the current balance between the need for governments to be able to implement their plans and policies and the opportunities granted to the opposition not only to express their public criticism of them, but also to present themselves to the electorate as a future alternative government—all these rest on convention. It is convention which protects them from arbitrary change and gives them their fundamental character. With none of these do the courts have any direct involvement.

C: Laws, sanctions, and conventions

In the passage by Dicey (see earlier in this chapter in Section 2A at p. 196), he distinguished between laws and conventions, stating that laws are enforced by the courts whereas conventions are not. Sir Ivor Jennings in *The Law and the Constitution* (5th edn, 1959), at pp. 103–36, takes issue with Dicey. Much of the argument is semantic, being centred on the issue whether all laws are enforced by the courts. Jennings chose to interpret Dicey as suggesting that courts would apply sanctions for the breach of any and every law. Many laws are not enforced by the application of sanctions; but they are given effect by the courts, in that they are adhered to and applied. In this sense they are enforced, whereas conventions are treated differently. Other contrasts between laws and conventions have been noted by Munro.

C. R. Munro, *Studies in Constitutional Law*
(2nd edn, 1999), pp. 69–71

For example, instead of being concerned with the practical effects of breaches of rules, we might consider how the rules come into being. In a legal system, a certain number of sources are recognised as law-constitutive. So there are rules specifying what counts as law (or what, by implication, does not). In England, for instance, the courts accept as law only legislation made or authorised by Parliament and the body of rules evolved by the courts called common law. There are formal signs, such as the words of enactment used for Acts of Parliament, denoting that rules have passed a test for being laws. The point here is not merely to reiterate that conventions fall outside the categories recognised as law (which it has been the object of this section so far to show). Rather, what is significant is that conventions do not share the same qualities as laws. They do not come from a 'certain' number of sources: their origins are amorphous, and there are any number of dramatis personae whose behaviour may later be taken as evidence for the existence of a constitutional rule or practice. No body has the function of deciding whether conventions exist. There is no formal sign of their entitlement to be so regarded, and there are no agreed rules for deciding.

These points are related to a larger contrast which may be drawn. Rules of law form parts of a system. Included in the system are rules about the rules: there are provisions about entry to, and exit from, the system, and procedures for the determination and application of the rules. We cannot conceive of a single legal rule, in isolation from a system. However, conventions do not form a system. There is no unifying feature which they possess, and no apparatus of secondary rules. They merely evolve in isolation from each other.

Here, incidentally, lies the answer to Jennings' specious argument that laws and conventions are the same because both 'rest essentially upon general acquiescence'. That is quite misleading. Conventions rest entirely on acquiescence, but individually. If a supposed convention is not accepted as binding by those to whom it would apply, then there could not be said to be a convention, and this is a test on which each must be separately assessed. Laws do not depend upon acquiescence. Individual laws may be unpopular or widely disobeyed, but it does not mean that they are not laws. No doubt the system as a whole must possess some measure of de facto effectiveness for us to recognise it as valid, although it might be stretching language to describe the citizens of any country occupied by enemy forces or ruled by a brutal dictatorship as 'acquiescing' in the laws which govern them. In any event, it is obvious that the comparison is inapt.

When 'acquiescence' is properly analysed, another means of distinguishing emerges. Breaches of a legal rule do not bring into question the existence or validity of the rule; for example, however frequently motorists might exceed the speed limits, the road traffic laws are no less laws for that. However, according to a generally accepted definition, conventions are supposed to be 'rules of political practice which are regarded as binding by those to whom they apply'. If such rules are broken, it becomes appropriate to ask whether they are still 'regarded as binding', and if they are broken often, surely one cannot say that any obligatory rule exists? In other words, the breach of a convention carries a destructive effect, which is absent with laws. The reason for this is that 'feeling obliged' is a necessary condition for the existence of a convention, whereas it is neither a necessary nor a sufficient condition for the existence of laws.

■ QUESTION

If the courts do not apply sanctions for failure to observe a convention, why are conventions observed? A further potential explanation, based on the idea that reciprocal obligations exist between different political actors, is provided in the extract which follows.

J. Jaconelli, 'Do constitutional conventions bind?'

(2005) *Cambridge Law Journal* 149–76, pp. 170–3

Constitutional conventions are sometimes represented as arising from a form of contract or agreement between the various parties. If they were so founded, there would be no difficulty in giving an account of their obligatory force. For we regard freely entered agreements as giving rise to obligations between the contracting parties, even if they are not always obligations which a court of law would enforce. Yet constitutional conventions are founded on contract or agreement only if these terms are used in some loose, figurative sense. Rather, their essence is found to subsist in a stream of concordant actions and expectations deriving from such actions. In such a system of reciprocal acts and forbearances it is possible to derive the basis of obligation .... [This] analysis, adapted to our subject-matter, runs as follows: the [political] party that is in power at the moment respects the constraints that are imposed on it by constitutional conventions in the expectation that the opposition parties, when they attain office, will likewise respect the same constraints. When constitutional conventions are seen in this way the nearest analogy to them in legal doctrine is provided, not by the institution of contract, but by those unusual cases (predominantly to be found in land law) in which rights and duties have been held to spring up from positions of mutual benefit and burden. In this way those, for example, who wish to benefit from the performance by others of obligations contained in covenants must themselves accept the burdens imposed on them by those same covenants ....

This perspective provides at least one reason why the rotation of parties is (instrumentally) beneficial for democracy. Such a state of affairs, certainly, could be seen as good in itself. For it amounts to a form of *serial* power-sharing between the various political groupings in society and may thus embody some of the benefits that certain thinkers have associated with *concurrent* power-sharing. For our purpose, however, it might be accounted as instrumentally good, for as each party comes to government in turn it gains a schooling in the discipline of observing the constraints imposed by constitutional conventions and is allowed the opportunity to perform its side of the constitutional compact.

■ QUESTION

Does the idea that conventions might be underpinned by the attitudes of political actors suggest that the rules are too open to change? Does this focus on the benefits for elite level operators exclude from consideration the interests of wider groups, like the electorate, when determining the extent and force of constitutional conventions?

D: Conventions in the courts

It is clear that courts will not enforce conventions by imposing sanctions for their breach. Recognition of the existence of a convention by a court, however, can be significant in the court's determination of the issues before it. Conventions may be used as an aid to statutory interpretation, or to support judicial decisions not to review discretionary powers of the executive because of the Minister's accountability to Parliament (see *Liversidge* v *Anderson* [1942] AC 206). In *Carltona* v *Commissioners of Works* [1943] 2 All ER 560, Lord Greene MR placed considerable emphasis on the convention of ministerial responsibility in reaching his decision. He stated (at p. 563):

> In the administration of government in this country the functions which are given to ministers (and constitutionally properly given to ministers because they are constitutionally responsible) are functions so multifarious that no minister could ever personally attend to them. To take the example of the present case no doubt there have been thousands of requisitions in this country by individual ministries. It cannot be supposed that this regulation meant that, in each case, the minister in person should direct his mind to the matter. The duties imposed upon ministers and the powers given to ministers are normally exercised under the authority of the ministers by responsible officials of the department. Public business could not be carried on if that were not the case. Constitutionally, the decision of such an official is, of course, the decision of the minister. The minister is responsible. It is he who must answer before Parliament for anything that his officials have done under this authority, and, if for an important matter he selected an official of such junior standing that he could not be expected competently to perform the work, the minister would have to answer for that in Parliament. The whole system of departmental organisation and administration is based on the view that ministers, being responsible to Parliament, will see that important duties are committed to experienced officials. If they do not do that, Parliament is the place where complaint must be made against them.

One of the best examples of judicial consideration of conventions in a United Kingdom court is the case which follows.

Attorney-General v *Jonathan Cape Ltd*
[1976] QB 752, High Court

Between 1964 and 1970 Richard Crossman was a Cabinet Minister, and he kept a political diary. Following his death in 1974, his diary for 1964–66 was edited for publication. A copy was sent to the Secretary to the Cabinet for his approval but was rejected on the ground that publication was against the public interest, in that the doctrine of collective responsibility would be harmed by the disclosure of details of Cabinet decisions, the revelation of differences between members of the Cabinet, and the disclosure of advice given by, and discussions regarding the appointment of, civil servants. When Crossman's literary executors decided to publish extracts of the diary in the *Sunday Times*, the Attorney-General sought injunctions against the publishers, literary executors, and the *Sunday Times* to restrain publication of the book or extracts from it.

> LORD WIDGERY CJ: ... It has always been assumed by lawyers and, I suspect, by politicians, and the Civil Service, that Cabinet proceedings and Cabinet papers are secret, and cannot be publicly disclosed until they have passed into history. It is quite clear that no court will compel the production of Cabinet papers in the course of discovery in an action, and the Attorney-General contends that not only will the court refuse to compel the production of such matters, but it will go further and positively forbid the disclosure of such papers and proceedings if publication will be contrary to the public interest.
>
> The basis of this contention is the confidential character of these papers and proceedings, derived from the convention of joint Cabinet responsibility whereby any policy decision reached by the Cabinet has to be supported thereafter by all members of the Cabinet whether they approve of it or not, unless

they feel compelled to resign. It is contended that Cabinet decisions and papers are confidential for a period to the extent at least that they must not be referred to outside the Cabinet in such a way as to disclose the attitude of individual Ministers in the argument which preceded the decision. …

There is no doubt that Mr Crossman's manuscripts contain frequent references to individual opinions of Cabinet Ministers. … There have, as far as I know, been no previous attempts in any court to define the extent to which Cabinet proceedings should be treated as secret or confidential, and it is not surprising that different views on this subject are contained in the evidence before me. …

The Attorney-General contends that all Cabinet papers and discussions are prima facie confidential, and that the court should restrain any disclosure thereof if the public interest in concealment outweighs the public interest in a right to free publication. The Attorney-General further contends that, if it is shown that the public interest is involved, he has the right and duty to bring the matter before the court. In this contention he is well supported by Lord Salmon in *Reg* v *Lewes Justices, Ex parte Secretary of State for the Home Department* [1973] AC 388, 412, where Lord Salmon said:

> when it is in the public interest that confidentiality shall be safeguarded, then the party from whom the confidential document or the confidential information is being sought may lawfully refuse it. In such a case the Crown may also intervene to prevent production or disclosure of that which in the public interest ought to be protected.

I do not understand Lord Salmon to be saying, or the Attorney-General to be contending, that it is only necessary for him to evoke the public interest to obtain an order of the court. On the contrary, it must be for the court in every case to be satisfied that the public interest is involved, and that, after balancing all the factors which tell for or against publication, to decide whether suppression is necessary.

The defendants' main contention is that whatever the limits of the convention of joint Cabinet responsibility may be, there is no obligation enforceable at law to prevent the publication of Cabinet papers and proceedings, except in extreme cases where national security is involved. In other words, the defendants submit that the confidential character of Cabinet papers and discussions is based on a true convention as defined in the evidence of Professor Henry Wade, namely, an obligation founded in conscience only. Accordingly, the defendants contend that publication of these Diaries is not capable of control by any order of this court. …

However, the Attorney-General has a powerful reinforcement for his argument in the developing equitable doctrine that a man shall not profit from the wrongful publication of information received by him in confidence. …

It is not until the decision in *Duchess of Argyll* v *Duke of Argyll* [1967] Ch 302, that the same principle was applied to domestic secrets such as those passing between husband and wife during the marriage. …

Even so, these defendants argue that an extension of the principle of the *Argyll* case to the present dispute involves another large and unjustified leap forward, because in the present case the Attorney-General is seeking to apply the principle to public secrets made confidential in the interests of good government. I cannot see why the courts should be powerless to restrain the publication of public secrets, while enjoying the *Argyll* powers in regard to domestic secrets. Indeed, as already pointed out, the court must have power to deal with publication which threatens national security, and the difference between such a case and the present case is one of degree rather than kind. I conclude, therefore, that when a Cabinet Minister receives information in confidence the improper publication of such information can be restrained by the court, and his obligation is not merely to observe a gentleman's agreement to refrain from publication.

The Cabinet is at the very centre of national affairs, and must be in possession at all times of information which is secret or confidential. Secrets relating to national security may require to be preserved indefinitely. Secrets relating to new taxation proposals may be of the highest importance until Budget day, but public knowledge thereafter. To leak a Cabinet decision a day or so before it is officially announced is an accepted exercise in public relations, but to identify the Ministers who voted one way or another is objectionable because it undermines the doctrine of joint responsibility.

It is evident that there cannot be a single rule governing the publication of such a variety of matters. In these actions we are concerned with the publication of diaries at a time when 11 years have expired since the first recorded events. The Attorney-General must show (a) that such publication would be a breach of confidence; (b) that the public interest requires that the publication be restrained, and (c) that there are no other facts of the public interest contradictory of and more compelling than that relied upon. Moreover, the court, when asked to restrain such a publication, must closely examine the extent to which relief is necessary to ensure that restrictions are not imposed beyond the strict requirement of public need.

Applying those principles to the present case, what do we find? In my judgment, the Attorney-General has made out his claim that the expression of individual opinions by Cabinet Ministers in the course of Cabinet discussion are matters of confidence, the publication of which can be restrained by the court when this is clearly necessary in the public interest.

The maintenance of the doctrine of joint responsibility within the Cabinet is in the public interest, and the application of that doctrine might be prejudiced by premature disclosure of the views of individual Ministers.

There must, however, be a limit in time after which the confidential character of the information, and the duty of the court to restrain publication, will lapse. Since the conclusion of the hearing in this case I have had the opportunity to read the whole of volume one of the Diaries, and my considered view is that I cannot believe that the publication at this interval of anything in volume one would inhibit free discussion in the Cabinet of today, even though the individuals involved are the same, and the national problems have a distressing similarity with those of a decade ago. It is unnecessary to elaborate the evils which might flow if at the close of a Cabinet meeting a Minister proceeded to give the press an analysis of the voting, but we are dealing in this case with a disclosure of information nearly 10 years later.

It may, of course, be intensely difficult in a particular case, to say at what point the material loses its confidential character, on the ground that publication will no longer undermine the doctrine of joint Cabinet responsibility. It is this difficulty which prompts some to argue that Cabinet discussions should retain their confidential character for a longer and arbitrary period such as 30 years, or even for all time, but this seems to me to be excessively restrictive. The court should intervene only in the clearest of cases where the continuing confidentiality of the material can be demonstrated. In less clear cases— and this, in my view, is certainly one—reliance must be placed on the good sense and good taste of the Minister or ex-Minister concerned.

In the present case there is nothing in Mr Crossman's work to suggest that he did not support the doctrine of joint Cabinet responsibility. The question for the court is whether it is shown that publication now might damage the doctrine notwithstanding that much of the action is up to 10 years old and three general elections have been held meanwhile. So far as the Attorney-General relies in his argument on the disclosure of individual ministerial opinions, he has not satisfied me that publication would in any way inhibit free and open discussion in Cabinet hereafter.

It remains to deal with the Attorney-General's two further arguments, namely, (a) that the Diaries disclose advice given by senior civil servants who cannot be expected to advise frankly if their advice is not treated as confidential; (b) the Diaries disclose observations made by Ministers on the capacity of individual senior civil servants and their suitability for specific appointments. I can see no ground in law which entitles the court to restrain publication of these matters. A Minister is, no doubt, responsible for his department and accountable for its errors even though the individual fault is to be found in his subordinates. In these circumstances, to disclose the fault of the subordinate may amount to cowardice or bad taste, but I can find no ground for saying that either the Crown or the individual civil servant has an enforceable right to have the advice which he gives treated as confidential for all time.

For these reasons I do not think that the court should interfere with the publication of volume one of the Diaries, and I propose, therefore, to refuse the injunction sought but to grant liberty to apply in regard to material other than volume one if it is alleged that different considerations may there have to be applied.

Injunction refused.

NOTE: Following the decision in the case, a committee of privy councillors considered the problem of memoirs of former Cabinet Ministers (Cmnd 6386, 1976). The Radcliffe Committee drew a distinction between secret information relating to national security and international relations, and other confidential material about relationships between Ministers, or between Ministers and civil servants. In the former case the Minister must accept the decision of the Cabinet Secretary, while in the latter case there should be no publication within 15 years except with approval of the Cabinet Secretary but, in the event of a dispute, the final decision would lie with the former Minister as to what to publish. The Committee did not consider that legislation would be appropriate. The Ministerial Code (2016) confirms, in para. 8.10, that the principles established by the Radcliffe Committee still govern the publication of memoirs by former Ministers.

■ QUESTIONS

1. What is the relationship between the law protecting breach of confidence, and the conventional requirement that Ministers should not disclose what is discussed in the Cabinet? What role did the convention of collective responsibility play in Lord Widgery CJ's decision? (See further, on collective responsibility in Chapter 6, Section 2A at pp. 222–5.)

2. To what extent are courts equipped to establish the extent of particular constitutional conventions that may be relevant to deciding a case before them? In *Jonathan Cape* the court was dealing with a very well-established convention, but what about where there is uncertainty about the scope of a convention?

Courts have also made influential statements as to the nature and scope of conventions, even where they are not enforcing these non-legal rules in formal terms. The nature of conventions received considerable attention in a famous Canadian case. This case arose because of a special procedure in Canada whereby an issue may be referred to court for an advisory opinion; no such procedure exists for the United Kingdom.

Reference Re Amendment of the Constitution of Canada
(1982) 125 DLR (3d) 1, Supreme Court of Canada

In 1980, after failing to reach agreement with the provinces on constitutional reform, the Federal Government decided to press ahead with a scheme which would patriate the Canadian Constitution by ending the link with Westminster, establish a new procedure for constitutional amendment, and create a new Charter of Rights which would be binding on both federal and provincial legislatures. Eight of the ten provinces opposed the scheme. The question arose whether the federal authorities were entitled to request Westminster to enact the proposed scheme (as was then required to effect an amendment of the existing constitution) in the absence of unanimous approval from the provinces. The issue progressed to the Canadian Supreme Court when Manitoba, Newfoundland, and Quebec (three of the dissenting provinces) instituted proceedings to obtain a ruling on the constitutionality of the action being taken by the Federal Government.

Two important questions arose for determination. Was there a convention that the Federal Parliament would not request an amendment to the constitution affecting federal–provincial relationships without prior consultation and agreement with the provinces? And could the Federal Government *legally* request an amendment in the absence of such agreement (in other words, could the convention, if it existed, be enforced by the courts)? The judgment of the majority also addressed the purpose of conventions more broadly.

The main purpose of constitutional conventions is to ensure that the legal framework of the Constitution will be operated in accordance with the prevailing constitutional values or principles of the period. For example, the constitutional value which is the pivot of the conventions stated above and relating to responsible government is the democratic principle: the powers of the State must be exercised in accordance with the wishes of the electorate; and the constitutional value or principle which anchors the conventions regulating the relationship between the members of the Commonwealth is the independence of the former British colonies.

Being based on custom and precedent, constitutional conventions are usually unwritten rules. Some of them, however, may be reduced to writing and expressed in the proceedings and documents of Imperial conferences, or in the preamble of statutes such as the *Statute of Westminster, 1931*, or in the proceedings and documents of federal-provincial conferences. They are often referred to and recognized in statements made by members of governments.

The conventional rules of the Constitution present one striking peculiarity. In contradistinction to the laws of the Constitution, they are not enforced by the Courts. One reason for this situation is that, unlike common law rules, conventions are not judge-made rules. They are not based on judicial precedents but on precedents established by the institutions of government themselves. Nor are they in the nature of statutory commands which it is the function and duty of the Courts to obey and enforce. Furthermore, to enforce them would mean to administer some formal sanction when they are breached. But the legal system from which they are distinct does not contemplate formal sanctions for their breach.

Perhaps the main reason why conventional rules cannot be enforced by the Courts is that they are generally in conflict with the legal rules which they postulate and the Courts are bound to enforce the legal rules. The conflict is not of a type which would entail the commission of any illegality. It results from the fact that legal rules create wide powers, discretions and rights which conventions prescribe should be exercised only in a certain limited manner, if at all.

Nevertheless, the majority went on to consider whether the existence of a particular convention is purely a political question or one upon which a court may adjudicate. They concluded that this was a constitutional question which it was proper for a court to decide.

In so recognizing conventional rules, the Courts have described them, sometimes commented upon them and given them such precision as is derived from the written form of a judgment. They did not shrink from doing so on account of the political aspects of conventions, nor because of their supposed vagueness, uncertainty or flexibility.

In our view, we should not, in a constitutional reference, decline to accomplish a type of exercise that Courts have been doing of their own motion for years. ...

The requirements for establishing a convention bear some resemblance with those which apply to customary law. Precedents and usage are necessary but do not suffice. They must be normative. We adopt the following passage of Sir W. Ivor Jennings in *The Law and the Constitution*, 5th edn. (1959), p. 136:

> We have to ask ourselves three questions: first, what are the precedents; secondly, did the actors in the precedents believe that they were bound by a rule; and thirdly, is there a reason for the rule? A single precedent with a good reason may be enough to establish the rule. A whole string of precedents without such a reason will be of no avail, unless it is perfectly certain that the persons concerned regarded them as bound by it.

Applying the three-part Jennings test, the majority concluded that there was an accumulation of precedents in support of the convention, that the relevant actors treated the rule as binding, and that there was a reason for the rule: that Canada is a federal union.

The purpose of this conventional rule is to protect the federal character of the Canadian Constitution and prevent the anomaly that the House of Commons and Senate could obtain by simple resolutions what they could not validly accomplish by statute. ...

We have reached the conclusion that the agreement of the Provinces of Canada, no views being expressed as to its quantification, is constitutionally required for the passing of the 'Proposed Resolution for a joint Address to Her Majesty respecting the Constitution of Canada' and that the passing of this Resolution without such agreement would be unconstitutional in the conventional sense.

NOTE: In response to the Supreme Court's decision the Federal Government decided not to press on with the request to Westminster to enact legislation. Further discussions were held with the provinces and concessions were offered. In response, nine provinces agreed to the revised proposals. A new request was made, and the Canada Act 1982 was duly enacted at Westminster following a recommendation from the House of Commons Select Committee on Foreign Affairs (the 'Kershaw Committee') that consent from nine out of ten provinces constituted a substantial measure of support for the proposals.

Foreign Affairs Committee, *Third report on the British North America Acts: the role of Parliament* (Kershaw Report)
HC 128 of 1981–2, paras 6–7

6. The criteria suggested in our First Report for assessing the appropriate level of Provincial support were put forward, not as minima required by any existing constitutional rule or convention, but rather as indications of what 'Parliament would be justified in regarding as sufficient' or of what 'it would not be inappropriate for the UK Parliament to expect'. Since then, the Supreme Court of Canada has determined that what is constitutionally required is 'at least a substantial measure of Provincial consent'. The Court decided that unanimity is not required, but did not define or quantify 'a substantial measure'. The Government of Quebec have, we understand, commenced litigation to establish whether their concurrence is constitutionally required. So it is important to observe that the Supreme Court has stated, 'It will be for the political actors, not this Court, to determine the degree of provincial consent required'. The Federal-Provincial Agreement of 5 November 1981, made in the wake of the Supreme Court's judgement and accepted by nine of the ten Provinces, appears to us to amount to a determination by the political actors in Canada that the concurrence of nine Provinces is constitutionally sufficient, albeit the dissenting Province be Quebec.

7. In this situation, what we said in our First Report seems applicable: 'the UK Parliament is bound to exercise its best judgement in deciding whether the request, in all the circumstances, conveys the clearly expressed wishes of Canada as a federally structured whole'. In our view, the present request does this.

■ QUESTIONS

1. Do you accept the distinction drawn by the Supreme Court of Canada between recognizing the applicability of a convention, and the judicial enforcement of the rule? What would have been the consequences if the Canadian Federal Government had disregarded the judgment of the Court and continued with 'unconstitutional' conduct regardless? Could the legitimacy of the Court have been damaged if the political institutions had reacted differently to the judgment?

2. Are courts well equipped to consider—and decide—questions as to the scope of constitutional conventions, which are in large part highly political rules? This issue is relevant in the following case.

Evans v Information Commissioner
[2012] UKUT 313 (AAC), Upper Tribunal

Evans appealed against the decision of the Information Commissioner not to order the disclosure of letters written by the heir to the throne, Prince Charles, to a number of government departments under the Freedom of Information Act 2000. Evans sought the disclosure in particular of what was described as 'advocacy correspondence' between Prince Charles and the government departments: correspondence which sought to express to Ministers a particular policy preference of the heir to the throne. By s. 37 of the Act, communications 'with Her Majesty' or 'with other members of the Royal Family' were subject to a qualified exemption from disclosure, which would have effect if the public interest in maintaining the exemption outweighed the public interest in disclosure. By s. 41 of the Act, disclosure of information would be exempt if it would constitute a breach of confidence to do so, which would also be determined by reference to whether such disclosure would be in the public interest. As part of its determination of whether the disclosure of Prince Charles' advocacy correspondence was in the public interest, the Upper Tribunal was required to consider the scope of the constitutional convention that the heir to the throne is entitled to be confidentially instructed in the business of government in preparation for rule ('the education convention').

G1. Constitutional conventions generally

…

66. What are constitutional conventions? The first thing to stress is that they are not law. They are not enforced by courts.

…

68. The third thing to stress follows in part from the first. The parties invite us to decide the extent of the constitutional convention. It is only rarely that a court or tribunal has to decide a question of that kind, and it is a task which we undertake with circumspection. We are not deciding an issue of law. Questions about constitutional conventions have been the subject of much academic and political debate. So it is important to understand precisely what we were invited to do.

69. On the question of how far the constitutional convention extended the parties made reference to the test for identifying whether a constitutional convention exists at all. In his statement Professor Brazier said that there was no general agreement, but identified two tests which "enjoy considerable support":

8 Sir Ivor Jennings has suggested [at p. 131 of *The Law and the Constitution* (5th ed., 1959)] (in summary) that a constitutional convention exists if (i) there are precedents underpinning it, (ii) the parties to the relevant practice consider themselves to be bound by it, and (iii) there is a reason for the existence of the convention.

9 Other writers [for example G. Marshall and G. Moodie, *Some Problems of the Constitution* (5th ed., 1971), pp. 22–26] have said that a convention is a non-legal rule of constitutional behaviour which has been consistently accepted by those affected by it as binding on them, but which is not enforceable in the courts.

70. Mr Swift suggested to Professor Tomkins that these tests represented different "schools of thought". That suggestion was not accepted. Professor Tomkins responded firmly that Sir Ivor Jennings's test has been accepted by constitutional legal scholarship throughout the 80year period since the first edition of his book was published. Moreover, Professor Tomkins added that there was in fact nothing said by Marshall and Moodie which was inconsistent with what was said by Jennings.

71. Under questioning by Mr Fordham, Professor Brazier stood by his position that Jennings was not the only test. However for the purposes of this case he was content to adopt Jennings. He did not suggest that it would be enough to have something which failed Jennings but met some other test.

72. The first element of the Jennings test is summarised by Professor Brazier as being that before something can be held to be a constitutional convention there must be "precedents underpinning it". The use of the plural here may be misleading. Jennings described constitutional conventions connected with internal government as arising "by the gradual crystallisation of practice into binding rules." When explaining the third element of the test he stressed that neither precedents nor dicta were conclusive. In that context he added that:

A single precedent with a good reason may be enough to establish the rule.

73. The second element of the Jennings test is summarised by Professor Brazier as being that the parties to the relevant practice consider themselves to be bound by it. In oral evidence Professor Brazier

made it clear that this requirement applied to both sides. In the present case, accordingly, in order for the departments to make good their case it would be necessary for both Prince Charles and government ministers to consider themselves to be bound to treat Prince Charles's education in the business of government, with its special constitutional status and associated special degree of confidentiality, as extending not merely – as Mr Evans accepts – to government informing Prince Charles about what it is doing and responding to queries from him.

74. The third element of the Jennings test is summarised by Professor Brazier as being that there is a reason for the existence of the convention. In response to questions from Mr Fordham Professor Brazier agreed that in the present case this means that there must be a good constitutional reason for the reach of the convention, i.e. for its scope. In that regard Professor Brazier accepted what Jennings himself had said about the third element in the test:

> As in the creation of law, the creation of a convention must be due to the reason of the thing because it accords with the prevailing political philosophy, it helps to make the democratic system operate, it enables the machinery of state to run more smoothly and, if it were not there, friction would result.

75. Accordingly for the purposes of the present case, the answer to the question we posed above is that a particular constitutional obligation will be a constitutional convention if the Jennings test is met. As regards the scope of the education convention, we must apply the three elements of that test. First, we must consider whether there is at least one precedent underpinning such a scope. Second, we must consider whether both parties to it considered themselves to be bound to treat Prince Charles's education in the business of government, with its special constitutional status and associated special degree of confidentiality, as extending not merely – as Mr Evans accepts – to government informing Prince Charles about what it is doing and responding to queries from him. Third, we must consider whether there is a reason, in the sense used by Jennings and described above, for the convention to have that scope.

…

G4. The education convention and its scope

…

103. In our view the new approach as advanced by Professor Brazier in his witness statement would involve a massive extension of the education convention. The new approach seemed to involve a proposition that whenever Prince Charles interacted with government this helped to prepare him to be king and was therefore part of the education convention. The logical consequence of this proposition would be that the education convention extended both to advocacy correspondence and to correspondence on charitable or social matters without any advocacy element.

…

105. The massive extension of the convention advanced by the Departments, and the less massive extension identified by the Commissioner, would both have to meet the second element of the Jennings test. In the context of the education convention this would require that both sides considered that as part of Prince Charles's preparation to be king they were bound to permit correspondence with government in the manner contemplated by the extension. … The submissions for Mr Evans accepted that the traditional education convention involved informing Prince Charles about governmental matters and responding to queries from him about that information. The evidence before us, as examined in open session, demonstrates that interaction between Prince Charles and government went far beyond this, but not "as part of preparation to be king". Published advocacy correspondence shows Prince Charles using his access to government ministers, and no doubt considering himself entitled to use that access, in order to set up and drive forward charities and to promote views – but not as part

of his preparation for kingship. Ministers responded, and no doubt felt themselves obliged to respond, but again not as part of Prince Charles's preparation for kingship. Indeed Prince Charles himself accepts, and government acknowledges, that his role as king would be very different. The inevitable conclusion is that while correspondence going beyond the traditional education convention may well be confidential, and is not (despite Professor Tomkins's concerns) said by Mr Evans in these proceedings to be unconstitutional, it does not have the special status of correspondence falling within a constitutional convention.

106. There is another element in the Jennings test which leads to the same conclusion. It is the third element: there must be good reason for the suggested extension. … In our view, however, there is an overwhelming difficulty in suggesting that there is good reason for regarding advocacy correspondence by Prince Charles as falling within a constitutional convention. It is a difficulty that was recognised in Professor Brazier's answer cited earlier: it is the constitutional role of the monarch, not the heir to the throne, to encourage or warn government. Accordingly it is fundamental that advocacy by Prince Charles cannot have constitutional status.

Having established the scope of the education convention, the Upper Tribunal turned to the balancing of the public interest arguments in favour of disclosure against the public interest arguments in favour of the advocacy correspondence being exempted from disclosure, one of which was the importance in maintaining the education convention.

J. Analysis of the public interest

123. In the decision notices the Commissioner identified specific public interests in disclosure of the information and in its non-disclosure. For convenience we identify these factors in this way:

Factors in favour of disclosure

IC(1) governmental accountability and transparency;

IC(2) the increased understanding of the interaction between government and monarchy;

IC(3) a public understanding of the influence, if any, of Prince Charles on matters of public policy;

IC(4) a particular significance in the light of media stories focusing on Prince Charles's alleged inappropriate interference/lobbying;

IC(5) furthering the public debate regarding the constitutional role of the monarchy and, in particular, the heir to the throne; and

IC(6) informing the broader debate surrounding constitutional reform.

Factors against disclosure

IC(7) potential to undermine the operation of the education convention;

IC(8) an inherent and weighty public interest in the maintenance of confidences;

IC(9) potential to undermine Prince Charles's perceived political neutrality;

IC(10) interference with Prince Charles's right to respect for private life under article 8; and

IC(11) a resultant chilling effect on the frankness of communication between Prince Charles and government ministers.

J8. General aspects of the overall balance

...

210. Turning to the particular considerations said to affect Prince Charles, the Commissioner's analysis identified a need for exceptionally strong arguments in favour of disclosure. This analysis is dependent upon substantial weight being given (a) to an education convention going beyond its previously identified scope or alternatively to an element of preparation for kingship in parts of the disputed information not falling within the education convention; (b) to the danger of "misperception" by the public of Prince Charles's political neutrality and other matters; and (c) to a "truly personal" characterisation of the disputed information. For reasons given in sections J4, J5, and J7 none of these matters, as regards advocacy correspondence, is likely in the absence of special circumstances (for example, information falling within the true scope of the education convention, or which is properly to be regarded as part of preparation for kingship) to give rise to weighty public interest considerations favouring non-disclosure. We are not persuaded that they warrant giving correspondence between ministers and Prince Charles greater protection from disclosure than would be afforded to correspondence with others who have dealings with government in a context where those others are seeking to advance the work of charities or to promote views. ...

Appeal allowed.

NOTES

1. Section 37 of the Freedom of Information Act 2000 has now been amended by the Constitutional Reform and Governance Act 2010 to confer an absolute exemption on correspondence between government departments and the heir to the throne. Future 'advocacy correspondence' between Prince Charles and Ministers will, therefore, be protected from disclosure absolutely, rather than subject to a public interest test of the kind carried out by the Upper Tribunal in *Evans*.
2. Following the decision of the Upper Tribunal, the Attorney-General exercised the Government's power under s. 53(2) of the Freedom of Information Act 2000 to veto disclosure of the advocacy correspondence. This veto was challenged by Evans, who sought judicial review on the grounds that its use in these circumstances was 'unreasonable'. This argument was upheld in the Supreme Court [2015] UKSC 21 (see Chapter 3, Section 5 at pp. 137–40). For Lord Mance and Lady Hale (in the majority as to the result), the fact that the Attorney General's certificate of veto reached a different view as to the scope of the education convention from the Upper Tribunal, and did not adequately justify this alternative position, was a crucial reason that this exercise of power was unreasonable, and therefore unlawful.

■ QUESTIONS

1. The Upper Tribunal endorsed the Jennings tripartite test for establishing the existence of constitutional conventions. Does this bind politicians and officials to use this test when seeking to establish whether a convention has been created? Does the requirement that there be a 'reason' for a convention pose potential problems in this regard, if there is disagreement among officials as to whether a conventional rule *ought* to exist?
2. To what extent does the Upper Tribunal's decision as to the limited scope of the 'education convention' bind future governments? While the amendment of s. 37 of the 2000 Act (noted earlier) ensures that future correspondence between the heir to the throne and Ministers will be confidential, could a Minister rely on the decision in *Evans* to refuse to read or engage with 'advocacy correspondence' from Prince Charles or his successors?
3. Does the seemingly definitive statement of the Upper Tribunal establishing the scope of the 'education convention' prevent it from changing in the future? Do judicial decisions ascertaining the content of conventions (whether in *Evans* or in the other cases considered in this chapter) restrict their flexibility?

E: Can conventions obtain legal force?

The nature and effect of the Sewel convention, which establishes the requirement that the UK Parliament will obtain the consent of the devolved legislatures in Scotland, Wales, and Northern Ireland when legislating on a devolved matter or to alter the competence of the devolved institutions (see Chapter 8, Section 2B at pp. 364–6), was considered by the Supreme Court in *R (Miller)* v *Secretary of State for Exiting the European Union* [2017] UKSC 5. In addition to the argument (accepted by an 8–3 majority of the Court) that the royal prerogative power to notify an intention to withdraw from the EU under Art. 50 TEU had been displaced by statute, it was also argued, in a joined appeal from Northern Ireland (*Re McCord* [2016] NIQB 85), that the Sewel convention operated so as to require the consent of the devolved legislatures to an Act of the UK Parliament providing authorization for the triggering of exit negotiations. The Supreme Court rejected this argument unanimously.

R (Miller) v Secretary of State for Exiting the European Union
[2017] UKSC 5, Supreme Court

141.…. [I]t is necessary to consider the role of the courts in relation to constitutional conventions. It is well established that the courts of law cannot enforce a political convention. In *Re Resolution to Amend the Constitution* [1981] 1 SCR 753, the Supreme Court of Canada addressed the nature of political conventions. In the majority judgment the Chief Justice (Laskin) and Dickson, Beetz, Estey, McIntyre, Chouinard and Lamer JJ stated at pp 774 to 775:

"The very nature of a convention, as political in inception and as depending on a consistent course of political recognition by those for whose benefit and to whose detriment (if any) the convention developed over a considerable period of time is inconsistent with its legal enforcement." …

145. While the UK government and the devolved executives have agreed the mechanisms for implementing the convention in the Memorandum of Understanding, the convention operates as a political restriction on the activity of the UK Parliament. Article 9 of the Bill of Rights, which provides that "Proceedings in Parliament ought not to be impeached or questioned in any Court or Place out of Parliament", provides a further reason why the courts cannot adjudicate on the operation of this convention.

146. Judges therefore are neither the parents nor the guardians of political conventions; they are merely observers. As such, they can recognise the operation of a political convention in the context of deciding a legal question (as in the Crossman diaries case – *Attorney General v Jonathan Cape Ltd* [1976] 1 QB 752), but they cannot give legal rulings on its operation or scope, because those matters are determined within the political world….

The Sewel convention had, however, also been recognized in statute: while the unlimited legislative power of the UK Parliament is explicitly preserved in s. 28(7), s. 28(8) of the Scotland Act 1998 (which is essentially duplicated in the Wales Bill 2016–17) provides that 'it is recognised that the Parliament of the United Kingdom will not normally legislate with regard to devolved matters without the consent of the Scottish Parliament'. It was therefore argued in *Miller* that the reflection of the convention in statute gave legal force to this rule, which was capable of judicial enforcement. All 11 Justices of the Supreme Court also rejected this argument.

148. As the Advocate General submitted, by such provisions, the UK Parliament is not seeking to convert the Sewel Convention into a rule which can be interpreted, let alone enforced, by the courts; rather, it is recognising the convention for what it is, namely a political convention, and is effectively declaring that it is a permanent feature of the relevant devolution settlement. That follows from the nature of the content, and is acknowledged by the words ("it is recognised" and "will not normally"), of

the relevant subsection. We would have expected UK Parliament to have used other words if it were seeking to convert a convention into a legal rule justiciable by the courts.

149. In the Scotland Act 2016, the recognition of the Sewel Convention occurs alongside the provision in section 1 of that Act. That section, by inserting section 63A into the Scotland Act 1998, makes the Scottish Parliament and the Scottish government a permanent part of the United Kingdom's constitutional arrangements, signifies the commitment of the UK Parliament and government to those devolved institutions, and declares that those institutions are not to be abolished except on the basis of a decision of the people of Scotland voting in a referendum. This context supports our view that the purpose of the legislative recognition of the convention was to entrench it as a convention.

■ QUESTIONS

1. Was the Supreme Court right to regard the Sewel convention as legally unenforceable, despite recognizing its fundamental constitutional importance? Could the Court have taken a broader understanding of the domestic 'constitutional requirements' (as Art. 50 provides) for authorizing notice of the UK's intention to withdraw from the EU, recognizing the political as well as the legal rules of the UK constitution? Or would this have taken the court into difficult political territory, and therefore beyond its jurisdiction?

2. If a convention which has been explicitly recognized in statute will not be enforced by the Supreme Court, could you think of any other ways in which the courts might rule on the applicability of conventions? Could the Supreme Court have ruled on the *scope* of the Sewel convention, while accepting it could not *enforce* this?

F: Codification of conventions

As part of the process of reform of the House of Lords, a Joint Lords-Commons select committee was created and asked to codify the conventions regulating the relations between the two Houses of Parliament.

Joint Committee on Conventions, *Conventions of the UK Parliament*
HL 265/ HC1212 of 2005–06, paras 253–6, 263–9, 272–9

253. "Codification" may be taken in at least two senses: (i) the broad sense of an authoritative statement, and (ii) the narrow sense of reduction to a literal code or system. In the context of Parliament, an authoritative statement could take any of the following forms:

a) a statement made anywhere, e.g. in a book
b) some form of concordat or memorandum of understanding
c) a statement made in Parliament, e.g. in Hansard or in evidence to a Committee
d) a Committee report
e) a report agreed to by one or both Houses of Parliament
f) a resolution of one or both Houses of Parliament
g) a literal Code, such as each House's Code of Conduct for Members
h) a statement in the House of Lords' *Companion to Standing Orders*
i) words in *Erskine May*
j) a Standing Order
k) an Act of Parliament

254. It might be felt that only the most formal of these–a Code, a Standing Order or an Act–would really constitute codification. But the Leader of the House of Commons appeared to have a broader definition in mind when he noted, in the Commons debate on setting up this Committee, that "[t]he

manner in which the conventions could be codified ranges from a codification in the body of the Committee's report, to a code that has been negotiated by both Houses and which we endorse in resolutions, through to its inclusion in Standing Orders or its enshrinement in law. That is a subsequent matter". He later said that, in his opinion, "it would be a grave error to put any description of the convention[s] into legislation".

255. We are aware that our remit is to an extent self-fulfilling. The authoritative statements about conventions, by our witnesses and in this report, will be cited in future, even if the report leads to no further action.

256. As well as the end product of codification, there is the question of process. Some of the items in the above list have their own process (e.g. a resolution is preceded by debate), but additional steps are possible, e.g. a Speakers' Conference.

...

263. The Clerk of the Parliaments distinguishes conventions from rules. Conventions evolve; rules are fixed. Rules require enforcement and sanctions; conventions have no sanctions. Conventions may evolve into fixed rules; those under consideration are "too new to have become fixed". If they were codified and fixed, they would cease to be conventions and become rules.

264. He gives examples of conventions described as such and set out in the *Companion*. One of them, the target rising time of 10pm, was substantially breached 53 times between its introduction in 2002 and the Whitsun recess 2006, showing that recording a convention in an agreed form may introduce clarity without ensuring observance.

265. The Clerk of the Parliaments draws attention to the question of who is bound by a convention and is in a position to deliver observance. For the Salisbury-Addison Convention, his answer is, the Leader of the Opposition. But for the reasonable time and delegated legislation conventions it is less clear, and in a self-regulating House any backbencher could provoke a breach.

266. If it were intended to embody a convention in a Standing Order or an Act, new clarity would be needed, e.g. in defining a manifesto Bill for the purposes of the Salisbury-Addison Convention. Formally defined powers might be used to the limit, rather than with restraint—though, as he pointed out, the Parliament Acts give the Lords a month to pass a Money Bill but they often do so within days. And legislation would raise the possibility of intervention by the courts, which would be undesirable and "uncomfortable for both sides".

267. In oral evidence, the Clerk of the Parliaments canvassed the more acceptable option of a unanimous report from this Committee endorsed by resolutions of both Houses. "It does not mean to say that one cannot depart from the norm, but the clearer the norm is the more the House would have to justify, in the forum of public opinion, taking a different line". Peer pressure would also operate. He denied that doing this would inhibit evolution.

268. The Clerk of the House of Commons, Sir Roger Sands, observed first that "conventions must be understood in the context of the constitutional and political circumstances in which they have been forged ... The 'practicality' of codification ... is not merely a matter of reviewing the technical options; it is a matter of considering whether the settled and predictable constitutional circumstances exist which would provide the necessary context for codification".

269. He gave his own list of arguments against turning conventions into rules. This would involve difficulties of definition, and lead to loss of flexibility. It would imply a need for adjudication; for conventions governing relations between the Houses, this would have to be by either an extraparliamentary body or some kind of Conference of the two Houses. Paradoxically, codifying the conventions could lead to increased delay, while awaiting adjudication. And if codification took the form of statute law, it would create a possibility of court intervention, which in his opinion could not be excluded, and which

might be more likely with the creation of the new Supreme Court in 2009. Sir Roger agreed that this would be a "substantial constitutional change". Commenting on the notion of embodying an agreed description of the conventions in resolutions, the Clerk of the House of Commons confirmed that this would be a weak form of codification. It would warrant entries in *Erskine May* and the *Companion*, "but no more; and so the Speaker would find it very difficult to give rulings just on the basis of a codification in that form". This is the process proposed by the Hunt report for codifying the Salisbury-Addison Convention, and the Hunt report envisaged eliminating "any doubt or ambiguity as to their [the conventions'] application in all circumstances". The Clerk of the House of Commons did not think that was "a viable proposition".

...

272. According to Lord Norton of Louth "'codifying conventions' is a contradiction in terms ... If conventions are codified, they cease to be conventions". This is because in his view codification by definition involves enforceability and a convention is by definition unenforceable. He admits however that one could adopt "a soft definition of codification", i.e. "simply listing what are agreed to be conventions"; but in his view this exercise would be "nugatory". He also admits that "strong" codification, i.e. turning the conventions into enforceable rules, would be possible; but he argues against it. It would change the relationship between the Houses by taking from the Lords the leverage derived from reserve powers; it would require an enforcement mechanism; and in any case the present system works "reasonably well". Also it would reduce the capacity of the constitution to evolve in response to political reality.

273. Dr Russell observed that there is "nowhere comparable" to this Parliament for reliance on conventions as opposed to written rules. Likewise Professor Bogdanor observed, "Conventions are bound to play a most important role in an uncodified constitution such as that of the United Kingdom".

274. Professor Bradley likewise sees two possible forms of codification: "merely summarising past practice or an exercise in formulating rules for future conduct". He argues against the rule-making approach. "The British system is dynamic and flexible, rather than rigid". Its lack of clarity may sometimes seem a nuisance, but it enables it to evolve as circumstances change. A convention may be the practical expression of a principle; in a certain situation it may be possible, even necessary, to appear to breach the convention while upholding the principle. The sovereignty of Parliament means that exceptions must be expected: "a bill may raise a fundamental constitutional question such that it is not possible in advance to predict how the Lords should respond". In the absence of rules, all this can "come out in the political wash".

275. Professor Bogdanor agrees with Professor Bradley in seeing the conventions as defined by, and changing in response to, the political situation, in which he includes public opinion. He agrees with Sir Roger Sands that now, "when the constitution is in ferment", is a bad time to try to pin conventions down.

276. According to the Clerk of the Australian Senate, relations between the Houses in Canberra are governed entirely by the constitution and by standing orders. "Various participants in the parliamentary processes have attempted at various times to invent conventions to suit their purposes, but no conventions have been established". The Acting Clerk of the Australian House of Representatives provides an interesting illustration of the fact that a written constitution may still leave room for doubt and disagreement on important matters.

277. In Australia, a Constitutional Convention met in 1983–85 to "recognise and declare" constitutional conventions previously unwritten. But this concerned the relationship between the Governor-General and the Prime Minister (and in particular the power of the Governor-General to call an Election), not relations between the Houses. Professor Bogdanor commented, "It declared that 'the following principles and practices shall be observed in Australia'. It is not clear what authority the Commission had for making such a statement".

278. The Clerk of the Canadian Senate says, "In many respects, the relations between the contemporary Senate and the House of Commons, as in the UK Parliament, have followed certain recognisable practices. These practices have never been codified and are not usually identified as conventions" …

279. In our view the word "codification" is unhelpful, since to most people it implies rule-making, with definitions and enforcement mechanisms. Conventions, by their very nature, are unenforceable. In this sense, therefore, codifying conventions is a contradiction in terms. It would raise issues of definition, reduce flexibility, and inhibit the capacity to evolve. It might create a need for adjudication, and the presence of an adjudicator, whether the courts or some new body, is incompatible with parliamentary sovereignty. Even if an adjudicator could be found, the possibility of adjudication would introduce uncertainty and delay into the business of Parliament. In these ways, far from reducing the risk of conflict, codification might actually damage the relationship between the two Houses, making it more confrontational and less capable of moderation through the usual channels. This would benefit neither the Government nor Parliament.

NOTE: The report was approved in resolutions in identical terms in both Houses. See further C. J. G Sampford, 'Recognise and Declare: An Australian Experiment in Codifying Constitutional Conventions' (1987) 7 *Oxford Journal of Legal Studies* 369.

■ QUESTIONS

1. If the committee did not codify the conventions of the United Kingdom Parliament, what did they do and was it worthwhile?

2. The broader question of whether the UK constitution should be codified was the subject of a long-term inquiry by the House of Commons Political and Constitutional Reform Committee between 2010 and 2015. One of the three possible models explored by the Committee was a 'Constitutional Consolidation Act' which would be a 'consolidation of existing laws of a constitutional nature in statute, the common law and parliamentary practice, together with a codification of essential constitutional conventions' (see *A New Magna Carta?* HC 463 of 2014–15, p. 10). If codification were to be recommended, and pursued by a future government, should constitutional conventions be included in such an exercise? Or should conventions be left outside any legal codification of the constitution? Would the codification of conventions within a Consolidation Act change their non-legal character?

6

Parliament: Scrutiny of Policy and Administration

OVERVIEW

In this chapter, which examines the operation of our parliamentary style of government, we focus on the House of Commons with an emphasis upon the responsibility and accountability of the Government. The most important constitutional convention is that of responsible government, the idea that the Executive will be responsible for its exercise of power and be accountable to Parliament and thence to the electorate. Having set out the theory we look at the practice and the various procedures in select committees, on the floor of the Commons and in correspondence, ending with the review of some reforms intended to re-balance power to enhance Parliament and back-bench MPs.

SECTION 1: THE ROLE OF PARLIAMENT

The UK Parliament has many functions: it makes law, represents the people, debates and scrutinizes policy, provides the state with a government, and holds that government to account. An understanding of the role of Parliament must therefore be sensitive to the fact that it actually has a number of roles, which sometimes may be in tension with each other.

P. Norton (ed.), *Parliament in the 1980s*

(1985), pp. 4–6, 8

Some observers identify a variety of functions, others list only two or three. An analysis of writings on Parliament, of constitutional practice and of parliamentary behaviour would suggest three primary ones: those of providing the personnel of government, of legitimization, and of subjecting measures of public policy to scrutiny and influence. This is to identify them in rather bald terms. Each is in need of qualification and amplification.

Providing the personnel of government

This is the least problematic of the functions. By convention, ministers are drawn from and remain within Parliament. Again by convention, most ministers—including the Prime Minister and most members of the Cabinet—are drawn from the elected chamber. (No less than two but rarely more than four peers are appointed now to the Cabinet.) There is no formal prohibition on a Prime Minister appointing as a minister someone who is neither an MP or a peer; such occasions are rare but not unknown. However, those given office are normally then elevated to the peerage or (more riskily) seek a Commons seat through the medium of a by-election. In practice, most ministers have served a parliamentary apprenticeship of several years before their appointments. Parliament provides both the personnel of government and the forum in which those seeking office can make their mark. Though there are occasional calls for non-parliamentarians (businessmen, industrialists and the like) to be brought into government, this function of Parliament arouses no serious debate or controversy.

Legitimization

Most national assemblies exist for the purpose of giving assent to measures of public policy. Indeed, this constitutes the primary purpose for which representatives of the local English communities (*communes*) were first summoned in the thirteenth century. Today, the broad rubric of legitimization encompasses different elements. The most obvious and the most significant is that of manifest legitimization. This constitutes the formal giving of assent to measures, enabling them to be designated Acts of Parliament; such Acts are accepted as having general and binding applicability by virtue of having been passed by the country's elected or part-elected national assembly (the elected chamber now having dominance within that assembly). A second element is that of latent legitimization. The government derives its primary political legitimacy from being elected through (if no longer by) the House of Commons. The collectivity of ministers that form the government enjoy enhanced legitimacy also by being drawn from and remaining in Parliament. For Parliament as an institution, this of course constitutes an essentially passive function.

There are two other sub-functions that fall under the heading of legitimization: those of tension-release and support-mobilization. By meeting and debating issues, Parliament provides an outlet, an authoritative outlet, for the expression of different views within society. Thus it plays an important part in the dissipation of tension. For example, during the Falklands crisis in 1982, Parliament provided the authoritative forum for the expression of public feelings on the issue. In Argentina, by contrast, citizens enjoyed no such body through which their views could be expressed and were forced instead to take to the streets to make their feelings known. Parliament also seeks to mobilize public support for measures which it has approved. In essence, these two sub-functions constitute a two-way process between electors and the elected, the views of citizens being channelled through Parliament (tension-release) and Parliament then mobilizing support for those measures which it has approved (support-mobilization). In practice, the extent to which Parliament is capable of fulfilling these functions has been much overlooked and, when considered by writers, has often been found wanting.

Scrutiny and influence

Parliament ceased to be a policy-making legislature in the nineteenth century. Instead it acquired the characteristics of what I have elsewhere termed a policy-influencing legislature. It ceased to be involved in the making of public policy, but it was expected to subject such policy to a process of scrutiny and influence. Scrutiny and influence are analytically separable terms, but scrutiny without any consequent sanction to effect influence is of little worth; and influence is best and most confidently attempted when derived from prior scrutiny. Hence, scrutiny and influence may be conjoined as a single function of Parliament. It is, in practice, its most debated and contentious function.

The exercise of scrutiny and influence can be seen to operate at two levels. These, in simple terms, may be characterized as being at the macro and the micro level of public policy. At the macro level, Parliament is expected to subject measures of public policy, embodied in legislative bills or in executive actions, to scrutiny and influence prior to giving assent to them. It is essentially a reactive function, exercised at a moderately late stage in the policy cycle ... It is one which is most often carried out through the party elements in both Houses, the official Opposition or, nowadays, opposition parties seeking to exert the most sustained scrutiny of government measures. However, Parliament is but one of many influences at work in the policy cycle and, by virtue of what is usually an assured government majority at the end of the scrutinizing process, is rarely deemed to be the most important. Indeed, in some analyses, it is of no great importance at all.

At the micro level, Parliament is expected to scrutinize and respond to the effects of policy on the community. In practice, this task is exercised less through the party elements and Parliament as a collective entity, and more through Members of Parliament as Constituency representatives. Members represent territorially designated areas (constituencies) and seek to defend and pursue the interests of their constituents and groups within their constituencies. Whereas at the macro level MPs will be concerned to debate the principle of public policy, usually within the context of party ideology, at the micro level they are much more concerned with the policy's practical implications for their constituents.

In terms of the working life of Parliament, scrutiny and influence constitute its most demanding function. Seeking to subject government actions and legislative measures to scrutiny and a degree of influence occupies most of Parliament's time and energies. It is also the function that attracts the most debate and criticism. At best, effective fulfilment of the function allows Parliament to set the broad limits within which government can govern. (At the end of the day, it retains the formal sanction to deny assent to the government's legislative proposals and its request for supply.) At worst, the function may be fulfilled in the most superficial of ways, providing no effective check upon the executive.

NOTES

1. Norton does not say that the House of Commons controls the Executive. Michael Ryle in *The Commons Today* (1981) says that it is a popular misapprehension to regard the Commons as a governmental rather than a critical body. As he puts it, 'Parliament is the forum where the exercise of government is publicly displayed and is open to scrutiny and criticism'.
2. There is much contemporary debate about the influence and effectiveness of Parliament over the Executive. It is increasingly becoming clear that the idea that Parliament is a weak institution with limited power to challenge or influence the Government is at best simplistic, and contradicted by available evidence, as the following extract discusses.

M. Russell and P. Cowley, 'The Policy Power of the Westminster Parliament: "The Parliamentary State" and the Empirical Evidence'

(2016) *Governance* pp. 132–4

In a recent book on policy failures in British government, two well-respected political scientists claimed that as a legislative assembly, "the parliament of the United Kingdom is, much of the time, either peripheral or totally irrelevant. It might as well not exist" (King and Crewe 2013, 361). This may be in line with the conventional "parliamentary decline thesis" and comparative views of Westminster, but is inconsistent with the empirical evidence. The data that we have presented make clear that the British parliament has significant influence, at all stages of the policy process.

We have reviewed influence through some of Westminster's most central mechanisms – intraparty negotiation on the government side, intercameral negotiation between Commons and Lords, the legislative process, and select committees. Our coverage is nonetheless not exhaustive, and other potential mechanisms of influence exist. These include parliamentary questions (where ministers must explain themselves publicly), Private Members' Bills (which rarely pass, but have at least some agenda-setting capacity), and nonlegislative debates (which can do the same, and also—as indicated below—sometimes force decisions). These mechanisms have been subjected to relatively less empirical study—in part because of assumptions of their powerlessness, and in part because of measurement problems—but may well have additional effects.

Our analysis has demonstrated that there are two primary weaknesses in the arguments of parliamentary detractors, which insights from the public policy and the legislative studies literature can respectively help to address. The first is that detractors tend to focus on the policy decision-making stage, to the exclusion of parliament's role at the earlier and later stages widely recognized in the public policy literature (e.g., John 2012). The second weakness is that detractors focus on visible and measurable influence, overlooking the behind-the-scenes negotiations and "anticipated reactions" that legislative studies scholars have long deemed important (e.g., Mezey 1979). Our research demonstrates that parliament is powerful at the decision-making stage, but that much of that power is exercised through anticipated reactions, in terms of ministers facilitating last-minute negotiations to avert rebellions and defeats. This anticipated reactions function is also important in shaping policy formulation. Meanwhile, executive accountability mechanisms—particularly the select committees—contribute throughout the other stages of the process, influencing government agenda setting, policy formulation, implementation, and evaluation. Select committees also provide a key site of influence for external pressure groups. That is, at the very point when Richardson and Jordan (1979) claimed policy networks had sidelined parliament, a reform took place that led to far greater interest group involvement with parliament.

In parliamentary systems such as that in Britain, less visible influence is always likely to be the norm. Indeed, examination of some visible reversals readily illustrates how these represent the system failing to work as it should. Governments take constant account of parliamentary opinion, and in normal circumstances, do not put proposals to parliament that it will not accept. Commons defeats are rare and generally a sign that party managers have misjudged the situation. A recent high-profile example was Prime Minister David Cameron's defeat over proposed military action in Syria, following a nonlegislative debate in August 2013. Parliament had been recalled from its summer recess, and so whips lacked their usual day-to-day contact with members. The defeat was unexpected and embarrassing to government. In contrast, most policy is made in a more planned manner, where procedures to consider likely parliamentary responses are well developed, and compromise is preferred.

Hence, if conflict within a parliament is limited, and defeats unusual, this does not necessarily indicate the institution's weakness—but instead potentially its strength…. The downside, however, is that this form of influence demonstrates few outward signs that citizens' elected representatives are doing an effective job.

Responding to the claims of a "post-parliamentary democracy" in Britain, Judge (1993, 125–126) observed that "if the core of policy-making is policy communities comprised of government departments and institutionalised interest groups, it is surrounded, encompassed and ultimately delimited by the legitimating frame of the parliamentary system itself." This is true, but understates the case. Parliaments are not just legitimating frames, providing democratic cover for governments to act as they wish; they must also approve government decisions, and—in parliamentary systems— the government's continued existence itself. Ministers' dependence on parliamentary confidence in Britain means that they take backbenchers' views into account on both policy direction and detail, and while the Lords does not enjoy the same kind of confidence relationship with the executive, it provides an uncertain multiparty environment where ministers will struggle if policy is not adequately explained. Importantly, defeats in the Lords force ministers to choose between risking explicitly presenting the Commons with controversial policies or abandoning them. This empowers nongovernment peers, as well as the government's own Commons supporters.

NOTE: See also Russell, Gover, and Wollter, 'Does the Executive Dominate the Westminster Legislative Process?: Six Reasons for Doubt' (2016) *Parliamentary Affairs* 286–308. The study considered in detail amendments to a sample of government bills. The resulting reasons for doubt about Executive domination offered by the authors are:

- Government success is overstated because: (i) most government amendments have little substance; and (ii) most substantive government amendments respond to parliamentary pressure.
- Non-government failure is overstated because: (i) there may be several non-government amendments on the same issue at multiple stages of the legislative process, which may only in combination produce an effect; and (ii) many non-government amendments do not aim to change the bill, as opposed to probing or highlighting a particular issue of difficulty.
- Parliament has influence at other policy stages: (i) Parliament influences legislation before the formal legislative process begins; and (ii) Parliament influences policy after the legislative process is complete.

The study concludes:

> This article has presented summary results from the largest study of the legislative process at Westminster for 40 years. The resulting evidence suggests that the British parliament is far less dominated by the executive than is often assumed, and that it exerts a significant influence on government policy….

A key reason for Westminster's reputation as weak is that it exhibits few visible signs of conflict with the executive: government defeats in the House of Commons are very rare, and few non-government amendments are passed in either chamber. In contrast, many hundreds of government amendments are agreed in both each year. This creates an impression not only of parliamentary weakness, but of executive dominance, with ministers freely changing their own legislation even after it has been introduced. But a more careful look at the amendment process shows that this is a misleading picture. The majority of government amendments have little substance, while most substantive changes made inside parliament in fact follow pressure from non-government parliamentarians. Meanwhile, many non-government amendments serve purposes other than seeking immediate policy change, such as 'probing', signalling to groups outside parliament, embarrassing the government or creating policy markers for the future...

Perhaps most importantly, however, parliament influences the shape of legislation long before it is introduced, and continues to influence policy implementation and future development once it has been formally passed.... In exploring more tangibly the power of parliament, it is clearly not sufficient to scour the official record or trace changes made within the institution. Because parliament's greatest power is one of 'anticipated reactions', detecting this requires discussion with insiders (particularly from the executive) about behind-the-scenes negotiations.

■ **QUESTIONS**

1. Does what Norton refers to as 'micro level' scrutiny by MPs include constituency work where the public can come to MPs' surgeries to complain about various matters? Is the redress of citizens' grievances against officialdom not a very important part of MPs' work? (See later in this chapter in Section 2D(a) at pp. 261–3.)

2. What exactly is meant by legitimization? Is legitimization real if Parliament approves the actions of the executive in the manner of a rubber stamp? Or is legitimacy to be obtained through engaging in a continuous process of accountability, regardless of the outcome of any particular vote?

3. In what ways—both formal and informal—does Parliament influence government policy? Is the absence of frequent, visible conflicts with the government, which the legislature can be seen to 'win', evidence of the strength or weakness of Parliament?

SECTION 2: POLICY AND ADMINISTRATION

A: Ministerial responsibility

The responsibility of ministers to Parliament is the foundation of representative, democratic, accountable government in the UK. There are two key (and related) elements to this constitutional convention: that ministers are responsible to Parliament collectively and individually.

C. Turpin, 'Ministerial Responsibility: Myth or Reality?' in J. Jowell and D. Oliver (eds), *The Changing Constitution*
(2nd edn, 1989), pp. 55–7

When it is said that ministers are collectively and individually responsible to Parliament, what is meant by 'responsible'? It may help us find the answer if we compare the idea of ministerial responsibility to Parliament with that of *control* by Parliament of the executive. Much contemporary discussion of the relations between Parliament and government is concerned with the reassertion of parliamentary control, and by this is generally meant a power to influence the decisions of government. Control, that is to say, is exercised a priori. On the other hand, when it is said that ministers are 'responsible' or 'answerable' or 'accountable'—terms not generally distinguished in meaning—to Parliament, reference is usually being made to the obligation of ministers to respond or answer or account for actions already performed (or left unperformed): responsibility is retrospective or a posteriori. There is, of course, an overlap between the parliamentary functions of 'controlling' and 'holding responsible' ('calling to account'). Some techniques, such as parliamentary questions and scrutiny by selected committees, are directed both to control and to the assertion of responsibility. An a posteriori investigation or check may have the aim of influencing future policy-making. The notion of 'responsible government' implies both acceptance of responsibility for things done and 'responsiveness' to influence, persuasion, and pressure for modifications of policy. Activist parliamentarians of our day aim to 'redress the balance' of the constitution in favour of Parliament by strengthening both control and responsibility of the executive, without making a fine discrimination between these concepts. This is not to say that equal progress is to be expected in establishing control and in extending responsibility. . . . A posteriori responsibility implies that certain obligations are owed by ministers to Parliament. What are these obligations?

It is demanded of ministers, in the first place, that they should *answer* or give account, discharging the essential 'obligation of Ministers, collectively and individually, to meet Parliament and provide information about their policies'. This includes a duty to provide financial accounts attesting to the regularity of government expenditure, as one element of a fuller 'explanatory accountability' which requires the giving of reasons and explanations for action taken, whether or not involving expenditure. That this is not a negligible aspect of responsibility was recognized by H. J. Laski: 'A Government that is compelled to explain itself under cross-examination will do its best to avoid the grounds of complaint. Nothing makes responsible government so sure.' The requirement to answer goes further: it imports an obligation to submit to scrutiny—to provide opportunities for Parliament to question, challenge, probe, and criticize. A duty to answer is something hollow if there are not apt procedures, respected by government, for such 'calling to account'.

The obligation to answer and submit to scrutiny is ancillary to what we may see as government's traditional obligation to redress grievances, which here means to take remedial action for revealed errors or defects of policy or administration, whether by compensating individuals, reversing or modifying policies or decisions, disciplining Civil Servants, or altering departmental procedures. This may be called 'amendatory accountability'; it presupposes an acknowledgement by ministers that they 'bear responsibility' to Parliament for what is shown to have gone wrong, whether or not they accept personal blame for the failure.

The obligations to answer, to submit to scrutiny, and to redress grievances may seem in practice to lack the support of any coercive rule or sanction. Undoubtedly these obligations are imperfect, resting as they do upon conventions, practices, and procedures which are liable to change and to be variously interpreted and applied, and which depend ultimately upon the political culture. But this is far from saying that the obligations in question lack substance, or that they can be flouted with impunity.

(a) Collective ministerial responsibility

Ministerial responsibility comprises both collective and individual responsibility. In his book on constitutional conventions, Marshall classifies the branches of collective ministerial responsibility as the confidence rule, the unanimity rule, and the confidentiality rule.

(i) *Confidence*

G. Marshall, *Constitutional Conventions*
(1984), pp. 55–6

It sometimes used to be said that a prime non-legal rule of the Constitution was that governments defeated by the House on central issues of policy were obliged to resign. But only one Prime Minister has resigned as the result of a defeat in the House in the twentieth century and that was immediately after being deprived of his majority by a General Election (Baldwin in January 1924). MacDonald was defeated on a confidence issue in 1924 and Callaghan in 1979, but neither resigned. Both fought the subsequent General Elections as leader of a government, having advised dissolution.

So the rule about a government that loses the confidence of the House seems to be that it must *either* resign *or* advise dissolution. Its right is only to advise, not to have, dissolution; since dissolution can, as we have seen, in some circumstances be refused. Resignation might therefore follow as the result of such a refusal (by the Queen), but that has not happened. As to what constitutes a loss of confidence there seems also to have been a development in doctrine. The books used to say that defeat on major legislative measures or policy proposals as well as on specifically worded confidence motions was fatal to the continuance of the government. But this no longer seems to be believed or acted on. In 1977 *The Times* propounded the view that 'there is no constitutional principle that requires a government to regard any specific policy defeat as evidence that it no longer possesses the necessary confidence of the House of Commons'. Some were greatly shocked by this doctrine and Professor Max Beloff wrote to *The Times* to say that it was inconsistent with the principles of the Constitution as hitherto understood. Sir Ivor Jennings, he pointed out, had said in *Cabinet Government* that the government must go if the House failed to approve its policy. What provoked the disagreement was that the Labour Government had just failed to carry a budget proposal about the rate of income tax and was proposing to remain in office in defiance of Sir Ivor Jennings's view of the established convention. Sir Ivor Jennings was of course dead, which is supposed to augment the authority of a textbook writer by allowing his views to be cited more freely in the course of litigation. Unfortunately there is a countervailing disadvantage in that his works may go out of print and are no longer constantly perused by Ministers, who are thereby enabled to fall into lax habits and disregard established constitutional conventions. In the 1960s and 1970s, in any event, governments seem to have been following a new rule, according to which only votes specifically stated by the Government to be matters of confidence, or votes of no confidence by the Opposition are allowed to count. Just conceivably one can imagine amongst recent Prime Ministers those who might have felt it their duty to soldier on in the general interest even in the face of such a vote.

NOTES

1. Government defeats on confidence motions are very rare, yet this does not diminish the importance of the rule: a government must retain the confidence of the House of Commons to be sustained in office. Defeats on major policy issues can be the trigger for a subsequent confidence vote, as with Prime Minister John Major's defeat on the Social Chapter of the Maastricht Treaty in 1993. Major's government won the confidence of the House, and remained in office until the 1997 general election.
2. See Chapter 5, Section 1B at pp. 180–3 for the effect of the Fixed-term Parliaments Act 2011 following the passing of a vote of no confidence.

(ii) Unanimity

House of Lords, HL Deb
Vol. 239, cols 833–4, 8 April 1878

THE MARQUESS OF SALISBURY: … My Lords, my noble Friend [the Earl of Derby] pointed out several measures of the Government to which in the public eye he was an assenting party. He did not, he said, in reality assent to all; one was a compromise, while to another, he was persuaded by some observations which fell from the Chancellor of the Exchequer, which appeared to be founded on a mistake. Now, my Lords, am I not defending a great Constitutional principle, when I say that, for all that passes in Cabinet, each member of it who does not resign is absolutely and irretrievably responsible, and that he has no right afterwards to say that he agreed in one case to a compromise, while in another he was persuaded by one of his Colleagues. Consider the inconvenience which will arise if such a great Constitutional law is not respected. … It is, I maintain, only on the principle that absolute responsibility is undertaken by every Member of a Cabinet who, after a decision is arrived at, remains a Member of it, that the joint responsibility of Ministers to Parliament can be upheld, and one of the most essential conditions of Parliamentary responsibility established.

In exceptional circumstances, the unanimity requirement may be set aside by the Prime Minister, as the following extract demonstrates.

House of Commons, HC Deb

Vol. 889, Written Answers, Mr H. Wilson, col. 351, 7 April 1975

THE PRIME MINISTER: In accordance with my statement in the House on 23rd January last, those Ministers who do not agree with the Government's recommendation in favour of continued membership of the European Community are, in the unique circumstances of the referendum, now free to advocate a different view during the referendum campaign in the country.

This freedom does not extend to parliamentary proceedings and official business. Government business in Parliament will continue to be handled by all Ministers in accordance with Government policy. Ministers responsible for European aspects of Government business who themselves differ from the Government's recommendation on membership of the European Community will state the Government's position and will not be drawn into making points against the Government recommendation. Wherever necessary Questions will be transferred to other Ministers. At meetings of the Council of Ministers of the European Community and at other Community meetings, the United Kingdom position in all fields will continue to reflect Government policy.

I have asked all Ministers to make their contributions to the public campaign in terms of issues, to avoid personalising or trivialising the argument, and not to allow themselves to appear in direct confrontation, on the same platform or programme, with another Minister who takes a different view on the Government recommendation.

NOTES

1. This breach or suspension of unanimity or Cabinet solidarity was criticized as being simply a device to keep the Labour Party together. The United Kingdom's membership of the European Communities has caused problems for the Labour Party. In 1977 the point at issue was the use of proportional representation as the method of voting in the direct elections to the European Parliament. As unanimity in Cabinet could not be achieved, collective responsibility was, once again, suspended. The then Prime Minister, Mr Callaghan, answering a question in the House of Commons about collective responsibility, said: 'I think the doctrine should apply except in cases where I announce that it does not.' (HC Deb, Vol. 993, col. 552, 16 June 1977.)

2. The occasions on which it has been formally announced that unanimity in a government would be suspended have been few. Ministers have resigned because they could not agree with their colleagues on governmental policy. Mr Ian Gow resigned as Junior Minister in the Treasury because he did not agree with the Anglo-Irish Agreement 1985. Mr Michael Heseltine resigned as Secretary of State for Defence in the Westland Affair because he could not accept the requirement that all Ministers should clear speeches about Westland with the Cabinet Office.

   The Coalition Agreement provided for situations in which the partners in the government which held office 2010–15 could differ, as with the commitment to legislate for a referendum on the Alternative Vote system for election to the House of Commons, but this was 'without prejudice to the positions the parties will take during the referendum'. This led to the Ministerial Code (2010) stipulating that '[T]he principle of collective responsibility, save where it is explicitly set aside, applies to all Government Ministers' and so the Coalition partners could be on opposing sides in the referendum campaign with the Liberal Democrats supporting and the Conservatives (successfully) opposing the change of voting system.

   Following the return of a Conservative majority government in 2015, the Ministerial Code was amended to remove the explicit recognition that the principle of collective responsibility could be set aside. Nevertheless, the Prime Minister David Cameron did allow Cabinet Ministers to differ on the question of EU membership in the referendum campaign in 2016. Five Cabinet Ministers campaigned to leave the EU while remaining in government (Chris Grayling, Michael Gove, Theresa Villiers, John Whittingdale, and Priti Patel). A further Minister, Iain Duncan Smith, also campaigned to leave, but after resigning as Work and Pensions Secretary in March 2016, citing disagreement with government policies on austerity and cuts to disability benefits, which he had been instrumental in delivering to that point.

■ **QUESTION**

What purpose does Cabinet solidarity serve, and whom does it (and its suspension) benefit?

(iii) Confidentiality

The confidentiality of Cabinet proceedings is, of course, related to unanimity in that body. Disclosures of what happened in Cabinet do occur. Ministers may 'leak', i.e. brief journalists, on the basis that they do not name their source, or they may publish their memoirs. The publication of the Crossman Diaries has changed the practice, if not the convention, of confidentiality. (See *Attorney-General* v *Jonathan Cape Ltd* [1976] QB 752 and Lord Widgery CJ's judgment in Chapter 5, Section 2D at pp. 202–5.)

Subsequently the Report of the Radcliffe Committee of Privy Councillors on Ministerial Memoirs (Cmnd 6386) was published. According to its guidelines, Ministers should not disclose what happened in Cabinet until 15 years have passed where the material concerns national security; or where foreign relations would be adversely affected; or where it would reveal relationships between Ministers and (a) officials, or (b) Ministers' outside advisers. The Ministerial Code (2016) continues to require Ministers to conform to these requirements (para 8.10).

(b) Individual ministerial responsibility

Ministers are individually responsible for their personal conduct, decisions taken in their department, and the acts of civil servants within it. The Ministerial Code (2016) requires:

> 1.1 Ministers of the Crown are expected to behave in a way that upholds the highest standards of propriety.
>
> 1.2 The Ministerial Code should be read against the background of the overarching duty on Ministers to comply with the law and to protect the integrity of public life. They are expected to observe the Seven Principles of Public Life [Selflessness, Integrity, Objectivity, Accountability, Openness, Honesty, and Leadership], and the following principles of Ministerial conduct: …
>
>   b. Ministers have a duty to Parliament to account, and be held to account, for the policies, decisions and actions of their departments and agencies; …
>   f. Ministers must ensure that no conflict arises, or appears to arise, between their public duties and their private interests;

These general principles are context-dependent, and may be applied in different ways in different circumstances. There can be uncertainty as to what should prompt the resignation of an individual Minister. In 1982 Lord Carrington, the Secretary of State, and two of his junior ministers, resigned from the Foreign and Commonwealth Office after Argentinean troops had invaded the Falkland Islands. Lord Carrington wrote in his letter of resignation:

> The Argentine invasion of the Falkland Islands has led to strong criticism in Parliament and in the press on the Government's policy. In my view, much of the criticism is unfounded. But I have been responsible for the conduct of that policy and I think it right that I should resign … [T]he invasion of the Falkland Islands has been a humiliating affront to this country.

This is an example of a classic case of a Minister accepting that the faults in a Department were his responsibility and then resigning. As such it is unusual.

In the following year there was a mass breakout from the Maze Prison in County Down, Northern Ireland. There was an inquiry into the circumstances of the escape by Her Majesty's Chief Inspector of Prisons (HC 203 of 1983–84), which found that the prison governor must be held accountable for a major failure in the prison's security arrangements. This report, the Hennessy Report, was debated in the House of Commons.

House of Commons, HC Deb

Vol. 53, cols 1042, 1060–1, 9 February 1984

THE SECRETARY OF STATE FOR NORTHERN IRELAND (MR J. PRIOR): There are those who, while they accept this policy, have nevertheless suggested that the circumstances of the escape demand ministerial resignation. I take that view seriously and have given it the most careful consideration. I share hon. Members' concern about the honour of public life and the maintenance of the highest standards. I said at the time of my statement to the House on 24 October, without any pre-knowledge of what Hennessy would find:

> It would be a matter for resignation if the report of the Hennessy inquiry showed that what happened was the result of some act of policy that was my responsibility, or that I failed to implement something that I had been asked to implement, or should have implemented. In that case, I should resign.—[*Official Report*, 24 October 1983, Vol. 47, c. 23–24.]

In putting the emphasis that I did on the issue of 'policy', I was not seeking to map out some new doctrine of ministerial responsibility. I was responding to the accusations made at the time that it was policy decisions, reached at the end of the hunger strike, that made the escape possible.

Since the report was published, the nature of the charges levelled at my hon. Friend and myself has changed. It is now argued in some quarters that Ministers are responsible for everything that happens in their Departments and should resign if anything goes wrong. My position has not changed, and I want to make it quite clear that if there were any evidence in the Hennessy report that Ministers were to blame for the escape, I would not hesitate to accept that blame and act accordingly, and so I know, would my hon. Friend. However, I do not accept—and I do not think it right for the House to accept—that there is any constitutional or other principle that requires ministerial resignations in the face of failure, either by others to carry out orders or procedures or by their supervisors to ensure that staff carried out those orders. Let the House be clear: the Hennessy report finds that the escape would not have succeeded if orders and procedures had been properly carried out that Sunday afternoon.

Of course, I have looked carefully at the precedents. There are those who quote the Crichel Down case. I do not believe that it is a precedent or that it establishes a firm convention. It is the only case of its sort in the past 50 years, and constitutional lawyers have concluded that the resignation was not required by convention and was exceptional.

Whatever some may wish, there is no clear rule and no established convention. Rightly, it is a matter of judgment in the light of individual circumstances….

MR J. ENOCH POWELL (Down, South): The Secretary of State, from the beginning of his speech, recognised the central issue in this debate, that of ministerial responsibility, without which the House scarcely has a real function or any real service that it can perform for the people whom it represents. We are concerned with the nature of the responsibility, the ministerial responsibility, for an event which, even in isolation from its actual context, was a major disaster….

As the Secretary of State reminded us this afternoon, even before the publication of the report he drew a distinction, which I believe to be invalid, between responsibility for policy and responsibility for administration. I believe that this is a wholly fallacious view of the nature of ministerial responsibility. I shall argue presently that there is a policy element in the event that we are considering and that it cannot be understood fully except in its policy framework. But even if all considerations of policy could be eliminated, the responsibility for the administration of a Department remains irrevocably with the Minister in charge. It is impossible for him to say to the House or to the country, 'The policy was excellent and that was mine, but the execution was defective or disastrous and that has nothing to do with me.' If that were to be the accepted position, there would be no political source to which the public could complain about administration or from which it could seek redress for failings of administration.

What happened was an immense administrative disaster. It was not a disaster in a peripheral area of the responsibilities of the Northern Ireland Department. It was a disaster that occurred in an area which was quite clearly central to the Department's responsibilities. If the responsibility for administration so central to a Department can be abjured by a Minister, a great deal of our proceedings in the House is a beating of the air because we are talking to people who, in the last resort, disclaim the responsibility for the administration.

NOTE: Mr Powell's view is not one, it would appear, which is shared by Ministers. The classic statement about the circumstances in which a Minister will be responsible for the action of his officials was given in 1954 by Sir David Maxwell-Fyfe, who was Home Secretary at the time. He made his statement on the occasion of the debate of the report into the Crichel Down affair. Some land had been compulsorily acquired by the Air Ministry. It was later transferred to the Ministry of Agriculture, which then leased the land to a tenant in breach of promises made about the way in which such a disposal of the land would be carried out. The Minister for Agriculture, Sir Thomas Dugdale, resigned.

House of Commons, HC Deb
Vol. 530, cols 1285–8, 10 July 1954

THE SECRETARY OF STATE FOR THE HOME DEPARTMENT (SIR DAVID MAXWELL-FYFE): … There has been criticism that the principle [of Ministerial responsibility] operates so as to oblige Ministers to extend total protection to their officials and to endorse their acts, and to cause the position that civil servants cannot be called to account and are effectively responsible to no one. That is a position which I believe is quite wrong…. It is quite untrue that well-justified public criticism of the actions of civil servants cannot be made on a suitable occasion. The position of the civil servant is that he is wholly and directly responsible to his Minister. It is worth stating again that he holds his office 'at pleasure' and can be dismissed at any time by the Minister; and that power is none the less real because it is seldom used. The only exception relates to a small number of senior posts, like permanent secretary, deputy secretary, and principal financial officer, where, since 1920, it has been necessary for the Minister to consult the Prime Minister, as he does on appointment,

I would like to put the different categories where different considerations apply … [I]n the case where there is an explicit order by a Minister, the Minister must protect the civil servant who has carried out his order. Equally, where the civil servant acts properly in accordance with the policy laid down by the Minister, the Minister must protect and defend him.

I come to the third category, which is different…. Where an official makes a mistake or causes some delay, but not on an important issue of policy and not where a claim to individual rights is seriously involved, the Minister acknowledges the mistake and he accepts the responsibility, although he is not personally involved. He states that he will take corrective action in the Department. I agree with the right hon. Gentleman that he would not, in those circumstances, expose the official to public criticism….

But when one comes to the fourth category, where action has been taken by a civil servant of which the Minister disapproves and has no prior knowledge, and the conduct of the official is reprehensible, then there is no obligation on the part of the Minister to endorse what he believes to be wrong, or to defend what are clearly shown to be errors of his officers. The Minister is not bound to defend action of which he did not know, or of which he disapproves. But, of course, he remains constitutionally responsible to Parliament for the fact that something has gone wrong, and he alone can tell Parliament what has occurred and render an account of his stewardship. The fact that a Minister has to do that does not affect his power to control and discipline his staff. One could sum it up by saying that it is part of a Minister's responsibility to Parliament to take necessary action to ensure efficiency and the proper discharge of the duties of his Department. On that, only the Minister can decide what it is right and just to do, and he alone can hear all sides, including the defence.

NOTES
1. It has been held by some that Sir Thomas's resignation was one in which he accepted responsibility for the wrongdoing of his officials. However, the current view seems to be that the resignation occurred because Sir Thomas had lost the support of his ministerial and party colleagues.

See, for example, I. F. Nicolson, *The Mystery of Crichel Down* (1986), and J. A. G. Griffith, 'Crichel Down: The Most Famous Farm in British Constitutional History' (1987) 1 *Contemporary Record* 35. Perhaps this explains James Prior's view—expressed when defending his decision not to resign as a result of the Maze Prison breakouts—that Crichel Down did not set a precedent for resignation.

2. If Sir Thomas Dugdale did resign as a result of broader political factors, this would conform with the classic analysis of Finer, that resignations only result 'if the minister is yielding, his Prime Minister unbending, and his party is out for blood' ('The Individual Responsibility of Ministers' (1956) *Public Administration* 377–96, p. 383). In addition to recognizing the importance of the political judgements made by the Minister, Prime Minister, and party, the modern (perhaps constitutional) role of the media in generating or amplifying political pressure must also be acknowledged. As Woodhouse notes, 'Most cases of resignation in the last 50 years owe something to the media', and 'a sustained campaign by the media against a minister may be sufficient to bring him or her down' (Woodhouse, 'UK Ministerial Responsibility in 2002' (2004) *Public Administration* 1–19, p. 16). Ultimately, as the Ministerial Code (2016) notes (para.1.5):

> … Ministers only remain in office for so long as they retain the confidence of the Prime Minister. She is the ultimate judge of the standards of behaviour expected of a Minister and the appropriate consequences of a breach of those standards.

Nevertheless, the Prime Minister may also be vulnerable to accepting ultimate responsibility for government failures: after the defeat of the Government-led 'Remain' campaign in the 2016 EU Referendum, the then Prime Minister David Cameron resigned from office, indicating that 'the country requires fresh leadership to take it in this direction'.

3. The uncertainty as to what conduct exactly will necessitate a ministerial resignation has not abated in the contemporary constitution. Some Ministers may make a virtue out of their continuation in office. Alastair Darling was Chancellor of Exchequer when, in 2007, two CDs containing the sensitive personal information of millions of child benefit claimants were lost in the post, due a mistake made by a civil servant employed by HM Revenue and Customs, for which Darling was constitutionally responsible. The senior civil servant in charge of HMRC resigned, but Darling did not, and argued in the House of Commons that he was taking steps to rectify mistakes.

House of Commons, HC Deb
Vol. 467, cols 1107–8, 20 November 2007

DR CABLE: … Finally, I want to raise the issue of the principles governing resignation from Government when administrative disasters occur. One senior official, Paul Gray [the then Chairman of HMRC], has now resigned as a matter of honour; another, the Metropolitan Police Commissioner, declined to do so. Home Office Ministers have resigned on matters of honour; Treasury Ministers decline to do so. Where does the buck stop in this Government?

MR DARLING: The hon. Gentleman asks a number of questions and I agree with him that this information should not have been downloaded in the way that it was; it certainly should not have been sent in the way that it was, without any readily available means of identifying where it was. It was password-protected, but that was inadequate. However, the hon. Gentleman needs to bear it in mind that the key problem is that HMRC has clear instructions, rules and procedures on requesting, downloading and transmitting information, and that the individuals concerned ignored those instructions. That is the difficulty, and that is what we need to make sure does not happen again.

HMRC is operationally responsible for the collection and making of payments. It is, quite properly, independent of Government, because it is involved in dealing with personal data. That is why it is a responsibility, which this House recently agreed to, of a board of commissioners and the chairman. They are accountable to Parliament through me, which is why I am making this statement today, but there is no doubt in my mind that what we have here is an extremely serious breach. It should never have happened, and the problem is that individuals within HMRC ignored the procedures that were there. That should not have happened and that is what we need to put right.

The precise provisions of the Ministerial Code may have considerable importance when attempting to determine whether a Minister should resign. In 2011, it was revealed that the Defence Secretary Liam Fox had been accompanied by a personal friend, Adam Werritty, when engaged in official business in the UK and abroad. In meetings with the representatives of foreign governments, Werritty, who was a private 'adviser' to Fox, was presented as a Government official. Werritty's attendance on these trips was funded by influential Conservative Party donors and lobbyists. Fox initially refused to resign, but the Cabinet Secretary, Gus O'Donnell, was asked to conduct an investigation. O'Donnell's report is interesting in that it paid close attention to the provisions of the Ministerial Code, in identifying whether Fox's conduct had been deficient.

Allegations against Rt Hon Dr Liam Fox MP, Report by the Cabinet Secretary
October 2011

21. Dr Fox has already accepted that his actions and judgement fell short of the standards of conduct required in the Ministerial Code and the evidence in this report supports the conclusion of a clear breach of the Ministerial Code. He should have declared to his Permanent Secretary that Mr Werritty was a friend who had a company, Pargav, which was funded by a number of donors, some of whom had provided funding to Dr Fox when in Opposition.

22. The Ministerial Code requires Ministers to ensure that no conflict arises, or could reasonably be perceived to arise, between their public duties and their private interests, financial or otherwise. Dr Fox's actions clearly constitute a breach of the Ministerial Code which Dr Fox has already acknowledged. This was a failure of judgement on his part for which he has taken the ultimate responsibility in resigning office. Your foreword to the Ministerial Code makes clear that you expect Ministers to act in the national interest, above improper influence, and to serve to the highest standards of conduct. The Ministerial Code sets out very clearly the standards of behaviour required from Ministers. Dr Fox did not live up to these standards which he has since acknowledged.

23. Dr Fox's close and visible association with Mr Werritty in the UK and overseas, and the latter's use of misleading business cards, has fuelled a general impression that Mr Werritty spoke on behalf of the UK Government. The risks of Dr Fox's association with Mr Werritty were raised with Dr Fox by both his private office and the Permanent Secretary. Dr Fox took action in respect of business cards but clearly made a judgement that his contact with Mr Werritty should continue. This may have been a reasonable judgement had the contacts been minimal and purely personal and had not involved Mr Werritty's frequent attendance at meetings in the MoD main building and on overseas visits. The damage arose because the frequency, range and extent of these contacts were not regulated as well as they should have been and this was exacerbated by the fact that Dr Fox did not make his department aware of all the various contacts. I also conclude that the links and a lack of clarity of roles means that the donations given to Mr Werritty could be seen as giving rise to the perception of a conflict of interest.

24. In this case there was an inappropriate blurring of lines between official and personal relationships. Mr Werritty should not have been provided with access to Dr Fox's diary and itinerary. Nor should he have been allowed to participate in the social elements of the then Defence Secretary's overseas trips in a way which might have given rise to the impression that he was part of the official party. He should not have had meetings in the MOD with such frequency as did occur, as this access may have provided others with a belief that Mr Werritty was speaking for Government and was part of an official entourage. This impression was of course reinforced by the business cards which Mr Werritty provided to people. However, I have found no evidence that Dr Fox gained financially in any way from this relationship.

Fox resigned prior to publication of O'Donnell's report, but returned to Government in 2016, under new Prime Minister Theresa May, as Secretary of State for International Trade.

(c) Ministerial responsibility and accountability

Ministerial responsibility and accountability were considered by the Public Administration Select Committee in an inquiry which had initially focused upon fears that the civil service was becoming politicized, through political involvement in appointment and promotion of civil servants, but was subsequently widened out to explore aspects of the governing relationship between ministers and officials. Between the beginning of the inquiry and the report there were a series of political and administrative failures, and arguments about where responsibility lay. The Department for the Environment, Food and Rural Affairs failed to implement the new system of farm payments; the Home Office failed to keep track of foreign prisoners who should have been considered for deportation; and the National Health Service failed to make its budget balance. The committee quoted from a speech by William Waldegrave in the Government's response to the Public Service Select Committee's report on *Ministerial Responsibility and Accountability* in HC of 1996–07, Appendix, para. 4:

There is a clear democratic line of accountability which runs from the electorate through MPs to the Government which commands the confidence of a majority of those MPs in Parliament. The duly constituted government—whatever its political complexion—is assisted by the Civil Service which is permanent and politically impartial. Hence, Ministers are accountable to Parliament; civil servants are accountable to Ministers. That is the system we have in this country.

Third Report from the Public Administration Select Committee,
Politics and Administration: Ministers and Civil Servants
HC 122 of 2006–07, paras 21–4, 58–9, 62, 66, 68

The Accountability Gap

21. The tradition of civil service impartiality in the United Kingdom runs so strong that the rationale for such impartiality is rarely questioned. It can seem an end in itself rather than a means to good governance. Yet the Northcote Trevelyan report that ended patronage and opened up appointment on merit to the civil service was clear that a system in which posts were obtained by patronage would deter "able young men" from the civil service as a career. In other words, the argument for an impartial civil service was one of operational effectiveness.

22. Recent events have suggested that permanence, independence and impartiality do not necessarily secure an operationally effective civil service. In fact, it is possible to go further. Some have suggested that the current arrangements actively militate against effectiveness by blurring the division of ministerial and civil service accountability. It has been held that they create a system in which politicians and civil servants can hide behind each other, so that no one is really held to account. Ministers are politically accountable to Parliament, but although civil servants are theoretically accountable to ministers, the doctrine of independence makes it difficult for this accountability to be exercised effectively, and may prevent a minister from dismissing or disciplining individual civil servants.

23. There is no consensus about the respective responsibilities of ministers and civil servants. Indeed, Janet Paraskeva, the First Civil Service Commissioner told us "I believe that the doctrine of ministerial responsibility needs to be reviewed…. We no longer understand what it means … ". It has been possible to reconcile a doctrine of ministerial accountability which holds that ministers are ultimately accountable for everything done on their behalf (whether by civil servants or other public employees) with the doctrine of civil service independence for over a century. Why has it now become more problematic?

There are many reasons for this, but it is likely that the new attention to transparency, accountability and performance has played a major part. Indeed, the development of scrutiny by Parliamentary Committees has exposed the difficulties of assigning responsibilities. Senior civil servants have been made more visible by their regular appearances before Committees, supposedly on ministers' behalf. At the same time, Permanent Secretaries continue to appear before the Public Accounts Committee in their role as Accounting Officers, where they are individually responsible.

24. If ideas about ministerial and civil service responsibilities are varied and inconsistent, it is no wonder that the public service bargain is no longer as straightforward as once it seemed. We try here to tease out some of the theory and reality of civil service and ministerial responsibility. This is a complex area, where different kinds of responsibility and accountability are closely interrelated, and where assumptions about the proper roles of ministers and civil servants are contested. We look at:

- the doctrine of ministerial accountability to Parliament;
- the extent to which civil servants are responsible to ministers and to what extent they have wider responsibilities;
- the effect of civil service independence on ministers' ability to run their departments;
- where authority and accountability should lie;
- the extent to which clear division between political and administrative responsibilities is possible; and
- the benefits of impartiality and the extent to which they are effectively secured.

This brief survey will give some idea of the muddle that is reality. We then consider whether there are ways in which the muddle could at least be tidied up.

A new Public Service Bargain

58. There are good reasons for having an independent and impartial civil service. Sir Robin Mountfield set these out succinctly:

It is a defence against corruption: 'jobs for the boys' or the 'spoils system' invite abuse.

It provides continuity, especially after a change of government.

It maintains deep expertise and 'institutional memory' of the background to policy issues.

It provides real knowledge of how the machinery of government works, making it possible for a government to achieve the results it wants.

It provides a loyal and supportive, but detached and politically-neutral, analytical challenge to political enthusiasm: an essential health-check in a democratic process.

It entrenches a deeply-rooted and distinctive ethical base to the public service.

We agree with this analysis. However, we heard evidence that these claimed benefits might not always be achieved in practice.

59. For example, some former ministers told us that, although individuals might be excellent, the service as a whole was not good at retaining collective memory. This is made worse where there is a rapid turnover of ministers themselves. The administrative structures deliberately encouraged circulation of staff, but this could be at the expense of experience and expertise. In other words, one of the key advantages of a permanent and impartial civil service was not in fact secured....

62. A high degree of independence has not prevented accusations that the civil service has neglected its traditional skills, and failed in its duty to ensure that ministers are properly briefed. The Butler and Hutton Reports have been cited as revealing the way in which good government is undermined by inadequate procedures. The ability to speak truth unto power seems to have been lacking, together with a willingness or ability to hold a constitutional line. Clearly, there can be pressures which prevent the full advantages of independence from being secured. There is no easy answer to the division of

responsibility between ministers and officials, but the relationship between ministers and their senior civil servants, particularly their Permanent Secretaries, is crucial to effective government. That relationship will necessarily be complex. It will depend on political context, personal styles, and different approaches to the job. Sir Gus O'Donnell told us that even principles of accountability were worked out in different ways with different ministers and civil servants. Some ministers will want (as Baroness Shephard told us she had wanted) to be more administratively active than others. Above all, it will depend on the current understanding of what has been described as the "public service bargain"….

66. Under its provisions, civil servants would expect to have their access to ministers safeguarded and their right to give advice, however unpalatable, protected. Their role in procedural and propriety matters should be made explicit. Just as Accounting Officers have a right to give clear advice about expenditure, and to be absolved from responsibility if it is overridden, so Permanent Secretaries should have a right to advise on procedure and propriety. Civil servants have a right to expect clear and consistent political leadership and that programmes will be matched by resources, and a right not to be made public scapegoats when things go wrong for which they are not responsible. For their part, ministers should expect professional and committed service to their governing objectives, along with good advice. They have a right to expect that poor performance will be dealt with effectively, that there is a robust system of performance management, and that civil servants will have the skills and experience to enable them to support ministers efficiently. It should be accepted that ministers may have a role in organising departments if they wish….

68. A clearer understanding of the public service bargain should be accompanied by an increased willingness to give a full account of operational errors to Parliament, and an acceptance that civil servants do have some direct accountability to Parliament. That will only be possible if Committees accept that a blame culture will not lead to good administration. There will be circumstances in which individual responsibility cannot be overlooked, and ministers need to be held to account, but investigations of policy should not routinely become a political blame game. If that happens we will have swapped a culture in which ministers and civil servants can hide behind each other for one in which they push the other into the firing line.

NOTES

1. The Public Administration Committee at para. 68 seem to have taken a view similar to that of D. Woodhouse in 'The Reconstruction of Constitutional Accountability' [2002] *Public Law* 72, which suggested that attention should be moved away from 'causal' responsibility, with its focus upon direct ministerial involvement, towards 'role' responsibility which concentrates upon the requirements of the job of a Minister, including supervision of a department, explaining actions carried out in its name, and correcting any deficiencies. This would avoid the confusion introduced by managerial accountability with its 'responsibility/accountability' and 'policy/operations' distinctions. Woodhouse suggests that the actions of some Ministers seem to be based upon this 'role' conception: the setting up of an inquiry and the implementation of the reforms proposed in 1998 following allegations that Foreign Office officials had sanctioned the supply of military equipment to Sierra, and the Home Secretary apologizing for the backlog in processing and issuing passports by the executive agency, the Passport Office, in 1999.

2. The concern about identifying responsibility and accountability when things go wrong was addressed in the Environment, Food and Rural Affairs select committee report on the Rural Payments Agency and the implementation of the single payment scheme. In its thorough report (HC 107 of 2006–07) the committee highlighted problems and suggested improvements, and expressed the view that it was odd that only the Chief Executive of the agency was removed from his post. The committee pointed out that another official was specified in the governance arrangements as sharing responsibility and suggested that in a company the chairman and senior executives would face dismissal over such an operational failure, so that it was surprised that the Permanent Secretary was still in place and it noted the Secretary of State had been promoted. The committee was very unimpressed with the delay in the Government's response to its report, and called its content 'shoddy'. On accountability, the Government response regretted

that the committee had criticized named officials, as select committees in the Government's view are not concerned with discipline inside departments, and stated on the publication of the report that the Prime Minister and Head of the Civil Service had expressed their confidence in the Permanent Secretary, and that the guidance on ministerial responsibilities in the Ministerial Code did not require any supplement (HC 956 of 2006–07).

3. The Coalition Government produced *The Civil Service Reform Plan* (2012) which included proposals dealing with accountability and the relationship between ministers and officials. The House of Commons Public Administration Select Committee criticized the plan for failing to take a strategic approach, calling for a Parliamentary Commission from both Houses to undertake a strategic review of the nature, role, and purpose of the Civil Service, which would consider relationships not only with Ministers but also with Parliament, the public, local government, and the wider public sector, as well as the relationship between the centre of government and departments, and the impact of devolution. While supporting the importance of a politically impartial civil service, it thought that the Haldane model of Ministers being accountable for everything in their department should be reviewed. The committee concluded that (HC 74 of 2013–14, at pp. 57–8):

> ... Much has changed since the Haldane model of ministerial accountability became established nearly a century ago, not least the size, role and complexity of departments for which ministers are accountable. In recent decades, citizens as consumers have hugely increased their demands and expectations of what Government should be able to deliver. Technology has transformed the way business operates, which has adopted new structures and management practices which would seem unrecognisable to previous generations. Modern business structures have far fewer tiers of management, and delegate far more to empowered, autonomous managers who are accountable for standards and performance, but this has hardly happened at all in the Civil Service, despite the fact that many believe in these principles. At the same time, the demands of 24-7 media, Parliamentary select committees, the Freedom of Information Act, and the demand for open data, openness and transparency now subject the system and the people and their relationships within it to unparalleled scrutiny and exposure. Furthermore, society has changed; we no longer live in an age of deference which tended to respect established institutions and cultures, but in a new 'age of reference', in which anyone can obtain almost unlimited information about almost everything, empowering individuals to challenge people with power and their motives.
>
> Ministers say they want to strengthen ministerial accountability, but a comprehensive reassessment of how the Haldane doctrine can operate in today's world is long overdue. Much of the rhetoric of the present administration was about embracing change of this nature—the word 'change' was the watchword of the Prime Minister's approach to his new Government—but this has exposed an increasing dysfunctionality in aspects of the Civil Service key skills: procurement, IT, strategic thinking, and implementation. Ministers tend to blame failures in defence procurement or the Borders Agency on civil servants or previous governments and we believe that Civil Servants may attribute such failures to inexperienced ministers with party political agendas. Either way, few ministers or officials seem to be held accountable when things go wrong. More importantly, there is a risk that an atmosphere of blame overshadows acknowledgement of excellent work. The need to address this may not invalidate the traditional doctrine of ministerial responsibility, but it needs to be redefined and adapted in order to serve good process and effective government in the modern context.

4. The House of Lords Committee on the Constitution, in its report on the accountability of civil servants, reaffirmed ministerial responsibility for the civil service (HL 61 of 2012–13, para. 12):

> We conclude that the convention that ministers are constitutionally responsible for all aspects of their departments' business is an essential principle underlying the arrangements that enable Parliament properly to perform its function of holding the Government to account. The convention is clear, straightforward and leaves no gaps.

The Committee also think that 'there is no constitutional difference between the terms responsibility and accountability' (para. 17).

In relation to appointment and disciplining of civil servants, it thought ministers might be able to play a greater role in appointing Permanent Secretaries and temporary senior civil servants but that the constitutional principles now enshrined in the Constitutional Reform and Governance Act 2010 of integrity, honesty, objectivity, and impartiality, must be respected (paras 20–35). The Committee thought it 'entirely inappropriate' for ministers to make disciplinary decisions about officials in their departments, but that they could contribute to the appraisal process for officials whose work they see and who manage projects for which ministers are accountable (paras 36–9).

5. The Conservative Government elected in 2015 published *The Civil Service Workforce 2016–2020*, aimed at accelerating the pace of change, and responding further to the challenges and opportunities posed for administration by new technologies. In November 2016, the (reconfigured) Public Administration and Constitutional Affairs Committee of the House of Commons launched an inquiry into the work of the civil service, which considers key issues especially in the light of the impact of the decision taken to leave the EU. As the inquiry's terms of reference indicated:

> This has significant implications for Whitehall, which now faces new challenges and a host of new tasks, including:
>
> * Handling negotiations of the withdrawal agreement with the EU
> * Examining the legislative implications of leaving
> * Formulating the UK's new trade policy
> * Taking back responsibility for policy and regulation in a wide range of areas including agriculture and financial services
> * Considering how the return of powers and functions from the EU will affect the devolution settlement in the UK and relations between the governments and parliaments of the UK
> * Establishing post-EU membership relations with the EU and each of the member states.
>
> These challenges make it all the more important that the Civil Service is clear about its mission and role, and that it understands the principles upon which it is based and the institutional framework within which it operates. They also mean that it is essential that issues affecting Civil Service effectiveness and capabilities are addressed.

■ QUESTIONS

1. Would it be possible to draft clearly the respective duties of Ministers and Chief Executives, thus ending the current ambiguity about policy and operations which seems to enable Ministers to choose what is, and is not, policy and therefore those things for which they can be held responsible?

2. How different is Woodhouse's 'role' responsibility from Enoch Powell's conception of ministerial responsibility? See the House of Commons, HC Deb earlier in this chapter in Section 2A(b) at pp. 226–7.

3. The accountability of government to Parliament is of clear importance, and very prominent, from the perspective of constitutional principle. But are other forms of accountability just as significant to the effective operation of administration in the state? See the extracts which follow.

Public Service Committee, *Ministerial Accountability and Responsibility*
HC 313 of 1995–96, paras 170–2, 174

IX. DIFFERENT SORTS OF ACCOUNTABILITY

170. In this Report, we have been mainly concerned with Parliamentary accountability. But we are well aware that government are not accountable only through Parliament. Mr David Faulkner of St John's College, Oxford, put this point in his evidence to us:

> Accountability can also take different forms—political, financial, managerial, operational, legal, professional. It can be to different authorities, institutions or individuals—Parliament, Ministers, managers, the courts, auditors, inspectors, regulators, users, customers or the general public.... Accountability can operate through direct supervision or contact, through formal arrangements for reporting or consultation (in public or in private), through procedures (such as complaints) which can be activated when required, and in various other ways ... accountability—or responsibility— should lie, not just to central government and Parliament, but also to the organisations with which they work and on which they may depend; to local communities; to users; and to the wider public. Accountability should take multiple forms and operate through multiple, and often reciprocal, channels.

171. In recent years, three institutions or developments have tended to increase the extent to which the public is able to ensure that public services are properly accountable. The growth of judicial review is one of them. The Treasury and Civil Service Committee noted in 1994, the accountability of the executive through the Courts has been enhanced in recent years by the growth of judicial review. That Committee also noted the Government's observation that 'existence of judicial review has clearly and substantially increased the work of both lawyers and administrators, in effect to "judicial review-proof" departmental decisions, but it has also improved the quality of decision-making by making it more structured and consistent'. Judicial review was 'a contribution to upholding the values of fairness, reasonableness and objectivity in the conduct of public business'. in addition to judicial review, statutory right of appeal against many types of administrative decision—such as on asylum applications, or planning applications—is now provided. Many of these are on essentially the same grounds as might be claimed in an application for judicial review.

172. Another is the role of the Parliamentary Commissioner for Administration (the Ombudsman) in investigating complaints from persons or organisations who contend that there is prima facie evidence of maladministration, by a body within his jurisdiction (generally speaking, government departments and bodies), which has led to hardship or injustice ....

174. Recent changes in the management of the public service have had an impact, in many ways, on the extent to which it is effectively publicly accountable. Delegation and privatisation are reducing the extent to which effective political accountability can be provided through Parliament. Accountability might be provided by some other mechanism, by Charters, through the Ombudsman, through the courts, even; and we welcome that. Accountability, however, should be a broad obligation, to many different bodies. Accountability to Parliament should not preclude accountability to the public; and *vice versa*. Parliament needs to retain and protect its role; and to do so, it has to be more effective in fulfilling it. A number of our recommendations involve changes to (or implications for) the House's practices and procedures. We hope that these will be further considered by the appropriate Committees of the House, particularly the Procedure Committee and the Liaison Committee. We have considered, in this Report, mainly what government does to comply with its obligation of accountability to Parliament; we hope that others will carry this forward by considering what Parliament can do to enforce it.

■ QUESTION

Would the imposition of legal liability upon Chief Executives improve their accountability?

C. Scott, 'Accountability in the Regulatory State'

(2000) 27 *Journal of Law and Society* 38, 41–3, 50–4, 57–60

It is helpful to keep distinct the three sets of accountability questions: 'who is accountable?'; 'to whom?'; and 'for what?' With the 'who is accountable'? question, the courts have been willing to review all decisions involving the exercise of public power, even where exercised by bodies in private ownership. In the utilities sectors the exercise of public privileges, such as monopoly rights, by private companies carry with them responsibilities to account for their activities, both in domestic fora and EC law. In some instances, the receipt of public funds by private bodies renders recipients liable to public accountability through audit mechanisms. Considerable attention has been paid to this issue in the literature, with a consensus for the view that simple distinctions between private actors (not publicly accountable) and public actors (subject to full public accountability) are thus not sustainable.

For what?	Economic Values	Social/Procedural Values	Continuity/ Security Values
To whom?			
'Upwards' accountability	Of departments to treasury for expenditure	Of administrative decision-makers to courts/tribunals	Of utility companies to regulators
'Horizontal' accountability	Of public bodies to external and internal audit for probity and VFM	Review of decisions by grievance-handlers	Third-party accreditation of safety standards
'Downwards' accountability	Of utility companies to financial markets	Of public/privatized service providers to users	Consultation requirements re: universal service requirements

Figure 1 Examples of linkages between values and accountability institutions

The 'to whom?' question has often been mingled with the 'for what?' question, for example in the distinction between legal accountability (to the courts in respect of the juridical values of fairness, rationality and legality) and political accountability (to ministers and to Parliament or other elected bodies such as local authorities and via these institutions ultimately to the electorate). Furthermore, while it might be helpful to think of 'administrative accountability' as accountability to administrative bodies such as grievance [handlers] and auditors, in fact these mechanisms for accountability have conventionally been distinguished, with administrative accountability only indicating the former, while financial accountability is used for the latter.

Separating the 'to whom?' and 'for what?' we find three broad classes within each category. Thus accountability may be rendered to a higher authority ('upwards accountability'), to a broadly parallel institution ('horizontal accountability') or to lower level institutions and groups (such as consumers) ('downwards accountability'). The range of values for which accountability is rendered can be placed in three categories: economic values (including financial probity and value for money (VFM)); social and procedural values (such as fairness, equality, and legality); continuity/security values (such as social cohesion, universal service, and safety). Figure 1 sets out the possible configurations of the 'to whom?' and 'for what?' questions, producing nine possible pairs of co-ordinates.

… If we think of traditional accountability as encompassing the 'upwards' mechanisms of accountability to ministers, Parliament, and courts, with some recognition of the more formal horizontal mechanisms (such as grievance-handlers and auditors) then it is possible to conceive of a concept of 'extended accountability' within which traditional accountability is only part of a cluster of mechanisms through which public bodies are in fact held to account.

… Close exploration of the structures of extended accountability in the United Kingdom reveals at least two different models which have developed which feature overlapping and fuzzy responsibility and accountability: interdependence and redundancy. No domain is likely to precisely correspond to one or other of these models. There are likely to be elements of both identifiable in many policy domains but, for reasons of clarity, the examples used in the following sections are presented in somewhat simplified and ideal-type form.

1. Interdependence

The identification and mapping out of relationships of interdependence within policy domains has been one of the key contributions of the recent pluralist literature in public policy. The identification of interdependence has important implications for accountability structures. Interdependence provides a model of accountability in which the formal parliamentary, judicial, and administrative methods of traditional accountability are supplemented by an extended accountability. Interdependent actors are dependent on each other in their actions because of the dispersal of key resources of authority (formal and informal), information, expertise, and capacity to bestow legitimacy such that each of the principal actors has constantly to account for at least some of its actions to others within the space, as a precondition to action. The executive generally, and the Treasury in particular, has long had a central role in calling public bodies to account over a range of values, in a way that is often less transparent in the case of the more dignified, but arguably less efficient parliamentary mechanisms of accountability. But these less formal and more hidden accountability mechanisms extend well beyond the capacities of central government, extending potentially to any actors, public or private, within a domain with the practical capacity to make another actor, public or private, account for its actions. Within the pluralist political science literature this conception is sometimes referred to as 'constituency relations' or 'mutual accountability'. Indeed it may be that the simple monolithic structures presented as the welfare state model are too simple, that they disguise intricate internal and opaque webs of control and accountability that are functionally equivalent to the new instruments of the regulatory state, but are less formal and transparent. Among the more obvious examples were the consumer committees established for the nationalized industries with a brief to hold those public corporations to account from a collective consumer viewpoint.

This model is exemplified by the United Kingdom telecommunications sector (Figure 4). Figure 4 shows that though BT is subject to diminished upwards accountability to parliament and courts (noted above), it has a new forms of accountability in each dimension—upwards to a new regulator, horizontally to the mechanisms of corporate governance, and downwards to shareholders (and possibly also the market for corporate control) and users. The financial markets arguably provide a more rigorous form of financial accountability than applies to public bodies because there are so many individual and institutional actors with a stake in scrutinizing BT's financial performance. The accountability of BT to the regulator, OFTEL, is also more focused, in the sense that OFTEL has a considerable stake in getting its regulatory scrutiny right, being itself scrutinized closely by BT, by other licensees, and by ministers, in addition to the more traditional scrutiny by the courts and by public audit institutions. OFTEL's quest for legitimacy has caused it to develop novel consultative procedures, and to publish a very wide range of documents on such matters as competition investigations and enforcement practices. Each of these other actors has powers or capacities which constrain the capacities of the others and require a day-to-day accounting for actions, more intense in character than the accountability typically applied within traditional upwards accountability mechanisms. This form of accountability, premised upon interdependence, is not linear, but more like a servo-mechanism holding the regime in a broadly acceptable place through the opposing tensions and forces generated. Such a model creates the potential to use the shifting of balances in order to change the way the model works in any particular case.

2. Redundancy

A second extended accountability model is that of redundancy, in which overlapping (and ostensibly superfluous) accountability mechanisms reduce the centrality of any one of them. In common parlance, redundancy is represented by the 'belt and braces' approach, within which two independent mechanisms are deployed to ensure the system does not fail, both of which are capable of working on their own. Where one fails the other will still prevent disaster. Redundancy in failsafe mechanisms is a common characteristic of public sector activities generally, and can be threatened by privatization. Equally explicit concern about risks associated with change may cause redundancy to be built in to oversight structures. Redundancy can be an unintended effect of certain institutional configurations. In practice, examples of redundancy in accountability regimes appear to be a product of a mixture of design and contingency.

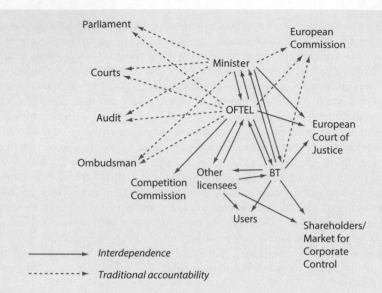

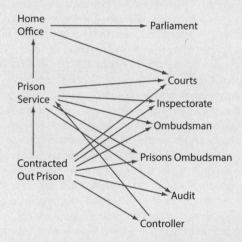

Figure 4 Accountability for provision of telecoms services 2: Interdependence model

Figure 5 Accountability for prisons provision: redundancy mode

There are at least two forms to the redundancy model: traditional and multi-level governance. The traditional redundancy model is exemplified by the accountability mechanisms for contracted-out prisons in the United Kingdom (Figure 5). Directors of contracted-out prisons are subject to all the forms of accountability directed at publicly operated prisons: upwards (legal, to the courts); financial (to the National Audit Office); and horizontal (to the Prisons Inspectorate, the Prisons Ombudsman, and prison visitors). But, contracted-out prisons are additionally subject to a further form of horizontal accountability with a requirement to account, day-to-day to an on-site regulator (called a controller), appointed by the Prison Service to monitor compliance with contract specification. Unusually within the prisons sector, controllers wield the capacity to levy formal sanctions for breach of contract. Some commentators have suggested that there is a structural risk with on-site regulators of capture by the director, in the sense of controllers over-identifying with the needs and limits to the capacities of those they are supposed to regulate. However, with the redundancy model of accountability were such capture to occur it would likely be identified by one or more of the others holding the director to account....

The multi-level governance redundancy model of extended accountability is likely to see further development in the United Kingdom arising out the devolution of considerable powers to a new Scottish Parliament and Northern Irish and Welsh Assemblies. In each of these jurisdictions new executives and parliamentary/assembly committees have the potential to develop and reinvent the parliamentary oversight already exercised over United Kingdom-wide or multi-jurisdiction public functions.

...

The transformation of public administration in the United Kingdom has made more transparent the dense networks of accountability within which public power is exercised. The constitutional significance of this observation is to suggest that there is a potential to harness these networks for the purposes of achieving effective accountability or control, even as public power continues to be exercised in more fragmented ways. Outstanding questions for this analysis are whether there are other models of accountability in the regulatory state not captured by the interdependence and redundancy models, and whether it is possible to capture the complete set within an overall theory of extended accountability. Areas requiring further exploration are the role of voluntary organizations (such as prisons campaigners and consumer groups) and the media in rendering public and quasi-public bodies accountable.

NOTES

1. Scott points out some of the deficiencies in his two models of extended accountability, and it would seem that the situation is improved if the different mechanisms are all operating. This ideal may not happen in practice. In 'Accountability, New Public Management, and the Problems of the Child Support Agency' (1999) 26 *Journal of Law and Society* 150, Carol Harlow concluded that while the external accountability provided by the Social Security Committee, the Select Committee on the Parliamentary Commissioner for Administration, and the Public Accounts Committee was very good, many of the operational problems they dealt with had their roots in policy which was not given a sufficiently rigorous scrutiny by Parliament during the passage of legislation. This fault of inadequate consultation is known; see the Hansard Society in Chapter 7, Section 1B(a) at pp. 286–8, and the revised guidance on it in Chapter 7, Section 1B(c)(i) at pp. 288–9. Thus it seemed unfair that the only resignation was that of the Child Support Agency's first chief executive who arrived after the policy had been formulated by Ministers. Internal accountability procedures associated with the New Public Management, such as business plans and performance indicators, were of no assistance to clients when things went wrong. Harlow also pointed out that judicial review in child support was like the 'dog which never barked'. She wondered if an explanation may be found in the fact that the child support cases were heard by judges in the family law division rather than the public law division.

2. The Hansard Society's report *The Challenge for Parliament: Making Government Accountable* (2001) agreed with Harlow's analysis as to the partial success of Parliament's engagements with the Child Support Agency. The vast majority of the report's case studies showed inadequacies in Parliament's oversight; e.g., despite the availability of early warning about problems in the Passport Office in Spring 1999, the Public Accounts Committee's report in Summer 2000 was full but, as is usual, the relevant departmental select committee (Home Affairs) had not conducted a watching brief, and the debating opportunities tend to be used for party political matters rather than one of public interest. It was noted that Parliament is unclear about its relationship with regulators, inspectorates, and other outside bodies. Parliament should use the information provided by individual cases, draw out the lessons from this work, and give greater worth to their investigations by using them as a basis for holding Government to account. The report recommends that Parliament should be at the apex of a network of regulatory bodies and alternative scrutiny mechanisms. A culture of scrutiny should be developed and improvements made to work done in committee and the chamber in the House of Commons with more emphasis given to financial scrutiny. The House of Lords should complement the Commons and there should be better communication between Parliament and the public.

B: Select committees

An account of the genesis of the reforms of the Select Committee system can be found in G. Drewry (ed.), *The New Select Committees* (2nd edn, 1989) ch. 1. Select Committees have become since their reform in 1979, 'the principal mechanism through which the House of Commons hold the executive to account', according to the Hansard Society, a body dedicated to promoting the parliamentary system of government. This has been reflected in the chairs of select committees being paid an amount in addition to their MP's salary and opening up the prospect of an alternative career path to that of ministerial office. While it was a government which initially promoted the reform, governments tend not to be too enthusiastic about enhancing the powers of bodies which hold them to account and can cause difficulties. It can, therefore, be appreciated why it took some time for the removal of party control over membership of select committees by replacing nomination with election. This significant change followed acceptance of the proposals of the House of Commons Reform Committee (known as the 'Wright Committee' after its chair). The Wright Committee, which had been created as a response to the loss of public confidence in Parliament and politics after the MPs' expenses scandal, sought generally to redress the balance of power between the House and Government (see later in this chapter in Section 2E at pp. 269–73). In relation to select committees, they proposed that chairs of select committees be elected by the whole House and that members be elected within their party groups by secret ballot. The Government has a majority in the House and this is reflected in most but not all committees' membership. The Wright reforms were agreed in 2010, in the last session of the Parliament elected in 2005 and were implemented in the first session of the Parliament elected in 2010. The Liaison Committee reviewed the committees after two years and made recommendations on their effectiveness, resources, and powers.

Liaison Committee, *Select Committee effectiveness, resources and powers*
HC 697 of 2012–13, paras 12–14, 20, 70, 105–8, 112–13

… 12 … select committees should influence policy and have an impact on Government departments and the agencies to which their functions may be devolved. This is our first objective. The extent of this influence and impact is the primary measure of the effectiveness of select committees.

13. But committees are not only concerned with influencing Government. Many reports contain recommendations targeted at bodies outside Government: the European Commission, for example, professional bodies and occasionally private sector companies.

And, in a growing number of cases, third parties — including private sector bodies — can be the focus of committee inquiries. Increasingly, the private sector is involved in delivering public services, and committees have a legitimate interest in scrutinising how taxpayers' money is spent. And some private sector services are of such concern that the public expect the committee to intervene, filling the accountability gap. The inquiries by the Transport Committee into the cost of motor insurance, and the Treasury Committee into retail banking are examples. While committees' primary purpose is to scrutinise Government, it is sometimes in the public interest for them to extend their scrutiny to other organisations.

14. A further important function of committees is to act as a forum for discussion and informed debate, raising issues in the public consciousness and giving a public platform to experts and affected individuals.

…

20. We set out in Table 2 below revised core tasks, which we encourage committees to take into account when planning their programmes. They will not all be relevant to every committee; and some committees — those with a large amount of legislation, for example — will not have the time to cover everything.

…

Table 2 Revised select committee core tasks for departmental select committees

Overall aim: To hold Ministers and Departments to account for their policy and decision-making and to support the House in its control of the supply of public money and scrutiny of legislation

STRATEGY

Task 1   To examine the strategy of the department, how it has identified its key objectives and priorities and whether it has the means to achieve them, in terms of plans, resources, skills, capabilities and management information

POLICY

Task 2   To examine policy proposals by the department, and areas of emerging policy, or where existing policy is deficient, and make proposals

EXPENDITURE AND PERFORMANCE

Task 3   To examine the expenditure plans, outturn and performance of the department and its arm's length bodies, and the relationships between spending and delivery of outcomes

DRAFT BILLS

Task 4   To conduct scrutiny of draft bills within the committee's responsibilities

BILLS AND DELEGATED LEGISLATION

Task 5   To assist the House in its consideration of bills and statutory instruments, including draft orders under the Public Bodies Act

POST-LEGISLATIVE SCRUTINY

Task 6   To examine the implementation of legislation and scrutinise the department's post-legislative assessments

EUROPEAN SCRUTINY

Task 7   To scrutinise policy developments at the European level and EU legislative proposals

APPOINTMENTS

Task 8   To scrutinise major appointments made by the department and to hold pre-appointment hearings where appropriate

SUPPORT FOR THE HOUSE

Task 9   To produce timely reports to inform debate in the House, including Westminster Hall, or debating committees, and to examine petitions tabled

PUBLIC ENGAGEMENT

Task 10   To assist the House of Commons in better engaging with the public by ensuring that the work of the committee is accessible to the public

70. . . . We agree that committees should be proactive and forward-looking — and devote less effort to raking over the coals of past events unless there are lessons to be learnt and changes to be recommended.

. . .

Departments' record of co-operation

105. More effective scrutiny also requires the co-operation of Government. The memoranda from committees demonstrate varying degrees of co-operation from departments at present. Some enjoy a positive and co-operative relationship with their department; others record a number of problems. Some common themes emerge.

Government responses

106. Several committees complain about the timeliness of Government responses to reports. The Government's guidance to departments ("the Osmotherly Rules") states that departments should aim to respond to reports within two months, but responses are quite frequently late....

107. Other committees — and some outside observers — complain about the content of responses. The Defence Committee said that "departmental replies to reports are usually very defensive, often late, and show little appetite for dialogue with the Committee".... The Regulatory Policy Institute's Better Government Programme described government responses as "models of evasion".

108. An increasing number of committees are taking action when a response is unsatisfactory, by publishing a substantive critical report with the response, or by calling the Minister in for a further evidence session to explain it. We, the Liaison Committee, have recently issued a second report highlighting the inadequacy of the Government's response to our report on Public Appointments and Select Committees... If a government response is inadequate, a committee can and should draw attention to this when it reports and publishes the response.

...

112. Other committees have had difficulties in securing the attendance of particular officials. In some cases, the responsible official has moved on to another job, or has retired. The Defence Committee reported an instance in which it was told by the department that the witness it had asked for was not the appropriate person only to be told by his replacement and the Minister at the evidence session that they were surprised he was not there....

113. ... We do not accept that the Osmotherly rules should have any bearing on whom a select committee should choose to summon as a witness. The Osmotherly rules are merely internal for Government. They have never been accepted by Parliament. Where the inquiry relates to departmental delivery rather than ministerial decision-making, it is vital that committees should be able to question the responsible official directly — even if they have moved on to another job. It does of course remain the case that an official can decline to answer for matters of policy, on the basis that it is for the minister to answer for the policy, but officials owe a direct obligation to Parliament to report on matters of fact and implementation. This does not alter the doctrine of ministerial accountability in any way. Ministers should never require an official to withhold information from a select committee. It cannot be a breach of the principle of ministerial responsibility for an official to give a truthful answer to a select committee question. No official should seek to protect his or her minister by refusing to do so.

NOTE: The Liaison Committee made a further report (HC 911 of 2012–13) in which it commented on the responses received from the Speaker, and senior House officials, and the Government. The responses from within the House were positive with recommendations being accepted, and select committees discussing implications of recommendations on best practice and taking up enthusiastically the recommendations on professional development. On the other hand:

3. The response from Government is mixed. It welcomes our review as timely and thorough, and it is positive in tone.... The Government recognises our interest and says it is keen to work with us; but this is phrased as consulting us on the Government's proposals for reform, rather than clearly accepting our recommendation of a joint approach, aimed at joint guidelines. While we welcome, and will respond positively to, the Government's willingness to engage with us, we are not yet convinced that the Government has fully accepted the case for a new approach. Our scepticism is reinforced by the further response which we have received from the Government to our reports on Select Committees and Public Appointments (published separately as our First Special Report of Session 2012–13, HC 912), which — though friendly in tone — gives disappointingly little ground. We believe that the Government has not yet recognised the changed mood in the House and the strength of our resolve to achieve change.

The Osmotherly rules, mentioned in para. 113 in the extract, provide guidance for civil servants giving evidence to select committees. The most recent version will now be considered.

Cabinet Office: *Giving Evidence to Select Committees: Guidance for Civil Servants*
October 2014

Role of Select Committee

1. Select Committees have an important role in ensuring the full and proper accountability of the Executive to Parliament. Ministers have emphasised that, when officials represent them before Select Committees, they should be as forthcoming and helpful as they can in providing information relevant to Committee inquiries. In giving evidence to Select Committees, officials should take care to ensure that no information is withheld which would not be exempted if a parallel request were made to the Department under the Freedom of Information Act....

General Principles

4. The Civil Service Code makes clear that civil servants are accountable to Ministers who in turn are accountable to Parliament. It therefore follows that when civil servants give evidence to a Select Committee they are doing so, not in a personal capacity, but as representatives of their Ministers.

5. This does not mean that officials may not be called upon to give a full account of government policies, or the justification, objectives and effects of these policies, but their purpose in doing so is to contribute to the process of ministerial accountability not to offer personal views or judgements on matters of government policy - to do so could undermine their political impartiality.

Civil Service Code obligations

9. Civil servants who give evidence to Select Committees do so on behalf of their Ministers and under their directions.

10. This is in accordance with the principle that it is Ministers who are accountable to Parliament for the policies and actions of their Departments. Civil servants are accountable to Ministers....

Summoning of Named Officials

11. Parliament has powers to call any individual to give evidence. However, in accordance with Ministerial accountability, where evidence relates to Government policy or action, it is given by Ministers or officials on their behalf. Officials providing evidence to Select Committees do so under Ministerial agreement and instruction....

12. When a Select Committee indicates that it wishes to take evidence from any particular named official, including special advisers, the presumption is that Ministers will seek to agree such a request. However, the decision on who is best able to represent the Minister rests with the Minister concerned. It remains the right of a Minister to suggest an alternative civil servant, or additional civil servant(s), to the person named by the Committee if he or she feels that would be a better way to represent them. If there is no agreement about which official should most appropriately give evidence, the Minister can offer to appear personally before the Committee.

13. If a Committee nonetheless insists on a named official appearing before them, contrary to the Minister's wishes, the formal position remains that it could issue an order for attendance, and request the House to enforce it. In such an event the official, as any other individual would have to appear before the Committee but, in all circumstances, would remain subject to Ministerial instruction and the Civil Service Code. This would be a very exceptional action.

NOTES

1. The revised Osmotherly rules were considered by the Liaison Committee (a committee composed of the elected chairs of all other Commons select committees) in its *Legacy Report* (HC 954 of 2014–15). It noted there had been 'a long delay' and the revised version contained 'little radical change', [14]. It also confirmed:

> 15. It remains our approach that it is not for the Liaison Committee or the House to endorse Whitehall's own rules about giving evidence to Parliament. These are the Government's rules— not Parliament's rules—and Parliament reserves the right to depart from them when necessary.

2. Whilst committees have powers to call persons, backed by resolution of the House, there is a convention that MPs and Peers are not summoned to appear. The select committee dealing with transport has complained about occasions when they were not able to see witnesses despite having requested that they attend the committee. The committee issued two special reports on this in 2002. The first (HC 655 of 2001–02) concerned Lord Birt who was acting as a special adviser to the Prime Minister. The Government made a general case against committees seeing advisers:

- If they had to appear before Select Committees and answer questions, advisers would be unwilling to take on the job.
- They are unpaid.
- If the Prime Minister's advisers were to appear before Select Committees the system of Cabinet Government would be undermined.
- The advice given by advisers to Ministers should be confidential.

But the Committee pointed out that in the past other advisers had given evidence. It could not compel Lord Birt's attendance because of the convention against compelling Peers to attend a select committee, and so it wished that the convention be modified as it was inappropriate for advisers to the Prime Minister and other Ministers to be able to avoid the committee. In the end the committee did not think Lord Birt was a significant adviser on the particular matter, but it was concerned about advisers in general and those advising the Prime Minister in particular, a point taken up by the Liaison Committee (HC 446 of 2003–04, para. 90).

The second report (HC 771 of 2001–02) concerned the failure of a Treasury Minister to appear before the committee during its inquiry into the London Underground to give evidence on the Public–Private Partnership financial arrangements. The committee felt that the Treasury was pushing this particular policy and so wished the House to make an order requiring a Treasury minister to give evidence to them on this matter.

The Government response to the report on Treasury Ministers (HC 1241 of 2001–02) argued that it was inappropriate for the House to make the requested order as the Secretary of State for Transport speaks for the Government on transport matters and it is he who should appear before the committee on this matter. Treasury Ministers would appear on matters where they have responsibility and a Treasury Minister had appeared to give evidence on taxation policy in the transport committee's inquiry into the Ten-Year Plan for Transport in March 2002.

Nonetheless, the Liaison Committee's *Legacy Report* (HC 954 of 2014–15) presents a generally positive picture of recent Government engagement with select committees:

> 16. Our overall impression is that government departments are taking committees seriously and engaging positively with them. While there have been occasions of late replies to reports and disagreements about witnesses and evidence, most relationships between select committees and departments appear to be constructive.

The *Legacy Report* also notes the role of the Liaison Committee as a 'guarantor' of government engagement with the House of Commons:

> 12. Less visibly, the Liaison Committee plays a fundamental role as the protector of the House's backbench and committee scrutiny of the Government. On occasions when individual committees have difficulty—perhaps in securing the attendance of witnesses or in getting a timely reply from a government department—the collective support of the Liaison Committee can reinforce the rights of individual committees to carry out their scrutiny function.

3. Prime Minister Blair had declined to attend committees, claiming precedent, but agreed in May 2002 to meet the Liaison Committee twice a year. Subsequent Prime Ministers have also agreed to these biannual meetings with the Liaison Committee.

■ QUESTION

Given the immense range of activities carried out by the modern administrative state, how important is the work of specialist select committees in ensuring that government is held to account in detail?

C: The floor of the House of Commons

The passage of legislation, which is considered in Chapter 7, Section 1A(a) at pp. 278–80, is the activity which takes up a significant amount of time for business in the House of Commons. In the 2013–14, 2014–15, and 2015–16 sessions it accounted for 34 per cent, 30 per cent, and 33 per cent of time in the Commons. The following table shows how the rest of the time was spent.

House of Commons Sessional Returns
2013–14, 2014–15, 2015–16, pp. 42–3, 31–2, 35–6

Distribution of time on the floor of the House between principal types of business	Total time spent (hours:minutes)		
	2013–14	2014–15	2015–16
Addresses, other than Motions to annul or revoke Statutory Instruments	37:29	35:24	39:17
Government motions			
European Union Documents	15.26	3:43	4:07
Business motions	1:02	2:18	0:04
General	44:81	46:34	43:30
Opposition days	132:37	109:13	125:12
Backbench business	174:38	132:26	130:19
Private Members' Motions	13:25	11:28	12:20
Adjournment, general and topical debates			
General Debates	-	-	12:19
Daily	77:31	63:49	74:00
Standing Order No. 24 debate	-	2:59	11.34
Estimates (debates on Select Committee Reports under Standing Order No 54)	15:36	13:51	8:56
Questions to ministers	113:11	90:59	109:52
Topical Questions	28:17	22:38	25:57
Urgent Questions	23:01	29:18	47:39
Statements	82:38	62:04	82:50
Business Statements	31:27	22:30	32:27
Standing Order No. 24 Applications	0:04	0:05	0:25

Distribution of time on the floor of the House between principal types of business

	Total time spent (hours:minutes)		
	2013–14	2014–15	2015–16
Points of Order	9:19	11:30	11:51
Public Petitions	2:56	2:18	1:58
Daily Prayers	13:22	10:50	12:23
Miscellaneous (including suspension of proceedings of the House)	14:05	3:02	16:00

NOTES

1. The General Election in May 2015 meant that the 2014–15 session was shorter than average, running to ten months. The 2013–14 and 2015–16 sessions lasted 12 months each.
2. Standing Order No. 24 (previously SO 20) is a procedure under which there is an adjournment of the House in order to discuss an urgent and important matter. It is considered later in this chapter in Section 2C(iii) at pp. 257–8.

(a) Debate

R. Blackburn and A. Kennon, *Griffith & Ryle on Parliament Functions, Practice and Procedures*
(2003), p. 286

The process of debate, as established by basic procedures … is the main process used for most of the House's business—but not all; it is not used in questions or ministerial statements, or in select committee proceedings, for example. The process is essentially simple: a motion is made ('That this House approves … '); a question is proposed by the Chair in the same form; debate arises; the question is put; it is agreed to or negatived; if agreed a resolution (expressing an opinion) or an order (requiring action by the House, or a committee or individual Members or officers) results. There are all sorts of variations or modern qualifications of this basic process; amendments may be moved on which a question is again proposed and each amendment must be disposed of separately, before the main question (as amended if it has been) is put; there may be amendments to amendments; some motions may not, by standing order, be amended or others may not be debated; debate on motions or amendments may be adjourned; debate may be closured; and motions or amendments may be withdrawn. But the essentials are plain; only one motion is considered at a time and in the end all motions (and amendments) must either be agreed to, negatived, or withdrawn.

The logic of this procedure is binary. Decisions are taken in sequence, singly, and each decision on each motion and each amendment is a simple 'yes' or 'no.' With a few exceptions there are no qualified majorities:

(i) 100 members must vote in the majority for a closure to be effective.
(ii) If a division shows that fewer than 40 Members are present, the business concerned stands over until another day.
(iii) 20 or more Members can block a motion to refer a bill to a second reading committee (and thereby insist on second reading on the floor of the House).

There is no requirement on any question for an absolute majority, and, as we will see, there are not even any procedures for registering abstentions in a division. This binary process is mirrored in—or is a reflection of—the two-sided, confrontational nature of the House's proceedings.… The systematic logic of these procedures protects the clarity of decision taking.

P. Norton, *The Commons in Perspective*
(1981), p. 119

[G]eneral debates are nevertheless not without some uses in helping to ensure a measure of scrutiny and influence, however limited. A debate prevents a Government from remaining mute. Ministers have to explain and justify the Government's position. They may want to reveal as little as possible, but the Government cannot afford to hold back too much for fear of letting the Opposition appear to have the better argument. The involvement of Opposition spokesman and backbenchers ensures that any perceived cracks in the Government's position will be exploited. If it has failed to carry its own side privately, the Government may suffer the embarrassment of the publicly expressed dissent of some of its own supporters, dissent which provides good copy for the press. On some occasions, Ministers may even be influenced by comments made in debate. They will not necessarily approach an issue with closed minds, and will normally not wish to be totally unreceptive to the comments of the Opposition (whose co-operation they need for the efficient despatch of business) or of their own Members (whose support they need in the lobbies, and among whom morale needs to be maintained); a Minister who creates a good impression by listening attentively to views expressed by Members may enhance his own prospects of advancement. The likelihood of a Minister's being influenced may be greatest when he is at the despatch box. Though the House may be nearly empty for much of a debate, it fills up during the front-bench speeches, and this is when the atmosphere of the House becomes important. A Minister faced by a baying Opposition and silence behind him may be unnerved and realise that he is not carrying Members on either side with him, and in consequence may moderate or even, in extreme cases, reverse his position. On such an occasion, the debate-vote relationship may become important, the fear of defeat concentrating the minds of Ministers. A recent example of such a debate was that on Members' pay in 1979, when the Leader of the House, Norman St John-Stevas, received such a rough reception at the despatch box that the Cabinet realised it did not have the support of the House and changed its previous decision.

In addition, debates may act as useful channels for the expression of views held by the general interests and specific bodies represented by Members. If a Member with a known constituency interest in a certain subject rises to speak, he will invariably be listened to with greater respect than one who seeks solely to score party political points, and may even have some influence on the Minister's thinking; all MPs—Ministers and backbenchers—represent constituencies, and will normally have at least a degree of empathy for a Member seeking conscientiously to defend the interests of his constituents.

NOTE: Debates may be on motions proposed by the Government, the Opposition, and the various committees of the House. Debates may also be proposed by backbench MPs, with the creation of the Backbench Business Committee in 2010 tasked with deciding how the time available for this should be allocated. The following extracts are taken from the debate on the second reading of a Bill when general principles are usually discussed.

House of Commons, HC Deb
Vol. 596, cols 1047–52, 9 June 2015

European Union Referendum Bill
Second Reading

Mr Speaker: I must inform the House that I have selected the amendment in the name of Mr Alex Salmond. Before I ask the Foreign Secretary to move the Second Reading of the Bill, the House will not be surprised to hear that some dozens of colleagues are seeking to catch my eye and a time limit will have to be imposed. Front Benchers are not constrained by it, of course, but the Foreign Secretary and his shadow are nothing if not sensitive to the wishes of the House and I am sure they will want to balance the need to cover the subject thoroughly and take interventions with the interests of other colleagues in having the chance to contribute.

12.41 pm

The Secretary of State for Foreign and Commonwealth Affairs (Mr Philip Hammond): I beg to move, That the Bill be now read a Second time.

This is a simple, but vital, piece of legislation. It has one clear purpose: to deliver on our promise to give the British people the final say on our EU membership in an in/out referendum by the end of 2017. For those who were present in the last Parliament, today's debate will be tinged with a sense of déjà vu: we have, of course, debated this Bill before. So before I start, I would like to pay tribute to my hon. Friend the Member for Stockton South (James Wharton). His European Union (Referendum) Bill in the last Parliament was passed by this House, but sadly was blocked in the other place by the opposition parties. He deserves the credit for paving the way for the Bill we are debating today.

Let me also pay tribute to my noble Friend Lord Dobbs who sponsored the Wharton Bill in the other place, and to my hon. Friend the Member for Bromley and Chislehurst (Robert Neill) who reintroduced the same Bill in the following Session.

The commitment on the Government side of the House to giving the British people their say has deep roots.

Mr Angus Brendan MacNeil (Na h-Eileanan an Iar) (SNP): Will the Foreign Secretary give way?

Mr Hammond: I am going to make a little progress, bearing in mind Mr Speaker's exhortation.

It is almost four decades ago to the day that I, along with millions of others in Britain, cast my vote in favour of our membership of the European Communities, and like millions of others I believed then that I was voting for an economic community that would bring significant economic benefits to Britain, but without undermining our national sovereignty. I do not remember anyone saying anything about ever-closer union or a single currency. But the institution that the clear majority of the British people voted to join has changed almost beyond recognition in the decades since then.

Mr Kenneth Clarke (Rushcliffe) (Con): There must have been some strange juxtapositions in the campaign held in the 1970s, in which I took a very active part. Most of the debates I took part in were about the pooling of sovereignty and the direct applicability of European legislation without parliamentary intervention, which was a very controversial subject, and, besides, ever-closer union was in the treaty to which we were acceding.

9 Jun 2015 : Column 1048

Mr Hammond: Call me negligent, but as an 18-year-old voter in that election, I did not actually read the treaty before I cast my vote.

Treaty after treaty—the Single European Act, Maastricht, Amsterdam, Nice and Lisbon—individually and collectively have added hugely to the European Union's powers, often in areas that would have been unthinkable in 1975, and that change has eroded the democratic mandate for our membership to the point where it is wafer-thin and demands to be renewed.

Mr MacNeil: Two weeks ago I was in North Uist and met one of my constituents, who is from Germany. She has lived in North Uist for 25 years and she voted in the Scottish referendum, but she cannot vote in this referendum. Why were the Scottish Government more generous to and more understanding of her rights as a citizen for 25 years than the Tory Government? Why is she excluded?

Mr Hammond: If the hon. Gentleman can bear to stop wagging his finger and wait a little, I will come to the question of franchise.

To many people, not only in the UK, but across Europe, the European Union has come to feel like something that is done to them, not for them. Turnout in last year's European Parliament elections was the lowest ever, dropping to 13% in Slovakia. The fragility of the European Union's democratic legitimacy is felt particularly acutely by the British people. Since our referendum in 1975, citizens across Europe from Denmark and Ireland to France and Spain have been asked their views on crucial aspects of their country's relationships with the EU in more than 30 different national referendums—but not in the UK.

We have had referendums on Scottish devolution, Welsh devolution, our electoral system and a regional assembly for the north-east, but an entire generation of British voters has been denied the chance to have a say on our relationship with the European Union. Today we are putting that right. After fighting and winning the general election as the only major party committed to an in/out referendum, in the face of relentless opposition from the other parties, today we are delivering on our promise to give that generation its say.

Mike Gapes (Ilford South) (Lab/Co-op): In the Foreign Secretary's opening remarks, he referred to the number of changes that have taken place since 1975, when there was last a referendum. Can I take it from what he said that unless the British people have a right to reject all those changes brought about without a referendum he will not be satisfied? Or, can he at least set out today what it is that the Government wish to take back, rather than simply condemning his and all previous Governments since 1975?

Mr Hammond: The answer to question No. 1 is no and the answer to question No. 2 is that the Prime Minister has set out in a series of speeches, articles and interviews, and in the Conservative party manifesto, the key areas where we require change to the way that Britain's relationship with the European Union works if we are to be able to get the consent of the British people to our future membership.

Conservative Members have long been clear that the European Union needs to change and that Britain's relationship with the European Union needs to change.

9 Jun 2015 : Column 1049

Unlike the Labour party, we believe that Brussels has too much power and that some of those powers need to be brought back to national capitals. In a world whose centre of economic gravity is shifting fast, Europe faces a serious challenge. If we are to continue to earn our way in the world and to secure European living standards for future generations, the EU needs to focus relentlessly on jobs, growth and competitiveness. Bluntly, it needs to become far less bureaucratic and far more competitive.

With the European electorate more disenchanted with the EU than ever before and with anti-EU parties on the rise across the continent, it is time to bring Europe back to the people, ensuring that decisions are made as close to them as possible and giving national Parliaments a greater role in overseeing the European Union. Such issues resonate across all member states. Change is needed for the benefit of all to make the EU fit for the purpose of the 21st century.

Sir William Cash (Stone) (Con): I applaud my right hon. Friend's opening remarks and the Prime Minister for making certain that we had the Bill. May I ask the Foreign Secretary one question? In the last statement made by the Prime Minister in the previous Parliament, he clearly said that he wanted reform and a fundamental change in our relationship with the EU. Will he explain what the second part of that means in practice and in relation to the debate?

Mr Hammond: My hon. Friend's question is germane to the point I am making.

For the good of all 28 countries, there are things that need to be done to reform the way in which the European Union works to make it more competitive, effective and democratically accountable. However, the British people have particular concerns, borne of our history and circumstances. For example, we are not part of the single currency and, so long as there is a Conservative Government, we never will be. We made that decision because we will not accept the further integration of our fiscal, economic, financial and social policy—[Hon. Members: "We made it!"] The hon. Member for Eltham (Clive Efford) says that Labour made that decision. Is it the position of the Labour party that we will never join the single currency? I have not heard that position being articulated from the Labour Benches. It would be a seminal moment in our parliamentary history if Labour was able to make that commitment today.

We made that decision because we will not accept the further integration of our fiscal, economic, financial and social policy that will inevitably be required to make the eurozone a success. So, in answer to the point raised by my hon. Friend the Member for Stone (Sir William Cash), we need to agree a framework with our partners that will allow further integration of the eurozone while protecting Britain's interests and those of the other "euro-outs" within the EU. Because we occupy a crowded island with a population that is growing, even before net migration, and a welfare system that is more accessible than most and more generous than many in Europe, we are far more sensitive than many member states to the impact of migration from the EU and the distorting effects of easy access to benefits and services and of in-work welfare top-ups to wages that are already high by comparison with many EU countries.

9 Jun 2015 : Column 1050

In the Conservative party manifesto, we therefore committed to negotiate a new settlement for Britain in Europe—a settlement that addresses the concerns of the British people and sets the European Union on a course that will benefit all its people. The Prime Minister has already begun that process by meeting 15 European leaders, and at the European Council in June he will set out formally the key elements of our proposals.

Daniel Kawczynski (Shrewsbury and Atcham) (Con): I understand my right hon. Friend's point about the pressures of increased numbers coming to work in the United Kingdom, but will he take a moment to pay tribute to the hard-working eastern Europeans from Poland and elsewhere who have come here, worked hard, paid their taxes and contributed to our society?

Mr Hammond: I am very happy to do so. I do not think anybody—or at least not very many people—in this country has a problem with those who come here to work hard, pay their dues and make a better life for themselves while contributing to the UK economy. They are the not the focus of our concern. Our focus is on the distorting effect of easy access to our welfare system.

Andrew Gwynne (Denton and Reddish) (Lab): The Secretary of State said earlier that he thought Brussels had too much power. Will he tell the House which powers affecting the United Kingdom Brussels has too much of? Will he also tell us whether he would consider it a success or a failure if the Prime Minister failed to repatriate those powers?

Mr Hammond: I am afraid that the hon. Gentleman has just fallen into the obvious trap. He knows that a negotiation is a negotiation. He asks me to set out a list of powers for repatriation, then invites me to say that the Prime Minister would have failed if we did not achieve the repatriation of every single one of them. No sensible person with any negotiating experience would approach a complex negotiation in that way.

Several hon. Members *rose—*

Mr Hammond: I need to make some progress.

There are those who will say that this process cannot succeed, that Europe will never change, and that our negotiations will not be successful. Looking at the record of the last Labour Government, I can see why they would say that. Under that Labour Government, there was a one-way transfer of powers from Westminster to Brussels. They gave away £7 billion of the hard-fought-for British rebate but got absolutely nothing in return. They presided over a massive increase in the EU budget, they signed us up to the eurozone bail-out funds and they failed to deliver on their promise to give the British people a say before ratifying the Lisbon treaty. Labour's record on Europe was one of dismal failure.

In the last Parliament, however, we showed what could be done. We showed that, even in coalition with the Liberal Democrats, change could be achieved by adopting a tough negotiating stance and a laser-like focus on our national interest. We cut the EU budget for the first time ever, saving British taxpayers billions of pounds. We took Britain out of the eurozone bail-outs that Labour signed us up to—the first ever return of powers

9 Jun 2015 : Column 1051

from Brussels. We vetoed an EU treaty that would have damaged Britain's interests, we brought back control of more than 100 police and criminal justice measures and we secured exemptions for the smallest businesses from EU regulation. Our record in the past five years shows that we can deliver change in Europe that is in Britain's national interest.

Steve Brine (Winchester) (Con): The Foreign Secretary is taking a lot of noise and advice from those on the Labour Benches, but many of my colleagues and I remember sitting here, Friday after Friday, while they bitterly opposed the European Union (Referendum) Bill introduced by my hon. Friend the Member for Stockton South (James Wharton). I presume that my right hon. Friend welcomes the sinner who repents today, but as he takes all that advice will he just remember that if we had taken the advice of Labour, Scottish National party and Liberal Democrat Members, Britain would now be languishing in the euro?

Mr Hammond: My hon. Friend is absolutely right. When the electorate considers the stated positions of the parties, I would advise them to look not only at the positions they hold today but at the depth of the roots that sustain those positions.

Paul Farrelly (Newcastle-under-Lyme) (Lab): Does the Foreign Secretary believe that, when the Prime Minister completes these unspecified negotiations and decides to campaign for a yes in the referendum, my next-door neighbour the hon. Member for Stone (Sir William Cash) and his allies who held the Major Government hostage will ever be satisfied?

Mr Hammond: I will let my hon. Friend the Member for Stone speak for himself in the course of the debate. I am sure, however, that he will await—with a healthily sceptical approach—the return of the Prime Minister from Brussels with that package, and that he will consider it carefully and analytically, safe in the knowledge that underpinning this whole process is an absolute commitment to allow the British people to have the final say on this issue in an in/out referendum.

Mr Bernard Jenkin (Harwich and North Essex) (Con): None of the concessions that the Prime Minister has so far obtained from the European Union, including the veto of the fiscal union treaty, has fundamentally changed our relationship with the EU. How does he intend fundamentally to change that relationship?

Mr Hammond: My hon. Friend is right, of course. I have already mentioned an area in which we need fundamental change in the way in which the European Union operates. It is now a Union with a euro-zone of 19 member states at its core, and those states will integrate more closely together. There needs to be an explicit recognition that those who are not part of that core do not need to pursue ever-closer union. There needs to be an explicit protection of the interests of those non-eurozone members as the EU goes forward. That is an example of an area in which we need specific structural change to the way in which the European Union operates.

Ian Austin (Dudley North) (Lab) *rose—*

Bill Esterson (Sefton Central) (Lab) *rose—*

Clive Efford (Eltham) (Lab) *rose—*

9 Jun 2015 : Column 1052

Mr Hammond: I must make some progress.

Of course, negotiating with 27 member states will not be easy and it will not happen overnight, but we expect to be able to negotiate a new deal that will address the concerns of the British people about Britain's relationship with Europe, which we will put to them in the promised referendum. The Bill provides the mechanism to do that. It sets in stone our commitment to hold the referendum before the end of 2017. Of course, if the process is completed sooner, the referendum could be held sooner. So the Bill allows for the date of the referendum to be determined by regulations, made by affirmative resolution.

The Bill provides for the wording of the referendum question on its face. In 2013, the Electoral Commission assessed the referendum question posed by the Wharton Bill. The Commission recommended two possible formulations. This Bill specifies the simpler of the two:

"Should the United Kingdom remain a member of the European Union?",

with a yes/no answer. *[Interruption.]* Hon. Members need not answer now; they can wait until the designated referendum day. The Electoral Commission will of course report again on this Bill and we look forward to its assessment.

Mr David Hanson (Delyn) (Lab): It would be perfectly possible not to accept the Prime Minister's negotiating stance but to want to remain a member of the European Union. Should we not have a specific vote on the Prime Minister's recommendations as well as on the retention of membership of the European Union?

Mr Hammond: No. We made a proposal to the British people, it was put to the test in the general election and we have received an overwhelming mandate to progress. That is what we will do.

NOTES

1. The final legislation—the European Union (Referendum) Act 2015—provided the legal authority for the 2016 referendum at which a majority of the electorate voted to leave the EU. The question proposed by the Foreign Secretary in the debate above was not the question which appeared on the final ballot. Instead, the Electoral Commission (which has a statutory responsibility to report on the intelligibility of a question included in a referendum Bill once laid before Parliament, under the Political Parties, Elections and Referendums Act 2000) recommended an alternative question, which was seen to avoid the potential for perceived bias:

   'Should the United Kingdom remain a member of the European Union or leave the European Union?'
   Responses: 'Remain a member of the European Union' / 'Leave the European Union'
   The Bill was amended on the basis of this advice by government amendment.

2. Debates in the Commons should both reflect and lead broader public discussion of key political issues, given the constitutional centrality of the elected chamber of the UK Parliament. A number of themes emerging in the extract from the Second Reading debate on the Bill remained of considerable importance during the referendum campaign, and during subsequent discussion of withdrawal from the EU: for example, the exclusion of EU citizens from the referendum franchise and their future status in the UK after 'Brexit', the scale of the powers the UK can reclaim from Brussels and the implications for sovereignty, and the ease of negotiation with the 27 other Member States. The party political dimension of parliamentary debates is also evident in the extract, especially concerning responsibility for the decision not to join the European Single Currency.

(b) Parliamentary questions

Questions may be divided into those to be answered orally, or in writing. Written answers to Parliamentary Questions, or PQs, will be dealt with later in this section at pp. 264–9.

In its report on PQs the Procedure Committee put forward the following objectives of PQs:

> (a) a vehicle for individual backbenchers to raise their constituents' grievances;
>
> (b) an opportunity for the House of Commons to probe the detailed actions of the Executive;
>
> (c) a means of illuminating differences of policy on major issues between the various political parties or of judging the Parliamentary skills of individual MPs on both sides of the House;
>
> (d) a combination of these or any other purposes, for example a way of enabling the Government to disseminate information about particular policy decisions; and
>
> (e) the obtaining of information by the House from the Government and its subsequent publication (HC 178 of 1990–91, para. 26).

PQs for oral answer must be tabled in advance giving at least three days notice to the Minister (five days for questions to the Northern Ireland, Scotland, and Wales Offices). The Prime Minister answers PQs now on Wednesdays, previously on Tuesdays and Thursdays, whereas question time for other Ministers is determined by a rota. The dates of forthcoming ministerial question sessions, according to the rota, are published online by the Commons Table Office, along with deadlines for the submission of oral questions (see e.g. https://www.parliament.uk/documents/commons-table-office/Oral-questions-rota.pdf).

There are quite detailed rules on the form and content of PQs. These rules have derived from the rulings of the Speaker and are collected in *Erskine May's Treatise on the Law, Privileges, Proceedings and Usage of Parliament* (24th edn, 2011). PQs which deal with matters under consideration by Royal Commissions, parliamentary committees, or which are *sub judice* are inadmissible. Ministers only answer PQs on matters for which they are responsible.

This can create a problem as Ministers vary in their practice in answering questions which relate to other public bodies. The rule in *Erskine May* is that PQs 'should relate to the public affairs with which they are officially concerned, to proceedings in Parliament or to matters for which they are responsible (p. 295)'. The Committee recommended that the Table Office, which receives PQs, should give the benefit of the doubt to MPs when they want to ask a PQ about one of these public bodies which operates at 'arm's length' from the Minister.

The aim of most MPs tabling a PQ for an oral answer is to be able to pose a supplementary question for which no notice is necessary. Thus the tabled question may be quite general, or open, in nature. This is particularly so of PQs directed at the Prime Minister. A typical open PQ to the Prime Minister will inquire about the Prime Minister's engagements for that day. The Leader of Her Majesty's Opposition does not table PQs but is called by the Speaker to up to six supplementary questions. The leader of the third largest party in the Commons (from 2015, the Scottish National Party) is called to ask two questions.

R. Blackburn and A. Kennon, *Griffith & Ryle on Parliament Functions, Practice and Procedures*

(2003), p. 370

The formula which is nowadays almost uniformly adopted is 'To ask the Prime Minister if he will list his official engagements for [the day of answer.]' Every Wednesday some 200 questions of this kind are tabled but only the top 20 appear on the Order Paper, with only one or two on specific topics and a few questions 'To ask the Prime Minister if he will pay an official visit to [somewhere in the Member's constituency]' (which is a geographically narrowed form of open question). Despite the change in May 1997, there is usually no more than one substantive question to the Prime Minister in the top 20 listed on the Order Paper each Wednesday. Those who, by the luck of the shuffle, come in the first eight on the list will have an opportunity to fire a supplementary at the Prime Minister on a subject of their own choosing; but the Prime Minister only reads out a standard answer about his engagements in reply to the first question—he no longer refers 'the Hon. Member to the reply I gave some moments ago'. Those who have tabled 'engagements' questions are called by the Speaker and proceed at once to ask their substantive question, *e.g.* 'will the Prime Minister give consideration to the rising unemployment caused by the shut down of factories in any constituency, and what is he doing about it … ?'. Any Member who has tabled a substantive question simply calls the number of the question, to which the Prime Minister replies, before the Member asks a supplementary and receives a reply to that. This underlines the difference between substantive and open questions to the Prime Minister.

6–201 Again the Speaker controls the calling of additional Members to ask supplementaries, but here he has further factors to take into account. First, very many Members want to join in and this causes considerable pressure on the Chair. The Speaker calls Members, in turn, from either side. Records are kept showing how many times back-benchers have been called, so as to be as fair as possible. …

Secondly, the leader of the opposition is allowed up to six questions to the Prime Minister; and the leader of the second largest opposition party (recently the Liberal Democrats) has been allowed two questions; no-one else has more than one. The leader of the opposition sometimes takes his questions in two separate batches of three at the start and towards the end of Prime Minister's Questions. This is a prime opportunity for the leader of the opposition to put on the political agenda the issue of the day.

NOTE: The political points made in PQs directed to ministers can vary significantly, in substance, scope, and tone, as this extract from *Hansard* shows on a day when it was the turn of ministers at the Department for Education to answer questions. The extracts are taken from the first oral questions session held for the Department since the appointment of ministers to their posts in the new Government of Prime Minister Theresa May.

House of Commons, HC Deb

Vol. 615, cols 18–24, 10 October 2016

Topical Questions

Alison Thewliss (Glasgow Central) (SNP): T1. If she will make a statement on her departmental responsibilities. [906479]

The Secretary of State for Education (Justine Greening): This Government are determined to make this a country that works for everyone, and education is at of the heart of that ambition. I have already had the opportunity to see some of the excellent work being carried out in our classrooms. As my hon. Friend the Minister for Schools has said, there are now 1.4 million more children in good or outstanding schools than there were in 2010. The Department for Education has an expanded role, taking in higher education, further education and skills. That was reflected in my first announcement as Secretary of State, of the six opportunity areas where we are going to trial a new approach to boosting attainment and outcomes in social mobility coldspots that have been identified by the Social Mobility Commission. We will work inside schools and outside them, with communities and businesses, to make sure that we can turbo-charge those children's opportunities.

…

Alison Thewliss: I welcome the Secretary of State to her place. The reputation of Scotland's higher education sector is of huge significance at home and in the wider world. What assessment has she made of the damage that could be caused to that reputation by the marketisation of the HE sector opening it up to unknown and disreputable new providers?

Justine Greening: That is not at all what the Higher Education and Research Bill seeks to do. It is about opening up the higher education sector, so that we have the next wave of institutions that can provide fantastic degrees, and about making sure that there is teaching excellence. It is a strong Bill that will move the sector forward for the first time in 25 years.

...

Tulip Siddiq (Hampstead and Kilburn) (Lab): I would like to come back to a point made by my hon. Friend the Member for Manchester Central (Lucy Powell). The fairer early years funding plan has created a ticking time bomb for nurseries. Figures revealed by the Secretary of State's own Department show that 25% of local authorities across the country will lose out financially. I am afraid that her earlier answer will do nothing to reassure the National Association of Head Teachers, which believes that that will lead to the closure of hundreds of nurseries. Will she today commit to a funding pledge for nurseries for provision for after the first two years, so that the pledge of 30 hours of free childcare will be honoured for all?

The Parliamentary Under-Secretary of State for Education (Caroline Dinenage): I would like to take this opportunity to welcome the hon. Lady to her place on the Opposition Front Bench. I can reassure her that the funding formula that we have consulted on will make funding fairer, more transparent and more sustainable. Indeed, she is misinformed: our proposals mean that 88% of local authorities and their providers can expect to see their funding rates increase.

Stephen Hammond (Wimbledon) (Con): T5. As part of local democracy week, I visited two excellent primary schools, Hillcross and The Priory, in my constituency this morning. As I left, the headteacher of one of them asked me about the primary school assessment framework. Can the Minister confirm to the House how long he expects the transitional arrangements to be in place? [906484]

The Minister for Schools (Mr Nick Gibb): We will be announcing the response to the primary assessment arrangements shortly. It was important that we raised academic standards in our primary schools, and that is why we had a new curriculum introduced by 2014, after two or three years of preparation and consultation. We are raising standards in reading—there are now 147,000 more six-year-olds reading more effectively than they otherwise would be—and we are raising academic standards in maths and in grammar, punctuation and spelling. That is very important, and we will make further announcements about the details of the assessment soon.

Margaret Greenwood (Wirral West) (Lab): T2. In the Higher Education and Research Bill, the Government will allow universities simply to shut down if they fail in the HE marketplace, as though their role in local communities was a matter of no significance or concern to Government. That takes no account of the impact that closures will have on students and lecturers or the businesses and communities around them. Will the Government think again? [906481]

The Minister for Universities, Science, Research and Innovation (Joseph Johnson): The Higher Education and Research Bill will make student protection plans mandatory for the first time, putting in place systematic protection for students, which at present is very patchy and partial across our higher education system.

Sir Desmond Swayne (New Forest West) (Con): T7. How is our proper and welcome focus on phonics progressing? [906487]

Mr Gibb: I am grateful to my right hon. Friend for that question; it is progressing extremely well. In 2012, 58% of six-year-olds passed the check. This year, 81% passed the check. That is a huge improvement in the quality of the teaching of reading in our primary schools.

Daniel Zeichner (Cambridge) (Lab): T4. Can the Secretary of State explain how allowing schools to select all their pupils by religion, abolishing the 50% cap, will in any way help to bring communities together? [906483]

Justine Greening: The current rule is generally inoperative for many free schools when they begin, because they are not over-subscribed and it only kicks in if they are. We are proposing to put in place much stronger, more effective controls to ensure that faith schools that are opening will be community schools. I would very much encourage the hon. Gentleman to read the consultation document, which sets out proposals, including that those schools should demonstrate clear parental demand from parents of other faiths or no faith and that they should twin with primary schools and other schools.

…

Stephen Twigg (Liverpool, West Derby) (Lab/Co-op): The Secretary of State has spoken about social mobility. Where is the evidence, from this country or other parts of the world, that bringing back selection at 11 will increase social mobility? I think the evidence shows the opposite. May I urge her once again to think again about this plan to extend grammar schools and instead work together to raise standards for all children in all our schools?

Justine Greening: Of course, the two objectives are not mutually exclusive. Indeed, our school reforms will continue, and they have already seen the best part of 1.5 million children now in good or outstanding schools who were not in 2010. We see attainment driven through grammar schools in places such as Northern Ireland. It is just wrong simply to set on one side schools that are closing the attainment gap for children on free school meals and not look at how we can make that option available to more parents and more children.

…

Caroline Ansell (Eastbourne) (Con): On mandarin, I know my hon. Friend will be impressed of the work of St Catherine's College's Confucius school and the Eastbourne District Chinese Association. It is clearly important to promote language learning at home. I am pleased to note the uptake in Mandarin, even though I am a French teacher by profession. Can my hon. Friend assure me that we will continue to value opportunities for British students to study abroad?

Mr Gibb: On the last point, yes. We continue to value travel abroad. Learning a language is key to being able to travel and work abroad, and that is what the Mandarin Excellence Programme is all about. We hope 5,000 students will be fluent in Mandarin, reaching levels of HSK4 and HSK5, which go beyond A-level. We want more young people to take languages in our schools—including the language my hon. Friend teaches—following the fall in GCSEs thanks to the Labour party.

…

Karin Smyth (Bristol South) (Lab) *rose—[Interruption.]*

Mr Speaker: Order. Shrieking from a sedentary position is very unfair on the Member who is trying to secure a hearing from the House. Let us hear Karin Smyth.

Karin Smyth: Thank you, Mr Speaker. Following the report by the Public Accounts Committee on entitlement to free early years education and childcare and a Westminster Hall debate on the subject that I initiated in July, the then Minister promised me that the Department was due to publish the early years workforce strategy document, addressing the shortfall in qualified staff to deliver the 30 hours of free childcare. What progress has been made?

> **Caroline Dinenage:** The hon. Lady asks an important question. I am clear that we need to help employers to attract, retain and develop their staff to the very highest possible quality of early years provision. The workforce strategy will be published very shortly.
>
> **Several hon. Members** *rose—*
>
> **Mr Speaker:** Order. I am sorry to disappoint colleagues, but as usual demand has exceeded supply.

(c) Urgent questions

These are questions which refer to points which are urgent matters of public importance, or which relate to the arrangement of business in the House. Application is made to the Speaker on the day on which the MP wishes to ask the question, and, if granted, the urgent notice question will be asked at the conclusion of the normal Question Time.

In the sessions 2013–14, 2014–15, and 2015–16 the numbers of urgent questions (excluding business questions) asked were 35, 45, and 77 respectively. Session 2014–15 was shorter than average because of the General Election in May 2015.

(d) Adjournment debates

There are four types of adjournment debate, but only two will be covered here. These are the daily adjournment debate and the emergency adjournment debate.

Adjournment debates do not involve a division as they are a method by which an MP may raise a matter for a Minister who has responsibility. There is a ballot for the daily adjournment debate. The emergency adjournment debate is a relatively rare event which deals with an urgent matter not otherwise covered in the current business of the House. The table which follows gives an indication of the incidence of, and topics discussed in, emergency adjournment debates.

UK Parliament (data as at 14 January 2017)

http://www.parliament.uk/about/how/business/application-for-emergency-debates/

Applications for emergency debates in the House of Commons since May 2012

MP	Debate Title	Date	Decision	Proposal for debate
Mr Andrew Mitchell	Humanitarian Catastrophe in Aleppo and Syria	11.10.16	Agreed	c.72
Mrs Anne Main	Tobacco and Related Products Regulations 2016	08.06.16	Declined	c1205
Ms Angela Eagle	UK steel industry	11.04.16	Agreed	c93
Dr Eilidh Whiteford	Tax Credits	27.10.15	Declined	c197
Chris Bryant	The Operation of the Wilson Doctrine	15.10.15	Agreed	c515
Yvette Cooper	The Refugee Crisis in Europe	07.09.15	Agreed	c66
Mr Alistair Carmichael	Means of delivery of English votes on English laws	06.07.15	Agreed	c55
Sir Richard Ottaway	Ban by China on the Foreign Affairs Committee visit to Hong Kong	01.12.14	Agreed	c68

MP	Debate Title	Date	Decision	Proposal for debate
Nigel Adams	UK Coal's proposed closure of Kellingley and Thoresby collieries	08.04.14	Declined	c135
Mr David Cameron	Royal Charter on Press Conduct	18.03.13	Agreed	c630
Jeremy Lefroy	Mid Staffordshire NHS Foundation Trust special administrator	05.03.13	Declined	c863
Caroline Nokes	The closure of the Ford assembly plant at Swaythling	29.10.12	Declined	c52
Tim Farron	West Coast Main Line	03.09.12	Declined	c69
Mr Peter Bone	Wellingborough Prison	17.06.12	Declined	c854

(e) Early day motions

[The following extract is taken from the UK Parliament website and is available at http://www.parliament.uk/business/publications/business-papers/commons/early-day-motions]

What are Early day motions?
Early day motions (EDMs) are formal motions submitted for debate in the House of Commons. However, very few EDMs are actually debated.

How are EDMs used?
EDMs are used for reasons such as publicising the views of individual MPs, drawing attention to specific events or campaigns, and demonstrating the extent of parliamentary support for a particular cause or point of view.

Do they get debated?
Although there is very little prospect of EDMs being debated, many attract a great deal of public interest and frequently receive media coverage.

Do they have to comply to a format?
EDMs have a strict format. Each one has a short title, like 'Internet Gambling', and a sentence no longer than 250 words detailing the motion.

What are the rules?
Other than following the above format, EDMs must abide by certain rules about their subject matter. The main ones are:
- EDMs may only criticise other MPs, Lords, judges or members of the royal family if that is the main subject of the motion
- no reference should be made to matters before the courts
- no unparliamentary language or irony should be used
- titles must be purely descriptive

Types of EDMs
- EDMs against statutory instruments (are known as 'prayer') - generally the only type of EDM that leads to a debate.
- Internal party groups - put forward by party members to express a different view on an issue to the official party position.

- All-party EDMs - usually promote an issue, such as animal welfare, across party divides. Generally, only all-party EDMs attract a large number of signatures.
- Critical - occasionally EDMs are tabled criticising another Member of the House, or a member of the House of Lords.
- Promotion - of an outside campaign or report (often by the voluntary sector).
- Constituency issue - drawing attention to and commenting on.
- Commenting on deficiencies in other parties' policies - often by government MPs as they can't criticise the Opposition at question time.

Signatures

In an average session only six or seven EDMs reach over two hundred signatures. Around seventy or eighty get over one hundred signatures. The majority will attract only one or two signatures.

An EDM is not likely to be debated even if it gains a large number of signatures.

Who will not sign?

The following people in Parliament normally will not sign EDMs:
- Ministers and government whips
- Parliamentary Private Secretaries
- The Speaker and his deputies

Ministers and whips do not normally sign EDMs. The 2005 Ministerial Code stated that Parliamentary Private Secretaries "must not associate themselves with particular groups advocating special policies", and they do not normally sign EDMs. Neither the Speaker nor Deputy Speakers will sign EDMs. Internal party rules may also affect who can sign early day motions.

Amendments to EDMs

After an EDM has been tabled, other Members can then table amendments to the original EDM. Proposed amendments must not increase the motion's length beyond 250 words and any names of Members signing an amendment are automatically withdrawn from the main motion.

EDM's that are amendments to a previous motion have an 'A' after their number followed by a further number to indicate whether it is the first amendment, second etc.

Withdrawal of EDMs

The Member in charge of an EDM (i.e. the first signatory) may withdraw it even if other Members have signed it. Individual names may also be withdrawn.

The following extracts provide examples of EDMs taken from the UK Parliament's online database to January 2017.

Early Day Motion 828: UN INTERNATIONAL MIGRANTS DAY

- Session: 2016-17
- Date tabled: 19.12.2016
- Primary sponsor: McDonald, Stuart
- Sponsors: Durkan, Mark; Bottomley, Peter; Thewliss, Alison; Grady, Patrick; Shannon, Jim

That this House acknowledges the significant contribution that migrants make to all parts of the UK; welcomes those who choose to call the UK their home whether they are joining family, studying, working or seeking refuge or asylum; remembers all those migrants that have lost their lives fleeing persecution; and joins in celebrating UN International Migrants Day, 18 December 2016, as an opportunity to raise awareness of the rights of migrants in this country and the UK's duty to provide a place of protection and safety.

Total number of signatures: 19

Early Day Motion 396: CONCENTRIX

- Session: 2016-17
- Date tabled: 05.09.2016
- Primary sponsor: Law, Chris
- Sponsors: Mullin, Roger; Wishart, Pete; McCaig, Callum; Day, Martyn; Monaghan, Paul

That this House condemns the treatment of UK citizens by Concentrix, a multi-billion pound American business services company contracted by HM Revenue and Customs to investigate alleged benefit fraud, paid on a results basis when it cuts the tax credit bill, profiting from stopping payments to those most in need; notes that thousands of people on low incomes, including many residents in Dundee West constituency, have been unfairly hounded by Concentrix and accused of cheating the benefits system by being wrongly accused of having a partner living with them and contributing to household income, and have had their tax credits suddenly cut off without warning causing an immense amount of stress and hardship and pushing many families into poverty; further notes that to reverse the sanctions families are required to gather an extensive amount of paperwork which can be difficult and can take a long time to collect leading to extended periods of sanctions; and urges the Government to investigate the conduct of Concentrix before more people experience the appalling consequences of the brutal and disrespectful approach toward the legitimate needs of that company on behalf of the Government.

Total number of signatures: 54

Early Day Motion 1861: EVERTON FOOTBALL CLUB

- Session: 2001-02
- Date tabled: 06.11.2002
- Primary sponsor: Kilfoyle, Peter

That this House congratulates Everton FC on being the first club to enjoy 100 seasons in English football's top division; believes that the unique loyalty of generations of Everton supporters has provided the foundation for this great achievement; calls on the British sports media to recognise this outstanding success; and expects the People's Club to forge ever stronger links with its supporters, to maintain a record in the 21st century consistent with that of the 20th century.

Total number of signatures: 10

NOTE: In sessions 2013–14, 2014–15, and 2015–16 the total number of EDMs tabled were 1,336, 919, and 1,474 respectively.

(f) Westminster Hall

Following a report made by the Select Committee on the Modernisation of the House of Commons (HC 194 of 1998–99) an experiment was agreed for the 1999–2000 session in which a parallel chamber would be established to be known as, and to take place in, Westminster Hall. The idea behind this initiative, modelled on the Main Committee in the House of Representatives in Canberra, was to allow the House of Commons to deal with business which couldn't be conducted on the floor of the House, because of lack of time, and with business which was not currently taken. Westminster Hall was to be chaired by Deputy Speakers and the layout of the room was to be a wide hemicycle. The business which was to be conducted in Westminster Hall was to differ from the Chamber in that there would not be any divisions. If there were to be a decision made in a sitting in Westminster Hall then it would have to be unanimous. There would be sittings on Tuesday and Wednesday mornings which would deal with private Members' business, and a third sitting on Thursday afternoon which would deal with business agreed through the usual channels (the Whips). The business which could take place in Westminster Hall would include additional opportunities for adjournment debates, debates on the reports of select committees, and new business such as opportunities for regular debates on (a) different regions of the world to augment the annual adjournment debate on foreign affairs, and (b) Green Papers and other consultative documents.

The experiment was a success and became permanent. The House of Commons Procedure Committee, in its report *Business in Westminster Hall* (HC 236 of 2014–15), p. 3, noted that 'sittings have evolved principally into a forum for backbench business. Westminster Hall is widely held to be a success and provides expanded opportunities for backbench MPs and for oversight of the executive.' The Committee made a number of recommendations for minor change to the use of Westminster Hall, including the introduction of one hour debates (complementing the existing 90- and 30-minute debates), use of neutral 'general debate' motions instead of adjournment-style motions, and the allocation of overall responsibility for all business at Westminster Hall sittings to the Chair of Ways and Means. While rejecting some of the Committee's recommendations, these changes were accepted by the Government.

D: Correspondence

(a) Constituents' grievances

Much of the correspondence conducted by MPs is concerned with their role as the persons who attempt to remedy the grievances of their constituents.

R. Rawlings, 'Parliamentary Redress of Grievance' in C. Harlow (ed.),
Public Law and Politics

(1986), p. 120

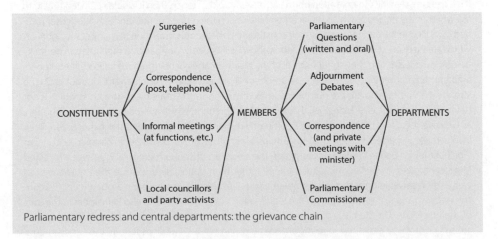

Parliamentary redress and central departments: the grievance chain

NOTE: Rawlings ('Parliamentary Redress of Grievance', pp. 128–9) points out that MPs as intermediaries can act in different ways in chasing grievances on behalf of constituents. They may act as *gatekeepers*, which means that they filter out some kinds of complaint; or they may be *letterboxes*, simply passing on complaints; or they may perform the role of *advocate*, actively taking up the complaint and using whatever means they wish in order to have it resolved in the constituent's favour. An MP can, of course, act in all of these roles, depending upon expertise in the matter, availability of time, sympathy for the complainant, and party political/electoral considerations.

Some studies have attempted to gauge the number of letters which MPs write to public authorities, including Ministers, on their constituents' behalf. Ridley's conservative estimate was that public authorities received more than half a million letters from MPs annually (F. Ridley (1984) 37 *Parliamentary Affairs* 24). Norton projected that between 156,000 and 830,000 were written to Ministers by MPs each year (P. Norton (1982) 35 *Parliamentary Affairs* 60). The advent of email and social media makes MPs more readily contactable than ever. In 2010, Dominic Raab MP complained that the volume of email correspondence—particularly from lobbying websites that provide the facility for citizens to send template emails about a specific issue direct to MPs in large numbers—was creating an 'undue administrative burden'. The increasing accessibility of MPs to a range of methods of communication may have significant implications—both positive and negative—for the way in which they are able to represent their constituents, and engage with their grievances (see discussion in Power, *Global Parliamentary Report: The Changing Nature of Parliamentary Representation* (2012), pp. 55–6).

A. Page, 'MPs and the Redress of Grievances'

[1985] *Public Law* 1, 6–9

That MPs through their intervention do succeed in getting decisions changed there is no doubt. The impression, however, is that this is a relatively infrequent outcome: ' … most letters do not result in a changed decision or new course of action being pursued.' Moreover, even where a decision is changed, it is by no means clear that the same result could not have been achieved without the intervention of the MP. Indeed, the strict tradition is that the Member's letter does not call forth a different decision from that which would be given to any other analogous case, unless very rarely it induces a Minister to initiate a change in policy.

The only advantage of an MP's intervention which can be pointed to is that because MPs' letters are normally considered at a higher level within departments, the chances of an inappropriate routine response being made to a case are reduced.

Comment

If it is the case that MPs' intervention normally makes little difference, then it would seem legitimate to ask whether the emphasis which is placed on MPs' role in the redress of grievances is altogether justified or indeed in the best interests of their constituents. Their status in relation to many of the agencies which are the subject of complaint is uncertain, how well or badly they perform their role can normally be only guessed at, and they suffer from all of the disadvantages of being 'unspecialised, ill-equipped, amateurish and over-worked.' In reply, a number of arguments can be put forward. Undoubtedly the strongest is that, in handling the number of cases which they do, MPs are meeting a need which is not being met by anyone else. Moreover, they are doing something which is expected of them, although, as we have seen, MPs themselves have been partly responsible for generating this expectation. Their involvement in personal cases, therefore, helps MPs to keep their constituents satisfied, a concern which although understandable does create the risk of an unspoken conspiracy between MPs and Ministers to keep aggrieved individuals happy rather than genuinely to pursue their grievances, as well as themselves informed of local problems and difficulties. It has also been argued that MPs' constituency work is an important part of the legitimation not only of MPs but also Parliament in the eyes of the electorate. On the basis of these arguments, the only question which arises is whether MPs are sufficiently well-equipped in terms of secretarial and research facilities to fulfil their constituents' expectations of them. Accepting that they are not, additional assistance might conceivably increase their effectiveness in the redress of grievances. It is at this point that one comes back to the fact that the PCA was intended to help MPs to carry out more effectively their role in the protection of the individual against government. However, MPs are supposed to regard the PCA as of only limited value and as the least effective of the available means of pursuing their constituents' grievances. This is no doubt partly attributable to the restrictions on his jurisdiction, but MPs' views are less than disinterested. Thus, a condition of the acceptance of the PCA by MPs was the insertion of the 'MP filter' to allay their fears that the PCA might come to supplant their own role in the redress of grievances, and the fact that MPs continue to oppose removal of the filter suggests that they remain extremely jealous of their own perceived primacy in the redress of grievances. MPs' welfare role, however, is not without its costs. It represents a substantial burden for MPs themselves and for the administration. In the view of the Fulton Committee, Parliament should 'take fully into account the cumulative cost (not only in time but in the quality of the administration) that the raising of minutiae imposes … ' Whether MPs' insistence on their primacy in the redress of grievances is in the best interests of aggrieved individuals is also questionable. Certainly in his most recent Annual Report, the PCA questions whether it always is:

> I have often employed the familiar arguments in defence of our system, chief of which is that every Member of Parliament is an ombudsman for his constituents and that the body of Members makes a natural and valuable filter for discriminating between simple and complex cases, the worthy and the unworthy. But five years' experience has led me to doubt the validity of these arguments, at any rate in opposition to some modification of our arrangements. At present the Member may, and often does, ask the Minister for the appropriate Department to let him have, in the familiar phrase, 'an answer which I can send to my constituent' about his grievance. But on receipt of that reply, the Member has neither the time, nor the resources, nor the powers to verify by examination of departmental papers or witnesses the explanations offered, which must of necessity be composed on the basis of facts and opinions advanced by those against whom the complaint is laid. When Members do send me their files, it sometimes happens that the Minister's letter of response is the starting point of an investigation which shows that there is more to the case than the letter might be thought to suggest. [HC 322, 1983–84, para. 7.]

The PCA went on to recommend that an individual who had first asked his MP to take up his case but who was dissatisfied with the ultimate response should have the right to invite the PCA to examine the progress made. Whether this recommendation will be acted upon remains to be seen. If MPs, rather than the Government, were to oppose its implementation, their motives would be open to question, for the point which emerges from this survey is not that MPs should not act on behalf of their constituents, but that what they do should be kept firmly in perspective, and inflated claims, such as 'the primary responsibility for defending the citizen against the executive rests with the Member of Parliament,' should not be allowed to stifle the development of other forms of redress. As Mitchell observed:

> The problem of finding a place in the sun for the backbench MP is essentially different from the problem of finding effective means of redress for the individual who has suffered injustice.

NOTE: See Chapter 12 on Ombudsmen at p. 609.

■ QUESTIONS

1. Is there competition between the Ombudsman and MPs in remedying citizens' grievances? Should they not work together? See Rawlings, 'Parliamentary Redress of Grievance' at pp. 137–41, for a proposal which seeks to use the casework of MPs as a means of external oversight and, therefore, adding to the House of Commons function of scrutiny and influence.
2. Is writing a letter to a Minister more effective than asking a PQ or seeking an adjournment debate, or does an MP have resort to these parliamentary procedures if a letter does not satisfactorily resolve the situation?

(b) Parliamentary Questions for Written Answer

House of Commons, *Sessional Returns*
2013–2014, 2014–15, and 2015–16, p. 5, p. 6, and p. 5 respectively.

Questions appearing on the Order Paper calculated by the Journal Office

	2013–14	2014–15	2015–16
Appearing on the Order Paper for written answer on a named day	13,010	11,638	13,283
for ordinary written answer	30,227	18,548	22,673
for oral answer	5,037	4,240	4,742
Number reached for answer in the House	3,822	3,044	3,603
Total number of Questions	**48,274**	**34,426**	**40,698**

NOTE: The General Election in May 2015 meant that the 2014–15 session was shorter than average at ten months, as compared with 12 months for the two other sessions above.

Questions for Written Answer are used mainly to seek information and are usually more specific than the 'open' PQ for Oral Answer. Since 12 September 2014, Written Questions and Answers are published in a database on the Parliament website, rather than in *Hansard* (as previously, and which remains the case for historical Written Questions and Answers).

UK Parliament, Written Questions and Answers
http://www.parliament.uk/writtenanswers

5 September 2016

TREASURY

River Mersey: Bridges

Maria Eagle: [43666] To ask Mr Chancellor of the Exchequer, if he will extend the local discount scheme to residents across Merseyside to allow them to travel toll-free across the Mersey Gateway and Silver Jubilee bridges when they open in 2017.

Mr David Gauke: My officials continue to work with the Department for Transport on the financial and contractual implications of any further extension of user discounts. A decision will be made on this in due course.

...

DEFENCE

Ministry of Defence: Living Wage

Frank Field: [43516] To ask the Secretary of State for Defence, how many people working for his Department or its executive agencies on a (a) directly employed, (b) agency or (c) outsourced basis are paid less than the living wage as defined by the Living Wage Foundation; and how many of those people are employed on zero-hours contracts.

Mark Lancaster: The Ministry of Defence (MOD) pays over and above the New National Living Wage across all of our business areas (£7.20 per hour).

In 2015 the Secretary of State for Defence agreed that London-based staff should be paid the London Living Wage rate (£9.40 per hour). This is in line with the rate defined by the Living Wage Foundation. This rate includes basic pay and any applicable allowances. It is regularly reviewed and where an individual's rate falls under this they are paid specific enhancements.

The MOD has not formally signed up to the National Living Wage rate as defined by the Living Wage Foundation (£8.25 per hour). The table below details those directly employed by the Ministry of Defence (MOD) and its agencies who are paid less than this rate.

ANSWERS NATIONAL LIVING WAGE	
MOD (outside London)	1,017
Defence Equipment & Support (outside London)	93
Defence Science & Technology Laboratory	107
United Kingdom Hydrographic Office	55
Defence Electronics and Components Agency	0

Contracted workers' rates of pay, where paid by their parent company or recruitment agency, are not visible to the MOD.

The MOD does not employ individuals on zero-hours contracts.

...

EXITING THE EUROPEAN UNION

Department for Exiting the European Union: Legal Opinion

Diana Johnson: [43742] To ask the Secretary of State for Exiting the European Union, how much his Department has spent to date on legal advice; and how much he estimates will be so spent during 2016-17.

Mr David Jones: The Department has been billed for £12,711 in relation to legal fees since it was established. Detailed work is underway to establish the Department's future budget requirements, including for legal advice.

Department for Exiting the European Union: Recruitment

Jonathan Ashworth: [43634] To ask the Secretary of State for Exiting the European Union, what the recruitment process is for employing an official from another government department in a new role in his Department.

Mr David Jones: The new Department for Exiting the European Union will be made up of staff from various departments across Government, including from the UK's Permanent Representation to the EU. The department has already started drawing together expertise from a wide range of departments where there is specific relevant knowledge. The overall size and scope of the new department, including staffing and budget, are now being considered – the department now has over 180 staff.

NOTES

1. The Freedom of Information Act 2000 provides for a right to recorded information held by public authorities, and is an important alternative route to obtain official records and data. The duty covers confirming, or denying, that the requested information is held by the public authority and, if the requested information is held, communicating it to the applicant. A request for

information may be subject to a fee and can be refused if the cost of providing it is disproportionate. There are time limits within which compliance with a request must be carried out. Public authorities have a duty to advise and assist applicants and to publish publication schemes which outline the information which they publish or intend to publish and which information will be free or subject to a fee. Public authorities must give the basis for their refusal to provide information and this may be challenged by the applicant before the Information Commissioner who, on finding that the public authority has not met its duty, may issue an enforcement notice which requires steps to be taken in order to comply with the statute. There are various types of information which are exempt and may not be provided. Some exemptions are absolute:

- information accessible by other means—s. 21,
- supplied by, or relating to bodies dealing with security—s. 23;
- court records—s. 32;
- Parliamentary privilege—s. 34;
- prejudice to the conduct of public affairs—s. 36;
- personal information—s. 40(1)(2),
- information provided in confidence—s. 41;
- disclosure is prohibited by another statute, Community law obligation, or would be a contempt of court—s. 44.

Other categories of information will be exempt if the public interest in maintaining the exemption outweighs disclosure:

- information intended for future publication—s. 22;
- national security—s. 24;
- defence—s. 26;
- international relations—s. 27;
- relations within the UK—s. 28;
- the economy—s. 29;
- investigations and proceedings conducted by public authorities—s. 30;
- law enforcement—s. 31;
- audit functions—s. 33;
- formulation of government policy—s. 35;
- communications with Her Majesty, etc. and honours—s. 37;
- health and safety—s. 38;
- legal professional privilege—s. 42;
- commercial interests—s. 43.

Notices issued by the Information Commissioner may be appealed to the Upper Tribunal. By s. 53, an accountable officer may issue a certificate which excepts the public authority from compliance with those notices. The accountable officer is the First and Deputy First Minister acting together in relation to a Northern Ireland Assembly department or public authority; the First Minister in relation to National Assembly for Wales department or public authority in Wales or, for any other public authority, a Cabinet Minister or Attorney General or Advocate General for Scotland or Northern Ireland. The scope of the s. 53 'veto' was significantly, and controversially, reduced by the decision of the Supreme Court in *R (Evans)* v *Attorney General* [2015] UKSC 21—on the interpretation of the majority, the veto cannot reasonably be used simply where the accountable person takes a different view of the requirements of the public interest from that reached by the Upper Tribunal (see Chapter 3, Section 5 at pp. 137–40). An Independent Commission began a review of the operation of the Freedom of Information Act in July 2015, issuing its final report in March 2016. The Commission concluded that the Act was 'generally working well', and was 'one of a number of measures that have helped to change the culture of the public sector', generating 'enhanced openness and transparency'. It recommended little radical legislative change to the Act, and that new fees for requests should not be introduced; the Government accepted these recommendations.

2. The Ministerial Code (2016) requires, by para 1.2:

> (c) It is of paramount importance that Ministers give accurate and truthful information to Parliament, correcting any inadvertent error at the earliest opportunity. Ministers who knowingly mislead Parliament will be expected to offer their resignation to the Prime Minister;
>
> (d) Ministers should be as open as possible with Parliament and the public, refusing to provide information only when disclosure would not be in the public interest, which should be decided in accordance with the relevant statutes and the Freedom of Information Act 2000.

3. The general principles to be adopted by departments are in the central guidance on drafting answers to Parliamentary Questions which was revised in March 2016.

Handling Correspondence from Members of Parliament, Members of the House of Lords, MEPs and Members of Devolved Administrations: Guidance for Departments
Cabinet Office, 2016

Introduction

1. The Prime Minister and Cabinet colleagues attach great importance to the effective and timely handling of correspondence. This vitally important interface with members of the public, Members of Parliament (MPs) and Peers should be given the highest priority....

Performance Targets

5. All departments should set targets for replying to correspondence from MPs. These targets (which may be different to the targets set for other types of correspondence) will be published in the annual correspondence report coordinated by the Cabinet Office .... Individual departments' targets for routine correspondence from MPs should be a maximum of 20 working days. Departments should consider setting themselves more challenging targets. When calculating the target date for reply, the clock should start the day after (Day 1) the correspondence was received ....

'Treat Official' Correspondence

9. Although this guidance is primarily aimed at handling correspondence from MPs, Peers, MEPs and the devolved administrations, departments should adhere to the principles set out in this guidance when handling correspondence from members of the public ....

10. Treat official correspondence is considered to be letters, faxes or emails replied to by officials, normally from members of the public ....

Substantive Replies

12. The right of MPs to take up constituents' cases and other issues directly with Government is an important part of the democratic process and underlines the accountability of Ministers to Parliament. It is essential that MPs receive carefully considered and prompt responses to their enquiries, addressing constituents' concerns. Every effort should be made to provide an MP with a substantive reply within the deadline.

13. A 'substantive reply' is where the response answers all or most of the points or questions raised in any correspondence.

14. Departments must ensure that:
   (i)   all replies to letters from MPs are of the highest quality - accurate, clear and helpful;
   (ii) every effort is made to reply promptly and in line with departments' own published standards for answering ministerial correspondence.

Campaign Letters

34. MPs may write to departments as part of a larger policy campaign. All types of correspondence from MPs should be treated equally and any response should be sent within departmental targets. Departments may wish to consider the use of a formulated standard reply when responding to similar or identical campaign letters on a particular subject. Departments should consider setting a threshold level for the drafting of a standard reply (for example 50 letters received on the same subject). MPs should be aware that they may not receive an individual tailored response to every piece of identical campaign correspondence ....

Email Correspondence

38. Some MPs prefer to correspond by e-mail. Departments should ensure systems are in place for those MPs who wish to do so. E-mails should be treated and monitored in the same way and subject to the same response targets as formal written correspondence. Replies should either be in the form of an e-mail or letter. Departments should agree to any requests from MPs to correspond solely via electronic mail.

39. Departments may wish to consider offering the public the ability to submit issues via an online web form on their Gov.uk website as alternative to e-mailing or sending in 'treat official' correspondence. Submissions via online forms should be handled in the same manner as all other treat official correspondence ....

Freedom of Information (Access to Information)

51. **All requests for information under the FOI Act including letters from MPs and Peers should be handled in accordance with the requirements of the Act.** Guidance for Departments on the handling of FOI requests is available separately at www.justice.gov.uk/guidance/guidancefoi.htm. Requests for environmental information should be treated in accordance with requirements of the Environmental Information Regulations (EIR) 2004, guidance on the handling of EIR requests can be obtained at www.defra.gov.uk/corporate/opengov/eir/index.htm.

52. Departments should ensure that they adhere to guidance produced by the Information Commissioner on dealing with requests for MPs' correspondence 12 relating to constituents. Guidance can be accessed at http://www.ico.gov.uk/upload/documents/library/freedom_of_information/detailed_specialist_guides/guidance_on_dealing_with_requests_for_mps_6_august_version1.pdf

■ QUESTION

How real is the commitment to openness given the rules and practice on answering PQs? Will the Freedom of Information Act and its exceptions, improve matters? How important is formal monitoring of the performance of Government departments?

NOTE: The Commons Procedure Committee monitors the response of departments to written PQs. In their report (HC 1095 of 2012–13) they outlined the trial exercise which had been conducted in monitoring unsatisfactory and late answers to written PQs. They followed up answers which MPs had referred to them in which the relevant department: failed to provide the information requested; the question had been misinterpreted; inadequate information had been provided in response to questions, particularly when answers referred to websites; and inappropriate content was given in answers—as well as late answers. The response to the committee's follow-up has either produced a more satisfactory answer or an explanation as to why it was not possible to provide one. In relation to late answers they obtained responses and apologies where they had been unreasonably delayed. The committee considered the trial a success and will now permanently accept and, where appropriate, pursue MPs' complaints about unsatisfactory and late responses to written PQs to try to maintain general improvement in government performance. Statistics on the timeliness of responses were produced by the Committee, which were shared with the Leader of the House, and letters written to ministers whose departments had a poor record. In relation to the worst performer, the Department for Education, a formal session was held with a junior minister and a senior official. This was not satisfactory so the Committee invited the Secretary of State and the Permanent Secretary to a follow-up formal session. The invitation prompted the release of an action plan which was discussed at the session.

In the most recent monitoring report covering session 2015–16 (HC 191 of 2016–17), the Procedure Committee noted it had received 21 complaints about the quality or timeliness of answers, ten of which were sufficiently serious to investigate. They included (para. 5):

- Not answering all or part of the question asked: one response failed to provide a direct response to the question asked. The Minister responsible later issued a correction, updating the answer to include the information requested. Responses to a series of questions asked concerning a particular policy area were found to be incomplete: the Department undertook a review of the responses and provided further information.
- Referring a Member to data on a website: one response referred a Member to a website where the information sought was said to be available: in fact the information was not available. The Department conceded the point and undertook to provide the information to the Member.
- Providing vague or imprecise details of meetings held: a series of questions drafted in order to elicit specific information about meetings between two Government departments received identical and non-specific answers. The Department concerned agreed to provide more specific information about the meetings.
- Late answers: on several occasions the Chair was asked to write to a Department to secure answers to questions which were weeks overdue.

The Committee also identified the worst-performing departments in terms of timeliness of response: the Home Office, the Department of Culture, Media and Sport and the (now) Department of Business, Energy and Industrial Strategy. The Committee expects a commitment from the new ministerial teams in these departments 'to a marked increase in performance in the timely answering of questions' (para. 20).

E: Reviewing rebalancing reforms

The House of Commons has been undergoing a series of reforms since 2005, designed to enhance the power of Parliament in holding the Government to account and to improve the opportunities for backbenchers to contribute to the work of the House. The House's own review of the impact of two sets of reforms will now be considered: the Wright committee report and the role of Parliament in public appointments.

(a) Wright committee report

In the aftermath of the scandal over MPs' expenses, a Select Committee on Reform of the House of Commons was established, chaired by Dr Tony Wright MP, who was chair of the Public Administration Committee. The report *Rebuilding the House* (HC 1117 of 2008–09) outlined the principles which guided their work:

(a) We should seek to enhance the House of Commons' control over its own agenda, timetable and procedures, in consultation with Government and Opposition, whilst doing nothing to reduce or compromise such powers where they already exist;

(b) We should seek to enhance the collective power of the Chamber as a whole, and to promote non-adversarial ways of working, without impeding the ability of the parties to debate key issues of their choosing; and to give individual Members greater opportunities;

(c) We should seek to enhance the transparency of the House's decision making to Members and to the public, and to increase the ability of the public to influence and understand parliamentary proceedings;

(d) We should recognise that the Government is entitled to a guarantee of having its own business, and in particular Ministerial legislation, considered at a time of its own choosing, and concluded by a set date;

(e) We should recognise that time in the Chamber, Westminster Hall and committees is necessarily limited, and therefore should work broadly within the existing framework of sitting days and sitting hours;

(f) Changes should be devised with sensitivity to real-world political constraints, and in a way which maximises the likelihood of achieving majority support in the House.

Their recommendations dealt with select committees, business in the House, and greater involvement of the public through petitions. In relation to select committees, their proposals about electing chairs and members, rather than having them selected by the party whips, and establishing them quickly after the beginning of a new Parliament were accepted and implemented. The major innovations in their proposals on the conduct of business in the House were for a House Business Committee and a Backbench Business Committee. The latter would schedule a specified amount of backbench business. Standing Orders were amended and, under SO 14(3A), 35 days were allocated in each session to backbench business in the House and Westminster Hall with at least 27 days to be in the House. Topical debates would be decided by this new Committee and it would also schedule business in Westminster Hall on Thursdays. The proposals for a House Business Committee sought to bring together the key ideas that the House should control its time and that the Government should be entitled to put forward legislation at a time of its choosing and for it to be concluded by a set date. The House Business Committee would have Government and Opposition representatives, as well as those of the Backbench Business Committee, and would be chaired by the Chair of Ways and Means, the Deputy Speaker. Together they would draw up a draft agenda for the next week's business which would then be put before the House for its agreement. This proposal was not implemented: the 2010 Coalition Agreement contained a pledge that the issue would be considered in the third year of the Parliament, the outcome is discussed as follows.

The proposals to extend public involvement were for enhanced participation—for a measure of direct democracy to 'nourish' representative democracy so that the public might be able to initiate debates and other proceedings in the House. The committee recommended that those involved in developing an e-petitions scheme should bring proposals forward urgently; that in the next Parliament consideration should be given as to how the public might (a) be able to influence draft legislation and (b) initiate proceedings in Parliament by applying at the national level the procedures applied to local authorities for 'petitions requiring debate', drawing on local and international experience, including the appropriate thresholds to be applied. The typical threshold for local authorities is that 5 per cent of the local authority population should have signed the petition to trigger a debate.

The Commons Procedure Committee reported on the operation of the Backbench Business Committee (HC 168 of 2012–13). The committee, as did others, regarded the innovation as a success and made only minor recommendations for change, including seeking a reassurance that an allocation of 35 days for Backbench business be increased pro rata if a session exceeded a calendar year. The Government Response (HC 978 of 2012–13) accepted some points and not others: in particular, it rejected as inflexible the proposal about pro rata increases of 35 days, reasoning that it was not appropriate to single out only this type of business for that approach to the allocation of time.

The Political and Constitutional Reform Committee produced a report considering the impact of the Wright reforms (HC 82 of 2013–14). The focus here will be on their consideration of a House Business Committee and e-petitions. The Committee was in favour of a House Business Committee but recognized that there was a range of opinion including that of the Leader of the House who had decided there was insufficient consensus and so was not going to bring forward proposals. The Committee proposed how to take forward their preferred model for a House Business Committee, which they thought met the tests for effectiveness outlined in evidence by the Leader of the House.

Political and Constitutional Reform Committee, *Revisiting Rebuilding the House: the impact of the Wright reforms*
HC 82 of 2013–14, paras 105, 120–1, 124, and 132

D. A Consultative House Business Committee

Formal select committee meeting in private, with published summary Minutes: membership established by House with representatives of all sides of House and not dominated by Whips, but separate from Backbench Business Committee; chaired by the Chairman of Ways and Means; purely consultative—Leader determines agenda actually announced to House; some House secretariat and access to forward plans to enable Committee to give timely consideration to Government's proposals.

PROS

- Could enhance House's control (Principle 1 (a)) and collective power (Principle 1(b)), possibly over Government business
- Would improve transparency modestly (Principle 1 (c))
- Recognizes real world constraints (Principle 1 (f) and Principle 1 (d)) because consultative only. Would provide opportunity for appropriate backbench influence
- Properly constituted and with the right remit, would avoid risk of undermining Backbench Business Committee

CONS

- Transparency limited by private nature of proceedings
- Possible risk of politicisation of role of Chairman of Ways and Means

....

105. *We believe that there must be a continuing conversation about the House Business Committee which recognises that Parliament and Government each have a strong interest in effective scrutiny. To initiate this process of engagement, we will seek time from the Backbench Business Committee for a debate in the autumn on the response to our report, with a particular emphasis on the House Business Committee. Recognising that there will inevitably be questions raised about how the House Business Committee would work, we see no reason why the Leader should not invite the chairs of backbench party committees to join a business managers' meeting on an informal trial basis. This would enable any issues to be addressed, so that the proposed new Standing Order for the establishment of the Committee can be refined if necessary.*

The position in regard to public engagement was focused on e-petitions, where things had developed quickly, due to the Government's separate initiative to create an e-petitions website. This had some notable successes, including a half-day debate on 17 October 2011 to press the Government on its commitment to the disclosure of all papers associated with the Hillsborough football disaster in 1989 to the independent panel overseeing the release of official documents, after an e-petition was supported by 156,218 signatories (HC Deb 17 October 2011, Vol. 533, col. 662–724). The Constitutional and Political Reform Committee report nevertheless identified potential for reform.

120. Most of the Committee's proposals on petitions were however overtaken by the unexpected Coalition Agreement commitment to a 100,000 signature threshold for possible debate following an e-petition, and the establishment of a website in the summer of 2011. Our evidence made clear that many people have made use of the opportunity to sign e-petitions. As Ms Engel put it, "The public now … has an indirect power to influence Parliamentary time with the introduction of e-petitions." Catherine Bochel of the University of Lincoln told us that, to judge from the number of e-petitions submitted, "it is clearly a popular development with the public." Once an e-petition reaches 100,000 signatures, if a Member makes representations in its favour to the Backbench Business Committee, up to three hours in Westminster Hall might be allocated to it, or it might even be debated on the floor of the House on a votable motion, although there is no guarantee of either. The Committee only considers an e-petition for a debate if an MP comes to make a case for the subject to be debated.

121. However, a number of witnesses told us that, despite its apparent popularity, experience of the e-petitions system could increase—and perhaps already had increased—public disillusionment with the House. Ms Engel, Chair of the Backbench Business Committee, acknowledged that the number of people who have signed e-petitions is "absolutely phenomenal." But she did not think that this translated into positive, active engagement with Parliament. Ms Engel said that the House had raised expectations that if an e-petition reached 100,000 signatures, not only would there be a debate, but there would be a vote and a change in the law—the instant that the 100,000th signature goes on to the e-petition. She said: "That obviously is not true and is not something that we can deliver, but that is what the public perception is. I think that has been quite damaging".

Other problems include that those without access to computers are excluded …

124. There is also a constitutional question mark over the current practice. Ms Bochel criticised the e-petitions system as 'hybrid' and a source of confusion about the roles of Government and Parliament: "petitions are submitted to Government but are then passed to the Backbench Business Committee once they reach the 100,000 signature threshold, because the system does not belong to the House of Commons." She called for the ownership of the system to be transferred to the House.

...

132. *We believe that there must be a clear separation between petitions intended to prompt action by Government and petitions aimed at Parliament. The Parliamentary petitions system must in future belong unequivocally to Parliament. This means that all e-petitions for consideration by Parliament must be hosted on the Parliamentary website. We also believe that numbers thresholds should not be used to determine whether a petition should be debated.*

NOTES

1. The Government response to these particular points was made in HC 910 of 2013–14. On the House Business Committee, the response was that 'On balance, the proposal put forward by the Committee does not appear to be one upon which a consensus can be built within the House' (para. 61). The Government's objections include the risk of politicizing the neutral Chairman of Ways and Means, who was proposed to chair the House Business Committee, and that it is also not appropriate for a Committee which is concerned with Government business to be chaired by a member of the Opposition, even one serving in a politically neutral post. Much of the information that governs the scheduling of business is politically sensitive (para. 63) and the Committee's proposals did not include provision for accommodating the interests of Backbench Business Committee and for taking account of the progress of business in the House of Lords, both essential elements of current arrangements (para. 65). The Government elected following the 2015 general election confirmed that consensus was still not possible, and, as such, it would not bring forward proposals to establish a House Business Committee (HC Deb 9 July 2015, Vol. 598, col. 448).

2. On e-petitions the Government accepted the recommendation for a clearer system, in which it collaborated with the Commons. The Procedure Committee made proposals for the creation of a new House of Commons Petitions Committee to take responsibility for the system (HC 235 of 2014–15); the new committee was introduced in 2015. The table below indicates the subjects debated following petitions in the first year of the committee's operation (via Petitions Committee, *Your Petitions: A Year of Action*, July 2015–July 2016):

PETITIONS WHICH WERE SCHEDULED FOR DEBATE BY THE PETITIONS COMMITTEE IN ITS FIRST YEAR:	
14/09/2015	To debate a vote of no confidence in Health Secretary the Right Hon Jeremy Hunt (Contracts and conditions in the NHS)
12/10/2015	Make the production, sale and use of cannabis legal
19/10/2015	Stop allowing immigrants into the UK
26/10/2015	Make an allowance for up to 2 weeks term time leave from school for holiday
30/11/2015	Introduce a tax on sugary drinks in the UK to improve our children's health
07/12/2015	Don't kill our bees! Immediately halt the use of Neonicotinoids on crops
11/01/2016	Keep the NHS Bursary
18/01/2016	Block Donald J Trump from UK entry; Don't ban Trump from the United Kingdom
25/01/2016	Scrap plans forcing self employed & small business to do 4 tax returns yearly
01/02/2016	Make fair transitional state pension arrangements for 1950s women
07/03/2016	Scrap the £35k threshold for non-EU citizens settling in the UK
21/03/2016	Jeremy Hunt to resume meaningful contract negotiations with the BMA
18/04/2016	Fund more research into brain tumours, the biggest cancer killer of under-40s
25/04/2016	Give the Meningitis B vaccine to ALL children, not just newborn babies
09/05/2016	Stop Cameron spending British taxpayers' money on Pro-EU Referendum leaflets
06/06/2016	Restrict the use of fireworks to reduce stress and fear in animals and pets
13/06/2016	Stop spending a fixed 0.7 per cent slice of our national wealth on Foreign Aid
04/07/2016	Include expressive arts subjects in the Ebacc
11/07/2016	No more school penalty fines and bring back the 10 day authorised absence
18/07/2016	Stop retrospective changes to the student loans agreement

The Petitions Committee has responsibility for ensuring that registered petitions meet the appropriate standards—in the first year of the committee's operation, petitions were most commonly rejected for duplicating matters covered in existing petitions, requesting something not within the responsibility of the UK Government or Parliament, or for being unclear. The Petitions Committee also has the power to conduct its own investigations into matters raised by a petition where they do not consider the issues to have been adequately addressed, as with, for example, a special inquiry conducted into *Funding for Research for Brain Tumours* (HC 554 of 2015–16), which led to the Government committing to convene a working group of experts to address the issue.

3. The Backbench Business Committee, which was established following the original recommendations by the Wright Committee, issued a report on its work during the 2010–15 Parliament (HC 1106 of 2014–15). It concluded 'the Backbench Business Committee has made a positive difference to the work of the House by providing new opportunities for self-expression by backbenchers and making Parliament more relevant to the outside world'. It noted that there had been changes in Government policy seemingly as a result of backbench debates (including, in 2011, in relation to compensation for victims of contaminated blood and blood products, funding of the BBC World Service, and freezing of fuel duty), and that '[a]lthough there have been numerous occasions when both the government and opposition business managers would have preferred us not to schedule certain debates, we have maintained good working relationships with the front benches. The Government has provided us with sufficient time in the Chamber for backbench debate, giving us as much advance notice of dates as they realistically can.' The Committee also supported the creation of the (now established) Petitions Committee, noting that it would have 'a separate but complementary role to our own'.

(b) Public appointments

As part of its constitutional reform programme the Labour government, under Prime Minister Gordon Brown, announced proposals in 2007 for enhancing the role Parliament could play in public appointments.

The Governance of Britain

Cm 7170, para. 76

[The Government] proposes that the Government nominee for key positions such as those listed below should be subject to a pre-appointment hearing with the relevant select committee. The hearing would be non-binding, but in the light of the report from the committee, Ministers would decide whether to proceed. The hearings would cover issues such as the candidate's suitability for the role, his or her key priorities, and the process used in selection.

The Liaison Committee reported in September 2011 on three years' experience of pre-appointment hearings of preferred candidates for public appointments and made some proposals (HC 1230 of 2010–12). The Government response was nine months later in June 2012, which was seven months after the Government's own deadline for responses to select committee reports. The Liaison Committee were disappointed by this response. They noted that the response had some positive elements but 'overall, the response fails to engage with our recommendations, and is somewhat dismissive in tone, even where the Government declares itself in agreement with us'. In the extracts which follow the Liaison Committee comments on that disappointing response to their proposals published in September 2012 and then the Government's response to that report received and published without comment by the Liaison Committee in January 2013.

Liaison Committee, *Select Committees and Public appointments: the Government's response*

HC 394 of 2012–13, paras 8, 11, 14–16, 18

What are pre-appointment hearings for?

8. While the Government agrees with the Committee that the pre-appointment hearing system requires a clearer statement of purpose, it fails to endorse unequivocally the four clear statements of purpose we set out in our report:

- scrutiny of the quality of ministerial decision-making, which is a proper part of ministerial accountability;
- providing public reassurance (in addition to the private processes of the Office of the Commissioner for Public Appointments) that those appointed to key public offices are selected on merit;
- enhancing the appointee's legitimacy in undertaking their function;
- providing public evidence of the independence of mind of the candidate.

The Government agrees that greater clarity over the role and purpose of pre-appointment hearings should be at the centre of new guidance for departments on pre-appointment hearings, but it is difficult to see where these statements are made explicit in the guidance documents annexed to the Government response.

…

Power of veto

11. The Government response rejects the three category approach we proposed for pre-appointment hearings. It rejects our proposal for a top tier of constitutional posts over which the House should have formal control of appointment and dismissal, except for the three where this is already firmly established: the Comptroller and Auditor General, the Parliamentary and Health Services Ombudsman (both posts which are Officers of the House) and the Chair of the Office for Budget Responsibility (for which the veto is established in statute). The Government does not, for instance, include the post of Chair of the UK Statistics Authority, which is surprising given that the Government has agreed that that appointment should be subject to a vote in the House. The Government merely asserts it would not be appropriate for Parliament to be an equal partner in appointment decisions.

The guidance on pre-appointment hearings annexed to the Government response emphasises that Committee recommendations are "non-binding" on Ministers. It says that Ministers should give "careful consideration" to Committee reports and reasons but notes the "considerable legal constraints" as to what the Minister can take into account in reaching a final decision. These constraints are not elaborated upon. We find it odd that these constraints were not raised at an earlier stage in our dialogue with Government …

…

Political appointments

14. The response entirely ignores our recommendation that political appointments, such as the UK's European Commissioner, or ambassadors or High Commissioners appointed from outside the career diplomatic service, should be subject to pre-appointment scrutiny by an appropriate select committee. The fact that these very important appointments have not been subject to normal appointment processes strengthens the case for parliamentary scrutiny.

Guidance on process

15. The response merely "notes" our draft guidance "with thanks". It says that the Government has been reviewing its guidance and wishes to adopt a "more principles-based approach". It encloses new guidance which the Cabinet Office appears to have sent out to Government Departments in June 2012 on public appointments, itself enclosing two appendices: the new OCPA Code of Practice for Ministerial Appointments to Public Bodies and new Cabinet Office guidance on pre-appointment scrutiny by select committees. It states that this last draws on our draft, but the connection is slight. We have two principal objections to this guidance. It appears to have been issued to Departments without consulting us and without much reference to our proposed draft guidance. The response states that the guidance is still to be "agreed between Government and Parliament" but the Government does not appear to be seeking our agreement to it. Moreover, there are a number of inconsistencies in the three documents which have the potential to cause confusion.

16. It worries us the Government appears to have disengaged from the process in which the Liaison Committee and the Cabinet Office had been engaged over recent years of devising a joint way forward on public appointments, specifically in respect of consolidated guidance, clarity over the lists of posts and the scope of pre-appointment hearings.

...

Conclusion

18. The Government's response to our report on Select Committees and Public Appointments misjudges the mood of this Committee and—we believe—the mood of the House and the expectations of the public. It is unacceptable that it is seven months late. It is inexcusable, given the time taken, that it does not take us further forward in strengthening the accountability of ministerial appointments. We will be pursuing this matter with Ministers and we draw our concern to the attention of the House.

Liaison Committee, *Select Committee effectiveness, resources and powers: responses to the Committee's second report*
HC 912 of 2012–13, pp. 1–4

Purpose of pre-appointment hearings

... This Government is firmly committed to ensuring the proper scrutiny exists on public appointments and we believe the key to this is to ensure transparency and accountability.

The Government's original response agreed with the objectives set out by the Liaison Committee and we believe we have ensured that their spirit is incorporated within the Government's guidance.

... Power of veto

Pre-appointment scrutiny by Select Committees has an invaluable role in the appointment process for those public appointments it is relevant for. The Government's position remains that we cannot agree to Select Committees having an effective veto on a wider range of positions. As we stated in the original Government response, these are Ministerial appointments and the direct line of accountability and responsibility between the appointee and the Minister must be preserved.

The Government does agree that in exceptional circumstances, it is appropriate for Parliament to exercise a formal control over some appointments. These were listed as being the Chair of the Office for Budget Responsibility and the Comptroller and Auditor General. We added the Parliamentary and Health Ombudsman. The Liaison Committee also recommended inclusion of the UK Statistics Authority. We do not agree with this recommendation as the UK Statistics Authority does not have a remit associated with the functions of Parliament in the same way as, for example, the Parliamentary and Health Ombudsman .... The Liaison Committee report also questions the references in the Government's guidance on how Ministers should take Select Committee considerations into account when making their final appointment decisions. The guidance separates out statutory and non-statutory appointments, as there may be examples of statutory appointments where the recruitment process is set out clearly in legislation. What Ministers can therefore take into account when appointing an individual in these circumstances may be more constrained than in other recruitments. We would expect this to be relevant in only a very small number of cases. An example of where this may be the case is in the appointment of the Chair of the Judicial Appointments Commission. The Constitutional Reform Act 2005 is clear that the Chair is appointed by Her Majesty on the recommendation of the Lord Chancellor, following the recommendations of a selection panel that involves obtaining the agreement of the Lord Chief Justice. Schedule 12 to the Act goes as far as to specify the make up of the selection panel for the selection of the Chair. Legislation for other appointments, however, is less prescriptive.

In the majority of cases, as stated in the guidance, we would expect that the select committee will agree with the appointment of the Government's preferred candidate where an open and transparent process has been followed, the candidate has been selected on merit, and the relevant committee has been engaged.

...

Political appointments

The Liaison Committee's latest report notes that the Government response did not cover political appointments. As you have rightly pointed out, political appointments are not public appointments and are not covered by OCPA regulation. These appointments would be to a role representing a Minister, rather than bringing the element of independence to a role that is a characteristic of a public appointment.

The appointments referenced in the Liaison Committee's report include ambassadorial and high commissioner appointments where these are outside of the diplomatic service. These appointments are civil service appointments and therefore would not be appropriate for inclusion in our guidance on public appointments.

In addition, the report references the UK's European Commissioner. This is a unique international appointment — more akin to a ministerial appointment — and would also not be suitable for inclusion in our guidance on domestic UK public appointments.

Guidance on process

We welcomed the work done by the Committee in producing a version of guidance, but we have been clear to match the Government's guidance with the light-touch, principles based change is to ensure that departments are focused on achieving the right outcome from the recruitment, and are not just following a standard process. However, I am happy for my officials to discuss with yours the potential for addressing some of your Committee's concerns in the Government's guidance which they will do over the next few weeks. Cabinet Office officials will be working closely with departments to ensure this guidance is implemented effectively.

The Government is working toward the same objectives as the Liaison Committee in ensuring that Select Committees are able to rightly scrutinise major public appointments and to hold Ministers to account for their decisions. We very much welcome the work that the Liaison Committee have done on this and I hope that this further explanation of the Government's position is helpful.

NOTES

1. There remain two separate sources of guidance concerning parliamentary hearings relating to public appointments. The parliamentary and the Government guidance differ particularly in the emphasis placed on the effect of a select committee's decision. The Cabinet Office guidance states:

> 6. It is for Ministers to decide whether or not to accept a committee's recommendations relating to an appointment. Ministers must consider any relevant observations made by the committee before deciding whether to go ahead with the appointment (subject to the provisions regarding any statutory appointment outlined in paragraph 18 below). If a committee recommendation in relation to an appointment is not accepted, the Minister responsible should respond to the Committee explaining the reason(s) why....
> 17. In relation to the findings of the Committee, Ministers should weigh the views of the committee carefully against the evidence from the appointments procedure to reach a final view to ensure that the decision is made fairly and taking all relevant considerations into account.

The House of Commons Liaison Committee guidance, in contrast, states:

> 5. While committee observations on a candidate's suitability are, in most cases, not binding on Ministers, it is expected that the appointing Minister will consider any relevant observations made by a committee before deciding whether to proceed with an appointment....
> 25. The appointing Minister is expected to ensure that the decision on appointment is made fairly and takes all relevant considerations into account. Such considerations should include the views of the relevant select committee on the suitability of the candidate (particularly if they are negative).

The difference in emphasis may simply be explained by the different—and competing—objectives that Parliament and the Government may be pursuing through subjecting public appointments to parliamentary hearings.

2. Public appointments hearings have become a well-established part of parliamentary select committee activity, and an opportunity to exert influence over Government policy and those who are appointed to develop it. Between July 2007 and July 2016, there were 87 pre-appointment hearings by select committees. Five reports were negative; of those, four appointments were nonetheless made—Dr Maggie Atkinson as Children's Commissioner for England in 2009; Diana Fulbrook as HM Chief Inspector of Probation; Prof Leslie Ebdon as Director for the Office of Fair Access in 2012; and Amanda Spielman as HM Chief Inspector for OFSTED in 2016. One candidate subject to a negative report withdrew—Dominic Dodd for Monitor Chair in 2013. A further candidate withdrew following a parliamentary hearing before a report could be issued—Dame Janet Finch for Chair of UK Statistics Authority in 2011. One neutral report was also issued in this period—by the Joint Committee on Human Rights and the Women and Equalities Committee working together in relation to the appointment of David Isaac as the Chair of the Equality and Human Rights Commission. The appointment was subsequently made.

■ QUESTIONS

1. Will the reforms relating to backbench business encourage a more independent approach or simply contain it within the allocated periods? Does the continued failure to establish a House Business Committee demonstrate the limits of an approach to parliamentary reform which is dependent on the Government for change?

2. Is the offer to the public of a chance to initiate a debate a sufficient degree of participation to improve the public perception of Parliament?

3. Is it preferable for select committees to hold persons in public office to account rather than seeking influence in their appointment? Is the purpose of such hearings, where they occur, undermined by the absence of a parliamentary veto, or is the process of pre-appointment scrutiny designed instead to make the Government consider its candidates very carefully in advance, and to make the prospective appointees to public office aware of their location in a broader network of accountability?

7

Parliament: Law-making

OVERVIEW

In this chapter we first consider the different types of legislative measures, then the methods of control used before, and during, their consideration by Parliament and finally judicial review of delegated legislation.

SECTION 1: LAW-MAKING

There are many varieties of legislation: statutes, delegated legislation, and what may be called quasi-legislation which can encompass administrative rules and guidance. Quasi-legislation can take the form, for example, of circulars from central departments, or codes of practice. The Americans refer to legislative activity carried out by administrative bodies as rule-making, and this includes what the British call delegated and quasi-legislation. It is important to realize that not all legislation will be made by Parliament. Our consideration of law-making will focus, first, on the assorted types of legislative measures and their rationale, and then on the methods for, and issues concerning, control of these legislative measures.

One of the characteristics of legislation is that it is empowering, that is it gives a public body the power to carry out tasks which the legislation also imposes upon the public body.

A: Types of legislative measure

(a) Statute

R. Rose, 'Law as a Resource of Public Policy'
(1986) 39 *Parliamentary Affairs* 297, 302–5

LAWS are a fundamental and unique resource of government. Without Acts of Parliament, force, personal preferences or momentary whim would justify the actions of government. Without laws, citizens would have no protection against arbitrary authority, no entitlements to social benefits, and no obligation to pay taxes. Without laws, civil servants would have no authority to act, or procedures to follow. Without laws, elections could not be held, for there would be no rules about who could vote, how votes should be counted, and who should be elected as MPs. In order to understand government, we must understand the uses of laws.

Until the growth of the twentieth-century welfare state, MPs viewed law as the principal resource of government. The characteristic concern of Parliament was not with public expenditure issues, but with the principles to be embodied in Acts of Parliament that involved questions of civil and political rights such as the franchise …

Once the importance of laws is recognised, the next question to address is: In what ways are laws important? The distinctive feature of law is that it is an expression of authority. It is not coercive in the sense that actions by the police may be coercive. Nor does the law consist of cash incentives to actions, as do the wages paid civil servants.

Statute laws establish parameters within which individuals and organisations may carry out their activities. Since the activities of society are heterogeneous, the parameters of laws are multiple. In order to understand the broad effect of laws, we need to understand the nature of laws as parameters; the extent of discretion that can be exercised within legal parameters; and then, whose activities have bounds set upon them by the statute book.

Parameters: more route maps than tethers. The traditional idea of laws as a set of commands and prohibitions ('Thou shalt … ' or 'Thou shalt not … ') presents a misleading picture of the uses of laws in the contemporary state. While there are some compelling and forbidding laws about crime, public health and safety, nine-tenths of statutes concern ways in which individuals or organisations may proceed of their own volition.

When a law sets parameters upon behaviour in society, it neither commands nor compels. Rules are promulgated which remain constant while the facts of specific circumstances vary. For example, laws governing marriage are hardly affected by characteristics of the partners of the marriage. Nor does the existence of such laws compel everyone to get married. Procedures are laid down which describe the actions that a pair of individuals should take if they want their union to be legally valid. There are few prohibitions, e.g. a minimum age, but these constrain the behaviour of a very, very small proportion of the population.

Most laws about the everyday activities of citizens are virtually unnoticed. For example, laws affecting property rights in a house; the content of foods; the conditions of driving a motor car or being a passenger on public transport, conditions of employment; or laws concerning broadcasting. This is not to say that such laws are unnecessary. Instead of involving the compulsion and prohibition of acts, most laws give guidance about ways to maintain a well ordered society.

Most contemporary laws are best conceived as a route map, laying down conditions by which one may proceed. Their relevance is contingent, taking the form of 'If … then' propositions. For example, 'If you want to drive a car, then you must have a driver's licence, the car must be licensed and insured, and you must drive within the traffic code'. Most laws do not tether behaviour in the sense of confining a person to act within narrowly circumscribed limits.

Scope for discretion. Both jurisprudential and sociological analyses emphasise that even the most carefully stated statute cannot control 100 per cent of behaviour. Violations of the law occur in every society. Yet violations are only a small proportion of total social activity, e.g. fraud arises in only a very small percentage of market transactions, and violent assault or murder in an infinitesimal proportion of social interactions.

The most significant limitation upon law is the existence of 'gaps' that give some latitude for discretion, i.e. choice within the parameters of the statute book. In the real world, the statute book is subject to multiple imperfections—vagueness of language, omissions, and the incapacity to anticipate every possible concatenation of events. In falling short of the perfection of an ideal-type, it is no different from administration, markets, or democracy itself. Discretion can be found in four main areas.

(a) *Judges* inevitably are faced with 'hard' cases, that is, circumstances in which lawyers dispute how the law is to be interpreted and applied to the facts of a particular case. Bell describes judges as acting as interstitial legislators: 'There are situations where the legal audience would recognise that there is no single clear solution to a case and that several possible solutions are at least arguable. At the same time, it must be recognised that, in presenting his decision, the judge has to justify himself within the legal materials, showing how the solution fits within existing legal prescriptions and standards. It is thus somewhat misleading to suggest that the law in such situations 'runs out', as if anything at all could be used to fill the 'gap.'

(b) *Executive lawmaking* occurs through the issuance of a variety of rules and regulations that can be made pursuant to Acts of Parliament; in Britain these measures can conveniently be described as Statutory Instruments. Acts of Parliament establish the parameters within which executive rule-making may be done; these are necessarily more confined than those of the Act itself. Statutory instruments typically affect procedures for putting an Act into effect, or fill out details that may be negotiated with subjects of regulation, or are likely to vary from time to time in relation to changing economic or social conditions. The limited political significance of this form of executive rule-making is shown by the fact that less than one per cent of Statutory Instruments are deemed worthy of careful scrutiny by the parliamentary committee exercising oversight of them. The chief reason is that these regulations are likely to be agreed with affected parties in advance of their promulgation…

(c) *Administrative discretion* is an element in the implementation of a new Act of Parliament, and in the routine operation of many acts. The degree of discretion depends upon the extent to which laws and regulations can prescribe the parameters of action. The extent is variable: pensions officials, postal clerks and airline pilots have much less discretion than public employees who deliver services to citizens in conditions in which the services provided cannot be tightly circumscribed nor their behaviour closely monitored, for example policemen, teachers, doctors and social workers.

Lipsky argues that 'street-level' public employees are not rule-bound bureaucrats but individuals with a significant degree of discretion to decide how to treat individuals seeking their services … While awareness of an element of discretion is an important caution against excessive legalism, it does not justify Lipsky writing as if public policies could be carried out by ignoring or flouting the parameters of the law.

(d) *Adaptive behaviour* can be undertaken by citizens in ways that recognise the parameters of the law, but may not be what was anticipated by lawmakers. Within the parameters of any Act of Parliament citizens are free to behave in many ways. Adaptive behaviour is most familiar in tax avoidance, that is, the alteration of behaviour to lessen the legal liability to taxation. By definition, tax avoidance (e.g. working a limited number of hours a week to avoid national insurance tax, or converting income subject to a high marginal income tax rate into a capital gain subject to a lower rate) is within the law. But it is also action taken to avoid what would otherwise be undesirable consequences.

In a mixed society the role of law is not so much that of telling people what they must and must not do; it is to establish rules and regulations under which individuals and organisations can carry out their everyday affairs in ways that are orderly, predictable and recognised and accepted by all concerned. Only in a totalitarian society could the law claim to be all-powerful. A major contribution of law to public policy in a free society is that it establishes parameters within which individuals and organisations can then be free to pursue what they regard as their own wellbeing and interests. This liberal idea of the limits of laws poses problems for democratic socialists who want certain outcomes, for example, equality of educational opportunity, but do not want to use laws to prohibit private education or compel everyone to have their children educated at state schools.

NOTE: Legislation can be divided into public and private. Rose discussed public statutes, which are normally initiated by the Government but may be introduced by MPs as a Private Member's Bill. Private legislation may confer powers or benefits on particular individuals or bodies, which may be in addition to, or in conflict with, the general law. Such measures will be promoted by the relevant individuals or bodies such as local authorities, universities, or companies. A hybrid bill is one, usually initiated by the Government, which is public in nature but will affect private rights. As, for example, with the Channel Tunnel, where power may be given to a Minister to acquire specified land.

(b) Delegated legislation

Report of the Committee on Ministers' Powers
Cmd 4046, pp. 51–2

Necessity for Delegation

We have already expressed the view that the system of delegated legislation is both legitimate and constitutionally desirable for certain purposes, within certain limits, and under certain safeguards. We proceed to set out briefly—mostly by way of recapitulation—the reasons which have led us to this conclusion:—

(1) Pressure upon Parliamentary time is great. The more procedure and subordinate matters can be withdrawn from detailed Parliamentary discussion, the greater will be the time which Parliament can devote to the consideration of essential principles in legislation.

(2) The subject matter of modern legislation is very often of a technical nature. Apart from the broad principles involved, technical matters are difficult to include in a Bill, since they cannot be effectively discussed in Parliament....

(3) If large and complex schemes of reform are to be given technical shape, it is difficult to work out the administrative machinery in time to insert in the Bill all the provisions required; it is impossible to foresee all the contingencies and local conditions for which provision must eventually be made....

(4) The practice, further, is valuable because it provides for a power of constant adaptation to unknown future conditions without the necessity of amending legislation. Flexibility is essential. The method of delegated legislation permits of the rapid utilisation of experience, and enables the results of consultation with interests affected by the operation of new Acts to be translated into practice....

(5) The practice, again, permits of experiment being made and thus affords an opportunity, otherwise difficult to ensure, of utilising the lessons of experience. The advantage of this in matters, for instance, like town planning, is ... obvious....

(6) In a modern State there are many occasions when there is a sudden need of legislative action. For many such needs delegated legislation is the only convenient or even possible remedy. No doubt, where there is time, on legislative issues of great magnitude, it is right that Parliament itself should either decide what the broad outlines of the legislation shall be, or at least indicate the general scope of the delegated powers which it considers are called for by the occasion.

But emergency and urgency are matters of degree; and the type of need may be of greater or less national importance. It may be not only prudent but vital for Parliament to arm the executive Government in advance with almost plenary power to meet occasions of emergency, which affect the whole nation—as in the extreme case of the Defence of the Realm Acts in the Great War, where the exigency had arisen; or in the less extreme case of the Emergency Powers Act, 1920, where the exigency had not arisen but power was conferred to meet emergencies that might arise in future....

But the measure of the need should be the measure alike of the power and of its limitation. It is of the essence of constitutional Government that the normal control of Parliament should not be suspended either to a greater degree, or for a longer time, than the exigency demands....

NOTE: Delegated legislation may take several forms—regulations, Orders in Council, rules, and orders. Parliament usually makes delegated legislation as statutory instruments, the passage of which is governed by the Statutory Instruments Act 1946. The more important pieces of delegated legislation are Orders in Council. Legislative measures which would have been passed as Acts of the Northern Ireland Assembly and its predecessor were passed as Orders in Council when the devolved institutions were suspended.

(c) Quasi-legislation

There is an overlap between delegated legislation and administrative rules of quasi-legislation, even though the legal forms of these measures differ. A classification of administrative rules based on function was proposed by R. Baldwin and J. Houghton, in 'Circular Arguments: The Status and Legitimacy of Administrative Rules' ([1986] *Public Law* 239, 241–5). They suggested eight categories: (1) Procedural rules; (2) Interpretative guides; (3) Instructions to officials; (4) Prescriptive/evidential rules; (5) Commendatory rules; (6) Voluntary Codes; (7) Rules of practice, management, or operation; (8) Consultative devices and administrative pronouncements. The rules in (1) may be mandatory or directory. The difference between (2) and (3) is that the focus is on the public body, to maintain order and consistency rather than informing the citizen. The Highway Code is an example of (4) prescriptive rules for road users, and non-compliance could lead to a sanction by the criminal law or liability under the civil law. Non-compliance by police officers with codes of practice under the Police and Criminal Evidence Act 1984 could lead to disciplinary action but not legal liability. The regulation of health and safety has a hierarchy with statutory duties at the top and moving to (5) advice about safety. Self-regulation using (6) has often been used to prevent the imposition of governmental regulation. Take-overs and mergers are subject to such a code, as are advertising and consumer standards. An example of (7) would be an extra-statutory concession made by HMRC or indeed its opposite, cancelling a tax advantage (but see substantive legitimate expectations in Chapter 10, Section 2E at p. 547). The final category (8) is described as a safety net in which the pronouncement has a significance beyond an individual case and a prime example would be a consultative statement.

NOTE: See also G. Ganz, *Quasi-Legislation: Some Recent Developments in Secondary Legislation* (1987) and R. Baldwin, *Rules and Government* (1995).

(d) Prerogative

The royal prerogative provides a further source of legislative and executive power. This residual source of government authority derives from the historic powers of the Crown to perform specific functions, including the conduct of foreign affairs, declaration of war, the appointment of Ministers and Privy Councillors, and conferral of peerages and honours. The prerogative can be displaced by statute, and cannot be exercised in a way which frustrates the purpose of an Act of Parliament; see Chapter 5, Section 1D at pp. 191–5.

(e) European Union legislation

While the UK remains a Member State of the EU and subject to EU law—this includes a continuing obligation to make the EU part of domestic law. The legislative powers of the EU are laid down in Art. 288 of the Treaty on the Functioning of the European Union (TFEU). Regulations, directives, and decisions are binding, but recommendations and opinions are not. The procedural requirements specified in Art. 296 must be carried out otherwise the measure could be annulled under Art. 19 of the Treaty on the European Union and Arts 263 and 264 of the TFEU. Although Art. 297 of the TFEU only requires publication of regulations and some directives, other directives are also published, as are many decisions.

Some legislation implementing EU measures will be passed by Parliament in the form of Orders in Council or rules and regulations. This is provided for in s. 2(2) of the European Communities Act 1972 (see Chapter 2, Section 3A(b) at p. 72).

Statutes are enacted to ratify treaty amendments, such as the Single European Act which was effected by the European Communities (Amendment) Act 1986.

B: Control

(a) Consultation

Consultation occurs within and outside Government in the policy-making and legislative processes. A topic becomes an issue and then is included in a policy agenda. The issue is investigated, problems and solutions identified, and the Government has to decide that it is going to legislate on the issue. Getting to that stage may have included the preparation of a Green Paper in which options are published for consultation. This may then be followed by a White Paper in which policy and proposals based on them are set out.

Sometimes there is a statutory requirement to consult. Such a requirement may be derogated from, as in social security, where the Minister need not consult the Social Security Advisory Committee about draft regulations if it is inexpedient to do so by reason of urgency (Social Security Administration Act 1992, s. 173(1)(a)).

Where a consultation obligation is imposed in respect of legislation, what will be considered to be sufficient consultation?

R v Secretary of State for Social Services, ex parte Association of Metropolitan Authorities
[1986] 1 WLR 1, Queen's Bench Division

Before making regulations constituting the housing benefits scheme, the Minister was required, by s. 36(1) of the Social Security and Housing Benefits Act 1982, to consult with organizations which appeared to him to be representative of the housing authorities concerned. The applicant was such an organization whose views had been sought by the Minister's officials on proposed amendments to the 1982 regulations. The consultative letter was written on 16 November 1984 and received by the applicant on 22 November. A response was requested by 30 November. The applicant complained about the shortness of time and asked for an extension so that its advisers could be consulted. On 4 December officials wrote to the applicant seeking its views on further proposed amendments. No draft of the proposals was forwarded and no mention was made of a material feature which required local authorities to investigate whether housing benefit claimants had created joint tenancies so as to gain from the housing benefit scheme. A response was requested by 12 December. The applicant answered the first letter on 7 December and sent brief comments about the second letter on 13 December. The Housing Benefits Amendment (No. 4) Order Regulations 1984 were made on 17 December and came into effect on 19 December. The applicant sought, *inter alia*, a declaration that the Minister had not exercised his duty under s. 36(1) of the Act of 1982, and an order of *certiorari* to quash the regulations because of the failure to consult.

WEBSTER J: ... There is no general principle to be extracted from the case law as to what kind or amount of consultation is required before delegated legislation, of which consultation is a precondition, can validly be made. But in any context the essence of consultation is the communication of a genuine invitation to give advice and a genuine receipt of that advice. In my view it must go without saying that to achieve consultation sufficient information must be supplied by the consulting to the consulted party to enable it to tender helpful advice. Sufficient time must be given by the consulting to the consulted party to enable it to do that, and sufficient time must be available for such advice to be considered by the consulting party. Sufficient, in that context, does not mean ample, but at least enough to enable the relevant purpose to be fulfilled. By helpful advice, in this context, I mean sufficiently informed and considered information or advice about aspects of the form or substance of the proposals, or their implications for the consulted party, being aspects material to the implementation of the proposal as to which the Secretary of State might not be fully informed or advised and as to which the party consulted might have relevant information or advice to offer ...

… In the present case, looking at the 'whole scope and purpose' of the Act of 1982, one matter which stands out is that its day-to-day administration is in the hands of local housing authorities who bear 10 per cent of the cost of the scheme. It is common ground that in them resides the direct expertise necessary to administer schemes made under the Act on a day-to-day basis. For these reasons, if for no other, I conclude that the obligation laid on the Secretary of State to consult organisations representative of those authorities is mandatory, not directory …

[T]o what extent is it for the Secretary of State, not the court, to judge how much consultation is necessary and how long is to be given for it? The answer to that question may qualify the word 'sufficient' in the requirements of consultation which I have set out above.…

… [T]he first point to note is that the power to make the regulations is conferred on the Secretary of State and that his is the duty to consult. Save for those consulted, no one else is involved in the making of the regulations. Secondly, both the form or substance of new regulations and the time allowed for consulting, before making them, may well depend in whole or in part on matters of a political nature, as to the force and implications of which it would be reasonable to expect the Secretary of State, rather than the court, to be the best judge. Thirdly, issues may well be raised after the making of the regulations as to the detailed merits of one or other reason for making them, or as to the precise degree of urgency required in their making, issues which have been raised on this application. Those issues cannot be said to be wholly irrelevant to a challenge to the vires of the regulations … In my view, therefore, the court, when considering the question whether the consultation required by section 36(1) was in substance carried out, should have regard not so much to the actual facts which preceded the making of the regulations as to the material before the Secretary of State when he made the regulations, that material including facts or information as it appeared or must have appeared to him acting in good faith, and any judgments made or opinions expressed to him before the making of the regulations about those facts which appear or could have appeared to him to be reasonable …

The effect of [this] … is to give a certain flexibility to the notions of sufficiency, sufficient information, sufficient time and sufficiently informed and considered information and advice … Thus, it can have the effect that what would be sufficient information or time in one case might be more or less than sufficient in another, depending on the relative degrees of urgency and the nature of the proposed regulation. There is no degree of urgency, however, which absolves the Secretary of State from the obligation to consult at all.

Upon consideration of the facts, his Lordship said that the Minister's view on the urgency of the need for the amending regulations and the nature of the proposed amendments justified requiring comments to be expressed quickly, but not in so short a period that the comments would be insufficiently informed or insufficiently considered. When account was also taken of the fact that the applicant had no notice of a material feature until after the regulations were made, his Lordship concluded that the Minister had not discharged his duty to consult before making the regulations.

… [I]n principle I treat the matter as one of pure discretion and so treating it decline to revoke the instrument for the following reasons, no particular significance being attached to the order in which I state them.

Although six organisations were and are habitually consulted in this context, only one of them has applied for revocation of the instrument and that one applies only on the ground that it was not properly consulted … Although the association complains about the substance of the regulations, it is apparent that its principal complaint throughout is, and has been, the absence of proper consultation and it and other organisations were able to express some, albeit in a sense piecemeal, views about the proposal which apparently the department took into account before making the regulations, but without, be it noted, any effort whatsoever on the November or December amendments. The regulations have been in force for about six months and, although their implementation creates difficulties for some at least of the housing authorities who have to administer them, those authorities must by now have adapted themselves as best they can to those difficulties. If, however, the regulations were to be revoked all applicants who had been refused benefit because of the new regulations would be entitled to make fresh claims, and all authorities would be required to consider each such claim.

Finally, the Housing Benefits Amendment (No. 4) Regulations 1984 have been consolidated into the Housing Benefits Regulations 1985 (S.I. 1985 No. 677), which were made on 29 April 1985, laid before Parliament on 30 April and came into operation and indeed have come into operation for the most part, today, 21 May. Those regulations are not at present challenged. If, therefore, the Housing Benefits Amendment (No. 4) Regulations 1984 were to be revoked, and so long as the Regulations of 1985 remain valid, any person entitled to reconsideration of his claim to benefit would, if successful, at best be entitled to benefits for about six months. For all these reasons, I refuse, in the exercise of my discretion, to revoke the Housing Benefits Amendment (No. 4) Regulations 1984.

I can see no reason whatsoever, however, for refusing the association the declaration for which they ask....

Declaration accordingly. Application for order of certiorari refused.

■ QUESTIONS

1. Consultation is not generally required for legislation, although central governmental practice is usually to conduct consultation amongst interested bodies and consultation exercises are regulated by governmental guidance. From 2008 to 2014 the *Code of Practice on Consultation* stated that it 'does not have legal force' but it further stated that 'the Code and the criteria within it apply to all UK public consultations by government departments and agencies'. In the following case the argument concerned a change in policy (a) to cease a discretionary compensation scheme which was more generous than a statutory one, and (b) to use a different and less generous assessment for fees, the Court of Appeal ruled on the general applicability of legitimate expectations and dismissed the appeal contending that the consultation was unlawful (see also *R (Greenpeace) v Secretary of State for Trade and Industry* [2007] EWHC 311 (Admin), in Chapter 10, Section 2C(b) at p. 539).

R (Bhatt Murphy) v The Independent Assessor
[2008] EWCA Civ 755, Court of Appeal

50. A very broad summary of the place of legitimate expectations in public law might be expressed as follows. The power of public authorities to change policy is constrained by the legal duty to be fair (and other constraints which the law imposes). A change of policy which would otherwise be legally unexceptionable may be held unfair by reason of prior action, or inaction, by the authority. If it has distinctly promised to consult those affected or potentially affected, then ordinarily it must consult (the paradigm case of procedural expectation). If it has distinctly promised to preserve existing policy for a specific person or group who would be substantially affected by the change, then ordinarily it must keep its promise (substantive expectation). If, without any promise, it has established a policy distinctly and substantially affecting a specific person or group who in the circumstances was in reason entitled to rely on its continuance and did so, then ordinarily it must consult before effecting any change (the secondary case of procedural expectation). To do otherwise, in any of these instances, would be to act so unfairly as to perpetrate an abuse of power …

54. As regards the Code of Practice I agree entirely with the Divisional Court. May LJ said:

23 … The Introduction states that the Code and the criteria apply to all public consultations by government departments and agencies. Mr Swift submits, correctly in my view, that this means that the Code is to apply whenever it is decided as a matter of policy to have a public consultation; not that public consultation is a required prelude to every policy change. The Code states that it does not have legal force but should generally be regarded as binding on United Kingdom departments and their agencies unless Ministers conclude that exceptional circumstances require a departure from it. Ministers retain their existing discretion not to conduct a formal written consultation exercise under the terms of the Code, for example where the issue is very specialised and

where there is a very limited number of so-called stakeholders who have been directly involved in the policy development process.

24 For the reasons given by Mr Swift, I do not consider that it is possible to read this document as any form of governmental promise or undertaking that policy changes will never be made without consultation. It would be very surprising if it could be so read, not least because a decision in a particular case whether to consult is itself a policy decision. Rather the Code prescribes how generally public consultation should be conducted if there is to be public consultation.

This leaves the area of quasi-legislation produced by other public authorities and agencies. Bearing in mind that the courts seem to have regard to the distinctions between legislative, executive, and administrative action, should there be a general statutory obligation imposed on all public bodies who make any measures, whether they take the form of primary, delegated, or quasi-legislation?

2. What are the benefits and disadvantages of consultation, and would the benefits outweigh the disadvantages:
   (a) generally;
   (b) only for some types of quasi-legislation?
3. If such a general duty of consultation were required, would it be in conflict with the representative nature of our parliamentary democratic constitution?
4. For the purposes of a duty to consult, should we make a distinction between those measures which are subject to parliamentary oversight and those which are not?

NOTE: The Hansard Society produced a report on the legislative process. In this they proposed guiding principles which underpinned their recommendations for reform. The evidence which they received indicated that the current arrangements for consultation were unsatisfactory.

The Hansard Society, *Making the Law*
(1993), pp. 139–41

[W]e have agreed five central principles which guide and govern all the recommendations we make:

- Laws are made for the benefit of the citizens of the state. All citizens directly affected should be involved as fully and openly as possible in the process by which statute law is prepared.
- Statute law should be as certain as possible and as intelligible and clear as possible, for the benefit of the citizens to whom it applies.
- Statute law must be rooted in the authority of Parliament and thoroughly exposed to open democratic scrutiny by the representatives of the people in Parliament.
- Ignorance of the law is no excuse, therefore the current statute law must be as accessible as possible to all who need to know it.
- The Government needs to be able to secure the passage of its legislation, but to get the law right and intelligible, for the benefit of citizens, is as important as to get it passed quickly.

[Recommendations on consultation]

Primary Legislation

4. The overwhelming impression from the evidence is that many of those most directly affected are deeply dissatisfied with the extent, nature, timing and conduct of consultation on bills as at present practised … the Government must heed this criticism and seek to meet it ….

5. The Government should always seek the fullest advice from those affected on the problems of implementing and enforcing proposed legislation….

6. Although some bills are inevitably required in a hurry, getting a bill right should always have priority over passing it quickly....

7. The Government should make every effort to get bills in a form fit for enactment, without major alteration, before they are presented to Parliament; in the Government's review of the legislative process, this should be a first and overriding objective....

8. Proper consultation should play a central part in the preparation of bills....

9. Good consultation practice requires that when a bill is being prepared, bodies with relevant experience or interests—particularly those directly affected—should be given all the relevant information and an opportunity to make their views known or to give information or advice, at each level of decision-taking....

10. Consultation should be as open as possible....

11. Secrecy regarding the content and results of consultations should be minimised and feedback maximised....

12. When major reviews are required of how the current law is operating and of the need for reform, we would welcome more frequent appointment of independent inquiries, including Royal Commissions. If the Government is not prepared to accept the advice of such inquiries, it would be expected to publish its reasons....

13. Consultative documents should be as clear and precise as possible. They should be specific about the questions on which departments want responses, while leaving opportunity for bodies to put forward further ideas of their own on relevant points. Green Papers should set out the facts fully and, as far as possible, the options being considered. White Papers should normally be preceded by Green Papers. White Papers should, where possible, systematically detail changes from Green Papers, indicating why these changes had been made....

14. Departments should offer more consultations on draft texts, especially in so far as they relate to practical questions of the implementation and enforcement of legislation....

16. Where there is no great urgency for a bill, the whole bill might sometimes be published in draft in a Green Paper, as the basis for further consultation and possibly parliamentary scrutiny....

17. Government departments should consult the main bodies concerned in each case and seek to agree how much time should be allowed for their responses to a consultation document....

18. Consultation should not be delayed....

19. Bodies invited by Government departments to respond to consultative documents on proposed legislation, and other bodies with a *bona fide* interest, should be given, free of charge, as many copies of those documents as they can show they need....

20. Bodies which have contributed to consultation on proposed legislation should be supplied, free of charge, with copies of the resulting bills, Acts and statutory instruments....

21. The Government should, drawing on best practice, prepare consultation guidelines which would be applicable to all Government departments when preparing legislation....

22. We recommend that—

(a) the Government's guidelines on consultation should be published;
(b) each department when applying to the Future Legislation Committee for inclusion of a bill in the Government's legislative programme should submit a check-list indicating how far it has been able to comply with the guidelines, and give details of the consultations it has already carried out or proposes to conduct; and

(c) an up-dated version of the check-list and this information should be submitted with the draft bill to the Legislation Committee and published with the bill....

Delegated Legislation

23. There should be consultation where appropriate at the formative stage of delegated legislation, but wherever possible departments should also consult outside experts and affected bodies on drafts of the actual instruments that they propose to lay before Parliament....

24. The Government's guidelines that we have recommended regarding consultation on bills, should be applied with appropriate modifications to consultation on delegated legislation....

NOTE: In a subsequent Hansard Society report (see A. Brazier et al, *Law in the Making: Influence and Change in the Legislative Process* (2008), p. 179) there was criticism by some groups that some consultation exercises were simply 'going through the motions', and that they were designed to produce a particular outcome or only the views of certain 'trusted' groups were really considered.

■ QUESTIONS

1. Does consultation operate more as an attempt to legitimise rather than control legislation?
2. Do the Hansard Society's proposals focus more on the workability of legislation when made, whereas the government concentrates more on the processes and politics of making legislation?

Consultation Principles

A. Consultations should be clear and concise

Use plain English and avoid acronyms. Be clear what questions you are asking and limit the number of questions to those that are necessary. Make them easy to understand and easy to answer. Avoid lengthy documents when possible and consider merging those on related topics.

B. Consultations should have a purpose

Do not consult for the sake of it. Ask departmental lawyers whether you have a legal duty to consult. Take consultation responses into account when taking policy forward. Consult about policies or implementation plans when the development of the policies or plans is at a formative stage. Do not ask questions about issues on which you already have a final view.

C. Consultations should be informative

Give enough information to ensure that those consulted understand the issues and can give informed responses. Include validated assessments of the costs and benefits of the options being considered when possible; this might be required where proposals have an impact on business or the voluntary sector.

D. Consultations are only part of a process of engagement

Consider whether informal iterative consultation is appropriate, using new digital tools and open, collaborative approaches. Consultation is not just about formal documents and responses. It is an on-going process.

E. Consultations should last for a proportionate amount of time

Judge the length of the consultation on the basis of legal advice and taking into account the nature and impact of the proposal. Consulting for too long will unnecessarily delay policy development. Consulting too quickly will not give enough time for consideration and will reduce the quality of responses.

F. Consultations should be targeted

Consider the full range of people, business and voluntary bodies affected by the policy, and whether representative groups exist. Consider targeting specific groups if appropriate. Ensure they are aware of the consultation and can access it. Consider how to tailor consultation to the needs and preferences of particular groups, such as older people, younger people or people with disabilities that may not respond to traditional consultation methods.

G. Consultations should take account of the groups being consulted

Consult stakeholders in a way that suits them. Charities may need more time to respond than businesses, for example. When the consultation spans all or part of a holiday period, consider how this may affect consultation and take appropriate mitigating action.

H. Consultations should be agreed before publication

Seek collective agreement before publishing a written consultation, particularly when consulting on new policy proposals. Consultations should be published on gov.uk.

I. Consultation should facilitate scrutiny

Publish any response on the same page on gov.uk as the original consultation, and ensure it is clear when the government has responded to the consultation. Explain the responses that have been received from consultees and how these have informed the policy. State how many responses have been received.

J. Government responses to consultations should be published in a timely fashion

Publish responses within 12 weeks of the consultation or provide an explanation why this is not possible. Where consultation concerns a statutory instrument publish responses before or at the same time as the instrument is laid, except in exceptional circumstances. Allow appropriate time between closing the consultation and implementing policy or legislation.

K. Consultation exercises should not generally be launched during local or national election periods

If exceptional circumstances make a consultation absolutely essential (for example, for safeguarding public health), departments should seek advice from the Propriety and Ethics team in the Cabinet Office.

NOTE: These principles are revisions to a new approach to consultation announced in July 2012. The revisions followed the report of the House of Lords Secondary Legislation Committee on this new approach published in February 2013 which called for a review of the consultation principles to be conducted by a unit independent of government (HL 100 of 2012–13). The review was conducted by Cabinet Office officials who involved an independent panel and was reported upon by the Lords Committee in November (HL 75 of 2013–14). They welcomed, amongst other points, the earlier engagement with groups before consultation and the earlier publication of Government evidence to enable challenge. They remained of the view that the minimum duration of a consultation should be six weeks and that holiday periods should be avoided. Guidance to consider taking mitigating action if the consultation spanned a holiday was too vague, and if it was unavoidable they liked the independent panel's idea of adding two weeks. The Government had not addressed in the revision some points made in February, including the need for active monitoring across Government of consultation approaches and for a redress mechanism for stakeholders in relation to a consultation which does not comply with the principles. Overall the Committee felt that the Government's approach to timetabling was to prefer administrative convenience over the ability of respondents to make a reasoned response and they feared this would undermine the public's belief that their comments will be properly taken into account.

(b) Publicity

All statutes are published, as is delegated legislation governed by the Statutory Instruments Act 1946, but this does leave open the possibility of other legislative measures not being readily available or known about.

Statutory Instruments Act 1946

1.—(1) Where by this Act or any Act passed after the commencement of this Act power to make, confirm or approve orders, rules, regulations or other subordinate legislation is conferred on His Majesty in Council or on any Minister of the Crown then, if the power is expressed—

(a) in the case of a power conferred on His Majesty, to be exercisable by Order in Council;

(b) in the case of a power conferred on a Minister of the Crown, to be exercisable by statutory instrument,

any document by which that power is exercised shall be known as a 'statutory instrument' and the provisions of this Act shall apply thereto accordingly….

2.—(1) Immediately after the making of any statutory instrument, it shall be sent to the King's printer of Acts of Parliament and numbered in accordance with regulations made under this Act, and except in such cases as may be provided by any Act passed after the commencement of this Act or prescribed by regulations made under this Act, copies thereof shall as soon as possible be printed and sold by the King's printer of Acts of Parliament….

3. —(1) Regulations made for the purposes of this Act shall make provision for the publication by His Majesty's Stationery Office of lists showing the date upon which every statutory instrument printed and sold by the King's printer of Acts of Parliament was first issued by that office; and in any legal proceedings a copy of any list so published purporting to bear the imprint of the King's printer shall be received in evidence as a true copy, and an entry therein shall be conclusive evidence of the date on which any statutory instrument was first issued by His Majesty's Stationery Office.

(2) In any proceedings against any person for an offence consisting of a contravention of any such statutory instrument, it shall be a defence to prove that the instrument had not been issued by His Majesty's Stationery Office at the date of the alleged contravention unless it is proved that at that date reasonable steps had been taken for the purpose of bringing the purport of the instrument to the notice of the public, or of persons likely to be affected by it, or of the person charged.

(3) Save as therein otherwise expressly provided, nothing in this section shall affect any enactment or rule of law relating to the time at which any statutory instrument comes into operation….

8.—(1) The Treasury may, with the concurrence of the Lord Chancellor and the Speaker of the House of Commons, by statutory instrument make regulations for the purposes of this Act, and such regulations may, in particular:— …

(c) provide with respect to any classes or descriptions of statutory instrument that they shall be exempt, either altogether or to such extent as may be determined by or under the regulations, from the requirement of being printed and of being sold by the King's printer of Acts of Parliament, or from either of those requirements: …

NOTE: Under the Statutory Instruments Regulations 1947, regs 5–8 some regulations are exempted from the publication requirements of the 1946 Act. These are: local instruments and those otherwise published regularly (reg. 5); temporary instruments (reg. 6); schedules to rules which are too bulky and where other steps have been taken to bring them to the notice of the public (reg. 7); cases in which it would be contrary to the public interest for publication to occur before the rules came into operation (reg. 8). The Minister making rules subject to the exceptions in regs 6–8 must certify that the conditions are satisfied.

R v Sheer Metalcraft Ltd

[1954] 1 QB 586, Kingston-upon-Thames Assizes

STREATFIELD J: … This matter comes before the court in the form of an objection to the admissibility in evidence of a statutory instrument known as the Iron and Steel Prices Order, 1951. It appears that part and parcel of that instrument consisted of certain deposited schedules in which maximum prices for different commodities of steel were set out. The instrument is said to have been made by the Minister of Supply on February 16, 1951; laid before Parliament on February 20, 1951; and to have come into operation on February 21, 1951. It is under that statutory instrument that the present charges are made against the two defendants in this case.

The point which has been taken is that by reason of the deposited schedules not having been printed and not having been certified by the Minister as being exempt from printing, the instrument is not a valid instrument under the Statutory Instruments Act, 1946. That point was taken in *Simmonds* v *Newell* [1953] 1 WLR 826, but it was expressly left open in view of a certain admission then made by the Solicitor-General, which, however, does not apply to the present case. The point arises in this way: under regulation 55AB of the Defence (General) Regulations, 1939, as amended, a competent authority, which in this case is the Minister of Supply, may by statutory instrument provide for controlling the prices to be charged for goods of any description or the charges to be made for services of any description, and for any incidental and supplementary matters for which the competent authority thinks it expedient for the purposes of the instrument to provide. It is said in the statutory instrument here that it was made in exercise of the powers conferred upon the Minister by regulations 55AB and 98 of the Defence (General) Regulations, and other statutory authorities.

The contention is that the making of that instrument is governed by the provisions of the Statutory Instruments Act, 1946 …

[His Lordship read sections 1 and 2 of the Act of 1946 and regulation 7 of the Statutory Instruments Regulations, 1947, and continued:] Section 1 visualizes the making of what is called a statutory instrument by a Minister of the Crown; section 2 visualizes that after the making of a statutory instrument it shall be sent to the King's Printer to be printed, except in so far as under regulations made under the Act it may be unnecessary to have it printed. It is said here that the Minister did not certify that the printing of these very bulky deposited schedules was unnecessary within the meaning of regulation 7. It is contended, therefore, that as he did not so certify it, it became an obligation under the Act that the deposited schedules as well as the instrument itself should be printed under section 2 of the Act of 1946, and in the absence of their having been printed as part of the instrument, the instrument cannot be regarded as being validly made.

To test that matter it is necessary to examine section 3 of the Act of 1946. By subsection (1) [see p. 290] … There does not appear to be any definition of what is meant by 'issue,' but presumably it does mean some act by the Queen's Printer of Acts of Parliament which follows the printing of the instrument. That section, therefore, requires that the Queen's Printer shall keep lists showing the date upon which statutory instruments are printed and issued.

Subsection (2) is important and provides [see p. 290] … It seems to follow from the wording of this subsection that the making of an instrument is one thing and the issue of it is another. If it is made it can be contravened; if it has not been issued then that provides a defence to a person charged with its contravention. It is then upon the Crown to prove that, although it has not been issued, reasonable steps have been taken for the purpose of bringing the instrument to the notice of the public or persons likely to be affected by it … In my judgment the making of an instrument is complete when it is first of all made by the Minister concerned and after it has been laid before Parliament. When that has been done it then becomes a valid statutory instrument, totally made under the provisions of the Act.

The remaining provisions to which my attention has been drawn, in my view, are purely procedure for the issue of an instrument validly made—namely, that in the first instance it must be printed by the Queen's Printer unless it is certified to be unnecessary to print it; it must then be included in a list published by Her Majesty's Stationery Office showing the dates when it is issued and it may be issued by the Queen's Printer of Acts of Parliament. Those matters, in my judgment, are matters of procedure. If they were not and if they were stages in the perfection of a valid statutory instrument, I cannot see that section 3(2) would be necessary, because if each one of those stages were necessary to make a statutory instrument valid, it would follow that there could be no infringement of an unissued instrument and therefore it would be quite unnecessary to provide a defence to a contravention of any such instrument …

In those circumstances I hold that this instrument was validly made and approved and that it was made by or signed on behalf of the Minister on its being laid before Parliament; that so appears on the fact of the instrument itself. In my view, the fact that the Minister failed to certify under regulation 7 does not invalidate the instrument as an instrument but lays the burden upon the Crown to prove that at the date of the alleged contraventions reasonable steps had been taken for bringing the instrument to the notice of the public or persons likely to be affected by it. I, therefore, rule that this is admissible. . . .

Verdict: Guilty on all counts.

NOTE: For a critical analysis of this case and s. 3 of the 1946 Act, see articles by Lanham at (1974) 37 *Modern Law Review* 510 and [1983] *Public Law* 395.

■ QUESTIONS

1. The publication requirements in the 1946 Act affect only statutory instruments in respect of which no exemption has been made. Should there be a general duty of publication?

2. With respect to publication of quasi-legislation:

    (a) should it only be required if it is reasonable and non-disclosure would prejudice the public; and

    (b) when would non-disclosure be reasonable?

(c) Parliamentary oversight

House of Commons Sessional Returns
2013–14, 2014–15, 2015–16, pp. 42–3, 31–2, 35–6 respectively

Distribution of time on the floor of the House between principal types of business

	Total time spent (hours:minutes)		
	2013–14	2014–15	2015–16
Government Bills			
Second readings: committed to a public bill committee	79.10	39.21	71.30
Second readings: committed to Committee of whole House (wholly or partly)	26.10	18.46	31.01
Committee of the whole House	47.26	29.19	57.57
Consideration	138.31	71.00	87.08
Third Reading	11.01	10.42	11.45
Lords amendments	28.46	22.25	24.33
Allocation of time motions	1.47	0.02	0.58
Committal & carry-over motions/Other stages	4.36	2.19	4.54
Private Members' Bills			
Motions for the introduction of Ten Minute Rule Bills	11.53	9.43	11.14
Second readings (and all stages)	40.50	42.38	49.38

	Total time spent (hours:minutes)		
Later stages	21.14	18.18	11.51
Money Resolutions	0.38	1.06	0.58
Ways and Means motions	22.03	22.45	46.09
Motions for approval of Statutory Instruments	5.56	15.36	7.27
Motions to annul or revoke Statutory Instruments	—	1.43	—

(i) Primary legislation

House of Lords Library Note 2013/008 *Volume of Legislation*

Year	No of Acts	No of Pages	Average No Pages
1931	51	322	6
1941	43	400	9
1951	59	628	11
1961	61	938	15
1971	66	1300	20
1981	56	1490	27
1991	58	1492	26
2001	21	1363	65
2002	39	2730	70
2003	41	3221	79
2004	34	3291	97
2005	19	2150	113
2006	46	3342	73
2007	28	3066	110
2008	27	3088	114
2009	23	2800	122
2010	30	2224	74
2011	22	2121	96
2012*	20	1886	94

1987 Change in size of Queen's Printer's bound volumes from A5 to A4
*Provisional figures
[These are selected statistics]
Source: House of Lords Library

House of Commons, Background Paper: *Public Bills in Parliament*

SN/PC/0657, 2012, p. 5

Figure 1 Progress of legislation through Parliament

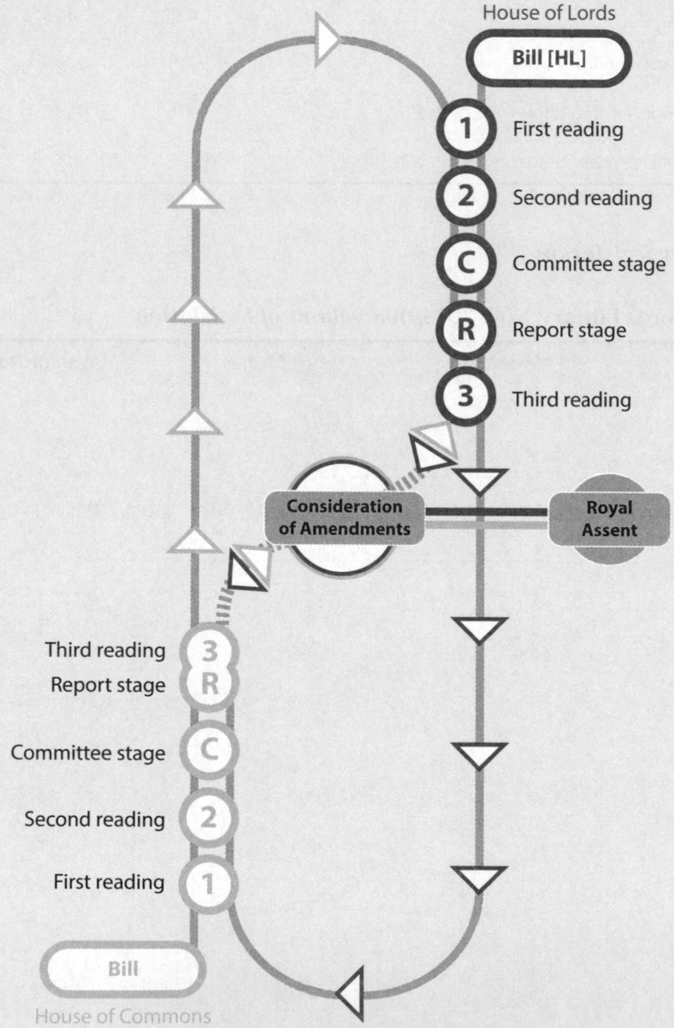

NOTE: Bills can be introduced into *either* the House of Commons or the House of Lords. In either case, a bill will pass through a number of stages in one house, followed by similar stages in the other house: it will then return to the first house for consideration of amendments.

Within the first month of the new Parliament elected in 1997, the House of Commons established a Select Committee to examine ways in which the House might be modernized. In its first report, it focused upon the legislative process in relation to primary legislation.

Committee on Modernisation of the House of Commons, *The Legislative Process*

HC 190 of 1997–98, paras 4–14, 84–8, 91–2, 94–102

Perceived Defects in the Present System

4. Previous inquiries into the legislative process have consistently identified a number of defects in the way in which Parliament considers legislation. Criticisms are made not only of the procedures used but of the pattern and timing of legislative scrutiny during a typical parliamentary session.

5. The first criticism made is that there has hitherto been little, if any, consultation with Members or with the House as a whole before Bills are formally introduced. In recent years some draft Bills have been produced for prior consultation, and the present Government has specifically undertaken in the Queen's Speech to extend this process. The House itself has however made no attempt to undertake any systematic consideration of such draft Bills.

6. There has as a result been no formal channel to allow time and opportunity for Members to receive representations from interested parties. Consultations between Government and those outside Parliament with a legitimate concern in the legislation has also been criticised as patchy and spasmodic.

7. Once Bills are formally introduced they are largely set in concrete. There has been a distinct culture prevalent throughout Whitehall that the standing and reputation of Ministers have been dependent on their Bills getting through largely unchanged. As a result there has been an inevitable disposition to resist alteration, not only on the main issues of substance, but also on matters of detail.

8. The Committee stage of a Bill, which is meant to be the occasion when the details of the legislation are scrutinised, has often tended to be devoted to political partisan debate rather than constructive and systematic scrutiny. On Bills where policy differences are great, the role of Government backbenchers on a Standing Committee has been primarily to remain silent and to vote as directed. By contrast the Opposition has often set out to devise methods designed simply to extend debate. The Government has then been forced to bring in a guillotine which has often been draconian, as a result of which large sections of the Bill have not been considered.

9. Special Standing Committees, which were designed to encourage more informed discussion on Bills which were not highly politically controversial, have rarely been used. This has almost certainly been because of the perceived amount of extra time involved and the consequent pressure on the legislative timetable, although evidence from those concerned, including Ministers, suggests that such a perception is in fact misconceived.

10. Report stages have frequently been equally unconstructive. So far as the Opposition has been concerned, they have often been seen as an opportunity to debate on the floor of the House issues which they regard as of major political importance. Amendments and new clauses are tabled as a peg on which to hang a particular debate, not always closely related to the provisions of the Bill. By contrast the Government has frequently taken the opportunity to table literally hundreds of amendments, some very technical, some very long, possibly as a consequence of the Bill being, as First Parliamentary Counsel put it, 'produced too quickly to get the policy and drafting right'.

11. Turning to the pattern of legislation, critics regularly point to the marked imbalance in the legislative activity at different times in the session. Early on in a typical parliamentary year, the House is usually swamped with major Bills in Committee as Ministers seek to get a head start for their own measures. The recent change in the timing of the Budget and the subsequent Finance Bill has made this worse. By contrast the House of Lords is under extreme pressure at the latter end of the session as it receives the major Commons Bills.

12. This pattern, combined with the absolute cut-off imposed by prorogation, frequently makes the last few days of a session particularly chaotic as attempts are made to complete the Government's legislative programme. Bills go to and fro between the Houses, both of which are asked to agree (or disagree) usually with minimal notice to a large number of amendments. Few, if any Members, are able to know what is going on, and there is potential scope for error. The House has in the past even been asked to debate Lords Amendments of which there has been no available text.

The Essential Requirements of a Reformed System

13. We do not dissent from the general thrust of the criticisms outlined in the previous paragraphs. We do however note the considered view of the chairmen of standing committees, as conveyed to us by the Chairman of Ways and Means, that there has been a marked improvement in recent years, particularly since the adoption of the informal timetabling of bills following the Jopling reforms. The Chairman also suggested that the system also had some notable strengths: in particular, the system of appointing a committee with a separate membership for each bill, the fact that the process of detailed consideration and confrontation is carried out in public, and the tradition of impartial chairmanship.

14. Before considering ways in which the House's procedures and practices could be changed to meet the criticisms, we set out what in our view are the essential criteria which must be met in making any reforms. These may be summarised as follows:

(a) The Government of the day must be assured of getting its legislation through in reasonable time (provided that it obtains the approval of the House).

(b) The Opposition in particular and Members in general must have a full opportunity to discuss and seek to change provisions to which they attach importance.

(c) All parts of a Bill must be properly considered.

(d) The time and expertise of Members must be used to better effect.

(e) The House as a whole, and its legislative Committees in particular, must be given full and direct information on the meaning and effect of the proposed legislation from those most directly concerned, and full published explanations from the Government on the detailed provisions of its Bill.

(f) Throughout the legislative process there must be greater accessibility to the public, and legislation should, so far as possible, be readily understandable and in plain English.

(g) The legislative programme needs to be spread as evenly as possible throughout the session in both Houses.

(h) There must be sufficient flexibility in any procedures to cope with, for example, emergency legislation.

(i) Monitoring and, if necessary, amending legislation which has come into force should become a vital part of the role of Parliament.

…

Conclusions

84. There is general agreement that more thorough parliamentary scrutiny of legislation is necessary and long overdue. We have tried in this Report to begin to set out how best to achieve this end. We have concluded that it would be wrong to prescribe a single approach for all types of legislation. We have stated some broad principles, in particular that the Government of the day must be assured of getting its legislation through in reasonable time (provided that it has the approval of the House), and that the Opposition and all Members must have a full opportunity to discuss and seek to change provisions to which they attach importance. Each bill will be different and its treatment should reflect this, with its passage to the statute book designed to recognise the broad principles to which we have referred. A higher quality of legislation must have substantial benefits for all.

85. There is much that can already be done by using to greater effect and with greater imagination the existing procedures and practices of the House. Beyond that, relatively minor changes could significantly improve the scrutiny of legislation. We recommend greater use in appropriate cases of more of the options already available and of others that could easily be brought forward. Fundamental to this is a willingness on the part of Government to experiment with such options. It equally entails some greater flexibility on the part of the House. If the new opportunities offered are wasted or abused, the chance will have been missed.

86. If significant changes are made to the scrutiny of legislation in the longer term, there would be consequences for the overall framework within which Parliament legislates. These could include in defined circumstances consideration of the 'rollover' of Bills from one parliamentary year to another, and the shape and form of that year. Such matters are in any event subject to alteration: for example, the Budget was moved in 1993 from March to November, whereas it has recently been announced that in 1998 there will be a spring Budget.

87. Flexibility is an inherent strength of our system, and any attempt to impose a straitjacket on it should be resisted.

88. The recommendations we make below are based on options either already available, or which would involve small changes in procedures.

…

Pre-legislative scrutiny

91. We welcome the Government's intention to publish 7 draft bills in the course of this Session, and recommend that some, or even all, be considered by the House, using one of the easily available avenues—

(i) an ad hoc Select Committee to consider a particular draft bill: or

(ii) following a discussion with the House of Lords, an ad hoc Joint Select Committee to consider a particular draft bill: or

(iii) consideration of a particular draft bill by the appropriate departmental select committee.

Presentation and First Reading

92. (i) We have invited First Parliamentary Counsel to explore as soon as possible ways in which the explanatory memorandum accompanying each bill can be made more user-friendly.

(ii) We recommend that the Government should also consider the production of a simpler explanatory guide, along the lines of that produced by the Chancellor of the Exchequer for the Budget, to be made available to interested parties, including via the Internet.…

Second Reading

94. We agree that the great majority of bills should be subject to a Second Reading debate on the floor of the House. We also consider however that greater use should be made of Second Reading Committees to consider 'non-controversial bills which do not raise substantial issues of principle', or those non-controversial Bills which may have been subject to previous committee scrutiny. To facilitate this the Government should bring forward proposals to amend Standing Order No. 90 so as to relax some of the provisions governing the procedures for sending bills to Second Reading Committees, and to permit all Members of the House to attend and speak.

Committee Stage

95. The committee stage of any bill should be handled in whatever way is most appropriate for that bill. Following the Second Reading of a bill, there is a range of committal options open to Government with decisions usually being taken following discussions. These options have been used very sparingly in the past, and we recommend greater use in future of:

(i) committal of appropriate bills to a Special Standing Committee, under Standing Order No. 91, which should be amended so as to give these committees greater flexibility in their operations; or

(ii) committal of appropriate bills to ad hoc Select Committees; or

(iii) splitting a bill on committal between the floor of the House and a Standing Committee, a procedure which we consider could be extended to make it possible, subject to agreement, to split bills between different sorts of committees, as deemed appropriate.

96. Where a pre-legislative or First Reading Committee has been used the Committee of Selection should so far as possible nominate the same core of Members to the subsequent committee stage, supplemented as necessary.

97. There are several changes to existing procedures and practices in Standing Committee which could lead to a more effective use of time, including:

(i) a sensible agreement to ensure that all parts of a Bill are discussed;

(ii) an amendment to Standing Orders so that the consideration of the existing Clauses of a bill can follow the practice currently used for new Clauses;

(iii) removal of many of the constraints and conventions on the times during which a committee may meet and the number of timings of sittings, including the extension to Standing Committees of the facility available to select committees to meet during recesses; and

(iv) the Chairman to be given powers similar to those given to the Speaker under Standing Order No. 47 to impose a limit on the length of speeches.

98. Notes on Clauses should be available to members of Standing Committees in time for them to be able to frame and table amendments which would be open to selection.

Report Stage

99. We recommend that, for a certain number of appropriate bills, the Standing Committee which had considered the bill should be reconvened to consider non-controversial Government amendments, such as those giving effect to assurances given at committee stage, with the reported Bill considered as at present on the floor of the House.

Lords Amendments

100. We recommend that the House should also explore the possibility of referring appropriate Lords Amendments to the Standing Committee which considered the bill. This would be followed by consideration in the House, normally on a formal motion to agree with the Committee's resolutions.

Post-legislative scrutiny

101. The Liaison Committee should encourage the monitoring by departmentally-related Select Committees of legislation newly in force. The option should remain open for the appointment of ad hoc Select Committees to consider and report on the operation of a particular piece of legislation causing concern which affects more than one Department.

The sessional cycle

102. (i) The Committee agrees the principle that, in defined circumstances and subject to certain safeguards, Government Bills may be carried over from one session to the next in the same way as hybrid and private Bills. Discussions should begin between the appropriate authorities in both Houses to determine how this might best be achieved, without infringing the constitutional implications of prorogation.

(ii) In drawing up detailed proposals the appropriate authorities should consider in particular the need to ensure (a) the identification by the Government as early as possible of any Bill it wished to be subject to a carry-over procedure (b) that the procedure should only be used for Bills which are either to be subject to select committee type scrutiny or are introduced after a certain period in the session and (c) that no Bill should be carried over more than once.

NOTE: A report by the Committee (HC 543 of 1997–98) led to agreement that in defined circumstances Government bills not passed by the end of a session could be carried over in the next session. The first Government bill to be carried over was the Financial Services and Markets Bill 1998–99. A new Order was agreed on carry-over on 22 October 2002 (HC Debs, Vol. 391, cols. 827–8, 29 October 2002).

■ QUESTION

How far does the Modernisation Select Committee's report meet the concerns of the Hansard Society Commission's report?

The Committee revisited the legislative process with a view to improving the opportunities for the general public, lobbyists and stakeholders to influence Parliament's consideration of bills. The extracts concentrate on the pre-legislative stage, where it is feared that recent good progress has faltered, and on the committee stage.

Committee on Modernisation of the House of Commons, *The Legislative Process*
HC 1097 of 2005–06, paras 16–33, 50–7, 62, 67–73

Impact of pre-legislative scrutiny

16. The impact of pre-legislative scrutiny can be assessed against the three related purposes identified by the Modernisation Committee in 1997:

   a) connecting with the public by involving outside bodies and individuals in the legislative process;
   b) changing the bill to produce better law; and
   c) achieving consensus so that the bill completes its passage through the House more smoothly.

Connecting with the public

17. A major theme of this inquiry has been the question of how to involve the public more closely in the legislative process. By 'the public', we mean not only individuals, but also the non-governmental organisations, lobby groups and interest groups who seek to influence the form and content of laws. It is an important matter of principle, in a democracy, that citizens should be able to make their views known to legislators, and an accessible legislative process provides access to the many thousands of smaller groups as well as to the larger, better-organised interests.

18. Pre-legislative scrutiny is an effective way of drawing all those who have a point of view to put across into the legislative process. Inquiries are usually well-publicised (though some are inevitably higher profile than others) and there are clear and well-understood routes for submitting evidence to committees considering draft bills. The Joint Committee on the draft Charities Bill, for example, received more than 360 written submissions and heard oral evidence from 34 individuals representing 28 organisations. This is also the only part of the legislative process in which innovative ways of connecting with the public, such as on-line consultation, can effectively be tried out.

19. Meetings where committees take evidence are, for a variety of reasons, generally more media-friendly than standing committee proceedings, so pre-legislative scrutiny also has the potential to stimulate and inform public debate in a way that other proceedings on a bill do not. It can therefore be effective in putting Parliament at the centre of the national debate on forthcoming legislation.

Improving the law

20. There is little doubt that pre-legislative scrutiny produces better laws. As the Law Society told us, 'it would probably be difficult to prove scientifically that more pre-legislative scrutiny has improved legislation, but it would seem unarguable in practice that it has…. Effective consultation procedures and processes such as publication and consideration of Bills in draft would appear to have greatly improved the text which is presented to Parliament or to have identified drawbacks in the draft text which require its rethinking'. This view was echoed by the Hansard Society, the Members of Parliament who gave evidence to us, and by academic witnesses. Witnesses from the CBI, the TUC and the Law Society all suggested that pre-legislative scrutiny could play a significant part in improving the quality of bills.

21. Examples of pre-legislative scrutiny having a major impact on a bill include the draft Communications Bill, where the Government accepted 120 of the Joint Committee's 148 recommendations and the Civil Contingencies Bill, which the Minister acknowledged at second reading was 'now stronger in a number of important ways' than the original draft, the Government having accepted in full 13 of the Joint Committee's 50 recommendations, including some key concessions and significant changes in policy. In the case of the Disability Discrimination Bill, the Government initially accepted 32 of the Committee's 75 recommendations at the pre-legislative stage, but by the time it had completed its passage in the Lords and reached the Commons, it had accepted a total of 61.

22. Even where there has been extensive consultation by Government and others during the production of a bill, pre-legislative scrutiny by Parliament can still make a valuable contribution to the

process. A good example is the draft Corruption Bill, which was based on recommendations from the Royal Commission on Standards in Public Life in 1976 and further developed in a Law Commission Report of 1998. It had in the meantime been the subject of numerous reports and consultations of one kind or another. Despite the bill's leisurely journey in the direction of the statute book and the amount of expert interest that had been taken in it, the Joint Committee on the draft Bill was critical, noting 'many adverse comments on the approach adopted in the Bill and its drafting, clarity and comprehensibility'. They concluded that 'modifying the bill by trying to improve it marginally' would still leave it 'obscure and unsatisfactory' and recommend that it be completely re-drafted.

23. The Home Office accepted the Committee's recommendations and scrapped the bill, issuing a new consultation paper on bribery in December 2005, acknowledging that, in the light of the Joint Committee's Report, there 'no longer [seemed] to be broad consensus' on the approach proposed by the Law Commission.

24. In the case of the Company Law Reform Bill [*Lords*], the CBI argued that it should have been published in draft. The DTI had resisted this on the ground that the bill had been the product of a lengthy consultation exercise run by Government, but the bill as introduced contained some significant deviation from what had been agreed in that exercise, including important new material. Parliamentary scrutiny at the pre-legislative stage can play an important role in improving the law, even where there has already been lengthy and extensive external consultation by Government.

Smoothing the passage of legislation

25. Our predecessor Committee suggested that pre-legislative scrutiny should lead to less time being needed at later stages of the legislative process. If a consensus has been reached before a bill is introduced, and any points of disagreement or controversy have been resolved, then it would not seem unreasonable to assume that the subsequent passage of the bill through Parliament will be faster than it otherwise would have been. However, research into this question has failed to provide conclusive evidence of this. Jennifer Smookler, a Committee Specialist working with pre-legislative scrutiny committees in the House of Lords, argued that the process of pre-legislative scrutiny may cause a bill to be challenged on a greater number of issues precisely because of the level of knowledge gained by parliamentarians as a result of the inquiry. She cited the example of the Civil Contingencies Bill, which spent ten months in Parliament and saw two key amendments relating to the pre-legislative Committee's recommendations going to an exchange of Messages between the two Houses.

26. Whatever its impact on the passage of legislation, the purpose of pre-legislative scrutiny is not to secure an easy ride for the Government's legislative programme, it is to make better laws by improving the scrutiny of bills and drawing the wider public more effectively into the Parliamentary process. Some bills may enjoy a swifter progress through the two Houses as a result of pre-legislative scrutiny, whilst others may well take longer. If the result is a better Act, then that is a good thing. In an earlier Report, this Committee made the connection between pre-legislative scrutiny and carry-over of public bills. If a bill is to undergo an additional Parliamentary stage, without any guarantee that this will expedite the subsequent stages, then the one-Session time limit arguably becomes more of a burden than a safeguard.

27. The Law Society told us that carry-over had undoubtedly been useful in allowing greater and more considered attention to be given to bill, and getting legislation right, as opposed to getting it through within a given time-scale should be the priority for both sides of the House. Philip Cowley, Reader in Parliamentary Government at the University of Nottingham, went a step further: 'let us stop trying to legislate everything within a year and take instead the norm that we take two years for a run-of-the-mill bill to pass through its legislative stages'. The House of Lords Constitution Committee has also recommended that carry-over should be the norm for bills that have been subject to pre-legislative scrutiny, a suggestion that was also put to us by David Kidney MP.

28. It is important to note that carry-over does not increase the House's overall capacity to deal with bills, since a bill which is carried over in one Session adds to the total volume of material to be

considered in the next one. It does allow longer gaps to be left between stages, providing more time for consideration, reflection and informal discussions and negotiations during the bill's passage. It also allows greater flexibility in deciding how to divide the available Parliamentary time between bills.

29. The Sessional clock does not start ticking until a bill is formally presented in the first House, so pre-legislative scrutiny does not necessarily mean that a bill needs to be carried over if it is considered in draft in one Session and presented in the next. However, it is possible that the Sessional time-limit is placing some strain on the pre-legislative stage itself, as there is pressure for bills published in draft in the spring to have completed the pre-legislative stage and so be ready for presentation by the late Autumn, early in the following Session. Two chairmen of committees engaged in pre-legislative scrutiny of the draft Legal Services Bill and the draft Coroners Bill have expressed concern to us about the time available for their committees to complete their work. We recommend that, where a bill is introduced late in a Session because it has been subject to pre-legislative scrutiny, the assumption should be that it will be carried over to the next Session, subject to the same restrictions which currently apply, including the twelve-month time-limit. It is hoped and expected that this would be done with cross-party support. The purpose of carrying over these bills is to relieve pressure of time on both the pre-legislative and legislative stages. We would still expect to see them pass reasonably quickly from second reading to committee to report, with adequate time allowed at each stage.

Making pre-legislative scrutiny more effective

Volume of draft bills

30. The Government and Parliament are both committed to expanding the use of pre-legislative scrutiny. Publication of bills in draft rose from three in 1997–98, to a peak of 12 in 2003–04, equivalent to more than a third of the total number of Government bills that were passed in that Session, though a reduction in the number of draft Bills is to be expected in the Session following a general election, even where there has been no change of Government. It has more recently dropped off, to six in the pre-election 2004–05 Session and just two so far in the current Session, though a reduction in the number of draft Bills is to be expected in the Session following a general election, even where there has been no change of Government. Many witnesses have argued that pre-legislative scrutiny should be the norm for Government bills, with the exception of the Finance Bill and legislation which needs to be passed urgently. In 2003, this Committee said,

'We recognise that it will never be possible to have every Bill published in draft. There will always be occasions when new developments require urgent legislation. However, we hope eventually to see publication in draft become the norm. We recommend that the Government continue to increase with each Session the proportion of Bills published in draft'.

We welcome the Government's progress in increasing the proportion of legislation published in draft between 1997–98 and 2003–04. We are however concerned by the reduction in the number of draft bills since then, and we urge the Government to increase further the proportion of legislation published in draft. It will never be possible to produce all legislation in draft and there may be occasions, such as the Session following election of a new Government, when very little pre-legislative scrutiny is possible. But we believe that pre-legislative scrutiny should be the usual course for major Government bills.

31. Pre-legislative scrutiny has so far been used for bills which do not deal primarily with matters of party political controversy. That is not to say that the bills have all been uncontroversial—animal welfare, gambling and nuclear decommissioning, for example, are often the subject of lively public debate—only that they have not tended to deal with areas where there have been significant differences in the settled policies of the main political parties. Professor Robert Hazell of the Constitution Unit, UCL, has noted that pre-legislative scrutiny is rarely used for bills of constitutional significance, having been used in only three of the 55 constitutional bills he identifies in the last two Parliaments.

32. It might be that pre-legislative scrutiny is most useful for bills which are not controversial in the party-political sense but we would not like to see its use confined exclusively to bills of that kind. We recommend that, in increasing the number of bills published in draft, the Government include bills that are likely to be the subject of party-political controversy.

Continuity of membership

33. In 1997, the Committee recommended that where a pre-legislative committee had been used the Committee of Selection should so far as possible nominate the same core of Members to the subsequent committee stage, supplemented as necessary. With a few exceptions, this recommendation has not been followed.

...

Committee Stage

50. Early in the inquiry, we decided to focus on the committee stage of bills. There were three main reasons for this:

a) First, the committee stage is where a great deal of the substance of the House's consideration of a bill takes place, and where most of the detail of the bill is settled.

b) Second, the committee stage permits of several variations—committal to a standing committee, a Committee of the whole House, and split committal between the two are all regularly used. Committal to a select committee is used every five years for the Armed Forces Bill and special standing committees have been used on a few occasions since 1980. We are therefore able to draw on the House's own experiences in evaluating different approaches to the committee stage.

c) Third, the work of standing committees has been one of the most criticised aspects of the legislative process. This criticism was summarised by the Hansard Society, who told us that standing committees 'fail to deliver genuine and analytical scrutiny of [bills], their political functions are neutered, dominated almost exclusively by government ... , they fail to engage with the public and the media (in contrast to select committees) and they do not adequately utilise the evidence of experts or interested parties'.

51. Although some of this criticism of standing committees is valid, it is important not to over-state the weaknesses of the system. Partisan debates can be a useful way of testing the provisions of a bill, of identifying its weaknesses and the case for change. Whilst it is unusual for the Government to accept back-bench or opposition amendments in standing committee, it is not unusual for the Government to table amendments at report stage which are intended to rectify problems identified in committee. We do believe that there is a strong case for introducing a more collaborative, evidence-based approach to the legislative process (see paragraphs 58–62, below), but it should supplement, rather than supplant, traditional standing committee debates.

52. We have considered two parallel sets of questions relating to standing committees: what are the alternatives to the traditional standing committee; and how might the existing standing committee system be improved? ...

53. Most of our witnesses favoured those committee arrangements which provided for an evidence-taking, as well as a deliberative stage. There are several benefits that an evidence taking stage could provide. It is first and foremost a mechanism for ensuring that Members are informed about the subject of the bill and that there is some evidential basis for the debate on the bill. Evidence-gathering is also, by its nature, a more consensual and collective activity than debate, and there is evidence that those outside Parliament have a more positive view of select committee proceedings than of debate. So there is a reputational benefit to Parliament in being seen to engage in a more open, questioning and consensual style of law-making, before moving on to the necessary partisan debate.

54. An evidence-taking stage is also an effective way of engaging the wider public directly in the legislative process. The Law Society argued that it is important that the process for influencing a committee's thinking was as straightforward as possible and suggested that many organisations would value the opportunity to give evidence to a committee considering a bill, even if they had contributed to the Government's consultation exercise. A good example of this is the inquiry into the draft Corporate Manslaughter Bill by the Work and Pensions and Home Affairs Committees. They received over 150 submissions from organisations including victims' groups, trade unions, lawyers, and business representatives.

55. Witnesses from the CBI and the TUC, two organisations which are at the forefront of consultation and lobbying on proposed legislation, told us that they did not always find it easy to influence the standing committee process and that, as a consequence, they devoted more resources to trying to influence the process at other stages. Both organisations strongly favoured increasing the emphasis on formal evidence-taking as a way of improving the involvement of outside bodies in the process.

56. All these benefits, of course, are there to be had at the pre-legislative stage and pre-legislative committees usually (though not always) allow a rather longer inquiry than is possible once a bill has begun its passage through the House. But, as we have already noted, there is often a disjunction between the pre-legislative stage and the legislative stage, with few Members of pre-legislative committees finding their way onto the standing committee considering the bill. Furthermore, the bill which is presented is might differ significantly from the original draft, so that parts of it will not have been subject to the pre-legislative stage. Unlike the other stages of a bill, pre-legislative scrutiny is in the gift of the Government. As we have seen since the 2003–04 peak of draft bills, with the best will in the world, extensive pre-legislative scrutiny can never be guaranteed.

57. We do not wish to detract from the success of pre-legislative scrutiny, but we believe that, even with its further development, there is a compelling case for integrating evidence taking into the legislative process itself. Both the Deputy Director-General of the CBI and the TUC's Head of Campaigns and Communications argued that introducing oral evidence into the standing committee process itself was the single most important change that they would like to see made to the primary legislative process.

…

62. We recommend that Standing Order No. 83A (Programme motions) be amended so that the definition of 'programme motion' includes a requirement that it provides for committal of the bill to a public bill committee with the power to take evidence, to a Committee of the whole House, or split committal between the two. Private Members' bills would continue to stand referred to an ordinary standing committee under Standing Order No. 63, as would any Government bills which were not programmed (e.g. the Finance Bill).

…

Making public bill committees more flexible

67. Under the current Standing Order, a special standing committee considers a bill in two phases:

a) The evidence-taking phase. This must be completed within 28 days of the bill's committal, during which time the committee may hold one private deliberative, meeting (to decide when to meet, which witnesses to invite, etc.) and up to three public evidence sessions of not more than three hours each. The committee is chaired for this phase by the chairman of the relevant select committee and has the same powers as a select committee to call for evidence.

b) The standing committee phase. Having completed the evidence-taking phase, the committee proceeds to go through the bill in the normal way. This phase is chaired by a member of the Chairmen's Panel. The Minister in charge of the bill is a member of the committee, though he or she may also appear as a witness during the evidence-taking phase.

The evidence-taking phase

68. The time restrictions on the evidence-taking phase were proposed in the original Procedure Committee Report which recommended the establishment of such committees. The Committee was

> 'anxious that the House should proceed cautiously with this new and potentially most useful reform. If experience showed that the standard allocation of three sittings could be enlarged, this could be done later in the light of that experience … the addition of three morning sittings for the investigative stage of each bill would be offset by a reduction in the "amendment" stage whereas a longer allocation of investigative time would be bound to add considerably to the total time taken by each bill in committee'.

The requirement that the sittings be held in the morning was presumably to avoid clashing with the sittings of the House.

69. It is indeed likely that providing for evidence sessions on the bill will reduce the time needed and taken for debate on the bill. For example, many of the 'probing' amendments tabled in standing committee for the purpose of testing a particular piece of wording, most of which are in any event withdrawn, could be dispensed with if Members had an opportunity at the outset to question the Minister and officials on the bill. Direct questioning is perhaps a more efficient means for Members to examine the bill than the use of probing amendments, which often require officials to guess what the amendment might be getting at when preparing the Minister's brief, and then lead to debate on the technical merits of the proposed amendment rather than on the merits of the bill.

70. However, we are not confident that the right equilibrium between investigation and debate will always be reached with three evidence sessions. Some bills might require more evidence to do them justice. Others might require fewer, a single session with the Minister and officials being sufficient. The same applies to the length of the evidence sessions; and the requirement that they be held in the mornings, which was anyway waived in the most recent case of the Adoption and Children Bill, is out-of-date given the introduction of the new sitting hours of the House.

71. The simple purpose of these restrictions—to stop the evidence-taking phase of the committee from becoming unduly drawn-out and unnecessarily delaying the passage of the bill—can now adequately be met by a sensible programme order. We recommend that public bill committees should hold at least one evidence session, with the Minister and officials, in all cases. Beyond that, the general restrictions on the number, duration and timing of oral evidence sessions held by public bill committees should be lifted. Appropriate out-dates should be applied instead on a case-by-case basis in the programme order. The programming sub-committee of the public bill committee should decide on how the committee uses the time available to it, including the division of time between evidence-taking and debate.

Chairing public bill committees

72. As we have already noted, the evidence-taking phase of the special standing committee has usually been chaired by the chairman of the relevant departmental select committee. There are good reasons for this practice, which provides a degree of continuity between select and standing committee work but, if all government bills are to go to a special standing committee, it could become an intolerable burden on some select committee chairmen. All departmental select committee chairmen should expect to chair the evidence-taking phase of a public bill committee from time to time but, in committees whose departments have a heavy legislative workload, we suggest that this work might be shared between the members of the committee. It might also be appropriate for the chairman of a non-departmental committee, such as Environmental Audit or Public Administration, to take the chair in some cases.

Public bill committees and pre-legislative scrutiny

73. The purpose of a public bill committee is not to replicate the pre-legislative inquiry, nor should it be seen as a substitute for a proper pre-legislative stage. The need to complete both the evidence-taking and the consideration of the bill in reasonable time means that these committees are not a suitable vehicle for exhaustive inquiries, nor are they a substitute for the consultation exercises under-taken by Government before a bill is presented. Where there has been a pre-legislative inquiry, we would expect the public bill committee to take the pre-legislative report as its starting point and not to re-examine the same witnesses on the same issues. In some cases, a more substantial series of evi-dence sessions will be appropriate but in many cases, it might be that only one investigative meeting is required.

NOTES

1. Further recommendations on committee consideration of bills included improving the quality and format of information to committee members to enable them to keep track of amendments and their effect on the bill and it was suggested that IT could be used as is the case in the Scottish Parliament and National Assembly for Wales. It was also proposed that the public should have access to better information gateways to the legislation.
2. The proposal that standing committees which consider public bills be renamed public bill com-mittees was accepted. Government bills which are programmed (have a timetable for the various legislative stages) will be sent to these committees which will have the power to send 'for persons, papers and records'. Oral evidence shall be printed in the official report of the committee's debates and the committee shall have power to report written evidence to the House as if it were a select committee. It is expected that the committees will have around 17 members including at least one minister from the relevant department and front benchers from the opposition parties. A pilot scheme on the publication of explanatory material on amendments to bills is to be conducted.
3. At para. 30 the Committee expressed concern about the Government's commitment to pre-legislative scrutiny, in relation to the number of draft bills. This has been reiterated by various committees. The Political and Constitutional Reform Committee in its review of the Wright reforms (HC 82 of 2013–14) made a recommendation on the scale of pre-legislative scrutiny, to amend Standing Orders so that:

> *No public bill shall be presented unless* a) a draft of the bill has received pre-legislative scrutiny by a committee of the House or a joint committee of both Houses, or b) it has been certified by the Speaker as a bill that requires immediate scrutiny and pre-legislative scrutiny would be inexpedi-ent. (para. 35)

They also agree with the Commons Liaison Committee that Commons' committees be given 'first refusal' of conducting pre-legislative scrutiny of a draft bill, rather than the Government suggesting that it be conducted by a joint committee. This not only reflects a preference for the primacy of the Commons but also the membership of such joint committees is nominated rather than elected and they also want Commons Public Bill Committees to be elected like the Commons departmental select committees (para. 36).
4. The House of Commons Modernisation Committee also thought that Parliament should conduct more post-legislative scrutiny but deferred for a report which was being carried out by the Law Commission. Its conclusions were as follows.

Law Commission, *Post-Legislative Scrutiny*

Law Com 302 (2006) pp. 46–7

6.2 For the purposes of this report, we understand post-legislative scrutiny to refer to a broad form of review the purpose of which is to address the effects of the legislation in terms of whether the intended policy objectives have been met by the legislation and, if so, how effectively. However, this does not preclude consideration of narrow questions of a purely legal or technical nature. [para. 2.4]

6.3 The headline reasons for having more systematic post-legislative scrutiny are as follows:

- to see whether legislation is working out in practice as intended;
- to contribute to better regulation;
- to improve the focus on implementation and delivery of policy aims;
- to identify and disseminate good practice so that lessons may be drawn from the successes and failures revealed by the scrutiny work.

We recognise the real value of these arguments and are persuaded that together these reasons provide a strong case for more systematic post-legislative scrutiny. However, we also recognise the limitations. We acknowledge there are difficult challenges in relation to post-legislative scrutiny, namely: how to avoid a replay of policy arguments, how to make it workable within resource constraints and how to foster political will for it. [para. 2.24]

6.4 We consider that the clarification of policy objectives is critical. RIAs provide a good place for the clarification of policy objectives and the setting out of criteria for monitoring and review. Therefore RIAs should be enhanced in order to incorporate these considerations more effectively. [para. 3.16]

6.5 We consider that strengthened guidance from the centre of Government to departments will help to ensure that there is greater commitment from departments to post-enactment review work and that this would also strengthen the link between departmental review work and the Government's better regulation agenda. [para. 3.29]

6.6 We recommend that consideration be given to the setting up of a new Parliamentary joint committee on post-legislative scrutiny. Select committees would retain the power to undertake post-legislative review, but, if they decided not to exercise that power, the potential for review would then pass to a dedicated committee. The committee, supported by the Scrutiny Unit, could be involved at pre-legislative as well as post-legislative stages in considering what should be reviewed, could undertake the review work itself or commission others to do so and would develop organically within its broad terms of reference. [para. 3.47]

6.7 It already happens that legislation may provide for review by an external reviewer (for example in the Charities Bill). A new joint committee may wish to involve independent experts in its review work and in this context we do see a potential role for the National Audit Office. However, we do not see the need to create a new body independent of Parliament to carry out post-legislative scrutiny. [para. 3.54]

6.8 Whether or not a Bill has formal pre-legislative scrutiny, we suggest that departments should give routine consideration to whether and if so how legislation will be monitored and reviewed. This can be addressed through strengthened guidance on RIAs. If there is a new joint committee on post-legislative scrutiny, it might also consider Bills and whether and if so how they should be reviewed post-enactment. The committee might recommend that, in certain cases, a carefully thought-out review clause would be appropriate. [para. 3.59]

6.9 We believe that any system of post-legislative scrutiny should ensure that interested parties are able to channel their concerns about the operation of legislation to the reviewing body and play a part in any subsequent review through consultation or by giving evidence. [para. 3.68]

6.10 For Parliamentary review, we consider that a new joint committee will be best placed to decide which legislation should be reviewed. For departmental review, the decision should be for the department in accordance with guidance from the centre of Government. [paras 3.72 and 3.81]

6.11 We remain of the opinion that the timescale for review should not be prescribed in order to allow for flexibility of approach depending on the type of legislation under review and the type of review. [para. 3.75]

6.12 We invite the Government to consider whether departmental reviews should be published and possibly laid before Parliament. [para. 3.77]

6.13 We suggest that in the light of experience of post-legislative scrutiny of primary legislation by a new committee serving this purpose, there is scope for the development of Parliamentary post-legislative scrutiny of secondary legislation. [para. 4.7]

5. The Government broadly endorsed the Law Commission's proposals in the response made by the Leader of the House of Commons in 2008 (Cm 7320). The Government did not wish to see a joint committee but rather proposed that the department responsible for a statute should between three and five years after Royal Assent prepare a memorandum which would include:

- information on when and how different provisions of the Act had been brought into operation;
- information highlighting any provisions which had not been brought into force, or enabling powers not used, and explaining why not;
- a brief description or list of the associated delegated legislation, guidance documents or other relevant material prepared or issued in connection with the Act;
- an indication of any specific legal or drafting difficulties which had been matters of public concern (e.g. issues which had been the subject of actual litigation or of comment from parliamentary committees) and had been addressed;
- a summary of any other known post-legislative reviews or assessments of the Act conducted in Government, by Parliament, or elsewhere;
- a short preliminary assessment of how the Act has worked out in practice, relative to objectives and benchmarks identified at the time of the passage of the bill.

It would then be open to the relevant Commons departmental select committee to decide if it wished to conduct a post-legislative review. Yet it seems that despite this approach which the Coalition Government has affirmed, this type of scrutiny has not been a significant part of the work of select committees. The Liaison Committee's review of select committees noted that not much post-legislative scrutiny had been conducted as such, but that select committees had included it in wider reviews of government policy. Nonetheless the Committee thought it likely that this sort of scrutiny would place a greater demand on committee time in the future (HC 697 of 2010–112, para. 47). In its response to this point, the Government stated (HC 911 of 2012–13, p. 12):

The Government will keep under review the use made of these memoranda; if only a small minority of them are proving to be of value to select committees it may be a more efficient use of resources to adopt a more targeted approach, on the basis of discussions between departments and committees.

■ QUESTION

Do these proposals and initiatives in relation to both pre- and post-legislative scrutiny suggest a real change towards a more thorough approach to law-making and, if so, what might the implications be for House of Lords reform, where the House of Lords has tended to conduct a more painstaking technical approach to scrutiny of legislation than the current, more politically driven approach, adopted in the Commons?

There had been criticism of the quantity and quality of legislation. The Liaison Committee asked the Political and Constitutional Reform Committee (PCR Committee) to lead on the issue. In their report (HC 85 of 2013–14) the PCR Committee quoted, with approval, the view of the Hansard Society:

There is no single cause for this deficient legislation. The explanation lies in a complex confluence of factors primarily related to volume, attitude, preparation and deliberation.

The PCR Committee made five key recommendations:

i.   that there should be a Code of Legislative Standards for good quality legislation agreed between Parliament and the Government;

ii. that a Joint Legislative Standards Committee with an oversight role should be created;

iii. that a week should elapse between the conclusion of Public Bill Committee evidence sessions and the start of line by line scrutiny, to allow Members enough time to consider the evidence they have heard, and for amendments to be drafted and selected for debate;

iv. that a test for identifying constitutional legislation should be agreed between Parliament and the Government;

v. that the Government should publish the reasons why a bill has not been published in draft and cannot therefore be subject to pre-legislative scrutiny.

The Government in its response rejected most of these five key recommendations. The Government was, however, in favour of both pre- and post-legislative scrutiny. In relation to the recommendation to explain why there had not been a published draft bill, the Government said that in its review of the Explanatory Notes the Government is 'considering how information on the pre-introduction stages of a bill can best be included'. The Government did suggest that the creation of House of Lords committees on an ad hoc basis to conduct post-legislative review was an alternative to the limited work on this carried out in the Commons.

In the following extracts from the Government response, the reasons are given for rejecting the key PCR Committee's recommendations.

Political and Constitutional Reform Committee, *Ensuring standards in the quality of legislation: Government Response to the Committee's First Report of Session 2013–14*
HC 611 of 2013–14, paras 12–15, 17–20, 27, 58–60

12. The Government does not believe that a Code of Legislative Standards is necessary or would be effective in ensuring quality legislation. It is the responsibility of government to bring forward legislation of a high standard and it has comprehensive and regularly updated guidance to meet this objective. This is publicly available and can be used by parliamentarians in fulfilling their role of scrutinising legislation. Following a recent review, existing guidance for Parliamentary Counsel will be consolidated in the Cabinet Office's Guide to Making Legislation to further improve accessibility. We undertake annual lessons learned exercises within Government designed to capture best legislative practice and we would be happy to engage with parliamentarians on this exercise if that would be of interest. Ultimately, it is for Ministers to defend both the quality of the legislation they introduce and the supporting material provided to Parliament to aid scrutiny.

13. As the Committee acknowledges, many of the suggestions in its draft Code are already included in Explanatory Notes. For example, it is standard practice for the Explanatory Notes to refer to any consultation documents which the Government has issued. It is also standard practice for the Government to publish the response to any consultation, whether in a White Paper accompanying a Bill or as a separate document, and to make reference in the Explanatory Notes to where that response can be found. Explanatory Notes also routinely explain what the impact of the proposed legislation on existing arrangements will be, and where it is possible to access a wider assessment of the economic impact, the impact on the third sector and business.

14. The Government is committed to ensuring that Explanatory Notes, and Impact Assessments, are as helpful as they can be in meeting the needs of users and are of a consistently high standard. In pursuit of this aim, the Office of Parliamentary Counsel has been asked, as part of the Good Law initiative, to conduct a comprehensive review of Explanatory Notes. A comprehensive survey of users is being undertaken to establish exactly what users think should be included in revised Notes and how this information should be presented. Without wishing to pre-empt this work, we are minded to agree

with the Committee's view that there is logic in combining most information on a bill in one document. Members of the Committee will have an opportunity to comment on the outcome of this work and other proposals emanating from the Good Law initiative about the drafting of legislation.

15. The aim of the revised Explanatory Notes will be to provide bill documentation that contains the information that is most helpful to users, including both parliamentarians scrutinising the bill and the public seeking to understand and contribute to debate on it. Good Explanatory Notes explain why the legislation is needed and the process leading up to its introduction, as well as the meaning of each clause. But every bill is different and it is up to Government to provide the right material on a case-by-case basis. A Code of Legislative Standards with lists of requirements risks encouraging a tick-box mentality which does little to support effective scrutiny. Nor can a Code, as proposed by the Committee, provide the degree of objectivity it envisages: questions such as "is it understandable and accessible?" and "whether the change is politically or legally important" indicate the extent to which the quality of legislation is a subjective judgement. Similarly, whether purpose clauses or sunset clauses are required to meet the expected "standard" will always be a matter for debate on a case-by-case basis rather than an objective test. This underlines the difficulty any committee would have in separating the quality of legislation from the policy underlying it.

...

17. The Government does not believe that a Legislative Standards Committee, as proposed by the Committee, is either necessary or would be effective in improving legislation.

18. Without a Code of Legislative Standards, the case for a Committee, part of whose remit is to monitor compliance with the Code, weakens significantly. As has been explained, revised Explanatory Notes will set out necessary information relating to the preparation and content of the bill and Ministers will account directly to Parliament for any perceived deficiencies.

19. Another proposed purpose of the Committee – to monitor the work of the Cabinet Committee on Parliamentary Business and Legislation – would not be appropriate. Paragraph 2.3 of the Ministerial Code states that the internal process through which a decision is made or the level of committee by which it was taken should not be disclosed. It is essential that time and space be allowed for Ministers to debate and stress test legislation within Government before presenting its final position. A bill when it is published is the collectively agreed view of the whole Government on how it wishes to proceed. The process by which it has arrived at that view is a matter for the Government, not for Parliament.

20. Whilst the model advocated by the Committee would meet concerns about introducing further delay to the legislative process, it has notable shortcomings. By normally examining legislation shortly after Royal Assent, its intervention would come too late to amend the bill but too early to conduct meaningful post-legislative scrutiny. Any deficiencies in legislation are unlikely to become apparent until it has been fully implemented and in use for a reasonable period: hence the 3–5 year window agreed between Government and Parliament for post-legislative scrutiny.

...

27. If, as the Committee asserts, the majority of poor quality legislation results from inadequate policy preparation or insufficient time allowed for drafting, it is difficult to see how a Code and Legislative Standards Committee would address this. Whilst the Committee recognises that "legislation is not made in a vacuum" it underplays the degree to which it is an iterative process, with policies being refined and adjusted under the light of Parliamentary scrutiny and changing circumstances. Nor is legislative scrutiny an objective, academic exercise, the sole purpose of which is deliver high quality law. Good legislative practice may be put under pressure by wider political considerations from time to time. No Legislative Standards Committee, however formed, would be immune from such political considerations.

...

58. The Government does not accept that it would be helpful to seek to define "constitutional" legislation, nor that it should automatically be subject to a different standard of scrutiny. The tests suggested by Lord Norton and the list of characteristics suggested by Professor Sir John Baker are themselves subjective: whether something raises an important issue of principle, or represents a "substantial" alteration to the liberties of the subject, for example, are matters more for political rather than technical judgement.

59. The Government does not accept that the process of identifying bills to take on the floor of the House of Commons lacks transparency. It is up to each House to agree to what is proposed on each bill or, if not content, to propose alternatives. It is usually a matter of common sense and therefore uncontroversial, although not all bills that might be deemed constitutional are taken on the Floor in Committee. The Leader of the House of Commons answers questions on forthcoming business each week and has seldom been asked to provide an explanation of the rationale behind the type of committee stage proposed for a bill.

60. The Government does not agree with the Committee's assertion that "constitutional law is qualitatively different from other types of legislation". Constitutional legislation, like all legislation, varies in its importance, complexity and impact. It may form a small part of a wider and otherwise "non-constitutional" bill. In some cases, a non-constitutional bill might bring about fundamental social change, with greater impact on daily life, than what might be deemed a constitutional bill, and warrant more thorough scrutiny on this basis. Current legislative processes provide sufficient flexibility to allow an assessment to be made on the bill in question and the Government to propose the appropriate method and level of scrutiny.

■ QUESTION

Is the Government's rejection of the idea that constitutional legislation is qualitatively different from other legislation contradicted by the convention that constitutional bills have their committee stage on the floor of the House?

(d) Revising parliamentary procedure

The fact that MPs representing Scottish constituencies could participate fully in the procedures at Westminster to make legislation applying only to England, or England and Wales, while MPs in English (or Welsh) constituencies could not vote for legislation applying only to Scotland under the powers devolved to the Scottish Parliament was an anomaly which was recognized (as the 'West Lothian question') when devolution was first legislated for in the late 1970s. Since the implementation of the Scotland Act 1998 the number of people sharing the perception that this is unfair has increased and so has the associated sense of grievance. This prompted the appointment by the Coalition Government in 2012 of The Commission on the Consequences of Devolution for the House of Commons. Its report (2013) had the guiding principle 'decisions at the United Kingdom level with a separate and distinct effect for England (or for England-and-Wales) should normally be taken only with the consent of a majority of MPs for constituencies in England (or England-and-Wales)'. The Conservative Party's England Manifesto for the 2015 General Election included a proposal for English Votes for English Laws (EVEL). Following their election success this promise was implemented via a change to the Standing Orders of the Commons rather than through primary legislation. The changed legislative process gives rights of veto to MPs representing English constituencies, or English and Welsh constituencies (as applicable), over legislation which (i) relates only to England, or England and Wales, or (in more limited circumstances concerning financial measures in England, Wales, and Northern Ireland); and (ii) concerns topics for which responsibility has been devolved to Scotland, Wales, or Northern Ireland (as appropriate). The amended Standing Order 83 requires the Speaker of the House of Commons, before a bill receives its Second Reading, to identify and certify those clauses which satisfy the two conditions above. When a certified bill then comes for detailed consideration in Committee Stage, it will be considered in a public bill committee composed of only English MPs, or English and Welsh MPs, depending on where it will have effect. Crucially, following Report Stage—at which the agreement of a majority of all MPs is required—before the bill can be given its Third Reading in the Commons, a new stage is inserted: a Legislative Grand Committee for England, or England and Wales (or, exceptionally, England, Wales, and Northern Ireland) must pass a Legislative Consent Motion to indicate that the bill (or relevant clauses) also has the approval of a majority of MPs representing the constituencies which the legislation will affect. Clauses (or bills) which do not, even after reconsideration, meet the requirement would fail to progress. The House of Lords legislative process has not been changed, but if a bill is amended in the Lords, any amendments which are certified by the Speaker must be approved by a double majority of all MPs, and, within that, all English/English and Welsh MPs, in the Commons. Secondary legislation must also (where applicable) be approved by a double majority. (See Figure 7.1.)

The new EVEL law-making procedure does not therefore remove the right of all MPs—regardless of constituency—to vote on any bill, but it inserts additional requirements into the legislative process. This has resulted in considerable complexity, and the EVEL process has been criticized on this basis.

Procedure Committee, *English Votes for English Laws Standing Orders: reports of the Committee's technical evaluation*
HC 189 of 2016–17, paras 69, 71–2, 75–6, 31–2, 45, 73

69. … In short, the standing orders and the procedure they provide for are undesirable and inconsistent with the House's traditions. The House has developed and adopted standing orders to regulate its own procedures in ways which its Members can interpret and comprehend. The drafting of the October 2015 package has grafted onto the House's existing standing orders procedures which, in their drafting, are alien to the House's traditions. It is wholly unacceptable that their drafting is so opaque as to defy interpretation by Members. They fly in the face of any attempt by the House to make its procedures more open and accessible.…

71. We expect the Government, in its technical review of the EVEL procedures, to give serious attention both to the unsatisfactory design of the present system and to the overelaborate means whereby it is implemented. We recommend that the Government, as a matter of urgency, should commission a project to redraft the present EVEL standing orders to make them more accessible and comprehensible, and to deliver a package more likely to command respect, support and understanding from all sides of the House.

Conclusion

72. On 22 October 2015 the House agreed to implement, through Standing Orders, new procedures which have had far-reaching implications for the preparation of legislation and its passage through the legislative process, the role of the Speaker in making determinations on the content of bills and amendments, the systems used by the House to record votes cast in divisions, and the use of the Chamber itself. The level of complexity added to the formal proceedings of the House on legislation has been substantial. Standing Orders have increased in number by 15 and in length by twelve per cent.…

75. … We have not pronounced on the merits of the policy which the Government has sought to implement through standing order changes, though we trust the Government will reflect on the implications of the technical issues we have raised for the feasibility of its broader policy objectives. The

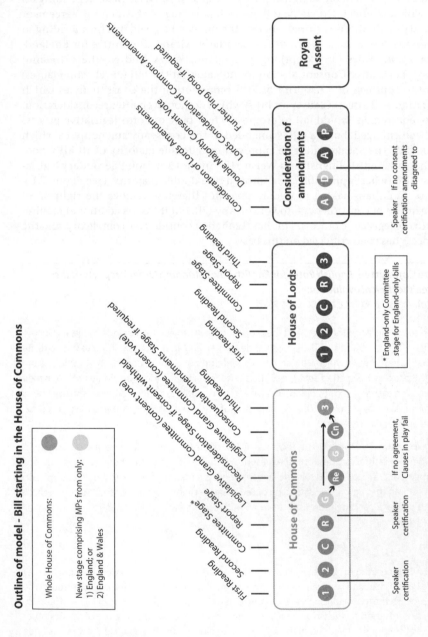

Figure 7.1 House of Commons Library, Briefing Note No 7339, *English Votes for English Laws* (2015)

complexity of a system which seeks to join two separate functions—a political voice and a legislative veto—has led to imperfect results. It is this contradiction at the heart of the system's design that the Government must urgently address.

76. We remain concerned that the substantial standing order changes made in October 2015 were not achieved by consensus. The House was sharply divided on their introduction: solely members of the Government party voted in favour, and members of six of the seven other parties represented in the House, together with one independent Member voted against…. One year on from their introduction, we find that the new EVEL procedures do not command the respect and support across all parties that they should if the system is to be sustainable through the political stresses it must expect to face in the future. This is not a sound basis for a major long-term change to the legislative process in this House. When reviewing the operation of the present system, and contemplating any change, it is vital that the Government seek consensus from Members representing constituencies in each constituent nation of the United Kingdom for the basis of a system which will meet its policy objectives.

The Committee also noted issues with the functioning of Legislative Grand Committees.

Legislative grand committees

31. One or more legislative grand committees have met on 12 occasions in relation to bills which have been certified either before Second Reading or after Report stage as containing provisions requiring the consent of Members from constituencies in England or England and Wales.

Debate and other proceedings in legislative grand committee

32. We have not been overwhelmed with evidence praising this procedural innovation. Genuine debate in such committees has been so scarce as to be almost non-existent. One individual Member has been responsible for over thirty minutes speaking time out of the total time of one hour and 23 minutes taken by the House in legislative grand committee. Apart from the formal moving of consent motions by Ministers, five other members have spoken in such debates….

45. Legislative grand committees were intended to give Members representing England or England and Wales a forum to debate, and to agree, whether to consent to, or withhold consent from, certified provisions of legislation. In practice, these committees are regularly brought into existence purely so that those Members may formally waive their rights to object to a motion consenting to certified provisions of bills. Legislative grand committees are at present performing a function which suits the Government—namely delivering decisions and validating certified elements of legislation—but are not effectively serving the broader objective of allowing Members from constituencies in England or England and Wales a separate voice on proposed legislation. The attempt to combine the twin functions of voice and veto in a single legislative stage is not delivering significant and worthwhile benefits to Members representing constituencies in England and Wales.

Nevertheless, despite these complexities, the Committee noted, concerns about the politicization of the Speaker had not been realized.

73. … There have been no instances where the Speaker's certification has been challenged by Ministers, even in areas where the Speaker has come to a decision on certification which differs from the view set out by the Government….

NOTE: While the report of the Procedure Committee provides much evidence of the complexity of the new arrangements, their contradictory objectives, and their largely superficial impact on parliamentary practice, the broader constitutional implication of EVEL may also be significant (see Chapter 8, Section 2B at p. 353). Noting the difficulty in drawing conclusions about the constitutional impact of EVEL on the Union at this early stage, the House of Lords Constitution Committee, *English Votes for English Laws* (HL Paper 61 of 2016–17) observed, pp. 3–4:

> We recommend that, following the Government's review in autumn 2016, the EVEL procedures—
> if they are retained—should be subject to an extended trial period for the remainder of this
> Parliament, with a final review taking place early in the next Parliament. The next few years will
> see a series of votes on matters relating to the UK's exit from the EU which may well provide a
> 'stress test' for the procedures. Following the extended trial period, the revised procedures should
> be subject to scrutiny by a Joint Committee examining both the technical and the constitutional
> aspects of EVEL.

NOTE: The Government commenced a 'technical review' of EVEL in October 2016.

■ QUESTION

Is the English Votes for English Laws system: (i) desirable; and (ii) workable? Could it have broader constitutional consequences if Scottish and Northern Irish MPs come to feel that they have a lower status than English (and where applicable, Welsh) MPs in the UK Parliament to which they were all similarly elected?

(e) Delegated legislation

House of Lords Library Note 2013/008 *Volume of Legislation*

Table 4 Statutory Instruments

Year	No of SIs	No of Pages	Average No Pages
1961	747	4525	6
1971	1116	6305	6
1981	1047	6516	6
1987[†]	1176	6256	5
1991	1508	7506	5
1996	1800	10151	6
1997	1634	8522	5
1998	1534	7344	5
1999	1742	10602	6
2000	1582	8608	5
2001	1861	10711	6
2002	1574	9039	6
2003	1488	9328	6
2004	1470	9435	6
2005	1559	12758	8
2006	1408	11289	8
2007	1513	11961	8
2008	1395	10662	8
2009	1420	11414	8

[†]1987 Change in size of Queen's Printer's bound volumes from A5 to A4
[Selected statistics]
Source: House of Lords Library

NOTE: As detailed in Chapter 6, Section 2B-C, at pp. 240–61, it is possible to divide the work of the House of Commons between that which takes place on the floor and that which takes place in committee. The most detailed scrutiny of a bill or a statutory instrument will take place in committee.

There are various procedures by which statutory instruments are passed. The instrument may or may not be required to be laid before Parliament. If it is to be laid before Parliament, then there may or may not be provision for action by Parliament. The action to be taken by Parliament can be broadly divided into affirmative and negative procedures. Under the affirmative procedure Parliament must pass an affirmative resolution in order for the measure to become law or to continue as law. On the other hand, a measure will remain in force unless Parliament annuls it using the negative procedure. The negative resolution is by far the most frequently used procedure by which Parliament may supervise statutory instruments. In order to annul a statutory instrument the prayer for annulment must have been passed within 40 days of the laying of the instrument before Parliament.

The statute which enables the making of a statutory instrument will specify which procedure is to be used. Unlike the case with bills, it is extremely rare for a statutory instrument to be amended as only a very few enabling statutes provide for amendment.

Specialist committees. Parliament has created several specialist committees to examine delegated legislation and European Communities legislation. The committees dealing with delegated legislation are divided between those which deal with technical matters and those which deal with the merits. The technical committees are (i) the Joint Select Committee on Delegated Legislation; and (ii) the Commons Select Committee on Statutory Instruments, composed of the House of Commons members of the Joint Committee, which deals with instruments subject only to House of Commons oversight. The merits of an instrument may be referred to a House of Commons standing committee or be dealt with on the floor of the House.

Those committees dealing with the European Union are, in the House of Commons, the European Scrutiny Committee, and, in the House of Lords, the Select Committee on the European Communities. These committees consider both delegated legislation which is intended to implement EU legislation, and proposals from Brussels for future EU legislation.

The House of Commons Committee may refer matters to three European Standing Committees, two of which were established in 1990–91 and a third in 1998.

Procedure Select Committee, *Delegated Legislation*
HC 48 of 1999–2000, paras 10–12, 14, 17–18, 20–1, 23, 41, 43–5, 48–53

Criticisms of the Existing System, and the 1996 Report's Recommendations

10. In devising an effective system of scrutiny of delegated legislation, the key question is how best to target Parliament's over-stretched resources of time and expertise. There is widespread agreement that at present those resources are ineffectively targeted. There are three major areas of criticism.

11. Firstly it is argued that instruments do not receive scrutiny in proportion to their merits. The current system, as outlined in paragraphs 5 to 9 above, rests on the assumption that affirmative instruments are intrinsically more significant and debate-worthy than negative ones. This may be true of a majority of instruments, but it is generally acknowledged that there is a significant minority of affirmatives which deal with matters too trivial or technical to merit debate, and negatives which deal with important or sensitive matters where there is demand for a debate. This mismatch between the level of scrutiny provided for in the parent legislation and the level which is actually appropriate may arise from a variety of factors. Ministers may have up-graded procedure from negative to affirmative as a political concession during committee stage of a bill; contrariwise, the conferral of significant powers may have 'slipped through' Parliament without provision for proper scrutiny; whilst in other cases, circumstances may have changed during the years or decades since the passage of the parent legislation, rendering issues once regarded as important less so, and vice versa. Nonetheless, in the words of the Clerk of the House, 'the House is locked into a procedural approach to an instrument by provisions made sometimes many, many years before in the parent act'. As a result, the time and expertise of Members is frequently wasted in attendance at DL Committees to consider 'trivial affirmatives', often meeting for a few minutes only; whilst significant changes to the law may pass through Parliament unregarded and undebated because contained in negative instruments.

12. Our predecessors in 1996 [HC 152 of 1995–96] briefly considered the question of whether the existing distinction between affirmatives and negatives should be retained ... 14. The 1996 report concluded that the most satisfactory way forward would be for the House to establish a single 'Sifting Committee' to consider and assess all SIs laid before Parliament. The committee would have power to call for further information from government departments where necessary. Its key task would be to make recommendations on which negative instruments merited debate. The recommendations would be put to the House by the chairman of the committee in the form of a motion which could be opposed and indeed defeated (thus enabling the Government to retain its ultimate control of the process). The committee would also have powers to identify affirmative instruments which did *not* merit debate, and on which the question could be put forthwith unless at least six Members had earlier indicated they wished for a debate. In order to allow a reasonable time for scrutiny, the report recommended that praying time against negative instruments should be extended from 40 to 60 days (this would require amendment of the Statutory Instruments Act 1946). The Sifting Committee would require specialist staff back-up.

...

17. The 1996 report recommended that motions in DL Committee should be substantive and amendable, and that where the Government's motion is defeated there should be up to an hour's further debate on the Floor. It also proposed that aspects of European Standing Committee procedure should be adopted for DL Committees, in particular that proceedings should begin with a Ministerial statement and questions, and that debate should last for up to two and a half hours, rather than one and a half as at present.

18. The 1996 report considered the question of whether statutory instruments themselves should be amendable during their passage. At present instruments cannot be amended unless the parent legislation allows for it, and virtually no legislation currently in force so allows. The Committee concluded that the complications that would ensue from any change in this position would greatly outweigh any likely benefits.

...

20. The existing system of scrutiny has also been criticised for containing no provision for a higher level of scrutiny for a small number of very complex SIs. The 1996 Committee proposed a new category of 'super-affirmatives', whereby proposals for draft Orders would be laid for pre-legislative scrutiny by the relevant departmental select committee. This would be an adaptation of the existing procedure for considering draft Deregulation proposals.

21. The 1996 report contained a number of further recommendations. The most important of these was that a standing order should be passed to provide that no decision on a statutory instrument should be made by the House until the instrument had been considered by the Joint Committee on Statutory Instruments. A similar standing order already exists in the House of Lords. The report pointed out that it would always be open to the House to override the standing order by resolution if the Government could persuade it that this was justified in a particular case. This recommendation to create a 'scrutiny reserve' has been strongly supported by the Chairman and members of the present JCSI.

...

Developments since 1996

23. We have considered whether developments since publication of the 1996 report have affected the validity of its conclusions.

...

41. With regard to the Royal Commission's proposal that the sifting of SIs should be entrusted to a Joint Committee, we consider that this might be a sensible way of avoiding duplication of effort, but

measures would need to be taken to ensure that recommendations relating to Commons business were taken by the Commons members of any such committee alone.

...

43. Of equal, perhaps even greater, significance for our present purposes has been the extent to which other, permanent committees both of the Commons and the Lords have been developing techniques of scrutiny in recent years. Several deserve to be highlighted.

44. The *House of Lords Select Committee on Delegated Powers and Deregulation* was set up (as the Select Committee on Delegated Powers) on an experimental basis in 1992–93, and since 1993–94 has been routinely reappointed on a sessional basis. In 1994 it was given the additional role of scrutinising deregulation proposals. Its ... concern is ... 'with the justification for and appropriateness of the secondary powers' ... and it [noted] that 'we have never needed to divide in the seven sessions of our existence'. It added that when it had advised the House that bills should be amended, this advice had 'almost always been accepted by the Government and the House'. The Government has undertaken to respond quickly to the Committee's reports, if practicable.

45. In the Commons, the *Deregulation Committee* was first set up in 1994, to consider proposals for orders and draft Orders laid under the Deregulation and Contracting Out Act 1994. In each case the Committee conducts its examination both at the pre-legislative stage (proposals for orders) and, if it is reached, the legislative stage (draft Orders). Within a fixed timetable the Committee can take written or oral evidence, and report to the House its opinion on whether or not the proposal should proceed or the draft Order be approved. What happens to draft Orders in the House depends on the nature of the Committee's report: if it has reported unanimously that the draft Order should be approved, a motion to that effect is put in the House and the Question put forthwith; if it has agreed on Division that the draft Order should be approved, a motion is moved and the Question put after a maximum of one and a half hours' debate; and if it has recommended that the draft Order should not be approved, the Government may move a motion to disagree with the Committee's report on which the Question can be put after a maximum of 3 hours' debate, with the Question on the draft Order put forthwith if that motion is agreed to. . . .

48. The *European Scrutiny Committee* (until 1998 the European Legislation Committee) is charged with the task of considering a range of EU documents, as defined in Standing Order No. 143. These include EU Regulations, Directives, Decisions of the Council, budgetary documents, Commission proposals, reports and recommendations, documents submitted to the European Central Bank, various inter-governmental proposals, and reports of the Court of Auditors. About 1,000 EU documents a year are deposited in Parliament for scrutiny. The Committee's functions are to assess the political and/or legal importance of these documents and decide which merit further scrutiny, either in European Standing Committee or on the Floor; to report in detail on each document the Committee considers important (some 475 a year), taking written and oral evidence if necessary; to monitor business in the Council of Ministers and the negotiating position of UK Ministers; to review EU legal, procedural and institutional developments which may have implications for the UK and the House; and to police the scrutiny system.

49. When a document is referred by the Committee to one of the three *European Standing Committees*, that committee will meet to hear a Government Minister make a statement and answer questions put by Members for up to one hour (extendable by a further 30 minutes at the Chairman's discretion); this is followed by a debate on an amendable motion for up to a further one hour 30 minutes. The Chairman reports to the House any resolution to which the committee has come, or that it has come to no resolution. A Government motion couched in similar terms is usually moved in the House a few days later; the Question on this is put forthwith.

50. Some aspects of this European scrutiny process have potential implications for the House's consideration of delegated legislation. First, the European Scrutiny Committee acts as a 'filter' on behalf of the House. It assesses a large number of documents and reaches judgements on whether they merit further debate, either on the Floor of the House or in one of the European Standing Committees. This role would be similar to that envisaged in the 1996 report for the Sifting Committee on delegated legislation. The European Scrutiny Committee performs this role with the assistance of a comparatively large complement of staff and advisers. Second, the 1996 report recommended that certain aspects of European Standing Committee procedure be transferred to DL committees—in particular, beginning proceedings with a statement and questions, allowing debate on a substantive amendable motion, and extending the period of debate to two and a half hours from the present one and a half.

51. The 1996 report commented that 'the European Legislation Committee and the Deregulation Committee have demonstrated that scrutiny by committees can work, and can engage Members' attention and commitment'. We have taken evidence from the Chairman of both Committees, and are happy to endorse that view. The activities of the European Scrutiny Committee, European Standing Committees, the Deregulation Committee and the House of Lords Delegated Powers and Deregulation Committee have continued to develop during the four years since our predecessors reported, and form a valuable contribution to the effectiveness of Parliament. In particular, it has been demonstrated that committees working within the Westminster tradition can successfully develop modes of scrutiny involving the sifting of complex documents, the targeted use of specialist staff resources, the maintenance where appropriate of traditions of non-partisanship, and the holding of Ministers to account in public committee meetings through question-and-answer sessions as well as through debate on amendable and substantive motions. They have also demonstrated the ability of select committees, appropriately resourced, to combine the examination of technical detail which is characteristic of the Joint Committee on Statutory Instruments with the exercise of political judgement. In short, almost every element of the 1996 report's proposed reforms in the field of delegated legislation has been pioneered in one or other of these committees and shown to be eminently workable.

Conclusions

52. The package of proposals first put forward in 1996, which we endorse, was deliberately designed to be realistic, not Utopian. Taken as a whole, the proposals recognise the constraints imposed both by the Government's need to make progress with its legislative programme and the House's wish that minor business should not take up valuable time on the Floor. We recognise that it is in the nature of secondary legislation that it should receive less protracted and intensive scrutiny than primary legislation.

53. Nonetheless, the existing system of scrutinising delegated legislation is urgently in need of reform. We concur with our predecessors' description of that system as 'palpably unsatisfactory' . . .

NOTES

1. In relation to the proposal of sifting statutory instruments the House of Lords established a committee to do this but the House of Commons did not. The House of Lords appointed its Merits of Statutory Instruments Committee in December 2003 and began reporting weekly on SIs in April 2004. The Secondary Legislation Scrutiny Committee (SLSC) is the successor to the Merits of Statutory Instruments Committee, which was established in 2003 and existed until the end of the 2010–12 session. The SLSC considers the policy merits of regulations and other types of secondary legislation subject to parliamentary procedure; the Committee will consider all statutory instruments which are subject to parliamentary procedure (negative and affirmative). The Committee reports on an S.I. within 12–16 days of it being laid before Parliament, to allow time for any Member of the House to pursue the issues raised by asking a question or tabling a motion for debate within the 40-day 'prayer' period for negative instruments. Affirmative instruments have to be considered by the SLSC before they can be debated in House of Lords. The Committee meets weekly when the House is in session and aims to publish reports of its

activities by the following week. Reports indicate statutory instruments that the Committee has determined should be drawn to the attention of the House, including the reasons for that decision—examples may be instruments are poorly drafted or inadequately explained; statutory instruments which the Committee considers may be of special interest to the House, and instruments which the Committee has considered and has determined that the special attention of the House need not be drawn.

2. In the Commons the Procedure Committee proposed that a joint sifting committee should be created (HC 501 of 2002–03). The Government rejected this and the Committee was unimpressed with the reasons given: the increase in time spent on debating instruments, the desirability of considering the experience of the Lords' committee, and that the matter was one for the Modernisation Committee, arguing that the extra time would result in more systematic scrutiny; that the arguments for accepting sifting in the Lords were just as applicable in the Commons and working jointly would be more effective, and that the Modernisation Committee had agreed to the Procedure Committee taking the lead on this topic.

3. The Regulatory Reform Order is a type of delegated legislation which is unusual in that it (a) may amend primary legislation and (b) may itself be amended during its parliamentary passage if the super-affirmative procedure is used. This is provided for by the Legislative and Regulatory Reform Act 2006 which replaced the Regulatory Reform Act 2001. Its aim is to ease regulatory burdens but the initial proposals were thought to confer too much power on Ministers and met with strong opposition both inside and outside Parliament. Several select committees reported adversely. In the Commons the committees were: Regulatory Reform (HC 878 of 2005–06); Procedure (HC 894 of 2005–06); Public Administration (HC 1033 of 2005–06); and in the Lords, Delegated Powers and Regulatory Reform (HL 192 of 2005–06) and Constitution (HL 194 of 2005–06). A group of Cambridge Law professors wrote a letter to *The Times*, 16 February 2006, raising their concern about the 'drastic power' and its 'weak limits'. Section 1 of the Regulatory Reform Act 2006 gives Ministers the power by order to remove or reduce burdens in legislation which are imposed directly or indirectly on any person. The burden may be (a) a financial cost; (b) an administrative inconvenience; (c) an obstacle to efficiency, productivity or profitability; or (d) a sanction, criminal or otherwise, which affects the carrying on of any lawful activity. The preconditions for such regulatory reform orders are (a) the policy objective intended to be secured by the provision could not be satisfactorily secured by non-legislative means; (b) the effect of the provision is proportionate to the policy objective; (c) the provision, taken as a whole, strikes a fair balance between the public interest and the interests of any person adversely affected by it; (d) the provision does not remove any necessary protection; (e) the provision does not prevent any person from continuing to exercise any right or freedom which that person might reasonably expect to continue to exercise; (f) the provision is not of constitutional significance. Before a Minister may make a regulatory reform order, there must be a consultation process involving those affected by the proposals and others. If it is felt appropriate to proceed then a draft order with an explanatory document are to be laid before Parliament. The explanatory document as well as explaining the need for the order and the details and result of the consultation, including if any changes were made as a consequence of representations received, must make a reasoned recommendation as to which procedure should be following in making the order. The procedures are (a) the negative resolution procedure; (b) the affirmative resolution procedure; and (c) the super-affirmative procedure. Within 30 days of the laying of the draft order either House of Parliament can resolve that the procedure to be applied to a draft order can be 'upgraded' and thus require more Parliamentary control. The negative resolution procedure could be upgraded to either the affirmative or super-affirmative and the affirmative resolution procedure to the super-affirmative. The Commons' Regulatory Reform Committee and the Lords Delegated Powers and Regulatory Reform Committee will consider the draft order. Under the negative resolution procedure the Minister may make an order in the terms of the draft after 40 days from the laying of the draft order unless either House of Parliament resolves that it not be made. The committees which scrutinize the order may after 30 days and before 40 days from laying recommend that it not be made in the terms of the draft. This 'veto' may be overturned in the same session by a resolution of that committee's House. Under the affirmative resolution procedure the Minister makes the order in terms of the draft if it has been approved in a resolution by each House of Parliament. Under the super-affirmative procedure, the Minister is to have regard to any representations, any resolution of either House and the recommendation of any committee scrutinizing the draft made in the 60-day period following its laying. If the Minister seeks to make the order in terms of the draft,

then a statement is to be laid which gives details of representations and recommendations made in the 60 days and the Minister may make the order if both Houses of Parliament so resolve. Either of the committees scrutinizing the order may recommend taking no further proceedings after the statement has been laid and this may be overturned in the same session by the relevant House. The Minister may after the 60-day period decide to revise the draft order, in which case this is laid with details of representations and the revisions. If this revised draft is approved by both Houses then the Minister may make it in those revised terms but a committee can recommend not proceeding with it and that can be overturned by resolution of the relevant House. Each House's Standing Orders specify the procedures to be followed when a committee has made a recommendation on a draft order.

4. Another type of delegated legislation which may amend primary legislation is an order provided for by the Public Bodies Act 2011. The policy the statute is implementing is the reform of public bodies, checking if they are needed and, if they are, whether they might be merged with other bodies or otherwise modified. In schedules 1–5 were listed 285 public bodies established by statute and ss 1–5 provide for orders which may abolish, merge, or modify constitutional arrangements, funding arrangements and the modifying or transferring of functions. Section 8 sets out tests for the purpose to be achieved by orders, Consultation requirements are imposed by s. 10 and the procedure is outlined in s. 11. This procedure may be summarized:

- a draft public bodies order is laid before both Houses by the Minister, together with an Explanatory Document;
- a 40-day scrutiny period is thereby initiated, after which the draft order can be put to both Houses for approval;
- during the first 30 days of the scrutiny period, the nominated committee in each House, or either House itself, can trigger the 60-day 'enhanced affirmative' procedure;
- if the 60-day enhanced affirmative procedure is triggered, the nominated committee in either House can make recommendations on the draft order, or either House can pass resolutions relating to the draft order; and the Minister has a statutory duty to have regard to those recommendations or resolutions;
- once the 60-day period is completed, the Minister may either submit the draft order in its original form for approval by resolution of each House of Parliament or, if he wishes to make material changes to the draft order, he may lay a revised draft before both Houses together with a statement summarising the changes proposed.

The report discussed in Note 5 below, also pointed out that the experience of using Regulatory Reform and Public Bodies Orders was taking rather longer than anticipated and that it was suggested that Government departments acknowledge it would be preferable to use primary legislation.

5. The Hansard Society produced a report *The Devil is in the Detail: Parliament and Delegated Legislation*, which was extremely critical of the way in which Parliament scrutinized delegated legislation as well as the confusing nomenclature and procedure which meant the public had very little understanding or appreciation of its significance. It called for an independent inquiry to conduct a thorough examination of the entire legislative process for the preparation and scrutiny of primary and secondary legislation, which would consider, amongst other points, the balance between administrative and political convenience and good legislative practice, criteria for what Members want to consider in delegated legislation and how this can be best achieved, whether there could individual or independent bodies with particular expertise in various policy areas, and whether the House of Lords might take up more of the burden in scrutinizing delegated legislation. Indeed, the report had suggested reforming Commons Delegated Legislation Committees along the lines of the Lords' arrangements for European scrutiny, a committee with specialist policy area sub-committees, and that the House of Lords should make greater but judicious use of its veto. The following year the Government reacted to a cleverly worded delaying motion by the Lords, and the ensuing events are considered next.

(f) Strathclyde review

Following a defeat in the House of Lords on the Draft Tax Credits (Income Thresholds and Determination of Rates) (Amendment) Regulations 2015, the Government asked Lord Strathclyde to examine how the Government might 'secure their business in

Parliament' and to consider how to ensure 'the decisive role of the elected House of Commons in relation to its primacy on financial matters, and secondary legislation'.

The Review (*The Strathclyde Review: Secondary Legislation and the primacy of the House of Commons*, Cm 2015, 2015) sets out three options: option 1 would remove the Lords from secondary legislation procedure altogether; option 2 would entail the reframing of the convention governing the exercise of the power of the Lords so that the 'veto is left unused'; and, option 3—the option recommended by Lord Strathclyde—would create a new statutory procedure which would remove the power of the Lords to reject an instrument but would allow the Lords to invite the Commons to 'think again' in an unspecified way.

Three House of Lords and one House of Commons select committees made critical reports and the Government, in its response to the committees (Cm 9396, 2016), said that '... the Government does not intend to introduce legislation in this parliamentary session.' This is not surprising given the tenor of the committees' reports. For example, the conclusion of the Commons Public Administration and Constitutional Affairs Committee, *The Strathclyde Review: Statutory Instruments and the House of Lords*, HC752 of 2015–16, at para. 56:

> The Government should not produce legislative proposals aimed at implementing the Strathclyde Review's recommendations. Such legislation would be an overreaction and entirely disproportionate to the House of Lords' legitimate exercise of a power that even Lord Strathclyde has admitted is rarely used. The Government's time would be better spent in rethinking the way it relies on secondary legislation for implementing its policy objectives and in building better relations with the other groupings in the House of Lords.

There was a consensus amongst the four committees as to the real issue being the balance of power between the Executive and Parliament and the proper scrutiny of the large volume of delegated legislation. In the extracts which follow, analysis is provided by the Lords Constitution Committee on the issues of whether there was a convention on the Lords vetoing delegated legislation and financial privilege; by the Lords Deregulatory Powers and Regulatory Reform Committee on the proper boundary between primary and delegated legislation; and by the Lords Secondary Legislation Scrutiny Committee on the Strathclyde options.

Constitution Committee, *Delegated Legislation and Parliament: A response to the Strathclyde Review,*
HL 116 of 2015–16, paras 23–32

Conventions and established practice in relation to delegated legislation

23. While the House of Lords has previously resolved "That this House affirms its unfettered freedom to vote on any subordinate legislation submitted for its consideration", it has rarely been the House's practice to reject delegated legislation. In 2006, the Joint Committee on Conventions of the UK Parliament scrutinised various elements of relations between the two Houses. On delegated legislation, it concluded "that the House of Lords should not regularly reject Statutory Instruments, but that in exceptional circumstances it may be appropriate for it to do so". The report then set out a non-prescriptive list of 'exceptional circumstances'. It noted that in the absence of any exceptional or special circumstances, "opposition parties should not use their numbers in the House of Lords to defeat an SI simply because they disagree with it."

24. There is no doubt that rejecting a statutory instrument is a significant act. The 2011 report of the Leader's Group on Working Practices, chaired by Lord Goodlad, stated that "the use by Parliament of

its statutory power either to annul or to decline to approve SIs is seen as a 'nuclear option', to be used rarely, or not at all."

25. The Strathclyde Review set out the difficulty faced by members of the House:

"The convention that the House of Lords should not, or should not regularly, reject SIs is long-standing but has been interpreted in different ways, has not been understood by all, and has never been accepted by some members of the House."

26. Some members argue that the defeat of the Tax Credits Regulations was covered by the 'exceptional circumstances' qualification set out in the Joint Committee's description of the convention. Others suggest that since the motion was arguably not fatal the convention did not apply. **What is clear is that conventions can only govern proceedings when there is a common understanding as to their meaning—and that is no longer the case, if it ever were. We are wary of describing the House's pattern of behaviour in relation to statutory instruments as constituting a constitutional convention at all; it might better be described as long established practice.**

27. It is clear that motions to reject delegated legislation are still uncommon. The House has divided on delegated legislation over 150 times since 1950; slightly over half have been on fatal motions. These resulted in six statutory instruments being defeated (if one includes the Tax Credits Regulations), five of them since 1997. The Government has won over 90% of divisions on fatal motions since 1950; including 84% since 1997.

28. It should be acknowledged, however, that the number of instruments subject to divisions on fatal motions in the current Session has been relatively high … There have been divisions on fatal motions on five instruments so far in this Session. The only sessions in which more instruments have been the subject of fatal motions were the 2006–07 Session, when six divisions took place and one instrument was not approved, and the long 1979–80 Session, when the Government faced and won nine divisions on fatal motions.

29. The number of divisions and rejections of instruments should be considered in the context of the huge scale of delegated legislation. In the last ten full sessions (2004–05 to 2014–15), the House considered over 2,000 motions on delegated legislation, nearly 13,000 statutory instruments were laid before Parliament, and some 36,000 statutory instruments became law. In that same period, the House of Lords rejected two instruments.

Financial privilege

30. The final point of contention was over the extent to which the House of Commons' financial privilege applies to delegated legislation. As John Penrose MP stated when announcing the Strathclyde Review: "By longstanding convention the House of Lords does not seek to challenge the primacy of the elected House on spending and taxation". This primacy is based on a resolution of the House of Commons of 1671 which states "That in all aids given to the King by the Commons, the rate of tax ought not to be altered by the Lords", and on a further resolution of 1678 which restates the "undoubted and sole right of the Commons" to deal with all bills of aids and supplies. It was confirmed in the 1911 Parliament Act in relation to primary financial legislation relating to taxing and spending.

31. The Strathclyde Review states that Commons financial privilege applies to delegated legislation: "There is nothing in the history or practice of the claims by the House of Commons to a special privilege in relation to taxation and spending and connected financial matters that would justify any argument that it should be regarded as irrelevant to statutory instruments." Many members in the chamber supported his view in the debate on the Tax Credits Regulations. Former Lord Chancellor Lord Mackay of Clashfern, for example, stated: "It is clear that these tax credit payments are made out of the supply raised by taxation and that the other place has decided that the Tax Credits Act 2002 should be amended in terms of the approved draft. I am clearly of the opinion that a failure on the part of this

House to approve the draft of this instrument would be a breach of the fundamental privileges of the elected Chamber."

32. Others have disagreed. Dr Ruth Fox, Director of the Hansard Society, told the Secondary Legislation Scrutiny Committee that financial privilege does not apply to secondary legislation. Professor Russell told PACAC that the Review had offered no evidence for the assertion financial privilege applied to delegated legislation. Professor Russell concluded that: "there never has been any kind of a clear convention of financial privilege applying to secondary legislation. I have never been aware of a convention on financial privilege on statutory instruments. This is a new issue that has come to the agenda in this context."

House of Lords Delegated Powers and Regulatory Reform Committee,
Special Report: Response to the Strathclyde Review
HL 119 of 2015–16, paras 31, 33, 39–41

Skeleton bills and skeleton provision

31. A skeleton, or framework, bill is one which is principally made up of delegations of powers, leaving most of the legislative content to be set out in delegated legislation made under the bill once it has become an Act of Parliament. Sometimes whole bills are "skeleton"; sometimes the description applies to only a part of a bill. The problem of skeleton bills and skeleton provision is not new. In its first report in 1992–93 the Committee referred to "the more extreme use of delegated powers that [are] contained in so-called 'skeleton bills'".

Examples of the use of skeleton bills and skeleton provision

33. The following is a list of examples, along with a short extract from the Committee's report on the bill, covering a number of governments since the Committee was established:

- **Jobseekers Bill** (1994–95): "It could be … argued that the bill leaves so much power in the hands of Ministers, and that the powers are so fundamental, that the bill is no more than a 'skeleton bill'."
- **Pollution Prevention and Control Bill** (1998–99): "… our fundamental concern is as to whether it can ever be right to legislate on a topic of such importance … leaving everything of substance to be determined either by or under … regulations. We are bound to report … that … this is a 'skeleton' bill and so is an inappropriate delegation …"
- **Age-related Payments Bill** (2003–04): "… a skeleton provision only, setting out neither a sufficient statement of principle nor appropriate limitations on the face of the bill … an inappropriate delegation of legislative power." …
- **Planning Bill** (2007–08): "Part 11 of the bill is skeleton in its current form and … a considerable amount of legislation which is currently proposed to be delegated should instead appear on the face of the bill."
- **Energy Bill** (2013–14): "… the true nature of very significant new arrangements concerned with aspects of the reform of the electricity market is virtually indiscernible from the provision on the face of the Bill." And, "… not enough has been done to redress the imbalance between the scarcity of provision on the face of the Bill and the preponderance of delegated powers." …

Prevalence of Henry VIII powers

39. Given the difference between parliamentary scrutiny procedures for primary and for delegated legislation, Henry VIII powers are bound to be potentially controversial. During the debate on the Strathclyde Review, a number of members of the House deprecated their use. Lord Judge, in particular, spoke powerfully about his "nightmare": "we have too many Henry VIII clauses, and we call them Henry VIII clauses because they are draconian and potentially tyrannical". Examples of Henry VIII powers on which we have commented across the years are:

- **Local Government (Wales) Bill** (1993–94): "The Bill contains a number of provisions which confer a power to amend or modify primary legislation. Some are clearly Henry VIII powers and others could be so labelled…. [we] invite the House to consider with care any proposal that a Henry VIII clause should be subject to the negative procedure."
- **Company Law Reform Bill** (later the Companies Bill) (2005–06): "… if the Bill is passed, the power would enable the Secretary of State to repeal and replace most of one of the longest Acts ever passed … The power is, in effect, one to rewrite company law, including policy changes … Despite the limitations … and the super-affirmative procedure, we consider that the proposed delegation of power … is inappropriate and we recommend … its removal from the Bill."
- **Banking No.2 Bill** (2008–09): "… an extremely wide power … by order to disapply or modify the effect of any enactment (other than Part 1 of the Bill) or of any rule of law not in legislation, for the purpose of enabling the powers in Part 1 of the Bill … to be used effectively … we draw it to the attention of the House, so that it might satisfy itself that the rather unusual context for which Part 1 of this Bill makes provision justifies the extremely wide power."
- **Pensions Bill** (2013–14): "… enables the amendment or other modification of legislation ("whenever passed or made") … the memorandum does not explain why the power extends to the amendment of future Acts. We recommend that such extension is inappropriate, unless the House can be satisfied by the Minister that there are compelling reasons why it should be retained."

…

What steps can be taken to re-set the boundary between primary and delegated legislation?

40. During the debate on the Strathclyde Review, Lord Beith said:

"This is much more than a minor procedural issue. Governments of all kinds use delegated legislation to enact new policies and principles to change the impact of the criminal law, and amend the very legislation on which the instrument is based, as a number of noble Lords have mentioned. Committees of your Lordships' House have produced egregious examples of this, such as the Childcare Bill 2015–16, which was described by the delegated legislation committee as little more than a mission statement. Yet even the mildest of the alternative proposals in the report of the noble Lord, Lord Strathclyde, rests on the utterly implausible hope that Governments will "take steps to ensure that Bills contain an appropriate level of detail and that too much is not left for implementation by statutory instrument". That will never happen. It would be like relying on an alcoholic promising to drink only moderately in future. It is just not realistic."

41. We acknowledge that there are grounds for pessimism given the Committee's recent experience of Government bills, and also the incentive for governments of all persuasions to seek as much flexibility and future-proofing of legislation as possible. However, we do not accept Lord Beith's view that change will never happen and that steps cannot be taken to correct the current misalignment.

Secondary Legislation Scrutiny Committee, *Response to the Strathclyde Review: Effective parliamentary scrutiny of secondary legislation*
HL 126 of 2015-16, pp. 3–4

[W]e do not support any of the three Strathclyde options. Options 1 and 3 would, by statute, remove the Lords power to reject secondary legislation; and although, without statutory change, option 2 does not remove that power, it would it appears involve the Lords agreeing to a convention under which the power to reject would not be used.

In our report, we consider the options in some detail. We received no evidence at all, either from Lord Strathclyde or anyone else, in favour of option 1. Option 2 has the advantage of being non-statutory but it is ill-defined and appears to assume that the Lords power to reject secondary legislation will never be used. Option 3 has a number of practical problems and carries with it the risks associated with implementation by primary legislation. More importantly, it would involve a fundamental change in the role of the Lords in scrutinizing secondary legislation and would weaken the ability of Parliament as a whole to challenge the Government. If a bill were to be introduced as a result of the Strathclyde Review, we recommend that it should first be subject to prelegislative scrutiny in order to ensure that the Government were not "carving out a smooth legislative path for themselves".

Having reflected on the Strathclyde options and also the evidence we received, we conclude that there are strong arguments in favour of re-affirming what we consider to be the current convention as set out in the report of the Joint Committee on Conventions of the UK Parliament (under the chairmanship of the Rt Hon. Lord Cunningham of Felling), namely that the Lords should retain its power to reject an instrument but that that power should be used only in exceptional circumstances, and we recommend accordingly.

Lord Strathclyde ends his review with the comment that, "to mitigate against excessive use" of the proposed procedure under option 3, it would be appropriate for the Government "to take steps to ensure that bills contain an appropriate level of detail and that too much is not left for implementation by statutory instrument". We welcome this sentiment and suggest that if the Government were, in the future, to exercise greater caution in using secondary legislation for significant policy change, then a likely concomitant would be a reduction in challenges to secondary legislation.

Finally, we make recommendations about wider issues relating to parliamentary scrutiny of secondary legislation. During the course of our inquiry we received a range of evidence about how scrutiny of secondary legislation might be improved. We recommend that further work should be undertaken by some appropriate form of collaborative group to consider what procedural changes in both Houses could be introduced to make parliamentary scrutiny more effective.

NOTES

1. The three Lords' committees made a joint response to the Government response to their reports (HL90 of 2016–17). The committees welcomed the Government's decision not to introduce legislation along the lines of Lord Strathclyde's option 3 in the current session but noted that the decision may change should certain circumstances arise. They agreed with the statement to the House of Lords on 17 November 2016, by the Leader of the House, the Rt Hon. Baroness Evans of Bowes Park, who said that the Government were therefore 'reliant on the discipline and self-regulation that this House imposes upon itself'. They therefore regret the more minatory tone of the Government's response which stated at para. 23: '... if the House of Lords puts itself in a position where it seeks to vote against SIs approved by the House of Commons, then Lord Strathclyde's recommendation provides a clear mechanism for the House of Commons to be able to assert its primacy over SIs'. This is contrary to the conclusion of the Joint Committee on Conventions of the UK Parliament, a report which was noted with approval by both Houses of Parliament and which envisaged rejection of instruments in 'exceptional circumstances'.

    The committees were disappointed that the Government's response devoted only 4 out of 23 paragraphs to the four select committee reports and did not address the point expressed by two of the committees and by Lord Strathclyde himself that Government departments should more effectively ensure that 'bills contain an appropriate level of detail and that too much is not left for implementation by statutory instrument'.

2. It is likely that the work entailed in implementing Brexit may (partially) explain why the Government is not implementing option 3 in the 2015–20 parliamentary session. Yet the volume of this legislative work involving the proposed Great Repeal Bill will have to use an extensive amount of very technical secondary legislation. The Hansard Society had already pointed out, in its 2014 report, that the existing arrangements for making secondary legislation were simply inadequate, and will be even worse for the extensive volume of hugely important and highly detailed work involved in considering proposals to retain and remove EU law from domestic law. Prior to this will be the work in making and unmaking treaties and Parliament's role in overseeing that as well as the passage of legislation. The Hansard Society suggests alternative scenarios of an 'empowered Executive' or an enhanced Parliament and intends to conduct work to promote

the latter. (See blog posts on 22 October 2016 http://blog.hansardsociety.org.uk/will-the-great-repeal-bill-be-another-abolition-of-parliament-bill/ and on 20 January 2017 http://blog.hansardsociety.org.uk/why-parliament-needs-a-good-brexit/.)

■ QUESTIONS

1. Is Parliamentary oversight of law-making more illusory than real, given that the Government controls the passage of primary legislation, and that the scrutiny of delegated legislation is limited and non-existent for some quasi-legislation?

2. As there is so much pressure on parliamentary time, can consultation and publicity be improved so as to control quasi-legislation?

3. Is there a need for (a) a Code of Legislative Standards and/or (b) principles and guidance about the content of legislative power which it delegates, thereby discouraging inappropriate resort to secondary legislation as well as facilitating judicial review?

(g) Judicial review

Control of law-making by the courts through judicial review has increased beyond delegated legislation and quasi-legislation. The basis of this review is the doctrine of *ultra vires* (see generally Chapters 10 and 11 on judicial review) as well as the Human Rights Act 1998 where primary legislation may be declared to be incompatible with Convention rights (see Chapter 9).

Council of Civil Service Unions v Minister for the Civil Service
[1985] AC 374, House of Lords

(For the facts of this case see Chapter 10, Section 2C(b) at p. 538.)

LORD FRASER OF TULLYBELTON: … As *De Keyser's* case shows, the courts will inquire into whether a particular prerogative power exists or not, and, if it does exist, into its extent. But once the existence and the extent of a power are established to the satisfaction of the court, the court cannot inquire into the propriety of its exercise. That is undoubtedly the position as laid down in the authorities to which I have briefly referred and it is plainly reasonable in relation to many of the most important prerogative powers which are concerned with control of the armed forces and with foreign policy and with other matters which are unsuitable for discussion or review in the law courts. In the present case the prerogative power involved is power to regulate the Home Civil Service, and I recognise there is no obvious reason why the mode of exercise of that power should be immune from review by the courts. Nevertheless to permit such review would run counter to the great weight of authority to which I have briefly referred. Having regard to the opinion I have reached on Mr. Alexander's second proposition, it is unnecessary to decide whether his first proposition is sound or not and I prefer to leave that question open until it arises in a case where a decision upon it is necessary. I therefore assume, without deciding, that his first proposition is correct and that all powers exercised directly under the prerogative are immune from challenge in the courts. I pass to consider his second proposition….

LORD SCARMAN: … My Lords, I would wish to add a few, very few, words on the reviewability of the exercise of the royal prerogative. Like my noble and learned friend Lord Diplock, I believe that the law relating to judicial review has now reached the stage where it can be said with confidence that, if the subject matter in respect of which prerogative power is exercised is justiciable, that is to say if it is a matter upon which the court can adjudicate, the exercise of the power is subject to review in accordance with the principles developed in respect of the review of the exercise of statutory power. Without usurping the role of legal historian, for which I claim no special qualification, I would observe that the royal prerogative has always been regarded as part of the common law, and that Sir Edward Coke had no doubt that it was subject to the common law: *Prohibitions del Roy* (1608) 12 Co Rep 63 and the *Proclamations Case* (1611) 12 Co Rep 74. In the latter case he declared, at p. 76, that 'the King hath no prerogative, but that which the law of the land allows him.' It is, of course, beyond doubt that in Coke's time and thereafter judicial review of the exercise of prerogative power was limited to inquiring into whether a particular power existed and, if it did, into its extent: *Attorney-General* v *De Keyser's Royal Hotel Ltd* [1920] AC 508. But this limitation has now gone, overwhelmed by the developing modern law of judicial review: *Reg.* v *Criminal Injuries Compensation Board, Ex parte Lain* [1967] 2 QB 864 (a landmark case comparable in its generation with the *Proclamations Case*, 12 Co Rep 74) and *Reg.* v *Secretary of State for Home Affairs, Ex parte Hosenball* [1977] 1 WLR 766. Just as ancient restrictions in the law relating to the prerogative writs and orders have not prevented the courts from extending the requirement of natural justice, namely the duty to act fairly, so that it is required of a purely administrative act, so also has the modern law, a vivid sketch of which my noble and learned friend Lord Diplock has included in his speech, extended the range of judicial review in respect of the exercise of prerogative power. Today, therefore, the controlling factor in determining whether the exercise of prerogative power is subject to judicial review is not its source but its subject matter. . . .

LORD DIPLOCK: . . . My Lords, that a decision of which the ultimate source of power to make it is not a statute but the common law (whether or not the common law is for this purpose given the label of 'the prerogative') may be the subject of judicial review on the ground of illegality is, I think, established by the cases cited by my noble and learned friend, Lord Roskill, and this extends to cases where the field of law to which the decision relates is national security, as the decision of this House itself in *Burmah Oil Co. Ltd* v *Lord Advocate*, 1964 SC (HL) 117 shows. While I see no *a priori* reason to rule out 'irrationality' as a ground for judicial review of a ministerial decision taken in the exercise of 'prerogative' powers, I find it difficult to envisage in any of the various fields in which the prerogative remains the only source of the relevant decision-making power a decision of a kind that would be open to attack through the judicial process upon this ground. Such decisions will generally involve the application of government policy. The reasons for the decision-maker taking one course rather than another do not normally involve questions to which, if disputed, the judicial process is adapted to provide the right answer, by which I mean that the kind of evidence that is admissible under judicial procedures and the way in which it has to be adduced tend to exclude from the attention of the court competing policy considerations which, if the executive discretion is to be wisely exercised, need to be weighed against one another—a balancing exercise which judges by their upbringing and experience are ill-qualified to perform. So I leave this as an open question to be dealt with on a case to case basis if, indeed, the case should ever arise.

As respects 'procedural propriety' I see no reason why it should not be a ground for judicial review of a decision made under powers of which the ultimate source is the prerogative. Such indeed was one of the grounds that formed the subject matter of judicial review in *Reg.* v *Criminal Injuries Compensation Board, Ex parte Lain* [1967] 2 QB 864. Indeed, where the decision is one which does not alter rights or obligations enforceable in private law but only deprives a person of legitimate expectations, 'procedural impropriety' will normally provide the only ground on which the decision is open to judicial review. But in any event what procedure will satisfy the public law requirement of procedural propriety depends upon the subject matter of the decision, the executive functions of the decision-maker (if the decision is not that of an administrative tribunal) and the particular circumstances in which the decision came to be made. . . .

LORD ROSKILL: . . . My Lords, the right of the executive to do a lawful act affecting the rights of the citizen, whether adversely or beneficially, is founded upon the giving to the executive of a power enabling it to do that act. The giving of such a power usually carries with it legal sanctions to enable that power if necessary to be enforced by the courts. In most cases that power is derived from statute though in some cases, as indeed in the present case, it may still be derived from the prerogative. In yet other cases, as the decisions show, the two powers may coexist or the statutory power may by necessary implication have replaced the former prerogative power. If the executive in pursuance of the statutory power does an act affecting the rights of the citizen, it is beyond question that in principle the manner of the exercise of that power may today be challenged on one or more of the three grounds which I have mentioned earlier in this speech. If the executive instead of acting under a statutory power acts under a prerogative power and in particular a prerogative power delegated to the respondent under article 4 of the Order in Council of 1982, so as to affect the rights of the citizen, I am unable to see, subject to what I shall say later, that there is any logical reason why the fact that the source of the power is the prerogative and not statute should today deprive the citizen of that right of challenge to the manner of its exercise which he would possess were the source of the power statutory. In either case the act in question is the act of the executive. To talk of that act as the act of the sovereign savours of the archaism of past centuries. In reaching this conclusion I find myself in agreement with my noble and learned friends Lord Scarman and Lord Diplock whose speeches I have had the advantage of reading in draft since completing the preparation of this speech.

But I do not think that that right of challenge can be unqualified. It must, I think, depend upon the subject matter of the prerogative power which is exercised. Many examples were given during the argument of prerogative powers which as at present advised I do not think could properly be made the subject of judicial review. Prerogative powers such as those relating to the making of treaties, the defence of the realm, the prerogative of mercy, the grant of honours, the dissolution of Parliament and the appointment of ministers as well as others are not, I think, susceptible to judicial review because their nature and subject matter are such as not to be amenable to the judicial process. The courts are not the place wherein to determine whether a treaty should be concluded or the armed forces disposed in a particular manner or Parliament dissolved on one date rather than another.

In my view the exercise of the prerogative which enabled the oral instructions of 22 December 1983 to be given does not by reason of its subject matter fall within what for want of a better phrase I would call the 'excluded categories' some of which I have just mentioned. It follows that in principle I can see no reason why those instructions should not be the subject of judicial review. . . .

LORD BRIGHTMAN agreed with LORD FRASER on this point about the prerogative.

R v Secretary of State for the Home Department, ex parte Fire Brigades Union
[1995] 2 AC 513, House of Lords

The Criminal Injuries Compensation Scheme had been introduced under the prerogative. Under the Criminal Justice Act 1988, ss 108–17, Schs 6 and 7 the scheme was enacted and would come into force on 'such day as the Secretary of State may ... appoint'—s. 171(1). No day was appointed and the non-statutory scheme continued. In 1993 the Secretary of State indicated that the enacted provisions would not be brought into force and that the existing scheme would be replaced by another non-statutory scheme under which the basis for the determination of compensation awards would be changed from common law principles to a tariff fixed according to particular categories of injury. The Appropriation Act 1994 approved supply estimates which contained an amount for criminal injury compensation under the tariff scheme. The applicants, representing people likely to be the victims of violent crime, sought declarations that the Secretary of State was in breach of a duty under the 1988 Act by (1) not bringing into force the enacted provisions, and (2) that the introduction of the tariff scheme was in breach of the duty and an abuse of prerogative power. The Divisional Court dismissed the application but the Court of Appeal allowed an appeal on the second declaration by a majority. On appeal their Lordships dismissed the cross-appeal that there was a legally enforceable duty to bring ss 108–17 into force.

LORD BROWNE-WILKINSON: ... It does not follow that, because the Secretary of State is not under any duty to bring the section into effect, he has an absolute and unfettered discretion whether or not to do so. So to hold would lead to the conclusion that both Houses of Parliament had passed the Bill through all its stages and the Act received the Royal Assent merely to confer an enabling power on the executive to decide at will whether or not to make the parliamentary provisions a part of the law. Such a conclusion, drawn from a section to which the sidenote is 'Commencement,' is not only constitutionally dangerous but flies in the face of common sense. The provisions for bringing sections into force under section 171(1) apply not only to the statutory scheme but to many other provisions. In the absence of express provisions to the contrary in the Act, the plain intention of Parliament in conferring on the Secretary of State the power to bring certain sections into force is that such power is to be exercised so as to bring those sections into force when it is appropriate and unless there is a subsequent change of circumstances which would render it inappropriate to do so.

If, as I think, that is the clear purpose for which the power in section 171(1) was conferred on the Secretary of State, two things follow. First, the Secretary of State comes under a clear duty to keep under consideration from time to time the question whether or not to bring the sections (and therefore the statutory scheme) into force. In my judgment he cannot lawfully surrender or release the power contained in section 171(1) so as to purport to exclude its future exercise either by himself or by his successors. In the course of argument, the Lord Advocate accepted that this was the correct view of the legal position. It follows that the decision of the Secretary of State to give effect to the statement in paragraph 38 of the White Paper (Cm. 2434) that 'the provisions in the Act of 1988 will not now be implemented' was unlawful. The Lord Advocate contended, correctly, that the attempt by the Secretary of State to abandon or release the power conferred on him by section 171(1), being unlawful, did not bind either the present Secretary of State or any successor in that office. It was a nullity. But, in my judgment, that does not alter the fact that the Secretary of State made the attempt to bind himself not to exercise the power conferred by section 171(1) and such attempt was an unlawful act.

… In claiming that the introduction of the new tariff scheme renders it undesirable now to bring the statutory scheme into force, the Secretary of State is, in effect, claiming that the purpose of the statutory power has been frustrated by his own act in choosing to introduce a scheme inconsistent with the statutory scheme approved by Parliament.

…

My Lords, it would be most surprising if, at the present day, prerogative powers could be validly exercised by the executive so as to frustrate the will of Parliament expressed in a statute and, to an extent, to pre-empt the decision of Parliament whether or not to continue with the statutory scheme even though the old scheme has been abandoned. It is not for the executive, as the Lord Advocate accepted, to state as it did in the White Paper (paragraph 38) that the provisions in the Act of 1988 'will accordingly be repealed when a suitable legislative opportunity occurs.' It is for Parliament, not the executive, to repeal legislation. The constitutional history of this country is the history of the prerogative powers of the Crown being made subject to the overriding powers of the democratically elected legislature as the sovereign body. The prerogative powers of the Crown remain in existence to the extent that Parliament has not expressly or by implication extinguished them. But under the principle in *Attorney-General* v *De Keyser's Royal Hotel Ltd* [1920] AC 508, if Parliament has conferred on the executive statutory powers to do a particular act, that act can only thereafter be done under the statutory powers so conferred: any pre-existing prerogative power to do the same act is pro tanto excluded.

How then is it suggested that the executive has power in the present case to introduce under the prerogative power a scheme inconsistent with the statutory scheme? … The *De Keyser* principle does not apply since it only operates to the extent that Parliament has conferred statutory powers which in fact replace pre-existing powers: unless and until the statutory provisions are brought into force, no statutory powers have been conferred and therefore the prerogative powers remain. Moreover, the abandonment of the old scheme and the introduction of the new tariff scheme does not involve any interference by the executive with private rights. The old scheme, being a scheme for ex gratia payments, conferred no legal rights on the victims of crime. The new tariff scheme, being also an ex gratia scheme, confers benefits not detriments on the victims of crime. …

In my judgment, these arguments overlook the fact that this case is concerned with public, not private, law. If this were an action in which some victim of crime were suing for the benefits to which he was entitled under the old scheme … such a victim has no legal right to any benefits. But these are proceedings for judicial review of the decisions of the Secretary of State in the discharge of his public functions. The well known passage in the speech of Lord Diplock in the G.C.H.Q. case, *Council of Civil Service Unions* v *Minister for the Civil Service* [1985] AC 374, 408–410, demonstrates two points relevant to the present case. First, an executive decision which affects the legitimate expectations of the applicant (even though it does not infringe his legal rights) is subject to judicial review. Second, judicial review is as applicable to decisions taken under prerogative powers as to decisions taken under statutory powers save to the extent that the legality of the exercise of certain prerogative powers (e.g. treaty-making) may not be justiciable.

The G.C.H.Q. case demonstrates that the argument based on the ex gratia and voluntary nature of the old scheme and the tariff scheme is erroneous. Although the victim of a crime committed immediately before the White Paper was published had no legal right to receive compensation in accordance with the old scheme, he certainly had a legitimate expectation that he would do so. Moreover, he had a legitimate expectation that, unless there were proper reasons for further delay in bringing sections 108 to 117 of the Act into force, his expectation would be converted into a statutory right. If those legitimate expectations were defeated by the composite decision of the Secretary of State to discontinue the old scheme and not to bring the statutory scheme into force and those decisions were unlawfully taken, he has locus standi in proceedings for judicial review to complain of such illegality.

… In his powerful dissenting judgment in the Court of Appeal Hobhouse LJ decided that, since the statutory provisions had not been brought into force, they had no legal significance of any kind. He held, in my judgment correctly, that the *De Keyser* principle did not apply to the present case: since the statutory provisions were not in force they could not have excluded the pre-existing prerogative powers. Therefore the prerogative powers remained. He then turned to consider whether it could be said that the Secretary of State had abused those prerogative powers and again approached the matter on the basis that since the sections were not in force they had no significance in deciding whether or not the Secretary of State had acted lawfully. I cannot agree with this last step. In public law the fact that a scheme approved by Parliament was on the statute book and would come into force as law if and when the Secretary of State so determined is in my judgment directly relevant to the question whether the Secretary of State could in the lawful exercise of prerogative powers both decide to bring in the tariff scheme and refuse properly to exercise his discretion under section 171(1) to bring the statutory provisions into force.

I turn to consider whether the Secretary of State's decisions were unlawful as being an abuse of power. In this case there are two powers under consideration: first, the statutory power conferred by section 171(1); second, the prerogative power. In order first to test the validity of the exercise of the prerogative power, I will assume that the Act of 1988, instead of conferring a discretion on the Secretary of State to bring the statutory scheme into effect, had specified that it was to come into force one year after that date of the Royal Assent. As Hobhouse LJ held, during that year the *De Keyser* principle would not apply and the prerogative powers would remain exercisable. But in my judgment it would plainly have been an improper use of the prerogative powers if, during that year, the Secretary of State had discontinued the old scheme and introduced the tariff scheme. It would have been improper because in exercising the prerogative power the Secretary of State would have had to have regard to the fact that the statutory scheme was about to come into force: to dismantle the machinery of the old scheme in the meantime would have given rise to further disruption and expense when, on the first anniversary, the statutory scheme had to be put into operation. This hypothetical case shows that, although during the suspension of the coming into force of the statutory provisions the old prerogative powers continue to exist, the existence of such legislation basically affects the mode in which such prerogative powers can be lawfully exercised.

Does it make any difference that the statutory provisions are to come into effect, not automatically at the end of the year as in the hypothetical case I have put, but on such day as the Secretary of State specifies under a power conferred on him by Parliament for the purpose of bringing the statutory provisions into force? In my judgment it does not. The Secretary of State could only validly exercise the prerogative power to abandon the old scheme and introduce the tariff scheme if, at the same time, he could validly resolve never to bring the statutory provisions and the inconsistent statutory scheme into effect. For the reasons I have already given, he could not validly so resolve to give up his statutory duty to consider from time to time whether to bring the statutory scheme into force. His attempt to do so, being a necessary part of the composite decision which he took, was itself unlawful. By introducing the tariff scheme he debars himself from exercising the statutory power for the purpose and on the basis which Parliament intended. For these reasons, in my judgment the decision to introduce the tariff scheme at a time when the statutory provisions and his power under section 171(1) were on the statute book was unlawful and an abuse of the prerogative power....

LORD MUSTILL: ... I turn to the second area of complaint, which relates to the implementation of the new scheme in a form which differs radically from that contained in Part VII of the Act. This complaint is advanced in two ways, first that the actions and statements of the Secretary of State were an abuse of the powers conferred by section 171(1), secondly, that the powers exercisable under the Royal Prerogative were limited by the presence in the background of the statutory scheme.

At first sight a negative answer to each of these averments seems inevitable, once given the premise that section 171(1) creates no duty to appoint a day. As regards the Act, in a perspective which may never yield a statutory scheme, the possibility of substituting one non-statutory scheme for another must have been just as much envisaged and tolerated as was the continuation of the existing non-statutory scheme, or indeed the termination of any scheme at all. The interval between the passing of the Act and the bringing into force of Part VII, if it ever happened, was simply a statutory blank.

So too, it would appear, as regards the argument based on the Royal Prerogative. The case does not fall within the principle of *Attorney-General* v *De Keyser's Royal Hotel* ... Once the superior power of Parliament has occupied the territory the prerogative must quit the field. In the present case, however, the territory is quite untouched. There is no Parliamentary dominion over compensation for criminal injuries, since Parliament has chosen to allow its control to be exercised today, or some day, or never, at the choice of the Secretary of State. Until he chooses to call the Parliamentary scheme into existence there is a legislative void, and the prerogative subsists untouched. The position is just the same as if Part VII had never been enacted, or had been repealed soon afterwards.

This is not to say that the decisions of the Secretary of State in the exercise of the prerogative power to continue, modify or abolish the scheme which his predecessor in the exercise of the same power had called into existence are immune from process. They can be called into question on the familiar grounds: *Reg.* v *Criminal Injuries Compensation Board, Ex parte Lain* [1976] 2 QB 864. But no question of irrationality arises here, and the decision to inaugurate a new scheme cannot be rendered unlawful simply because of its conflict on paper with a statutory scheme which is not part of the law.

... [I]t is said, there is no statutory void; for although Part VII is not itself in force, section 171(1) is in force and must not be ignored. The continued existence of section 171(1) means that, even if there is no present duty to appoint a day, there is a continuing duty, which will subsist until either a day is appointed or the relevant provisions are repealed, to address in a rational manner the question whether the power created by section 171(1) should be exercised. This continuing duty overshadows the exercise by the Secretary of State of his powers under the Royal Prerogative.

... Pending the appointment of a day it is impossible for the Secretary of State to remain completely inactive. He has no choice but to do something about compensation for criminal injuries: whether wind up the existing scheme and put nothing in its place; or keep the existing scheme in force; or modify it; or copy the statutory scheme. It seems to me inevitable, once it is acknowledged that it may be proper at any given time for the Secretary of State to say, 'It is inappropriate at present to put the statutory scheme into force' that it can be proper for him to install something different from the statutory scheme. Otherwise there would be the absurdity that the Secretary of State is obliged to do something under the Royal Prerogative which he is not obliged to do under the statute. Thus, merely to introduce a cheaper scheme cannot in itself be an abuse of the prerogative powers which subsist in the interim. If the Secretary of State had made an announcement as follows: 'I have come to the conclusion after careful study that for the reasons which I have explained the Parliamentary scheme must now be seen as too expensive, slow and top-heavy; that its priority is not sufficiently high to justify the great expense when there are other calls on the country's resources; that the scheme which I propose will do substantial justice in a more efficient way; and that accordingly I shall run the scheme for a while to see how it works and if, as I confidently expect, it is a success I will ask Parliament to agree with me and repeal the statutory scheme … ' it is hard to see what objection could have been taken. Does not the minister's actual stance, although perhaps more likely to provoke hostility, really come to the same thing?

The applicants reply that it does not, essentially for two reasons. First, they contend that the Secretary of State has renounced the statutory duty which still dominates the prerogative in this field: not the duty, as under the argument already discussed and rejected, to bring Part VII into force, but the duty to keep under review the powers conferred by section 171(1). I would reject this argument. Perhaps the Secretary of State has laid himself open to attack more than he need have done by the tone of his announcement, but I cannot read him as having said that however much circumstances may change he will never think again; and even if he had said this his statement would have been meaningless since, leaving aside questions arising from the doctrine of 'legitimate expectation' which do not arise here, nothing that he says on one day could bind him in law, or bind his successor, not to say and do the opposite the next day.

Furthermore, even if the argument were sound it would not yield any useful relief. The most that the court could do would be to grant a declaration that the Secretary of State is now and in the future obliged to keep the power under review in a spirit of good faith: something which the Lord Advocate on his behalf has not denied….

The applicants' second contention is that the Secretary of State has frustrated the intentions of Parliament by bringing in his own inconsistent scheme and hence nullifying any realistic possibility that he will perform his continuing duty to keep the implementation of the statutory scheme under review. I do not accept this. No doubt if Part VII had been the subject of section 171(1) and hence due to come into force inevitably on a fixed date the creation of any different scheme otherwise than purely as an interim measure would have been a breach of duty. It is also possible to imagine cases where the provisions to be brought into force on an appointed day are such as to become incapable of execution if irreversible changes have been made in the meantime, and it may be that to make such changes would be an abuse of the prerogative. But this is not so here. The new scheme is not in tablets of stone. Certainly, it would be an inconvenient, time-consuming and expensive business to dismantle the scheme and return to something on the former lines. But it would be feasible to do so, just as it proved feasible to pull down the original scheme which has been firmly established over many years. Nothing is certain in politics…. If a successor Minister] made an order under section 171(1), accompanied by the necessary regulations and by executive action to wind up the new scheme, there is nothing in what the present Secretary of State has done that could stand in his way. His words have no lasting effect; he has not put an end to the statutory scheme; only Parliament can do that. So long as he and his successors in office perform in good faith the duty to keep the implementation of Part VII under review there is in my opinion no ground for the court to interfere …

[Lords LLOYD OF BERWICK and NICHOLLS OF BIRKENHEAD gave speeches concurring with Lord BROWNE-WILKINSON, and Lord KEITH OF KINKEL concurred with Lord Mustill].

Appeal dismissed.

NOTE: See the discussion on this case in Chapter 4, Section 1A at p. 142.

■ QUESTION

Are the majority buttressing legislative supremacy against improper executive intervention by way of the prerogative, or is their intervention improper?

The courts' general approach. When the courts review delegated legislation the approach they take is to look at the purposes of the enabling statute in order to check if the delegated legislation is *intra vires* or not. The courts presume that certain things may not be done by delegated legislation without express authorization by the enabling statute. Thus delegated legislation has been found to be *ultra vires* where it purported to:

  (a) impose taxation (*Attorney-General* v *Wilts United Dairies Ltd* (1921) 37 TLR 884);

(b) deny the citizen access to the courts to determine rights and obligations (*Customs & Excise Commissioners* v *Cure & Deely Ltd* [1962] 1 QB 340; *R* v *Lord Chancellor, ex parte Witham* [1998] QB 575);

(c) interfere with the liberty of the citizen (*Chester* v *Bateson* [1920] 1 KB 829).

Circumstances can change such a presumption, as in *Liversidge* v *Anderson* [1942] AC 206, in which a Defence of the Realm regulation was upheld which allowed a Minister to order detention of persons whom he had reasonable cause to believe to be of hostile origin or associations and in need of subjection to preventive control. The fact that this case was decided during the Second World War may explain its illiberality. See the powerful dissent by Lord Atkin, at pp. 225–46.

Procedural ultra vires. Delegated legislation can be challenged on the ground that specified procedures were not followed in making the legislative measure. This is part of the procedural impropriety class of judicial review (see Chapter 10, Section 2C at p. 520). For an example of this ground of review, see *R* v *Secretary of State for Social Services, ex parte Association of Metropolitan Authorities* [1986] 1 WLR 1 discussed earlier in this chapter in Section 1B(a) at p. 561. An important distinction is whether the procedural requirement is mandatory or directory.

Substantive ultra vires. See Chapter 10, Sections 2B and 2D at pp. 499 and 540 on the illegality and irrationality grounds of review. Where irrationality or reasonableness is the ground of challenge, its chances of success would appear to be lower the more legislative in character the measure is. See *Nottinghamshire CC* v *Secretary of State for the Environment*, Chapter 10, Section 2D at p. 543. There also appears to be a distinction drawn between Parliamentary measures and local authority bye-laws, with bye laws being less immune from challenge. There is still a presumption that bye-laws passed for general welfare will be benevolently construed (see *Kruse* v *Johnson* [1898] 2 QB 91).

The grounds of judicial review which seem to be most important with respect to quasi-legislation are legitimate expectations and unreasonableness. See G. Ganz, *Quasi-Legislation: Some Recent Developments in Secondary Legislation* (1987), pp. 41–6 and R. Baldwin and J. Houghton, 'Circular Arguments: The Status and Legitimacy of Administrative Rules' [1986] *Public Law* 239.

It seems that vagueness of regulations would, in a suitable case, be a ground of review.

McEldowney v *Forde*
[1971] AC 632, House of Lords

By the Civil Authorities (Special Powers) Act (Northern Ireland) 1922, s. 1:

(1) The civil authority shall have power, in respect of persons, matters and things within the jurisdiction of the Government of Northern Ireland to take all such steps and issue all such orders as may be necessary for preserving the peace and maintaining order, according to and in the execution of this Act and the regulations contained in the Schedule thereto, or such regulations as may be made in accordance with the provisions of this Act (which regulations, whether contained in the said Schedule or made as aforesaid, are in this Act referred to as 'the regulations'): Provided that the ordinary course of law and avocations of life and the enjoyment of property shall be interfered with as little as may be permitted by the exigencies of the steps required to be taken under this Act.

(2) For the purposes of this Act the civil authority shall be the Minister of Home Affairs for Northern Ireland....

(3) The Minister of Home Affairs shall have power to make regulations—(a) for making further provision for the preservation of the peace and maintenance of order, and (b) for varying or revoking any provision of the regulations, and any regulations made as aforesaid shall, subject to the provisions of this Act, have effect and be enforced in like manner as regulations contained in the Schedule to this Act....

On 22 May 1922 the Minister of Home Affairs made a regulation under the powers conferred by s. 1(3) of the Act. This provided that:

24A Any person who becomes or remains a member of an unlawful association or who does any act with a view to promoting or calculated to promote the objects of an unlawful association or seditious conspiracy shall be guilty of an offence against these regulations....

The following organisations shall for the purposes of this regulation be deemed to be unlawful associations:

The Irish Republican Brotherhood, The Irish Republican Army, The Irish Volunteers, The Cumann na m'Ban, The Fianna na h'Eireann.

The named organizations were existing organizations of a militant type and it was conceded before the House of Lords, as it had been before the Court of Appeal in Northern Ireland, that they were in fact unlawful organizations.

On 7 March 1967 the Minister of Home Affairs made a further regulation under s. 1(3) of the Act. After reciting that it was expedient to make further provision for the preservation of the peace and maintenance of order, this stated:

1. Regulation 24A of the principal regulations shall have effect as if the following organisations were added to the list of organisations which for the purpose of that regulation are deemed to be unlawful associations:

'The organisations at the date of this regulation or at any time thereafter describing themselves as "republican clubs" or any like organisation howsoever described.'

The appellant was charged in the magistrates' court with being a member of the Slaughtneil Republican Club contrary to reg. 24A as amended. The magistrates found that he was a member of the Club but that no evidence was given that he or the club was at any time a threat to peace, law, and order and that in so far as the police were aware there was nothing seditious in its pursuits or those of its members. The charge was dismissed but the Court of Appeal of Northern Ireland (Lord MacDermott CJ, dissenting) held that the amended regulation was *intra vires* the Act of 1922 and remitted the case to the magistrates. On appeal to the House of Lords:

LORD HODSON: ... The proscription of present and future 'republican clubs' including 'any like organisations howsoever described' is said to be something outside the scope and meaning of the Act and so incapable of being related to the prescribed purposes of the Act. Accepting that the word 'republican' is an innocent word and need not connote anything contrary to law, I cannot escape the conclusion that in its context, added to the list of admittedly unlawful organisations of a militant type, the word 'republican' is capable of fitting the description of a club which in the opinion of the Minister should be proscribed as a subversive organisation of a type akin to those previously named in the list of admittedly unlawful organisations. The context in which the word is used shows the type of club which the Minister had in mind and there is no doubt that the mischief aimed at is an association which had subversive objects. On this matter, in my opinion, the court should not substitute its judgment for that of the Minister, on the ground that the banning of 'republican clubs' is too remote. I agree that the use of the words 'any like organisation howsoever described' lends some support to the contention that the regulation is vague and for that reason invalid, but on consideration I do not accept the argument based on vagueness. It is not difficult to see why the Minister, in order to avoid subterfuge, was not anxious to restrict himself to the description 'republican' seeing that there might be similar clubs which he might seek to proscribe whatever they called themselves. If and when any case based on the words 'any like organisation' arises it will have to be decided, but I do not, by reason of the use of those words, condemn the regulation as being too vague or uncertain to be supported. I would dismiss the appeal.

LORD GUEST: … The final argument for the appellant related to the third category of organisations which it is said the regulation covered, namely, 'or any like organisation howsoever described.' It was submitted that this would cover any club whatever its name and whatever its objects and that such an exercise of the Minister's power was unreasonable, arbitrary and capricious. In my view this argument is not well founded. The regulation first of all embraces republican clubs eo nomine and they are caught by their very description. If they do not bear the name 'republican,' it would be a question of interpretation after evidence whether any particular club was covered by the words 'any like organisation howsoever described.' It is indeed not necessary for the purposes of this case where the organisation bore the name 'republican club' to examine this question in any great detail. But my provisional view is that the regulation would cover any organisation having similar objects to those of a republican club or of any of the named organisations or of any organisation whose objects included the absorption of Northern Ireland in the Republic of Ireland.

Having regard to all these matters I cannot say that the class of 'like organisations' is either ambiguous or arbitrary so as to invalidate the regulation. In my view this ground of attack also fails. … I would therefore dismiss the appeal.

LORD PEARCE: … Further, the 1967 regulation is too vague and ambiguous. A man may not be put in peril on an ambiguity under the criminal law. When the 1967 regulation was issued the citizen ought to have been able to know whether he could or could not remain a member of his club without being subject to a criminal prosecution. Yet I doubt if one could have said with certainty that any man or woman was safe in remaining a member of any club in Northern Ireland, however named or whatever its activities or objects.

Had the final phrase 'or any like organisation howsoever described' been absent, the regulation would have simply been an attack on the description 'republican,' however innocent the club's activities. Presumably the justification for it would have to be that the mere existence of the word republican in the name of a club was so inflammatory that its suppression was 'necessary for preserving the peace and maintaining order' and that the 'exigencies' of the need for its suppression did not permit the citizen's right in that respect to prevail. For the reasons given by the Lord Chief Justice I do not accept that such a justification could suffice. But be that as it may, the final phrase shows that this is more than an attack on nomenclature, since the club is deemed equally unlawful if it is a like organisation, whatever be the name under which it goes.

  And what is the 'likeness' to a republican club which makes an organisation unlawful 'howsoever described'? Since a republican club is banned whatever may be its activities, the likeness cannot consist in its activities. And since the organisation is unlawful, howsoever described, the 'likeness' cannot consist in a likeness of nomenclature. The only possibility left seems to be that the 'likeness' may consist in the mere fact of being a club. In which case all clubs, however named, are unlawful—which is absurd.

  One cannot disregard the final phrase, since that would wholly alter the meaning of the regulation. Without the final phrase it is simply an attack on nomenclature. But with the final phrase it cannot simply be an attack on nomenclature. One cannot sever the bad from the good by omitting a phrase when the omission must alter the meaning of the rest. One must take the whole sentence as it stands. And as it stands it is too vague and ambiguous to be valid.

  I would therefore allow the appeal.

LORD PEARSON: … There is one further argument against the validity of this regulation, and it is the most formidable one. It is that the regulation is too vague, because it includes the words 'or any like organisation howsoever described.' I have had doubts on this point, but in the end I think the argument against the validity of the regulation ought not to prevail. The Minister's intention evidently was (if I may use a convenient short phrase) to ban republican clubs. He had to exclude in advance two subterfuges which might defeat his intention. First, an existing republican club might be dissolved, and a new one created. The words 'or at any time thereafter' would exclude that subterfuge as well as applying to new republican clubs generally. Secondly, a new club, having the characteristic object of a republican club, might be created with some other title such as 'New Constitution Group' or 'Society for the alteration of the Constitution.' The words 'or any like organisation however described' would exclude that subterfuge.

In construing this regulation one has to bear in mind that it authorises very drastic interference with freedom of association, freedom of speech and in some circumstances the liberty of the subject. Therefore it should be narrowly interpreted. Also it should if possible be so construed as to have sufficient certainty to be valid—ut res magis valeat quam pereat.

In my opinion the proper construction of the regulation is that the organisations to be deemed unlawful are—

(i) any organisation describing itself as a 'republican club,' whatever its actual objects may be, and

(ii) any organisation which has the characteristic object of a republican club—namely, to introduce republican government into Northern Ireland—whatever its name may be.

I would dismiss the appeal.

LORD DIPLOCK: … But there is another reason for rejecting this construction of the regulation which I find compelling. It is not, in my view, permissible to treat the regulation as severable in the way adopted by the majority of the Court of Appeal. To do so is to treat it as striking at more than one unrelated mischief whereas the inclusion in the description of the organisations deemed to be unlawful association of the words 'any like organisation' makes it plain that it is organisations possessing a common mischievous characteristic that are intended to be proscribed.

What then is that characteristic? Even if it were legitimate to infer that the Minister had knowledge of the objects of 'republican clubs' in existence at the date of the regulation he could not have knowledge of what would be the objects of clubs to be formed in the future which would describe themselves as 'republican clubs.' The characteristic struck at, therefore, cannot be the possession *in fact* of unlawful objects by the organisations proscribed. Nor for the reasons previously indicated can the common characteristic struck at be the use of the name 'republican club.' It is conceivable that the adoption of a particular name might of itself be so inflammatory in Northern Ireland as to endanger the preservation of peace and the maintenance of order, but the regulation proscribes 'like organisations' which do not adopt this name.

But there are no other ascertainable common characteristics of the organisations described in the regulation except that they are composed of members and possess objects of some kind or other and describe themselves by some name or other. If the Minister's intention was to proscribe all clubs and associations in Northern Ireland whatever their objects and name the regulation plainly falls outside the power delegated to him by section 1(3) of the Special Powers Act to make regulations 'for making further provision for the preservation of the peace and the maintenance of order.' It makes unlawful conduct which cannot have the effect of endangering the preservation of the peace or the maintenance of order. But if the Minister's intention was to proscribe some narrower category of organisations the suppression of which would have the effect of preserving the peace and maintaining order he has in my view failed to disclose in the regulation what the narrower category is. A regulation whose meaning is so vague that it cannot be ascertained with reasonable certainty cannot fall within the words of delegation.

It is possible to speculate that the Minister when he made the regulation now challenged bona fide believed that the sort of club which at that date described itself as a 'republican club' was likely to have unlawful objects which would endanger the preservation of the peace and the maintenance of order and by the words that he added he may have intended to do no more than to prevent such clubs from evading the regulation by dissolving and re-forming or by changing their names. If this was his intention he signally failed to express it in the regulation, for by no process of construction can it be given this limited effect. Or he may have thought it administratively convenient to insert in the regulation a description of proscribed organisations so wide as to include also those with lawful objects in order to be sure that none with unlawful objects should be omitted, and to rely upon the administrative discretion of the Attorney-General under section 3(2) of the Act not to enforce the regulation. But to do this, however, if administratively convenient, would be outside his delegated legislative powers.

But this is speculation not construction and your Lordships' function is limited to construing the words which the Minister has used. In my view the words used by the Minister in the regulation are either too wide to fall within the description of the regulations which he is empowered to make under section 1(3) of the Special Powers Act or are too vague and uncertain in their meaning to be enforceable.

I would allow this appeal.

Appeal dismissed.

NOTE: For criticism of this case, see MacCormick (1970) 86 *Law Quarterly Review* 171. Today under the Human Rights Act, even when the UK has derogated from the European Convention on Human Rights, the courts are likely to be more searching in their examination—see *A and ors* v *Secretary of State for the Home Department* [2004] UKHL 56, dealing with the provision for indeterminate detention without trial of suspected international suspects. The House of Lords quashed the derogating of the UK from the ECHR, and issued a declaration of incompatibility which was made in relation to the Anti-Terrorism, Crime and Security Act 2001, s. 23 in relation to Arts 5, 14 ECHR.

■ QUESTIONS

1. Do you think that the context of the 'troubles' in Northern Ireland helps explain the decision of the majority?

2. Is it not more important in that kind of situation for the courts to examine very carefully regulations which interfere with the liberty of the citizen?

(i) Exclusion of judicial review

The exclusion of judicial review of delegated legislation has been the subject of a variety of decisions. On the one hand *Institute of Patent Agents* v *Lockwood* [1894] AC 347 indicated that it was possible, whilst *Minister of Health* v *R, ex parte Yaffe* [1931] AC 494 determined that judicial review was not excluded. See also Chapter 11, Section 7 at p. 606.

(ii) Discretionary nature of judicial review

See *R* v *Secretary of State for Social Services, ex parte Association of Metropolitan Authorities* [1986] 1 WLR 1, discussed earlier in this chapter in Section 1B(a) at p. 283.

See also Chapter 11, Section 6 at p. 600, on the discretionary nature of judicial review.

■ QUESTIONS

1. Is it more likely that delegated legislation which has been in existence for a little time will not be struck down by the courts than is the case with the various types of quasi-legislation and administrative action?

2. What kinds of delegated legislation might be struck down even if they had been in existence for some time?

3. Is judicial wariness in striking down delegated legislation satisfactory given the lack of real parliamentary oversight?

(iii) Partial invalidity

DPP v Hutchinson
[1990] 2 AC 783, House of Lords

The Secretary of State was empowered to make bye-laws for land appropriated for military purposes under the Military Lands Act 1892, s. 14(1). The power allowed for bye-laws which could prohibit intrusion onto such land but did not permit any prejudicial effect on any right in common. The Secretary of State made the RAF Greenham Common Bye-laws 1985 in respect of common land which had been appropriated for military purposes. Bye-law 2(b) provided that no person could enter or remain in the protected area without the permission of an authorized person. Protestors against nuclear weapons who camped on the protected land were charged and convicted of infringing bye-law 2(b). The Crown Court allowed the appeal on the basis that it was *ultra vires* as it prejudiced the rights of commoners. This decision was overturned by the Divisional Court on an appeal by case stated. The defendants appealed to the House of Lords.

LORD BRIDGE: My Lords, these two appeals raise important questions as to the tests to be applied in determining whether delegated legislation which on its face exceeds the power conferred upon the legislator may nevertheless be upheld and enforced by the courts in part on the basis that the legislation is divisible into good and bad parts and that the good is independent of, and untainted by, the bad.

When a legislative instrument made by a law-maker with limited powers is challenged, the only function of the court is to determine whether there has been a valid exercise of that limited legislative power in relation to the matter which is the subject of disputed enforcement. If a law-maker has validly exercised his power, the court may give effect to the law validly made. But if the court sees only an invalid law made in excess of the law-maker's power, it has no jurisdiction to modify or adapt the law to bring it within the scope of the law-maker's power.

…

The application of these principles leads naturally and logically to what has traditionally been regarded as the test of severability. It is often referred to inelegantly as the 'blue pencil' test …What is involved is in truth a double test. I shall refer to the two aspects of the test as textual severability and substantial severability. A legislative instrument is textually severable if a clause, a sentence, a phrase or a single word may be disregarded, as exceeding the law-maker's power, and what remains of the text is still grammatical and coherent. A legislative instrument is substantially severable if the substance of what remains after severance is essentially unchanged in its legislative purpose, operation and effect.

…

The test of textual severability has the great merit of simplicity and certainty. When it is satisfied the court can readily see whether the omission from the legislative text of so much as exceeds the law-maker's power leaves in place a valid text which is capable of operating and was evidently intended to operate independently of the invalid text. But I have reached the conclusion, though not without hesitation, that a rigid insistence that the test of textual severability must always be satisfied if a provision is to be upheld and enforced as partially valid will in some cases, of which *Dunkley* v *Evans* and *Daymond* v *Plymouth City Council* are good examples, have the unreasonable consequence of defeating subordinate legislation of which the substantial purpose and effect was clearly within the law-maker's power when, by some oversight or misapprehension of the scope of that power, the text, as written, has a range of application which exceeds that scope. It is important, however, that in all cases an appropriate test of substantial severability should be applied. When textual severance is possible, the test of substantial severability will be satisfied when the valid text is unaffected by, and independent of, the invalid. The law which the court may then uphold and enforce is the very law which the legislator has enacted, not a different law. But when the court must modify the text in order to achieve severance,

this can only be done when the court is satisfied that it is effecting no change in the substantial purpose and effect of the impugned provision. Thus, in *Dunkley* v *Evans*, the legislative purpose and effect
of the prohibition of fishing in the large area of the sea in relation to which the minister was authorised
to legislate was unaffected by the obviously inadvertent inclusion of the small area of sea to which his
power did not extend. In *Daymond* v *Plymouth City Council* the draftsman of the Order had evidently
construed the enabling provision as authorising the imposition of charges for sewerage services upon
occupiers of property irrespective of whether or not they were connected to sewers. In this error he
was in the good company of two members of your Lordships' House. But this extension of the scope
of the charging power, which, as the majority held, exceeded its proper limit, in no way affected the
legislative purpose and effect of the charging power as applied to occupiers of properties which were
connected to sewers.

To appreciate the full extent of the problem presented by the Greenham byelaws it is necessary to
set out the full text of the prohibitions imposed by byelaw 2 which provides:

> No person shall: (a) enter or leave or attempt to enter or leave the protected area except by way of
> an authorised entrance or exit. (b) enter, pass through or over or remain in or over the protected
> area without authority or permission given by or on behalf of one of the persons mentioned in
> byelaw 5(1). (c) cause or permit any vehicle, animal, aircraft or thing to enter into or upon or to
> pass through or over or to be or remain in or upon or over the protected area without authority
> or permission given by or on behalf of one of the persons mentioned in byelaw 5(1). (d) remain
> in the protected area after having been directed to leave by any of the persons mentioned in
> byelaw 4. (e) make any false statement, either orally or in writing, or employ any other form of
> misrepresentation in order to obtain entry to any part of the protected area or to any building or
> premises within the protected area. (f) obstruct any constable (including a constable under the
> control of the Defence Council) or any other person acting in the proper exercise or execution
> of his duty within the protected area. (g) enter any part of the protected area which is shown by
> a notice as being prohibited or restricted. (h) board, attempt to board, or interfere with, or inter-
> fere with the movement or passage, of any vehicle, aircraft or other installation in the protected
> area. (i) distribute or display any handbill, leaflet, sign, advertisement, circular, poster, bill, notice or
> object within the protected area or affix the same to either side of the perimeter fences without
> authority or permission given by or on behalf of one of the persons mentioned in byelaw 5(1).
> (j) interfere with or remove from the protected area any property under the control of the Crown
> or the service authorities of a visiting force or, in either case, their agents or contractors. (k) wilfully
> damage, destroy, deface or remove any notice board or sign within the protected area. (l) wilfully
> damage, soil, deface or mark any wall, fence, structure, floor, pavement, or other surface within the
> protected area.

It is at once apparent that paragraphs (a), (b), (c), (d), (g), (j) and (l) are ultra vires as they stand. Paragraphs
(e), (f), (i) and (k) appear to be valid and paragraph (h) is probably good in part and bad in part, since
the exercise by a commoner of his rights may well interfere with the movement or passage of vehicles.
Textual severance can achieve nothing since it is apparent that the valid provisions are merely ancillary
to the invalid provisions….

I think the proper test to be applied when textual severance is impossible, following in this respect
the Australian authorities, is to abjure speculation as to what the maker of the law might have done
if he had applied his mind to the relevant limitation on his powers and to ask whether the legislative
instrument

> with the invalid portions omitted would be substantially a different law as to the subject matter
> dealt with by what remains from what it would be with the omitted portions forming part of it: *Rex*
> v *Commonwealth Court of Conciliation and Arbitration, Ex parte Whybrow & Co.* 11 CLR 1, 27.

In applying this test the purpose of the legislation can only be inferred from the text as applied to
the factual situation to which its provisions relate. Considering the Greenham byelaws as a whole it is
clear that the absolute prohibition which they impose upon all unauthorised access to the protected

area is no less than is required to maintain the security of an establishment operated as a military air-base and wholly enclosed by a perimeter fence. Byelaws drawn in such a way as to permit free access to all parts of the base to persons exercising rights of common and their animals would be byelaws of a totally different character. They might serve some different legislative purpose in a different factual situation, as do some other byelaws to which our attention has been drawn relating to areas used as military exercise grounds or as military firing ranges. But they would be quite incapable of serving the legislative purpose which the Greenham byelaws, as drawn, are intended to serve.

For these reasons I conclude that the invalidity of byelaw 2(b) cannot be cured by severance. It follows that the appellants were wrongly convicted and I would allow their appeals, set aside the order of the Divisional Court and restore the order of the Crown Court at Reading.

[Lords Griffith, Goff, and Oliver concurred with Lord Bridge.]

LORD LOWRY: … That problem has traditionally been resolved by applying first the textual, and then the substantial, severability test. If the legislation failed the first test, it was condemned in its entirety. If it passed that test, it had to face the next hurdle. This approach, in my opinion, has a great deal in its favour.

The basic principle is that an ultra vires enactment, such as a byelaw, is void ab initio and of no effect. The so-called blue pencil test is a concession to practicality and ought not to be extended or weakened. In its traditional form it is acceptable because, once the offending words are ignored, no word or phrase needs to be given a meaning different from, or more restrictive than, its original meaning. Therefore the court has not legislated; it merely continues to apply that part of the existing legislation which is good.

…

1. The blue pencil test already represents a concession to the erring law-maker, the justification for which I have tried to explain.

2. When applying the blue pencil test (which actually means ignoring the offending words), the court cannot cause the text of the instrument to be altered. It will remain as the ostensible law of the land unless and until it is replaced by something else. It is too late now to think of abandoning the blue pencil method, which has much to commend it, but the disadvantage inherent in the method ought not to be enlarged.

3. It is up to the law-maker to keep within his powers and it is in the public interest that he should take care, in order that the public may be able to rely on the written word as representing the law. Further enlargement of the court's power to validate what is partially invalid will encourage the law-maker to enact what he pleases, or at least to enact what may or may not be valid, without having to fear any worse result than merely being brought back within bounds.

…

5. To liberalise the test would, in my view, be anarchic, not progressive. It would tend in the wrong direction, unlike some developments in the law of negligence, which have promoted justice for physically or economically injured persons, or the sounder aspects of judicial review, which have promoted freedom and have afforded protection from power.

6. The current of decisions and relevant authority has flowed in favour of the traditional doctrine.

This last observation brings me back to *Daymond* v *Plymouth City Council* [1976] AC 609, the case in which, as my noble and learned friend has said, it appears to have been taken for granted that severance was possible, and the question is, what significance should be attached to that fact when reviewing the doctrine of textual severability?

[Lord Lowry thought that textual severability would have been of no assistance to either the majority or minority judgments.]

I am therefore very reluctant to treat the case as an authority which by implication contradicts the established doctrine of textual severability for the purposes of the present appeal. Accordingly, I would allow this appeal on two grounds, (1) that there is no valid part of byelaw 2(b) which can be severed from the invalid part and stand by itself and (2) that the byelaw would not in any event survive the test of substantial severability.

Appeal allowed.

NOTE: In *The Confederation of Passenger Transport UK* v *The Humber Bridge Board and the Secretary of State for Transport, Local Government and the Regions* [2003] EWCA Civ 842, it was held that it was possible to correct a drafting error in delegated legislation applying the principles outlined by Lord Nicholls in interpreting primary legislation in *Inco Europe Limited* v *First Choice Distribution* [2000] 1 WLR 586, 592c–593a:

> This power is confined to plain cases of drafting mistakes. The courts are ever mindful that their constitutional role in this field is interpretative. They must abstain from any course which might have the appearance of judicial legislation. A statute is expressed in language approved and enacted by the legislature. So the courts exercise considerable caution before adding or omitting or substituting words. Before interpreting a statute in this way the court must be abundantly sure of three matters: (1) the intended purpose of the statute or provision in question; (2) that by inadvertence the draftsman and Parliament failed to give effect to that purpose in the provision in question; and (3) the substance of the provision Parliament would have made, although not necessarily the precise words Parliament would have used, had the error in the bill been noticed. The third of these conditions is of crucial importance. Otherwise any attempt to determine the meaning of the enactment would cross the boundary between construction and legislation: see per Lord Diplock in *Jones* v *Wrotham Park Settled Estates* [1980] AC 74, 105–106.

■ QUESTIONS

1. Is the majority giving the courts a wide power to amend delegated legislation by severing invalid portions?

2. Is such a power to amend constitutional or desirable, given that Parliament can rarely amend delegated legislation?

8

Devolution

OVERVIEW

In this chapter, we examine the topic of devolution, a central part of the constitutional reform programme implemented by the New Labour government after being elected to office in 1997. Legislative and executive power has been devolved to Scotland, Wales, and Northern Ireland, and we consider the background to devolution and outline the nature of this asymmetrical devolution settlement. We then explore some of the issues related to devolution which have been raised in the courts, and the extent to which the current devolution settlement is dynamic and continuing to change.

SECTION 1: BACKGROUND TO DEVOLUTION

Of all of the constitutional reform implemented by New Labour following their election to government in 1997, devolution has perhaps had the greatest impact on both the UK constitution and the UK as a unitary nation state. By Acts of the Westminster Parliament, new institutions of government were created in Scotland, Wales, and Northern Ireland, with legislative and executive power devolved to those three constituent nations of the UK.

B. Hadfield, 'Devolution: A National Conversation?' in J. Jowell and D. Oliver (eds), *The Changing Constitution*
(7th edn, 2011), pp. 213–14

A consideration of the devolved UK constitution may be placed within the perspective of the UK as a unitary state; that is, one in which popular power flows to and political power flows from the centrally located Parliament and government in London. Devolution then is viewed as a means of the granting or 'delegation' of power from the centre to new regional institutions which then exercise whatever power is devolved for as long as it is devolved. Alternatively, a wider political and historical perspective would emphasise the centuries' old formation of the UK through the various Acts of Union involving England, Wales, Scotland and (Northern) Ireland and their terms and conditions. Devolution then is viewed as an (incomplete) reversion to a status quo *ante* or, better, a dynamic renewal of an *'ancien regime'*. One value of the latter perspective is to accentuate the different histories, legal systems, educational and local government structures, cultures and traditions within the component parts of the UK and to negate an apparently dominant perspective of a constitutional and historico-political monolith composed mainly of the sovereign Westminster Parliament and central government based on support (at least until the 2010 general election) for one of only two nationally based political parties. Elements of both perspectives may be seen in the introduction and evolution of devolution since New Labour's key legislation of 1998.

Thus there is more than one model of devolution and more than one set of principles to be served by it. Devolution for Scotland and Wales, for example, was presented by the Labour government of the late 1990s as a way of strengthening the Union through decentralization and subsidiarity and consequently of weakening any separatist tendencies. By contrast, devolution for Northern Ireland was part of both a peace and a political process accommodating internal cross-community and all-Ireland dimensions, the principle of parity of esteem across a wide range of factors, and with statutory provision made for the termination of the Union under certain specified conditions.

If it is accurate to state that devolution may serve a variety of constitutional and political purposes, whatever the similarities of the delivered statutory models, it is equally accurate to state that the founding principles cannot constrain its development. The actual introduction of devolution itself creates the probability of alternative political conceptions of its evolution which may run counter to its original design. These alternative conceptions may emerge from either the devolved institutions themselves or from the electorate. A central aspect of all the devolution packages was the requirement that the relevant nation's electorate should endorse the government's proposals before their enactment in legislation, thus adding the third element of popular sovereignty to the 'equation for change', alongside the Westminster Parliament and the devolved authorities. It is a possible, if not probable, hypothesis, that the development of devolution in real terms, as opposed to the formal conferment of powers, will be more influenced by the devolved authorities and their electorate than by Westminster.

P. Leyland, 'The Multifaceted Constitutional Dynamics of UK Devolution'

(2011) 9(1) *International Journal of Constitutional Law* 251–3

The introduction of devolution under the new Labour government elected in 1997 was a radical constitutional change; however, it was not undertaken as part of a wider strategy of constitutional transformation. Rather, the package of measures contained in each devolution statute and subsequently ratified by referenda represented a distinct and pragmatic attempt to solve particular problems and aspirations associated with Scotland, Wales, and Northern Ireland. The schemes set in place, under the 1998 legislation, were meant to confer sufficient power to satisfy local political conditions while also addressing the dissatisfaction felt in the most far-flung parts of the United Kingdom with the centralizing tendencies that had been emanating from Westminster under the previous Conservative administration. In its effect, devolution has also contributed significantly to creating what has been termed "a multi-layered constitution," featuring a hollowing out of central government power, which has come to be located at several different levels and which is exercised in many different ways, adding greatly to the complexity of modern governance.

The discussion that follows demonstrates how devolution has been employed in the United Kingdom in a somewhat different way from federalism as a mechanism for organizing the division of powers and functions between national and subnational government. However, it is mainly argued here that it is incorrect to regard these changes as forming a new constitutional settlement. While it is true that the nature of the Constitution has been transformed in fundamental respects, and that certain local aspirations in Scotland, Wales, and Northern Ireland have been met, devolution has triggered a process of ongoing constitutional change at many levels. There was a lack of any overall reflection on the wider constitutional impact that would be caused by the extreme asymmetry in the way power has been distributed and exercised. For example, we will see that the Scottish government, now under the control of the Scottish National Party, only views the current arrangements as a staging post on the road to full independence. The Government of Wales Act (GWA) 2006 put the seal on a second phase of Welsh devolution by granting the devolved bodies enhanced lawmaking powers; however, this was also an acknowledgment of the limitations of the original scheme. Devolution in Northern Ireland has been plagued with difficulties, leading to suspension on three occasions up until its most recent and so far sustained relaunch in 2007. More generally, the funding arrangements for devolution under the

Barnett formula, which have remained in place since its launch in 1999, have been called into question and may soon be replaced by an alternative method of revenue raising.

Perhaps the most serious constitutional imbalance has concerned the implications for Westminster and the lack of any equivalent form of government for England. In constitutional terms, it is as if each nation comprising the U.K. has embarked on a journey with an uncertain destination. Viewed from a rather different perspective, it will also become apparent that devolution has not only involved the introduction of innovative legislative and oversight processes in Scotland, Wales and Northern Ireland, which have so far proved more resistant to executive domination than their counterparts at Westminster, but it has also had unanticipated consequences here, as well. One such result... has concerned the continuing importance of Westminster legislation in the devolved areas of the United Kingdom. In view of the many changes in the form of devolution alluded to in this essay, it is suggested that not only is devolution itself a dynamic process but that it has also exerted a major influence on the development of the U.K. constitutional system.

NOTE: These extracts identify two key characteristics of the existing UK devolution settlement which will be under consideration in this chapter:

(1) Devolution in the UK is *asymmetrical*, with power devolved to Scotland, Wales, and Northern Ireland to different extents. This is a consequence of the fact that, as Hadfield indicates, devolution to these three constituent parts of the UK was carried out for different reasons. As a result, the powers devolved could be tailored to the objectives which devolution sought to achieve with respect to each particular nation.

(2) Devolution in the UK is *dynamic*, with each of the three devolution regimes having subsequently been altered from its original state, and further changes the subject of ongoing political debate.

Perhaps just as important as the nature of the existing devolution settlement is what it does not include: devolution of power to England, discussed in the following extract.

B. Hadfield, 'Devolution, Westminster and the English Question'

[2005] *Public Law* 286, 291

This brings us to the second significant element of the present devolution arrangements [the first being asymmetry]—the omission of devolution to England. England is the only UK nation *all* of whose laws are made and *all* of whose policies are formulated by a UK body and *never* by a solely English-elected body. Consequently, and also, all of its laws are always made by a sovereign legislature. Given the nature, extent and continuity of Scottish devolution, these issues are particularly acute with regard to Scottish M.P.s and English affairs at Westminster. This has been vividly illustrated by the passing of legislation to introduce foundation hospitals and top-up students' fees in England. Crucial votes carried overall in the House of Commons received the support of only a minority of English M.P.s. That, on its own, seems to be sufficient to highlight the English Question. If, however, (lack of) reciprocity is to be factored in also, then it is relevant to indicate that the Labour-dominated Scottish Executive has rejected both policies. The specific English Question to be considered here, therefore, is this: how acceptable is it, in the devolved United Kingdom, for M.P.s representing the devolved nations (particularly Scotland) to "vote" on English affairs at Westminster? Here the word "vote" is used loosely to cover three distinct processes: (a) to contribute to the debate in the House of Commons on an English matter; (b) actually to vote on the matter; and (c) to resolve the outcome of the vote against the wishes of the majority of English M.P.s. The last possibility may be predicted on the basis of certain factors—the overall balance between the parties; whether or not the government is dependent for its majority on the votes of Scottish M.P.s; the likelihood of a back-bench rebellion and so forth--but it cannot, of course, be definitely known in advance of a vote.

NOTES

1. While power was not devolved directly to England as a nation, there were some notable developments under New Labour. The Greater London Authority Act 1999 established a London Assembly and a directly elected Mayor for the city. Further, a referendum was held in the northeast of England in 2004 on whether an elected assembly should be established for that region—78 per cent of those voting rejected the notion, on a 48 per cent turnout. This overwhelming defeat signalled the end of New Labour's attempts to devolve further power within England, although the Conservative–Liberal Democrat coalition encouraged other cities to alter their local government arrangements to introduce directly elected mayors. Few cities moved quickly to adopted this model—of the 12 largest cities in England, Liverpool and Leicester introduced directly elected mayors by resolution of their city councils; the remaining ten held referendums on the proposal in May 2012, with it being rejected in all with the sole exception of Bristol.

2. The Coalition Government nevertheless attempted to facilitate further devolution *within* England. The then Chancellor, George Osborne, led the development of the 'Northern Powerhouse' policy—designed to redress the economic imbalance between the North and South of England—beginning in 2014 with a deal for the devolution of a broad range of powers over (and funding for) transport, housing, policing, business support and skills, and health and social care to an elected mayor for the Greater Manchester Combined Authority, a model which brings together multiple local councils in new governance arrangements to make collective decisions. Similar deals to establish and empower Combined Authorities have been agreed for the Liverpool City Region, the Sheffield City Region, West Yorkshire, Cornwall, Tees Valley, the West Midlands, Cambridgeshire and Peterborough, and the West of England. Deals initially agreed for the North East, Norfolk and Suffolk, and Greater Lincolnshire collapsed when they were rejected in one or more constituent local authorities, and the election of a major for the Sheffield City Region was to be delayed from 2017 (the election year for the other Combined Authority mayors) to 2018 to allow an unlawful consultation over the boundaries of the area to be rerun. The Conservative Government elected in 2015 has affirmed its commitment to this programme of local devolution within England, reforming the statutory framework for such deals via the Cities and Local Government Devolution Act 2016. In many ways, this scheme of local devolution within England reflects the scheme of devolution to the nations of the UK more broadly: it is asymmetrical, with different powers and levels of funding agreed with different areas (and with many areas of England not covered by any such Combined Authority deal), and has been fast-moving and dynamic, with further powers agreed for devolution from central government to Combined Authorities after the initial deals (most notably in relation to Greater Manchester, the original and most far-reaching of all the agreed Combined Authorities, in terms of powers and funding).

   There have, nevertheless, been questions raised about the 'very significant lack' of consultation with and engagement of the public when agreeing these deals, and whether negotiations between central and local government have been sufficiently transparent (see House of Commons Communities and Local Government Committee, *Devolution: the Next Five Years and Beyond* (HC 369 of 2015–16)). There are also concerns about whether the funding provided will be adequate, or represent the further devolution of cuts in public services to the local level. Additionally, there is debate about whether this truly constitutes 'devolution' (let alone 'a devolution revolution', as it was described by George Osborne in November 2015) given it may arguably be driven by economic imperatives—to boost growth and development outside London—rather than a constitutional desire to reshape the institutional architecture of the UK, or a political belief in the virtue of self-government. This uncertainty of motive is reflected to some extent in the Communities and Local Government Committee's conclusion (para. 18):

   > We believe that the Government should set out the aims of its devolution policy more clearly, preferably in a way that would, over time, allow success to be measured. The Government needs a clear hierarchy for the many things it is trying to achieve through devolution—promoting local growth at minimum cost, achieving a better balanced economy, improving integration of public services, enhancing local freedom to experiment, bringing decision-making closer to local communities and enhancing the democratic process. It also needs to be clear how the forms of devolution it favours are intended to achieve them, while recognising that there may be a different balance and mix of objectives in different areas.

3. The problems posed by the English Question (or 'West Lothian Question', after the then MP for West Lothian, Tam Dalyell, who raised the issue when devolution was under consideration by

James Callaghan's Labour government in 1977) have been the subject of much discussion. While the difficulties caused by this aspect of the existing asymmetrical devolution settlement—the lack of devolution of power to England—can be readily identified, it remains far from clear how they might be solved (if indeed a 'solution' is required). A recent official assessment of these issues was the McKay Commission, an independent commission announced by the Government on 17 January 2012, and which reported on 25 March 2013.

Report of the Commission on the Consequences of Devolution for the House of Commons ('The McKay Commission')

March 2013, paras 1, 3–8, 12, 15–16, 19–20

Executive Summary

1. The Commission was asked to consider **how the House of Commons might deal with legislation which affects only part of the United Kingdom, following the devolution of certain legislative powers to the Scottish Parliament, the Northern Ireland Assembly and the National Assembly for Wales**. ...

3. The powers and institutional form of the devolved institutions in Northern Ireland, Scotland and Wales vary substantially and asymmetrically. Each now has wide-ranging legislative and executive responsibilities across many fields of domestic policy. The "West Lothian Question" raises the situation that then arises when MPs from outside England could help determine laws that apply in England while MPs from England would have no reciprocal influence on laws outside England in policy fields for which the devolved institutions are now responsible.

4. Some see this as an anomaly which is unfair to people in England, requiring remedial action to give MPs in England a fuller or decisive, even unique, role in making laws for England in policy areas which are devolved outside England. Specifically it raises the possibility that a majority opinion among MPs from England on such laws could be outvoted by a UK-wide majority of all UK MPs. But it is extremely rare for this to happen. Since 1919, only in the short-lived parliaments of 1964–66 and February–October 1974 has the party or coalition forming the UK Government not also enjoyed a majority in England.

5. The governing arrangements for England in the post-devolution era are emerging by default, a residual consequence of devolution elsewhere. While the UK Parliament is set to focus increasingly on England, its procedures for making laws for England have changed little post devolution, and do not differentiate between English and UK-wide matters.

6. Survey research on public attitudes in England reveals *differences of interest* that people in England perceive as distinct from the interests of other parts of the UK. Evidence suggests a significant level of grievance among the people of England, sparked by the perception that Scotland enjoys advantages relative to England under current governing arrangements, particularly in the distribution of public spending and economic benefit. There is a clear and enduring sense that England is materially disadvantaged relative to the other parts of the UK, especially Scotland.

7. In addition, there is a consistent message that the people of England do not think it right that MPs from Scotland should be allowed to vote in the House of Commons on laws that affect England only. The current institutional arrangements for making laws for England are seen fairly uniformly across England as wanting, and they need to be modified to establish some form of England-specific legislative process. More than 50% of respondents supported some form of England-specific procedure for making laws for England, and some 60% did not trust any UK Government "very much" or "at all" to pursue the interests of England. The West Lothian Question, then, has a strong negative resonance in the surveys. Although its salience in practice may be much reduced, respondents want a significant response to their concerns – a voice for England.

8. None of the following potential solutions is a sustainable response:

   • Abolishing devolution is not on the political agenda.
   • Maintaining the status quo is a long-term risk.
   • Strengthening local government in England does not tackle the governance of England.
   • Federalism, both England-wide with an English parliament or with English regions, has compelling objections.
   • Electoral reform, including proportional representation and reduction in the number of MPs returned for seats outside England, is not realistic and fails to tackle the underlying issue.

   …

A principle to inform a response

12. A principle common to the devolution arrangements for Northern Ireland, Scotland and Wales exists on which to base proposals for modifying the procedures of the House of Commons to mitigate the unfairness felt by people in England. The constitutional principle that should be adopted for England (and for England-and-Wales) is that:

decisions at the United Kingdom level with a separate and distinct effect for England (or for England-and-Wales) should normally be taken only with the consent of a majority of MPs for constituencies in England (or England-and-Wales).

   …

15. **MPs from outside England should not be prevented from voting on matters before Parliament**. This would create different classes of MP and could provoke deadlock between the UK Government and the majority of MPs in England. The concerns of England should be met without provoking an adverse reaction outside England. MPs from all parts of the UK need to have the opportunity to participate in the adoption of legislation, whatever the limits of its territorial effect. Instead, MPs from England (or England-and-Wales) should have new or additional ways to assert their interests. But MPs from outside England would then continue to vote on all legislation but with prior knowledge of what the view from England is.

NOTES

1. 'Legislative consent motions' are considered later in this chapter in Section 2B at pp. 364–6: they are a process by which one of the devolved legislatures can consent to the UK Parliament legislating for a devolved nation on a devolved matter and are required, by convention, prior to such legislation being enacted.

2. In 2015, the Conservative majority Government elected subsequent to the publication of the McKay Commission's report decided to introduce a scheme of English Votes for English Laws ('EVEL') through change to the Standing Orders of the House of Commons. The changed legislative process establishes an additional power of veto for MPs representing English constituencies, or English and Welsh constituencies (as appropriate), but does not remove the requirement that a majority of all MPs vote to approve an Act of Parliament; see Chapter 7, Section 1B(d) at pp. 310–14 for full details. The broader constitutional impact of EVEL on the Union could be significant. While noting the difficulty in reaching conclusions at this early stage, the House of Lords Constitution Committee, *English Votes for English Laws* (HL Paper 61 of 2016–17), observed, pp. 3–4:

   The public's desire for England to have a voice and decision-making capacity equal to the devolved nations' in relation to matters which affect only England is understandable. And there are, currently, no viable alternatives other than to provide that voice through the House of Commons. However, attempting to provide a separate voice for England through the membership and institutions of the UK Parliament carries risks. Parliament is a unifying body at the centre of the political union, where all citizens, regardless of where they live, have the same say in the laws and policies that govern them. Using the same institution to provide a separate and distinct role for England could risk undermining Parliament's position as a UK, rather than English, institution—a position which is already under threat given the growth of distinct and separate political party systems and political discourse within each of the devolved nations....

Similarly, the House of Commons Public Administration and Constitutional Affairs Committee expressed concern about the constitutional implications of EVEL, and its place within the wider architecture of devolution, *The Future of the Union, part 1: English Votes for English Laws* (HC 523 of 2015–16), para. 70:

> The ad-hoc approach to change in the constitution of the Union, that dates back to the devolution reforms initiated by the then Labour Government in 1997, and has treated each of Scotland, Wales and Northern Ireland in different ways at different times, has been characteristic of constitutional reform since the 1990s. [The problems with EVEL illustrate] the need for Government to abandon this ad-hoc approach and to explore a comprehensive strategy for the future of relationships between the Westminster Parliament and the component parts of the United Kingdom. The Government should be working towards a new and durable constitutional settlement for the United Kingdom that reflects the scale of constitutional change since the 1997 devolution referendums. This will be the subject of our continuing inquiry into the Future of the Union and of our subsequent Reports on the subject.

■ QUESTIONS

1. Is the existing asymmetrical devolution settlement unsatisfactory in so far as it fails to devolve any power to new institutions with responsibility for England as a whole? Or given England dominates the UK in population terms—based on the 2011 census, 84 per cent of the UK population is English—is concern about the extent to which English interests fail to be represented in the UK institutions of government unjustified?

2. Would the creation of an English Parliament and government undermine the authority of UK institutions? Is the extension of local devolution through Combined Authority deals, in combination with EVEL, a satisfactory alternative?

SECTION 2: THE ASYMMETRICAL REGIMES

Devolution has resulted in the creation of new democratic institutions in Scotland, Wales, and Northern Ireland exercising legislative and executive power to differing extents. This has been achieved by Acts of the Westminster Parliament. In this section, we highlight selected provisions in this legislation which (a) create legislative and executive institutions; (b) devolve power, in particular law-making competence; and (c) offer some specific examples of the asymmetry at the core of the existing settlement(s).

A: Institutions

Scotland Act 1998

1. The Scottish Parliament

(1) There shall be a Scottish Parliament.

(2) One member of the Parliament shall be returned for each constituency (under the simple majority system) at an election held in the constituency.

(3) Members of the Parliament for each region shall be returned at a general election under the additional member system of proportional representation provided for in this Part and vacancies among such members shall be filled in accordance with this Part.

(4) The validity of any proceedings of the Parliament is not affected by any vacancy in its membership.

(5) Schedule 1 (which makes provision for the constituencies and regions for the purposes of this Act and the number of regional members) shall have effect.

...

44. The Scottish Government

(1) There shall be a Scottish Government, whose members shall be—

    (a) the First Minister,

    (b) such Ministers as the First Minister may appoint under section 47, and

    (c) the Lord Advocate and the Solicitor General for Scotland.

(2) The members of the Scottish Government are referred to collectively as the Scottish Ministers.

(3) A person who holds a Ministerial office may not be appointed a member of the Scottish Government; and if a member of the Scottish Government is appointed to a Ministerial office he shall cease to hold office as a member of the Scottish Government.

(4) In subsection (3), references to a member of the Scottish Government include a junior Scottish Minister and "Ministerial office" has the same meaning as in section 2 of the House of Commons Disqualification Act 1975.

NOTES

1. The Scotland Act 1998 originally referred to a 'Scottish Executive'. This was amended by s. 12(2)(a) of the Scotland Act 2012, which substituted 'Government' for 'Executive', reflecting a change in terminology which had been adopted in practice by the Scottish National Party minority administration after its election to office in 2007.

2. The First Minister is 'appointed by Her Majesty from among the members of the Parliament and shall hold office at Her Majesty's pleasure', but is nominated for appointment by the Scottish Parliament (s. 46). The First Minister appoints Ministers from among the members of the Parliament 'with the approval of Her Majesty'. But approval will not be sought for appointment of a Minister without the approval of the Parliament (s. 47). The First Minister may resign the office at any time, but 'shall do so if the Parliament resolves that the Scottish Government no longer enjoys the confidence of the Parliament' (s. 45).

3. Prior to devolution, Scotland already had a judicial system which was largely separate from that of the rest of the UK, preserved in the Acts of Union 1707. Appeals from the Inner House of the Court of Session, Scotland's highest civil court, can be heard in the UK Supreme Court. The High Court of Justiciary is Scotland's supreme criminal court; appeals on criminal matters are not heard by the UK Supreme Court. The jurisdiction of the UK Supreme Court over devolution issues (transferred from the Judicial Committee of the Privy Council by s. 40(4)(b) of the Constitutional Reform Act 2005) has, however, complicated this state of affairs. For decisions of the High Court in Scotland as to the compatibility of Scots criminal law with the European Convention on Human Rights raise what can be understood to be devolution issues, and can thus be appealed to the UK Supreme Court. A controversial example of this can be seen in *Cadder* v *HM Advocate* [2010] UKSC 43, in which the Supreme Court held that, when prosecuting a criminal offence, the Crown's reliance on admissions obtained from a detainee while being interviewed by police without access to legal advice was incompatible with his Art. 6 right to a fair trial. A second controversial case, which led to members of the Scottish Government publicly, and extensively, criticizing the Supreme Court for intervening in Scots criminal matters, was *Fraser* v *HM Advocate* [2011] UKSC 24, in which it had been held that non-disclosure of evidence had violated the right to a fair trial protected by Art. 6. The law in relation to devolution issues, compatibility with European Convention on Human Rights (ECHR) rights, and Scots criminal proceedings has subsequently been amended by ss 34–7 of the Scotland Act 2012, which creates a new procedure by which compatibility matters can be referred to the UK Supreme Court, while providing that such matters will not also be devolution issues, and preventing the Supreme Court from granting remedies after determining a compatibility issue, by requiring such decisions to be remitted to the High Court of Justiciary for consideration.

4. The institutions created by the Scotland Act 1998 are now recognized in that statute as 'a permanent part of the United Kingdom's constitutional arrangements', as a result of amendments made by the Scotland Act 2016, s. 1. The newly established s. 63A of the Scotland Act 1998 signifies the commitment of the UK Parliament and Government to the Scottish Parliament and Government, and declares that these institutions cannot be abolished unless authorized in a referendum of the people of Scotland; on the development and legal status of this provision, see later in this chapter in Section 4A at p. 389.

Government of Wales Act 2006

1. The Assembly

(1) There is to be an Assembly for Wales to be known as the National Assembly for Wales or Cynulliad Cenedlaethol Cymru (referred to in this Act as "the Assembly").

(2) The Assembly is to consist of–

(a) one member for each Assembly constituency (referred to in this Act as "Assembly constituency members"), and

(b) members for each Assembly electoral region (referred to in this Act as "Assembly regional members").

(3) Members of the Assembly (referred to in this Act as "Assembly members") are to be returned in accordance with the provision made by and under this Act for–

(a) the holding of general elections of Assembly members (for the return of the entire Assembly), and

(b) the filling of vacancies in Assembly seats.

(4) The validity of any Assembly proceedings is not affected by any vacancy in its membership.

(5) In this Act "Assembly proceedings" means any proceedings of–

(a) the Assembly,

(b) committees of the Assembly, or

(c) sub-committees of such committees.

…

45. Welsh Government

(1) There is to be a Welsh Government, or Llywodraeth Cymru, whose members are–

(a) the First Minister or Prif Weinidog (see sections 46 and 47),

(b) the Welsh Ministers, or Gweini dogion Cymru, appointed under section 48,

(c) the Counsel General to the Welsh Government or Cwnsler Cyffredinol i Lywodraeth Cymru (see section 49) (referred to in this Act as "the Counsel General"), and

(d) the Deputy Welsh Ministers or Dirprwy Weinidogion Cymru (see section 50).

(2) In this Act and in any other enactment or instrument the First Minister and the Welsh Ministers appointed under section 48 are referred to collectively as the Welsh Ministers.

NOTES

1. Devolution of power to Wales was originally executed and governed by the Government of Wales Act 1998. The Welsh Assembly, unlike the Scottish Parliament, did not initially possess the power to enact primary legislation, but was instead the recipient of powers previously exercised by UK Government ministers, including powers to make subordinate legislation relating to Wales. The 2006 Act, as will be seen later in this chapter in Section 2B at pp. 356–9, extended the legislative power of the Assembly significantly.

2. The office of First Minister for Wales and the Welsh Assembly Government were created by the 2006 Act; the Welsh Assembly Government was then renamed the Welsh Government by the Wales Act 2014, s. 4. Prior to this, the 1998 Act had created the post of Assembly First Secretary, who could appoint further Assembly Secretaries, and Assembly functions could be delegated to these office-holders or Assembly committees. The extension of the legislative power of the Assembly by the 2006 Act produced an institutional arrangement which more closely reflects that adopted in Scotland, with a clearer distinction between a legislature (the Assembly) and an executive (the Welsh Government, led by the First Minister). As in relation to Scotland, the First Minister for Wales is appointed by the Queen, on the nomination of the Assembly (ss 46–7). The First Minister may appoint Welsh Ministers from among the members of the Assembly, again formally 'with the approval of Her Majesty' (s. 48).

Northern Ireland (Elections) Act 1998

1. The New Northern Ireland Assembly

(1) There shall be an Assembly called the New Northern Ireland Assembly, for the purpose of taking part in preparations to give effect to the agreement reached at the multi-party talks on Northern Ireland set out in Command Paper 3883.

(2) The Secretary of State may refer to the Assembly—

  (a) specific matters arising from that agreement, and

  (b) such other matters as he thinks fit.

(3) The Assembly shall consist of 108 members.

(4) The initial members shall be returned at an election for the constituencies in Northern Ireland which would return members to the Parliament of the United Kingdom if a general election were held on the date of the passing of this Act.

(5) Each constituency shall return six members.

(6) The Schedule to this Act (which makes supplementary provision about the Assembly) shall have effect.

NOTE: The Northern Ireland Assembly created in 1998 was 'new' because, unlike Scotland and Wales, there had been previous experience of devolution in Northern Ireland, with a Parliament of Northern Ireland having been created by the Government of Ireland Act 1920, and a previous Assembly established under the Northern Ireland Constitution Act 1973. The present Assembly was created in the aftermath of the Good Friday Agreement, signed on 10 April 1998 by the main Northern Irish political parties and the UK and Irish governments (referred to in the extract earlier as 'Command Paper 3883'). The Good Friday Agreement made provision for the future governance of Northern Ireland and its terms, after being approved in referendums held in Northern Ireland and the Republic of Ireland, were given effect in the Northern Ireland Act 1998 (which also, by Sch. 15, repealed the Northern Ireland (Elections) Act 1998).

Northern Ireland Act 1998

...

4. Transferred, excepted and reserved matters

...

(5) In this Act–

  "the Assembly" means the New Northern Ireland Assembly, which after the appointed day shall be known as the Northern Ireland Assembly;

...

16A. Appointment of First Minister, deputy First Minister and Northern Ireland Ministers following Assembly election

(1) This section applies where an Assembly is elected under section 31 or 32.

(2) All Northern Ireland Ministers shall cease to hold office.

(3) Within a period of 14 days beginning with the first meeting of the Assembly–

  (a) the offices of First Minister and deputy First Minister shall be filled by applying subsections (4) to (7); and

  (b) the Ministerial offices to be held by Northern Ireland Ministers shall be filled by applying section 18(2) to (6).

(4) The nominating officer of the largest political party of the largest political designation shall nominate a member of the Assembly to be the First Minister.

(5) The nominating officer of the largest political party of the second largest political designation shall nominate a member of the Assembly to be the deputy First Minister.

(6) If the persons nominated do not take up office within a period specified in standing orders, further nominations shall be made under subsections (4) and (5).

(7) Subsections (4) to (6) shall be applied as many times as may be necessary to secure that the offices of First Minister and deputy First Minister are filled.

(8) But no person may take up office as First Minister, deputy First Minister or Northern Ireland Minister by virtue of this section after the end of the period mentioned in subsection (3) (see further section 32(3)).

(9) The persons nominated under subsections (4) and (5) shall not take up office until each of them has affirmed the terms of the pledge of office....

(12) This section shall be construed in accordance with, and is subject to, section 16C. ...

16C. Sections 16A and 16B: supplementary

...

(3) For the purposes of sections 16A and 16B and this section, a political party to which one or more members of the Assembly belong is to be taken–

(a) to be of the political designation "Nationalist" if, at the relevant time (see subsection (11)), more than half of the members of the Assembly who belonged to the party were designated Nationalists;

(b) to be of the political designation "Unionist" if, at the relevant time, more than half of the members of the Assembly who belonged to the party were designated Unionists;

(c) otherwise, to be of the political designation "Other".

(4) For the purposes of sections 16A and 16B and this section–

(a) the size of the political designation "Nationalist" is to be taken to be equal to the number of members of the Assembly who, at the relevant time, were designated Nationalists;

(b) the size of the political designation "Unionist" is to be taken to be equal to the number of members of the Assembly who, at the relevant time, were designated Unionists;

(c) the size of the political designation "Other" is to be taken to be equal to the number of members of the Assembly who, at the relevant time, were neither designated Nationalists nor designated Unionists. ...

17. Ministerial offices

(1) The First Minister and the deputy First Minister acting jointly may at any time, and shall where subsection (2) applies, determine—

(a) the number of Ministerial offices to be held by Northern Ireland Ministers; and

(b) the functions to be exercisable by the holder of each such office.

(2) This subsection applies where provision is made by an Act of the Assembly for establishing a new Northern Ireland department or dissolving an existing one.

(3) In making a determination under subsection (1), the First Minister and the deputy First Minister shall ensure that the functions exercisable by those in charge of the different Northern Ireland departments existing at the date of the determination are exercisable by the holders of different Ministerial offices.

(4) The number of Ministerial offices shall not exceed 10 or such greater number as the Secretary of State may by order provide.

(5) A determination under subsection (1) shall not have effect unless it is approved by a resolution of the Assembly passed with cross-community support.

20. The Executive Committee

(1) There shall be an Executive Committee of each Assembly consisting of the First Minister, the deputy First Minister and the Northern Ireland Ministers.

(2) The First Minister and the deputy First Minister shall be chairmen of the Committee….

(4) The Committee shall also have the function of discussing and agreeing upon—….

(b) significant or controversial matters that the First Minister and deputy First Minister acting jointly have determined to be matters that should be considered by the Executive Committee.

NOTES

1. These extracts are as amended by the Northern Ireland (Monitoring Commission etc.) Act 2003, the Northern Ireland (St Andrews Agreement) Act 2006, and the Northern Ireland (Stormont Agreement and Implementation Plan) Act 2016.

2. A number of provisions relating to the legislative and executive institutions are specifically designed for the government of Northern Ireland: the provisions as to the appointment of the First Minister and Deputy First Minister (s. 16A); their joint determination of the Ministerial Offices which will exist, to a maximum of ten, and the functions which will be exercised (s. 17); the appointment of Ministers to those offices in accordance with a statutory 'd'Hondt' formula which seeks to fix the number of Ministers drawn from a party against the number of seats that party has won in the Assembly (s. 18); and the potential exclusion from government on a temporary basis of Ministers or parties not committed to non-violence (s. 30). The effect of these provisions is to require that the Executive Committee is cross-party, bringing together the parties designated as Nationalist and Unionist (s. 16C) to share the exercise of governmental power devolved to Northern Ireland—a crucial element in the process of uniting communities divided by political and religious conflict in the decades prior to devolution.

B: Legislative competence

Scotland Act 1998

28. Acts of the Scottish Parliament

(1) Subject to section 29, the Parliament may make laws, to be known as Acts of the Scottish Parliament.

(2) Proposed Acts of the Scottish Parliament shall be known as Bills; and a Bill shall become an Act of the Scottish Parliament when it has been passed by the Parliament and has received Royal Assent.

(3) A Bill receives Royal Assent at the beginning of the day on which Letters Patent under the Scottish Seal signed with Her Majesty's own hand signifying Her Assent are recorded in the Register of the Great Seal.

(4) The date of Royal Assent shall be written on the Act of the Scottish Parliament by the Clerk, and shall form part of the Act.

(5) The validity of an Act of the Scottish Parliament is not affected by any invalidity in the proceedings of the Parliament leading to its enactment.

(6) Every Act of the Scottish Parliament shall be judicially noticed.

(7) This section does not affect the power of the Parliament of the United Kingdom to make laws for Scotland.

(8) But it is recognised that the Parliament of the United Kingdom will not normally legislate with regard to devolved matters without the consent of the Scottish Parliament.

29. Legislative competence

(1) An Act of the Scottish Parliament is not law so far as any provision of the Act is outside the legislative competence of the Parliament.

(2) A provision is outside that competence so far as any of the following paragraphs apply—

(a) it would form part of the law of a country or territory other than Scotland, or confer or remove functions exercisable otherwise than in or as regards Scotland,

(b) it relates to reserved matters,

(c) it is in breach of the restrictions in Schedule 4,

(d) it is incompatible with any of the Convention rights or with EU law,

(e) it would remove the Lord Advocate from his position as head of the systems of criminal prosecution and investigation of deaths in Scotland.

(3) For the purposes of this section, the question whether a provision of an Act of the Scottish Parliament relates to a reserved matter is to be determined, subject to subsection (4), by reference to the purpose of the provision, having regard (among other things) to its effect in all the circumstances.

(4) A provision which—

(a) would otherwise not relate to reserved matters, but

(b) makes modifications of Scots private law, or Scots criminal law, as it applies to reserved matters, is to be treated as relating to reserved matters unless the purpose of the provision is to make the law in question apply consistently to reserved matters and otherwise.

(5) Subsection (1) is subject to section 30(6).

30. Legislative competence: supplementary

(1) Schedule 5 (which defines reserved matters) shall have effect.

(2) Her Majesty may by Order in Council make any modifications of Schedule 4 or 5 which She considers necessary or expedient. ...

(5) Subsection (6) applies where any alteration is made—

(a) to the matters which are reserved matters, or

(b) to Schedule 4,

(whether by virtue of the making, revocation or expiry of an Order in Council under this section or otherwise).

(6) Where the effect of the alteration is that a provision of an Act of the Scottish Parliament ceases to be within the legislative competence of the Parliament, the provision does not for that reason cease to have effect (unless an enactment provides otherwise).

31. Scrutiny of Bills before introduction

(1) A person in charge of a Bill shall, on or before introduction of the Bill in the Parliament, state that in his view the provisions of the Bill would be within the legislative competence of the Parliament.

(2) The Presiding Officer shall, on or before the introduction of a Bill in the Parliament, decide whether or not in his view the provisions of the Bill would be within the legislative competence of the Parliament and state his decision.

(3) The form of any statement, and the manner in which it is to be made, shall be determined under standing orders, and standing orders may provide for any statement to be published.

...

33. Scrutiny of Bills by the Supreme Court

(1) The Advocate General, the Lord Advocate or the Attorney General may refer the question of whether a Bill or any provision of a Bill would be within the legislative competence of the Parliament to the Supreme Court for decision.

(2) Subject to subsection (3), he may make a reference in relation to a Bill at any time during—

(a) the period of four weeks beginning with the passing of the Bill, and

(b) any period of four weeks beginning with any subsequent approval of the Bill in accordance with standing orders made by virtue of section 36(5).

NOTES

1. The extracts reproduced earlier in this section are as amended by the Constitutional Reform Act 2005 and the Scotland Act 2012.
2. The power of the UK Parliament to legislate for Scotland is explicitly preserved (and as will be seen later in this section, similar provisions are included in the legislation applicable to Wales and Northern Ireland), which in principle ensures there can be no clash between the devolution settlement and the doctrine of parliamentary sovereignty. In practice, however, the power of the UK Parliament to repeal the Scotland Act 1998 unilaterally, and reverse the effects of devolution, must be understood to be severely limited. In particular, the fact that devolution of legislative and executive power to Scotland was approved by the Scottish electorate at a referendum provides direct democratic legitimacy to the devolved institutions (74.3 per cent of voters in favour of establishing a Scottish Parliament on a turnout of 60.4 per cent), making it near impossible in political terms for the UK Parliament to legislate to abolish the devolution settlement unless acting on an alternative democratic mandate derived from Scottish voters. This reality is now reflected in s. 63A of the Scotland Act 1998 (as amended by s. 1 of the Scotland Act 2016) which recognizes the 'permanence' of the Scottish Parliament and Government; see later in this chapter in Section 4A at p. 389.
3. The 'reserved powers' model of legislative competence established in relation to Scotland is defined on an exclusionary basis. The Scottish Parliament has power to legislate, except in relation to those matters stated to be outside its competence: in particular, this includes legislation which violates EU law or the ECHR, and legislation which concerns a reserved matter. Matters which are reserved to the UK Parliament are set out in detail in Sch. 5 to the Scotland Act 1998; the following extract provide an indication of some of the crucial topics *outside* the legislative competence of the Scottish Parliament.

Scotland Act 1998

Schedule 5 – Reserved Matters

Part I – General Reservations

The Constitution
Para 1 The following aspects of the constitution are reserved matters, that is –

(a) the Crown, including succession to the Crown and a regency,
(b) the Union of the Kingdoms of Scotland and England,
(c) the Parliament of the United Kingdom,
(d) the continued existence of the High Court of Justiciary as a criminal court of first instance and of appeal,
(e) the continued existence of the Court of Session as a civil court of first instance and of appeal.

Political Parties ...
Foreign Affairs etc. ....
Public Service ...
Defence ...
Treason ...

Part II – Specific Reservations

Head A – Financial and Economic Matters

Para A1 Fiscal, economic and monetary policy
Para A2 The currency

Head B – Home Affairs

Para B1 Misuse of drugs
Para B2 Data Protection

Para B4   Firearms

Para B6   Immigration and nationality

Para B8   National security, interception of communications, official secrets and terrorism

Para B11   Extradition

Para B13   Access to information

Head C – Trade and Industry

Para C7   Consumer Protection

Para C8   Product standards, safety and liability

Para C9   Weights and measures

Head D – Energy…
Head E – Transport…
Head F – Social Security…
Head G – Regulation of the Professions…
Head H – Employment…
Head J – Health and Medicines…
Head K – Media and Culture…
Head L – Miscellaneous…

Para L1   Judicial remuneration

Para L2   Equal opportunities

Para L3   Control of weapons

Para L5   Time

Para L6   Outer space

Para L7   Antarctica

NOTE: Within the broad categories above, specific matters are identified as being reserved to the Westminster Parliament. The reservations on the legislative power of the Scottish Parliament continue to change since the 1998 settlement. Most recently, the Scotland Act 2016 will remove reservations in a range of areas, most notably in relation to significant policy areas like elections, welfare benefits, employment support, abortion rights, onshore petroleum exploration, and will devolve further fiscal control over taxation and borrowing; see later in this chapter in Section 4A at pp. 388–9.

Government of Wales Act 2006

107. Acts of the Assembly

(1) The Assembly may make laws, to be known as Acts of the National Assembly for Wales or Deddfau Cynulliad Cenedlaethol Cymru (referred to in this Act as "Acts of the Assembly").

(2) Proposed Acts of the Assembly are to be known as Bills; and a Bill becomes an Act of the Assembly when it has been passed by the Assembly and has received Royal Assent.

(3) The validity of an Act of the Assembly is not affected by any invalidity in the Assembly proceedings leading to its enactment.

(4) Every Act of the Assembly is to be judicially noticed.

(5) This Part does not affect the power of the Parliament of the United Kingdom to make laws for Wales.

108. Legislative competence

(1) Subject to the provisions of this Part, an Act of the Assembly may make any provision that could be made by an Act of Parliament.

(2) An Act of the Assembly is not law so far as any provision of the Act is outside the Assembly's legislative competence.

(3) A provision of an Act of the Assembly is within the Assembly's legislative competence only if it falls within subsection (4) or (5).

(4) A provision of an Act of the Assembly falls within this subsection if–

(a) it relates to one or more of the subjects listed under any of the headings in Part 1 of Schedule 7 and, subject to subsection (4A), does not fall within any of the exceptions specified in that Part of that Schedule (whether or not under that heading or any of those headings), and

(b) it neither applies otherwise than in relation to Wales nor confers, imposes, modifies or removes (or gives power to confer, impose, modify or remove) functions exercisable otherwise than in relation to Wales.

(4A) Provision relating to a devolved tax (as listed under the heading "Taxation" in Part 1 of Schedule 7) is not outside the Assembly's legislative competence by reason only of the fact that it falls within an exception specified under another heading in that Part of that Schedule.

(5) A provision of an Act of the Assembly falls within this subsection if–

(a) it provides for the enforcement of a provision (of that or any other Act of the Assembly) which falls within subsection (4) or a provision of an Assembly Measure or it is otherwise appropriate for making such a provision effective, or

(b) it is otherwise incidental to, or consequential on, such a provision.

(6) But a provision which falls within subsection (4) or (5) is outside the Assembly's legislative competence if–

(a) it breaches any of the restrictions in Part 2 of Schedule 7, having regard to any exception in Part 3 of that Schedule from those restrictions,

(b) it extends otherwise than only to England and Wales, or

(c) it is incompatible with the Convention rights or with EU law.

(7) For the purposes of this section the question whether a provision of an Act of the Assembly relates to one or more of the subjects listed in Part 1 of Schedule 7 (or falls within any of the exceptions specified in that Part of that Schedule) is to be determined by reference to the purpose of the provision, having regard (among other things) to its effect in all the circumstances.

109 Legislative competence: supplementary

(1) Her Majesty may by Order in Council amend Schedule 7.

(2) An Order in Council under this section may make such modifications of–

(a) any enactment (including any enactment comprised in or made under this Act) or prerogative instrument, or

(b) any other instrument or document, as Her Majesty considers appropriate in connection with the provision made by the Order in Council.

(3) An Order in Council under this section may make provision having retrospective effect. …

(5) The amendment of Schedule 7 by an Order in Council under this section does not affect–

(a) the validity of an Act of the Assembly passed before the amendment comes into force, or

(b) the previous or continuing operation of such an Act of the Assembly.

110 Introduction of Bills

(1) A Bill may, subject to the standing orders, be introduced in the Assembly–

(a) by the First Minister, any Welsh Minister appointed under section 48 any Deputy Welsh Minister or the Counsel General, or

(b) by any other Assembly member.

(2) The person in charge of a Bill must, on or before the introduction of the Bill, state that, in that person's view, its provisions would be within the Assembly's legislative competence.

(3) The Presiding Officer must, on or before the introduction of a Bill in the Assembly–

(a) decide whether or not, in the view of the Presiding Officer, the provisions of the Bill would be within the Assembly's legislative competence, and

(b) state that decision. …

112 Scrutiny of Bills by Supreme Court

(1) The Counsel General or the Attorney General may refer the question whether a Bill, or any provision of a Bill, would be within the Assembly's legislative competence to the Supreme Court for decision.

(2) Subject to subsection (3), the Counsel General or the Attorney General may make a reference in relation to a Bill at any time during–

(a) the period of four weeks beginning with the passing of the Bill, and

(b) any period of four weeks beginning with any subsequent approval of the Bill in accordance with provision included in the standing orders in compliance with section 111(7). …

NOTES

1. On enactment of the Government of Wales Act 2006, the Welsh Assembly did not initially possess the power to pass Assembly Acts in accordance with the provisions highlighted earlier. Instead, Part 3 of the 2006 Act initially permitted the Assembly to pass 'Assembly Measures', in accordance with ss 93–102. The authority to enact Assembly Measures was still a significant advance on the limited powers initially devolved to Wales under the 1998 Act (discussed earlier), for such Measures had the status of primary legislation. Yet for a Measure to be within the competence of the Assembly, it had to relate to a specific 'matter' within a broad 'field', with competence for such 'matters' transferred by Legislative Competence Orders made by the Crown in Council. In effect, the system meant that competence for the Assembly to legislate had to be approved in relation to the specific issue which was to be the subject of a Measure by the UK Parliament and Government.

   The 2006 Act provided by s. 103, however, for the Measures system to be replaced by the current Acts system (set out in Part 4 of the 2006 Act) upon its approval by the Welsh electorate at a referendum. This referendum was held on 3 March 2011, with a larger percentage of those voting approving the extension of the Assembly's legislative power than had voted in favour of devolution initially being established in 1997 (in 2011, 63.5 per cent of voters elected to increase the power of the Assembly, as compared with the 50.3 per cent of voters who approved the creation of the Assembly in 1997—the turnout in 2011 was, however, considerably lower: only 35.2 per cent of registered voters took part, compared with 50.1 per cent of voters in 1997).

2. Under this system, the competence of the Assembly to enact Acts no longer depended on specific Legislative Competence Orders. Instead, the Assembly had the power to legislate in the 20 broad 'fields', now re-designated as 'subjects', within which specific 'matters' had previously had to be located. This approach to legislative competence, while more generous than that which existed under the Assembly Measures system, still differed from that in place in Scotland. Whereas the legislative competence of the Scottish Parliament is defined on an exclusionary basis (power to legislate is given in general, subject to specific reservations), the competence of the Assembly has been defined on an inclusionary basis—the Assembly can *only* legislate in relation to those subjects explicitly stated to be *within* its competence, defined in Sch. 7 of the 2006 Act. These subjects are set out in the following extract.

Government of Wales Act 2006

Schedule 7 – Part 1

Para 1 Agriculture, forestry, animals, plants and rural development
Para 2 Ancient monuments and historic buildings
Para 3 Culture
Para 4 Economic development
Para 5 Education and training
Para 6 Environment
Para 7 Fire and rescue services and fire safety
Para 8 Food
Para 9 Health and health services
Para 10 Highways and transport
Para 11 Housing
Para 12 Local government
Para 13 National Assembly for Wales
Para 14 Public administration
Para 15 Social welfare
Para 16 Sport and recreation
Para 17 Tourism
Para 18 Town and country planning
Para 19 Water and flood defence
Para 20 Welsh language

NOTE: Specific exceptions still operate in relation to many of these subject matters; the Assembly does not have unlimited power even in these designated areas. The overall design and effect of the Assembly Acts scheme has been to provide the Welsh Assembly with legislative competence which is still more limited than that possessed by the Scottish Parliament, albeit much less so than as compared to the powers devolved in the original Government of Wales Act 1998. Nevertheless, further legislative change has been executed—in the Wales Act 2014—and more is planned—through the draft Wales Bill 2016–17, under consideration by the UK Parliament—to bring Welsh devolution arrangements into closer alignment with the more extensive scheme in operation in Scotland; see later in this chapter in Section 4B at pp. 389–91.

Northern Ireland Act 1998

4. Transferred, excepted and reserved matters.

(1) In this Act—

"excepted matter" means any matter falling within a description specified in Schedule 2;
"reserved matter" means any matter falling within a description specified in Schedule 3;
"transferred matter" means any matter which is not an excepted or reserved matter.

(2) If at any time after the appointed day it appears to the Secretary of State—

(a) that any reserved matter should become a transferred matter; or
(b) that any transferred matter should become a reserved matter,
  he may, subject to subsections (2A) to (3D), lay before Parliament the draft of an Order in Council amending Schedule 3 so that the matter ceases to be or, as the case may be, becomes a reserved matter with effect from such date as may be specified in the Order.

...

(3) The Secretary of State shall not lay before Parliament under subsection (2) the draft of any other Order unless the Assembly has passed with cross-community support a resolution praying that the matter concerned should cease to be or, as the case may be, should become a reserved matter….

(4) If the draft of an Order laid before Parliament under subsection (2) is approved by resolution of each House of Parliament, the Secretary of State shall submit it to Her Majesty in Council and Her Majesty in Council may make the Order.

(5) In this Act—

"the Assembly" means the New Northern Ireland Assembly, which after the appointed day shall be known as the Northern Ireland Assembly;

"cross-community support", in relation to a vote on any matter, means—

    (a) the support of a majority of the members voting, a majority of the designated Nationalists voting and a majority of the designated Unionists voting; or

    (b) the support of 60 per cent of the members voting, 40 per cent of the designated Nationalists voting and 40 per cent of the designated Unionists voting;

"designated Nationalist" means a member designated as a Nationalist in accordance with standing orders of the Assembly and *"designated Unionist"* shall be construed accordingly.

…

5. Acts of the Northern Ireland Assembly.

(1) Subject to sections 6 to 8, the Assembly may make laws, to be known as Acts.

(2) A Bill shall become an Act when it has been passed by the Assembly and has received Royal Assent.

(3) A Bill receives Royal Assent at the beginning of the day on which Letters Patent under the Great Seal of Northern Ireland signed with Her Majesty's own hand signifying Her Assent are notified to the Presiding Officer.

(4) The date of Royal Assent shall be written on the Act by the Presiding Officer, and shall form part of the Act.

(5) The validity of any proceedings leading to the enactment of an Act of the Assembly shall not be called into question in any legal proceedings.

(6) This section does not affect the power of the Parliament of the United Kingdom to make laws for Northern Ireland, but an Act of the Assembly may modify any provision made by or under an Act of Parliament in so far as it is part of the law of Northern Ireland.

6. Legislative competence.

(1) A provision of an Act is not law if it is outside the legislative competence of the Assembly.

(2) A provision is outside that competence if any of the following paragraphs apply—

    (a) it would form part of the law of a country or territory other than Northern Ireland, or confer or remove functions exercisable otherwise than in or as regards Northern Ireland;

    (b) it deals with an excepted matter and is not ancillary to other provisions (whether in the Act or previously enacted) dealing with reserved or transferred matters;

    (c) it is incompatible with any of the Convention rights;

    (d) it is incompatible with EU law;

    (e) it discriminates against any person or class of person on the ground of religious belief or political opinion;

    (f) it modifies an enactment in breach of section 7.

(3) For the purposes of this Act, a provision is ancillary to other provisions if it is a provision—

    (a) which provides for the enforcement of those other provisions or is otherwise necessary or expedient for making those other provisions effective; or

    (b) which is otherwise incidental to, or consequential on, those provisions;

and references in this Act to provisions previously enacted are references to provisions contained in, or in any instrument made under, other Northern Ireland legislation or an Act of Parliament.

(4) Her Majesty may by Order in Council specify functions which are to be treated, for such purposes of this Act as may be specified, as being, or as not being, functions which are exercisable in or as regards Northern Ireland.

(5) No recommendation shall be made to Her Majesty to make an Order in Council under subsection (4) unless a draft of the Order has been laid before and approved by resolution of each House of Parliament.. . .

8. Consent of Secretary of State required in certain cases.

The consent of the Secretary of State shall be required in relation to a Bill which contains—

(a) a provision which deals with an excepted matter and is ancillary to other provisions (whether in the Bill or previously enacted) dealing with reserved or transferred matters; or

(b) a provision which deals with a reserved matter.

9. Scrutiny by Ministers.

(1) A Minister in charge of a Bill shall, on or before introduction of it in the Assembly, make a statement to the effect that in his view the Bill would be within the legislative competence of the Assembly.

(2) The statement shall be in writing and shall be published in such manner as the Minister making the statement considers appropriate.

10. Scrutiny by Presiding Officer.

(1) Standing orders shall ensure that a Bill is not introduced in the Assembly if the Presiding Officer decides that any provision of it would not be within the legislative competence of the Assembly.

(2) Subject to subsection (3)—

(a) the Presiding Officer shall consider a Bill both on its introduction and before the Assembly enters on its final stage; and

(b) if he considers that the Bill contains—

(i) any provision which deals with an excepted matter and is ancillary to other provisions (whether in the Bill or previously enacted) dealing with reserved or transferred matters; or

(ii) any provision which deals with a reserved matter, he shall refer it to the Secretary of State; and

(c) the Assembly shall not proceed with the Bill or, as the case may be, enter on its final stage unless—

(i) the Secretary of State's consent to the consideration of the Bill by the Assembly is signified; or

(ii) The Assembly is informed that in his opinion the Bill does not contain any such provision as is mentioned in paragraph (b)(i) or (ii).

(3) Subsection (2)(b) and (c) shall not apply—

(a) where, in the opinion of the Presiding Officer, each provision of the Bill which deals with an excepted or reserved matter is ancillary to other provisions (whether in the Bill or previously enacted) dealing with transferred matters only; or

(b) on the introduction of a Bill, where the Bill has been endorsed with a statement that the Secretary of State has consented to the Assembly considering the Bill.

11. Scrutiny by the Supreme Court.

(1) The Advocate General for Northern Ireland or the Attorney General for Northern Ireland may refer the question of whether a provision of a Bill would be within the legislative competence of the Assembly to the Supreme Court for decision.

(2) Subject to subsection (3), he may make a reference in relation to a provision of a Bill at any time during—

   (a) the period of four weeks beginning with the passing of the Bill; and

   (b) the period of four weeks beginning with any subsequent approval of the Bill in accordance with standing orders made by virtue of section 13(6).

(3) If he notifies the Presiding Officer that he does not intend to make a reference in relation to a provision of a Bill, he shall not make such a reference unless, after the notification, the Bill is approved as mentioned in subsection (2)(b).

(4) If the Supreme Court decides that any provision of a Bill would be within the legislative competence of the Assembly, its decision shall be taken as applying also to that provision if contained in the Act when enacted.

NOTES

1. These extracts are as amended by the Justice (Northern Ireland) Act 2002, the Constitutional Reform Act 2005, the Northern Ireland (Miscellaneous Provisions) Act 2006, and the Northern Ireland (Miscellaneous Provisions) Act 2014.

2. The Northern Irish provisions regarding legislative competence contain a number of mechanisms also contained in the Scottish and Welsh devolution arrangements considered in the earlier extracts (mechanisms which do not exist in relation to the sovereign UK Parliament, although comparable—but less extensive—statements of compatibility with ECHR rights are required when legislation is introduced in Westminster by s. 19 of the Human Rights Act 1998); in particular:

   • the need for a statement to be made by the person introducing the Bill that it would be within legislative competence;

   • the requirement that any Bill be scrutinized by the Presiding Officer to ascertain whether it is within legislative competence;

   • the possibility of references to the Supreme Court to consider whether proposed legislation is within legislative competence.

   While there are broad similarities, the specific mechanisms applicable to the Northern Ireland Assembly differ to some extent, however, from those applicable in Scotland and Wales. In particular, there is an additional role for a UK Secretary of State, in consenting to certain kinds of Bill, and in determining whether legislation should be submitted for royal assent. In addition to an assessment as to whether it is within legislative competence, this can involve, in accordance with s. 14(5), a substantive assessment of the content of the legislation: if the Secretary of State considers a Bill would be 'incompatible with any international obligations, with the interests of defence or national security or with the protection of public safety or public order', or would 'have an adverse effect on the operation of the single market in goods and services' within the UK.

3. The Northern Ireland Act 1998 provides yet another model of legislative competence. Transferred matters fall within the competence of the Northern Ireland Assembly, excepted matters do not, reserved matters may be the subject of legislation with the consent of a UK government minister ('the Secretary of State'). Transferred matters are defined as any matter which is not excepted or reserved, which is in this sense comparable with the Scottish exclusionary model of legislative competence. Reserved matters may become transferred matters if the necessary conditions are met, including attracting cross-community support (the particularly controversial example of the originally reserved matter of policing and justice powers being transferred will be considered later in this chapter in Section 4C at pp. 392–4). In substantive terms, legislation (as with Scotland and Wales) may not violate EU law or the ECHR, but a further substantive limit is introduced, preventing legislation which discriminates against people or groups on the grounds of religious belief or political opinion. The following extract highlights a number of the broad topics which are excepted and reserved matters in relation to the Assembly.

Northern Ireland Act 1998

Schedule 2 – Excepted Matters

Para 1 The Crown

Para 2 The Parliament of the United Kingdom

Para 3 International relations

Para 4 The defence of the realm

Para 5 Control of nuclear, biological and chemical weapons and other weapons of mass destruction

Para 6 Dignities and titles of honour

Para 7 Treason but not powers of arrest or criminal procedure

Para 8 Nationality; immigration

Para 9 Taxation applicable to the United Kingdom as a whole

Para 9A Child Trust Funds

Para 9C The operation of the Small Charitable Donations Act 2012

Para 9D Bonuses under the Savings (Government Contributions) Act 2017

Para 10 National insurance contributions

Para 10A Tax credits

Para 10B Health in pregnancy grant, Child benefit and guardian's allowance

Para 10C The operation of the Childcare Payments Act 2014

Para 11 Remuneration of judges

Para 11A The Supreme Court

Para 12 Elections

Para 13 The subject-matter of the Political Parties, Elections and Referendums Act 2000

Para 14 Coinage, legal tender and bank notes

Para 15 The National Savings Bank

Para 16 The subject-matter of the Protection of Trading Interests Act 1980

Para 17 National security

Para 18 Nuclear energy and nuclear installations

Para 19 Regulation of sea fishing outside the Northern Ireland zone

Para 20 Regulation of activities in outer space

Para 20A Regulation of activities in Antarctica

Para 21 Any matter with which a provision of the Northern Ireland Constitution Act 1973, other than section 36(1)(c), solely or mainly deals

Para 21A The office and functions of the Advocate General for Northern Ireland

Para 22 Any matter with which specified provisions of this Act solely or mainly deals

Schedule 3 – Reserved Matters

Para 1 The conferral of functions in relation to Northern Ireland on any Minister of the Crown

Para 2 Property belonging to Her Majesty in right of the Crown or belonging to a department of the Government of the United Kingdom

Para 3 Navigation, including merchant shipping, but not harbours or inland waters

Para 4 Civil aviation but not aerodromes

Para 5 The foreshore and the sea bed and subsoil and their natural resources

Para 6 Domicile …

Para 10(1) The subject-matter of the Public Processions (Northern Ireland) Act 1998

Para 10(2) In relation to the maintenance of public order, the armed forces of the Crown …

Para 12(1) Items for the time being specified in Article 45(1) or (2) of the Firearms (Northern Ireland) Order 2004; and the subject-matter of Article 45(10) of that Order.

Para 12(2) The security of explosives, including—

  (a) the prevention of loss or theft of explosives,
  (b) the prevention of the use of explosives for wrongful purposes, and
  (c) the detection, identification and traceability of explosives.

This sub-paragraph does not include the security of fireworks, or the licensing of shotfirers, or the subject-matter of section 2 of the Explosives Act (Northern Ireland) 1970.

Para 13 Civil defence …

Para 28 Units of measurement and United Kingdom primary standards …

Para 34 Human genetics …

Para 37 Consumer safety in relation to goods …

■ QUESTIONS

1. Are the differences in institutions and legislative competence between Scotland, Wales, and Northern Ireland justifiable?

2. Is the asymmetrical nature of the devolution settlements established in Scotland, Wales, and Northern Ireland beneficial, in so far as it offers the flexibility to create institutions, and devolve power, which can be tailored to the differing circumstances of each of these three nations? Or is it problematic, in so far as it makes the entire devolution settlement more difficult to navigate and understand from a UK perspective?

3. Would a uniform model of devolution—establishing identical institutions with identical competences in each of the nations—be preferable? Would such a 'federal' model of devolution have implications for England?

4. Are there any aspects of the devolution settlements which should be extended to the UK? In particular, could the general mechanisms designed to ensure that Bills are within the competence of each devolved legislature be applied to the UK Parliament? Would such mechanisms challenge the doctrine of parliamentary sovereignty?

NOTE: To ensure that the sovereignty of Parliament is preserved, the devolution statutes affirm that the power of the UK Parliament to legislate for Scotland, Wales, and Northern Ireland on devolved or transferred matters remains unaffected. By convention, however, the Westminster Parliament will not legislate in relation to devolved matters without the consent of the devolved legislature. This is commonly known as the 'Sewel convention', for when the Scotland Bill was being debated in the House of Lords, Lord Sewel announced on behalf of the Government (HL Deb, Vol. 592, col. 791, 21 July 1998) that the Government:

> ... would expect a convention to be established that Westminster would not normally legislate with regard to devolved matters in Scotland without the consent of the Scottish Parliament.

Such a convention also governed legislation by Westminster for former dependent territories which had become independent members of the Commonwealth (see the preamble to and s. 4 of the Statute of Westminster 1931). The convention is now formally recognized in a *Memorandum of Understanding*, the most recent version of which was agreed and published in September 2012, although essentially reiterating principles established in Cm 5240, published in December 2001.

Memorandum of Understanding and Supplementary Agreements

September 2012, paras 1–2, 14–15

Between the United Kingdom Government, the Scottish Ministers, the Welsh Ministers, and the Northern Ireland Executive Committee

Presented to Parliament by Command of Her Majesty and presented to the Scottish Parliament and the Northern Ireland Assembly and laid before the National Assembly for Wales.

PART I: MEMORANDUM OF UNDERSTANDING

Introduction

1. This Memorandum sets out the understanding of, on the one hand, the United Kingdom Government, and on the other, the Scottish Ministers, the Welsh Ministers, and the Northern Ireland Executive Committee ("the devolved administrations") of the principles that will underlie relations between them. The UK Government represents the UK interest in matters which are not devolved in Scotland, Wales or Northern Ireland. Policy responsibility for these non-devolved areas is within the exclusive responsibility of the relevant UK Ministers and Departments. It is recognised by these Ministers and Departments that, within the UK Government, the Secretaries of State for Scotland, Wales and Northern Ireland are responsible for ensuring that the interests of those parts of the UK in non-devolved matters are properly represented and considered. Other UK Ministers and their departments represent the interests of England in all matters.

2. This Memorandum is a statement of political intent, and should not be interpreted as a binding agreement. It does not create legal obligations between the parties. ...

Parliamentary Business

14. The United Kingdom Parliament retains authority to legislate on any issue, whether devolved or not. It is ultimately for Parliament to decide what use to make of that power. However, the UK Government will proceed in accordance with the convention that the UK Parliament would not normally legislate with regard to devolved matters except with the agreement of the devolved legislature. The devolved administrations will be responsible for seeking such agreement as may be required for this purpose on an approach from the UK Government.

15. The United Kingdom Parliament retains the absolute right to debate, enquire into or make representations about devolved matters. It is ultimately for Parliament to decide what use to make of that power, but the UK Government will encourage the UK Parliament to bear in mind the primary

responsibility of devolved legislatures and administrations in these fields and to recognise that it is a consequence of Parliament's decision to devolve certain matters that Parliament itself will in future be more restricted in its field of operation.

NOTES

1. The Sewel convention provides an interesting example of the flexibility and variation of constitutional conventions in the UK, a topic discussed generally in Chapter 5. It is written and was deliberately created—indeed, as the quote from Lord Sewel demonstrates, its creation was envisaged even before the devolution legislation had actually been enacted—rather than unwritten and having evolved over time. It is also a convention of considerable importance, which conditions the effect of the formal legal power retained by the UK Parliament, and thus demonstrates the central role that conventions can play in the UK constitution. Indeed, the use of 'legislative consent motions' in the Scottish Parliament and the Assemblies in Northern Ireland and Wales, to indicate their consent in the circumstances where the Sewel convention applies, may have been more frequent than was initially anticipated (although there is debate about what initial expectations actually were, as noted in the Scottish Parliament Procedures Committee Report which led to the formalization of procedures associated with legislative consent motions; SP Paper 428, 7th Report of 2005, 43–5). It is now clear that the convention is not an exceptional mechanism, but a central part of regulating the relationships between the UK Government and the devolved institutions.

2. There is, nevertheless, debate about the extent of this convention—in practice, legislative consent has been sought from the devolved institutions not simply in relation to substantive legislation by the UK Parliament which relates to devolved matters (as envisaged in the Sewel convention as originally set out), but also in relation to changes to the scope of the devolution arrangements themselves. This broader formulation of the scope of the convention is captured in Devolution Guidance Note 10 (DGN 10) on *Post-Devolution Legislation Affecting Scotland* (2005), one of a number of official documents published by the UK Cabinet Office on working arrangements between the UK Government and devolved administrations. According to DGN 10, para. 4.III, Bills subject to the convention requiring the consent of the Scottish Parliament are those which:

> contains provisions applying to Scotland and which are for devolved purposes, or which alter the legislative competence of the Parliament or the executive competence of the Scottish Ministers.

This may generate uncertainty as to the application of the convention in relation to significant constitutional change for which responsibility is explicitly reserved to the UK Parliament—in particular, withdrawal from the EU or the ECHR—but which would inevitably affect the legislative competence of the Scottish Parliament, in so far as existing limits on law-making power, defined by reference to these bodies of supranational legal rules in s. 29(2)(d) of the Scotland Act 1998, would need to be removed. See further C. McCorkindale, 'Echo Chamber: the 2015 General Election at Holyrood—a word on Sewel', *Scottish Constitutional Futures Forum Blog* (13 May 2015).

3. The operation of the Sewel convention in normal circumstances—although only in its original, narrower formulation, as concerning UK legislation relating to devolved matters—has now been 'recognized' in statute; see s. 28(8) of the Scotland Act 1998, at p. 353 earlier in this section. This sub-section was introduced by s. 1 of the Scotland Act 2016, and raises questions about whether the convention has now obtained legal force. Such claims were, however, unanimously rejected by the Supreme Court when considering the domestic constitutional requirements for beginning the process of negotiating UK withdrawal from the EU in *R (Miller)* v *Secretary of State for Exiting the European Union* [2017] UKSC 5 [148]:

> by such provisions, the UK Parliament is not seeking to convert the Sewel Convention into a rule which can be interpreted, let alone enforced, by the courts; rather, it is recognising the convention for what it is, namely a political convention, and is effectively declaring that it is a permanent feature of the relevant devolution settlement.

C: Key specific examples of asymmetry

Scotland Act 1998

80C Power to set Scottish rates for Scottish taxpayers

(1) The Scottish Parliament may by resolution (a "Scottish rate resolution") set the Scottish basic rate, and any other rates, for the purposes of section 11A of the Income Tax Act 2007 (which provides for the income of Scottish taxpayers which is charged at those rates).

(2A) Where a Scottish rate resolution sets more than one rate it must also set limits or make other provision to enable it to be ascertained, for the purposes of that section, which rates apply in relation to a Scottish taxpayer.

(2B) But a Scottish rate resolution may not provide for different rates to apply in relation to different types of income.

(2C) In this Chapter a "Scottish rate" means a rate set by a Scottish rate resolution.

(3) A Scottish rate resolution applies—

   (a) for only one tax year, and
   (b) for the whole of that year.

(5) A Scottish rate must be a whole number or half a whole number, or zero.

(6) A Scottish rate resolution—

   (a) must specify the tax year for which it applies,
   (b) must be made before the start of that tax year, and
   (c) must not be made more than 12 months before the start of that year.

(7) If a Scottish rate resolution is cancelled before the start of the tax year for which it is to apply—

   (a) the Income Tax Acts have effect for that year as if the resolution had never been passed, and
   (b) the resolution may be replaced by another Scottish rate resolution.

(8) Standing orders must provide that only a member of the Scottish Government may move a motion for a Scottish rate resolution.

NOTES

1. This provision was initially inserted into the 1998 Act by the Scotland Act 2012, replacing and extending a previous power to vary (within limits) the basic rate of income tax applicable in Scotland, with a new power to establish a Scottish rate of income tax, representing a common baseline by reference to which a basic, higher and additional rate would then be calculated (and so ensuring the gaps between those varying tax bands would be the same as in the rest of the UK). The creation of a power to vary the basic rate of income had been explicitly approved by the Scottish electorate, with a specific question as to this included in the referendum held prior to the establishment of devolution in Scotland. This section was further amended by the Scotland Act 2016, s. 13, extending further the powers of the Scottish Parliament in relation to income tax: rather than simply establishing one baseline Scottish rate, from 2017/18 the Scottish Parliament will have the power to set all rates and tax band thresholds. The Scottish National Party Government proposes to use this power to maintain higher income tax rates in Scotland, in distinction from the current policy of the UK Government, which is to cut the higher rate threshold.

2. The Scotland Act 2012 further extended the financial powers of the Scottish Parliament in other ways, amending the 1998 Act to empower the devolved legislature to replace UK stamp duty with a Scottish tax on transactions involving interests in land (s. 80I), replace UK landfill tax with a Scottish tax on disposals of waste to landfill (s. 80K), and establishing a power to devolve responsibility for further existing taxes and create new devolved taxes (s. 80B). The Scotland Act 2012 also contained provisions to extend the borrowing powers of Scottish Ministers, and in

particular, permit borrowing of up to £2.2 billion to fund capital expenditure. These extended fiscal powers for the Scottish Government came into effect between April 2015 and April 2016, after Scotland voted to remain part of the UK. Yet there has been further devolution of fiscal power under the Scotland Act 2016, enacted in the aftermath of the close referendum decision, to provide an even more extensive devolution settlement for Scotland. These powers include the assignment to Scotland of funds from VAT (s. 63A of the amended 1998 Act), devolution of the tax on carriage of air passengers (s. 80L), and increasing the borrowing limit for capital expenditure to £3 billion (s. 67A). Significant powers in relation to welfare benefits and employment support are also being devolved under the Scotland Act 2016, ss 22–31, including a power to create new benefits in devolved areas (s. 28).

3. The fiscal powers devolved to Scotland are considerably greater than those devolved to Northern Ireland or Wales. The Scotland Act 2012, which made provision for their further extension was enacted in response to the recommendations of the Calman Commission, which reported in June 2009. The Commission had been tasked with conducting a review of the experience of devolution in Scotland, making recommendations which would strengthen the existing settlement and (as its terms of reference indicated) 'continue to secure the position of Scotland within the United Kingdom'. The further devolution of powers mapped out in the Scotland Act 2016 was also a response to the independence referendum, implementing recommendations made by the Smith Commission, which was established in 2014 to develop proposals to give effect to 'the vow' made by the main UK political parties in the days prior to the vote. This vow was a commitment to strengthen Scottish devolution if the people of Scotland voted to remain part of the UK, a result which was delivered by 55 per cent to 45 per cent in the September 2014 referendum; see later in this chapter in Section 4A at pp. 386–9. The extension of fiscal powers to Scotland has also provided a template for extension of fiscal powers to Northern Ireland and Wales; see later in this chapter in Section 4B at pp. 389–90.

Government of Wales Act 2006

78 The Welsh language

(1) The Welsh Ministers must adopt a strategy ("the Welsh language strategy") setting out how they propose to promote and facilitate the use of the Welsh language.

(4) The Welsh Ministers–

(a) must keep under review the Welsh language strategy, and

(b) may from time to time adopt a new strategy or scheme or revise it.

(5) Before adopting or revising a strategy, the Welsh Ministers must consult such persons as they consider appropriate.

(6) The Welsh Ministers must publish the Welsh language strategy when they first adopt it and–

(a) if they adopt a new strategy they must publish it, and

(b) if they revise the Welsh language strategy (rather than adopting a new strategy or scheme) they must publish either the revisions or the strategy as revised (as they consider appropriate).

(7) If the Welsh Ministers publish a strategy, or revisions, under subsection (6) they must lay a copy of the strategy, or revisions, before the Assembly.

(8) After each financial year the Welsh Ministers must publish a report of how the proposals set out in the Welsh language strategy were implemented in that financial year and how effective their implementation has been in promoting and facilitating the use of the Welsh language and must lay a copy of the report before the Assembly.

(9) For each financial year, the Welsh Ministers must publish a plan setting out how they will implement the proposals set out in the Welsh language strategy during that year.

(10) The plan must be published as soon as reasonably practicable before the commencement of the financial year to which it relates.

NOTE: This extract is as amended by the Welsh Language (Wales) Measure 2011 and the Welsh Language (Wales) Measure 2011 (Consequential Provisions) Order 2016/409. This specific provision requiring the promotion and facilitation of the use of the Welsh language by the Welsh Government demonstrates how important cultural differences can be reflected, and protected, in an asymmetrical devolution settlement. The amendment of the provision in the 2006 Act by Welsh legislation demonstrates the flexibility of the devolved arrangements, where many (although not all) of the provisions in the foundational statutes are open to amendment by the institutions they establish. The amendment of this provision—in particular, removing references to a Welsh language scheme—reflects the fact that far more extensive protection of the Welsh language is contained in devolved legislation: the Welsh Language (Wales) Measure 2011, among other things, gives official status to the Welsh language in Wales, including requiring that the language be treated no less favourably than English, and imposing duties to comply with standards of conduct relating to its use in the delivery of public services.

Northern Ireland Act 1998

1. Status of Northern Ireland

(1) It is hereby declared that Northern Ireland in its entirety remains part of the United Kingdom and shall not cease to be so without the consent of a majority of the people of Northern Ireland voting in a poll held for the purposes of this section in accordance with Schedule 1.

(2) But if the wish expressed by a majority in such a poll is that Northern Ireland should cease to be part of the United Kingdom and form part of a united Ireland, the Secretary of State shall lay before Parliament such proposals to give effect to that wish as may be agreed between Her Majesty's Government in the United Kingdom and the Government of Ireland.

...

Schedule 1

Polls for the Purpose of Section 1

1. The Secretary of State may by order direct the holding of a poll for the purposes of section 1 on a date specified in the order.

2. Subject to paragraph 3, the Secretary of State shall exercise the power under paragraph 1 if at any time it appears likely to him that a majority of those voting would express a wish that Northern Ireland should cease to be part of the United Kingdom and form part of a united Ireland.

3. The Secretary of State shall not make an order under paragraph 1 earlier than seven years after the holding of a previous poll under this Schedule.

4. —

  (1) An order under this Schedule directing the holding of a poll shall specify—
    (a) the persons entitled to vote; and
    (b) the question or questions to be asked.
  (2) An order—
    (a) may include any other provision about the poll which the Secretary of State thinks expedient (including the creation of criminal offences); and
    (b) may apply (with or without modification) any provision of, or made under, any enactment

NOTES

1. This provision gives effect to a key aspect of the Good Friday Agreement, and repeats a commitment contained in previous legislation regarding devolution to Northern Ireland (see in particular the Northern Ireland Constitution Act 1973, s. 1, and the Ireland Act 1949, s. 1(2), although the latter makes reference to the consent of the Parliament of Northern Ireland, whereas the former is more closely related to the 1998 Act in so far as it makes departure from the UK conditional upon a majority vote in a referendum). The provision is the only one in the current devolution settlement which puts in place a standing process for a nation to cease to be part of the UK,

although as will be seen later in this chapter in Section 4A at pp. 386–9, specific (but temporary) provision was made for a referendum to be held on Scottish independence.

2. The implications of this provision were considered in *R (Miller)* v *Secretary of State for Exiting the European Union* [2017] UKSC 5, in which one argument considered on appeal from Northern Ireland was whether beginning negotiations to withdraw from the EU without the consent of the people of Northern Ireland (who had voted to remain in the referendum on EU membership) would impede the operation of s. 1 of the 1998 Act. While acknowledging the significance of the provision, the Supreme Court rejected this argument:

> 135. In our view, this important provision, which arose out of the Belfast Agreement, gave the people of Northern Ireland the right to determine whether to remain part of the United Kingdom or to become part of a united Ireland. It neither regulated any other change in the constitutional status of Northern Ireland nor required the consent of a majority of the people of Northern Ireland to the withdrawal of the United Kingdom from the European Union. Contrary to the submission of Mr Lavery QC for Mr McCord, this section cannot support any legitimate expectation to that effect.

SECTION 3: DEVOLUTION ISSUES IN THE UK COURTS

Devolution to Scotland, Wales, and Northern Ireland has raised a number of legal issues in the UK courts. As we have seen earlier in this chapter in Section 2A at pp. 353–66, the UK Supreme Court has jurisdiction to hear appeals on devolution matters. In this section, we will consider a number of issues which are of broad relevance to all three devolution regimes, despite their asymmetry, and which may have a wider impact on the UK constitution as a whole. In particular, we will look at (a) the interpretation of the devolution Acts, (b) judicial review of legislation made by the devolved institutions, and (c) references to the Supreme Court as to whether Bills are within legislative competence.

A: Interpretation of the Devolution Acts

How are the Acts of the Westminster Parliament which established devolution in Scotland, Wales, and Northern Ireland to be interpreted? Does their constitutional significance mean that they must be interpreted in a way which differs from 'ordinary' Acts of Parliament?

Robinson v Secretary of State for Northern Ireland
[2002] UKHL 32, [2002] N.I. 390, House of Lords

Robinson, a member of the Democratic Unionist Party, sought to challenge the validity of the election of a First Minister and Deputy First Minister for Northern Ireland. By s. 16(8) of the Northern Ireland Act 1998, election to these offices was to take place within a six-week period. If the offices were not filled within this period, the Secretary of State for Northern Ireland was, by s. 32(3), to name a date for new elections to be held. A First Minister and Deputy First Minister having been elected outside of this six-week period, the Secretary of State announced that the next election would occur in approximately 18 months time, on the date already set for the next election by the Northern Ireland Act 1998. Robinson argued that the Assembly lacked the power to elect a First Minister and Deputy First Minister outside the six-week period, and that fresh elections should be called imminently.

LORD BINGHAM (WITH WHOM LORDS HOFFMANN AND MILLETT AGREED):

10. The 1998 Act, as already noted, was passed to implement the Belfast Agreement, which was itself reached, after much travail, in an attempt to end decades of bloodshed and centuries of antagonism. The solution was seen to lie in participation by the unionist and nationalist communities in shared political institutions, without precluding (see section 1 of the Act) a popular decision at some time in the future on the ultimate political status of Northern Ireland. If these shared institutions were to deliver the benefits which their progenitors intended, they had to have time to operate and take root.

11. The 1998 Act does not set out all the constitutional provisions applicable to Northern Ireland, but it is in effect a constitution. So to categorise the Act is not to relieve the courts of their duty to interpret the constitutional provisions in issue. But the provisions should, consistently with the language used, be interpreted generously and purposively, bearing in mind the values which the constitutional provisions are intended to embody. Mr Larkin submitted that the resolution of political problems by resort to the vote of the people in a free election lies at the heart of any democracy and that this democratic principle is one embodied in this constitution. He is of course correct. Sections 32(1) and (3) expressly contemplate such elections as a means of resolving political impasses. But elections held with undue frequency are not necessarily productive. While elections may produce solutions they can also deepen divisions. Nor is the democratic ideal the only constitutional ideal which this constitution should be understood to embody. It is in general desirable that the government should be carried on, that there be no governmental vacuum. And this constitution is also seeking to promote the values referred to in the preceding paragraph.

12. It would no doubt be possible, in theory at least, to devise a constitution in which all political contingencies would be the subject of predetermined mechanistic rules to be applied as and when the particular contingency arose. But such an approach would not be consistent with ordinary constitutional practice in Britain. There are of course certain fixed rules, such as those governing the maximum duration of parliaments or the period for which the House of Lords may delay the passage of legislation. But matters of potentially great importance are left to the judgment either of political leaders (whether and when to seek a dissolution, for instance) or, even if to a diminished extent, of the crown (whether to grant a dissolution). Where constitutional arrangements retain scope for the exercise of political judgment they permit a flexible response to differing and unpredictable events in a way which the application of strict rules would preclude.

...

LORD HOFFMANN:

33. Mr Larkin QC, in the course of his admirable argument for the appellant, politely but firmly reminded your Lordships that your function was to construe and apply the language of Parliament and not merely to choose what might appear on political grounds to be the most convenient solution. It is not for this House, in its judicial capacity, to say that new elections in Northern Ireland would be politically inexpedient. Mr Larkin cited Herbert Wechsler's famous Holmes Lecture, Towards Neutral Principles of Constitutional Law ((1959) 73 Harvard LR 1). My Lords, I unreservedly accept those principles. A judicial decision must, as Professor Wechsler said (at p. 19) rest on "reasons that in their generality and their neutrality transcend any immediate result that is involved." But I think that the construction which I favour satisfies those requirements. The long title of the Act is "to make new provision for the government of Northern Ireland for the purpose of implementing the agreement reached at multi-party talks on Northern Ireland ...". According to established principles of interpretation, the Act must be construed against the background of the political situation in Northern Ireland and the principles laid down by the Belfast Agreement for a new start. These facts and documents form part of the admissible background for the construction of the Act just as much as the Revolution, the Convention and the Federalist Papers are the background to construing the Constitution of the United States.

34. Mr Larkin said that the respondents' position was undemocratic: it denied the electorate of Northern Ireland the right to elect a new Assembly which was granted to them by the Act. But that of course begs the question, which is whether the Act requires an immediate election or not. On the

construction which I have adopted, the question of when the election should be held will be a matter for the Secretary of State and will be informed by his political judgment as to the likelihood of the Assembly being able to elect the Ministers. But that does not mean that your Lordships are making a political decision. Your Lordships are not expressing any views on whether holding an election immediately after 6 November 2001 would have been politically expedient or not. That was a matter for the Secretary of State.

...

LORD HUTTON (DISSENTING, WITH LORD HOBHOUSE):

47. On 6 November 2001 the Northern Ireland Assembly held a further election for the offices of First Minister and deputy First Minister. On this occasion, following the re-designation as unionists of a number of members of the Assembly who had previously been designated neither unionists nor nationalists, the two candidates, Mr Trimble and Mr Durkan, did receive the required number of votes and were elected as First Minister and deputy First Minister respectively and have acted in that capacity since that date. It is the validity of that election which is at issue in the present proceedings.

...

51. The principal argument advanced on behalf of the appellant is that section 16(8) requires the election to fill the vacant offices of First Minister and deputy First Minister to take place within the specified period of six weeks, and if the offices are not filled by election within that period section 32(3) imposes a duty on the Secretary of State to propose a date for the poll for the election of the next Assembly, and it is implicit in that duty that he must propose an early poll. The appellant submits that it is clear from the express provisions of the 1998 Act that an election of a First Minister and a deputy First Minister after the expiration of the period of six weeks specified in section 16(8) is invalid and void.

...

54. My Lords, despite the attractiveness of the respondents' argument based on the purpose of the Belfast Agreement, I have come to the conclusion that the appeal should succeed. The Northern Ireland Assembly is a body created by a Westminster statute and it has no powers other than those given to it by statute. Section 16(1) and section 16(8) expressly require that the election of the First Minister and deputy First Minster shall take place within a period of six weeks beginning either with the first meeting of the Assembly or, if the offices become vacant at any time, within a period of six weeks beginning with the time of the vacancy. Therefore once the period of six weeks has expired the Assembly has no express power under the Act to elect the First Minister and deputy First Minister. Does the Assembly then have an implied power to elect a First Minister and deputy First Minister outside the six weeks' period? Where a statute gives power to a statutory body to perform a certain act within a specified period the normal rule is that the body has no power to perform that act outside the period, and I see nothing in the provisions of the Act pointing to a different conclusion.

...

59. In my opinion the wording of section 32(3) read in conjunction with the other subsections of section 32 makes it clear that Parliament intended that if there was not a successful election within the six weeks' period, the Secretary of State would fix an early date for the poll. What has happened in this case, where the Secretary of State has fixed the date as being the date when a poll would have taken place under section 31 on the normal expiration of the life of the Assembly, appears to be a procedure which is contrived and artificial, particularly as the side note to section 32 refers to "Extraordinary elections" but the Secretary of State has proposed the date on which an ordinary election for the Assembly would take place under section 31. Moreover on the respondents' argument if the Assembly failed under section 16(1) to elect a First Minister and deputy First Minister within six weeks of its first meeting, the Secretary of State would be entitled in some circumstances to propose a date more than three years

beyond the expiration of the six weeks' period. I do not think that Parliament intended that section 32(3) could operate in that way and that the Secretary of State should have such a power.

60. I do not consider that constitutional practice in relation to the United Kingdom Parliament at Westminster assists in the interpretation of section 32. ... the Assembly is entirely a creation of statute and Parliament has laid down the procedure to be followed where the Assembly resolves that it should be dissolved or fails to elect a First Minister and deputy First Minister within the stipulated period of six weeks....

61. In considering the extent to which the purpose of the 1998 Act to implement the Belfast Agreement can affect the interpretation of section 16 and section 32 I think it is necessary to bear in mind that the Belfast Agreement was drafted in a spirit of hope that the cross-community institutions of government which it proposed would succeed. Whilst the Agreement contains a final section containing provisions for review by the British and Irish Governments in consultation with the parties in the Assembly if difficulties arise across the range of institutions, the Agreement contains no express provision stating what would happen if cross-community government was not established or did not continue. But Parliament had to provide for this contingency and it did so by the provisions of section 16(1), 16(8) and section 32. Parliament has laid down a procedure to be followed in the event of the Assembly resolving that it should be dissolved or failing to elect a First Minister or deputy First Minister within the specified period of six weeks, and whilst those sections continue in force unamended I consider that the objective of the Belfast Agreement cannot operate to alter the meaning of their words.

Appeal dismissed.

NOTE: The House of Lords in *Robinson* was divided as to the manner in which the Northern Ireland Act 1998 should be interpreted. For Lord Bingham and the majority, it was in effect a constitution which ought to be interpreted generously in light of its purpose (to establish power-sharing government in Northern Ireland), whereas for Lord Hutton and the minority, the provisions were to be interpreted literally, and applied as such. To do otherwise would be to extend the powers of the devolved institutions beyond those which they had been given by the sovereign UK Parliament. There has been much debate about the implications of the *Robinson* case, and whether it requires all devolution legislation to be interpreted generously and purposively, as will be seen in the following extracts. It is worth noting the aftermath of the decision in *Robinson*: the Northern Ireland Assembly was suspended 11 months after the election, which the House of Lords had held to be lawful, of David Trimble and Mark Durkan as First Minister and Deputy First Minister respectively. Power was eventually restored in May 2007 following an agreement between the Democratic Unionist Party and Sinn Fein to form a government.

Imperial Tobacco Limited v The Lord Advocate (Scotland)
[2012] CSIH 9, Inner House of the Court of Session, [2012] UKSC 61, Supreme Court

This case concerned a challenge to ss 1 and 9 of the Tobacco and Primary Medical Services (Scotland) Act 2010, which sought to restrict the display and retailing of tobacco products in specified circumstances. It was argued that the 2010 Act was outside the legislative competence of the Scottish Parliament. A submission was advanced that how the Scotland Act 1998 was to be interpreted would be significant, given it possessed a constitutional status. This argument was addressed in the Inner House of the Court of Session, and rejected by Lord Reed.

LORD REED:
69 [That there is no singular approach to constitutional interpretation] was made clear in *Boyce v The Queen* [2005] 1 AC 400, a case which concerned the Constitution of Barbados. As Lord Hoffmann, giving the judgment of the majority of the Board of the Privy Council, explained at para 28, the object of the interpretation of a constitutional provision is to arrive at its true meaning. That may call for a generous

interpretation, or it may not, depending on the terms of the provision and the context which is relevant to the interpretation of its terms. The same can be said of the interpretation of statutory provisions, which in modern practice is based upon a purposive approach and the construction of statutes as "always speaking" (see e.g. *R (Quintavalle) v Secretary of State for Health* [2003] 2 AC 687).

70 Lord Bingham's remarks in the case of *Robinson* are not inconsistent with this approach. In order to interpret a provision purposively, it is necessary first to identify the relevant purpose. Once that has been done, it may (as in *Robinson*) or may not be necessary to adopt a generous construction so as not to defeat the purpose. As Lord Bingham noted, such a construction must in any event be consistent with the language used.

71 The Scotland Act is not a constitution, but an Act of Parliament. There are material differences. The context of the devolution of legislative and executive power within the United Kingdom is evidently different from that of establishing a constitution for an independent state such as Jamaica or Barbados, or a British overseas territory such as Bermuda. In form, the Scotland Act does not resemble the fundamental rights provisions of a constitution: its provisions are dense and detailed. The Scotland Act can also be amended more easily than a constitution: a factor which is relevant, since the difficulty of amending a constitution is often a reason for concluding that it was intended to be given a flexible interpretation. Although the UK Government's stated policy on legislation concerning devolved matters... known colloquially as the Sewel Convention, may impose a political restriction upon Parliament's ability to amend the Scotland Act unilaterally, there have nevertheless been many amendments made to the Act. They include amendments to Schedules 4 and 5, which can be effected under section 30 by Order in Council. A Bill designed to effect more substantial amendments is currently in the course of its passage through Parliament.

72 A factor which appears to me to be of greater significance to the interpretation of the Scotland Act is that it established new constitutional arrangements which were intended to be stable and workable. The provisions defining the legislative competence of the Scottish Parliament, in particular, must have been intended, as Lord Walker observed in *Martin v Most* 2010 SC (UKSC) 40 at para 52, to create a rational and coherent scheme. In construing the provisions in issue in the present case, I have proceeded with these aims in mind. Beyond that, however, the interpretation of any specific provision will depend upon the language used, and the context which is relevant to understanding the meaning of that language.

On appeal to the Supreme Court, this question of the interpretation of the Scotland Act 1998 was addressed by Lord Hope (with whom Lord Walker, Lady Hale, Lord Kerr, and Lord Sumption agreed).

LORD HOPE:
The interpretation issue

10 Much of the discussion in the Court of Session was devoted to the question whether a different approach should be taken to the interpretation of the 1998 Act from that applicable to other statutes because it was said to be a constitutional instrument. I do not think that it is necessary to dwell on that issue at length at this stage. The Dean of Faculty accepted that the object was to arrive at the true meaning of the statute. Its content might influence the approach to be taken, but assertions about its constitutional nature were not in point. He acknowledged that the exercise to be undertaken was in essence no different from that which was applicable in the case of any other United Kingdom statute.

11 Mr Mure QC for the Lord Advocate and the Advocate General were, however, not entirely at one as to the approach that should be adopted. For the Lord Advocate it was stressed that a construction should be avoided which would render the endowment of plenary law-making powers on the Scottish Parliament futile. The Advocate General, for his part, said that it would be wrong to favour an expansive approach to the meaning and application of the provisions about legislative competence. Asserting

that the purpose of the 1998 Act was to devolve plenary legislative power on the Parliament did not assist in determining the actual scope of what it was designed to achieve. The Dean of Faculty said that the appellants were content to align themselves with the views of the Advocate General.

12 It is unsatisfactory that there should continue to be room for doubt on this matter. So it may be helpful to summarise, quite briefly, three principles that should be followed when undertaking the exercise of determining whether, according to the rules that the 1998 Act lays down, a provision of an Act of the Scottish Parliament is outside competence.

13 First, the question of competence must be determined in each case according to the particular rules that have been set out in section 29 of and Schedules 4 and 5 to the 1998 Act. It is not for the courts to say whether legislation on any particular issue is better made by the Scottish Parliament or by the Parliament of the United Kingdom at Westminster: *Martin v Most* 2010 SC (UKSC) 40, para 5. How that issue is to be dealt with has been addressed and determined by the United Kingdom Parliament. As Lord Walker observed in Martin, para 44, its task was to define the legislative competence of the Scottish Parliament, while itself continuing as the sovereign legislature of the United Kingdom. The statutory language was informed by principles that were applied to resolve questions that had arisen in federal systems, where the powers of various legislatures tend to overlap: see Martin, paras 11-15. But the intention was that it was to the 1998 Act itself, not to decisions as to how the problem was handled in other jurisdictions, that one should look for guidance. So it is to the rules that the 1998 Act lays down that the court must address its attention, bearing in mind that a provision may have a devolved purpose and yet be outside competence because it contravenes one of the rules. As Lord Atkin said in *Gallagher v Lynn* [1937] AC 863, 870, an Act may have a perfectly lawful object but may seek to achieve that object by invalid methods.

14 Second, those rules must be interpreted in the same way as any other rules that are found in a UK statute. The system that those rules laid down must, of course, be taken to have been intended to create a system for the exercise of legislative power by the Scottish Parliament that was coherent, stable and workable. This is a factor that it is proper to have in mind. But it is not a principle of construction that is peculiar to the 1998 Act. It is a factor that is common to any other statute that has been enacted by the legislature, whether at Westminster or at Holyrood. The best way of ensuring that a coherent, stable and workable outcome is achieved is to adopt an approach to the meaning of a statute that is constant and predictable. This will be achieved if the legislation is construed according to the ordinary meaning of the words used.

15 Third, the description of the Act as a constitutional statute cannot be taken, in itself, to be a guide to its interpretation. The statute must be interpreted like any other statute. But the purpose of the Act has informed the statutory language. Its concern must be taken to have been that the Scottish Parliament should be able to legislate effectively about matters that were intended to be devolved to it, while ensuring that there were adequate safeguards for those matters that were intended to be reserved. That purpose provides the context for any discussion about legislative competence. So it is proper to have regard to the purpose if help is needed as to what the words actually mean. The fact that section 29 provides a mechanism for determining whether a provision of an Act of the Scottish Parliament is outside, rather than inside, competence does not create a presumption in favour of competence. But it helps to show that one of the purposes of the 1998 Act was to enable the Parliament to make such laws within the powers given to it by section 28 as it thought fit. It was intended, within carefully defined limits, to be a generous settlement of legislative authority.

16 It will, of course, be necessary to identify the purpose of the provision if the challenge is brought under section 29(2)(b) on the ground that it relates to a reserved matter, bearing in mind that the phrase "relates to" indicates something more than a loose or consequential connection: see Lord Walker in *Martin v Most*, para 49. As Lord Rodger said in that case at para 75, the clearest indication of its purpose may be found in a report that gave rise to the legislation or in a report from one of the committees of the Parliament. But it may also be clear from its context. As is the case when any other

statute is being construed, the context will be relevant to understanding the meaning of the words used by the 1998 Act.

Appeal dismissed.

■ QUESTIONS

1. What is the status of the decision of the House of Lords in *Robinson* following *Imperial Tobacco*? Lord Reed in the Inner House of the Court of Session thought that his view was not necessarily inconsistent with the position set out by Lord Bingham in *Robinson*, but can the same be said of the clarification offered by Lord Hope in the Supreme Court?

2. Was the Supreme Court in *Imperial Tobacco* right to say that the devolution Acts should be interpreted in the same way as any other Act of Parliament? Does this have an impact on the status of the devolution Acts, or is it simply a necessary consequence of the fact that the UK constitution is uncodified and based on the doctrine of parliamentary sovereignty?

3. In *H* v *Lord Advocate* [2012] UKSC 24, [2013] 1 AC 413, Lord Hope said at [30]:

> [T]he effect of the Scotland Act is that the Scottish Ministers derive their existence only from that Act. As has been repeatedly pointed out by the court, they have no power to act other than in a way that is consistent with section 57(2) of that Act: see, eg, *HM Advocate v R* [2004] 1 AC 462, paras 46, 129; *McGowan v B* [2011] 1 WLR 3121, para 6. The functions that the [Extradition Act 2003] has conferred on the Scottish Ministers must be seen in that light. It would perhaps have been open to Parliament to override the provisions of section 57(2) so as to confer on them more ample powers than that subsection would permit in the exercise of their functions under the 2003 Act. But in my opinion only an express provision to that effect could be held to lead to such a result. This is because of the fundamental constitutional nature of the settlement that was achieved by the Scotland Act. This in itself must be held to render it incapable of being altered otherwise than by an express enactment. Its provisions cannot be regarded as vulnerable to alteration by implication from some other enactment in which an intention to alter the Scotland Act is not set forth expressly on the face of the statute.

The comments of Lord Hope as to the need for alteration of the Scotland Act 1998 to be by express enactment can be understood to be obiter dicta, because it was held in this case that there was no clash between the 1998 Act and the Extradition Act 2003, which could operate in 'parallel' (and thus the question of whether the 2003 Act had purported to repeal any part of the 1998 Act did not need to be determined). Nevertheless, is this position consistent in principle with Lord Hope's comments in *Imperial Tobacco* about the 'constitutional' nature of legislation being irrelevant to the manner in which it should be interpreted? Is it coherent to understand the constitutional nature of the devolution Acts as being relevant to the question of how they might be repealed or altered, but not as to how they are to be interpreted?

4. How does the discussion of the legal implications of the 'constitutional' status of the devolution Acts considered in this section relate with developments considered in Chapter 2, Section 3A(b) at pp. 78–84, in relation to EU membership? In particular, do the comments about 'constitutional instruments' contained in *HS2* [2014] UKSC 3 suggest that the UK Supreme Court may in future attach greater importance to the designation of statutes (including the devolution statutes) as 'constitutional'? Or is this simply rhetoric, with limited concrete legal consequences? See also the description of the European Communities Act 1972 as possessing a 'constitutional character' in *R (Miller)* v *Secretary of State for Exiting the European Union* [2017] UKSC 5, [67]. The judgment of the majority does not suggest that this description of the 1972 Act has any general legal implications, beyond the fact that the legislation has in substance had a profound impact on UK constitutional law (this position can be contrasted with the more extensive observations of the Divisional Court in *Miller* [2016] EWHC 2768 (Admin), where it was accepted that the designation of the 1972 Act as a constitutional statute was material to its interpretation: [43]–[44], [82]–[88]).

B: Judicial review of devolved legislation

As discussed earlier, the legislative competence of the Scottish Parliament, the Welsh Assembly, and Northern Ireland Assembly is expressly limited by the Acts of Parliament which constituted these devolved legislatures. Matters which are explicitly reserved to the Westminster Parliament, or in the case of Wales, subjects for which responsibility has not been devolved, are outside the competence of these legislatures, as is any Act which violates EU law or the ECHR.

These challenges to legislative competence are often considered in combination, with overlaps between the various statutory limits on the power of the devolved legislatures. For a recent example, see the challenge to the Children and Young People (Scotland) Act 2014, introducing the requirement that every child in Scotland would have a 'named person' to support their well-being, with the sharing of data between relevant public authorities crucial to enable each named person to fulfil their role. In a challenge to this legislation, in *Christian Institute* v *Lord Advocate* [2016] UKSC 51, 2016 SLT 805, the Supreme Court concluded, [106]:

that the information sharing provisions of Pt 4 of the Act (a) do not relate to reserved matters, namely the subject matter of the [Data Protection Act 1998] and [Directive 95/46/EC], (b) are incompatible with the rights of children, young persons and parents under art.8 of the ECHR because they are not "in accordance with the law" as that article requires, (c) may in practice result in a disproportionate interference with the art.8 rights of many children, young persons and their parents, through the sharing of private information, and (d) are not incompatible with EU law in any way which goes beyond their incompatibility with art.8 of the ECHR ... Conclusion (b) therefore means that the information sharing provisions of Pt 4 of the Act are not within the legislative competence of the Scottish Parliament.

But in addition to these expressly defined statutory limits, are there implied limits on the power of the devolved legislatures? The following case—decided in relation to the Scottish Parliament, but of general applicability—addresses this issue.

AXA General Insurance Ltd v Lord Advocate
[2011] UKSC 46, [2012] 1 AC 868, Supreme Court

The Damages (Asbestos-related Conditions) Scotland Act 2009 was enacted to reverse the effect of the decision of the House of Lords in *Rothwell* v *Chemical Insulating Co Ltd* [2008] AC 281. The 2009 Act provided that specified asbestos-related medical conditions would constitute (and be treated as always having constituted) actionable harm for personal injury for which damages could be awarded. Having rejected the argument that the 2009 Act was an unlawful violation of the right to peaceful enjoyment of possessions protected by Art. 1 of Protocol 1 to the ECHR (A1P1), and therefore within the competence of the Scottish Parliament as defined by s. 29 of the Scotland Act 1998, a common law challenge to the 2009 Act was considered.

LORD HOPE:

The common law grounds

42 The appellants' case at common law is that the 2009 Act was the result of an unreasonable, irrational and arbitrary exercise of the legislative authority conferred by the Scotland Act 1998 on the Scottish Parliament.... [T]he question as to whether Acts of the Scottish Parliament and measures passed under devolved powers by the legislatures in Wales and Northern Ireland are amenable to judicial review, and if so on what grounds, is a matter of very great constitutional importance. It goes to the root of the relationship between the democratically elected legislatures and the judiciary. At issue

is the part which the rule of law itself has to play in setting the boundaries of this relationship. I think therefore that the argument which this part of the appellants' case raises cannot be dismissed so easily.

43 The issue can be broken down into its component parts in this way. First, there is the question whether measures passed by the devolved legislatures are amenable to judicial review, other than in the respects expressly provided for by the devolution statutes, at all. If not, that will be the end of the argument. But if they are open to judicial review on common law grounds at all, there is the question as to what these grounds are. At the one extreme are the grounds that the appellants' second plea in law encapsulates: that the legislation is unreasonable, irrational or arbitrary. At the other is the proposition that judicial intervention is admissible only in the exceptional circumstances that Lord Steyn had in mind in *R (Jackson) v Attorney General* [2006] 1 AC 262, para 102; see also my own speech at paras 104–107 and Baroness Hale of Richmond's observations at para 159. To answer these questions in their proper context it is necessary to set out the background in a little more detail. Although I am conscious of the implications of what the court decides in this case for the other devolved legislatures, I shall concentrate on the position of the Scottish Parliament. As was common ground before us, I consider that, while there are some differences of detail between the Scotland Act 1998 and the corresponding legislation for Wales and Northern Ireland, these differences do not matter for present purposes. The essential nature of the legislatures that the legislation has created in each case is the same....

45 Devolution is an exercise of its law-making power by the United Kingdom Parliament at Westminster. It is a process of delegation by which, among other things, a power to legislate in areas that have not been reserved to the United Kingdom Parliament may be exercised by the devolved legislatures. The Scotland Act 1998 sets out the effect of the arrangement as it affects Scotland with admirable clarity. Section 1(1) of the Act declares: "There shall be a Scottish Parliament." Its democratic legitimacy is enshrined in the provisions of section 1(2) and section 1(3), which provide for the election of those who are to serve as its members as constituency members and by a system of proportional representation chosen from the regional lists. Section 28(1) provides that the Parliament may make laws, to be known as Acts of the Scottish Parliament, and section 28(2) provides for them to receive the Royal Assent. Section 28(5) provides that the validity of an Act of the Scottish Parliament is not affected by any invalidity in the proceedings of the Parliament leading to its enactment. Although section 28(7) provides that that section shall not affect the power of the United Kingdom to make laws for Scotland, in practice the Scottish Parliament enjoys the same law making powers for Scotland as the Westminster Parliament except as provided expressly for in section 29 which, in certain closely defined respects, limits its legislative competence. Section 29 does not, however, bear to be a complete or comprehensive statement of limitations on the powers of the Parliament. The Act as a whole has not adopted that approach: see *Somerville v Scottish Ministers (HM Advocate General for Scotland intervening)* [2007] 1 WLR 2734, para 28.

46 The carefully chosen language in which these provisions are expressed is not as important as the general message that the words convey. The Scottish Parliament takes its place under our constitutional arrangements as a self-standing democratically elected legislature. Its democratic mandate to make laws for the people of Scotland is beyond question. Acts that the Scottish Parliament enacts which are within its legislative competence enjoy, in that respect, the highest legal authority. The United Kingdom Parliament has vested in the Scottish Parliament the authority to make laws that are within its devolved competence. It is nevertheless a body to which decision making powers have been delegated. And it does not enjoy the sovereignty of the Crown in Parliament that, as Lord Bingham of Cornhill said in *Jackson*, para 9, is the bedrock of the British constitution. Sovereignty remains with the United Kingdom Parliament. The Scottish Parliament's power to legislate is not unconstrained. It cannot make or unmake any law it wishes....

47 Against this background, as there is no provision in the Scotland Act which excludes this possibility, I think that it must follow that in principle Acts of the Scottish Parliament are amenable to the supervisory jurisdiction of the Court of Session at common law. The much more important question is what the grounds are, if any, on which they may be subjected to review.

48 There is very little guidance as to how this question should be answered in the authorities.... The fact is that, as a challenge to primary legislation at common law was simply impossible while the only legislature was the sovereign Parliament of the United Kingdom at Westminster, we are in this case in uncharted territory. The issue has to be addressed as one of principle.

49 The dominant characteristic of the Scottish Parliament is its firm rooting in the traditions of a universal democracy. It draws its strength from the electorate. While the judges, who are not elected, are best placed to protect the rights of the individual, including those who are ignored or despised by the majority, the elected members of a legislature of this kind are best placed to judge what is in the country's best interests as a whole. A sovereign Parliament is, according to the traditional view, immune from judicial scrutiny because it is protected by the principle of sovereignty. But it shares with the devolved legislatures, which are not sovereign, the advantages that flow from the depth and width of the experience of its elected members and the mandate that has been given to them by the electorate. This suggests that the judges should intervene, if at all, only in the most exceptional circumstances. As Lord Bingham of Cornhill said in *R (Countryside Alliance) v Attorney General* [2008] AC 719, para 45, the democratic process is liable to be subverted if, on a question of political or moral judgment, opponents of an Act achieve through the courts what they could not achieve through Parliament....

51 We do not need, in this case, to resolve the question how these conflicting views about the relationship between the rule of law and the sovereignty of the United Kingdom Parliament may be reconciled. The fact that we are dealing here with a legislature that is not sovereign relieves us of that responsibility. It also makes our task that much easier. In our case the rule of law does not have to compete with the principle of sovereignty. As I said in *Jackson*, para 107, the rule of law enforced by the courts is the ultimate controlling factor on which our constitution is based. I would take that to be, for the purposes of this case, the guiding principle. Can it be said, then, that Lord Steyn's endorsement of Lord Hailsham's warning about the dominance over Parliament of a government elected with a large majority has no bearing because such a thing could never happen in the devolved legislatures? I am not prepared to make that assumption. We now have in Scotland a government which enjoys a large majority in the Scottish Parliament. Its party dominates the only chamber in that Parliament and the committees by which bills that are in progress are scrutinised. It is not entirely unthinkable that a government which has that power may seek to use it to abolish judicial review or to diminish the role of the courts in protecting the interests of the individual. Whether this is likely to happen is not the point. It is enough that it might conceivably do so. The rule of law requires that the judges must retain the power to insist that legislation of that extreme kind is not law which the courts will recognise.

52 As for the appellants' common law case, I would hold, in agreement with the judges in the Inner House (2011 SLT 439, para 88), that Acts of the Scottish Parliament are not subject to judicial review at common law on the grounds of irrationality, unreasonableness or arbitrariness. This is not needed, as there is already a statutory limit on the Parliament's legislative competence if a provision is incompatible with any of the Convention rights: section 29(2)(d) of the Scotland Act 1998. But it would also be quite wrong for the judges to substitute their views on these issues for the considered judgment of a democratically elected legislature unless authorised to do so, as in the case of the Convention rights, by the constitutional framework laid down by the United Kingdom Parliament.

...

LORD REED:

147 In these circumstances, it appears to me that it must have been Parliament's intention, when it established the Scottish Parliament, that that institution should have plenary powers within the limits upon its legislative competence which were created by section 29(2). Since its powers are plenary, they do not require to be exercised for any specific purpose or with regard to any specific considerations. It follows that grounds of review developed in relation to administrative bodies which have been given limited powers for identifiable purposes, and which are designed to prevent such bodies from exceeding their powers or using them for an improper purpose or being influenced by irrelevant

considerations, generally have no purchase in such circumstances, and cannot be applied. As a general rule, and subject to the qualification which I shall mention shortly, its decisions as to how to exercise its law-making powers require no justification in law other than the will of the Parliament. It is in principle accountable for the exercise of its powers, within the limits set by section 29(2), to the electorate rather than the courts.

...

149 There remains the question whether the court possesses the power to intervene, in exceptional circumstances, on grounds other than those specified in section 29(2) : as, for example, if it were shown that legislation offended against fundamental rights or the rule of law. In their submissions, counsel for the Lord Advocate accepted that devolved legislation was subject to review on such grounds, which they categorised as constitutional review, in distinction from administrative review.

150 Fundamental rights and the rule of law are protected by section 29(2) of the Act, in so far as it preserves Convention rights. But, as Lord Steyn pointed out in *R (Anufrijeva) v Secretary of State for the Home Department* [2004] 1 AC 604, para 27:

> "The Convention is not an exhaustive statement of fundamental rights under our system of law. Lord Hoffmann's dictum (in *Ex p Simms*) applies to fundamental rights beyond the four corners of the Convention."

The question is therefore not of purely academic significance.

...

152 The principle of legality means not only that Parliament cannot itself override fundamental rights or the rule of law by general or ambiguous words, but also that it cannot confer on another body, by general or ambiguous words, the power to do so. ...

153 The nature and purpose of the Scotland Act appear to me to be consistent with the application of that principle. As Lord Rodger of Earlsferry said in *HM Advocate v R* [2004] 1 AC 462, para 121, the Scotland Act is a major constitutional measure which altered the government of the United Kingdom; and his Lordship observed that it would seem surprising if it failed to provide effective public law remedies, since that would mark it out from other constitutional documents. In *Robinson v Secretary of State for Northern Ireland* [2002] N.I. 390, para 11, Lord Bingham of Cornhill said of the Northern Ireland Act 1998 that its provisions should be interpreted "bearing in mind the values which the constitutional provisions are intended to embody". That is equally true of the Scotland Act. Parliament did not legislate in a vacuum: it legislated for a liberal democracy founded on particular constitutional principles and traditions. That being so, Parliament cannot be taken to have intended to establish a body which was free to abrogate fundamental rights or to violate the rule of law.

154 There is however no suggestion in the present case that the Scottish Parliament has acted in such a manner. That being so, and review for irrationality being excluded, it follows that the challenge to the validity of the 2009 Act on common law grounds must be rejected.

Appeal dismissed.

■ QUESTIONS

1. On one hand, the common law jurisdiction of the courts to review devolved legislation was at issue in the *Axa* case; on the other hand (as Lord Reed noted at [154]), there was no question that the enactment of the 2009 Act was in violation of fundamental rights or the rule of law, and so did not constitute the kind of exceptional circumstances that were being discussed by the Justices of the Supreme Court. Are the comments of Lords Hope and Reed

(with which all the judges agreed) as to the fact that Acts of the Scottish Parliament are amenable to common law review in exceptional circumstances obiter dicta, or part of the ratio
in *Axa*?

2. Section 29 of the Scotland Act 1998 makes clear, extensive provision as to what is within,
and what is outside of, the legislative competence of the Scottish Parliament, including
providing greater protection for ECHR rights than is established in relation to Acts of the
Westminster Parliament under the Human Rights Act 1998. Given the constitutional significance of the Scotland Act 1998, and the desirability of constitutions being accessible to
citizens, can it be argued that the Supreme Court should have viewed s. 29 as setting out
exhaustive limits on the legislative competence of the Scottish Parliament?

3. Do Lords Hope and Reed give sufficient detail as to what sort of legislation might be considered so extreme or exceptional as to justify the courts invalidating it at common law? If
you were advising either the Scottish Government or affected citizens as to whether an Act
of the Scottish Parliament was valid at common law, how easy would this be using the judgments handed down in *Axa*?

4. Since the UK Parliament, the Scottish Parliament, the Welsh Assembly, and the Northern
Ireland Assembly are all democratically elected legislatures, is the fact that, following *Axa*,
Acts of the former are not subject to common law judicial review, whereas Acts of the others
are, something that can be justified? If not, does this mean the courts should use *Axa* (in
combination with the controversial obiter dicta of Lords Hope, Steyn, and Baroness Hale
in *Jackson*, discussed in Chapter 2, Section 3C at pp. 88–95) to challenge the sovereignty of
the UK Parliament? Or that the courts should be very reluctant to strike down Acts of the
devolved legislatures on common law grounds?

C: References to the Supreme Court

As we saw earlier, under the devolution Acts applicable to Scotland, Wales, and Northern
Ireland, references can be made to the Supreme Court to determine *in advance* whether
proposed legislation falls within the competence of a devolved legislature. There have
been a number of made in relation to Welsh Assembly Bills in particular. The first such
case to be heard by the Supreme Court concerned the question of whether s. 9 of the
Local Government Byelaws (Wales) Bill 2012 was within the legislative competence
of the National Assembly for Wales, in so far as it gave to Welsh Ministers a power to
add further byelaws to a list of those which could be enacted without confirmation of
the UK Secretary of State (as was previously required, and which was outside the competence of the Assembly, by Sch. 7 to the Government of Wales Act 2006, unless the
Secretary of State consented to its enactment, or the removal of functions was 'incidental to, or consequential on' the other provisions in the Bill). The Supreme Court held
that the Bill was within legislative competence, and Lord Hope addressed the question
of why a reference had been necessary in light of the structure of the Welsh devolution
system.

Attorney General v National Assembly for Wales Commission
[2012] UKSC 53, [2013] 1 AC 792, Supreme Court

LORD HOPE:

74 The reason why a reference has been made in this case, in contrast to the lack of use of the equivalent
provision in Scotland, is likely to lie in differences between the systems that have been used to devolve
legislative power to the devolved legislatures from the United Kingdom Parliament at Westminster and
executive power to the devolved governments from Ministers of the United Kingdom Government.
Under the Scottish system, the general power to make laws conferred on the Scottish Parliament by

section 28 is subject to section 29 of the 1998 Act, which provides that an Act of the Scottish Parliament is outside its competence so far as, among other things, it relates to matters reserved to Westminster or is in breach of the restrictions in Schedule 4. A list of the reserved matters is set out in Schedule 5 to the 1998 Act. These provisions were accompanied by a general transfer of functions conferred on Ministers of the Crown to the Scottish Ministers by section 53, so far as these functions are exercisable within devolved competence.

75 Under the Welsh system, section 108 of the 2006 Act provides that a provision of an Act of the Assembly is within competence only if it falls within subsections (4) or (5) of that section and complies with the requirements of subsection (6). It must relate to one or more of the subjects listed in Schedule 7 to be within competence. A transfer of functions from Ministers of the Crown to the Welsh Ministers is achieved by an Order in Council made under section 58 of the 2006 Act, which may direct among other things (i) that functions are to be exercisable by the Welsh Ministers, the First Minister or the Counsel General concurrently with the Minister of the Crown or (ii) that any function so far as exercisable by a Minister of the Crown in relation to Wales is to be exercisable by the Minister of the Crown only with the agreement of, or after consultation with, the Welsh Ministers, the First Minister or the Counsel General. This is a more cautious transfer of executive power than that which was thought appropriate for Scotland. Not surprisingly, the question where the balance has been struck between the functions of the Welsh Ministers on the one hand and the Ministers of the Crown on the other is a sensitive one.

NOTE: As Lord Hope notes at [87], while this was the first devolution reference actually to reach the Supreme Court, it was not the first to have been made:

> The only previous example of a reference being made to the Supreme Court of a Bill passed by a devolved legislature is a reference that was made by the Attorney General for Northern Ireland in 2011. As was noted in *AXA General Insurance Co Ltd v HM Advocate* [2012] 1 AC 868, para 15, he referred the question whether the Damages (Asbestos-related Conditions) (Northern Ireland) Bill was within the competence of the Northern Ireland Assembly for pre-enactment scrutiny under section 11 of the Northern Ireland Act 1998. ... But the reference was withdrawn before the hearing of the appeal in the *AXA* case took place.

Further references have been made in relation to the Agricultural Sector (Wales) Bill and in relation to the Recovery of Medical Costs for Asbestos Diseases (Wales) Bill. In the former reference [2014] UKSC 43, the Supreme Court decided that the bill to establish an Agricultural Advisory Panel for Wales (replacing the Agricultural Wages Board for England and Wales, which had been abolished by legislation of the UK Parliament) was within the legislative competence of the Welsh Assembly, because it crucially related to the devolved subject of agriculture, and it did not matter whether it also related in some way to a subject (in this case, employment) for which competence had not been devolved:

> [67] ... The legislation does not require that a provision should only be capable of being characterised as relating to a devolved subject.
> [68] ... Not only is [the alternative approach] impermissible in principle, but it would in practice restrict the powers of the Assembly to legislate on subjects which were intended to be devolved to it: as the present case demonstrates, a Bill which undoubtedly relates to a devolved subject may also be capable of being classified as relating to a subject which is not devolved. Such an interpretation of section 108 would therefore give rise to an uncertain scheme that was neither stable nor workable. In contrast, the application of the clear test in section 108 provides for a scheme that is coherent, stable and workable.

The third Welsh reference to reach the Supreme Court was more controversial.

Re Recovery of Medical Costs for Asbestos Diseases (Wales) Bill
[2015] UKSC 3; [2015] AC 1016, Supreme Court

The reference concerned a Bill which was intended to allow the National Health Service in Wales to recover the costs of treating asbestos-related diseases from an employer or insurer who was liable to compensate a person in receipt of medical treatment. The Counsel General for Wales referred the question of whether the Bill was within legislative competence to the Supreme Court; the Association of British Insurers received permission to intervene, and argued that the Bill was outside legislative competence as it did not relate to the devolved subject of 'health and health services', and violated the insurers' right to peaceful enjoyment of their possessions under Art. 1 of Protocol 1 to the ECHR, in particular due to its retrospective imposition of liability on insurers.

LORD MANCE (with whom LORD NEUBERGER and LORD HODGE agreed):

26 The provision of health services and the organisation and funding of the Welsh NHS clearly cannot permit the Welsh Assembly to raise moneys generally, by relying on the fact that any moneys raised from any source increase the funds available for all its spending, including spending on the Health Service. The question is whether the position is different if the moneys raised can be said to be specifically intended or hypothecated to provide funds for use in the Health Service. . . .

27 In these circumstances, any raising of charges permissible under paragraph 9 [of Pt.1 of Sch.7 to the Government of Wales Act 2006] would have, in my opinion, to be more directly connected with the service provided and its funding. The mere purpose and effect of raising money which can or will be used to cover part of the costs of the Welsh NHS could not constitute a sufficiently close connection. In the case of prescription or other charges to users of the Welsh NHS service, a direct connection with the service and its funding exists, in that users are directly involved with and benefitting by the service. In the case of charges under section 2, the argument would have to be that a sufficient connection can be found in the actual or alleged wrongdoing that led to a compensator making a compensation payment to or in respect of a sufferer from an asbestos related disease. But that is at best an indirect, loose or consequential connection. The expression "organisation and funding of national health service" could not, in my opinion, have been conceived with a view to covering what would amount in reality to rewriting the law of tort and breach of statutory duty by imposing on third persons (the compensators), having no other direct connection in law with the NHS, liability towards the Welsh Ministers to meet costs of NHS services provided to sufferers from asbestos-related diseases towards whom such third persons decide to make a compensation payment for liability which may or may not exist or have been established or admitted.

In relation to compatibility with Art. 1 of Protocol 1, the majority continued:

66 The Counsel General maintains that special justification exists for the retrospectivity involved in the Bill because, without it, the Bill cannot achieve its legitimate policy aim. That is a circular submission, which, if accepted, would eliminate the important balancing stage of the proportionality exercise identified by Lord Reed JSC in *Bank Mellat* (para 45 above), by Lord Hope DPSC in *AXA* (para 51 above), and by the Strasbourg court in its case law: paras 44-48 above. As a matter of legislative policy it could be thought appropriate by the relevant legislature that the Welsh NHS should be able to recover hospitalisation costs from those whose breach of tortious or statutory duty caused them to be incurred. But that is, as I have noted, a provision which could have been made by the United Kingdom when or at any time since the NHS was introduced. It is a provision which would no doubt have been proportionate if introduced in relation to future exposure to asbestos and future insurance contracts. But rewriting historically incurred obligations to impose it in relation to future Welsh NHS costs is a quite different step. It is a step for which, on the authorities and as the Counsel General accepts, special justification is necessary, and none is shown. I therefore conclude that, even assuming the Bill to satisfy section 108(4) and/or (5), it falls outside the legislative competence of the Welsh Assembly.

LORD THOMAS (dissenting, with whom BARONESS HALE agreed):

93 [T]here is a clear distinction between exercising general tax raising powers and charging for services provided by the NHS. A specific cost can be attributed to the services. The funds so raised can then be used to defer the costs of those services rather than utilising the grant provided to the Welsh Consolidated Fund. Thus it is entirely consistent with the grant to the Welsh Assembly of primary

legislative powers in respect of health under heading 9, that the Welsh Assembly was given competence to vary the NHS (Wales) Act and to charge for services provided without being constrained by the terms of that Act....

100 As the Welsh Assembly has, in my view, competence to impose such charges directly on the employees, I can see no objection to the competence of the Welsh Assembly under the provisions of section 108(4)(5) and heading 9 of Part 1 of Schedule 7 in imposing such charges directly on the employers to achieve the aims of the Bill.

On the question of retrospectivity:

108 ... [T]he Welsh Assembly's objective in making the tortfeasor pay rather than the public as a whole is a choice which can properly be regarded as having an economic and social purpose. This is clearly an objective on which different views can reasonably be held. However, it is in every respect pre-eminently a political judgment in relation to social and economic policy on which it is for the legislative branch of the state to reach a judgment. The judicial branch of the state should not therefore question this first and central aim of the Bill, as there are manifestly reasonable grounds for reaching the view which the Welsh Assembly has reached....

124 In the present case, as I have concluded that the view taken by the Welsh Assembly is a view which is reasonably open to it as a view of the public interest and of social justice on a matter of social and economic policy, I therefore consider great weight should be attached to the legislative choice made by the Welsh Assembly as expressed in the Bill enacted by it as primary legislation within its competence. It must follow therefore that the judgment of the Welsh Assembly as to the public interest and social justice should be preferred on matters of social and economic policy to a judicial view of what it regards as being in the public interest and representing social justice.

Nevertheless, while the aim of the policy was legitimate, in one respect the minority agreed that the bill would violate the right to peaceful enjoyment of possessions:

138 ... I can see no justification in the balancing exercise under A1P1 for extending the liability of insurers under section 14 further than the indemnity which insurers were bound to provide under their policies if the indemnity had been called on to indemnify the sums which would have been payable by the employers as damages.

(e) Conclusion in relation to insurers

139 It is for that reason, I have come to the conclusion that section 14 as drafted, besides being beyond the competence under section 108(4)(5), infringes A1P1. However if section 14 had been limited in the way I have suggested, I would have considered it as a provision that achieved a fair balance under A1P1. That is because the retrospectivity would have been limited to providing an indemnity solely in respect of the machinery of collection of sums that would have been otherwise due under the insurance policies if the charges imposed by the Welsh Assembly had been payable by way of damages by the employers as tortfeasors in the ordinary way.

140 For the reasons I have given, insurers, just as employers, have no legitimate interest which protects them against the withdrawal of the state benefit conferred in the provision of free medical treatment and care for diseases caused by negligence or breach of statutory duty, irrespective of whether that negligence or breach of statutory duty occurred in the past, particularly in circumstances where the consequences of such wrongdoing take many years to become manifest.

NOTE: The decision of the majority has been criticized on the grounds that it departs from previous devolution case law and takes too narrow a view of the competence of the Welsh Assembly, characterizing the purpose of the Bill in such a way as to place it outside the devolved responsibility for 'health and health services'. A further controversy relates to the extent the court was willing to question the policy choices made by the democratically elected legislature. For Lord Thomas:

> 122 I cannot see why in principle the United Kingdom Parliament in making legislative choices in relation to England (in relation to matters such as the funding of the NHS in England) is to be accorded a status which commands greater weight than would be accorded to the Scottish Parliament and the Northern Ireland and Welsh Assemblies in relation respectively to Scotland, Northern Ireland and Wales. As each democratically elected body must be entitled to form its own judgment about public interest and social justice in matters of social and economic policy within a field where, under the structure of devolution, it has sole primary legislative competence, there is no logical justification for treating the views of one such body in a different way to the others, given the constitutional structure that has been developed. The judgment of each must have the same effect and force. Although the weight to be accorded to the judgment of these legislative bodies will vary according to the matter in issue, there is no reason in determining weight to treat the judgment of the Scottish Parliament, the Northern Ireland Assembly and the Welsh Assembly in any way different to the United Kingdom Parliament.

Whereas Lord Mance took a more restrictive view, arguing that:

> 67 Lord Thomas of Cwmgiedd CJ attaches great weight to the judgment of the Welsh Assembly that this is a measure which should in the interests of Wales be enacted. I agree that weight should be given to the Welsh Assembly's judgment. But it is the court's function, under GOWA, to evaluate the relevant considerations and to form its own judgment, on the issue both of legislative competence and of consistency with the Convention rights.

For critical discussion, see A. Tomkins, 'Confusion and Retreat: The Supreme Court on Devolution', *UK Constitutional Law Association Blog* (19 February 2015).

■ QUESTIONS

1. Does the decision in *Re Recovery of Medical Costs for Asbestos Diseases (Wales) Bill* present difficulties in relation to the interpretation of the scope of the Welsh Assembly's competence? Compare with the approach of the Supreme Court in *Re Agricultural Sector (Wales) Bill*.

2. Are the democratically elected devolved legislatures comparable to the UK Parliament? What are the constitutional similarities and differences?

3. Should the courts defer to the decisions made by the devolved legislatures on difficult questions of social and economic policy, especially when challenged on human rights grounds? See also Chapter 9.

4. Is the reference process a useful mechanism? On the one hand, it enables clarity to be achieved about the validity of legislation prior to its enactment. On the other, it can delay the implementation of legislation which the devolved legislature was perfectly competent to enact. When the Supreme Court is required to engage in an assessment of the validity of legislation which is still yet to be enacted, is there a risk it could be viewed as a political actor interfering in political disputes, especially between the devolved and UK institutions of government?

SECTION 4: DEVOLUTION AS A DYNAMIC SETTLEMENT

In this final section, we consider key examples of the dynamic nature of devolution. That this is the case has already been demonstrated by the discussion to this point, with changes having already occurred in Scotland, Wales, and Northern Ireland since the modern devolution settlement was established in 1998. Here, we consider key recent or potential change to devolution in all three nations: (a) the Scottish independence referendum and its aftermath; (b) change to the model of devolution in Wales; and (c) devolution of Police and Justice powers to Northern Ireland.

A: The Scottish independence referendum and its aftermath

On its election with an overall majority as Scottish Government in 2011, the Scottish National Party administration sought to implement its core policy: the holding of a referendum on whether Scotland should leave the UK entirely, and become an independent nation. By Sch. 5 of the Scotland Act 1998, the constitution is a reserved matter, and in particular, by para. 1(b) of Part I, this includes 'the Union of the Kingdoms of Scotland and England'. This posed a constitutional problem—the election of the Scottish National Party gave it both an electoral mandate and the votes in the Scottish Parliament to pass legislation making provision for an independence referendum to be held; yet to do so appeared to be beyond the legislative competence of the Scottish Parliament. Whether it would be lawful to enact an Act of the Scottish Parliament which purported to authorize the holding of a *non-binding* referendum, the result of which could not directly affect the constitution or the Union, was a matter of much debate. The prospect of this being settled by the UK Supreme Court in London, whether on a reference or on appeal, threatened to exacerbate the controversy further. The matter was settled after negotiation between the UK and Scottish governments, which led to the UK Government making an order under s. 30 of the Scotland Act 1998—the Scotland Act 1998 (Modification of Schedule 5) Order 2013/242—extending to the Scottish Parliament, for a limited period of time, the competence to hold a referendum on Scottish independence. Acting on this power, the Scottish Parliament enacted legislation making provision for an independence referendum to be held.

Scottish Independence Referendum Act 2013

1. Referendum on Scottish independence

  (1) A referendum is to be held in Scotland on a question about the independence of Scotland.

  (2) The question is—

"Should Scotland be an independent country?"

  (3) The ballot paper to be used for the purpose of the referendum is to be printed—

    (a) in the form set out in schedule 1, and

    (b) according to the directions set out in that schedule.

  (4) The date on which the poll at the referendum is to be held is 18 September 2014, unless before then an order is made under subsection (6).

  (5) Subsection (6) applies if the Scottish Ministers are satisfied—

    (a) that it is impossible or impracticable for the poll at the referendum to be held on 18 September 2014, or

    (b) that it cannot be conducted properly if held on that date.

  (6) The Scottish Ministers may by order appoint a later day (being no later than 31 December 2014) as the day on which the poll at the referendum is to be held.

  (7) An order under subsection (6)—

    (a) may include supplementary or consequential provision,

    (b) may modify any enactment (including this Act), and

    (c) is subject to the affirmative procedure.

2. Those who are entitled to vote

Provision about who is entitled to vote in the referendum is made by the Scottish Independence Referendum (Franchise) Act 2013.

NOTES

1. The Scottish Independence Referendum (Franchise) Act 2013 referred to in s. 2 made provision for those aged 16 and above to vote in the referendum, whereas the usual minimum voting age in UK elections is 18. This was explained by reference to the national and constitutional significance of the referendum, which, it was been argued, justified an extension of the franchise to 16- to 18-year-old voters.

2. We were therefore in the remarkable position of having devolved legislative competence used to make provision for a referendum which could bring about a partial breakup of the UK, and an end to devolution in Scotland. When the New Labour government established the devolution settlement in 1998, some members of the Conservative Party objected that it could be a 'slippery slope' which could lead to the end of the Union. While the final result in the September 2014 referendum did not see this come about, with the Scottish electorate voting to remain an independent country by 55 per cent to 45 per cent, the prospect of a second independence referendum remains on the political horizon, as a result of the re-election in 2016 of a Scottish National Party government, and the UK-wide vote to leave the European Union, in which a majority of the Scottish people voted to remain. The arguments for and against independence cover a broad range of issues which are political, social, cultural, and economic in substance. Yet the nature and adequacy of devolution is also a key component of those debates, as the following extracts from the 2014 referendum campaign indicate. First, the UK Government's defence of the Union was based, to a significant extent, on the benefits that devolution offers. The Scottish Government, in contrast, argued that independence was a natural progression from devolution.

Scotland Analysis: Devolution and the Implications of Scottish Independence
Cm 8554, 2013, paras ix, xi–xii

Scotland's constitution today

ix The analysis in this paper makes the case that **devolution – Scotland's constitution today – offers people in Scotland the best of both worlds**. Scotland has always maintained its own distinctive identity, legal and education systems, and other aspects of civic life. But devolution has, in little more than a decade, brought political decision-making on key issues closer to the people affected by it, within the framework of a single UK.

xi. **Devolution is also a system of government that is flexible and responsive to changing needs and circumstances**. In 2012 the UK Parliament passed a second Scotland Act, which contained the single biggest devolution of financial powers since 1707. Between the landmark devolution Acts of 1998 and 2012, many other powers have been devolved. Most recently, the UK Government was able to deliver its commitment in the Edinburgh Agreement to transfer to the Scottish Parliament the power to hold a legal, fair and decisive referendum on independence.

xii. **That flexibility does not mean that independence would simply be an extension of devolution**. Legally and constitutionally, independence is a totally different proposition. Independence would mean the end of devolution. Devolution ensures that Scotland has a strong position within the UK. Independence would remove Scotland from the UK, along with the benefits that devolution brings.

Scottish Government, *Scotland's Future: from the Referendum to Independence and a Written Constitution*
February 2013, paras 1.1, 1.4, 2.16

Independence for Scotland

1.1 An independent Scotland will ensure that decisions about Scotland are taken by the people who care most about it – those who live and work here. The Scottish Parliament is already responsible for important issues such as the health service, education and the protection of the environment. Independence will complete the powers of the Parliament, making it fully responsible for the economy, welfare and international relations….

A written constitution

1.4 The Scottish Government's proposal is that an independent Scotland should have a written constitution which expresses our values, embeds the rights of its citizens and sets out clearly how institutions of state interact with each other and serve the people. This will contrast with the UK's largely unwritten constitution in which the Westminster Parliament can do anything except bind its successors. The Westminster system has sometimes led to major decisions being taken by the government without the possibility of challenge (for example, the decision to go to war in Iraq in 2003). There has long been a distinct Scottish constitutional tradition, affirmed by the Scottish Parliament as recently as January 2012–the sovereignty of the Scottish people and their right to choose the form of government best suited to their needs. ...

After independence

2.16 When the Scottish Parliament was reconvened in 1999, Scotland embarked on an historic journey. That journey will continue after a 'yes' vote in 2014. Independence will complete the powers of the Scottish Parliament and equip it to build a thriving, self-confident, democratic independent European country in the years to follow. Independence will allow the people of Scotland to elect a government and a Parliament that reflects their views and values, and allow our government and Parliament to make the best decisions for Scotland. Scotland's journey is not an event, but a process that continues, and independence will enable the sovereign people of Scotland to choose their future for themselves.

NOTE: In the aftermath of the referendum result, the Smith Commission was established to make recommendations to further strengthen devolution to Scotland, to give effect to a commitment made by the leaders of the three main UK parties (who all campaigned against independence) in the days prior to the referendum. The Commission comprised representatives from across the political spectrum, and reported in November 2014. Proposals for change were made across three Heads of Agreement.

Report of the Smith Commission for further Devolution of Powers to the Scottish Parliament

27 November 2014

16. The five political parties have agreed that new powers will be devolved to the Scottish Parliament and to Scottish Ministers. They have agreed to refer to this package of powers as 'the Smith Commission Agreement.' These powers are arranged within these heads of agreement according to three 'pillars'. These pillars are:

- pillar 1: providing a durable but responsive constitutional settlement for the governance of Scotland
- pillar 2: delivering prosperity, a healthy economy, jobs, and social justice
- pillar 3: strengthening the financial responsibility of the Scottish Parliament

17. The parties believe that Scotland's devolution settlement should be durable but responsive to the changing needs and aspirations of the people of Scotland within the United Kingdom. As a result, it may be appropriate to devolve further powers beyond those set out in the heads of agreement where doing so would aid the implementation of the consensus reached by the parties in this report.

18. It is agreed that nothing in this report prevents Scotland becoming an independent country in the future should the people of Scotland so choose.

NOTE: The Scotland Act 2016 was enacted to give effect to these proposals, and transferred significant further powers to the Scottish Parliament. This included the considerable extension of fiscal powers, and control over many aspects of social welfare and employment support (see earlier in this chapter in Section 2C at pp. 367–8). New powers including those over elections (subject in some instances to a super-majority legislative requirement, including in relation to the definition of the electorate), onshore oil and gas extraction, fuel poverty, and renewable energy were devolved, and powers in relation to transport were extended. Two provisions of constitutional significance were also introduced: the statutory recognition of the normal operation of the Sewel convention (discussed earlier in this chapter in Section 2B at pp. 364–6), and of the permanence of the Scottish institutions. In relation to the latter, the Scotland Act 2016, s. 1, amended the existing devolution scheme as follows.

Scotland Act 1998

63A Permanence of the Scottish Parliament and Scottish Government

(1) The Scottish Parliament and the Scottish Government are a permanent part of the United Kingdom's constitutional arrangements.

(2) The purpose of this section is, with due regard to the other provisions of this Act, to signify the commitment of the Parliament and Government of the United Kingdom to the Scottish Parliament and the Scottish Government.

(3) In view of that commitment it is declared that the Scottish Parliament and the Scottish Government are not to be abolished except on the basis of a decision of the people of Scotland voting in a referendum.

NOTE: A similar provision is proposed to be enacted with respect to Wales, in the Wales Bill 2016–17, draft clause 1. There is much scope for debate about the implications of this provision, which raises questions about the sovereignty of the UK Parliament as well as the devolution system. Is it simply a recognition of constitutional reality in statute, designed to signify commitment to devolution, rather than create any binding legal effects? Or is the referendum requirement set out in s. 63A(3) a legally enforceable limit on the power of future UK Parliaments?

■ QUESTIONS

1. Has the more extensive devolution to Scotland in the aftermath of the 2014 independence referendum created a durable and fixed settlement for the future? Or could further change to devolution be imminent, whether through a second independence referendum as the UK leaves the EU, or as powers reclaimed from the EU—perhaps including those over agriculture, the environment, consumer protection, and employment rights—are devolved to the Scottish Parliament?

2. If Scotland were to become an independent country, and established a written constitution, do you think this would have an impact on debates as to whether the UK should codify its constitution?

B: Change to the model of devolution in Wales

As discussed earlier, the Scotland Act 2012 greatly extended the fiscal powers of the Scottish Parliament and Government. The 2012 Act was enacted in response to recommendations made by the Calman Commission; a similar commission—known as the Silk Commission—was subsequently established in Wales to consider whether the fiscal powers of the Welsh Assembly and Government ought to be extended.

Commission on Devolution in Wales, *Empowerment and Responsibility: Financial Powers to Strengthen Wales*
November 2012, paras R1–R4, R26–R27

RECOMMENDATIONS

R.1. The current funding arrangements for the Welsh Government do not meet the requirements of a mature democracy and are anomalous in an international context. The funding model of a block grant and some devolved taxes best meets sound principles for funding the Welsh Government. We therefore recommend that part of the budget for the Welsh Government should be funded from devolved taxation under its control.

R.2. Business rates should be fully devolved subject to the Welsh and UK Governments agreeing the details and assessing any risks involved.

R.3. Stamp Duty Land Tax should be devolved to the Welsh Government with Welsh Ministers given control over all aspects of the tax in Wales. A fixed deduction should be made to the block grant with the value of this agreed between the Welsh and UK Governments taking due consideration of the volatility of receipts.

R.4. Landfill tax should be devolved to the Welsh Government with Welsh Ministers given control over all aspects of the tax in Wales. A fixed deduction should be made to the block grant with the value of this agreed between the Welsh and UK Governments taking due consideration of the declining taxable base....

R.26. Devolution of income tax should be subject to a referendum in Wales. Provision for such a referendum should be contained in the Act which introduces tax and borrowing powers.

R.27. A new Wales Bill should be introduced in this Parliament to devolve tax and borrowing powers....

NOTES

1. The extent to which the Silk Commission's recommendations were influenced by the further devolution of financial power to Scotland via the 2012 Act is clear. Yet in some respects, the Silk Commission proposals went further: one key example of this was R.16 (d), in which it was proposed that the Welsh Government should have the power to vary the different rates of income tax independently of one another, in contrast to the more restrictive Scottish 'lockstep' approach establish by the 2012 Act (whereby the rate of each tax band must be increased or decreased by the same amount, keeping the difference between bands the same as in relation to UK income tax). Indeed, this more expansive power to vary income tax rates—including the differences between the basic, higher, and additional bands—has now been devolved to Scotland by the 2016 Act, and will be in effect from 2017/18 (see earlier in this chapter in Section 2C at pp. 367–8). The report of the Silk Commission demonstrates how the asymmetrical devolution of power in the UK can be used to justify the 'levelling up' of devolved power overall—the differences of power between nations can be used as a basis for seeking extended competence where it is lacking, in multiple directions.

2. The recommendations of the Silk Commission were implemented in the Wales Act 2014. In addition to devolution of taxation and borrowing powers, a particular innovation—as recommended by the Commission—was s. 12, which made standing provision for income tax powers to come into force if approved at a referendum of the people of Wales. Nevertheless, the pace of change to devolution is such that this requirement is to be removed by further legislation extending powers to Wales, as proposed in clause 17 of the Wales Bill 2016–17. When enacted, this provision will allow the income tax powers to commence without approval at a referendum in Wales.

3. The Wales Bill 2016–17 has been controversial. In addition to devolving a range of new powers to Wales, it also aims to shift the model of Welsh devolution radically, amending the Government of Wales Act 2006 to create a reserved powers model comparable to that operating in Scotland (see earlier in this chapter in Section 2B at pp. 353–6). Yet the fact that England and Wales share a common legal jurisdiction has caused complexity. The application of a 'necessity test' before Welsh legislation could alter criminal or private law (the key levers by which public policy goals may be enforced) was much criticized. There were also concerns over new consent requirements in the original draft Bill, with the Welsh Affairs Committee concluding that extended requirements for the consent of a UK Minister to Welsh legislation which was to remove functions previously exercised by government ministers under the law of England and Wales actually amounted to a reduction in the legislative competence of the Assembly (HC 449 of 2015–16). The UK Government revisited the Bill in light of these criticisms, and made some amendments, including replacing the necessity tests required before changes to criminal or private law with a justice impact assessment, considering the impact of proposed legislation on the justice system in

England and Wales. The new Bill will also recognize a distinct body of 'Welsh law'—that which applies in Wales, made by the Assembly and the Welsh Ministers, yet which is also part of the law of England and Wales; for discussion see M. George and H. Pritchard, 'Take 2: The Wales Bill', *Centre on Constitutional Change Blog* (9 July 2016). The Welsh Assembly passed a legislative consent motion approving the amended Wales Bill on 17 January 2017, despite the continuing reservations of the First Minister Carwyn Jones that it was 'not possible to conclude that the reserved powers model, welcome though it is in theory, is fit for purpose in the long term', in particular due to the potential for difficulties caused by the commitment to a common legal jurisdiction for England and Wales.

Record of Proceedings, National Assembly for Wales
Legislative Consent Motion on the Wales Bill, NDM6203, 17 January 2017

The First Minister, Carwyn Jones

There are concerns about the limited scope of our powers and the impact of the restrictions in the new model. The weight of these concerns depends on an assessment of risk in relation to the 'relates to' test and the necessity test, and how far the Assembly's future legislative ambitions are likely to hit against the limitations of these tests.

The UK Government will claim that this Bill provides greater certainty, but it would undermine that certainty if, within a few months or years, we find ourselves back in front of the Supreme Court asking the Supreme Court to take a decision as to where the boundary lies in terms of devolved powers....

There is no other country that I know of where two legislatures exist in the same jurisdiction. It's unheard of anywhere else and it has an important practical effect. It is possible in the future that somebody might be arrested in Cardiff for something that is not an offence in Wales. It is possible that somebody might serve a sentence of imprisonment in a prison in England for something that isn't an offence in England. That to me makes no sense at all as far as the future is concerned. It also confuses the public and the professions. We're already having instances communicated to me by the Lord Chief Justice of lawyers turning up in Welsh courts and arguing the wrong law, because they assume the law is the same in both England and Wales.... But, of course, this complication is something that the UK Government have chosen to do.

The failure by the UK Government to engage with the fundamental questions of justice and the jurisdiction means that the Bill can't be a sustainable, long-term settlement. The future of justice in Wales with the growing body of devolved Welsh law providing a distinct Welsh legal jurisdiction is too important to be ignored. That's why we argued throughout the passage of the Bill that we need a commission to consider and report on the arrangements that need to be put in place to ensure we have a justice system in Wales that is fit for purpose and, of course, fit for the new devolution settlement. As the UK Government has been unwilling to take on that task, we will do so. The Welsh Government will make more announcements about this over the coming months.

■ QUESTIONS

1. Should the combined jurisdiction of the law of England and Wales be abandoned to bring greater clarity to the devolution settlement? Would this have broader constitutional implications for the position of England, given the lack of an English Parliament?

2. Does the extension of devolution to Wales—in both terms of extended fiscal powers, and the proposed introduction of a reserved powers model—indicate that the asymmetry of the UK's devolution arrangements is diminishing over time?

C: Devolution of police and justice powers to Northern Ireland

Responsibility for Policing and Justice has been a significant issue in the politics of devolution in Northern Ireland. As the Independent Commission on Policing in Northern Ireland (created in accordance with the Good Friday agreement) noted in its report in 1999, since being established in 1922 the Royal Ulster Constabulary (RUC) was 'disproportionately Protestant and Unionist', and thus had 'been identified by one section of the population not primarily as upholders of the law but as defenders of the state' (p. 2). The RUC was replaced by a reformed Police Service of Northern Ireland in 2001, but ongoing concern and further revelations as to the conduct of the police and other state security agencies during the Troubles meant that this continued to be a controversial part of the peace process and associated debates about the devolution of political power. This was reflected in the devolution legislation, which was amended by the Northern Ireland (Miscellaneous Provisions) Act 2006 to make specific provision as to how police and justice powers (then a reserved matter) could be transferred.

Northern Ireland Act 1998

4. …

(2A) The Secretary of State shall not lay before Parliament under subsection (2) the draft of an Order amending Schedule 3 so that a policing and justice matter ceases to be a reserved matter unless–
   (a) a motion for a resolution praying that the matter should cease to be a reserved matter is tabled by the First Minister and the deputy First Minister acting jointly; and
   (b) the resolution is passed by the Assembly with the support of a majority of the members voting on the motion, a majority of the designated Nationalists voting and a majority of the designated Unionists voting.

NOTE: Devolution in Northern Ireland having been suspended a number of times between 2000 and 2002 due to concerns about the decommissioning of weapons by the IRA, the Northern Ireland Assembly was then suspended for what would ultimately be almost five years on 14 October 2002. An agreement reached at St Andrews on 13 October 2006 paved the way for the restoration of devolution, and indicated that efforts would be made to request the devolution of police and criminal justice powers from the UK Government by May 2008. This target was not met, but agreement was ultimately reached in 2010.

Agreement at Hillsborough Castle
5 February 2010, paras 1–2, 4–5

Section 1 - Policing and Justice
Devolution timetable

   1. Following community consultation the First Minister and deputy First Minister will table jointly a resolution for a cross-community vote in the Assembly on 9 March. Following affirmation of the resolution they will support all necessary steps in the Assembly to ensure devolution of powers by the 12 April. The Government will set out publicly the Parliamentary schedule for the related transfer orders required to effect devolution. Policing and justice powers will be devolved on that day.

The Department of Justice - Model

   2. The Assembly's Department of Justice Bill, which completed its passage in December, establishes the new Department of Justice and sets out the arrangements for the appointment of the Justice

Minister. It provides that there will be a single Justice Minister in charge of the Department of Justice which will be responsible for devolved policing and justice policy and legislation. The Justice Minister will be elected by a cross community vote in the Assembly following a nomination by any MLA.

…

Independence of Judiciary and Chief Constable

4. We believe that the independence of the judiciary is essential in a democratic society which supports the rule of law. It is of paramount importance that the judicial function remains independent of Government and immune from any partisan or political interest. Public confidence requires that judicial decisions are taken in a fair, impartial, objective and consistent manner. This confidence can only be maintained if judges are able to act with independence.

5. As part of the devolved policing arrangements the Chief Constable will be operationally responsible for directing and controlling the police. The PSNI will have operational responsibility for policing, and for implementing the policies and objectives set by the Department of Justice and the Policing Board.

NOTES

1. Implementing the Hillsborough Castle Agreement, a Department of Justice was established, to which a range of executive functions were transferred by the Northern Ireland Act 1998 (Devolution of Policing and Justice Functions) Order 2010/976. The Northern Ireland Act 1998 (Amendment of Schedule 3) Order 2010/977 was also enacted to change specified policing and justice functions from reserved matters to transferred matters. This competence has been exercised by the Northern Ireland Assembly to enact the Justice Act (Northern Ireland) 2011 (which, among other things, makes provision for the establishment of Policing and Community Safety Partnerships) and the Criminal Justice (Northern Ireland) Act 2013. The Alliance Party leader David Ford held the position of Justice Minister from 2010 to 2016, but the party resolved not to take the post—elected on the basis of cross-community support—from that point onwards, resulting in the election of the independent unionist Claire Sugden to the office in May 2016.
2. While agreement was reached over the devolution of policing and justice powers to Northern Ireland, there has been disagreement in other areas. A particular area of difficulty was welfare reform, with the Northern Irish Assembly voting to reject UK-wide welfare cuts introduced by the UK Government in 2012, leaving the Executive with a financial shortfall. The *Stormont Agreement and Implementation Plan: Welfare Reform* (November 2015) determined that the UK Government should legislate for welfare reform in Northern Ireland to bypass this disagreement in the short term, which was quickly done in the form of the Northern Ireland (Welfare Reform) Act 2015. The welfare reform implemented by the Act was accompanied by £585 million in additional funding for the Northern Ireland Executive to top up UK tax credits and subsidize those subject to the 'bedroom tax' over a transitional period. Other issues agreed in the broader deal included measures on ending paramilitarism (with the creation of an Independent Reporting Commission in the Northern Ireland (Stormont Agreement and Implementation Plan) Act 2016) and committing to a start date of April 2018 for the devolution of corporation tax, responsibility for which had been transferred to Northern Ireland by the Corporation Tax (Northern Ireland) Act 2015.
3. The delicate position of devolution in Northern Ireland was further demonstrated in January 2017, by the resignation of Martin McGuinness as Deputy First Minister, in protest at the refusal of the First Minister, Arlene Foster, to resign over a scandal relating to major overpayments to participants in a Renewable Heat Incentive scheme. Foster had been the Minister in charge of the green energy scheme when it was set up in 2012, but the subsidies offered to businesses switching to environmentally friendly fuel sources were initially uncapped, leaving the programme nearly £500 million in deficit. The joint nature of the appointment of the First Minister and Deputy First Minister under the power-sharing devolution arrangements meant that Sinn Fein's decision not to nominate a successor to McGuinness brought down the Executive, with new elections to be held in March 2017. If the DUP and Sinn Fein are again returned as the largest unionist and nationalist parties respectively, the disagreement will need to be resolved if they are to form a

joint government. The UK Secretary of State for Northern Ireland, James Brokenshire, had indicated he is not contemplating alternatives to devolved government, such as the resumption of direct rule of Northern Ireland by the UK Government.

■ QUESTIONS

1. How important do you think the asymmetrical, flexible manner in which devolution has been pursued in the UK has been in allowing agreement over contentious matters eventually to be reached? Do the events surrounding the devolution of police and justice powers to Northern Ireland demonstrate that the imposition of a uniform model of devolution in all of the nations of the UK would have been inherently unworkable, and that asymmetrical devolution was the only realistic choice?

2. The Explanatory Memorandum to the two 2010 Orders which transferred legislative and executive policing and justice powers to Northern Ireland describes this as 'the final stage in the process of devolution' (para. 7.2). While this has undoubtedly been a critical part of concluding the peace process, do subsequent events suggest this was the end of devolution to Northern Ireland? Or, given the dynamic nature of the process, that yet further devolution of power or change to the structures of government is possible, or even likely?

Justice Committee, *Devolution: A Decade On*
HC 529 of 2008–09, pp. 3, 5

Summary

Devolution was a major component of the Government's package of proposed constitutional reform for the United Kingdom post 1997. The central purpose of devolution was to bring government closer to the people than had previously been the case under the centralised UK state. In doing so, not only has devolution fundamentally transformed politics within the devolved territories, but, alongside the other components in the programme of constitutional reform, it has also had a significant impact on the make-up and the constitution of the United Kingdom….

4. In summary, the system of government of the United Kingdom as a whole has changed irreversibly from that of an undifferentiated unitary state, and will continue to adapt to the changes already made; and the way in which England is currently governed may be unsustainable in this changed system.

House of Lords Committee on the Constitution, *The Union and Devolution*
HL Paper 149, 10th Report of 2015–16, p. 3

Power has been devolved to Scotland, Wales and Northern Ireland in an ad hoc, piecemeal fashion. Successive Governments have taken the Union for granted. Proper consideration of the cumulative impact of devolution on the integrity of the Union itself has been lacking.

Every system has limits. This haphazard approach to the UK's constitution, in which power has been devolved without any counter-balancing steps to protect the Union, recently culminated in an existential threat in the form of a referendum on Scottish independence.

An inattentive approach to the integrity of the Union cannot continue. Following the significant changes that the territorial constitution has undergone in recent years, the time has come to reflect and take stock. While the constitution should reflect the wishes and interests of the nations and regions, that must not be at the expense of the stability, coherence and viability of the Union as a whole. Should any proposals for further devolution arise in the future, they should be considered within an appropriate framework of constitutional principles that safeguard the integrity of the Union.

■ QUESTIONS

1. To what extent do the observations of the House of Commons Justice Committee in 2009 accurately describe the current devolution settlement in the UK? Has devolution brought government closer to the people?

2. Do you share the concerns of the House of Lords Constitution Committee about (i) the future of the Union, and (ii) the inadequacy of the process by which the devolution settlement has been reformed?

3. Has devolution had a significant impact on the make-up and constitution of the UK?

4. Is devolution now irreversible?

5. Is it still accurate to describe the UK as a unitary state?

6. Is the way England is governed unsustainable in this changed system? Has your response to the 'West Lothian Question' changed since the start of this chapter?

9

Human Rights

OVERVIEW

In this chapter we consider first the former position on human rights, then the European Convention on Human Rights and its incorporation into domestic law by the Human Rights Act 1998. We look at the extent of its application to private bodies performing public functions, and between private parties; how it affects the interpretation of legislation, when courts may find legislation compatible with Convention rights and when they may issue a declaration of incompatibility.

SECTION 1: INTRODUCTION

The area of human rights is so large that it would merit a book on its own. Consequently, treatment of this topic in this chapter will be selective, seeking to highlight certain issues.

In most constitutions there are declarations of particular rights or liberties to be accorded to citizens and respected by Government, such as freedom of speech, freedom of the person, freedom of conscience, freedom of movement, the right to privacy, and the right to equal treatment. Often these freedoms or rights have an entrenched or protected status so that they may not easily be restricted or overridden by temporary political majorities in control of the legislature. These rights or freedoms are seen as essential to the existence and maintenance of a liberal democracy. The position in the United Kingdom was very different and owed much to Dicey. With the enactment of the Human Rights Act 1998 major changes have been introduced. These will be examined later in the chapter, but to understand the significance of these changes it is necessary to understand the way in which rights were protected prior to the enactment of the 1998 Act.

A. V. Dicey, *An Introduction to the Study of the Law of the Constitution*
(10th edn, 1969), p. 203

[W]ith us the law of the constitution, the rules which in foreign countries naturally form part of a constitutional code, are not the source but the consequence of the rights of individuals, as defined and enforced by the courts; that, in short, the principles of private law have with us been by the action of the courts and Parliament so extended as to determine the position of the Crown and of its servants; thus the constitution is the result of the ordinary law of the land.

The former position in the United Kingdom was summarized as follows:

Legislation on Human Rights: A Discussion Document
(Home Office, 1976), paras 2.01–2.05

Our arrangements for the protection of human rights are different from those of most other countries. The differences are related to differences in our constitutional traditions. Although our present constitution may be regarded as deriving in part from the revolution settlement of 1688–89, consolidated by the Union of 1707, we, unlike our European neighbours and many Commonwealth countries, do not owe our present system of government either to a revolution or to a struggle for independence. The United Kingdom—

(a) has an omnicompetent Parliament, with absolute power to enact any law and change any previous law; the courts in England and Wales have not, since the seventeenth century, recognised even in theory any higher legal order by reference to which Acts of Parliament could be held void; in Scotland the courts, while reserving the right to treat an Act as void for breaching a fundamental term of the Treaty of Union [see *MacCormick* v *Lord Advocate* [1953] SC 396], have made it clear that they foresee no likely circumstances in which they would do so;

(b) unlike other modern democracies, has no written constitution;

(c) unlike countries in the civil law tradition, makes no fundamental distinction, as regards rights or remedies, between 'public law' governing the actions of the State and its agents, and 'private law' regulating the relationships of private citizens with one another; nor have we a coherent system of administrative law applied by specialised tribunals or courts and with its own appropriate remedies;

(d) has not generally codified its law, and our courts adopt a relatively narrow and literal approach to the interpretation of statutes;

(e) unlike the majority of EEC countries and the United States, does not, by ratifying a treaty or convention, make it automatically part of the domestic law (nor do we normally give effect to such an international agreement by incorporating the agreement itself into our law).

In other countries the rights of the citizen are usually (though not universally) to be found enunciated in general terms in a Bill of Rights or other constitutional document. The effectiveness of such instruments varies greatly. A Bill of Rights is not an automatic guarantee of liberty; its efficacy depends on the integrity of the institutions which apply it, and ultimately on the determination of the people that it should be maintained. The United Kingdom as such has no Bill of Rights of this kind. The Bill of Rights of 1688, though more concerned with the relationship between the English Parliament and the Crown, did contain some important safeguards for personal liberty—as did the Claim of Rights of 1689, its Scottish equivalent. Among the provisions common to both the Bill of Rights and the Claim of Rights are declarations that excessive bail is illegal and that it is the right of subjects to petition the Crown without incurring penalties. But the protection given by these instruments to the rights and liberties of the citizen is much narrower than the constitutional guarantees now afforded in many other democratic countries.

The effect of the United Kingdom system of law is to provide, through the development of the common law and by express statutory enactment, a diversity of specific rights with their accompanying remedies. Thus, to secure the individual's right to freedom from unlawful or arbitrary detention, our law provides specific and detailed remedies such as habeas corpus and the action for false imprisonment. The rights which have been afforded in this way are for the most part negative rights to be protected from interference from others, rather than positive rights to behave in a particular way. Those rights which have emerged in the common law can always be modified by Parliament. Parliament's role is all-pervasive—potentially, at least. It continually adapts existing rights and remedies and provides new ones, and no doubt this process would continue even if a comprehensive Bill of Rights were enacted.

The legal remedies provided for interference with the citizen's rights have in recent times been overlaid by procedures which are designed to afford not so much remedies in the strict sense of the term as facilities for obtaining independent and impartial scrutiny of action by public bodies about which an individual believes he has cause for complaint, even though the action may have been within the body's legal powers. For example, the actions of central government departments are open to scrutiny by the Parliamentary Commissioner for Administration; and complaints about the administration of the National Health Service are investigated by the Health Service Commissioners.

NOTES

1. 'Rights' and 'freedoms' were regarded negatively in the United Kingdom; they were the area of freedom which remained after legal restraints were subtracted. Thus a person was free to do anything subject to the provisions of the law. There was, however, no guarantee that the area of freedom would not be contracted by the incremental encroachment of legislation until little freedom remained. In *Entick* v *Carrington* (1765) 19 St Tr 1030 (see Chapter 3, Section 5 at p. 124), Lord Camden had made it clear that Government, if it is to be free to interfere with individual rights, must be able to point to specific statutory or common law powers. The problem with this was that if these powers did not exist, they could always be created by new legislation. Today, for example, the police and other officials, such as HM Revenue Inspectors and Officers, have considerable powers under various Acts to obtain warrants and enter and search premises and seize property. See, for example, Police and Criminal Evidence Act 1984, s. 8; Taxes Management Act 1970, s. 20C, inserted by Finance Act 1976; Customs and Excise Management Act 1979, s. 161; Official Secrets Act 1911, s. 9; Police Act 1997, ss. 92–108.

   While some statutes may seek to limit rights, others may accord protection which did not exist at common law. For example, at common law discrimination on the grounds of race or sex was not generally prohibited. Parliament intervened by means of the Race Relations Act 1976 and the Sex Discrimination Act 1975 to prohibit discrimination in certain circumstances, such as employment, housing, education, and the provision of goods and services. This is not equivalent, however, to creating a general right to be free from discrimination. This kind of legislative intervention by Parliament is limited as each piece of legislation represents a limited response to a perceived mischief. Until the enactment of the Human Rights Act 1998 the practice was to provide limited remedies against particular abuses but to stop short of providing any general declaration of particular rights.

2. The UK's constitutional culture was not one in which there was widespread appreciation of, and concern for, the protection of human rights. Some thought that everything was fine and those who took the contrary view were divided in how to improve the situation, particularly in the role which should be given to the courts. It seemed that there were cycles in which the judiciary were and were not active in protecting civil liberties. A contrast may be drawn between the first half of the twentieth century and its final decade. Ewing and Gearty argued in *The Struggle for Civil Liberties: Political Freedom and the Rule of Law 1914–45* (2000) that the judicial record was decidedly unimpressive whereas in the 1990s there was a reawakening of judicial interest in constitutional rights and a much greater willingness to conceive of their existence as a brake on the power of the Executive. In *R* v *Lord Chancellor, ex parte Witham* [1998] QB 575, a litigant in person, who was unemployed and in receipt of income support and who wished to sue for defamation (for which legal aid was not available), sought judicial review of Art. 3 of the Supreme Court Fees (Amendment) Order 1996 made by the Lord Chancellor under s. 130 of the Supreme Court Act 1981. Article 3 imposed a minimum fee of £120 for the issuing of a writ and removed a provision under a previous Order of 1980 which relieved litigants in person who were in receipt of income support from the obligation to pay fees. The Divisional Court granted the application for a declaration that Art. 3 was unlawful. Laws J stated:

   > [T]he right to a fair trial, which of necessity imports the right of access to the court, is as near to an absolute right as any which I can envisage. ... Access to the courts is a constitutional right; it can only be denied by the government if it persuades Parliament to pass legislation which specifically—in effect by express provision—permits the executive to turn people away from the court door. That has not been done in this case.

   There was nothing in s. 130 of the 1981 Act which provided expressly for the abrogation of this right. This willingness to recognize the added importance of human rights began to have an impact on the way in which the *Wednesbury* unreasonableness test was applied in judicial review proceedings. In *R* v *Ministry of Defence, ex parte Smith* [1996] QB 517, the Court of Appeal adopted the approach that 'the more substantial the interference with human rights, the more the court will require by way of justification before it is satisfied that the decision is reasonable'. This involves 'anxious scrutiny' or 'high-intensity review' in human rights cases. In *Chesterfield Properties plc v Secretary of State for the Environment* [1998] JPL 568, at 579–80, Laws J expressed the operation of this process as follows:

> Where an administrative decision abrogates or diminishes a constitutional or fundamental right, *Wednesbury* requires that the decision-maker provide a substantial justification in the public interest for doing so. ... The identification of any right as 'constitutional', however, means nothing in the absence of a written constitution unless it is defined by reference to some particular protection which the law affords it. The common law affords such protection by adopting, within *Wednesbury*, a variable standard of review. There is no question of the court exceeding the principle of reasonableness. It means only that reasonableness itself requires in such cases that in ordering the priorities which will drive his decision, the decision-maker must give a high place to the right in question. He cannot treat it merely as something to be taken into account, akin to any other relevant consideration; he must recognise it as a value to be kept, unless in his judgment there is a greater value which justifies its loss. In many arenas of public discretion, the force to be given to all and any factors which the decision-maker must confront is neutral in the eye of the law; he may make of each what he will, and the law will not interfere because the weight he attributes to any of them is for him and not the court. But where a constitutional right is involved, the law presumes it to carry substantial force. Only another interest, a public interest, of greater force may override it.

In *R v Lord Saville, ex parte A and Others* [1999] 4 All ER 860, the Court of Appeal applied the high-intensity review test. The Bloody Sunday Review Tribunal, chaired by Lord Saville of Newdigate, had denied anonymity to soldiers testifying before it although accepting that anonymity would not hamper it in finding the truth. The Tribunal concluded that anonymity would affect the openness of the inquiry. Seventeen soldiers applied for judicial review, claiming that disclosure of their identities would put them at risk and thus interfered with their right to life. Their application was allowed by the Divisional Court. The Tribunal appealed. Lord Woolf MR, delivering the judgment of the court, dismissing the appeal stated (at p. 872):

> [W]hen a fundamental right such as the right to life is engaged, the options available to the reasonable decision-maker are curtailed. They are curtailed because it is unreasonable to reach a decision which contravenes or could contravene human rights unless there are sufficiently significant countervailing considerations. In other words it is not open to the decision-maker to risk interfering with fundamental rights in the absence of compelling justification. Even the broadest discretion is constrained by the need for there to be countervailing circumstances justifying interference with human rights. The courts will anxiously scrutinise the strength of the countervailing circumstances and the degree of the interference with the human right involved and then apply the test accepted by Lord Bingham MR in *Smith*.

This judicial awakening to the existence of constitutional or fundamental rights ties in with the political developments of the late 1990s which resulted in the enactment of the Human Rights Act 1998, which incorporated the European Convention on Human Rights.

SECTION 2: THE EUROPEAN CONVENTION ON HUMAN RIGHTS

In 1950 Member States of the Council of Europe (which included the United Kingdom) drew up the European Convention on Human Rights and Fundamental Freedoms. This was based on the Universal Declaration of Human Rights and is designed to provide basic protection for human rights. The Convention was ratified by the United Kingdom in 1951 and came into force in 1953, but it was not until 1966 that the United Kingdom accorded to its citizens the right to individual petition, whereby a victim of abuse could, upon exhausting all domestic remedies, pursue a complaint before the European Commission of Human Rights and ultimately, if found admissible, before the European Court on Human Rights.

In some States the Convention has been incorporated into municipal law and is enforceable before the domestic courts of those States; in others equivalent protection is afforded by a domestic Bill of Rights. In the United Kingdom the Convention was not initially incorporated into domestic law and thus could not be directly enforced before domestic courts. The success of the Convention in protecting human rights is very much dependent upon the goodwill of the signatory State in complying with its provisions initially, or in complying with the decisions of the Committee of Ministers or Court if it has acted in contravention of the Convention. If a government ignores these decisions there is no sanction which can be invoked. The only hope is that international diplomatic pressure will encourage compliance. The United Kingdom has been found to be in breach of the Convention on many occasions but has generally complied with decisions against it by taking the necessary steps to amend domestic law to comply with the Convention. This may, however, take time, as the Government's response is rarely immediate and the legislative process is slow. In the calendar year 2016, the European Court of Human Rights found the United Kingdom to have violated the Convention in 7 cases out of 17 judgments decided and 373 applications alleging breaches of the Convention by the United Kingdom were allocated to a judicial formation, 360 were declared inadmissible or struck off, 51 were referred to the Government and 8 declared admissible (see European Court of Human Rights, *Analysis of Statistics 2016*).

Protocol No. 11 to the Convention for the Protection of Human Rights and Fundamental Freedoms, which entered into force on 1 November 1998, restructured the control machinery under the Convention. The pressure on the Commission and Court had increased greatly with the increase in the number of signatories to the Convention and the rising number of applications brought by individuals alleging a breach of the Convention. This led to a huge backlog of cases. The role of the European Commission in determining the admissibility of applications has ceased. In place of the previous procedure, all alleged violations of the rights of persons are referred directly to the new permanent Court. The number of judges in the Court is equivalent to the number of signatory States, which currently stands at 47. In the majority of cases, the Court will sit in Chambers of seven judges, but on occasions a Grand Chamber of 17 may be convened. The Court deals with individual and inter-State petitions. Initially a committee of three judges will determine admissibility, and by unanimous vote may declare manifestly ill-founded cases inadmissible. If the Court declares an application admissible, it will (in a Chamber of seven) pursue the examination of the case, together with the parties' representatives, and if necessary will undertake an investigation. The Court will also place itself at the disposal of the parties to seek to secure a friendly settlement on the basis of respect for human rights. (Where a case pending before a Chamber raises a serious question affecting the interpretation of the Convention or the protocols thereto, or where the resolution of a question before the Chamber might have a result inconsistent with a judgment previously delivered by the Court, the Chamber may, at any time before it has rendered its judgment, relinquish jurisdiction in favour of the Grand Chamber, unless one of the parties to the case objects.) If no friendly settlement has been arrived at the Court will deliver its judgment. Within a period of three months from the date of the judgment of the Chamber, any party to the case may, in exceptional cases (serious questions affecting the interpretation or application of the Convention or the protocols thereto, or serious issues of general importance), request that the case be referred to the Grand Chamber. If the request is accepted, the resulting judgment of the Grand Chamber will be final. Otherwise, judgments of Chambers will become final when the parties declare that they will not request that the case be referred to the Grand Chamber, or have made no request for reference three months after the date of the judgment; or, if such a request is made, when the panel of the Grand Chamber rejects the request to refer.

The changes brought about by the 11th Protocol have not been able to cope with the exponential increase in individual applications to the Court. Further work on reform on the control system culminated in the adoption of a 14th Protocol which entered into force on 1 June 2010. The new protocol seeks to manage the volume of cases by reinforcing the mechanisms which can filter out unmeritorious applications, applying new admissibility criteria in cases where the applicant has not suffered significant disadvantage, and dealing with repetitive cases. A single judge is now empowered to declare inadmissible or strike out an application, and it is now possible to declare inadmissible applications where the applicant has not suffered a significant disadvantage and which, in terms of respect for human rights, did not otherwise require an examination on the merits by the Court. This is subject to an explicit condition to ensure that it does not lead to rejection of cases which have not been duly considered by a domestic tribunal. The competence of committees of three judges is now extended to cover repetitive cases so they could rule, in a simplified procedure, not only on the admissibility but also on the merits of an application, if the underlying question in the case is already the subject of well-established case law of the Court.

European Convention for the Protection of Human Rights and Fundamental Freedoms

Article 1

The High Contracting Parties shall secure to everyone within their jurisdiction the rights and freedoms defined in section 1 of this Convention.

SECTION I

Article 2

1. Everyone's right to life shall be protected by law. No one shall be deprived of his life intentionally save in the execution of a sentence of a court following his conviction of a crime for which this penalty is provided by law.

2. Deprivation of life shall not be regarded as inflicted in contravention of this Article when it results from the use of force which is no more than absolutely necessary:

    (a) in defence of any person from unlawful violence;
    (b) in order to effect a lawful arrest or to prevent the escape of a person lawfully detained;
    (c) in action lawfully taken for the purpose of quelling a riot or insurrection.

Article 3

No one shall be subjected to torture or to inhuman or degrading treatment or punishment.

Article 4

1. No one shall be held in slavery or servitude.
2. No one shall be required to perform forced or compulsory labour.
3. For the purpose of this Article the term 'forced or compulsory labour' shall not include:

    (a) any work required to be done in the ordinary course of detention imposed according to the provisions of Article 5 of this Convention or during conditional release from such detention;
    (b) any service of a military character or, in case of conscientious objectors in countries where they are recognized, service exacted instead of compulsory military service;
    (c) any service exacted in case of an emergency or calamity threatening the life or well-being of the community;
    (d) any work or service which forms part of normal civic obligations.

Article 5

1. Everyone has the right to liberty and security of person. No one shall be deprived of his liberty save in the following cases and in accordance with a procedure prescribed by law;

    (a) the lawful detention of a person after conviction by a competent court;

    (b) the lawful arrest or detention of a person for non-compliance with the lawful order of a court or in order to secure the fulfilment of any obligation prescribed by law;

    (c) the lawful arrest or detention of a person effected for the purpose of bringing him before the competent legal authority on reasonable suspicion of having committed an offence or when it is reasonably considered necessary to prevent his committing an offence or fleeing after having done so;

    (d) the detention of a minor by lawful order for the purpose of educational supervision or his lawful detention for the purpose of bringing him before the competent legal authority;

    (e) the lawful detention of persons for the prevention of the spreading of infectious diseases, of persons of unsound mind, alcoholics or drug addicts, or vagrants;

    (f) the lawful arrest or detention of a person to prevent his effecting an unauthorized entry into the country or of a person against whom action is being taken with a view to deportation or extradition.

2. Everyone who is arrested shall be informed promptly, in a language which he understands, of the reasons for his arrest and of any charge against him.

3. Everyone arrested or detained in accordance with the provisions of paragraph 1 (c) of this Article shall be brought promptly before a judge or other officer authorized by law to exercise judicial power and shall be entitled to trial within a reasonable time or to release pending trial. Release may be conditioned by guarantees to appear for trial.

4. Everyone who is deprived of his liberty by arrest or detention shall be entitled to take proceedings by which the lawfulness of his detention shall be decided speedily by a court and his release ordered if the detention is not lawful.

5. Everyone who has been the victim of arrest or detention in contravention of the provisions of this Article shall have an enforceable right to compensation.

Article 6

1. In the determination of his civil rights and obligations or of any criminal charge against him, everyone is entitled to a fair and public hearing within a reasonable time by an independent and impartial tribunal established by law. Judgment shall be pronounced publicly but the press and public may be excluded from all or part of the trial in the interest of morals, public order or national security in a democratic society, where the interest of juveniles or the protection of the private life of the parties so require, or to the extent strictly necessary in the opinion of the court in special circumstances where publicity would prejudice the interests of justice.

2. Everyone charged with a criminal offence shall be presumed innocent until proved guilty according to law.

3. Everyone charged with a criminal offence has the following minimum rights:

    (a) to be informed promptly, in a language which he understands and in detail, of the nature and cause of the accusation against him;

    (b) to have adequate time and facilities for the preparation of his defence;

    (c) to defend himself in person or through legal assistance of his own choosing or, if he has not sufficient means to pay for legal assistance, to be given it free when the interests of justice so require;

    (d) to examine or have examined witnesses against him and to obtain the attendance and examination of witnesses on his behalf under the same conditions as witnesses against him;

    (e) to have the free assistance of an interpreter if he cannot understand or speak the language used in court.

Article 7

1. No one shall be held guilty of any criminal offence on account of any act or omission which did not constitute a criminal offence under national or international law at the time when it was committed. Nor shall a heavier penalty be imposed than the one that was applicable at the time the criminal offence was committed.

2. This Article shall not prejudice the trial and punishment of any person for any act or omission which, at the time when it was committed, was criminal according to the general principles of law recognized by civilized nations.

Article 8

1. Everyone has the right to respect for his private and family life, his home and his correspondence.

2. There shall be no interference by a public authority with the exercise of this right except such as is in accordance with the law and is necessary in a democratic society in the interests of national security, public safety or the economic well-being of the country, for the prevention of disorder or crime, for the protection of health or morals, or for the protection of the rights and freedoms of others.

Article 9

1. Everyone has the right to freedom of thought, conscience and religion; this right includes freedom to change his religion or belief, and freedom, either alone or in community with others and in public or private, to manifest his religion or belief, in worship, teaching, practice and observance.

2. Freedom to manifest one's religion or beliefs shall be subject only to such limitations as are prescribed by law and are necessary in a democratic society in the interests of public safety, for the protection of public order, health or morals, or for the protection of the rights and freedoms of others.

Article 10

1. Everyone has the right to freedom of expression. This right shall include freedom to hold opinions and to receive and impart information and ideas without interference by public authority and regardless of frontiers. This Article shall not prevent States from requiring the licensing of broadcasting, television or cinema enterprises.

2. The exercise of these freedoms, since it carries with it duties and responsibilities, may be subject to such formalities, conditions, restrictions or penalties as are prescribed by law and are necessary in a democratic society in the interests of national security, territorial integrity or public safety, for the prevention of disorder or crime, for the protection of health or morals, for the protection of the reputation or rights of others, for preventing the disclosure of information received in confidence, or for maintaining the authority and impartiality of the judiciary.

Article 11

1. Everyone has the right to freedom of peaceful assembly and to freedom of association with others, including the right to form and to join trade unions for the protection of his interests.

2. No restrictions shall be placed on the exercise of these rights other than such as are prescribed by law and are necessary in a democratic society in the interests of national security or public safety, for the prevention of disorder or crime, for the protection of health or morals or for the protection of the rights and freedoms of others. This Article shall not prevent the imposition of lawful restrictions on the exercise of these rights by members of the armed forces, of the police or of the administration of the State.

Article 12

Men and women of marriageable age have the right to marry and to found a family, according to the national laws governing the exercise of this right.

Article 13

Everyone whose rights and freedoms as set forth in this Convention are violated shall have an effective remedy before a national authority notwithstanding that the violation has been committed by persons acting in an official capacity.

Article 14

The enjoyment of the rights and freedoms set forth in this Convention shall be secured without discrimination on any ground such as sex, race, colour, language, religion, political or other opinion, national or social origin, association with a national minority, property, birth or other status.

Article 15

1. In time of war or other public emergency threatening the life of the nation any High Contracting Party may take measures derogating from its obligations under this Convention to the extent strictly required by the exigencies of the situation, provided that such measures are not inconsistent with its other obligations under international law.
2. No derogation from Article 2, except in respect of deaths resulting from lawful acts of war, or from Articles 3, 4 (paragraph 1) and 7 shall be made under this provision.
3. Any High Contracting Party availing itself of this right of derogation shall keep the Secretary-General of the Council of Europe fully informed of the measures which it has taken and the reasons therefore. It shall also inform the Secretary-General of the Council of Europe when such measures have ceased to operate and the provisions of the Convention are again being fully executed.

Article 16

Nothing in Articles 10, 11, and 14 shall be regarded as preventing the High Contracting Parties from imposing restrictions on the political activity of aliens.

Article 17

Nothing in this Convention may be interpreted as implying for any State, group or person any right to engage in any activity or perform any act aimed at the destruction of any of the rights and freedoms set forth herein or at their limitation to a greater extent than is provided for in the Convention.

Article 18

The restrictions permitted under this Convention to the said rights and freedoms shall not be applied for any purpose other than those for which they have been prescribed.

PROTOCOL 1—ENFORCEMENT OF CERTAIN RIGHTS AND FREEDOMS NOT INCLUDED IN SECTION I OF THE CONVENTION

Article 1

Every natural or legal person is entitled to the peaceful enjoyment of his possessions. No one shall be deprived of his possessions except in the public interest and subject to the conditions provided for by law and by the general principles of international law.

The preceding provisions shall not, however, in any way impair the right of a State to enforce such laws as it deems necessary to control the use of property in accordance with the general interest or to secure the payment of taxes or other contributions or penalties.

Article 2

No person shall be denied the right to education. In the exercise of any functions which it assumes in relation to education and to teaching, the State shall respect the right of parents to ensure such education and teaching in conformity with their own religious and philosophical convictions.

Article 3

The High Contracting Parties undertake to hold free elections at reasonable intervals by secret ballot, under conditions which will ensure the free expression of the opinion of the people in the choice of the legislature.

PROTOCOL 4—PROTECTING CERTAIN ADDITIONAL RIGHTS

Article 1

No one shall be deprived of his liberty merely on the ground of inability to fulfil a contractual obligation.

Article 2

1. Everyone lawfully within the territory of a State shall, within that territory, have the right to liberty of movement and freedom to choose his residence.

2. Everyone shall be free to leave any country, including his own.

3. No restrictions shall be placed on the exercise of these rights other than such as are in accordance with law and are necessary in a democratic society in the interests of national security or public safety, for the maintenance of 'order public', for the prevention of crime or for the protection of the rights and freedoms of others.

4. The rights set forth in paragraph 1 may also be subject, in particular areas, to restrictions imposed in accordance with law and justified by the public interest in a democratic society.

Article 3

1. No one shall be expelled, by means either of an individual or of a collective measure, from the territory of the State of which he is a national.

2. No one shall be deprived of the right to enter the territory of the State of which he is a national.

Article 4

Collective expulsion of aliens is prohibited.

PROTOCOL 6—CONCERNING THE ABOLITION OF THE DEATH PENALTY

Article 1

The death penalty shall be abolished. No one shall be condemned to such penalty or executed.

Article 2

A State may make provision in its law for the death penalty in respect of acts committed in time of war or of imminent threat of war; such penalty shall be applied only in the instances laid down in the law and in accordance with its provisions. The State shall communicate to the Secretary General of the Council of Europe the relevant provisions of that law.

Article 3

No derogation from the provisions of this Protocol shall be made under Article 15 of the Convention.

Article 4

No reservation may be made under Article 64 of the Convention in respect of the provisions of this Protocol.

PROTOCOL 7

Article 1

1. An alien lawfully resident in the territory of a State shall not be expelled therefrom except in pursuance of a decision reached in accordance with law and shall be allowed;

    (a) to submit reasons against his expulsion;
    (b) to have his case reviewed; and
    (c) to be represented for these purposes before the competent authority or a person or persons designated by that authority.

2. An alien may be expelled before the exercise of his rights under paragraph 1(a), (b) and (c) of this article, when such expulsion is necessary in the interests of public order or is grounded on reasons of national security.

Article 2

1. Everyone convicted of a criminal offence by a tribunal shall have the right to have his conviction or sentence reviewed by a higher tribunal. The exercise of this right, including the grounds on which it may be exercised, shall be governed by law.

2. This right may be subject to exceptions in regard to offences of a minor character, as prescribed by law, or in cases in which the person concerned was tried in the first instance by the highest tribunal or was convicted following an appeal against acquittal.

Article 3

When a person has by a final decision been convicted of a criminal offence and when subsequently his conviction has been reversed, or he has been pardoned, on the ground that a new or newly discovered fact shows conclusively that there has been a miscarriage of justice, the person who has suffered punishment as a result of such conviction shall be compensated according to the law or the practice of the State concerned, unless it is proved that the non-disclosure of the unknown fact in time is wholly or partly attributable to him.

Article 4

1. No one shall be liable to be tried or punished again in criminal proceedings under the jurisdiction of the same State for an offence for which he has already been finally acquitted or convicted in accordance with the law and penal procedure of that State.

2. The provisions of the preceding paragraph shall not prevent the reopening of the case in accordance with the law and penal procedure of the State concerned, if there is evidence of new or newly discovered facts, or if there has been a fundamental defect in the previous proceedings, which could affect the outcome of the case.

3. No derogation from this article shall be made under Article 15 of the Convention.

Article 5

Spouses shall enjoy equality of rights and responsibilities of a private law character between them, and in their relations with their children, as to marriage, during marriage and in the event of its dissolution. This article shall not prevent States from taking such measures as are necessary in the interests of the children.

NOTE: The United Kingdom has made the following reservation to Article 2 to Protocol 1:

... in view of certain provisions of the Education Acts in force in the United Kingdom, the principle affirmed in the second sentence of Article 2 is accepted by the United Kingdom only so far as it is compatible with the provision of efficient instruction and training, and the avoidance of unreasonable expenditure.

The United Kingdom has not ratified Protocol 4 or 7. Articles 1 and 2 of Protocol 6 which abolish the death penalty in most circumstances were initially in the list of 'convention rights' protected by the Human Rights Act, the Protocol being signed and ratified in 1999. Protocol 13 which abolished the death penalty in all circumstances has been ratified and replaced Articles 1 and 2 of Protocol 6 in the Schedule to the Human Rights Act.

It should be noted that the rights are guaranteed in Art. 6 (regarding the public nature of criminal trials) but that the rights guaranteed in Arts 8–12 are subject to a broad range of exceptions. In interpreting the Convention the Court adopts a teleological approach whereby it seeks to give effect to its 'object and purpose'.

In *Soering* v *United Kingdom* Series A No. 161, (1989) 11 EHRR 439, the Court stated:

87. In interpreting the Convention regard must be had to its special character as a treaty for the collective enforcement of human rights and fundamental freedoms (see the *Ireland* v *The United Kingdom* judgment of 18 January 1978, Series A no. 25, p. 90, § 239). Thus, the object and purpose of the Convention as an instrument for the protection of individual human beings require that its provisions be interpreted and applied so as to make its safeguards practical and effective (see, *inter alia*, the *Artico* judgment of 13 May 1980, Series A no. 37, p. 16, § 33). In addition, any interpretation of the rights and freedoms guaranteed has to be consistent with 'the general spirit of the Convention, an instrument designed to maintain and promote the ideals and values of a democratic society' (see the *Kjeldsen, Busk Madsen and Pedersen* judgment of 7 December 1976, Series A No. 23, p. 27, § 53).

This also means that the interpretation of the Convention will develop over time just as conceptions of the 'ideals and values of a democratic society' will develop. This was emphasized by the Court in *Tyrer* v *UK*, Series A No. 26, (1978) 2 EHRR 1, where the practice of corporal punishment in the Isle of Man was challenged as amounting to degrading treatment. The Court stated at para. 31:

The Court must ... recall that the Convention is a living instrument which, as the Commission rightly stressed, must be interpreted in the light of present-day conditions. In the case now before it the Court cannot but be influenced by the developments and commonly accepted standards in the penal policy of Member States of the Council of Europe in this field.

When applying the Convention the Court also recognizes the open-textured nature of the language used, Interpretation will always be required. In *Soering* at para. 89, the Court stated that 'inherent in the whole of the Convention is a search for a fair balance between the demands of the general interest of the community and the requirements of the protection of the individual's fundamental rights'. A principle which the Court has developed which flows from this is that of proportionality. This is particularly relevant where the Convention permits restrictions upon a right as in Articles 8–11. Any restrictions which a State places on these rights 'must be proportionate to the legitimate aim pursued' (see *Handyside* v *UK*, Series A, No. 24 (1976) 1 EHRR 737 para. 49).

When balancing individual claims against the needs of the community as a whole, a crucial qualification is that any limitation be 'necessary in a democratic society'. In *United Communist Party of Turkey* v *Turkey* (1998) 26 EHRR 121, the European Court of Human Rights emphasized (at p. 148) that democracy is the 'only political model contemplated by the Convention and, accordingly, the only one compatible with it'. The Court stated that freedom of expression and free elections are essential characteristics of a democracy and that political parties play an essential role in ensuring pluralism and the proper functioning of democracy. In *The Socialist Party* v *Turkey* (1998) 27 EHRR 51, the European Court of Human Rights stated (at pp. 84–5):

[O]ne of the principal characteristics of democracy is the possibility it offers of resolving a country's problems through dialogue, without recourse to violence, even when they are irksome. Democracy thrives on freedom of expression. ... It is the essence of democracy to allow diverse political programmes to be proposed and debated, even those that call into question the way a State is currently organised, provided that they do not harm democracy itself.

Diverse political parties, mass media which may freely criticize the *status quo*, and channels for public debate and participation are thus crucial to the existence of a democracy and at the centre of the values which the Convention is seeking to protect.

The Convention now applies in 47 countries, but these are far from homogeneous. The Court therefore tends to adopt an interpretative approach which recognizes differences and makes allowances for variations between States by means of the margin of appreciation doctrine. Harris, O'Boyle, and Warbrick, *Law of the European Convention on Human Rights* (1995) state (at p. 12):

> In general terms, it means that the state is allowed a certain measure of discretion, subject to European supervision, when it takes legislative, administrative or judicial action in the area of a Convention right.

This doctrine was explained by the Court in the *Handyside* case which arose from a prosecution of the publisher of *The Little Red Schoolbook* under the Obscene Publications Act 1959 for possessing obscene books for publication for gain. The applicant complained that his conviction and the forfeiture and destruction of the books amounted to a breach of his Art. 10 rights. The volume had also been published in eight other European countries without giving rise to any prosecutions. It was also published in Northern Ireland and Scotland, where no proceedings against the publisher were taken as the 1959 Act did not apply to those countries. Despite this the Court found that Art. 10 had not been breached by the UK as the limitation on freedom of expression could be justified as being necessary for the 'protection of morals'. The Court stated:

> 48. The Court points out that the machinery of protection established by the Convention is subsidiary to the national systems safeguarding human rights. The Convention leaves to each Contracting State, in the first place, the task of securing the rights and freedoms it enshrines. The institutions created by it make their own contribution to this task but they become involved only through contentious proceedings and once all domestic remedies have been exhausted (Art. 26).
>
> These observations apply, notably, to Article 10(2). In particular, it is not possible to find in the domestic law of the various Contracting States a uniform European conception of morals. The view taken by their respective laws of the requirements of morals varies from time to time and from place to place, especially in our era which is characterised by a rapid and far-reaching evolution of opinions on the subject. By reason of their direct and continuous contact with the vital forces of their countries, State authorities are in principle in a better position than the international judge to give an opinion on the exact content of these requirements as well as on the 'necessity' of a 'restriction' or 'penalty' intended to meet them. The Court notes at this juncture that, whilst the adjective 'necessary', within the meaning of Article 10(2), is not synonymous with 'indispensable', neither has it the flexibility of such expressions as 'admissible', 'ordinary', 'useful', 'reasonable' or 'desirable'. Nevertheless, it is for the national authorities to make the initial assessment of the reality of the pressing social need implied by the notion of 'necessity' in this context.
>
> Consequently, Article 10(2) leaves to the Contracting States a margin of appreciation. This margin is given both to the domestic legislator ('prescribed by law') and to the bodies, judicial amongst others, that are called upon to interpret and apply the laws in force.
>
> 49. Nevertheless, Article 10(2) does not give the Contracting States an unlimited power of appreciation. The Court, which, with the Commission, is responsible for ensuring the observance of those States' engagements, is empowered to give the final ruling on whether a 'restriction' or 'penalty' is reconcilable with freedom of expression as protected by Article 10. The domestic margin of appreciation thus goes hand in hand with a European supervision. Such supervision concerns both the aim of the measure challenged and its 'necessity'; it covers not only the basic legislation but also the decision applying it, even one given by an independent court. In this respect, the Court refers to Article 50 of the Convention ('decision or … measure taken by a legal authority or any other authority') as well as to its own case-law.
>
> The Court's supervisory functions oblige it to pay the utmost attention to the principles characterising a 'democratic society'. Freedom of expression constitutes one of the essential foundations of such a society, one of the basic conditions for its progress and for the development of every man. Subject to

Article 10(2), it is applicable not only to 'information' or 'ideas' that are favourably received or regarded as inoffensive or as a matter of indifference, but also to those that offend, shock or disturb the State or any sector of the population. Such are the demands of that pluralism, tolerance and broadmindedness without which there is no 'democratic society'. This means, amongst other things, that every 'formality', 'condition', 'restriction' or 'penalty' imposed in this sphere must be proportionate to the legitimate aim pursued.

From another standpoint, whoever exercises his freedom of expression undertakes 'duties' and 'responsibilities' the scope of which depends on his situation and the technical means he uses. The Court cannot overlook such a person's 'duties' and 'responsibilities' when it enquires, as in this case; whether 'restrictions' or 'penalties' were conducive to the 'protection of morals' which made them 'necessary' in a 'democratic society'.

This doctrine of 'margin of appreciation' will be applied differentially depending upon the context, but generally it derives from the fact that the Court is exercising a supervisory jurisdiction and that the responsibility for ensuring that human rights are protected and respected within States lies with the contracting parties themselves. This can mean that widely varying practices amongst the contracting parties are tolerated depending on the degree of laxity the Court displays; this can vary with the context, namely the Article under consideration.

SECTION 3: INCORPORATION OF THE EUROPEAN CONVENTION ON HUMAN RIGHTS INTO UK LAW

A: The Human Rights Act 1998

In October 1997 the Labour Government introduced the Human Rights Bill into Parliament and at the same time published the White Paper, *Rights Brought Home: The Human Rights Bill*, which explained the design of the Bill and the subsequent Act.

Rights Brought Home: The Human Rights Bill
Cm 3782, 1997, cll.1.14–1.16, 2.1–3.12

CHAPTER 1—THE CASE FOR CHANGE

...

The case for incorporation

1.14 The effect of non-incorporation on the British people is a very practical one. The rights, originally developed with major help from the United Kingdom Government, are no longer actually seen as British rights. And enforcing them takes too long and costs too much. It takes on average five years to get an action into the European Court of Human Rights once all domestic remedies have been exhausted; and it costs an average of £30,000. Bringing these rights home will mean that the British people will be able to argue for their rights in the British courts—without this inordinate delay and cost. It will also mean that the rights will be brought much more fully into the jurisprudence of the courts throughout the United Kingdom, and their interpretation will thus be far more subtly and powerfully woven into our law. And there will be another distinct benefit. British judges will be enabled to make a distinctively British contribution to the development of the jurisprudence of human rights in Europe.

1.15 Moreover, in the Government's view, the approach which the United Kingdom has so far adopted towards the Convention does not sufficiently reflect its importance and has not stood the test of time.

1.16 … It is plainly unsatisfactory that someone should be the victim of a breach of the Convention standards by the State yet cannot bring any case at all in the British courts, simply because British law does not recognise the right in the same terms as one contained in the Convention.

…

CHAPTER 2—THE GOVERNMENT'S PROPOSALS FOR ENFORCING THE CONVENTION RIGHTS

2.1 The essential feature of the Human Rights Bill is that the United Kingdom will not be bound to give effect to the Convention rights merely as a matter of international law, but will also give them further effect directly in our domestic law. But there is more than one way of achieving this. This Chapter explains the choices which the Government has made for the Bill.

A new requirement on public authorities

2.2 Although the United Kingdom has an international obligation to comply with the Convention, there at present is no requirement in our domestic law on central and local government, or others exercising similar executive powers, to exercise those powers in a way which is compatible with the Convention. This Bill will change that by making it unlawful for public authorities to act in a way which is incompatible with the Convention rights. The definition of what constitutes a public authority is in wide terms. Examples of persons or organisations whose acts or omissions it is intended should be able to be challenged include central government (including executive agencies); local government; the police; immigration officers; prisons; courts and tribunals themselves; and, to the extent that they are exercising public functions, companies responsible for areas of activity which were previously within the public sector, such as the privatised utilities. The actions of Parliament, however, are excluded.

2.3 A person who is aggrieved by an act or omission on the part of a public authority which is incompatible with the Convention rights will be able to challenge the act or omission in the courts. The effects will be wide-ranging. They will extend both to legal actions which a public authority pursues against individuals (for example, where a criminal prosecution is brought or where an administrative decision is being enforced through legal proceedings) and to cases which individuals pursue against a public authority (for example, for judicial review of an executive decision). Convention points will normally be taken in the context of proceedings instituted against individuals or already open to them, but, if none is available, it will be possible for people to bring cases on Convention grounds alone. Individuals or organisations seeking judicial review of decisions by public authorities on Convention grounds will need to show that they have been directly affected, as they must if they take a case to Strasbourg.

2.4 It is our intention that people or organisations should be able to argue that their Convention rights have been infringed by a public authority in our courts at any level. This will enable the Convention rights to be applied from the outset against the facts and background of a particular case, and the people concerned to obtain their remedy at the earliest possible moment. We think this is preferable to allowing cases to run their ordinary course but then referring them to some kind of separate constitutional court which, like the European Court of Human Rights, would simply review cases which had already passed through the regular legal machinery. In considering Convention points, our courts will be required to take account of relevant decisions of the European Commission and Court of Human Rights (although these will not be binding).

2.5 The Convention is often described as a 'living instrument' because it is interpreted by the European Court in the light of present day conditions and therefore reflects changing social attitudes and the changes in the circumstances of society. In future our judges will be able to contribute to this dynamic and evolving interpretation of the Convention. In particular, our courts will be required to balance the protection of individuals' fundamental rights against the demands of the general interest of the community, particularly in relation to Articles 8–11 where a State may restrict the protected right to the extent that this is 'necessary in a democratic society'.

Remedies for a failure to comply with the Convention

2.6 A public authority which is found to have acted unlawfully by failing to comply with the Convention will not be exposed to criminal penalties. But the court or tribunal will be able to grant the injured person any remedy which is within its normal powers to grant and which it considers appropriate and just in the circumstances. What remedy is appropriate will of course depend both on the facts of the case and on a proper balance between the rights of the individual and the public interest. In some cases, the right course may be for the decision of the public authority in the particular case to be quashed. In other cases, the only appropriate remedy may be an award of damages. The Bill provides that, in considering an award of damages on Convention grounds, the courts are to take into account the principles applied by the European Court of Human Rights in awarding compensation, so that people will be able to receive compensation from a domestic court equivalent to what they would have received in Strasbourg.

Interpretation of legislation

2.7 The Bill provides for legislation—both Acts of Parliament and secondary legislation—to be interpreted so far as possible so as to be compatible with the Convention. This goes far beyond the present rule which enables the courts to take the Convention into account in resolving any ambiguity in a legislative provision. The courts will be required to interpret legislation so as to uphold the Convention rights unless the legislation itself is so clearly incompatible with the Convention that it is impossible to do so.

2.8 This 'rule of construction' is to apply to past as well as to future legislation. To the extent that it affects the meaning of a legislative provision, the courts will not be bound by previous interpretations. They will be able to build a new body of case law, taking into account the Convention rights.

A declaration of incompatibility with the Convention rights

2.9 If the courts decide in any case that it is impossible to interpret an Act of Parliament in a way which is compatible with the Convention, the Bill enables a formal declaration to be made that its provisions are incompatible with the Convention. A declaration of incompatibility will be an important statement to make, and the power to make it will be reserved to the higher courts. They will be able to make a declaration in any proceedings before them, whether the case originated with them (as, in the High Court, on judicial review of an executive act) or in considering an appeal from a lower court or tribunal. The Government will have the right to intervene in any proceedings where such a declaration is a possible outcome. A decision by the High Court or Court of Appeal, determining whether or not such a declaration should be made, will itself be appealable.

Effect of court decisions on legislation

2.10 A declaration that legislation is incompatible with the Convention rights will not of itself have the effect of changing the law, which will continue to apply. But it will almost certainly prompt the Government and Parliament to change the law.

2.11 The Government has considered very carefully whether it would be right for the Bill to go further, and give to courts in the United Kingdom the power to set aside an Act of Parliament which they believe is incompatible with the Convention rights. In considering this question, we have looked at a number of models. The Canadian Charter of Rights and Freedoms 1982 enables the courts to strike down any legislation which is inconsistent with the Charter, unless the legislation contains an explicit statement that it is to apply 'notwithstanding' the provisions of the Charter. But legislation which has been struck down may be re-enacted with a 'notwithstanding' clause. In New Zealand, on the other hand, although there was an earlier proposal for legislation on lines similar to the Canadian Charter, the human rights legislation which was eventually enacted after wide consultation took a different form. The New Zealand Bill of Rights Act 1990 is an 'interpretative' statute which requires past and future legislation to be interpreted consistently with the rights contained in the Act as far as possible but provides that legislation stands if that is impossible. In Hong Kong, a middle course was adopted. The

Hong Kong Bill of Rights Ordinance 1991 distinguishes between legislation enacted before and after the Ordinance took effect: previous legislation is subordinated to the provisions of the Ordinance, but subsequent legislation takes precedence over it.

2.12 The Government has also considered the European Communities Act 1972 which provides for European law, in cases where that law has 'direct effect', to take precedence over domestic law. There is, however, an essential difference between European Community law and the European Convention on Human Rights, because it is a requirement of membership of the European Union that member States give priority to directly effective EC law in their own legal systems. There is no such requirement in the Convention.

2.13 The Government has reached the conclusion that courts should not have the power to set aside primary legislation, past or future, on the ground of incompatibility with the Convention. This conclusion arises from the importance which the Government attaches to Parliamentary sovereignty. In this context, Parliamentary sovereignty means that Parliament is competent to make any law on any matter of its choosing and no court may question the validity of any Act that it passes. In enacting legislation, Parliament is making decisions about important matters of public policy. The authority to make those decisions derives from a democratic mandate. Members of Parliament in the House of Commons possess such a mandate because they are elected, accountable and representative. To make provision in the Bill for the courts to set aside Acts of Parliament would confer on the judiciary a general power over the decisions of Parliament which under our present constitutional arrangements they do not possess, and would be likely on occasions to draw the judiciary into serious conflict with Parliament. There is no evidence to suggest that they desire this power, nor that the public wish them to have it. Certainly, this Government has no mandate for any such change.

2.14 It has been suggested that the courts should be able to uphold the rights in the Human Rights Bill in preference to any provisions of earlier legislation which are incompatible with those rights. This is on the basis that a later Act of Parliament takes precedence over an earlier Act if there is a conflict. But the Human Rights Bill is intended to provide a new basis for judicial interpretation of all legislation, not a basis for striking down any part of it.

2.15 The courts will, however, be able to strike down or set aside secondary legislation which is incompatible with the Convention, unless the terms of the parent statute make this impossible. The courts can already strike down or set aside secondary legislation when they consider it to be outside the powers conferred by the statute under which it is made, and it is right that they should be able to do so when it is incompatible with the Convention rights and could have been framed differently.

Entrenchment

2.16 On one view, human rights legislation is so important that it should be given added protection from subsequent amendment or repeal. The Constitution of the United States of America, for example, guarantees rights which can be amended or repealed only by securing qualified majorities in both the House of Representatives and the Senate, and among the States themselves. But an arrangement of this kind could not be reconciled with our own constitutional traditions, which allow any Act of Parliament to be amended or repealed by a subsequent Act of Parliament. We do not believe that it is necessary or would be desirable to attempt to devise such a special arrangement for this Bill.

Amending legislation

2.17 Although the Bill does not allow the courts to set aside Acts of Parliament, it will nevertheless have a profound impact on the way that legislation is interpreted and applied, and it will have the effect of putting the issues squarely to the Government and Parliament for further consideration. It is important to ensure that the Government and Parliament, for their part, can respond quickly. In the normal way, primary legislation can be amended only by further primary legislation, and this can take a long time. Given the volume of Government business, an early opportunity to legislate may not arise; and the process of legislating is itself protracted. Emergency legislation can be enacted very quickly indeed, but it is introduced only in the most exceptional circumstances.

2.18 The Bill provides for a fast-track procedure for changing legislation in response either to a declaration of incompatibility by our own higher courts or to a finding of a violation of the Convention in Strasbourg. The appropriate Government Minister will be able to amend the legislation by Order so as to make it compatible with the Convention. The Order will be subject to approval by both Houses of Parliament before taking effect, except where the need to amend the legislation is particularly urgent, when the Order will take effect immediately but will expire after a short period if not approved by Parliament.

2.19 There are already precedents for using secondary legislation to amend primary legislation in some circumstances, and we think the use of such a procedure is acceptable in this context and would be welcome as a means of improving the observance of human rights. Plainly the Minister would have to exercise this power only in relation to the provisions which contravene the Convention, together with any necessary consequential amendments. In other words, Ministers would not have carte blanche to amend unrelated parts of the Act in which the breach is discovered.

Scotland

2.20 In Scotland, the position with regard to Acts of the Westminster Parliament will be the same as in England and Wales. All courts will be required to interpret the legislation in a way which is compatible with the Convention so far as possible. If a provision is found to be incompatible with the Convention, the Court of Session or the High Court will be able to make a declarator to that effect, but this will not affect the validity or continuing operation of the provision.

2.21 The position will be different, however, in relation to Acts of the Scottish Parliament when it is established. The Government has decided that the Scottish Parliament will have no power to legislate in a way which is incompatible with the Convention; and similarly that the Scottish Executive will have no power to make subordinate legislation or to take executive action which is incompatible with the Convention. It will accordingly be possible to challenge such legislation and actions in the Scottish courts on the ground that the Scottish Parliament or Executive has incorrectly applied its powers. If the challenge is successful then the legislation or action would be held to be unlawful. As with other issues concerning the powers of the Scottish Parliament, there will be a procedure for inferior courts to refer such issues to the superior Scottish courts; and those courts in turn will be able to refer the matter to the Judicial Committee of the Privy Council. If such issues are decided by the superior Scottish courts, an appeal from their decision will be to the Judicial Committee. These arrangements are in line with the Government's general approach to devolution.

Wales

2.22 Similarly, the Welsh Assembly will not have power to make subordinate legislation or take executive action which is incompatible with the Convention. It will be possible to challenge such legislation and action in the courts, and for them to be quashed, on the ground that the Assembly has exceeded its powers.

Northern Ireland

2.23 Acts of the Westminster Parliament will be treated in the same way in Northern Ireland as in the rest of the United Kingdom. But Orders in Council and other related legislation will be treated as subordinate legislation. In other words, they will be struck down by the courts if they are incompatible with the Convention. Most such legislation is a temporary means of enacting legislation which would otherwise be done by measures of a devolved Northern Ireland legislature.

CHAPTER 3—IMPROVING COMPLIANCE WITH THE CONVENTION RIGHTS

3.1 The enforcement of Convention rights will be a matter for the courts, whilst the Government and Parliament will have the different but equally important responsibility of revising legislation where necessary. But it is also highly desirable for the Government to ensure as far as possible that legislation which it places before Parliament in the normal way is compatible with the Convention rights, and for Parliament to ensure that the human rights implications of legislation are subject to proper consideration before the legislation is enacted.

Government legislation

3.2 The Human Rights Bill introduces a new procedure to make the human rights implications of proposed Government legislation more transparent. The responsible Minister will be required to provide a statement that in his or her view the proposed Bill is compatible with the Convention. The Government intends to include this statement alongside the Explanatory and Financial Memorandum which accompanies a Bill when it is introduced into each House of Parliament.

3.3 There may be occasions where such a statement cannot be provided, for example because it is essential to legislate on a particular issue but the policy in question requires a risk to be taken in relation to the Convention, or because the arguments in relation to the Convention issues raised are not clear-cut. In such cases, the Minister will indicate that he or she cannot provide a positive statement but that the Government nevertheless wishes Parliament to proceed to consider the Bill. Parliament would expect the Minister to explain his or her reasons during the normal course of the proceedings on the Bill. This will ensure that the human rights implications are debated at the earliest opportunity.

Consideration of draft legislation within Government

3.4 The new requirement to make a statement about the compliance of draft legislation with the Convention will have a significant and beneficial impact on the preparation of draft legislation within Government before its introduction into Parliament. It will ensure that all Ministers, their departments and officials are fully seized of the gravity of the Convention's obligations in respect of human rights. But we also intend to strengthen collective Government procedures so as to ensure that a proper assessment is made of the human rights implications when collective approval is sought for a new policy, as well as when any draft Bill is considered by Ministers. Revised guidance to Departments on these procedures will, like the existing guidance, be publicly available.

3.5 Some central co-ordination will also be extremely desirable in considering the approach to be taken to Convention points in criminal or civil proceedings, or in proceedings for judicial review, to which a Government department is a party. This is likely to require an inter-departmental group of lawyers and administrators meeting on a regular basis to ensure that a consistent approach is taken and to ensure that developments in case law are well understood by all those in Government who are involved in proceedings on Convention points. We do not, however, see any need to make a particular Minister responsible for promoting human rights across Government, or to set up a separate new Unit for this purpose. The responsibility for complying with human rights requirements rests on the Government as a whole.

A Parliamentary Committee on Human Rights

3.6 *Rights Brought Home* suggested that 'Parliament itself should play a leading role in protecting the rights which are at the heart of a parliamentary democracy'. How this is achieved is a matter for Parliament to decide, but in the Government's view the best course would be to establish a new Parliamentary Committee with functions relating to human rights. This would not require legislation or any change in Parliamentary procedure. There could be a Joint Committee of both Houses of Parliament or each House could have its own Committee; or there could be a Committee which met jointly for some purposes and separately for others.

3.7 The new Committee might conduct enquiries on a range of human rights issues relating to the Convention, and produce reports so as to assist the Government and Parliament in deciding what action to take. It might also want to range more widely, and examine issues relating to the other international obligations of the United Kingdom such as proposals to accept new rights under other human rights treaties.

Should there be a Human Rights Commission?

3.8 *Rights Brought Home* canvassed views on the establishment of a Human Rights Commission, and this possibility has received a good deal of attention. No commitment to establish a Commission was, however, made in the Manifesto on which the Government was elected. The Government's priority is implementation of its Manifesto commitment to give further effect to the Convention rights in domestic law so that people can enforce those rights in United Kingdom courts. Establishment of a new Human Rights Commission is not central to that objective and does not need to form part of the current Bill.

3.9 Moreover, the idea of setting up a new human rights body is not universally acclaimed. Some reservations have been expressed, particularly from the point of view of the impact on existing bodies concerned with particular aspects of human rights, such as the Commission for Racial Equality and the Equal Opportunities Commission, whose primary concern is to protect the rights for which they were established. A quinquennial review is currently being conducted of the Equal Opportunities Commission, and the Government has also decided to establish a new Disability Rights Commission.

3.10 The Government's conclusion is that, before a Human Rights Commission could be established by legislation, more consideration needs to be given to how it would work in relation to such bodies, and to the new arrangements to be established for Parliamentary and Government scrutiny of human rights issues. This is necessary not only for the purposes of framing the legislation but also to justify the additional public expenditure needed to establish and run a new Commission. A range of organisational issues need more detailed consideration before the legislative and financial case for a new Commission is made, and there needs to be a greater degree of consensus on an appropriate model among existing human rights bodies.

3.11 However, the Government has not closed its mind to the idea of a new Human Rights Commission at some stage in the future in the light of practical experience of the working of the new legislation. If Parliament establishes a Committee on Human Rights, one of its main tasks might be to conduct an inquiry into whether a Human Rights Commission is needed and how it should operate. The Government would want to give full weight to the Committee's report in considering whether to create a statutory Human Rights Commission in future.

3.12 It has been suggested that a new Commission might be funded from non-Government sources. The Government would not wish to deter a move towards a non-statutory, privately-financed body if its role was limited to functions such as public education and advice to individuals. However, a non-statutory body could not absorb any of the functions of the existing statutory bodies concerned with aspects of human rights.

NOTE: See the Equality Act 2006 which established the Commission for Equality and Human Rights.

■ **QUESTIONS**

1. Does the existence of a democratic mandate entitle Parliament to pass laws which might threaten the very conditions essential to the existence of a democracy and which a Bill of Rights should protect (see cl. 2.13 in the preceding extract on p. 412)? Does the fact that courts were unable to declare statutes unconstitutional necessarily mean that they should not be able to do so in the future? Would giving to judges the power to determine the constitutionality of statutes necessarily make them more political than they currently are?

2. Is the Human Rights Act unnecessarily weakened by preventing it from impliedly repealing pre-existing statutes which conflict with its provisions? Would permitting the doctrine of implied repeal (see cl. 2.14 in the preceding extract on p. 412) to operate have undermined the supremacy of Parliament?

The Human Rights Act 1998

Introduction

1. The Convention and the First Protocol

(1) In this Act, 'the Convention rights' means the rights and fundamental freedoms set out in—

(a) Articles 2 to 12 and 14 of the Convention,
(b) Articles 1 to 3 of the First Protocol, and
(c) Articles 1 and 2 of the Sixth Protocol,

as read with Articles 16 to 18 of the Convention.

(2) Those Articles are to have effect for the purposes of this Act subject to any designated derogation or reservation (as to which see sections 14 and 15).

(3) The Articles are set out in Schedule 1.

(4) The Lord Chancellor may by order make such amendments to this section or Schedule 1 as he considers appropriate to reflect the effect, in relation to the United Kingdom, of a protocol.

(5) In subsection (4) 'protocol' means a protocol to the Convention—

(a) which the United Kingdom has ratified; or
(b) which the United Kingdom has signed with a view to ratification.

(6) No amendment may be made by an order under subsection (4) so as to come into force before the protocol concerned is in force in relation to the United Kingdom.

2. Interpretation of Convention rights

(1) A court or tribunal determining a question which has arisen under this Act in connection with a Convention right must take into account any—

(a) judgment, decision, declaration or advisory opinion of the European Court of Human Rights,
(b) opinion of the Commission given in a report adopted under Article 31 of the Convention,
(c) decision of the Commission in connection with Article 26 or 27(2) of the Convention, or
(d) decision of the Committee of Ministers taken under Article 46 of the Convention,

whenever made or given, so far as, in the opinion of the court or tribunal, it is relevant to the proceedings in which that question has arisen.

(2)–(3) …

Interpretation of legislation

3. Legislation

(1) So far as it is possible to do so, primary legislation and subordinate legislation must be read and given effect in a way which is compatible with the Convention rights.

(2) This section—

(a) applies to primary legislation and subordinate legislation whenever enacted;
(b) does not affect the validity, continuing operation or enforcement of any incompatible primary legislation; and
(c) does not affect the validity, continuing operation or enforcement of any incompatible subordinate legislation if (disregarding any possibility of revocation) primary legislation prevents removal of the incompatibility.

4. Declaration of incompatibility

(1) Subsection (2) applies in any proceedings in which a court determines whether a provision of primary legislation is compatible with a Convention right.

(2) If the court is satisfied that the provision is incompatible with a Convention right, it may make a declaration of that incompatibility.

(3) Subsection (4) applies in any proceedings in which a court determines whether a provision of subordinate legislation, made in the exercise of a power conferred by primary legislation, is compatible with a Convention right.

(4) If the court is satisfied—

(a) that the provision is incompatible with a Convention right, and
(b) that (disregarding any possibility of revocation) the primary legislation concerned prevents removal of the incompatibility,

it may make a declaration of that incompatibility.

(5) In this section 'court' means—

(a) the House of Lords;
(b) the Judicial Committee of the Privy Council;
(c) the Courts-Martial Appeal Court;
(d) in Scotland, the High Court of Justiciary sitting otherwise than as a trial court or the Court of Session;
(e) in England and Wales or Northern Ireland, the High Court or the Court of Appeal.

(6) A declaration under this section ('a declaration of incompatibility')—
(a) does not affect the validity, continuing operation or enforcement of the provision in respect of which it is given; and
(b) is not binding on the parties to the proceedings in which it is made.

5. Right of Crown to intervene

(1) Where a court is considering whether to make a declaration of incompatibility, the Crown is entitled to notice in accordance with rules of court.

(2) In any case to which subsection (1) applies—

(a) a Minister of the Crown (or a person nominated by him);
(b) a member of the Scottish executive;
(c) a Northern Ireland Minister;
(d) a Northern Ireland department, is entitled, on giving notice in accordance with rules of court, to be joined as a party to the proceedings.

(3) Notice under subsection (2) may be made at any time during the proceedings.

(4) A person who has been made a party to criminal proceedings (other than in Scotland) as the result of a notice under subsection (2) may, with leave, appeal to the House of Lords against any declaration of incompatibility made in the proceedings.

(5) …

Public authorities

6. Acts of public authorities

(1) It is unlawful for a public authority to act in a way which is incompatible with a Convention right.

(2) Subsection (1) does not apply to an act if—

(a) as the result of one or more provisions of primary legislation, the authority could not have acted differently; or
(b) in the case of one or more provisions of, or made under, primary legislation which cannot be read or given effect in a way which is compatible with the Convention rights, the authority was acting so as to give effect to or enforce those provisions.

(3) In this section, 'public authority' includes—

(a) a court or tribunal, and
(b) any person certain of whose functions are functions of a public nature, but does not include either House of Parliament or a person exercising functions in connection with proceedings in Parliament.

(4) In subsection (3) 'Parliament' does not include the House of Lords in its judicial capacity.

(5) In relation to a particular act, a person is not a public authority by virtue only of subsection (3)(b) if the nature of the act is private.

(6) 'An act' includes a failure to act but does not include a failure to—

(a) introduce in, or lay before, Parliament a proposal for legislation; or

(b) make any primary legislation or remedial order.

7. Proceedings

(1) A person who claims that a public authority has acted (or proposes to act) in a way which is made unlawful by section 6(1) may—

(a) bring proceedings against the authority under this Act in the appropriate court or tribunal, or

(b) rely on the Convention right or rights concerned in any legal proceedings, but only if he is (or would be) a victim of the unlawful act.

(2) In subsection (1)(a) 'appropriate court or tribunal' means such court or tribunal as may be determined in accordance with rules; and proceedings against an authority includes a counterclaim or similar proceeding.

(3) If the proceedings are brought on an application for judicial review, the applicant is to be taken to have a sufficient interest in relation to the unlawful act only if he is, or would be, a victim of that act.

(4) If the proceedings are made by way of a petition for judicial review in Scotland, the applicant shall be taken to have title and interest to sue in relation to the unlawful act only if he is, or would be, a victim of that act.

(5) Proceedings under subsection (1)(a) must be brought before the end of—

(a) the period of one year beginning with the date on which the act complained of took place; or

(b) such longer period as the court or tribunal considers equitable having regard to all the circumstances,

but that is subject to any rule imposing a stricter time limit in relation to the procedure in question.

(6) In subsection (1)(b) 'legal proceedings' includes—

(a) proceedings brought by or at the instigation of a public authority; and

(b) an appeal against the decision of a court or tribunal.

(7) For the purposes of this section, a person is a victim of an unlawful act only if he would be a victim for the purposes of Article 34 of the Convention if proceedings were brought in the European Court of Human Rights in respect of that act.

(8) Nothing in this Act creates a criminal offence.

(9)–(11) …

8. Judicial remedies

(1) In relation to any act (or proposed act) of a public authority which the court finds is (or would be) unlawful, it may grant such relief or remedy, or make such order, within its jurisdiction as it considers just and appropriate.

(2) But damages may be awarded only by a court which has power to award damages, or to order the payment of compensation, in civil proceedings.

(3) No award of damages is to be made unless, taking account of all the circumstances of the case, including—

(a) any other relief or remedy granted, or order made, in relation to the act in question (by that or any other court), and

(b) the consequences of any decision (of that or any other court) in respect of that act,

the court is satisfied that the award is necessary to afford just satisfaction to the person in whose favour it is made.

(4) In determining—

(a) whether to award damages, or

(b) the amount of an award,

the court must take into account the principles applied by the European Court of Human Rights in relation to the award of compensation under Article 41 of the Convention.

(5) …

(6) In this section—

'court' includes a tribunal;

'damages' means damages for an unlawful act of a public authority; and

'unlawful' means unlawful under section 6(1).

9. Judicial acts

(1) Proceedings under section 7(1)(a) in respect of a judicial act may be brought only—

(a) by exercising a right of appeal;

(b) on an application (in Scotland a petition) for judicial review; or

(c) in such other forum as may be prescribed by rules.

(2) That does not affect any rule of law which prevents a court from being the subject of judicial review.

(3) In proceedings under this Act in respect of a judicial act done in good faith, damages may not be awarded otherwise than to compensate a person to the extent required by Article 5(5) of the Convention.

(4) An award of damages permitted by subsection (3) is to be made against the Crown; but no award may be made unless the appropriate person, if not a party to the proceedings, is joined.

(5) In this section—

'appropriate person' means the Minister responsible for the court concerned, or a person or government department nominated by him;

'court' includes a tribunal;

'judge' includes a member of a tribunal, a justice of the peace and a clerk or other officer entitled to exercise the jurisdiction of a court;

'judicial act' means a judicial act of a court and includes an act done on the instructions, or on behalf, of a judge;

…

Remedial action

10. Power to take remedial action

(1) This section applies if—

(a) a provision of legislation has been declared under section 4 to be incompatible with a Convention right and, if an appeal lies—

(i) all persons who may appeal have stated that they do not intend to do so;

(ii) the time for bringing an appeal has expired and no appeal has been brought within that time; or

(iii) an appeal brought within that time has been determined or abandoned;

(b) it appears to a Minister of the Crown or Her Majesty in Council that, having regard to a finding of the European Court of Human Rights made after the coming into force of this section in proceedings against the United Kingdom, a provision of legislation is incompatible with an obligation of the United Kingdom arising from the Convention.

(2) If a Minister of the Crown considers that there are compelling reasons for proceeding under this section, he may by order make such amendments to the legislation as he considers necessary to remove the incompatibility.

(3) If, in the case of subordinate legislation, a Minister of the Crown considers—

   (a) that it is necessary to amend the primary legislation under which the subordinate legislation in question was made, in order to enable the incompatibility to be removed, and

   (b) that there are compelling reasons for proceeding under this section, he may by order make such amendments to the primary legislation as he considers necessary.

(4) This section also applies where the provision in question is in subordinate legislation and has been quashed, or declared invalid, by reason of incompatibility with a Convention right and the Minister proposes to proceed under paragraph 2(b) of Schedule 2.

(5) If the legislation is an Order in Council, the power conferred by subsection (2) or (3) is exercisable by Her Majesty in Council.

(6) In this section 'legislation' does not include a Measure of the Church Assembly or of the General Synod of the Church of England.

(7) …

Other rights and proceedings

11. Safeguard for existing human rights

A person's reliance on a Convention right does not restrict—

(a) any other right or freedom conferred on him by or under any law having effect in any part of the United Kingdom, or

(b) his right to make any claim or bring any proceedings which he could make or bring apart from sections 7 to 9.

12. Freedom of expression

(1) This section applies if a court is considering whether to grant any relief which, if granted, might affect the exercise of the Convention right to freedom of expression.

(2) If the person against whom the application for relief is made ('the respondent') is neither present nor represented, no such relief is to be granted unless the court is satisfied—

   (a) that the applicant has taken all practicable steps to notify the respondent; or

   (b) that there are compelling reasons why the respondent should not be notified.

(3) No such relief is to be granted so as to restrain publication before trial unless the court is satisfied that the applicant is likely to establish that publication should not be allowed.

(4) The court must have particular regard to the importance of the Convention right to freedom of expression and, where the proceedings relate to material which the respondent claims, or which appears to the court, to be journalistic, literary or artistic material (or to conduct connected with such material), to—

   (a) the extent to which—

      (i) the material has, or is about to, become available to the public; or

      (ii) it is, or would be, in the public interest for the material to be published;

   (b) any relevant privacy code.

(5) In this section—

'court' includes a tribunal; and

'relief' includes any remedy or order (other than in criminal proceedings).

13. Freedom of thought, conscience and religion

(1) If a court's determination of any question arising under this Act might affect the exercise by a religious organisation (itself or its members collectively) of the Convention right to freedom of thought, conscience and religion, it must have particular regard to the importance of that right.

(2) In this section, 'court' includes a tribunal.

Derogations and reservations

14. Derogations

(1) In this Act, 'designated derogation' means any derogation by the United Kingdom from an Article of the Convention, or of any protocol to the Convention, which is designated for the purposes of this Act in an order made by the Lord Chancellor.

(2) [*repealed*].

(3) If a designated derogation is amended or replaced it ceases to be a designated derogation.

(4) But subsection (3) does not prevent the Lord Chancellor from exercising his power under subsection (1) to make a fresh designation order in respect of the Article concerned.

(5) The Lord Chancellor must by order make such amendments to Schedule 2 as he considers appropriate to reflect—

  (a) any designation order; or

  (b) the effect of subsection (3).

(6) A designation order may be made in anticipation of the making by the United Kingdom of a proposed derogation.

15. Reservations

(1) In this Act, 'designated reservation' means—

  (a) the United Kingdom's reservation to Article 2 of the First Protocol to the Convention; and

  (b) any other reservation by the United Kingdom to an Article of the Convention, or of any protocol to the Convention, which is designated for the purposes of this Act in an order made by the Lord Chancellor.

(2) The text of the reservation referred to in subsection (1)(a) is set out in Part II of Schedule 3.

(3) If a designated reservation is withdrawn wholly or in part it ceases to be a designated reservation.

(4) But subsection (3) does not prevent the Lord Chancellor from exercising his power under subsection (1)(b) to make a fresh designation order in respect of the Article concerned.

(5) The Lord Chancellor must by order make such amendments to this Act as he considers appropriate to reflect—

  (a) any designation order; or

  (b) the effect of subsection (3).

16. Period for which designated derogations have effect

(1) If it has not already been withdrawn by the United Kingdom, a designated derogation ceases to have effect for the purposes of this Act at the end of the period of five years beginning with the date on which the order designating it was made.

(2) At any time before the period—

  (a) fixed by subsection (1), or

  (b) extended by an order under this subsection,

comes to an end, the Lord Chancellor may by order extend it by a further period of five years.

(3) An order under section 14(1) ceases to have effect at the end of the period for consideration, unless a resolution has been passed by each House approving the order.

(4) Subsection (3) does not affect—

  (a) anything done in reliance on the order; or

  (b) the power to make a fresh order under section 14(1).

(5) In subsection (3) 'period for consideration' means the period of forty days beginning with the day on which the order was made.

(6) In calculating the period for consideration, no account is to be taken of any time during which—

  (a) Parliament is dissolved or prorogued; or

  (b) both Houses are adjourned for more than four days.

(7) If a designated derogation is withdrawn by the United Kingdom, the Lord Chancellor must by order make such amendments to this Act as he considers are required to reflect that withdrawal.

17. Periodic review of designated reservations

(1) The appropriate Minister must review the designated reservation referred to in section 15(1)(a)—

(a) before the end of the period of five years beginning with the date on which section 1(2) came into force; and

(b) if that designation is still in force, before the end of the period of five years beginning with the date on which the last report relating to it was laid under subsection (3).

(2) The appropriate Minister must review each of the other designated reservations (if any)—

(a) before the end of the period of five years beginning with the date on which the order designating the reservation first came into force; and

(b) if the designation is still in force, before the end of the period of five years beginning with the date on which the last report relating to it was laid under subsection (3).

(3) The Minister conducting a review under this section must prepare a report on the result of the review and lay a copy of it before each House of Parliament.

Judges of the European Court of Human Rights

18. Appointment to European Court of Human Rights

(1) In this section 'judicial office' means the office of—

(a) Lord Justice of Appeal, Justice of the High Court or Circuit judge, in England and Wales;

(b) judge of the Court of Session or sheriff, in Scotland;

(c) Lord Justice of Appeal, judge of the High Court or county court judge, in Northern Ireland.

(2) The holder of a judicial office may become a judge of the European Court of Human Rights ('the Court') without being required to relinquish his office.

(3) But he is not required to perform the duties of his judicial office while he is a judge of the Court.

(4)–(7) …

Parliamentary procedure

19. Statements of compatibility

(1) A Minister of the Crown in charge of a Bill in either House of Parliament must, before Second Reading of the Bill—

(a) make a statement to the effect that in his view the provisions of the Bill are compatible with the Convention rights ('a statement of compatibility'); or

(b) make a statement to the effect that although he is unable to make a statement of compatibility the government nevertheless wishes the House to proceed with the Bill.

(2) The statement must be in writing and be published in such manner as the Minister making it considers appropriate.

SUPPLEMENTAL

20. Orders under this Act

(1) Any power to make an order under this Act is exercisable by statutory instrument.

(2) The power to make rules (other than rules of court) under section 2(3) or 7(9) is exercisable by statutory instrument.

(3) Any statutory instrument made under section 14, 15 or 16(7) must be laid before Parliament.

(4) No order may be made under section 1(4), 7(11) or 16(2) unless a draft of the order has been laid before, and approved by, each House of Parliament.

(5) Any statutory instrument made under section 18(7) or Schedule 4, or to which subsection (2) applies, shall be subject to annulment in pursuance of a resolution of either House of Parliament.

(6)–(8) …

21. Interpretation, etc

(1) In this Act—

…

'the appropriate Minister' means the Minister of the Crown having charge of the appropriate authorised government department (within the meaning of the Crown Proceedings Act 1947);

…

'primary legislation' means any—

(a) public general Act;
(b) local and personal Act;
(c) private Act;
(d) Measure of the Church Assembly;
(e) Measure of the General Synod of the Church of England;
(f) Order in Council—

  (i) made in exercise of Her Majesty's Royal Prerogative;
  (ii) made under section 38(1)(a) of the Northern Ireland Constitution Act 1973 or the corresponding provision of the Northern Ireland Act 1998; or
  (iii) amending an Act of a kind mentioned in paragraph (a), (b) or (c); and includes an order or other instrument made under primary legislation (otherwise than by the National Assembly for Wales, a member of the Scottish Executive, a Northern Ireland Minister or a Northern Ireland department) to the extent to which it operates to bring one or more provisions of that legislation into force or amends any primary legislation;

…

'remedial order' means an order under section 10;

'subordinate legislation' means any—

(a) Order in Council other than one—

  (i) made in exercise of Her Majesty's Royal Prerogative;
  (ii) made under section 38(1)(a) of the Northern Ireland Constitution Act 1973 or the corresponding provision of the Northern Ireland Act 1998; or
  (iii) amending an Act of a kind mentioned in the definition of primary legislation;

(b) Act of the Scottish Parliament;
(c) Act of the Parliament of Northern Ireland;
(d) Measure of the Assembly established under section 1 of the Northern Ireland Assembly Act 1973;
(e) Act of the Northern Ireland Assembly;
(f) order, rules, regulations, scheme, warrant, byelaw or other instrument made under primary legislation (except to the extent to which it operates to bring one or more provisions of that legislation into force or amends any primary legislation);
(g) order, rules, regulations, scheme, warrant, byelaw or other instrument made under legislation mentioned in paragraph (b), (c), (d) or (e) or made under an Order in Council applying only to Northern Ireland;
(h) order, rules, regulations, scheme, warrant, byelaw or other instrument made by a member of the Scottish Executive, a Northern Ireland Minister or a Northern Ireland department in exercise of prerogative or other executive functions of Her Majesty which are exercisable by such a person on behalf of Her Majesty;

'transferred matters' has the same meaning as in the Northern Ireland Act 1998; and 'tribunal' means any tribunal in which legal proceedings may be brought.

…

22. Short title, commencement, application and extent

(1) This Act may be cited as the Human Rights Act 1998.

(2) Sections 18 and 20 and this section come into force on the passing of this Act.

(3) The other provisions of this Act come into force on such day as the Secretary of State may by order appoint; and different days may be appointed for different purposes.

(4) Paragraph (b) of subsection (1) of section 7 applies to proceedings brought by or at the instigation of a public authority whenever the act in question took place; but otherwise that subsection does not apply to an act committed before the coming into force of that section.

(5) This Act binds the Crown.

(6) This Act extends to Northern Ireland.

(7) Section 21(5), so far as it relates to any provision contained in the Army Act 1955, the Air Force Act 1955 or the Naval Discipline Act 1957, extends to any place to which that provision extends.

B: The implications of the Human Rights Act for human rights

Lord Irvine of Lairg LC, The Tom Sargant Memorial Lecture, 'The Development of Human Rights in Britain under an Incorporated Convention on Human Rights'
16 December 1997

… The traditional freedom of the individual under an unwritten constitution to do himself that which is not prohibited by law gives no protection from misuse of power by the State, nor any protection from acts or omissions by public bodies which harm individuals in a way that is incompatible with their human rights under the Convention.

The implications of the change

What then are the practical implications of this change to a rights based system within the field of civil liberties?

First, the Act will give to the courts the tools to uphold freedoms at the very time their infringement is threatened. … The courts will now have the power to give effect to the Convention rights in the course of proceedings when they arise in this country and to grant relief against an unlawful act of a public authority (a necessarily widely drawn concept). The courts will not be able to strike down primary legislation. But they will be able to make a declaration of incompatibility where a piece of primary legislation conflicts with a Convention right. This will trigger the ability to use in Parliament a special fast-track procedure to bring the law into line with the Convention.

This innovative technique will provide the right balance between the judiciary and Parliament. Parliament is the democratically elected representative of the people and must remain sovereign. The judiciary will be able to exercise to the full the power to scrutinise legislation rigorously against the fundamental freedoms guaranteed by the Convention but without becoming politicised. The ultimate decision to amend legislation to bring it into line with the Convention, however, will rest with Parliament. The ultimate responsibility for compliance with the Convention must be Parliament's alone.

That point illustrates the second important effect of our new approach. If there are to be differences or departures from the principles of the Convention they should be conscious and reasoned departures, and not the product of rashness, muddle or ignorance. This will be guaranteed both by the powers given to the courts but also by other provisions which will be enacted. In particular, Ministers and administrators will be obliged to do all their work keeping clearly and directly in mind its impact on human rights, as expressed in the Convention and the jurisprudence which attaches to it. For, where any Bill is introduced in either House, the Minister of the Crown, in whose charge it is, will be required to make a written statement that, either, in his view, the provisions of the Bill are compatible with the Convention rights; or that he cannot make that statement but the Government nonetheless wishes the House to proceed with the Bill. In the latter case the Bill would inevitably be subject to close and critical scrutiny by Parliament. Human rights will not be a matter of fudge. The responsible Minister will have to ensure that the legislation does not infringe guaranteed freedoms, or be prepared to justify his decision openly and in the full glare of Parliamentary and public opinion.

That will be particularly important whenever there comes under consideration those articles of the Convention which lay down what I call principled rights, subject to possible limitation. I have in mind Articles 8–11, dealing with respect for private life; freedom of religion; freedom of expression; and freedom of assembly and association; which confer those freedoms subject to possible limitations, such as, for instance in the case of Article 10 (freedom of expression):

> are prescribed by law and are necessary in a democratic society in the interests of national security, territorial integrity or public safety, for the prevention of disorder or crime, for the protection of health or morals, for the protection of the reputation or rights of others, for preventing the disclosure of information received in confidence, or for maintaining the authority and impartiality of the judiciary.

In such cases, administrators and legislators, will have to think clearly about whether what they propose really is necessary in a democratic society and for what object it is necessary. Quite apart from the concentration on the Convention and its jurisprudence this will require, the process should produce better thought-out, clearer and more transparent administration.

The important requirements of transparency on Convention issues that will accompany the introduction of all future legislation will ensure that Parliament knows exactly what it is doing in a human rights context. I regard this improvement in both the efficiency and the openness of our legislative process as one of the main benefits produced by incorporation of the Convention.

Substantive rights

Thirdly, the Convention will enable the Courts to reach results in cases which give full effect to the substantive rights guaranteed by the Convention. … But the courts have only had limited ability to give effect to those rights. …

It is moreover likely—although individual cases will be for the Courts to determine and I should not attempt to prejudge them—that the position will in at least some cases be different from what it would have been under the pre-incorporation practice. The reason for this lies in the techniques to be followed once the Act is in force. Unlike the old Diceyan approach where the Court would go straight to what restriction had been imposed, the focus will first be on the positive right and then on the justifiability of the exception. Moreover, the Act will require the Courts to read and give effect to the legislation in a way compatible with the Convention rights 'so far as it is possible to do so.' This, as the White Paper makes clear, goes far beyond the present rule. It will not be necessary to find an ambiguity. On the contrary the Courts will be required to interpret legislation so as to uphold the Convention rights unless the legislation itself is so clearly incompatible with the Convention that it is impossible to do so. Moreover, it should be clear from the Parliamentary history, and in particular the Ministerial statement of compatibility which will be required by the Act, that Parliament did not intend to cut across a Convention right. Ministerial statements of compatibility will inevitably be a strong spur to the courts to find means of construing statutes compatibly with the Convention. …

The Court will interpret as consistent with the Convention not only those provisions which are ambiguous in the sense that the *language* used is capable of two different meanings but also those provisions where there is *no* ambiguity in that sense, unless a *clear* limitation is expressed. In the latter category of case it will be 'possible' (to use the statutory language) to read the legislation in a conforming sense because there will be no clear indication that a limitation on the protected rights was intended so as to make it 'impossible' to read it as conforming.

The morality of decisions

The fourth point may be shortly stated but is of immense importance. The Courts' decisions will be based on a more overtly principled, indeed moral, basis. The Court will look at the positive right. It will only accept an interference with that right where a justification, allowed under the Convention, is made out. The scrutiny will not be limited to seeing if the *words* of an exception can be satisfied. The Court will need to be satisfied that the *spirit* of this exception is made out. It will need to be satisfied that the interference with the protected right *is* justified in the public interests in a free democratic society. Moreover, the Courts will in this area have to apply the Convention principle of proportionality. This means the Court will be looking *substantively* at that question. It will not be limited to a secondary review of the decision making process but at the primary question of the merits of the decision itself.

In reaching its judgment, therefore, the Court will need to expand and explain its own view of whether the conduct is legitimate. It will produce in short a decision on the *morality* of the conduct and not simply its compliance with the bare letter of the law.

The influence on other areas of law

I believe, moreover, that the effects of the incorporation of the Convention will be felt way beyond the sphere of the application of the rights guaranteed by the Convention alone. As we move from the traditional Diceyan model of the common law to a rights based system, the effects will be felt throughout the common law and in the very process of judicial decision-making. This will be a healthy and dynamic development in our law.

...

Although the legislative technique adopted under the Human Rights Bill is different from that under the European Communities Act, the effect on the general process of deciding cases will, I believe, be as influential. Courts will, from time to time be required to determine if primary or secondary legislation is incompatible with the Convention rights. They will decide if the acts of public authorities are unlawful through contravention, perhaps even conscious contravention, of those rights. They may have to award damages as a result.

These are all new remedies for our courts to apply and, as they begin to develop the tools and techniques to apply them, an influence on other areas of law and judicial decision making is, I believe, inevitable.

...

So too it is becoming increasingly hard not explicitly to recognise in English administrative law the Community law doctrine of proportionality.

That doctrine, drawn from German Administrative law principles, is a tool for judging the lawfulness of administrative action. It amounts to this. Excessive means are not to be used to attain permissible objects. Or, as it was more pithily put by Lord Diplock, 'a steam hammer should not be used to crack a nut'. There has been much argument whether this principle now forms a part of the criteria for review of public decisions generally since Lord Diplock opened that door in 1985 [see *Council of Civil Service Unions* v *Minister for the Civil Service* [1985] AC 374]. It seemed to have been slammed shut in *Brind* in 1991. This is not the occasion to trace those developments. Yet, by whatever name, it seems undeniable that the traditional common law concepts converge with their continental cousins. This is but another example of the inevitable incremental effects of introducing another system of law to be applied alongside traditional common law principles.

C: How does the Human Rights Act operate in practice?

The introduction of the Human Rights Act is a major step forward in the protection of human rights. Gradually uncertainties as to how the Act will operate in practice are being resolved such as that the domestic system of precedent holds even though there is a subsequent inconsistent decision of the European Court of Human Rights (*Kay* v *Lambeth London Borough Council* [2006] UKHL 10 [2006] 2 AC 465), and that the Act extends beyond the territory of the UK where UK public authorities exercised control so that a military base in Iraq was within jurisdiction (*R (Al-Skeini)* v *Secretary of State for Defence* [2007] UKHL 26, [2007] 3 WLR 33).

In the following extracts, some of the major questions from academic and judicial writers and from decisions of the appellate courts are explored.

(a) What is a 'public authority'?

Joint Committee on Human Rights, *The Meaning of Public Authority under the Human Rights Act*
HL 39 / HC 382 of 2003–2004, paras 3–7, 39–41, 138–47

3. The intention of Parliament was that a wide range of bodies performing public functions would fall within the obligation under section 6 to act in a manner compatible with the 'Convention rights' established under the Act.

4. However, while the Convention had been designed to protect the individual from abuse of power by the State, the Human Rights Act was enacted at a time when the map of the public sector had been redrawn, as privatisation and contracting-out had, over several decades, increased the role of the private and voluntary sectors in the provision of public services. This development was acknowledged and considered by those who drafted and debated the Act. In particular, it was clearly envisaged that the Act would apply beyond activities undertaken by purely State bodies, to those functions performed on behalf of the State by private or voluntary sector bodies, acting under either statute or under contract. The Act was therefore designed to apply human rights guarantees beyond the obvious governmental bodies. Section 6 identified two distinct categories of 'public authorities' which would have a duty to comply with the Convention rights.

5. First, under section 6(3)(a), ['core'] public authorities (such as government departments, local authorities, or the police) are required to comply with Convention rights in all their activities, both when discharging intrinsically public functions and also when performing functions which could be done by any private body. So, for example, a local authority must as a pure public authority comply with the non-discrimination standards imposed by Article 14 of the Convention not only in its provision of public housing but also in its dealings with building contractors [Courts and tribunals are specifically stated to be public authorities (in all their activities) under section 6(3)(a)].

6. Second, under section 6(3)(b), those who exercise some public functions but are not ['core'] public authorities are required to comply with Convention human rights when they are exercising a 'function of a public nature' but not when doing something where the nature of the act is private (section 6(5)). So, for example, a private security firm would be required to comply with Convention rights in its running of a prison, but not in its provision of security to a supermarket. These bodies to which section 6(3)(b) applies have been termed 'hybrid' or 'functional' public authorities.

7. The term 'hybrid' public authority is unhelpful—it is not the *intrinsic* nature of these bodies which brings them within the ambit of the Act, it is the nature of the *functions* they perform which is determinative. A body could be liable under the Act one day while delivering functions under contract to a 'pure' public authority; the next day, if the contract had ended, it might become again a purely private body without any alteration to its intrinsic nature. In the remainder of this report we will use the term 'functional public authority' to refer to a body to which section 6(3)(b) of the Act might apply.

…

39. It seems therefore that the courts are likely to interpret the category of 'pure' public authority (all of the actions of which would be required to be compatible with the Convention rights) narrowly. In particular, the courts consider that they must exclude bodies capable of enforcing their Convention rights. But when it comes to interpreting the definition of a 'functional' public authority, which can be held to account under the Human Rights Act only in respect of its 'public' functions, it is not clear that the approach of the House of Lords in *Aston Cantlow* [[2003] UKHL 37, [2003] 3 WLR 283], which stressed the importance of analysing the character of the function concerned rather than the character of the institutional arrangements of the body performing the function, is being applied in the lower courts. This may be because the clear principles set out by the House of Lords were stated without reference

to, and without express disapproval or overruling of, the earlier cases—including *Poplar Homes* [[2001] EWCA Civ 595, [2002] QB 48] and *Leonard Cheshire* [[2002] EWCA Civ 366, [2002] 2 All ER 936], which took a predominantly 'institutional' rather than 'functional' approach to the question …

41. The tests being applied by the courts to determine whether a function is a 'public function' within the meaning of section 6(3)(b) of the Human Rights Act are, in human rights terms, highly problematic. Their application results in many instances where an organisation 'stands in the shoes of the State' and yet does not have responsibilities under the Human Rights Act. It means that the protection of human rights is dependent not on the type of power being exercised, nor on its capacity to interfere with human rights, but on the relatively arbitrary (in human rights terms) criterion of the body's administrative links with institutions of the State. The European Convention on Human Rights provides no basis for such a limitation, which calls into question the capacity of the Human Rights Act to bring rights home to the full extent envisaged by those who designed, debated and agreed the Act.

42. In our view, the principles set out by Lord Hope of Craighead in *Aston Cantlow* [[2003] UKHL 37, at para. 31] would provide an effective basis for protection of the Convention rights. Although the House of Lords in that case did not expressly overrule the decisions in *Poplar* and in *Leonard Cheshire*, it appears that the principles set out by Lord Hope in *Aston Cantlow* are at odds with those earlier decisions of the lower courts. In our view, the approach in *Aston Cantlow* is to be preferred.

[The committee considered four potential solutions, rejecting amendment of the Human Rights Act, using contract to secure protection of convention rights, and the use of guidance but preferring the use of principles of interpretation to assist with the key terms of 'public' and 'function'.]

…

138. In our view, a function is a public one when government has taken responsibility for it. Very few services or acts are in themselves inherently public. There is no doubt that caring for the sick, or educating children, do not involve acts that are inherently public. Health and education services can be and are provided by the State; they can equally well be provided by commercial enterprises, or charitable organisations, or families. To limit the meaning of public functions to those functions which can only (legally) be carried out by the State would be to confine its meaning to a narrow category hardly extending beyond coercive powers. This would leave the Human Rights Act far short of fulfilling the UK's obligation to protect and secure Convention rights effectively, forcing the victims of violations to rely on the Strasbourg court for redress.

139. The range of functions which are generally considered to be public, in that they are generally expected to be performed directly or indirectly by the State, varies over time. The State has in the past used direct delivery by government-owned or controlled bodies to effect the enlargement of the scope of its activities, but in the last 25 years or so has moved significantly in the direction of indirect delivery of many of these same functions, and some new ones.

140. The key test of whether a function is public is whether it is one for which the government has taken responsibility in the public interest. For example, although the various activities involved in care for the sick may be performed by anyone, the State has chosen, through a comprehensive social programme, to provide healthcare to those who wish to receive healthcare from the State rather than privately. This programme is undertaken in the public interest to provide what the government considers to be an important social service. In our view, discharge of duties necessary for provision of the government programme of healthcare is a public function. Discharge of healthcare services, in itself, is not. It is the doing of this work as part of a government programme which denotes a public function, rather than the provision of healthcare in itself. In performing duties as part of the State programme of healthcare, a private organisation is assisting in performing what the State itself has identified as the State's responsibilities …

Public functions and statute

142. On the principles set out above, for a body to discharge a public function, it does not need to do so under direct statutory authority. A State programme or policy, with a basis in statute or otherwise, may delegate its powers or duties through contractual arrangements without changing the public nature of those powers or duties. Under section 6 of the Human Rights Act, there should be no distinction between a body providing housing because it itself is required to do so by statute, and a body providing housing because it has contracted with a local authority which is required by statute to provide the service. The loss of a single step in proximity to the statutory duty does not change the nature of the function, nor the nature of its capacity to interfere with Convention rights.

Public functions and public institutions

143. Institutional links with a public body are not necessary to identifying a public function (although by contrast they are relevant to assessing whether a body as a whole is a 'pure public authority' under section 6, and to whether a body is amenable to judicial review). Although institutional proximity to the State may supply evidence that the organisation is delivering on a public or governmental programme, and is therefore performing a public function, it does not, in itself, determine the nature of the function being performed. An organisation could be closely administratively connected with a State authority, whilst performing only private functions, for example the recruitment of staff. Furthermore, the criterion of enmeshment or connection with a State authority has no basis in the jurisprudence of the European Court of Human Rights ...

NOTE: This analysis was accepted and adopted by the successor committee in its report HL 77/ HC 410 of 2006–07. In the intervening period the courts had not approached the interpretation of s. 6(3)(b) in its preferred manner and it had taken evidence to suggest that there was uncertainty. The Government did intervene in some cases arguing along the lines urged by the JCHR, however, by a three to two majority the House of Lords in *YL v Birmingham City Council* [2007] UKHL 27, [2007] 3 WLR 112, rejected this approach to interpretation. The case involved a resident of a care home, operated by Southern Cross a private company, whose place was paid for by the council. Lord Bingham and Baroness Hale did accept the point that this was a situation intended to be covered by s. 6(3)(b). Lord Bingham said:

20. When the 1998 Act was passed, it was very well known that a number of functions formerly carried out by public authorities were now carried out by private bodies. Section 6(3)(b) of the 1998 Act was clearly drafted with this well-known fact in mind. The performance by private body A by arrangement with public body B, and perhaps at the expense of B, of what would undoubtedly be a public function if carried out by B is, in my opinion, precisely the case which section 6(3)(b) was intended to embrace. It is, in my opinion, this case.

The contrary view of the majority is encapsulated by Lord Mance at [27]:

A number of the features which have been relied on by YL and the intervenors seems to me to carry little weight. It is said, correctly, that most of the residents in the Southern Cross care homes, including YL, are placed there by local authorities pursuant to their statutory duty under section 21 of the 1948 Act and that their fees are, either wholly or partly, paid by the local authorities or, where special nursing is required, by health authorities. But the fees charged by Southern Cross and paid by local or health authorities are charged and paid for a service. There is no element whatever of subsidy from public funds. It is a misuse of language and misleading to describe Southern Cross as publicly funded. If an outside private contractor is engaged on ordinary commercial terms to provide the cleaning services, or the catering and cooking services, or any other essential services at a local authority owned care home, it seems to me absurd to suggest that the private contractor, in earning its commercial fee for its business services, is publicly funded or is carrying on a function of a public nature. It is simply carrying on its private business with a customer who happens to be a public authority. The owner of a private care home taking local authority funded residents is in no different position. It is simply providing a service or services for which it charges a commercial fee...

29. An argument heavily relied on in support of the appeal has been a comparison of the management by a local authority care home with the management of a privately owned care home. There is no relevant difference, it is pointed out, between the activities of a local authority in managing its own care homes and those of the managers of privately owned care homes. The function of the local authority is unquestionably a function of a public nature, so how, at least in relation to residents the charges for whom are being paid by the local authority, can the nature of the function of the

managers of a privately owned care home be held to be different? So the argument goes. There are, in my opinion, very clear and fundamental differences. The local authority's activities are carried out pursuant to statutory duties and responsibilities imposed by public law. The costs of doing so are met by public funds, subject to the possibility of a means tested recovery from the resident. In the case of a privately owned care home the manager's duties to its residents are, whether contractual or tortious, duties governed by private law. In relation to those residents who are publicly funded, the local and health authorities become liable to pay charges agreed under private law contracts and for the recovery of which the care home has private law remedies. The recovery by the local authority of a means tested contribution from the resident is a matter of public law but is no concern of the care home.

Lord Neuberger concluded his speech [171]:

Finally, it is right to add this. It may well be thought to be desirable that residents in privately owned care homes should be given Convention rights against the proprietors. That is a subject on which there are no doubt opposing views, and I am in no position to express an opinion. However, if the legislature considers such a course appropriate, then it would be right to spell it out in terms, and, in the process, to make it clear whether the rights should be enjoyed by all residents of such care homes, or only certain classes (eg those whose care and accommodation is wholly or partly funded by a local authority).

The Government was persuaded to pass legislation which specifically reversed the decision in *YL*. Initially this was s. 145(1) of the Health and Social Care Act 2008 which has been superseded by s. 73 of the Social Care Act 2014. This stipulates that providers of personal care and of residential accommodation provided with nursing and personal care, will 'be taken for the purposes of section 6(3)(b) of the Human Rights Act 1998 (acts of public authorities) to be exercising a function of a public nature in providing the care or support' if certain conditions are met. These are that the care and support is arranged or paid for (directly or indirectly and in whole or part) by specified authorities under specified powers.

This legislative provision is limited to certain services under specific statutory powers. There are still difficulties in determining if a hybrid body is subject to the s. 6 duty not to infringe Convention rights. First, is the body performing a public function (s. 6(3)) and then is the act a public one or not (s. 6(5))? In *London & Quadrant Housing Trust v Weaver* [2009] EWCA Civ 587 there was a contrasting approach on whether the act is public or not in the provision of subsidized housing to those in need by the Trust, a Registered Social Landlord (RSL), in which it was held that the termination of a tenancy was a public act. The Trust conceded that it was a hybrid authority. For Elias LJ, the context is important in determining the nature of the act. Drawing on Lord Nicholls in *Aston Cantlow*, (i) the extent to which in carrying out the relevant function the body is publicly funded, or (ii) is exercising statutory powers, or (iii) is taking the place of central government or local authorities, or is (iv) providing a public service. Elias LJ decided that there is significant reliance on public finance as the trust receives a significant public subsidy; while not replacing local government, the Trust in allocating social housing is acting in close harmony with it under a statutory duty to cooperate; provision of social housing is to be a governmental activity and this provision of a subsidy to assist the poor is also a public service. He neither accepts the argument that an act was private because it involves the exercise of private rights, that is if it is essentially contractual, it necessarily involves the exercise of private rights; nor that it is supported by *Aston Cantlow* and *YL*.

London & Quadrant Housing Trust v Weaver

[2009] EWCA Civ 587, Court of Appeal

75. In my judgment, that would be a misreading of those decisions. The observations about private acts in *Aston Cantlow* and *YL* were in a context where it had already been determined that the function being exercised was not a public function. I do not consider that their Lordships would have reached

the same conclusion if they had found that the nature of the functions in issue in those cases were public functions.

76. In my judgment, the act of termination is so bound up with the provision of social housing that once the latter is seen, in the context of this particular body, as the exercise of a public function, then acts which are necessarily involved in the regulation of the function must also be public acts. The grant of a tenancy and its subsequent termination are part and parcel of determining who should be allowed to take advantage of this public benefit. This is not an act which is purely incidental or supplementary to the principal function, such as contracting out the cleaning of the windows of the Trust's properties. That could readily be seen as a private function of a kind carried on by both public and private bodies. No doubt the termination of such a contract would be a private act (unless the body were a core public authority.)

In his dissent Rix LJ did not think it was public function but even if it was, the act of terminating the tenancy was private. He disputes the contention that even if it is accepted that allocation of social housing is a public function then this is also true for termination.

151. … submissions have proceeded from the concept that "management and allocation" is an all-embracing public function which includes termination …I do not accept that that is a satisfactory way to analyse the housing function … "Management" is a vast and undifferentiated area which, as it seems to me, inevitably includes functions and acts which are most unlikely to be of a public nature: such as the commercial acquisition or even development of property, or the financing of it (even on the basis that public subsidy plays an important role, as to which see below), or the maintenance and repair of it, or the daily grind of administering a very substantial portfolio of property of all kinds …the divisional court has proceeded on the basis that management is essentially a function of either a public or a private nature and chosen between these extremes in favour of the former. It has seemed to me that both sides of this dispute have had an interest in advancing an argument which would dispose, once and for all, of the issue whether an RSL is for all purposes a hybrid public authority or not. I very much doubt, however, that such an issue can be debated in this way.

152. … my concern becomes increasingly acute when the proposition is that because management is a public function, then allocation is, or perhaps vice versa, and because allocation is, therefore termination is. YL is clear authority for the proposition that even where a public authority has a statutory duty both to arrange and to provide care and accommodation for the most vulnerable of our society, the fact that the arrangement may be of an inherently governmental or public nature does not mean that their provision is. It seems to me that, as compared with the case of care and accommodation in a care home, a fortiori that is true of the case of housing, even social housing. Moreover, in as much as it is suggested that because allocation is a function of a public nature, therefore termination is, I would respectfully disagree. Allocation arises under arrangements made between an RSL and a local authority, where the local authority makes use of such arrangements to fulfil their statutory duty to have an allocation policy. However, once an allocation has been made and a prospective tenant has been accepted by an RSL as its tenant, the tenant then enters into a contractual tenancy with the RSL, and their relationship thenceforward is governed, just like any tenant's relationship with his or her landlord, by private law. That remains the case despite the relevance of regulation. Moreover, the statutes which govern the recovery of possession apply to an RSL's social housing tenancies and other landlords' tenancies alike. All the authorities I have considered stress the importance of private contractual rights. Poplar's decision was driven by very special factors.

153. While it is inevitable that core public authorities who enter into contractual tenancies are subject to the Convention, it seems to me to require special circumstances to impose Convention solutions on top of the working out of private law contracts of private bodies, even if such bodies are also in some respects hybrid public authorities. Where, however, as here, the contract concerned is one so well known to private/commercial life as a tenancy agreement, where such contracts are being entered into in almost identical or standard form with social housing tenants and non social housing tenants alike,

it seems to me to be counter-intuitive to suppose that the working out of that contract as between a private (non-governmental) landlord and a tenant can depend on Convention rights. An exception might be where public functions fill the whole or a substantial space of that contract. I see no reason, however, for saying that that is the situation here. On the contrary, a contract like a tenancy contract, for all that it is hedged around by statutory provisions, is made for the specific purpose of determining the rights between the parties …

■ QUESTION

Is it contrary to constitutional principle that the protections contained in the HRA should vary with the method of service delivery, whether it is directly provided by a core public authority, or under contract?

(b) Does the Convention apply between private litigants?

A major question relating to the impact which the Human Rights Act will have is whether it imposes an obligation on courts to apply the Convention in determining cases between private litigants. As s. 6(3)(a) includes a court or tribunal within the definition of a 'public authority', this has given rise to speculation whether the Human Rights Act has horizontal effect between private individuals and bodies. The extracts which follow give a flavour of the differing views which existed prior to the implementation of the Human Rights Act and are followed by extracts from an important case before the High Court, Family Division, involving arguments based on the Convention Art. 8 right to privacy.

I. Leigh and L. Lustgarten, 'Making Rights Real: the Courts, Remedies and the Human Rights Act'
(1999) 58 *Cambridge Law Journal* 509, 512–13

… One of the most contested provisions of the Act is the apparently innocuous section (s. 6(3)(a)) which includes a court or tribunal within the definition of a 'public authority'. Since 'public authorities' act unlawfully where they violate a person's Convention rights unless clearly required to do so by legislation, there is some debate about whether the effect of including courts is to require re-interpretation of the common law, even that applicable between private parties, or whether the section has more limited impact. Space precludes full discussion here of the arguments concerning full horizontal effect, but a straightforward case can be made that wherever a court has a procedural, evidential, or remedial discretion, whether under common law or statute and in criminal or civil litigation, a decision about how to use the discretion will constitute a judicial 'act' under section 6. Convention rights are therefore relevant to a number of judicial decisions affecting a person's liberties in the course of proceedings, quite apart from the substantive law to be applied. In the criminal sphere these might include: extensions of detention in police custody, delay before prosecution, decisions to prosecute, the adjournment of proceedings, the grant of legal aid, imposition of bail conditions, orders relating to pre-trial disclosure, the imposition of publication restrictions or bans, the treatment of vulnerable or protected witnesses, the mandatory or discretionary exclusion of evidence (under Police and Criminal Evidence Act, ss. 76 & 78), evidential inferences from silence, and the effect of conditions imposed on community sentences such as probation, community service orders, curfews and tagging orders. In the civil sphere examples would include discretions arising under the wardship jurisdiction and concerning the best interests of the child under the Children Act 1989 in other contexts such as custody, under the Contempt of Court Act 1981, s. 10 (identification of sources of information in limited circumstances), and in the grant of equitable orders. Prior to the Act, English courts have already recognised that the Convention may be relevant to a number of these discretionary decisions, and in others the failure to do so has resulted in adverse rulings from Strasbourg. The approach has, however, been somewhat haphazard. While the Convention has been taken into account on occasion, it has rarely been decisive. If our interpretation of the reach of section 6 is accepted a more rigorous approach will be needed in future: the test will be the *impact* of the discretionary decision on a person's Convention rights. There will be no possibility of balancing prejudice to those rights against other factors, except within the permitted restrictions of the Convention articles themselves. This approach is closer to that of the ECtHR which has held in a number of instances that member states are liable for infringements of the Convention resulting solely from the terms of court orders or, indeed, the failure of a court to grant effective protection of a right.

Lord Irvine of Lairg LC, Address to the Third Clifford Chance Conference on the Impact of a Bill of Rights on English Law
28 November 1997

Clause 6 makes it clear that 'public authority' includes a court and a tribunal which exercises functions in relation to legal proceedings. That inclusion, as this audience will recognise, does more than asking the courts to interpret legislation compatibly with the Convention. It imposes on them to a duty to act compatibly with the Convention.

We believe that it is right as a matter of principle for the courts to have the duty of acting compatibly with the Convention. They will be under this duty not only in cases involving other public authorities but also in developing the common law in deciding cases between individuals. It has been suggested that the courts should exclude Convention considerations altogether from cases between individuals. We do not think that that would be justifiable. Nor, indeed, do we think it would be practicable. The courts already bring Convention considerations to bear in cases before them. I have no doubt that they will continue to do so in developing the common law. Clause 3 makes this clear by requiring the courts to interpret legislation compatibly with the Convention rights and to the fullest extent possible in all cases coming before them.

You would not expect me to leave this subject without touching on privacy.

I would not agree with any proposition that the courts as public authorities will be obliged to fashion a law on privacy because of the terms of the Bill. That is simply not so. If it were so, whenever a law cannot be found either in the statute book or as a rule of common law to protect a Convention right, the courts would in effect be obliged to legislate by way of judicial decision to make one. That is not the true position. If it were—in my view, it is not—the courts would also have in effect to legislate where Parliament had acted, but incompatibly, with the Convention. Let us suppose that an Act of Parliament provides for detention on suspicion of drug trafficking but that the legislation goes too far and conflicts with Article 5. The court would so hold and would make a declaration of incompatibility. The scheme of the Bill is that Parliament may act to remedy a failure where the judges cannot.

In my opinion, the court is not obliged to remedy the failure by legislating via the common law either wherever a Convention right is infringed by incompatible legislation or wherever, because of the absence of legislation—say, privacy legislation—a Convention right is left unprotected.

In my view, the courts may not act as legislators and grant new remedies for infringement of Convention rights unless the common law itself enables them to develop new rights or remedies. I believe that the true view is that the courts will be able to adapt and develop the common law by relying on existing domestic principles in the laws of trespass, nuisance, copyright, confidence and the like, to fashion a common law right to privacy. I say this because members of the higher judiciary have already themselves said so.

The experience of continental countries shows that their cautious development of privacy law has been based on domestic law case by case, although they have also had regard to the Convention. My view is that any privacy law developed by the judges will be a better law after incorporation of the Convention because the judges will have to balance and have regard to Articles 10 and 8, giving Article 10 its due high value.

M. Hunt, 'The "Horizontal Effect" of the Human Rights Act'
[1998] *Public Law* 423, 438–42

It is clear beyond argument that *direct* horizontal application is not intended. This much is immediately apparent from the fact that the obligation to act compatibly with the Convention in section 6(1) of the Act is expressed to be binding only on public authorities, and that section 6 goes on to give examples of what is included in the definition of public authority. The clear implication is that there are persons who are *not* bound to act compatibly with the Convention at all; and indeed, by virtue of section 6(5), even the hybrid bodies made public authorities by section 6(3)(b), and therefore subject to the section 6(1) obligation, are not bound by the Convention in respect of those of their acts which are of a private nature. This inference, that the Act does not have direct horizontal effect, is further reinforced by the absence of any references to private individuals or organisations anywhere in the Act.

To put the matter beyond doubt, the Lord Chancellor, in his speech on Second Reading explaining the main provisions of the Bill, made clear that the Government had decided that:

> a provision of this kind [cl. 6(1)] should apply only to public authorities, however defined, and not to private individuals. That reflects the arrangements for taking cases to the Convention institutions in Strasbourg. The Convention had its origins in a desire to protect people from the misuse of power by the state, rather than from the actions of private individuals. ... Clause 6 does not impose a liability on organisations which have no public functions at all.

Indeed, read in isolation, these explanatory comments about who is 'bound' by the Act might even be thought to give some sustenance to a vertical reading of the legislation's application. It is extremely important, however, that they are seen as precluding *direct* horizontal effect, rather than as endorsing a *vertical* approach. That this is the Government's intention is abundantly clear from the wider context provided not only by provisions in the rest of the Act, but by the parliamentary debates which preceded their adoption. In particular, the rejection of a purely vertical approach, and embrace of something more, is clear on the face of the provision that is without doubt the single most important feature of the legislation as far as determining the scope of its application is concerned: the express inclusion of courts and tribunals within the definition of public authorities obliged by section 6(1) to act compatibly with the Convention.

This inclusion of courts and tribunals in the definition of public authorities who are subject to the obligation in section 6(1) to act compatibly with the Convention is of great significance for the horizontality of Convention rights under the Human Rights Act. ... [T]he effect of making courts expressly bound is to give a greater degree of horizontal effect to fundamental rights. ...

It is true that there is no clause in the UK's Human Rights Act expressly saying that the Convention rights 'apply to all law', or some phrase capable of making clear that the common law is subject to the Convention. It is also true that the interpretive obligation contained in section 3(1) relates only to legislation and not to the common law. But neither of these could he characterised as significant omissions in view of the clarity about the overall purpose of the Act and the unequivocal nature of the obligation imposed on courts and tribunals by section 6. The whole scheme of the Human Rights Act is premised on the proposition that the only domestic law which is not to be subjected to Convention rights is legislation which cannot possibly be given a meaning compatible with Convention rights. The nature of the section 6(1) obligation on courts and tribunals is in keeping with that purpose. Whereas section 3(1) of the Act imposes an *interpretive* obligation on courts in relation to statute law, requiring courts to read and give effect to legislation in a way which is compatible with Convention rights, but subject to the limitation that the legislative language must be capable of bearing the meaning necessary to make it compatible, section 6 goes further. By making courts and tribunals 'public authorities' it imposes a *duty* on them to act compatibly with the Convention, including when they decide purely private disputes between private parties governed solely by the common law.

That this is the intention behind the inclusion of courts and tribunals in section 6(1) was confirmed in the strongest possible terms by both the Lord Chancellor and Lord Williams of Mostyn during the Bill's Committee stage in the House of Lords. An amendment was proposed by Lord Wakeham, the head of the Press Complaints Commission, designed specifically to preclude the possibility of the legislation having *any* horizontal effect. The amendment proposed that the obligation to act compatibly with the Convention in section 6(1) not apply 'where the public authority is a court or tribunal and the parties to the proceedings before it do not include any public authority'. Its purpose was avowedly to confine the Convention right to having vertical effect only: to prevent them being used by the courts in disputes between private individuals, and in particular 'to stop the development of a common law of privacy'.

The Lord Chancellor, responding at the end of the debate on this proposed amendment, left no doubt about the intention behind the inclusion of courts in section 6(1):

> We … believe that it is right as a matter of principle for the courts to have the duty of acting compatibly with the Convention not only in cases involving other public authorities but also in developing the common law in deciding cases between individuals. Why should they not? In preparing this Bill, we have taken the view that it is the other course, that of excluding Convention considerations altogether from cases between individuals, which would have to be justified. We do not think that that would be justifiable; nor, indeed, do we think it would be practicable.

Lord Williams similarly made clear, in response to a different amendment, the Government's view that courts and tribunals 'are in a very similar position to obvious public authorities, such as government departments, in that all their acts are to be treated as being of such a public nature as to engage the Convention'.

The explanatory statements leave no room for doubt as to the intention behind the inclusion of courts and tribunals within the definition of 'public authority' for the purposes of section 6(1). It is to ensure that all law, other than unavoidably incompatible legislation, is to be subjected to Convention rights, which thereby attain the all-pervasive status of which the White Paper boasts. There it is made explicit that the Convention rights 'will be brought much more fully into the jurisprudence of the courts throughout the United Kingdom, and their interpretation … far more subtly and powerfully woven into our law'. That is consistent also with the clear policy decision not to have a special court or separate procedure for human rights cases, but for the questions to be dealt with as they arise by the ordinary courts in ordinary cases. As Lord Irvine made clear in his Tom Sargant Memorial Lecture, the Government's explicit purpose in choosing the model it has introduced is that 'the Convention rights must *pervade all law* and all court systems'.

That a degree of horizontal effect in purely private disputes between private parties is explicitly envisaged by the Government is therefore without doubt, but that leaves one important question unanswered: how far towards full horizontality does it go? In particular, does it go beyond the present position, in which UK courts are undoubtedly free to 'take the Convention into account' when interpreting or developing the common law, or beyond even the indirect horizontal effect of the Canadian (and German) approach, in which courts are under an obligation to take human rights 'values' into account in interpreting the common law?

It seems quite clear that the model which has been chosen goes considerably further in the direction of horizontality than either of these. When the Act comes into force, courts will not merely have a power to 'consider' the Convention when interpreting the common law in private disputes. nor will they merely have an obligation to take into account Convention 'values'. Rather they will be under an unequivocal duty to act compatibly with Convention rights. In some cases, this will undoubtedly require them actively to modify or develop the common law in order to achieve such compatibility. Precisely where the line is drawn between legitimate judicial development of the common law and illegitimate judicial 'legislation' is a matter of degree and, ultimately, a matter of legal and political philosophy. The Lord Chancellor in the course of the parliamentary debates sought to indicate that courts will not be empowered by the Human Rights Act to go beyond their legitimate function of incremental common law development, for example by creating entirely new causes of action, for that would be to tread on Parliament's toes. But it remains to be seen whether judges will be as cautious as the Lord Chancellor envisages or more adventurous in plugging the gaps in the common law's scheme of remedies by imaginative analogising from existing causes of action.

The most likely position, then, is that the Convention will be regarded as applying to all law, and therefore as potentially relevant in proceedings between private parties, but will fall short of being *directly* horizontally effective, because it will not confer any new private causes of action against individuals in respect of breach of Convention rights. This requires a distinction to be drawn between the evolution of existing causes of action over time and the creation of entirely new causes of action against private parties. It is beyond argument that the Human Rights Act does not do the latter, but the courts will undoubtedly develop over time causes of action such as trespass, confidence, and copyright, as the Lord Chancellor himself accepted in Parliament. Law which already exists and governs private relationships must be interpreted, applied and if necessary developed so as to achieve compatibility with the Convention. But where no cause of action exists, and there is therefore no law to apply, the courts cannot invent new causes of action, as that would be to embrace full horizontality which has clearly been precluded by Parliament.

NOTE: In the case which follows the Family Division confirmed that the doctrine of confidence had developed into a privacy remedy, placing emphasis on the relevance of the Convention rights.

Thompson and Venables v News Group Newspapers Ltd
[2001] 2 WLR 1038, Family Division

T and V had been convicted as children of the murder of two-year-old James Bulger and sentenced to detention during Her Majesty's pleasure in 1993. They were protected by injunctions issued by the trial judge for an unlimited period restricting publication of further information about them. In July 2000, four newspapers applied to the court for clarification of the injunctions in light of T's and V's impending majority. Subsequently T and V issued the present proceedings in which they sought injunctions against specific newspapers and all the world to protect all information about, *inter alia*, their whereabouts, movements, appearance, and their new identities on release on the basis that such injunctions were necessary to protect their rights of confidentiality and their rights to life and freedom from persecution and harassment conferred by the European Convention. Dame Elizabeth Butler-Sloss P granted permanent injunctions against all the world because of the disastrous consequences such disclosure might have for them, not least the serious possibility of physical harm or death.

DAME ELIZABETH BUTLER-SLOSS P:

. . .

C. The law: jurisdiction to grant an injunction
Application of the Convention

24   Before turning to the question of whether there is jurisdiction to grant injunctions, the preliminary issue is whether the Convention applies to this case. It is clear that, although operating in the public domain and fulfilling a public service, the defendant newspapers cannot sensibly be said to come within the definition of public authority in section 6(1) of the Human Rights Act 1998. Consequently, Convention rights are not directly enforceable against the defendants: see section 7(1) and section 8 of the 1998 Act. That is not, however, the end of the matter, since the court is a public authority (see section 6(3)) and must itself act in a way compatible with the Convention (see section 6(1)) and have regard to European jurisprudence: see section 2. In a private family law case, *Glaser v United Kingdom* [2000] 3 FCR 193, the European Court of Human Rights, sitting as a Chamber, declared admissible an application by a father seeking the enforcement of contact orders made in private law proceedings between him and the mother of his children. They considered the potential breach of the father's rights under article 8 and article 6. The court said, at pp 208–209, para 63:

> 'The essential object of article 8 is to protect the individual against arbitrary interference by public authorities. There may, however, be positive obligations inherent in an effective "respect" for family life. Those obligations may involve the adoption of measures designed to secure respect for family life even in the sphere of relations between individuals, including both the provision of a regulatory framework of adjudicatory and enforcement machinery protecting individuals' rights

and the implementation, where appropriate, of specific steps (see among other authorities, *X and Y* v *The Netherlands* (1985) 8 EHRR 235 and mutatis mutandis, *Osman* v *United Kingdom* (1998) 29 EHRR 245). In both the negative and United Kingdom positive contexts, regard must be had to the fair balance which has to be struck between the competing interests of the individual and the community, including other concerned third parties, and the state's margin of appreciation (see, among other authorities, *Keegan* v *Ireland* (1994) 18 EHRR 342, 362, para 49).'

25 The court held that, in that case, the authorities, including the courts, struck a fair balance between the competing interests and did not fail in their responsibilities to protect the father's right to respect for family life. This decision underlines the positive obligations of the courts including, where necessary, the provision of a regulatory framework of adjudicatory and enforcement machinery in order to protect the rights of the individual. The decisions of the European Court of Human Rights in *Glaser's* case and *X and Y* v *The Netherlands* (1985) 8 EHRR 235, seem to dispose of any argument that a court is not to have regard to the Convention in private law cases. In *Douglas* v *Hello! Ltd* [2001] 2 WLR 992, 1027, para 133, Sedley LJ held that section 12(4) of the Human Rights Act 1998 'puts beyond question the direct applicability of at least one article of the Convention as between one private party to litigation and another—in the jargon, its horizontal effect'.

26 In the light of the judgments in *Douglas's* case, I am satisfied that I have to apply article 10 directly to the present case.

27 That obligation on the court does not seem to me to encompass the creation of a free-standing cause of action based directly upon the articles of the Convention, although that proposition is advanced by Mr Fitzgerald as a fall-back position, if all else fails. The duty on the court, in my view, is to act compatibly with Convention rights in adjudicating upon existing common law causes of action, and that includes a positive as well as a negative obligation.

The jurisdictional basis for an injunction

28 … The principal submission in favour of the existence of the court's power is based upon the law of confidence, taking into account the implementation of the Human Rights Act 1998.

…

The jurisdiction based on confidence

30 As I have already said, in my view, the claimants in private law proceedings cannot rely upon a free-standing application under the Convention. In their submissions, the claimants, supported by the Attorney General and the Official Solicitor, relied upon the common law right to confidence. The tort of breach of confidence is a recognised cause of action. Megarry J in *Coco* v *A N Clark (Engineers) Ltd* [1969] RPC 41, 47, identified three essentials of the tort of breach of confidence: (1) the evidence must have 'the necessary quality of confidence about it'; (2) the information 'must have been imparted in circumstances importing an obligation of confidence'; (3) there must be an 'unauthorised use of the information to the detriment of the party communicating it'.

31 In *Attorney General* v *Guardian Newspapers (No. 2)* [1990] 1 AC 109, 281 Lord Goff of Chieveley said:

'I start with the broad general principle (which I do not intend in any way to be definitive) that a duty of confidence arises when confidential information comes to the knowledge of a person (the confidant) in circumstances where he has notice, or is held to have agreed, that the information is confidential, with the effect that it would be just in all the circumstances that he should be precluded from disclosing the information to others … in the vast majority of cases … the duty of confidence will arise from a transaction or relationship between the parties … But it is well settled that a duty of confidence may arise in equity independently of such cases … '

32 He raised three limiting principles, at p 282:

'that the principle of confidentiality only applies to information to the extent that it is confidential. In particular, once it has entered what is usually called the public domain (which means no more than that the information in question is so generally accessible that, in all the circumstances, it cannot be regarded as confidential) then, as a general rule, the principle of confidentiality can have no application to it … The second limiting principle is that the duty of confidence applies neither to useless information, nor to trivia. There is no need for me to develop this point. The third limiting principle is of far greater importance. It is that, although the basis of the law's protection of confidence is that there is a public interest that confidences should be preserved and protected by the law, nevertheless that public interest may be outweighed by some other countervailing public interest which favours disclosure … It is this limiting principle which may require a court to carry out a balancing operation, weighing the public interest in maintaining confidence against a countervailing public interest favouring disclosure.'

33 The confidentiality sought to be protected in the present case is clearly not trivial. Lord Goff's third limiting principle cannot, I would respectfully suggest, now stand in the light of section 12 of the Human Rights Act 1998 and article 10(1) of the Convention, which together give an enhanced importance to freedom of expression and consequently to the right of the press to publish.

Article 10: freedom of expression

34 Article 10, as applied to the media, is central to this case. …

35 In section 12 of the Human Rights Act 1998, special provisions are made in relation to applications to restrict freedom of expression. Section 12(4) states: 'The court must have particular regard to the importance of the Convention right to freedom of expression … '

36 There is no doubt, therefore, that Parliament has placed great emphasis upon the importance of article 10 and the protection of freedom of expression, inter alia for the press and for the media. The Human Rights Act 1998 and the Convention do not, however, establish new law. They reinforce and give greater weight to the principles already established in our case law. In *R* v *Secretary of State for the Home Department, Ex p Simms* [2000] 2 AC 115, 126, Lord Steyn said:

'Freedom of expression is, of course, intrinsically important: it is valued for its own sake. But it is well recognised that it is also instrumentally important. It serves a number of broad objectives. First, it promotes the self-fulfilment of individuals in society. Secondly, in the famous words of Holmes J (echoing John Stuart Mill), "the best test of truth is the power of the thought to get itself accepted in the competition of the market": *Abrams* v *United States* (1919) 250 US 616, 630 per Holmes J (dissenting). Thirdly, freedom of speech is the lifeblood of democracy. The free flow of information and ideas informs political debate. It is a safety valve: people are more ready to accept decisions that go against them if they can in principle seek to influence them. It acts as a brake on the abuse of power by public officials. It facilitates the exposure of errors in the governance and administration of justice of the country: see Stone, Seidman, Sunstein & Tushnet, *Constitutional Law*, 3rd ed (1996), pp 1078–1086.'

Her Ladyship also quoted from the judgments of Hoffmann LJ in *R* v *Central Independent Television plc* [1994] Fam 192, 202–204 and Munby J in *Kelly* v *British Broadcasting Corpn* [2001] 2 WLR 253, 264 before continuing:

39 In *Sunday Times* v *United Kingdom* (1979) 2 EHRR 245 the European Court of Human Rights said, at p. 281, para 65: 'The court is faced not with a choice between two conflicting principles, but with a principle of freedom of expression that is subject to a number of exceptions which must be narrowly interpreted.'

40 However, more recently, in *Douglas* v *Hello! Ltd* [2001] IP & T 391 at 426–427 (paras 136–137), Sedley LJ said:

' …by virtue of s 12(1) and (4) [of the 1998 Act] the qualifications set out in art 10(2) are as relevant as the right set out in art 10(1). This means, for example, the reputations and rights of others—not only but not least their convention rights—are as material as the defendant's right of free expression. So is the prohibition on the use of one party's convention rights to injure the convention rights of others. Any other approach to s 12 would in my judgment violate s 3 …the much-quoted remark of Hoffmann J in *R* v *Central Independent Television plc* [1994] 3 All ER 641 at 652, [1994] Fam 192 at 203 that freedom of speech "is a trump card which always wins" came in a passage which expressly qualified the proposition as lying "outside the established exceptions (or any new ones which parliament may enact in accordance with its obligations under the convention)". If freedom of expression is to be impeded, in other words, it must be on a cogent ground recognised by law …s 12 of the 1998 Act requires the court to have regard to art 10 …this cannot …give the art 10(1) right to freedom of expression a presumptive priority over other rights. What it does require the court to consider is art 10(2) along with 10(1), and by doing so bring into the frame the conflicting right to privacy. This right, contained in art 8 and reflected in English law, is in turn qualified in both contexts by the right of others to free expression. The outcome, which self evidently has to be the same under both articles, is determined principally by considerations of proportionality.'

41 In his Goodman Lecture on 22 May 1996, Lord Hoffmann referred to his judgment in *R* v *Central Television plc* [1994] Fam 192 and said:

'Some people have read that to mean that freedom of speech always trumps other rights and values. But that is not what I said. I said only that in order to be put [in] the balance against freedom of speech, another interest must fall within some established exception which could be justified under article 10 of the European Convention.'

42 Mr Desmond Browne [counsel for the defendants] submitted that it was not a balancing operation between the right to freedom of expression against any legitimate aim falling within article 10(2). It would seem to me however that, whether it is called a balancing process or any other description, the conflict that may arise between article 10(1) and article 10(2) has to be resolved and the legitimate aim in restricting freedom of expression within the exceptions in article 10(2) given appropriate weight according to the facts of the individual case. Sedley LJ said, in *Douglas*'s case, at p 1028G–H, para 136: 'the qualifications set out in article 10(2) are as relevant as the right set out in article 10(1)'.

43 There would not however be such a juggling act in a case which did not fall within the exceptions set out in article 10(2). It is clear however that, to obtain an injunction to restrain the media from publication of information, it requires a strong case. Brooke LJ said in *Douglas*'s case, at p 1006, para 49: 'Although the right to freedom of expression is not in every case the ace of trumps, it is a powerful card to which the courts of this country must always pay appropriate respect.' And Sedley LJ said, at p 1029, para 136: 'If freedom of expression is to be impeded … it must be on cogent grounds recognised by law.'

44 The onus of proving the case that freedom of expression must be restricted is firmly upon the applicant seeking the relief. The restrictions sought must, in the circumstances of the present case, be shown to be in accordance with the law, justifiable as necessary to satisfy a strong and pressing social need, convincingly demonstrated, to restrain the press in order to protect the rights of the claimants to confidentiality, and proportionate to the legitimate aim pursued. The right to confidence is, however, a recognised exception within article 10(2) and the tort of breach of confidence was the domestic remedy upon which the European Commission, in *Earl Spencer* v *United Kingdom* (1998) 25 EHRR CD 105, declared inadmissible an application by Lord and Lady Spencer on the basis that they had not exhausted their domestic remedies.

45 I turn to the three other articles of the Convention which are said by the claimants to be engaged in this case, and which clearly I must consider alongside article 10.

Article 2: right to life

46 If the claimants' case is made out, article 2 is clearly engaged. In *Osman* v *United Kingdom* (1998) 29 EHRR 245, the European Court of Human Rights held that the provisions of article 2 enjoined a positive obligation upon contracting states to take measures to secure the right to life. In that case it was

the failure of the police to act to protect a family from criminal acts including murder. The European Court said, at p 305, paras 115–116:

'The court notes that the first sentence of article 2(1) enjoins the state not only to refrain from the intentional and unlawful taking of life, but also to take appropriate steps to safeguard the lives of those within its jurisdiction … it must be established to its satisfaction that the authorities knew or ought to have known at the time of the existence of a real and immediate risk to the life of an identified individual or individuals from the criminal acts of a third party and that they failed to take measures within the scope of their powers which, judged reasonably, might have been expected to avoid that risk.'

Article 3: prohibition of torture

47 Article 3 is equally potentially applicable, if I am satisfied as to the strength of the claimants' case. Other than in the specified exceptions in article 2, there is to be no derogation from the rights set out in these two articles.

Article 8: right to respect for private and family life

48 Article 8 is also potentially applicable. …

49 In *X and Y* v *The Netherlands* (1985) 8 EHRR 235, the European Court of Human Rights held that, in a case where the prosecutor took no action on a complaint by a father of a sexual assault on his mentally incapacitated daughter of 16, that the state had failed to protect a vulnerable individual from a criminal violation of her physical and moral integrity by another private individual. A violation of article 8 was found. The court said, at pp 239–240, para 23:

'The court recalls that although the object of article 8 is essentially that of protecting the individual against arbitrary interference by the public authorities, it does not merely compel the state to abstain from such interference: in addition to this primarily negative undertaking, there may be positive obligations inherent in an effective respect for private or family life. These obligations may involve the adoption of measures designed to secure respect for private life even in the sphere of the relations of individuals between themselves.'

50 Sedley LJ said in *Douglas* v *Hello! Ltd* [2001] IP & T 391 at 425–426 (paras 133–134):

'The other point, well made by Mr Tugendhat, is that it is "the convention right" to freedom of expression which both triggers the section (see s 12(1) [of the 1998 Act]) and to which particular regard is to be had. That convention right, when one turns to it, is qualified in favour of the reputation and rights of others and the protection of information received in confidence. In other words you cannot have particular regard to art 10 without having equally particular regard at the very least to art 8 …[Mr Carr] balked at what Mr Tugendhat submitted, and I agree, was the necessary extension of the subsection's logic. A newspaper, say, intends to publish an article about an individual who learns of it and fears, on tenable grounds, that it will put his life in danger. The newspaper, also on tenable grounds, considers his fear unrealistic …it seems to me inescapable that s 12(4) makes the right to life, which is protected by art 2 and implicitly recognised by art 10(2), as relevant as the right of free expression to the court's decision; and in so doing it also makes art 17 (which prohibits the abuse of rights) relevant.'

51 Although the Court of Appeal was concerned with an entirely different situation, the observations of Sedley LJ in *Douglas*'s case are highly relevant to and helpful in the task facing me in the present case where I have to resolve a potential conflict between article 10 on the one hand and articles 2, 3 and 8 on the other hand.

Her Ladyship went on to examine the evidence upon which the claimants relied in support of the applications for permanent injunctions and the evidence adduced by the defendant newspapers.

E. Conclusions on jurisdiction

75 My conclusions on the application of the principles of English law to the facts of this case, are based on the assumption that the case put forward by the claimants has been established.

76 I am, of course, well aware that, until now, the courts have not granted injunctions in the circumstances which arise in this case. It is equally true that the claimants are uniquely notorious. On the basis of the evidence presented to me, their case is exceptional. I recognise also that the threats to the life and physical safety of the claimants do not come from those against whom the injunctions are sought. But the media are uniquely placed to provide the information that would lead to the risk that others would take the law into their own hands and commit crimes against the claimants.

77 The starting point is, however, the well-recognised position of the press, and their right and duty to be free to publish, even in circumstances described by Hoffmann LJ in *R* v *Central Independent Television plc* [1994] Fam 192. As Brooke LJ said in *Douglas* v *Hello! Ltd* [2001] 2 WLR 992, it is a powerful card to which I must pay appropriate respect. I am being asked to extend the domestic law of confidence to grant injunctions in this case. I am satisfied that I can only restrict the freedom of the media to publish if the need for those restrictions can be shown to fall within the exceptions set out in article 10(2). In considering the limits to the law of confidence, and whether a remedy is available to the claimants within those limits, I must interpret narrowly those exceptions. In so doing and having regard to articles 2, 3 and 8 it is important to have regard to the fact that the rights under articles 2 and 3 are not capable of derogation, and the consequences to the claimants if those rights were to be breached. It is clear that, on the basis that there is a real possibility that the claimants may be the objects of revenge attacks, the potential breaches of articles 2, 3 and 8 have to be evaluated with great care.

78 What is the information sought to be protected and how important is it to protect it? The single most important element of the information is the detection of the future identity of the claimants in the community. All the other matters sought to be protected for the present, and for the future, are bound up in the risk of identification, whether by photographs, or by descriptions of identifying features of their appearance as adults, and their new names, addresses and similar information. That risk is potentially extreme if it became known what they look like, and where they are. The risk might come from any quarter, strangers such as vigilante groups, as well as the parents, family and friends of the murdered child. In the present case, the public authority, the court, has knowledge of the risk to the claimants. Does the risk displace the right of the media to publish information about the claimants without any restriction imposed by the court?

79 As I have set out, article 10(2) recognises the express exception, 'for preventing the disclosure of information received in confidence'. None the less, in order for it to be used to restrict freedom of expression, all the criteria in article 10(2), narrowly interpreted, must be met. Taking each limb in turn:

90 The evidence, which I have set out above, demonstrates to me the huge and intense media interest in this case, to an almost unparalleled extent, not only over the time of the murder, during the trial and subsequent litigation, but also that media attention remains intense seven years later. Not only is the media interest intense, it also demonstrates continued hostility towards the claimants. I am satisfied from the extracts from the newspapers: (a) that the press have accurately reported the horror, moral outrage and indignation still felt by many members of the public; (b) that there are members of the public, other than the family of the murdered boy, who continue to feel such hatred and revulsion at the shocking crime and a desire for revenge that some at least of them might well engage in vigilante or revenge attacks if they knew where either claimant was living and could identify him. There also remains a serious risk from the Bulger family, and the father was quoted as recently as October 2000 saying that upon their release he would 'hunt the boys down'; (c) that some sections of the press support this feeling of revulsion and hatred to the degree of encouraging the public to deny anonymity to the claimants. The inevitable conclusion to which I am driven, in particular, by the editorial from the 'News of the World' (one of the newspapers in the defendant group), is that sections of the press would

support, and might even initiate, efforts to find the claimants and to expose their identity and their addresses in their newspapers.

...

96 The Press Code, as applied by the Press Complaints Commission, is not, in the exceptional situation of the claimants, sufficient protection. Criticism of, or indeed sanctions imposed upon, the offending newspaper after the information is published would, in the circumstances of this case, be too late. The information would be in the public domain and the damage would be done. The Press Code cannot adequately protect in advance. The risk is too great for the court to rely upon the voluntary Press Code. To do so would not be a sufficient response to the principles enunciated in *Osman* v *United Kingdom* 29 EHRR 245. I do not consider that the provisions of the Protection from Harassment Act 1997 would or could be adequate to protect the claimants if their identities became known. Recourse to the courts after the event would be too late—for example because they would have by then, almost certainly, been photographed, and would then be recognised everywhere.

97 These uniquely notorious young men are and will, on release, be in a most exceptional situation and the risks to them of identification are real and substantial. It is therefore necessary, in the exceptional circumstances of this case, to place the right to confidence above the right of the media to publish freely information about the claimants. Although the crime of these two young men was especially heinous, they did not thereby forfeit their rights under English law and under the European Convention for the Protection of Human Rights and Fundamental Freedoms. They have served their tariff period and when they are released, they have the right of all citizens to the protection of the law. In order to give them the protection they need and are entitled to receive, I am compelled to grant injunctions.

G. The scope of the injunctions

99 In the present case I have come to the conclusion that I am compelled to grant injunctive relief for the protection of the claimants in respect of a special category of confidential information. For that information to be revealed by a newspaper or television programme, not a party to these proceedings, would have an equally devastating effect as disclosure by one of the defendant groups. It would cause equal harm. It would also, as Balcombe J recognised in *In re X (A Minor) (Wardship: Injunction)* [1984] 1 WLR 1422, be most unjust to the defendants if they were the only newspaper groups to be so restricted. The granting of the injunctions would not, however, have that limited effect. Mr Desmond Browne submitted that, since the decision of the House of Lords in *Attorney General* v *Times Newspapers Ltd* [1992] 1 AC 191, publication of the injunctions against the newspapers would, in practice, act in a similar way, and have the same effect, as injunctions against the media generally. He argued that it was not, therefore, necessary for the injunctions to be made against the world at large. It seems to me that to accept that position would be to achieve through the back door, that which it is submitted I cannot do through the front. I agree with Mr Caldecott that this is somewhat of an academic exercise. There is a *positive* duty on the court as a public authority to take steps to protect individuals from the criminal acts of others: see *Osman* v *United Kingdom* 29 EHRR 245.

100 Although the dictum of Lord Eldon in *Iveson*'s case 7 Ves 251 has been generally followed for nearly 200 years, in light of the implementation of the Human Rights Act 1998, we are entering a new era, and the requirement that the courts act in a way that is compatible with the Convention, and have regard to European jurisprudence, adds a new dimension to those principles. I am satisfied that the injunctive relief that I grant should, in this case, be granted openly against the world.

...

The information to be protected

104 In my judgment, there are compelling reasons to grant injunctions to protect, in the broadest terms, the following information. (i) Any information leading to the identity, or future whereabouts, of each claimant, which includes photographs, description of present appearance and so on. (ii) In order to protect the claimants on their release from detention, it is necessary to have injunctions to protect

their present whereabouts, any information about their present appearance and similar information. That protection must include any efforts by the media to solicit information from past or present carers, staff or co-detainees at their secure units until the claimants' release from detention. (iii) In order further to protect their future identity and whereabouts, no information may be made public or solicited from their secure units that might lead to the identification of the units for a reasonable period after their release. It would seem to me that 12 months from the date of the release of each claimant would be a sufficient period to protect that information, subject to any further argument from counsel. ...

105 I am, of course, aware that injunctions may not be fully effective to protect the claimants from acts committed outside England and Wales resulting information about them being placed on the Internet. The injunctions can, however, prevent wider circulation of that information through the newspapers or television and radio. To that end, therefore, I would be disposed to add, in relation to information in the public domain, a further proviso, suitably limited, which would protect the special quality of the new identity, appearance and addresses of the claimants or information leading to that identification, even after that information had entered the public domain to the extent that it had been published on the Internet or elsewhere such as outside the United Kingdom. I am also aware that the Parole Board will soon be making inquiries and compiling a report for consideration at the Parole Board hearing. It is, in my view, essential that the nature of the inquiries, the content of the report and the hearing itself must be covered by the injunctions.

Injunctions accordingly.

NOTES

1. Case law suggests that in relation to privacy we have indirect horizontal effect which can develop existing rights.
2. In *Campbell* v *Mirror Group Newspapers* [2004] UKHL 22, [2004] 2 WLR 1232, the model Naomi Campbell brought an action over the publication of a story about her attending meetings of Narcotics Anonymous, which included details of her treatment and was accompanied by a photograph. It was a majority decision in the House of Lords and the possible impact upon Ms Campbell's struggle with addiction appeared to be a strong factor for members of the majority. Baroness Hale said [132]:

> Neither party to this appeal has challenged the basic principles which have emerged from the Court of Appeal in the wake of the Human Rights Act 1998. The 1998 Act does not create any new cause of action between private persons. But if there is a relevant cause of action applicable, the court as a public authority must act compatibly with both parties' Convention rights. In a case such as this, the relevant vehicle will usually be the action for breach of confidence, as Lord Woolf CJ held in *A v B plc* [2002] EWCA Civ 337, [2003] QB 195] para. 4.

Convention privacy rights were expanded by the ECtHR in *von Hannover* v *Germany* 16 BHRC 545, which held that photographs of Princess Caroline of Monaco in public places published in German magazines infringed her Art. 8 rights.

3. Dame Elizabeth Butler-Sloss P granted another lifetime injunction in *X (Mary Bell) and another* v *News Group Newspapers and another* [2003] EWHC QB 1101, [2003] EMLR 37 which prohibited identifying the location of Mary Bell, who at the age of 11 had been found guilty of the murder of two young children. Unlike in the decision in *Venables and Thompson* v *News Group Newspapers*, the judge did not recognize any threat to the claimant's, or her daughter's, life but felt that the exceptional circumstances, which included the mental health of Mary Bell, justified the protection of their right to private and family life.
4. The House of Lords ruled against creating a new tort of invasion of privacy in *Wainwright* v *Home Office* [2003] UKHL 53, [2003] 3 WLR 1137, where the appellants complained about the strip searches carried out by prison officers.

■ QUESTION

PeJay, a famous pop star, has become the victim of a stalker who has issued threats against him. PeJay secretly moves home and stops making public appearances. Previously PeJay had courted publicity and had permitted various newspapers and magazines to have access to his previous home to photograph him and to do features on its design and décor. PeJay learns that *Pop Today*, a magazine, has discovered details about his new home and is planning a feature which will use photographs previously published in a property magazine and a photograph of PeJay in the grounds of the home. This photograph was taken by a birdwatcher using a telephoto lens from a position on a public right of way running next to the boundary of PeJay's property. The birdwatcher sold the photograph to *Pop Today*. PeJay applies to the High Court for an injunction against *Pop Today* and all the world forbidding publication of his address and any details or photographs of his home or grounds claiming that such would breach his right to privacy and put his life at risk. How might the Court decide the issue? Would your answer differ if there was no stalker and PeJay had simply decided to retire and withdraw from public life?

(c) How will the courts interpret legislation?

The task of interpreting legislation in actions brought under the Human Rights Act is a very sensitive one. Some of the factors are considered later:

NOTES

1. Section 2(1) of the 1998 Act requires a court or tribunal to 'take into account' the jurisprudence of the European Court of Human Rights and the decisions of other specified Strasbourg bodies.

   The jurisprudence of the European Court of Human Rights may be neither clear nor constant, or it may be subject to interpretation. In *Alconbury* the House of Lords differed in its interpretation of the jurisprudence of the European Court of Human Rights from the lower courts. The same occurred in *Brown* v *Stott (Procurator Fiscal, Dunfermline) and another* [2001] 2 WLR 817 (see later in this chapter in Section 3C(e) at p. 468), where the Privy Council differed in its interpretation of the Strasbourg jurisprudence from that adopted by the High Court of Justiciary. In *R* v *Horncastle* [2009] UKSC 14, Lord Philips said at [11]:

   > ... The requirement to "take into account" the Strasbourg jurisprudence will normally result in this Court applying principles that are clearly established by the Strasbourg Court. There will, however, be rare occasions where this court has concerns as to whether a decision of the Strasbourg Court sufficiently appreciates or accommodates particular aspects of our domestic process. In such circumstances it is open to this court to decline to follow the Strasbourg decision, giving reasons for adopting this course. This is likely to give the Strasbourg Court the opportunity to reconsider the particular aspect of the decision that is in issue, so that there takes place what may prove to be a valuable dialogue between this court and the Strasbourg Court.

2. Section 3(1) of the 1998 Act requires courts to interpret all legislation, regardless of when it was enacted (and thus also of how it may have been interpreted previously), 'So far as it is possible to do so ... in a way which is compatible with the Convention rights'. The New Zealand Bill of Rights Act 1990 contains a similar provision in s. 6, which reads: 'Wherever an enactment can be given a meaning that is consistent with the rights and freedoms contained in this Bill of Rights, that meaning shall be preferred to any other meaning.'

Lord Irvine of Lairg, 'Activism and Restraint: Human Rights and the Interpretative Process'

[1999] *European Human Rights Law Review* 350, 366–7

The Human Rights Legislation: A Constitutional Balancing Act

... The Human Rights Act is founded upon a division of functions between the different branches of government, which reflects the British conception of the separation of powers principle on which our constitution is based. Under the Act our courts have to interpret statutes 'so far as possible' to be compatible with Convention rights; if this is impossible they have been given a unique power to declare legislation to be incompatible, but then it is for the executive to initiate, and Parliament to enact, remedial legislation, with a fast track process available for that purpose. This balance which inheres in the text of the Act can be secured in practical terms only by a measured judicial response to the challenge of seeking, so far as is possible, to interpret national law consistently with the Convention.

If the courts were to adopt a very narrow view of this duty of consistent construction, their ability interpretatively to guarantee Convention rights would be severely curtailed. Instead of reading municipal law in a way which gave effect to individuals' rights, the courts would tend to discover irreconcilable conflicts between United Kingdom law and the Convention which would then require legislative correction. In contrast, a judiciary which took an extremely radical view of its interpretative duty would be likely to stretch legislative language, beyond breaking point, if necessary, in order to effect judicial vindication of Convention rights. Such an approach would yield virtually no declarations of incompatibility: the judges would, in effect, be taking it upon themselves to rewrite legislation in order to render it consistent with the Convention, and so excluding Parliament and the executive from the human rights enterprise.

Both of these approaches would be wrong. The constitutional theory on which the Human Rights Act rests is one of balance. It requires courts to recognise that they have a fundamental contribution to make in this area, while appreciating that the other elements of the constitution also have important roles to play in securing the effective protection of the Convention rights in domestic law. Thus the Act, while significantly changing the nature of the interpretative process, does not confer on the courts a licence to construe legislation in a way which is so radical and strained that it arrogates to the judges a power completely to rewrite existing law: that is a task for Parliament and the executive. The interpretative duty which the courts will soon begin to discharge in the human rights arena is therefore a strong one; but it is nevertheless subject to limits which the Act imposes, and which find still deeper resonance in the doctrine of the separation of powers on which the constitution is founded.

… A different, but related, challenge will arise once the Scottish Parliament begins to legislate. According to the Scotland Act 1998, s. 28(6), the courts must seek to avoid reaching the conclusion that Scottish legislation is invalid (on the ground of its being *ultra vires*) by construing it narrowly. Although this interpretative duty is different in nature from that which the Human Rights Act creates, the importance of balance will remain constant: the courts will have a fundamental contribution to make in seeking to ensure that the Scottish Parliament's legislation is effective (in the sense of being *intra vires*) while preserving the integrity of the distribution of legislative competence between Westminster and Edinburgh which the Scotland Act embodies. Thus, by utilising interpretative methodology to secure the protection of fundamental rights and the efficacy of Scottish legislation, both the Human Rights Act and the Scotland Act recognise that the interpretative process will be of central importance to the success of the constitutional reform programme.

R v Secretary of State for the Home Department, ex parte Simms and another
[1999] 3 WLR 328, House of Lords

(For the facts of this case see Chapter 10, Section 2B at p. 518.)

LORD HOFFMANN: … Parliamentary sovereignty means that Parliament can, if it chooses, legislate contrary to fundamental principles of human rights. The Human Rights Act 1998 will not detract from this power. The constraints upon its exercise by Parliament are ultimately political, not legal. But the principle of legality means that Parliament must squarely confront what it is doing and accept the political cost. Fundamental rights cannot be overridden by general or ambiguous words. This is because there is too great a risk that the full implications of their unqualified meaning may have passed unnoticed in the democratic process. In the absence of express language or necessary implication to the contrary, the courts therefore presume that even the most general words were intended to be subject to the basic rights of the individual. In this way the courts of the United Kingdom, though acknowledging the sovereignty of Parliament, apply principles of constitutionality little different from those which exist in countries where the power of the legislature is expressly limited by a constitutional document.

The Human Rights Act 1998 will make three changes to this scheme of things. First, the principles of fundamental human rights which exist at common law will be supplemented by a specific text, namely the European Convention. But much of the Convention reflects the common law: see

Derbyshire County Council v *Times Newspapers Ltd* [1993] AC 534, 551. That is why the United Kingdom government felt able in 1950 to accede to the Convention without domestic legislative change. So the adoption of the text as part of domestic law is unlikely to involve radical change in our notions of fundamental human rights. Secondly, the principle of legality will be expressly enacted as a rule of construction in section 3 and will gain further support from the obligation of the Minister in charge of a Bill to make a statement of compatibility under section 19. Thirdly, in those unusual cases in which the legislative infringement of fundamental human rights is so clearly expressed as not to yield to the principle of legality, the courts will be able to draw this to the attention of Parliament by making a declaration of incompatibility. It will then be for the sovereign Parliament to decide whether or not to remove the incompatibility.

NOTE: A number of appellate decisions have involved the courts in exploring the meaning of the interpretative obligation which s. 3 of the Human Rights Act 1998 places upon them. The impact of the section on the traditional approach to statutory interpretation is immense, as indicated by the following extract from the judgment of Lord Woolf CJ in *Poplar Housing Association Ltd* v *Donoghue* [2001] EWCA Civ 595:

75 It is difficult to overestimate the importance of section 3. It applies to legislation passed both before and after the Human Rights Act 1998 came into force. Subject to the section not requiring the court to go beyond that which is possible, it is mandatory in its terms. In the case of legislation predating the Human Rights Act 1998 where the legislation would otherwise conflict with the Convention, section 3 requires the court to now interpret legislation in a manner which it would not have done before the Human Rights Act 1998 came into force. When the court interprets legislation usually its primary task is to identify the intention of Parliament. Now, when section 3 applies, the courts have to adjust their traditional role in relation to interpretation so as to give effect to the direction contained in section 3. It is as though legislation which predates the Human Rights Act 1998 and conflicts with the Convention has to be treated as being subsequently amended to incorporate the language of section 3. However, the following points, which are probably self-evident, should be noted.

(a) Unless the legislation would otherwise be in breach of the Convention section 3 can be ignored (so courts should always first ascertain whether, absent section 3, there would be any breach of the Convention).

(b) If the court has to rely on section 3 it should limit the extent of the modified meaning to that which is necessary to achieve compatibility.

(c) Section 3 does not entitle the court to *legislate* (its task is still one of *interpretation*, but interpretation in accordance with the direction contained in section 3).

(d) The views of the parties and of the Crown as to whether a 'constructive' interpretation should be adopted cannot modify the task of the court (if section 3 applies the court is required to adopt the section 3 approach to interpretation).

(e) Where, despite the strong language of section 3, it is not possible to achieve a result which is compatible with the Convention, the court is not *required* to grant a declaration and presumably in exercising its discretion as to whether to grant a declaration or not it will be influenced by the usual considerations which apply to the grant of declarations.

The problem which courts confront, however, is determining where the line is to be drawn between interpreting the legislation and legislating themselves. The bolder the interpretative approach which the court adopts, the greater the risk that the line will be transgressed. Consider whether the House of Lords, in the case which follows, by reading words into the statute in question to achieve compatibility, crossed the line.

Ghaidan v *Godin-Mendoza*

[2004] UKHL 30, [2004] 2 AC 557, House of Lords

On the death of a protected tenant of a dwelling-house his or her surviving spouse, if then living in the house, becomes a statutory tenant by succession. But marriage is not essential for this purpose. A person who was living with the original tenant 'as his or her wife or husband' is treated as the spouse of the original tenant: see Rent Act 1977, Schedule 1, para. 2(2). In *Fitzpatrick* v *Sterling Housing Association Ltd* [2001] 1 AC 27, the House of Lords decided this provision did not include persons in a same-sex relationship. The question raised by this appeal is whether this reading of para. 2 can survive the coming into force of the Human Rights Act 1998. The county court held that it could, but this was overturned by the Court of Appeal. On appeal:

LORD STEYN: ... My Lords,

37. In my view the Court of Appeal came to the correct conclusion. I agree with the conclusions and reasons of my noble and learned friends Lord Nicholls of Birkenhead, Lord Rodger of Earlsferry and Baroness Hale of Richmond. In the light of those opinions, I will not comment on the case generally.

38. I confine my remarks to the question whether it is possible under section 3(1) of the Human Rights Act 1998 to read and give effect to paragraph 2(2) of Schedule 1 to the Rent Act 1977 in a way which is compatible with the European Convention on Human Rights. In my view the interpretation adopted by the Court of Appeal under section 3(1) was a classic illustration of the permissible use of this provision. But it became clear during oral argument, and from a subsequent study of the case law and academic discussion on the correct interpretation of section 3(1), that the role of that provision in the remedial scheme of the 1998 Act is not always correctly understood. I would therefore wish to examine the position in a general way...

40. My impression is that two factors are contributing to a misunderstanding of the remedial scheme of the 1998 Act. First, there is the constant refrain that a judicial reading down, or reading in, under section 3 would flout the will of Parliament as expressed in the statute under examination. This question cannot sensibly be considered without giving full weight to the countervailing will of Parliament as expressed in the 1998 Act.

41. The second factor may be an excessive concentration on linguistic features of the particular statute. Nowhere in our legal system is a literalistic approach more inappropriate than when considering whether a breach of a Convention right may be removed by interpretation under section 3. Section 3 requires a broad approach concentrating, amongst other things, in a purposive way on the importance of the fundamental right involved.

42. In enacting the 1998 Act Parliament legislated "to bring rights home" from the European Court of Human Rights to be determined in the courts of the United Kingdom. That is what the White Paper said: see Rights Brought Home: The Human Rights Bill (1997) (Cm 3782), para 2.7. That is what Parliament was told. The mischief to be addressed was the fact that Convention rights as set out in the ECHR, which Britain ratified in 1951, could not be vindicated in our courts. Critical to this purpose was the enactment of effective remedial provisions. [See sections 3(1), (2), 4(1), (2) at Section 3A, at p. 416.]

If Parliament disagrees with an interpretation by the courts under section 3(1), it is free to override it by amending the legislation and expressly reinstating the incompatibility.

44. It is necessary to state what section 3(1), and in particular the word 'possible', does not mean. First, section 3(1) applies even if there is no ambiguity in the language in the sense of it being capable of bearing two *possible* meanings. The word 'possible' in section 3(1) is used in a different and much stronger sense. Secondly, section 3(1) imposes a stronger and more radical obligation than to adopt a purposive interpretation in the light of the ECHR. Thirdly, the draftsman of the Act had before him the model of the New Zealand Bill of Rights Act which imposes a requirement that the interpretation to be adopted must be reasonable. Parliament specifically rejected the legislative model of requiring a reasonable interpretation.

45. Instead the draftsman had resort to the analogy of the obligation under the EEC Treaty on national courts, as far as possible, to interpret national legislation in the light of the wording and purpose of directives. In *Marleasing SA* v *La Comercial Internacional de Alimentación SA* (Case C–106/89) [1990] ECR I–4135, 4159 the European Court of Justice defined this obligation as follows:

'It follows that, in applying national law, whether the provisions in questions were adopted before or after the directive, the national court called upon to interpret it is required to do so, as far as possible, in light of the wording and the purpose of the directive in order to achieve the result pursued by the latter and thereby comply with the third paragraph of Article 189 of the Treaty.'

Given the undoubted strength of this interpretative obligation under EEC law, this is a significant signpost to the meaning of section 3(1) in the 1998 Act.

46.   Parliament had before it the mischief and objective sought to be addressed, viz the need 'to bring rights home'. The linch-pin of the legislative scheme to achieve this purpose was section 3(1). Rights could only be effectively brought home if section 3(1) was the prime remedial measure, and section 4 a measure of last resort. How the system modelled on the EEC interpretative obligation would work was graphically illustrated for Parliament during the progress of the Bill through both Houses. The Lord Chancellor observed that 'in 99% of the cases that will arise, there will be no need for judicial declarations of incompatibility' and the Home Secretary said 'We expect that, in almost all cases, the courts will be able to interpret the legislation compatibly with the Convention': Hansard (HL Debates,) 5 February 1998, col 840 (3rd reading) and Hansard (HC Debates,) 16 February 1998, col 778 (2nd reading). It was envisaged that the duty of the court would be to strive to find (if possible) a meaning which would best accord with Convention rights. This is the remedial scheme which Parliament adopted.

47.   Three decisions of the House can be cited to illustrate the strength of the interpretative obligation under section 3(1). The first is *R* v *A (No. 2)* [2002] 1 AC 45 which concerned the so-called rape shield legislation. The problem was the blanket exclusion of prior sexual history between the complainant and an accused in section 41(1) of the Youth Justice and Criminal Evidence Act 1999, subject to narrow specific categories in the remainder of section 41. In subsequent decisions, and in academic literature, there has been discussion about differences of emphasis in the various opinions in *A*. What has been largely overlooked is the unanimous conclusion of the House. The House unanimously agreed on an interpretation under section 3 which would ensure that section 41 would be compatible with the ECHR. The formulation was by agreement set out in paragraph 46 of my opinion in that case as follows:

'The effect of the decision today is that under section 41(3)(c) of the 1999 Act, construed where necessary by applying the interpretive obligation under section 3 of the Human Rights Act 1998, and due regard always being paid to the importance of seeking to protect the complainant from indignity and from humiliating questions, the test of admissibility is whether the evidence (and questioning in relation to it) is nevertheless so relevant to the issue of consent that to exclude it would endanger the fairness of the trial under article 6 of the Convention. If this test is satisfied the evidence should not be excluded.'

This formulation was endorsed by Lord Slynn of Hadley at p 56, para 13 of his opinion in identical wording. The other Law Lords sitting in the case expressly approved the formulation set out in para 46 of my opinion: Lord Hope of Craighead, at pp 87–88, para 110, Lord Clyde, at p 98, para 140; and Lord Hutton, at p 106, para 163. In so ruling the House rejected linguistic arguments in favour of a broader approach. In the subsequent decisions of the House in *In re S (Minors) (Care Order: Implementation of Care Plan)* [2002] 2 AC 291 and *Bellinger* v *Bellinger* [2003] 2 AC 467, which touched on the remedial structure of the 1998 Act, *the decision* of the House in the case of *A* was not questioned. And in the present case nobody suggested that *A* involved a heterodox exercise of the power under section 3.

48.   The second and third decisions of the House are *Pickstone* v *Freemans plc* [1989] AC 66 and *Litster* v *Forth Dry Dock & Engineering Co Ltd* [1990] 1 AC 546 which involve the interpretative obligation under EEC law. *Pickstone* concerned section 1(2) of the Equal Pay Act 1970, (as amended by section 8 of the Sex Discrimination Act 1975 and regulation 2 of the Equal Pay (Amendment) Regulations 1983 (SI 1983/1794) which implied into any contract without an equality clause one that modifies any term in a woman's contract which is less favourable than a term of a similar kind in the contract of a man:

(a) where the woman is employed on like work with a man in the same employment …

(b) where the woman is employed on work rated as equivalent with that of a man in the same employment …

(c) where a woman is employed on work which, not being work in 'relation to which paragraph (a) or (b) above applies, is, in terms of the demands made on her (for instance under such headings as effort, skill and decision), of equal value to that of a man in the same employment'.

Lord Templeman observed (at pp 120–121):

'In my opinion there must be implied in paragraph (c) after the word "applies" the words "as between the woman and the man with whom she claims equality." This construction is consistent with Community law. The employers' construction is inconsistent with Community law and creates a permitted form of discrimination without rhyme or reason.'

That was the ratio decidendi of the decision. *Litster* concerned regulations intended to implement an EC Directive, the purpose of which was to protect the workers in an undertaking when its ownership was transferred. However, the regulations only protected those who were employed 'immediately before' the transfer. Having enquired into the purpose of the Directive, the House of Lords interpreted the Regulations by reading in additional words to protect workers not only if they were employed 'immediately before' the time of transfer, but also when they would have been so employed if they had not been unfairly dismissed by reason of the transfer: see Lord Keith of Kinkel, at 554. In both cases the House eschewed linguistic arguments in favour of a broad approach. *Pickstone* and *Litster* involved national legislation which implemented EC Directives. *Marleasing* extended the scope of the interpretative obligation to unimplemented Directives. *Pickstone* and *Litster* reinforce the approach to section 3(1) which prevailed in the House in the rape shield case.

49. A study of the case law listed in the Appendix to this judgment reveals that there has sometimes been a tendency to approach the interpretative task under section 3(1) in too literal and technical a way. In practice there has been too much emphasis on linguistic features. If the core remedial purpose of section 3(1) is not to be undermined a broader approach is required. That is, of course, not to gainsay the obvious proposition that inherent in the use of the word 'possible' in section 3(1) is the idea that there is a Rubicon which courts may not cross. If it is not possible, within the meaning of section 3, to read or give effect to legislation in a way which is compatible with Convention rights, the only alternative is to exercise, where appropriate, the power to make a declaration of incompatibility. Usually, such cases should not be too difficult to identify. An obvious example is *R (Anderson)* v *Secretary of State for the Home Department* [2003] 1 AC 837. The House held that the Home Secretary was not competent under article 6 of the ECHR to decide on the tariff to be served by mandatory life sentence prisoners. The House found a section 3(1) interpretation not 'possible' and made a declaration under section 4. Interpretation could not provide a substitute scheme. *Bellinger* is another obvious example. As Lord Rodger of Earlsferry observed ' … in relation to the validity of marriage, Parliament regards gender as fixed and immutable': [2003] 2 WLR 1174, 1195, para 83. Section 3(1) of the 1998 Act could not be used.

50. Having had the opportunity to reconsider the matter in some depth, I am not disposed to try to formulate precise rules about where section 3 may not be used. Like the proverbial elephant such a case ought generally to be easily identifiable. What is necessary, however, is to emphasise that interpretation under section 3(1) is the prime remedial remedy and that resort to section 4 must always be an exceptional course. In practical effect there is a strong rebuttable presumption in favour of an interpretation consistent with Convention rights. Perhaps the opinions delivered in the House today will serve to ensure a balanced approach along such lines.

51. I now return to the circumstances of the case before the House. Applying section 3 the Court of Appeal interpreted 'as his or her wife or husband' in the statute to mean '*as if they were* his wife or husband'. While there has been some controversy about aspects of the reasoning of the Court of Appeal, I would endorse the reasoning of the Court of Appeal on the use of section 3(1) in this case. It was well within the power under this provision.

52. I would also dismiss the appeal.

LORD MILLETT: ...

55. I agree with all my noble and learned friends, whose speeches I have had the advantage of reading in draft, that such discriminatory treatment of homosexual couples is incompatible with their Convention rights and cannot be justified by any identifiable legitimate aim ...

56. It follows that, unless the court can apply section 3 of the Human Rights Act 1998 to extend the reach of para 2(2) to the survivor of a couple of the same sex, it must consider making a declaration of incompatibility under section 4. The making of such a declaration is in the court's discretion (section 4 provides only that the court 'may' make one); and it may be a matter for debate whether it would be appropriate to do so at a time when not merely has the Government announced its intention to bring forward corrective legislation in due course (as in *Bellinger* v *Bellinger* [2003] 2 AC 467) but Parliament is currently engaged in enacting remedial legislation. It is, however, unnecessary to enter upon this question, for there is a clear majority in favour of the view that section 3 can be applied to interpret para 2(2) in a way which renders legislative intervention unnecessary.

57. I have the misfortune to be unable to agree with this conclusion. I have given long and anxious consideration to the question whether, in the interests of unanimity, I should suppress my dissent, but I have come to the conclusion that I should not. The question is of great constitutional importance, for it goes to the relationship between the legislature and the judiciary, and hence ultimately to the supremacy of Parliament. Sections 3 and 4 of the Human Rights Act were carefully crafted to preserve the existing constitutional doctrine, and any application of the ambit of section 3 beyond its proper scope subverts it. This is not to say that the doctrine of Parliamentary supremacy is sacrosanct, but only that any change in a fundamental constitutional principle should be the consequence of deliberate legislative action and not judicial activism, however well meaning.

...

69. ... it may be helpful if I give some examples of the way in which I see section 3 as operating.

70. In the course of his helpful argument counsel for the Secretary of State, who did not resist the application of section 3, acknowledged that it could not be used to read 'black' as meaning 'white'. That must be correct. Words cannot *mean* their opposite; 'black' cannot *mean* 'not black'. But they may *include* their opposite. In some contexts it may be possible to read 'black' as meaning 'black or white'; in other contexts it may be impossible to do so. It all depends on whether 'blackness' is the essential feature of the statutory scheme; and while the court may look behind the words of the statute they cannot be disregarded or given no weight, for they are the medium by which Parliament expresses its intention.

71. Again, 'red, blue or green' cannot be read as meaning 'red, blue, green or yellow'; the specification of three only of the four primary colours indicates a deliberate omission of the fourth (unless, of course, this can be shown to be an error). Section 3 cannot be used to supply the missing colour, for this would be not to interpret the statutory language but to contradict it.

72. The limits on the application of section 3 may thus be in part at least linguistic, as in the examples I have given, but they may also be derived from a consideration of the legislative history of the offending statute. Thus, while it may be possible to read 'cats' as meaning 'cats or dogs' (on the footing that the essential concept is that of domestic pets generally rather than felines particularly), it would obviously not be possible to read 'Siamese cats' as meaning 'Siamese cats or dogs'. The particularity of the expression 'Siamese cats' would preclude its extension to other species of cat, let alone dogs. But suppose the statute merely said 'cats', and that this was the result of successive amendments to the statute as originally enacted. If this had said 'Siamese cats', and had twice been amended, first to read 'Siamese or Persian cats' and then to read simply 'cats', it would not, in my opinion, be possible to read the word 'cats' as including 'dogs'; the legislative history would demonstrate that, while Parliament had successively widened the scope of the statute, it had consistently legislated in relation to felines, and had left its possible extension to other domestic pets for future consideration. Reading the word 'cats' as meaning 'cats or dogs' in these circumstances would be to usurp the function of Parliament.

73. In *R v A* [2002] 1 AC 45 [*sic*] the offending statute had laid down an elaborate scheme to prevent the defendant to a charge of rape from adducing certain kinds of evidence at his trial. Read without qualification this could exclude logically relevant evidence favourable to the accused and deny him a fair trial contrary to article 6 of the Convention. The House read the statute as subject to the implied proviso that evidence or questioning which was required to ensure a fair trial should not be treated as inadmissible. The House supplied a missing qualification which significantly limited the operation of the statute but which did not contradict any of its fundamental features. As Lord Steyn observed (at p 68, para 45) it would be unrealistic to suppose that Parliament, if alerted to the problem, would have wished to deny an accused person the right to put forward a full and complete defence by advancing truly probative material.

74. For my own part, I have no difficulty with the conclusion which the House reached in that case. The qualification which it supplied glossed but did not contradict anything in the relevant statute. Neither expressly nor implicitly did the statute require logically probative evidence to be excluded if its exclusion would have the effect of denying the accused a fair trial. The meaning of the statute was not ambiguous, and in the absence of section 3 the proviso could not have been implied. But if it had been expressed it would not have made the statute self-contradictory or produced a nonsense.

[Lord Millett considered the legislative history.]

94. By 1988 Parliament, therefore, had successively widened the scope of paragraph 2(1). First applying only to the tenant's widow, it was extended first to his or her surviving spouse and later to a person who had lived with the tenant as his or her spouse though without actually contracting a legally binding marriage. The common feature of all these relationships is that they are open relationships between persons of the opposite sex. Persons who set up home together may be husband and wife or live together as husband and wife; they may be lovers; or brother and sister; or friends; or fellow students; or share a common economic interest; or one may be economically dependent on the other. But Parliament did not extend the right to persons who set up home together; but only to those who did so *as husband and wife*.

95. Couples of the same sex can no more live together as husband and wife than they can live together as brother and sister. To extend the paragraph to persons who set up home as lovers would have been a major category extension. It would have been highly controversial in 1988 and was not then required by the Convention. The practice of Contracting States was far from uniform; and Parliament was entitled to take the view that any further extension of paragraph (2) could wait for another day. One step at a time is a defensible legislative policy which the courts should respect. Housing Acts come before Parliament with some frequency; and Parliament was entitled to take the view that the question could be revisited without any great delay. It is just as important for legislatures not to proceed faster than society can accept as it is for judges; and under our constitutional arrangements the pace of change is for Parliament.

96. Parliament, as I have said, is now considering corrective legislation in the Civil Partnerships Bill currently before the House in its legislative capacity. The Bill creates a new legal relationship, called a civil partnership, which the persons of the same sex may enter into by registering themselves as civil partners. It inserts the words "or surviving civil partner" after the words 'surviving spouse' in paragraph 2(1), and adds a new paragraph (2)(b):

'(b) a person who was living with the original tenant as if they were civil partners shall be treated as the civil partner of the original tenant.'

97. There will thus be four categories of relationship covered if the Bill becomes law: (i) spouses, ie married persons (necessarily being persons of the opposite sex); (ii) persons who live together as husband and wife who are to be treated as if they were married (and who must therefore also be of the opposite sex); (iii) civil partners (who must be of the same sex) who are given the same rights as

but are not treated as if they were married persons; and (iv) persons who live together as if they were civil partners without having registered their relationship, who are treated as if they had done so. This is a rational and sensible scheme which does not involve pretending that couples of the same sex can marry or be treated as if they had done so.

98.   Among the matters which Parliament will have had to consider in debating the Civil Partnerships Bill are: (i) which statutes to amend by extending their reach to civil partners and persons living together as civil partners; (ii) whether such statutes should extend to unregistered civil partnerships in every case or whether in some cases it would be appropriate to require the parties to register their relationship before taking the benefits of the statute; (iii) whether the Bill should be retrospective to any and what extent; and (iv) from what date should the new provisions come into force. Presumably some time must elapse before a system of registration can be established: should unregistered civil partners have to wait until it is? These, and no doubt other matters, are questions of policy for the legislature.

99.   All this will be foreclosed by the majority. By what is claimed to be a process of interpretation of an existing statute framed in gender specific terms, and enacted at a time when homosexual relationships were not recognised by law, it is proposed to treat persons of the same sex living together as if they were living together as husband and wife and then to treat such persons as if they were lawfully married. It is to be left unclear as from what date this change in the law has taken place. If we were to decide this question we would be usurping the function of Parliament; and if we were to say that it was from the time when the European Court of Human Rights decided that such discrimination was unlawful we would be transferring the legislative power from Parliament to that court. It is, in my view, consonant with the Convention for the Contracting States to take time to consider its implications and to bring their laws into conformity with it. They do not demand retrospective legislation.

100.   Worse still, in support of their conclusion that the existing discrimination is incompatible with the Convention, there is a tendency in some of the speeches of the majority to refer to loving, stable and long-lasting homosexual relationships. It is left wholly unclear whether qualification for the successive tenancy is confined to couples enjoying such a relationship or, consistently with the legislative policy which Parliament has hitherto adopted, is dependent on status and not merit.

101.   In my opinion all these questions are essentially questions of social policy which should be left to Parliament. For the reasons I have endeavoured to state it is in my view not open to the courts to foreclose them by adopting an interpretation of the existing legislation which it not only does not bear but which is manifestly inconsistent with it.

102.   I would allow the appeal.

...

LORD RODGER OF EARLSFERRY:

122.   ... the key to what it is possible for the courts to imply into legislation without crossing the border from interpretation to amendment does not lie in the number of words that have to be read in. The key lies in a careful consideration of the essential principles and scope of the legislation being interpreted. If the insertion of one word contradicts those principles or goes beyond the scope of the legislation, it amounts to impermissible amendment. On the other hand, if the implication of a dozen words leaves the essential principles and scope of the legislation intact but allows it to be read in a way which is compatible with Convention rights, the implication is a legitimate exercise of the powers conferred by section 3(1). Of course, the greater the extent of the proposed implication, the greater the need to make sure that the court is not going beyond the scheme of the legislation and embarking upon amendment. Nevertheless, what matters is not the number of words but their effect

...

124.   Sometimes it may be possible to isolate a particular phrase which causes the difficulty and to read in words that modify it so as to remove the incompatibility. Or else the court may read in words that qualify the provision as a whole. At other times the appropriate solution may be to read down the provision so that it falls to be given effect in a way that is compatible with the Convention rights

in question. In other cases the easiest solution may be to put the offending part of the provision into different words which convey the meaning that will be compatible with those rights. The preferred technique will depend on the particular provision and also, in reality, on the person doing the interpreting. This does not matter since they are simply different means of achieving the same substantive result. However, precisely because section 3(1) is to be operated by many others besides the courts, and because it is concerned with interpreting and not with amending the offending provision, it respectfully seems to me that it would be going too far to insist that those using the section to interpret legislation should match the standards to be expected of a parliamentary draftsman amending the provision: cf *R* v *Lambert* [2002] 2 AC 545, 585, para 80 per Lord Hope of Craighead. It is enough that the interpretation placed on the provision should be clear, however it may be expressed and whatever the precise means adopted to achieve it.

Appeal disallowed.

NOTE: In *R* v *A (No. 2)* [2002] 1 AC 45, there was criticism that the Law Lords had gone too far and frustrated parliamentary intention, and this may explain the justifications of it in *Ghaidan*. For an interesting defence of *R* v *A* see A. Kavanagh 'Unlocking the Human Rights Act: the Radical Approach to section 3(1) Revisited' (2005) 3 *European Human Rights Law Review* 259.

■ QUESTION
By interpreting 'as his or her wife or husband' to include same-sex couples, have the majority gone beyond interpreting the legislation and, in effect, engaged in legislating, and, if yes, are the courts an appropriate institution to consider the various issues of policy?

In the following case the House of Lords shows some limits to making a Convention compatible interpretation under s. 3(1).

In re S (Minors) (Care Order: Implementation of Care Plan)
[2002] UKHL 10, House of Lords

LORD NICHOLLS OF BIRKENHEAD:
My Lords,
    1. These appeals concern the impact of the Human Rights Act 1998 on Parts III and IV of the Children Act 1989. The Court of Appeal (Thorpe, Sedley and Hale LJJ) made, in the words of Thorpe LJ, two major adjustments and innovations in the construction and application of the Children Act. The principal issue before your Lordships' House concerns the soundness of this judicial initiative.

    …

    17. Stated shortly, the two innovations fashioned by the Court of Appeal were these. First, the court enunciated guidelines intended to give trial judges a wider discretion to make an interim care order, rather than a final care order. The second innovation was more radical. It concerns the position after the court has made a care order. The Court of Appeal propounded a new procedure, by which at the trial the essential milestones of a care plan would be identified and elevated to a 'starred status'. If a starred milestone was not achieved within a reasonable time after the date set at trial, the local authority was obliged to 'reactivate the interdisciplinary process that contributed to the creation of the care plan'. At the least the local authority must inform the child's guardian of the position. Either the guardian or the local authority would then have the right to apply to the court for further directions: see the judgment of Thorpe LJ ([2000] EWCA Civ 757, at paragraphs 29 and 30).

    …

Starred milestones
    23. Two preliminary points can be made at the outset. First, a cardinal principle of the Children Act is that when the court makes a care order it becomes the duty of the local authority designated by the order to receive the child into its care while the order remains in force. So long as the care order is

in force the authority has parental responsibility for the child. The authority also has power to decide the extent to which a parent of the child may meet his responsibility for him: section 33. An authority might, for instance, not permit parents to change the school of a child living at home. While a care order is in force the court's powers, under its inherent jurisdiction, are expressly excluded: section 100(2)(c) and (d). Further, the court may not make a contact order, a prohibited steps order or a specific issue order: section 9(1).

24. There are limited exceptions to this principle of non-intervention by the court in the authority's discharge of its parental responsibility for a child in its care under a care order. The court retains jurisdiction to decide disputes about contact with children in care: section 34. The court may discharge a care order, either on an application made for the purpose under section 39 or as a consequence of making a residence order (sections 9(1) and 91(1)). The High Court's judicial review jurisdiction also remains available.

25. These exceptions do not detract significantly from the basic principle. The Act delineated the boundary of responsibility with complete clarity. Where a care order is made the responsibility for the child's care is with the authority rather than the court. The court retains no supervisory role, monitoring the authority's discharge of its responsibilities. That was the intention of Parliament.

...

31. In autumn 1998 the Government published its response to the children's safeguards review (Cm 4105) and launched its 'Quality Protects' programme, aimed at improving the public care system for children. Conferences have also been held, and many research studies undertaken, both private and public, on particular aspects of the problems. Some of the problems were discussed at the bi-annual President's Interdisciplinary Conference on family law 1997, attended by judges, child psychiatrists, social workers, social services personnel and other experts. The proceedings of the conference were subsequently published in book form, '*Divided Duties*' (1998). The sharpness of the divide between the court's powers before and after the making of a care order attracted criticism. The matters discussed included the need for a care plan to be open to review by the court in exceptional cases. One suggestion was that a court review could be triggered by failure to implement 'starred' key factors in the care plan within specified time-scales. The guardian ad litem would be the appropriate person to intervene.

32. This was the source of the innovation which found expression in the judgments of the Court of Appeal in the present appeals. The House was informed by counsel that the starred milestones guidance given by the Court of Appeal was not canvassed in argument before the court. This guidance appeared for the first time in the judgments of the court.

33. The jurisprudential route by which the Court of Appeal found itself able to bring about this development was primarily by recourse to section 3 of the Human Rights Act. Hale LJ said, at paragraphs 79-80:

'Where elements of the care plan are so fundamental that there is a real risk of a breach of Convention rights if they are not fulfilled, and where there is some reason to fear that they may not be fulfilled, it must be justifiable *to read into the Children Act* a power in the court to require a report on progress. ... the court would require a report, either to the court or to CAFCASS., who could then decide whether it was appropriate to return the case to court. ... [W]hen making a care order, the court is being asked to interfere in family life. If it perceives that the consequence of doing so will be to put at risk the Convention rights of either the parents or the child, the court *should be able* to impose this very limited requirement as a condition of its own interference.' (My emphasis)

Section 3 of the Human Rights Act

34. The judgments in the Court of Appeal are a clear and forceful statement of the continuing existence of serious problems in this field. In the nature of things, courts are likely to see more of the cases which go wrong. But the view, widespread among family judges, is that all too often local authorities'

discharge of their parental responsibilities falls short of an acceptable standard. A disturbing instance can be found in the recent case of *F v London Borough of Lambeth* (28 September 2001, unreported). Munby J said, in paragraph 38 of his judgment, that the 'blunt truth is that in this case the state has failed these parents and these boys'.

35. It is entirely understandable that the Court of Appeal should seek some means to alleviate these problems: some means by which the courts may assist children where care orders have been made but subsequently, for whatever reason, care plans have not been implemented as envisaged and, as a result, the welfare of the children is being prejudiced. This is entirely understandable. The courts, notably through their wardship jurisdiction, have long discharged an invaluable role in safeguarding the interests of children. But the question before the House is much more confined. The question is whether the courts have power to introduce into the working of the Children Act a range of rights and liabilities not sanctioned by Parliament.

36. On this I have to say at once, respectfully but emphatically, that I part company with the Court of Appeal. I am unable to agree that the court's introduction of a 'starring system' can be justified as a legitimate exercise in interpretation of the Children Act in accordance with section 3 of the Human Rights Act. Even if the Children Act is inconsistent with articles 6 or 8 of the Convention, which is a question I will consider later, section 3 does not in this case have the effect suggested by the Court of Appeal.

37. Section 3(1) provides:

 'So far as it is possible to do so, primary legislation … must be read and given effect in a way which is compatible with the Convention rights.'

This is a powerful tool whose use is obligatory. It is not an optional canon of construction. Nor is its use dependent on the existence of ambiguity. Further, the section applies retrospectively. So far as it is possible to do so, primary legislation 'must be read and given effect' to in a way which is compatible with Convention rights. This is forthright, uncompromising language.

38. But the reach of this tool is not unlimited. Section 3 is concerned with interpretation. This is apparent from the opening words of section 3(1): 'so far as it is possible to do so'. The side heading of the section is 'Interpretation of legislation'. Section 4 (power to make a declaration of incompatibility) and, indeed, section 3(2)(b) presuppose that not all provisions in primary legislation can be rendered Convention compliant by the application of section 3(1). The existence of this limit on the scope of section 3(1) has already been the subject of judicial confirmation, more than once: see, for instance, Lord Woolf CJ in *Poplar Housing and Regeneration Community Association Ltd v Donoghue* [2001] 3 WLR 183, 204, para 75 and Lord Hope of Craighead in *R v Lambert* [2001] 3 WLR 206, 233-235, paras 79-81.

39. In applying section 3 courts must be ever mindful of this outer limit. The Human Rights Act reserves the amendment of primary legislation to Parliament. By this means the Act seeks to preserve parliamentary sovereignty. The Act maintains the constitutional boundary. Interpretation of statutes is a matter for the courts; the enactment of statutes, and the amendment of statutes, are matters for Parliament.

40. Up to this point there is no difficulty. The area of real difficulty lies in identifying the limits of interpretation in a particular case. This is not a novel problem. If anything, the problem is more acute today than in past times. Nowadays courts are more 'liberal' in the interpretation of all manner of documents. The greater the latitude with which courts construe documents, the less readily defined is the boundary. What one person regards as sensible, if robust, interpretation, another regards as impermissibly creative. For present purposes it is sufficient to say that a meaning which departs substantially from a fundamental feature of an Act of Parliament is likely to have crossed the boundary between interpretation and amendment. This is especially so where the departure has important practical repercussions which the court is not equipped to evaluate. In such a case the overall contextual setting may leave no scope for rendering the statutory provision Convention compliant by legitimate use of the process of

interpretation. The boundary line may be crossed even though a limitation on Convention rights is not stated in express terms. Lord Steyn's observations in *R v A (No. 2)* [2002] 2 AC 45, 68D-E, para 44 are not to be read as meaning that a clear limitation on Convention rights in terms is the only circumstance in which an interpretation incompatible with Convention rights may arise.

41. I should add a further general observation in the light of what happened in the present case. Section 3 directs courts on how legislation shall, as far as possible, be interpreted. When a court, called upon to construe legislation, ascribes a meaning and effect to the legislation pursuant to its obligation under section 3, it is important the court should identify clearly the particular statutory provision or provisions whose interpretation leads to that result. Apart from all else, this should assist in ensuring the court does not inadvertently stray outside its interpretation jurisdiction.

42. I return to the Children Act. I have already noted, as a cardinal principle of the Act, that the courts are not empowered to intervene in the way local authorities discharge their parental responsibilities under final care orders. Parliament entrusted to local authorities, not the courts, the responsibility for looking after children who are the subject of care orders. To my mind the new starring system would depart substantially from this principle. Under the new system the court, when making a care order, is empowered to impose an obligation on an authority concerning the future care of the child. In future, the authority must submit a progress report, in circumstances identified by the court, either to the court or to the Children and Family Court Advisory and Support Service (CAFCASS). This is only the first step. The next step is that the court, when seised of what has happened after the care order was made, may then call for action. If it considers this necessary in the best interests of the child, the court may intervene and correct matters which are going wrong. In short, under the starring system the court will exercise a newly-created supervisory function.

43. In his judgment Thorpe LJ noted that the starring system 'seems to breach the fundamental boundary between the functions and responsibilities of the court and the local authority': see paragraph 31. I agree. I consider this judicial innovation passes well beyond the boundary of interpretation. I can see no provision in the Children Act which lends itself to the interpretation that Parliament was thereby conferring this supervisory function on the court. No such provision was identified by the Court of Appeal. On the contrary, the starring system is inconsistent in an important respect with the scheme of the Children Act. It would constitute amendment of the Children Act, not its interpretation. It would have far-reaching practical ramifications for local authorities and their care of children. The starring system would not come free from additional administrative work and expense. It would be likely to have a material effect on authorities' allocation of scarce financial and other resources. This in turn would affect authorities' discharge of their responsibilities to other children. Moreover, the need to produce a formal report whenever a care plan is significantly departed from, and then await the outcome of any subsequent court proceedings, would affect the whole manner in which authorities discharge, and are able to discharge, their parental responsibilities.

44. These are matters for decision by Parliament, not the courts. It is impossible for a court to attempt to evaluate these ramifications or assess what would be the views of Parliament if changes are needed... In my view, in the present case the Court of Appeal exceeded the bounds of its judicial jurisdiction under section 3 in introducing this new scheme.

NOTE Lord Nicholls ended his speech with the observation that while starred milestones could not be implied into the Children Act, the problems identified by the Court of Appeal must be attended to urgently by the Government. See s. 26 of the Children Act 1989 as amended by s. 118 of the Children and Adoption Act 2002.

(d) How do declarations of incompatibility operate?

Where there is a conflict between Convention rights and primary legislation which cannot be resolved by an interpretation which renders the legislation compatible with the Convention, a court at the level of the High Court or above may make a declaration of incompatibility (see s. 4(2) and (3)). In the following case the court could not make Convention compatible interpretations of primary legislation and had to make a declaration of incompatibility.

R v Secretary of State for the Home Department, ex parte Anderson

[2002] UKHL 46, House of Lords

The appellant prisoner was challenging the minimum period of a mandatory life sentence for murder. This tariff had been recommended to be 15 years by the trial judge and the Lord Chief Justice, but the Home Secretary increased it to 20 years. In the House of Lords it was argued that the power of the Home Secretary to set the tariff was incompatible with the prisoner's right to have sentence imposed by an independent and impartial tribunal under Art. 6(1).

LORD BINGHAM OF CORNHILL:...

19. In the agreed issue formulated for decision by the House attention was focused on the conduct of the Home Secretary in this case in setting the appellant's tariff substantially higher than that recommended by the trial judge and the Lord Chief Justice, and Mr Edward Fitzgerald QC devoted part of his argument to this aspect. He had good forensic reason for doing so. The appellant has served almost 15 years in prison. Were the judicial recommendations to be effective, he would be approaching the stage at which the Parole Board would consider whether it was safe to release him on licence. As it is, because of the higher tariff set by the Home Secretary, he has 5 years to serve before reaching that stage. So it would best serve the appellant's interest if the Home Secretary's increase were invalidated and the judicial recommendations stood. But the principles which Mr Fitzgerald must invoke to attack the setting of the tariff by the Home Secretary at a level higher than that recommended by the judges preclude consideration of the issues on so narrow a basis. As became clear in argument, the decision of the House must rest on a broader basis of principle.

20. Mr Fitzgerald's argument for the appellant involved the following steps:

(1) Under article 6(1) of the convention a criminal defendant has a right to a fair trial by an independent and impartial tribunal.
(2) The imposition of sentence is part of the trial.
(3) Therefore sentence should be imposed by an independent and impartial tribunal.
(4) The fixing of the tariff of a convicted murderer is legally indistinguishable from the imposition of sentence.
(5) Therefore the tariff should be fixed by an independent and impartial tribunal.
(6) The Home Secretary is not an independent and impartial tribunal.
(7) Therefore the Home Secretary should not fix the tariff of a convicted murderer.

I must review these steps in turn.

21. Step (1) is correct. The right to a fair trial by an independent and impartial tribunal is guaranteed by article 6(1) of the convention. It is one of the rights which the United Kingdom committed itself to protect when it ratified the convention and it is one of the most important rights to which domestic effect was given by the Human Rights Act 1998.

22. Step (2) is also correct. Strasbourg authority supporting the proposition is to be found in *Ringeisen v Austria (No. 1)* (1971) 1 EHRR 455; *Eckle v Germany* (1983) 5 EHRR 1, paras 76-77; *Bromfield v United Kingdom* (Application No. 32003/96, 1 July 1998, p 10); *V v United Kingdom* (1999) 30 EHRR 121 at pp 185-186, para 109. It makes good sense that the same procedural protections should apply to the imposition of sentence as to the determination of guilt.

23. Step (3) is a logical consequence of steps (1) and (2). But the point was clearly expressed by the Supreme Court of Ireland in *Deaton v Attorney-General and the Revenue Commissioners* [1963] IR 170 at 182-183:

"There is a clear distinction between the prescription of a fixed penalty and the selection of a penalty for a particular case. The prescription of a fixed penalty is the statement of a general rule, which is one of the characteristics of legislation; this is wholly different from the selection of a penalty to be imposed in a particular case...The Legislature does not prescribe the penalty to be imposed in an individual citizen's case; it states the general rule, and the application of that rule is for the Courts...the selection of punishment is an integral part of the administration of justice and, as such, cannot be committed to the hands of the Executive. ...".

24. Examination of the facts has already led me to accept the correctness of step (4): see paragraphs 17-18 above. The clearest authoritative statement of this proposition is in paragraph 79 of the European Court's judgment in *Stafford*, quoted in paragraph 17 above. But earlier authorities had laid the foundations for that conclusion: *R v Secretary of State for the Home Department, Ex p Doody* [1994] 1 AC 531 at 557; *R v Secretary of State for the Home Department, Ex p Venables and Thompson* [1998] AC 407 at 490, 526, 537; *R v Secretary of State for the Home Department, Ex p Pierson* [1998] AC 539 at 585; *R (Anderson) v Secretary of State for the Home Department* [2002] 2 WLR 1143, paras 57, 67 (the present case in the Court of Appeal). It is clear beyond doubt that the fixing of a convicted murderer's tariff, whether it be for the remainder of his days or for a relatively short time only, involves an assessment of the quantum of punishment he should undergo.

25. If it be assumed that steps (1) to (4) are correct, step (5) necessarily follows from them.

26. The correctness of step (6) was accepted on behalf of the Home Secretary, and rightly so. The European court has interpreted "independent" in the context of article 6(1) of the convention to mean "independent of the parties to the case and also of the executive": *V v United Kingdom* (1999) 30 EHRR 121, at 186-187, paragraph 114. Far from being independent of the executive, the Home Secretary and his junior ministers are important members of it. I need not linger on this point, since it is not controversial. Plainly, the Home Secretary is not independent of the executive and is not a tribunal.

27. Step (7) follows logically from the preceding steps and must be accepted. In *R v Secretary of State for the Home Department, Ex p Stafford* [1998] 1 WLR 503 at 518 the Court of Appeal expressed concern at the imposition of what was in effect a substantial term of imprisonment by the exercise of executive discretion, which in its view lay uneasily with ordinary concepts of the rule of law. This concern was echoed in the House of Lords ([1999] 2 AC 38 at 51), and again by the European Court (*Stafford v United Kingdom* (Application No. 46295/99, 28 May 2002) in paragraph 78 of its judgment quoted in paragraph 17 above. In *Benjamin and Wilson v United Kingdom* (Application No. 28212/95, 26 September 2002) the European Court took a step further: it held that the Home Secretary's role in the release of 2 "technical lifers" was objectionable because he was not independent of the executive and he could not save the day by showing that he always acted in accordance with the recommendation of the mental health review tribunal (paragraph 36). The European Court observed (paragraph 36):

"This is not a matter of form but impinges on the fundamental principle of separation of powers and detracts from a necessary guarantee against the possibility of abuse..."

The European Court was right to describe the complete functional separation of the judiciary from the executive as "fundamental", since the rule of law depends on it.

28. Thus I accept each of Mr Fitzgerald's steps (1) to (7) save that, in the light of *Benjamin and Wilson v United Kingdom* (Application No. 28212/95), it must now be held that the Home Secretary should play no part in fixing the tariff of a convicted murderer, even if he does no more than confirm what the judges have recommended. To that extent the appeal succeeds.

29. The conclusion that the Home Secretary should play no part in the fixing of convicted murderers' tariffs makes for much greater uniformity of treatment than now exists. The tariff term to be served by a discretionary life sentence prisoner is already determined by the trial judge in open court (subject to the accused's right of appeal under section 9 of the Criminal Appeal Act 1968 and the

Attorney General's right to apply to refer a sentence to the court as unduly lenient under section 36 of the Criminal Justice Act 1988) and the Parole Board decide whether it is safe to release the prisoner at the end of that tariff term. The Home Secretary has no role. The result of *V v United Kingdom* (1999) 30 EHRR 121 was to make plain that the Home Secretary should not fix the tariff of a young murderer ordered to be detained during Her Majesty's Pleasure. In Scotland, following an audit conducted by the Scottish Executive to identify procedures operating there which might fall foul of the convention, the Convention Rights (Compliance) (Scotland) Act 2001 was enacted: this provides that those convicted of murder in Scotland should be treated in very much the same way as discretionary life sentence prisoners, with no intervention by the executive. Similar arrangements have been adopted in Northern Ireland, doubtless with the same object of complying with the convention. It is the Home Secretary's role in relation to convicted murderers which has become anomalous.

30. The question of relief therefore arises. Section 29 of the Crime (Sentences) Act 1997, quoted in paragraph 6 above, appears to stand in the way of the appellant. It is unrepealed primary legislation. Mr Fitzgerald contended that it was possible to read and give effect to section 29 in a manner compatible with the convention, and that the House should do so in exercise of the interpretative power conferred by section 3(1) of the Human Rights Act 1998. Mr Pannick contended that, even if the House were to accept Mr Fitzgerald's argument summarised in paragraph 20 above, the only relief which the appellant could obtain would be a declaration of incompatibility under section 4 of the 1998 Act. On this point I am satisfied that Mr Pannick is right. As observed in paragraph 6 above, Parliament did not attempt to prescribe the procedures to be followed in fixing the tariff of a convicted murderer. But some things emerge clearly from this not very perspicuous section. The power to release a convicted murderer is conferred on the Home Secretary. He may not exercise that power unless recommended to do so by the Parole Board. But the Parole Board may not make such a recommendation unless the Home Secretary has referred the case to it. And the section imposes no duty on the Home Secretary either to refer a case to the board or to release a prisoner if the board recommends release. Since, therefore, the section leaves it to the Home Secretary to decide whether or when to refer a case to the board, and he is free to ignore its recommendation if it is favourable to the prisoner, the decision on how long the convicted murderer should remain in prison for punitive purposes is his alone. It cannot be doubted that Parliament intended this result when enacting section 29 and its predecessor sections. An entirely different regime was established, in the case of discretionary life sentence prisoners, in section 28. The contrast was plainly deliberate. In section 1(2) of the Murder (Abolition of Death Penalty) Act 1965, Parliament was at pains to give judges a power to recommend minimum periods of detention, but not to rule. That was for the Home Secretary. To read section 29 as precluding participation by the Home Secretary, if it were possible to do so, would not be judicial interpretation but judicial vandalism: it would give the section an effect quite different from that which Parliament intended and would go well beyond any interpretative process sanctioned by section 3 of the 1998 Act (*In re S (Minors) (Care Order: Implementation of Care Plan)* [2002] 2 WLR 720 at 731-732, para 41).

31. For these reasons and also for the reasons given by my noble and learned friends Lord Steyn and Lord Hutton I would accordingly allow the appeal to the extent already indicated with costs in the House and below and make a declaration of incompatibility in terms which have been agreed between the parties:

> "Section 29 of the Crime (Sentences) Act 1997 is incompatible with a Convention right (that is the right under Article 6 of the European Convention on Human Rights to have a sentence imposed by an independent and impartial tribunal) in that the Secretary of State for the Home Department is acting so as to give effect to section 29 when he himself decides on the minimum period which must be served by a mandatory life sentence prisoner before he is considered for release on life licence."

LORD STEYN: ...

In this way Parliamentary sovereignty was preserved.

59. Counsel for the appellant invited the House to use the interpretative obligation under section 3 to read into section 29 alleged Convention rights, viz to provide that the tariff set by the Home

Secretary may not exceed the judicial recommendation. It is impossible to follow this course. It would not be interpretation but interpolation inconsistent with the plain legislative intent to entrust the decision to the Home Secretary, who was intended to be free to follow or reject judicial advice. Section 3(1) is not available where the suggested interpretation is contrary to express statutory words or is by implication necessarily contradicted by the statute: *In re S (Minors) (Care Order: Implementation of Care Plan)* [2002] 2 WLR 720, 731-732, para 41 per Lord Nicholls of Birkenhead. It is therefore impossible to imply the suggested words into the statute or to secure the same result by a process of construction.

60. It follows that there must be a declaration of incompatibility.

Such a declaration has no impact, however, on the immediate proceedings; nor does it affect the validity or continuing enforcement of the impugned legislation (see s. 4(6)). As such the authority has not acted unlawfully and no remedies may be granted against it. The victim has, at best, a Pyrrhic victory. The declaration also casts the 'hot potato' into a politician's hands as the relevant Minister will have to determine whether the incompatible legislation should be amended. He may use the fast-track procedure in s. 10 and Sch. 2 to amend the legislation by means of a 'remedial order' which must be approved in draft by positive resolution of each House of Parliament. The response to the declaration of incompatibility in *Anderson* was to include in the Criminal Justice Act 2003 the repeal of the law and the making of transitional and new sentencing regulations. Should the Minister decide not to act (and there may be pragmatic political reasons for such a decision), the victim will have to resort to seeking to enforce his or her rights under the Convention machinery.

Sir W. Wade QC, 'The United Kingdom's Bill of Rights' in *Constitutional Reform in the United Kingdom: Practice and Principles*
(1998), pp. 66–7

Under clause 4 a declaration of incompatibility may be made by the court if it is satisfied that there is an unavoidable conflict between Convention rights and primary legislation; and the same is to apply in the case of subordinate legislation if it cannot be made compatible because of primary legislation. The declaration is not to affect the validity, continuing operation or enforcement of the offending provision, nor is it to be binding on the parties. But it may lead to a 'remedial order' amending the offending legislation which may be made by a minister of the Crown and must be approved in draft by positive resolution of each House of Parliament. There are, however, certain escape clauses. In case of urgency the Parliamentary resolutions may be dispensed with for up to 40 days. Furthermore, a minister may make a remedial order without a declaration by the court if it appears to him that a finding of the European Court of Human Rights produces an incompatibility with the UK's Convention obligations—a provision comparable to that of the European Communities Act 1972 under which ministers may amend legislation by Order in Council or regulations for the purpose of reconciling it with EU law.

A remedial order, like the provision of the European Communities Act, is an exceptionally drastic form of Henry VIII clause, of the kind that has recently worried the House of Lords' Delegated Powers Scrutiny Committee. It may well be the most drastic example yet seen, since it is expressly made capable of operating retrospectively, subject only to a ban on retrospective criminal liability. There is wide power to include 'such incidental, supplemental, consequential and transitional provisions' as may be thought appropriate by the minister and it may amend or repeal legislation, whether primary or subordinate, other than that containing the incompatibility. These extraordinary powers were the subject of protests in the House of Lords, Lord Simon of Glaisdale saying 'we cannot have Henry VIII trampling through the statute book in this way'. But, inevitably, such powers have to be accepted, however grudgingly, as part of the mechanism for adopting an external system of law, and in default of new and speedy Parliamentary procedures.

Reverence for the sovereignty of Parliament was the motive behind this remarkable amalgam of judicial and executive powers. But the sovereignty of Parliament is not what it was, having suffered severe diminution by its subjection to EU law. Lord Lester's earlier private member's bill had provided for the Convention rights to prevail over inconsistent legislation without intervention by the executive, but now he declared a change of mind and accepted the government's plan as 'an ingenious and successful reconciliation of principles of Parliamentary sovereignty and the need for effective domestic remedies'—though only, he added, 'after a good deal of arm-twisting by some members of this place rather more noble and learned than myself'. It is not surprising if the government resorted to some degree of intellectual harassment in order to secure the support of Lord Lester, with his immense experience and authority in this field.

If, then, a declaration of incompatibility is granted in some case, what is the likely result? A litigant has established that he ought to win his case because of the infringement of his human rights, but yet he loses it since the declaration does not affect the validity of the offending statute or regulation, or its enforceability. The appropriate minister must then consider whether to make a remedial order. It would seem inevitable that the court would grant a stay of execution while the minister considers whether to make an order, and whether it should be retrospective. If he makes a retrospective order, he deprives the victorious party of the fruits of his judgment. If he does not, he leaves the other party to suffer a violation of his human rights; and it is the same if the minister makes no order at all. The minister's position between these two fires is far from enviable. There may be a lot of money at stake and the government itself may be a party, so that the minister is compelled to be judge in his own cause. In such cases there is certain to be trouble in Parliament and a risk that the positive resolution will be opposed. There may be very difficult questions about the effect on third parties, even though clause 11 allows different provision to be made for different cases. It is hard to think of a more invidious position for a minister. And what, finally, about Article 6 of the Convention, which entitles everyone to a fair and public hearing by an independent and impartial tribunal in the determination of his civil rights and obligations? Will the Strasbourg court allow civil rights, and especially human rights, to be decided by discretionary executive order in this way? It seems highly unlikely.

In the House of Lords' second reading and committee debates there was no mention, I think, of the rule of law. Yet to allow questions of personal legal right to be decided by executive discretion offends against the rule of law in its most basic sense: the rule of law as opposed to the rule of discretionary power. Remedial orders will, indeed, be subject to judicial review and the Bill makes no attempt to exempt them. But the taking of human rights cases so far out of the course of ordinary law does not seem to be an adequately constitutional solution.

G. Marshall, 'Patriating Rights—with Reservations: the Human Rights Bill 1998'
in *Constitutional Reform in the United Kingdom: Practice and Principles*
(1998), pp. 81–2

Assessing Incompatibility

… [T]wo different questions can be distinguished. In the first place, all reviewing courts have to adopt some view of the relation of their function to that of the legislature. What standard of review or degree of deference, or presumption of constitutionality is appropriate? Should it be different for different kinds of legislation and so on? In this respect, how should United Kingdom courts take into account decisions of the European Court of Human Rights as the Bill requires? That court has applied to national legislatures a relatively low standard of scrutiny under the rubric of the margin of appreciation on the ground that state authorities are better able to judge national conditions and requirements than international judges. But that *rationale* does not apply within a state as between its legislature and judiciary. So in taking account of the decisions of the Strasbourg court, it would seem appropriate for British courts to subtract the effect of the margin of appreciation. In at least some cases this should lead to different and more activist decisions.

A second aspect of judicial review (or incompatibility assessment) relates to the substantive criteria that compatible legislation is required to meet. Here it can be seen that there are two analytically different, though sometimes confusingly related, reasons why a legislative provision might not contravene, or might not be incompatible, with the Convention. In the first place it might not be incompatible with an enumerated right because the Convention does not cover or relate to the disputed activity at all. A law restricting the use of firearms is not inconsistent with Convention rights, because nothing in the Convention guarantees the right to use firearms. In the second place, a legislative provision may be held to be compatible with the Convention because although the Convention is relevant and the disputed legislation appears to limit or impinge upon one or other of its rights, it is held to be a justified limitation in those cases where the Convention provides that limits may properly be imposed that are demonstrably justified by stated criteria or in a free and democratic society (the criterion found in some Convention rights and whose wording has been adopted in the general limitation sections of the Canadian and New Zealand rights legislation). Such limits may be said to place a restriction on, or involve a modification of, a right in its unqualified form, but they do not constitute a denial, negation, abridgement, curtailment, contravention, infringement or violation of a right.

…

A question for the future is the status of the Human Rights Bill when the European Convention is formally embodied in the law of the European Union. Within the area covered by the Treaties, United Kingdom courts may then find themselves obliged to disapply British statutes incompatible with Convention rights embodied in Community law whilst holding themselves unable to do so when the same provisions are alleged to conflict with the Convention rights included in the United Kingdom Human Rights legislation. At that point, the government's attitude to judicial review will appear even more bizarre and indefensible.

S. Kentridge QC, 'The Incorporation of the European Convention on Human Rights' in *Constitutional Reform in the United Kingdom: Practice and Principles*

(1998), p. 69

Some speakers regard the provision in the Bill for declarations of incompatibility as an inadequate remedy against legislative infringements of fundamental rights. I regard it as a subtle compromise between the concepts of parliamentary sovereignty and fundamental rights. I believe, moreover, that declarations of incompatibility with primary legislation are likely to be rare, at least in relation to future legislation. There are two main reasons for this. The first, a very practical one, is that the individual litigant 'the victim' is likely to get little direct benefit from such a declaration. It is difficult to visualise a situation in which a lawyer will advise his client to go to court to seek a declaration of incompatibility. The second reason, a politico-legal one, is that Parliament, the executive and the courts will all strive to avoid the necessity for such declarations. The executive in introducing legislation, and Parliament in passing it, will do their utmost to ensure that there is no incompatibility with the Convention. The courts in compliance with clause 3 will, so far as it is possible to do so, read and give effect to legislation in a way which is compatible with the Convention rights. The executive, as litigant, will also in most instances prefer a 'reading down' of contested legislation to a declaration of incompatibility.

■ QUESTIONS

1. If Kentridge is correct that the individual litigant is likely to get little direct benefit from a declaration of incompatibility, is this not a cause for concern? Further, if a victim of a violation of the Convention is blocked from obtaining an effective remedy, is this not a further breach of the Convention, namely Art. 13? It should be noted that Art. 13 is excluded from those rights which are incorporated by the Human Rights Act.

2. What is the consequence of a statement by a Minister in charge of a Bill at Second Reading that although he is unable to make a 'statement of compatibility' the Government nevertheless wishes the House to proceed with the Bill (see s. 19(1)) if the Bill is ultimately enacted and challenged before a United Kingdom court resulting in a declaration of incompatibility?

3. Is Marshall correct when he states that 'the Human Rights Bill contains a major contradiction of purpose and is attempting to marry two inconsistent principles of action. The rights principle is in essence anti-majoritarian. You cannot successfully combine the effective protection of rights against the majority with unfettered Parliamentary supremacy'?

NOTE: A summary of cases up to July 2016, where a declaration of incompatibility was made under the Human Rights Act, follows.

(i) Responding to human rights judgments

Report to the Joint Committee on Human Rights on the Government response to Human Rights judgments 2014–16
Cm 9360, 2016

Annex A: Declarations of incompatibility

Since the Human Rights Act 1998 came into force on 2 October 2000 until the end of July 2016, 34 declarations of incompatibility have been made. Of these:

- 22 have become final (in whole or in part) and are not subject to further appeal;
- 4 are or may be subject to appeal; and
- 8 have been overturned on appeal.

Of the 22 declarations of incompatibility that have become final:

- 13 have been remedied by later primary or secondary legislation;
- 3 have been remedied by a remedial order under section 10 of the Human Rights Act;
- 4 related to provisions that had already been remedied by primary legislation at the time of the declaration;
- 1 the Government has notified the JCHR that it intends to address the incompatibility through a remedial order; and
- 1 is under consideration as to how to remedy the incompatibility.

(e) How will the Human Rights Act affect the way in which judges decide cases?

Lord Irvine of Lairg LC, The Tom Sargant Memorial Lecture, 'The Development of Human Rights in Britain under an Incorporated Convention on Human Rights'
16 December 1997

The Emergence of a new approach

I have referred to the effect the introduction of European Community law has had on the development of our own domestic law. I believe that incorporating into our own law the Convention rights will have an equally healthy effect.

Any court or tribunal determining any question relating to a Convention Right will be obliged to take into account the body of jurisprudence of the Court and Commission of Human rights and of the Council of Ministers. This is obviously right. It gives British courts both the benefit of 50 years careful analysis of the Convention rights and ensures British Courts interpret the Convention consistently with Strasbourg. The British courts will therefore need to apply the same techniques of interpretation and decision-making as the Strasbourg bodies. I have already mentioned recourse to Parliamentary materials such as Hansard—where we are now closer in line with our continental colleagues. I will mention three more aspects. As I do so, it should be remembered that the courts which will be applying these techniques will be the ordinary courts of the land; we have not considered it right to create some special human rights court alongside the ordinary system; the Convention rights must pervade all law and all the courts systems. Our courts will therefore learn these techniques and inevitably will consider their utility in deciding other non-Convention cases.

First there is the approach to statutory interpretation. The tools of construction in use in mainland Europe are known to be different from those the English courts have traditionally used. I will refer to just one: the so-called teleological approach which is concerned with giving the instrument its presumed legislative intent. It is less concerned with the textual analysis usual to the common law tradition of interpretation. It is a process of moulding the law to what the Court believes the law should be trying to achieve. It is undoubtedly the case that our own domestic approach to interpretation of statutes has become more purposive. Lord Diplock had already identified this trend 20 years ago when he noted that:

> If one looks back to the actual decisions of the [House of Lords] on questions of statutory construction over the last 30 years one cannot fail to be struck by the evidence of a trend away from the purely literal towards the purposive construction of statutory provisions.

This trend has not diminished since then, although there are cases where the Courts have declined to adopt what was in one case described as an 'over purposive' approach.

Yet as the Courts, through familiarity with the Convention jurisprudence, become more exposed to methods of interpretation which pay more heed to the purpose, and less to whether the words were felicitously chosen to achieve that end, the balance is likely to swing more firmly yet in the direction of the purposive approach.

Secondly, there is the doctrine of proportionality … This doctrine is applied by the European Court of Human Rights. Its application is to ensure that a measure imposes no greater restriction upon a Convention right than is absolutely necessary to achieve its objectives. Although not identical to the principle as applied in Luxembourg, it shares the feature that it raises questions foreign to the traditional *Wednesbury* approach to judicial review. Under the *Wednesbury* doctrine an administrative decision will only be struck down if it is so bad that no reasonable decision-maker could have taken it.

Closely allied with the doctrine of proportionality is the concept of the margin of appreciation. The Court of Human Rights has developed this doctrine which permits national courts a discretion in the application of the requirements of the Convention to their own national conditions. This discretion is not absolute, since the Court of Human Rights reserves the power to review any act of a national authority or court; and the discretion is more likely to be recognised in the application of those articles of the Convention which expressly include generally stated conditions or exceptions, such as Articles 8–11, rather than in the area of obligations which in any civilised society should be absolute, such as the rights to life, freedom from torture and freedom from slavery and forced labour that are provided by Articles 2–4.

This 'margin of appreciation', was first developed by the Court in a British case, *Handyside* v *UK*. It concerned whether a conviction for possessing an obscene article could be justified under Article 10(2) of the Convention as a limitation upon freedom of expression that was necessary for the 'protection of morals'. The court said:

> By reason of their direct and continuous contact with the vital forces of their countries, state authorities are in principle in a better position than the international judge to give an opinion on the exact content of those requirements [of morals] as well as on the 'necessity' of a 'restriction' or 'penalty' intended to meet them …

Although there is some encouragement in British decisions for the view that the margin of appreciation under the Convention is simply the *Wednesbury* test under another guise statements by the Court of Human Rights seem to draw a significant distinction. The Court of Human Rights has said in terms that its review is not limited to checking that the national authority 'exercised its discretion reasonably, carefully and in good faith'. It has to go further. It has to satisfy itself that the decision was based on an 'acceptable assessment of the relevant facts' and that the interference was no more than reasonably necessary to achieve the legitimate aim pursued.

That approach shows that there is a profound difference between the Convention margin of appreciation and the common law test of rationality. The latter would be satisfied by an exercise of discretion done 'reasonably, carefully and in good faith' although the passage I have cited indicates that the Court of Human Rights' review of action is not so restricted. In these cases a more rigorous scrutiny than traditional judicial review will be required. An illustration of the difference may be found in the speech of Simon Brown LJ in *ex p Smith* (the armed forces homosexual policy case)

> If the Convention for the Protection of Human Rights and Fundamental Freedoms were part of our law and we were accordingly entitled to ask whether the policy answers a pressing social need and whether the restriction on human rights involved can be shown proportionate to its benefits, then clearly the primary judgement (subject only to a limited 'margin of appreciation') would be for us and not for others; the constitutional balance would shift. But that is not the position. In exercising merely a secondary judgement, this court is bound, even though adjudicating in a human rights context, to act with some reticence.

The question I pose is how long the courts will restrict their review to a narrow *Wednesbury* approach in non-Convention cases, if used to inquiring more deeply in Convention cases? There will remain distinctions of importance between the two categories of case which should be respected. But some blurring of line may be inevitable.

I have expressed my views in my Administrative Law Bar Association Lecture in 1995 on how the Courts ought properly to regard the dividing line between their function and that of Parliament. But the process is not one way. British influence on the application of the Convention rights is likely to increase. British officials were closely involved in the drafting of the Convention. When our British courts make their own pronouncements on the Convention, their views will be studied in other Convention countries and in Strasbourg itself with great respect. I am sure that British judges' influence for the good of the Convention will be considerable. They will bring to the application of the Convention their great skills of analysis and interpretation. But they will also bring to it our proud British traditions of liberty.

The Shift from form to substance

So there is room to predict some decisive and far reaching changes in future judicial decision making. The major shift may be away from a concern with form to a concern with substance. Let me summarise the reasons.

In the field of review by judges of administrative action, the courts' decisions to date have been largely based on something akin to the application of a set of rules. If the rules are broken, the conduct will be condemned. But if the rules are obeyed, (the right factors are taken into account, no irrelevant factors taken into account, no misdirection of law and no out and out irrationality) the decision will be upheld, usually irrespective of the overall objective merits of the policy. In some cases much may turn—or at least appear to turn—on the form in which a decision is expressed rather than its substance. Does the decision as expressed show that the right reasons have been taken into account? Does it disclose potentially irrational reasoning? Might the court's review be different if the reasoning were expressed differently so as to avoid the court's *Wednesbury* scrutiny?

Now, in areas where the Convention applies, the Court will be less concerned whether there has been a failure in this sense but will inquire more closely into the merits of the decision to see for example that necessity justified the limitation of a positive right, and that it was no more … of a limitation than was needed. There is a discernible shift which may be seen in essence as a shift from form to substance. If, as I have suggested, there is a spillover into other areas of law, then that shift from form to substance will become more marked.

This may be seen as a progression of an existing and now long standing trend. In modern times, the emphasis on identifying the true substance at issue has been seen in diverse areas: in tax where new techniques have developed to view the substance of a transaction overall rather than to be mesmerised by the form of an isolated step, or in the areas of statutory control of leases, where the Courts are astute to prevent form being used to obscure the reality of the underlying transaction. In what may seem at first blush a very different area, that of interpretation of contracts, recent decisions also emphasise the need to cast away the baggage of older years where literal and semantic analysis was allowed to override the real intent of the parties.

In a very broad sense we can see here a similarity of approach: to get to the substance of the issue and not be distracted by the form.

These are trends already well developed but I believe they will gain impetus from incorporation of the Convention. In addition the Courts will be making decisions founded more explicitly and frequently on considerations of morality and justifiability.

This Bill will therefore create a more explicitly moral approach to decisions and decision making; will promote both a culture where positive rights and liberties become the focus and concern of legislators, administrators and judges alike; and a culture in judicial decision making where there will be a greater concentration on substance rather than form.

P. Duffy QC, 'The European Convention on Human Rights, Issues Relating to its Interpretation in the Light of the Human Rights Bill' in *Constitutional Reform in the United Kingdom: Practice and Principles*
(1998), pp. 100–2

Several of the rights in the Convention, notably Article 8 (right to respect for private and family life, home and correspondence), Article 9 (freedom of thought, conscience and religion), Article 10 (freedom of expression) and Article 11 (freedom of assembly and association) are stated in general terms in a first paragraph and can be subject to restrictions in the interests of other legitimate interests provided such restriction is regulated by the law and is, in the language of the Convention, 'necessary in a democratic society'. The case law of the Court provides well established guidance on the approach to be taken.

First, a generous approach is to be taken when determining what comes within the scope of the protected fundamental rights. The Court has pointed out that to construe the scope of the rights protected broadly is consonant with the essential object and purpose of the ECHR [*Niemietz* v *Germany*, 16 EHRR 97, para. 31] which, of course, is 'an instrument for the protection of individual human beings', accordingly 'its provisions [should] be interpreted and applied so as to make its safeguards practical and effective' [*Loizidou* v *Turkey* (1995) 20 EHRR 99, para. 71]. Adopting a narrow construction of the rights protected risks denying Convention scrutiny in cases where a fundamental right may be affected, albeit indirectly. The Court has rightly stressed that giving a broad construction to the rights protected does not unduly hamper public bodies for they retain their entitlement to 'interfere' provided the conditions of the Convention are respected [*Niemietz*, para. 31].

The conditions under which restrictions are permitted vary somewhat from right to right but important underlying principles are well established in the Court's case law and practice. For an interference to be justified, four conditions must be fulfilled. These are that (i) the interference is 'lawful', (ii) it serves a legitimate purpose, (iii) it is 'necessary in a democratic society'; and (iv) it is not discriminatory. Each of these requirements is outlined in turn below.

First, the lawfulness requirement, this does not merely mean that interference with a fundamental right is permitted under domestic law. The Court has consistently stated that 'it [is] contrary to the rule of law for the legal discretion granted to the executive to be in the form of unfettered power':

> The law must indicate the scope of any such discretion conferred on the competent authorities and the manner of its exercise with sufficient clarity, having regard to the legitimate aim of the measure in question, to give the individual adequate protection against arbitrary interference [*Malone* v *United Kingdom* (1985) 7 EHRR 14, para. 68].

The condition of 'lawfulness' is unlikely to detain British courts much where legislation circumscribes the powers of public authorities. Where it will make a difference, once the Human Rights Act enters into force, is to the Diceyan rule of law concept that public bodies are permitted to do anything which is not specifically prohibited by law. This has led in a number of cases to British courts being unable to provide redress when intrusive powers were unregulated. In *Malone* v *Metropolitan Police Commissioner (No. 2)* [[1979] 1 Ch 344 at 380], Sir Robert Megarry V-C described interception of communications as 'a subject which cries out for legislation' yet, without ECHR incorporation and under the old concept of the rule of law, he could not provide relief. The case proceeded to Strasbourg and the finding, as Sir Robert had predicted, that English law then failed to provide 'the minimum degree of legal protection to which citizens are entitled under the rule of law in a democratic society.'

The second condition is that the reason for an interference is a proper one. In very few cases under the ECHR has an improper purpose been shown. In the vast majority of cases, it is common ground that the public authority had a proper purpose. Forensic and judicial attention focuses instead on the third and fourth conditions, namely whether the interference for a proper purpose was 'necessary in a democratic society' and was done without any impermissible discrimination.

For an interference to be 'necessary in a democratic society', the courts must be satisfied that the public body can convincingly demonstrate the need for the interference and that the interference is 'fair'.

The fourth and final condition to mention is that any action undertaken by public bodies which gives effect to or interferes with Convention rights and freedoms must be done in a non-discriminatory manner. Not every difference of treatment amounts to discrimination. Discrimination occurs if 'the distinction has no objectives and reasonable justification' [*Belgian Linguistic* (1968) 1 EHRR 252, para. 10]. Checking this requirement also involves testing proportionality, similar to considering 'necessity in a democratic society'. This is not surprising as unjustified discrimination cannot sensibly be described as necessary in a democratic society. It is worth emphasising, however, that some grounds of distinction, particularly race or gender, cannot normally be accepted and that discriminatory treatment on such grounds is regarded as especially serious and that it can rarely be accepted and must be particularly closely scrutinised. This represents a significant change from the piece-meal protection against discrimination in existing British legislative schemes.

For incorporation to be effective, as Parliament intends, British courts will have to engage in an effective control of the reasons given for interference and their sufficiency. The courts have already emphasised that greater scrutiny is needed when fundamental rights are in play. In *R v Ministry of Defence, ex parte Smith* [[1996] QB 517], the case on dismissal of homosexuals and lesbians from the armed services, Sir Thomas Bingham MR (as he then was) stated [at p. 554] that:

> The court may not interfere with the exercise of an administrative discretion on substantive grounds save where the court is satisfied that the decision is unreasonable in the sense that it is beyond the range of responses open to a reasonable decision maker. But in judging whether the decision maker has exceeded this margin of appreciation the human rights context is important. The more substantial the interference with human rights, the more the court will require by way of justification before it is satisfied that the decision is reasonable in the sense outlined above.

For ECHR incorporation to be effective, the British courts in such cases will have to go beyond a heightened *Wednesbury* review, whilst still respecting the decision making discretion of the primary decision maker. The Lord Chancellor again explained this point with clarity in his 1997 Tom Sargant Lecture. In striking the balance, the Convention's case law uses phrases such as 'fair balance' and 'proportionate'. Domestic courts, of course, frequently exercise discretion that call for decisions on what is fair and reasonable in all circumstances. That experience, including that of applying principles of equity, can be drawn upon in ensuring that incorporation is made effective.

NOTE: Section 2(1) of the Human Rights Act 1998 requires a court when determining an issue relating to a Convention right to take into account any relevant jurisprudence from the European Court of Human Rights. Such decisions are not, however, binding—they simply have to be considered—but the Convention rights are binding. In arriving at their decisions the European Court of Human Rights has developed the doctrine of the margin of appreciation (see earlier in this chapter in Section 2A at p. 408) to reflect diversity within Europe and also the fact that the Court is performing a supervisory function as the primary responsibility for ensuring that human rights are protected lies with the State. Could the courts within a state seek to apply or develop their own version of the doctrine of margin of appreciation? Sir John Laws, 'The Limitations of Human Rights' [1998] *Public Law* 254, at 258, states:

> The margin of appreciation ... will necessarily be inapt to the administration of the Convention in the domestic courts for the very reason that they are domestic; they will not be subject to an objective inhibition generated by any cultural distance between themselves and the state organs whose decisions are impleaded before them.

There is a possibility, however, that Convention rights may be diluted if courts show undue deference to Parliament or the Executive or if they ignore the influence of the doctrine on decisions of the European Court of Human Rights when considering their relevance to the United Kingdom. That there is a notion of judicial deference is evidenced by dicta in several cases. In *R v Director of Public Prosecutions, ex parte Kebilene and Others* [2000] 2 AC 326, Lord Hope stated:

> [The doctrine of margin of appreciation] is an integral part of the supervisory jurisdiction which is exercised over state conduct by the international court. By conceding a margin of appreciation to each national system, the court has recognised that the Convention, as a living system, does not need to be applied uniformly by all states but may vary in its application according to local needs and conditions. This technique is not available to the national courts when they are considering Convention issues arising within their own countries. But in the hands of the national courts also the Convention should be seen as an expression of fundamental principles rather than as a set of mere rules. The question which the courts will have to decide in the application of these principles will involve questions of balance between competing interests and issues of proportionality.
>
> In this area difficult choices may have to be made by the executive or the legislature between the rights of the individual and the needs of society. In some circumstances it will be appropriate for the courts to recognise that there is an area of judgment within which the judiciary will defer, on democratic grounds, to the considered opinion of the elected body or person whose act or decision is said to be incompatible with the Convention. This point is well made at p. 74, para 3.21 of *Human Rights Law and Practice* (1999) ... where the area in which these choices may arise is conveniently and appropriately described as the 'discretionary area of judgment'. It will be easier for such an area of judgment to be recognised where the Convention itself requires a balance to be struck, much less so where the right is stated in terms which are unqualified. It will be easier for it to be recognised where the issues involve questions of social or economic policy, much less so where the rights are of high constitutional importance or are of a kind where the courts are especially well placed to assess the need for protection.

In *R v Lambert, Ali and Jordan* [2001] 1 All ER 1014, Lord Woolf CJ stated (at para. 16):

> It is also important to have in mind that legislation is passed by a democratically elected Parliament and therefore the courts under the convention are entitled to and should, as a matter of constitutional principle, pay a degree of deference to the view of Parliament as to what is in the interest of the public generally when upholding the rights of the individual under the convention. The courts are required to balance the competing interests involved.

In according deference to Parliament or the Executive a key consideration will be the question of proportionality which featured in their Lordships' deliberations in the following two cases. In the second case a major shift in the test for judicial review, at least where Convention rights are involved, suggests that the proportionality principle may result in significantly less deference being accorded to the views of decision-makers than prior to the enactment of the Human Rights Act 1998, even under the 'anxious scrutiny' test adopted in *R v Ministry of Defence, ex parte Smith* [1996] QB 517 (see earlier in this chapter in Section 1 at p. 398).

Brown v Stott (Procurator Fiscal, Dunfermline) and Another
[2001] 2 WLR 817, Privy Council

B was suspected of stealing a bottle of gin from a supermarket to which she had travelled by car. The police were called to the store. Her breath smelled of alcohol which prompted the police officer to ask her how she had travelled there. B replied that she had travelled by car and subsequently pointed out her car in the car park. By virtue of powers under s. 172(2)(a) of the Road Traffic Act 1988 she was required to say who had been driving the car. B admitted that she had. A breath test proved positive. B was charged both with theft and with driving her car after consuming an excess of alcohol contrary to s. 5(1)(a) of the 1988 Act. B sought to claim that use at her trial of the admission compulsorily obtained from her would be incompatible with her right to a fair hearing under Art. 6(1) of the Convention. The sheriff ruled against B but the High Court of Justiciary allowed her appeal declaring that the procurator fiscal had no power at her trial to lead evidence of, and rely on, the admission B had been compelled to make. The procurator fiscal and Advocate General appealed.

LORD BINGHAM OF CORNHILL: ...

Section 172 of the Road Traffic Act 1988

So far as material, s 172 of the 1988 Act at the relevant time provided:

> (2) Where the driver of a vehicle is alleged to be guilty of an offence to which this section applies—
> (a) the person keeping the vehicle shall give such information as to the identity of the driver as he may be required to give by or on behalf of a chief officer of police. ...
> (3) Subject to the following provisions, a person who fails to comply with a requirement under subsection (2) above shall be guilty of an offence.

It is evident that the power of the police to require information to be given as to the identity of the driver of a vehicle only arises where the driver is alleged to be guilty of an offence to which the section applies. Those offences include the most serious of driving offences, such as manslaughter or culpable homicide, causing death by dangerous driving, dangerous and careless driving, causing death by careless driving when under the influence of drugs or drink, and driving a vehicle after consuming alcohol above the prescribed limit. They also include the offence, in Scotland, of taking and driving away a vehicle without consent or lawful authority. The offences excluded are of a less serious and more regulatory nature. They include offences in relation to driving instruction, the holding of motoring events on public ways, the wearing of protective headgear, driving with uncorrected defective eyesight and offences pertaining to the testing, design, inspection and licensing of vehicles. The penalty for failing to comply with a requirement under sub-s (2) is a fine of (currently) not more than £1,000: in the case of an individual, disqualification from driving is discretionary but endorsement of the licence is mandatory. The requirement to supply information under sub-s (2) may be made of 'the person keeping the vehicle' or 'any other person', irrespective of whether either of them is suspected of being the driver alleged to have committed the relevant offence. In this case, it is clear that the respondent, when required to give information, was suspected of committing the offence for which she was later prosecuted. ...

Article 6 of the convention

Attention has often, and rightly, been drawn to contrasts between different articles of the convention. Some (such as arts 3 and 4) permit no restriction by national authorities. Others (such as arts 8, 9, 10 and 11) permit a measure of restriction if certain stringent and closely prescribed conditions are satisfied ...

[Article 6] has more in common with the first group of articles mentioned above than the second. The only express qualification relates to the requirement of a 'public hearing'. But there is nothing to suggest that the fairness of the trial itself may be qualified, compromised or restricted in any way, whatever the circumstances and whatever the public interest in convicting the offender. If the trial as a whole is judged to be unfair, a conviction cannot stand.

What a fair trial requires cannot, however, be the subject of a single, unvarying rule or collection of rules. It is proper to take account of the facts and circumstances of particular cases, as the European Court has consistently done.

Conclusions

The convention is an international treaty by which the contracting states mutually undertake to secure to all within their respective jurisdictions certain rights and freedoms. The fundamental nature of these rights and freedoms is clear, not only from the full title and the content of the convention but from its preamble in which the signatory governments declared:

> their profound belief in those fundamental freedoms which are the foundation of justice and peace in the world and are best maintained on the one hand by an effective political democracy and on the other by a common understanding and observance of the human rights upon which they depend.

Judicial recognition and assertion of the human rights defined in the convention is not a substitute for the processes of democratic government but a complement to them. While a national court does not accord the margin of appreciation recognised by the European Court as a supra-national court, it will give weight to the decisions of a representative legislature and a democratic government within the discretionary area of judgment accorded to those bodies (see Lester and Pannick, *Human Rights Law and Practice* (1999) pp 73–76). The convention is concerned with rights and freedoms which are of real importance in a modern democracy governed by the rule of law. It does not, as is sometimes mistakenly thought, offer relief from 'The heart-ache and the thousand natural shocks That flesh is heir to'.

In interpreting the convention, as any other treaty, it is generally to be assumed that the parties have included the terms which they wished to include and on which they were able to agree, omitting other terms which they did not wish to include or on which they were not able to agree. Thus particular regard must be had and reliance placed on the express terms of the convention, which define the rights and freedoms which the contracting parties have undertaken to secure. This does not mean that nothing can be implied into the convention. The language of the convention is for the most part so general that some implication of terms is necessary, and the case law of the European Court shows that the court has been willing to imply terms into the convention when it was judged necessary or plainly right to do so. But the process of implication is one to be carried out with caution, if the risk is to be averted that the contracting parties may, by judicial interpretation, become bound by obligations which they did not expressly accept and might not have been willing to accept. As an important constitutional instrument the convention is to be seen as a 'living tree capable of growth and expansion within its natural limits' (*Edwards* v *A-G for Canada* [1930] AC 124, 136 per Lord Sankey LC), but those limits will often call for very careful consideration.

Effect has been given to the right not to incriminate oneself in a variety of different ways. … [It] is an implied right. While it cannot be doubted that such a right must be implied, there is no treaty provision which expressly governs the effect or extent of what is to be implied.

The jurisprudence of the European Court very clearly establishes that while the overall fairness of a criminal trial cannot be compromised, the constituent rights comprised, whether expressly or implicitly, within article 6 are not themselves absolute. Limited qualification of these rights is acceptable if reasonably directed by national authorities towards a clear and proper public objective and if representing no greater qualification than the situation calls for. The general language of the convention could have led to the formulation of hard-edged and inflexible statements of principle from which no departure could be sanctioned whatever the background or the circumstances. But this approach has been consistently eschewed by the court throughout its history. The case law shows that the court has paid very close attention to the facts of particular cases coming before it, giving effect to factual differences and recognising differences of degree. Ex facto oritur jus. The court has also recognised the need for a fair balance between the general interest of the community and the personal rights of the individual, the search for which balance has been described as inherent in the whole of the convention (see *Sporrong* v *Sweden* (1982) 5 EHRR 35, 52, para 69; *Sheffield* v *UK* (1998) 27 EHRR 163, 191, para 52).

The high incidence of death and injury on the roads caused by the misuse of motor vehicles is a very serious problem common to almost all developed societies. The need to address it in an effective way, for the benefit of the public, cannot be doubted. Among other ways in which democratic governments have sought to address it is by subjecting the use of motor vehicles to a regime of regulation and making provision for enforcement by identifying, prosecuting and punishing offending drivers. Materials laid before the Board, incomplete though they are, reveal different responses to the problem of enforcement. Under some legal systems (Spain, Belgium and France are examples) the registered owner of a vehicle is assumed to be the driver guilty of minor traffic infractions unless he shows that some other person was driving at the relevant time or establishes some other ground of exoneration. There being a clear public interest in enforcement of road traffic legislation the crucial question in the present case is whether s 172 of the 1988 Act represents a disproportionate response, or one that undermines a defendant's right to a fair trial, if an admission of being the driver is relied on at trial.

I do not for my part consider that s 172, properly applied, does represent a disproportionate response to this serious social problem, nor do I think that reliance on the respondent's admission, in the present case, would undermine her right to a fair trial. I reach that conclusion for a number of reasons.

(1) Section 172 of the 1988 Act provides for the putting of a single, simple question. The answer cannot of itself incriminate the suspect, since it is not without more an offence to drive a car. An admission of driving may, of course, as here, provide proof of a fact necessary to convict, but the section does

not sanction prolonged questioning about the facts alleged to give rise to criminal offences such as was understandably held to be objectionable in *Saunders v UK* (1997) 23 EHRR 313, and the penalty for declining to answer under the section is moderate and non-custodial. There is in the present case no suggestion of improper coercion or oppression such as might give rise to unreliable admissions and so contribute to a miscarriage of justice, and if there were evidence of such conduct the trial judge would have ample power to exclude evidence of the admission.

(2) While the High Court was entitled to distinguish … between the giving of an answer under s 172 and the provision of physical samples, and had the authority of the European Court in *Saunders* (1997) 23 EHRR 313, 337–338, para 69, for doing so, this distinction should not in my opinion be pushed too far. It is true that the respondent's answer, whether given orally or in writing, would create new evidence which did not exist until she spoke or wrote. In contrast, it may be acknowledged, the percentage of alcohol in her breath was a fact, existing before she blew into the breathalyser machine. But the whole purpose of requiring her to blow into the machine (on pain of a criminal penalty if she refused) was to obtain evidence not available until she did so and the reading so obtained could, in all save exceptional circumstances, be enough to convict a driver of an offence. If one applies the language of *Wigmore on Evidence* (McNaughton revision 1961) vol 8, p 318, quoted by the High Court that an individual should 'not be conscripted by his opponent to defeat himself' it is not easy to see why a requirement to answer a question is objectionable and a requirement to undergo a breath test is not. Yet no criticism is made of the requirement that the respondent undergo a breath test.

(3) All who own or drive motor cars know that by doing so they subject themselves to a regulatory regime which does not apply to members of the public who do neither. Section 172 of the 1988 Act forms part of that regulatory regime. This regime is imposed not because owning or driving cars is a privilege or indulgence granted by the state but because the possession and use of cars (like, for example, shotguns, the possession of which is very closely regulated) are recognised to have the potential to cause grave injury. It is true that s 172(2)(b) permits a question to be asked of 'any other person' who, if not the owner or driver, might not be said to have impliedly accepted the regulatory regime, but someone who was not the owner or the driver would not incriminate himself whatever answer he gave. If, viewing this situation in the round, one asks whether s 172 represents a disproportionate legislative response to the problem of maintaining road safety, whether the balance between the interests of the community at large and the interests of the individual is struck in a manner unduly prejudicial to the individual, whether (in short) the leading of this evidence would infringe a basic human right of the respondent, I would feel bound to give negative answers. If the present argument is a good one it has been available to British citizens since 1966, but no one in this country has to my knowledge, criticised the legislation as unfair at any time up to now.

… In the present case the High Court came very close to treating the right not to incriminate oneself as absolute, describing it as a 'central right' which permitted no gradations of fairness depending on the seriousness of the charge or the circumstances of the case. The High Court interpreted the decision in *Saunders* as laying down more absolute a standard than I think the European Court intended, and nowhere in the High Court judgments does one find any recognition of the need to balance the general interests of the community against the interests of the individual or to ask whether s 172 represents a proportionate response to what is undoubtedly a serious social problem.

In my opinion the procurator fiscal is entitled at the respondent's forthcoming trial to lead evidence of her answer given under s 172. I would allow the appeal and quash the declaration made by the High Court.

LORD STEYN: …

VI. What deference may be accorded to the legislature?

Under the convention system the primary duty is placed on domestic courts to secure and protect convention rights. The function of the European Court is essential but supervisory. In that capacity it accords to domestic courts a margin of appreciation, which recognises that national institutions are in principle better placed than an international court to evaluate local needs and conditions. That principle is logically not applicable to domestic courts. On the other hand, national courts may accord to the decisions of national legislatures some deference where the context justifies it (see *R* v *DPP, ex p Kebilene* [1999] 4 All ER 801 at 844, [2000] 2 AC 326 at 381 per Lord Hope of Craighead …)

In my view this factor is of some relevance in the present case. Here s 172(2) addresses a pressing social problem, namely the difficulty of law enforcement in the face of statistics revealing a high accident rate resulting in death and serious injuries. The legislature was entitled to regard the figures of serious accidents as unacceptably high. It would also have been entitled to take into account that it was necessary to protect other convention rights, viz the right to life of members of the public exposed to the danger of accidents (see art 2(1)). On this aspect the legislature was in as good a position as a court to assess the gravity of the problem and the public interest in addressing it. It really then boils down to the question whether in adopting the procedure enshrined in s 172(2), rather than a reverse burden technique, it took more drastic action than was justified. While this is ultimately a question for the court, it is not unreasonable to regard both techniques as permissible in the field of the driving of vehicles. After all, the subject invites special regulation; objectively the interference is narrowly circumscribed; and it is qualitatively not very different from requiring, for example, a breath specimen from a driver. Moreover, it is less invasive than an essential modern tool of crime detection such as the taking of samples from a suspect for DNA profiling. If the matter was not covered by authority, I would have concluded that s 172(2) is compatible with art 6.

VII. *Saunders* v *UK*

The decision of the European Court in *Saunders* v *UK* (1997) 23 EHRR 313 gave some support to the view of the High Court of Justiciary. With due respect I have to say that the reasoning in *Saunders* v *UK* is unsatisfactory and less than clear. The European Court did not rule that the privilege against self incrimination is absolute. Surprisingly in view of its decision in *Murray* v *UK* (1996) 22 EHRR 29 that the linked right of silence is not absolute it left the point open in respect of the privilege against self-incrimination. On the other hand, the substance of its reasoning treats both privileges as not absolute. The court observed, at p 373, para 68:

> The Court recalls that, although not specifically mentioned in article 6 of the convention, the right to silence and the right not to incriminate oneself are generally recognised international standards which lie at the heart of the notion of a fair procedure under article 6. Their rationale lies, inter alia, in the protection of the accused from improper compulsion by the authorities thereby contributing to the avoidance of miscarriages of justice and to the fulfilment of the aims of article 6 …

The court emphasised the rationale of improper compulsion. It does not hold that *anything* said under compulsion of law is inadmissible. Admittedly, the court also observed, at para 68:

> The right not to incriminate oneself, in particular, presupposes that the prosecution in a criminal case seek to prove their case against the accused without resort to evidence obtained through methods of coercion or oppression in defiance of the will of the accused. In this sense the right is closely linked to the presumption of innocence contained in article 6(2) of the convention.

Again one finds the link with the non-absolute right of silence. In any event 'methods of coercion or oppression in defiance of the will of the accused' is probably another way of referring to improper compulsion. This is consistent with the following passage, at p 338, para 69:

> In the present case the Court is only called upon to decide whether the use made by the prosecution of the statements obtained from the applicant by the inspectors amounted to an unjustifiable infringement of the right. This question must be examined by the Court in the light of all the circumstances of the case. In particular, it must be determined whether the applicant has been subject to compulsion to give evidence and whether the use made of the resulting testimony at his trial offended the basic principles of a fair procedure inherent in article 6(1) of which the right not to incriminate oneself is a constituent element.

The expression 'unjustifiable infringement of the right' implies that some infringements may be justified. In my view the observations in *Saunders* do not support an absolutist view of the privilege against self incrimination. It may be that the observations in *Saunders* will have to be clarified in a further case by the European Court. As things stand, however, I consider that the High Court of Justiciary put too great weight on these observations. In my view they were never intended to apply to a case such as the present.

VIII. Conclusion on art 6

That brings me back to the decision of the High Court of Justiciary. It treated the privilege against self incrimination as virtually absolute. That conclusion fits uneasily into the balanced convention system, and cannot be reconciled with art 6 of the convention in all its constituent parts and the spectrum of jurisprudence of the European Court on the various facets of art 6.

I would hold that the decision of the High Court of Justiciary on the merits was wrong. The procurator fiscal is entitled to lead the evidence of Miss Brown's admission under s 172(2) of the 1988 Act.

Appeal allowed.

■ QUESTION

Did the Privy Council strike the balance between the protection of individual rights and the interests of the community at large, in the right place?

Huang v Secretary of State for the Home Department and *Kashmiri v Secretary of State for the Home Department*
[2007] UKHL 11, [2007] 2 AC 167, House of Lords

The two appeals raise the question as to what is the decision-making role or function of appellate immigration authorities (adjudicators, the Immigration Appeal Tribunal, immigration judges) when deciding appeals, on Convention grounds, against refusal of leave to enter or remain, under s. 65 of the Immigration and Asylum Act 1999 and Part III of Sch. 4 to that Act.

LORD BINGHAM of CORNHILL, LORD HOFFMANN, BARONESS HALE of RICHMOND, LORD CARSWELL and LORD BROWN of EATON-UNDER-HEYWOOD: ...

11. These provisions, read purposively and in context, make it plain that the task of the appellate immigration authority, on an appeal on a Convention ground against a decision of the primary official decision-maker refusing leave to enter or remain in this country, is to decide whether the challenged decision is unlawful as incompatible with a Convention right or compatible and so lawful. It is not a secondary, reviewing, function dependent on establishing that the primary decision-maker misdirected himself or acted irrationally or was guilty of procedural impropriety. The appellate immigration authority must decide for itself whether the impugned decision is lawful and, if not, but only if not, reverse it. This is the decision reached by the Court of Appeal (Judge, Laws and Latham LJJ) in these conjoined appeals, and it is correct: [2005] EWCA Civ 105, [2006] QB 1 ...

13. In the course of his justly-celebrated and much-quoted opinion in *R (Daly) v Secretary of State for the Home Department* [2001] UKHL26, [2001] 2 AC 532, paras 26–28, Lord Steyn pointed out that neither the traditional approach to judicial review formulated in *Associated Provincial Picture Houses Ltd v Wednesbury Corporation* [1948] 1 KB 223 nor the heightened scrutiny approach adopted in *R v Ministry of Defence, Ex p Smith* [1996] QB 517 had provided adequate protection of Convention rights, as held by the Strasbourg court in *Smith and Grady v United Kingdom* (1999) 29 EHRR 493. Having referred to a material difference between the *Wednesbury* and *Smith* approach on the one hand and the proportionality approach applicable where Convention rights are at stake on the other, he said (para 28): "This does not mean that there has been a shift to merits review". This statement has, it seems, given rise to some misunderstanding. The policy attacked in *Daly* was held to be ultra vires the Prison Act 1952 (para 21) and also a breach of article 8. With both those conclusions Lord Steyn agreed (para 24). They depended on questions of pure legal principle, on which the House ruled. *Ex p Smith* was different. It

raised a rationality challenge to the recruitment policy adopted by the Ministry of Defence which both the Divisional Court and the Court of Appeal felt themselves bound to dismiss. The point which, as we understand, Lord Steyn wished to make was that, although the Convention calls for a more exacting standard of review, it remains the case that the judge is not the primary decision-maker. It is not for him to decide what the recruitment policy for the armed forces should be. In proceedings under the Human Rights Act, of course, the court would have to scrutinise the policy and any justification advanced for it to see whether there was sufficient justification for the discriminatory treatment. By contrast, the appellate immigration authority, deciding an appeal under section 65, is not reviewing the decision of another decision-maker. It is deciding whether or not it is unlawful to refuse leave to enter or remain, and it is doing so on the basis of up to date facts.

The task of the appellate immigration authority

14. Much argument was directed on the hearing of these appeals, and much authority cited, on the appellate immigration authority's proper approach to its task, due deference, discretionary areas of judgment, the margin of appreciation, democratic accountability, relative institutional competence, a distinction drawn by the Court of Appeal between decisions based on policy and decisions not so based, and so on. We think, with respect, that there has been a tendency, both in the arguments addressed to the courts and in the judgments of the courts, to complicate and mystify what is not, in principle, a hard task to define, however difficult the task is, in practice, to perform. In describing it, we continue to assume that the applicant does not qualify for leave to enter or remain under the Rules, and that reliance is placed on the family life component of article 8.

15. The first task of the appellate immigration authority is to establish the relevant facts. These may well have changed since the original decision was made. In any event, particularly where the applicant has not been interviewed, the authority will be much better placed to investigate the facts, test the evidence, assess the sincerity of the applicant's evidence and the genuineness of his or her concerns and evaluate the nature and strength of the family bond in the particular case. It is important that the facts are explored, and summarised in the decision, with care, since they will always be important and often decisive.

16. The authority will wish to consider and weigh all that tells in favour of the refusal of leave which is challenged, with particular reference to justification under article 8(2). There will, in almost any case, be certain general considerations to bear in mind: the general administrative desirability of applying known rules if a system of immigration control is to be workable, predictable, consistent and fair as between one applicant and another; the damage to good administration and effective control if a system is perceived by applicants internationally to be unduly porous, unpredictable or perfunctory; the need to discourage non-nationals admitted to the country temporarily from believing that they can commit serious crimes and yet be allowed to remain; the need to discourage fraud, deception and deliberate breaches of the law; and so on. In some cases much more particular reasons will be relied on to justify refusal, as in *Samaroo v Secretary of State for the Home Department* [2001] EWCA Civ 1139, [2002] INLR 55 where attention was paid to the Secretary of State's judgment that deportation was a valuable deterrent to actual or prospective drug traffickers, or *R (Farrakhan) v Secretary of State for the Home Department* [2002] EWCA Civ 606, [2002] QB 1391, an article 10 case, in which note was taken of the Home Secretary's judgment that the applicant posed a threat to community relations between Muslims and Jews and a potential threat to public order for that reason. The giving of weight to factors such as these is not, in our opinion, aptly described as deference: it is performance of the ordinary judicial task of weighing up the competing considerations on each side and according appropriate weight to the judgment of a person with responsibility for a given subject matter and access to special sources of knowledge and advice. That is how any rational judicial decision-maker is likely to proceed. It is to be noted that both *Samaroo* and *Farrakhan* (cases on which the Secretary of State seeks to place especial reliance as examples of the court attaching very considerable weight to decisions of his taken in an immigration context) were not merely challenges by way of judicial review rather than appeals but cases where Parliament had specifically excluded any right of appeal.

17. Counsel for the Secretary of State nevertheless put his case much higher even than that. She relied by analogy on the decision of the House in *Kay v Lambeth London Borough Council* [2006] UKHL 10, [2006] 2 AC 465, where the House considered the article 8 right to respect for the home. It held that the right of a public authority landlord to enforce a claim for possession under domestic law against an occupier whose right to occupy (if any) had ended and who was entitled to no protection in domestic law would in most cases automatically supply the justification required by article 8(2), and the courts would assume that domestic law struck the proper balance, at any rate unless the contrary were shown. So here, it was said, the appellate immigration authority should assume that the Immigration Rules and supplementary instructions, made by the responsible minister and laid before Parliament, had the imprimatur of democratic approval and should be taken to strike the right balance between the interests of the individual and those of the community. The analogy is unpersuasive. Domestic housing policy has been a continuing subject of discussion and debate in Parliament over very many years, with the competing interests of landlords and tenants fully represented, as also the public interest in securing accommodation for the indigent, averting homelessness and making the best use of finite public resources. The outcome, changed from time to time, may truly be said to represent a considered democratic compromise. This cannot be said in the same way of the Immigration Rules and supplementary instructions, which are not the product of active debate in Parliament, where non-nationals seeking leave to enter or remain are not in any event represented. It must be remembered that if an applicant qualifies for the grant of leave to enter or remain under the Rules and is refused leave, the immigration appeal authority must allow such applicant's appeal by virtue of paragraph 21(1)(a) of Part III of Schedule 4 to the 1999 Act. It is a premise of the statutory scheme enacted by Parliament that an applicant may fail to qualify under the Rules and yet may have a valid claim by virtue of article 8.

18. The authority must of course take account, as enjoined by section 2 of the 1998 Act, of Strasbourg jurisprudence on the meaning and effect of article 8. While the case law of the Strasbourg court is not strictly binding, it has been held that domestic courts and tribunals should, in the absence of special circumstances, follow the clear and constant jurisprudence of that court: *R (Alconbury Developments Ltd) v Secretary of State for the Environment, Transport and the Regions* [2001] UKHL 23, [2003] 2 AC 295, para 26; *R (Ullah) v Special Adjudicator* [2004] UKHL 26, [2004] 2 AC 323, para 20. It is unnecessary for present purposes to attempt to summarise the Convention jurisprudence on article 8, save to record that the article imposes on member states not only a negative duty to refrain from unjustified interference with a person's right to respect for his or her family but also a positive duty to show respect for it. The reported cases are of value in showing where, in many different factual situations, the Strasbourg court, as the ultimate guardian of Convention rights, has drawn the line, thus guiding national authorities in making their own decisions. But the main importance of the case law is in illuminating the core value which article 8 exists to protect. This is not, perhaps, hard to recognise. Human beings are social animals. They depend on others. Their family, or extended family, is the group on which many people most heavily depend, socially, emotionally and often financially. There comes a point at which, for some, prolonged and unavoidable separation from this group seriously inhibits their ability to live full and fulfilling lives. Matters such as the age, health and vulnerability of the applicant, the closeness and previous history of the family, the applicant's dependence on the financial and emotional support of the family, the prevailing cultural tradition and conditions in the country of origin and many other factors may all be relevant. The Strasbourg court has repeatedly recognised the general right of states to control the entry and residence of non-nationals, and repeatedly acknowledged that the Convention confers no right on individuals or families to choose where they prefer to live. In most cases where the applicants complain of a violation of their article 8 rights, in a case where the impugned decision is authorised by law for a legitimate object and the interference (or lack of respect) is of sufficient seriousness to engage the operation of article 8, the crucial question is likely to be whether the interference (or lack of respect) complained of is proportionate to the legitimate end sought to be achieved. Proportionality is a subject of such importance as to require separate treatment.

Proportionality

19. In *de Freitas v Permanent Secretary of Ministry of Agriculture, Fisheries, Lands and Housing* [1999] 1 AC 69, 80, the Privy Council, drawing on South African, Canadian and Zimbabwean authority, defined the questions generally to be asked in deciding whether a measure is proportionate:

> "whether: (i) the legislative objective is sufficiently important to justify limiting a fundamental right; (ii) the measures designed to meet the legislative objective are rationally connected to it; and (iii) the means used to impair the right or freedom are no more than is necessary to accomplish the objective."

This formulation has been widely cited and applied. But counsel for the applicants (with the support of Liberty, in a valuable written intervention) suggested that the formulation was deficient in omitting reference to an overriding requirement which featured in the judgment of Dickson CJ in *R v Oakes* [1986] 1 SCR 103, from which thivs approach to proportionality derives. This feature is (p 139) the need to balance the interests of society with those of individuals and groups. This is indeed an aspect which should never be overlooked or discounted. The House recognised as much in *R (Razgar) v Secretary of State for the Home Department* [2004] UKHL 27, [2004] 2 AC 368, paras 17–20, 26, 27, 60, 77, when, having suggested a series of questions which an adjudicator would have to ask and answer in deciding a Convention question, it said that the judgment on proportionality must always involve the striking of a fair balance between the rights of the individual and the interests of the community which is inherent in the whole of the Convention. The severity and consequences of the interference will call for careful assessment at this stage" (see para 20).

If, as counsel suggest, insufficient attention has been paid to this requirement, the failure should be made good.

20. In an article 8 case where this question is reached, the ultimate question for the appellate immigration authority is whether the refusal of leave to enter or remain, in circumstances where the life of the family cannot reasonably be expected to be enjoyed elsewhere, taking full account of all considerations weighing in favour of the refusal, prejudices the family life of the applicant in a manner sufficiently serious to amount to a breach of the fundamental right protected by article 8. If the answer to this question is affirmative, the refusal is unlawful and the authority must so decide. It is not necessary that the appellate immigration authority, directing itself along the lines indicated in this opinion, need ask in addition whether the case meets a test of exceptionality. The suggestion that it should is based on an observation of Lord Bingham in *Razgar* above, para 20. He was there expressing an expectation, shared with the Immigration Appeal Tribunal, that the number of claimants not covered by the Rules and supplementary directions but entitled to succeed under article 8 would be a very small minority. That is still his expectation. But he was not purporting to lay down a legal test.

NOTES

1. The significance of *Huang* and *Kashmiri* may be recognized in its single unanimous opinion. The decision seeks to clarify two issues from Lord Steyn's speech in *Daly*, merits review and deference. On the first in [11] their Lordships say that human rights adjudication involves the immigration appellate authority deciding for itself if the primary decision-maker's decision is lawful (Convention-compatible) and, if it is not, to reverse it. This is neither merits review nor judicial review directed at illegality, irrationality or procedural irregularity. It is not merits review because the appellate authority is not the primary decision-maker and while the standard of review is different from that used in judicial review, this does not mean the determination of policy is being removed from the primary decision-maker, so as, to use the instance of *Smith*, to decide what the recruitment policy of the armed forces should be. On deference, their Lordships at [16] preferred to say this was the weighing-up of competing considerations with appropriate weight given to a person responsible for a subject matter with access to special sources of knowledge and advice.
2. Is the human rights adjudication discussed by their Lordships restricted to the immigration appellate authority considering a s. 65 appeal and not applicable to the courts hearing a human rights

challenge brought by way of judicial review? M. Amos in 'Separating Human Rights Adjudication from Judicial Review—*Huang* v *Secretary of State for the Home Department* and *Kashmiri* v *Secretary of State for the Home Department*', (2007) 5 *European Human Rights Law Review* 679, argues that it is applicable on the basis of two House of Lords decisions where the approach of the Court of Appeal was criticized, *R* v *(Begum) Headteacher and Governors of Denbigh High School* [2006] UKHL 15, [2007] 1 AC 100 and *Belfast City Council* v *Miss Behavin' Ltd* [2007] UKHL 19, [2007] 1WLR 1420. In the latter case Baroness Hale said at [31]:

> The first, and most straightforward, question is who decides whether or not a claimant's Convention rights have been infringed. The answer is that it is the court before which the issue is raised. The role of the court in human rights adjudication is quite different from the role of the court in an ordinary judicial review of administrative action. In human rights adjudication, the court is concerned with whether the human rights of the claimant have in fact been infringed, not with whether the administrative decision-maker properly took them into account. If it were otherwise, every policy decision taken before the Human Rights Act 1998 which came into force but which engaged a convention right would be open to challenge, no matter how obviously compliant with the right in question it was. That cannot be right.

3. Their Lordships' re-formulation of deference at [16], as taking into account the views of a person responsible with special access to knowledge and advice, could suggest that the courts give weight to primary decision-makers because of their institutional capacity and expertise, however, the discussion at [17] about Parliamentary involvement in housing policy in relation to the House's decision *Kay* v *Lambeth London Borough Council* [2006] UKHL 10, [2006] 2 AC 465, compared with the Immigration Rules seems to suggest that the 'democratic compromise' in the housing policy is significant. Commentators including J. Jowell, 'Judicial Deference: Servility, Civility or Institutional Capacity' [2003] *Public Law* 592 and M. Hunt, 'Sovereignty's Blight: Why Contemporary Public Law Needs the Concept of "Due Deference"' in N. Bamforth and P. Leyland (eds), *Public Law in a Multi-Layered Constitution* (2003), p. 337; have taken issue with the idea that democratic arguments should pre-empt judicial involvement. The judiciary must not abdicate their responsibilities of deciding Convention rights, a view also shared by Lord Steyn, 'Deference: A Tangled Story' [2005] *Public Law* 346. Amos argues that it is implicit in their Lordships' arguments about *Kay* that weight is properly accorded to a primary decision-maker who had done its job properly in relation to Convention rights. Amos again draws on *Begum* and *Belfast City Council* for support. In *Begum* the Court of Appeal had found that the school had not followed a formal approach in devising its policy on uniform which specifically recognized that pupils' Art. 9 Convention right was engaged. Lord Bingham said at [34] in relation to the assessment of the proportionality of the interference with the claimant's Art. 9 right that it would be

> ... irresponsible of any court, lacking the experience, background and detailed knowledge of the head teacher, staff and governors, to overrule their judgment on a matter as sensitive as this.

In *Belfast City Council* the council in the exercise of its licensing powers had not explicitly or implicitly considered the proportionality of its interference with Convention rights, Baroness Hale said at [37]:

> ... the court has to decide whether the authority has violated the convention rights. In doing so, it is bound to acknowledge that the local authority is much better placed than the court to decide whether the right of sex shop owners to sell pornographic literature and images should be restricted—for the prevention of disorder or crime, for the protection of health or morals, of for the protection of the rights of others. But the views of the local authority are bound to carry less weight where the local authority has made no attempt to address that question. Had the Belfast City Council expressly set itself the task of balancing the rights of individuals to sell and buy pornographic literature and images against the interests of the wider community, a court would find it hard to upset the balance which the local authority had struck. But where there is no indication that this has been done, the court has no alternative but to strike the balance for itself, giving due weight to the judgments made by those who are in much closer touch with the people and the places involved that the court could ever be.

■ QUESTION

Does the *Huang* approach to deference set clear and appropriate boundaries to the courts' review function or does it seek to make palatable a significant shift in power to the judges?

Huang also developed the test for proportionality used by the courts in the UK when dealing with Convention rights under the Human Rights Act 1998. In the following cases we see in *R* v *(Daly) Secretary of State for the Home Department*, the initial recognition and articulation of proportionality as the appropriate test instead of the different domestic standard of unreasonableness or irrationality (see the extract which follows). Proportionality along with legality forms the test which the ECHR provides for determining if restrictions upon qualified Convention rights are lawful. The components of legality test are outlined in *R* v *Shayler* and then in *R (British Broadcasting Corporation)* v *Secretary of State for Justice* we see the application of the proportionality test in a challenge to a ministerial decision successfully arguing that it constituted a breach of the freedom of expression in Art. 10 (see the extracts which follow).

R (Daly) v Secretary of State for the Home Department

[2001] UKHL 26, House of Lords

D, a prisoner, stored correspondence with his solicitor in his cell. He was subject to a standard cell searching policy under paras 17.69–17.74 of a Security Manual issued by the Secretary of State to prison governors under his power to make rules for the regulation and control of prisoners under s. 47(1) of the Prison Act 1952. The policy required prisoners to be excluded during cell searches to prevent intimidation and to prevent prisoners acquiring knowledge of the search techniques. Prison officers were to examine any legal correspondence to ensure it contained nothing likely to endanger prison security but they were not to read it. D sought judicial review of the decision that prisoners' legally privileged correspondence could be examined in their absence. The application was dismissed by the Court of Appeal. D appealed to the House of Lords. He did not contest the need for correspondence to be examined but contended that such examination should ordinarily take place in the presence of the prisoner.

LORD BINGHAM OF CORNHILL: …

[His Lordship referred to the origins of the policy in the report of the Woodcock Inquiry following the escape of six dangerous prisoners from HMP Whitemoor in 1994. The report recommended that cells and property should be searched at frequent but irregular intervals. His Lordship examined the restrictions on rights which imprisonment involves and the case law relating thereto before quoting with approval from the speech by Lord Browne-Wilkinson in *R* v *Secretary of State for the Home Department, ex p Pierson* [1998] AC 539, 575:]

> From these authorities I think the following proposition is established. A power conferred by Parliament in general terms is not to be taken to authorise the doing of acts by the donee of the power which adversely affect the legal rights of the citizen or the basic principles on which the law of the United Kingdom is based unless the statute conferring the power makes it clear that such was the intention of Parliament.

The argument

…

15 It is necessary, first, to ask whether the policy infringes in a significant way Mr Daly's common law right that the confidentiality of privileged legal correspondence be maintained. He submits that it does for two related reasons: first, because knowledge that such correspondence may be looked at by prison officers in the absence of the prisoner inhibits the prisoner's willingness to communicate with his legal adviser in terms of unreserved candour; and secondly, because there must be a risk, if the prisoner is not present, that the officers will stray beyond their limited role in examining legal correspondence, particularly if, for instance, they see some name or reference familiar to them, as would be the case if the prisoner were bringing or contemplating bringing proceedings against officers in

the prison. For the Home Secretary it is argued that the policy involves no infringement of a prisoner's common law right since his privileged correspondence is not read in his absence but only examined.

16 I have no doubt that the policy infringes Mr Daly's common law right to legal professional privilege. This was the view of two very experienced judges in *R* v *Secretary of State for the Home Department, Ex p Simms* [1999] QB 349, against which decision the present appeal is effectively brought. At p 366, Kennedy LJ said:

> In my judgment legal professional privilege does attach to correspondence with legal advisers which is stored by a prisoner in his cell, and accordingly such correspondence is to be protected from any unnecessary interference by prison staff. Even if the correspondence is only inspected to see that it is what it purports to be that is likely to impair the free flow of communication between a convicted or remand prisoner on the one hand and his legal adviser on the other, and therefore it constitutes an impairment of the privilege.

Judge LJ was of the same opinion. At p 373, he said:

> Prisoners whose cells are searched in their absence will find it difficult to believe that their correspondence has been searched but not read. The governor's order will sometimes be disobeyed. Accordingly I am prepared to accept the potential 'chilling effect' of such searches.

In an imperfect world there will necessarily be occasions when prison officers will do more than merely examine prisoners' legal documents, and apprehension that they may do so is bound to inhibit a prisoner's willingness to communicate freely with his legal adviser.

17 The next question is whether there can be any ground for infringing in any way a prisoner's right to maintain the confidentiality of his privileged legal correspondence. Plainly there can. Some examination may well be necessary to establish that privileged legal correspondence is what it appears to be and is not a hiding place for illicit materials or information prejudicial to security or good order.

18 It is then necessary to ask whether, to the extent that it infringes a prisoner's common law right to privilege, the policy can be justified as a necessary and proper response to the acknowledged need to maintain security, order and discipline in prisons and to prevent crime. Mr Daly's challenge at this point is directed to the blanket nature of the policy, applicable as it is to all prisoners of whatever category in all closed prisons in England and Wales, irrespective of a prisoner's past or present conduct and of any operational emergency or urgent intelligence. The Home Secretary's justification rests firmly on the points already mentioned: the risk of intimidation, the risk that staff may be conditioned by prisoners to relax security and the danger of disclosing searching methods.

19 In considering these justifications, based as they are on the extensive experience of the prison service, it must be recognised that the prison population includes a core of dangerous, disruptive and manipulative prisoners, hostile to authority and ready to exploit for their own advantage any concession granted to them. Any search policy must accommodate this inescapable fact. I cannot however accept that the reasons put forward justify the policy in its present blanket form. Any prisoner who attempts to intimidate or disrupt a search of his cell, or whose past conduct shows that he is likely to do so, may properly be excluded even while his privileged correspondence is examined so as to ensure the efficacy of the search, but no justification is shown for routinely excluding all prisoners, whether intimidatory or disruptive or not, while that part of the search is conducted. Save in the extraordinary conditions prevailing at Whitemoor before September 1994, it is hard to regard the conditioning of staff as a problem which could not be met by employing dedicated search teams. It is not suggested that prison officers when examining legal correspondence employ any sophisticated technique which would be revealed to the prisoner if he were present, although he might no doubt be encouraged to secrete illicit materials among his legal papers if the examination were obviously very cursory. The policy cannot in my opinion be justified in its present blanket form. The infringement of prisoners' rights to maintain the confidentiality of their privileged legal correspondence is greater than is shown

to be necessary to serve the legitimate public objectives already identified. I accept Mr Daly's submission on this point.

[His Lordship was fortified in reaching his view by four considerations, namely, (i) that the Prisons Ombudsman had upheld a similar complaint by another prisoner in 1996 resulting in Security Group (the company which ran the prison concerned) adopting revised procedures which permitted the prisoner to remain in his cell while his legal documents were searched; (ii) the Ombudsman's report also revealed a procedure adopted in HMP Full Sutton to accommodate a similar complaint from a prisoner there; (iii) the procedures in Scotland involved the prisoner being present during examination of his privileged legal correspondence; (iv) in only two cases have illicit items been found hidden in legally privileged documents.]

21 In *R* v *Secretary of State for the Home Department, Ex p Simms* [1999] QB 349 and again in the present case, the Court of Appeal held that the policy represented the minimum intrusion into the rights of prisoners consistent with the need to maintain security, order and discipline in prisons. That is a conclusion which I respect but cannot share. In my opinion the policy provides for a degree of intrusion into the privileged legal correspondence of prisoners which is greater than is justified by the objectives the policy is intended to serve, and so violates the common law rights of prisoners. Section 47(1) of the 1952 Act does not authorise such excessive intrusion, and the Home Secretary accordingly had no power to lay down or implement the policy in its present form. I would accordingly declare paragraphs 17.69 to 17.74 of the Security Manual to be unlawful and void in so far as they provide that prisoners must always be absent when privileged legal correspondence held by them in their cells is examined by prison officers.

...

23 I have reached the conclusions so far expressed on an orthodox application of common law principles derived from the authorities and an orthodox domestic approach to judicial review. But the same result is achieved by reliance on the European Convention. Article 8(1) gives Mr Daly a right to respect for his correspondence. While interference with that right by a public authority may be permitted if in accordance with the law and necessary in a democratic society in the interests of national security, public safety, the prevention of disorder or crime or for protection of the rights and freedoms of others, the policy interferes with Mr Daly's exercise of his right under article 8(1) to an extent much greater than necessity requires. In this instance, therefore, the common law and the Convention yield the same result. But this need not always be so. In *Smith and Grady* v *United Kingdom* (1999) 29 EHRR 493, the European Court held that the orthodox domestic approach of the English courts had not given the applicants an effective remedy for the breach of their rights under article 8 of the Convention because the threshold of review had been set too high. Now, following the incorporation of the Convention by the Human Rights Act 1998 and the bringing of that Act fully into force, domestic courts must themselves form a judgment whether a Convention right has been breached (conducting such inquiry as is necessary to form that judgment) and, so far as permissible under the Act, grant an effective remedy. On this aspect of the case, I agree with and adopt the observations of my noble and learned friend Lord Steyn which I have had the opportunity of reading in draft.

LORD STEYN: ...

24 My Lords, I am in complete agreement with the reasons given by Lord Bingham of Cornhill in his speech. For the reasons he gives I would also allow the appeal. Except on one narrow but important point I have nothing to add.

25 There was written and oral argument on the question whether certain observations of Lord Phillips of Worth Matravers MR in *R (Mahmood)* v *Secretary of State for the Home Department* [2001] 1 WLR 840 were correct. The context was an immigration case involving a decision of the Secretary of State made before the Human Rights Act 1998 came into effect. The Master of the Rolls nevertheless

approached the case as if the Act had been in force when the Secretary of State reached his decision. He explained the new approach to be adopted. The Master of the Rolls concluded, at p 857, para 40:

> When anxiously scrutinising an executive decision that interferes with human rights, the court will ask the question, applying an objective test, whether the decision-maker could reasonably have concluded that the interference was necessary to achieve one or more of the legitimate aims recognised by the Convention. When considering the test of necessity in the relevant context, the court must take into account the European jurisprudence in accordance with section 2 of the 1998 Act.

> ...

26 The explanation of the Master of the Rolls in the first sentence of the cited passage requires clarification. It is couched in language reminiscent of the traditional *Wednesbury* ground of review (*Associated Provincial Picture Houses Ltd* v *Wednesbury Corpn* [1948] 1 KB 223), and in particular the adaptation of that test in terms of heightened scrutiny in cases involving fundamental rights as formulated in *R* v *Ministry of Defence, Ex p Smith* [1996] QB 517, 554E–G per Sir Thomas Bingham MR. There is a material difference between the *Wednesbury* and *Smith* grounds of review and the approach of proportionality applicable in respect of review where Convention rights are at stake.

27 The contours of the principle of proportionality are familiar. In *de Freitas* v *Permanent Secretary of Ministry of Agriculture, Fisheries, Lands and Housing* [1999] 1 AC 69 the Privy Council adopted a three-stage test. Lord Clyde observed, at p 80, that in determining whether a limitation (by an act, rule or decision) is arbitrary or excessive the court should ask itself:

> whether: (i) the legislative objective is sufficiently important to justify limiting a fundamental right; (ii) the measures designed to meet the legislative objective are rationally connected to it; and (iii) the means used to impair the right or freedom are no more than is necessary to accomplish the objective.

Clearly, these criteria are more precise and more sophisticated than the traditional grounds of review. What is the difference for the disposal of concrete cases? ... The starting point is that there is an overlap between the traditional grounds of review and the approach of proportionality. Most cases would be decided in the same way whichever approach is adopted. But the intensity of review is somewhat greater under the proportionality approach. Making due allowance for important structural differences between various convention rights, which I do not propose to discuss, a few generalisations are perhaps permissible. I would mention three concrete differences without suggesting that my statement is exhaustive. First, the doctrine of proportionality may require the reviewing court to assess the balance which the decision maker has struck, not merely whether it is within the range of rational or reasonable decisions. Secondly, the proportionality test may go further than the traditional grounds of review inasmuch as it may require attention to be directed to the relative weight accorded to interests and considerations. Thirdly, even the heightened scrutiny test developed in *R* v *Ministry of Defence, Ex p Smith* [1996] QB 517, 554 is not necessarily appropriate to the protection of human rights. It will be recalled that in *Smith* the Court of Appeal reluctantly felt compelled to reject a limitation on homosexuals in the army. The challenge based on article 8 of the Convention for the Protection of Human Rights and Fundamental Freedoms (the right to respect for private and family life) foundered on the threshold required even by the anxious scrutiny test. The European Court of Human Rights came to the opposite conclusion: *Smith and Grady* v *United Kingdom* (1999) 29 EHRR 493. The court concluded, at p 543, para 138:

> the threshold at which the High Court and the Court of Appeal could find the Ministry of Defence policy irrational was placed so high that it effectively excluded any consideration by the domestic courts of the question of whether the interference with the applicants' rights answered a pressing social need or was proportionate to the national security and public order aims pursued, principles which lie at the heart of the court's analysis of complaints under article 8 of the Convention.

In other words, the intensity of the review, in similar cases, is guaranteed by the twin requirements that the limitation of the right was necessary in a democratic society, in the sense of meeting a pressing social need, and the question whether the interference was really proportionate to the legitimate aim being pursued.

28 The differences in approach between the traditional grounds of review and the proportionality approach may therefore sometimes yield different results. It is therefore important that cases involving Convention rights must be analysed in the correct way. This does not mean that there has been a shift to merits review. On the contrary, as Professor Jowell [2000] PL 671, 681 has pointed out the respective roles of judges and administrators are fundamentally distinct and will remain so. To this extent the general tenor of the observations in *Mahmood* [2001] 1 WLR 840 are correct. And Laws LJ rightly emphasised in *Mahmood*, at p 847, para 18, 'that the intensity of review in a public law case will depend on the subject matter in hand'. That is so even in cases involving Convention rights. In law context is everything.

Appeal allowed.

R v Shayler

[2002] UKHL 11, House of Lords

LORD HOPE OF CRAIGHEAD: ...

54. Article 10(1) of the Convention states that the right to freedom of expression includes the right to impart information and ideas without interference by public authorities. Article 10(2) states, by way of qualification, that the exercise of this right,

> "... since it carries with it duties and responsibilities, may be subject to such formalities, conditions, restrictions or penalties as are prescribed by law and are necessary ... in the interests of national security ..."

55. The wording of article 10(2) as applied to this case indicates that any such restriction, if it is to be compatible with the Convention right, must satisfy two basic requirements. First, the restriction must be "prescribed by law". So it must satisfy the principle of legality. The second is that it must be such as is "necessary" in the interests of national security. This raises the question of proportionality. The jurisprudence of the European Court of Human Rights explains how these principles are to be understood and applied in the context of the facts of this case. As any restriction with the right to freedom of expression must be subjected to very close scrutiny, it is important to identify the requirements of that jurisprudence before undertaking that exercise.

56. The principle of legality requires the court to address itself to three distinct questions. The first is whether there is a legal basis in domestic law for the restriction. The second is whether the law or rule in question is sufficiently accessible to the individual who is affected by the restriction, and sufficiently precise to enable him to understand its scope and foresee the consequences of his actions so that he can regulate his conduct without breaking the law. The third is whether, assuming that these two requirements are satisfied, it is nevertheless open to the criticism on the Convention ground that it was applied in a way that is arbitrary because, for example, it has been resorted to in bad faith or in a way that is not proportionate. I derive these principles, which have been mentioned many times in subsequent cases, from *The Sunday Times v United Kingdom* (1979–1980) 2 EHRR 245, para 49 and also from *Winterwerp v The Netherlands* (1979) 2 EHRR 387, 402–403, para 39 and *Engel v The Netherlands (No. 1)*(1976) 1 EHRR 647, 669, paras 58–59 which were concerned with the principle of legality in the context of article 5(1): see also *A v The Scottish Ministers* 2001 SLT 1331, 1336L-1337B (PC).

In the next case we see an example of judgment finding unlawful restriction upon freedom of expression. Note the structure of the judgment in which:

(a) the importance of freedom of expression is outlined and the significant impact of television at [37]–[45];
(b) the outlining of the legality and proportionality tests derived from Art. 10(2) to determine if the restrictions are lawful and that reasons must be convincing [46]–[54]; and
(c) the application of those tests to the facts and the reasoning supporting the finding at [76]–[97].

R (British Broadcasting Corporation) v *Secretary of State for Justice*
[2012] EWHC 12 (Admin), Divisional Court

The BBC challenged the refusal to grant permission for a face-to-face interview with a prisoner and to broadcast that interview in a television programme, arguing that it breached freedom of expression under Art. 10. The policy document relied upon by the Minister for the decision, PSI 37/2010, outlined criteria for visits by journalists: the interview must relate to an alleged miscarriage of justice and the prisoner had exhausted all appeals, or that there was some other sufficiently strong public interest issue which would be raised during the visit.

SINGH J: ...

37. It is clear from the text of article 10(1) that it confers not only the right to "impart" information and ideas but also the right to "receive" them: see *Sunday Times v United Kingdom* (1979) 2 EHRR 245, at paras. 65-66. The claimants emphasise this because they submit that there is a particularly strong public interest in the case of Mr Ahmad and that the public have a right to see a programme about it which would include extracts from a recorded interview with him.

38. It is also important to recall that the press and broadcasting media are not given special rights under article 10 as privileges. Rather, as has frequently been said by the European Court of Human Rights, they enjoy these rights on behalf of all of us as members of the public. The media are regarded as essential in a democracy as the "watchdog" of the public: see e.g. *Bladet Tromso and Stensaas v Norway* (2000) 29 EHRR 125 at para. 59.

39. In a case which preceded the coming into force of the HRA Lord Steyn emphasised the reasons why the right to freedom of expression is so important. In *R v Secretary of State for the Home Department, ex parte Simms* [2000] 2 AC 115 at 126, he said:

"Freedom of expression is, of course intrinsically important: it is valued for its own sake. But it is well recognised that it is also instrumentally important. It serves a number of broad objectives. First, it promotes the self-fulfilment of individuals in society. Secondly, in the famous words of Holmes J (echoing John Stuart Mill), 'The best test of truth is the power of the thought to get itself accepted in the competition of the market': *Abrams v United States* (1919) 250 US 616, 630, per Holmes J (dissenting). Thirdly, freedom of speech is the lifeblood of democracy. The free flow of information and ideas informs political debate. It is a safety valve: people are more ready to accept decisions that go against them if they can in principle seek to influence them. It acts as a brake on the abuse of power by public officials. It facilitates the exposure of errors in the governance and administration of justice of the country. ..."

40. One important aspect of the right to freedom of expression is that the state may not normally prescribe the content of what may be said or received by members of the public. In American constitutional jurisprudence such "content-based" restrictions are viewed with particular suspicion under the First Amendment, although they are not absolutely prohibited. As Jackson J put it in *West Virginia State Board of Education v Barnette* (1943) 319 US 624 (a freedom of religion case), at 642:

"If there is any fixed star in our constitutional constellation, it is that no official, high or petty, can prescribe what shall be orthodox in politics, nationalism, religion or other matters of opinion to force citizens to confess by word or act their faith therein."

41. One reason for this is to be found in the "marketplace of ideas" rationale mentioned by Lord Steyn in *Simms*. History has taught us that, in fields as diverse as politics, religion, science and the law, what starts as a heresy may well end up as the orthodoxy. Indeed, that is what happened to the views on the First Amendment of Holmes J in *Abrams* (cited by Lord Steyn in *Simms*), which were expressed in a dissenting judgment in the US Supreme Court. Society benefits when there is free trade in ideas.

42. The Secretary of State fairly points out that in the present case he has not sought to impose a content-based restriction. He notes that Mr Ahmad and others speaking on his behalf have had plenty of opportunity to contribute to public debate about his case, for example in newspaper articles and on the internet, and may do so in the future. He also observes that there is nothing to prevent the claimants from making a programme about Mr Ahmad's case and the more general issues of public interest which it raises.

43. The claimants emphasise that the rights in article 10 include the right to choose not just the content of what is to be expressed but also the form of such expression. They submit that this is especially important as an aspect of journalistic and editorial freedom. In *News Verlags GmbH and CoKG v Austria* (2001) 31 EHRR 8, at para. 39, the European Court of Human Rights said:

"The Court recalls that it is not for the Court, or for the national courts for that matter, to substitute their own views for those of the press as to what technique of reporting should be adopted by journalists. Article 10 protects not only the substance of ideas and information but also the form in which they are conveyed."

44. The claimants submit that, in the present case, it is important for them to be able to exercise their professional judgment in deciding whether a face-to-face interview with Mr Ahmad is necessary and whether they should include extracts from that interview in a programme about his case. The Secretary of State submits that it is sufficient that they may correspond with Mr Ahmad in writing.

45. In this context it is worth recalling the particular power that television has in modern life. This can cut both ways. The claimants submit that a broadcast interview will bring home to the public the real human story of Mr Ahmad's case, for example the impact on his appearance, voice and manner of many years of detention without trial. On the other hand, the Secretary of State points out that it is precisely because of the greater impact that television can have that it needs to be more carefully regulated, for example because of the distress it could cause to the victim of a prisoner's crime. In *R (Pro Life Alliance) v British Broadcasting Corporation* [2004] 1 AC 185, at para. 20, Lord Hoffmann explained that the power of the medium is the reason why broadcasting has been required to conform to standards of taste and decency which in the case of other media would nowadays be thought to be an unwarranted restriction on freedom of expression:

"The main reason for singling out television and, to a lesser extent, radio for the imposition of standards of taste and decency is the intimate relationship which these media establish between the broadcaster and the viewer or listener in his home. Television in particular makes the viewer feel a participant in the events it depicts and acquainted with the people (real or fictitious) whom he regularly sees. The visual image brings home the reality which lies behind words."

46. As is well-known, the right to freedom of expression in article 10 is not absolute. In principle it can be limited provided the conditions in article 10(2) are satisfied.

47. First, the limitation must be prescribed by law: there is no dispute about that in the present case.

48. Secondly, the limitation must have one or more of the legitimate aims set out in article 10(2): again, there has been no dispute about that in the present case. In particular, the Secretary of

State relies upon the legitimate aims of the protection of the rights of others and the protection of their health. There are hints in the evidence before the Court that the Secretary of State also relies upon the legitimate aims of the prevention of crime and the maintenance of the authority of the judiciary.

49. Thirdly, the limitation must be necessary in a democratic society. This requires in turn that the limitation must meet a pressing social need and satisfy the principle of proportionality, to which we will return in more detail. It is important not to lose sight of the phrase "in a democratic society." These words, which appear in many of the articles of the Convention, are not superfluous. The framers of the Convention, arising as it did out of the ashes of European conflict in the 1930s and 1940s, recognised that not everything that the state asserts to be necessary will be acceptable in a democratic society. The jurisprudence of the European Court of Human Rights has frequently stressed that the hallmarks of a democratic society are pluralism, tolerance and broad-mindedness: e.g. *Handyside v United Kingdom* 1 EHRR 737, at para. 49.

50. In this context, the Court has said in many cases that, since freedom of expression constitutes one of the essential foundations of a democratic society, "it is applicable not only to information or ideas that are favourably received or regarded as inoffensive or as a matter of indifference, but also to those that offend, shock or disturb the State or any sector of the population": *Sunday Times*, at para. 65.

51. The principle of proportionality was explained by the House of Lords in *Huang v Secretary of State for the Home Department* [2007] 2 AC 167, at para. 19, in a single opinion of the appellate committee which was given by Lord Bingham of Cornhill. Although that was a case about article 8 (the right to respect for private and family life), the structure of that article is similar to article 10 and the principles which Lord Bingham set out were derived from comparative law relating to human rights generally. After drawing on well-known authority from the Privy Council, the Supreme Court of Canada and other Commonwealth jurisdictions, Lord Bingham summarised the requirements of proportionality as follows (we adapt the language slightly to make it pertinent to cases such as the present):

(i)   the objective is sufficiently important to justify limiting a fundamental right;
(ii) the means used to achieve that objective are rationally connected to it;
(iii) the means used to impair the right or freedom are no more than is necessary to accomplish that objective; and
(iv) there is maintained a fair balance between the rights of individuals or groups and the interests of the community.

52. Also in *Huang* Lord Bingham gave important guidance as to the relevance of the judgment of the Secretary of State when a court is called upon to adjudicate on the question of proportionality. At para. 16 he said:

"The giving of weight to factors such as these is not, in our opinion, aptly described as deference: it is performance of the ordinary judicial task of weighing up the competing considerations on each side and according appropriate weight to the judgment of a person with responsibility for a given subject matter and access to special sources of knowledge and advice. That is how any rational judicial decision-maker is likely to proceed."

53. As has been observed in the past, the concept of "deference" is inapt in this context since it has "overtones of servility": e.g. the *Pro Life Alliance* case, at para. 75 (Lord Hoffmann). More often used are phrases such as the "margin of appreciation" or the "discretionary area of judgment". The former should not be used in the domestic context as it is a concept of international law, more appropriate in the Strasbourg Court: *R v Director of Public Prosecutions, ex parte Kebilene* [2000] 2 AC 326, at 380 (Lord Hope of Craighead). We have found helpful the concept of "appropriate weight" to which Lord Bingham referred in *Huang*. As the passage from which we have quoted makes clear, how much weight should be given to the judgment of a person such as the Secretary of State will vary according to the subject matter and the extent of their expertise and access to specialist sources of knowledge and advice. As we understand it, this is what is meant by "institutional competence", about which there was some

debate at the hearing before us. The passage we have quoted from *Huang* also makes it clear that, at the end of the day, the assessment of proportionality under the HRA is a judicial task, once all the material has been taken into account and appropriate weight given to the views of others, including those of the decision-maker. As Lord Bingham observed in his opinion in *A v Secretary of State for the Home Department* [2005] 2 AC 68, at para. 42, the HRA "gives the courts a very specific, wholly democratic mandate" to adjudicate on human rights issues.

54. The European Court of Human Rights has frequently stressed that, in view of the importance of the right to freedom of expression, restrictions upon it have to be "established convincingly": see e.g. *Bergens Tidende v Norway* (2001) 31 EHRR 16, at para. 48. Furthermore, in *Sunday Times* the Court made it clear that the assessment of proportionality will in article 10 cases be highly fact-specific. It will not suffice to demonstrate that, in principle, a legislative or other measure complies with the principle of proportionality; it will also be necessary to show that the decision applying it to the facts of a particular case does so. At para. 65, the Court said:

". . . . the Court's supervision under article 10 covers not only the basic legislation but also the decision applying it. It is not sufficient that the interference involved belongs to that class of the exceptions listed in article 10(2) which has been invoked; neither is it sufficient that the interference was imposed because its subject matter fell within a particular category or was caught by a legal rule formulated in general or absolute terms: the Court has to be satisfied that the interference was necessary having regard to the facts and circumstances prevailing in the specific case before it."

. . .

76. In our judgment, and even after giving appropriate weight to the views of the Secretary of State, the decision of 22 September 2011 constitutes a disproportionate interference with the right to freedom of expression in article 10. In the circumstances of this particular case, the justification for that interference has not been "convincingly established", as the jurisprudence on article 10 requires.

77. The Secretary of State's own policy in PSI 37/2010 recognises that there may be instances where a face-to-face interview will be permitted. The policy does not envisage that permission to conduct such an interview will normally be refused. Rather, it envisages that there may well be cases in which such an interview should be permitted either because its purpose is to highlight a potential miscarriage of justice or because there is some other sufficiently strong public interest: see para. 4.5 of PSI 37/2010. However, under the policy, permission for a face-to-face interview will only be given when the conditions set out in para. 4.6 are met.

[4.6 *In respect of either reason for a visit mentioned above the Secretary of State must also be satisfied that*:

(i) a visit is the only suitable method of communication; and the journalist and prisoner have previously communicated by written correspondence, which has proved to be inadequate; and

(ii) the journalist intends a serious attempt to investigate or bring to public attention the prisoner's case or the other issue with a sufficiently strong public interest raised by the prisoner; and

(iii) permitting the visit will not pose a threat to security, or to good order or discipline (this will include a consideration of the prisoner's behaviour in prison)." (Italics in original)]

78. In our judgment, the claimants have demonstrated on the evidence before the Court that they do require a face-to-face interview with Mr Ahmad and that they have achieved as much as they can by written correspondence. . . .

79. The practical considerations which form part of the rationale for the Secretary of State's policy in PSI 37/2010 do not justify the decision in the present case, although they may well do so in many cases. It was essentially because of such practical considerations that the (former) European Commission of Human Rights held to be inadmissible the application in *Bamber v United Kingdom* (App. No. 33742/96, 11 September 1997, BAILII [1997] ECHR 205).

80. If the decision of Mr Blunt of 15 July 2011 had stood, there can be little doubt that the authorities would have found practical ways of permitting the face-to-face interview with Mr Ahmad to take place. As counsel for the Secretary of State fairly accepted during the hearing before us, the nub of the Secretary of State's reasoning for refusing the claimant's request in the present case can be found in paragraph 32 of Mr Elder's first witness statement. The two reasons which are given there are essentially reasons of principle and not ones that turn on practical considerations. They focus on the Secretary of State's policy that permission will normally be refused for the broadcasting of any interview where recording is allowed. It is because the claimants wished to broadcast the interview that the initial decision of 15 July 2011 to permit an interview was revoked on 22 September 2011.

81. Turning to the question of whether the claimants should be permitted to broadcast the product of any recorded interview, the policy in PSI 37/201 does envisage that this will normally be refused: see para. 4.27. However, the policy is not absolute, nor could it be as a matter of administrative law, since a rigid and inflexible policy would be unlawful. The policy on its face admits of the possibility in exceptional cases of permitting such an interview to be recorded for the purpose of broadcasting.

82. In our judgment, it is difficult to think of a case which would fall within the exception if not the present one. We accept the claimants' contention that, as a result of the particular combination of circumstances, this case is highly exceptional. By saying that we make it clear that we do not consider that the present case should be regarded as setting any precedent for other cases. It is because of the unusual combination of facts that the present case, in our view, justifies departure from the normal policy. More than that, in our view, the claimants' rights under article 10 require that departure in the exceptional circumstances of this case, and the Secretary of State has not been able to justify denying those rights on the facts of this case. However, the Secretary of State is entitled to maintain the policy which he does: no challenge has been made to his entitlement to have such a policy in principle and to apply it to the great majority of cases. It is on the unusual facts of the present case that its application constituted a disproportionate interference with the right to freedom of expression.

83. As we have mentioned, and as counsel for the Secretary of State accepted, the nub of the reasoning which is said to support his decision in this case is set out at paragraph 32 of Mr Elder's first witness statement. In our judgment, while that reasoning tends to justify the general policy which the Secretary of State is entitled to adopt and maintain, it does not amount to a sufficient justification for the interference with the right to freedom of expression on the particular facts of the present case.

84. The first of the reasons advanced by Mr Elder, at paragraph 32(a), is that the restriction on the right to freedom of expression is necessary in the present case in order to protect the victims of terrorism from distress.

85. In our judgment, this reason does not stand up to scrutiny in the circumstances of the present case, having regard to the principle of proportionality, which we have outlined earlier. As is accepted by the Secretary of State, mere offence is not sufficient to justify a restriction on the right to freedom of expression: see *Sunday Times*, at para. 65, which we have quoted earlier. If it is to justify a restriction on the right to freedom of expression, distress must, therefore, be something more than offence. It is important to recall that Mr Ahmad has not been convicted of any offence; he has not been charged in this jurisdiction even though in principle he could have been if the CPS had considered there was sufficient evidence; and no *prima facie* case has to be demonstrated to a court in this country before he can be extradited. We also remind ourselves in this context of what we have said earlier about the nature of a democratic society: it is one which is characterised by pluralism, tolerance and broad-mindedness. This country has a proud and well-known tradition of fairness, which includes the presumption of innocence, that everyone is presumed to be innocent until proved guilty, a presumption which also finds its place in article 6(2) of the Convention rights.

86. The case of *Nilsen v United Kingdom* (App. No. 36882/05, 9 March 2010, BAILII [2010] ECHR 470) on which the Secretary of State placed some reliance, is distinguishable. In that case the European Court

of Human Rights held the application to be inadmissible as it was manifestly ill-founded. The application was brought not by a reputable organisation like the BBC but by a notorious murderer who was serving a whole-life tariff. The applicant in that case had been convicted of the most serious offences and wished to publish his autobiography. He had nothing serious to say in the public interest, although the policy applied in his case would not have prevented even him from engaging in such serious debate: see paragraph 51 of the admissibility decision. To the contrary, the applicant wished to use his memoirs as a platform to seek to justify his conduct and denigrate people he disliked and his manuscript contained "several lurid and pornographic passages" and highly personal details of a number of his offences: see paragraph 53. The applicant did not take issue with the description of his crimes as being "as grave and depraved as it is possible to imagine": see paragraph 54. Even in such an extreme case, the Court was careful to distinguish between the causing of offence to members of the public, which would not be a sufficient justification for restricting article 10 rights, and "an affront to human dignity", which would, that being itself a fundamental value in the Convention: see paragraph 54.

87. When the policy in PSI 37/2010 refers, towards the end of para. 4.5, to the need to give consideration to the possible impact of permitting an interview on "the victim" or "the victim's family", it clearly envisages that there is a specific victim of the particular offence committed by the prisoner. That entails that it has already been established that the prisoner has in fact committed that offence. That passage in para. 4.5 does not appear to have in mind the notion of "victims" of crime more generally and in the abstract.

88. However, we do not say that there can never be cases in which the Secretary of State can properly apply the policy in PSI 37/2010 to a person who has not yet been convicted of an offence. Counsel for the Secretary of State submitted that, if the claimants succeeded in the present case, there would be nothing to stop every prisoner on remand insisting on a face-to-face interview to be broadcast on television. We do not agree. Most prisoners on remand in this country will be there because there was thought to be sufficient evidence for them to be charged, which is not the case with Mr Ahmad; and because they are awaiting trial in this country, usually for a relatively short period, certainly nothing like the more than seven years that Mr Ahmad has been in detention.

89. The second reason advanced by Mr Elder to justify the restriction in the present case, at paragraph 32(b) of his statement, is that a broadcast interview with Mr Ahmad would undermine the public's confidence in the criminal justice system. We have no doubt that, in many cases, the Secretary of State would be perfectly entitled to rely upon this rationale to justify application of his normal policy in PSI 37/2010 to a prisoner. If the only purpose of an interview, or a broadcast of it, were to enable a prisoner to argue his innocence, either in place of, or in parallel with, the ordinary processes of the courts, whether in this country or elsewhere, application of the normal policy would ordinarily be proportionate and compatible with article 10. However, as we have already emphasised, the present case is far from ordinary: it is, as the claimants submit, highly exceptional. This is because of the combination of circumstances which we have set out earlier. Together, those circumstances mean that the public interest in the claimants' right to freedom of expression is especially strong on one side of the balance. On the other side of the balance, this second reason advanced by Mr Elder is relatively weaker on the facts of this case. We note, in this context, what Mr Casciani says, at paragraph 17 of his statement, that the BBC has no intention of being "used" by Mr Ahmad to suit his own ends. Quite apart from his professed innocence, there are many wider issues which the claimants wish to explore in the public interest.

90. A major plank of the Secretary of State's submissions included reliance on the decision of the House of Lords in the *Pro Life Alliance* case. In that case the House of Lords had to consider a decision by the BBC, which happened in that case to be the defendant to proceedings brought under the HRA, to prevent the claimant, a political party opposed to abortion, from including highly graphic images of terminations of pregnancy in a party election broadcast in Wales. That decision was taken under the requirement which prevents material which is offensive on grounds of taste and decency being broadcast on television in this country.

91. We do not accept the suggested analogy with the *Pro Life Alliance* case. The requirement in that case, as embodied either in primary legislation (section 6(1)(a) of the Broadcasting Act 1990) or, in the BBC's case, in its licence agreement with the Secretary of State for National Heritage, was absolute. It did not permit of exceptions. No challenge was made by the claimant organisation in that case to the legislation itself, as in principle it might have been, since a declaration of incompatibility could have been sought under section 4 of the HRA. Since there was no such challenge to the legislation (or the agreement applicable to the BBC) itself, the only question was whether the BBC had been entitled to apply the requirement on taste and decency on the facts of the particular case. The House of Lords held that it had been so entitled and the courts could not properly, in the exercise of their supervisory jurisdiction, disturb the BBC's judgment on that issue: see in particular paras. 9-16 (Lord Nicholls of Birkenhead) and paras. 49-51 and 78-81 (Lord Hoffmann).

92. The present case is different in material respects. There is no primary legislation or the equivalent: this case concerns an administrative policy, in PSI 37/2010. Most importantly, that policy is not absolute, nor could it properly be: it envisages that there may be exceptions. The question in the present case is not whether the Court is entitled to interfere with the application of a policy to a given set of facts but whether an exception to that policy must be made on the facts of the present case in order to comply with article 10 and, in particular, to comply with the principle of proportionality. In our judgment, it must, in the highly exceptional circumstances of this case, for reasons we have set out earlier.

93. The Secretary of State filed evidence, exhibited to Mr Elder's second witness statement, about the practice adopted in various European states in relation to similar issues as arise in the present case. As counsel for the Secretary of State fairly accepted, that evidence discloses that there is no uniformity even among the states referred to (it had not been possible to obtain evidence about every member of the Council of Europe). He submitted that it assisted his case in that it showed that reasonable people could take different views. In our view, the evidence as to the variety of practices in different states does not assist in answering the crucial question in the present case. As we have already said, the Secretary of State is entitled to adopt and maintain the general policy that he does in PSI 37/2010. The crucial question is whether, in the very unusual circumstances of the present case, when taken together, an exception must be made. We have come to the conclusion that it must.

94. We remind ourselves of the main requirements of the principle of proportionality, as summarised earlier by reference to *Huang*. In our judgment, while in principle (i) the reasons advanced by the Secretary of State to justify his decision in the present case disclose objectives that are sufficiently important to justify restricting the right to freedom of expression; and (ii) the means used to achieve those objectives are rationally connected to them; (iii) it has not been demonstrated by the Secretary of State that the means used are no more than is necessary to accomplish their objectives; and (iv) it has not been shown that a fair balance has been maintained between the right to freedom of expression and the general interests of the community.

95. As to (iii), there are less restrictive alternatives available in principle to achieve the policy's objectives. For example, it could have been agreed with the claimants that any broadcast of an interview with Mr Ahmad must not allow him to use the programme as a platform to mount a media campaign to protest his innocence or to cause distress to the victims of terrorism. It is not certain what stance the claimants would have taken to such a proposal but it is likely, in the light of Mr Casciani's statement, in particular at paragraph 17, that they would have had no objection in principle to such an agreement, since it is not their wish to be "used", as Mr Casciani puts it, in that way. We remind ourselves that the BBC has a worldwide reputation for integrity and independence, and we have no reason to doubt what Mr Casciani says in his evidence about the kind of programme the BBC wishes to make and broadcast about Mr Ahmad's case.

96. However, the stance which the Secretary of State took on 22 September 2011 and has maintained to date is not to envisage the conditional grant of permission to the claimants but rather to refuse them permission as a matter of principle. In other words, when they made clear that the reason they wished to conduct a face-to-face interview with Mr Ahmad was with a view to broadcasting

recorded extracts of it, he did not say "Yes but …"; he simply said "No." In our judgment, on the facts of the present case, that stance goes beyond what is necessary to achieve the Secretary of State's legitimate objectives and, for that reason, breaches the principle of proportionality.

97. Turning to issue (iv), for reasons that we have already set out, we have come to the clear conclusion that the Secretary of State has not established that a fair balance has been maintained on the facts of this case. This is not a case where the public interest lies only on one side of the balance. The public interest in preventing distress to victims of terrorist offences is important, as is the public interest in maintaining confidence in the criminal justice system. However, there are powerful public interests on the other side of the balance too. Article 10 confers a right on the public to receive information, in particular about matters of public concern in a democratic society, such as the treatment of a prisoner who has been in detention for a very long time without charge; and the extradition arrangements applied in this case. It is not for this Court to pronounce on the rights and wrongs of different views that may be held in debate about such matters. The importance of the rights in article 10 is that, in principle, the public should be able to engage in such debates and be as fully informed as possible and make their own minds up. For this reason too, the failure to maintain a fair balance, the Secretary of State's decision breaches the principle of proportionality.

Since the Secretary of State's decision of 22 September 2011 was disproportionate, it was incompatible with the right to freedom of expression in article 10. Accordingly, by virtue of section 6(1) of the HRA, the Secretary of State's decision was unlawful.

NOTES

1. The significance of freedom of expression for a democratic society is strongly emphasized in the judgment, bringing out not only the interest of those wanting to express their views but also the interest of others in receiving those views.
2. It was important to distinguish the *Pro Life* case. This concerned images of an abortion which were sought to be included in a party election broadcast. The House of Lords, while emphasizing the enhanced importance of freedom of expression during an election, nevertheless took the view that legislation which regulated matters of taste and decency justified and required the broadcasters to refuse to broadcast the images. As Singh J. pointed out, in that case the challenge did not press for the legislation to be declared incompatible with the Convention right.
3. In *Bank Mellat v Her Majesty's Treasury (No. 1)* [2013] UKSC 38 Lord Sumption at [20] restated in slightly different wording the proportionality test. Lord Reed at [74] offered a more expansive formulation of the fourth criterion:

> (4) whether, balancing the severity of the measure's effects on the rights of the persons to whom it applies against the importance of the objective, to the extent that the measure will contribute to its achievement, the former outweighs the latter.

   In this case Singh J's interpretation of the *Huang* formulation was very important and it does seem to be in keeping with Lord Reed's version.
4. The circumstances of this case, which contributed to its exceptional nature, included that the prisoner Mr Ahmad, who was a British citizen, had been arrested and released in relation to possible charges under the Terrorism Act 2000 but the Crown Prosecution Service had determined there was insufficient evidence for a successful prosecution. He had brought a civil claim against the Metropolitan Police alleging excessive force in arresting him and the police admitted liability. In subsequent criminal proceeding the officers were acquitted. A Federal Grand Jury in Connecticut had requested extradition of Mr Ahmad on four charges including two relating to terrorism. Mr Ahmad was arrested and was still detained at the time of the BBC's case. Following a determination that there was no bar to extradition, the Home Secretary authorized the extradition and challenges in domestic courts were unsuccessful. He made an application to the European Court of Human Rights which ordered that he must not be deported until his case had been determined by the Court. Later the application was found to be partly admissible but it was not clear (a) if the Court would require a hearing or determine the case on the papers, nor (b) when the case would be determined. It was discovered that conversations Mr Ahmad had

with his MP in prison visits were secretly recorded but a later inquiry determined that the recording was not unlawful. The Joint Committee on Human Rights published a report in which they were critical of the lack of human rights protection provided under the Extradition Act 2003. Subsequently an independent panel appointed by the government reported that human rights under the Extradition Act was satisfactory. An e-petition with over 140,000 signatures calling for Mr Ahmad to be tried in the UK, rather than in the US, and 100 lawyers signed a letter to the Leader of the House of Commons asking that there should be a debate about Mr Ahmad.

■ QUESTION

Does the standard of review in the tests of 'prescribed by law' and 'necessary in a democratic society' take the judges outside their constitutional role and specialist knowledge?

10

Judicial Review: The Grounds

OVERVIEW

In this chapter the nature and constitutional role of judicial review is introduced before considering the various grounds of review which have been placed in three classes: illegality, procedural impropriety, and irrationality. The consideration of irrationality also looks at proportionality and substantive legitimate expectations and the relationship between irrationality and proportionality in pure domestic law.

SECTION 1: INTRODUCTION

A: The role of judicial review in the constitution

In some countries, for example in the United States, the judges are permitted to review legislation in order to establish whether it complies with the terms of the constitution. In the United Kingdom, the absence of a written constitution with the status of a higher law and the doctrine of parliamentary supremacy prevent the judges from exercising this role. They may, however, review the manner in which public authorities exercise the powers which have been conferred upon them by the legislature.

This power of judicial review may be defined as the jurisdiction of the superior courts (the High Court, the Court of Appeal, and the Supreme Court) to review the acts, decisions, and omissions of public authorities in order to establish whether they have exceeded or abused their powers. The courts have developed a number of principles in order to establish whether there has been an excess or abuse of power. For example, a public authority must direct itself properly on the law, it must not use its powers for improper purposes, and it must not act in breach of the rules of natural justice.

What is the justification for permitting such judicial control? One theory, discussed in the following extract, is that the courts are simply giving effect to the intentions of Parliament.

P. Cane, *Administrative Law*

(2011), pp. 36–41

It is the task of the courts to interpret and enforce the provisions of statutes, which impose duties and confer powers on public administrators, in the light of the principles embodied in the norms of administrative law. In so doing they are giving effect to the intention of Parliament.

Four problems with the ultra vires interpretation of the principle of legality are worth mentioning. The first is a general problem with applying and interpreting statutes: statutory provisions, including those that create institutions of public administration and confer powers and impose duties on them, may be unclear, ambiguous, or incomplete. When they are, it is unrealistic to treat the process of interpreting statutes, resolving ambiguities and lack of clarity, and filling gaps, as always being a matter of discerning and giving effect to the intention of Parliament. Even assuming that we can make sense of the notion of intention when applied to a multi-member body following a simple majority voting rule, there will be many cases in which Parliament did not think about the question relevant to resolving the ambiguity or lack of clarity, or filling the gap—on the contrary, the unclearness, ambiguity or gap may have been deliberate and designed to offload onto the bureaucracy the choice involved in how to resolve it. In such cases statutory interpretation is inevitably a creative activity. The weakness of the intention theory of statutory interpretation is made clear by the notion of 'purposive interpretation'. Especially (but not only) in the contexts of interpreting statutes passed to give effect to EU law and of protecting Convention rights (ie rights recognized by the ECHR), courts may go beyond interpreting the words actually used in statutes and insert (or 'imply') into legislative provisions words or phrases needed to give effect to what the court perceives to be the true purpose or aim of the provision in question. It makes little sense to describe this process in terms of giving effect to what Parliament actually intended all along.

A technique for giving meaning to the idea of the intention of the legislature is for courts to pay attention to what are sometimes called 'travaux préparatoires'—that is, policy documents and statements (including Parliamentary debates) that preceded the enactment of the relevant legislation and might throw some light on its intended meaning or, at least, the purpose for which it was enacted. In *Pepper v Hart* [[1993] AC 593] the House of Lords held that where a statutory provision is ambiguous or obscure or leads to an absurdity, a court required to interpret the provision can refer to clear statements, made in Parliament by a Minister or promoter of the bill, as to its intended meaning and effect, and to other Parliamentary material that might be necessary to understand such statements. This decision was of considerable constitutional significance because it implied that the relevant intention was not that of Parliament in enacting the legislation but rather that of the government in promoting it. The court seemed to acknowledge the effective reality that Parliament does not legislate but rather legitimizes the government's legislation. In so doing, it further undermined the notion that in interpreting legislation, the courts were giving effect to the intention of Parliament. In an influential article critical of the decision in *Pepper v Hart*, Lord Steyn made these implications explicit; and in its wake the House of Lords embarked on a process of re-interpreting *Pepper v Hart* so as to avoid undermining the principles that the job of interpreting legislation belongs ultimately to the courts, not to the government, and that the question for the court is what the statutory words mean, not what the government or anyone else thinks they mean. Although theoretically based on a distinction between the government and the legislature, this approach actually asserts an independent role for the judiciary in determining what the law is—not only the common law but also statute law.

A second problem with the 'intention-of-Parliament' interpretation of the principle of legality is that it does not accurately reflect the law. As already noted, the power of courts to control the administration and the principles of administrative law on the basis of which they exercise this power are judicial creations. Courts go to great lengths to preserve their jurisdiction to supervise the administration by applying these principles. Perhaps the most striking modern example of this is the case of *Anisminic Ltd v Foreign Compensation Commission* [[1969] 2 AC 147]. The main question in this case was whether a section in the Foreign Compensation Act, purporting to 'oust' ('exclude') the jurisdiction of the court to review 'determinations' of the Commission, was effective to that end. The House of Lords held that the word 'determination' must be read so as to exclude ultra vires (ie illegal) determinations. It then went on to extend considerably the notion of ultra vires as it applied to decisions on questions of law, the final result being to reduce the application of the 'ouster clause' almost to vanishing point, despite the fact that it had arguably been meant to have wide effect.

Another example is provided by the law concerning the role of statute in determining the requirements of procedural fairness. In the face of legislative silence on the question of whether an applicant before an administrative body is entitled to fair procedure as defined by the common law, two approaches are possible. It could be said that the common law rules of procedural fairness will apply only if there is evidence of a legislative intention that they should; alternatively, it could be argued that silence should be construed as an invitation to the courts to apply common law procedural standards.

On the whole the courts have tended to the latter view, thus asserting the independent force of the common law rules of procedural fairness. Moreover, the 'right to a fair trial' is now guaranteed by Art 6 of the ECHR, further undermining the ability of Parliament to regulate administrative procedure even expressly.

A third problem with the ultra vires interpretation of the principle of legality is that it does not justify regulation of the performance of non-statutory functions. As we have seen (1.3), in the *GCHQ* case the House of Lords rejected the proposition that the common law (prerogative) powers of central government are beyond the province of administrative law in favour of the proposition that exercise of a common law power will be reviewable provided the power is justiciable. We have also seen that the province of administrative law has been extended to embrace the exercise, for public purposes, of de facto power which has no identifiable legal source either in common law or statute. Whatever the administrative law principles applicable to the exercise of non-statutory powers, they cannot, by definition, be derived from a power-conferring statute.

A fourth problem with 'the doctrine of ultra vires' is, perhaps, the most significant. The doctrine assumes that Parliamentary legislation is the highest form of law in the system. However, to all intents and purposes, this is no longer true. The European Communities Act 1972 provides that conflicts between EU law and UK law (even primary legislation) must be resolved in favour of EU law. A provision of primary legislation that cannot be given an interpretation consistent with the ECHR can be declared to be incompatible with the Convention. Such a declaration does not render the provision invalid or inoperative but it does impose an obligation on the government to bring the legislation into compliance with the ECHR and renders the government liable to being sued in the ECtHR for breach of the Convention if it does not do so.

These two qualifications on the supremacy of primary legislation affect the ultra vires doctrine in different ways. The effect of EU law is that a decision or action of a public administrator may be unlawful even if it complies with all relevant provisions of UK statute law. The impact of the HRA is more subtle but also more pervasive. The ultra vires doctrine (even as modified by EU law) focuses attention on exercise of public functions and asks whether or not it complies with the law. By contrast, the HRA directs attention to the rights of citizens and asks whether or not those rights have been infringed. As we will see, the approach to answering this latter question adopted by the ECtHR and English courts is significantly different from the approach traditionally taken to answering the ultra vires question. Under the influence of the ECHR and as a result of the enactment of the HRA, English administrative law is experiencing a 'rights revolution'; but it is not yet clear to what extent the language of rights and the techniques of rights protection will supplant the conduct-oriented understanding of the legality principle.

One thing is clear, however. The normative framework of public administration in England is a product of the activities of various institutions including the legislature, courts (and tribunals), the law-making authorities of the EU, and the institutions of the ECHR—the Council of Europe and the ECtHR. Although the common law contribution to the framework made by the courts must be consistent with that of these other institutions, it is an autonomous contribution that cannot be fully captured by saying that in holding the administration accountable and in developing principles of administrative law, the courts are merely giving expression to 'the intention' or 'the will' of some other institution such as the UK legislature or the European Commission. This is because the documents in which such institutions express their 'intentions' may be unclear, ambiguous, or incomplete; and the institutions responsible for interpreting those documents—ultimately the courts—must sometimes exercise independent and creative choice in resolving lack of clarity and ambiguity, and filling gaps. By virtue of their power to hold the administration accountable, courts play a significant and independent role in establishing the normative framework of public administration.

All this having been said, however, the fact is that the great bulk of public administration involves the implementation of statutory programmes, the performance of statutory functions, the exercise of statutory powers, and the discharge of statutory duties. Although statutes are not the whole legal framework of public administration, in very many cases statutory provisions are the source of the administrator's power and define the task to be performed. Moreover, common law principles of administrative law must be applied in the context of and consistently with relevant statutory provisions.

One final point about statutory interpretation: although courts have the ultimate power to interpret legislative documents, they do so relatively rarely. Public administrators are much more central to the process of interpreting and applying legislation. Not only do they do so much more often than courts, but most of the time they do so without any judicial supervision: only a miniscule proportion of administrative applications and interpretations of legislation is ever challenged. In English law, the principle of legality means that administrators have to get the law right; and 'right' means what the courts say is right.

Although we know very little about how, in practice, administrators go about the task of interpreting statutes, we can assume that they follow basically the same approach as courts because they know that if they do not, their decision may be held unlawful if it is challenged.

NOTES

1. The election of Parliament gives democratic legitimacy to its legislation but because the legislative and executive branches are 'integrated' in our separation of powers, Cane argues that '[t]o counterbalance the combined force of the other two branches, the citizen needs a truly independent judicial branch that can "speak truth to power". This is found in the traditional judiciary' (p. 45). He further contends that the constitutional significance of the independence of courts and tribunals has been increased because of the Human Rights Act which requires interpretation of legislation to be compatible with the ECHR, confers on the higher courts, the power to make a declaration of incompatibility and the HRA played a part in removing our top court from the House of Lords and establishing it as the UK Supreme Court (p. 46). (See Chapter 6, Section 2 at p. 221 for a discussion of the mechanisms of political accountability and Chapter 9, Section 3C at p. 426 for statutory interpretation using the Human Rights Act.)

   The links between judicial review and democracy are also explored by T. R. S. Allan in 'Legislative Supremacy and the Rule of Law' (1985) 44 *Cambridge Law Journal*, 111–43 at 129–33. In this extract Allan argues that judicial review is not inconsistent with the legislative supremacy of Parliament because the courts will give effect to the clear and unambiguous words of statutes. He also argues that judicial review functions to protect the democratic principle of the political sovereignty of the people. Unless prevented from doing so by the clear and unambiguous words of statutes, the courts in judicial review proceedings will give effect to common standards of morality and the natural expectations of the citizen. Allan thus differs from Cane in that he claims that ultimately judicial review poses no threat to the doctrine of parliamentary supremacy. Further, while Cane raises the possibility that judicial review may be more justifiable because of the inadequacies of other means of scrutinizing the Executive, he does not claim, as Allan does, that judicial review actually promotes democracy because it gives effect to common standards of morality and the natural expectations of the citizen.

2. Cane's discussion is primarily concerned with judicial review of statutory powers, but he points out that it has been expanded and refers to *Council of Civil Service Unions v Minister for the Civil Service* [1985] AC 374 which allows for review of the exercise of powers conferred by the royal prerogative. It has been clearly established that, in certain circumstances, the courts may review the exercise of powers which are not conferred by either statute or the royal prerogative but which depend on the consent of those who are subject to them (see *R v Panel on Take-overs and Mergers, ex parte Datafin Plc* [1987] QB 815 in Chapter 11, Section 4 at p. 594). Can any of the justifications which have been put forward for judicial review of statutory powers be used to justify judicial review of powers derived from other sources?

B: The distinction between review and appeal

The courts have been concerned to emphasize that, in judicial review proceedings, they are exercising a supervisory, not an appellate, jurisdiction. Where statute provides for an appeal and the grounds of appeal are not restricted by the statute itself, the court is generally required to decide whether the decision under appeal was right or wrong. If it decides that the decision was wrong, the court hearing the appeal is generally permitted to substitute its decision for that of the authority which first determined the matter in question. What is the position in judicial review proceedings?

Chief Constable of the North Wales Police v Evans

[1982] 1 WLR 1155, House of Lords

The Chief Constable of North Wales decided that Evans, a probationer constable in the force, should be required to resign or, if he refused, be discharged from the force. Evans resigned but subsequently challenged the decision on the ground that it was taken in breach of natural justice because he was not told of the allegations which had led to the decision and had not been given an opportunity to offer any explanation. The House of Lords agreed with the decision of the Court of Appeal that there had been a breach of natural justice, but in the light of comments made in the Court of Appeal, felt it necessary to make some general comments on the scope of judicial review.

LORD HAILSHAM: The first observation I wish to make is by way of criticism of some remarks of Lord Denning MR which seem to me to be capable of an erroneous construction of the purpose and the remedy by way of judicial review under RSC Ord 53. This remedy, vastly increased in extent, and rendered, over a long period in recent years, of infinitely more convenient access than that provided by the old prerogative writs and actions for a declaration, is intended to protect the individual against the abuse of power by a wide range of authorities, judicial, quasi-judicial, and, as would originally have been thought when I first practised at the Bar, administrative. It is not intended to take away from those authorities the powers and discretions properly vested in them by law and to substitute the courts as the bodies making the decisions. It is intended to see that the relevant authorities use their powers in a proper manner.

Since the range of authorities, and the circumstances of the use of their power, are almost infinitely various, it is of course unwise to lay down rules for the application of the remedy which appear to be of universal validity in every type of case. But it is important to remember in every case that the purpose of the remedies is to ensure that the individual is given fair treatment by the authority to which he has been subjected and that it is no part of that purpose to substitute the opinion of the judiciary or of individual judges for that of the authority constituted by law to decide the matters in question. The function of the court is to see the lawful authority is not abused by unfair treatment and not to attempt itself the task entrusted to that authority by the law. There are passages in the judgment of Lord Denning MR (and perhaps in the other judgments of the Court of Appeal) in the instant case and quoted by my noble and learned friend which might be read as giving the courts carte blanche to review the decision of the authority on the basis of what the courts themselves consider fair and reasonable on the merits. I am not sure whether the Master of the Rolls really intended his remarks to be construed in such a way as to permit the courts to examine, as for instance in the present case, the reasoning of the subordinate body with a view to substituting its own opinion. If so, I do not think this is a correct statement of principle. The purpose of judicial review is to ensure that the individual receives fair treatment, and not to ensure that the authority, after according fair treatment, reaches on a matter which it is authorised by law to decide for itself a conclusion which is correct in the eyes of the court. ...

LORD BRIGHTMAN: ... I turn secondly to the proper purpose of the remedy of judicial review, what it is and what it is not. In my opinion the law was correctly stated in the speech of Lord Evershed [in *Ridge* v *Baldwin* [1964] AC 40], at p. 96. His was a dissenting judgment but the dissent was not concerned with this point. Lord Evershed referred to 'a danger of usurpation of power on the part of the courts ... under the pretext of having regard to the principles of natural justice.' He added:

> I do observe again that it is not the decision as such which is liable to review; it is only the circumstances in which the decision was reached, and particularly in such a case as the present the need for giving the party dismissed an opportunity for putting his case.

Judicial review is concerned, not with the decision, but with the decision-making process. Unless that restriction on the power of the court is observed, the court will in my view, under the guise of preventing the abuse of power, be itself guilty of usurping power.

■ QUESTIONS

1. What, then, are the differences between appeal and review?
2. This case concerned the principles of natural justice. The other grounds for judicial review are summarized later in this chapter in Section 2 at p. 499. Do you think they could all be said to be concerned not with 'the decision but with the decision-making process'? Do you think their Lordships intended their remarks to apply to all the grounds for judicial review?

C: The use of judicial review

Table 10.1 Number of judicial review applications lodged, granted, and found in favour of claimant

Year	Applications	Permission granted		Cases found in claimant's favour	
2011	11,360	1,292	11%	177	2%
2012	12,432	1,473	20%	174	1%
2013	15,594	1,613	10%	145	3%
2014	4,062	748	18%	90	2%
2015	4,679	608	13%	81	2%

Source: Civil Justice and Judicial Review Tables

NOTES

1. Table 10.1 shows a dramatic fall in applications from 2013 caused by the transfer of immigration and asylum judicial review cases to the Upper Tribunal following the decision to reverse its domination of the Administrative Court caseload (see Chapter 13, Section 2A at p. 655). The Ministry of Justice is now the largest single defendant in the judicial review work of the Administrative Court followed closely by the Home Office and then local authorities.
2. Table 10.1 also shows that the majority of permission applications are not successful and only a small number of cases have a hearing: see V. Bondy and M. Sunkin, *The Dynamics of Judicial Review Litigation: The Resolution of Public Law Challenges Before Final Hearing* (2009). See also the debate about Government proposals to reform judicial review in Chapter 11, Section 1 at p. 571.

SECTION 2: THE GROUNDS FOR JUDICIAL REVIEW

This chapter is concerned with the grounds for judicial review. The extracts which are included do, however, contain a number of references to the remedies which are available where there is a breach of the principles of judicial review. Before reading the cases, students should acquaint themselves with the following terms.

Subject to certain qualifications, which will be examined in further detail in Chapter 11, the normal method of seeking review is through making a claim for judicial review. In the claim for judicial review the court may grant one or more of the following remedies which have been renamed by the Civil Procedure Rules, Part 54 (see Chapter 11, Section 1 at p. 572).

A: The prerogative orders

These are:

(1) Quashing order, formerly *certiorari*: this remedy quashes an unlawful decision of a public authority.

(2) Prohibiting order, formerly prohibition: this remedy prohibits an unlawful act which a public authority is proposing to perform.

(3) Mandatory order, formerly *mandamus*: this remedy compels a public authority to perform a public duty.

Prerogative orders may not be granted against the Crown, although they may be granted against individual ministers of the Crown. They may not be used to challenge delegated legislation.

Injunctions. Injunctions may be prohibitory (restraining unlawful action) or mandatory (compelling the performance of a duty). An interim injunction is one granted before trial in order to preserve the status quo until the issues have been determined. In an emergency an injunction may be granted without hearing the defendant. Note, however, that s. 21 of the Crown Proceedings Act 1947 prevents the grant of injunctions against the Crown. So far as Ministers of the Crown are concerned, injunctions can be granted against them, both in matters of European Union law (see *R* v *Secretary of State for Transport, ex parte Factortame (No. 2)* [1990] 1 AC 603) and in domestic law (see *In re M* [1993] 3 WLR 433, Chapter 3, Section 4B at p. 108).

Declarations. Declarations are a very flexible remedy. They may, for instance, simply state the parties' rights, set out the true construction of a statute, or state that an administrative act is invalid.

Damages. Damages may be awarded in an application for judicial review provided the applicant has claimed one or more of the remedies specified earlier. Damages are not available simply because one of the principles of judicial review has been breached. The applicant must show, in addition, that the authority has breached a right of his for which damages are available (e.g. that the authority has committed a tort or breach of contract).

There has been an exchange of views on the basis and justification of judicial review between broadly those who argue for a common law basis and those who advocate *ultra vires* and legislative intent. In the common law group are D. Oliver, 'Is the Ultra Vires Rules the Basis of Judicial Review?' [1987] *Public Law* 543; Sir John Laws 'Illegality: The Problem of Jurisdiction' in M. Supperstone and J. Goudie (eds), *Judicial Review* (1997); P. Craig, 'Ultra Vires and the Foundations of Judicial Review' [1998] CLJ 63 and 'Competing Models of Judicial Review' [1999] *Public Law* 428; and J. Jowell, 'Of Vires and Vacuums: The Constitutional Context of Judicial Review' [1999] *Public Law* 448. The defenders of *ultra vires* are C. Forsyth, 'Of Fig Leaves and Fairy Tales: The *Ultra Vires* Doctrine, the Sovereignty of Parliament and Judicial Review' [1996] *Cambridge Law Journal* 122 and M. Elliott, 'The Demise of Parliamentary Sovereignty? The Implications for Justifying Judicial Review' (1999) 115 *Law Quarterly Review* 119 and 'The *Ultra Vires* Doctrine in A Constitutional Setting: Still the Central Principle of Administrative Law' [1999] *Cambridge Law Journal* 129. All of these extracts, except for those asterisked, are reprinted in C. Forsyth (ed.), *Judicial Review and the Constitution* (2000). The debate has continued with M. Elliott, *The Constitutional Foundations of Judicial Review* (2001); P. Craig and N. Bamforth, 'Constitutional Analysis, Constitutional Principle and Judicial Review' [2001] *Public Law* 763; T. Allan, 'The Constitutional Foundations of Judicial Review, Conceptual Conundrum or Interpretative Inquiry?' [2002] *Cambridge*

Law Journal 87; P. Craig, 'Constitutional Foundations, The Rule of Law and Supremacy' [2003] *Public Law* 92, C. Forsyth & M. Elliott, 'The Legitimacy of Judicial Review' [2003] *Public Law* 286.

Council of Civil Service Unions v Minister for the Civil Service

[1985] AC 374, House of Lords

[The facts are stated later in this chapter in Section 2 at p. 538.]

LORD DIPLOCK: ... Judicial review has I think developed to a state today when, without reiterating any analysis of the steps by which the development has come about, one can conveniently classify under three heads the grounds on which administrative action is subject to control by judicial review. The first ground I would call 'illegality', the second 'irrationality' and the third 'procedural impropriety'. That is not to say that further development on a case by case basis may not in course of time add further grounds. I have in mind particularly the possible adoption in the future of the principle of 'proportionality' which is recognised in the administrative law of several of our fellow members of the European Economic Community; but to dispose of the instant case the three already well-established heads that I have mentioned will suffice.

By illegality as a ground for judicial review I mean that the decision-maker must understand correctly the law that regulates his decision-making power and must give effect to it. Whether he has or not is par excellence a justiciable question to be decided in the event of dispute, by those persons, the judges, by whom the judicial power of the state is exercisable.

By irrationality I mean what can by now be succinctly referred to as '*Wednesbury* unreasonableness' (see *Associated Provincial Picture Houses Ltd v Wednesbury Corp* [1948] 1 KB 223). It applies to a decision which is so outrageous in its defiance of logic or accepted moral standards that no sensible person who had applied his mind to the question to be decided could have arrived at it. Whether a decision falls within the category is a question that judges by their training and experience should be well-equipped to answer, or else there would be something badly wrong with our judicial system. To justify the court's exercise of this role, resort I think today is no longer needed to Viscount Radcliffe's ingenious explanation in *Edwards v Bairstow* [1956] AC 14 of irrationality as a ground for a court's reversal of a decision by ascribing it to an inferred though identifiable mistake of law by the decision-maker. 'Irrationality' by now can stand on its own feet as an accepted ground on which a decision may be attacked by judicial review.

I have described the third head as 'procedural impropriety' rather than failure to observe basic rules of natural justice or failure to act with procedural fairness towards the person who will be affected by the decision. This is because susceptibility to judicial review under this head covers also failure by an administrative tribunal to observe procedural rules that are expressly laid down in the legislative instrument by which its jurisdiction is conferred, even where such failure does not involve any denial of natural justice.

NOTE: Lord Diplock's threefold classification of the grounds for judicial review has been cited in many subsequent cases. The classification will be followed in this chapter, where each of the three categories will be examined in more detail. Proportionality will be considered later in this chapter in Section 2F, on irrationality, at p. 562.

B: Illegality

Lord Diplock used this phrase to cover a number of different grounds which are frequently treated separately. The most important are:

(1) An authority must not exceed its jurisdiction by purporting to exercise powers which it does not possess.

(2) An authority must direct itself properly on the law.

(3) An authority must not use its power for an improper purpose.

(4) An authority must take into account all relevant considerations and disregard all irrelevant considerations.

(5) An authority to which the exercise of a discretion has been entrusted cannot delegate the exercise of its discretion to another unless clearly authorized to do so.

(6) An authority must not fetter its discretion.

(7) An authority acts unlawfully if it fails to fulfil a statutory duty.

(8) An authority must not make a mistake of fact.

(9) An authority must not excessively interfere with fundamental rights.

It should be noted that this list is not exhaustive and that the grounds clearly overlap to some extent. Consider the following cases.

Anisminic Ltd v Foreign Compensation Commission
[1969] 2 AC 147, House of Lords

Anisminic Ltd owned property in Egypt which was sequestrated in 1956 by the Egyptian government. In 1957 Anisminic sold the property, for substantially less than its real value, to TEDO, an Egyptian organization.

Under a treaty, the United Arab Republic paid to the United Kingdom £27.5 million as compensation for property confiscated in Egypt in 1956. Responsibility for distributing the compensation money was vested in the Foreign Compensation Commission (FCC). Anisminic Ltd submitted a claim for compensation to the FCC.

Article 4 of the Foreign Compensation (Egypt) (Determination and Registration of Claims) Order 1962 provided that the Commission shall treat a claim as established if satisfied of the following matters:

(a) the applicant is the person referred to in the relevant part of Annex E of the Order as 'the owner of the property or is the successor in title of such a person';

(b) the person referred to in the relevant part of Annex E 'and any person who became successor in title of such person on or before February 28, 1959, were British nationals on October 31, 1956, and February 28, 1959.'

The Commission's provisional determination was that Anisminic Ltd had failed to establish its claim because TEDO, its successor in title, was not a British national.

Anisminic Ltd sought a declaration that the Commission had misconstrued the Order.

LORD REID: It has sometimes been said that it is only where a tribunal acts without jurisdiction that its decision is a nullity. But in such cases the word 'jurisdiction' has been used in a very wide sense, and I have come to the conclusion that it is better not to use the term except in the narrow and original sense of the tribunal being entitled to enter on the inquiry in question. But there are many cases where, although the tribunal had jurisdiction to enter on the inquiry, it has done or failed to do something in the course of inquiry which is of such nature that its decision is a nullity. It may have given its decision in bad faith. It may have made a decision which it had no power to make. It may have failed in the course of the inquiry to comply with the requirements of natural justice. It may in perfect good faith have misconstrued the provisions giving it power to act so that it failed to deal with the question remitted to it and decided some question which was not remitted to it. It may have refused to take into account something which it was required to take into account. Or it may have based its decision on some matter which, under the provisions setting it up, it had no right to take into account. I do not intend this list to be exhaustive. But if it decides a question remitted to it for decision without committing any of these errors it is as much entitled to decide that question wrongly as it is to decide it rightly. I understand that some confusion has been caused by my having said in *Reg v Governor of Brixton Prison, Ex parte Armah*

[1968] AC 192, 234 that if a tribunal has jurisdiction to go right it has jurisdiction to go wrong. So it has, if one uses 'jurisdiction' in the narrow original sense. If it is entitled to enter on the inquiry and does not do any of those things which I have mentioned in the course of the proceedings, then its decision is equally valid whether it is right or wrong subject only to the power of the court in certain circumstances to correct an error of law. I think that, if these views are correct, the only case cited which was plainly wrongly decided is *Davies* v *Price* [1958] 1 WLR 434. But in a number of other cases some of the grounds of judgment are questionable.

I can now turn to the provisions of the Order under which the commission acted, and to the way in which the commission reached their decision. It was said in the Court of Appeal that publication of their reasons was unnecessary and perhaps undesirable. Whether or not they could have been required to publish their reasons, I dissent emphatically from the view that publication may have been undesirable. In my view, the commission acted with complete propriety, as one would expect looking to its membership.

The meaning of the important parts of this Order is extremely difficult to discover, and, in my view, a main cause of this is the deplorable modern drafting practice of compressing to the point of obscurity provisions which would not be difficult to understand if written out at rather greater length. ...

So the question is whether on a true construction of the Order the applicants did or did not have to prove anything with regard to successors in title. If the commission were entitled to enter on the inquiry whether the applicants had a successor in title, then their decision as to whether TEDO was their successor in title would I think be unassailable whether it was right or wrong: it would be a decision on a matter remitted to them for their decision. The question I have to consider is not whether they made a wrong decision but whether they inquired into and decided a matter which they had no right to consider.

I have great difficulty in seeing how in the circumstances there could be a successor in title of a person who is still in existence. This provision is dealing with the period before the Order was made when the original owner had no title to anything: he had nothing but a hope that some day somehow he might get some compensation... In themselves the words 'successor in title' are, in my opinion, inappropriate in the circumstances of this Order to denote any person while the original owner is still in existence, and I think it most improbable that they were ever intended to denote any such person. There is no necessity to stretch them to cover any such person. I would therefore hold that the words 'and any person who became successor in title to such person' in article 4(1)(b)(ii) have no application to a case where the applicant is the original owner. It follows that the commission rejected the appellants' claim on a ground which they had no right to take into account and that their decision was a nullity. I would allow this appeal.

LORD PEARCE: Lack of jurisdiction may arise in various ways. There may be an absence of those formalities or things which are conditions precedent to the tribunal having any jurisdiction to embark on an inquiry. Or the tribunal may at the end make an order that it has no jurisdiction to make. Or in the intervening stage, while engaged on a proper inquiry, the tribunal may depart from the rules of natural justice; or it may ask itself the wrong questions; or it may take into account matters which it was not directed to take into account. Thereby it would step outside its jurisdiction. It would turn its inquiry into something not directed by Parliament and fail to make the inquiry which Parliament did direct. Any of these things would cause its purported decision to be a nullity. ...

LORD WILBERFORCE: In every case, whatever the character of a tribunal, however wide the range of questions remitted to it, however great the permissible margin of mistakes, the essential point remains that the tribunal has a derived authority, derived, that is, from statute: at some point, and to be found from a consideration of the legislation, the field within which it operates is marked out and limited. There is always an area, narrow or wide, which is the tribunal's area; a residual area, wide or narrow, in which the legislature has previously expressed its will and into which the tribunal may not enter. Equally, though this is not something that arises in the present case, there are certain fundamental assumptions, which without explicit restatement in every case, necessarily underlie the remission of power to decide such as (I do not attempt more than a general reference, since the strength and shade of these matters will depend upon the nature of the tribunal and the kind of question it has to decide) the requirement that a decision must be made in accordance with principles of natural justice and good faith. The principle that failure to fulfil these assumptions may be equivalent to a departure from the remitted area must be taken to follow from the decision of this House in *Ridge* v *Baldwin* [1964] AC 40. Although, in theory perhaps, it may be possible for Parliament to set up a tribunal which has full and autonomous powers to fix its own area of operation, that has, so far, not been done in this country. The question, what is the tribunal's proper area, is one which it has always been permissible to ask and to answer, and it must follow that examination of its extent is not precluded by a clause conferring conclusiveness, finality, or unquestionability upon its decisions. These clauses in their nature can only relate to decisions given within the field of operation entrusted to the tribunal. They may, according to the width and emphasis of their formulation, help to ascertain the extent of that field, to narrow it or to enlarge it, but unless one is to deny the statutory origin of the tribunal and of its powers, they cannot preclude examination of that extent. ...

The extent of the interpretatory power conferred upon the tribunal may sometimes be difficult to ascertain and argument may be possible whether this or that question of construction has been left to the tribunal, that is, is within the tribunal's field, or whether, because it pertains to the delimitation of the tribunal's area by the legislature, it is reserved for decision by the courts. Sometimes it will be possible to form a conclusion from the form and subject-matter of the legislation. In one case it may be seen that the legislature, while stating general objectives, is prepared to concede a wide area to the authority it establishes: this will often be the case where the decision involves a degree of policy-making rather than fact-finding, especially if the authority is a department of government or the Minister at its head. I think that we have reached a stage in our administrative law when we can view this question quite objectively, without any necessary predisposition towards one that questions of law, or questions of construction, are necessarily for the courts. In the kind of case I have mentioned there is no need to make this assumption. In another type of case it may be apparent that Parliament is itself directly and closely concerned with the definition and delimitation of certain matters of comparative detail and has marked by its language the intention that these shall accurately be observed. ... The present case, by contrast, as examination of the relevant Order in Council will show, is clearly of the latter category. ...

Lord Pearce and Lord Wilberforce also agreed with Lord Reid's interpretation of the Order.

Lord Morris and Lord Pearson dissented.

■ QUESTION

On what ground or grounds did the court grant judicial review?

NOTES

1. The Foreign Compensation Act 1950 purported to oust the jurisdiction of the courts to question any determination of the Commission. This aspect of the case is considered in Chapter 11, Section 7 at p. 606.

2. Since *Anisminic*, there has been considerable dispute as to whether all errors of law take a public authority outside its jurisdiction. In *Re Racal Communications Ltd* [1981] AC 374 Lord Diplock stated, at p. 383:

> The break-through made by *Anisminic* [1969] 2 AC 147 was that, as respects administrative tribunals and authorities, the old distinction between errors of law that went to jurisdiction and errors of law that did not, was for practical purposes abolished. Any error of law that could be shown to have been made by them in the course of reaching their decision on matters of fact or of administrative policy would result in their having asked themselves the wrong question with the result that the decision they reached would be a nullity. ...
>
> But there is no similar presumption that where a decision-making power is conferred by statute upon a court of law, Parliament did not intend to confer upon it power to decide questions of law as well as questions of fact. Whether it did or did not and, in the case of inferior courts, what

limits are imposed on the kinds of questions of law they are empowered to decide, depends upon the construction of the statute unencumbered by any such presumption. In the case of inferior courts where the decision of the court is made final and conclusive by the statute, this may involve the survival of those subtle distinctions formerly drawn between errors of law which go to jurisdiction and errors of law which do not that did so much to confuse English administrative law before *Anisminic* [1969] 2 AC 147; but upon any application for judicial review of a decision of an inferior court in a matter which involves, as so many do, interrelated questions of law, fact and degree the superior court conducting the review should not be astute to hold that Parliament did not intend the inferior court to have jurisdiction to decide for itself the meaning of the ordinary words used in the statute to define the question which it has to decide.

In *O'Reilly* v *Mackman* [1983] 2 AC 237, at p. 278, Lord Diplock referred to the *Anisminic* case as liberating English public law 'from the fetters that the courts had theretofore imposed upon themselves so far as determinations of inferior courts and statutory tribunals were concerned by drawing esoteric distinctions between errors of law committed by such tribunals that went to their jurisdiction, and errors of law committed by them within their jurisdiction'.

There is division of opinion on the point as to whether inferior courts, but not administrative tribunals, may be immune from judicial review for errors of law within jurisdiction. In *R* v *Lord President of the Privy Council, ex parte Page* [1993] AC 682 (a case concerning the jurisdiction of a university visitor), the majority of Lords Keith, Griffiths, and Browne-Wilkinson affirmed Lord Diplock's dicta in *Re Racal Communications* on inferior courts.

■ QUESTION

What light is thrown on judicial thinking on the boundaries and basis of judicial review by:

(a) the erosion of the difference between jurisdictional errors and errors of law within jurisdiction; and

(b) the exception to this for inferior courts and visitors but not administrative tribunals, even those staffed by lawyers?

Wheeler v Leicester City Council
[1985] AC 1054, House of Lords

Leicester Football Club had a licence to use a recreation ground administered by the local council. Under s. 10 of the Open Spaces Act the council held and administered the recreation ground in trust to allow, and with a view to, its enjoyment by the public as an open space. Section 76 of the Public Health (Amendment) Act 1907 gave the council power to set apart pitches for the purpose of playing football. Section 56 of the Public Health Act 1925 gave the council power to permit the exclusive use by any club of such a pitch, subject to such charges and conditions as the local authority thought fit.

In April 1984 three members of the club were invited to join the English rugby football team selected to tour South Africa. The council supported a Commonwealth Agreement to withhold support for and discourage sporting links with South Africa. It put four questions to the club and indicated that only an affirmative answer to each of them would be acceptable:

(a) Does the Leicester Football Club support the Government opposition to the tour?

(b) Does the Leicester Football Club agree that the tour is an insult to a large proportion of the Leicester population?

(c) Will the Leicester Football Club press the Rugby Football Union to call off the tour?

(d) Will the Leicester Football Club press the players to pull out of the tour?

The club stated that, while it agreed with the council in condemning apartheid in South Africa, it was not unlawful for members to participate in the tour, nor was it contrary to the rules of the Rugby Football Union or the club. The club's role was purely advisory and it had asked the members to consider the memorandum to the Rugby Football Union prepared by the anti-apartheid movement. The three members subsequently took part in the tour. In August 1984 the council passed a resolution banning the club and its members from using the recreation ground for 12 months. The club applied for an order of *certiorari* to quash the decision. The judge refused the application and his decision was upheld by the Court of Appeal.

ACKNER LJ: . . . [Counsel], for the council, has submitted, and I entirely accept, that in exercising their discretion the council are entitled to take into account the effect that such an exercise would have on the performance of their other statutory functions. He gave us instances where the use of the pitch might potentially contravene the council's policies under the Town and Country Planning Acts, or interfere with their obligations under the Housing Acts, or contravene the Public Health Acts. In all such cases obviously the council, in considering how to exercise its discretion in relation to the recreation ground, would be entitled to and indeed be under a duty to have regard to their other statutory functions and duties.

The statutory function which [counsel] submits the council were fully entitled to take into account in exercising their discretionary powers in relation to this recreation ground, is to be found in section 71 of the Race Relations Act 1976. . . . The relevant words of the section read as follows:

. . . it shall be the duty of every local authority to make appropriate arrangements with a view to securing that their various functions are carried out with due regard to the need . . . (b) to promote . . . good relations, between different persons of different racial groups.

[Counsel] for the club accepts that a local authority are, vis a vis race relations, in a very special position. It is the local authority that provides many of the social services, they are a substantial employer of labour and are thus capable of setting an example in regard to race relations conduct and policies which is likely to be followed. Notwithstanding this concession, [counsel] submits that this section is what he describes as an 'inward-looking' section, directed to requiring that the local authority themselves maintain the standards laid down by the Act, that is to say their codes of practice in regard to their own internal behaviour so as to comply with the requirements of the Act. It is a section whose function is limited to ensuring that the local authority put their own house in order.

I consider this to be too narrow a construction. To my mind the section is imposing an obligation on the local authority, when they consider discharging any of their functions which might have a race relations content, to do so in such a manner as would tend to promote good relations between persons of different racial groups. Accordingly, in my judgment, the council were fully entitled when exercising their discretionary powers in relation to this recreation ground to have regard to the purposes expressed in section 71. . . .

If I am right so far, this leaves only one final question to consider. Can it be said in the circumstances of this case that no reasonable local authority could properly conclude that temporarily banning from the use of their recreational ground an important local rugger club, which declined to condemn a South African tour and declined actively to discourage its members from participating therein, could promote good relations between persons of different racial groups? (see the well-known Wednesbury test: *Associated Provincial Picture Houses Ltd v Wednesbury Corp* [1948] 1 KB 223).

Ackner LJ decided that the answer to this question was no. Sir George Waller also dismissed the club's appeal, but Browne-Wilkinson LJ dissented. The club then appealed to the House of Lords.

LORD TEMPLEMAN: . . . My Lords, the laws of this country are not like the laws of Nazi Germany. A private individual or a private organisation cannot be obliged to display zeal in the pursuit of an object sought by a public authority and cannot be obliged to publish views dictated by a public authority.

The club having committed no wrong, the council could not use their statutory powers in the management of their property or any other statutory powers in order to punish the club. There is no doubt that the council intended to punish and have punished the club. When the club were presented by the council with four questions it was made clear that the club's response would only be acceptable if, in effect, all four questions were answered in the affirmative. When the club committee made their dignified and responsible response to these questions, a response which the council find unsatisfactory to the council, the council commissioned a report on possible sanctions that might be taken against the club. That report suggested that delaying tactics could be used to hold up the grant of a lease then being negotiated by the club. It suggested that land could be excluded from the lease as it was 'thought that this could embarrass the club because it had apparently granted sub-leases ... ' It was suggested that the council's consent, which had already been given for advertisements by the club's sponsors, could be withdrawn although according to the report 'the actual effect of this measure on the club is difficult to assess.' It was suggested that 'a further course is to insist upon strict observance of the tenant's covenants in the lease. However, the city estate's surveyor, having inspected the premises, is of the opinion that the tenant's covenants are all being complied with.' Finally, it was suggested that 'the council could terminate the club's use of the recreation ground.' This might cause some financial loss to the council and might 'form the basis of a legal challenge to the council's decision. The club may contend that the council has taken an unreasonable action against the club in response to personal decisions of members of its team over which it had no control.' Notwithstanding this warning, the council accepted the last suggestion and terminated the club's use of the recreation ground. In my opinion, this use by the council of its statutory powers was a misuse of power. The council could not properly seek to use its statutory powers of management or any other statutory powers for the purposes of punishing the club when the club had done no wrong.

In *Congreve* v *Home Office* [1976] 1 QB 629 the Home Secretary had a statutory power to revoke television licences. In exercise of that statutory power he revoked the television licences of individuals who had lawfully surrendered an existing licence and taken out a new licence before an increase in the licence fee was due to take effect. Lord Denning MR said at p. 651:

> If the licence is to be revoked—and his money forfeited—the Minister would have to give good reasons to justify it. Of course, if the licensee had done anything wrong—if he had given a cheque for £12 which was dishonoured, or if he had broken the conditions of the licence—the Minister could revoke it. But when the licensee has done nothing wrong at all, I do not think the Minister can lawfully revoke the licence, at any rate, not without offering him his money back, and not even then except for good cause. If he should revoke it without giving reasons, or for no good reason, the courts can set aside the revocation and restore the licence. It would be a misuse of the power conferred on him by Parliament: and these courts have the authority—and I would add the duty—to correct a misuse of power by a Minister or his department, no matter how much he may resent it or warn us of the consequences if we do.

Similar considerations apply, in my opinion, to the present case. Of course this does not mean that the council is bound to allow its property to be used by a racist organisation or by any organisation which, by its actions or its words, infringes the letter or the spirit of the Race Relations Act 1976. But the attitude of the club and of the committee of the club was a perfectly proper attitude, caught as they were in a political controversy which was not of their making.

For these reasons and the reasons given by my noble and learned friend Lord Roskill I would allow this appeal.

Lord Roskill decided that the council had made a decision which was so unreasonable that no reasonable authority could have come to it. The other Law Lords agreed with both Lord Templeman and Lord Roskill.

■ **QUESTIONS**

1. On which ground(s) for judicial review did each of the judges base his decision?
2. How did (a) Ackner LJ and (b) Lord Templeman decide which purposes the council was/ was not entitled to pursue? Did they find assistance in the statutes under which the council managed the recreation ground or in the Race Relations Act 1976? What other matters did they refer to in determining this issue?

3. How did they decide which purposes the club had pursued?

4. Would it have made any difference to the decision of Lord Templeman if the club had espoused racist views in its reply to the council's request?

5. Does this case provide support for Allan's view that in judicial review proceedings the judges are furthering the political sovereignty of the people by giving effect to common standards of morality or the natural expectations of citizens?

NOTE: Lord Templeman based his decision on the ground that the council had acted for an improper purpose. Difficulties may arise when an authority acts for more than one purpose, some of which are lawful and others unlawful. The courts have not always been consistent in deciding how to deal with this conflict. Consider the approach adopted in the following extract.

R v Inner London Education Authority, ex parte Westminster City Council

[1986] 1 WLR 28, High Court

The Inner London Education Authority (ILEA) determined the rates for education spending precepted on rating authorities in Inner London, including Westminster City Council. ILEA was opposed to the Government's policies, announced in 1983, of limiting the amount of rates levied by local authorities, a process known as rate-capping. By s. 142(2) of the Local Government Act 1972 ILEA was empowered to incur expenditure on arranging for the publication within their area of information on matters relating to local government. In July 1983 an education sub-committee of ILEA agreed to retain an advertising agency, referred to in the extract following as AMV, at a cost of £651,000, to mount a media and poster campaign to 'gain awareness of the authority's views of the needs of the education service and to alter the basis of the public debate about the effect of ... Government actions.' Westminster City Council sought a declaration that the decision of the sub-committee was *ultra vires* because ILEA sought to persuade the public to support ILEA's views on rate-capping. ILEA accepted that the decision was made with the dual purpose of informing and persuading.

GLIDEWELL LJ: ...

Two purposes

This brings me to what I regard as being the most difficult point in the case, namely, if a local authority resolves to expend its ratepayers' money in order to achieve two purposes, one of which it is authorised to achieve by statute but for the other of which it has no authority, is that decision invalid?

I was referred to the following authorities.

(i) *Westminster Corp* v *London and North Western Rly Co* [1905] AC 426. Westminster City Council had power to provide public lavatories under the Public Health (London) Act 1891, section 44. They constructed public lavatories underground, under the centre of the south end of Whitehall. The lavatories were approached from each side of the street by a subway, which could also be used as a pedestrian subway for people who wished to cross the street and not to use the lavatories. The London and North Western Railway Co., who owned the land at the east end of the subway, challenged the construction of the lavatories and subway, alleging that the main purpose of the Corporation was to construct a pedestrian subway which did not fall within the power of the Act. The Court of Appeal found for the railway company. By a majority, the House of Lords allowed the appeal, but did so on the facts, i.e., by holding that the Court of Appeal had drawn a wrong inference from the affidavits and documents before the court. In his speech, the Earl of Halsbury LC said at p. 428:

> I quite agree that if the power to make one kind of building was fraudulently used for the purpose of making another kind of building, the power given by the legislature for one purpose could not be used for another.

Lord Macnaghten said at p. 433:

> I entirely agree with Joyce J at first instance that the primary object of the council was the construction of the conveniences with the requisite and proper means of approach thereto and exit therefrom.

This suggests that a test for answering the question is, if the authorised purpose is the primary purpose, the resolution is within the power.

(ii) .... [is omitted]

(iii) More recently in *Hanks v Minister of Housing and Local Government* [1963] 1 QB 999, Megaw J did have to deal with a case in which it was alleged that a compulsory purchase order had been made for two purposes, one of which did not fall within the empowering Act. ... [He stated] at [1963] 1 QB 999 at 1020–1021:

> I confess that I think confusion can arise from the multiplicity of words which have been used in this case as suggested criteria for the testing of the validity of the exercise of a statutory power. The words have included 'objects', 'purposes', 'motives', 'motivation', 'reasons', 'grounds' and 'considerations'. In the end, it seems to me, the simplest and clearest way to state the matter is by reference to 'considerations'. A 'consideration', I apprehend, is something which one takes into account as a factor in arriving at a decision. I am prepared to assume, for the purposes of the case, that, if it be shown that an authority exercising a power has taken into account as a relevant factor something which it could not properly take into account in deciding whether or not to exercise the power, then the exercise of the power, normally at least, is bad. Similarly, if the authority fails to take into account as a relevant factor something which is relevant, and which is or ought to be known to it, and which it ought to have taken into account, the exercise of that power is normally bad. I say 'normally', because I can conceive that there may be cases where the factor wrongly taken into account, or omitted, is insignificant, or where the wrong taking-into-account, or omission, actually operated in favour of the person who later claims to be aggrieved by the decision.

... I have considered also the views of the learned authors of the textbooks on this. Professor Wade in his book *Administrative Law* 5th edn (1982) under the heading Duality of Purpose says at p. 388:

> Sometimes an act may serve two or more purposes, some authorised and some not, and it may be a question whether the public authority may kill two birds with one stone. The general rule is that its action will be lawful provided the permitted purpose is the true and dominant purpose behind the act, even though some secondary or incidental advantage may be gained for some purpose which is outside the authority's powers.

Professor Evans, in *de Smith's Judicial Review of Administrative Action* 4th edn (1980) p. 329, comforts me by describing the general problem of plurality of purpose as 'a legal porcupine which bristles with difficulties as soon as it is touched.' He distils from the decisions of the courts five different tests on which reliance has been placed at one time or another, including, at pp. 330–332:

> (1) What was the *true purpose* for which the power was exercised? If the actor has in truth used his power for the purposes for which it was conferred, it is immaterial that he was thus enabled to achieve a subsidiary object ... (5) Was any of the purposes pursued an unauthorised purpose? If so, and if the unauthorised purpose has materially influenced the actor's conduct, the power has been invalidly exercised because irrelevant considerations have been taken into account.

These two tests, and Professor Evans's comment on them, seem to me to achieve much the same result and to be similar to that put forward by Megaw J in *Hanks v Minister of Housing and Local Government* [1963] 1 QB 999 in the first paragraph of the passage I have quoted from his judgment. That is the part that includes the sentence: 'In the end, it seems to me, the simplest and clearest way to state the matter is by reference to considerations.' I gratefully adopt the guidance of Megaw J and the two tests I have referred to from *de Smith's Judicial Review of Administrative Action*.

It thus becomes a question of fact for me to decide, on the material before me, whether, in reaching its decision of 23 July 1984, the staff and general sub-committee of ILEA was pursuing an unauthorised purpose, namely that of persuasion, which has materially influenced the making of its decision. I have already said that I find that one of the sub-committee's purposes was the giving of information. But I also find that it had the purpose of seeking to persuade members of the public to a view identical with that of the authority itself, and indeed I believe that this was a, if not the, major purpose of the decision. In reaching this decision of fact, I have taken into account in particular the material to which

I have referred above in AMV's 'presentation' of 18 July 1984, the passages I have quoted from the report of the Education Officer to the sub-committee, particularly the reference to changing 'the basis of public debate', and the various documents which have been published by AMV since 23 July with the approval of ILEA. I accept that some of the documents do inform, but in my view some of them contain little or no information and are designed only to persuade. This is true in particular, in my view, of the poster slogan 'Education Cuts Never Heal' (skilful though I think it is) and it is also true of the advertisement 'What do you get if you subtract £75 million from London's education budget?'

Adopting the test referred to above, I thus hold that ILEA's sub-committee did, when making its decision of 23 July 1984, take into account an irrelevant consideration, and thus that decision was not validly reached.

■ QUESTIONS

1. On which of the grounds for judicial review did the Court base its decision?
2. Glidewell LJ quoted part of a passage from de Smith. Do you agree with his comment that the two tests set out in this passage achieve much the same result? On the facts of *Westminster Corporation* v *London and North Western Railway Co* [1905] AC 426, might it have been possible to say that, although the construction of a subway was not a primary object, the desire to provide such a subway was a material influence on the council's decision?

NOTE: In *R* v *Greenwich London Borough Council, ex parte Lovelace* [1991] 3 All ER 511, Staughton LJ in the Court of Appeal stated that, in cases of 'mixed motives', the question was whether the improper motive had exercised a 'substantial influence' on the decision.

Although *R* v *ILEA, ex parte Westminster City Council* was argued on the basis that the authority had acted for an improper purpose, Glidewell LJ stated that he felt the case was best approached on the basis of whether the authority had been materially influenced by an irrelevant consideration. This ground for judicial review is dealt with in more detail in the following extract.

Padfield v *Minister for Agriculture, Fisheries and Food*
[1968] AC 997, House of Lords

The Agricultural Marketing Act 1958 regulated the marketing of various agricultural products, including milk. Section 19(3) provided: 'A committee of investigation shall … (b) be charged with the duty, if the Minister in any case so directs, of considering and reporting to the Minister … any complaint made to the Minister as to the operation of any scheme which, in the opinion of the Minister, could not be considered by a consumers' committee … '. The south-eastern dairy farmers complained to the Minister about the operation of a scheme involving the fixing of price differentials by the Milk Marketing Board, but the Minister refused to refer the complaint to a committee of investigation. They accordingly applied for an order of *mandamus*.

The Divisional Court made an order against the Minister which was set aside by the Court of Appeal.

LORD REID: … The question at issue in this appeal is the nature and extent of the Minister's duty under section 19(3)(b) of the Act of 1958 in deciding whether to refer to the committee of investigation a complaint as to the operation of any scheme made by persons adversely affected by the scheme. The respondent contends that his only duty is to consider a complaint fairly and that he is given an unfettered discretion with regard to every complaint either to refer it or not to refer it to the committee as he may think fit. The appellants contend that it is his duty to refer every genuine and substantial complaint, or alternatively that his discretion is not unfettered and that in this case he failed to exercise his discretion according to law because his refusal was caused or influenced by his having misdirected himself in law or by his having taken into account extraneous or irrelevant considerations.

In my view, the appellants' first contention goes too far. There are a number of reasons which would justify the Minister in refusing to refer a complaint. For example, he might consider it more suitable for arbitration, or he might consider that in an earlier case the committee of investigation had already rejected a substantially similar complaint or he might think the complaint to be frivolous or vexatious. So he must have at least some measure of discretion. But is it unfettered?

It is implicit in the argument for the Minister that there are only two possible interpretations of this provision—either he must refer every complaint or he has an unfettered discretion to refuse to refer in any case. I do not think that is right. Parliament must have conferred the discretion with the intention that it should be used to promote the policy and objects of the Act; the policy and objects of the Act must be determined by construing the Act as a whole and construction is always a matter of law for the court. In a matter of this kind it is not possible to draw a hard and fast line, but if the Minister, by reason of his having misconstrued the Act or for any other reason, so uses his discretion so as to thwart or run counter to the policy and objects of the Act, then our law would be very defective if persons aggrieved were not entitled to the protection of the court. So it is first necessary to construe the Act. …

The approval of Parliament shows that this scheme was thought to be in the public interest, and in so far as it necessarily involved detriment to some persons, it must have been thought to be in the public interest that they should suffer it. But in sections 19 and 20 Parliament drew a line. They provide machinery for investigating and determining whether the scheme is operating or the board is acting in a manner contrary to the public interest.

The effect of these sections is that if, but only if, the Minister and the committee of investigation concur in the view that something is being done contrary to the public interest the Minister can step in. Section 20 enables the Minister to take the initiative. Section 19 deals with complaints by individuals who are aggrieved. I need not deal with the provisions which apply to consumers. We are concerned with other persons who may be distributors or producers. If the Minister directs that a complaint by any of them shall be referred to the committee of investigation, that committee will make a report which must be published. If they report that any provision of this scheme or any act or omission of the Board is contrary to interests of the complainers *and* is not in the public interest, then the Minister is empowered to take action but not otherwise. He may disagree with the view of the committee as to public interest, and, if he thinks that there are other public interests which outweigh the public interest that justice should be done to the complainers, he would be not only entitled but bound to refuse to take action. Whether he takes action or not, he may be criticised and held accountable in Parliament but the court cannot interfere.

I must now examine the Minister's reasons for refusing to refer the appellant's complaint to the committee. I have already set out the letters of March 23 and May 3, 1965. I think it is right also to refer to a letter sent from the Ministry on May 1 1964, because in his affidavit the Minister says he has read this letter and there is no indication that he disagrees with any part of it.

[Lord Reid read the letter and continued.] The first reason which the Minister gave in his letter of March 23, 1965, was that this complaint was unsuitable for investigation because it raised wide issues. Here it appears to me that the Minister has clearly misdirected himself. Section 19(6) contemplates the raising of issues so wide that it may be necessary for the Minister to amend a scheme or even to revoke it. Narrower issues may be suitable for arbitration but section 19 affords the only method of investigating wide issues. In my view it is plainly the intention of the Act that even the widest issues should be investigated if the complaint is genuine and substantial, as this complaint certainly is.

Then it is said that the issue should be 'resolved through the arrangements available to producers and the board within the framework of the scheme itself.' This re-states in a condensed form the reasons given in paragraph 4 of the letter of May 1, 1964, where it is said 'the Minister owes no duty to producers in any particular region,' and reference is made to the 'status of the Milk Marketing Scheme as an instrument for the self-government of the industry,' and to the Minister 'assuming an inappropriate degree of responsibility.' But as I have already pointed out, the Act imposes on the Minister a responsibility whenever there is a relevant and substantial complaint that the board are acting in a manner inconsistent with the public interest, and that has been relevantly alleged in this case. I can find nothing in the Act to limit this responsibility or to justify the statement that the Minister owes no duty to producers in a particular region. The Minister is, I think, correct in saying that the board is an instrument of the self-government of the industry. So long as it does not act contrary to the public interest the Minister cannot interfere. But if it does act contrary to what both the committee of investigation and the Minister hold to be the public interest the Minister has a duty to act. And if a complaint relevantly alleges that the board has so acted, as this complaint does, then it appears to me that the Act does impose a duty on the Minister to have it investigated. If he does not do that he is rendering nugatory a safeguard provided by the Act and depriving complainers of a remedy which I am satisfied that Parliament intended them to have. ...

The House of Lords by a majority allowed the appeal and granted an order of mandamus (Lord Morris of Borth-y-Gest dissenting).

NOTE: The aftermath of this case provides a good illustration of the point that success in a judicial review application does not require that the authority whose actions have been challenged must reach a decision which is favourable to the applicant. After this case the Minister submitted a complaint for investigation to the investigative committee. The Minister then rejected the committee's advice. Commenting on this Carol Harlow stated that 'The remedy had proved illusory; the same decision could be reached with only nominal deference to the court, and the waste of time and money entailed is a deterrent to future complainants' (C. Harlow, 'Administrative Reaction to Judicial Review' [1976] *Public Law* 116). Do you agree?

■ QUESTIONS

1. How did the House of Lords decide which considerations were relevant and which were irrelevant?

2. How did the House of Lords decide which considerations had been taken into account?

3. Are there any circumstances in which the taking into account of an irrelevant consideration will not render the decision unlawful. Does *R v Inner London Education Authority* (see earlier in this chapter in Section 2B at p. 506) suggest an answer? (See also *R v BBC, ex parte Owen* [1985] 2 All ER 522.)

NOTES

1. Public bodies will have various duties and powers and responsibilities. Are they entitled to take into account their own financial resources in making decisions involving expenditure? In *R v Gloucestershire County Council, ex parte Barry* [1997] AC 584, the removal of cleaning and laundry services by the council on the ground of lack of resources was challenged. The House of Lords by a 3:2 majority held that it was a relevant consideration for a council to take into account the resources it had available when carrying out its statutory duty under the Chronically Sick and Disabled Persons Act 1970, s. 2(1), to consider the needs of chronically sick and disabled persons in its area. Lord Nicholls said that 'needs for services cannot be sensibly assessed without having some regard to the cost of providing them. A person's need for a particular type or level of service cannot be decided in a vacuum from which all considerations of cost have been expelled'. In a subsequent decision the Court of Appeal held in *R v Sefton Metropolitan Borough Council, ex parte Help the Aged* [1997] 4 All ER 532, that a council making decisions under National Assistance Act 1948, s. 21(1) as to whether an elderly person was in need of care and attention, was entitled to have regard to its own resources. Where it was decided that a person was in such need then a lack of resources was no excuse if arrangements were not made to provide for the identified needs. Subsequently *ex parte Barry* has been distinguished by the House of Lords in *R v East Sussex County Council, ex parte Tandy* [1998] 2 All ER 769, where it was held that a local education authority's resources were an irrelevant consideration in determining what constituted suitable education for the purposes of the Education Act 1993, s. 298. This section imposed a duty to make arrangements for suitable education for children in specified circumstances. Their Lordships also held that if there was more than one way of providing suitable education, then it would be permissible for a local education authority to have regard to its resources in choosing between different ways of making such provision. See E. Palmer, 'Resource Allocation, Welfare Rights—Mapping the Boundaries of Judicial Control in Public Administrative Law' (2000) 20 *Oxford Journal of Legal Studies* 63, and J. A. King 'The Justiciability of Resource Allocation' (2007) 70 *Modern Law Review* 197.

A Chief Constable may have regard to available resources when determining policing priorities: see *R v Chief Constable of Sussex, ex parte International Trader's Ferry Ltd* [1999] 2 AC 418, later in chapter in Section 2F at p. 562.

2. Failure to consider a legitimate expectation is a failure to consider a relevant consideration: see *R (Bibi) v Newham London Borough Council* [2001] EWCA Civ 607, [2002] 1 WLR 237, later in this chapter in Section 2E at p. 544.

3. It has been held to be an irrelevant consideration for the Home Secretary to take into account a public campaign urging a long period of minimum detention for boys who had murdered a younger child. The majority of the House of Lords held in *R v Secretary of State for the Home Department, ex parte Venables* [1997] 3 WLR 23, that in this position of determining the minimum period of detention or tariff, it was permissible to take into account general considerations of public confidence in the administration of justice. In making this decision the Home Secretary was acting like a judge determining sentence. It was further held that the consideration of the public campaign in a particular case would also amount to a breach of natural justice.

4. *R (Corner House Research) v Director of the Serious Fraud Office* [2008] UKHL 60, has been considered in Chapter 3, Section 5 at p. 135 on the rule of law. When the Supreme Court overturned the decision of the Divisional Court, it was clear that the threat of the withdrawal of Saudi cooperation was a relevant factor to be considered by the Director when deciding on whether to proceed with or discontinue the prosecutions.

5. It will be clear that the court is required to address some difficult issues in deciding upon the legality of an authority's decisions. For example, how do the courts decide what considerations were taken into account? How do they decide whether an irrelevant consideration has had only an insignificant or insubstantial influence on a decision? Two points in particular should be noted. First, the burden of proof in an application for judicial review generally falls on the applicant. Hence, for example, the onus was on the complainants in *Padfield* to prove that irrelevant consideration(s) were taken into account. Secondly, there is no general requirement that the authority should give reasons for its decision. In the course of argument in *Padfield* it was submitted that the Minister may properly refuse to act on a complaint without giving any reasons, and that in such a case a complainant would have no remedy and the decision could not be questioned. Lord Pearce stated at pp. 1053–4:

> I do not regard a Minister's failure or refusal to give any reasons as a sufficient exclusion of the court's surveillance. If all the prima facie reasons seem to point in favour of his taking a certain course to carry out the intention of Parliament in respect of a power which it has been given to him in that regard, and he gives no reason whatever for taking a contrary course, the court may infer that he has no good reason and that he is not using the power given by Parliament to carry out its intentions. In the present case, however, the Minister has given reasons which show that he was not exercising his discretion in accordance with the intentions of the Act.

(See also the comments of Lord Reid, at pp. 1032(G)–1033(A) and Lord Upjohn, at pp. 1061(G)–62(A).)

After citing this passage in the case of *Lonrho plc v Secretary of State* [1989] 2 All ER 609, at p. 620, Lord Keith, with whom the other Law Lords agreed, stated:

> The absence of reasons for a decision where there is no duty to give them cannot of itself provide any support for the suggested irrationality of the decision. The only significance of the absence of reasons is that if all other known facts and circumstances appear to point overwhelmingly in favour of a different decision, the decision-maker who has given no reasons cannot complain if the court draws the inference that he had no rational reason for his decision.

While there is no general duty to provide reasons authorities are sometimes obliged by statute to provide them (see, in particular, s. 10 of the Tribunal and Inquiries Act 1992). It has also been recently accepted that natural justice could, in exceptional cases, require the provision of reasons (see *R v Civil Service Appeal Board, ex parte Cunningham* [1991] 4 All ER 310, discussed at [1991] *Public Law*, 340–6). In *Doody v Secretary of State for the Home Department* [1993] 3 All ER 92 the House of Lords held that the Secretary of State was obliged to give reasons to prisoners when he proposed to depart from the periods recommended by the judiciary for the purposes of retribution and deterrence. Yet in *R v Higher Education Funding Council, ex parte Institute of Dental Surgery* [1994] 1 All ER 651, although the Council's reasons for refusing to give reasons for its decision to lower the institute's research rating were not well grounded, this was not a case in which the law might require reasons. In *R v Ministry of Defence, ex parte Murray* [1998] COD 134 the principles from those three cases were drawn together by Hooper J. While there was as yet no general duty to give reasons, the courts will seek to ensure that bodies given power to make decisions affecting individuals act fairly and it may be that a procedure of not giving reasons is unfair, even if there is no requirement to do so. Particular concern will arise if a tribunal's decisions affect personal liberty. In deciding if fairness requires a tribunal to give reasons, then regard will be had to the initial hearing but also to the availability of any appeal or judicial review and the absence of such a remedy could be a point in favour of requiring reasons. Reasons will not be required where considerations of public interest would outweigh the advantages of requiring reasons or if the procedures of a particular decision-maker would be frustrated if required to give reasons, even short reasons. In summary, factors in favour of requiring reasons are: 'the giving of reasons may among other things concentrate the decision-maker's mind on the right questions; demonstrate to the recipient that this is so; show that the issues have been conscientiously addressed and how the result has been reached; or alternatively alert the recipient to a justiciable flaw in the process'. On the other hand factors not requiring the giving of reasons include where: 'it may place an undue burden on decision-makers; demand an appearance of unanimity where there is diversity; call for articulation of sometimes inexpressible value judgments; and offer an invitation to the captious to comb the reasons for previously unsuspected grounds of challenge'.

In *R v Secretary of State for the Home Department, ex parte Fayed* [1997] 1 All ER 228, British Nationality Act 1981, s. 44(2) allowed the Home Secretary not to give reasons when deciding applications for naturalization as British citizens. By a majority the Court of Appeal held that the Minister had to be fair and that an applicant should be given sufficient information about the Minister's concerns to allow the applicant to make representations. If that would involve disclosing matters not in the public interest then this should be indicated so that the applicant could challenge the justification for the refusal to give reasons in the courts. Note that the section did not ban the giving of reasons.

British Oxygen Co Ltd v *Minister of Technology*
[1971] AC 610, House of Lords

British Oxygen Co Ltd used metal cylinders to store pressurized gases which it manufactured. It applied for a grant in respect of the cylinders under s. 1(1) of the Industrial Development Act 1966, which provided that the Board of Trade 'may make to any person carrying on a business in Great Britain a grant towards approved capital expenditure incurred by that person in providing new machinery or plant'. The Board had a policy of denying grants for any item of plant costing less than £25 and, in pursuance of that policy, rejected British Oxygen's application as the gas cylinders cost just under £20 each. British Oxygen sought declarations that (*inter alia*) the cylinders were eligible for grant.

LORD REID: Section 1 of the Act provides that the Board of Trade 'may' make grants. It was not argued that 'may' in this context means 'shall', and it seems to me clear the Board were intended to have a discretion. But how were the Board intended to operate that discretion? Does the Act read as a whole indicate any policy which the Board is to follow or even give any guidance to the Board? If it does then the Board must exercise its discretion in accordance with such policy or guidance (*Padfield* v *Minister of Agriculture, Fisheries and Food* [1986] AC 997). One generally expects to find that Parliament has given some indication as to how public money is to be distributed. In this Act Parliament has clearly laid down the conditions for eligibility for grants and it has clearly given to the Board a discretion so that the Board is not bound to pay to every person who is eligible to receive such a grant. But I can find nothing to guide the Board as to the circumstances in which they should pay or the circumstances in which they should not pay grants to such persons. ...

There are two general grounds on which the exercise of an unqualified discretion can be attacked. It must not be exercised in bad faith, and it must not be so unreasonably exercised as to show that there cannot have been any real or genuine exercise of the discretion. But, apart from that, if the Minister thinks that policy or good administration requires the operation of some limiting rule, I find nothing to stop him.

It was argued on the authority of *Rex* v *Port of London Authority ex parte Kynoch* [1919] 1 KB 176 that the Minister is not entitled to make a rule for himself as to how he will in future exercise his discretion. In that case Kynoch owned land adjoining the Thames and wished to construct a deep water wharf. For this they had to get the permission of the authority. Permission was refused on the ground that Parliament had charged the authority with the duty of providing such facilities. It appeared that before reaching their decision the authority had fully considered the case on its merits and in relation to the public interest. So their decision was upheld.

Bankes LJ said at p. 184:

> There are on the one hand cases where a tribunal in the honest exercise of its discretion has adopted a policy, and, without refusing to hear an applicant, intimates to him what its policy is, and that after hearing him it will in accordance with its policy decide against him, unless there is something exceptional in his case. I think counsel for the applicants would admit that, if the policy has been adopted for reasons which the tribunal may legitimately entertain, no objection could be taken to such a course. On the other hand there are cases where a tribunal has passed a rule, or come to a determination, not to hear any application of a particular character by whomsoever made. There is a wide distinction to be drawn between these two classes.

I see nothing wrong with that. But the circumstances in which discretions are exercised vary enormously and that passage cannot be applied literally in every case. The general rule is that anyone who has to exercise a statutory discretion must not 'shut his ears to an application' (to adapt from Bankes LJ on p. 183). I do not think there is any great difference between a policy and a rule. There may be cases where an officer or authority ought to listen to a substantial argument reasonably presented urging a change of policy. What the authority must not do is to refuse to listen at all. But a ministry or large authority may have had to deal already with a multitude of similar applications and then they will almost certainly have evolved a policy so precise that it could well be called a rule. There can be no objection to that, provided the authority is always willing to listen to anyone with something new to say—of course I do not mean to say that there need be an oral hearing. In the present case the respondent's officers have carefully considered all that the appellants have had to say and I have no doubt that they will continue to do so. ...

VISCOUNT DILHORNE: ... [T]he distinction between a policy decision and a rule may not be easy to draw. In this case it was not challenged that it was within the power of the Board to adopt a policy not to make a grant in respect of such an item. The policy might equally well be described as a rule. It was both reasonable and right that the Board should make known to those interested the policy it was going to follow. By doing so fruitless applications involving expense and expenditure of time might be avoided. The Board says that it has not refused to consider any application. It considered the appellants'. In these circumstances it is not necessary to decide in this case whether, if it had refused to consider an application on the ground that it related to an item costing less than £25, it would have acted wrongly.

I must confess that I feel some doubt whether the words used by Bankes LJ in the passage cited above [see p. 548, *ante*] are really applicable to a case of this kind. It seems somewhat pointless and a waste of time that the Board should have to consider applications which are bound as a result of its policy decision to fail. Representations could of course be made that the policy should be changed. ...

Lord Morris of Borth-y-gest, Lord Wilberforce and Lord Diplock agreed with Lord Reid.

■ QUESTIONS

1. On which ground(s) was the decision of the House of Lords based?

2. Under the Children Act 1989 local authorities have a duty to safeguard and promote the welfare of children within their area who are in need 'by providing a range and level of services appropriate to those children's needs' (s. 17). The services may include giving assistance in kind or, in exceptional circumstances, in cash. Assume that a local authority has made certain policies to govern the provision of such assistance. An applicant for assistance in cash is told that her application will be refused under the general policies operated by the council (of which she is aware) unless she wishes to make representations that the policies should be altered and the authority is prepared to accept the representations. Would the applicant be able to challenge this decision? (See *Attorney-General ex relator Tilley* v *Wandsworth LBC* [1981] 1 WLR 854.)

NOTES

1. In *R (P)* v *Secretary of State for the Home Department* and *R (Q)* v *Secretary of State for the Home Department* [2001] EWCA Civ 1151, [2001] 1 WLR 2002 the Court of Appeal demonstrated how to deal with a rigid or blanket policy when human rights were engaged. In these cases the Prison Service's policy requiring babies to be separated from their prisoner mothers on reaching 18 months of age was considered in the light of the mother's, and particularly the child's, right to family life. The Prison Service was required to consider whether the interference with the right was justified by the legitimate aims in Art. 8(2). Factors to be taken into account include necessary limitations upon the mother's rights because of her imprisonment, how relaxation of the policy might affect the good order and discipline of the prison, the length of the mother's sentence, the welfare of the child including the extent of harm likely to be caused by separation, the extent of harm likely to be caused by remaining in prison, and the quality of alternative arrangements. The Court concluded that in most cases separation before 18 months would be justified but there could be cases in which the interests of mother and child outweighed other factors. In the case of P the application of the policy would be lawful but so far as Q was concerned there were factors which led to the court to remit the case to the Prison Service for reconsideration. On the application of this test with pressing social need see Chapter 9, Section 3B(b) at p. 481, and for its relationship with *Wednesbury* unreasonableness/irrationality and proportionality see Chapter 9, Section 3C at p. 482.

2. See C. Hilson, 'Judicial Review, Policies and the Fettering of Discretion' [2002] *Public Law* 111 for a thorough examination of the 'no fettering' doctrine in which the doctrine and its application by the courts are criticized and an argument is made for a more nuanced approach which allows for justifiable rigid policies and also for more individualized decision-making where required and, where human rights are engaged, for a relationship in which the newer human rights approach can be combined with the older doctrine.

3. The application of a policy may result in breaches of the duty to be fair (see later in this section at p. 531). For example, in *R* v *Secretary of State for the Environment, ex parte Brent LBC* [1982] QB 593 the Secretary of State failed to consider any of the representations made to him to change his policy on reducing the rate support grant to certain authorities. The Divisional Court held that he had both unlawfully fettered his discretion and failed to discharge the duty of fairness.

E v *Secretary of State for the Home Department*

[2004] EWCA Civ 49, [2004] 2 WLR 1351, Court of Appeal

Two asylum cases were joined in the appeal. The asylum claims had been rejected by the Secretary of State and the appeals to the Adjudicator and Immigration Appeal Tribunal (IAT) had been unsuccessful, however, new evidence had come to light between the hearing and the promulgation of the decision by the IAT and the appellants had not been able to persuade the IAT to hear appeals based on this evidence which would show the mistake, as the IAT took the view it could not take the new evidence into account. On appeal on a point of law to the Court of Appeal.

CARNWATH LJ: …

Incorrect basis of fact

44.   Can a decision reached on an incorrect basis of fact be challenged on an appeal limited to points of law? This apparently paradoxical question has a long history in academic discussion, but has never received a decisive answer from the courts. The answer is not made easier by the notorious difficulty of drawing a clear distinction between issues of law and fact (see, Craig *op cit* p488; *Moyna v Secretary of State for Work and Pensions* [2003] UKHL 44 para 22 ff, per Lord Hoffmann).

45.   The debate received new life following the affirmative answer given by Lord Slynn in *R v Criminal Injuries Compensation Board ex parte A* [1999] 2AC 330. In that case the claimant had claimed compensation on the basis that in the course of a burglary she had been the victim of rape and buggery. She was examined five days after the burglary by a police doctor who reported that her findings were consistent with the allegation of buggery. However, at the hearing of her claim that report was not included in the evidence, and the Board was given the impression by the police witnesses that there was nothing in the medical evidence to support her case. The claimant did not ask for the report, but, in Lord Slynn's words:

> " … having been told that she should not ask for police statements as they would be produced by the police, it would not be surprising that she assumed that if there was a report from the police doctor, it would be made available with the police report" (p 343F).

46.   One of the issues discussed in detail in argument was whether the decision could be quashed on the basis of a mistake, in relation to material which was or ought to have been within the knowledge of the decision maker (see p 333–336). Lord Slynn thought it could. He said:

> Your Lordships have been asked to say that there is jurisdiction to quash the Board's decision because that decision was reached on a material error of fact. Reference has been made to "Administrative Law" (Wade and Forsyth (7th edition)) in which it is said at pp. 316–318 that:
>
> Mere factual mistake has become a ground of judicial review, described as 'misunderstanding or ignorance of an established and relevant fact,' [*Secretary of State for Education v Tameside* [1977] AC 1014, 1030] or acting 'upon an incorrect basis of fact.' … This ground of review has long been familiar in French law and it has been adopted by statute in Australia. It is no less needed in this country, since decisions based upon wrong fact are a cause of injustice which the courts should be able to remedy. If a 'wrong factual basis' doctrine should become established, it would apparently be a new branch of the ultra vires doctrine, analogous to finding facts based upon no evidence or acting upon a misapprehension of law.
>
> De Smith, Woolf and Jowell *Judicial Review of Administrative Action* 5th ed., at p. 288
>
> The taking into account of a mistaken fact can just as easily be absorbed into a traditional legal ground of review by referring to the taking into account of an irrelevant consideration, or the failure to provide reasons that are adequate or intelligible, or the failure to base the decision on any evidence. In this limited context material error of fact has always been a recognised ground for judicial intervention.
>
> For my part, I would accept that there is jurisdiction to quash on that ground in this case … (p 344G–345E).

47.   However, Lord Slynn "preferred" to decide the instant case on the alternative basis that there had been a breach of the rules of natural justice amounting to "unfairness." As to that he said: …
He concluded:

> I consider therefore, on the special facts of this case and in the light of the importance of the role of the police in co-operating with the Board in the obtaining of the evidence, that there was unfairness in the failure to put the doctor's evidence before the board and if necessary to grant an adjournment for that purpose. I do not think it possible to say here that justice was done or seen to be done. (p 347B).

48. The other members of the House agreed with Lord Slynn's reasoning, thereby (as I read the speeches) endorsing his "preferred" basis of unfairness. Only Lord Hobhouse made any direct reference to the question of review for "error of fact", specifically reserving that issue for consideration in the future (p 348E).

49. The same statement on that question was repeated by Lord Slynn, in another context, in *R v Secretary of State for the Environment ex p Alconbury* [2003] 2 AC 295, [2001] UKHL 23 para. 53. He referred to the jurisdiction to quash for "misunderstanding or ignorance of an established and relevant fact", as part of his reasons for holding that the court's powers of review (under a statutory procedure to quash for excess of power) met the requirements of the European Convention on Human Rights. This part of his reasoning was not in terms adopted by the other members of the House of Lords. The point was mentioned by Lord Nolan and Lord Clyde. Lord Nolan put it in somewhat narrower terms; he said:

> But a review of the merits of the decision-making process is fundamental to the Court's jurisdiction. The power of review may even extend to a decision on a question of fact. As long ago as 1955 your Lordships' House, in *Edwards v Bairstow* [1956] AC 14, a case in which an appeal (from General Commissioners of Income Tax) could only be brought on a question of law, upheld the right and duty of the appellate court to reverse a finding of fact which had no justifiable basis. (para. 61).

> He saw *Edwards v Bairstow* as an illustration of "the generosity" with which the Courts have interpreted the power to review questions of law, corresponding to "a similarly broad and generous" approach in the development of judicial review (para 62). Lord Clyde referred to Lord Slynn's statement on this issue in *CICB*, commenting that it was:

> ... sufficient to note ... the extent to which the factual areas of a decision may be penetrated by a review of the account taken by a decision-maker of facts which are irrelevant or even mistaken. (para. 169)

50. In the present case the appellants rely on Lord Slynn's statement as representing the law. Mr Kovats, for the Secretary of State, contents himself with the observation that the *CICB* case is "not in point" because it was a judicial review case, and Lord Slynn's statement was *obiter*. For the reasons already given, we do not think the fact that *CICB* was a judicial review case is an adequate ground of distinction. Indeed, Lord Slynn himself (and Lord Clyde) treated it as no less relevant to a statutory review procedure in *Alconbury*. The fact that the statement was *obiter* means of course that it is not binding on us, but does not detract from its persuasive force, bearing in mind also the authority of the textbooks cited by him.

51. Although none of the parties found it necessary to examine in any detail the authorities referred to in argument in the *CICB* case or in the textbooks, it seems to us difficult to avoid such examination, if we are to address properly the issue in these appeals. Fortunately the ground is very well-covered, not only in the textbooks, but also in two excellent articles: by Timothy Jones, "Mistake of fact in Administrative Law" [1990] PL 507; and by Michael Kent QC (no doubt stimulated by his unsuccessful advocacy in *CICB* itself) "Widening the scope of review for error of fact" [1999] JR 239. The authorities are helpfully summarised in Michael Fordham's invaluable *Judicial Review Handbook* 3rd Ed pp 730–2 (see also Demetriou and Houseman *Review for Error of fact—a brief guide* [1997] JR 27). ...

52. ... Before reaching a conclusion that mistake of fact is now a ground for judicial review in its own right, it is necessary to review briefly the authorities mentioned in those articles. Two main points emerge: first, that widely differing views have been expressed as to the existence or scope of this ground of review; but, secondly, that, in practice, this uncertainty has not deterred administrative court judges from setting aside decisions on the grounds of mistake of fact, when justice required it. ...

63. In our view, the *CICB* case points the way to a separate ground of review, based on the principle of fairness. It is true that Lord Slynn distinguished between "ignorance of fact" and "unfairness" as grounds of review. However, we doubt if there is a real distinction. The decision turned, not on issues of fault or lack of fault on either side; it was sufficient that "objectively" there was unfairness. On analysis, the "unfairness" arose from the combination of five factors:

i)   An erroneous impression created by a mistake as to, or ignorance of, a relevant fact (the availability of reliable evidence to support her case);

ii) The fact was "established", in the sense that, if attention had been drawn to the point, the correct position could have been shown by objective and uncontentious evidence;

iii) The claimant could not fairly be held responsible for the error;

iv) Although there was no duty on the Board itself, or the police, to do the claimant's work of proving her case, all the participants had a shared interest in co-operating to achieve the correct result;

v)   The mistaken impression played a material part in the reasoning.

64. If that is the correct analysis, then it provides a convincing explanation of the cases where decisions have been set aside on grounds of mistake of fact. Although planning inquiries are also adversarial, the planning authority has a public interest, shared with the Secretary of State through his inspector, in ensuring that development control is carried out on the correct factual basis. Similarly, in *Tameside*, the Council and the Secretary of State, notwithstanding their policy differences, had a shared interest in decisions being made on correct information as to practicalities. The same thinking can be applied to asylum cases. Although the Secretary of State has no general duty to assist the appellant by providing information about conditions in other countries (see *Abdi and Gawe v Secretary of State* [1996] 1 WLR 298, he has a shared interest with the appellant and the Tribunal in ensuring that decisions are reached on the best information. It is in the interest of all parties that decisions should be made on the best available information (see the comments of Sedley LJ in *Batayav*, quoted above).

(We have also taken account of the judgment of Maurice Kay J in *R (Cindo) v Secretary of State* [2002] EWHC 246 para 8–11, drawn to our attention since the hearing by Mr Gill, in which some of these issues were discussed.)

65. The apparent unfairness in *CICB* was accentuated because the police had in their possession the relevant information and failed to produce it. But, as we read the speeches, "fault" on their part was not essential to the reasoning of the House. What mattered was that, because of their failure, and through no fault of her own, the claimant had not had "a fair crack of the whip". (See *Fairmount Investments v Secretary of State* [1976] 1 WLR 1255, 1266A, per Lord Russell.) If it is said that this is taking "fairness" beyond its traditional role as an aspect of procedural irregularity, it is no further than its use in cases such as *HTV Ltd v Price Commission* [1976] ICR 170, approved by the House of Lords in *R v IRC ex p Preston* [1985] AC 835, 865–6.)

66. In our view, the time has now come to accept that a mistake of fact giving rise to unfairness is a separate head of challenge in an appeal on a point of law, at least in those statutory contexts where the parties share an interest in co-operating to achieve the correct result. Asylum law is undoubtedly such an area. Without seeking to lay down a precise code, the ordinary requirements for a finding of unfairness are apparent from the above analysis of *CICB*. First, there must have been a mistake as to an existing fact, including a mistake as to the availability of evidence on a particular matter. Secondly, the fact or evidence must have been "established", in the sense that it was uncontentious and objectively verifiable. Thirdly, the appellant (or his advisers) must not been have been responsible for the mistake. Fourthly, the mistake must have played a material (not necessarily decisive) part in the Tribunal's reasoning.

67. Accordingly, we would accept the submissions of each of the present appellants, that, if the new evidence is admitted, the Court will be entitled to consider whether it gives rise to an error of law in the sense outlined above.

Appeals allowed.

NOTE: The court was seeking to show that mistake of fact was a ground of challenge available both in an appeal on a point of law and in a claim for judicial review and this required that it be regarded as an error of law. The chosen rationale is that the mistake of fact leads to unfairness which can amount to an error of law. See P. Craig, 'Judicial Review, Appeal and Factual Error' [2004] *Public Law* 788.

R v Secretary of State for the Home Department, ex parte Simms
[1999] 3 WLR 328, House of Lords

The applicants were prisoners who were convicted of murder and who continued to protest their innocence after they had been refused permission to appeal against their convictions. On becoming aware that some of the applicants' visitors were journalists who were interested in publicizing the applicants' stories, the prison authorities refused to allow journalists to visit the prisoners unless they signed an undertaking that no material obtained in the visits would be used for professional purposes. The authority for this was para. 37 of section A of the Prison Service Standing Order No. 5 of 1996. The journalists did not seek permission under para. 37A where, exceptionally, professional visits could be permitted conditionally. The Home Secretary had a blanket policy excluding professional visits on the basis that they tended to undermine proper control and discipline. The applicants successfully sought judicial review arguing that the blanket ban on the use of information was an excessive interference with the right of free speech. The Court of Appeal reversed this decision. On appeal to the House of Lords.

LORD STEYN: … Two important inferences can and should be drawn. First, until the Home Secretary imposed a blanket ban on oral interviews between prisoners and journalists in or about 1995, such interviews had taken place from time to time and had served to identify and undo a substantial number of miscarriages of justice. There is no evidence that any of these interviews had resulted in any adverse impact on prison discipline. Secondly, the evidence establishes clearly that without oral interviews it is now virtually impossible under the Home Secretary's blanket ban for a journalist to take up the case of a prisoner who alleges a miscarriage of justice. In the process a means of correcting errors in the functioning of the criminal justice system has been lost.

(c) The counter-arguments on behalf of the Home Secretary

For my part I am reasonably confident that once it is accepted that oral interviews with prisoners serve a useful purpose in exposing potential miscarriages of justice the Home Secretary would not wish his present policy to be maintained. But, if I am mistaken in that supposition, my view is that investigative journalism, based on oral interviews with prisoners, fulfils an important corrective role, with wider implications than the undoing of particular miscarriages of justice. Nevertheless, I must directly address the counter arguments advance by the Home Secretary.

Latham J was unimpressed with the reasons advanced in opposition to the applicants' limited claim in the first affidavit of Audrey Wickington. In my judgment the judge was right. The two new affidavits make a case that any oral interviews between prisoners and journalist will tend to disrupt discipline and order in prisons. In my view these affidavits do not take sufficient account of the limited nature of the applicants' claims, viz to have interviews for the purpose of obtaining a thorough investigation of their cases as a first step to possibly gaining access through the Criminal Cases Review Commission to the Court of Appeal (Criminal Division). The affidavits do not refute the case that until 1995 such interviews enabled a substantial number of miscarriages to be undone. Moreover, they do not establish that interviews confined to such limited purposes caused disruption to prison life. In any event, the affidavits do not establish a case of pressing need which might prevail over the prisoners' attempt to gain access to justice: see decision of the Court of Appeal in *Reg.* v *Secretary of State for the Home Department, Ex parte Leech* [1994] QB 198, the correctness of which was expressly accepted by counsel for the Home Secretary.

Counsel for the Home Secretary relied on the decision of the United States Supreme Court in *Pell* v *Procunier* (1974) 417 US 817. The case involved a ban by prison authorities of face to face interviews between journalists and inmates. The background was a relatively small number of inmates who as a result of press attention became virtual 'public figures' within prison society and gained a disproportionate notoriety and influence among their fellow inmates. The evidence showed that the interviews caused severe disciplinary problems. By a majority of five to four the Supreme Court held the ban to be constitutional. The majority enunciated an approach of a 'measure of judicial deference owed to corrections officials'. This approach was followed in *Turner* v *Safley* (1987) 482 US 78 where the Supreme Court upheld restrictions on correspondence between inmates. In *Pell* v *Procunier* the Supreme Court was faced with a very particular and intolerable situation in the Californian prison service where there had been virtually unlimited access by journalists to inmates. Nobody suggests anything of the kind in the present case. While the inmates in *Pell* v *Procunier* no doubt wished to air their general grievances, there is nothing in the report to indicate that the prisoners wanted interviews with journalists for the specific purpose of obtaining access to an appeal process to challenge their convictions. And, in any event, the approach of judicial deference to the views of prison authorities enunciated in *Pell* v *Procunier* does not accord with the approach under English law. It is at variance with the principle that only a pressing social need can defeat freedom of expression as explained in the *Derbyshire* case [*Derbyshire County Council* v *Times Newspapers*] [1993] AC 534, 550H–551A, the *Leech* case [1994] QB 198, 212 E–F, and *Silver* v *United Kingdom* (1980) 3 EHRR 475, 514–515, paras 372–375 (the commission): (1983) 5 EHRR 347, 377, para. 99(e) (the court). It is also inconsistent with the principle that the more substantial the interference with fundamental rights the more the court will require by way of justification before it can be satisfied that the interference is reasonable in a public law sense: *Reg.* v *Ministry of Defence, Ex parte Smith* [1996] QB 517, 554E–F. In my view *Pell* v *Procunier* does not assist.

(d) Conclusion

On the assumption that paragraphs 37 and 37A should be construed as the Home Secretary contends, I have no doubt that these provisions are exorbitant in width in so far as they would undermine the fundamental rights invoked by the applicants in the present proceedings and are therefore ultra vires.

2. The interpretation of paragraphs 37 and 37A

It is now necessary to examine the correctness of the interpretation of paragraphs 37 and 37A, involving a blanket ban on interviews, as advanced by the Home Secretary. Literally construed there is force in the extensive construction put forward. But one cannot lose sight that there is at stake a fundamental or basic right, namely the right of a prisoner to seek through oral interviews to persuade a journalist to investigate the safety of the prisoner's conviction and to publicise his findings in an effort to gain access to justice for the prisoner. In these circumstances even in the absence of an ambiguity there comes into play a presumption of general application operating as a constitutional principle as Sir Rupert Cross explained in successive editions of his classic work: *Statutory Interpretation*, 3rd ed. (1995), pp. 165–166. This is called 'the principle of legality': *Halsbury's Laws of England*, 4th ed. reissue, Vol. 8(2) (1996), pp. 13–14, para. 6. Ample illustrations of the application of this principle are given in the speech of Lord Browne-Wilkinson, and in my speech, in *Reg.* v *Secretary of State for the Home Department, Ex parte Pierson* [1998] AC 539, 573G–575D, 587C–590A. Applying this principle I would hold that paragraphs 37 and 37A leave untouched the fundamental and basic rights asserted by the applicants in the present case.

The only relevant issue in the present proceedings is whether paragraphs 37 and 37A are ultra vires because they are in conflict with the fundamental and basic rights claimed by the applicants. The principle of legality justifies the conclusion that paragraphs 37 and 37A have not been demonstrated to be ultra vires in the cases under consideration.

3. The disposal of the appeal

My Lords, my judgment does not involve tearing up the rule book governing prisons. On the contrary I have taken full account of the essential public interest in maintaining order and discipline in prisons. But, I am satisfied that consistently with order and discipline in prisons it is administratively workable to allow prisoners to be interviewed for the narrow purposes here at stake notably if a proper foundation is laid in correspondence for the requested interview or interviews. One has to recognise that oral interviews with journalists are not in the same category as visits by relatives and friends and require more careful control and regulation. That is achievable. This view is supported by the favourable judgment of past experience. Moreover, in reality an oral interview is simply a necessary and practical extension of the right of a prisoner to correspond to journalists about his conviction: compare *Silver* v *United*

Kingdom (1980) 3 EHRR 475 (the commission): 5 EHRR, 347 (the court) and Livingstone & Owen, *Prison Law*, 2nd ed. (1999), pp. 228–230, paras 7.30–7.33.

The criminal justice system has been shown to be fallible. Yet the effect of the judgment of the Court of Appeal is to outlaw the safety valve of effective investigative journalism. In my judgment the conclusions and reasoning of the Court of Appeal were wrong.

Declarations should be granted in both cases to the effect that the Home Secretary's current policy is unlawful, and that the governors' administrative decisions pursuant to that policy were also unlawful. I would allow both appeals.

While the rules were *intra vires*, the policy was unlawful.

NOTES

1. The decision is based on common law and not the Human Rights Act 1998, the entry into force of which it pre-dated by some 14 months.
2. In *R (Daly)* v *Secretary of State for the Home Department* [2001] UKHL 26, [2001] 2 AC 532, Chapter 9, Section 3C at p. 478 and later in this section at p. 546, their Lordships accepted that there were some fundamental rights recognized by the common law which included access to a court; access to legal advice; and the right to communicate confidentially with a legal adviser under the seal of legal professional privilege, which only the express words of a statute could restrict. Accordingly the policy on searching cells including papers covered by legal professional privilege without the prisoner being present was unlawful under both the common law and the Human Rights Acts 1998.
3. Just as the Human Rights Act 1998 provides for a challenge based on the duty imposed on public authorities not to infringe Convention rights, so s. 149 of the Equality Act 2010 imposes a duty which can also provide a ground of challenge in judicial review. The public sector equality duty (PSED) requires public authorities, and others, who exercise public functions to have due regard to: (a) eliminate discrimination, harassment, victimization, and any other conduct that is prohibited by or under this Act; (b) advance equality of opportunity between persons who share a relevant protected characteristic and persons who do not share it; and (c) foster good relations between persons who share a relevant protected characteristic and persons who do not share it. The protected characteristics are age; disability; gender reassignment; pregnancy and maternity; race; religion or belief; sex; and sexual orientation.

    Advancing equality of opportunity includes: (i) removing or minimizing disadvantages suffered by people with protected characteristics due to having that characteristic; (ii) taking steps to meet the needs of people with protected characteristics that are different from people who do not have that characteristic (including taking account of a disability); and (iii) encouraging protected groups to participate in public life and in any other activity where participation is disproportionately low. Fostering good relations involves tackling prejudice and promoting understanding. In the climate of austerity, campaigners have used the PSED to challenge decisions to cut services but it has also been used in planning matters affecting travellers; immigration; and school uniforms and admission policies. See A. McColgan, 'Litigating the Public Sector Equality Duty: The Story So Far' (2015) 35 *Oxford Journal of Legal Studies*, 435–85. One high-profile 'cuts' case involved the Independent Living Fund which helped disabled people. In *Bracking* v *Secretary of State for Work and Pensions* [2013] EWCA Civ 1345, the Court of Appeal upheld a successful challenge to the decision to close the fund on the basis that the Minister did not have enough information on the impact upon disabled recipients of the fund and there was no evidence of a focus on the PSED's specific duties. A subsequent decision to close the fund survived another PSED-based challenge: *Aspinall, Pepper & Ors* v *Secretary of State for Work and Pensions* [2014] EWHC 4143.

C: Procedural impropriety

In *Council of Civil Service Unions* v *Minister for the Civil Service* (see immediately following) Lord Roskill used this phrase specifically to include a breach both of express statutory procedural requirements and the common law rules of natural justice. Express statutory requirements include, for example, a requirement to give notice or to consult certain persons before a decision is made. Whether or not a breach of a statutory requirement will render the resulting decision invalid depends on a number of circumstances, including the importance of the provision which has been disregarded in the light of the objects of the statute, whether there was total or only partial breach of the requirement, and whether or not the breach caused any prejudice (see, e.g., *Coney* v *Choyce* [1975] 1 All ER 979; *Bradbury* v *London Borough of Enfield* [1967] 3 All ER 434; *London and Clydeside Estates Ltd* v *Aberdeen DC* [1979] 2 All ER 876). This section will focus on the common law rules of natural justice. Despite the requirements of the Human Rights Act 1998, the protection under Convention rights 'did not supersede the protection of the common law or statute, or create a discrete body of law based on the judgments of the European court. Human rights continue to be protected by our domestic law, interpreted and developed in accordance with the Act when appropriate', per Lord Reed, *Osborn* v *The Parole Board* [2013] UKSC 61, at [57].

Council of Civil Service Unions v *Minister for the Civil Service*
[1985] AC 374, House of Lords

[The facts are set out later in this section at p. 538.]

LORD ROSKILL: . . . the use of this phrase [natural justice] is no doubt hallowed by time and much judicial repetition, but it is a phrase often widely misunderstood and therefore as often misused. The phrase perhaps might now be allowed to find a permanent resting place and be better replaced by speaking of a duty to act fairly. But the latter phrase must not in its turn be misunderstood or misused. It is not for the courts to determine whether a particular policy or particular decisions taken in fulfilment of that policy are fair. They are only concerned with the manner in which those decision have been taken and the extent of the duty to act fairly will vary greatly from case to case as indeed the decided cases since 1950 consistently show. Many features will come into play including the nature of the decision and the relationship of those involved on either side before the decision was taken.

NOTE: The use of the phrase 'duty to act fairly' rather than 'natural justice' is frequently traced to the decision in *Re HK* [1967] 2 QB 617 where it was held that, although immigration officers were not obliged to hold a hearing before determining an immigrant's status, they were obliged to act fairly. Since then there has been a difference of opinion on the correct use of the two phrases. In *McInnes* v *Onslow Fane* [1978] 1 WLR 1520 Megarry V-C stated that 'the further the situation is away from anything that resembles a judicial or quasi-judicial decision, and the further the question is removed from what may reasonably be called a justiciable question, the more appropriate it is to reject an expression which includes the word justice and to use instead terms such as "fairness" or "the duty to act fairly".' Other judges have used the phrases interchangeably. What did Lord Roskill state on this point and why?

A related difficulty is whether there is any difference between the content of natural justice and the content of the duty to be fair. On one view, which appears to be that of both Lord Roskill and Megarry V-C, there is no difference: the content of natural justice and the content of the duty to be fair are both flexible and depend on all the circumstances of the case. Another view, however, is that the duty to be fair might include requirements which were not part of the traditional concept of natural justice, for example a duty to act on evidence (see *R* v *Deputy Industrial Injuries Commissioner, ex parte Moore* [1965] 1 QB 456).

In the notes and questions which follow, reference will be made to the duty to be fair. The cases cited will, however, contain references to both concepts for the reasons explained earlier.

What then is required of the duty to be fair? As Lord Fraser indicated in *Council of the Civil Service Unions* v *Minister for the Civil Service*, the requirements of fairness depend on all the circumstances of the case. In an earlier case, *Russell* v *Duke of Norfolk* [1949] 1 All ER 109, in which the term natural justice was used, Tucker LJ stated, at p. 118:

... There are, in my view, no words which are of universal application to every kind of inquiry and every kind of domestic tribunal. The requirements of natural justice must depend on the circumstances of the case, the nature of the inquiry, the rules under which the tribunal is acting, the subject matter which is being dealt with and so forth. Accordingly, I do not derive much assistance from the definitions of natural justice which have been from time to time used. ...

The requirements of the duty to be fair are generally divided into two general principles, the rule against bias and the right to a fair hearing.

(a) The rule against bias

R v Bow Street Metropolitan Stipendiary Magistrate, ex parte Pinochet Ugarte (No. 2)
[2000] 1 AC 119, House of Lords

The applicant was the former head of state of Chile. Extradition proceedings were brought at the request of a Spanish judge in respect of allegations of crimes against humanity committed when the applicant was President of Chile. Two arrest warrants had been issued by the magistrate, but then quashed in an application for judicial review; however, the quashing of the second was stayed so that an appeal could be heard by the House of Lords on the scope of immunity of a former head of state from arrest and extradition proceedings in the United Kingdom in respect of acts committed while he was head of state. Amnesty International (AI) was permitted to act as a third-party intervenor in these proceedings. By a 3:2 majority the appeal was allowed on 25 November 1998 and the second warrant was restored. Afterwards the applicant learnt that Lord Hoffmann, who was a member of the majority in the appeal before the House of Lords, was a member and chairman of Amnesty International Charity Ltd (AICL), a body which carried out AI's charitable purposes. The applicant petitioned the House to set aside the order of 25 November.

LORD BROWNE-WILKINSON: ... The contention is that there was a real danger or reasonable apprehension or suspicion that Lord Hoffmann might have been biased, that is to say, it is alleged that there is an appearance of bias not actual bias.

The fundamental principle is that a man may not be a judge in his own cause. This principle, as developed by the courts, has two very similar but not identical implications. First it may be applied literally: if a judge is in fact a party to the litigation or has a financial or proprietary interest in its outcome then he is indeed sitting as a judge in his own cause. In that case, the mere fact that he is a party to the action or has a financial or proprietary interest in its outcome is sufficient to cause his automatic disqualification. The second application of the principle is where a judge is not a party to the suit and does not have a financial interest in its outcome, but in some other way his conduct or behaviour may give rise to a suspicion that he is not impartial, for example because of his friendship with a party. This second type of case is not strictly speaking an application of the principle that a man must not be judge in his own cause, since the judge will not normally be himself benefiting, but providing a benefit for another by failing to be impartial.

In my judgment, this case falls within the first category of case, viz. where the judge is disqualified because he is a judge in his own cause. In such a case, once it is shown that the judge is himself a party to the cause, or has a relevant interest in its subject matter, he is disqualified without any investigation into whether there was a likelihood or suspicion of bias. The mere fact of his interest is sufficient to disqualify him unless he has made sufficient disclosure: see Shetreet, *Judges on Trial* (1976), p. 303; De Smith, Woolf and Jowell, *Judicial Review of Administrative Action*, 5th ed. (1995) p. 525, I will call this 'automatic disqualification'.

In *Dimes* v *Proprietors of Grand Junction Canal* (1852) 3 HL Cas 759, the then Lord Chancellor, Lord Cottenham, owned a substantial shareholding in the defendant canal which was an incorporated body. In the action the Lord Chancellor sat on appeal from the Vice-Chancellor, whose judgment in favour of the company he affirmed. There was an appeal to your Lordships' House on the grounds that the Lord Chancellor was disqualified. Their Lordships consulted the judges who advised, at p. 786, that Lord Cottenham was disqualified from sitting as a judge in the cause because he had an interest in the suit … The authorities cited in the *Dimes* case show how the principle developed. The starting-point was the case in which a judge was indeed purporting to decide a case in which he was a party. This was held to be absolutely prohibited. That absolute prohibition was then extended to cases where, although not nominally a party, the judge had an interest in the outcome.

The importance of this point in the present ease is this. Neither AI, nor AICL have any financial interest in the outcome of this litigation. We are here confronted, as was Lord Hoffmann, with a novel situation where the outcome of the litigation did not lead to financial benefit to anyone. The interest of AI in the litigation was not financial: it was its interest in achieving the trial and possible conviction of Senator Pinochet for crimes against humanity.

By seeking to intervene in this appeal and being allowed so to intervene, in practice AI became a party to the appeal. Therefore if, in the circumstances, it is right to treat Lord Hoffmann as being the alter ego of AI and therefore a judge in his own cause, then he must have been automatically disqualified on the grounds that he was a party to the appeal. Alternatively, even if it be not right to say that Lord Hoffmann was a party to the appeal as such, the question then arises whether, in non-financial litigation, anything other than a financial or proprietary interest in the outcome is sufficient automatically to disqualify a man from sitting as judge in the cause …

Then is this a case in which it can be said that Lord Hoffmann had an 'interest' which must lead to his automatic disqualification? Hitherto only pecuniary and proprietary interests have led to automatic disqualification. [T]here is no good reason in principle for so limiting automatic disqualification. The rationale of the whole rule is that a man cannot be a judge in his own cause. In civil litigation the matters in issue will normally have an economic impact; therefore a judge is automatically disqualified if he stands to make a financial gain as a consequence of his own decision of the case. But if, as in the present case, the matter at issue does not relate to money or economic advantage but is concerned with the promotion of the cause, the rationale disqualifying a judge applies just as much if the judge's decision will lead to the promotion of a cause in which the judge is involved together with one of the parties. Thus in my opinion if Lord Hoffmann had been at member of AI he would have been automatically disqualified because of his non-pecuniary interest in establishing that Senator Pinochet was not entitled to immunity …

The substance of the matter is that AI, AIL and AICL are all various parts of an entity or movement working in different fields towards the same goals. If the absolute impartiality of the judiciary is to be maintained, there must be a rule which automatically disqualifies a judge who is involved, whether personally or as a director of a company, in promoting the same causes in the same organisation as is a party to the suit. There is no room for fine distinctions if Lord Hewart CJ's famous dictum is to be observed: it is 'of fundamental importance that justice should not only be done, but should manifestly and undoubtedly be seen to be done': see *Rex* v *Sussex Justices, Ex parte McCarthy* [1924] 1 KB 256, 259.

…

It is important not to overstate what is being decided. It was suggested in argument that a decision setting aside the order of 25 November 1998 would lead to a position where judges would be unable to sit on cases involving charities in whose work they are involved. It is suggested that, because of such involvement, a judge would be disqualified. That is not correct. The facts of this present case are exceptional. The critical elements are (1) that AI was a party to the appeal; (2) that AI was joined in order to argue for a particular result; (3) the judge was a director of a charity closely allied to AI and sharing, in this respect, AI's objects. Only in cases where a judge is taking an active role as trustee or director of a charity which is closely allied to and acting with a party to the litigation should a judge normally be concerned either to recuse himself or disclose the position to the parties. However, there may well be other exceptional cases in which the judge would be well advised to disclose a possible interest …

Election, waiver, abuse of process

Mr Alun Jones submitted that by raising with the Home Secretary the possible bias of Lord Hoffmann as a ground for not authorising the extradition to proceed, Senator Pinochet had elected to choose the Home Secretary rather than your Lordships' House as the arbiter as to whether such bias did or did not exist. Consequently, he submitted, Senator Pinochet had waived his right to petition your Lordships and, by doing so immediately after the Home Secretary had rejected the submission, was committing an abuse of the process of the House.

This submission is bound to fail on a number of different grounds, of which I need mention only two. First, Senator Pinochet would only be put to his election as between two alternative courses to adopt. I cannot see that there are two such courses in the present case, since the Home Secretary had no power in the matter. He could not set aside the order of 25 November and as long as such order stood, the Home Secretary was bound to accept it as stating the law. Secondly, all three concepts—election, waiver and abuse of process require that the person said to have elected etc. has acted freely and in full knowledge of the facts. Not until 8 December 1998 did Senator Pinochet's solicitors know anything of Lord Hoffmann's position as a director and chairman of AICL. Even then they did not know anything about AICL and its constitution. To say that by hurriedly notifying the Home Secretary of the contents of the letter from AI's solicitors Senator Pinochet had elected to pursue the point solely before the Home Secretary is unrealistic. Senator Pinochet had not yet had time to find out anything about the circumstances beyond the bare facts disclosed in the letter.

...

Petition granted.

Locabail (UK) Ltd v Bayfield Properties Ltd

[2000] QB 451, Court of Appeal

LORD BINGHAM of CORNHILL CJ, LORD WOOLF MR and SIR RICHARD SCOTT V-C: ...

25. It would be dangerous and futile to attempt to define or list the factors which may or may not give rise to a real danger of bias. Everything will depend on the facts, which may include the nature of the issue to be decided. We cannot, however, conceive of circumstances in which an objection could be soundly based on the religion, ethnic or national origin, gender, age, class, means or sexual orientation of the judge. Nor, at any rate ordinarily, could an objection be soundly based on the judge's social or educational or service or employment background or history, nor that of any member of the judge's family; or previous political associations; or membership of social or sporting or charitable bodies; or Masonic associations; or previous judicial decisions; or extra-curricular utterances (whether in textbooks, lectures, speeches, articles, interviews, reports or responses to consultation papers); or previous receipt of instructions to act for or against any party, solicitor or advocate engaged in a case before him; or membership of the same Inn, circuit, local Law Society or chambers (*KFTCIC* v *Icori Estero SpA* (Court of Appeal of Paris, 28 June 1991, International Arbitration Report, vol 6, 8/91)). By contrast, a real danger of bias might well be thought to arise if there were personal friendship or animosity between the judge and any member of the public involved in the case; or if the judge were closely acquainted with any member of the public involved in the case, particularly if the credibility of that individual could be significant in the decision of the case; or if, in a case where the credibility of any individual were an issue to be decided by the judge, he had in a previous case rejected the evidence of that person in such outspoken terms as to throw doubt on his ability to approach such person's evidence with an open mind on any later occasion; or if on any question at issue in the proceedings before him the judge had expressed views, particularly in the course of the hearing, in such extreme and unbalanced terms as to throw doubt on his ability to try the issue with an objective judicial mind (see *Vakauta* v *Kelly* (1989) 167 CLR 568); or if, for any other reason, there were real ground for doubting the ability of the judge to

ignore extraneous considerations, prejudices and predilections and bring an objective judgment to bear on the issues before him. The mere fact that a judge, earlier in the same case or in a previous case, had commented adversely on a party or witness, or found the evidence of a party or witness to be unreliable, would not without more found a sustainable objection. In most cases, we think, the answer, one way or the other, will be obvious. But if in any case there is real ground for doubt, that doubt should be resolved in favour of recusal. We repeat: every application must be decided on the facts and circumstances of the individual case. The greater the passage of time between the event relied on as showing a danger of bias and the case in which the objection is raised, the weaker (other things being equal) the objection will be.

26. We do not consider that waiver, in this context, raises special problems (*Shrager* v *Basil Dighton Ltd* [1924] 1 KB 274 at 293; *R* v *Essex Justices, ex p Perkins* [1927] 2 KB 475 at 489; *Ex parte Pinochet (No. 2)* [2000] 1 AC 119, 136–137, the *Auckland Casino* case [1995] 1 NZLR 142 at 150–151 and *Vakauta* v *Kelly* (1989) 167 CLR 568 at 572, 577). If, appropriate disclosure having been made by the judge, a party raises no objection to the judge hearing or continuing to hear a case, that party cannot thereafter complain of the matter disclosed as giving rise to a real danger of bias. It would be unjust to the other party and undermine both the reality and the appearance of justice to allow him to do so. What disclosure is appropriate depends in large measure on the stage that the matter has reached. If, before a hearing has begun, the judge is alerted to some matter which might, depending on the full facts, throw doubt on his fitness to sit, the judge should in our view inquire into the full facts, so far as they are ascertainable, in order to make disclosure in the light of them. But if a judge has embarked on a hearing in ignorance of a matter which emerges during the hearing, it is in our view enough if the judge discloses what he then knows. He has no obligation to disclose what he does not know. Nor is he bound to fill any gaps in his knowledge which, if filled, might provide stronger grounds for objection to his hearing or continuing to hear the case. If, of course, he does make further inquiry and learn additional facts not known to him before, then he must make disclosure of those facts also. It is, however, generally undesirable that hearings should be aborted unless the reality or the appearance of justice requires that they should.

NOTES

1. The specially staffed Court of Appeal was here dealing with five applications for permission to appeal on the ground of bias of the judge. The listing and hearing together of these applications enabled the court to give this guidance. In *Locabail (UK) Ltd* v *Bayfield Properties Ltd, Locabail (UK) Ltd* v *Waldorf Investment Corp; Williams* v *HM Inspector of Taxes*, and *R* v *Bristol Betting and Gaming Licensing Committee, ex parte O'Callaghan*, permission to appeal was not granted. In *Timmins* v *Gormley*, the defendant in a personal injuries case successfully argued that the articles in legal publications written by the recorder who heard the case, in which he expressed pronounced pro-claimant anti-insurer views, allowed for the possibility that the recorder might lean in favour of the claimant and against the defendant. The Court held that it was not wrong for the recorder to be engaged in writing but that it is 'inappropriate for a judge to use intemperate language about subjects on which he has adjudicated or will have to adjudicate'.
2. There has been debate over what is the appropriate test for apparent bias.

Porter v *Magill*
[2001] UKHL 67, [2002] 2 AC 357, House of Lords

LORD HOPE OF CRAIGHEAD: …

101. The English courts have been reluctant, for obvious reasons, to depart from the test which Lord Goff of Chieveley so carefully formulated in *R* v *Gough*. In *R* v *Bow Street Metropolitan Stipendiary Magistrate, Ex p Pinochet Ugarte (No 2)* [2000] 1 AC 119, 136A–C Lord Browne-Wilkinson said that it was unnecessary in that case to determine whether it needed to be reviewed in the light of subsequent decisions in Canada, New Zealand and Australia. I said, at p 142F–G, that, although the tests in Scotland

and England were described differently, their application was likely in practice to lead to results that were so similar as to be indistinguishable. The Court of Appeal, having examined the question whether the "real danger" test might lead to a different result from that which the informed observer would reach on the same facts, concluded in *Locabail (UK) Ltd v Bayfield Properties Ltd* [2000] QB 451, 477 that in the overwhelming majority of cases the application of the two tests would lead to the same outcome.

102. In my opinion however it is now possible to set this debate to rest. The Court of Appeal took the opportunity in *In re Medicaments and Related Classes of Goods (No. 2)* [2001] 1 WLR 700 to reconsider the whole question. Lord Phillips of Worth Matravers MR, giving the judgment of the court, observed, at p 711A–B, that the precise test to be applied when determining whether a decision should be set aside on account of bias had given rise to difficulty, reflected in judicial decisions that had appeared in conflict, and that the attempt to resolve that conflict in *R v Gough* had not commanded universal approval. At p 711B–C he said that, as the alternative test had been thought to be more closely in line with Strasbourg jurisprudence which since 2 October 2000 the English courts were required to take into account, the occasion should now be taken to review *R v Gough* to see whether the test it lays down is, indeed, in conflict with Strasbourg jurisprudence. Having conducted that review he summarised the court's conclusions, at pp 726H–727C:

> 85 When the Strasbourg jurisprudence is taken into account, we believe that a modest adjustment of the test in *R v Gough* is called for, which makes it plain that it is, in effect, no different from the test applied in most of the Commonwealth and in Scotland. The court must first ascertain all the circumstances which have a bearing on the suggestion that the judge was biased. It must then ask whether those circumstances would lead a fair-minded and informed observer to conclude that there was a real possibility, or a real danger, the two being the same, that the tribunal was biased.

103. I respectfully suggest that your Lordships should now approve the modest adjustment of the test in *R v Gough* set out in that paragraph. It expresses in clear and simple language a test which is in harmony with the objective test which the Strasbourg court applies when it is considering whether the circumstances give rise to a reasonable apprehension of bias. It removes any possible conflict with the test which is now applied in most Commonwealth countries and in Scotland. I would however delete from it the reference to "a real danger". Those words no longer serve a useful purpose here, and they are not used in the jurisprudence of the Strasbourg court. The question is whether the fair-minded and informed observer, having considered the facts, would conclude that there was a real possibility that the tribunal was biased.

R v Abdroikov, R v Green, R v Williamson

[2007] UKHL 37, [2007] 1 WLR 2679, House of Lords

Bias was raised to challenge convictions where a member of the jury in criminal trials was a police officer in the first two cases, and a solicitor in the Crown Prosecution Service in the third.

LORD BINGHAM OF CORNHILL: . . . 25. In the case of the first appellant, it was unfortunate that the identity of the officer became known at such a late stage in the trial, and on very short notice to the judge and defence counsel. But had the matter been ventilated at the outset of the trial, it is difficult to see what argument defence counsel could have urged other than the general undesirability of police officers serving on juries, a difficult argument to advance in face of the parliamentary enactment. It was not a case which turned on a contest between the evidence of the police and that of the appellant, and it would have been hard to suggest that the case was one in which unconscious prejudice, even if present, would have been likely to operate to the disadvantage of the appellant, and it makes no difference that the officer was the foreman of the jury. In the event, confronted with this question at very short notice, defence counsel raised no objection. I conclude, not without unease, that having regard to the parliamentary enactment the Court of Appeal reached the right conclusion in this case, and I would dismiss the appeal.

26. The second appellant's case is different. Here, there was a crucial dispute on the evidence between the appellant and the police sergeant, and the sergeant and the juror, although not personally known to each other, shared the same local service background. In this context the instinct (however unconscious) of a police officer on the jury to prefer the evidence of a brother officer to that of a drug-addicted defendant would be judged by the fair-minded and informed observer to be a real and possible source of unfairness, beyond the reach of standard judicial warnings and directions. The second appellant was not tried by a tribunal which was and appeared to be impartial. It cannot be supposed that Parliament intended to infringe the rule in the *Sussex Justices* case, still less to do so without express language. I would allow this appeal, and quash the second appellant's conviction.

27. In the case of the third appellant, no possible criticism is to be made of Mr McKay-Smith, who acted in strict compliance with the guidance given to him and left the matter to the judge. But the judge gave no serious consideration to the objection of defence counsel, who himself had little opportunity to review the law on this subject. It must, perhaps, be doubted whether Lord Justice Auld or Parliament contemplated that employed Crown prosecutors would sit as jurors in prosecutions brought by their own authority. It is in my opinion clear that justice is not seen to be done if one discharging the very important neutral role of juror is a full-time, salaried, long-serving employee of the prosecutor. This is a much stronger case than *Pullar v United Kingdom* (1996) 22 EHRR 391 (see para 17 above): it is as if, on the facts of that case, F had been employed in the department of the procurator fiscal. Had that been so, one may be sure the court would have agreed with the commission. The third appellant was entitled to be tried by a tribunal that was and appeared to be impartial, and in my opinion he was not. The consequence is that his convictions must be quashed. This is a most unfortunate outcome, since the third appellant was accused of very grave crimes, of which he may have been guilty. But even a guilty defendant is entitled to be tried by an impartial tribunal and the consequence is inescapable. I would allow the appeal and remit the case to the Court of Appeal with an invitation to quash the convictions and rule on any application which may be made for a retrial.

NOTE: Lords Rodger and Carswell dissented on the second and third appeals arguing that the Criminal Justice Act 2003 in amending the qualifications on jurors had added to the existing risk that people of similar backgrounds to parties in a trial might unconsciously favour them and that the fair-minded and informed observer would have realized that given there are 12 members of a jury, while there is a possible risk of one juror being partial this does not meant that there is a real possibility that the jury is incapable of reaching an impartial verdict.

(b) Right to a fair hearing

Ridge v Baldwin
[1964] AC 40, House of Lords

Following his arrest and charge for conspiracy to obstruct the course of justice, Ridge, the Chief Constable of Brighton, was suspended from duty. At his trial Ridge was acquitted but the judge was critical of his leadership of the force. A further charge of corruption was brought against Ridge and the judge repeated these comments when directing Ridge's acquittal.

Under the Municipal Corporations Act 1882, s. 191(4) a watch committee could dismiss 'any borough constable whom they think negligent in the discharge of his duty, or otherwise unfit for the same'. After Ridge's acquittal the watch committee met and decided that Ridge should be dismissed. Ridge was not asked to attend the meeting, but at the request of his solicitor the watch committee reconvened some days later and decided not to change its original decision. Before this second meeting Ridge gave notice of appeal to the Home Secretary against the original decision under the Police (Appeals) Act 1927. He also stated, however, that this was without prejudice to his right to argue that the procedure adopted by the committee was in breach of the relevant statutory provisions and of the rules of natural justice. The Home Secretary dismissed his appeal and Ridge appealed to the courts, seeking a declaration that the purported dismissal was *ultra vires*. Ridge, whose case failed before Streatfield J and the Court of Appeal, appealed to the House of Lords. The following extract deals with his claim that there was a breach of natural justice.

LORD REID: The appellant's case is that in proceeding under the Act of 1882 the watch committee were bound to observe what are commonly called the principles of natural justice. Before attempting to reach any decision they were bound to inform him of the grounds on which they proposed to act and give him a fair opportunity of being heard in his own defence. The authorities on the applicability of the principles of natural justice are in some confusion, and so I find it necessary to examine this matter in some detail. The principle audi alteram partem goes back many centuries in our law and appears in a multitude of judgments of judges of the highest authority. In modern times opinions have sometimes been expressed to the effect that natural justice is so vague as to be almost meaningless. But I would regard these as tainted by the perennial fallacy that because something cannot be cut and dried or nicely weighed and measured therefore it does not exist. … It appears to me that one reason why the authorities on natural justice have been found difficult to reconcile is that insufficient attention has been paid to the great difference between various kinds of cases in which it has been sought to apply the principle. What a minister ought to do in considering objections to a scheme may be very different from what a watch committee ought to do in considering whether to dismiss a chief constable. So I shall deal first with cases of dismissal. These appear to fall into three classes: dismissal of a servant by his master, dismissal from an office held during pleasure, and dismissal from an office where there must be something against a man to warrant his dismissal.

Lord Reid then went on to consider the three different cases and concluded that, in the case of the third category (into which *Ridge* fell), there was an unbroken line of authority to the effect that an officer cannot lawfully be dismissed without first telling him what is alleged against him and hearing his defence or explanation.

Stopping there, I would think that authority was wholly in favour of the appellant, but the respondent's argument was mainly based on what has been said in a number of fairly recent cases dealing with different subject-matter. Those cases deal with decisions by ministers, officials and bodies of various kinds which adversely affected property rights or privileges of persons who had no opportunity or no proper opportunity of presenting their cases before the decisions were given. And it is necessary to examine those cases for another reason. The question which was or ought to have been considered by the watch committee on March 7, 1958, was not a simple question whether or not the appellant should be dismissed. There were three possible courses open to the watch committee— reinstating the appellant as chief constable, dismissing him, or requiring him to resign. The difference between the latter two is that dismissal involved forfeiture of pension rights, whereas requiring him to resign did not. Indeed, it is now clear that the appellant's real interest in this appeal is to try to save his pension rights. …

I would start an examination of the authorities dealing with property rights and privileges with *Cooper v Wandsworth Board of Works* (1863) 14 CBNS 180. Where an owner had failed to give proper notice to the Board they had under an Act of 1855 authority to demolish any building he had erected and recover the cost from him. This action was brought against the board because they had used that power without giving the owner an opportunity of being heard. The board maintained that their discretion to order demolition was not a judicial discretion and that any appeal should have been to the Metropolitan Board of Works. But the Court decided unanimously in favour of the owner. …

[Lord Reid examined a number of other authorities and continued.] … It appears to me that if the present case had arisen thirty or forty years ago the court would have had no difficulty in deciding this issue in favour of the appellant on these authorities which I have cited. So far as I am aware none of these authorities has ever been disapproved or even doubted. Yet the Court of Appeal have decided this issue against the appellant on more recent authorities which apparently justify that result. How has this come about?

At least three things appear to have contributed. In the first place there have been many cases where it has been sought to apply the principles of natural justice to the wider duties imposed on Ministers and other organs of government by modern legislation. For reasons which I shall attempt to state, it has been held that those principles have a limited application in such cases and those limitations have tended to be reflected in other decisions on matters to which in principle they do not appear to me to apply. Secondly, again for reasons which I shall attempt to state, those principles have been held to have a limited application in cases arising out of war-time legislation; and again such limitations have tended to be reflected in other cases. And, thirdly, there has, I think, been a misunderstanding of the judgment of Atkin LJ in *Rex* v *Electricity Commissioners ex parte London Electricity Joint Committee Co.* [1924] 1 KB 171.

In cases of the kind I have been dealing with the Board of Works or the Governor of the club committee was dealing with a single isolated case. It was not deciding, like a judge in a lawsuit, what were the rights of the person before it. But it was deciding how he should be treated—something analogous to a judge's duty in imposing a penalty. No doubt policy would play some part in the decision—but so it might when a judge is imposing a sentence. So it was easy to say that such a body is performing a quasi-judicial task in considering and deciding such a matter, and to require it to observe the essentials of all proceedings of a judicial character—the principles of natural justice.

Sometimes the functions of a minister or department may also be of that character, and then the rules of natural justice can apply in much the same way. But more often their functions are of a very different character. If a minister is considering whether to make such a scheme for, say, an important new road, his primary concern will not be with the damage which its construction will do to the rights of individual owners of land. He will have to consider all manner of questions of public interest and, it may be, a number of alternative schemes. He cannot be prevented from attaching more importance to the fulfilment of his policy than to the fate of individual objectors, and it would be quite wrong for the courts to say that the minister should or could act in the same kind of way as a board of works deciding whether a house should be pulled down. And there is another important difference. As explained in *Local Government Board* v *Arlidge* [1915] AC 120 a minister cannot do everything himself. His officers will have to gather and sift all the facts, including objections by individuals, and no individual can complain if the ordinary accepted methods of carrying on public business do not give him as good protection as would be given by the principles of natural justice in a different kind of case.

Lord Reid continued to discuss cases decided under the Defence Regulations made in wartime and concluded that the fact that the rules of natural justice were not applied should not be regarded as of any great weight in cases arising under the 1882 Act because it was a reasonable inference in the former case that it was Parliament's intention to exclude the application of the rules of natural justice.

The matter has been further complicated by what I believe to be a misunderstanding of a much-quoted passage in the judgment of Atkin LJ in *Rex* v *Electricity Commissioners, ex parte London Electricity Joint Committee Co.* [1925] 1 KB 171. He said ' ... the operation of the writs [of prohibition and certiorari] has extended to control the proceedings of bodies which do not claim to be, and would not be recognised as courts of justice. Wherever any body of persons having legal authority to determine questions affecting the rights of subjects, and having the duty to act judicially, act in excess of their legal authority, they are subject to the controlling jurisdiction of the King's Bench Division exercised in these writs.'

A gloss was put on this by Lord Hewart CJ in *Rex* v *Legislative Committee of the Church Assembly, ex parte Haynes-Smith* [1928] 1 KB 411. ... Lord Hewart said, having quoted the passage from Atkin LJ's judgment: ' ... It is to be observed that in the last sentence which I have quoted ... the word is not "or", but "and". In order that a body may satisfy the required test it is not enough that it should have legal authority to determine questions affecting the rights of subjects; there must be superadded to that characteristic the further characteristic that the body has the duty to act judicially. The duty to act judicially is an ingredient which, if the test is to be satisfied, must be present. As these writs in the earlier days were issued only to bodies which without any harshness of construction could be called, and naturally would be called courts, so also today these writs do not issue except to bodies which act or are under a duty to act in a judicial capacity.'

... If Lord Hewart meant that it is never enough that a body simply has a duty to determine what the rights of an individual should be, but that there must always be something more to impose on it a duty to act judicially before it can be found to observe the principles of natural justice, then that appears to me impossible to reconcile with the earlier authorities. ...

There is not a word in Atkin LJ's judgment to suggest disapproval of the earlier line of authority which I have cited. On the contrary, he goes further than those authorities. I have already stated my view that it is more difficult for the courts to control an exercise of power on a large scale where the treatment to be meted out to a particular individual is only one of many matters to be considered. This was a case of that kind, and, if Atkin LJ was prepared to infer a judicial element from the nature of the power in this case, he could hardly disapprove such an inference when the power relates solely to the treatment of a particular individual.

I would sum up my opinion in this way. Between 1882 and the making of police regulations in 1920, section 191(4) had to be applied to every kind of case. The respondents' contention is that, even where there was a doubtful question whether a constable was guilty of a particular act of misconduct, the watch committee were under no obligation to hear his defence before dismissing him. In my judgment it is abundantly clear from the authorities I have quoted that at that time the courts would have rejected any such contention. In later cases dealing with different subject-matter opinions have been expressed in wide terms so as to appear to conflict with those earlier authorities. But learned judges who expressed those opinions generally had no power to overrule those authorities, and in any event it is a salutary rule that a judge is not to be assumed to have intended to overrule or disapprove of an authority which has not been cited to him and which he does not even mention. So I would hold that the power of dismissal in the Act of 1882 could not then have been exercised and cannot now be exercised until the watch committee have informed the constable of the grounds on which they propose to proceed and given him a proper opportunity to present his case in defence. ...

Lord Reid decided that this failure was not made good by the reconvening of the watch committee because this did not provide for a full rehearing and granted a declaration that the dismissal was unlawful. Lord Morris, Lord Hodson, and Lord Devlin delivered judgments in favour of allowing the appeal. Lord Evershed delivered a speech in favour of dismissing the appeal.

NOTES

1. The significance of *Ridge* v *Baldwin* is that it helped to free the rules of natural justice from strict limitations which had been imposed in earlier decisions, in particular from the requirement that the decision-making body must be under a duty to act judicially. The decision in the case may be compared with that in *Nakkuda Ali* v *Jayaratne* [1951] AC 66 which was disapproved in *Ridge* v *Baldwin*.
2. The requirements of a fair hearing depend on all the circumstances. They may include:
   (a) the right to notice, but restrictions may be placed on this where the public interest so requires (see, for example, *R* v *Gaming Board of Great Britain, ex parte Benaim and Khaida* [1970] 2 QB 417);
   (b) the right to make representations, whether in writing or orally; oral hearings are not required in all circumstances where the rules of natural justice apply (see, for example, *Lloyd* v *McMahon* [1987] 1 All ER 1118);
   (c) where an oral hearing is held—
       (i) the right to comment on any evidence presented;
       (ii) where evidence is given orally by witnesses, the right to put questions to those witnesses (see, for example, *R* v *Deputy Industrial Injuries Commissioner, ex parte Moore* [1965] 1 QB 456);
   (d) legal representation (see later in this section at pp. 537–38).

In order to understand the flexibility of the principles, consider the following cases.

R v Board of Visitors of Hull Prison, ex parte St Germain (No. 2)
[1979] 1 WLR 1401, Divisional Court

Following a riot in Hull Prison in 1976, numerous charges of breaches of the Prison Rules 1964 were heard by the prison's board of visitors. During the hearing reference was made to a number of statements by prison officers, who were not available to give evidence, to support the evidence given by a witness. Seven of the prisoners who were found guilty of offences against prison discipline sought an order of *certiorari* on the grounds that the proceedings before the prison's board of visitors breached the rules of natural justice. The following extracts relate to the prisoners' complaint that hearsay evidence was taken into account.

GEOFFREY LANE LJ: … [W]e now turn to the suggestion that hearsay evidence is not permissible in a hearing before a board of visitors. It is of course common ground that the board of visitors must base their decisions on evidence. But must such evidence be restricted to that which would be admissible in a criminal court of law? Viscount Simon LC in *General Medical Council* v *Spackman* [1943] AC 627, 634, considered there was no such restriction. That was also clearly the view of the Privy Council in *Ceylon University* v *Fernando* [1960] 1 WLR 223, 234. The matter was dealt with in more detail by Diplock LJ in *Reg.* v *Deputy Industrial Injuries Commissioner ex parte Moore* [1965] 1 QB 456, 488:

> These technical rules of evidence, however, form no part of the rules of natural justice. The require-ment that a person exercising quasi-judicial functions must base his decision on evidence means no more than it must be based upon material which tends logically to show the existence or non-existence of facts relevant to the issue to be determined, or to show the likelihood or unlikelihood of the occurrence of some future event the occurrence of which would be relevant. It means that he must not spin a coin or consult an astrologer, but he may take into account any material which, as a matter of reason, has some probative value in the sense mentioned above. If it is capable of having any probative value, the weight to be attached to it is a matter for the person to whom Parliament has entrusted the responsibility of deciding the issue. The supervisory jurisdiction of the High Court does not entitle it to usurp this responsibility and to substitute its own view for his.

However, it is clear that the entitlement of the board to admit hearsay evidence is subject to the over-riding obligation to provide the accused with a fair hearing. Depending upon the facts of the particular case and the nature of the hearsay evidence provided to the board, the obligation to give the accused a fair chance to exculpate himself, or a fair opportunity to controvert the charge—to quote the phrases used in the passages cited above—or a proper or full opportunity of presenting his case—to quote the language of section 47 or rule 49—may oblige the board not only to inform the accused of the hear-say evidence but also to give the accused a sufficient opportunity to deal with that evidence. Again, depending upon the nature of that evidence and the particular circumstances of the case, a sufficient opportunity to deal with the hearsay evidence may well involve the cross-examination of the witness whose evidence is initially before the board in the form of hearsay.

We again take by way of example the case in which the defence is an alibi. The prisoner contends that he was not the man identified on the roof. He, the prisoner, was at the material time elsewhere. In short the prisoner has been mistakenly identified. The evidence of identification given by way of hearsay may be of the 'fleeting glance' type as exemplified by the well-known case of *Reg* v *Turnbull* [1977] QB 224. The prisoner may well wish to elicit by way of questions all manner of detail, e.g. the poorness of the light, the state of the confusion, the brevity of the observation, the absence of any contemporaneous record, etc., all designed to show the unreliability of the witness. To deprive him of the opportunity of cross-examination would be tantamount to depriving him of a fair hearing.

We appreciate that there may well be occasions when the burden of calling the witness whose hearsay evidence is readily available may impose a near impossible burden upon the board. However, it has not been suggested that hearsay evidence should be resorted to in the total absence of any first-hand evidence. In the instant cases hearsay evidence was only resorted to supplement the first-hand evidence and this is the usual practice. Accordingly where a prisoner desires to dispute the hearsay evidence and for this purpose to question the witness, and where there are insuperable or very grave difficulties in arranging for his attendance, the board should refuse to admit that evidence, or, if it has already come to their notice, should expressly dismiss it from their consideration. ...

The findings of guilt which were based on hearsay evidence were quashed by orders of certiorari.

R v *Commissioner for Racial Equality, ex parte Cottrell and Rothon*
[1980] 1 WLR 1580, Court of Appeal

The Commission for Racial Equality received a complaint that a firm of estate agents, Messrs Cottrell & Rothon, was committing acts of unlawful discrimination in the course of its business as an estate agent. Under s. 48 of the Race Relations Act 1976, the Commission nominated two of its members to conduct an investigation. When the Commission were minded to issue a non-discrimination notice, they notified the firm under s. 58(5) of the Act of their intention, and gave the firm an opportunity to make written and oral representations to the nominated commissioners. The firm took the opportunity to make both oral and written representations. At the hearing before the commissioners, no witnesses were available to give evidence to sustain the complaint or be cross-examined on behalf of the firm. The Commission decided to issue the notice. The firm applied for an order of *certiorari* on the ground, *inter alia*, that witnesses ought to have been available for cross-examination.

LORD LANE CJ: Of course there is a wealth of authority on what are and what are not the rules of natural justice. The rules have been described in various ways, as an 'unruly horse,' I think, in one decision, and there is no doubt that what may be the rules of natural justice in one case may well not be the rules of natural justice in another. As has frequently been said, and there is no harm in repeating it, all that the rules of natural justice mean is that the proceedings must be conducted in a way which is fair to the firm in this case, fair in all the circumstances. All the circumstances include a number of different considerations: first of all, the penalties, if any. There are no penalties under the Race Relations Act in the form of fines or imprisonment or anything like that, but what [counsel for the firm] has drawn to our attention, quite correctly, is that under the terms of the Estate Agents Act 1979 (and no one has been able to discover whether that has come into operation yet or not) there is no doubt that a person on whom a non-discriminatory notice has been served may, if he is an estate agent, suffer, if certain procedural steps are taken, grave disadvantages because it is open, under a number of safeguards into which I do not propose to go, for the Director General of Fair Trading to take steps to see that a person against whom this action had been taken under the Race Relations Act 1976 does not practise in business as an estate agent. Of course it is a very long call from saying that a person who has this non-discriminatory notice served on him is necessarily going to suffer in his business by the action of the Director General of Fair Trading. Many procedures have to be gone through before that can take place, but there is a danger there, and that is one of the matters which is a circumstance to be taken into account.

The next matter, and possibly the most important matter, is the nature of the provisions of the Race Relations Act 1976 itself. I have read sufficient of the contents of section 58 of that Act to indicate that there is no mention in that section, or indeed in any other section, of any right to cross-examine any of the witnesses. That perhaps is a surprising omission if it was the intention of Parliament to allow a person in the position of the firm in this case the full panoply of legal rights which would take place at a judicial hearing.

It seems to me that there are degrees of judicial hearing, and those degrees run from the borders of pure administration to the borders of the full hearing of a criminal cause or matter in the Crown Court. It does not profit one to try to pigeon-hole the particular set of circumstances either into the administrative pigeon-hole or into the judicial pigeon-hole. Each case will inevitably differ, and one must ask oneself what is the basic nature of the proceeding which was going on here. It seems to me that, basically, this was an investigation being carried out by the commission. It is true that in the course of the investigation the commission may form a view, but it does not seem to me that is a proceeding which requires, in the name of fairness, any right in the firm in this case to be able to cross-examine witnesses whom the commission have seen and from whom they have taken statements. ...

[Counsel for the firms] sought to derive assistance from some of the passages of the decision of this court in *Reg v Hull Prison Board of Visitors ex parte St Germain* [1979] QB 425, but it seems to me that the decision there was based on facts widely differing from those in the present case. That was truly a judicial proceeding carried out by the prison visitors and the complaint there was that there had been no opportunity to cross-examine prison officers in hotly disputed questions of identity. Speaking for myself, I derive little assistance from any dicta in that case.

... It seems to me for the reasons I have endeavoured to set out that in this case there was no breach of the rules of fairness in that cross-examination was not permitted or that the witnesses did not attend. ...

Woolf J agreed with Lord Lane LJ.

R v Army Board of the Defence Council, ex parte Anderson
[1991] 3 WLR 42, Divisional Court

In this case the court had to scrutinize the procedures adopted by the Army Board in deciding upon complaints of racial discrimination by soldiers under the Race Relations Act 1976. (Complaints of racial discrimination in employment are normally dealt with by industrial tribunals but special procedures apply to complaints by soldiers.) The applicant was a former soldier who alleged that he had been subjected to forms of racial abuse which caused him to go absent without leave. The papers relating to the complaint were seen separately by two members of the Army Board who reached individual conclusions that, although there was some truth in the applicant's claim, there was no basis for making an apology to him or awarding him compensation. The applicant's requests for disclosure of documents relating to investigations into his complaints were refused, as was his request for an oral hearing. He applied for judicial review of the Board's decision.

TAYLOR LJ: ...

Procedural requirements

What procedural requirements are necessary to achieve fairness when the Army Board considers a complaint of this kind? In addressing this issue, counsel made much of the distinction between judicial and administrative functions. Were it necessary to decide in those terms the functions of the Army Board when considering a race discrimination complaint, I would characterise it as judicial rather than administrative. The board is required to adjudicate on an alleged breach of a soldier's rights under the 1976 Act and, if it be proved, to take any necessary steps by way of redress. It is accepted that the board has the power, inter alia, to award compensation. A body required to consider and adjudicate upon an alleged breach of statutory rights and to grant redress when necessary seems to me to be exercising an essentially judicial function. It matters not that the body has other functions which are non-judicial: see *R v Secretary of State for the Home Dept, ex p Tarrant* [1985] QB 251, 268.

However, to label the board's function either 'judicial' or 'administrative' for the purpose of determining the appropriate procedural regime is to adopt too inflexible an approach. ...

What, then, are the criteria by which to decide the requirements of fairness in any given proceeding? Authoritative guidance as to this was given by Lord Bridge in *Lloyd v McMahon* [1987] AC 625, 702. He said:

My Lords, the so-called rules of natural justice are not engraved on tablets of stone. To use the phrase which better expresses the underlying concept, what the requirements of fairness demand when any body, domestic, administrative or judicial, has to make a decision which will affect the rights of individuals depends on the character of the decision-making body, the kind of decision it has to make and the statutory or other framework in which it operates. In particular, it is well established that when a statute has conferred on any body the power to make decisions affecting individuals, the courts will not only require the procedure prescribed by the statute to be followed, but will readily imply so much and no more to be introduced by way of additional procedural safeguards as will ensure the attainment of fairness.

Applying these principles to the present case, the character of the Army Board and its role in this context have already been described. It is pertinent, however, to note that its decision is final apart from the possibility of judicial review. There is no appeal from its findings. The kind of decision it has to make has also been described. [Mr Sedley, counsel for the applicant] argues from that and from the statutory framework that all the procedural features to be found in a court trial are required—full discovery of documents, an oral hearing and cross-examination. As to the statutory framework, he points out that complaints of racial discrimination under Pt III of the 1976 Act relating to goods and services go before the county court with all the incidents of court procedure. Most civilian complaints of racial discrimination contrary to s. 4 of the 1976 Act go to an industrial tribunal under s. 54(1). There they are subject to rules requiring the procedures Mr Sedley claims here. Thus, if Mr Anderson had been seeking entry to the army, and had been turned down on allegedly racial grounds, his case could have been presented to the industrial tribunal under s. 4(1)(c), and he would have enjoyed all the procedures claimed here. Why should he be worse off simply because he is actually in the army and s. 54(2) requires his complaint to be considered by a different body?

Against this, [Mr Pannick, counsel for the Army Board] contends that Parliament has expressly provided that a soldier's complaint shall not go before an industrial tribunal but shall instead be subject to the army procedures pursuant to s. 181 of the 1955 Act. Parliament must, he submits, have been aware of the procedures normally followed in regard to other complaints under that section. Moreover, had Parliament wished to impose a more rigid and rigorous procedure, still in an army context, it could have directed that complaints of racial discrimination should be subject to s. 135 (board of inquiry), s. 137 (regimental inquiry) or even ss. 92 to 103 (court-martial). Process under each of those sections would have afforded the complainant the procedural formalities contended for here.

I should say that the existence of those forms of inquiry and their procedure undercuts [the] suggestion that exigencies of the service would make oral hearings impracticable.

In my judgment, there is force in Mr Pannick's argument. Since Parliament has deliberately excluded soldiers' complaints from industrial tribunals and thus from the procedures laid down for such tribunals, it cannot be axiomatic that by analogy all those procedures must be made available by the Army Board. Had Parliament wished to impose those detailed procedures on the Army Board, it could have done so.

However, Mr Pannick went on to contend that the Army Board's duty of fairness required no more than that it should act bona fide, not capriciously or in a biased manner, and that it should afford the complainant a chance to respond to the basic points put against him. In my judgment, this does not go far enough. The Army Board as the forum of last resort, dealing with an individual's fundamental statutory rights, must by its procedures achieve a high standard of fairness. I would list the principles as follows.

(1) There must be a proper hearing of the complaint in the sense that the board must consider, as a single adjudicating body, all the relevant evidence and contentions before reaching its conclusions. This means, in my view, that the members of the board must meet. It is unsatisfactory that the members should consider the papers and reach their individual conclusions in isolation and, perhaps as here, having received the concluded views of another member. Since there are ten members of the Army Board and any two can exercise the board's powers to consider a complaint of this kind, there should be no difficulty in achieving a meeting for the purpose.

(2) The hearing does not necessarily have to be an oral hearing in all cases. There is ample authority that decision-making bodies other than courts and bodies whose procedures are laid down by statute are masters of their own procedure. Provided that they achieve the degree of fairness appropriate to their task it is for them to decide how they will proceed and there is no rule that fairness always requires

an oral hearing: see *Local Government Board* v *Arlidge* [1915] AC 120, 132–133, *Selvarajan* v *Race Relations Board* [1975] 1 WLR 1686, 1694 and *R* v *Immigration Appeal Tribunal, ex parte Jones* [1988] 1 WLR 477, 481. Whether an oral hearing is necessary will depend upon the subject matter and circumstances of the particular case and upon the nature of the decision to be made. It will also depend upon whether there are substantial issues of fact which cannot be satisfactorily resolved on the available written evidence. This does not mean that, whenever there is a conflict of evidence in the statements taken, an oral hearing must be held to resolve it. Sometimes such a conflict can be resolved merely by the inherent unlikelihood of one version or the other. Sometimes the conflict is not central to the issue for determination and would not justify an oral hearing. Even when such a hearing is necessary, it may only require one or two witnesses to be called and cross-examined.

Mr Sedley submits that, whatever the position regarding other complaints under s. 181, an oral hearing should be obligatory where the complaint is of race discrimination. He submits that experience shows proof of discrimination to be elusive. Discriminatory motivation can be innocent and subconscious. Without cross-examination at an oral hearing it may not emerge. I recognise the difficulties of proving discrimination in many cases, but I do not accept that a general rule requiring oral hearings must be applied by the Army Board to all complaints of discrimination. In the present case, for example, the direct and crude nature of the alleged racial abuse hardly raises any specially subtle possibility of subconscious motivation. Either the racial attacks, oral and physical, took place or they did not. Whether, when the Army Board sees all the statements and transcripts, it considers it necessary to hold an oral hearing to decide that issue or whether it can resolve it on the written material will be for it to decide in its discretion. What it cannot do, at the other extreme from Mr Sedley's submission, is to have an inflexible policy not to hold oral hearings. The findings of the two members in this case suggest that is what they did. …

[T]he board fettered its discretion and failed to consider the request for an oral hearing in the present case on its own merits.

(3) The opportunity to have the evidence tested by cross-examination is again within the Army Board's discretion. The decision whether to allow it will usually be inseparable from the decision whether to have an oral hearing. The object of the latter will usually be to enable witnesses to be tested in cross-examination, although it would be possible to have an oral hearing simply to hear submissions.

(4) Whether oral or not, there must be what amounts to a hearing of any complaint under the 1976 Act. This means that the Army Board must have such a complaint investigated, consider all the material gathered in the investigation, give the complainant an opportunity to respond to it and consider his response.

But what is the board obliged to disclose to the complainant to obtain his response? Is it sufficient to indicate the gist of any material adverse to his case or should he be shown all the material seen by the board?

Mr Pannick submits that there is no obligation to show all to the complainant. He relies upon three authorities, *R* v *Secretary of State, ex parte Mughal* [1974] QB 313 *R* v *Secretary of State, ex parte Santillo* [1981] QB 778 and *R* v *Monopolies and Mergers Commission, ex parte Matthew Brown plc* [1987] 1 WLR 1235. However, in each of those cases, the function of the decision-making body was towards the administrative end of the spectrum. Because of the nature of the Army Board's function pursuant to the 1976 Act, already analysed above, I consider that a soldier complainant under that Act should be shown all the material seen by the board, apart from any documents for which public interest immunity can properly be claimed. The board is not simply making an administrative decision requiring it to consult interested parties and hear their representations. It has a duty to adjudicate on a specific complaint of breach of a statutory right. Except where public interest immunity is established, I see no reason why on such an adjudication the board should consider material withheld from the complainant.

In the present case it is true that Mr Anderson was shown a summary of the SIB report, though not the report itself. He also received the commanding officer's letter of 20 July which summarised points made against him, but he did not see the statements of other soldiers. Nor was he shown the information obtained individually by each of the board members. Thus, the response he made to the commanding officer's letter was hampered by a lack of full information. …

The Divisional Court granted an order of certiorari to quash the Board's decision.

NOTES

1. A commentary on the use of judicial review in the context of racial discrimination in the public sector may be found at [1991] *Public Law*, at pp. 317–25.
2. *Ex parte St Germain (No. 2)* and *ex parte Cottrell and Rothon* have been used by H. F. Rawlings to illustrate a particular criticism of the rules of natural justice.

H. F. Rawlings, 'Judicial Review and the Control of Government'

(1986) 64 *Public Administration* 135, 140–1

... It has long been the concern of many academic administrative lawyers that our system of judicial review is for various reasons not adequate to ensure protection of the citizen against government excess. ... In contrast, the adequacy of our administrative law principles from the point of view of the civil or public servant has rarely been considered. I suggest that the principles which have been developed by the courts over the last twenty years are quite simply not sufficiently precise to offer any meaningful guidance to administrators in their day-to-day decision-making, even if those administrators are aware of the existence of administrative law. ...

What, then, are those principles? In essence there are two (I leave out of account here the question of illegality, which is not germane to the present discussion). First, there is the obligation to observe the rules of natural justice. Here we may return to *Ridge* v *Baldwin* [1964] AC 40. That case establishes that in a far wider category of situations than had previously been thought true, a public authority had, in exercising statutory functions, to observe the natural justice requirement. But what is that requirement? It must be remembered that the content of the natural justice rule derives from the court proceedings paradigm—judges must be unbiased, and parties must be given an opportunity to present their cases. How might these rules be applied in the infinite variety of administrative practices to which *Ridge* v *Baldwin* now extends them?

Two possibilities were open to the courts, given this new activist approach to the applicability of natural justice. ... [W]e might characterise these as the 'formal activist' and the 'informal activist' approaches. Under the former, the courts could seek, by firm application of the rules, to force the administrative process into a more judicial mould, to follow the formal procedures of the courts so far as possible. Under the latter, the courts could permit administrators a greater degree of latitude in their procedures and allow the applicability of the rules of natural justice in particular circumstances to be determined by the realities of administration, while all the time insisting that compliance with the rules was necessary. As is now well-known, the courts adopted the latter approach— natural justice was to be flexibly applied, to fit the circumstances of the case. In the result, observation of the rules of natural justice came to mean that the procedure required of the administrator had to be, in all the circumstances of the case, 'fair' (see, for example *Re HK* [1967] 2 QB 617 and *R* v *Commission for Racial Equality ex parte Cottrell and Rothon* [1980] 1 WLR 1580).

Now it may be that this was an inevitable result, although potentially pregnant with danger for the individual citizen asserting a right to be heard. It seems to me, however, that in their understandable desire to avoid over-judicialising administrative procedures, the courts have thrown out the baby with the bath-water. Flexible natural justice, or 'fairness', has come to have no fixed or settled content that an administrator should know must be observed in exercising decision-making powers. All he knows ... is that he must be 'fair'—and what 'fairness' requires in the particular circumstances he can only ultimately find out when the court, on judicial review, tells him that he has, or has not, been fair. Is this an adequate administrative law principle, from the point of view of the administrator?

The point may briefly be illustrated by considering a specific issue in natural justice. It is sometimes said that, before any administrative decision is taken, a party who is likely to be affected by it shall have the right to hear what evidence against his interests has been given by someone else, and shall have the opportunity to question that person on the assertions contained therein ... Decided cases, tell us, to take just two examples, that in the context of prison disciplinary proceedings, 'fairness' requires that such cross-examination is permitted (*R* v *Hull Prison Visitors ex parte St Germain (No. 2)* [1979] 1 WLR 1401), whereas in the context of issuance of a non-discrimination notice against a private estate agency under the Race Relations Act, 'fairness' does not require that such cross-examination is permitted (*R* v *CRE ex parte Cottrell and Rothon* [1980] 1 WLR 1580).

Now these results can be defended, because as Lord Lane CJ says in the *Cottrell and Rothon case*, there are 'degrees of judicial hearing, and those degrees run from the borders of pure administration to the borders of a full hearing of a criminal cause or matter'. The precise requirements of fairness depend upon how far along that continuum is the particular administrative process to be placed—the closer to 'pure administration' it is, the less onerous will be the procedural requirements imposed on administrators. This, as I have said, is defensible as a matter of theory, but I suggest that as guidance to administrative practice it is hopelessly imprecise from the point of view of those who want to know what procedural requirements the law lays down for them to observe.

■ QUESTIONS

1. What distinctions did Lord Lane CJ draw between the circumstances in *ex parte St Germain* and those in *ex parte Cottrell and Rothon*? Do you consider that the distinctions justify the different decisions reached in each case?

2. Cane, in the extract earlier in this chapter in Section 1 at p. 497, has suggested that there are two possible approaches which the court might adopt in the face of legislative silence on the precise content of the rules of natural justice/procedural fairness. 'It could be said that the common law rules of natural justice will apply only if there is evidence of a legislative intention that they should; alternatively, it could be argued that silence should be construed as an invitation by the courts to apply common law procedural standards.' Which approach did the courts adopt in *ex parte St Germain*, *ex parte Cottrell and Rothon*, and *ex parte Anderson*?

3. Write a paragraph to guide public administrators on the circumstances in which public authorities should be willing (a) to permit oral hearings and (b) to permit the cross-examination of witnesses.

4. Is there any solution to the problems identified by Rawlings?

5. Can there be a breach of the rules of natural justice where an applicant has been deprived of an opportunity to present his case, not through the fault of the decision-making body, but through the fault of his own advisers? (See *Al-Mehdawi* v *Secretary of State for the Home Department* [1990] AC 876, noted at [1990] *Public Law* 467–75.)

NOTE: One problem which has been discussed in a number of cases is that of legal representation. In *R* v *Board of Visitors of HM Prison, The Maze, ex parte Hone* [1988] 2 WLR 177 the House of Lords rejected the argument that a prisoner facing a disciplinary charge before a prison board of visitors had a right to legal representation. The House of Lords did, however, approve the decision in *R* v *Secretary of State for the Home Department, ex parte Tarrant* [1985] QB 251 that a board of visitors still has a discretion to allow legal representation and that in certain circumstances it would be wrong not to allow it. Webster J specified a number of points which are to be taken into account, including the seriousness of the charge and potential penalty, whether points of law are likely to arise, the particular prisoner's ability to present his case and the need for reasonable speed in reaching a decision.

The rules governing hearings before the prison board of visitors did not state that legal representation was prohibited. What is the position where the rules governing a particular hearing *do* prohibit legal representation? In *Enderby Town Football Club Ltd* v *Football Association Ltd* [1971] Ch 591, Lord Denning MR stated, at p. 607:

> Seeing that the courts can inquire into the validity of the rule, I turn to the next question: Is it lawful for a body to stipulate in its rules that its domestic tribunal shall not permit legal representation? Such a stipulation is, I think, clearly valid so long as it is construed as directory and not imperative: for that leaves it open to the tribunal to permit legal representation in an exceptional case when the justice of the case so requires. But I have some doubt whether it is legitimate to make

> a rule which is so imperative in its terms as to exclude legal representation altogether, without giving the tribunal any discretion to admit it, even when the justice of the case so requires.

Lord Denning has repeated this view on other occasions (see e.g. *Edwards* v *SOGAT* [1971] Ch 354). In *Enderby Town* itself, however, Cairns LJ took a contrary view.

> In *Maynard* v *Osmond* [1977] QB 240 Lord Denning was a member of the Court of Appeal which was required to consider the validity of police discipline regulations prohibiting legal representation. The regulations were made under statutory powers. It was held unanimously that the regulations were not *ultra vires*, and in particular that they were not in breach of natural justice. In this case Lord Denning stated, obiter, that it is permissible for a domestic tribunal to adopt a rule forbidding legal representation, and Orr LJ endorsed the view of Cairns LJ in *Enderby Town*.

The two principles so far discussed have been concerned with procedural fairness. In recent years the courts have begun to develop a principle of fairness which may require public authorities to reach a particular decision rather than simply to follow a fair procedure. The concept of legitimate expectation, which is explained in *Council of the Civil Service Unions* v *Minister for the Civil Service*, has been important in the development of this principle.

Council of the Civil Service Unions v Minister for the Civil Service
[1985] AC 374, House of Lords

Government Communications Headquarters, a branch of the civil service, is responsible for the security of the United Kingdom military and official communications and the provision of signals intelligence for the Government. Since the formation of GCHQ in 1947, all the staff had been permitted to belong to trade unions. There was an established practice of consultation between the management and the civil service unions at GCHQ. Following incidents of industrial action at GCHQ the Minister for the Civil Service, the Prime Minister, issued an oral instruction to the effect that the terms and conditions of civil servants at GCHQ should be revised to exclude membership of any trade union other than a departmental staff association approved by the Minister. The instruction was issued under art. 4 of the Civil Service Order in Council 1982 'to give instructions ... for controlling the conduct of the Service, and providing for the ... conditions of service', the Order itself having been made under the royal prerogative. The union applied for judicial review, seeking a declaration that the Minister had acted unfairly in removing their fundamental right to belong to a trade union without consultation. The Court of Appeal allowed the Minister's appeal against the judge's decision that the Minister had acted unlawfully. The appellants appealed to the House of Lords. Having held that the courts could review the exercise of a power delegated to the decision-maker under the royal prerogative, Lord Fraser went on to consider whether there was a duty to consult the unions.

LORD FRASER:

The duty to consult

[Counsel for the appellants] submitted that the Minister had a duty to consult the CCSU, on behalf of employees at GCHQ, before giving the instruction on 22 December 1983 for making an important change in their conditions of service. His main reason for so submitting was that the employees had a legitimate, or reasonable, expectation that there would be such prior consultation before any important change was made in their conditions.

It is clear that the employees did not have a legal right to prior consultation. The Order in Council confers no such right and article 4 makes no reference at all to consultation. ... But even where a person claiming some benefit or privilege has no legal right to it, as a matter of private law, he may have a legitimate expectation of receiving the benefit or privilege, and, if so, the courts will protect his expectation by judicial review as a matter of public law. This subject has been fully explained by

Lord Diplock, in *O'Reilly* v *Mackman* [1983] 2 AC 237 and I need not repeat what he has so recently said. Legitimate, or reasonable, expectation may arise either from an express promise given on behalf of a public authority or from the existence of a regular practice which the claimant can reasonably expect to continue. Examples of the former type of expectation are *Reg* v *Liverpool Corporation, ex parte Liverpool Taxi Fleet Operators Association* [1972] 2 QB 299 and *A-G of Hong Kong* v *Ng Yuen Shiu* [1983] 2 AC 629. (I agree with Lord Diplock's view, expressed in the speech in this appeal, that 'legitimate' is to be preferred to the word 'reasonable' in this context. I was responsible for using the word 'reasonable' for the reason explained in *Ng Yuen Shiu*, but it was intended only to be exegetical of 'legitimate'.) An example of the latter is *Reg* v *Hull Prison Board of Visitors ex parte St Germain* [1979] 1 All ER 701, [1979] QB 425, approved by this House in *O'Reilly* v *Mackman* [1982] 3 All ER 1124 at 1126, [1983] 2 AC 237 at 274. The submission on behalf of the appellants is that the present case is of the latter type. The test of that is whether the practice of prior consultation of the staff on significant changes in their conditions of service was so well established by 1983 that it would be unfair or inconsistent with good administration for the Government to depart from the practice in this case. Legitimate expectations such as are now under consideration will always relate to a benefit or privilege to which the claimant has no right in private law, and it may even be to one which conflicts with his private law rights. In the present case the evidence shows that, ever since GCHQ began in 1947, prior consultation has been the invariable rule when conditions of service were to be significantly altered. Accordingly in my opinion if there had been no question of national security involved, the appellants would have had a legitimate expectation that the Minister would consult them before issuing the instruction of 22 December 1983.

NOTES

1. A majority of their Lordships held that the exercise of prerogative powers could be challenged in judicial review proceedings provided that the subject matter was justiciable. (On the issue of justiciability, see Chapter 11, Section 5 at p. 597.) Lord Fraser and Lord Brightman left open the question whether a direct exercise of the prerogative powers could be subject to judicial review, but they did accept that powers which had been delegated to decision-makers by an Order in Council made under prerogative powers were subject to judicial review. All their Lordships agreed that, had issues of national security not been involved, the unions would have been entitled to consultation. (On the issues of national security which arose in this case, see Chapter 11, Section 5 at p. 598.) This was applied to the making of Orders in Council for a colony as well as to the exercise of the powers thus conferred in *R (Bancoult) Secretary of State for Foreign and Commonwealth Affairs* v *The Queen* [2008] UKHL 61, [2009] 1 AC 453.

2. There have been various cases on consultations. One high-profile case was *R (Greenpeace)* v *Secretary of State for Trade and Industry* [2007] EWHC 311 (Admin), [2007] in which Greenpeace successfully challenged the policy on building new nuclear power stations as it did not met their expectation of being the fullest public consultation. The consultation exercise had a paper which was adequate as an issues paper but not as a consultation paper because it contained no proposals as such, the information provided was wholly insufficient to enable an intelligent response and contained nothing on two issues which had been identified as being of critical importance, the economics of new nuclear build and the disposal of nuclear waste. Indeed on the latter point it was wholly misleading about the position of the Committee on Radioactive Waste Management. Material on these two issues was produced after the close of the consultation period so it was procedural unfairness to make a decision on this material when consultees did not have a chance to respond to it. The decision was given in February 2007 and in May the Government launched a new Energy White Paper and consultation process which ran from May until October (see *Meeting the Energy Challenge: A White Paper on Energy*, Cm 7124, and *The Future of Nuclear Power: The Role of Nuclear Power in A Low Carbon UK Economy, A Consultation Paper*, Department of Trade and Industry). In January 2008 the result of the consultation and the new policy were announced. Nuclear power had a place in the energy policy and invitations were being made to energy companies to produce plans for building and operating new nuclear power stations (see *Meeting the Energy Challenge: A White Paper on Nuclear Power*, Cm 7296, and *The Future of Nuclear Power: An Analysis of Consultation Responses*, Department for Business Enterprise and Regulatory Reform). Therefore Greenpeace's challenge brought about a fuller consultation process but did not prevent new nuclear build.

3. The concept of legitimate expectation has been discussed by a number of writers (see, for example, C. Forsyth, 'The Provenance and Protection of Legitimate Expectations' (1988) 47 CLJ 238–60; B. Hadfield, 'Judicial Review and the Concept of Legitimate Expectation' (1988) 39 *Northern Ireland Legal Quarterly* 103–19; Ganz, 'Legitimate Expectation' in C. Harlow (ed.), *Public Law and Politics* (1986), 145; P. Craig, 'Legitimate Expectations: A Conceptual Analysis' (1992) 108 *Law Quarterly Review* 79); P. Sales and K. Steyn, 'Legitimate Expectations in English Public Law: An Analysis' [2004] *Public Law* 564. They have highlighted the different ways in which the concept is used by the courts. Predominantly, the legitimate expectation has related to fair procedures but see later in this section at p. 547, for substantive legitimate expectations.

D: Irrationality

Prior to the decision in *Council of the Civil Service Unions* v *Minister for the Civil Service* this ground was often expressed in the principle that an authority must not reach a decision which is so unreasonable that no reasonable body could have come to it. After *CCSU* the use of the term 'irrationality' has become more common, but in *R* v *Devon CC, ex parte G* [1988] 3 WLR 49, at p. 51, the Master of the Rolls stated that he preferred the older test because the term 'irrationality' could be widely misunderstood as casting doubt on the mental capacity of the decision-maker. Subsequent cases have used both terms.

Wheeler v *Leicester City Council*
[1985] AC 1054, House of Lords

(The facts are set out earlier in this chapter in Section 1B at p. 503.)

LORD ROSKILL: It is important to emphasise that there was nothing illegal in the action of the three members in joining the tour. The government policy recorded in the well-known Gleneagles agreement has never been given the force of law at the instance of any government, whatever its political complexion, and a person who acts otherwise than in accordance with the principles of that agreement, commits no offence even though he may by his action earn the moral disapprobation of large numbers of his fellow citizens. That the club condemns apartheid, as does the council, admits of no doubt. But the council's actions against the club were not taken, as already pointed out, because the club took no action against its three members. They were taken, according to Mr Soulsby, because the club failed to condemn the tour and to discourage its members from playing. The same point was put more succinctly by Mr Sullivan QC, who appeared for the council—'The club failed to align themselves whole-heartedly with the council on a controversial issue.' The club did not condemn the tour. They did not give specific affirmative answers to the first two questions. Thus, so the argument ran, the council, legitimately bitterly hostile to the policy of apartheid, were justified in exercising their statutory discretion to determine by whom the recreation ground should be used so as to exclude those, such as the club, who would not support the council's policy on the council's terms. The club had, however, circulated to those involved the powerfully reasoned and impressive memorandum which had been sent to the RFU [the Rugby Football Union] on 12 March 1984 by the anti-apartheid movement. Of the club's own opposition to apartheid as expressed in its memorandum which was given to Mr Soulsby, there is no doubt. But the club recognised that those views, like those of the council, however passionately held by some, were by no means universally held, especially by those who sincerely believed that the evils of apartheid were enhanced rather than diminished by a total prohibition of all sporting links with South Africa.

The council's main defence rested on section 71 of the Race Relations Act 1976. That section appears as the first section in Part X of the Act under the cross-heading 'Supplemental.' For ease of reference I will set out the section in full:

> Without prejudice to their obligation to comply with any other provision of this Act, it shall be the duty of every local authority to make appropriate arrangements with a view to securing that their

various functions are carried out with due regard to the need—(a) to eliminate unlawful racial discrimination; and (b) to promote equality of opportunity, and good relations, between persons of different racial groups.

My Lords, it was strenuously argued on behalf of the club that this section should be given what was called a 'narrow' construction. It was suggested that the section was only concerned with the actions of the council as regards its own internal behaviour and was what was described as 'inward looking.' The section had no relevance to the general exercise by the council or indeed of any local authority of their statutory functions, as for example in relation to the control of open spaces or in determining who should be entitled to use a recreation ground and on what terms. It was said that the section was expressed in terms of a 'duty.' But it did not impose any duty so as to compel the exercise by a local authority of other statutory functions in order to achieve the objectives of the Act of 1976.

My Lords, in respectful agreement with the courts below, I unhesitatingly reject this argument. I think the whole purpose of the section is to see that in employment, and in Part III, education, local authorities must in relation to 'their various functions' make 'appropriate arrangements' to secure that those functions are carried out 'with due regard to the need' mentioned in the section.

It follows that I do not doubt that the council were fully entitled in exercising their statutory discretion under, for example, the Open Spaces Act 1906 and the various Public Health Acts, which are all referred to in the judgments below, to pay regard to what they thought to be in the best interests of race relations.

The only question is, therefore, whether the action of the council of which the club complains is susceptible of attack by way of judicial review. It was forcibly argued by Mr Sullivan QC for the council, that once it was accepted, as I do accept, that section 71 bears the construction for which the council contended, the matter became one of political judgment only, and that by interfering the courts would be trespassing across that line which divides a proper exercise of a statutory discretion based on a political judgment, in relation to which the courts will not interfere, from an improper exercise of such a discretion in relation to which the courts will interfere.

Lord Roskill referred to the judgment in *Council of the Civil Service Unions* v *Minister for the Civil Service* (see earlier in this chapter in Section 2C at p. 499) and continued:

To my mind the crucial question is whether the conduct of the council in trying by their four questions, whether taken individually or collectively, to force acceptance by the club of their own policy (however proper that policy may be) on their own terms, as for example, by forcing them to lend their considerable prestige to a public condemnation of the tour, can be said either to be so 'unreasonable' as to give rise to '*Wednesbury* unreasonableness' (*Associated Provincial Picture Houses Ltd* v *Wednesbury Corporation* [1948] 1 KB 223) or to be so fundamental a breach of the duty to act fairly which rests upon every local authority in matters of this kind and thus to justify interference by the courts.

I do not doubt for one moment the great importance which the council attach to the presence in its midst of a 25 per cent population of persons who are either Asian or of Afro-Caribbean origin. Nor do I doubt for one moment the sincerity of the view expressed in Mr Soulsby's affidavit regarding the need for the council to distance itself from bodies who hold important positions and who do not actively discourage sporting contacts with South Africa. Persuasion, even powerful persuasion, is always a permissible way of seeking to obtain an objective. But in a field where other views can equally legitimately be held, persuasion, however powerful, must not be allowed to cross that line where it moves into the field of illegitimate pressure coupled with the threat of sanctions. The four questions, coupled with the insistence that only affirmative answers to all four would be acceptable, are suggestive of more than powerful persuasion. The second question is to my mind open to particular criticism. What, in the context, is meant by the 'club?' The committee? 90 playing members? 4,300 non-playing members? It by no means follows that the committee would all have agreed on an affirmative answer to the question and still less that a majority of their members, playing or non-playing, would have done so. Nor would any of these groups of members necessarily have known whether 'the large proportion,' whatever that phrase may mean in the context, of the Leicester population would have regarded the tour as 'an insult' to them.

None of the learned judges in the court below have felt able to hold that the action of the club was unreasonable or perverse in the *Wednesbury* sense. They do not appear to have been invited to consider whether those actions, even if not unreasonable on *Wednesbury* principles, were assailable on the grounds of procedural impropriety or unfairness by the council in the manner in which, in the light of the facts I have outlined, they took their decision to suspend for 12 months the use by the club of the Welford Road recreation ground.

I greatly hesitate to differ from four learned judges on the *Wednesbury* issue but for myself I would have been disposed respectfully to do this and to say that the actions of the council were unreasonable in the *Wednesbury* sense. But even if I am wrong in this view, I am clearly of the opinion that the manner in which the council took that decision was in all the circumstances of the case unfair within the third of the principles stated in *Council for the Civil Service Unions* v *Minister for the Civil Service* [1985] AC 374. The council formulated those four questions in the manner of which I have spoken and indicated that only such affirmative answers would be acceptable. They received reasoned and reasonable answers which went a long way in support of the policy which the council had accepted and desired to see accepted. The views expressed in these reasoned and reasonable answers were lawful views and the views which, as the evidence shows, many people sincerely hold and believe to be correct. If the club had adopted a different and hostile attitude, different considerations might well have arisen. But the club did not adopt any such attitude. ...

I would therefore allow the appeal.

NOTE: The judgment of Lord Roskill may be compared to that of Ackner LJ in the Court of Appeal in *Wheeler*. Having decided that the council were lawfully entitled to take into account the purposes expressed in s. 71 of the Race Relations Act 1976, Ackner LJ continued:

If I am right so far, this leaves only one final question to consider. Can it be said in the circumstances of the case that no reasonable local authority could properly conclude that temporarily banning from the use of its recreation grounds an important local rugger club, which declined to condemn a South African tour and declined actively to discourage its members from participating therein, could promote good relations between persons of different racial groups? (The well-known *Wednesbury* test: see *Associated Provincial Picture Houses Ltd* v *Wednesbury Corp.* [1947] 2 All ER 680, [1948] 1 KB 223.) Forbes J was at pains to point out, as I certainly would wish also to do, that courts are not concerned with the merits of the two rival views, no doubt equally honestly held, as to the value of severing sporting links with South Africa. I am fully prepared to accept that, even amongst those who feel strongly that sporting links should be severed, there may be some who could take the view that the club acted wholly reasonably in the action it took and should not have been expected to go further. But to accept the mere existence of such a school of thought does not establish that the council's decision was perverse and this is what the club is obliged to do to succeed under this head. Nor is the club's case advanced by emphasising that the council were imposing a sanction against members of the club for refusing publicly to endorse the reasonable views of the council and thereby interfering with the club's freedom of speech. The view which the council held as to the importance of severing sporting links with South Africa had clearly been fully considered by the council well before the events of 1984, and in view of the make-up of the population of the city it was a view which understandably was very strongly supported. It represented no more than that clearly recorded in the Gleneagles Agreement. In my judgment it would be quite wrong to categorise as perverse the council's decision to give an outward and visible manifestation of their disapproval of the club's failure, indeed refusal, 'to take every practical step to discourage' the tour, and in particular the participation of its members.

I would accordingly dismiss this appeal.

■ QUESTIONS

1. On the question of whether the council had acted in a way in which no reasonable council could have acted, do you find the reasoning of Lord Roskill or that of Ackner LJ more convincing?

2. Does Lord Roskill explain which of the particular aspects of Lord Diplock's third category, procedural impropriety, he considered to have been breached?

Nottinghamshire CC v Secretary of State for the Environment
[1986] 1 AC 240, House of Lords

In 1984 the Secretary of State issued a report containing the guidance for expenditure by local authorities for 1985–86. The guidance was based on the 1984–85 budgets of local authorities and an amount known as 'grant-related expenditure' (GRE). Grant-related expenditure is the notional expenditure which an authority might incur if all authorities provided the same standard of service with the same degree of efficiency at a level consistent with the Government's aggregate spending plans for local authorities. The guidance for 1985–86 stated that authorities which had budgeted to spend at or below the GRE expenditure in 1984–85 could budget in 1985–86 for the 1984/85 GRE plus 3.75 per cent. Those which had budgeted at above their GRE for 1984/85 could budget for the figure in the 1984–85 guidance plus 3.75 per cent. Under the scheme established by the Local Government Planning and Land Act 1980, if a local authority's expenditure exceeded that set in the guidance to it, the Secretary of State was empowered to reduce the amount of the rate support grant made by central government to the authority.

The report was laid before the House of Commons pursuant to s. 60 of the Act, and was approved by an affirmative resolution of the House. Nottinghamshire CC and the City of Bradford MC applied for an order of *certiorari* to quash the decision of the Secretary of State contained in the report and for declarations that the expenditure guidance contained in the report was invalid. They based their application on two grounds. First, the Secretary of State's guidance did not comply with the requirement in s. 59(11A) of the 1980 Act that 'any guidance issued ... be framed by reference to principles applicable to all local authorities ... ' because it differentiated between authorities budgeting to spend above or below the GRE. Secondly, they argued that the decision of the Secretary was unreasonable because the guidance was disproportionately disadvantageous to a small group of public authorities whose 1984–85 guidance was below GRE and who were budgeting to spend above GRE.

At first instance, the application was dismissed but the Court of Appeal allowed the authority's appeal. On appeal to the House of Lords the first ground was rejected; it was held that, on the true construction of the Act, while there had to be one set of principles applicable to all local authorities, it was permissible for those principles to identify and reflect differences between local authorities, including their past expenditure records. The following extracts deal with the second ground.

LORD SCARMAN: ... Their second submission is that, even if the guidance complies with the words of the statute, it offends a principle of public law in that the burden which the guidance imposes on some authorities, including Nottingham and Bradford, is so disproportionately disadvantageous when compared with its effect upon others that it is a perversely unreasonable exercise of the power conferred by the statute upon the Secretary of State. The respondents rely on what has become known to lawyers as the 'Wednesbury principles'—by which is meant the judgment of Lord Greene MR in *Associated Provincial Picture House Ltd* v *Wednesbury Corporation* [1948] 1 KB 223, 229. ...

The submission raises an important question as to the limits of judicial review. We are in the field of public financial administration and we are being asked to review the exercise by the Secretary of State of an administrative discretion which inevitably requires a political judgment on his part and which cannot lead to action by him against a local authority unless that action is first approved by the House of Commons.

... My Lords, I think the courts below were absolutely right to decline the invitation to intervene. I can understand that there may well be a justiciable issue as to the true construction of the words of the statute and that, if the Secretary of State has issued guidance which fails to comply with the requirement of subsection (11 A) of section 59 of the Act of 1980 the guidance can be quashed. But I cannot accept that it is constitutionally appropriate, save in very exceptionable circumstances, for the courts to intervene on the ground of 'unreasonableness' to quash guidance framed by the Secretary of State and by necessary implication approved by the House of Commons, the guidance being concerned with the limits of public expenditure by local authorities and the incidence of the tax burden as between taxpayers and ratepayers. Unless and until a statute provides otherwise, or it is established that the Secretary of State has abused his power, these are matters of political judgment for him and for the House of Commons. They are not for the judges or your Lordships' House in its judicial capacity.

For myself, I refuse in this case to examine the detail of the guidance or its consequences. My reasons are these. Such an examination by a court would be justified only if a prima facie case were to be shown for holding that the Secretary of State has acted in bad faith, or for an improper motive, or that the consequences of his guidance were so absurd that he must have taken leave of his senses. The evidence comes nowhere near establishing any of these propositions. Nobody in the case has ever suggested bad faith on the part of the Secretary of State. Nobody suggests, nor could it be suggested in the light of the evidence as to the matters he considered before reaching his decision, that he had acted for an improper motive. Nobody now suggests that the Secretary of State failed to consult local authorities in the manner required by statute. It is plain that the timetable, to which the Secretary of State in the preparation of the guidance was required by statute and compelled by circumstances to adhere, involved him necessarily in framing guidance on the basis of the past spending record of authorities. It is recognised that the Secretary of State and his advisers were well aware that there would be inequalities in the distribution of the burden between local authorities but believed the guidance upon which he decided would by discouraging the high spending and encouraging the low spending be the best course of action in the circumstances. And as my noble and learned friend, Lord Bridge of Harwich, demonstrates, it was guidance which complied with the terms of the statute. This view of the language of the statute has inevitably a significant bearing upon the conclusion of 'unreasonableness' in the *Wednesbury* sense. If, as your Lordships are holding, the guidance was based on principles applicable to all authorities, the principles would have to be either a pattern of perversity or an absurdity of such proportions that the guidance could not have been framed by a bona fide exercise of political judgment on the part of the Secretary of State. And it would be necessary to find as a fact that the House of Commons had been misled: for their approval was necessary and was obtained to the action that he proposed to take to implement the guidance.

… The present case raises in acute form the constitutional problem of the separation of powers between Parliament, the executive, and the courts. In this case, Parliament has enacted that an executive power is not to be exercised save with the consent and approval of one of its Houses. It is true that the framing of the guidance is for the Secretary of State alone after consultation with local authorities; but he cannot act on the guidance so as to discriminate between local authorities without reporting to, and obtaining the approval of, the House of Commons. That House has, therefore, a role and responsibility not only at the legislative stage when the Act was passed but in the action to be taken by the Secretary of State in the exercise of the power conferred upon him by the legislation.

To sum it up, the levels of public expenditure and the incidence and distribution of taxation are matters for Parliament and, within Parliament, especially for the House of Commons. If Parliament legislates, the courts have their interpretative role: they must, if called upon to do so, construe the statute. If a minister exercises a power conferred on him by the legislation, the courts can investigate whether he has abused his power. But if, as in this case, effect cannot be given to the Secretary of State's determination without the consent of the House of Commons and the House of Commons has consented, it is not open to the courts to intervene unless the minister and the House must have misconstrued the statute or the minister has—to put it bluntly—deceived the House. The courts can properly rule that a minister has acted unlawfully if he has erred in law as to the limits of his power even when his action has the approval of the House of Commons, itself acting not legislatively but within the limits set by a statute. But, if a statute, as in this case, requires the House of Commons to approve a minister's decision before he can lawfully enforce it, and if the action proposed complies with the terms of the statute (as your Lordships, I understand, are convinced that it does in the present case), it is not for the judges to say that the action has such unreasonable consequences that the guidance upon which the action is based and on which the House of Commons had notice was perverse and must be set aside. For that is a question of policy for the minister and the Commons, unless there has been bad faith or misconduct by the minister. Where Parliament has legislated that the action to be taken by the Secretary of State must, before it is taken, be approved by the House of Commons, it is no part of the judge's role to declare that the action proposed is unfair, unless it constitutes an abuse of power in the sense which I have explained; for Parliament has enacted that one of its Houses is responsible. Judicial review is a great weapon in the hands of the judges: but the judges must observe the constitutional limits set by our parliamentary system upon their exercise of this beneficent power. …

Lord Bridge and Lord Templeman delivered judgments in which they agreed with Lord Scarman. Lord Roskill and Lord Griffiths agreed with Lord Scarman.

NOTE: Lord Scarman's judgment was discussed and followed by the House of Lords in *R* v *Secretary of State for the Environment, ex parte Hammersmith and Fulham LBC* [1990] 3 All ER 589, a case which also involved a dispute between central and local government over finances. The House of Lords held that the Secretary of State had acted lawfully in setting a maximum amount for the budgets of a number of authorities under the Local Government Finance Act 1988.

■ QUESTIONS

1. Do you interpret Lord Scarman's judgment as stating that judicial review of a decision of this nature on the ground of unreasonableness is excluded?
2. Would judicial review be available on any other grounds, for example that the Minister had acted for an improper purpose or on the basis of irrelevant considerations?
3. Which constitutional theory did his Lordship rely on in this case?
4. Commenting on this decision in (1986) 45 *Cambridge Law Journal* (169–73), Colin Reid sees it, at p. 171:

> … as an affirmation of our traditional constitutional theory. There may be no formal separation of powers in this country, but the basic notions of our constitution, such as parliamentary sovereignty, the rule of law and responsibility of the Executive to Parliament, do create a fundamental distribution of powers and functions between the various elements of the state. It is to Parliament that one must look to control the executive on matters of policy and principle, *a fortiori* in cases where it has been enacted that the Executive must seek parliamentary approval for the exercise of the powers conferred on it. …

The question must be asked, though, how well this structure serves us in the political realities of today. Can we rely on Parliament to provide an adequate check on the powers of the Executive?

If the answer is no, can judicial review provide a solution? Note that Reid's view is that it cannot:

> …the way to achieve greater control over the Executive must lie in far-reaching reforms to our constitutional structure, rather than to a continued extension, or rather distortion, of judicial review to embrace issues and arguments not suited to judicial resolution.

NOTE: The *Nottinghamshire* and *Hammersmith & Fulham* cases have been described as being super-*Wednesbury* because their approach imposes a higher threshold. The appropriate standard of *Wednesbury* review was at issue in the next case.

R (Daly) v Secretary of State for the Home Department

[2001] UKHL 26, [2001] 2 AC 532, House of Lords

LORD STEYN: …

My Lords,

24. I am in complete agreement with the reasons given by Lord Bingham of Cornhill in his speech. For the reasons he gives I would also allow the appeal. Except on one narrow but important point I have nothing to add.

25. There was written and oral argument on the question whether certain observations of Lord Phillips of Worth Matravers MR in *R (Mahmood)* v *Secretary of State for the Home Department* [2001] 1 WLR 840 were correct. The context was an immigration case involving a decision of the Secretary of State made before the Human Rights Act 1998 came into effect. The Master of the Rolls nevertheless approached the case as if the Act had been in force when the Secretary of State reached his decision. He explained the new approach to be adopted. The Master of the Rolls concluded, at p 857, para 40:

> When anxiously scrutinising an executive decision that interferes with human rights, the court will ask the question, applying an objective test, whether the decision-maker could reasonably have concluded that the interference was necessary to achieve one or more of the legitimate aims recognised by the Convention. When considering the test of necessity in the relevant context, the court must take into account the European jurisprudence in accordance with section 2 of the 1998 Act.

These observations have been followed by the Court of Appeal in *R* v *Secretary of State for the Home Department, Ex p Isiko* (unreported), 20 December 2000 and by Thomas J in *R* v *Secretary of State for the Home Department, Ex p Samaroo* (unreported), 20 December 2000.

26. The explanation of the Master of the Rolls in the first sentence of the cited passage requires clarification. It is couched in language reminiscent of the traditional *Wednesbury* ground of review (*Associated Provincial Picture Houses Ltd* v *Wednesbury Corporation* [1948] 1 KB 223), and in particular the adaptation of that test in terms of heightened scrutiny in cases involving fundamental rights as formulated in *R* v *Ministry of Defence, Ex p Smith* [1996] QB 517, 554E–G per Sir Thomas Bingham MR. There is a material difference between the *Wednesbury* and *Smith* grounds of review and the approach of proportionality applicable in respect of review where convention rights are at stake.

27. The contours of the principle of proportionality are familiar. In *de Freitas* v *Permanent Secretary of Ministry of Agriculture, Fisheries, Lands and Housing* [1999] 1 AC 69 the Privy Council adopted a three stage test. Lord Clyde observed, at p 80, that in determining whether a limitation (by an act, rule or decision) is arbitrary or excessive the court should ask itself:

> whether: (i) the legislative objective is sufficiently important to justify limiting a fundamental right; (ii) the measures designed to meet the legislative objective are rationally connected to it; and (iii) the means used to impair the right or freedom are no more than is necessary to accomplish the objective.

Clearly, these criteria are more precise and more sophisticated than the traditional grounds of review. What is the difference for the disposal of concrete cases? Academic public lawyers have in remarkably similar terms elucidated the difference between the traditional grounds of review and the proportionality approach: see Professor Jeffrey Jowell QC, 'Beyond the Rule of Law: Towards Constitutional Judicial Review' [2000] PL 671; Craig, *Administrative Law*, 4th ed (1999), 561–563; Professor David Feldman, 'Proportionality and the Human Rights Act 1998', essay in *The Principle of Proportionality in the Laws of Europe* (1999), pp 117, 127 et seq. The starting point is that there is an overlap between the traditional grounds of review and the approach of proportionality. Most cases would be decided in the same way whichever approach is adopted. But the intensity of review is somewhat greater under the proportionality approach. Making due allowance for important structural differences between various convention rights, which I do not propose to discuss, a few generalisations are perhaps permissible. I would mention three concrete differences without suggesting that my statement is exhaustive. First, the doctrine of proportionality may require the reviewing court to assess the balance which the decision maker has struck, not merely whether it is within the range of rational or reasonable decisions. Secondly, the proportionality test may go further than the traditional grounds of review inasmuch as it may require attention to be directed to the relative weight accorded to interests and considerations. Thirdly, even the heightened scrutiny test developed in *R* v *Ministry of Defence, Ex p Smith* [1996] QB 517, 554 is not necessarily appropriate to the protection of human rights. It will be recalled that in *Smith* the Court of Appeal reluctantly felt compelled to reject a limitation on homosexuals in the army. The challenge based on article 8 of the Convention for the Protection of Human Rights and Fundamental Freedoms (the right to respect for private and family life) foundered on the threshold required even by the anxious scrutiny test. The European Court of Human Rights came to the opposite conclusion: *Smith and Grady* v *United Kingdom* (1999) 29 EHRR 493. The court concluded, at p 543, para. 138:

> the threshold at which the High Court and the Court of Appeal could find the Ministry of Defence policy irrational was placed so high that it effectively excluded any consideration by the domestic courts of the question of whether the interference with the applicants' rights answered a pressing social need or was proportionate to the national security and public order aims pursued, principles which lie at the heart of the court's analysis of complaints under article 8 of the Convention.

In other words, the intensity of the review, in similar cases, is guaranteed by the twin requirements that the limitation of the right was necessary in a democratic society, in the sense of meeting a pressing social need, and the question whether the interference was really proportionate to the legitimate aim being pursued.

28. The differences in approach between the traditional grounds of review and the proportionality approach may therefore sometimes yield different results. It is therefore important that cases involving convention rights must be analysed in the correct way. This does not mean that there has been a shift to merits review. On the contrary, as Professor Jowell [2000] PL 671, 681 has pointed out the respective roles of judges and administrators are fundamentally distinct and will remain so. To this extent the general tenor of the observations in *Mahmood* [2001] 1 WLR 840 are correct. And Laws LJ rightly emphasised in *Mahmood*, at p 847, para 18, 'that the intensity of review in a public law case will depend on the subject matter in hand'. That is so even in cases involving Convention rights. In law context is everything.

NOTE: We appear to have ordinary *Wednesbury* unreasonableness, super-*Wednesbury*, which is less intensive and, when human rights are at issue, a distinction between fundamental rights recognized at common law, which uses 'anxious scrutiny' and, for convention rights under the Human Rights Act, a more searching scrutiny by the courts which is closer to proportionality. After considering substantive legitimate expectations, where proportionality is used, we will return to *Wednesbury* unreasonableness and its relationship with proportionality.

In *Brind*, some members of the House of Lords were clear that proportionality was very different from *Wednesbury* unreasonableness and might overstep the legality/merits boundary. This view is changing, in part because the judges have more experience in applying it in cases involving European Union law.

E: Substantive legitimate expectations

NOTE: Earlier we saw how the concept of legitimate expectations had initially been concerned with procedure. It has been held to have a substantive aspect, but there has been doubt about the test which should be used—*Wednesbury* unreasonableness or proportionality. Consider the following case.

R v North and East Devon Health Authority, ex parte Coughlan
[2000] 2 WLR 622, Court of Appeal

The applicant was severely disabled in a road accident. In 1993 she and other disabled patients had been moved from a hospital to Mardon House. The health authority had promised that this would be their home for life. Following the issue of criteria by the Department of Health, the authority concluded that the applicant did not qualify for specialist nursing services to be provided by the authority but for general nursing care to be purchased by local authorities. Subsequently the health authority, following a public consultation, decided to close Mardon House and to transfer the applicant to the local authority for long-term general nursing care. In a successful application for judicial review of the decision to close Mardon House, it was held that the applicant and others had received a clear promise that Mardon House would be their home for life; that no overriding public interest had been established to justify breaking that promise; that the closure decision was flawed as no alternative placement for the applicant had been identified; that all nursing care was an NHS responsibility and that it was not open to the health authority to transfer general nursing care responsibility to a local authority, and that the health authority's eligibility criteria for long-term health care were flawed. On appeal to the Court of Appeal:

LORD WOOLF MR, MUMMERY and SEDLEY LJJ: …

56. What is still the subject of some controversy is the court's role when a member of the public, as a result of a promise or other conduct, has a legitimate expectation that he will be treated in one way and the public body wishes to treat him or her in a different way. Here the starting point has to be to ask what in the circumstances the member of the public could legitimately expect. In the words of Lord Scarman in *In re Findlay* [1985] AC 318, 338, 'But what was their *legitimate* expectation?' Where there is a dispute as to this, the dispute has to be determined by the court, as happened in *In re Findlay*. This can involve a detailed examination of the precise terms of the promise or representation made, the circumstances in which the promise was made and the nature of the statutory or other discretion.

57. There are at least three possible outcomes. (a) The court may decide that the public authority is only required to bear in mind its previous policy or other representation, giving it the weight it thinks right, but no more, before deciding whether to change course. Here the court is confined to reviewing the decision on *Wednesbury* grounds (*Associated Provincial Picture Houses Ltd* v *Wednesbury Corporation* [1948] 1 KB 223). This has been held to be the effect of changes of policy in cases involving the early release of prisoners: see *In re Findlay* [1985] AC 318; *Reg.* v *Secretary of State for the Home Department, Ex parte Hargreaves* [1997] 1 WLR 906. (b) On the other hand the court may decide that the promise or practice induces a legitimate expectation of, for example, being consulted before a particular decision is taken. Here it is uncontentious that the court itself will require *the opportunity for consultation* to be given unless there is an overriding reason to resile from it (see *Attorney-General of Hong Kong* v *Ng Yuen Shiu* [1983] 2 AC 629) in which case the court will itself judge the adequacy of the reason advanced for the change of policy, taking into account what fairness requires. (c) Where the court considers that a lawful promise or practice has induced a legitimate expectation of a *benefit which is substantive*, not simply procedural, authority now establishes that here too the court will in a proper case decide whether to frustrate the expectation is so unfair that to take a new and different course will amount to an abuse of power. Here, once the legitimacy of the expectation is established, the court will have the task of weighing the requirements of fairness against any overriding interest relied upon for the change of policy.

58. The court having decided which of the categories is appropriate, the court's role in the case of the second and third categories is different from that in the first. In the case of the first, the court is restricted to reviewing the decision on conventional grounds. The test will be rationality and whether the public body has given proper weight to the implications of not fulfilling the promise. In the case of the second category the court's task is the conventional one of determining whether the decision was procedurally fair. In the case of the third, the court has when necessary to determine whether there is a sufficient overriding interest to justify a departure from what has been previously promised.

59. In many cases the difficult task will be to decide into which category the decision should be allotted. In what is still a developing field of law, attention will have to be given to what it is in the first

category of case which limits the applicant's legitimate expectation (in Lord Scarman's words in *In re Findlay* [1985] AC 318) to an expectation that whatever policy is in force at the time will be applied to him. As to the second and third categories, the difficulty of segregating the procedural from the substantive is illustrated by the line of cases arising out of decisions of justices not to commit a defendant to the Crown Court for sentence, or assurances given to a defendant by the court: here to resile from such a decision or assurance may involve the breach of legitimate expectation: see *Reg.* v *Grice* (1977) 66 Cr App R 167; cf. *Reg.* v *Reilly* [1982] QB 1208, *Reg.* v *Dover Magistrates' Court, Ex parte Pamment* (1994) 15 Cr App R (S) 778, 782. No attempt is made in those cases, rightly in our view, to draw the distinction. Nevertheless, most cases of an enforceable expectation of a substantive benefit (the third category) are likely in the nature of things to be cases where the expectation is confined to one person or a few people, giving the promise or representation the character of a contract....

60. We consider that Mr Goudie and Mr Gordon are correct, as was the judge, in regarding the facts of this case as coming into the third category. (Even if this were not correct because of the nature of the promise, and even if the case fell within the second category, the health authority in exercising its discretion and in due course the court would have to take into account that only an overriding public interest would justify resiling from the promise.) Our reasons are as follow. First, the importance of what was promised to Miss Coughlan (as we will explain later, this is a matter underlined by the Human Rights Act 1998); second, the fact that promise was limited to a few individuals, and the fact that the consequences to the health authority of requiring it to honour its promise are likely to be financial only.

...

64. It is axiomatic that a public authority which derives its existence and its powers from statute cannot validly act outside those powers. This is the familiar ultra vires doctrine adopted by public law from company law (*Colman* v *Eastern Counties Railway Co.* (1846) 10 Beav 1). Since such powers will ordinarily include anything fairly incidental to the express remit, a statutory body may lawfully adopt and follow policies (*British Oxygen Co. Ltd* v *Board of Trade* [1971] AC 610) and enter into formal undertakings. But since it cannot abdicate its general remit, not only must it remain free to change policy; its undertakings are correspondingly open to modification or abandonment. The recurrent question is when and where and how the courts are to intervene to protect the public from unwarranted harm in this process. The problem can readily be seen to go wider than the exercise of statutory powers. It may equally arise in relation to the exercise of the prerogative power, which at least since *Reg.* v *Criminal Injuries Compensation Board, Ex parte Lain* [1967] 2 QB 864, has been subject to judicial review, and in relation to private monopoly powers: *Reg.* v *Panel on Take-overs and Mergers, Ex parte Datafin Plc* [1987] QB 815.

65. The court's task in all these cases is not to impede executive activity but to reconcile its continuing need to initiate or respond to change with the legitimate interests or expectations of citizens or strangers who have relied, and have been justified in relying, on a current policy or an extant promise. The critical question is by what standard the court is to resolve such conflicts. It is when one examines the implications for a case like the present of the proposition that, so long as the decision-making process has been lawful, the court's only ground of intervention is the intrinsic rationality of the decision, that the problem becomes apparent. Rationality, as it has developed in modern public law, has two faces: one is the barely known decision which simply defies comprehension; the other is a decision which can be seen to have proceeded by flawed logic (though this can often be equally well allocated to the intrusion of an irrelevant factor). The present decision may well pass a rationality test; the health authority knew of the promise and its seriousness; it was aware of its new policies and the reasons for them; it knew that one had to yield, and it made a choice which, whatever else can be said of it, may not easily be challenged as irrational. As Lord Diplock said in *Secretary of State for Education and Science* v *Tameside Metropolitan Borough Council* [1977] AC 1014, 1064:

> The very concept of administrative discretion involves a right to choose between more than one possible course of action upon which there is room for reasonable people to hold differing opinions as to which is to be preferred.

But to limit the court's power of supervision to this is to exclude from consideration another aspect of the decision which is equally the concern of the law.

66. In the ordinary case there is no space for intervention on grounds of abuse of power once a rational decision directed to a proper purpose has been reached by lawful process. The present class of case is visibly different. It involves not one but two lawful exercises of power (the promise and the policy change) by the same public authority, with consequences for individuals trapped between the two. The policy decision may well, and often does, make as many exceptions as are proper and feasible to protect individual expectations. The departmental decision in *Ex parte Hamble (Offshore) Fisheries Ltd* [1995] 2 All ER 714 is a good example. If it does not, as in *Ex parte Unilever Plc* [1996] STC 681, the court is there to ensure that the power to make and alter policy has not been abused by unfairly frustrating legitimate individual expectations. In such a situation a bare rationality test would constitute the public authority judge in its own cause, for a decision to prioritise a policy change over legitimate expectations will almost always be rational from where the authority stands, even if objectively it is arbitrary or unfair. It is in response to this dilemma that two distinct but related approaches have developed in the modern cases.

67. One approach is to ask not whether the decision is ultra vires in the restricted *Wednesbury* sense but whether, for example through unfairness or arbitrariness it amounts to an abuse of power. The leading case on the existence of this principle is *Ex parte Preston* [1985] AC 835. It concerned an allegation, not in the event made out, that the Inland Revenue Commissioners had gone back impermissibly on their promise not to reinvestigate certain aspects of an individual taxpayer's affairs. Lord Scarman, expressing his agreement with the single fully reasoned speech (that of Lord Templeman) advanced a number of important general propositions. First, he said, at p. 851:

> ... I must make clear my view that the principle of fairness has an important place in the law of judicial review: and that in an appropriate case it is a ground upon which the court can intervene to quash a decision made by a public officer or authority in purported exercise of a power conferred by law.

Second, Lord Scarman reiterated, citing the decision of the House of Lords in *Reg.* v *Inland Revenue Commissioners, Ex parte National Federation of Self-Employed and Small Businesses Ltd* [1982] AC 617, that a claim for judicial review may arise where the Commissioners have failed to discharge their statutory duty to an individual or 'have abused their powers or acted outside them'. Third, that 'unfairness in the purported exercise of a power can be such that it is an abuse or excess of power.'

...

69. Abuses of power may take many forms. One, not considered in the *Wednesbury* case [1948] 1 KB 223 (even though it was arguably what the case was about), was the use of a power for a collateral purpose. Another, as cases like *Ex parte Preston* [1985] AC 835 now make clear, is reneging without adequate justification, by an otherwise lawful decision, on a lawful promise or practice adopted towards a limited number of individuals.

There is no suggestion in *Ex parte Preston* or elsewhere that the final arbiter of justification, rationality apart, is the decision-maker rather than the court. Lord Templeman ... reached this conclusion, at pp. 866–867: ...

> In the present case, however, I consider that the [taxpayer] is entitled to relief by way of judicial review for 'unfairness' amounting to abuse of power if the commissioners have been guilty of conduct equivalent to a breach of contract or breach of representations on their part.

The entire passage, too long to set out here, merits close attention. It may be observed that Lord Templeman's final formulation, taken by itself, would allow no room for a test of overriding public interest....

70. This approach, in our view, embraces all the principles of public law which we have been considering. It recognises the primacy of the public authority both in administration and in policy development but it insists, where these functions come into tension, upon the adjudicative role of

the court to ensure fairness to the individual. It does not overlook the passage in the speech of Lord Browne-Wilkinson in *Reg.* v *Hull University Visitor, Ex parte Page* [1993] AC 682, 701, that the basis of the 'fundamental principle ... that the courts will intervene to ensure that the powers of public decision-making bodies are exercised lawfully' is the *Wednesbury* limit on the exercise of powers; but it follows the authority not only of *Ex parte Preston* [1985] AC 835 but of Lord Scarman's speech in *Reg.* v *Secretary of State for the Environment, Ex parte Nottinghamshire County Council* [1986] AC 240, 249, in treating a power which is abused as a power which has not been lawfully exercised.

71. Fairness in such a situation, if it is to mean anything, must for the reasons we have considered include fairness of outcome. This in turn is why the doctrine of legitimate expectation has emerged as a distinct application of the concept of abuse of power in relation to substantive as well as procedural benefits, representing a second approach to the same problem. If this is the position in the case of the third category, why is it not also the position in relation to the first category? May it be (though this was not considered in *In re Findlay* [1985] AC 318 or *Ex parte Hargreaves* [1997] 1 WLR 906) that, when a promise is made to a category of individuals who have the same interest, it is more likely to be considered to have binding effect than a promise which is made generally or to a diverse class, when the interests of those to whom the promise is made may differ or, indeed, may be in conflict? Legitimate expectation may play different parts in different aspects of public law. The limits to its role have yet to be finally determined by the courts. Its application is still being developed on a case by case basis. Even where it reflects procedural expectations, for example concerning consultation, it may be affected by an overriding public interest. It may operate as an aspect of good administration, qualifying the intrinsic rationality of policy choices. And without injury to the *Wednesbury* doctrine it may furnish a proper basis for the application of the now established concept of abuse of power.

78. It is from the revenue cases that, in relation to the third category, the proper test emerges. Thus in *Ex parte Unilever Plc* [1996] STC 681 this court concluded that for the Crown to enforce a time limit which for years it had not insisted upon would be so unfair as to amount to an abuse of power. As in other tax cases, there was no question of the court's deferring to the Inland Revenue's view of what was fair. The court also concluded that the Inland Revenue's conduct passed the 'notoriously high' threshold of irrationality; but the finding of abuse through unfairness was not dependent on this.

...

80. In *Ex parte Unilever Plc* [1996] STC 681, 695 Simon Brown LJ proposed a valuable reconciliation of the existing strands of public law:

'Unfairness amounting to an abuse of power' as ... in *Preston* and the other revenue cases is unlawful not because it involves conduct such as would offend some equivalent private law principle, not principally indeed because it breaches a legitimate expectation that some different substantive decision will be taken, but rather because it is illogical or immoral or both for a public authority to act with conspicuous unfairness and in that sense abuse its power. As Lord Donaldson MR said in *Reg.* v *Independent Television Commission, Ex parte T.S.W. Broadcasting Ltd, The Times,* 7 February 1992: 'The test in public law is fairness, not an adaption of the law of contract or estoppel.' In short, I regard the *M.F.K.* category of legitimate expectation as essentially but a head of *Wednesbury* unreasonableness, not necessarily exhaustive of the grounds upon which a successful substantive unfairness challenge may be based.

81. For our part, in relation to this category of legitimate expectation, we do not consider it necessary to explain the modern doctrine in *Wednesbury* terms, helpful though this is in terms of received jurisprudence (cf. Dunn LJ in *Reg.* v *Secretary of State for the Home Department, Ex parte Asif Mahmood Khan* [1984] 1 WLR 1337, 1352: 'an unfair action can seldom be a reasonable one'). We would prefer to regard the *Wednesbury* categories themselves as the major instances (not necessarily the sole ones: see *Council of Civil Service Unions* v *Minister for the Civil Service* [1985] AC 374, 410, *per* Lord Diplock) of how public power may be misused. Once it is recognised that conduct which is an abuse of power is contrary to law its existence must be for the court to determine.

82. The fact that the court will only give effect to a legitimate expectation within the statutory context in which it has arisen should avoid jeopardising the important principle that the executive's policy-making powers should not be trammelled by the courts: see *Hughes* v *Department of Health and Social Security* [1985] AC 766, 788 *per* Lord Diplock. Policy being (within the law) for the public authority alone, both it and the reasons for adopting or changing it will be accepted by the courts as part of the factual data—in other words, as not ordinarily open to judicial review. The court's task—and this is not always understood is then limited to asking whether the application of the policy to an individual who has been led to expect something different is a just exercise of power. In many cases the authority will already have considered this and made appropriate exceptions (as was envisaged in *British Oxygen Co. Ltd* v *Board of Trade* [1971] AC 610 and as had happened in *Ex parte Hamble (Offshore) Fisheries Ltd* [1995] 2 All ER 714), or resolved to pay compensation where money alone will suffice. But where no such accommodation is made, it is for the court to say whether the consequent frustration of the individual's expectation is so unfair as to be a misuse of the authority's power.

Fairness and the decision to close

83. How are fairness and the overriding public interest in this particular context to be judged? The question arises concretely in the present case. Mr Goudie argued, with detailed references, that all the indicators, apart from the promise itself, pointed to an overriding public interest, so that the court ought to endorse the health authority's decision. Mr Gordon contended, likewise with detailed references, that the data before the health authority were far from uniform. But this is not what matters. What matters is that, having taken it all into account, the health authority voted for closure in spite of the promise. The propriety of such an exercise of power should be tested by asking whether the need which the health authority judged to exist to move Miss Coughlan to a local authority facility was such as to outweigh its promise that Mardon House would be her home for life.

84. That a promise was made is confirmed by the evidence of the health authority that:

the applicant and her fellow residents were justified in treating certain statements made by the health authority's predecessor, coupled with the way in which the authority's predecessor conducted itself at the time of the residents' move from Newcourt Hospital, as amounting to an assurance that, having moved to Mardon House, Mardon House would be a permanent home for them.

And the letter of 7 June 1994 sent to the residents by Mr Peter Jackson, the then general manager of the predecessor of the health authority, following the withdrawal of John Grooms stated:

… I am writing to confirm therefore, that the health authority has made it clear to the community trust that it expects the trust to continue to provide good quality care for you at Mardon House for as long as you choose to live there. …

As has been pointed out by the health authority, the letter did not actually use the expression 'home for life.'

85. The health authority had, according to its evidence, formed the view that it should give considerable weight to the assurances given to Miss Coughlan; that those assurances had given rise to expectations which should not, in the ordinary course of things, be disappointed; but that it should not treat those assurances as giving rise to an absolute and unqualified entitlement on the part of the Miss Coughlan and her co-residents since that would be unreasonable and unrealistic; and that:

If there were compelling reasons which indicated overwhelmingly that closure was the reasonable and—other things being equal—the right course to take, provided that steps could be taken to meet the applicant's (and her fellow residents') expectations to the greatest degree possible following closure, it was open to the authority, weighing up all these matters with care and sensitivity, to decide in favour of the option of closure.

Although the first consultation paper made no reference to the 'home for life' promise, it was referred to in the second consultation paper as set out above.

86. ... This was an express promise or representation made on a number of occasions in precise terms. It was made to a small group of severely disabled individuals who had been housed and cared for over a substantial period in the health authority's predecessor's premises at Newcourt. It specifically related to identified premises which it was represented would be their home for as long as they chose. It was in unqualified terms. It was repeated and confirmed to reassure the residents. It was made by the health authority's predecessor for its own purposes, namely to encourage Miss Coughlan and her fellow residents to move out of Newcourt and into Mardon House, a specially built substitute home in which they would continue to receive nursing care. The promise was relied on by Miss Coughlan. Strong reasons are required to justify resiling from a promise given in those circumstances. This is not a case where the health authority would, in keeping the promise, be acting inconsistently with its statutory or other public law duties. A decision not to honour it would be equivalent to a breach of contract in private law.

87. The health authority treated the promise as the 'starting point' from which the consultation process and the deliberations proceeded. It was a factor which should be given 'considerable weight', but it could be outweighed by 'compelling reasons which indicated overwhelmingly that closure was the reasonable and the right course to take'. The health authority, though 'mindful of the history behind the residents' move to Mardon House and their understandable expectation that it would be their permanent home', formed the view that there were 'overriding reasons' why closure should nonetheless proceed. The health authority wanted to improve the provision of reablement services and considered that the mix of a long stay residential service and a reablement service at Mardon House was inappropriate and detrimental to the interests of both users of the service. The acute reablement service could not be supported there without an uneconomic investment which would have produced a second class reablement service. It was argued that there was a compelling public interest which justified the health authority's prioritisation of the reablement service.

88. It is, however, clear from the health authority's evidence and submissions that it did not consider that it had a legal responsibility or commitment to provide a *home*, as distinct from care or funding of care, for the applicant and her fellow residents. It considered that, following the withdrawal of the John Grooms Association, the provision of care services to the current residents had become 'excessively expensive', having regard to the needs of the majority of disabled people in the authority's area and the 'insuperable problems' involved in the mix of long-term residential care and reablement services at Mardon House. Mardon House ... did not represent value for money and left fewer resources for other services.

The health authority's attitude was that:

> It was because of our appreciation of the residents' expectation that they would remain at Mardon House for the rest of their lives that the board agreed that the authority should accept a continuing commitment to finance the care of the residents of Mardon for whom it was responsible.

But the cheaper option favoured by the health authority misses the essential point of the promise which had been given. The fact is that the health authority has not offered to the applicant an equivalent facility to replace what was promised to her. The health authority's undertaking to fund her care for the remainder of her life is substantially different in nature and effect from the earlier promise that care for her would be provided *at Mardon House*. That place would be her home for as long as she chose to live there.

89. We have no hesitation in concluding that the decision to move Miss Coughlan against her will and in breach of the health authority's own promise was in the circumstances unfair. It was unfair because it frustrated her legitimate expectation of having a home for life in Mardon House. There was no overriding public interest which justified it. In drawing the balance of conflicting interests the court will not only accept the policy change without demur but will pay the closest attention to the assessment made by the public body itself. Here, however, as we have already indicated, the health authority failed to weigh the conflicting interests correctly. Furthermore, we do not know (for reasons we will

explain later) the quality of the alternative accommodation and services which will be offered to Miss Coughlan. We cannot prejudge what would be the result if there was on offer accommodation which could be said to be reasonably equivalent to Mardon House and the health authority made a properly considered decision in favour of closure in the light of that offer. However, absent such an offer, here there was unfairness amounting to an abuse of power by the health authority.

…

Appeal dismissed.

NOTE: The Court also held that the closure decision amounted to an unlawful interference with the right to respect for one's home under Art. 8 of the ECHR.

■ QUESTIONS

1. If the health authority had found cheaper accommodation for the applicant, would this have overridden the promise made to her?

2. Did the Court move from considering legality to the merits in this case?

NOTE: In the next case the Court considers whether there should be detrimental reliance by the claimant upon the legitimate expectation and what relief might be provided.

R (Bibi) v Newham London Borough Council

[2001] EWCA Civ 607, [2002] 1 WLR 237, Court of Appeal

The applicants had been given a promise that, as unintentionally homeless persons in priority need of accommodation, they would be provided with accommodation with security of tenure. Whilst they were provided with accommodation, this did not have security of tenure. They successfully sought judicial review that the accommodation provided did not discharge the housing authority's obligations to them. The Court found that the obligation was founded on a legitimate expectation and not a statutory duty, as the promise was made on a misunderstanding of what the statute (then the Housing (Homeless Persons) Act 1977) required. The authority appealed.

SCHIEMANN LJ: …

19. In all legitimate expectation cases … practical questions arise, [including] … whether the authority has acted or proposes to act unlawfully in relation to its commitment … [and] what the court should do. …

22. Two problems face a court in answering these questions. The first is to find one or more measuring rods by which it can be objectively determined whether a certain action or inaction is an abuse of power. The second is what order to make once an abuse of power has been discerned—can the court come to a substantive decision itself or should it send the matter back to the decision taker to decide afresh according to law?

23. To a degree the answer to the second depends on the approach one takes to the first. As Laws LJ pointed out in *R v Secretary of State for Education and Employment, ex parte Begbie* [2000] 1 WLR 1115 at page 1131C:

The more the decision challenged lies in what may inelegantly be called the macro-political field, the less intrusive will be the court's supervision. More than this: in that field, true abuse of power is less likely to be found, since within it changes of policy, fuelled by broad conceptions of the public interest, may more readily be accepted as taking precedence over the interests of groups which enjoyed expectations generated by an earlier policy.

Has the authority acted unlawfully? Introduction

24. ... [I]t is important to recognise that there is often a tension between several values in these cases. A choice may need to be made as to which good we attain and which we forego. There are administrative and democratic gains in preserving for the authority the possibility in the future of coming to different conclusions as to the allocation of resources from those to which it is currently wedded. On the other hand there is value in holding authorities to promises which they have made, thus upholding responsible public administration and allowing people to plan their lives sensibly. The task for the law in this area is to establish who makes the choice of priorities and what principles are to be followed.

...

Has the authority acted unlawfully? The relevance of reliance on the promise

26. Mr Matthias submits that, in cases where the expectation which has been generated is of a substantive as opposed to a procedural benefit, authority limits the court to enforcing it only if (a) the motive for resiling from it was improper, or (b) there has been detrimental reliance on it. Only then, he submits, can the departure be said to amount, as it must, to an abuse of power. Founding on the distinction between procedural and substantive expectations identified in *Coughlan* para. 57, on the reasoning in *Ex parte Preston* [1985] AC 835, 866–7 and on the cases reported to date, he argues that (absent bad faith) a substantive legitimate expectation can only arise where a situation analogous to a private law wrong, and therefore involving detrimental reliance, exists.

27. We would not accept this formulation. As Sir Thomas Bingham MR observed in *R* v *Inland Revenue Commissioners, ex p. Unilever plc* [1996] STC p. 681 at page 690f.

The categories of unfairness are not closed, and precedent should act as a guide and not as a cage.

28. As indicated in *R* v *Secretary of State for Education and Employment, ex parte Begbie* [2000] 1 WLR 1115 reliance, though potentially relevant in most cases, is not essential. In that case a letter sent to the parents of one child affected by legislative and policy changes concerning assisted school places came to the knowledge of another child's parent, who relied on it in judicial review proceedings. Peter Gibson LJ, giving the leading judgment, said at page 1123H:

> Mr. Beloff submits ... (v) it is not necessary for a person to have changed his position as a result of such representations for an obligation to fulfil a legitimate expectation to subsist; the principle of good administration prima facie requires adherence by public authorities to their promises. He cites authority in support of all these submissions and for my part I am prepared to accept them as correct, so far as they go. I would however add a few words by way of comment on his fifth proposition, as in my judgment it would be wrong to understate the significance of reliance in this area of the law. It is very much the exception, rather than the rule, that detrimental reliance will not be present when the court finds unfairness in the defeating of a legitimate expectation.

29. In the light of this, we respectfully adopt what Professor Craig has proposed in this regard in Craig, *Administrative Law* [1999] at p. 619:

> Detrimental reliance will normally be required in order for the claimant to show that it would be unlawful to go back on a representation. This is in accord with policy, since if the individual has suffered no hardship there is no reason based on legal certainty to hold the agency to its representation. It should not, however, be necessary to show any monetary loss, or anything equivalent thereto.

30. But he gives the following instance of a case where reliance is not essential —

> Where an agency seeks to depart from an established policy in relation to a particular person detrimental reliance should not be required. Consistency of treatment and equality are at stake in such cases, and these values should be protected irrespective of whether there has been any reliance as such.

31. In our judgment the significance of reliance and of consequent detriment is factual, not legal. In *Begbie* both aspects were in the event critical: there had been no true reliance on the misrepresentation of policy and therefore no detriment suffered specifically in consequence of it. In a strong case, no doubt, there will be both reliance and detriment; but it does not follow that reliance (that is, credence) without measurable detriment cannot render it unfair to thwart a legitimate expectation. ...

...

The role of the court

40. The court has two functions—assessing the legality of actions by administrators and, if it finds unlawfulness on the administrators' part, deciding what relief it should give. It is in our judgment a mistake to isolate from the rest of administrative law cases those which turn on representations made by authorities. The same constitutional principles apply to the exercise by the court of each of these two functions.

41. The court, even where it finds that the applicant has a legitimate expectation of some benefit, will not order the authority to honour its promise where to do so would be to assume the powers of the executive. Once the court has established such an abuse it may ask the decision taker to take the legitimate expectation properly into account in the decision making process.

42. Only part of the relevant material upon consideration of which any decision must be made is before the court. Because of the need to bear in mind more than the interests of the individual before the court, relevant facts are always changing. As Lord Bingham said in *R* v *Cambridge Health Authority, ex parte B* [1995] 2 All ER 129:

> ... it would be totally unrealistic to require the authority to come to the court with its accounts and seek to demonstrate that if this treatment were provided for B then there would be a patient, C, who would have to go without treatment. No major authority could run its financial affairs in a way which would permit such a demonstration.

43. While in some cases there can be only one lawful ultimate answer to the question whether the authority should honour its promise, at any rate in cases involving a legitimate expectation of a substantive benefit, this will not invariably be the case.

The present case

...

48. We proceed therefore on the basis that the Authority has lawfully committed itself to providing the applicants with suitable accommodation with secure tenure.

Has the authority acted unlawfully?

...

53. The fact that someone has not changed his position after a promise has been made to him does not mean that he has not relied on the promise. An actor in a play where another actor points a gun at him may refrain from changing his position just because he has been given a promise that the gun only contains blanks.

...

55. The present case is one of reliance without concrete detriment. We use this phrase because there is moral detriment, which should not be dismissed lightly, in the prolonged disappointment which has ensued; and potential detriment in the deflection of the possibility, for a refugee family, of seeking at the start to settle somewhere in the United Kingdom where secure housing was less hard to come by. In our view these things matter in public law, even though they might not found an estoppel or actionable misrepresentation in private law, because they go to fairness and through fairness to possible abuse of power. To disregard the legitimate expectation because no concrete detriment can be

shown would be to place the weakest in society at a particular disadvantage. It would mean that those who have a choice and the means to exercise it in reliance on some official practice or promise would gain a legal toehold inaccessible to those who, lacking any means of escape, are compelled simply to place their trust in what has been represented to them.

56. A further element for the Authority to bear in mind is the possibility of monetary compensation or assistance. As this court indicated in *Coughlan* para 82 [earlier at p. 552], a legitimate expectation may in some cases be appropriately taken into account by such a payment.

57. An element which may tell against giving effect to the legitimate expectation is the effect on others on the housing list of giving the present applicants special preference. Mr Matthias understandably relies on this both as a reason why Newham's stance is not unfair and, in the alternative, as an overriding policy reason why effect should not be given to the representation. Ostensibly powerful as this is it faces the obstacle, as Mr Luba has argued, that nothing unlawful would necessarily be involved in allocating secure housing to the applicants. For example, the Authority could change the allocation scheme to give weight to its representation to the applicants and the 115 others in their situation. Changing the scheme might not in truth be so simple—but it does not seem to have been considered by the Authority.

58. When considering the legitimate expectations which it has created, the Authority is entitled to take into account the current statutory framework, the allocation scheme, the legitimate expectations of other people, its assets both in terms of what housing it has at its disposal and in terms of what assets it has or could have available. It should consider whether, if it considers it inappropriate to grant the applicants secure tenancies of a council house, it should adopt any other way of helping the applicants to obtain secure housing whether by cash or other aid or by amending the allocation scheme so as to give some weight to legitimate expectations in cases similar to the present, of which we understand there to be a number.

59. But when the Authority looks at the matter again it must take into account the legitimate expectations. Unless there are reasons recognised by law for not giving effect to those legitimate expectations then effect should be given to them. In circumstances such as the present where the conduct of the Authority has given rise to a legitimate expectation then fairness requires that, if the Authority decides not to give effect to that expectation, the Authority articulate its reasons so that their propriety may be tested by the court if that is what the disappointed person requires.

What should the court do?

60. *Coughlan* emphasised the importance of considering these questions in their statutory context. ...

61. In the context of housing Lord Brightman said of the Act of 1977 in *R v Hillingdon LBC, ex parte Puhlhofer* [1986] AC 484, p. 517,

It is an Act to assist persons who are homeless, not an act to provide them with homes ... It is intended to provide for the homeless a lifeline of last resort; not to enable them to make inroads into the local authority's waiting list of applicants for housing. Some inroads there are probably bound to be, but in the end the local authority will have to balance the priority needs of the homeless on the one hand and the legitimate aspirations of those on their housing waiting list on the other hand.

...

63. The present case illustrates a potential conflict between the 'legitimate aspirations' of those who have been told where they are on the housing waiting list and what the Authority's allocation scheme is on the one hand and the 'legitimate expectations' of those to whom promises have been made by the Authority the fulfilment of which conflicts with the priorities contained in the allocation scheme on the other.

64. In an area such as the provision of housing at public expense where decisions are informed by social and political value judgments as to priorities of expenditure the court will start with a recognition that such invidious choices are essentially political rather than judicial. In our judgment the appropriate body to make that choice in the context of the present case is the authority. However, it must do so in the light of the legitimate expectations of the respondents.

65. Turner J declared that the Authority were 'bound to treat the duties originally owed by them to both applicants under section 65(2) as not discharged until the applicants be provided by them with suitable accommodation on a secure tenancy'. Rightly, he did not direct that they be given priority over everyone else who was on the housing register and was seeking the same type of accommodation. The applicants' counsel have not suggested that he should have so directed. They wish merely to hold the declaration which was made.

66. The Judge accepted that the applicants each have a legitimate expectation that they would be provided with suitable accommodation on a secure tenancy. We agree. However, we consider that the Judge went too far in the form of declaration which he made since it seems implicit in his declaration that there cannot be factors which inhibit the fulfilment of the legitimate expectations, even where the Authority has never so concluded.

67. We consider that it would be better simply to declare that the Authority is under a duty to consider the applicants' applications for suitable housing on the basis that they have a legitimate expectation that they will be provided by the Authority with suitable accommodation on a secure tenancy.

Appeal allowed in part.

NOTES

1. In requiring the authority to reconsider the matter the Court is taking notice of the fact that there are others on the housing list and this time the authority must take into account the representation they made to the claimant, and as is stated in [58] there may be other ways in which the claimants could be assisted. Nonetheless, the assumption is in [59] that the authority will meet the expectation and if not reasons must be given which could then be challenged.
2. In the next case attention is directed to the suitability of 'abuse of power' as a principle. Like 'unreasonable' or 'irrational', it is conclusionary and does not articulate its basis. See early comments on this aspect of *Coughlan* by Elliott [2000] *Judicial Review* 27; Craig and Schønberg [2000] *Public Law* 684.

Nadarajah v Secretary of State for the Home Department
[2005] EWCA Civ 1363, Court of Appeal

The appellant's claim for asylum had been rejected. In a subsequent unsuccessful challenge in the High Court it was held that the Secretary of State had misconstrued his 'family links' policy. The policy had been revised between the rejection of asylum and the court's decision. On appeal it was argued that the misconstruction of the original policy and the failure to apply it to the appellant amounted to an error of law and so the appellant then had an expectation that this would lead to the mistake being corrected by the application of the original policy rather than a reconsideration of the case applying the current policy which is unfavourable to the appellant.

LAWS LJ: ...

67. ... So far as it appears to rest on principle, with respect to Mr Underwood I think it superficial to hold that for a legitimate expectation to bite there must be something more than failure to honour the promise in question, and then to list a range of possible additional factors which might make the difference. It is superficial because in truth it reveals no principle. Principle is not in my judgment supplied by the call to arms of abuse of power. Abuse of power is a name for any act of a public authority that is not legally

justified. It is a useful name, for it catches the moral impetus of the rule of law. It may be, as I ventured to put it in *Begbie*, "the root concept which governs and conditions our general principles of public law". But it goes no distance to tell you, case by case, what is lawful and what is not. I accept, of course, that there is no formula which tells you that; if there were, the law would be nothing but a checklist. Legal principle lies ·between the overarching rubric of abuse of power and the concrete imperatives of a rule-book.

68. The search for principle surely starts with the theme that is current through the legitimate expectation cases. It may be expressed thus. Where a public authority has issued a promise or adopted a practice which represents how it proposes to act in a given area, the law will require the promise or practice to be honoured unless there is good reason not to do so. What is the principle behind this proposition? It is not far to seek. It is said to be grounded in fairness, and no doubt in general terms that is so. I would prefer to express it rather more broadly as a requirement of good administration, by which public bodies ought to deal straightforwardly and consistently with the public. In my judgment this is a legal standard which, although not found in terms in the European Convention on Human Rights, takes its place alongside such rights as fair trial, and no punishment without law. That being so there is every reason to articulate the limits of this requirement—to describe what may count as good reason to depart from it—as we have come to articulate the limits of other constitutional principles overtly found in the European Convention. Accordingly a public body's promise or practice as to future conduct may only be denied, and thus the standard I have expressed may only be departed from, in circumstances where to do so is the public body's legal duty, or is otherwise, to use a now familiar vocabulary, a proportionate response (of which the court is the judge, or the last judge) having regard to a legitimate aim pursued by the public body in the public interest. The principle that good administration requires public authorities to be held to their promises would be undermined if the law did not insist that any failure or refusal to comply is objectively justified as a proportionate measure in the circumstances.

69. This approach makes no distinction between procedural and substantive expectations. Nor should it. The dichotomy between procedure and substance has nothing to say about the reach of the duty of good administration. Of course there will be cases where the public body in question justifiably concludes that its statutory duty (it will be statutory in nearly every case) requires it to override an expectation of substantive benefit which it has itself generated. So also there will be cases where a procedural benefit may justifiably be overridden. The difference between the two is not a difference of principle. Statutory duty may perhaps more often dictate the frustration of a substantive expectation. Otherwise the question in either case will be whether denial of the expectation is in the circumstances proportionate to a legitimate aim pursued. Proportionality will be judged, as it is generally to be judged, by the respective force of the competing interests arising in the case. Thus where the representation relied on amounts to an unambiguous promise; where there is detrimental reliance; where the promise is made to an individual or specific group; these are instances where denial of the expectation is likely to be harder to justify as a proportionate measure. They are included in Mr Underwood's list of factors, all of which will be material, where they arise, to the assessment of proportionality. On the other hand where the government decision-maker is concerned to raise wide-ranging or "macro-political" issues of policy, the expectation's enforcement in the courts will encounter a steeper climb. All these considerations, whatever their direction, are pointers not rules. The balance between an individual's fair treatment in particular circumstances, and the vindication of other ends having a proper claim on the public interest (which is the essential dilemma posed by the law of legitimate expectation) is not precisely calculable, its measurement not exact. It is no surprise that, as I ventured to suggest in *Begbie*, "the first and third categories explained in the *Coughlan* case … are not hermetically sealed". These cases have to be judged in the round.

70. There is nothing original in my description of the operative principle as a requirement of good administration. The expression was used in this context at least as long ago as the *Ng Yuen Shiu* case, in which Lord Fraser of Tullybelton, delivering the judgment of the Privy Council, said this (638F):

It is in the interest of good administration that [a public authority] should act fairly and should implement its promise, so long as implementation does not interfere with its statutory duty.

My aim in outlining this approach has been to see if we can conform the shape of the law of legitimate expectations with that of other constitutional principles; and also to go some small distance in providing a synthesis, or at least a backdrop, within or against which the authorities in this area may be related to each other. I would make these observations on the learning I have summarised earlier. First, there are some cases where, on a proper apprehension of the facts, there is in truth no promise for the future: *Ex p. Hargreaves*; see also *In re Findlay* [1985] AC 318. Then in *Ng Yuen Shiu* and *Ex p. Khan* the breach of legitimate expectations—of the standard of good administration—could not be justified as a proportionate response to any dictate of the public interest; indeed I think it may be said that there was no public interest to compete with the expectation. In *Coughlan* the promise's denial could not be justified as a proportionate measure. The three categories of case there described by Lord Woolf represent, I would respectfully suggest, varying scenarios in which the question whether denial of the expectation was proportionate to the public interest aim in view may call for different answers. In *Begbie*, the legitimate expectation was frustrated by the operation of statute. *Bibi* went off essentially on the basis that the authority had "simply not acknowledged that the promises were a relevant consideration in coming to a conclusion as to whether they should be honoured". Its primary importance arises from the court's comments on reliance, including its citation of Professor Craig. That there is no hard and fast rule about reliance to my mind illustrates the fact, which I have already sought to emphasise, that it is in principle no more than a factor to be considered in weighing the question whether denial of the expectation is justified—justified, as I would suggest, as a proportionate act or measure.

71. Applying this approach to the present case, I would arrive at the same result as I have reached on the arguments as they were presented. I am clear that the Secretary of State was entitled to decline to apply the original policy, construed as Stanley Burnton J construed it, in the appellant's case. I have already said that the Secretary of State acted consistently throughout. The appellant knew nothing of the Family Links Policy at the time of the February 2002 decision. He seeks the benefit, not of a government policy intended to apply to persons in his position but unfairly denied him, but the windfall of the Secretary of State's misinterpretation. There is nothing disproportionate, or unfair, in his being refused it. Nothing in Mr Husain's points seems to me to shift that position.

Appeal dismissed.

NOTES

1. In *Nadarajah* at para [68] the principle of good administration gives rise to an obligation that an authority should be held to its promise or practice on how it proposes to act unless it can be objectively justified, was invoked to justify substantive legitimate expectations. It was also relied on in *Mandalia* v *Secretary of State for the Home Department* [2015] UKSC 59, to justify relief in the different but related situation where someone subsequently challenged the departure from an existing policy when unaware of that policy at the time of the decision or action. Such ignorance was felt to strain the concept of legitimate expectations but it was appropriate that the authority should be held to its promise or policy.

2. See this summary of the case law made by Cranston J in *United Kingdom Association of Fish Producer Organisations* v *Secretary of State for Environment, Food and Rural Affairs* [2013] EWHC 1959 (Admin):

> 92. The threads of the English doctrine of substantive legitimate expectation can be drawn together in the following propositions:
>
> 1. The undertaking must be clear, unambiguous and without relevant qualification: *R (Bancoult) v Secretary of State for Foreign and Commonwealth Affairs* [2008] UKHL 61, at [60].
> 2. On ordinary principles an undertaking can derive from a representation or a course of conduct. However, the mere existence of a scheme is inadequate in itself to generate a substantive legitimate expectation: *R (Bhatt Murphy) v Independent Assessor* [2008] EWCA Civ 755, at [63].

3. Whether there is such an undertaking is ascertained by asking how, on a fair reading, the representation or course of conduct would reasonably have been understood by those to whom it was made: *R (Patel) v General Medical Council* [2013] EWCA Civ 327, at [44]-[45], applying *Paponette v Attorney General of Trinidad and Tobago* [2010] UKPC 32, at [30].

4. Although in theory the defined class being large is no bar to their having a substantive legitimate expectation, in reality it is likely to be small if the expectation is to be made good: *Bhatt Murphy*, at [46]. In *Paponette* the successful class to whom a collective promise had been made was some 2000.

5. Detrimental reliance is not an essential requirement. However, it may be necessary where the issue is in the macro-political field or a person-specific undertaking is alleged: *Bancoult*, at [60]; *R v Secretary of State for Education and Employment, ex p Begbie* [1999] EWCA Civ 2100, at [48], [101].

6. To justify frustration of a substantive legitimate expectation, the decision maker must have taken into account as a relevant consideration the undertaking and the fact that it will be frustrated: *Paponette*, at [45]-[46].

7. Legitimate expectation is concerned with exceptional situations: *Bhatt Murphy*, at [41].

8. Justification turns on issues of fairness and good administration, whether frustrating the substantive legitimate expectation can be objectively justified in the public interest and as a proportionate response. Abuse of power is not an adequate guide: *R (Nadarajah) v Secretary of State for the Home Department* [2005] EWCA Civ 1363, at [70].

9. The intensity of review depends on the character of the decision. There will be a more rigorous standard than *Wednesbury* review, with a decision being judged by the court's own view of fairness. A public body will not often be held bound to maintain a policy which on reasonable grounds it has chosen to change. There will be less intrusive review in the macro-political field. As well, respect will be accorded to the relative expertise of a decision-maker: *Bhatt Murphy*, at [35], [41]; *Patel* at [60]-[62], [83].

10. Transitional arrangements, and whether there has been a warning of possible change, are not essential but may be relevant to the court's assessment of justification: *Bhatt Murphy* at [18]-[20], [56]-[57], [60]-[61], [65]-[70]; *Patel* at [77], [83].

3. The development of legitimate expectations has led the House of Lords to say that estoppel should be confined to private law (*R (Reprotech (Pebsham) Ltd) v East Sussex CC* [2002] UKHL 8, [2003] 1 WLR 348). There is a problem where a body makes an *ultra vires* representation, in that can a legitimate expectation be based on it? The position in common law was that the lack of legal capacity by the public body would frustrate the enforcement of the expectation against it, but where an ECHR right is concerned, it is less clear. In *Stretch v UK* (2004) 38 EHRR 12, which concerned an option to renew a lease, the ECtHR held that the option was a factor which could attach to property rights arising under the lease and be protected by Art. 1, Protocol 1. Unlike the Court of Appeal who found that the lack of legal capacity to grant the option was conclusive, the ECtHR held that this was a factor which would be included in the balancing exercise the court conducts when deciding if the expectation should be enforced or frustrated. It decided that damages could be awarded as the unlawful grant of the option did not prejudice the authority's statutory functions or third parties. Subsequently a different approach was used in *Rowland v Environment Agency* [2003] EWCA Civ 1885, a case about a stretch of the River Thames and the incorrect representations by the Agency that it did not have a public right of navigation. At common law, the Agency could not be required to act on its representations, but as Art. 1, Protocol 1 was engaged, the Court felt that the Agency could 'alleviate any injustice by benevolent exercise of its powers' by, as the Agency had offered, not promoting public use of the stretch of river. Damages were not sought, and some argue that it is a better method to reconcile the competing public and private interests: e.g., H. W. R. Wade and C. F. Forsyth, *Administrative Law* (2004), p. 314, whereas May LJ in *Rowland* thought that if, after conducting the balancing exercise, it was appropriate to enforce an unlawfully generated expectation, this was preferable to compensation from the public purse. Elliott argues that in principle there is no reason why the approach adopted in *Rowland* could not be adopted where Convention rights are not engaged (2004) 63 *Cambridge Law Journal* 261 (see also Craig (1999), at 611–49; (2016), at 694–708, whose 1999 discussion was considered by Peter Gibson and May LJJ in *Rowland*).

F: Irrationality and/or proportionality

Having considered the use of proportionality in substantive legitimate expectations and earlier in litigation under the Human Rights Act 1998 in Chapter 9, Section 3C at pp. 476–82, this helps in comparing proportionality with irrationality or *Wednesbury* unreasonableness. The law of the European Union also introduced the principle of proportionality which was to be used in situations where EU law had been transposed or produced direct effect in domestic law. In the following case a comparison was made between reasonableness and proportionality.

R v Chief Constable of Sussex, ex parte International Trader's Ferry Ltd
[1999] 2 AC 418, House of Lords

The applicant company (ITF) was engaged in exporting live animals. People who were opposed to this demonstrated at ports seeking to stop the transport of the livestock. The police operations enabled five sailings a week to be operated out of Shoreham. The Chief Constable reviewed the situation and, after taking into account his resources, decided to deploy officers at Shoreham on two consecutive days a week, or four consecutive days a fortnight. The applicants challenged this decision by judicial review. In the Divisional Court the Chief Constable's decision was quashed on the basis that it breached Art. 34 (now 35 TFEU) of the EC Treaty, as it was a measure having equivalent effect to a quantitative restriction on exports. In domestic law it was a lawful exercise of his discretion. On appeal the Court of Appeal held that if this decision was within the scope of Art. 34 (now 35 TFEU) it was covered by Art. 36 (now 36 TFEU) and was justified on grounds of public policy, the pursuit of effective policing. The applicants appealed.

LORD SLYNN: … What is required in a case like the present where the Chief Constable has statutory and common law duties to perform is to ask whether he did all that proportionately and reasonably he could be expected to do with the resources available to him. He is after all dealing with an emergency situation and there is no question of funds being deliberately withheld by the state to hamper his work. The budget for the authority was a very large one and it was for him to decide how he would use the moneys apportioned to him. These decisions have to be taken on the information available at the time. It is not right, in my view, that there should be an ex post facto examination of accounts to see whether, in some way or another, in the event moneys did prove to be available which perhaps could have been used. Thus, in the present case, I do not consider that the fact that the amount attributed to reserves in the final accounts in the 1995–96 year (£13.13m.) meant that, at the time he had to take his decision, the Chief Constable should have assumed that the police authorities would allocate more money to this particular task than appeared as reserves in the budget (£7.25m.). It seems to me that at the end of the day it is all a question of considering whether 'appropriate measures' have been taken. That in turn involves an inquiry as to whether the steps taken were proportionate.

In *Reg.* v *Secretary of State for the Home Department, Ex parte Brind* [1991] 1 AC 696 the House treated *Wednesbury* reasonableness and proportionality as being different. So in some ways they are though the distinction between the two tests in practice is in any event much less than is sometimes suggested. The cautious way in which the European Court usually applies this test, recognising the importance of respecting the national authority's margin of appreciation, may mean that whichever test is adopted, and even allowing for a difference in onus, the result is the same.

I am satisfied, as was the Court of Appeal, that the Chief Constable has shown here that what he did in providing police assistance was proportionate to what was required. To protect the lorries, in the way he did, was a suitable and necessary way of dealing with potentially violent demonstrators. To limit the occasions when sufficient police could be made available was, in the light of the resources available to him to deal with immediate and foreseeable events at the port, and at the same time to carry out all his other police duties, necessary and in no way disproportionate to the restrictions which were involved. Unlike the authorities in *Commission of the European Communities* v *French Republic* (Case C–265/95) [1997] ECR I–6959 he was controlling and arresting violent offenders. He was, moreover, not dealing with a situation where no other way of exporting the animals was available. Dover was available and there were and might be other occasions when the lorries could get through. Far from failing to protect the applicant's trade he was seeking to do it in the most effective way available to him with his finite resources. It was only on rare and necessary, even dangerous, occasions that lorries were turned back. In the light of article 36 [now 36] it is not open to ITF to say, as they at times seem to be saying, that they had an absolute right to export animals on seven days a week and there is no suggestion that with such a short Channel crossing their claim was necessarily limited to one sailing a day. This case is quite different from *Commission of the European Communities* v *French Republic* where 'manifest and persistent failure' to control those interfering with imports was shown and where there was no evidence to show that those responsible could have acted. Since this case involves the application of the principles laid down in the *French Republic* case, where clearly the European Court left a considerable discretion to national authorities in dealing with issues of this sort, I do not find it necessary, nor are your Lordships obliged, to refer a question concerning article 36 [now 30] to the European Court of Justice under article 177 [now 267] of the EC Treaty.

I am satisfied that here the Chief Constable has shown that the steps that he took were justified on grounds of public order and I would dismiss this appeal.

NOTES

1. Lord Cooke was also of the view that in this case 'the European concepts of proportionality and margin of appreciation produce the same result as what are commonly called *Wednesbury* principles'. He seemed to prefer a simpler test than the tautologous formula in *Wednesbury*—'so unreasonable that no reasonable authority could ever have come to it'—'whether the decision in question was one which a reasonable authority could reach'.

   Subsequent developments were summarized by Lord Mance in *Kennedy* v *The Charity Commission* [2014] UKSC 20:

   > 51....The common law no longer insists on the uniform application of the rigid test of irrationality once thought applicable under the so-called *Wednesbury* principle. The nature of judicial review in every case depends upon the context ...

   Lord Mance drawing on the judgment of Carnwath LJ in *IBA Health Ltd* v *Office of Fair Trading* [2004] EWCA Civ 142, at [91] based his summary on a type of what might be called a sliding scale produced by the case law where common law unreasonableness seems to be similar to proportionality as developed in the law of the EU and ECHR. Thus in the common law there is low-intensity review which is conducted in relation to 'macro-political' issues such as national economic policy in *R* v *Secretary of State, Ex p Hammersmith and Fulham London Borough Council* [1991] 1 AC 521, where the court would not intervene outside 'the extremes of bad faith, improper motive or manifest absurdity' (per Lord Bridge of Harwich, at pp. 596–7). At the other end of the spectrum review is conducted at a higher intensity when dealing with interference to rights; fundamental rights recognized by the common law 'anxious scrutiny' rather than perversity or absurdity.

Mark Elliot, 'Proportionality and contextualism in common-law review: The Supreme Court's judgment in *Pham*'

(2015) https://publiclawforeveryone.com/2015/04/17/proportionality-and-contextualism-in-common-law-review-the-supreme-courts-judgment-in-pham/

The recent decision of the UK Supreme Court in *Pham v Secretary of State for the Home Department* [2015] UKSC 19 marks a turning-point in the role of proportionality as a common-law ground of judicial review. Although the case did not ultimately turn upon proportionality, the judgments contain detailed discussion of the doctrine, and evidence judicial support for its availability as a ground of judicial review irrespective of whether the case has a European Union or ECHR dimension to it. And while this judgment does not come out of the blue—other cases have hinted at this development—*Pham* is particularly explicit and direct. In this way, it arguably represents a landmark in the emergence of proportionality as common-law head of review….

Background

The key issue in *Pham* was whether it was lawful for the Home Secretary to strip the appellant of British citizenship and deport him to Vietnam, where he had been born …

All four of the judgments given in the Supreme Court embraced the possibility—indeed, the likelihood—that it was unnecessary to decide the EU point because whether EU law was applicable would make no difference to the outcome of the case. The appellant's argument on this matter turned upon the assumption that establishing the applicability of EU law would unlock the door to a form of judicial review—i.e. review on proportionality grounds—that would otherwise be unavailable at common law. The Supreme Court, however, doubted the veracity of this assumption. It was against this backdrop that the Justices turned to consider the availability of proportionality review in purely "domestic" cases.

Lord Carnwath: Correspondence between *Wednesbury* and proportionality

Lord Carnwath discussed this matter relatively briefly. In doing so, he placed weight upon the Supreme Court's judgment in *Kennedy v The Charity Commission* [2014] UKSC 20 which, he said, endorsed "a flexible approach to principles of judicial review, particularly where important rights are at stake". He also referred to Paul Craig's 2013 *Current Legal Problems* lecture ['The Nature of Reasonableness Review'] in which Craig argues that "both reasonableness review and proportionality involve considerations of weight and balance, with the intensity of the scrutiny and the weight to be given to any primary decision maker's view depending on the context". Lord Carnwath indicated that this flexible approach should operate in favour of more stringent scrutiny where the removal of a "fundamental status" such as citizenship is concerned.

Lord Carnwath does not go so far as to endorse explicitly the availability of proportionality in cases where an "important right" or a "fundamental status" is at stake. However, he arguably indicates, at least implicitly, that the relationship between proportionality and rationality is such that the choice of label does not matter a great deal, and that the common law is capable, in appropriate cases, of supplying scrutiny equivalent to that which is available under proportionality.

Lords Mance, Sumption and Reed, however, went further. Like Lord Carnwath, Lord Mance invoked both *Kennedy* and Craig. However, he went on not simply to note a degree of correspondence between *Wednesbury* and proportionality, but explicitly to endorse the application of the latter at common law: [at para. 98]

> Removal of British citizenship under the power provided by section 40(2) of the British Nationality Act 1981 is, on any view, a radical step, particularly if the person affected has little real attachment to the country of any other nationality that he possesses and is unlikely to be able to return there. A correspondingly strict standard of judicial review must apply to any exercise of the power contained in section 40(2), and the tool of proportionality is one which would, in my view and for the reasons explained in *Kennedy* …, be both available and valuable for the purposes of such a review.

This unambiguous endorsement of proportionality as a common-law ground of review is important. Equally, important, however is the fact that Lord Mance's embrace of proportionality was accompanied by a nuanced account of what proportionality review amounts to. Lord Mance introduced this nuance by disaggregating two distinct but often conflated features of substantive review—namely, *intensity* and *structure*. Proportionality is often taken to be more intense *because* it is more structured, but Lord Mance argued—correctly—that this is not so. Instead, he endorsed Lübbe-Wolff's view that whether proportionality intensifies review "is not determined by the structure of the test but by the degree of judicial restraint practised in applying it". The purpose of this discussion was presumably to establish that proportionality can exist as common-law ground of review without threatening fundamental constitutional considerations such as the distinction between appeal and review. In this way, Lord Mance tackles the sort of criticisms levelled at proportionality by Lords Ackner and Lowry in *R v Secretary of State for the Home Department, ex parte Brind* [1991] 1 AC 696, by showing that its adoption need not herald a shift to uniformly more intensive review.

Lord Reed: Proportionality and the principle of legality

If Lord Mance's judgment demonstrates greater doctrinal depth than Lord Carnwath's, it is fair to say that Lord Reed's goes further still. In particular, Lord Reed distinguished between two senses in which the term proportionality is used. In the first place, he observed, it may simply connote a general ground of judicial review that—as cases like *R v Barnsley Metropolitan Borough Council, ex parte Hook* [1976] 1 WLR 1052 demonstrate—are of relatively long standing. Viewed in this way, however, proportionality is concerned with nothing more than the question of means-ends fit, and does not obviously differ from *Wednesbury*, given that the use of a sledgehammer to crack a nut—likely with deleterious collateral disadvantages—is readily characterisable as irrational.

However, Lord Reed distinguished this from proportionality as a vehicle for "the scrutiny of justifications advanced for interferences with legal rights". He argued that proportionality in this sense can be seen to have operated at common law in cases such as *R v Secretary of State for the Home Department, ex parte Leech (No 2)* [1994] QB 198 and *R v Secretary of State for the Home Department, ex parte Daly* [2001] UKHL 26. In those cases, the principle of legality—a principle of statutory construction—facilitated proportionality review by means of the reading into the statute of implied prohibitions upon disproportionate interference with rights …

> [119] One can infer from these cases that, where Parliament authorises significant interferences with important legal rights, the courts may interpret the legislation as requiring that any such interference should be no greater than is objectively established to be necessary to achieve the legitimate aim of the interference: *in substance, a requirement of proportionality*. [Emphasis added]

Significantly, Lord Reed suggested that this interpretative methodology—including its facilitating of proportionality review—might be appropriate in a case such as *Pham*:

> [120] Given the fundamental importance of citizenship, it may be arguable that the power to deprive a British citizen of that status should be interpreted as being subject to an implied requirement that its exercise should be justified as being necessary to achieve the legitimate aim pursued. Such an argument has not however been advanced at the hearing of this appeal, and it would be inappropriate to express any view on it.

This goes further than either *Leech* or *Daly*, given that proportionality was never *explicitly* used in the former, and given that the Convention rights were in play in the latter (albeit that it was decided principally on the basis of common-law rights). In this way, Lord Reed's analysis in *Daly* represents the most explicit and authoritative judicial acknowledgment to date of the capacity of the principle of legality to operate as a vehicle for proportionality review in cases lacking any EU or ECHR dimension.

Lord Sumption: A Damascene conversion?

Lord Sumption (with whom Lords Neuberger and Wilson and Lady Hale agreed) was also willing to countenance the possibility of proportionality review at common law. He observed that

> [105] although English law has not adopted the principle of proportionality generally, it has for many years stumbled towards a concept which is in significant respects similar, and over the last three decades has been influenced by European jurisprudence even in areas of law lying beyond the domains of EU and international human rights law. Starting with the decision of the House of Lords in *R v Secretary of State for the Home Department, Ex p Bugdaycay* [1987] AC 514 it has recognised the need, even in the context of rights arising wholly from domestic law, to differentiate between rights of greater or lesser importance and interference with them of greater or lesser degree. This is essentially the same problem as the one to which proportionality analysis is directed. The solution adopted, albeit sometimes without acknowledgment, was to expand

the scope of rationality review so as to incorporate at common law significant elements of the principle of proportionality.

It is important to acknowledge that Lord Sumption was not merely describing these developments; he was endorsing them. Indeed, he pointed to what he considered to be the "arbitrariness" of dealing with domestic matters by reference to *Wednesbury* and cases in which EU or Convention rights are implicated by means of proportionality review. That said, Lord Sumption does not go quite as far as Lord Mance or Lord Reed, in that he does not explicitly support the use of "proportionality" as a domestic head of review. Rather, his approach is closer to Lord Carnwath's, according to which any rigid distinction between the two grounds of review is somewhat arid, the crucial question being where a given right falls on a "sliding scale, in which the cogency of the justification required for interfering with a right will be proportionate to its perceived importance and the extent of the interference".

Conclusion: The opportunities and risks of contextualism

…

Pham is important because it reconceives the way in which the [judicial] toolbox is organised. In particular, it rejects the compartmentalisation sketched above, according to which *Wednesbury* and proportionality are viewed as rigidly separate; it evidences a contextualist approach which echoes that which underpinned the diversification of *Wednesbury*; and it extends such contextualism such that proportionality (or something that is its functional equivalent) becomes available at common law where circumstances warrant it. In this way, *Pham* eschews rigid distinctions between "domestic" and "European" cases, between "rights" and "non-rights" cases, and between *Wednesbury* and proportionality themselves. This approach is to be welcomed. Indeed, it is of a piece with an approach that I have advocated elsewhere, according to which substantive judicial review is to be understood as a contextualist endeavour that cannot be undertaken by reference to the sort of crude distinctions sketched above.

There are, however, risks associated with such an approach. Those risks track the two key changes that *Pham* implies, namely the extension of the range of substantive-review tools to include proportionality and the adoption of contextual criteria to determine the operative approach to review. The first point is that, for all its faults, *Wednesbury* operated as an important safeguard against judicial overreach. Once it is joined by proportionality—which, if not necessarily more intrusive, is potentially more intrusive—that safeguard is removed. Instead, it becomes necessary to rely upon judicial wisdom both in terms of deciding when recourse to proportionality is in the first place warranted and, when it is, to what extent its intrusiveness should be moderated by recourse to deference. The second point relates to the contextualist approach that, according to *Pham*, ought now to prevail. Sensibly deployed, such an approach is capable of forming the foundation of a mature, nuanced and sophisticated body of substantive-review doctrine—one that is the servant of principle, rather than a Procrustean bed based on bald categorisation, and one that reflects the full complexity of this area of the law in normative, institutional and constitutional terms. The risk, however, is that such contextualism may collapse into a chaotic regime of single instances that renders substantive review little more than a vehicle for dispensing palm-tree justice in an unpredictable fashion.

NOTES

1. It might have been thought following *Pham* that the Supreme Court might have been prepared to reconsider rationality review in domestic law and replace it with proportionality. This was one of the arguments made by the appellants in *Keyu* v *Secretary of State for Foreign and Commonwealth Affairs* [2015] UKSC 69 who were challenging the decision taken by the Foreign and Defence Secretaries of State, to refuse a public inquiry into events which had occurred in Malaysia when it was a British colony. The opportunity was not taken. Lord Neuberger said at para. [132]:

> It would not be appropriate for a five-Justice panel of this court to accept, or indeed to reject, this argument, which potentially has implications which are profound in constitutional terms and very wide in applicable scope.

Lord Kerr at para. [271] agreed that this issue was not appropriate for a five-judge panel but did not seem to think that the constitutional significance was as great as some thought, and said he believed that in the past the width of some of the implications of such a change had been overestimated.

He outlines some of the issues which could be considered at para. [278]:

> Final conclusions on a number of interesting issues that arise in this area must await a case where they can be more fully explored. These include whether irrationality and proportionality are forms of review which are bluntly opposed to each other and mutually exclusive; whether intensity of review operates on a sliding scale, dependent on the nature of the decision under challenge and that, in consequence, the debate about a 'choice' between proportionality and rationality is no longer relevant; whether there is any place in modern administrative law for a 'pure' irrationality ground of review ie one which poses the question, 'could any reasonable decision-maker, acting reasonably, have reached this conclusion'; and whether proportionality provides a more structured and transparent means of review.

One topic which Lord Kerr does address is the suitability of the proportionality four-criteria test in cases in which there are no rights at stake, as in *Keyu* where the appellants had no right to an inquiry. He suggests at para. [282]:

> I envisage a more loosely structured proportionality challenge where a fundamental right is not involved. As Lord Mance said in *Kennedy*, this involves a testing of the decision in terms of its "suitability or appropriateness, necessity and the balance or imbalance of benefits and disadvantages".

This restructuring is derived from Craig who is an advocate of proportionality as a general criterion of review (see the latest edition of his *Administrative Law* (2016) at pp. 660–8).

2. Elliott, in his blog post on *Keyu* 'Q: How many Supreme Court Justices does it take to perform the *Wednesbury* doctrine's burial rites? A: More than five' (https://publiclawforeveryone.com/2015/11/27/q-how-many-supreme-court-justices-does-it-take-to-perform-the-wednesbury-doctrines-burial-rites-a-more-than-five/), thinks that 'whether proportionality should supplant *Wednesbury*' is to ask the wrong question. He would ask how the range of approaches embodied in those concepts should relate to each other and argues that Lord Kerr's reimagining of a looser proportionality challenge, and the fact that in *Keyu* Lady Hale's dissent would have allowed the appeal on basis of a *Wednesbury* review which he felt in part resembled the fair balance stage of the proportionality test.

3. In *Youssef* v *Secretary of State for Foreign and Commonwealth Affairs* [2016] UKSC 3, in which Lord Carnwath gave the sole judgment, the Supreme Court took account of *Pham* and *Keyu* and at para. 56 said that in 'advance of a comprehensive review of the tests to be applied to administrative decisions generally, there is a measure of support for the use of proportionality as a test in relation to interference with "fundamental" rights'. He cited from *Keyu*, Lord Kerr [280]–[282] and Lady Hale [305] and in *Pham* himself [60], Lord Mance [95]–[98], and Lord Sumption [105]–[109].

■ **QUESTION**

Is the question to be asked whether under irrationality or proportionality, does the intensity of review, in any of the contexts, actually cross the line into full merits review and is this justifiable?

11

The Availability of Judicial Review

OVERVIEW

In this chapter we consider some questions in order to determine the availability of judicial review and its significance in the constitution. What is the nature of the procedure to seek judicial review and is it exclusive? Who can apply for judicial review? Against whom and in respect of what matters may judicial review be sought? Then comes a consideration of the discretionary nature of the remedies available in judicial review proceedings and the manner in which the courts exercise this discretion. We end with an examination of the courts' approach to legislative attempts to exclude judicial review.

SECTION 1: THE CLAIM FOR JUDICIAL REVIEW

In 1969 the Law Commission was asked to 'review the existing remedies for the judicial control of administrative acts or omissions with a view to evolving a simpler and more effective procedure'. At that time litigants seeking to challenge administrative acts or omissions had a choice of two procedures. They could begin an action by writ or originating summons seeking an injunction, declaration, and, if appropriate, damages. This is the normal way of commencing an action to establish a breach of a private law right, but the courts also allowed it to be used to challenge the decisions of public authorities on the ground that they had acted beyond their powers. Alternatively, litigants could use a special procedure to seek one or more of the prerogative orders, *certiorari*, prohibition, or *mandamus*. The difficulties surrounding the old prerogative order procedure are set out in the judgment of Lord Diplock in *O'Reilly* v *Mackman* (see later in this chapter in Section 2 at p. 581).

The result of the review was the Report on Remedies in Administrative Law (Law Com. No. 73, Cmnd 6407) which made a number of recommendations. It was assumed that implementation of the recommendations would require legislation, but the bulk of the changes contained in the proposals were in fact made by an amendment in 1977 to Ord. 53 of the Rules of the Supreme Court (S.I. 1977 No. 1955). Some of these provisions were themselves amended in 1980 by S.I. 1980 No. 2000. A number of provisions relevant to the application for judicial review were subsequently enacted in the Supreme Court Act 1981, which was renamed the Senior Courts Act 1981 by the Constitutional Reform Act 2005, s. 59, Sch. 11. Following Lord Woolf's review of civil justice, new Civil Procedure Rules were made, but judicial review was not initially reformed according to the new philosophy. A subsequent review of the Crown Office List chaired by Sir Jeffery Bowman led to various changes. The judicial review procedure was amended, becoming a claim for judicial review under Part 54 of the Civil Procedure Rules (CPR). The Crown Office List was renamed the Administrative Court, which was a recognition that the great bulk of cases assigned to it involved issues of public law. These changes took effect on 2 October 2000, the day the Human Rights Act 1998 came into force. A pre-action protocol for CPR, Part 54 came into force on 4 March 2002.

Senior Courts Act 1981

31. —(1) An application to the High Court for one or more of the following forms of relief, namely—

(a) a mandatory, prohibiting or quashing order;
(b) a declaration or injunction under subsection (2); …

shall be made in accordance with rules of court by a procedure to be known as an application for judicial review.

(2) A declaration may be made or an injunction granted under this subsection in any case where an application for judicial review, seeking that relief, has been made and the High Court considers that, having regard to—

(a) the nature of the matters in respect of which relief may be granted by orders of mandamus, prohibition or certiorari;
(b) the nature of the persons and bodies against whom relief may be granted by such orders; and
(c) all the circumstances of the case, it would be just and convenient for the declaration to be made or the injunction to be granted, as the case may be.

(2A) The High Court—

(a) must refuse to grant relief on an application for judicial review, and
(b) may not make an award under subsection (4) on such an application,

if it appears to the court to be highly likely that the outcome for the applicant would not have been substantially different if the conduct complained of had not occurred.

(2B) The court may disregard the requirements in subsection (2A)(a) and (b) if it considers that it is appropriate to do so for reasons of exceptional public interest.

(2C) If the court grants relief or makes an award in reliance on subsection (2B), the court must certify that the condition in subsection (2B) is satisfied.

(3) No application for judicial review shall be made unless the leave of the High Court has been obtained in accordance with rules of court; and the court shall not grant leave to make such an application unless

(a) it considers that the applicant has a sufficient interest in the matter to which the application relates, and
(b) the applicant has provided the court with any information about the financing of the application that is specified in rules of court for the purposes of this paragraph

(3A) The information that may be specified for the purposes of subsection (3)(b) includes—

(a) information about the source, nature and extent of financial resources available, or likely to be available, to the applicant to meet liabilities arising in connection with the application, and
(b) if the applicant is a body corporate that is unable to demonstrate that it is likely to have financial resources available to meet such liabilities, information about its members and about their ability to provide financial support for the purposes of the application.

(3B) Rules of court under subsection (3)(b) that specify information identifying those who are, or are likely to be, sources of financial support must provide that only a person whose financial support (whether direct or indirect) exceeds, or is likely to exceed, a level set out in the rules has to be identified. This subsection does not apply to rules that specify information described in subsection (3A)(b).

(3C) When considering whether to grant leave to make an application for judicial review, the High Court—

    (a) may of its own motion consider whether the outcome for the applicant would have been substantially different if the conduct complained of had not occurred, and

    (b) must consider that question if the defendant asks it to do so.

(3D) If, on considering that question, it appears to the High Court to be highly likely that the outcome for the applicant would not have been substantially different, the court must refuse to grant leave.

(3E) The court may disregard the requirement in subsection (3D) if it considers that it is appropriate to do so for reasons of exceptional public interest.

(3F) If the court grants leave in reliance on subsection (3E), the court must certify that the condition in subsection (3E) is satisfied.

(4) On an application for judicial review the High Court may award to the applicant damages, restitution or the recovery of a sum due if—

    (a) the application includes a claim for such an award arising from any matter to which the application relates; and

    (b) the court is satisfied that such an award would have been made if the claim had been made in an action begun by the applicant at the time of making the application.

(5) If, on an application for judicial review, the High Court quashes the decision to which the application relates, it may in addition—

    (a) remit the matter to the court, tribunal or authority which made the decision, with a direction to reconsider the matter and reach a decision in accordance with the findings of the High Court, or

    (b) substitute its own decision for the decision in question.

(5A) But the power conferred by subsection (5)(b) is exercisable only if—

    (a) the decision in question was made by a court or tribunal,

    (b) the decision is quashed on the ground that there has been an error of law, and

    (c) without the error, there would have been only one decision which the court or tribunal could have reached.

(5B) Unless the High Court otherwise directs, a decision substituted by it under subsection (5)(b) has effect as if it were a decision of the relevant court or tribunal.

(6) Where the High Court considers that there has been undue delay in making an application for judicial review, the court may refuse to grant—

    (a) leave for the making of the application; or

    (b) any relief sought on the application,

if it considers that the granting of the relief sought would be likely to cause substantial hardship to, or substantially prejudice the rights of, any person or would be detrimental to good administration.

(7) Subsection (6) is without prejudice to any enactment or rule of court which has the effect of limiting the time within which an application for judicial review may be made.

(8) In this section "the conduct complained of", in relation to an application for judicial review, means the conduct (or alleged conduct) of the defendant that the applicant claims justifies the High Court in granting relief.

NOTES

1. Provisions were added to s. 31 by Part 4 of the Criminal Justice and Courts Act 2015 following consultations on reforms of judicial review. The Government was concerned that it was taking too long to weed out weak judicial review applications; there was a growth in judicial review proceedings and this was causing delays, in some cases this was frustrating proposals for economic growth. The consultation included proposals on time limits and the procedure seeking permission to bring a judicial review, and the fees in judicial review proceedings (Ministry of Justice, *Judicial Review: Proposals for Reform*, Cm 8515, 2012). The proposals attracted a lot of criticism and the empirical data on judicial reviews presented by V. Bondy and M. Sunkin in 'Judicial Review Reform: Who is Afraid of Judicial Review? Debunking the Myths of Growth and Abuse', *UK Constitutional Law Blog*, 10 January 2013 (available at http://ukconstitutionallaw.org), supported their conclusion that the Government's concerns had not been substantiated. Economic growth was not endangered by judicial review, as the great majority of proceedings challenged central government decisions in immigration, asylum, and in criminal justice matters about prisoners and parole. Nonetheless, in the Government response the Lord Chancellor announced that most of them would be taken forward while acknowledging that the proposals drew more opposition than support (Cm 8611, 2013). Further consultation proposals were published, including planning cases, the requirements for standing to be able to bring judicial review, arrangements for costs, and the scope for greater use of 'leap-frogging' orders to move cases more quickly to the Supreme Court (see *Judicial Review: Proposals for further reform*, Cm 8703, 2013). The consultation response on standing provoked opposition and it was not pursued. We will consider changes made to the threshold test for relief, and the new requirements for providing financial information.

2. In s. 31(2A), the new test of materiality requires refusal of the grant of relief 'if it appears to the court that the outcome for the applicant would not have been substantially different if the conduct complained of had not occurred'. The test has been changed from inevitability to high likelihood; however, s. 31(2B) allows the court to disregard the new duty to refuse relief, if it is appropriate for reasons of exceptional public interest. This is aimed at, but not only to, procedural defects, which would not affect the decision made, such as some cases of public consultation (HC Deb, 13 Jan 2015, Col 812). In an analysis of the new test (The Bingham Centre for the Rule of Law, the Public Law Project and Justice, *Judicial Review and the Rule of Law: An Introduction to the Criminal Justice and Courts Act 2015, Part 4*, 2015), it is argued that the 'highly likely' test should mean that a court in refusing permission or relief should be satisfied that the possibility of a different outcome is very remote. When this is considered at the permission stage under s. 31(3C–F), it is contended that only if the court can confidently conclude without detailed enquiry that the 'highly likely' test is a 'knock-out blow', should permission be refused, citing *R (Mencap)* v *Parliamentary & Health Service Ombudsman* [2010] EWCA Civ 875, [15]; *R (Ewing)* v *Office of the Deputy Prime Minister* [2005] EWCA Civ 1583.

3. The provisions on financial disclosure in s. 31(3)(b), (3A–B), which have not yet come into force, have the policy objective of providing greater transparency about the financing of claimants' judicial reviews which the courts must take into account when deciding whether to make a costs order. In a consultation, *Reform of judicial review: proposals for the provision and use of financial information* (Cm 9117, 2015), it was proposed that where third parties' contributions or likely contributions would exceed a threshold of £1,500, then the details would be included in the claimant's declaration. Many responses contested the Government's rationale of the strength of the link between a contribution to and thereby control of the conduct of the proceedings, and thought this threshold was too low. In its response the Government consulted on a new threshold of £3,000 (Cm 9303, 2016). There is a concern generally about the possible impact on access to a court and the right to privacy under Art. 8 of the ECHR, as well as concerns about the possibility of disclosure of members of corporate bodies or charities which are claimants where the body could not demonstrate it had the resources to meet its liabilities. The analysis by The Bingham Centre et al. includes recommendations to safeguard access to court and privacy. It remains to be seen what policy the Government will adopt when inviting the bodies to make the rules for courts and tribunals on these disclosures provided for in s. 31(3)(b).

4. The text of s. 31A is not included here but in discussion of the powers of tribunals, see s. 19 of the Tribunals, Courts and Enforcement Act 2007, Chapter 13, Section 2C at p. 665.

Civil Procedure Rules

The full text of the latest update is available at http://www.justice.gov.uk/courts/procedure-rules/civil/rules.

Note source still refers to Supreme Court Act 1981 and not Senior Courts Act 1981.

Part 54

I. JUDICIAL REVIEW AND STATUTORY REVIEW

SCOPE AND INTERPRETATION

54.1 (1) This Section of this Part contains rules about judicial review.

(2) In this Section—

> (a) a 'claim for judicial review' means a claim to review the lawfulness of—
>> (i)   an enactment; or
>> (ii) a decision, action or failure to act in relation to the exercise of a public function; ...
> (e) 'the judicial review procedure' means the Part 8 procedure as modified by this Part;
> (f)   'interested party' means any person (other than the claimant and defendant) who is directly affected by the claim; and
> (g) 'court' means the High Court, unless otherwise stated ...

WHEN THIS SECTION MUST BE USED

54.2 The judicial review procedure must be used in a claim for judicial review where the claimant is seeking—

> (a) a mandatory order;
> (b) a prohibiting order;
> (c) a quashing order; or
> (d) an injunction under section 30 of the Supreme Court Act 1981 (restraining a person from acting in any office in which he is not entitled to act)...

PERMISSION REQUIRED

54.4 The court's permission to proceed is required in a claim for judicial review whether started under this Part or transferred to the Administrative Court.

TIME LIMIT FOR FILING CLAIM FORM

...

54.5

> (1) The claim form must be filed—
>> (a) promptly; and
>> (b) in any event not later than 3 months after the grounds to make the claim first arose.

> (2) The time limit in this rule may not be extended by agreement between the parties.
> (3) This rule does not apply when any other enactment specifies a shorter time limit for making the claim for judicial review.
> (4) Paragraph (1) does not apply in the cases specified in paragraphs (5) and (6).
> (5) Where the application for judicial review relates to a decision made by the Secretary of State or local planning authority under the planning acts, the claim form must be filed not later than six weeks after the grounds to make the claim first arose.
> (6) Where the application for judicial review relates to a decision governed by the Public Contracts Regulations 2006, the claim form must be filed within the time within which an economic operator would have been required by regulation 47D(2) of those Regulations (and disregarding the rest of that regulation) to start any proceedings under those Regulations in respect of that decision ...

PERMISSION GIVEN

54.10(1)   Where permission to proceed is given the court may also give directions.

(2)   Directions under paragraph (1) may include—

(a)   a stay of proceedings to which the claim relates;

(b)   directions requiring the proceedings to be heard by a Divisional Court …

SERVICE OF ORDER GIVING OR REFUSING PERMISSION

54.11   The court will serve—

(a)   the order giving or refusing permission; and

(ai)   any certificate (if not included in the order) that permission has been granted for reasons of exceptional public interest in accordance with section 31(3F) of the Senior Courts Act 1981; and

(b)   any directions, on—

(i)   the claimant;

(ii)   the defendant; and

(iii)   any other person who filed an acknowledgment of service.

Permission decision where court requires a hearing

54.11A

(1)   This rule applies where the court wishes to hear submissions on—

(a)   whether it is highly likely that the outcome for the claimant would not have been substantially different if the conduct complained of had not occurred; and if so

(b)   whether there are reasons of exceptional public interest which make it nevertheless appropriate to give permission.

(2)   The court may direct a hearing to determine whether to give permission.

(3)   The claimant, defendant and any other person who has filed an acknowledgment of service must be given at least 2 days' notice of the hearing date.

(4)   The court may give directions requiring the proceedings to be heard by a Divisional Court.

(5)   The court must give its reasons for giving or refusing permission.

PERMISSION DECISION WITHOUT A HEARING

54.12   (1)   This rule applies where the court, without a hearing—

(a)   refuses permission to proceed; or

(b)   gives permission to proceed—

(i)   subject to conditions; or

(ii)   on certain grounds only.

(2)   The court will serve its reasons for making the decision when it serves the order giving or refusing permission in accordance with rule 54.11.

(3)   The claimant may not appeal but may request the decision to be reconsidered at a hearing.

(4)   A request under paragraph (3) must be filed within 7 days after service of the reasons under paragraph (2).

(5)   The claimant, defendant and any other person who has filed an acknowledgment of service will be given at least 2 days' notice of the hearing date.

(6)   The court may give directions requiring the proceedings to be heard by a Divisional Court.

(7)   Where the court refuses permission to proceed and records the fact that the application is totally without merit in accordance with rule 23.12, the claimant may not request that decision to be reconsidered at a hearing.

DEFENDANT ETC. MAY NOT APPLY TO SET ASIDE

54.13 Neither the defendant nor any other person served with the claim form may apply to set aside an order giving permission to proceed.

RESPONSE

54.14 (1) A defendant and any other person served with the claim form who wishes to contest the claim or support it on additional grounds must file and serve—

(a) detailed grounds for contesting the claim or supporting it on additional grounds; and

(b) any written evidence,

within 35 days after service of the order giving permission …

WHERE CLAIMANT SEEKS TO RELY ON ADDITIONAL GROUNDS

54.15 The court's permission is required if a claimant seeks to rely on grounds other than those for which he has been given permission to proceed.

EVIDENCE

54.16(1) Rule 8.6 does not apply.

(2) No written evidence may be relied on unless—

(a) it has been served in accordance with any—

(i) rule under this Part; or

(ii) direction of the court; or

(b) the court gives permission.

COURT'S POWERS TO HEAR ANY PERSON

54.17 (1) Any person may apply for permission—

(a) to file evidence; or

(b) make representations at the hearing of the judicial review.

(2) An application under paragraph (1) should be made promptly.

JUDICIAL REVIEW MAY BE DECIDED WITHOUT A HEARING

54.18 The court may decide the claim for judicial review without a hearing where all the parties agree.

COURT'S POWERS IN RESPECT OF QUASHING ORDERS

54.19 (1) This rule applies where the court makes a quashing order in respect of the decision to which the claim relates.

(2) The court may—

(a) (i) remit the matter to the decision-maker; and

(ii) direct it to reconsider the matter and reach a decision in accordance with the Judgment of the court; or

(b) in so far as any enactment permits, substitute its own decision for the decision to which the claim relates …

TRANSFER

54.20 The court may

(a) order a claim to continue as if it had not been started under this Section; and

(b) where it does so, give directions about the future management of the claim.

(Part 30 (transfer) applies to transfers to and from the Administrative Court.)

NOTES

1. Following the consultation on proposed reforms (see note 1 above following s. 31 of the Senior Court Act 1981) the Government response, announced that there would be shorter time limits in planning and procurement cases (Cm 8611, 2013). These were implemented by Rule 54.5(5)–(6).
2. Rules 54.6–54.9 (not included) deal with requirements for the details of the claim form, its service and acknowledgement of service, and failure to acknowledge service. The claim form not only identifies the defendant but also interested parties and, unless the court directs otherwise, the claim form should also be served on interested parties. Parties not acknowledging service may not, unless the court otherwise directs, appear in the permission hearing. Where permission is granted they may, subject to complying with Rule 54.14, appear in the substantive hearing. Rule 54.7(A) deals with judicial review of specific decisions of the Upper Tribunal.
3. Rules 54.21–54.24 (not included) provide for a Planning Court to hear a specialist list of claims relating to specified planning and environmental issues, and a Practice Direction 54E.

Pre-action Protocol for Judicial Review

INTRODUCTION

1. This Protocol applies to proceedings **within England and Wales only**. It does not affect the time limit specified by Rule 54.5(1) of the Civil Procedure Rules (CPR), which requires that any claim form in an application for judicial review must be filed promptly and in any event not later than 3 months after the grounds to make the claim first arose. Nor does it form for certain planning judicial reviews must be filed within 6 weeks and the claim form for certain procurement judicial reviews must be filed within 30 days.
2. This Protocol sets out a code of good practice and contains the steps which parties should generally follow before making a claim for judicial review.
3. The aims of the protocol are to enable parties to prospective claims to—

   (a) understand and properly identify the issues in dispute in the proposed claim and share information and relevant documents;
   (b) make informed decisions as to whether and how to proceed;
   (c) try to settle the dispute without proceedings or reduce the issues in dispute;
   (d) avoid unnecessary expense and keep down the costs of resolving the dispute; and
   (e) support the efficient management of proceedings where litigation cannot be avoided …

5. Judicial review should only be used where no adequate alternative remedy, such as a right of appeal, is available. Even then, judicial review may not be appropriate in every instance. Claimants are strongly advised to seek appropriate legal advice as soon as possible when considering proceedings. Although the Legal Aid Agency will not normally grant full representation before a letter before claim has been sent and the proposed defendant given a reasonable time to respond, initial funding may be available, for eligible claimants, to cover the work necessary to write this. (See Annex C for more information.)
6. This protocol will not be appropriate in very urgent cases. In this sort of case, a claim should be made immediately. Examples are where directions have been set for the claimant's removal from the UK or where there is an urgent need for an interim order to compel a public body to act where it has unlawfully refused to do so, such as where a local housing authority fails to secure interim accommodation for a homeless claimant. A letter before claim, and a claim itself, will not stop the implementation of a disputed decision, though a proposed defendant may agree to take no action until its response letter has been provided. In other cases, the claimant may need to apply to the court for an urgent interim order. Even in very urgent cases, it is good practice to alert the defendant by telephone and to send by email (or fax) to the defendant the draft Claim Form which the claimant intends to issue. A claimant is also normally required to notify a defendant when an interim order is being sought.

7. All claimants will need to satisfy themselves whether they should follow the protocol, depending upon the circumstances of the case. Where the use of the protocol is appropriate, the court will normally expect all parties to have complied with it in good time before proceedings are issued and will take into account compliance or non-compliance when giving directions for case management of proceedings or when making orders for costs.

8. The Upper Tribunal Immigration and Asylum Chamber (UTIAC) has jurisdiction in respect of judicial review proceedings in relation to most immigration decisions. The President of UTIAC has issued a Practice Statement to the effect that, in judicial review proceedings in UTIAC, the parties will be expected to follow this protocol, where appropriate, as they would for proceedings in the High Court.

Alternative Dispute Resolution

9. The courts take the view that litigation should be a last resort. The parties should consider whether some form of alternative dispute resolution ('ADR') or complaints procedure would be more suitable than litigation, and if so, endeavour to agree which to adopt. Both the claimant and defendant may be required by the court to provide evidence that alternative means of resolving their dispute were considered. Parties are warned that if the protocol is not followed (including this paragraph) then the court must have regard to such conduct when determining costs. However, parties should also note that a claim for judicial review should comply with the time limits set out in the Introduction above. Exploring ADR may not excuse failure to comply with the time limits. If it is appropriate to issue a claim to ensure compliance with a time limit, but the parties agree there should be a stay of proceedings to explore settlement or narrowing the issues in dispute, a joint application for appropriate directions can be made to the court.

10. It is not practicable in this protocol to address in detail how the parties might decide which method to adopt to resolve their particular dispute. However, summarised below are some of the options for resolving disputes without litigation which may be appropriate, depending on the circumstances—

   • Discussion and negotiation.
   • Using relevant public authority complaints or review procedures.
   • Ombudsmen – the Parliamentary and Health Service and the Local Government Ombudsmen have discretion to deal with complaints relating to maladministration. The British and Irish Ombudsman Association provide information about Ombudsman schemes and other complaint handling bodies and this is available from their website at www.bioa.org.uk. Parties may wish to note that the Ombudsmen are not able to look into a complaint once court action has been commenced.
   • Mediation – a form of facilitated negotiation assisted by an independent neutral party.

11. The Civil Justice Council and Judicial College have endorsed The Jackson ADR Handbook by Susan Blake, Julie Browne and Stuart Sime (2013, Oxford University Press). The Citizens Advice Bureaux website also provides information about ADR: http://www.ad viceguide.org.uk/england/law_e/law_legal_system_e/law_taking_legal_action_e/alternatives_to_court.htm.Information is also available at: http://www.civilmediation.justice.gov.uk/

12. If proceedings are issued, the parties may be required by the court to provide evidence that ADR has been considered. A party's silence in response to an invitation to participate in ADR or refusal to participate in ADR might be considered unreasonable by the court and could lead to the court ordering that party to pay additional court costs.

Requests for information and documents at the pre-action stage

13. Requests for information and documents made at the pre-action stage should be proportionate and should be limited to what is properly necessary for the claimant to understand why the challenged decision has been taken and/or to present the claim in a manner that will properly identify the issues. The defendant should comply with any request which meets these requirements

unless there is good reason for it not to do so. Where the court considers that a public body should have provided relevant documents and/or information, particularly where this failure is a breach of a statutory or common law requirement, it may impose costs sanctions.

The letter before claim

14. In good time before making a claim, the claimant should send a letter to the defendant. The purpose of this letter is to identify the issues in dispute and establish whether they can be narrowed or litigation can be avoided.

15. Claimants should normally use the suggested standard format for the letter outlined at Annex A. For Immigration, Nationality and Asylum cases, the Home Office has a standardised form which can be used …

16. The letter should contain the date and details of the decision, act or omission being challenged, a clear summary of the facts and the legal basis for the claim. It should also contain the details of any information that the claimant is seeking and an explanation of why this is considered relevant. If the claim is considered to be an Aarhus Convention claim (see Rules 45.41 to 45.44 and Practice Direction 45), the letter should state this clearly and explain the reasons, since specific rules as to costs apply to such claims. If the claim is considered appropriate for allocation to the Planning Court and/or for classification as "significant" within that court, the letter should state this clearly and explain the reasons.

17. The letter should normally contain the details of any person known to the claimant who is an Interested Party. An Interested Party is any person directly affected by the claim. They should be sent a copy of the letter before claim for information. Claimants are strongly advised to seek appropriate legal advice when considering proceedings which involve an Interested Party and, in particular, before sending the letter before claim to an Interested Party or making a claim.

18. A claim should not normally be made until the proposed reply date given in the letter before the claim has passed, unless the circumstances of the case require more immediate action to be taken. The claimant should send the letter before claim in good time so as to enable a response which can then be taken into account before the time limit for issuing the claim expires, unless there are good reasons why this is not possible …

The letter of response

20. Defendants should normally respond within 14 days using the standard format at Annex B. Failure to do so will be taken into account by the court and sanctions may be imposed unless there are good reasons. Where the claimant is a litigant in person, the defendant should enclose a copy of this Protocol with its letter.

21. Where it is not possible to reply within the proposed time limit, the defendant should send an interim reply and propose a reasonable extension, giving a date by which the defendant expects to respond substantively. Where an extension is sought, reasons should be given and, where required, additional information requested. This will not affect the time limit for making a claim for judicial review nor will it bind the claimant where he or she considers this to be unreasonable. However, where the court considers that a subsequent claim is made prematurely it may impose sanctions.

22. If the claim is being conceded in full, the reply should say so in clear and unambiguous terms.

23. If the claim is being conceded in part or not being conceded at all, the reply should say so in clear and unambiguous terms, and—

    (a) where appropriate, contain a new decision, clearly identifying what aspects of the claim are being conceded and what are not, or, give a clear timescale within which the new decision will be issued;

    (b) provide a fuller explanation for the decision, if considered appropriate to do so;

    (c) address any points of dispute, or explain why they cannot be addressed;

    (d) enclose any relevant documentation requested by the claimant, or explain why the documents are not being enclosed;

(e) where documents cannot be provided within the time scales required, then give a clear time-scale for provision. The claimant should avoid making any formal application for the provision of documentation/information during this period unless there are good grounds to show that the timescale proposed is unreasonable;

(f) where appropriate, confirm whether or not they will oppose any application for an interim remedy; and

(g) if the claimant has stated an intention to ask for a protective costs order, the defendant's response to this should be explained.

If the letter before claim has stated that the claim is an Aarhus Convention claim but the defendant does not accept this, the reply should state this clearly and explain the reasons. If the letter before claim has stated that the claim is suitable for the Planning Court and/or categorisation as "significant" within that court but the defendant does not accept this, the reply should state this clearly and explain the reasons.

24. The response should be sent to all Interested Parties identified by the claimant and contain details of any other persons who the defendant considers are Interested Parties

NOTES

1. The aims of this pre-action protocol (see para. 3) can be summarized as seeking to enable parties to avoid litigation by settling, and failing that to support efficient management of proceedings before a claim begins. Settlement is an important consideration (see later in this chapter in Section 6A at p. 600). Yet para. 1 says the protocol does not affect time limits and para. 9 expressly prioritizes them over ADR.

2. This clash of priorities was mentioned in responses to the consultation proposal to shorten the time limits in planning and procurement cases, to the effect that the shorter time limit militated against ADR and made litigation more likely. Presumably the Government preferred the view expressed by others, particularly made about procurement, that negotiation was a delaying tactic (see Cm. 8611, 2013). Some procurement cases now have a 30-day limit and it is six weeks for most planning cases.

3. Where the use of the protocol is considered appropriate, then failure to follow it can result in the application of sanctions by making orders of costs against parties not complying with case-management directions (para. 7), unreasonable failure to consider or participate in ADR (para. 12), failure to provide documents (para. 13), and where a claim is thought to have been brought prematurely (para. 21).

Practice Direction 54D Administrative Court (Venue)

This Practice Direction supplements Part 54

SCOPE AND PURPOSE

1.1 This Practice Direction concerns the place in which a claim before the Administrative Court should be started and administered and the venue at which it will be determined.

1.2 This Practice Direction is intended to facilitate access to justice by enabling cases to be administered and determined in the most appropriate location. To achieve this purpose it provides flexibility in relation to where claims are to be administered and enables claims to be transferred to different venues.

VENUE—GENERAL PROVISIONS

2.1 The claim form in proceedings in the Administrative Court may be issued at the Administrative Court Office of the High Court at –

(1) the Royal Courts of Justice in London; or

(2) at the District Registry of the High Court at Birmingham, Cardiff, Leeds, or Manchester unless the claim is one of the excepted classes of claim set out in paragraph 3 of this Practice Direction which may only be started and determined at the Royal Courts of Justice in London.

2.2 Any claim started in Birmingham will normally be determined at a court in the Midland region (geographically covering the area of the Midland Circuit); in Cardiff in Wales; in Leeds in the North-Eastern Region (geographically covering the area of the North Eastern Circuit); in London at the Royal Courts of Justice; and in Manchester, in the North-Western Region (geographically covering the Northern Circuit).

EXCEPTED CLASSES OF CLAIM

3.1 The excepted classes of claim referred to in paragraph 2.1(2) are –

(1) proceedings to which Part 76 or Part 79 applies, and for the avoidance of doubt –

    (a) proceedings relating to control orders (within the meaning of Part 76);

    (b) financial restrictions proceedings (within the meaning of Part 79);

    (c) proceedings relating to terrorism or alleged terrorists (where that is a relevant feature of the claim); and

    (d) proceedings in which a special advocate is or is to be instructed;

(2) proceedings to which RSC Order 115 applies;

(3) proceedings under the Proceeds of Crime Act 2002;

(4) appeals to the Administrative Court under the Extradition Act 2003;

(5) proceedings which must be heard by a Divisional Court; and

(6) proceedings relating to the discipline of solicitors.

3.2 If a claim form is issued at an Administrative Court office other than in London and includes one of the excepted classes of claim, the proceedings will be transferred to London.

URGENT APPLICATIONS

4.1 During the hours when the court is open, where an urgent application needs to be made to the Administrative Court outside London, the application must be made to the judge designated to deal with such applications in the relevant District Registry.

4.2 Any urgent application to the Administrative Court during the hours when the court is closed, must be made to the duty out of hours High Court judge by telephoning 020 7947 6000.

ASSIGNMENT TO ANOTHER VENUE

5.1 The proceedings may be transferred from the office at which the claim form was issued to another office. Such transfer is a judicial act.

5.2 The general expectation is that proceedings will be administered and determined in the region with which the claimant has the closest connection, subject to the following considerations as applicable –

(1) any reason expressed by any party for preferring a particular venue;

(2) the region in which the defendant, or any relevant office or department of the defendant, is based;

(3) the region in which the claimant's legal representatives are based;

(4) the ease and cost of travel to a hearing;

(5) the availability and suitability of alternative means of attending a hearing (for example, by videolink);

(6) the extent and nature of media interest in the proceedings in any particular locality;

(7) the time within which it is appropriate for the proceedings to be determined;

(8) whether it is desirable to administer or determine the claim in another region in the light of the volume of claims issued at, and the capacity, resources and workload of, the court at which it is issued;

(9) whether the claim raises issues sufficiently similar to those in another outstanding claim to make it desirable that it should be determined together with, or immediately following, that other claim; and

(10) whether the claim raises devolution issues and for that reason whether it should more appropriately be determined in London or Cardiff.

5.3 (1) When an urgent application is made under paragraph 4.1 or 4.2, this will not by itself decide the venue for the further administration or determination of the claim.

(2) The court dealing with the urgent application may direct that the case be assigned to a particular venue.

(3) When an urgent application is made under paragraph 4.2, and the court does not make a direction under sub-paragraph (2), the claim will be assigned in the first place to London but may be reassigned to another venue at a later date.

5.4 The court may on an application by a party or of its own initiative direct that the claim be determined in a region other than that of the venue in which the claim is currently assigned. The considerations in paragraph 5.2 apply.

5.5 Once assigned to a venue, the proceedings will be both administered from that venue and determined by a judge of the Administrative Court at a suitable court within that region, or, if the venue is in London, at the Royal Courts of Justice. The choice of which court (of those within the region which are identified by the Presiding Judge of the circuit suitable for such hearing) will be decided, subject to availability, by the considerations in paragraph 5.2.

5.6 When giving directions under rule 54.10, the court may direct that proceedings be reassigned to another region for hearing (applying the considerations in paragraph 5.2). If no such direction is given, the claim will be heard in the same region as that in which the permission application was determined (whether on paper or at a hearing).

NOTE: Practice Direction 54D on the venue followed a report by a judicial working group entitled, *Justice Outside London* (2007) chaired by Lord Justice May. The Direction came into effect on 6 April 2009 with the intention of improving access to justice for claimants outside London and the southeast in judicial review and other aspects of the jurisdiction of the Administrative Court. Research on the caseload of the Administrative Court has been conducted since regionalization by Nason. In 'Justice Outside London? An Update on "Regional" Judicial Review', *UK Constitutional Law Blog* (16 November 2016) (available at https://ukconstitutionallaw.org/), she concludes that the concerns developed with Sunkin on earlier data about regionalization leaving the wider needs of regional communities unaddressed continue to be well founded. They believed that market forces and public funding policies were encouraging specialization in the provision of legal services and that regionalization was reinforcing this, prompting their concern that the broader needs of 'regional' populations would go unmet. A specialization developed by a concentration of solicitors' firms in the north of England related to proceedings about prisoners. As the subject of claims this had collapsed from 24 per cent of all ordinary civil judicial reviews (non-immigration and asylum) in the period 1 May 2009 to 30 April 2011 inclusive, to just 8 per cent of all Administrative Court ordinary civil judicial reviews in 2015–16. Nason suggests this is a likely explanation for the decline in claims originating in the north of England. She and Sunkin had speculated that the cuts in legal aid partially explain the increase in the proportion of judicial reviews brought by litigants in person and decline in the activities of more generalist 'regional' solicitors. One topic which is on the rise is judicial review of certain un-appealable Upper Tribunal decisions outside immigration and asylum. In 2015–16 this constituted 3 per cent of the Administrative Court's total ordinary civil judicial review caseload. Of these 50 claims, 88 per cent were issued in London, and 90 per cent were issued by litigants in person.

SECTION 2: THE EXCLUSIVITY PRINCIPLE

As stated earlier, prior to the introduction of the revised Ord. 53, the courts frequently permitted litigants to commence an action by way of a claim for a declaration or injunction as an alternative to using the special procedure for obtaining orders of *certiorari, mandamus,* and prohibition. Would the courts continue to offer litigants this choice following the introduction of the reformed procedure in 1977?

O'Reilly v Mackman
[1983] 2 AC 237, House of Lords

A number of prisoners at Hull Prison wished to challenge decisions reached by the prison's board of visitors on the ground that they were in breach of the rules of natural justice. They did not make use of Ord. 53, but instead began proceedings by writ or originating summons, asking for a declaration that the findings and subsequent penalties were null and void. The application was refused by the judge at first instance but the Court of Appeal allowed an appeal by the board. On appeal to the House of Lords:

LORD DIPLOCK: … All that is at issue in the instant appeal is the procedure by which such relief ought to be sought. Put in a single sentence the question for your Lordships is: whether in 1980 after RSC Ord. 53 in its new form, adopted in 1977, had come into operation it was an abuse of the process of the court to apply for such declarations by using the procedure laid down in the Rules for proceedings begun by writ or by originating summons instead of using the procedure laid down by Ord. 53 for an application for judicial review of the awards of forfeiture of remission of sentence made against them by the board which the appellants are seeking to impugn?

In their respective actions, the appellants claim only declaratory relief … So the first thing to note is that the relief sought in the action is discretionary only.

It is not, and it could not be, contended that the decision of the board awarding him forfeiture of remission had infringed or threatened to infringe any right of the appellant derived from private law, whether a common law right or one created by statute… So far as private law is concerned all that each appellant had was a legitimate expectation, based upon his knowledge of what is the general practice, that he would be granted the maximum remission permitted by rule 5(2) of the Prison Rules, of one third of his sentence if by that time no disciplinary award of forfeiture of remission had been made against him. So the second thing to be noted is that none of the appellants had any remedy in private law.

In public law, as distinguished from private law, however, such legitimate expectation gave to each appellant a sufficient interest to challenge the legality of the adverse disciplinary award made against him by the board on the ground that in one way or another the board in reaching its decision had acted without the powers conferred upon it by the legislation under which it was acting; and such grounds would include the board's failure to observe the rules of natural justice: which means no more than to act fairly towards him in carrying out their decision-making process, and I prefer so to put it.

Lord Diplock went on to outline the disadvantages of the procedure for applying for prerogative orders prior to 1977. These were:

(1) the absence of any provision for discovery;
(2) the absence of any express provision for cross-examination.

His Lordship continued to outline, on the other hand, the protections which the procedure for applying for prerogative orders afforded to public bodies:

(1) the requirement to obtain leave;
(2) the time-limits on the grant of certiorari.

His Lordship continued:

> ... I accept that having regard to disadvantages ... [of the prerogative order procedure], it could not be regarded as an abuse of the process of the court, before the amendments made to Order 53 in 1977, to proceed against the authority by an action for a declaration of nullity of the impugned decision with an injunction to prevent the authority from acting on it, instead of applying for an order of certiorari; and this despite the fact that, by adopting this course, the plaintiff evaded the safeguards imposed in the public interest against groundless, unmeritorious or tardy attacks upon the validity of decisions made by public authorities in the field of public law.
>
> Those disadvantages, which formerly might have resulted in an applicant's being unable to obtain justice in an application for certiorari under Order 53, have all been removed by the new Order introduced in 1977.

Lord Diplock discussed the provisions of the new Order which allow for interlocutory applications for discovery and cross-examination. He also discussed the provisions which permit claims for damages and applications for declarations and injunctions to be included in applications under the Order.

His Lordship continued:

> So Order 53 since 1977 has provided a procedure by which every type of remedy for infringement of the rights of individuals that are entitled to protection in public law can be obtained in one and the same proceeding by way of an application for judicial review, and whichever remedy is found to be the most appropriate in the light of what has emerged upon the hearing of the application, can be granted to him. If what should emerge is that his complaint is not of an infringement of any of his rights that are entitled to protection in public law, but may be an infringement of his rights in private law and thus not a proper subject for judicial review, the court has power under rule 9(5), instead of refusing the application, to order the proceedings to continue as if they had begun by writ. There is no such converse power under the RSC to permit an action begun by writ to continue as if it were an application for judicial review; and I respectfully disagree with that part of the judgment of Lord Denning MR which suggests that such a power may exist; nor do I see the need to amend the rules in order to create one.
>
> My Lords, Order 53 does not expressly provide that procedure by application for judicial review shall be the exclusive procedure available by which the remedy of a declaration or injunction may be obtained for infringement of rights that are entitled to protection under public law; nor does section 31 of the Supreme Court Act 1981. There is great variation between individual cases that fall within Order 53 and the Rules Committee and subsequently the legislature were, I think, for this reason content to rely upon the express and the inherent power of the High Court, exercised upon a case to case basis, to prevent abuse of its process whatever might be the form taken by that abuse. Accordingly, I do not think that your Lordships would be wise to use this as an occasion to lay down categories of cases in which it would necessarily always be an abuse to seek in an action begun by writ or originating summons a remedy against infringement of rights of the individual that are entitled to protection in public law. ...
>
> Now that those disadvantages to applicants have been removed and all remedies for infringements of rights protected by public law can be obtained upon an application for judicial review, as can also remedies for infringements of rights under private law if such infringements should also be involved, it would in my view as a general rule be contrary to public policy and, as such an abuse of the process of the court, to permit a person seeking to establish that a decision of a public authority infringed rights to which he was entitled to protection under public law to proceed by way of an ordinary action and by this means to evade the provisions of Order 53 for the protection of such authorities.
>
> My Lords, I have described this as a general rule; for though it may normally be appropriate to apply it by the summary process of striking out the action, there may be exceptions, particularly where the invalidity of the decision arises as a collateral issue in a claim for infringement of a right of the plaintiff arising under private law, or where none of the parties objects to the adoption of the procedure by writ

or originating summons. Whether there should be other exceptions should, in my view, at this stage in the development of procedural public law, be left to be decided on a case to case basis—a process that your Lordships will be continuing in the next case in which judgment is to be delivered today [*Cocks* v *Thanet District Council* [1983] 2 AC 286].

In the instant cases where the only relief sought is a declaration of nullity of the decisions of a statutory tribunal, the Board of Visitors of Hull Prison, as in any other case in which a similar declaration of nullity in public law is the only relief claimed, I have no hesitation, in agreement with the Court of Appeal, in holding that to allow the actions to proceed would be an abuse of the process of the court. They are blatant attempts to avoid the protections for the defendants for which Order 53 provides.

The other Law Lords agreed with Lord Diplock.

■ QUESTION

The Law Commission's Report on Administrative Law Remedies (Law Com. No. 73, Cmnd 6407) stated in para. 34 that 'we are clearly of the opinion that the new procedure we envisage in respect of applications to the Divisional Court should not be exclusive in the sense that it would become the only way by which issues relating to the acts or omissions of public authorities should come before the courts'.

The *JUSTICE–All Souls Report on Administrative Law* (1988) criticizes the decision in *O'Reilly* v *Mackman* on the ground 'that it has all the appearance of judicial legislation without the benefit of the consultation and debating process normally associated with legislation' (para. 6.19).

Do you agree?

NOTES

The procedural safeguards referred to in *O'Reilly* v *Mackman* and which are to be found in CPR, Part 54 require some further explanation.

1. *Permission* (see Senior Courts Act 1981, s. 31(3); and now CPR, r. 54.4, earlier in this chapter in Section 1 at p. 572). The requirement that an applicant for judicial review must obtain permission has been criticized. The *JUSTICE–All Souls Report* recommended that it should be abolished for several reasons:
   (a) Permission is not required in private law proceedings. A particular category of litigants, namely those seeking judicial review, should not be subjected to an impediment which is not placed before litigants generally.
   (b) The administration can be protected from 'groundless, unmeritorious or tardy harassment' by the procedure which allows parties to apply to strike out a case. A statement of case may be struck out under the rules CPR r. 34 if they disclose no reasonable cause of action, are likely to obstruct the just disposed of proceedings or if they otherwise constitute an abuse of the process of the courts, and the claim may be dismissed.
   (c) Issues of standing are no longer conclusively determined at the stage of the application for leave (see *IRC* v *National Federation of Self-Employed and Small Businesses Ltd* [1982] AC 617, later in this chapter in Section 3 at p. 591).
2. Despite criticism from academics (e.g. A. Le Sueur and M. Sunkin, 'Applications for Judicial Review: The Requirement of Leave' [1992] *Public Law* 102), the requirement for permission was retained in CPR, Part 54 but it was changed from an *ex parte* (without notice) to an *inter partes* (with notice) proceeding decided by the judge on the papers. The thinking behind this was that because of the significant number of cases which, after obtaining permission, were either settled or withdrawn, it would be better to allow defendants to make an initial outline of their defence so that weak cases would be recognized and claimants ejected at this early stage. In two articles, V. Bondy and M. Sunkin reported on their research on the dynamics of judicial review litigation 'Accessing Judicial Review' [2008] *Public Law* 647, and 'Settlement in Judicial Review Proceedings' [2009] *Public Law* 237. They found that while the success rate of claims for permission for judicial review had declined, there was an increasing number of claimants achieving successful outcomes without the need to have an adjudication in the Administrative Court. It would seem that the reforms have assisted in changing the culture to increase early dialogue between the parties and encourage timely settlement. They found that there were still barriers to early dialogue which included, in some public bodies, structural, procedural and policy factors delaying the

involvement of their lawyers. It would also seem that there was a significant degree of variability amongst the judges deciding permission.

3. *Time limits*. Problems have arisen as to the relationship between the provisions in the Senior Courts Act 1981, s. 31(6) and the RSC Ord. 53, r. 4, now CPR r. 54.5 (see earlier in this chapter in Section 1 at p. 572). The House of Lords dealt with time limits in *R v Dairy Produce Quota Tribunal, ex parte Caswell* [1990] 2 AC 738.

   (a) At the stage of the application for permission the court considers whether the application has been made promptly. The fact that an application has been made within three months does not necessarily mean that it has been made promptly.

   (b) If the application has not been made promptly or within three months the court will have to consider whether there is good reason for the delay.

   (c) Where there is a finding of promptness at the permission stage, this does not preclude a finding of undue delay at the substantive hearing.

   (d) Whenever there is a failure to act promptly or within three months there is undue delay, and the court may either refuse to grant permission for the making of the application or, at the hearing, refuse to grant relief if it considers that the granting of the relief sought would be likely to cause substantial hardship to, or substantially prejudice the rights of, any person or would be detrimental to good administration.

   It is open to the court to deliberate upon undue delay under s. 31(6) at the substantive hearing even where promptness under CPR, r. 54.5 was considered at the permission stage if new relevant material is brought forward or a relevant point was overlooked (*R v Lichfield DC, ex parte Lichfield Securities Ltd* [2001] 3 LGLR 35).

4. The *JUSTICE–All Souls Report* (1988) criticized the three-month period as too short, and recommended that Ord. 53, r. 4 (now CPR, r. 54.5) be removed, thus leaving the question of delay to be dealt with by reference to the statutory test in s. 31(6) of the 1981 Act (see paras 6.28–6.31). The Law Commission concluded that certainty was desirable and recommended the continuance of the three-month time limit. A case could move to a substantive hearing if the reason for the delay in making the application for permission was the pursuit of an alternative remedy—*R v Rochdale Metropolitan Borough Council, ex parte Cromer Ring Mill Ltd* [1982] 3 All ER 761.

5. Lords Steyn and Hope have wondered whether the use of the term 'promptly' in CPR 54.5(1) (a) is sufficiently certain to comply with both EU law and Art 6(1) ECHR (*R v London Borough of Hammersmith and Fulham and Others, ex parte Burkett* [2002] UKHL 23, [2002] 1 WLR 593). The CJEU held that 'promptly' breached EU law on public procurement by causing uncertainty and should not be applied (Case C-406/08 *Uniplex* [2010] ECR I-817).

■ QUESTION

Do the criticisms made of the procedural safeguards in the CPR, Part 54 procedure undermine the basis of the decision in *O'Reilly* v *Mackman*?

NOTES

Lord Diplock mentioned that there may be certain exceptions to the general exclusivity principle. The courts have been required to consider the scope of the exclusivity rule, and the exceptions to it, in a number of cases.

1. In *Wandsworth London Borough Council* v *Winder* [1985] AC 461 it was held that a council tenant could, in defending proceedings for rent arrears, seek a declaration that the rent increases were *ultra vires*. It was subsequently held that the rent increases were in fact valid and an appeal to the Court of Appeal was dismissed (see *London Borough of Wandsworth* v *Winder (No. 2)* (1987) 19 HLR 204, (1988) 20 HLR 400).

2. The principle of raising a public law issue as a defence in civil litigation has been applied to criminal prosecution. Such a collateral challenge to the validity of a bye-law or administrative action was approved in the House of Lords in *Boddington* v *British Transport Police* [1997] 2 AC 143. Their Lordships overruled *Bugg* v *DPP* [1993] QB 473, which allowed a collateral challenge of a bye-law for substantive but not procedural invalidity. There is an exception, in that if legislation specified an appeal process then collateral challenge is not permitted (see *R v Wicks* [1998] AC 92—enforcement notices under the planning legislation).

Roy v Kensington and Chelsea FPC
[1992] 2 WLR 239, House of Lords

The Kensington and Chelsea and Westminster Family Practitioner Committee (FPC) was responsible, under the National Health Service (General Medical and Pharmaceutical Services) Regulations 1974, for making payments to general practitioners undertaking National Health Service work within its area. Dr Roy was on the list of doctors undertaking National Health Service work within the FPC's area. The FPC decided to use its powers under the Regulations to reduce Dr Roy's basic practice allowance by 20 per cent on the basis that he was not devoting a substantial amount of time to general practice under the National Health Service. Dr Roy issued a writ claiming the full amount of the basic practice allowance. In the same writ he also claimed repayment of sums due to him in relation to the employment of ancillary staff. The FPC argued that the inclusion of the claim relating to the basic practice allowance was an abuse of the process of the court. The judge decided that, as the committee's decision was clearly a public law decision, it could only be challenged by judicial review. His decision was reversed by the Court of Appeal and the FPC appealed to the House of Lords. (In the meantime Dr Roy proceeded with his claim in relation to the employment of ancillary staff and obtained an order for repayment.)

LORD BRIDGE OF HARWICH: … Agreeing, as I do, with the conclusion he reaches, I shall state my own reasons briefly.

The decisions of this House in *O'Reilly* v *Mackman* [1983] 2 AC 237 and *Cocks* v *Thanet District Council* [1983] 2 AC 286, have been the subject of much academic criticism.… I have not been persuaded that the essential principle embodied in the decisions requires to be significantly modified, let alone overturned. But if it is important, as I believe, to maintain the principle, it is certainly no less important that its application should be confined within proper limits. It is appropriate that an issue which depends exclusively on the existence of a purely public law right should be determined in judicial review proceedings and not otherwise. But where a litigant asserts his entitlement to a subsisting right in private law, whether by way of claim or defence, the circumstance that the existence and extent of the private right asserted may incidentally involve the examination of a public law issue cannot prevent the litigant from seeking to establish his right by action commenced by writ or originating summons, any more than it can prevent him from setting up his private law right in proceedings brought against him. I think this proposition necessarily follows from the decisions of this House in *Davy* v *Spelthorne Borough Council* [1984] AC 262 and *Wandsworth London Borough Council* v *Winder* [1985] AC 461. In the latter case Robert Goff LJ in the Court of Appeal, commenting on a passage from the speech of Lord Fraser of Tullybelton in the former case, said, at p. 480:

> For my part, I find it difficult to conceive of a case where a citizen's invocation of the ordinary procedure of the courts in order to enforce his private law rights, or his reliance on his private law rights by way of defence in an action brought against him, could, as such, amount to an abuse of the process of the court.

I entirely agree with this.…

I do not think the issue in the appeal turns on whether the doctor provides services pursuant to a contract with the family practitioner committee. I doubt if he does and am content to assume that there is no contract. Nevertheless, the terms which govern the obligations of the doctor on the one hand, as to the services he is to provide, and of the family practitioner committee on the other hand, as to the payments which it is required to make to the doctor, are all prescribed in the relevant legislation and it seems to me that the statutory terms are just as effective as they would be if they were contractual to confer upon the doctor an enforceable right in private law to receive the remuneration to which the terms entitle him. It must follow, in my view, that in any case of dispute the doctor is entitled to claim and recover in an action commenced by writ the amount of remuneration which he is able to prove as being due to him. Whatever remuneration he is entitled to under the statement is remuneration he has duly earned by the services he has rendered. The circumstance that the quantum of that remuneration, in the case of a particular dispute, is affected by the discretionary decision made by the committee cannot deny the doctor his private law right of recovery or subject him to the constraints which the necessity to seek judicial review would impose upon that right.

LORD LOWRY: [Lord Lowry reviewed a number of authorities including *Wandsworth Borough Council* v *Winder* [1985] AC 461 and *Cocks* v *Thanet DC* [1983] 2 AC 286 and continued.] …

[T]he actual or possible absence of a contract is not decisive against Dr Roy. He has in my opinion a bundle of rights which should be regarded as his individual private law rights against the committee, arising from the statute and regulations and including the very important private law right to be paid for the work that he has done. As Judge White put it [1989] 1 Med LR 10, 12:

> Private law rights flow from the statutory provisions and are enforceable, as such, in the courts but no contractual relations come into existence.

The judge, however, held that, *even if the doctor's rights to full payments under the scheme were contractually based*, the committee's duty was a public law duty and could be challenged only on judicial review. Mr Collins admitted that, if the doctor had a *contractual* right, he could … vindicate it by action. But, my Lords, I go further: if Dr Roy has any kind of *private law right*, even though not contractual, he can sue for its alleged breach… In any event, a successful application by judicial review could not lead directly, as it would in an action, to an order for payment of the full basic practice allowance. Other proceedings would be needed.

… even if one accepts the full rigour of *O'Reilly* v *Mackman*, there is ample room to hold that this case comes within the exceptions allowed for by Lord Diplock. It is concerned with a private law right, it involves a question which *could* in some circumstances give rise to a dispute of fact and one object of the plaintiff is to obtain an order for the payment (not by way of damages) of an ascertained or ascertainable sum of money. If it is wrong to allow such a claim to be litigated by action, what is to be said of other disputed claims for remuneration? I think it is right to consider the whole spectrum of claims which a doctor might make against the committee. The existence of any dispute as to entitlement means that he will be alleging a breach of his private law rights through a failure by the committee to perform their public duty. If the committee's argument prevails, the doctor must in all these cases go by judicial review, even when the facts are not clear. I scarcely think that this can be the right answer. …

The 'broad approach' was that the rule in *O'Reilly* v *Mackman* did not apply generally against bringing actions to vindicate private rights in all circumstances in which those actions involved a challenge to a public law act or decision, but that it merely required the aggrieved person to proceed by judicial review only when private law rights were not at stake. The 'narrow approach' assumed that the rule applied generally to *all* proceedings in which public law acts or decisions were challenged, subject to some exceptions when private law rights were involved. There was no need in *O'Reilly* v *Mackman* to choose between these approaches, but it seems clear that Lord Diplock considered himself to be stating a general rule with exceptions. For my part, I much prefer the broad approach, which is both traditionally orthodox and consistent with the *Pyx Granite* principle [1960] AC 260, 286, as applied in *Davy* v *Spelthorne Borough Council* [1984] AC 262, 274 and in *Wandsworth London Borough Council* v *Winder* [1985] AC 461, 510. It would also, if adopted, have the practical merit of getting rid of a procedural minefield. I shall, however, be content for the purpose of this appeal to adopt the narrow approach …

Whichever approach one adopts, the arguments for excluding the present case from the ambit of the rule or, in the alternative, making an exception of it are similar and to my mind convincing.

(1) Dr Roy has either a contractual or a statutory private law right to his remuneration in accordance with his statutory terms of service.
(2) Although he seeks to enforce performance of a public law duty … his private law rights dominate the proceedings.

(3) The type of claim and other claims for remuneration (although not this particular claim) may involve disputed issues of fact.

(4) The order sought (for the payment of money due) could not be granted on judicial review.

(5) The claim is joined with another claim which is fit to be brought in an action (and has already been successfully prosecuted).

(6) When individual rights are claimed, there should not be a need for leave or a special time limit, nor should the relief be discretionary.

(7) The action should be allowed to proceed unless it is plainly an abuse of process.

(8) The cases I have cited show that the rule in *O'Reilly* v *Mackman* [1983] 2 AC 237, assuming it to be a rule of general application, is subject to many exceptions based on the nature of the claim and on the undesirability of erecting procedural barriers.

My Lords, I have already disclaimed the intention of discussing the scope of the rule in *O'Reilly* v *Mackman* but, even if I treat it as a general rule, there are many indications in favour of a liberal attitude towards the exceptions contemplated but not spelt out by Lord Diplock. For example: first, the Law Commission, when recommending the new judicial review procedure, contemplated the continued coexistence of judicial review proceedings and actions for a declaration with regard to public law issues. *Associated Provincial Picture Houses Ltd* v *Wednesbury Corporation* [1948] 1 KB 223 is a famous prototype of the latter. Secondly, this House has expressly approved actions for a declaration of nullity as alternative to applications for certiorari to quash, where private law rights were concerned: *Wandsworth London Borough Council* v *Winder* [1985] AC 461, 477 *per* Robert Goff LJ. Thirdly:

'The principle remains intact that public authorities and public servants are, unless clearly exempted, answerable in the ordinary courts for wrongs done to individuals ... We have not yet reached the point at which mere characterisation of a claim as a claim in public law is sufficient to exclude it from consideration by the ordinary courts: to permit this would be to create a dual system of law with the rigidity and procedural hardship for plaintiffs which it was the purpose of the recent reforms to remove': *Davy* v *Spelthorne Borough Council* [1984] AC 262, 276, *per* Lord Wilberforce.

In conclusion, my Lords, it seems to me that, unless the procedure adopted by the moving party is ill suited to dispose of the question at issue, there is much to be said in favour of the proposition that a court having jurisdiction ought to let a case be heard rather than entertain a debate concerning the form of the proceedings.

For the reasons already given I would dismiss this appeal.

The other Law Lords agreed with Lord Bridge and Lord Lowry.

Clarke v University of Lincolnshire and Humberside
[2000] 1 WLR 1988, Court of Appeal

A student was in dispute over an examination matter with her university, which as a new university under the Education Reform Act 1988 had neither a charter nor visitor. She attended the university from 1992–95 and in 1998 began proceedings alleging breach of contract. The claim was struck out on the grounds that such disputes between students and universities were not justiciable but on appeal she was allowed to amend her pleadings. The university contended that the student should have proceeded by judicial review and so it was an abuse of process to bring an action outside the three-month time limit.

Sedley LJ, with whom Ward LJ and Lord Woolf agreed, ruled that there were issues of academic judgment which would not be justiciable but the amended pleadings did not fall into that category and involved contractual issues which the courts were capable of adjudicating.

LORD WOOLF MR:

The effect of the Civil Procedure Rules on O'Reilly v Mackman

22. It is over eighteen years ago that Lord Diplock made his speech in *O'Reilly* v *Mackman* [1983] 2 AC 237, which has had such a strong influence on the development of public law in this jurisdiction. Generally, since that time, the courts have continued to follow the statement as to the practice which should be adopted when bringing a claim against a public body that Lord Diplock made in that case. Lord Diplock indicated, at p 285, that in his view it would:

> as a general rule be contrary to public policy, and as such an abuse of the process of the court, to permit a person seeking to establish that a decision of a public authority to infringe rights of which he was entitled to protection under public law to proceed by way of an ordinary action and by this means to evade the provisions of Order 53 for the protection of such authorities.

23. . . . First it is to be noted that counsel for the plaintiffs had:

> conceded that the fact that by adopting the procedure of an action begun by writ or by originating summons instead of an application for judicial review under Order 53 ... the plaintiffs had thereby been able to evade those protections against groundless, unmeritorious or tardy harassment that were afforded to statutory tribunals or decision making public authorities by Order 53. (p. 284)

Lord Diplock also pointed out that an advantage of Order 53 was that the court had an opportunity to exercise its discretion at the outset of the proceedings rather than would have happened at that time in proceedings begun by originating summons at the end of the proceedings. This was an important protection in the interests of good administration and for third parties who may be indirectly affected by the proceedings ...

24. Lord Diplock went on to indicate that why Order 53 was not made an exclusive procedure was because he considered that the Rules Committee and the Legislature were content to rely upon the inherent power of the High Court to prevent abuse of its process whatever might be the form taken by that abuse: at pp. 285 A–D.

25. Lord Diplock was however at pains to point out that what he had said with regard to the exclusivity of Order 53 was a *general* rule. He recognised that there could be exceptions. He identified an exception in the case of collateral issues and went on to say that other exceptions should in his view be developed on a case by case basis. This is what has since happened.

26. . . . The proceedings now have to be initiated by use of a 'claim form', maintaining the principle that all proceedings under the CPR are to be commenced in the same way (see Ord. 53 r5 (2)(A). In relation to the protection of the public and the interests of the administration which it provides, Order 53 has not been amended. However already Order 53 is part of the new code of civil procedure created by the CPR. It is subject to the general over-riding principles contained in Part 1.

27. In addition, if proceedings involving public law issues are commenced by an ordinary action under Part 7 or Part 8 they are now subject to Part 24 ... This is a markedly different position from that which existed when *O'Reilly* v *Mackman* [1983] 2 AC 237 was decided. If a defendant public body or an interested person considers that a claim has no real prospect of success an application can now be made under Part 24. This restricts the inconvenience to third parties and the administration of public bodies caused by a hopeless claim to which Lord Diplock referred.

28. The distinction between proceedings under Order 53 and an ordinary claim are now limited. Under Order 53 the claimant has to obtain permission to bring the proceedings so the onus is upon him to establish he has a real prospect of success. In the case of ordinary proceedings the defendant has to establish that the proceedings do not have a real prospect of success.

29. A university is a public body ... Court proceedings would, therefore, normally be expected to be commenced under Order 53. If the university is subject to the supervision of a visitor there is little scope for those proceedings (*Page* v *Hull University Visitor* [1993] AC 682). Where a claim is brought against a

university by one of its students, if because the university is a 'new university' created by statute, it does not have a visitor, the role of the court will frequently amount to performing the reviewing role which would otherwise be performed by the visitor. The court, for reasons which have been explained, will not involve itself with issues that involve making academic judgments. Summary judgment dismissing a claim, which if it were to be entertained, would require the court to make academic judgments should be capable of being obtained in the majority of situations. Similarly, the court has now power to stay the proceedings if it came to the conclusion that, in accordance with the over-riding objective, it would be desirable for a student to use an internal disciplinary process before coming to the court: see CPR 1.4(1)(e).

30. One of Lord Diplock's reasons which he gave in *O'Reilly* v *Mackman* [1983] 2 AC 237 for his concern about an ordinary civil action being commenced against public bodies when a more appropriate procedure was under Order 53 [but now] subject to the court's discretion to extend time, under Order 53 proceedings have to be commenced promptly and in any event within three months. If a student could bypass this requirement to bring proceedings promptly by issuing civil proceedings based on a contract, this could have a very adverse affect on administration of universities.

31.…. Grievances against universities are preferably resolved within the grievance procedure which universities have today. If they cannot be resolved in that way, where there is a visitor, they then have (except in exceptional circumstances) to be resolved by the visitor. The courts will not usually intervene.

32.…. If it is not possible to resolve the dispute internally, and there is no visitor, then the courts may have no alternative but to become involved. If they do so, the preferable procedure would usually be by way of judicial review. If, on the other hand, the proceedings are based on the contract between the student and the university then they do not have to be brought by way of judicial review …

34. The courts' approach to what is an abuse of process has to be considered today in the light of the changes brought about by the CPR. Those changes include a requirement that a party to proceedings should behave reasonably both before and after they have commenced proceedings. Parties are now under an obligation to help the court further the over-riding objectives which include ensuring that cases are dealt with expeditiously and fairly. (CPR 1.1(2)(d) and 1.3) They should not allow the choice of procedure to achieve procedural advantages …

35.…. If proceedings of a type which would normally be brought by judicial review are instead brought by bringing an ordinary claim, the court in deciding whether the commencement of the proceedings is an abuse of process can take into account whether there has been unjustified delay in initiating the proceedings.

36. When considering whether proceedings can continue the nature of the claim can be relevant. If the court is required to perform a reviewing role or what is being claimed is a discretionary remedy, whether it be a prerogative remedy or an injunction or a declaration the position is different from when the claim is for damages or a sum of money for breach of contract or a tort irrespective of the procedure adopted. Delay in bringing proceedings for a discretionary remedy has always been a factor which a court could take into account in deciding whether it should grant that remedy. Delay can now be taken into account on an application for summary judgment under CPR Part 24 if its effect means that the claim has no real prospect of success.

37. Similarly if what is being claimed could affect the public generally the approach of the court will be stricter than if the proceedings only affect the immediate parties. It must not be forgotten that a court can extend time to bring proceedings under Order 53. The intention of the CPR is to harmonise procedures as far as possible and to avoid barren procedural disputes which generate satellite litigation …

39. The emphasis can therefore be said to have changed since *O'Reilly* v *Mackman* [1983] 2 AC 237. What is likely to be important when proceedings are not brought by a student against a new university under Order 53, will not be whether the right procedure has been adopted but whether the protection

provided by Order 53 has been flouted in circumstances which are inconsistent with the proceedings being able to be conducted justly in accordance with the general principles contained in Part 1. Those principles are now central to determining what is due process. A visitor is not required to entertain a complaint when there has been undue delay and a court in the absence of a visitor should exercise its jurisdiction in a similar way. The courts are far from being the ideal forum in which to resolve the great majority of disputes between a student and his or her university. The courts should be vigilant to ensure their procedures are not misused. The courts must be equally vigilant to discourage summary applications which have no real prospect of success.

Appeal allowed.

NOTE: T. Cornford, 'The New Rules of Procedure for Judicial Review' [2000] 5 Web JCLI (home page available at http://www.webjcli.org//index) argues that the logic of having a special procedure for judicial review means that (predominantly) public law issues should be brought under it and that Lord Woolf's views on how the CPR can protect public authorities from abuse still leave the problem that some claimants may wrongly identify their claim as a private one and not use CPR, Part 54. They will not be able to transfer to Part 54 if they are outside the time limit.

■ QUESTION

Why do public authorities need safeguards in litigation involving public law issues but not private law ones?

SECTION 3: WHO MAY APPLY FOR JUDICIAL REVIEW?

The principles of standing or sufficient interest determine *who* is entitled to bring a particular dispute before the courts. They can thus be distinguished from the principles which determine whether a particular matter is suitable for adjudication in the courts (see later in this chapter in Section 5, on justiciability, at p. 597), whether a particular matter is one of public law (see p. 594), and what proceedings may be used to challenge the decision (see earlier in this chapter in Section 2 at p. 581).

There are many people who may consider that they are affected or have an interest in an administrative decision. Consider, for example, the range of persons who might be said to have an interest in a decision to close a school because of falling numbers. The list will obviously include persons whose children will have to start a new school, but it could also include a number of others, for example persons who are opposed in principle to the closure of small schools and persons who are concerned about the financial implications of the closure for the local education authority. The principles of standing have the function of determining which interests merit access to the courts.

What arguments might be put forward in favour of the courts' power to select the interests which merit access to the courts? Cane (2011) suggests a number of possible functions. First to restrict access to judicial review. This can be to protect public bodies from those acting vexatiously or meddling paternalistically in others' affairs. Other reasons for limiting access include: to curb the likelihood of public officials acting too cautiously, or otherwise being adversely affected by unwarranted litigation, and to promote challenge by those best placed to bring it and argue it (*Administrative Law*, 2011, p. 295).

What, then, are the principles of standing in judicial review proceedings?

Inland Revenue Commissioners v National Federation of Self-Employed and Small Businesses Ltd (NFSESB)

[1982] AC 617, House of Lords

The National Federation of Self-Employed and Small Businesses (NFSESB) sought an order of *mandamus* requiring the Inland Revenue Commissioners to assess and collect arrears of income tax due from a number of workers in the printing industry, known as the Fleet Street Casuals. This group had for some years been engaged in practices which deprived the Revenue of tax due in respect of their casual earnings. The Inland Revenue, on becoming aware of this, made an arrangement under which the workers were required to register in respect of their casual employment, so that in future tax could be collected in the normal way. Arrears of tax from 1977–78 were to be paid and current investigations to proceed, but investigations in respect of earlier years were not to take place. The House of Lords considered whether the Federation had standing. At that time the relevant rule was r. 3(5) of the Rules of the Supreme Court. Section 31(3) of the Supreme Court Act 1981 (now Senior Courts Act 1981, see earlier in this chapter in Section 1 at p. 569).

LORD WILBERFORCE: ... There may be simple cases in which it can be seen at the earliest stage that the person applying for judicial review has no interest at all or no sufficient interest to support the application: then it would be quite correct at the threshold to refuse him leave to apply. The right to do so is an important safeguard against the courts being flooded and public bodies being harassed by irresponsible applications. But in other cases this will not be so. In these it will be necessary to consider the powers or the duties in law of those against whom the relief is asked, the position of the applicant in relation to those powers or duties, and to the breach of those said to have been committed. In other words, the question of sufficient interest cannot, in such cases, be considered in the abstract, or as an isolated point: it must be taken together with legal and factual context. The rule requires sufficient interest in the matter to which the application relates. This, in the present case, necessarily involves the whole question of the duties of the Inland Revenue and the breaches for failure of those duties of which the respondents complain. ...

[After examining the relevant statutory provisions, his Lordship continued.]

The position of other taxpayers—other than the taxpayers whose assessment is in question—and their right to challenge the revenue's assessment or non-assessment of that taxpayer, must be judged according to whether, consistently with the legislation, they can be considered as having sufficient interest to complain of what has been done or omitted. I proceed therefore to examine the revenue's duties in that light.

These duties are expressed in very general terms and it is necessary to take account also of the framework of the income tax legislation. This established that the commissioners must assess each individual taxpayer in relation to his circumstances. Such assessments and all information regarding a taxpayer's affairs are strictly confidential ... No other person is given any right to make proposals about the tax payable by any individual: he cannot even inquire as to such tax. The total confidentiality of assessments and of negotiations between individuals and the revenue is a vital element in the working of the system. As a matter of general principle I would hold that one taxpayer has no sufficient interest in asking the court to investigate the tax affairs of another taxpayer or to complain that the latter has been under-assessed or over-assessed: indeed, there is a strong public interest that he should not. And this principle applies equally to groups of taxpayers ...

That a case can never arise in which the acts or abstentions of the revenue can be brought before the court I am certainly not prepared to assert, nor that, in a case of sufficient gravity, the court might not be able to hold that another taxpayer or other taxpayers could challenge them...

[After considering the evidence his Lordship decided that the Federation had no sufficient interest.]

LORD DIPLOCK:

[His Lordship began by saying he would allow the appeal on the basis that the commissioners had not acted unlawfully in exercising their wide managerial discretion. He nonetheless went on to consider the question of standing.]

The procedure under the new Order 53 involves two stages: (1) the application for leave to apply for judicial review, and (2) if leave is granted, the hearing of the application itself. The former, or 'threshold' stage is regulated by rule 3. The application for leave to apply for judicial review is made ex parte, but may be adjourned for the persons or bodies against whom relief is sought to be represented. This did not happen in the instant case. Rule 3(5) specifically requires the court to consider at this stage whether 'it considers that the applicant has a sufficient interest in the matter to which the application relates.' So this is a 'threshold' question in the sense that the court must direct its mind to it and form a prima facie view about it upon the material that is available at the first stage. The prima facie view so formed, if favourable to the applicant, may alter on further consideration in the light of further evidence that may be before the court at the second stage, the hearing of the application for judicial review itself.

The need for leave to start proceedings for remedies in public law is not new … Its purpose is to prevent the time of the court being wasted by busybodies with misguided or trivial complaints of administrative error, and to remove the uncertainty in which public officers and authorities might be left as to whether they could safely proceed with administrative action while proceedings for judicial review of it were actually pending even though misconceived. …

My Lords, at the threshold stage, for the Federation to make out a prima facie case of reasonable suspicion that the board in showing a discriminatory leniency to a substantial class of taxpayers had done so for ulterior reasons extraneous to good management, and thereby deprived the national exchequer of considerable sums of money, constituted what was in my view reason enough for the Divisional Court to consider that the Federation or, for that matter, any taxpayer, had a sufficient interest to apply to have the question whether the board was acting *ultra vires* reviewed by the court. The whole purpose of requiring that leave should first be obtained to make the application for judicial review would be defeated if the court were to go into the matter in any depth at that stage. If, on a quick perusal of the material then available, the court thinks that it discloses what might on further consideration turn out to be an arguable case in favour of granting to the applicant the relief claimed, it ought, in the exercise of a judicial discretion, to give him leave to apply for that relief. The discretion that the court is exercising at this stage is not the same as that which it is called upon to exercise when all the evidence is in and the matter has been fully argued at the hearing of the application. …

[T]he requirement of confidentiality which would be broken if one taxpayer could complain that another taxpayer was being treated by the revenue more favourably than himself, mean that occasions will be very rare on which an individual taxpayer (or pressure group of taxpayers) will be able to show a sufficient interest to justify an application for judicial review of the way in which the revenue has dealt with the tax affairs of any taxpayer other than the applicant himself.

Rare though they may be, however, if, in the instant case, what at the threshold stage was suspicion only had been proved at the hearing of the application for judicial review to be true in fact (instead of being utterly destroyed), I would have held that this was a matter in which the federation had a sufficient interest in obtaining an appropriate order, whether by way of declaration or mandamus, to require performance by the board of statutory duties which for reasons shown to be *ultra vires* it was failing to perform.

It would, in my view, be a grave lacuna in our system of public law if a pressure group, like the Federation, or even a single public-spirited taxpayer, were prevented by outdated technical rules of *locus standi* from bringing the matter to the attention of the court to vindicate the rule of law and get the unlawful conduct stopped. The Attorney-General, although he occasionally applies for prerogative orders against public authorities that do not form part of central government, in practice never does so against government departments. It is not, in my view, a sufficient answer to say that judicial review of the actions of officers or departments of central government is unnecessary because they are accountable to Parliament for the way in which they carry out their functions. They are accountable to Parliament for what they do so far as regards efficiency and policy, and of that Parliament is the only judge; they are responsible to a court of justice for the lawfulness of what they do, and of that the court is the only judge.

Lord Fraser and Lord Roskill delivered judgments in which they agreed with Lord Wilberforce. Lord Scarman delivered a judgment which agreed in general with that of Lord Diplock.

NOTE: Lord Diplock refers, in his judgment, to the role of the Attorney-General. The Attorney-General has a discretion to institute legal proceedings in the public interest. He may do so on his own initiative or upon the request of an individual or organization. Where the Attorney-General institutes litigation at the request of an individual or organization, this is known as a relator action. The Attorney-General's decision whether to bring a relator action cannot be challenged (see *Gouriet v Union of Post Office Workers* [1978] AC 435).

■ QUESTIONS

1. What are the differences, if any, between the approaches of Lord Diplock and Lord Wilberforce ?

2. Do the judgments suggest what their Lordships perceived to be the justification for standing rules (see Cane, earlier in this chapter in Section 3 at p. 590)?

3. Do the judgments suggest that the function of judicial review is:
   (a) to protect the individual who is specially affected by the decision;
   (b) to protect the public interest in rooting out administrative illegality?

NOTES

1. In *R v The Attorney-General, ex parte ICI plc* [1987] 1 CMLR 72 the applicant, ICI, was held to have standing to question the validity of the Inland Revenue's assessment of the tax payable by one of its competitors. The fact that ICI was challenging the assessment of a competitor was held to distinguish the application from that of the NFSESB in the *National Federation* case. Furthermore, the issue of confidentiality did not arise because the Revenue had already agreed voluntarily to disclose the basis of its assessment.

2. The Law Commission in its 1994 report favoured the broadly liberal approach of the courts on sufficient interest. They were concerned about the effect of *R v Secretary of State for the Environment, ex parte Rose Theatre Trust* [1990] 1 QB 504 on challenges brought by people who were concerned about, but not directly affected by, the administrative action. The Law Commission recommended that public interest applications be treated as having sufficient interest. Subsequently the courts have taken this approach. In *R v HM Inspector of Pollution, ex parte Greenpeace Ltd (No. 2)* [1994] 4 All ER 329 Otton J declined to follow *Rose Theatre Trust*. Greenpeace, an environmental pressure group, not only had a genuine interest in the issues involved (disposal of radioactive waste) but it had some 2,500 supporters in the area where the plant was situated and it if was not permitted to seek judicial review, then those who Greenpeace represents, who would have sufficient interest, e.g. neighbours, would not be able to command the expertise which Greenpeace has. A less well-informed challenge would not render the court the assistance which it needs in order to do justice between the parties. In *R v Secretary of State for Foreign Affairs, ex parte World Development Movement Ltd* [1995] 1 WLR 386 the applicant pressure group was regarded as having sufficient interest to challenge the decision by the Foreign Secretary to make a payment of aid under the Overseas Development and Co-operation Act 1980 to the Malaysian Government towards the construction of the Pergau dam and hydro-electric scheme. This was despite the fact that, unlike Greenpeace, it was unlikely that any of the applicant's individual members had a direct interest in the issue. The significant factors listed by Rose LJ were that the issue was important; it involved the vindication of the rule of law; there appeared to be no other responsible challenger; the nature of the breach of duty against which relief was sought, and the prominent role of these applications in giving advice, guidance, and assistance with regard to aid. See S. Chakrabati, J. Stephens, and C. Gallagher [2003] *Public Law* 697 on costs and groups litigating in the public interest.

SECTION 4: AGAINST WHOM, AND IN RESPECT OF WHAT ACTIVITIES, MAY JUDICIAL REVIEW BE SOUGHT?

O'Reilly v *Mackman* was a case in which the litigants attempted to use the procedure by way of writ instead of the application for judicial review. Conversely, there have been a number of cases in which the courts have held that litigants are not entitled to use the procedure for judicial review because their cases do not raise issues of 'public law'.

In *R* v *BBC, ex parte Lavelle* [1983] 1 WLR 23, the applicant sought to challenge a decision of a disciplinary board within the BBC suspending her from her employment. Woolf LJ considered that the scope of Ord. 53 was not necessarily confined to that of the old prerogative orders but depended solely on the criteria set out in Ord. 53, r. 1(2) (now Part 54.3(1)). He did, however, hold that Ord. 53 could not be used to challenge the decisions of purely private or domestic tribunals such as the disciplinary body within the BBC which derived its power solely from the contract between Miss Lavelle and the BBC.

In the case which follows, the applicants sought to use judicial review to challenge the decision of an unincorporated association which exercised no statutory or prerogative powers.

R v *Panel on Take-overs and Mergers, ex parte Datafin plc*
[1987] QB 815, Court of Appeal

The Take-over Panel is an unincorporated association which represents a wide range of institutional bodies operating in the financial market, for example, the Stock Exchange. It has a regulatory function concerning take-overs and mergers. In this role it makes, administers, and enforces a code of conduct known as the City Code.

The applicants, Datafin plc, were involved in a competitive take-over and complained to the Panel that their rivals, Norton Opax plc, had breached the City Code. The Panel dismissed the complaint and Datafin unsuccessfully sought leave in the High Court to apply for judicial review, seeking *certiorari*, prohibition, *mandamus*, and an injunction. Leave was granted on appeal by the Court of Appeal. The Court of Appeal considered three main issues:

(a) the susceptibility of the Panel's decisions to judicial review;

(b) the manner in which any jurisdiction was to be exercised; and

(c) whether, if there was jurisdiction, relief should be granted in the present case.

The following extracts are concerned only with the first question.

SIR JOHN DONALDSON MR: The Panel on Take-overs and Mergers ... oversees and regulates a very important part of the United Kingdom financial market. Yet it performs this function without any visible means of legal support. ... 'Self-regulation'... can connote a system whereby a group of people, acting in concert, use their collective power to force themselves and others to comply with a code of conduct of their own devising. This is not necessarily morally wrong or contrary to the public interest, unlawful or even undesirable. But it is very different.

The panel is a self-regulating body in [that] ... sense. Lacking any authority de jure, it exercises immense power de facto by devising, promulgating, amending and interpreting the City Code on Take-overs and Mergers, by waiving or modifying the application of the code in particular circumstances, by investigating and reporting on alleged breaches of the code and by the application or threat of sanctions. The sanctions are no less effective because they are applied indirectly and lack a legally enforceable base ...

The unspoken assumption, which I do not doubt is a reality, is that the Department of Trade and Industry or, as the case may be, the Stock Exchange or other appropriate body would in fact exercise statutory or contractual powers to penalise the transgressors. …

The principal issue in this appeal, and the only issue which may matter in the long term is whether this remarkable body is above the law. Its respectability is beyond question. So is its bona fides. I do not doubt for one moment that it is intended to and does operate in the public interest and that the enormously wide discretion which it arrogates to itself is necessary if it is to function efficiently and effectively. But … what is to happen if the panel goes off the rails? Suppose … that it were to use its powers in a way which was manifestly unfair. What then? [Counsel for the panel] submits that the panel would lose the support of public opinion in the financial markets and would be unable to operate. Further or alternatively, Parliament could and would intervene. Maybe, but how long would that take and who in the meantime could or would come to the assistance of those who were being oppressed by such conduct? …

The jurisdictional issue

… The picture which emerges is clear. As an act of government it was decided that, in relation to take-overs, there should be a central self-regulatory body which would be supported and sustained by a periphery of statutory powers and penalties wherever non-statutory powers and penalties were insufficient or non-existent or where EEC requirements called for statutory provisions. …

The issue is whether the historic supervisory jurisdiction of the Queen's courts extends to such a body discharging such functions, including some which are quasi-judicial in their nature, as part of such a system. [Counsel] for the panel, submits that it does not. He says that this jurisdiction only extends to bodies whose power is derived from legislation or the exercise of the prerogative. [Counsel for the applicants] submits that this is too narrow a view and that regard has to be had not only to the source of the body's power, but also to whether it operates as an integral part of a system which has a public law character, is supported by public law in that public law sanctions are applied if its edicts are ignored and performs what might be described as public law functions.

After discussing a number of cases, *R v Criminal Injuries Compensation Board, ex parte Lain* [1967] 2 QB 864, *O'Reilly v Mackman* [1983] 2 AC 237, *Council for the Civil Service Unions v Minister for the Civil Service* [1985] AC 374 and *Gillick v West Norfolk and Wisbech Area Health Authority* [1986] AC 112, the Master of Rolls continued:

In fact, given its novelty, the panel fits surprisingly well into the format which this court had in mind in the *Criminal Injuries Compensation Board* case. It is without doubt performing a public duty and an important one. This is clear from the expressed willingness of the Secretary of State for Trade and Industry to limit legislation in the field of take-overs and mergers and to use the panel as the centre-piece of his regulation of that market. The rights of citizens are indirectly affected by its decisions, some, but by no means all of whom, may in a technical sense be said to have assented to this situation, e.g. the members of the Stock Exchange. At least in its determination of whether there has been a breach of the code it has a duty to act judicially and it asserts that its raison d'être is to do equity between one shareholder and another. Its source of power is only partly based upon moral persuasion and the assent of institutions and their members, the bottom line being the statutory powers exercised by the Department of Trade and Industry and the Bank of England. In this context I should be very disappointed if the courts could not recognise the realities of executive power and allowed their vision to be clouded by the subtlety and sometimes the complexity of the way in which it can be exerted …

[W]e sought to investigate whether it could conveniently be controlled by established forms of private law, e.g. torts such as actionable combinations in restraint of trade, and, to this end, pressed [counsel for the applicants] to draft a writ. Suffice it to say that the result was wholly unconvincing and, not surprisingly, [counsel for the panel] did not admit that it would be in the least effective. …

LLOYD LJ: … I add only a few words on the important question whether the Panel on Take-overs and Mergers is a body which is subject to judicial review. In my judgment it is. …

On this part of the case counsel for the panel has advanced arguments on two levels. On the level of pure policy he submits that it is undesirable for decisions or rulings of the panel to be reviewable. The intervention of the court would at best impede, at worst frustrate, the purposes for which the panel exists. Secondly, on a more technical level, he submits that to hold that the panel is subject to the supervisory jurisdiction of the High Court would be to extend that jurisdiction further than it has ever been extended before.

On the policy level, I find myself unpersuaded ... I was unable to see why the mere fact that a body is self-regulating makes it less appropriate for judicial review... The panel wields enormous power. It has a giant's strength. The fact that it is self-regulating, which means, presumably, that it is not subject to regulation by others, and in particular the Department of Trade and Industry, makes it not less but more appropriate that it should be subject to judicial review by the courts. ...

The courts must remain ready, willing and able to hear a legitimate complaint in this as in any other field of our national life. I am not persuaded that this particular field is one in which the courts do not belong, or from which they should retire, on grounds of policy. And if the courts are to remain in the field, then it is clearly better, as a matter of policy, that legal proceedings should remain in the realm of public law rather than private law, not only because they are quicker, but also because the requirement of leave under Ord. 53 will exclude claims which are clearly unmeritorious.

So I turn to [counsel for the panel's] more technical argument. ...

After referring to Lord Diplock's speech in *Council of Civil Service Unions* v *Minister for the Civil Service* [1985] AC 374 Lloyd LJ continued:

I do not agree that the source of the power is the sole test whether a body is subject to judicial review, nor do I so read Lord Diplock's speech. Of course the source of power will often, perhaps usually, be decisive. If the source of power is a statute, or subordinate legislation under a statute, then clearly the body in question will be subject to judicial review. If, at the other end of the scale, the source of power is contractual, as in the case of private arbitration, then clearly the arbitrator is not subject to judicial review: see *R* v *National Joint Council for the Craft of Dental Technicians (Disputes Committee), ex parte Neate* [1953] 1 QB 704.

But in between these extremes there is an area in which it is helpful to look not just at the source of the power but at the nature of the power. If the body in question is exercising public law functions, or if the exercise of its functions have public law consequences, then that may, as counsel for the applicants submitted, be sufficient to bring the body within the reach of judicial review. ...

[S]uppose that the courts are indeed confined to looking at the source of the power, as [counsel for the panel] submits. Then I would accept the submission of counsel for the applicants that the source of the power in the present case is indeed governmental, at least in part. [Counsel for the panel] argued that ... this is a case where the government has deliberately abstained from exercising power ... I agree with [counsel for the applicants] when he says there has been an implied devolution of power. Power exercised behind the scenes is power nonetheless ... Having regard to the way in which the panel came to be established, the fact that the Governor of the Bank of England appoints both the chairman and the deputy chairman, and the other matters to which Sir John Donaldson MR has referred, I am persuaded that the panel was established under the authority of the government, to use the language of Diplock LJ in *Lain's* case. If in addition to looking at the source of the power we are entitled to look at the nature of the power, as I believe we are, then the case is all the stronger. ...

NICHOLLS LJ: ...

Jurisdiction

I take as my starting point *Reg* v *Criminal Injuries Compensation Board, ex parte Lain* [1967] 2 QB 864, 882, where Lord Parker CJ noted that the only constant limits on the ancient remedy of certiorari were that the tribunal in question was performing a public duty. He contrasted private or domestic tribunals whose authority is derived solely from the agreement of the parties concerned. ...

In my view, and quite apart from any other factors which point in the same direction, given the leading and continuing role played by the Bank of England in the affairs of the panel, the statutory source of the powers and duties of the Council of the Stock Exchange, the wide-ranging nature and importance of the matters covered by the code, and the public law consequences of non-compliance, the panel is performing a public duty in prescribing and operating the code (including ruling on complaints).

■ QUESTIONS

1. Is it correct to say, after *Datafin*, that the only criterion for deciding whether an authority is subject to judicial review is whether it performs a public function?

2. Would judicial review be available to challenge the decisions of the following:

    (a) the Advertising Standards Authority (see *R v Advertising Standards Authority Limited, ex parte The Insurance Service* (1989) 133 SJ 1545);

    (b) the National Greyhound Racing Club (see *Law v National Greyhound Racing Club* [1983] 1 WLR 1302, but note that this case was decided before *ex parte Datafin*. Do you think it would be decided any differently after *ex parte Datafin*?);

    (c) the Jockey Club (see *R v Disciplinary Committee of the Jockey Club, ex parte Aga Khan* [1993] 1 WLR 909);

    (d) the Association of the British Pharmaceutical Industry (see *R v Code of Practice Committee of the Association of the British Pharmaceutical Industry, The Times*, 7 November 1990);

    (e) a university (see *Page v Hull University Visitor* [1993] AC 682).

NOTE: There have been a number of cases in which the courts considered whether the decisions of statutory bodies to dismiss an employee/employees could be challenged under Ord. 53. In *R v East Berkshire Health Authority, ex parte Walsh* [1985] QB 152 the Court of Appeal held that this question depended on whether the employment had sufficient 'statutory underpinning'. The health authority was required by statute to contract with its employees on terms which included the conditions agreed by the Whitley Council for the Health Service and approved by the Secretary of State. The Court of Appeal decided that this did not provide a sufficient statutory underpinning. On the other hand, in *R v Secretary of State for the Home Department, ex parte Benwell* [1985] QB 152 Hodgson J granted judicial review of a decision to dismiss a prison officer. Benwell was not in a contractual relationship with his employers and Hodgson J considered that, because his employment was governed by a code of discipline issued under statutory authority, there was sufficient statutory underpinning to provide a public law element. See also *Roy v Kensington and Chelsea FPC* [1992] earlier in Section 2, p. 585. Ordinary civil servants have now been held to have contracts of employment (*R v Lord Chancellor's Department, ex parte Nangle* [1992] 1 All ER 897).

For further discussion of the distinction between public law and private law, see J. Beatson, '"Public" and "Private" in English Administrative Law' (1987) 103 *Law Quarterly Review*, 34–65.

Although the courts might decide that the claim for judicial review is not available because the dispute does not raise issues of public law, this does not mean that the principles of judicial review are irrelevant. The rules of natural justice are frequently applied to bodies (such as sporting clubs) which could not be challenged under the application for judicial review procedure (see, for example, *R v BBC, ex parte Lavelle* [1983] 1 WLR 23). In such cases the judges may describe their role as one of exercising judicial review. This means that it is important to bear in mind that there may be a distinction between the scope of judicial review at the substantive level (that is, the scope of the principles of judicial review) and the scope of judicial review at the procedural level (the scope of the application for judicial review).

SECTION 5: JUSTICIABILITY

Even if a matter raises an issue of public law, the courts may nonetheless refuse to review it on the ground that the matter is not justiciable. This generally means that the courts consider judicial procedures are unsuitable to control the exercise of discretion. This may be for a variety of reasons, for example because of lack of expertise on the part of the court or because of the constitutional inappropriateness of judicial intervention.

Council of Civil Service Unions v Minister for the Civil Service
[1985] AC 374, House of Lords

The facts of this case are in Chapter 10, Section 2C at p. 538. In it, the court accepted that prerogative powers were subject to judicial review. The question of whether public powers are subject to judicial review was not therefore to be established on the basis of whether the source of the powers was statute or the prerogative (see further *R* v *Panel on Take-overs and Mergers*). Review of the exercise of powers might, however, be denied if the subject matter of the dispute raised issues which were not justiciable.

LORD FRASER OF TULLYBELTON: … The respondent's case is that she deliberately made the decision without prior consultation because prior consultation 'would involve a real risk that it would occasion the very kind of disruption [at GCHQ] which was a threat to national security and which it was intended to avoid.' …

The question is one of evidence. The decision on whether the requirements of national security outweigh the duty of fairness in any particular case is for the Government and not for the courts; the Government alone has access to the necessary information, and in any event the judicial process is unsuitable for reaching decisions on national security. But if the decision is successfully challenged, on the ground that it has been reached by a process which is unfair, then the Government is under an obligation to produce evidence that the decision was in fact based on grounds of national security. …

[After considering *The Zamora* [1916] 2 AC 77 and the speeches of Lord Reid and Viscount Radcliffe in *Chandler* v *Director of Public Prosecutions* [1964] AC 763 his Lordship concluded that] … The affidavit [of Sir Robert Armstrong], read as a whole, does in my opinion undoubtedly constitute evidence that the Minister did indeed consider that prior consultation would have involved a risk of precipitating disruption at GCHQ. I am accordingly of opinion that the respondent has shown that her decision was one which not only could reasonably have been based, but was in fact based, on considerations of national security, which outweighed what would otherwise have been the reasonable expectation on the part of the appellants for prior consultation. …

LORD SCARMAN: My Lords, I would dismiss this appeal for one reason only. I am satisfied that the respondent has made out a case on the ground of national security. Notwithstanding the criticisms which can be made of the evidence and despite the fact that the point was not raised, or, if it was, was not clearly made before the case reached the Court of Appeal, I have no doubt that the respondent refused to consult the unions before issuing her instruction of the 22 December 1983 because she feared that, if she did, union-organised disruption of the monitoring services of GCHQ could well result. I am further satisfied that the fear was one which a reasonable minister in the circumstances in which she found herself could reasonably entertain. I am also satisfied that a reasonable minister could reasonably consider such disruption to constitute a threat to national security. I would, therefore, deny relief to the appellants upon their application for judicial review of the instruction, the effect of which was that staff at GCHQ would no longer be permitted to belong to a national trade union.

The point of principle in the appeal is as to the duty of the court when in proceedings properly brought before it a question arises as to what is required in the interest of national security. The question may arise in ordinary litigation between private persons as to their private rights and obligations: and it can arise, as in this case, in proceedings for judicial review of a decision by a public authority. The question can take one of several forms. It may be a question of fact which Parliament has left to the court to determine: see for an example section 10 of the Contempt of Court Act 1981. It may arise for consideration as a factor in the exercise of an executive discretionary power. But, however it arises, it is a matter to be considered by the court in the circumstances and context of the case. Though there are limits dictated by law and common sense which the court must observe in dealing with the question, the court does not abdicate its judicial function. If the question arises as a matter of fact, the court requires evidence to be given. If it arises as a factor to be considered in reviewing the exercise of a discretionary power, evidence is also needed so that the court may determine whether it should intervene to correct excess or abuse of the power. …

Lord Scarman, after discussing *The Zamora, Chandler* v *Director of Public Prosecutions,* and *Secretary of State for Defence* v *Guardian Newspapers Ltd* [1985] AC 339, continued:

My Lords, I conclude, therefore, that where a question as to the interests of national security arises in judicial proceedings the court has to act on evidence. In some cases a judge or jury is required by law to be satisfied that the interest is proved to exist: in others, the interest is a factor to be considered in the review of the exercise of an executive discretionary power. Once the factual basis is established by evidence so that the court is satisfied that the interest of national security is a relevant factor to be considered in the determination of the case, the court will accept the opinion of the Crown or its responsible officer as to what is required to meet it, unless it is possible to show that the opinion was one which no reasonable minister advising the Crown could in the circumstances reasonably have held. There is no abdication of the judicial function, but there is a common sense limitation recognised by the judges as to what is justiciable: and the limitation is entirely consistent with the general development of the modern case law of judicial review. ...

LORD ROSKILL: My Lords, the conflict between private rights and the rights of the state is not novel either in our political history or in our courts. Historically, at least since 1688, the courts have sought to present a barrier to inordinate claims by the executive. But they have also been obliged to recognise that in some fields that barrier must be lowered and that on occasions, albeit with reluctance, the courts must accept that the claims of executive power must take precedence over those of the individual. One such field is that of national security. The courts have long shown themselves sensitive to the assertion by the executive that considerations of national security must preclude judicial investigation of a particular individual grievance. But even in that field the courts will not act on a mere assertion that questions of national security are involved. Evidence is required that the decision under challenge was in fact founded on those grounds. That that principle exists is I think beyond doubt. In a famous passage in *The Zamora* [1916] 2 AC 77, 107 Lord Parker of Waddington, delivering the opinion of the Judicial Committee, said:

> Those who are responsible for the national security must be the sole judges of what the national security requires. It would be obviously undesirable that such matters should be the subject of evidence in a court of law or otherwise discussed in public.

The Judicial Committee were there asserting what I have already sought to say, namely that some matters, of which national security is one, are not amenable to the judicial process. ...

Lord Diplock and Lord Brightman delivered judgments in favour of dismissing the appeals.

■ QUESTION

What differences, if any, are there between the speeches of Lord Fraser and Lord Roskill on the one hand, and Lord Scarman on the other?

NOTES

1. In *R* v *Secretary of State for the Home Department, ex parte Ruddock* [1987] 1 WLR 1482, at p. 1490 it was said that 'credible evidence' was required in support of a plea of national security before judicial investigation of a factual issue (in this case whether a warrant had been issued to tap Mrs Ruddock's telephone) is precluded. Taylor J rejected the argument that the court should decline jurisdiction because a Minister states that to do so would be detrimental to national security. He did, however, accept that in an extreme case where there was 'cogent', 'very strong and specific' evidence of potential damage to national security flowing from the trial of the issues a court might have to decline to try factual issues.

2. In other cases the courts have held that certain decisions cannot be challenged on particular grounds (see *Nottinghamshire CC* v *Secretary of State for the Environment* [1986] AC 240, Chapter 10, Section 2D at p. 543).

3. In *R v Secretary of State for the Home Department, ex parte Bentley* [1994] QB 349 the exercise of the prerogative of mercy was successfully challenged, albeit on a narrow ground. The court held the Minister approached the question of a posthumous pardon on the wrong basis that a grant of a free pardon required moral and technical innocence, rather than considering whether, in all the circumstances, the appropriate punishment had been suffered.

The challenge to the Treaty on European Union was not successful (*R v Secretary of State for Foreign and Commonwealth Affairs, ex parte Rees-Mogg* [1994] QB 552).

4. In *Clark v University of Lincolnshire and Humberside* (see earlier in this chapter in Section 2 at p. 587) Sedley LJ said that issues of academic or pastoral judgement were ones which universities were better placed to judge than the courts and instanced the particular mark or class a student ought to be awarded or whether an aegrotat is justified. He also said that religious or aesthetic matters might fall within such a class of non-justiciable matters (para. 12).

■ QUESTION

Consider whether you think each of the following issues is justiciable and why/why not? Then read the cases cited to establish the views of the courts. What reasons did the courts give?

(a) A British citizen residing in Spain applied for a British passport. The application was refused, and he was told that the reason for this was that a warrant for his arrest had been issued in the United Kingdom and the Secretary of State would not issue a passport in such circumstances (see *R v Secretary of State for Foreign and Commonwealth Affairs, ex parte Everett* [1989] 2 WLR 224).

(b) The Attorney-General has power to stop or institute prosecutions and to issue directions to the Director of Public Prosecutions to take over the conduct of prosecutions. He or she may also give, or refuse to give, consent to the institution of relator actions (actions brought at the instance of a relator by the Attorney-General to restrain infringements of public rights). (See *Gouriet v UPOW* [1978] AC 435.)

SECTION 6: JUDICIAL REVIEW AS A DISCRETIONARY REMEDY

NOTE: It is important to remember that judicial review is a discretionary remedy. Hence, the effective scope of the principles of judicial review will depend on how the court chooses to exercise its discretion.

There are a number of factors which are relevant to the exercise of the court's discretion: the availability of alternative remedies and the question whether the applicant has suffered injustice have been particularly important in recent years.

A: The availability of alternative remedies

In the Practice Statement (Administrative Court: Listing and Urgent Cases) the then Lead judge of the Administrative Court Scott Baker J stated at para. 5:

Use of alternative means of resolution

I draw the attention of litigants and their advisers to the decision of the Court of Appeal in *R (Cowl)* v *Plymouth City Council (Practice Note)* [2001] EWCA Civ 1935, [2002] 1 WLR 803. The nominated judges are fully committed to resolving disputes by alternative means where appropriate and are exploring ways of promoting this.

R (Cowl) v Plymouth City Council (Practice Note)
[2001] EWCA Civ 1935, [2002] 1 WLR 803, Court of Appeal

The claimants, who were residents of a residential home, appealed the refusal of permission to grant judicial review of the decision by the council to confirm its social services committee's decision to close the residential home. The council had offered to convene a complaints panel under Local Authority Social Services Act 1970, s. 7B as inserted by National Health Service and Community Care Act 1990, s. 50.

LORD WOOLF CJ:

1 The importance of this appeal is that it illustrates that, even in disputes between public authorities and the members of the public for whom they are responsible, insufficient attention is paid to the paramount importance of avoiding litigation whenever this is possible. Particularly in the case of these disputes both sides must by now be acutely conscious of the contribution alternative dispute resolution can make to resolving disputes in a manner which both meets the needs of the parties and the public and saves time, expense and stress.

2 The appeal also demonstrates that courts should scrutinise extremely carefully applications for judicial review in the case of applications of the class with which this appeal is concerned. The courts should then make appropriate use of their ample powers under the Civil Procedure Rules to ensure that the parties try to resolve the dispute with the minimum involvement of the courts. The legal aid authorities should co-operate in support of this approach.

3 To achieve this objective the court may have to hold, on its own initiative, an inter partes hearing at which the parties ... should be asked why a complaints procedure or some other form of alternative dispute resolution has not been used or adapted to resolve or reduce the issues which are in dispute. If litigation is necessary the courts should deter the parties from adopting an unnecessarily confrontational approach to the litigation. If this had happened in this case many thousands of pounds in costs could have been saved and considerable stress to the parties could have been avoided.

...

14 It appears that ... both parties were under the impression that unless they agreed otherwise the claimants were *entitled* to proceed with their application for judicial review unless the complaints procedure on offer technically constituted an 'alternative remedy' which would fulfil all the functions of judicial review ... The parties do not today, under the Civil Procedure Rules, have a right to have a resolution of their respective contentions by judicial review in the absence of an alternative procedure which would cover exactly the same ground as judicial review. The courts should not permit, except for good reason, proceedings for judicial review to proceed if a significant part of the issues between the parties could be resolved outside the litigation process. The disadvantages of doing so are limited. If subsequently it becomes apparent that there is a legal issue to be resolved, that can thereafter be examined by the courts which may be considerably assisted by the findings made by the complaints panel.

...

21 Having read the numerous witness statements placed before us and the substantial skeleton arguments prior to the hearing, the members of this court came to the clear conclusion that the appeal raised no point of legal principle. However, while this was the position, the claimants were intent on examining in detail the previous decisions of courts, primarily at first instance, involving the closure of care homes in order to erect a series of legal hoops which it was contended Plymouth had to proceed through before it could close Granby Way. In reality, however, there was no legal principle which divided the parties. It was common ground that there has to be the fullest assessment of the effect of a possible move on the claimants before a decision whether to move the claimants could be reached. Plymouth were perfectly prepared to carry out such an assessment, and recognise that as yet it has not been carried out and that it has to be carried out. This does not satisfy the claimants. They contend

that as a matter of law the assessment is required to take place before closure. But absent any statutory requirement what is important is that an assessment takes place, not the time at which it takes place.

22 We understand the reason why the claimants attach such importance to the assessment being carried out before the decision to close. They do not want an assessment as to the propriety of moving the individual claimants to be taken against a decision that the home is to be closed as that could, they fear, prejudge the outcome. This is why they submit that the full assessment should take place before the decision to close the home is taken. The position of Plymouth now, whatever may have been the position in the past, is clearly to regard the decision to close as merely a decision in principle; that is, to close Granby Way subject to the full assessment of the impact upon the residents of their having to move. This approach on the part of Plymouth is understandable. Plymouth needed to make financial savings. The closure of Granby Way and another home would produce the required financial saving. From Plymouth's point of view therefore the first step was to consider whether closure would be a viable option. For this purpose they needed a limited assessment of the impact on the residents and of the practicality of their being rehoused, but no more than this. This exercise was carried out. The decision was made to proceed with this option. Detailed examination of what is involved in rehousing was then required so that a final decision could be made. The final decision would only be made after the full assessment of the impact upon the residents. Such an approach could be beneficial to the residents because, if the closure option was not viable, there was no need to subject them to the stress which would be involved in determining what would happen to them if they had to move.

23 Unfortunately Plymouth failed to make their strategy clear. They should have done this at the outset. Initially, therefore, there was justification for the claimants' concern that they were to be moved without any proper assessment being made before a final decision to close had taken place.

24 Nonetheless the decision which was taken did not have the technicality the claimants attached to it. There was nothing wrong with Plymouth adopting a two-stage process, with the detailed assessment being part of the second process. However, if this was what they were doing, it is regrettable that far from explaining it they obscured the fact that this was their intention. On the other hand, those who were acting on behalf of the claimants adopted a far too technical approach ...

25 We do not single out either side's lawyers for particular criticism. What followed was due to the unfortunate culture in litigation of this nature of over-judicialising the processes which are involved. It is indeed unfortunate that, that process having started, instead of the parties focusing on the future they insisted on arguing about what had occurred in the past ...Without the need for the vast costs which must have been incurred in this case already being incurred, the parties should have been able to come to a sensible conclusion as to how to dispose the issues which divided them. If they could not do this without help, then an independent mediator should have been recruited to assist. That would have been a far cheaper course to adopt. Today sufficient should be known about alternative dispute resolution to make the failure to adopt it, in particular when public money is involved, indefensible.

26 The disadvantages of what happened instead were apparent to the trial judge. They were also apparent to this court ... Having made clear our views, building on the proposal which had been made in the 23 May letter, the parties had no difficulty in coming to a sensible agreement in the terms which are annexed to this judgment and will form part of the order of the court. The terms go beyond what Plymouth was required to do under the statutory complaint procedure. This does not however, matter because it is always open to the parties to agree to go beyond their statutory obligations ...

27 This case will have served some purpose if it makes it clear that the lawyers acting on both sides of a dispute of this sort are under a heavy obligation to resort to litigation only if it is really unavoidable. If they cannot resolve the whole of the dispute by the use of the complaints procedure they should resolve the dispute so far as is practicable without involving litigation. At least in this way some of the expense and delay will be avoided.

Appeal dismissed.

NOTES

1. *Cowl* and the Practice Statement seem, at least, to be reiterating in the strongest terms the case law which requires exhaustion of alternative remedies. The actual facts of *Cowl* suggest that review was premature and Beatson argues that many of the cases on exhaustion of alternatives are not really concerned with the tests of adequacy and relative expertise of the alternative remedies, but rather the prematurity of review proceedings ('Prematurity and Ripeness for Review' in C. Forsyth and I. Hare (eds), *The Golden Metwand and the Crooked Cord* (1998), 221 at 234). See *R v Inland Revenue Commissioners, ex parte Preston*, [1985] AC 835 for a presumption that appellate procedures should be used and see Chapter 12, Section 3A at p. 621, for the Law Commission's proposal on the relationship between public services ombudsmen and the courts.

2. The previous case law on exhaustion did allow for exceptions. In *R v Chief Constable of Merseyside Police, ex parte Calvely* [1986] 2 WLR 144 some police officers had been found guilty of disciplinary offences by their Chief Constable. They had initiated a statutory appeal to the Home Secretary but also sought judicial review on the basis that there had been a breach of reg. 7, Police (Discipline) Regulations. Sir John Donaldson MR said:

[Counsel] for the Chief Constable, submits that the application for judicial review was rightly dismissed, not upon the ground that it was premature, but because judicial review is not an available remedy when another avenue of appeal is open. In this context he referred to *Reg v Epping and Harlow General Commissioners, ex parte Goldstraw* [1983] 3 All ER 257 where, with the agreement of Purchas LJ, I said, at p. 262:

> it is a cardinal principle that, save in the most exceptionable circumstances, [the judicial review] jurisdiction will not be exercised where other remedies were available and have not been used.

This, like other judicial pronouncements on the interrelationship between remedies by way of judicial review on the one hand and appeal procedures on the other, is not to be regarded or construed as a statute. It does not support the proposition that judicial review is not available where there is an alternative remedy by way of appeal. It asserts simply that the court, in the exercise of its discretion, will very rarely make this remedy available in these circumstances.

In other cases courts have asserted the existence of this discretion, albeit with varying emphasis on the reluctance to grant judicial review. Thus in *Reg v Paddington Valuation Officer, ex parte Peachey Property Corporation Ltd* [1966] 1 QB 380, 400, Lord Denning MR, with the agreement of Danckwerts and Salmon LJJ, held that certiorari and mandamus were available where the alternative statutory remedy was 'nowhere near so convenient, beneficial and effectual.' In *Reg v Hillingdon London Borough Council, ex parte Royco Homes Ltd* [1974] QB 720, 728 Lord Widgery CJ said: 'it has always been a principle that certiorari will go only where there is no other equally effective and convenient remedy.' In *Ex parte Waldron* [1985] 3 WLR 1090, 1108, Glidewell LJ, after referring to this passage, said:

> Whether the alternative statutory remedy will resolve the question at issue fully and directly; whether the statutory procedure would be quicker, or slower, than procedure by way of judicial review; whether the matter depends on some particular or technical knowledge which is more readily available to the alternative appellate body; these are amongst the matters which a court should take into account when deciding whether to grant relief by judicial review when an alternative remedy is available.

Finally, this approach is, I think, consistent with *Reg v Inland Revenue Commissioners, ex parte Preston* [1985] AC 835. …

The statutory scheme for police discipline contained in the Police (Discipline) Regulations 1977 and the Police (Appeals) Rules 1977 (SI 1977 No. 759) contemplates a right of appeal to the Secretary of State from a determination by the Chief Constable. … However, it is not speedy and, even if there had been no application for judicial review, it is not certain that the appeal would have been determined much before the present time. The application for judicial review in fact caused the appeal to be stayed and, on the most optimistic view, it could not be determined in less than five to six months from now.

Mr Livesey submits that the applicants' complaint of delay in serving the regulation 7 notices and of consequential prejudice should be determined by the appeal procedure provided by Parliament. The appeal tribunal would have a specialised expertise rendering it better able than a court to assess the prejudice. Furthermore, the applicants would be able to raise new points and call fresh evidence directed to the disciplinary charges themselves.

I acknowledge the specialised expertise of such a tribunal, but I think Mr Livesey's submission overlooks the fact that a police officer's submission to police disciplinary procedures is not unconditional. He agrees and is bound by these procedures taking them as a whole. Just as his right of appeal is constrained by the requirement that he give prompt notice of appeal, so he is not to be put in peril in respect of disciplinary, as contrasted with criminal, proceedings unless there is substantial compliance with the police disciplinary regulations. That has not occurred in this case. Whether in all the circumstances the Chief Constable, and the Secretary of State on appeal, is to be regarded as being without jurisdiction to hear and determine the charges which are not processed in accordance with the statutory scheme or whether, in natural justice, the Chief Constable and the Secretary of State would, if they directed themselves correctly in law, be bound to rule in favour of the applicants on the preliminary point, is perhaps only of academic interest. The substance of the matter is that, against the background of the requirement of regulation 7 that the applicants be informed of the complaint and given an opportunity to reply within days rather than weeks, the applicants had no formal notice of the complaints for well over two years. This is so serious a departure from the police disciplinary procedure that, in my judgment, the court should, in the exercise of its discretion, grant judicial review and set aside the determination of the Chief Constable.

I would allow the appeal accordingly.

■ **QUESTIONS**

1. In *Calvely* how important was the length of time of the statutory appeal to the decision of the court?
2. Is the convenience of the alternative remedy compatible with *Cowl*?

B: Needs of good administration

R v Monopolies and Mergers Commission, ex parte Argyll Group plc
[1986] 1 WLR 763, Court of Appeal

Argyll Group plc and Guinness plc were rivals in a bid to take over another company, Distillers. The Secretary of State for Trade and Industry referred the Guinness proposal to the Monopolies and Mergers Commission for inquiry and report. One week later the Chairman of the Monopolies and Mergers Commission sought and obtained the consent of the Secretary of State for Trade and Industry to the withdrawal of the reference on the ground that the proposal to make the arrangements had been abandoned. Argyll sought judicial review of this decision, seeking an order of *certiorari*. The Court of Appeal accepted that the Chairman of the Commission did not have the power to act alone in the matter. The following extracts relate to the court's discretion whether to grant a remedy.

SIR JOHN DONALDSON MR: ...

Discretion

... We are sitting as a public law court concerned to review an administrative decision, albeit one which has to be reached by the application of judicial or quasi-judicial principles. We have to approach our duties with a proper awareness of the needs of public administration. I cannot catalogue them all, but, in the present context, would draw attention to a few which are relevant.

Good public administration is concerned with substance rather than form. Difficult although the decision upon the fact of abandonment may or may not have been, I have little doubt that the commission, or a group of members charged with the conduct of the reference, would have reached and would now reach the same conclusion as did their experienced chairman.

Good public administration is concerned with speed of decision, particularly in the financial field. The decision to lay aside the reference was reached on 20 February 1986. If relief is granted, it must be some days before a new decision is reached.

Good public administration requires a proper consideration of the public interest. In this context, the Secretary of State is the guardian of the public interest. He consented to the reference being laid aside, although he need not have done so if he considered it to be in the public interest that the original proposals be further investigated. He could have made a further reference of the new proposals, if such they be, but has not done so.

Good public administration requires a proper consideration of the legitimate interests of individual citizens ... But in judging the relevance of an interest, however legitimate, regard has to be had to the purpose of the administrative process concerned. Argyll has a strong and legitimate interest in putting Guinness in baulk, but that is not the purpose of the administrative process under the Fair Trading Act 1973. To that extent their interest is not therefore of any great, or possibly any, weight.

Lastly good public administration requires decisiveness and finality unless there are compelling reasons to the contrary. The financial public has been entitled to rely upon the finality of the announced decision to set aside the reference and upon the consequence that, subject to any further reference, Guinness were back in the ring, from 20 February until at least 25 February when leave to apply for judicial review was granted, and possibly longer in the light of the judge's decision. This is a very long time in terms of a volatile market and account must be taken of the probability that deals have been done in reliance upon the validity of the decisions now impugned.

Taking account of all these factors, I do not consider that this is a case in which judicial review should be granted. Accordingly, I would dismiss the appeal.

Dillon LJ and Neill LJ delivered judgments in favour of dismissing the appeal.

NOTES

1. *R v Panel on Take-overs and Mergers, ex parte Datafin plc* [1987] QB 815 also illustrates the use of discretion in the grant of remedies. Sir John Donaldson MR stated (at p. 841) that the court would decide what order, if any, needed to be made, bearing in mind 'the likely outcome of the proceedings which will depend partly upon the facts as they appear from the information available to the court, but also in part upon the public administrative purpose which the panel is designed to serve'.

2. An example of a judicial review being successful in arguing illegality, but not leading to a remedy, is provided by a challenge to the regulation increasing university tuition fees based on non-compliance with the Public Sector Equality Duty in *R (Hurley & Moore) v Secretary of State for Business, Innovation & Skills* [2012] EWHC 201 (Admin), Elias LJ at [99].

> In my view, taking into account all these considerations, I do not consider that it would be a proportionate remedy to quash the regulations themselves. Whilst I have come to the conclusion that the Secretary of State did not give the rigorous attention required to the package of measures overall, and to that extent the breach is not simply technical, I am satisfied that the particular decision to fix the fees at the level reflected in the regulations was the subject of an appropriate analysis. Moreover, all the parties affected by these decisions – Government, universities and students – have been making plans on the assumption that the fees would be charged. It would cause administrative chaos, and would inevitably have significant economic implications, if the regulations were now to be quashed. I emphasise that those considerations would not of themselves begin to justify a refusal to quash the orders if the breach was sufficiently significant. It will be a very rare case, I suspect, where a substantial breach of the PSEDs would not lead to a quashing of the relevant decision, however inconvenient that might be. But in circumstances where, for reasons I have given, there has been very substantial compliance in fact, and an adequate analysis of implications on protected groups of the fee structure itself, these considerations reinforce my very clear conclusion that quashing the orders would not be appropriate.

■ QUESTIONS

1. Commenting on the factors referred to by Sir John Donaldson, S. Lee writes in (1987) 103 *Law Quarterly Review*, 166–8, at 167 that:

> If these are only a few of the possible reasons for judicial restraint, then their discretion is indeed very wide. There are obvious dangers to good public administration, let alone to aggrieved citizens, in such broad judicial discretion. Firstly, there is the danger that administrators will come to

> believe that they can get away with a breach of the principles of administrative action. Secondly, the prospect of winning the argument on abuse of administrative discretion but failing to secure a remedy through the exercise of judicial discretion may well act as a disincentive to bring applications for judicial review.

Do you agree that decisions such as *R* v *Monopolies and Mergers Commission* carry such risks?

2. Contrast the approach adopted in this case to arguments based on the interests of good administration with *O'Reilly* v *Mackman* (see earlier in this chapter in Section 2 at p. 581) and *Wandsworth Borough Council* v *Winder* (see earlier in this chapter in Section 2 at p. 584).

NOTE: The relevance of the argument that a fair hearing would make no difference has been considered by the courts in recent years. There are, in fact, a number of contrasting cases. Of these, *Glynn* v *Keele University* [1971] 1 WLR 487 provides an example of a case which accepts, as in *R* v *Monopolies and Mergers Commission, ex parte Argyll Group plc*, that a remedy may be denied where a fair hearing 'would make no difference'. In that case the claimant had been fined and excluded from residence on a university campus for a particular period. Pennycuick V-C found that there had been a breach of the rules of natural justice, but he refused to grant an injunction since he thought that the claimant had only lost a chance to make a plea in mitigation, and this was not a sufficient reason to set aside a decision which he believed to be perfectly proper. In contrast Megarry J in *John* v *Rees* [1970] Ch 345, at 402 stated:

> It may be that there are some who would decry the importance which the courts attach to the observance of the rules of natural justice. 'When something is obvious,' they may say, 'why force everybody to go through the tiresome waste of time involved in framing charges and giving an opportunity to be heard? The result is obvious from the start.' ... As everybody who has anything to do with the law well knows, the path of the law is strewn with open and shut cases which, somehow, were not; of unanswerable charges which, in the event, were completely answered; of inexplicable conduct which was fully explained; of fixed and unalterable determinations that, by discussion, suffered a change. Nor are those with any knowledge of human nature who pause to think for a moment likely to underestimate the feelings of resentment of those who find that a decision against them has been made without their being afforded any opportunity to influence the course of events.

SECTION 7: EXCLUSION OF JUDICIAL REVIEW

The legislature has sometimes attempted to protect public authorities from judicial review by inserting clauses which appear to be intended to exclude the jurisdiction of the court. For example, in *Anisminic Ltd* v *Foreign Compensation Commission* [1969] 2 AC 147, Anisminic Ltd wished to challenge a decision of the Foreign Compensation Commission that it was not entitled to compensation in respect of the sequestration of property which it had owned in Egypt, and accordingly applied for a declaration (see Chapter 10, Section 2B at p. 500). The legislation, however, provided that any determination by the Commission of an application 'shall not be called in question in any court of law' (Foreign Compensation Act 1950, s. 4(4)). The House of Lords considered the effect of this clause.

Anisminic Ltd v Foreign Compensation Commission
[1969] 2 AC 147, House of Lords

LORD REID: ... The next argument was that, by reason of the provisions of section 4(4) of the 1950 Act, the courts are precluded from considering whether the respondent's determination was a nullity, and therefore it must be treated as valid whether or not inquiry would disclose that it was a nullity. ...

The respondent maintains that these are plain words only capable of having one meaning. Here is a determination which is apparently valid: there is nothing on the face of the document to cast any doubt on its validity. If it is a nullity, that could only be established by raising some kind of proceedings in court. But that would be calling the determination in question, and that is expressly prohibited by statute. The appellants … say that 'determination' means a real determination and does not include an apparent or purported determination which in the eyes of the law has no existence because it is a nullity…. It is one thing to question a determination which does not exist: it is quite another to say that there is nothing to be questioned.

Let me illustrate the matter by supposing a simple case. A statute provides that a certain order may be made by a person who holds a specified qualification or appointment, and it contains a provision similar to section 4(4), that such an order made by such a person shall not be questioned in any court of law. A person aggrieved by an order alleges that it is a forgery or that the person who made the order did not hold that qualification or appointment. Does such a provision require the court to treat that order as a valid order? It is a well-established principle that a provision ousting the ordinary jurisdiction of the court must be construed strictly—meaning, I think, that, if such provision is reasonably capable of having two meanings, that meaning shall be taken which preserves the ordinary jurisdiction of the court.

Statutory provisions which seek to limit the ordinary jurisdiction of the court have a long history. No case has been cited in which any other form of words limiting the jurisdiction of the court has been held to protect a nullity. If the draftsman or Parliament had intended to introduce a new kind of ouster clause so as to prevent any inquiry as to whether the document relied on was a forgery, I would have expected to find something much more specific than the bald statement that a determination shall not be called in question in any court of law. Undoubtedly such a provision protects every determination which is not a nullity. But I do not think that it is necessary or even reasonable to construe the word 'determination' as including everything which purports to be a determination but which is in fact no determination at all. …

The other Law Lords delivered speeches in which they agreed that the ouster clause would not protect a decision from challenge if the FCC had acted outside its jurisdiction. A majority of their Lordships also held that Anisminic Ltd was entitled to the declaration which it sought because the FCC had made an error of law which took it outside its jurisdiction, see Chapter 10, Section 2B at p. 500.

NOTE: After the decision in *Anisminic* the Foreign Compensation Act 1969 was passed. Section 3 provided that a person aggrieved by a determination of the Commission on any question of law had a right to require the Commission to state and sign a case for the Court of Appeal. It was provided, however, that there was to be no appeal to the House of Lords from a decision of the Court of Appeal. Section 3(9) stated that, except as provided by the section and in respect of claims that the Commission had breached the rules of natural justice, no determination by the Commission on any claim under the Foreign Compensation Act 1950 shall be called in question in any court of law. Determination was defined as including a purported determination.

■ QUESTION

If these provisions had been in force at the time of the decision in *Anisminic*, do you think the House of Lords would have granted the declaration sought?

NOTE: The Tribunals and Inquiries Act 1992, s. 12(1) (formerly s. 11 of the Tribunal and Inquiries Act 1958) provides that, as respects England and Wales:

… any provision in an Act passed before 1 August 1958 that any order or determination shall not be called in question in any court, or any provision in such an Act which by similar words excludes any of the powers of the High Court, shall not have effect so as to prevent the removal of the proceedings into the High Court by order of certiorari or to prejudice the powers of the High Court to make orders of mandamus.

(Section 11 of the 1958 Act expressly excluded orders or determinations of the Foreign Compensation Commission from this general provision; in *Anisminic*, however, Lord Pearce specifically stated that s. 11 had no bearing on the issue which the court was required to consider.)

■ QUESTION

Why do you think this provision was confined to Acts passed before 1 August 1958?

NOTES

1. *Anisminic* concerned an absolute ouster clause. Partial or limited ouster clauses sometimes appear in certain statutory provisions. For example, in planning law persons aggrieved by a compulsory purchase order are permitted to appeal to the High Court on certain grounds within six weeks of publication of the order. Apart from this it is provided that a compulsory purchase order 'shall not ... be questioned in any legal proceedings whatsoever' (see Acquisition of Land Act 1981, ss. 23–5). The courts have upheld the validity of the partial or limited ouster clauses which attempt to protect decisions from challenge after the expiry of a time limit (see *R* v *Secretary of State for the Environment, ex parte Ostler* [1977] QB 122).

2. Where a legislative provision stipulates that the issuing of a certificate 'shall be conclusive evidence' that the conditions for the issue of the certificate had been satisfied, it seems that this can exclude review of the decision to issue the certificate—*R* v *Registrar of Companies, ex parte Central Bank of India* [1986] QB 1114.

3. An example of a significant ouster clause is the Security Services Act 1989, s. 5(4) 'decisions of the Tribunal ... (including any decisions as to their jurisdiction) shall not be subject to appeal or liable to be questioned in any court'.

4. The inclusion of an ouster clause in the Asylum and Immigration (Treatment of Claimants) Bill might, if it had been preserved in the 2004 Act, have led to a constitutional crisis. The Government was concerned that the two tiers of tribunal appeals followed by claims for judicial review were being abused, and so sought to create a single tribunal and severely restrict judicial review of the tribunal's determinations. Part of the ouster clause stipulated:

> (3) Subsections (1) and (2)—
>> (a) prevent a court, in particular, from entertaining proceedings to determine whether a purported determination, decision or action of the Tribunal was a nullity by reason of—
>>> (i) lack of jurisdiction,
>>> (ii) irregularity,
>>> (iii) error of law,
>>> (iv) breach of natural justice, or
>>> (v) any other matter....

The clause was comprehensive. In the view of the Commons Constitutional Affairs Select Committee its extensiveness was without precedent (HC 211 of 2003–04, para. 70). This was achieved ... said Lord Woolf CJ, in a speech ... as a result of the Government's consultations with him and other members of the judiciary, so that 'the clause was extended to close the loopholes we had identified instead of being abandoned as we had argued' ([2004] *Cambridge Law Journal*, 317, at 328). Another parliamentary committee, the Joint Committee on Human Rights (JCHR), also criticized the ouster clause, along with other provisions in the Bill, on human rights grounds. All of the critics argued that the ouster clause's degree of restriction of access to the courts was a serious breach of the rule of law. The Government decided to withdraw the clause and amendments were enacted. The JCHR's opinion of the amendments was that they could lead to violations of ECHR Arts 2, 3, 8 and 13, and 14 in conjunction with 2, 3, 6(1), 8, and 13 (HL 102/HC 240 of 2003–04). See R. Rawlings 'Review, Revenge and Retreat' (2005) 68 *Modern Law Review* 378 who doubts that the courts would have disapplied the ouster clause had it been enacted, a suggestion proposed by M. Fordham that Parliament would have been trespassing on the separation of powers and the courts' constitutional function of controlling administrative action (see 'Common Law Illegality of Ousting Judicial Review' [2004] *Judicial Review* 86. Despite the amendments a great deal of the Administrative Court's time was spent on asylum and immigration matters and a review by judges and administrators led to the proposal that Immigration and Asylum Chambers should be created in the First-tier and Upper Tribunals. This return to a two-stage tribunal process came into effect in February 2010: see Chapter 13, Section 2A at p. 655.

5. Concern about the volume of immigration and asylum judicial review cases has led to action which came into effect in November 2013 transferring most judicial reviews in this area from the Administrative Court to the Upper Tribunal (s. 22 of the Crime and Courts Act 2013 and a direction made by the Lord Chief Justice under s. 31A(2).

12

Ombudsmen

OVERVIEW

In this chapter we look at the institution of the ombudsman, its origins, the conditions of access, and the range of matters within the jurisdiction of the parliamentary and local government ombudsmen. We then consider the key terms of maladministration and injustice with which the ombudsmen are concerned, how they investigate and resolve complaints, seek improvements, the outcome of the investigations, and remedies recommended by the ombudsmen. We end with their arrangements for dealing with dissatisfied complainants.

SECTION 1: INTRODUCTION

In 1961 an influential report by the JUSTICE organization recommended that an impartial officer, to be known as a Parliamentary Commissioner, should be established and report on complaints of maladministration in central government. It argued that:

> ... there appears to be a continuous flow of relatively minor complaints, not sufficient in themselves to attract public interest but nevertheless of great importance to the individuals concerned, which give rise to feelings of frustration and resentment because of the inadequacy of the existing means of seeking redress. (JUSTICE, *The Citizen and the Administration* (1961), para. 76.)

The report outlined the weaknesses in the parliamentary question procedure and in adjournment debates as mechanisms for the investigation of complaints (on parliamentary questions and adjournment debates, see Chapter 6, Section 2C at pp. 253–8). The report envisaged that the Parliamentary Commissioner would be independent of the Executive and responsible only to Parliament. He would conduct investigations informally, in order to ensure that there would be no serious interference with the working of a department, and have access to departmental files. A Select Committee would be established to consider the annual reports of the Parliamentary Commissioner and any special reports which he might issue on particular issues. On the controversial question of whether the establishment of a Parliamentary Commissioner would have any implications for the doctrine of ministerial responsibility, the Report stated, at para. 155:

> It is a principle of such fundamental importance in our constitution that we think it would be wrong to make any proposal which might seem to qualify it and therefore we have suggested that a Minister should have the power to veto any proposed investigation by the Parliamentary Commissioner against his Department. We would expect, however, that as so often has happened in our constitutional history, a convention would grow up that the Minister would not exercise his power of veto unreasonably.

The report was also careful to stress that 'any additional procedure should not disturb the basic position of Parliament as a channel for complaint against the Executive and should not even appear to interfere with the relations between individual members and their constituents' (para. 156). With this in mind it recommended that, during an initial testing period, complaints should only be considered on reference from a Member of either House of Parliament. It did, however, anticipate that, after a period of about five years, the Commissioner should be empowered to receive complaints direct from the public. 'The ultimate object', according to the report, 'should be to establish a channel by which the investigation of administrative grievances should take place initially outside the political sphere. Parliament would, however, always be able to take up grievances in the last resort if the Commissioner's investigation failed to procure justice' (para. 157).

Following the publication of *The Citizen and the Administration*, the Conservative Lord Chancellor, Lord Dilhorne, argued that 'a Parliamentary Commissioner would seriously interfere with the prompt and efficient dispatch of public business' (HL Deb., Vol. 244, cols 384–5). Subsequently, however, a new government accepted, with certain modifications, the introduction of the Parliamentary Commissioner as a development and reinforcement of 'our existing constitutional arrangements for the protection of the individual' (see *The Parliamentary Commissioner for Administration*, (Cmnd 2767, 1965). On the introduction of the ombudsman system in the United Kingdom, see further, R. Gregory and P. Giddings, *The Ombudsman, the Citizen and Parliament* (2002).

The office of the Parliamentary Commissioner for Administration (or Parliamentary Ombudsman PO) was created in 1967. Since then there has been steady growth of ombudsmen in the United Kingdom. In 1969 two ombudsman offices were established in Northern Ireland, the Parliamentary Commissioner for Administration and the Commissioner for Complaints; the latter extending coverage to local government and the NHS. The offices of Health Service Commissioners of England, Wales, and Scotland were created by legislation in 1972 and 1973 and amended in 1993 and 1996. Before devolution all three posts were held by the person who was the PO. In 1974 Local Commissioners were established to deal with maladministration in local government in England and Wales and for Scotland in 1975. The establishment of the Scottish Parliament and the National Assembly for Wales has also led to the creation of new Public Services Ombudsmen. When the Scottish Public Services Ombudsman Act 2002 and Public Services Ombudsman (Wales) Act 2005 came into force 'one-stop shops' were created for complaints about devolved and local government, public/social housing and the National Health Service in Scotland and Wales. Similar amalgamating arrangements had initially been proposed for England in 2000, but instead the legislation for the separate ombudsmen operating in England was amended so that they could work in collaboration (see Regulatory Reform (Collaboration etc. Between Ombudsmen) Reform Order 2007). A report by the House of Commons Public Administration Select Committee (PASC), *Time for People's Ombudsman Service*, HC 65 of 2013–14, which renewed the call for merging the different public sector ombudsmen in England, led to the Cabinet Office commissioning a review, R. Gordon, *Better to Serve the Public: Proposals to restructure, reform, renew and reinvigorate public services ombudsmen* (2014). This review formed the basis of consultation proposals in March 2015, and in turn the Government response in December 2015 promised a draft Public Service Ombudsman Bill, which was published in December 2016. If these proposals are enacted the UK's first ombudsman will be the last one to become a merged institution following the amalgamation of the second and third oldest UK ombudsman offices provided for by the Public Services Ombudsman Act (Northern Ireland) 2016.

In addition to central and local government and the health service, public sector ombudsmen now include part of the police with the Police Ombudsman for Northern

Ireland (Police (Northern Ireland) Act 1998, s. 51). There is a Prisons & Probation Ombudsman, but unlike all of the aforementioned ombudsmen this officer does not have the same status of independence from the Executive and is more like the Adjudicator in HM Revenue and Customs, or the Independent Case Examiner in the various agencies in the Department of Work and Pensions, being above the internal departmental procedure and below the PO in the complaints-handling chain.

In the private sector some ombudsmen deal with aspects of financial services such as (a) banking, building societies, and insurance; and (b) legal services have statutory frameworks (respectively the Financial Services and Markets Act 2000; and Legal Services Act 2007).

This chapter focuses on the Parliamentary Ombudsman, and the Health Service Ombudsman for England (PHSO) and the Local Government Ombudsman for England (LGO) who will be merged if the proposals in the draft Bill are enacted.

The main legislative provisions governing the PO are contained in the Parliamentary Commissioner Act 1967. The provisions governing the LGO are set out in the Local Government Act 1974. Both pieces of legislation have been amended on a number of occasions.

The following extracts from the reports of the PHSO and the LGO provide some indication of the work which they carry out.

Parliamentary and Health Service Ombudsman, *The Ombudsman's Annual Report and Accounts 2015–16*

HC 779 of 2016–17, pp. 31–2

Patient's death not linked to medication change

Mr W had a history of high blood pressure and bipolar disorder and took regular medication to treat his illness. His GP increased his medication to treat high blood pressure. When Mr W reported symptoms, he received treatment promptly. He went to hospital, where his physical illness was treated, and he was seen by mental health specialists. His condition appeared to be stable but within 18 months his mental health had deteriorated and he died a few months later. Mrs W complained to the Practice about her husband's care. She believed that he had never fully recovered from his earlier illness and that Mr W's GP had caused the problem by increasing his blood pressure medication. The GP said that Mr W had been taking blood pressure medication for a long time and there were several factors which could have caused his illness. Mrs W remained dissatisfied with the Practice's response, and complained to us. We partly upheld this complaint. We found it was appropriate for the GP to increase Mr W's blood pressure medication. However, the GP should have arranged prompt blood tests to check that Mr W was not suffering a reaction to the increase. But the delay in arranging blood tests did not lead to Mr W's death. The Practice acknowledged the delay in arranging blood tests following the increase in Mr W's blood pressure medication. It apologised to Mrs W for the distress she had experienced due to not knowing whether her husband could have been treated differently if it had done so.

Border Force complaint handling was poor

Ms W came to the UK to study English, so that she could then apply for a visa to come and live here with her British husband. Before being granted entry, she was questioned by Border Force officers at Heathrow Airport about her proposed visit. She complained to Border Force that one of the officers had been aggressive and intimidating. Border Force investigated Ms W's complaint, but as the officer in question could not recall the incident, which had happened less than a month before, it could not substantiate the complaint. We looked into Border Force's investigation of Ms W's complaint and we found that it was poor. It took no further action when the officer said she did not remember the incident, and did not speak to a second officer who had been present when the officer had questioned Ms W. It also made no attempt to find out if CCTV footage of the incident still existed. Although CCTV footage had no sound, it may have helped Border Force with its investigation because Ms W had said that the officer had stood very close to her in an intimidating manner. Border Force also did not try to identify the senior officer who had been dismissive when Ms W had raised the complaint at the airport. Following our own investigation, Border Force apologised to Ms W and paid her £150. It also agreed to review its guidance on complaint handling to improve the way it investigates complaints.

HS2 Ltd

We reported on how HS2 Ltd could better communicate and engage with communities impacted by its routes, following an investigation into its treatment of a small, tight-knit community in Staffordshire. We found that a catalogue of errors by HS2 unnecessarily prolonged the uncertainty, stress and worry that families were experiencing. HS2's actions fell far below the reasonable standards we would expect. For instance, the company wrongly told complainants that moving forward with their relocation plans was conditional on them withdrawing their complaint to us. We recommended that HS2 publish an independent review of its current processes around engagement, communication and complaint handling; and demonstrate how it was going to make improvements. Our report prompted an inquiry by the Public Administration and Constitutional Affairs Committee, which called the Minister of State for the Department for Transport and HS2's Chief Executive to give evidence. As a result, HS2 took several significant steps to improve its complaint handling and communication, including increasing resource for its engagement and community relations teams, and introducing a 24-hour helpdesk to better engage with the public.

Local Government Ombudsman, *Annual Review of Local Government Complaints 2015–16*
(2016) pp. 14, 16, 20

Child protection – not following the children's complaints process

Petra became the adopted mother of two young girls, aged four and five. The children told her that their former foster carer had smacked them. Petra approached the council with the allegations … the council failed to convene the correct planning meetings and social workers recorded the concern as 'unsubstantiated'. Petra later raised further concerns made by the children. She also claimed that some of the children's belongings and memory boxes were not passed on from the foster carer. The council held a meeting chaired by an independent officer to look at whether the council had investigated the allegations properly. The meeting decided that any investigation could be traumatic for the children and doubted whether sufficient evidence would be gained. Petra tried to pursue her complaint with the council, but it refused progress it to the second stage, so she approached us. We found the council at fault for not following the statutory children's social care complaints process. And while the council claimed it did weigh up the evidence it may get from interviewing the children over the potential harm it may cause, it also failed to follow its own policy which said that any child or adult that reports a concern must be consulted. The council agreed to our recommendations to apologise and agree a clear plan for interviewing the children. It also agreed to train staff, and review its procedures for how it investigates allegations, how it progresses complaints through the statutory process quickly, and how it works with foster carers to impress the importance of keeping photographs and possessions safe.

We also recommended a small financial payment to Petra and her two daughters to recognise the avoidable frustration and distress they were caused

Traffic fines – failure to reverse fine

Dan and Kirsty received a penalty charge notice by post from the council for a moving traffic contravention. It contained a photograph of the car involved, but its vehicle registration was not the same as that on the notice itself. The council had clearly sent the notice to the couple in error and they wrote to point this out. Although it was correctly addressed, Dan and Kirsty's' letter to the council was returned marked 'addressee gone away'. Despite several letters and phone calls, the couple could not resolve the matter with the council and complained to us. At our intervention, the council accepted it had been at fault and cancelled the penalty charge. It agreed to pay Dan and Kirsty £25 to recognise their time and trouble. However, this complaint should have been resolved earlier. The council's error was readily apparent and it should not have required the couple to come to us to get things sorted.

Planning enforcement – failure to retain planning control

Johan complained that a neighbour's large terrace balcony affected his privacy by overlooking his garden. The council approved the neighbour's planning application, subject to a condition requiring him to submit detailed plans of screening measures, and build according to those plans. The council had intended the condition to also reserve the right for it to decide whether the screening was satisfactory, but failed to do this. It had assured Johan that a 1.8 metre high screen would protect his privacy. The neighbour submitted plans that the council found unsatisfactory. After it chased the neighbour for revised plans and got no response, it decided to start enforcement action. It was at this point, that it realised the planning condition was not worded as intended and the council had lost planning control. The neighbour had met its obligations by submitting plans and building to them. Johan decided to plant a large number of trees in an effort to protect his privacy. It is estimated it would take 3 to 5 years for them to grow to the 6 metres needed to begin to screen the impact of the balcony. The council agreed to our recommendations. These were to make a payment to Johan for the cost of planting the trees, for the impact of the balcony on his amenities until the trees provide screening, and for his time and trouble in pursuing the complaint.

SECTION 2: ACCESS TO THE OMBUDSMAN

Before we consider the statutory provisions regulating access to the PO and LGO there is the issue as to whether people think it is worthwhile complaining about public services. The PO in *The Annual Report and Accounts 2012–13* (HC 361 of 2013–14) reported on research the office had conducted into complaints about services (at p. 8):

Our research shows that most of the public (81%) are happy with public services. But of those who wanted to complain (18%), many found it difficult or felt it didn't make a difference. Here, we highlight what the public told us about complaining about public services…

Complaining can be hard to do

- It can be difficult to find out where to complain
- People fear that complaining will lead to a worse service
- For those who are ill, or struggling, complaining can be even harder
- Young people, those with learning difficulties and people from black and minority ethnic communities are less likely to complain

People lack confidence in complaining

- Over half of people who complained said they were not listened to or not kept up to date
- 46% felt they were not taken seriously
- 64% said they did not think their complaint would change anything
- Only a third of people who complained were happy with the outcome

Parliamentary Commissioner Act 1967

5. —(1) Subject to the provisions of this section, the Commissioner may investigate any action taken by or on behalf of a government department or other authority to which this Act applies, being action taken in the exercise of administrative functions of that department or authority, in any case where—

(a) a written complaint is duly made to a member of the House of Commons by a member of the public who claims to have sustained injustice in consequence of maladministration in connection with the action so taken; and

(b) the complaint is referred to the Commissioner, with the consent of the person who made it, by a member of that House with a request to conduct an investigation thereon.

6. — …

(3) A complaint shall not be entertained under this Act unless it is made to a member of the House of Commons not later than twelve months from the day on which the person aggrieved first had notice of the matters alleged in the complaint; but the Commissioner may conduct an investigation pursuant to a complaint not made within that period if he considers that there are special circumstances which make it proper to do so.

Local Government Act 1974

26. —(5) Before proceeding to investigate a complaint, a Local Commissioner shall satisfy himself that

(a) a matter has been brought, by or on behalf of the person affected, to the notice of the authority to which it relates and that that authority has been afforded a reasonable opportunity to investigate, the matter and to respond; or

(b) in the particular circumstances, it is not reasonable to expect the matter to be brought to the notice of that authority or for that authority to be afforded a reasonable opportunity to investigate the matter and to respond.

26A Who can complain

(1) Under this Part of this Act, a complaint about a matter may only be made—

(a) by a member of the public who claims to have sustained injustice in consequence of the matter,

(b) by a person authorised in writing by such a member of the public to act on his behalf, or

(c) in accordance with subsection (2).

(2) Where a member of the public by whom a complaint about a matter might have been made under this Part of this Act has died or is otherwise unable to authorise a person to act on his behalf, the complaint may be made—

(a) by his personal representative (if any), or

(b) by a person who appears to a Local Commissioner to be suitable to represent him.

26B Procedure for making complaints

(1) Subject to subsection (3), a complaint about a matter under this Part of this Act must be made—

(a) in writing, and

(b) before the end of the permitted period.

(2) In subsection (1)(b), "the permitted period" means the period of 12 months beginning with—

    (a) the day on which the person affected first had notice of the matter, or

    (b) if the person affected has died without having notice of the matter—

        (i) the day on which the personal representatives of the person affected first had notice of the matter, or

        (ii) if earlier, the day on which the complainant first had notice of the matter.

(3) A Local Commissioner may disapply either or both of the requirements in subsection (1)(a) and (b) in relation to a particular complaint.

26C Referral of complaints by authorities

(1) This section applies where a complaint about a matter is made to a member of an authority to which this Part of this Act applies.

(2) If the complainant consents, the complaint may be referred to a Local Commissioner by—

    (a) the member of the authority to whom the complaint was made,

    (b) any other member of that authority, or

    (c) a member of any other authority to which this Part of this Act applies which is alleged in the complaint to have taken or authorised the action complained of.

(3) Subject to subsection (4), a referral under this section must be made in writing.

(4) A Local Commissioner may disapply the requirement in subsection (3) in relation to a particular referral.

(5) If a Local Commissioner is satisfied that the complainant asked a member of an authority mentioned in subsection (2) to refer the complaint to a Local Commissioner, he may treat the complaint as if it had been referred to him under this section. …

26D Matters coming to attention of Local Commissioner

(1) This section applies to a matter which has come to the attention of a Local Commissioner if—

    (a) the matter came to his attention during the course of an investigation under this Part of this Act,

    (b) (subject to subsection (3)) the matter came to his attention—

        (i) before the person affected or his personal representatives had notice of the matter, or

        (ii) in any other case, before the end of the permitted period, and

    (c) it appears to the Local Commissioner that a member of the public has, or may have, suffered injustice in consequence of the matter.

(2) In subsection (1)(b)(ii), "the permitted period" means the period of 12 months beginning with—

    (a) the day on which the person affected first had notice of the matter, or

    (b) if the person affected has died without having notice of the matter, the day on which the personal representatives of the person affected first had notice of the matter.

(3) A Local Commissioner may disapply the requirement in subsection (1)(b) in relation to a particular matter.

NOTE: There has been concern about the public's awareness of ombudsmen. Survey research conducted for the ombudsmen indicates that poorer people, the young, and those in ethnic minority groups are the least aware of ombudsmen. In the 2006–07 Annual Report the PO stated:

> Moreover, the multitude of complaints systems in force across the public services can make it difficult for potential complainants to know where to turn. For these reasons, we consider it a priority to improve awareness of our service and make putting a complaint to the Ombudsman as simple and straightforward as possible. Since we cannot reach all the people who might want to use our service directly, we have developed close contacts with advocacy and advice bodies. These include Citizens' Advice and the Independent Complaints Advocacy Service of the NHS. We intend to strengthen our contacts with these bodies, and are developing an outreach strategy to help us achieve this.

■ QUESTION

Can you think of any ways of publicizing the work of the ombudsmen?

R. Gordon, *Better to Serve the Public: Proposals to restructure, reform, renew and reinvigorate public services ombudsmen*

(2014) paras 127–32

MP filter

127. The Whyatt report which originally proposed a Parliamentary Commissioner envisaged that after 5 years direct access for the public would be introduced. However, the then Government decided against the trial period and provided that complaints to the PCA should be routed through the constituency MP. It is now embedded into the concept and culture of the PHSO. The overwhelming majority of organisations and individuals who have commented on this issue propose that the MP filter should be removed and PASC's report underlined the number of recent reports that have recommended this course of action. PASC has now added its own voice recommending that any reforms include provision to abolish the filter.

128. For all, the key is the extent to which the filter inhibits the relationship between ombudsmen and public. It would not be right (or necessary) to lose altogether the valuable role MPs can play in supporting their constituents and there is value in maintaining their interest as a means of supporting the wider push to increase focus on value of complaints – and as an additional level at which trends emerging from complaints can be identified, escalated and acted upon.

129. **However, the requirement to route complaints to the ombudsman as Parliamentary Commissioner through a third party seems out of step with both practice elsewhere and the desire to have an accessible and responsive service able to engage flexibly with its customers and promoting a variety of contemporary modes of communication** …

130…. The PHSO's own 2010 opinion surveys on this issue revealed a particular concern amongst those who saw the filter as a deterrent which would build unnecessary delay in to the process. Those surveys showed that for some this is about efficiency, for some privacy, and for others it represents the insertion of what they perceive as an unwelcome political dynamic into what should be a wholly neutral and personal transaction.

131. I do not suggest that the removal of the filter alone would provide a complete answer to all these concerns. I absolutely accept too that there are circumstances in which it would be beneficial for a complainant to engage their MP and this should not be inhibited. However, I **recommend that it should not be a requirement that complaints to the Parliamentary commissioner (or UKPO) are addressed through an MP and that the PSO should receive complaints in its role as UKPO in the same way as those arising in all other areas of its jurisdiction.**

132. Alongside this, PASC has highlighted the similar impact of the current requirement that the PHSO can only receive complaints in writing. Having the ability to make optimum use of available technologies will ensure the PSO seems more immediately relevant to the public – but will also enhance the extent to which it is able to capture and analyse the valuable data. This in turn, will be critical in developing its public service delivery improvement function and will ensure the PSO is better able to prioritise the focus of its investigations. Professor Dunleavy has emphasised the powerful impact more modern forms of engagement with the public can have for the ombudsman, and the extent to which new technologies would allow a PSO to deal with any significant increase in the volume of complaints which might arise from such changes, whilst maximising the benefit from it (by quickly improving the quality of MI available, and adding weight to reports by being able to point to a much wider picture). This will be critical if the PSO is going to gain credibility as the benchmark for others in this area, and in a world in which Government is looking at similar technological solutions at the Departmental level.

■ QUESTION

Apart from discontinuing the MP filter and not requiring complaints to be made in writing, by what other means can access to the PO be strengthened?

SECTION 3: JURISDICTION OF THE OMBUDSMAN

Parliamentary Commissioner Act 1967

4.—(1) Subject to the provisions of this section and to the notes contained in Schedule 2 to this Act, this Act applies to the government departments, corporations and unincorporated bodies listed in that Schedule; and references in this Act to an authority to which this Act applies are references to any such corporation or body.

(2) Her Majesty may by Order in Council amend Schedule 2 to this Act by the alteration of any entry or note, the removal of any entry or note or the insertion of any additional entry or note.

(3) An Order in Council may only insert an entry if—

(a) it relates —

(i) to a government department; or

(ii) to a corporation or body whose functions are exercised on behalf of the Crown; or

(b) it relates to a corporation or body—

(i) which is established by virtue of Her Majesty's prerogative or by an Act of Parliament or an Order in Council or order made under an Act of Parliament or which is established in any other way by a Minister of the Crown in his capacity as a Minister or by a government department;

(ii) at least half of whose revenues derive directly from money provided by Parliament, a levy authorised by an enactment, a fee or charge of any other description so authorised or more than one of those sources; and

(iii) which is wholly or partly constituted by appointment made by Her Majesty or a Minister of the Crown or government department.

(3A) No entry shall be made if the result of making it would be that the Parliamentary Commissioner could investigate action which can be investigated by the Public Services Ombudsman for Wales under the Public Services Ombudsman (Wales) Act 2005.

(3B) No entry shall be made in respect of—

(a) the Scottish Administration or any part of it;

(b) any Scottish public authority with mixed functions or no reserved functions within the meaning of the Scotland Act 1998; or

(c) the Scottish Parliamentary Corporate Body.

(4) No entry shall be made in respect of a corporation or body whose sole activity is, or whose main activities are, included among the activities specified in subsection (5) below.

(5) The activities mentioned in subsection (4) above are—

(a) the provision of education, or the provision of training otherwise than under the Industrial Training Act 1982;

(b) the development of curricula, the conduct of examinations or the validation of educational courses;

(c) the control of entry to any profession or the regulation of the conduct of members of any profession;

(d) the investigation of complaints by members of the public regarding the actions of any person or body, or the supervision or review of such investigations or of steps taken following them.

(6) No entry shall be made in respect of a corporation or body operating in an exclusively or pre-dominantly commercial manner or a corporation carrying on under national ownership an industry or undertaking or part of an industry or undertaking.

(7) Any statutory instrument made by virtue of this section shall be subject to annulment in pursu-ance of a resolution of either House of Parliament ...

5.— ...

(2) Except as hereinafter provided, the Commissioner shall not conduct an investigation under this Act in respect of any of the following matters, that is to say—

   (a) any action in respect of which the person aggrieved has or had a right of appeal, reference or review to or before a tribunal constituted by or under any enactment or by virtue of Her Majesty's prerogative;

   (b) any action in respect of which the person aggrieved has or had a remedy by way of proceed-ings in any court of law:

Provided that the Commissioner may conduct an investigation notwithstanding that the person aggrieved has or had such a right or remedy if satisfied that in the particular circumstances it is not reasonable to expect him to resort or have resorted to it.

(3) Without prejudice to subsection (2) of this section, the Commissioner shall not conduct an inves-tigation under this Act in respect of any such action or matter as is described in Schedule 3 to this Act.

(4) Her Majesty may by Order in Council amend the said Schedule 3 so as to exclude from the provi-sions of that Schedule such actions or matters as may be described in the Order; and any statu-tory instrument made by virtue of this subsection shall be subject to annulment in pursuance of a resolution of either House of Parliament.

(5) In determining whether to initiate, continue or discontinue an investigation under this Act, the Commissioner shall, subject to the foregoing provisions of this section, act in accordance with his own discretion; and any question whether a complaint is duly made under this Act shall be determined by the Commissioner.

(5A) For the purposes of this section, administrative functions of a government department to which this Act applies include functions exercised by the department on behalf of the Scottish Ministers by virtue of section 93 of the Scotland Act 1998.

(5B) The Commissioner shall not conduct an investigation under this Act in respect of any action concerning Scotland and not relating to reserved matters which is taken by or on behalf of a cross-border public authority within the meaning of the Scotland Act 1998.

(6) For the purposes of this section, the administrative functions exercisable by any person appointed by the Lord Chancellor as a member of the administrative staff of any court or tribunal shall be taken to be administrative functions of the Lord Chancellor's Department. ...

NOTE: Schedule 3 specifies matters not subject to investigation: international matters including certified actions affecting dealings with other governments and international organizations, action relating to passports; legal and administrative matters include investigation or prevention of crime, the commencement of proceedings in a court; exercise of the prerogative of mercy, action by an official of a court or tribunal at the direction of a judge or member of a tribunal; employment matters include matters concerning appointment, removal, pay discipline, and superannuation of those employed by the Crown in the armed forces or service in any office or employment under the Crown; commercial or contractual matters unless concerning the acquisition or disposal of land; health matters include specified NHS contracts; and the grant of honours, awards, or privileges within the gift of the Crown including the grant of Royal Charters.

Local Government Act 1974

25. — (1) This Part of this Act applies to the following authorities—

[these include councils, National Park Authorities, fire and rescue authorities, police authorities]

(2) Her Majesty may by Order in Council provide that this Part of this Act shall also apply, subject to any modifications or exceptions specified in the Order, to any authority specified in the Order, being an authority which is established by or under an Act of Parliament, and which has power to levy a rate, or to issue a precept.

(3) An Order made by virtue of subsection (2) above may be varied or revoked by a subsequent Order so made and shall be subject to annulment in pursuance of a resolution of either House of Parliament.

(4) Any reference to an authority to which this Part of this Act applies includes a reference—
  (a) to the members and officers of that authority, and
  (b) to any person or body of persons acting for the authority under section 101, or
  (c) any committee mentioned in section 101(9) of the said Act.

(4A) Any reference to an authority to which this Part of this Act applies also includes, in the case of the Greater London Authority, a reference to each of the following—
  (a) the London Assembly;
  (b) any committee of the London Assembly;
  (c) any body or person exercising functions on behalf of the Greater London Authority.

(4B) Any reference to an authority to which this Part of this Act applies also includes, in the case of the London Transport Users' Committee, a reference to a sub-committee of that Committee.

(5) Any reference to an authority to which this Part of this Act applies also includes a reference to—
  (a) a school organisation committee constituted in accordance with section 24 of the School Standards and Framework Act 1998,
  (b) an exclusion appeals panel constituted in accordance with Schedule 18 to that Act,
  (c) an admission appeals panel constituted in accordance with Schedule 24 or paragraph 3 of Schedule 25 to that Act, and
  (d) the governing body of any community, foundation or voluntary school so far as acting in connection with the admission of pupils to the school or otherwise performing any of their functions under Chapter I of Part III of that Act. ...

26. — ... (6) A Local Commissioner shall not conduct an investigation under this Part of this Act in respect of any of the following matters, that is to say:
  (a) any action in respect of which the person affected has or had a right of appeal, reference or review to or before a tribunal constituted by or under any enactment;
  (b) any action in respect of which the person affected has or had a right of appeal to a Minister of the Crown or the National Assembly for Wales; or
  (c) any action in respect of which the person affected has or had a remedy by way of proceedings in any court of law:
  Provided that a Local Commissioner may conduct an investigation notwithstanding the existence of such a right or remedy if satisfied that in the particular circumstances it is not reasonable to expect the person aggrieved to resort or have resorted to it.

(7) A Local Commissioner shall not conduct an investigation in respect of any action which in his opinion affects all or most of the inhabitants of the ... area of the authority concerned.

(8) Without prejudice to the preceding provisions of this section, a Local Commissioner shall not conduct an investigation under this Part of this Act in respect of any such action or matter as is described in Schedule 5 to this Act.

(9) Her Majesty may by Order in Council amend the said Schedule 5 so as to add to or exclude from the provisions of that Schedule ... such actions or matters as may be described in the Order;
  Schedule 5 contains a number of exclusions, including in particular: legal proceedings; investigation or prevention of crime, contractual or commercial transactions (but the acquisition or disposal of land and the procurement of goods and services are within jurisdiction); personnel matters, and some educational matters.

(10) In determining whether to initiate, continue or discontinue an investigation, a Local Commissioner shall, subject to the preceding provisions of this section, act at discretion; and any questions whether a complaint is duly made under this Part of this Act shall be determined by the Local Commissioner.

NOTE: There is a great winnowing of the inquiries which the Ombudsmen receive as they are assessed to determine if they first come within jurisdiction and, if they do, whether it is an appropriate case to take-up. The following criteria must be met:

- It has been brought within the time limit (unless there are good reasons to waive) by
- a person or their representative/family who is entitled to raise the issue which
- is about in/action which can be considered involving a body within jurisdiction which
- is not premature because it has been fully considered by that body first, or
- it could not, or has not been pursued by another remedy unless there is a good reason for the Ombudsman to accept the case.

If it is a complaint to the Parliamentary Ombudsman it also has to be in writing and referred by an MP but if it is otherwise eligible the person can be assisted to meet these requirements.

The Local Government Ombudsman's second stage of assessment is outlined in their Assessment Code (available on their website at http://www.lgo.org.uk/information-centre/staff-guidance/assessment-code).

STAGE TWO: The discretionary stage
The discretionary stage uses four inter-related tests:

- **The Injustice Test** – This assesses the level of personal injustice the complainant claims to have been caused as a direct result of the actions or inactions of the service provider.
- **The Fault Test** – This assesses the scale and nature of the fault, that the complainant alleges has occurred and whether it is directly linked to the injustice claimed.
- **The Remedy Test** – This assesses how likely it is we will be able to achieve a meaningful outcome to the complaint.
- **The Public Interest Test** – This assesses the level of wider public interest arising from the individual case.

In some cases we will consider the combined impact of all four tests when deciding whether we will investigate. In other situations the significance of one particular test may be enough to determine what action is appropriate.

Our staff will use their experience and judgement to carry out this balancing exercise to apply these tests to the unique facts of each case. Complaints are not scored, weighted or rated according to any numerical formula.

The PHSO and LGO have similar stages in their process, an initial check on whether a case is within their jurisdiction, then assessment to determine if they should investigate and then investigating. The statistics for 2015–16:

Ombudsman	Contacts	Received	Assessed	Investigations completed	Upheld fully/ partially
PHSO	133,909	29,046	8,125	3,861	40%
LGO	65,000	20,102	11,833	4,792	51%

At the first stage where a case is not taken up there will be an explanation on why it is out of jurisdiction or why a detailed investigation will not be helpful. Advice will be given if it has been made prematurely or if another body may be able to help. If the investigation upholds the complaint, then failings will have been identified and agreement secured to put things right or a report is issued with recommendations on remedying the issue. If it is not upheld this means that the body had acted correctly or that action did not have adverse consequences.

In 2015–16 the various recommended remedies which the Ombudsmen made included:

PHSO: 1,338 apologies; 827 payments to make up for financial loss or recognize the impact of what went wrong; 955 service improvements, such as changing procedures or training staff; 336 other actions to put things right—for example, asking a Government department to review a decision; asking a GP practice to correct errors in medical records.

LGO: 255 providing reassurance that the local authority offered satisfactory remedy; 633 on preventing injustice for many—e.g. staff training, procedure change; 2,641 remedying injustice for individuals—e.g. apologies, financial redress, providing services.

Parliamentary and Health Service Ombudsman, *The Ombudsman's Annual Report and Accounts 2012–13, Aiming for Impact*
HC 361 of 2013–14, p. 20

Investigating more complaints

Our research among the public shows a significant need for our service. To help us meet this need in future, in 2012-13 groups of our staff reviewed the way we resolve complaints. Our new complaints process, which went live in April 2013, means we will be able to investigate thousands more complaints each year. Previously, we did a lot of preliminary work on complaints before deciding whether or not to carry out a full investigation. If we decided not to investigate a complaint, we could still provide answers and explanations, but our decisions at this stage were not formal and final findings. Now, under our new process, complaints that meet some basic criteria will usually be investigated straight away. This means that more of our customers will have their complaints investigated and will receive an independent, formal and final ruling. The NHS, UK government departments and other public organisations will also benefit, as we will share more information about complaints with them to help them.

NOTES

1. Investigations conducted by the PHSO annually from 2013–14 to 2015–16 with NHS investigations in brackets: 2013–14: 2,199 (NHS 1,715); 2014–15: 4,159 (NHS 3,274); 2015–16: 3,861 (NHS 3,185).
2. Where a complaint is outside jurisdiction the ombudsmen staff may be able to redirect the complainant to a more appropriate source of assistance. The jurisdiction of the LGO has been amended with the gain of Public Health matters which have been transferred from the NHS to local government; the transfer out of complaints about local authority housing to the Housing Ombudsman; and the reversal of a previous change, which had not been fully implemented, to consider complaints about the governing bodies and specified functions of head teachers in schools.

A: Overlap with alternative remedies

Law Commission, *Public Services Ombudsmen*
Law Com 329 (2011), paras 3.23, 3.25–6, 3.28, 3.39–49

STATUTORY BARS

Consultation paper proposals

3.23 By "statutory bars", we mean the statutory provisions, based on section 5(2) of the Parliamentary Commissioner Act 1967, whereby a public services ombudsman cannot open an investigation where the complainant has or had the possibility of recourse to a court, tribunal or other mechanism for review, unless it was not reasonable to expect the complainant to resort or to have resorted to it.

...

3.25 The first statutory bar was enacted in the Parliamentary Commissioner Act 1967, its purpose being to prevent an overlap between the jurisdiction of the courts and that of the ombudsmen.

3.26 Since then, however, there has been a considerable expansion in the ambit of judicial review, such that there is now a clear overlap between the jurisdiction of the ombudsmen and the courts. However, the approach adopted in each of the public services ombudsmen's current statutory bars is identical to that adopted originally in 1967. The effect of this is to create a preference in favour of the Administrative Court, where (but for the existence of the statutory bar) both the Administrative Court and the ombudsman could potentially consider a particular matter ...

3.28 Specifically, we made three provisional proposals in relation to the statutory bars:

(1) We provisionally proposed that the existing statutory bars be reformed, creating a general presumption in favour of a public services ombudsman being able to open an investigation.
(2) We provisionally proposed that this should be coupled with a broad discretion allowing the public services ombudsmen to decline to open an investigation.
(3) We provisionally proposed that in deciding whether to exercise that discretion the public services ombudsmen should ask themselves whether the complainant has already had or should have had recourse to a court or tribunal.

Discussion

3.39 The provisionally proposed reforms of the statutory bar, as they related to court-based mechanisms for administrative redress, met with substantial approval.

3.40 We are, therefore, recommending that the statutory bars as they relate to courts be repealed and replaced with the discretion for the ombudsmen to open an investigation, or otherwise dispose of a matter (for instance by referring it to mediation). This would give complainants greater freedom of choice over the institution, and related procedure, for administrative redress they can use.

3.41 In relation to statutory appeals and the issue raised by the Law Reform Committee of the Bar Council, we have not been persuaded that this argument should alter our stated position.

3.42 We think the appropriate way of considering a statutory appeal is in the context of the statute within which it is situated. At one level the creation of a statutory appeal can be taken as the drafting expression of an appeal preference, or the granting of a defined route for appeals, which need not exclude other methods of redress or dispute resolution.

3.43 A statutory appeal allows individuals to challenge the legality of a decision made concerning them. The core of this is, therefore, different to the primary role of the ombudsmen in investigating injustice caused to an individual as a result of maladministration.

3.44 Our reform would not alter statutory appeals or the possibility of recourse to them. Our recommended reform offers complainants a wider choice of options where previously there was a restriction on the use of ombudsmen.

3.45 Our recommended reform in no way reduces the discretion that the ombudsmen have to refuse to take a complaint where there is an alternative mechanism for administrative redress, which could be a statutory appeal, that it sees as more appropriate.

3.46 Following consultation, we do not think that it is necessary to define in statute the discretion available to the public services ombudsmen when deciding not to investigate a complaint. Whilst we are recommending a broad discretion, decisions would be susceptible to challenge on normal public law grounds. We think that this would provide sufficient protection from irrational decision-making.

3.47 In responses to our consultation paper, concerns were raised that individuals may not know which redress mechanism to use. By submitting an inappropriate complaint to an ombudsman, an individual may lose the opportunity to use a court or tribunal owing to the limitation periods of those institutions. Given the fact that many individuals will seek legal advice on important matters, we do not think that this is a significant problem. However, we accept that there is the potential for a limited number of individuals to be affected.

3.48 In order to reduce the chance of an individual being detrimentally affected by the removal of the statutory bars, we recommend that the ombudsmen publish guidance as to whether they are the appropriate mechanism for particular classes or sorts of complaint or whether it would be advisable for complainants to use other institutions. We think that the ombudsmen are ideally placed to publish such guidance. We appreciate that this happens already, but the situation will be different without the statutory bars and new guidance should reflect this.

3.49 Where the public services ombudsmen decide not to open an investigation, if our proposals in Part 5 are adopted, they should communicate a statement of reasons to the complainant directly.

NOTES

1. There is less of a problem if the complainant has a possible choice between pursuing a remedy in the court or with the ombudsman as the complainant's desired outcome may only be achieved in one. The Court of Appeal in *R* v *Local Commissioner for Administration in North and North East England, ex parte Liverpool City Council* [2001] All ER 462, held that it was permissible to take into account that complaining to the LGO is free whereas going to court is not. The Court said that this case was one better suited to the LGO, as her powers of investigation were better equipped for gathering facts than the judicial review process and so she was more likely to provide a just remedy.
2. In the draft Public Service Ombudsman Bill, cl. 7 does not implement the Law Commission's recommendation but would amend the existing provisions by adding a second discretionary power to accept a case if it is felt appropriate that the matter should be investigated even though the complainant had resorted to an alternative right or remedy and it would not matter whether resort to that right or remedy had been completed.

SECTION 4: MEANING OF INJUSTICE IN CONSEQUENCE OF MALADMINISTRATION

Parliamentary Commissioner Act 1967
[See s. 5(1), earlier in this chapter in Section 2 at p. 614]

12.—(3) It is hereby declared that nothing in this Act authorises or requires the Commissioner to question the merits of a decision taken without maladministration by a government department or other authority in the exercise of a discretion vested in that department or authority. . . .

Local Government Act 1974

26. For the purposes of section 24A(1)(b), in relation to an authority to which this Part of this Act applies, the following matters are subject to investigation by a Local Commissioner under this Part of this Act—

(a) alleged or apparent maladministration in connection with the exercise of the authority's administrative functions;
(b) an alleged or apparent failure in a service which it was the authority's function to provide;
(c) an alleged or apparent failure to provide such a service.

. . .

34.—(3) It is hereby declared that nothing in this Part of this Act authorises or requires a Local Commissioner to question the merits of a decision taken without maladministration by an authority in the exercise of a discretion vested in that authority.

Debate on the Second Reading of the Parliamentary Commissioner Bill, House of Commons, HC Deb

Vol. 734, col. 51, 18 October 1966

MR CROSSMAN: We might have made an attempt ... to define, by catalogue, all of the qualities which make up maladministration by a civil servant. It would be a wonderful exercise—bias, neglect, inattention, delay, incompetence, inaptitude, perversity, turpitude, arbitrariness and so on. It would be a long and interesting list.

In the following case note the different approach to considering the legality of the ombudsman's finding of maladministration and injustice between the majority and Lord Donaldson, who is much more accommodating to the ombudsman's analysis and expression of findings.

R v Local Commissioner, ex parte Eastleigh Borough Council

[1988] 3 WLR 116, Court of Appeal

Eastleigh Borough Council challenged an adverse report of the LGO on the basis that it sought to challenge a decision taken without maladministration by an authority in the exercise of a discretion vested in the authority. Nolan J held that the ombudsman had indeed exceeded its jurisdiction, but that it would be wrong to make a declaration to that effect. The authority appealed to the Court of Appeal and the Local Commissioner cross-appealed. There were three main issues in the appeal:

(a) Had the Commissioner acted contrary to law in concluding that the council had been guilty of maladministration?

(b) Had the Commissioner acted contrary to law in concluding that such maladministration, if it had occurred, had caused injustice to the complainant?

(c) If the Commissioner had acted contrary to law in one or both of these respects, should the court grant a remedy?

In the extract we will only consider (b).

LORD DONALDSON OF LYMINGTON MR: This appeal is about drains and an ombudsman. Most of the time the drains served six houses in Hampshire. However, on occasion they backed up to the discomfiture of the householders. On the complaint of one of the householders, [the ombudsman] investigated and concluded that the continued existence of the defect in the drains was caused by maladministration upon the part of the Eastleigh Borough Council. The council was not amused and sought judicial review of the ombudsman's report.

Nolan J held that the council had cause for complaint on two grounds. Second, the ombudsman had acted contrary to section 26(1) of the Act in that he had made a report on a complaint when it had not been established that the complainant had suffered injustice in consequence of the maladministration which was the subject of that complaint. However the judge refused to quash the report or to grant the council a declaration that the ombudsman had exceeded his jurisdiction. The council now appeals against this refusal and the ombudsman cross-appeals against the finding that he exceeded his powers.

Although this might be dismissed as a storm in a sewer, in fact it raises issues of some importance concerning the relationship between the courts and the local government ombudsmen.

The ombudsman's conclusions are stated in paragraphs 30 and 31 of his report:

31. I find, therefore, that the complainant has sustained injustice as a result of the council's maladministration. However, I cannot say, categorically, whether had the council carried out the final inspection in
accordance with the dictates of good administration the trouble at the centre of this complaint would
not have arisen. Equally, I have taken account of the argument that with synthetic piping of the sort
employed in this case soil compaction can cause undulation at a later date. I have also considered the
fact that the original fault was the builder's and that that (and the council's fault) occurred some years
ago. On the other hand the final inspection was, in my view, incomplete and the council could have
become aware of the problem at an early stage because of the difficulties experienced by the owner
of house 3. Having considered these factors I feel on balance it would be inequitable to ask the council
to defray the whole cost of the necessary remedial work. Accordingly, upon the residents' agreement
to pay a proportion of the reasonable cost, I consider that the council themselves should take the
action which the Assistant Director of Technical Services commended to the residents.

Section 26(1)

This subsection is in the following terms:

Subject to the provisions of this Part of this Act where a written complaint is made by or on behalf
of a member of the public who claims to have sustained injustice in consequence of maladministration in connection with action taken by or on behalf of an authority to which this Part of this
Act applies, being action taken in the exercise of administrative functions of that authority, a Local
Commissioner may investigate that complaint.

Clearly this subsection does not prevent the ombudsman from investigating a complaint of maladministration which prima facie may have led the complainant to sustain consequential injustice (see
the *Bradford Council* case [1979] QB 287), but it does mean that he cannot report adversely upon an
authority unless his investigation reveals not only maladministration, but injustice to the complainant
sustained as a consequence of that maladministration.

The mischief at which this subsection is directed is not difficult to detect. Every local authority has
living within its boundaries a small cadre of citizens who would like nothing better than to spend
their spare time complaining of maladministration. The subsection limits the extent to which they can
involve the ombudsman by requiring, as a condition precedent to his involvement, that the complainant shall personally have been adversely affected by the alleged maladministration. If he was not so
affected, he did not himself suffer injustice. If he was, he did. ...

It is his reference in paragraph 31 to the fact that he could not affirm categorically that a proper
inspection would have revealed the defects and to the argument that the synthetic piping soil compaction can cause undulation at a later date which has cast doubt on his finding. This point has given
me some concern, but in the end I have come to the conclusion that the ombudsman was intending to
say that, whilst there could be no absolute certainty that a proper inspection would have revealed the
defects and it was a possibility that the undulation occurred after the date of the inspection, on the balance of probabilities he was satisfied that the defects were present at the time of the inspection, that a
proper inspection would have revealed them and that he was therefore satisfied that the complainant
had suffered injustice in consequence of the maladministration.

An ombudsman's report is neither a statute nor a judgment. It is a report to the council and to the
ratepayers of the area. It has to be written in everyday language and convey a message. This report
has been subjected to a microscopic and somewhat legalistic analysis which it was not intended to
undergo. Valid criticisms have been made, particularly of paragraph 31, but in my judgment they go
to form rather than substance and, notwithstanding occasional dicta to the contrary, judicial review is
concerned with substance. I would therefore allow the ombudsman's cross-appeal.

PARKER LJ: The only question of difficulty arises on the cross-appeal of the ombudsman.

I turn to the second question raised on the cross-appeal, namely, whether the conclusion that the
complainant had suffered injustice as a result of the maladministration can be sustained. This depends
upon paragraph 31 of the report. Had the ombudsman stopped at the first sentence, I should have had
no doubt that the decision was sustainable. It seems to me abundantly clear that the complainant had

suffered injustice if the failure to inspect properly led to the subsequent expenditure and the ombudsman could in my view easily have determined that it had. It is submitted however that, having stated his conclusion in the opening sentence, he proceeds to negate it and that the paragraph read as a whole really amounts to this: 'I cannot say whether the failure to inspect led to the expenditure, but as the council were at fault it would be fair that they should contribute to the cost of remedial measures.' For the ombudsman it is submitted that this is not so and that on a fair reading the paragraph says no more than: 'I cannot be absolutely sure, but on the balance of probabilities I conclude … '.

I regret to say that, unlike Lord Donaldson MR I cannot accept this construction. It appears to me that to do so involves applying legal concepts of differing standards of proof in order to uphold a paragraph which, like its predecessor, must be broadly considered. I have, despite its opening words, been able, by a broad reading and the correctness of the ombudsman's directions to himself on the law, to uphold the conclusion in paragraph 30. In the case of paragraph 31 I am unable to do so.

I would therefore dismiss the cross-appeal and allow the appeal.

TAYLOR LJ:
As to paragraph 31, I agree with Parker LJ. Only by straining the language used by the ombudsman and attributing to him speculatively considerations as to the burden of proof, could one render his finding on causation sound. I do not think such straining and speculation is justified.

■ QUESTIONS

1. Do you think that the majority construed the Ombudsman's report as if it were a statute, and would that be appropriate bearing in mind the role of the Ombudsman?

2. What advice would you give to Ombudsmen on the drawing up of their reports after this case?

NOTES

1. In its *Second Report for the Session 1967–68* (HC 350) the Select Committee encouraged the PO to investigate complaints relating to 'bad decisions' and 'bad rules'. In respect of the 'bad decision' the Select Committee (at para. 14) stated that if the PO

> … finds a decision which, judged by its effect upon the aggrieved person, appears to him to be thoroughly bad in quality, he might infer from the quality of the decision itself that there had been an element of maladministration in the taking of it and ask for its review.

In respect of the 'bad rule', where an administrative rule, despite being applied properly, has caused hardship and injustice, the PO was urged

> … to enquire whether, given the effect of the rule in the case under his investigation, the Department had taken any action to review the rule. If found defective and revised, what action had been taken to remedy the hardship sustained by the complainant? If not revised, whether there had been due consideration by the Department of the grounds for maintaining the rule?

The PO accepted these suggestions, but it has been argued that they have had little impact on the number of cases in which he has been willing to find maladministration. In relation to the 'bad rule', Gregory in 'The Select Committee on the PCA 1967–80' [1982] *Public Law* 49, at p. 69 points out that 'only an extraordinarily inept department might be expected to conduct its review of a rule [so] that the Commissioner would find defects in the process subsequently described to him'.

2. A number of the cases considered by the PO and LGOs have involved allegations that authorities have failed to give proper advice; for a discussion of the Parliamentary Commissioner's approach to such cases, see A. Mowbray, 'A Right to Official Advice: The Parliamentary Commissioner's Perspective' [1990] *Public Law* 68–9.

3. In *Our Fettered Ombudsman* (1977), ch. VII, JUSTICE suggested that, following the New Zealand model, the jurisdiction of the PO should be extended to allow him to investigate any action which is 'unreasonable, unjust or oppressive … instead of maladministration'. The PO responded to this suggestion in his *Annual Report for 1977* (HC 157 of 1977–78) by stating that he believed he already had power to investigate complaints that actions by Government Departments are unjust or oppressive. He continued:

21. What the Act certainly does exclude from my jurisdiction are complaints about discretionary decisions taken 'without maladministration'. I believe this to be right. It is no part of my function to substitute my judgment for that of a Minister or one of his officials if I see no evidence of 'maladministration' either in the way the decision was taken or in the nature of the decision itself.

22. I believe therefore that the difficulty which has been detected in the limitation of my investigation powers to cases of 'maladministration' is more theoretical than practical. But if there is thought to be some semantic difficulty which confuses members of the public or members of parliament than I should see no objection to seeing my powers redefined in the sort of language suggested by JUSTICE. I think that in practice it would make very little difference.

Subsequently JUSTICE adopted the view that the definition of maladministration was not a source of much difficulty, bearing in mind the approach which the Commissioner took to his jurisdiction (see the reference to this in the *Fourth Report from the Select Committee*, HC 615 of 1977–78). The *JUSTICE–All Souls Report on Administrative Law* (1988) did not recommend any change in the definition (see pp. 92–3 and 133–4).

4. Sir Cecil Clothier, who was PO from 1979 to 1985, stated that he did not wish to be dragged into a review of political decision-making; and he suggested that a complaint is political if it has been debated in Parliament or where a very large proportion of the population is affected as well as the person making the complaint (see Clothier (1984) 81 *Law Society Gazette* 3108–9). On this ground he refused to investigate complaints relating to the Inland Revenue's agreement concerning Fleet Street casual workers who evaded their tax arrangements. This agreement subsequently gave rise to *Inland Revenue Commissioners* v *National Federation of Self-Employed and Small Businesses Ltd* [1982] AC 617 (see Chapter 11, Section 3 at p. 591). Section 26(7) of the Local Government Act 1974 specifically provides that a local commissioner shall not conduct an investigation in respect of any action which in his opinion affects all or most of the inhabitants in the area of the authority concerned.

5. One of the areas in which the ombudsmen can assist is in human rights, and the Health Service Ombudsman and the LGO have conducted joint investigations in which they found that a failure to take into account human rights issues was maladministration: for example, the 2009 report *Six Lives—The Provision of Public Services to People with Learning Disabilities* (HC 203 of 2008–09). The PO has suggested that as the concept of maladministration and remedy by the ombudsman has enabled people to have more convenient redress from public bodies the same can also be true in human rights. In A. Abraham, 'The Ombudsman and Individual Rights,' (2008) 61 *Parliamentary Affairs* 370, at pp. 377–8:

If a human rights culture is to be realised on the ground, public servants can reasonably expect to be judged against standards that expressly acknowledge the place that human rights principles should play in public administration. Good administration will invariably show signs of a human rights culture. For the Ombudsman, as protector on behalf of Parliament of those features of good administration, the task of making findings of maladministration is unavoidably implicated with human rights considerations, and in a way that is far less feasible for the High Court, which will find many of the relevant disputes well beneath its elevated horizon.

See also on the suitability of the ombudsman approach to the protection of rights and social rights, N. O'Brien, 'Ombudsmen and Social rights Adjudication' [2009] *Public Law* 466 and N. O'Brien and B. Thompson, 'Human Rights Accountability in the UK: Deliberative Democracy and the Role of the Ombudsman' (2010) *European Human Rights Law Review* 504.

SECTION 5: INVESTIGATION, RESOLUTION, AND IMPROVEMENT

A: Investigation and resolution

Parliamentary Commissioner Act 1967

7. — (1) Where the Commissioner proposes to conduct an investigation pursuant to a complaint under this Act, he shall afford to the principal officer of the department or authority concerned, and to any other person who is alleged in the complaint to have taken or authorised the action complained of, an opportunity to comment on any allegations contained in the complaint.

(2) Every such investigation shall be conducted in private, but except as aforesaid the procedure for conducting an investigation shall be such as the Commissioner considers appropriate in the circumstances of the case; and without prejudice to the generality of the foregoing provision the Commissioner may obtain information from such persons and in such manner, and make such inquiries, as he thinks fit, and may determine whether any person may be represented, by counsel or solicitor or otherwise, in the investigation.

(3) The Commissioner may, if he thinks fit, pay to the person by whom the complaint was made and to any other person who attends or furnishes information for the purposes of an investigation under this Act—

(a) sums in respect of expenses properly incurred by them;

(b) allowances by way of compensation for the loss of their time, in accordance with such scales and subject to such conditions as may be determined by the Treasury.

(4) The conduct of an investigation under this Act shall not affect any action taken by the department or authority concerned, or any power or duty of that department or authority to take further action with respect to any matters subject to the investigation …

8.—(1) For the purposes of an investigation under this Act the Commissioner may require any Minister, officer or member of the department or authority concerned or any other person who in his opinion is able to furnish information or produce documents relevant to the investigation to furnish any such information or produce any such document.

(2) For the purposes of any such investigation the Commissioner shall have the same powers as the Court in respect of the attendance and examination of witnesses (including the administration of oaths or affirmations and the examination of witnesses abroad) and in respect of the production of documents.

(3) No obligation to maintain secrecy or other restriction upon the disclosure of information obtained by or furnished to persons in Her Majesty's service, whether imposed by any enactment or by any rule of law, shall apply to the disclosure of information for the purposes of an investigation under this Act; and the Crown shall not be entitled in relation to any such investigation to any such privilege in respect of the production of documents or the giving of evidence as is allowed by law in legal proceedings.

(4) No person shall be required or authorised by virtue of this Act to furnish any information or answer any question relating to proceedings of the Cabinet or of any committee of the Cabinet or to produce so much of any document as relates to such proceedings; and for the purposes of this subsection a certificate issued by the Secretary of the Cabinet with the approval of the Prime Minister and certifying that any information, question, document or part of a document so relates shall be conclusive.

(5) Subject to subsection (3) of this section, no person shall be compelled for the purposes of any investigation under this Act to give any evidence or produce any document which he could not be compelled to give or produce in civil proceedings before the Court.

9.—(1) If any person without lawful excuse obstructs the Commissioner or any officer of the Commissioner in the performance of his functions under this Act, or is guilty of any act or omission in relation to an investigation under this Act which, if that investigation were a proceeding in the Court, would constitute contempt of court, the Commissioner may certify the offence to the Court. …

NOTES

1. Similar provisions regarding the conduct of investigations by the LGO are set out in the Local Government Act 1974, ss 26(5), 28–9.

2. The Regulatory Reform (Collaboration etc. Between Ombudsmen) Reform Order 2007 amends the principal statutes of the PO, LGO, and HSO in England to allow them to work together, with the consent of the complainant, where a complaint has elements which overlap their separate

jurisdictions, e.g. the PHSO could deal with health care and the LGO with social care. The amendments also allow delegation to, and the sharing of information amongst, the officers of the various ombudsmen.

3. Investigation was the method by which ombudsmen dealt with citizens' complaints to determine if there was injustice caused by maladministration and, if there was, to recommend redress. This was thorough but lengthy. In 1979–80 the LGO was the first ombudsman to interpret its statutory powers not to initiate or to discontinue an investigation so as to facilitate a local settlement of the case, rather than issuing a statutory investigation report. The PO did not introduce a similar change to its working practices until April 2000, prompted by a desire to achieve resolution, but also to speed up the average time taken to dispose of cases and reduce a burgeoning backlog. The Collcutt *Review of Public Sector Ombudsmen in England* (2000) was keen to see increased emphasis on resolving complaints more quickly and informally at para. 6.16:

> The elements of the new approach are therefore:
> - a focus on outcomes and in particular on complaints resolution;
> - clear recognition of when intervention is required;
> - a positive attitude to assisting complainants in progressing their complaint whether with the ombudsman or by other means;
> - initially an informal approach aiming to achieve co-operation and perhaps using a conciliatory approach;
> - investigation in the old sense to be used if informal methods do not work.

It would be wrong to imply that the ombudsmen are not using these methods—often they will but this concept of their role is not sufficiently reflected in their legislation.

4. The Regulatory Reform (Collaboration etc. Between Ombudsmen) Order 2007 also allows the PO, HSO, and LGO to appoint mediators in the conduct of their investigations. This type of resolution seems to differ from Scotland where the Scottish Public Service Ombudsmen Act 2002 provides:

> S.2 (4) The Ombudsman may take such action in connection with the complaint or request as the Ombudsman thinks may be of assistance in reaching any such decision.
> (5) Such action may, in particular, include action with a view to resolving the complaint or request.

This approach was extended by the Public Services Ombudsman (Wales) Act 2005:

> 3 Alternative resolution of complaints
>
> (1) The Ombudsman may take any action he thinks appropriate with a view to resolving a complaint which he has power to investigate under section 2.
> (2) The Ombudsman may take action under this section in addition to or instead of conducting an investigation into the complaint.
> (3) Any action under this section must be taken in private.

5. The Law Commission in its report *Public Services Ombudsmen*, (2013, paras 5.7–5.31) has proposed that (1) the PO and LGO be given specific powers to allow them to dispose of complaints in ways other than by conducting an investigation, and they have a preference for the more broadly drawn power in s. 3 of the Public Services Ombudsman (Wales) Act 2005, and (2) the ombudsmen publish digests giving anonymized details of cases disposed of by alternative dispute resolution. The draft Bill does not include a provision equivalent to s. 3 in the Welsh statute.

6. There is a concern that emphasizing resolving complaints rather than investigating them fully, carries the possibility that wider administrative issues raised by a case are not pursued. The ombudsmen all say that they are aware of this and do seek to continue work on cases where they think there may be systemic issues even though the parties are happy to resolve them.

■ QUESTION

Are the possible problems associated with resolution of complaints worse than the problem of the time taken to conduct formal investigations?

B: Improvement

A. Abraham, 'The Ombudsman as Part of the UK Constitution: A Contested Role?'

(2008) 61 *Parliamentary Affairs* 206, 209–12

There is, though, another essential aspect of my role that transcends the limitations that are common both to ADR and to conventional litigation: the ability to codify good practice and to recommend systemic change. The contemporary fluorescence of codification in the public sector can be traced back at least to John Major's experiment with the Citizens' Charter as a device for re-articulating the social contract between state and citizen, between the provider and the consumer of services. The Human Rights Act 1998 itself on one construction of its import represents the culmination of such an approach. Rightly characterised as more mission statement than reforming legislation of the usual black-letter sort, the Human Rights Act seeks to make explicit those fundamental and generic principles that must inform the most basic encounter between citizen and state, from which all other particular standards, codes and charters must derive their authority and to which they must be subservient.

In the sphere of public administration there are, of course, many recent and concrete manifestations of this phenomenon: the Committee on Standards in Public Life is currently reviewing its Seven Principles of Public Life; the British and Irish Ombudsman Association in April 2007 published its Guide to Principles of Good Complaint Handling; and the Civil Service Code, revised in June 2006, describes the values and behaviours which the Civil Service is expected to espouse. For my own part, the Principles of Good Administration that I published in March 2007 were intended not as a checklist but as a broad statement of what I believe public authorities within my jurisdiction should be doing to deliver good administration and customer service. The production of such principles (getting it right; being customer focused; being open and accountable; acting fairly and proportionately; putting things right; seeking continuous improvement) is entirely symbiotic with my function of investigating complaints, the one effortlessly informing the other. The grievances that citizens bring to my Office put me on notice of where things are going wrong and of where improvement is most needed; they make it possible for me to prescribe values and behaviours that will reduce the likelihood of repetition; and they also enable me to tackle future breaches. In this way a virtuous circle is established, the ultimate objective being not so much the retrospective eradication of maladministration but the prospective promotion of good administration, prevention rather than cure.

This codifying function, albeit derived from and closely implicated with my core complaint-investigating function, marks out a very distinctive role that sets me apart from either the courts and tribunals or other forms of ADR. It is a function that is also complementary to my ability to issue 'special reports', concerned not so much with individual grievances but rather with the underlying and systemic defects that have given rise to an entire cluster of complaints. It is the sort of function to which the common law mentality with its inherent individualism is a stranger, constrained from looking beyond the facts of the particular case, compelled invariably to resort to a simplistic 'rotten apple' theory of organisational malfunction instead of a more realistic analysis that makes room for systemic and institutional failure. It is this ability of the Ombudsman to transcend the individualism of the common law, to get behind the camouflage of apparently esoteric detail so often presented by an individual complaint and instead penetrate to the underlying structure of what has really gone wrong that makes most acute the question of where the Ombudsman's authentic identity resides: in the ability to deliver tangible benefit to individuals or in the ability to serve a much broader public benefit remit? The ability to deliver meaningful redress to individuals, albeit through a process significantly different from that of the courts and tribunals, certainly casts the Ombudsman in the role of servant of the people (or more particularly of individual citizens) and establishes the Ombudsman's credentials as a system of justice.

…

The founding legislation of 1967 in effect established the Ombudsman as an aid to Parliament in its constitutional scrutiny of the Executive. That role has evolved to comprise the distinct but inter-related functions of dispute resolution, guardian of good public administration, and of systemic check on the

Executive's effectiveness. It is the core activity of investigating complaints that makes operational those strategic priorities and makes possible the broader public interest remit that so characterises the role of Ombudsman. It does so in three ways in particular.

First, there is the ability of the Ombudsman ... to codify and share expertise on good administrative practice and on good complaint handling. This is my special territory, the field of expertise to which I lay special claim. In addition to recommending ways in which the particular complaint might be avoided in future, I have the capacity to identify patterns of maladministration disclosed by an entire sequence of complaints and so to propose principles of practice that will bring about substantive future improvement of administration and complaint handling, either within a particular organisation or even a whole sector. In other cases, an individual complaint will itself exemplify how a particular policy, system or statutory framework is being administered, pointing without further ado towards the need for systemic change. Secondly, there is my wider-reaching ability to influence and contribute to the improvement, not just of administration and complaint handling, but of public service delivery itself. In part, this ability is the natural concomitant of improving internal administration: there is a necessary link between good administration and the improvement of service delivery. Yet beyond that, there is also scope to extract the lessons yielded by a comprehensive 'database' of complaints in such a way that I can present a compelling narrative of ineffective service delivery and so bring about insight, a shift in awareness and, if necessary, a change of 'culture' within the public sector. This 'influencing' work is no doubt more remote from the resolution of individual complaints than a more conventional 'system of justice' role might entail, but it is nevertheless part and parcel of the remedial action available to me and ultimately rooted in the core activity of complaint handling. Thirdly, and most ambitiously, there is the prospect of drawing upon the experience of complaint handling not just to improve administration and change culture, but to inform policy debate on aspects of a particular case or sequence of cases is greater still. Yet it still finds its origins in the bedrock of complaints handling, whilst nevertheless having as its target the highest level of policy direction and of sustainable impact. This is in effect the gilt-edged Ombudsman 'dividend' that can transcend the limits of individual redress and effect real and sustainable change for the entire citizen body, the users of public services at large.

A recent example suggests how this cumulative remedial action can work in practice to the public benefit. In June 2005, I completed a special report into the UK Government's then new system for operating tax credits. That report focused in particular on the social group intended to benefit from the reform: low-income families with children, and low-income earners. Drawing directly on the experience of the individual complaints referred to me, I identified an underlying pattern of dissatisfaction that stemmed to a large extent from the Government having adopted a 'one size fits all' system, a system designed to require minimum human intervention and relying instead on IT. In short, I found that this 'blanket' approach took no account of the very different circumstances and needs within the target group. The result was that the new system often had harsh and unintended consequences for the most vulnerable users of the system, frequently leading to debt recovery action by the Government to retrieve overpayments caused by the malfunctioning of its own reforms and, irony of ironies, casting into debt those most in need of financial support and intended to benefit from the reform in the first place.

On top of investigating individual complaints (which at one stage accounted for a quarter of all complaints referred to my Office), I made twelve detailed recommendations aimed at improving the administration of the system in its entirety. But I did not stop there: instead, I felt compelled to ask the bigger policy question of whether a financial support system that included a degree of inbuilt financial insecurity could ever in practice meet the needs of very low-income families and earners. Now, two years later, in a second follow-up report published on 9 October 2007, I have drawn attention to the impact of that financial insecurity on that especially vulnerable client group and to how it is leading to confusion and hardship, and in some cases even to a desire to opt out of the tax credits system altogether. The picture that emerges is one of a tax credits system that, even when working as intended, in some respects runs counter to the key policy objectives of helping tackle child poverty and of encouraging more people to work by 'making work pay'.

As I said in my 2005 report, the design of the tax credits system is, in the end, a matter for Government and Parliament, not for me. It is certainly not the place of the Ombudsman to usurp the function of the legislature and the Executive. It is, however, very much the role of the Ombudsman, as the purveyor of public benefit, to invite further public service delivery. Here the degree of abstraction from the facts of reflection on the empirical evidence disclosed by complaints that these unintended, but nonetheless adverse, consequences continue to occur and must be recognised in future policy development.

Parliamentary and Health Service Ombudsman, *Principles of Good Administration*
(2009), pp. 2–3

Good administration by public bodies means:

1. Getting it right
   - Acting in accordance with the law and with regard for the rights of those concerned.
   - Acting in accordance with the public body's policy and guidance (published or internal).
   - Taking proper account of established good practice.
   - Providing effective services, using appropriately trained and competent staff.
   - Taking reasonable decisions, based on all relevant considerations.
2. Being customer focused
   - Ensuring people can access services easily.
   - Informing customers what they can expect and what the public body expects of them.
   - Keeping to its commitments, including any published service standards.
   - Dealing with people helpfully, promptly and sensitively, bearing in mind their individual circumstances.
   - Responding to customers' needs flexibly, including, where appropriate, co-ordinating a response with other service providers.
3. Being open and accountable
   - Being open and clear about policies and procedures and ensuring that information, and any advice provided, is clear, accurate and complete.
   - Stating its criteria for decision making and giving reasons for decisions.
   - Handling information properly and appropriately.
   - Keeping proper and appropriate records.
   - Taking responsibility for its actions.
4. Acting fairly and proportionately
   - Treating people impartially, with respect and courtesy.
   - Treating people without unlawful discrimination or prejudice, and ensuring no conflict of interests.
   - Dealing with people and issues objectively and consistently.
   - Ensuring that decisions and actions are proportionate, appropriate and fair.
5. Putting things right
   - Acknowledging mistakes and apologising where appropriate.
   - Putting mistakes right quickly and effectively.
   - Providing clear and timely information on how and when to appeal or complain.
   - Operating an effective complaints procedure, which includes offering a fair and appropriate remedy when a complaint is upheld.
6. Seeking continuous improvement
   - Reviewing policies and procedures regularly to ensure they are effective.
   - Asking for feedback and using it to improve services and performance.
   - Ensuring that the public body learns lessons from complaints and uses these to improve services and performance.

Parliamentary and Health Service Ombudsman, *Principles of Good Complaint Handling*
(2009), pp. 2–3

Good complaint handling by public bodies means:

1. Getting it right
   - Acting in accordance with the law and relevant guidance, and with regard for the rights of those concerned.
   - Ensuring that those at the top of the public body provide leadership to support good complaint management and develop an organisational culture that values complaints.
   - Having clear governance arrangements, which set out roles and responsibilities, and ensure lessons are learnt from complaints.
   - Including complaint management as an integral part of service design.
   - Ensuring that staff are equipped and empowered to act decisively to resolve complaints.
   - Focusing on the outcomes for the complainant and the public body.
   - Signposting to the next stage of the complaints procedure, in the right way and at the right time.
2. Being customer focused
   - Having clear and simple procedures.
   - Ensuring that complainants can easily access the service dealing with complaints, and informing them about advice and advocacy services where appropriate.
   - Dealing with complainants promptly and sensitively, bearing in mind their individual circumstances.
   - Listening to complainants to understand the complaint and the outcome they are seeking.
   - Responding flexibly, including co-ordinating responses with any other bodies involved in the same complaint, where appropriate.
3. Being open and accountable
   - Publishing clear, accurate and complete information about how to complain, and how and when to take complaints further.
   - Publishing service standards for handling complaints.
   - Providing honest, evidence-based explanations and giving reasons for decisions.
   - Keeping full and accurate records.
4. Acting fairly and proportionately
   - Treating the complainant impartially, and without unlawful discrimination or prejudice.
   - Ensuring that complaints are investigated thoroughly and fairly to establish the facts of the case.
   - Ensuring that decisions are proportionate, appropriate and fair.
   - Ensuring that complaints are reviewed by someone not involved in the events leading to the complaint.
   - Acting fairly towards staff complained about as well as towards complainants.
5. Putting things right
   - Acknowledging mistakes and apologising where appropriate.
   - Providing prompt, appropriate and proportionate remedies.
   - Considering all the relevant factors of the case when offering remedies.
   - Taking account of any injustice or hardship that results from pursuing the complaint as well as from the original dispute.
6. Seeking continuous improvement
   - Using all feedback and the lessons learnt from complaints to improve service design and delivery.
   - Having systems in place to record, analyse and report on the learning from complaints.
   - Regularly reviewing the lessons to be learnt from complaints.
   - Where appropriate, telling the complainant about the lessons learnt and changes made to services, guidance or policy.

Parliamentary and Health Service Ombudsman, *Principles for Remedy*
(2009), pp. 2–3

Good practice with regard to remedies means:

1. Getting it right
   - Quickly acknowledging and putting right cases of maladministration or poor service that have led to injustice or hardship.
   - Considering all relevant factors when deciding the appropriate remedy, ensuring fairness for the complainant and, where appropriate, for others who have suffered injustice or hardship as a result of the same maladministration or poor service.
2. Being customer focused
   - Apologising for and explaining the maladministration or poor service.
   - Understanding and managing people's expectations and needs.
   - Dealing with people professionally and sensitively.
   - Providing remedies that take account of people's individual circumstances.
3. Being open and accountable
   - Being open and clear about how public bodies decide remedies.
   - Operating a proper system of accountability and delegation in providing remedies.
   - Keeping a clear record of what public bodies have decided on remedies and why.
4. Acting fairly and proportionately
   - Offering remedies that are fair and proportionate to the complainant's injustice or hardship.
   - Providing remedies to others who have suffered injustice or hardship as a result of the same maladministration or poor service, where appropriate.
   - Treating people without bias, unlawful discrimination or prejudice.
5. Putting things right
   - If possible, returning the complainant and, where appropriate, others who have suffered similar injustice or hardship, to the position they would have been in if the maladministration or poor service had not occurred.
   - If that is not possible, compensating the complainant and such others appropriately.
   - Considering fully and seriously all forms of remedy (such as an apology, an explanation, remedial action, or financial compensation).
   - Providing the appropriate remedy in each case.
6. Seeking continuous improvement
   - Using the lessons learned from complaints to ensure that maladministration or poor service is not repeated.
   - Recording and using information on the outcome of complaints to improve services.

NOTE: Each set of principles has advice to the effect that they are not a checklist to be applied mechanically. Public bodies should use their judgement in applying them to produce reasonable, fair, and proportionate results or remedies in all the circumstances of the case. The ombudsman will adopt a similar approach when deciding if maladministration or service failure has occurred and when considering the standard of complaint handling by public bodies in her jurisdiction and when recommending remedies.

Parliamentary and Health Service Ombudsman, *The Ombudsman's Annual Report and Accounts 2015–16*
HC 361 of 2013–14, p. 43

Evidence of change resulting from influencing programmes

- Parliament held a hearing on our Time to Act report on sepsis and since then our recommendations have been steadily adopted. The Health Secretary announced new action to tackle sepsis in

January 2015, an NHS England action plan was introduced in December 2015, NICE guidelines were published in July 2016, and the Department of Health and Public Health England announced a UK-wide awareness campaign to improve public recognition of sepsis in August 2016.

- Since publishing our report into midwifery supervision and regulation, the Nursing and Midwifery Council have voted to take direct responsibility and accountability for all activity regulating midwives. The Government recently closed its consultation on proposed changes to the law from 2017.
- Age UK, the Alzheimer's Society, Independent Age and others supported Breaking Down the Barriers, which highlighted the significant problems that older people can face when looking to complain about their care.
- Our report of investigations into unsafe discharge from hospital led to an inquiry by the Public Administration and Constitutional Affairs Committee. Their subsequent report added Parliament's authority to the need to address the social care funding gap.
- HS2 introduced a 24-hour helpdesk to better engage with the public following our investigation.

Local Government Ombudsman, *Annual Review of Local Government Complaints 2015-16*

(2016) pp. 20, 23–4

Where a council or care provider is refusing to provide a suitable remedy we will issue a public report on the complaint, as required by legislation. We will also decide to issue such a public report where the circumstances of the individual complaint highlight issues of wider public interest. This can be where there is:

- Recurrent fault
- Significant fault, injustice or remedy
- High volume of complaints about one subject
- Significant topical issue (e.g. new legislation)
- Systemic problems and/or wider lessons to be learnt.

In total we published 28 detailed public interest reports of investigations. By publishing such cases we seek to ensure that all local authorities and care providers apply the lessons to their own services and learn from the experiences of people in one area to inform service improvement in another …

Our investigations will often highlight issues or themes that we see time and time again across different councils or providers. We have used Focus Reports as a vehicle to highlight learning opportunities to bodies in our jurisdiction, to encourage democratic scrutiny of the issues and to encourage policy makers to use the lessons from complaints to inform their work. Over the last 12 months we have published three Focus Reports: *Making a house a home: Local Authorities and disabled adaptations* (March 2016); *Full house: Councils' role in allocating social housing* (January 2016) and *Counting the cost of care: the council's role in informing public choices about care homes* (September 2015) …

We also continue to publish our sector wide reviews of complaints across both local public services and social care. These reviews not only set out where services need to improve but, alongside our annual letters to chief executives, place into the public domain the complaints records of every council and care provider that we have received a complaint about.

For a number of years we have offered more direct support for local complaints systems by providing training to local authorities on effective complaint handling. In the last year we delivered 40 courses, training over 600 front line council complaints staff. In last year's Annual Report we announced that, for the first time, we had also started to offer training to private social care providers. This year, in addition to the training delivered to councils, we have also trained 115 people who work in the independent care sector.

NOTE: There have been innovations in these more systemic ombudsman activities.

R. Gordon, *Better to Serve the Public: Proposals to restructure, reform, renew and reinvigorate public services ombudsmen*
(2014) paras 25–9, 134–9

25. In Scotland, following independent reviews of complaint handling which concluded that there was a clear need for a quicker, more consistent, more user focussed approach to handling complaints, the Scottish Parliament passed legislation placing new obligations on the SPSO and establishing a Complaints Standards Authority to work with public bodies to standardise and simplify complaints handling procedures and to help drive improvement. This legislation gives the SPSO the power to publish standard complaints handling procedures for most public authorities including local authorities and the NHS. The SPSO is also under a duty to monitor and promote best practice in complaints handling. Audit Scotland and the Care Commission have a role in monitoring compliance.

26. In the course of my discussions, some have pointed to challenges of scale in seeking to apply to England models or features of arrangements from the smaller constituent parts of the UK. **I think the prize of significantly improved upstream complaint handling in terms of the benefit to citizens of earlier resolution of their complaints as well as in terms of savings to public bodies themselves bears serious consideration and I recommend action.** This may not involve a direct transposition to England of the precise arrangements applying elsewhere in the UK but the progress made, for instance by the SPSO and public bodies in Scotland over only a few years, does highlight the kind of value adding function a reformed and enhanced ombudsman service could play in a reformed complaints handling landscape.

27. There is **a real opportunity also to consider what role the ombudsman might play in supporting and, potentially, policing any new systems.** The kind of cultural and institutional change the Minister for Government Policy has articulated cannot be driven by an ombudsman alone – but I would argue that **a new public services ombudsman should have at its heart a duty to set the expected standards in complaint handling, to support organisations in making the shift towards best practice and, ultimately, to support Parliament, Ministers, local authorities, and ALB Boards (in short the 'oversight bodies') in holding organisations to account for their performance.** As part of this, the Government may wish to consider whether the ombudsman should have a "kite-marking" or "passporting" function, acting as an assurer of practice or proposed complaint handling schemes in organisations within jurisdiction.

28. Both PASC and the PHSO have suggested that leadership is critical in driving improvements – and in ensuring that complaints are given appropriate priority. This is particularly important at Board level within public service organisations. **I consider that a renewed ombudsman function should play an important part in supporting and challenging the commitment of leaders to prioritise complaint handling and resolution in all bodies within the ombudsman's jurisdiction from government departments and local authorities, to the boards of bodies providing service to the public.**

29. There is a question for Government about the extent to which such obligations should be set down in statute – as they are in Scotland – or should be part of an MOU or similar agreement between Government or another part of the public sector and any new ombudsman. The ombudsman would be well placed to contribute by providing support and encouragement by highlighting best practice within the system, whilst retaining the ability to challenge, publishing details of an organisation's performance around complaint handling or highlighting trends which reveal concerns about particular areas of service delivery. Parliament has a role here too.

Own Initiative Power

134. PASC highlighted concerns that the ombudsman's ability to add value is fettered by an absence of such powers. This view is one expressed most strongly by the PHSO who has highlighted the fact that their absence places unnecessary restrictions on its ability to provide an early warning system or to better engage with those least likely to complain.

135. Previous consideration of this issue has encountered a reluctance to open up an additional channel of investigation, and perhaps led to concern that such a move might divert the ombudsman from his or her main task – that of delivering redress for the individual – whilst resource is channelled in to more wide-ranging reports or investigations (or indeed whether such a move alters the fundamental constitutional position of the ombudsman). This concern may have been heightened by the apparent absence of appropriate checks and balances in a system where the power could be exercised by a single office holder.

136. Own-initiative investigation powers have traditionally been used sparingly, accounting for just 3% of the caseload of the European Ombudsman and 1% of the complaints investigated by the Swedish Ombudsman, but they can deliver high levels of impact and the subsequent reports provide valuable research and further evidence with which to inform decision making and service delivery improvements.

137. **These powers go directly to the extent to which the PSO is able to play a full and enhanced role in driving up public delivery standards**. The issue then is how to frame such a power so as to ensure that its well-considered and responsible use adds value; avoids duplicating or crossing in to the well-established role of regulators or others in the administrative justice landscape and leads to early interventions which address emerging problems and produce early policy or delivery reforms.

138. **The framework within which such an investigation could be triggered needs to be clearly articulated and understood from the outset.** Specific proposals would need to be tested and I suggest that the framework would include:

- a published statement setting out the ombudsman's general approach to own-initiative investigations;
- a decision framework that is used to document in a systemic way the detailed reasoning that informs the decision to launch an own initiative investigation, covering the rationale and evidence base for the investigation, any relevant jurisdictional issues (and in particular why the ombudsman is better placed than others to act) and other background, the methodology to be used and the proposed timeline; and
- a protocol that commits the ombudsman to notify the leadership of the relevant organisation that it will be subject of an own-initiative investigation. The notification would specify the legal basis and reason for the investigation, as well as the scope or terms of reference of the investigation.
- The Board of the PSO should be required to sign off any proposal, having taken account of any views of the body or bodies in question. A report should then be made to the proposed Public Administration Commission recording the case put to the Board and including any comments received from the leadership of the organisation.

139. There will inevitably be some concern about the nature of any findings arising from such inquiries or investigations. I do not propose here that they should be underpinned by a statutory requirement for bodies to comply. I consider that a significant and high quality investigation and report from an enhanced PSO, supported by the necessary complementary scrutiny from Parliament, would inevitably create an environment in which there would be a strong public interest in seeing an adequate response from those bodies in jurisdiction to findings of fault.

NOTE: The Cabinet Office consultation included these proposals but the Government Response to the consultation was not quite so supportive of the range of activities which the SPSO has in enhancing complaint handling. The Response ruled out conferring an own-initiative investigation power on the grounds that it did not want to detract from the Ombudsman's role in remedying individual's complaints. The Public Services Ombudsman Act (Northern Ireland) 2016, s. 8, does confer this power, and it is also included in a draft bill prepared by the Welsh Assembly's Finance Committee in 2015. Both the Northern Ireland statute and the Welsh draft bill also include equivalent provisions to those in the Scottish statute on model complaints-handling procedures.

■ QUESTION

Bearing in mind that public service ombudsmen in most other countries have an own-initiative investigation power, and that it was recommended by PASC, Gordon, and in the Cabinet Office's consultation, is the Government's focus on individuals, neglecting the wider systemic role for improvement which the Ombudsman, can and ought to pursue?

SECTION 6: OUTCOME OF INVESTIGATIONS AND REMEDIES

Parliamentary Commissioner Act 1967

10.—(1) In any case where the Commissioner conducts an investigation under this Act or decides not to conduct such an investigation, he shall send to the member of the House of Commons by whom the request for investigation was made (or if he is no longer a member of that House, to such member of that House as the Commissioner thinks appropriate) a report of the results of the investigation or, as the case may be, a statement of his reasons for not conducting an investigation.

(2) In any case where the Commissioner conducts an investigation under this Act, he shall also send a report of the results of the investigation to the principal officer of the department or authority concerned and to any other person who is alleged in the relevant complaint to have taken or authorised the action complained of.

(3) [see later in this chapter in Section 6A at p. 642]

(4) The Commissioner shall annually lay before each House of Parliament a general report on the performance of his functions under this Act and may from time to time lay before each House of Parliament such other reports with respect to those functions as he thinks fit.

11.—(2) Information obtained by the Commissioner or his officers in the course of or for the purposes of an investigation under this Act shall not be disclosed except—

(a) for the purposes of the investigation and of any report to be made thereon under this Act;

(b) for the purposes of any proceedings for an offence under the Official Secrets Acts 1911 to 1939 alleged to have been committed in respect of information obtained by the Commissioner or any of his officers by virtue of this Act or for an offence of perjury alleged to have been committed in the course of an investigation under this Act or for the purposes of an inquiry with a view to the taking of such proceedings; or

(c) for the purposes of any proceedings under section 9 of this Act; and the Commissioner and his officers shall not be called upon to give evidence in any proceedings (other than such proceedings as aforesaid) of matters coming to his or their knowledge in the course of an investigation under this Act.

(3) A Minister of the Crown may give notice in writing to the Commissioner, with respect to any document or information specified in the notice, or any class of documents or information so specified, that in the opinion of the Minister the disclosure of that document or information, or of documents or information of that class, would be prejudicial to the safety of the State or otherwise contrary to the public interest; and where such a notice is given nothing in this Act shall be construed as authorising or requiring the Commissioner or any officer of the Commissioner to communicate to any person or for any purpose any document or information specified in the notice, or any document or information of a class so specified.

Local Government Act 1974

30 Reports on investigations

(1) If a Local Commissioner completes an investigation of a matter under this Part of this Act, he shall prepare a report of the results of the investigation and send a copy to each of the persons concerned (subject to subsection (1B)).

 (1A) A Local Commissioner may include in a report on a matter under subsection (1) any recommendations that he could include in a further report on the matter by virtue of section 31(2A) to (2BA).

 (1B) If, after the investigation of a matter is completed, the Local Commissioner decides—

  (a) that he is satisfied with action which the authority concerned have taken or propose to take, and

  (b) that it is not appropriate to prepare and send a copy of a report under subsection (1),

  he may instead prepare a statement of his reasons for the decision and send a copy to each of the persons concerned.

 (1C) If a Local Commissioner decides—

  (a) not to investigate a matter, or

  (b) to discontinue an investigation of a matter,

  he shall prepare a statement of his reasons for the decision and send a copy to each of the persons concerned.

 (1D) For the purposes of subsections (1) to (1C), the persons concerned are—

  (a) the complainant (if any),

  (b) any person who referred the matter under section 26C(2),

  (c) the authority concerned, and

  (d) any other authority or person who is alleged in the complaint, or who otherwise appears to the Local Commissioner, to have taken or authorised the action which is or would be the subject of the investigation.

NOTE: In the following extracts from PHSO and LGO reports, data are presented about reported investigations and the outcomes.

Parliamentary and Health Service Ombudsman, *Complaints about UK Government departments and agencies, and some UK public organisations 2015–16*
(2016) pp. 5, 8

Number of completed investigations

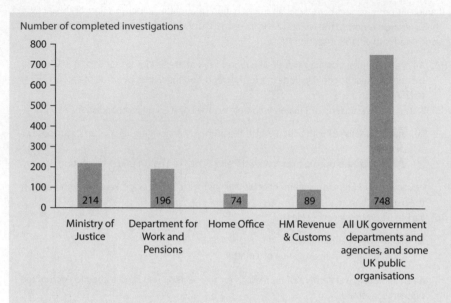

Outcome of investigations, 2015–16

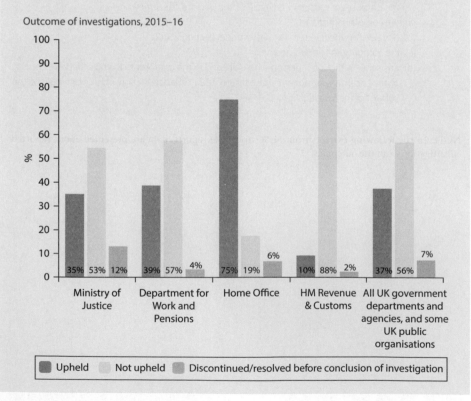

Local Government Ombudsman, *Review of Local Government Complaints 2015–16*

(2016) pp. 34, 47

Data sheets—complaints & enquiries received (by category) 2015–16

Adult Social Care	Benefits & tax	Corporate & other services	Education & children's services	Environmental services, public protection, & regulation
2,526	2,550	960	3,234	1,699

Highways & transport	Housing	Planning & development	Other	Total
2,085	2,232	2,522	167	1,7975

Data sheets—complaints & enquiries decided (by outcome) 2015–16

Invalid or incomplete	Advice given	Referred back for local resolution	Closed after initial enquiries	Not upheld
876	569	7406	4,968	2,162

Upheld	Uphold rate (%)	Total	Complaints remedied by LGO	Complaints remedied by Authority	Compliance rate (%)
2,237	51	18,218	1,648	155	99.94

NOTE: The range of remedies offered by ombudsmen is much wider than could be obtained in the courts.

A: Compliance with ombudsmen's reports

Usually reports by the PO are accepted and the recommendations are to a greater or lesser extent implemented.

Parliamentary Commissioner Act 1967

10. (3) If, after conducting an investigation under this Act, it appears to the Commissioner that injustice has been caused to the person aggrieved in consequence of maladministration and that the injustice has not been, or will not be, remedied, he may, if he thinks fit, lay before each House of Parliament a special report upon the case.

There have been six reports produced under this power (see the table summarizing these reports later in this section at p. 643) with four of them published in the period 2005–09. In the Foreword to the 2003–04 Annual Report (HC 702 of 2003–04) the PO stated:

... there is a clear reluctance among some government departments and agencies to accept my findings and recommendations for redress. I will be looking for significant changes in mindset among such government bodies and, as a result, an improvement in their response in the coming year.

After the fourth one had been published in 2006, the second in consecutive years, the Public Administration Select Committee produced a report, *The Ombudsman in Question: the Ombudsman's report on pensions and its constitutional implications* (HC1081 of 2005–6). In its conclusions the select committee stated:

8. It is not unprecedented for the Government to contest an Ombudsman's finding of maladministration. It is, however, unprecedented for there to be so many problems, in such a short space of time. Our scrutiny leads us to conclude that the fault lies with the Government, not the Ombudsman. (Paragraph 70)

9. We share the Ombudsman's concern that the Government has been far too ready to dismiss her findings of maladministration. Our investigations have shown that these findings were sound. It would be extremely damaging if government became accustomed simply to reject findings of maladministration, especially if an investigation by this Committee proved there was indeed a case to answer. It would raise fundamental constitutional issues about the position of the Ombudsman and the relationship between Parliament and the Executive. (Paragraph 78)

10. We trust that this Report will act as a warning to the Government. We will continue to monitor the Government's responses to the Parliamentary Commissioner's reports. If necessary we will seek a debate on the floor of the House, so that all Members can discuss these issues, and re-establish the Parliamentary Commissioner's role. The Parliamentary Commissioner is Parliament's Ombudsman: Government must respect her. (Paragraph 79)

Normal relations were restored but only for three years as two more s. 10(3) reports were published, the fifth and sixth, within seven months of each other in 2009. The response to every s. 10(3) report is that the select committee which oversees the PO produces a report. In all six cases the select committee, after conducting its own inquiry, has supported the PO and the political process has led to an outcome which has satisfied the PO. In the fifth case, however, *Equitable Life*, action has to be taken to implement the commitment given in the *Programme for Government* by the Coalition Government to provide more compensation. (See the table summarizing the PO's s. 10(3) reports, later in this section at p. 643.)

The trend in compliance has been different in LGO cases. Historically, there had been difficulties and the Widdicombe Report (*The Conduct of Local Authority Business*, Cmnd 9797, 1986) had suggested enacting provisions similar to those relating to the Commissioner for Complaints in Northern Ireland (see later in this section at p. 645). This recommendation was not accepted instead the Local Government Act 1974 was amended by the Local Government and Housing Act 1989, ss. 26 and 28, to provide that authorities must notify the Local Government Ombudsman of the action which they propose to take within three months from the date of an adverse report (Local Government Act 1974, s. 31(2), as amended). Similar time limits apply in respect of the consideration of a further report (s. 31(2)–(2c)). If an authority proposes not to accept the recommendation of the LGO in a further report, the report must generally be considered by the authority as a whole (s. 31A(1)). If, in considering the report, the authority take into account a report by a person or body with an interest in the LGO's report, they must also take into account a report by a person or body without an interest in the report (s. 31A(4)). No member of the council is entitled to vote on any question with respect to a report or a further report in which he is named and criticized (s. 31A(5)). If the authority do not satisfy the LGO with respect to a further report, he may require the authority to publish a statement, in a form agreed between the local authority and the Ombudsman, consisting of the details of the action recommended by the Local Government Ombudsman, such supporting material as he may require, and, if the authority so require, a statement of the reasons for non-compliance with the LGO's recommendations. The statement must be published in two editions of a local newspaper within a fortnight, the first publication to be as soon as possible. If the authority do not arrange for publication, the LGO may do so at their expense (s. 31(2D)–(2H)).

It would seem that the number of occasions in which the LGO has been dissatisfied and required a statement to be published following a further report have reduced. The Annual Report until 2006–07 included a table on compliance with recommendations, showing the number of cases in which reports recommending remedies for injustice had resulted in an outcome unsatisfactory to the LGO. Perhaps it can be inferred from that the absence of this table on compliance from the annual report indicates that it is no longer a problem.

T. Buck, R. Kirkham, and B. Thompson, *The Ombudsman Enterprise and Administrative Justice* (2011), pp. 252–3

Appendix 7 Parliamentary Ombudsman's section 10(3) reports

Name/Issue/Year/Dept	Disputed PO Findings and/or Recommendations	Governmental Objections	Select Committee View	Outcome/Reason
Rochester Way, Road Administration of compensation, 1978 Dept of Transport	Defective arrangements for publicizing details of compensation scheme led to applications being rejected as out of time	To make *exgratia* payments would override the will of Parliament	The commitment to inform people about the compensation scheme was not met	Amendments made to the legislation authorizing payments for late claims
Channel Tunnel Rail Link, planning blight, 1994 Dept of Transport	There was exceptional uncertainty about an unusual project which gave rise to general blight but this caused exceptional hardship for some people	The project the uncertainty and the hardship were not so exceptional as to override policy of not compensating for general blight	Dept had not considered identifying those who were inequitably affected by rigid adherence to the letter of law	Ombudsman satisfied as government indicated it was prepared to discuss terms of compensation but nothing done until change of government in 1997
Wartime Detainees, Administration of Compensation, 2005 Ministry of Defence	Both the scheme's terms and its announcement were unclear; new criterion not reviewed to check for equal treatment; no information provided to applicants on clarification of criteria; no review undertaken	Challenged PO's decision to investigate new 'bloodlink' criterion given an unsuccessful judicial review; complainant's case should not have been accepted	in preparing for select committee appearance, new evidence found suggesting unequal treatment; committee hoped MOD would pay	Ombudsman satisfied following the subsequent ministerial statement
Occupational Pensions, Compensation for poor regulation, 2006 Dept for Work and Pensions, Treasury, National Insurance Contributions Office (HMRC), Occupational Pensions Regulatory Authority	Misleading information on degree of protection; maladministration in not following advice on disclosing risks; maladmin in changing Minimum Funding Requirement and so contributed to losses in winding-up process	Rejected findings which were not substantiated; leaflet not comprehensive guide and no causal link to loss in the winding-up of companies	Agreed that maladmin had occurred, govt should engage properly with PO's recommendations rather than assuming too large a burden on the public purse	Ombudsman satisfied as Government actuary department (GAD) review found ways to improve Financial Assistance Scheme

Name/Issue/Year/Dept	Disputed PO Findings and/or Recommendations	Governmental Objections	Select Committee View	Outcome/Reason
Equitable Life, Compensation for poor regulation, 2009 HM Treasury	PO found a total of 10 instances of maladmin by DTI, GAD, FSA and recommended apology and compensation scheme. In s.10(3) report the terms of reference for the judge's advice will restrict those eligible for compensation and the likely amount will not be adequate	Accepted most findings, not accepting proposed compensation but asking judge to advise on a narrower ex gratia scheme for those who had suffered disproportionate impact	Select Committee supported PO's initial report before govt response report; their reaction to it made before s.10(3) report; disliked disproportionate impact test, not simple or quick	Ombudsman satisfied as following 2010 election new coalition proposed better terms
Single Payments Scheme and Rural Land Register, 2009 Department for Environment, Food and Rural Affairs (Defra)	Maladmin by not determining issues in stipulated period; did not react appropriately following indications of problems which led to delay and these two cases were representative, so apply recommendations to 22 others similarly placed	Dept concerned that indications on targets for decisions had become legitimate expectations; compensation had been paid, which was adequate and to provide the recommended compensation for other cases was a distraction	Following its evidence session with permanent secretary, the chair wrote to minister advising the dept had misunderstood basis for PO's decisions on targets; compensation for other 22 cases within Treasury guidance	Ombudsman satisfied as minister completely accepted recommendations following select committee chair's letter

NOTE: There has been one more report laid under s. 10(3) concerning a complaint against the Electoral Commission (HC 540 of 2014–15). This case was not considered by the select committee and it seems that the Electoral Commission was able to satisfy the Ombudsman about one of three findings of maladministration which the Commission did not accept and had prompted the report.

Where the Commissioner for Complaints in Northern Ireland makes a finding that an individual has sustained injustice in consequence of maladministration, the individual may apply to the county court, and the court may award 'such damages as the court may think just in all the circumstances to compensate' the applicant for loss or injury suffered on account of (a) expenses reasonabl y incurred, and (b) lost opportunity of acquiring benefit (Commissioner for Complaints Order (Northern Ireland) 1996, art. 16(2)). If it appears to the court that justice can only be done by ordering that body to take or refrain from taking some action, then the court may, if satisfied that in all the circumstances it is reasonable so to do, grant a mandatory or other injunction (art. 16(5)). In addition, where maladministration coupled with injustice has been found, and it appears to the Commissioner for Complaints that the body concerned has previously engaged in conduct of the same kind and is likely to continue to engage in future in conduct of the type which he has condemned, he may request the Attorney-General to apply to the High Court for appropriate relief, such as an injunction to restrain the continuation of the maladministration (art. 17). From 1978 to 1988 there were on average three applications each year to the county court by successful complainants. The Attorney-General has, however, never been asked to make an application (see the *JUSTICE–All Souls Report on Administrative Law* (1988), pp. 123–5, for a discussion of the role of the Commissioner for Complaints in Northern Ireland and C. White (1994) 45 *Northern Ireland Legal Quarterly* 395 on the Northern Ireland enforcement provision).

No action has been brought by a dissatisfied claimant in 26 years and in the consultation paper on proposed legislation, issued by a committee of the Northern Ireland Assembly in September 2010, it is asked if this 'enforcement provision' should be retained. Nonetheless, not only was this provision included in the Public Services Ombudsman Act (Northern Ireland) 2016, but it was also extended to cover other aspects of the former Commissioner for Complaints remit as well as that of the former Assembly Ombudsman's jurisdiction.

Both the Scottish Public Services Ombudsman Act 2002 and the Public Services Ombudsman (Wales) Act 2005 continue the tradition of non-binding investigation reports, and allow the Ombudsmen to issue special reports if dissatisfied with the remedy taken or proposed. During the passage of the Welsh statute there was concern about non-compliance which led to an amendment which became s. 20. This provision would allow the Ombudsman to issue a certificate to the High Court if of the view that a listed authority had without lawful excuse wilfully disregarded a report which upheld a complaint. This provision has not been brought into force by the commencement order made by the National Assembly for Wales (S.I. 2005 No. 2800 (W.119)).

B: Findings and recommendations

Although the fourth and fifth cases involving s. 10(3) reports (*Occupational Pensions* and *Equitable Life*) were settled in the political arena, the complainants sought judicial review of the Government's rejection of the PO's reports. In the *Occupational Pensions* case *R (Bradley) v Secretary of State for Work & Pensions* it was conceded that recommendations for remedy could not be binding upon the Government. However, in the Administrative Court Bean J held that it was irrational for the Minister to reject the first finding of maladministration ([2007] EWHC 242 (Admin) at [66]). On appeal the Court of Appeal accepted ([2008] EWCA Civ 36 at [72]) the argument that:

> The question is not whether the defendant himself considers that there was maladministration, but whether in the circumstances his rejection of the ombudsman's finding to this effect is based on cogent reasons.

The Court of Appeal held that the position in relation to findings was different for the LGO whose findings would be binding unless successfully challenged in a judicial review.

The reason for the distinction was the difference between the ombudsmen's respective statutes, the Parliamentary Commissioner Act 1967 and the Local Government Act 1974 ([2008] EWCA Civ 36 at [40]):

> The purpose for which the legislation was introduced was to give Members of Parliament—in particular, Members of the House of Commons—access to the services of an independent and authoritative investigator as "a better instrument which they can use to protect the citizen".

In *R (Equitable Members Action Group)* v *HM Treasury* [2009] EWHC 2495 (Admin), the Administrative Court held that no cogent reasons had been put forward to reject some of the PO's findings of maladministration and injustice, but that there were cogent reasons for departing from other findings, and reaffirmed that the enforcement of the PO's recommendations was a matter for Parliament.

The requirement of cogent reasons for a Minister to reject the PO's finding of maladministration is an extension of the irrationality ground of judicial review. It has been attacked as inappropriate by J. Varuhas, 'Governmental rejections of ombudsman findings: what role for the courts?' (2009) 72 *Modern Law Review* 102, and T. Endicott, *Administrative Law* (2009), pp. 495–6 and has been defended by T. Buck, R. Kirkham, and B. Thompson, *The Ombudsman Enterprise and Administrative Justice* (2011), pp. 217–19.

The Law Commission has considered ombudsmen findings and recommendations, proposing that these terms should be used and that findings should be statutorily defined. They agree that enforcing recommendations should be part of the political process.

Law Commission, *Public Services Ombudsmen*

Law Com 329 (2011) paras 5.117, 5.132–3

> **STATUS OF FINDINGS AND RECOMMENDATIONS**
>
> 5.117 Our approach to the public services ombudsmen recognises that they are not courts and we do not think that they should be made into court substitutes. Given this, and the way that ombudsmen seek to influence public bodies through repeated interactions, we did not think that there would be benefit in changing the current approach to recommendations – that they are not binding on public bodies....
>
> 5.132 Findings, we suggest, are of a very different nature to recommendations. Findings are findings of fact and maladministration on complaints made to the ombudsmen and are the result of their investigatory procedure. The ombudsmen's schemes, including the closed nature of their investigations, were designed specifically to facilitate processes leading to such findings. We think, therefore, that it would weaken unnecessarily the ombudsmen's processes if their findings could be dismissed with a mere statement of "cogent reasons", and that it would undermine an individual's decision to opt for an ombudsman rather than an alternative mechanism for administrative justice.
>
> 5.133 We, therefore, make the following recommendation.
>
> **Recommendation 12: We recommend that recommendations of the public services ombudsmen continue to be part of the political process. We recommend that findings of the public services ombudsmen be binding unless successfully challenged by way of judicial review.**

■ QUESTION

Do you agree with the Law Commission's proposals that (a) ombudsmen's findings of maladministration and injustice should be binding unless successfully challenged by way of judicial review, and (b) that the enforcement of recommendations for remedying injustice should be confined to the political arena?

SECTION 7: ARRANGEMENTS FOR DISSATISIFIED COMPLAINANTS

The ombudsmen's legislation does not provide arrangements for complainants who are dissatisfied with the treatment of their complaints. The ombudsmen have developed a non-statutory process.

Parliamentary and Health Service Ombudsman, *The Ombudsman's Annual Report and Accounts 2015–16*
HC 779 of 2016–17, p. 21

Complaints about how we reach decisions

Day to day our staff follow a robust process and make hundreds of sound decisions. These decisions are final, but we will take another look if someone is able to show us that:

- we may have made our decision based on inaccurate facts that could change our decision,
- we may have overlooked or misunderstood parts of the complaint or did not take account of relevant information, which could change our decision, or
- they have new and relevant information that was not previously available and which might change our decision.

If, having looked again at the process we followed to handle the complaint, we think we may have made an error; we will take action to put that right. This can sometimes involve reopening an investigation. In 2015-16, of the 33,316 decisions made at the initial checks, assessment and investigation steps, we reviewed 218 and upheld 14 of them. In 2014-15 we reviewed 392 decisions and upheld 78. The significant decline in the number of complaints needing review may be a result of our more consistent criteria and ways of working at every stage of our casework process.

Local Government Ombudsman, *Annual Report & Accounts 2015–16*
(2016) p. 19

There has been a slight reduction in the number of review requests we have received this year. Last year we received 1,212 requests compared with 1,185 this year. Encouragingly we have also seen a reduction in the number of reviews we have upheld and which required us to provide clarification or undertake further work. Last year we upheld 97 reviews (8% of the number received) compared with 69 (6% of the number received) this year. This represents just 0.6% of the complaints we decided.

NOTES
1. Understandably complainants dissatisfied with an ombudsman's decision want an independent appeal but that is not what these arrangements conducted by the ombudsmen's own staff provide. This is justified by the authors of the external evaluation of the LGO. In their recommendations they did propose, however, that the LGO employ an external reviewer to consider complaints about their service.

> The benefits of doing so would be that it would provide an element of external oversight of the LGO, make it more likely that poor performance is correctly identified and add to the pressures on LGO staff to maintain high standards.

Some other ombudsmen schemes do this, including the Scottish Public Services Ombudsman, who was one of the external team conducting the first annual evaluation. The evaluation of the LGO had been proposed in a report on the work of the LGO by the House of Commons Communities and Local Government Committee (HC 431 of 2012–13, para. 72).

2. The statistics for judicial review of the PHSO and the LGO as reported in the 2015–16 annual reports show the PHSO faced five applications for permission to make an application for judicial

review. Two were withdrawn, and in one of these, the PHSO agreed to reopen the case. Three were refused permission and of those two are awaiting decision by (a) the Court of Appeal on an appeal and (b) the High Court for an oral renewal of the application for permission. For the LGO there were 15 letters before claim and none of those which became applications for permission were successful.

3. Most judicial reviews against the ombudsmen are unsuccessful but one complainant was successful in three successive judicial reviews as first the initial PO report was challenged and then the subsequent reconsiderations were found to be flawed.

■ QUESTION

Is it appropriate that the ombudsmen should review their service in dissatisfied complainants' cases with judicial review as the final possibility for challenge?

13

Statutory Tribunals

OVERVIEW

In this chapter we consider the rationale for giving the task of resolving disputes to statutory tribunals rather than courts, the new structure and organization for most tribunals, and how they conduct dispute resolution. In the final section the idea of looking at tribunals as part of an administrative justice system is considered with attention given to a report on redress across complaints and tribunals and a focus on the needs of people seeking such redress.

SECTION 1: INTRODUCTION: THE RATIONALE FOR TRIBUNALS

Concern about the growth of tribunals and their functions and procedures prompted the formation of the Committee on Administrative Tribunals and Inquiries in 1955. The Committee reported in 1957, and its recommendations led to important reforms in the Tribunal and Inquiries Act 1958 and there were amendments to this framework in the Tribunals and Inquiries Act 1971 and the Tribunals and Inquiries Act 1992. The Committee and its report are often named after the chair, Sir Oliver, later Lord, Franks. The question of the reasons why tribunals are created was considered.

Report of the Committee on Administrative Tribunals and Enquiries
Cmnd 218, 1957, paras 20–2, 26–7, 29–32

20. It is noteworthy that Parliament, having decided that the decisions with which we are concerned should not be remitted to the ordinary courts, should also have decided that they should not be left to be reached in the normal course of administration. Parliament has considered it essential to lay down special procedures for them.

Good administration
21. This must have been to promote good administration. Administration must not only be efficient in the sense that the objectives of policy are securely attained without delay. It must also satisfy the general body of citizens that it is proceeding with reasonable regard to the balance between the public interest which it promotes and the private interest which it disturbs. Parliament has, we infer, intended in relation to the subject-matter of our terms of reference that the further decisions or, as they may rightly be termed in this context, adjudications must be acceptable as having been properly made.

22. It is natural that Parliament should have taken this view of what constitutes good administration. In this country government rests fundamentally upon the consent of the governed. The general acceptability of these adjudications is one of the vital elements in sustaining that consent.
...

26. At this stage another question naturally arises. On what principle has it been decided that some adjudications should be made by tribunals and some by Ministers? If from a study of the history of the subject we could discover such a principle, we should have a criterion which would be a guide for any future allocation of these decisions between tribunals and Ministers.

27. The search for this principle has usually involved the application of one or both notions, each with its antithesis. Both notions are famous and have long histories. They are the notion of what is judicial, its antithesis being what is administrative, and the notion of what is according to the rule of law, its antithesis being what is arbitrary.

...

29. The rule of law stands for the view that decisions should be made by the application of known principles or laws. In general such decisions will be predictable, and the citizen will know where he is. On the other hand there is what is arbitrary. A decision may be without principle, without any rules. It is therefore unpredictable, the antithesis of a decision taken in accordance with the rule of law.

30. Nothing that we say diminishes the importance of these pairs of antitheses. But it must be confessed that neither pair yields a valid principle on which one can decide whether the duty of making a certain decision should be laid upon a tribunal or upon a Minister or whether the existing allocation of decisions between tribunals and Ministers is appropriate. But even if there is no such principle and we cannot explain all the facts, we can at least start with them. An empirical approach may be the most useful.

31. Starting with the facts, we observe that the methods of adjudication by tribunals are in general not the same as those of adjudication by Ministers. All or nearly all tribunals apply rules. No ministerial decision of the kind denoted by the second part of our terms of reference is reached in this way. Many matters remitted to tribunals and Ministers appear to have, as it were, a natural affinity with one or other method of adjudication. Sometimes the policy of the legislation can be embodied in a system of detailed regulations. Particular decisions cannot, single case by single case, alter the Minister's policy. Where this is so, it is natural to entrust the decisions to a tribunal, if not to the courts. On the other hand it is sometimes desirable to preserve flexibility of decision in the pursuance of public policy. Then a wise expediency is the proper basis of right adjudication, and the decision must be left with a Minister.

32. But in other instances there seems to be no such natural affinity. For example, there seems to be no natural affinity which makes it clearly appropriate for appeals in goods vehicles cases to be decided by the Transport Tribunal when appeals in a number of road passenger cases are decided by the Minister.

NOTE: The authors of the Franks Report have candidly confessed that the principles they cite do not yield an explanation for why a particular decision should be laid upon a tribunal rather than upon a Minister. Other factors which may come into play are explored by Keith Hendry in the following extract.

K. H. Hendry, 'The Tasks of Tribunals: Some Thoughts'
(1982) 1 *Civil Justice Quarterly* 253, 256–9

Tribunals as components of administration schemes
A peremptory glance at the governmental picture in a modern welfare state such as the United Kingdom, will show a multiplicity of tribunals each operating within the bounds of a confined jurisdiction and each directed toward disposing of claims and arguments arising out of a particular statutory scheme. So, for example ... the many disputes that arise from the grant or withholding of [a social security] benefit; similarly under section 40 of the Finance Act 1972 (as amended) Value Added Tax Tribunals hear disagreements between tax officials and those liable to pay VAT. Many more examples could be given.

Parliament's enactment of various schemes and the inclusion within these schemes of specialist tribunals recognises firstly the social need for that scheme and secondly a social need for having machinery to dispose of disputes arising under that scheme. It is insufficiently stressed that as such tribunals have a task as essential parts of the machinery of administrative government.

So we see in particular the Council on Tribunals stressing that 'tribunals are bodies set up to *adjudicate* between the State and the individual … ' with little mention of a tribunal's role in the administrative field. This is not to belittle their role as adjudicatory machinery, but at the same time their responsibilities to their schemes will be vitally important to administration. To take an example: under section 3 of the Mental Health Act 1959, 14 Mental Health Review Tribunals are constituted. They disposed of 696 cases in 1978. The gravity of these tribunals should not be underestimated—they are empowered to determine whether a patient shall be compulsorily detained, and so lose his personal liberty. As such they are vital to the administration of a particular social necessity recognised by legislation.

The Franks Report expressly recognises this factor, albeit in a somewhat guarded way. Having noted that 'Parliament' decided that certain decisions should not be dealt with by the ordinary courts, nor in the normal course of administration, the Report sees tribunals existing so as to 'promote good administration,' that is 'efficient in the sense that the objectives of policy are securely attained without delay,' but at the same time 'with reasonable regard to the balance between the public interest … and the private interest' ' … adjudications must be acceptable as having been properly made.' Already we can see the emergence of the Franks bias, carried on today by its offspring, the Council on Tribunals, namely that what was important was the *correctness* of administration to the detriment of *administration* itself. Had more attention been paid to this task of tribunals one might have seen a greater recognition of its central importance and a consequent appreciation of tribunals as instruments of government. Having devised special procedures as essential elements of administration it can be inferred that tribunals have two further linked, but not quite so obvious, tasks. These are to avoid Ministerial Responsibility and to ease the workload of Governmental Departments.

Under the United Kingdom constitution, a Minister is primarily responsible to Parliament for his and his department's activities. Ultimately he is responsible to public opinion. Under a new legislative scheme it is a matter of choice as to whether decisions will be left to the Minister personally or to his Department. In both cases he remains responsible. However, if a dispute is to be decided outside the Department, for present purposes by a tribunal, the Minister will be able to disclaim responsibility for it. Furthermore, it will not be possible to bring political pressure to bear in order to affect that decision. The creation of a tribunal may therefore have as one of its purposes the evasion of Ministerial responsibility and the easing of Departmental workloads. So under section 12 of the Immigration Act 1971, one sees a two-tier appeal system; at first instance, adjudicators, and above them Immigration Tribunals. The volume of work done by these tribunals indicates the extent to which particularly the Home Office's workload is eased, and how a very politically sensitive decision is hived off to tribunals.

The decision to retain a decision within Departmental/Ministerial hands or to turn it over to a tribunal will, of course, be motivated by a number of factors: a 1980 Council on Tribunals Special Report felt that 'Parliament's' selection of subjects to be referred to tribunals does not form a regular pattern although basic guidelines and various factors included the nature of the decision, historical accidents, Departmental preferences and political consideration. The last-mentioned consideration could operate in both ways—one could give a matter which is potentially sensitive to a tribunal to desensitise it (the system of Immigration Tribunals is an example), or alternatively retain it for that reason within Departmental/Ministerial hands. Other factors would include the likely number of disputes, national interest, the level of discretion involved and so on, but one is forced to agree with the Council on Tribunals that there is no application of a set of coherent principles.

It seems, therefore, that the use of tribunals is a convenient means for affording Ministers immunity from responsibility to Parliament and public opinion for certain kinds of decision. It might even be argued that it is an aspect of 'good administration' for Departments to be denied and/or relieved of certain kinds of decisions which could expose them to pressures of many kinds—not least political.

The Franks Committee stressed that tribunals were not to be seen as 'appendages of Government Departments' … 'Parliament has deliberately provided for a decision outside and independent of the

Department concerned' … 'the intention of Parliament to provide for the independence of tribunals is clear and unmistakable.' With respect, there seems to be a rather large degree of unadulterated constitutional fiction here. John Griffith argues strongly that it is completely wrong to refer to some theoretic notion of Parliamentary intention; tribunals he says are instituted in reality by the Government of the day and in effect it is the relevant Department which will make the rules. The Council on Tribunals expressly cited Departmental preferences as one of the factors relevant to the creation of a tribunal. In their Annual Report for 1975–76 the Council states specifically that the detailed arrangements for tribunals remains the responsibility of Departments. To say, therefore, that tribunals are created to ensure that decisions should be made independently of Departments is simply not valid. Griffith suggests that Departments simply do not want to be bothered with the sorts of decisions tribunals will make: the policy is settled; it only has to be administered and disputes sorted out.

I introduce all this merely to stress the important role of tribunals as rudimentary but nevertheless vital components of administration. Writers today still insist on taking issue with the term *'administrative* tribunals' as giving too much emphasis to the administrative associations that tribunals have: ever since Franks the 'machinery for adjudication' theme has been predominant. In particular the Council of Tribunals has seen its most important contribution as being 'our constant effort to translate the general ideals of the Franks Committee into workable codes of principle and practice … ' As I have suggested it is my view that the Franks Report seriously underplayed the task of tribunals to be instruments of their respective administrative schemes. Be that as it may the Council on Tribunals continues the ideals of Franks with some zeal despite the fact that the Tribunals and Enquiries Act simply asks that they keep under review the constitution and working of Schedule 1 tribunals, report thereon and consider and report on matters as may be referred to them in respect of any tribunals other than courts of law. Is there not here some leeway for a more expansive notion of what tribunals are supposed to be doing?

NOTE: The creation of a statutory advisory body, the Council on Tribunals, was recommended by the Franks Report. The Franks Report referred to the natural affinity between, on the one hand, cases where the policy of legislation can be set out in detailed regulations and adjudication by tribunals and, on the other hand, cases where it is necessary to preserve flexibility in the pursuance of policy and ministerial decision-making. There are, however, tribunals which operate largely for the purposes of developing and applying policy (see, for example, the Civil Aviation Authority and the Competition and Markets Authority). This has led some commentators to draw a distinction between court-substitute and policy-oriented tribunals (on this distinction see further, B. Abel-Smith and R. Stevens, *In Search of Justice* (1968), pp. 20–21 and J. A. Farmer, *Tribunals and Government* (1974), chap. 8).

■ QUESTION

The extracts from the Franks Report, see earlier in this section at p. 649, have been concerned with the choice between providing an appeal to a Minister and providing an appeal to a tribunal. Assuming, then, that a decision has been made to establish a form of adjudication independently of the Department, what explains the decision to establish a tribunal rather than provide a statutory right of appeal to the courts?

Report of the Committee on Administrative Tribunals and Enquiries
Cmnd 218, 1957, paras 38–9

The choice between tribunals and courts of law

38. We agree with the Donoughmore Committee that tribunals have certain characteristics which often give them advantages over the courts. These are cheapness, accessibility, freedom from technicality, expedition and expert knowledge of their particular subject … But as a matter of general principle we are firmly of the opinion that a decision should be entrusted to a court rather than to a tribunal in the absence of special considerations which make a tribunal more suitable.

39. Moreover, if all decisions arising from new legislation were automatically vested in the ordinary courts the judiciary would by now have been grossly overburdened ... We agree with the Permanent Secretary to the Lord Chancellor that any wholesale transfer to the courts of the work of tribunals would be undesirable.

Report of the Review of Tribunals, *Tribunals for Users: One System, One Service*
(2001), paras 1.10–13

Tribunals or courts

1.10 It is important to be clear what work should be done by tribunals, rather than by courts. Franks did not consider in detail what principles should guide the allocation of cases to tribunals, accepting that the already large number of cases decided by tribunals in 1957 made the amalgamation of tribunals and courts impracticable. As the areas in which some kind of appeal is required proliferate, Parliament, policymakers and users should have principles to guide that allocation. We suggest that there should be three tests of whether tribunals rather than courts should decide cases.

Participation

1.11 First, the widest common theme in current tribunals is the aim that users should be able to prepare and present their own cases effectively, if helped by good-quality, imaginatively presented information, and by expert procedural help from tribunal staff and substantive assistance from advice services. We think the element of direct participation is particularly important in the field of disputes between the citizen and the state. ... The use of tribunals to decide disputes should be considered when the factual and legal issues raised by the majority of cases to be brought under proposed legislation are unlikely to be so complex as to prevent users from preparing their own cases and presenting them to the tribunal themselves, if properly helped.

The need for special expertise

1.12 Where the civil courts require expert opinion on the facts of the case, they generally rely on the evidence produced by the parties—increasingly jointly—or on a court-appointed assessor. Tribunals offer a different opportunity, by permitting decisions to be reached by a panel of people with a range of qualifications and expertise. A larger decision-taking body is obviously likely to be more expensive. But users clearly feel that the greater expertise makes for better decisions. They also say that having more members, and non-lawyers, on the panel makes it easier for at least some users to present their cases. The second reason why cases should be considered for allocation to a tribunal is if expertise, or accessibility to users, is a major issue in the resolution of the relevant disputes.

Expertise in administrative law

1.13 Thirdly, tribunals can be particularly effective in dealing with the mixture of fact and law often required to consider decisions taken by administrative or regulatory authorities. Our recommendations for a more coherent system will increase that effectiveness. Where any legislation establishes a statutory scheme involving decisions by an arm of government, the responsible minister should explicitly consider whether a right of appeal is required, on the basis that there should be strong specific arguments if an appeal route is not to be created, and that a tribunal route, rather than redress in the courts, should be the normal option in the interests of accessibility. It should not be regarded as satisfactory to leave judicial review as the citizen's only recourse, since that is expensive and difficult for the unassisted.

NOTE: The Donoughmore Committee produced a *Report on Ministers' Powers* (Cmd 4060, 1932) which concerned delegated legislation and tribunals and inquiries.

■ **QUESTIONS**

1. Are the two reports consistent with each other? Is the objective of not overburdening the judiciary a special consideration in favour of establishing a tribunal?
2. What do these passages indicate about the desirable qualities of tribunals and, in particular, how those qualities should differ from those of the courts? See later in this chapter in Section 3B at p. 669.

SECTION 2: THE STRUCTURE AND ORGANIZATION OF TRIBUNALS

Tribunals were well established by the end of the last century, but their proliferation caused problems. In May 2000 a former Lord Justice of Appeal, Sir Andrew Leggatt, was commissioned to chair a review of tribunals. The terms of reference required the review 'to look at the administrative justice system as a whole: its coherence, its accessibility, its organisation ... '. Their report *Tribunals for Users: One System, One Service* was published in 2001 along with a consultation paper by the Lord Chancellor's Department (LCD, now the Ministry of Justice). As the title of the report suggests, the review's recommendations proposed bringing the various tribunals together, to be supported administratively by an executive agency and for judicial leadership to be provided by a Senior President of Tribunals, who would be assisted by presidents responsible for various tribunals grouped into nine divisions. The benefits to users would be a clearly independent and more efficient tribunals system which was more focused on the users' needs with better information, advice and support. The hotchpotch of appeal and review routes would be streamlined to an appellate tribunal.

The Government accepted the main thrust of the Leggatt recommendations and in a White Paper, *Transforming Public Services: Complaints, Redress and Tribunals* (Cm 6243, 2004) expanded its coverage beyond tribunals to the whole of administrative justice. A graduated programme of incorporating tribunals into the Tribunals Service was begun. It was formally launched in 2006 and did not require legislation; however, statutory authority was needed to create a two-tier structure with judicial leadership and the rationalization of procedure and onward appeals and judicial review.

A: The two-tier structure

Tribunals, Courts And Enforcement Act 2007

3 The First-tier Tribunal and the Upper Tribunal

(1) There is to be a tribunal, known as the First-tier Tribunal, for the purpose of exercising the functions conferred on it under or by virtue of this Act or any other Act.

(2) There is to be a tribunal, known as the Upper Tribunal, for the purpose of exercising the functions conferred on it under or by virtue of this Act or any other Act.

(3) Each of the First-tier Tribunal, and the Upper Tribunal, is to consist of its judges and other members.

(4) The Senior President of Tribunals is to preside over both of the First-tier Tribunal and the Upper Tribunal.

(5) The Upper Tribunal is to be a superior court of record....

7 Chambers: jurisdiction and Presidents

(1) The Lord Chancellor may, with the concurrence of the Senior President of Tribunals, by order make provision for the organisation of each of the First-tier Tribunal and the Upper Tribunal into a number of chambers.

(2) There is—

    (a) for each chamber of the First-tier Tribunal, and

    (b) for each chamber of the Upper Tribunal, to be a person, or two persons, to preside over that chamber.

(3) A person may not at any particular time preside over more than one chamber of the First-tier Tribunal and may not at any particular time preside over more than one chamber of the Upper Tribunal (but may at the same time preside over one chamber of the First-tier Tribunal and over one chamber of the Upper Tribunal).

(4) A person appointed under this section to preside over a chamber is to be known as a Chamber President.

(5) Where two persons are appointed under this section to preside over the same chamber, any reference in an enactment to the Chamber President of the chamber is a reference to a person appointed under this section to preside over the chamber.

(6) The Senior President of Tribunals may (consistently with subsections (2) and (3)) appoint a person who is the Chamber President of a chamber to preside instead, or to preside also, over another chamber.

(7) The Lord Chancellor may (consistently with subsections (2) and (3)) appoint a person who is not a Chamber President to preside over a chamber.

(8) Schedule 4 (eligibility for appointment under subsection (7), appointment of Deputy Chamber Presidents and Acting Chamber Presidents, assignment of judges and other members of the First-tier Tribunal and Upper Tribunal, and further provision about Chamber Presidents and chambers) has effect.

(9) Each of the Lord Chancellor and the Senior President of Tribunals may, with the concurrence of the other, by order—

    (a) make provision for the allocation of the First-tier Tribunal's functions between its chambers;

    (b) make provision for the allocation of the Upper Tribunal's functions between its chambers;

    (c) amend or revoke any order made under this subsection.

NOTES

1. Figure 13.1 on p. 656 shows the two tribunal tiers and their chambers and the tribunal jurisdictions in those chambers. It is an evolving process, because it was planned in phases and it is a structure which is designed to accommodate additions. It was envisaged that the first-tier Tribunal would have a Property Chamber and this was eventually launched in July 2013. Formerly the residential property tribunal service, which was to be moved to it, was administered by the Department for Communities and Local Government. The General Regulatory Chamber had its remit expanded following the implementation of the Regulatory Enforcement and Sanctions Act 2008.

2. Not all tribunals are included within the new structure. The largest omission is employment, which has its own two-tier structure with Employment Tribunals and the Employment Appeal Tribunal. It was not felt appropriate to include these tribunals, in part because they determine disputes between private parties (party and party) rather than between the state and individuals (party and state). Some other tribunals including those dealing with appeals concerning admission to, and reviews of exclusion from, schools, and parking in London and the rest of the country are administered by local councils. Leggatt recommended that they be included (para. 3.15) but the Government decided to exclude them initially from the Tribunal Service and then to review the position (Cm 6243).

3. The biggest change was the addition of two Immigration and Asylum Chambers in 2010. This amounted to a complete reversal of policy which had been intended to streamline challenges by having only one appeal instead of two and a limited reconsideration in the Administrative Court. This had not worked and resulted in the Administrative Court being overwhelmed with asylum and immigration cases causing backlogs across the whole range of judicial review cases in the court.

4. In April 2011 the new HM Courts and Tribunals Service brought together the two previous agencies responsible for running the courts and tribunals. It is unusual in that the courts are those of England and Wales but the tribunals include those jurisdictions of the First-tier and Upper Tribunals also operating in Scotland and Northern Ireland.

5. Following the result of the Scottish Independence Referendum in 2014 that Scotland should remain in the UK, more powers were to be devolved to Scotland. Section 39 of the Scotland

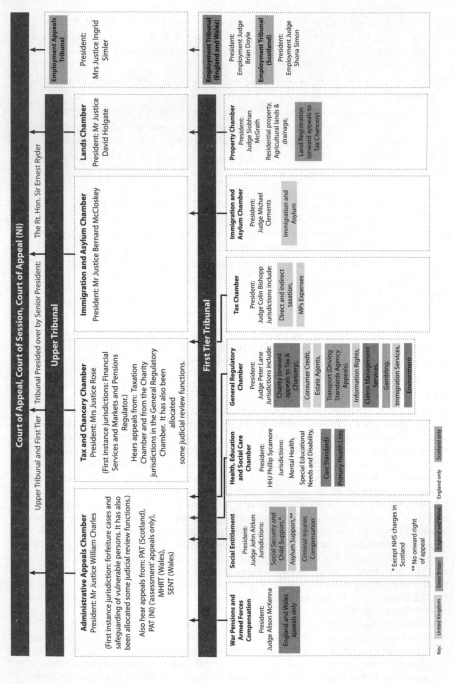

Figure 13.1 Tribunals Structure Chart

Source: Senior President of Tribunals' Annual Report 2016

Act 2016 makes provision for tribunal functions relating to reserved matters in Scottish cases to be exercised by a Scottish tribunal. These tribunals will only have functions in or as regards Scotland. There will be a two-stage process with an Order in Council conferring legislative competence on the Scottish Parliament which could then legislate to transfer specified functions to specified Scottish tribunals. The scope of reserved tribunal jurisdictions likely to be transferred range from those dealing with individuals challenging decisions of the state on personal welfare benefit claims to claims against private sector employers for breach of contract.

The Senior President of Tribunals Annual Report, *Tribunals Transformed*

(2010), para. 45

45. The Transfer of Functions of the Asylum and Immigration Tribunal Order 2010 comes into force on 15 February 2010, abolishing the Asylum and Immigration Tribunal and transferring its functions to the First-tier Tribunal. Also on that day, the Upper Tribunal assumes jurisdiction in respect of appeals against decisions of the First-tier Tribunal in immigration and asylum cases. What was a single tier jurisdiction thus becomes a two tier one, in common with other tribunal jurisdictions.

This is perhaps an appropriate moment to reflect on how the decision came about to bring the AIT wholly within the scheme of the TCEA. By 2007, the volume of immigration and asylum work in the Administrative Court was causing serious concern, particularly as regards the number of applications to that Court for reconsideration of AIT decisions, following initial refusal by that tribunal under s. 103A of the Nationality, Immigration and Asylum Act 2002. A small working group, jointly chaired by Richards LJ and Lin Homer, was formed in order to examine (amongst other things) how best to handle applications that sought to challenge first instance decisions of immigration judges.

The working group concluded that there would be advantages in replacing the system of reconsideration of single-tier decisions with a two-tier appellate process, whereby initial judicial decisions in immigration and asylum cases could be appealed (with permission) to the Upper Tribunal. As well as having the benefit of placing ultimate responsibility for permission applications with a specialist tribunal (which would nevertheless be able to call on High Court input, where appropriate), the creation of a two-tier system was seen to have the advantage of enabling initially legally erroneous decisions to be remade in the Upper Tribunal, thereby leading to a reduction in the immigration and asylum workload of the Court of Appeal, which had also increased to levels that were causing concern.

The Government welcomed the working group's recommendations, which it saw as leading to a more efficient but nevertheless fair and expert system. In August 2008 a consultation paper was published, inviting responses on the proposal to transfer the jurisdiction of the AIT in the manner just described. Following what was seen as a generally favourable response, the government announced in May 2009 that the necessary legislation would be brought forward. The Transfer Order is a key part of that legislative package; but other legislation also creates dedicated Immigration and Asylum Chambers in both the First-tier Tribunal and the Upper Tribunal, and provides the necessary procedure rules for both tiers.

NOTE Following the Security and Courts Act 2013, permission to seek judicial review and applications for judicial review in certain immigration, asylum, and nationality matters was transferred from the Administrative Court to the Immigration and Asylum Chamber of the Upper Tribunal.

B: Judicial leadership and tribunal composition

The Leggatt recommendations sought to ensure that the tribunals were independent of the departments whose decisions were under challenge and judicial leadership which, in the larger tribunal systems had been provided by presidents, was to be carried into the new structure. This leadership would be responsible for tribunal composition and thus ensuring that the classic tribunal characteristic of expertise, both legal and specialist in relation to the work which the tribunal carries out, would be available.

Tribunals, Courts and Enforcement Act 2007

1 Independence of tribunal judiciary

In section 3 of the Constitutional Reform Act 2005 (c. 4) (guarantee of continued judicial independence), after subsection (7) insert—

'(7A) In this section "the judiciary" also includes every person who—

(a) holds an office listed in Schedule 14 or holds an office listed in subsection (7B), and

(b) but for this subsection would not be a member of the judiciary for the purposes of this section.

(7B) The offices are those of—

(a) Senior President of Tribunals;

(b) President of Employment Tribunals (Scotland);

(c) Vice President of Employment Tribunals (Scotland);

(d) member of a panel of chairmen of Employment Tribunals (Scotland);

(e) member of a panel of members of employment tribunals that is not a panel of chairmen;

(f) adjudicator appointed under section 5 of the Criminal Injuries Compensation Act 1995.'

2 Senior President of Tribunals

(1) Her Majesty may, on the recommendation of the Lord Chancellor, appoint a person to the office of Senior President of Tribunals.

(2) Schedule 1 makes further provision about the Senior President of Tribunals and about recommendations for appointment under subsection (1).

(3) A holder of the office of Senior President of Tribunals must, in carrying out the functions of that office, have regard to—

(a) the need for tribunals to be accessible,

(b) the need for proceedings before tribunals—

(i) to be fair, and

(ii) to be handled quickly and efficiently,

(c) the need for members of tribunals to be experts in the subject-matter of, or the law to be applied in, cases in which they decide matters, and

(d) the need to develop innovative methods of resolving disputes that are of a type that may be brought before tribunals.

(4) In subsection (3) "tribunals" means—

(a) the First-tier Tribunal,

(b) the Upper Tribunal,

(c) employment tribunals,

(d) the Employment Appeal Tribunal, ...

7 Chambers: jurisdiction and Presidents

(1) The Lord Chancellor may, with the concurrence of the Senior President of Tribunals, by order make provision for the organisation of each of the First-tier Tribunal and the Upper Tribunal into a number of chambers.

(2) There is—

(a) for each chamber of the First-tier Tribunal, and
(b) for each chamber of the Upper Tribunal,

to be a person, or two persons, to preside over that chamber.

(3) A person may not at any particular time preside over more than one chamber of the First-tier Tribunal and may not at any particular time preside over more than one chamber of the Upper Tribunal (but may at the same time preside over one chamber of the First-tier Tribunal and over one chamber of the Upper Tribunal).

(4) A person appointed under this section to preside over a chamber is to be known as a Chamber President.

(5) Where two persons are appointed under this section to preside over the same chamber, any reference in an enactment to the Chamber President of the chamber is a reference to a person appointed under this section to preside over the chamber.

(6) The Senior President of Tribunals may (consistently with subsections (2) and (3)) appoint a person who is the Chamber President of a chamber to preside instead, or to preside also, over another chamber.

(7) The Senior President may (consistently with subsections (2) and (3)) appoint a person who is not a Chamber President to preside over a chamber.

(8) Schedule 4 (eligibility for appointment under subsection (7), appointment of Deputy Chamber Presidents and Acting Chamber Presidents, assignment of judges and other members of the First-tier Tribunal and Upper Tribunal, and further provision about Chamber Presidents and chambers) has effect.

(9) Each of the Lord Chancellor and the Senior President of Tribunals may, with the concurrence of the other, by order—

(a) make provision for the allocation of the First-tier Tribunal's functions between its chambers;
(b) make provision for the allocation of the Upper Tribunal's functions between its chambers;
(c) amend or revoke any order made under this subsection.

8 Senior President of Tribunals: power to delegate

(1) The Senior President of Tribunals may delegate any function he has in his capacity as Senior President of Tribunals—

(a) to any judge, or other member, of the Upper Tribunal or First-tier Tribunal;
(b) to staff appointed under section 40(1).

(1A) A function under paragraph 1(1) or 2(1) of Schedule 2 may be delegated under subsection (1) only to a Chamber President of a chamber of the Upper Tribunal.

(2) Subsection (1) does not apply to functions of the Senior President of Tribunals under [seven specific provisions].

(3) A delegation under subsection (1) is not revoked by the delegator's becoming incapacitated.

(4) Any delegation under subsection (1) that is in force immediately before a person ceases to be Senior President of Tribunals continues in force until varied or revoked by a subsequent holder of the office of Senior President of Tribunals.

(5) The delegation under this section of a function shall not prevent the exercise of the function by the Senior President of Tribunals.

Ministry of Justice, *Transforming Tribunals: Implementing Part 1 of the Tribunals, Courts and Enforcement Act 2007*

(2007), paras 141–3, 146, 157–8, 160–4, 227–8, 230–2

The Senior President's Functions

141 The functions of the Senior President are set out in the 2007 Act. These will be commenced when the new tribunal structures are populated with judges, members and jurisdictions. The principal functions will include:

- responsibility for representing the views of tribunal judiciary to Parliament and Ministers
- responsibility, within the resources provided by the Lord Chancellor, for the maintenance of appropriate arrangements for the training; guidance and welfare of judges and other members of the First-tier and Upper Tribunals as well as those of the AIT, ET and EAT (for which purpose he shares mutual duties of co-operation with the Lord Chief Justices of England and Wales, and of Northern Ireland, and the Lord President
- concurrence (with the Lord Chancellor) in relation to the chambers structure for the First-tier Tribunal and the Upper Tribunal, the allocation of functions between chambers, and the making of orders prescribing the qualifications required for appointment of members of the First-tier Tribunal and the Upper Tribunal
- assigning judges and members to chambers, for which purpose he is required to publish a policy agreed with the Lord Chancellor
- reporting to the Lord Chancellor in relation to tribunal cases on matters which the Senior President wishes to bring to the attention of the Lord Chancellor and matters which the Lord Chancellor has asked the Senior President to cover
- requesting court judges (with the agreement of the relevant chief justice) to act as a judge of the First-tier or Upper Tribunal
- taking oaths of allegiance and judicial oaths (or nominating someone to do so) from tribunal judges and other members, and
- acting as (or nominating) a member of the Tribunal Procedure Committee (it is expected that the Senior President or his nominee will chair the Committee).

142 Many of the responsibilities described above are completely new (for example those in relation to the organisation of the First-tier and Upper Tribunals), but judicial heads of the existing tribunal jurisdictions may already undertake many of these functions. The 2007 Act brings them together under the Senior President (subject to a power to delegate), but gives them a statutory basis and imposes an obligation on the Lord Chancellor to provide the necessary resources.

143 ... [T]he Lord Chief Justice can already delegate to [the Senior President of Tribunals] certain functions in relation to judicial discipline and complaints under the CRA and the Judicial Discipline (Prescribed Procedures) Regulations 2006. The provisions in the 2007 Act make those functions delegable to the Senior President of Tribunals. The Lord Chief Justice's role in relation to tribunal appointments under the CRA remains unchanged ...

Training

146 The Senior President is responsible for maintaining appropriate arrangements for judicial training. His Judicial Office, the Tribunals Service and the Judicial Studies Board will work together to devise and maintain these arrangements, having particular regard to the value of shared training where there is sufficient in common, such as with general tribunal practice and judicial leadership. Common proposals for appraisal of judicial members will also be developed.

...

Deployment of Judges and Non-Legal Members

157 The deployment of judges is a judicial matter. Under the 2007 Act the Senior President will have oversight of the process and, with Chamber Presidents, will determine the role of individual judges and members within the tribunal system.

158 Legally qualified and non-legal members of existing tribunals will be transferred into the new generic offices of 'judge of the First-tier Tribunal' and 'member of the First-tier Tribunal'. Judges and members will initially be assigned to Chambers on the basis of their previous tribunal-specific appointments. This may mean that those who held several tribunal appointments may be assigned to more than one Chamber …

'Ticketing'

160 It will be for the Chamber Presidents to decide how best to use the judges and members *within* a Chamber in order to match their experience and expertise to the needs of the Chamber.

161 Judges and members will be given a 'ticket' by the Chamber President indicating their suitability to sit in a particular jurisdiction. This will be subject to business need, and before being allowed to sit in additional jurisdictions within the Chamber, judges and members will require training and induction in areas with which they are unfamiliar (this may, for example, include training to enable them to deal effectively with cultural differences, where these are relevant to the decisions they have to take). There will be some jurisdictions which generate comparatively few cases and where it will be necessary for cases to be dealt with by a more limited number of judges and members. But as Chambers will group similar subject matter and skills together there is an expectation that, over time, judges and members will increase the number of 'tickets' they hold, widening the pool of expertise within their Chambers.

Assignment

162 A decision as to whether a judge or member should sit in a *different* Chamber follows a different process, known as assignment. It is important to bear in mind that the 2007 Act introduces the concept of appointment to a generic office of judge or member. This is different to the historical position of appointment to a particular jurisdiction. The assignment process will thus allow those judges and members appointed through the JAC [Judicial Appointments Commission] to be deployed to a number of Chambers where the need arises.

163 Assignment will only take place with the consent of the Chamber President and the individual judge or member. The actual process for assignment may depend on whether the assignment is to meet a long or short term need.

164 Under the 2007 Act the Senior President is required to publish a document, to which the Lord Chancellor has to agree, setting out his policy on assignment. The overriding principles will be:

- that the judge or member has the necessary skills and ability to hear cases within the Chamber to which they are assigned
- that the assignment process is open and transparent
- that assignment will be based on merit, with a link to judicial appraisal where appropriate
- that the assignment process will not be used for promotion. Promotion opportunities will be advertised and subject to the JAC processes, and
- that, subject to business need, the process must also balance opportunities for judges and members to develop their judicial careers while at the same time retaining their skills and expertise.…

Appointments and Tribunal Composition

227 In future, members of the First-tier Tribunal will be appointed under paragraph 2(1) of Schedule 2 to the 2007 Act, and to the Upper Tribunal under paragraph 2(1) of Schedule 3. Members of the

Asylum and Immigration Tribunal and the Employment Tribunals will become *ex officio* members of the First-tier Tribunal by virtue of sections 4(3)(c) and (d) … Similarly, members of the Employment Appeal Tribunal and the AIT will become *ex officio* members of the Upper Tribunal (by virtue of section 5(2) (c) and (d)). It is these provisions that will allow members to be pooled together and deployed across jurisdictions in the same way as tribunal judges. However, there is no general expectation that *ex officio* members will automatically sit on cases—they will only sit if requested to do so by the Senior President.

228 Under the 2007 Act the general rules on composition of tribunals for hearings will be laid down by an order or orders made by the Lord Chancellor, with the concurrence of the Senior President and subject to Parliamentary approval. The 2007 Act also allows the Lord Chancellor to delegate his duty in relation to regulating tribunal composition to the Senior President or to a Chamber President. The government considers it important to identify what principles should underlie tribunal composition and the orders to be made …

230 The government intends to map existing tribunal non-legal members into the new roles in a way which maximises the opportunity for their flexible use in appeals. The overriding principle will be that the use of non-legal members on a particular hearing should bring to the table skills, experience or knowledge that tribunal judges cannot provide (in certain employment tribunal cases, for example, there can arguably be circumstances in which little value is added by their presence. However, there is a clear body of opinion in support of their use in more complex cases).

231 To put that overriding principle into practice the government intends that the order stipulating tribunal composition will reflect the following:

- The maximum number hearing a case is three.
- Hearings with more than one judge are appropriate only where there is a significant question of law to be considered, or for training purposes.
- In tribunals of two the Chair has the deciding vote.
- Non-legal members are there to provide expertise. They should therefore be deployed selectively on the basis of the needs of the case following the Leggatt principle set out above. The needs of the case include the likely skills and understanding of the parties.
- Expertise comes in many forms: it is not confined to those with professional qualifications.
- Analytical and chairing skills are not confined to judges, so non-legal members may be able to chair hearings or conduct cases alone.
- Non-legal experts can and should be used outside formal hearings, such as by providing reports or chairing meetings of expert witnesses or advising generally, subject always to the rules of natural justice.
- Tribunal composition is not to change during a hearing except with the consent of the parties.
- Case management arrangements need to be in place to ensure that composition is geared to the needs of the individual case.

232 The government intends that the order will set a default position close to the present rules for the composition of existing tribunals but, in line with the principles above, it will also provide for a general discretion to order a tribunal to be composed in a different way for a particular hearing. It may also provide for non-legal expertise to be brought to bear in ways other than sitting in a hearing—for instance, by providing an independent examination and report or by leading a discussion between expert witnesses. If expertise is being provided in this way it would be open to the judiciary to conclude that the presence of the expert at a hearing was not always necessary.

NOTES

1. The Senior President has a crucial role and this is reflected in the arrangements for appointment which can be either by (a) agreement amongst the Lord Chancellor, the Lord Chief Justice of England and Wales, the Lord President of the Court of Session and the Lord Chief Justice of Northern Ireland on a Lord or Lady Justice of Appeal or a member of the Inner House of the Court

of Session, or (b) in the absence of such agreement the Lord Chancellor asks the JAC to select someone for recommendation for appointment. The eligibility criteria for the Senior President are the same as those for a Lord or Lady Justice of Appeal and the JAC process to be followed is that which would be used to appoint a Head of Division of the High Court with appropriate modifications.

2. Similarly, Chamber Presidents have an important role, and it appears that the Senior President will rely on them to manage the work of their chambers. The appointment process, as with that for the Senior President, may be one in which there is consensus about a person from a defined group of judges, or be a recommendation following a selection process organized by the JAC. If the former, a candidate is a member of the High Court or the Court of Session, or in Northern Ireland the High Court and the Court of Appeal, who would be nominated by the relevant Chief Justice and the Senior President would be consulted by the Lord Chancellor.

3. The involvement of the Lord Chancellor in various functions alongside the Senior President provides for accountability, as in the policy for assigning tribunal judges and members to chambers other than the one to which they were appointed, but the allocation of tribunal members to hear particular cases is a matter solely for judicial leadership. Examples of the flexibility afforded by the statute include judges of the (a) Upper Tribunal, with some in the Administrative Appeals Chamber, sitting in cases heard by the Immigration and Asylum Chamber where welfare benefits are at issue and (b) First-tier Tribunal, with judges in the Immigration and Asylum Chamber, assigned to the Health, Education, and Social Care Chamber, and ticketed to the Special Educational Needs and Disability jurisdiction in the busiest period of April and July due to the need to resolve matters before children join new schools in September.

4. In September 2016 the Ministry of Justice opened a consultation on various matters arising out of the reform programme *Transforming our justice system* (see later in this chapter in Section 3E at p. 684). The proposals included one to give the Senior President of Tribunals

> greater freedom to adopt a more proportionate and flexible approach to panel composition, by:
>
> - Providing that a tribunal panel in the First-tier Tribunal is to consist of a single member unless otherwise determined by the SPT; and
> - Removing the existing requirement to consider the arrangements that were in place before the tribunal transferred into the unified system.

It is stated that the aim is to allow the Senior President of Tribunals to

> be able to consider more flexible allocation of the important specialist resource provided by non-legal members. For example, they could be used as a pool of specialist experts who could be deployed across various Chambers and jurisdictions who would benefit from their expertise, answering specific queries from judges or helping people work through the process by sharing their skills and knowledge.
>
> This would facilitate another of the aims of the reform which is using technology to support innovation 'with a greater focus on online engagement and ongoing conversation outside of traditional hearings between the parties and the tribunal.'

C: Appeals and judicial review

Ministry of Justice, *Transforming Tribunals: Implementing Part 1 of the Tribunals, Courts and Enforcement Act 2007*

(2007), paras 177–9

> 177 The creation of the Upper Tribunal is probably the most significant innovation in the tribunal system. The need to rationalise the hotchpotch of appeal routes from administrative tribunals has been highlighted by a number of reports, including the Law Commission report on Administrative Law, the Woolf report on Civil Justice, and the Leggatt report. The present arrangements are illogical and incoherent, reflecting the piecemeal historical development of the tribunal system. Appeals routes

from first instance tribunals in England and Wales vary between specialised tribunals, the High Court (Administrative Court or Chancery Division), and the Court of Appeal. In some cases there is no statutory right of appeal, but judicial review provides an alternative remedy in the Administrative Court; or judicial review may be required to fill the gaps in a restricted statutory scheme. There are similar variations in the form and nature of the appeal, for example: whether on law only, or on law and fact; whether leave is required; and whether the procedure is primarily oral or written.

178 The creation of the Upper Tribunal provides the opportunity not only to rationalise the procedures, but also to establish a strong and dedicated appellate body at the head of the new system. Its authority will derive from its specialist skills, and its status as a superior court of record, with judicial review powers, presided over by the Senior President. It is expected that the Upper Tribunal will come to play a central, innovative and defining role in the new system, enjoying a position in the judicial hierarchy at least equivalent to that of the Administrative Court in England and Wales. The government expects it to benefit from the participation of senior judges from the courts in all parts of the United Kingdom. Appeal from the Upper Tribunal will be to the Court of Appeal with permission. The Lord Chancellor intends to exercise his power to prescribe that such appeals in England and Wales will only be permitted in cases of general importance or for other special reason (as for second appeals from the courts).

179 The structure of the Upper Tribunal will need to reflect the variety of jurisdictions within its remit. It will work alongside the existing dedicated appeal systems, respectively, for asylum and immigration and for employment. These will continue as separate pillars of the new structure, each presided over by a High Court judge, but under the general supervision of the Senior President.

Tribunals, Courts and Enforcement Act 2007

18 Limits of jurisdiction under section 15(1)

(1) This section applies where an application made to the Upper Tribunal seeks (whether or not alone)—

    (a) relief under section 15(1), or
    (b) permission (or, in a case arising under the law of Northern Ireland, leave) to apply for relief under section 15(1).

(2) If Conditions 1 to 4 are met, the tribunal has the function of deciding the application.
(3) If the tribunal does not have the function of deciding the application, it must by order transfer the application to the High Court.
(4) Condition 1 is that the application does not seek anything other than—

    (a) relief under section 15(1);
    (b) permission (or, in a case arising under the law of Northern Ireland, leave) to apply for relief under section 15(1);
    (c) an award under section 16(6);
    (d) interest;
    (e) costs.

(5) Condition 2 is that the application does not call into question anything done by the Crown Court.
(6) Condition 3 is that the application falls within a class specified for the purposes of this subsection in a direction given in accordance with Part 1 of Schedule 2 to the Constitutional Reform Act 2005 (c. 4).
(7) The power to give directions under subsection (6) includes—

    (a) power to vary or revoke directions made in exercise of the power, and
    (b) power to make different provision for different purposes.

(8) Condition 4 is that the judge presiding at the hearing of the application is either—

(a) a judge of the High Court or the Court of Appeal in England and Wales or Northern Ireland, or a judge of the Court of Session, or

(b) such other persons as may be agreed from time to time between the Lord Chief Justice, the Lord President, or the Lord Chief Justice of Northern Ireland, as the case may be, and the Senior President of Tribunals.

(9) Where the application is transferred to the High Court under subsection (3)—

(a) the application is to be treated for all purposes as if it—
(i) had been made to the High Court, and
(ii) sought things corresponding to those sought from the tribunal, and

(b) any steps taken, permission (or leave) given or orders made by the tribunal in relation to the application are to be treated as taken, given or made by the High Court.

(10) Rules of court may make provision for the purpose of supplementing subsection (9)....

19 Transfer of judicial review applications from High Court

...

(3) Where an application is transferred to the Upper Tribunal under 31A of the Senior Courts Act 1981 (c. 54) or section 25A of the Judicature (Northern Ireland) Act 1978 (transfer from the High Court of judicial review applications)—

(a) the application is to be treated for all purposes as if it—
(b) had been made to the tribunal, and
(c) sought things corresponding to those sought from the High Court,

(4) Where—

(a) an application for permission is transferred to the Upper Tribunal under section 31A of the Senior Courts Act 1981 (c. 54) and the tribunal grants permission, or

(b) an application for leave is transferred to the Upper Tribunal under section 25A of the Judicature (Northern Ireland) Act 1978 (c. 23) and the tribunal grants leave, the tribunal has the function of deciding any subsequent application brought under the permission or leave, even if the subsequent application does not fall within a class specified under section 18(6).

(5) Tribunal Procedure Rules may make further provision for the purposes of supplementing subsections (3) and (4).

NOTES
1. Sections 9 and 10 allow for the First-tier and Upper Tribunals to review their own decisions without the need for an appeal. If the tribunals decide that there was an accidental error in the record or the reasoning then this may be corrected or the decision may be set aside. If a decision is set aside the tribunal may re-decide the matter or if it is the First-tier Tribunal it may refer it to the Upper Tribunal. Review may be instigated by the tribunal itself or by a party who has a right of appeal.
2. A party has, under s. 11, a right to an appeal on a point of law from the First-tier Tribunal to the Upper Tribunal. Permission to appeal is required from either the First-tier Tribunal or the Upper Tribunal. Some decisions are excluded from appeal under s. 11(5) and include: appeals against decisions on reviews in relation to criminal injuries compensation; appeals against national security certificates under the Data Protection Act 1998 and the Freedom of Information Act 2000; a decision by the First-tier Tribunal under s. 9 to review or not to review, to take or not take any action in the light of an earlier review, or to refer or not to refer a decision to the Upper Tribunal; and any decision of the First-tier Tribunal of a description specified in an order made by the Lord Chancellor.
3. On appeal the Upper Tribunal must set aside the decision if it finds an error of law and may remit to the First-tier Tribunal with directions for reconsideration, or make the decision which should

have been made. If the Upper Tribunal finds that the error does not invalidate the decision then it may let the decision stand.

4. Under s. 13 there may be an appeal to the relevant appellate court, Court of Appeal, Court of Session, Court of Appeal of Northern Ireland. Permission is required from the Upper Tribunal or the relevant appellate court specified by the Upper Tribunal. Some decisions are excluded from appeal replicating those in s. 11(5) substituting Upper for First-tier Tribunal (see note 2, earlier).

5. The 'revolutionary' jurisdiction conferred on the Upper Tribunal is that of judicial review. Section 15 confers this jurisdiction on the Upper Tribunal and s. 19 allows for the transfer of judicial review applications from the High Court (s. 21 from the Court of Session). The Upper Tribunal, where it has jurisdiction, will be able to grant the same relief as if it were the High Court (Court of Session in Scotland) applying the same principles of judicial review in relation to permission, sufficient interest in the matter, delay in applying and grant of remedy. Where the Upper Tribunal makes a quashing order under s. 15(1) it may remit the matter to body which made the decision or substitute its own decision. The power to substitute its own decision is conditional on the decision in question having been made by a court or tribunal, the decision was quashed on the ground of error of law and, without the error, there is only one decision the court or tribunal could have made.

6. Section 19(1) inserts s. 31A in to the Senior Courts Act 1981 specifying the condition for required and discretionary transfer of judicial review applications to the Upper Tribunal. Section 19(2) and, ss 20 and 21 provide for Northern Ireland and Scotland respectively. A Practice Direction (2009) specifies two classes of judicial review cases which should be transferred from the Administrative Court to the Upper Tribunal. They are (1) any decision of the First-tier Tribunal concerning criminal injuries compensation, in respect of which there is no right of appeal to the Upper Tribunal and (2) any decision of the First-tier Tribunal for which there is no right of appeal. These do not apply if a declaration of incompatibility is sought under the Human Rights Act 1998. A second Practice Direction (2012) provides for certain immigration and asylum cases coming within the Upper Tribunal's judicial review jurisdiction.

7. The Supreme Court has held in *R (Cart)* v *Upper Tribunal* [2011] UKSC 28, that the Upper Tribunal is itself amenable to judicial review of its unappealable decision to refuse to allow permission to appeal to it from the First-tier Tribunal on limited grounds which are (a) that it would raise some important point of principle or practice; or (b) that there is some other compelling reason for the relevant appellate court to review the case. These criteria are drawn from second-tier appeals which apply to appeals on a point of law from the Upper Tribunal to the Court of Appeal in England and Wales, and also apply in Scotland and Northern Ireland, and were originally directed to regulate appeals to the Court of Appeal following a first appeal to the county court or High Court in England and Wales (Access to Justice Act 1999, s. 55). As Lady Hale SCJ said at para. 51:

> ... the adoption of the second-tier appeals criteria would be a rational and proportionate restriction upon the availability of judicial review of the refusal by the Upper Tribunal of permission to appeal to itself. It would recognize that the new and in many ways enhanced tribunal structure deserves a more restrained approach to judicial review than has previously been the case, while ensuring that important errors can still be corrected.

See M. Elliot and R. Thomas, 'Tribunal Justice and Proportionate Dispute Resolution' (2012) 71 *Cambridge Law Journal*, 297–324.

SECTION 3: **TRIBUNALS AND DISPUTE RESOLUTION**

A: **Tribunal caseload statistics**

Table 13.1 shows the volume of cases which is rising again after a significant fall.

Table 13.1 Receipts and Disposals by Jurisdiction

	Receipts			Disposals		
Financial Years	2013/14	2014/15	2015/16	2013/14	2014/15ʳ	2015/16
Tribunals Overall	**699838**	**360842**	**408315**	**876775**	**648186**	**372225**
First Tier Tribunal (Immigration and Asylum Chamber)[1,2]	104996	91627	76857	100122	91421	69696
Upper Tribunal (Immigration and Asylum Chamber)[1,3]	7712	9202	7964	8902	8654	8068
UTIAC Judicial Reviews[3,4]	7841	15179	15727	2324	15084	19192
Employment Tribunals Total	105803	61308	83032	148387	312773	49391
Single	34219	16420	16986	42165	18839	15250
Multiple	71584	44888	66046	106222	293934	34141
Employment Appeal	1721	1207	970	1684	1406	1055
Social Security and Child Support	401896	112082	157180	543609	150978	156535
Upper Tribunal (Administrative Appeals Chamber)	7040	7371	4603	6968	7462	5359
Mental Health	30701	32101	33067	31614	31971	33286
Land Registration[5]	1203	959	987	1231	1141	894
Agricultural Land and Drainage[5]	194	169	146	211	167	131
Professional Regulation[5,6]	0	6	26	0	-	26
Asylum Support	1306	1103	1984	1211	1182	1761
Care Standards	162	160	191	142	163	161
Charity[5]	19	30	14	17	27	15
Claims Management Services	3	1	4	4	1	2
Community Right To Bid[5]	12	22	27	8	18	12
Consumer Credit[5]	14	2	0	21	4	4
Copyright Licensing[7]	..	0	0	0	-	-
Criminal Injuries Compensation	1941	1463	1332	2655	2495	1232

(continued)

Table 13.1 Continued

Financial Years	Receipts			Disposals		
	2013/14	2014/15	2015/16	2013/14	2014/15[r]	2015/16
Electronic Communications & Postal Services[8]	..	0	0	0	-	-
Environment[5]	0	0	11	25	-	6
Estate Agents[5]	2	8	5	2	5	4
Examination Board[5]	..	0	0	0	-	-
Financial Services and Markets & Pensions Regulator	19	13	21	10	17	20
Food[9]	0	0	0	0	-	-
Immigration Services	14	13	13	10	21	14
Gambling Appeals	4	5	1	4	7	1
Gangmasters Licensing Appeals[5]	25	24	8	18	24	21
Gender Recognition Panel	311	336	374	371	283	375
Individual Electoral Registration[10]	..	0	0	..	-	-
Information Rights	295	374	321	278	361	343
Upper Tribunal (Lands)	624	685	633	696	658	799
Local Government Standards in England[5]	0	0	0	1	-	-
Pensions Regulation[11]	..	0	42	..	-	19
Primary Health Lists[5]	34	58	51	40	61	48
Reserve Forces Appeal Tribunals[5]	6	6	3	7	1	7
Residential Property Tribunals[5]	9597	10005	8914	9608	9292	10377
Special Commissioners (Income Tax)[12]	..	..	0	..	..	-
Special Educational Needs and Disability	4155	3734	3236	3615	3631	3141
First tier Tax Chamber[5]	9291	8282	7386	10227	5846	7083
Transport[13]	360	395	409	387	334	450
Upper Tribunal (Tax & Chancery)[14]	267	398	288	200	338	371
VAT & Duties[12]	..	..	0	..	..	-

Table 13.1 Continued

	Receipts			Disposals		
Financial Years	2013/14	2014/15	2015/16	2013/14	2014/15ʳ	2015/16
War Pensions and Armed Forces Compensation Chamber	2264	2514	2490	2166	2360	2314
Welfare of Animals[15]	..	0	0	..	-	-

Source: Tribunals Quarterly and Annual reconciled returns

Notes
1) The 'First Tier Tribunal Immigration and Asylum Chamber' and 'Upper Tribunal Immigration and Asylum Chamber' (FTTIAC and UTIAC), replaced the Asylum and Immigration Tribunal (AIT) on 15 February 2010.
2) Figures for 2009/10 relate to appeals dealt with by Immigration Judges at the AIT or FTTIAC.
3) The Upper Tribunal, Immigration and Asylum Chamber decides applications for judicial review of certain decisions made by the Secretary of State for the Home Department, entry clearance officers and others, under immigration legislation, since November 2013.
4) All figures for UTIAC Judicial Reviews have been revised to include cases which took place in regional courts (Q3 2014/15).
5) Prior to 2010/11 Employment Appeal Tribunal disposals exclude appeals rejected, struck out or withdrawn prior to registration.
6) Historic disposal figures for Social Security and Child Benefit have been revised. Please see Revisions section (Annex A) in publication for more details.
7) Details of those Tribunals that have become part of HMCTS or changed name are detailed in Table B.1.
8) Formerly Alternative Business Structures.
9) From April 2014. Hears appeals against decisions made by the Secretary of State for Business Innovation and Skills under the Copyright (Regulation of Relevant Licensing Bodies) Regulations 2014.
10) From April 2013. Hears appeals against decisions made by the Interception of Communications Commissioner under the Regulation of Investigatory Powers (Monetary Penalty Notices and Consents for Interceptions) Regulations 2011.
11) The food jurisdiction of the General Regulatory Chamber was established in January 2013 and hears appeals against decisions taken by these certain regulators
13) From October 2014. New legislation requires individuals to register to vote rather than relying on a member of the household registering for all household members. The Tribunals hears appeals against the issuing of a penalty notice by an Electoral Registration Officer.
13) From January 2015. Hears appeals against decisions made under the Pension Schemes Act 2015.
14) The VAT and Duties, and Special Commissioners (Income Tax) tribunals were replaced by the first tier Tax Chamber and Upper Tribunal (Tax Chamber), see Table B.1.
15) Includes appeals against decisions of the Registrar of Approved Driving Instructors and Traffic Commissioner appeals (heard by the Upper Tribunal (Administrative Appeals Chamber)).
.. Not available
- zero
r = figures have been revised as part of an annual reconciliation

B: Tribunal characteristics

Tribunals as 'court substitutes' were thought to have some advantages over the courts because of their characteristics. These were identified in the Franks Report.

Report of the Committee on Administrative Tribunals and Enquiries
Cmnd 218, 1957, paras 40–2, 62–4, 71–2, 76–7, 90

[See also paras 38–9, earlier in this chapter in Section 1 at pp. 652–3.]

40. Tribunals are not ordinary courts, but neither are they appendages of Government Departments. Much of the official evidence, including that of the Joint Permanent Secretary to the Treasury, appeared

to reflect the view that tribunals should properly be regarded as part of the machinery of administration, for which the Government must retain a close and continuing responsibility. Thus, for example, tribunals in the social services field would be regarded as adjuncts to the administration of the services themselves. We do not accept this view. We consider that tribunals should be regarded as machinery provided by Parliament for adjudication rather than as part of the machinery for administration. The essential point is that in all these cases Parliament has deliberately provided for a decision outside and independent of the Department concerned, either at first instance (for example, in the case of Rent Tribunals and the Licensing Authorities for Public Service and Goods Vehicles) or on appeal from a decision of a Minister or of an official in a special statutory position (for example a valuation officer or an insurance officer). Although the relevant statutes do not in all cases expressly enact that tribunals are to consist entirely of persons outside the Government service, the use of the term 'tribunal' in legislation undoubtedly bears this connotation, and the intention of Parliament to provide for the independence of tribunals is clear and unmistakeable.

The application of the principle of openness, fairness and impartiality

41. We have already expressed our belief, in Part 1, that Parliament in deciding that certain decisions should be reached only after a special procedure must have intended that they should manifest three basic characteristics: openness, fairness and impartiality. The choice of a tribunal rather than a Minister as the deciding authority is itself a considerable step towards the realisation of these objectives, particularly the third. But in some cases the statutory provisions and the regulations thereunder fall short of what is required to secure these objectives …

42. In the field of tribunals openness appears to us to require the publicity of proceedings and knowledge of the essential reasoning underlying the decisions; fairness to require the adoption of a clear procedure which enables parties to know their rights, to present their case fully and to know the case which they have to meet; and impartiality to require the freedom of tribunals from the influence, real or apparent, of Departments concerned with the subject-matter of their decisions.

…

Codes of procedure

62. Most of the evidence we have received concerning tribunals has placed great emphasis upon procedure, not only at the hearing itself but also before and after it. There has been general agreement on the broad essentials which the procedure, in this wider sense, should contain, for example provision for notice of the right to apply to a tribunal, notice of the case which the applicant has to meet, a reasoned decision by the tribunal and notice of any further right of appeal.

63. We agree that procedure is of the greatest importance and that it should be clearly laid down in a statute or statutory instrument. Because of the great variety of the purposes for which tribunals are established, however, we do not think it would be appropriate to rely upon either a single code or a small number of codes. We think that there is a case for greater procedural differentiation and prefer that the detailed procedure for each type of tribunal should be designed to meet the particular circumstances. …

Informality of atmosphere

64. There has been considerable emphasis, in much of the evidence we have received, upon the importance of preserving informality of atmosphere in hearings before tribunals, though it is generally conceded that in some tribunals, for example the Lands Tribunal, informality is not an over-riding necessity. We endorse this view, but we are convinced that an attempt which has been made to secure informality in the general run of tribunals has in some instances been at the expense of an orderly

procedure. Informality without rules of procedure may be positively inimical to right adjudication, since the proceedings may well assume an unordered character which makes it difficult, if not impossible, for the tribunal properly to sift the facts and weigh the evidence. It should be remembered that by their very nature tribunals may be less skilled in adjudication than courts of law. None of our witnesses would seek to make tribunals in all respects like courts of law, but there is a wide measure of agreement that in many instances their procedure could be made more orderly without impairing the desired informality of atmosphere. The object to be aimed at in most tribunals is the combination of a formal procedure with an informal atmosphere. We see no reason why this cannot be achieved. On the one hand it means a manifestly sympathetic attitude on the part of the tribunal and the absence of the trappings of a court, but on the other hand such prescription of procedure as makes the proceedings clear and orderly.

...

Knowledge of the case to be met

71. The second most important requirement before the hearing is that citizens should know in good time the case which they will have to meet. ...

72. We do not suggest that the procedure should be formalised to the extent of requiring documents in the nature of legal pleadings. What is needed is that the citizen should receive in good time beforehand a document setting out the main points of the opposing case. It should not be necessary and indeed in view of the type of person frequently appearing before tribunals it would in many cases be positively undesirable, to require the parties to adhere rigidly at the hearing to the case previously set out, provided always that the interests of another party are not prejudiced by such flexibility.

...

Public hearings

76. We have already said that we regard openness as one of the three essential features of the satisfactory working of tribunals. Openness includes the promulgation of reasoned decisions, but its most important constituent is that the proceedings should be in public. The consensus of opinion in the evidence received is that hearings before tribunals should take place in public except in special circumstances.

77. We are in no doubt that if adjudicating bodies, whether courts or tribunals, are to inspire that confidence in the administration of justice which is a condition of civil liberty they should, in general, sit in public. But just as on occasion the courts are prepared to try certain types of case wholly or partly *in camera* so, in the wide field covered by tribunals, there are occasions on which we think that justice may be better done, and the interests of the citizen better served, by privacy.

The Committee went on to outline three types of case: where considerations of public security are involved, where intimate personal or financial circumstances have to be disclosed, and where there are preliminary hearings involving professional capacity and reputation.

Evidence

90. Tribunals are so varied that it is impossible to lay down any general guidance on the requirement of evidence at hearings. In the more formal tribunals, for example, the Lands Tribunal, there seems no good reason why some of the rules of evidence as in courts of law should not apply. In the majority of tribunals, however, we think it would be a mistake to introduce the strict rules of evidence of the courts. The presence of a legally qualified chairman should enable the tribunal to attach the proper weight to such matters as hearsay and written evidence.

■ QUESTION

Are the Franks Committee's recommendations on the characteristics of tribunals consistent with its statement of the reasons for adjudication by tribunals rather than by the courts (see earlier in this chapter in Section 1 at p. 650)?

The Franks view of tribunals as part of the machinery of justice and not of the machinery of administration has been soundly criticized (see for example K. H. Hendry, 'The Tasks of Tribunals: Some Thoughts' (1982) 1 *Civil Justice Quarterly* 253) and as we shall see the Government's conception of dispute resolution views tribunals not solely as a means of securing justice but also of improving administration. The supposed advantages of the characteristics identified have also been challenged.

H. Genn, 'Tribunal Review of Administrative Decision-Making' in G. Richardson and H. Genn (eds), *Administrative Law and Government Action*

(1994), pp. 284–6

This chapter has attempted to show that there are considerable limits to the effectiveness of tribunals as a check on administrative decision-making and that these limitations stem at least in part from the design of tribunals and the low levels of representation at tribunals. In order for tribunals to act as an *effective* means of review they must be capable of conducting an accurate and fair review of administrative decisions. This requires time, expertise, and full information. It also requires that those who appear before tribunals are capable of understanding the relevance of regulations and the basis of their entitlement, and can provide relevant information and evidence of facts, largely without the benefit of advice or representation.

Given the weakness of first-line administrative decision-making, tribunals theoretically represent an important means of minimizing administrative injustice. However, evidence collected from recipients of adverse administrative decisions, although not conclusive, suggests that even when a relatively straightforward mechanism exists for review of decisions the opportunity is not taken because those affected may assume that the original decision was 'correct' or that it is unlikely to be changed. Thus, even if tribunal hearings provided perfect conditions for effective review of administrative decisions, they could only every afford a partial corrective to poor decision-making and administrative injustice. In practice, however, from the perspective of tribunal applicants, the conditions that operate in many tribunals are far from perfect. Despite their conventional characterization as informal, accessible, and non-technical, frequently tribunals are not particularly quick, there is considerable variation in the degrees of informality, and the issues dealt with are highly complex in terms of both the regulations to be applied and the factual situations of applicants. This study of tribunal processes and decision-making has highlighted the complexity of many areas of law with which tribunals must deal and the impact of this complexity on decision-making. Although tribunal procedures are generally more flexible and straightforward than court hearings, the nature of tribunal adjudication means that those who appear before tribunals without representation are often at a disadvantage. The short-comings of tribunals as effective checks on administrative decisions are the result of misdescription of procedures as informal and misconceptions about simple decision-making and the scope for unrepresented applicants to prepare, present, and advocate convincing cases.

The analysis of factors influencing the outcome of tribunal hearings suggests that increased advice and representation for applicants, and improved training and monitoring of tribunals, would be likely to increase the rate at which cases reviewed at tribunal hearings were allowed. This may not, of course, be the desired objective. It has been argued that tribunals were never intended to act as 'effective review mechanisms' and that their primary role is to provide a cloak of legitimacy for unpopular social regulation. If, however, there is a genuine intention that tribunals should provide a check on administrative decision-making, rather than merely providing a forum in which disappointed and disgruntled applicants can let off steam, their deficiencies must be addressed. It is not sufficient to assume or to assert that tribunals operate well. In order to achieve their theoretical objectives and to attain the qualities claimed for tribunals, consideration must be given to their procedures and to standards of tribunal adjudication. Finally, and most importantly, explicit attention must be paid to the means by which a balance can be struck between the conflicting demands of procedural simplicity and legal precision, in order to achieve substantive justice.

In the two extracts that follow conclusions are drawn from research on the users of tribunals. In the first extract Adler and Gulland have reviewed the research literature and in the second extract Genn et al.'s later study focuses upon the users of three tribunals: the Appeals Service (TAS) which dealt with social security and child support appeals; the Criminal Injuries Compensation Appeals Panel (CICAP); and the Special Educational Needs and Disability Tribunal (SENDIST).

M. Adler, J. Gulland, *Tribunal Users' Experiences, Perceptions and Expectations: A Literature Review*

(available at http://webarchive.nationalarchives.gov.uk/20100910235604/http://www.council-on-tribunals.gov.uk/docs/other_adler(2).pdf)

(2003), pp. 24–8

Practical barriers that prevent potential users from accessing tribunals

Most of the research on users' experiences looks at appellants rather than those who do not appeal. This means that most research is based on those who were *not* deterred by barriers that can prevent users from accessing the tribunal system and makes it difficult to gauge the full extent of these potential barriers.

Ignorance of rights or procedures

There are two types of ignorance which can prevent an appellant from making an appeal—ignorance of the fact that there may be grounds for appealing against the original decision and ignorance of the procedures which need to be followed. The general conclusion, supported by much of the research evidence, is that ignorance of the possible grounds of appeal is often more important than ignorance of procedures. Most appellants appear to have little understanding of the appeals procedure or the powers of tribunals but this does not, in itself, appear to be a barrier to appealing, since the procedures for appealing to most tribunals are fairly straight forward. Many researchers found that people appeal because they think the original decision s unjust, without necessarily understanding the legal basis for the decision or what their chances of success would be. There is, however, some variation between different tribunals.

Cost

There are five types of cost which can act as a deterrent for users: tribunal fees, the cost of advice and/or representation, the cost of obtaining independent assessments, the cost of attending a hearing and the risk of having costs awarded against them if they lose. Although cost is currently not an issue in most tribunals, a number of recent developments involving fees and awards of costs suggest that it may become more of an issue in future. There is little evidence from the research about whether the cost of representation acts as a barrier because most research has studied those who did appeal rather than those who did not. Non-financial costs (for example stress and time commitment) are also a concern for some appellants.

The complexity of the appeal process and absence of appropriate help

Research on many different tribunals makes it clear that many appellants are confused by the appeal process and have little idea of what will happen at a tribunal hearing. In some cases, they do not even realise that there will be a hearing and they are often confused by the paperwork they are sent. There are frequent references to the difficulties people find in obtaining advice about their appeals—this problem is especially acute in areas like child support and special educational needs where there is a shortage of specialist agencies that are able to provide representation. In addition, there is evidence that people often experience difficulties in accessing free sources of advice (such as Citizens Advice Bureaux) due to limited opening hours which necessitate taking time off work, waiting times for appointments, and difficulties in making telephone contact to arrange appointments. These are likely to disadvantage members of the public with 'low levels of competence in terms of education, income, confidence, verbal skills literacy skills and emotional fortitude' …

Physical barriers

There are a number of references to the difficulties faced by physically disabled appellants in accessing tribunal venues. Most of the research refers to the Appeals Service, i.e. to social security appeals but this is because there has been a good deal of research on appeals relating to disability benefits that has involved a high proportion of disabled appellants. On the other hand, there were favourable references to the use by the SENT of local hotels as venues since they can provide easy access for people with disabilities. Most other research on appeals has not looked specifically at appellants with disabilities, who, in most cases, constitute only a relatively small proportion of appellants.

    …

The balance between speed, quality and cost

There are many references in the literature to long delays before hearings are held and to the problems they cause, especially in social security appeals where people may have had their benefit stopped or reduced, in educational appeals where a delay can constitute a significant proportion of a child's school education and in mental health reviews where civil liberties are at stake. Even where appellants may appear to benefit from a delay, for example, in social security overpayments and asylum appeals, they may suffer because of the stress involved in waiting for a tribunal hearing. There does not appear to have been any research which has examined users' views about the optimum balance between speed, quality and cost.

Informality of hearings

There are many references to the fact that users find tribunals more formal than they had expected and to the problems that this sometimes causes. However, there are clearly substantial variations in formality, not only between different types of tribunal but also between different sittings (with different chairs) of the same tribunal. Some appellants confuse the formality of tribunal hearings with the fact that they are bound by legislation.

The value of representation

Most of the research concludes that appellants find it difficult to represent themselves. When people have the opportunity to be represented (because they are able to afford legal representation, because they are able to obtain legal aid, or because free lay representation is available) they tend to make use of it. Although some appellants choose to represent themselves, they often find that the process is more complex and legalistic than they had imagined and regret their decision afterwards. There is little research-based support for one of the central tenets of the Leggatt Report, namely that 'a combination of good quality information and advice, effective procedures and well-conducted hearings, and competent and well-trained tribunal members' would make it possible for 'the vast majority of appellants to put their cases properly themselves', i.e. without representation.

    …

Users' views on the independence and impartiality of tribunals

There is little research evidence to suggest that users question the independence or impartiality of tribunal proceedings. However, there are some exceptions to this general finding. Although the existence of strong 'outcome effects' confuses the issue, research indicates that some appellants feel that Employment tribunals are biased in favour of employers, that Rent Assessment Panels are biased in favour of landlords, that Exclusion Appeal Panels pre-judge cases and that Mental Health Review Tribunals are too dependent on the evidence of the RMO. Research also indicates that some appellants (particularly in social security and child support appeals) confuse the 'independence and impartiality' of tribunals with their duty to apply the law.

H. Genn, B. Lever, and L. Gray, *Tribunals For Diverse Users*
DCA Research Series 1/06, pp. ii–iii

Motivation and preparedness for tribunal hearings

A waiting room survey of tribunal users revealed that, across all ethnic groups, the principal motivation for appealing to tribunals was a sense of unfairness. Few users had known about the possibility of seeking redress from their general knowledge and in most cases information about the possibility of appealing to the tribunal had come from the initial decision letter sent by the Department or Authority.

Users' expectations of proceedings were relatively vague, with an unacceptably high proportion of users in TAS and CICAP not knowing what to expect. Some anticipated a judge and jury, others a friendly and informal chat. This presents a challenge to the new Tribunal Service in helping to prepare users for hearings so that they can present their cases effectively. In SENDIST, the practice of sending a video to users prior to their hearing appears to have been effective in framing users' expectations.

About half of the users interviewed at hearings were attending without representation, generally because it had not occurred to them to seek representation, or because they had tried and been unable to obtain representation. Unrepresented Minority Ethnic users attending hearings were more likely than White users to have tried and failed to obtain representation.

Delivering fair hearings

Observation of tribunal hearings revealed generally high levels of professionalism among tribunal judiciary, with most being able to combine authority with approachability. There were few examples of insensitive language and with rare exceptions tribunals treated users from all ethnic backgrounds with courtesy and respect. Tribunals used a wide range of techniques to enable users to participate effectively in hearings and to convey that they were listening to, and taking seriously, the user's case. Although, with the assistance of tribunals, most users were able to present their cases reasonably well, observation of users during hearings revealed deep and fundamental differences in language, literacy, culture, education, confidence and fluency, which traverse ethnic boundaries. These differences significantly affect users' ability to present their case. Even with the benefit of training, there are limits to the ability of tribunals to compensate for users' difficulties in presenting their case. In some circumstances, an advocate is not only helpful to the user and to the tribunal, but may be crucial to procedural and substantive fairness.

Users' assessments of hearings and outcome

Most users, interviewed after their hearing and before receiving their decision, made generally positive assessments of treatment during hearings and of their own ability to participate. Where dissatisfaction occurred, it tended to result from tribunals communicating the impression that they had already made up their mind or that they were not listening attentively to the user. This underlines the significance that users attach to feeling that they have been heard, that their arguments have been taken seriously and weighed by the tribunal. Lack of preparedness affected users' responses to the hearing and those startled by the relative formality of hearings tended to feel less comfortable and to express greater dissatisfaction. Despite users' generally positive assessments of hearings, about one in five, when prompted, raised concerns about perceived unfairness or lack of respect during the hearing. South Asian users and some other non-European users were consistently more negative than other groups in their assessments of hearings and were the most likely to perceive unfairness. Importantly, however, there was evidence that those Minority Ethnic groups most likely to perceive unfairness at hearings were less likely to do so when the tribunal was itself ethnically diverse. This suggests that increasing the ethnic diversity of tribunal panels might have a positive effect on perceptions of fairness among Minority Ethnic users.

Post-decision interviews revealed that about one-quarter of unsuccessful users had not understood the reason for the decision and this was more often the case among Minority Ethnic than White users. This presents a significant challenge to tribunals.

The outcome of tribunal hearings

Modelling the outcome of hearings in the three tribunals revealed that in TAS case type, representation and ethnic group independently influenced the outcome of hearings. Controlling for other factors, unrepresented TAS users were less likely to succeed at their hearing than represented TAS users and Minority Ethnic TAS users were slightly less likely to be successful at their hearing than White TAS users. By contrast, in CICAP and SENDIST only case type had a significant impact on the outcome of hearings, although the number of Minority Ethnic users in SENDIST is very small. Once case type had been controlled for, neither representation nor ethnic group appeared to affect outcome in either CICAP or SENDIST. The TAS outcome findings regarding representation and ethnicity raise some important questions.

Identifying the source of disadvantage that seems to flow from lack of representation and ethnicity would be valuable not only for TAS, but also more broadly for discussion about procedures and judicial training in other tribunals and in the courts. One clue may be that users' observed ability to argue their case was significantly associated with outcome at hearings. TAS users, who often come from among the most disadvantaged groups in society, were significantly less likely than CICAP or SENDIST users to present their cases well. This constitutes a general challenge to the enabling skills of TAS judiciary during relatively brief hearings, but in the case of some Minority Ethnic groups, language and cultural differences may present additional complications in enabling users to make the best of their case.

C: Alternative dispute resolution

These findings demonstrate that users did not find that some of the supposed advantages of tribunals over courts were realized. Despite the evidence suggesting that represented users are more successful than unrepresented users, Leggatt had recommended that users should normally be expected to present their cases themselves (para. 4.21). The Government took the view that users found oral hearings stressful and expounded a different strategy for people dealing with legal problems and disputes.

Transforming Public Services: Complaints, Redress and Tribunals
Cm 6243, 2004, paras 2.2–2.3, 2.11

2.2 … The aim is to develop a range of policies and services that, so far as possible, will help people to avoid problems and legal disputes in the first place; and where they cannot, provides tailored solutions to resolve the dispute as quickly and cost effectively as possible. It can be summed up as 'Proportionate Dispute Resolution'.

2.3 We want to:

- minimise the risk of people facing legal problems by ensuring that the framework of law defining people's rights and responsibilities is as fair, simple and clear as possible, and that State agencies, administering systems like tax and benefits, make better decisions and give clearer explanations;
- improve people's understanding of their rights and responsibilities, and the information available to them about what they can do and where they can go for help when problems do arise. This will help people to decide how to deal with the problem themselves if they can, and ensure they get the advice and other services they need if they cannot;
- ensure that people have ready access to early and appropriate advice and assistance when they need it, so that problems can be solved and potential disputes nipped in the bud long before they escalate into formal legal proceedings;
- promote the development of a range of tailored dispute resolution services, so that different types of dispute can be resolved fairly, quickly, efficiently and effectively, without recourse to the expense and formality of courts and tribunals where this is not necessary;
- but also deliver cost-effective court and tribunal services, that are better targeted on those cases where a hearing is the best option for resolving the dispute or enforcing the outcome.

One of the features of this new approach is the use of alternative dispute resolution methods.

2.11 There are a number of alternative dispute resolution (ADR) processes:

- adjudication involves an impartial, independent third party hearing the claims of both sides and issuing a decision to resolve the dispute. The outcome is determined by the adjudicator, not by the parties. Determinations are usually made on the basis of fairness, and the process used and means of decision-making are not bound by law. It can involve a hearing or be based on documents only;
- arbitration involves an impartial, independent third party hearing the claims of both sides and issuing a binding decision to resolve the dispute. The outcome is determined by the arbitrator, is final and legally binding, with limited grounds for appeal. It requires both parties' willing and informed consent to participate. It can involve a hearing or be based on documents only;
- conciliation involves an impartial third party helping the parties to resolve their dispute by hearing both sides and offering an opinion on settlement. It requires both parties' willing and informed consent to participate. The parties determine the outcome, usually with advice from the conciliator. An example is Acas conciliation;
- early neutral evaluation involves an independent person assessing the claims made by each side and giving an opinion on (a) the likely outcome in court or tribunal, (b) a fair outcome, and/or (c) a technical or legal point. It is non-binding, and the parties decide how to use the opinion in their negotiations. It requires both parties' willing and informed consent to participate. It can be useful to help moderate a party's unrealistic claims;
- mediation involves an independent third party helping parties to reach a voluntary, mutually agreed resolution. A key principle is that the parties, not the mediator, decide the outcome. It requires both parties' willing and informed consent to participate. It requires mediating skills, and it has a structured format;
- negotiation involves dealing directly with the person or the organisation in dispute. It is non-binding and can be done by the person in dispute or by a representative ('assisted negotiation'). The negotiator is not impartial but instead represents a party's interests. An example of negotiation is settlement discussions between solicitors; and
- ombudsmen are impartial, independent 'referees' who consider, investigate and resolve complaints about public and private organisations. Their decisions are made on the basis of what is fair and reasonable. They also have a role in influencing good practice in complaints handling.

M. Adler, 'Tribunal Reform: Proportionate Dispute Resolution and the Pursuit of Administrative Justice'

(2006) 69 *Modern Law Review* 958, 983–5

The ... White Paper is an ambitious document in that it sets out to turn on its head the Government's traditional emphasis on courts, judges and court procedure, and on legal aid to pay for litigation lawyers; to develop a range of policies and services that will help people to avoid problems and disputes in the first place; and to provide 'tailored solutions' to resolve disputes without necessarily seeking redress from a tribunal. In order to achieve these ends, it develops the principle of 'proportionate dispute resolution' and notes that, in order to put this principle into practice, the types of problems and disputes people have; the outcomes they wish to achieve; the various options available and the extent to which these options will promote administrative justice need to be considered. I have considered a number of policy options, each of which holds out the prospect of enhancing administrative justice, and my conclusions are summarised below.

As far as the types of problems and disputes people have are concerned, what is at issue is frequently contested by the parties in dispute—so called 'experts' think the issue about one thing while those who experienced the problem think it is about something else. However, I have pointed out that the distinctions invoked by the experts, e.g. between fact and law, rule and discretion, process and outcome, and law and policy, are more relevant to deciding how problems and disputes should be handled than the accounts of what is at issue that are given by those with grievances. It follows that more work needs to be done on refining a typology based on these 'top-down' distinctions. As far as the outcomes people wish to achieve are concerned, I have argued that it is by no means clear that it is always in the public interest that people's preferences should prevail. This is because those who just want an apology may have a strong legal case while those who seek a legal remedy may have a very weak case or no case at all. Thus, although there is a case for considering the remedies that people want, it may be in the public interest that cases are considered by a tribunal (or by a court or an ombudsman) so that there can be a clear and authoritative ruling on the issue in question. This outcome might be achieved if a 'one-door' approach, in which everyone who is dissatisfied with a decision or the way in which it was reached puts their concerns to an official who would then decide what kind of problem they have and directs them to the appropriate dispute resolution procedure.

I do not believe that effective external forms of accountability on their own will be sufficient to raise standards of first-instance decision making to acceptable levels and argue that effective internal forms of accountability, such as internal quality controls and quality assurance systems, are also required. I support the introduction of a 'one-door' approach, in which everyone who is dissatisfied with a decision, or with the way in which it is reached, would put their concerns to an official who would then decide what kind of problem they had and direct them to the appropriate dispute resolution procedure. This procedure ought to reduce the number of errors that individuals currently make when they select redress procedures for themselves.

It is my view that, if initial decisions were reviewed as a matter of routine by the line manager of the first-instance decision maker or by a specialist reviewing officer, many cases could probably be resolved at an early stage and I conclude that there is a very strong case for making departmental reviews mandatory. Although this would add to administrative costs, there would be administrative savings because, in the case of tribunals, there would be a reduction in the number of cases proceeding to a tribunal hearing. I argue that, providing the staff are of sufficient calibre, early-neutral evaluation would result in the identification of 'weak' cases on both sides and that, together with mandatory reviews of decisions that are complained about or appealed against, it would result in the 'filtering out' of a substantial proportion of the weak cases that are currently heard by tribunals. The costs of compulsory departmental review and early-neutral evaluation could be set against the savings, for government department or public bodies and the new Tribunals Service, which would result from a smaller number of tribunal hearings.

Because, in administrative disputes, citizens may settle for less than they are entitled to, I am somewhat skeptical about the contribution of mediation and conciliation (and likewise of negotiation) to the resolution of administrative disputes and I argue that tribunal hearings may be needed to protect the interests of the citizen. I am also, for different reasons, rather skeptical about the extent to which ombudsman techniques are transferable to many of the citizen versus state disputes that tribunals deal with and doubtful about whether the substitution of one mode of dispute resolution for another could be achieved in a smooth and orderly way. Thus, I conclude that the potential for mediation and conciliation, and for ombudsman techniques, in a tribunal system is rather limited. However, I do favour the provision of publicly-funded representation for appellants in second-tier appeal tribunals. I point out that, to the extent that cases are diverted from tribunals, the tribunal caseload should be smaller but argue that the need for representation in the smaller number of cases that still proceed to a tribunal hearing may actually be greater. Since this applies, in particular, to second-tier appeal tribunals, which will require leave and be limited to points of law, I conclude that there is a strong case for providing publicly-funded representation (not necessarily by lawyers) in such cases.

NOTES

1. Adler supports the use of internal review and early neutral evaluation. The Tribunals Service has undertaken two pilot projects in early dispute resolution. The first was conducted in three employment tribunal offices from August 2006 to July 2007. It involved a trained judicial member offering facilitative mediation with the aim of assisting the parties to resolve their dispute without the need for a hearing. Participation in this mediation was voluntary. There was a national roll out of judicial mediation before the publication of the evaluation which had not found it to be cost-effective and had not recommended a national roll out. See P. Urwin et al., *Evaluation of Early Neutral Evaluation Alternative Dispute Resolution in the Social Security and Child Support Tribunal* (Ministry of Justice Research Series 7/10, 2010).

   The second pilot examined whether a form of Early Neutral Evaluation can be effective as a means of dealing with some Disability Living Allowance and Attendance Allowance appeals. Here a designated judicial member assessed the case papers of appellants who had agreed to participate. The assessor formed a view on the likely outcome at hearing. The District Chairman then contacted the party who was assessed as the likely loser. If that was the Disability and Carers Service, they would be invited to reconsider the case. If it was the appellant then he or she was warned that the appeal would be likely to fail. Contact with the appellant might suggest that if the appellant had other evidence then it should be submitted, or advice should be sought, or focus put on the specific issues which the tribunal would need to consider. Thus, it was hoped, the weak cases would be discouraged or action taken to strengthen them. If the assessment was that the case was finely balanced then no contact was to be made with either party. The evaluation of this pilot found that 'Overall, therefore, there was evidence to conclude that ADR had achieved more proportionate resolution of cases to an extent but that it had impacted negatively on the speed of resolution of cases across the pilot as a whole'. This led to a recommendation to conduct a limited roll out and to adjust the procedure and monitor it. There has been no further action.

   (See C. Hay, K. McKennna, and T. Buck, *Evaluation of Early Neutral Evaluation Alternative Dispute Resolution in the Social Security and Child Support Tribunal* (Ministry of Justice Research Series 2/10, 2010).)

2. Concern about the rise of ADR has been expressed. One commentator notes the rise of informality and fears that it could create a transparency gap, 'There is a public, not merely a private interest in challenges brought by citizens against public authorities' (A. Le Sueur 'Administrative Justice and the Resolution of Disputes' in J. Jowell and D. Oliver (eds) *The Changing Constitution* (7th edn, 2011), p. 260 at 281). He is also concerned that parties might be compelled to use ADR.

3. Adler thinks that internal accountability mechanisms in administrative bodies such as quality assurance have to be supported by external mechanisms. Leggatt recommended that review

should be developed and supplemented by feedback from tribunals on systemic aspects of decision-making within departments (Ch. 9). The Government accepted this proposal, including it in the new approach to dispute resolution which would help departments to get decisions 'right first time' (Cm 6243, para. 6.32). The Senior President is required under s. 43 of the Tribunals, Courts and Enforcement Act 2007 to report annually to the Lord Chancellor on matters which he wishes to bring to the Lord Chancellor's attention and on matters which the Lord Chancellor has asked to be covered.

■ QUESTION

Bearing in mind the reservations of Adler and Le Sueur do you think there is (a) much scope for the use of the ADR in public law cases generally and tribunals in particular and (b) would the use of ADR be desirable?

D: Proportionate dispute resolution

Administrative Justice and Tribunals Council, *Putting it Right: A Strategic Approach to Resolving Administrative Disputes*
(2012), paras 11–12, 17–22

11. The 2004 White Paper *Transforming Public Services: Complaints, Redress and Tribunals* recognised the importance of an administrative justice system that is able to respond to the 'real world problems' faced by its users. The paper stated:

> *"The aim is to develop a range of policies and services that, so far as possible, will help people to avoid problems and legal disputes in the first place; and where they cannot, provides tailored solutions to resolve disputes as quickly and as cost efficiently as possible. It can be summed up as 'proportionate dispute resolution.'"*

12. The envisaged approach marked a move from the traditional focus on dispute *adjudication* by courts and tribunals to *resolution* of the dispute. This implies greater engagement with the parties in reaching a mutually accepted conclusion to the dispute rather than waiting for a judge to determine the matter one way or the other. Despite the approach being termed 'proportionate dispute resolution', it is as much about dispute avoidance and learning from mistakes as it is about resolution. Proportionate dispute resolution should therefore be seen as an end-to-end, whole system approach, not just as a collective name for techniques of dispute resolution.

...

The four-stage cycle of administrative justice

17. In 2009 the AJTC published a paper on 'The Developing Administrative Justice Landscape', which described the components of the administrative justice system. The paper suggested that the administrative justice system can be explained as a dynamic model, with links between its various components and stages, and used the following diagram to demonstrate its cyclical nature:

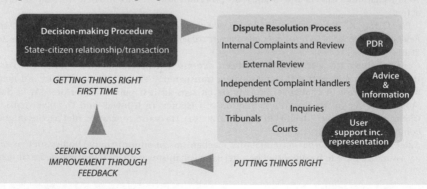

18. Building on this concept of the administrative justice system as a cycle, this report seeks to separate the cycle into four key stages.

Preventing disputes

19. The first stage comes pre-decision. It is easy to say that prevention is better than cure, but in the case of administrative justice prevention of a dispute still requires a significant effort and investment. Individuals must be able to understand their rights and entitlements and decision-makers must be trained to understand and to apply the applicable law, how to discover the relevant information and how to convey their decisions clearly. This relies on: the accessibility and clarity of legislation and regulations; the availability of information and guidance; and the investment in public education.

Reducing escalation of disputes

20. The second stage immediately follows the decision itself, aiming to avoid the escalation of the dispute to an external body. It is at this stage that individuals should be given the opportunity to raise a query, to correct an error or to ask for help in understanding the reasons for a decision without triggering a formal complaint or appeal process.

Resolving disputes

21. There will always be cases that cannot be avoided completely or resolved internally, and the third stage arises when an external organisation is involved in helping the parties to resolve a dispute. Some of the external organisations invoked will be statutory bodies, such as tribunals, and others will be non-statutory bodies that are nonetheless independent from the decision-making body itself. While some external organisations will be able to make binding decisions, others will not have that power. The procedure followed in some approaches will appear more or less formal than that in others. The dispute resolution methodologies that exist at stage three are diverse, and it is important that those seeking to improve the system build up a clear picture of which type of methodology is proportionate and appropriate to which type of case.

Learning from disputes

22. In a sense, gaining insight is not a discrete, final stage, as it should take place at each stage of the cycle. However, its importance requires that it be described separately, because in order to be effective, learning from the problems that arise must be seen as fundamental. Decision-makers and legislators need to understand where and why things went wrong and avoid the same mistake being made again and again. Information from decisions should be taken seriously so that insight is actively sought out and acted upon, and feedback systems should be embedded in organisations.

NOTES
1. In the AJTC's dispute cycle, the technique of internal or administrative review would be expected to be used at the second stage, that of reducing escalation of disputes through better communication for queries and corrections.

J Tomlinson and R. Thomas, *Administrative justice – A primer for policymakers and those working in the system*

(available at https://ukaji.org/2016/09/09/administrative-justice-a-primer-for-policymakers-and-those-working-in-the-system/)

2016 UKAJI

Different approaches to administrative review

There are different approaches to administrative review across government. There is no single coherent system of administrative review. "Administrative review" is an umbrella term for a variety of different processes e.g. mandatory reconsideration (operating in the social security context) and the various review systems in areas such as immigration, tax, FOI, homelessness, and criminal injuries compensation. However, administrative review will now handle more cases than tribunals and other forms of redress.

Examining the differences between three administrative review systems—those in tax, social security, and immigration—highlights divergent approaches to similar issues. These differences are set out in Figure 4. The different approaches show how different models can be deployed, and how different trade-offs can be made.

	Tax	Social Security	Immigration
Voluntary or mandatory?	AR is voluntary and alternative to tribunal appeal	Mandatory before tribunal appeal	AR has replaced many appeal rights
Who reviews?	AR undertaken by different decision-maker	AR undertaken by different decision-maker	AR undertaken by different decision-maker
Legal basis	Primary legislation	Secondary legislation	Immigration Rules and administrative guidance
Time limit for requesting review	30 day time-limit, unless reasonable excuse for late request	One month time-limit, with scope to extend for good reason	28 days for overseas decisions; 14 days for decisions taken in the UK; 7 days for detainees
Scope of review	To resolve case-working errors and to collect additional information	To resolve case-working errors and to collect additional information	To resolve case-working errors
Range of evidence considered	Additional evidence can be submitted	Additional evidence can be submitted. Reviewers contact claimants to explain decision and collect additional evidence	Additional evidence cannot be submitted
Fee	No fee	No fee	£80 fee (refundable)
Deadline to undertaken review	HMRC has 45 days to complete reviews (subject to variation); if exceeded, then decision treated is upheld and appealable	No formal deadline; straightforward cases expected to be completed within 14 days	No formal deadline; service standard of 28 days to complete reviews

Figure 4 Models of Administrative Review

2. Mandatory reconsideration has been used since 2013 in social security as a pre-requisite to an appeal before a tribunal where the person is dissatisfied with the determination of the application for a benefit. This has coincided with a dramatic reduction in social security appeals which was by far the jurisdiction with the largest volume of cases. An investigation by the Social Security Advisory Committee (SSAC) was unable to determine the contribution which mandatory reconsideration had made to this decrease. It had certainly been a policy aim that tribunal hearings would decline, but the scale had not been expected to be as large as this. The SSAC concluded:

Social Security Advisory Committee, *Occasional Paper 18: Decision making and mandatory reconsideration*
(available at https://www.gov.uk/government/publications/
ssac-occasional-paper-18-decision-making-and-mandatory-reconsideration)

(2016) p. 62

Properly conducted, Mandatory Reconsideration could be an efficient process that provides opportunity for timely review, the admission or reinterpretation of evidence and the avoidance of costly tribunals. It is certainly the case that tribunal numbers have fallen and from this perspective the policy may be seen as a success. However, this is only one angle, with much evidence provided from both stakeholders and staff conducting MR that the process does not work as well as it should. We have made a series of recommendations intended to improve the MR process as well as to improve decision making standards more generally.

3. The SSAC's recommendations totalled more than 30 and were put in four groups dealing with processes; advice and communications; training, feedback, and organizational learning; and medical issues. There were problems in requesting mandatory reconsiderations, the time limits were not felt to be long enough and there was inconsistency in the way in which requests for extensions were handled. There should be greater clarity in the communication of the notice of the decision made following mandatory reconsideration, including the implications for the claimant, the signposting of onward appeal rights, and the formatting of material so as to aid understanding of the complex reasoning. It was also recommended that the departments 'should identify and address the elements within the appeals process that claimants believe are too complex and consider further steps to help claimants better understand the appeals journey'. Training for those conducting mandatory reconsideration should be reviewed to ensure it met their needs, and the quality assurance framework should be reviewed 'to establish if it is fit for purpose in evaluating whether decisions are of a high quality'. In relation to feedback it was recommended that the annual report to the President of the Social Entitlement Chamber is published to improve understanding of how feedback is being used and what improvements are implemented as a result and that Decision Makers at DWP and HMRC are made aware of when their decisions are overturned at tribunal (and the reasons for this) to help identify where things could be done differently.

4. The Immigration Act 2014 removed some appeal rights to immigration decisions and replaced them with administrative review by the Home Office to provide 'a proportionate and less costly mechanism for resolving case working errors'. As MPs and Peers were concerned about this loss of an appeal to an independent tribunal, an amendment was passed which required the Home Secretary to commission a report from the Chief Inspector of Borders and Immigration which would address the following matters:

- 'the effectiveness of administrative review in identifying case working errors;
- the effectiveness of administrative review in correcting case working errors;
- the independence of persons conducting administrative review (in terms of their separation from the original decision-maker)'.

The report by the Independent Chief Inspector of Borders and Immigration, *An inspection of the Administrative Review processes introduced following the 2014 Immigration Act* (2016), found that case-working errors were not being identified and therefore not being corrected. There were three teams conducting administrative review: in-country, overseas, and at the border. There was clear separation between reviewers and original decision-makers for the in-country, but this separation was less easy to demonstrate in some of the smaller overseas posts and in the border team based at Heathrow airport. The Chief Inspector made 14 recommendations in four groups dealing with making applications for: consideration of, quality assurance of, and learning from administrative reviews.

■ QUESTION

If PDR is to be regarded as a staged journey do these reports on administrative review demonstrate the importance of independence not only in redressing disputes in the third stage but also for oversight of initial decision-making and administrative review?

E: The transformation of justice reforms

Reforms of courts and tribunals were announced in September 2016 with a vision to ensure that that they are just, proportionate and accessible. The statement continues and builds on the approach of avoiding and containing disputes as well as resolving them, which we have seen in PDR. Language and procedure are to be simplified and innovation is to be embraced with specially trained case officers handling basic case progression and case management, freeing up judges to concentrate on matters requiring their expertise.

The Lord Chancellor, The Lord Chief Justice, The Senior President of Tribunals, *The Transformation of Justice*
(2016)

Tomorrow's justice system

Over time, the work of the courts and tribunals will use online, virtual and traditional hearings as best meets the circumstances of the case. As new technologies bed down, we anticipate that more and more cases or parts of cases will be carried out virtually or online.

In certain circumstances, of course, justice will require that parties, their advisers and judges conduct hearings in physical courtrooms.

Meanwhile, those who use our courts and tribunals—including legal professionals—should expect two significant developments. The first is our aim for **all** cases to be started online, whether or not they are scheduled for the traditional system or for online resolution. The second will be the completion of some cases entirely online, which will be much more convenient for everyone involved. Suitable cases—initially lower value debt and damages claims and appeals to the Social Security and Child Support Tribunal—will be able to be managed through affordable and simple online services, specifically designed to meet user needs.

There will be a new, highly simplified procedural code. An online form will guide people through their application and the progress of their case. This new approach will be designed to promote more conciliatory approaches to dispute resolution, and to be understandable to non-lawyers, helping ordinary people resolve their issues in a low-key way, without needing expensive legal representation to help them understand what to do.

The use of technology will mean that fewer cases will require traditional hearings and this will decrease the need for court buildings. It is intended that fewer, more modern buildings will be designed to provide a service better adjusted to people's needs.

It is recognized that the objective of digital by default will present a challenge.

Although, in Great Britain, 86 per cent of homes had internet access in 2015, only 49 per cent of households with one adult aged 65 or over had internet access. One in ten adults, including a quarter of disabled adults, have never used the internet. Research shows that there is a small core of non-internet users who do not intend to get connected.

We will provide support for those who cannot access services digitally, or who need help to do so. In designing different services we will always tailor the support around the needs of those who will use them.

The reforms contain specific proposals for tribunals.

Tribunals

Tribunals are an essential component of the rule of law. They enable citizens to hold the state and employers to account for decisions that have a significant impact on people's lives. The hallmark of the tribunals system is the delivery of fair, specialist and innovative justice. That must not change.

The case for reform of the tribunals is nonetheless compelling. Over 400,000 claims a year come to tribunals. The necessary ingredients are already in place to help our judges and members to adopt a more inquisitorial and problem-solving approach, focused around the needs of individuals so that claimants can be more confident that their needs will be understood. This will be underpinned by a plan to create one system, one judiciary and better quality outcomes.

Innovative 'problem-solving' opportunities will be created to improve the determination of a range of issues which have historically been spread across courts and tribunals. This 'one stop shop' approach is being piloted with property disputes which can be dealt with before one specialist Judge, giving claimants a speedier and conclusive resolution to their complaint. The potential to extend this into other areas such as Mental Health and Employment will be explored.

Tribunals will be digital by default, with easy to use and intuitive online processes put in place to help people lodge a claim more easily, but with the right levels of help in place for anyone who needs it, making sure that nobody is denied justice. Once a claim is made, automatic sharing of digital documents with relevant government departments will mean that the tribunals and the parties will have all the right information to allow them to deal with claims promptly and effectively, saving time for both tribunal panels and claimants. Those who use tribunals will have access to specialist judicial expertise using tools and technology that they use routinely in other parts of their lives. This will allow the nub of a case to be identified quickly, wrong decisions resolved, and hopeless causes weeded out – improving justice for everyone involved.

In the next 18 months, online dispute resolution will be tested in Social Security & Child Support hearings, with people making their appeal and receiving a response online, and tribunal judges providing dispute resolution through "continuous online hearings". This ongoing process will enable judges to gather evidence and make informed decisions at a pace that is right for the case and the parties.

By 2020, tribunals will be part of a single justice system with a single judiciary. They will offer a range of choices to resolve appeals and claims with the needs of people who use the tribunals being put at the centre, from virtual hearings, online decision making, early evaluation, mediation and conciliation to the traditional face-to-face hearing. Cases will be resolved at the right level for the issues at hand, giving all parties better quality, faster and less stressful resolution of claims.

NOTES

1. It seems clear that it is expected that these reforms will produce savings. If they are to work then it must be more than a matter of digitizing existing procedures, they will have to redesigned.
2. While tribunals operating under current procedures are meant to be accessible to users who have no help or support, there is an increased chance of success if the user is represented. The Leggatt Review recommended that advice and assistance be made available so that users could be enabled to represent themselves. The plans to implement Leggatt included proposals for access to independent advice and support but these were not carried out. Indeed, as part of the 2010–15 Coalition Government's austerity measures, legal-aid spending was significantly reduced, and social welfare was removed from the scope of this reduced provision. The SSAC's investigation into mandatory reconsideration in social security noted the removal of legal aid and the resultant strain on welfare advice agencies with over 100 Citizen's Advice offices closing since 2009, partially caused by legal aid and local authority budget cuts, and an estimate that Citizen's Advice had seen 120,000 fewer people since the cuts. The SSAC recorded that this picture was less stark in Scotland and Northern Ireland.
3. The consultation on these proposals outlines the types of 'digital assistance' which will be provided to those people who have no computer skills and/or no access to computers. This is expected to include assistance offered face to face; by a telephone help service, by web chat, and by using paper channels for those who require it. There does not seem to be an intention to reverse the cuts in legal aid to provide advice and assistance directed to the substance of people's disputes which the new online tribunal processes are intended to resolve.
4. The SSAC published on its website its response to the consultation on digital assistance noting that many of the appellants to the Social Entitlement Chamber have vulnerabilities requiring support which will have to be adequately resourced. The SSAC say that their reports have shown

that using telephones is problematic for a significant number of appellants and that an advantage of a traditional tribunal hearing is that it facilitates the provision of new cogent oral information, which it is hoped will not be lost.

5. The proposals acknowledge some cases will require a traditional oral hearing. G. Richardson and H. Genn, in their article 'Tribunals in Transition: Adjudication or Resolution' [2007] *Public Law* 116, considered criteria for oral hearings. They noted there were instrumental reasons supporting oral hearings in both the law (common law and the jurisprudence on Art. 6(1) of the ECHR) and the research literature, to the effect that oral hearings could improve the accuracy of decisions, enhance transparency, and improve public confidence. There are other factors independent of the outcome of the decision, such as the dignity of the individual, democratic legitimacy, and participation. They also referred to the research on tribunal users' experiences, (including Genn et al., see earlier in this chapter in Section 3B at p. 673) highlighting T. Tyler, 'Social Justice: Outcome and Procedure' (2000) 35 *International Journal of Psychology* 117, who identified four primary factors: 'opportunities for participation (voice), the neutrality of the forum, the trust-worthiness of the authorities, and the degree to which people receive treatment with dignity and respect'. In the extract they draw on case law on due process from the US and on the guidance on what procedure is due in relation to a protected interest in *Mathews* v *Eldridge* 424 U.S. 319 (1976). In this case about the timing of a hearing on the determination of a benefit, the United States Supreme Court identified three factors which had to be balanced: 'the private interest affected, the risk of error, and the state's interest in minimising costs and additional burdens'.

They suggested that cases could be classed as involving fundamental rights; entitlements to a material benefit; and entitlements to an assessment or consideration. Applying these considerations, especially the factors in *Mathews* v *Eldridge*, they proposed that adjudication using oral hearings should be held in cases involving fundamental rights such as claims for asylum and reviewing compulsory detention and treatment in hospital on grounds of mental health. In these instances tribunals are not only checking the correct application of individuals' legal rights but also determining the boundaries of those rights. In cases involving an entitlement to a material benefits, such as a social security or criminal injuries compensation, the argue that both issues of eligibility for, and the amount or quantum of, the benefit are usually legislatively specified, so there is no scope for negotiation. Oral hearings may be required for testing of facts, such as degree of disability, on which eligibility will depend. In the third category they used the example of children with special educational needs and they suggest that while parents may have rights to have their children's needs assessed it is more of a right to an entitlement than a right to a material benefit as the extent of the material benefit can be highly contentious and resource dependent, and there is often no single outcome to be identified and imposed by a tribunal adjudication. The balancing of interests here might indicate that the procedure seeks an allocation of resources which appears fair and achievable to all sides. They acknowledge that some parents may be reluctant to compromise and that in such intractable cases a tribunal adjudication using an oral hearing should be used allowing for transparency in the process which could avoid further costs in onward appeal or judicial review. Indeed, in reforms made to special educational needs in the Children and Families Act 2014 made after publication of this article, the parents (or young person) who wished to appeal the local education authority's decision have to consider in some appeals using mediation, as a prerequisite to making the appeal. An adviser has to certify that information has been provided on mediation and the parent (or young person) has said that mediation will not be pursued (ss 51, 55). The initial proposal to require resort to mediation was withdrawn after opposition which was supported by the House of Commons Education select committee which had considered the draft proposals for legislation (HC 631 of 2012–13).

■ QUESTIONS

1. Do you think that it is adequate access to justice if tribunal users have limited or no access to advice and support for their appeal, and statistics demonstrate that the chances of success are increased if users opt for an oral hearing at which they are represented?

2. If a tribunal's procedure became more inquisitorial in which the tribunal decided what information it needed and had the power to require it to be submitted, rather than relying on the arguments and evidence provided by the parties, would that offset the disadvantage of the limited advice and support available to tribunal users?

SECTION 4: REVIEWING THE ADMINISTRATIVE JUSTICE SYSTEM

Tribunal reform was widened out to include administrative justice and the Council on Tribunals which had an oversight and advisory role was replaced by the Administrative Justice and Tribunals Council (AJTC), authorized by s. 44 of the Tribunals Courts and Enforcement Act 2007. Its roles included keeping under review the administrative justice system. The AJTC was abolished by the Public Bodies (Abolition of Administrative Justice and Tribunals Council) Order 2013 (S.I. 2013 No. 2042). In this section we will consider what is meant by this term, the administrative justice system, the suggested benefits of considering together, not separately, the different methods of resolving disputes with public bodies.

Administrative Justice and Tribunal Council, *The Future Oversight of Administrative Justice*

(2013), paras 14–18

14. The 'administrative justice system' was defined in the TCE Act as: "the overall system by which decisions of an administrative or executive nature are made in relation to particular persons, including – (a) the procedures for making such decisions, (b) the law under which such decisions are made, and 20 (c) the systems for resolving disputes and airing grievances in relation to such decisions". [Sch. 7, para. 13(4)]

15. The definition is very wide but also structurally cohesive. Its width means that it encapsulates the entire means by which the State exercises discretion in relation to individuals, complete with the processes for doing so and the various dispute-resolution systems which exist for when mistakes or misjudgements are alleged to have occurred. As such it includes within its scope the entire spheres of social security, education and health (amongst others), insofar as the State makes decisions affecting individual rights in these areas. PASC [Public Administration Select Committee] referred to the scale of this as "enormous" and the Justice Committee noted how the number of administrative cases "dwarfs" those of other areas of law. In terms of dispute resolution schemes, the system covers judicial review and related public law proceedings; statutory tribunals; ombudsmen and internal complaint-handling mechanisms.

16. The diversity of dispute resolution provision is an important feature, and there is perhaps more scope and appetite for innovative approaches than elsewhere in the machinery of justice. It includes the judicial means of seeking redress, of which the tribunals are most often used. But non-judicial methods are of equal importance and in some cases of greater utility given the advantages of securing proportionate dispute resolution wherever possible. Internal complaint-handling schemes need to be transparent and well led, fostering a culture in which public bodies seek to learn from mistakes and improve their performances. Ombudsmen as external complaint handlers provide a greater degree of independence and public accountability and are of fundamental importance…

17. The crucial point is that the statutory definition endorses a systematic approach to administrative justice, and no longer treated State decision-making as isolated from redress mechanisms which have been set up in response to it. This was achieved further to the recommendations of Sir Andrew Leggatt in his 2001 report *Tribunals for Users: One System, One Service*. The Leggatt Review paved the way for the co-ordinated tribunal system established by the 2007 Act and described the AJTC (as it became) as the "hub of the wheel of administrative justice".

18. That the State should provide for a fair, efficient and effective administrative justice system is of the utmost importance, as Parliament has recognised. In particular, PASC noted that the subject of administrative justice "may seem obscure and technical", but is greatly significant in that it "touches upon the lives, the standards of living, and rights of millions of citizens each year". This was an endorsement of an aspect of the justice system which we consider has long lacked the recognition it deserves,

given its impact upon society as a whole (and very often those of its members who are in a particularly vulnerable situation).

The AJTC's approach to administrative justice as a system led to their producing *Principles for Administrative Justice* (2010) as detailed in the following diagram:

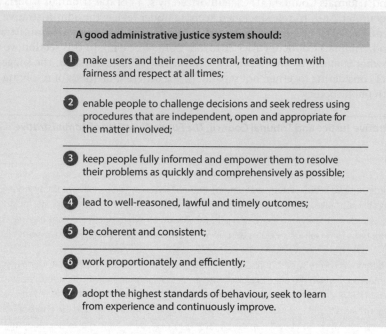

A good administrative justice system should:

1. make users and their needs central, treating them with fairness and respect at all times;

2. enable people to challenge decisions and seek redress using procedures that are independent, open and appropriate for the matter involved;

3. keep people fully informed and empower them to resolve their problems as quickly and comprehensively as possible;

4. lead to well-reasoned, lawful and timely outcomes;

5. be coherent and consistent;

6. work proportionately and efficiently;

7. adopt the highest standards of behaviour, seek to learn from experience and continuously improve.

These principles not only apply to initial decision-makers but also the providers of methods of redress. The AJTC was also keen to ensure that lessons are learnt so as to improve administration. It hoped that more feedback could be provided, as illustrated by the diagram from their 2012 report *Putting it Right: A Strategic Approach to Resolving Administrative Disputes*, see earlier at Section 3D, p. 680.

In the report the AJTC proposed an end-to-end, or holistic, approach to dispute resolution, with four stages. The action appropriate to those stages can apply whether a person is seeking redress by making a complaint or making an appeal to a tribunal. This dichotomy presents problems which the AJTC considers.

Administrative Justice and Tribunals Council, *Putting it Right: A Strategic Approach to Resolving Administrative Disputes*

(2012), paras 14–16, 135–9

...

Complaints and appeals

14. The current approach to resolving administrative justice disputes is not sufficiently sophisticated to address the varied and complex nature of grievances. These grievances tend to be categorised as one of two things: an appeal against a decision or a complaint about service, and two largely separate paths to redress have been built on the basis of this distinction, with most appeals being determined by tribunals and most complaints handled by ombudsmen as a last resort.

15. The difficulty with this approach is that users do not always want to challenge the elements in isolation – they may wish to complain and appeal. A further difficulty is that it may not actually be clear what the user wants to challenge, as the distinction between complaints and appeals is not always obvious. Complicating matters even further is that users may not know which institution they should turn to in order to make their challenge, and the links between the different institutions are not always sufficiently strong to ensure that cases are transferred to the correct channel.

16. This raises a number of questions that will have to be considered as the design of the administrative justice system is developed. First, is the distinction between complaints and appeals the correct one? Second, if it is, does it still follow that there need to be separate processes and institutions to deal with them? Third, even if separate processes and/or institutions are needed, how can the system be designed to ensure that users do not get lost in the maze?

…

Navigating the system

135. The overall system of administrative justice is composed of an increasingly diverse range of schemes and techniques. But, although the AJTC welcomes the flexibility and choice that this brings, there may be risks of fragmentation and confusion. Is there now a renewed need for the so-called "One Door" approach to receive further attention?

136. To inform its 2005 report on Citizen Redress, the National Audit Office conducted focus groups and a national opinion survey to examine how the public see redress options. The research suggested that the distinction between 'complaints' and 'appeals' was not well understood, and that one of the main problems encountered by users when trying to access and work through redress processes was finding the correct person to talk to in the first instance. In its report *When Citizens Complain*, the Public Administration Select Committee recommended that the government should explore providing a single point of contact for impartial information on where to make a complaint or seek redress. In the report *Administrative Justice in Scotland – The Way Forward* the Administrative Justice Steering Group built on these suggestions and raised the possibility of adopting a 'One Door' approach to redress in the public sector. In a 'One Door' approach, there would be a single point of entry to the grievance system, regardless of the nature of the grievance. The purpose of this would be to make it easier for users to know who to contact in the case of a problem, and would also allow an experienced professional to diagnose the nature of the grievance and to point the user towards the appropriate redress channel, leading to resolution of the dispute in a proportionate and appropriate manner.

137. The concept of filtering cases in order to work out the best way of resolving them was also considered by the Law Commission in its report 'Housing: Proportionate Dispute Resolution', which advocated the adoption of a 'Triage Plus' system.

138. The 'One Door' approach could operate at an agency level (for example, via a dedicated telephone line operated by decision-making departments) or even at a national level, with a single portal for all problems in the public sector. The NAO recommended that the Cabinet Office and the then Department for Constitutional Affairs should explore whether there was a value for money case to provide citizens' with a single point of contact. This does not appear to have been accepted and implemented yet, but the case may be even stronger now as modern technology improves the communication links between government and citizen.

139. The AJTC urges the UK government to give fresh consideration to the thinking behind a 'One Door' approach. This would appear to be a natural component of an appropriate and proportionate administrative justice system, with scope to operate as an important corollary to an approach which targets different mechanisms for resolving disputes. In the current economic climate it is not realistic to contemplate a new organisation to provide the 'One Door'. In any event, there would be sensitive and complex issues to address in terms of relationships with numerous statutory, judicial and voluntary bodies. The AJTC prefers to think in terms of a virtual One Door. This means:

- Developing a portal within the government's Directgov website which would direct individuals to the most appropriate place for their grievance (whether potentially a complaint, appeal or both) to be considered and resolved. We speculate that – as well as an FAQ approach – this could involve inter-active guidance which would take into account all the circumstances, not least the individual's own preferences about how they would like their case to be resolved.
- Active encouragement for all tribunals and other statutory, judicial and independent bodies which receive complaints or appeals to have triage systems which – as well as deciding which internal route to pursue – also permit cases (with the individual's consent) to be referred to another, more appropriate, institution. Even though this could not be mandatory, this may require changes to legislation and/or rules (e.g. to permit direct transfer of papers).
- As well as Citizens Advice and other advice services, a number of organisations in the administrative justice system already have considerable expertise at diagnosing problems (such as the Parliamentary and Health Service Ombudsman, the Local Government Ombudsman Advice Team and ICE which receive significant volumes of enquiries only to redirect the user elsewhere) and we envisage that this experience could be put to great use in designing and testing virtual 'One Door' approaches.

The Public Services Ombudsman for Wales already provides a web and telephone based complaints signposting service. The service gives independent and impartial advice on how to complain about a public service in Wales and could act as a useful template for the development of "one door" or triage systems across the UK.

NOTES

1. Administrative justice has been called the 'Cinderella' of the justice system, attracting much less attention and resources than criminal justice but yet as PASC noted, its reach is very wide. Perhaps this breadth is too much for a proper holistic view of the 'user journey' from the initial contact with a public body, the decision or action which causes dissatisfaction through to the completion of the redress process. There is fragmentation in relation to (a) the arrangements for redress, as complaints and appeals are different procedures, dealing with different issues and providing different remedies, and (b) between putting it right and getting it right first time. The SSAC study of mandatory reconsideration in social security shows that for the user this is all one transaction but responsibility is split between the DWP for the initial decision-making and second-stage reduction of dispute escalation, and the HMCTS and the MoJ operating the independent tribunals.

2. While users are central to the HMCTS and may well inform the development of the proposed online processes, there is no indication that a 'one door' approach will be pursued. Not only is there separation between departments responsible for different stages in the user journey, but also of parliamentary oversight. The cross-cutting select committee which deals with public administration, focuses upon complaints and does stress the importance of learning from disputes but tends not to consider tribunals and the Justice Committee has devoted the majority of its attention to criminal and then civil justice and is unlikely to consider what lessons might be derived from tribunals to improve initial decision-making even though one of HMCTS' objectives in its Framework Document is to 'work with government departments and agencies, as appropriate, to improve the quality and timeliness of their decision making in order to reduce the number of cases coming before tribunals and courts' (Cm 8882, p. 5).

■ QUESTION

Does the fact that in administrative justice the Government is a party in disputes require that there be an independent body acting as a focal point to avoid or minimize the fragmentation of oversight arrangements by making connections between the different parts of (a) Government conducting policy-making and operational roles, and (b) the legislatures performing law-making and oversight functions?

INDEX

Abraham, A. 630–2
Accountability
  debates on the floor of the House 246–52
  judiciary 161–3, 165–6
  limited government 24–5, 35–9
  ministerial responsibility
    Public Administration Select Committee
      (3rd Report) 230–4
    Public Service Committee Report 234–5
    regulatory state 235–9
  political constitutionalism 26–8
  public expectations 38–9
  rule of law 114–17
  select committees 240–5
Acts of Union
  legislative sovereignty 58–61
Adjournment debates 257–8
Adler, M. 673–5, 678–9
Administration see Maladministration
Administrative justice system 687–90
Administrative rules 282
Allan, T. R. S. 115
Alternative dispute resolution 676–80
Antecedent constitutions 1–2
Appeals
  alternative remedy to judicial review 600–4
  judicial review distinguished 495–7

Bagehot, W. 110
Baldwin, R. 282, 333
Barker, R. 20–1
Beetham, D. 11–14, 21–2
Bias, rule against 522–7
Bill of Rights
  Brazier, R. 4–5
  Parliament 49
  supreme law-making authority 47–50
Bingham, Lord 30
Blackburn, R. 246, 253–4
Blackstone, Sir W. 174, 191
Bolingbroke, Henry St John, Lord
  Bolingbroke 2–3
Bradley, A. 39, 117, 145–6
Brazier, R. 4–5, 174
'Brexit' 95
  Miller v Secretary of State for Exiting the
    European Union 192–5, 212–13
Buck, T. 643–4

Cabinet system 30
Calvert, H. 60–1
Cane, P. 492–5
Chief Executives 232, 234, 246
Civil liberties see Bill of rights;
  Human rights
Collective ministerial responsibility

confidence 222–3
confidentiality 225
unanimity 223–5
Commonwealth independence 61–5
Constitutional law
  see also Conventions
  democracy 16–23
  introduction 1–10
  legitimacy 10–16
  limited government 24–5
  State, the 39–45
Constitutionalism
  conditioning power 29–39
  democracy 25–6
  House of Lords Select Committee 6–7
  legal constitutionalism 23–6
  political constitutionalism 26–8
Consultation
  control over legislative powers 283–9
  procedural improprieties 539
Conventions
  codification 213–16
  contrasted with laws 200–1
  important rules of political
    behaviour 198–200
  Kershaw Report 207
  recognition by courts 202–13
  Sewel convention 213, 13, 366
  sources of constitution 196–8
Correspondence with MPs 261–3
Courts
  see also Jurisdiction; Tribunals
  conventions contrasted with laws 200–1
  judicial independence
    accountability to Parliament 161–3
    appointments 152–9, 167
    Constitutional Reform Act
      2005 142–6
    discipline 160–1
    effects of statutory reform 142–6
    expanded constitutional role 141–2
    legal constitutionalism 142
    Lord Chancellor 147–9
    media and public perceptions 164–8
    rule of law as political doctrine 113,
      114–17, 123
    Supreme Court 150–2
  recognition of conventions 202–13
  role in the constitution 30
  separation of powers 24, 29–35
Cowley, P. 219–21
Craig, P. 114–17

Davis, K.C. 106
Declarations of incompatibility
  operation of HRA 1998 456–63

Delegated legislation
control over legislative powers 314–26
law-making 280
Strathclyde Review 320–5
Democracy
comparative government 19–20
constitutional law in UK 3–6, 9–10,
16–23, 25–6
defined 16–19
elections 20–1
key principles 21–2
legitimacy 16–18
measured 20–1
relations of power 16–17
Devolution
asymmetry 343, 344, 346, 348, 367–70
background 342–8
dynamic nature 343–4, 385–95
'English Votes for English Laws' *x*, *xi*, 311–14, 344
institutions 348–53
interpretation of devolution Acts 370–6
judicial review 377–81
legislative competence 353–66
London Assembly 345
McKay Commission 346–7
Memorandum of Understanding 365
Northern Ireland 351–3, 359–65, 369–70,
370–3, 392–4
'Northern Powerhouse' *xi*, 345
regimes 348–70
Scotland 348–9, 353–6, 367–8, 373–6, 386–9
Supreme Court references 381–5
UK courts, in 370–85
Wales 350, 356–9, 368–9, 381–5, 389–91
'West Lothian Question' 310, 346
Dicey, A. V.
Commonwealth independence 62
conventions 196, 200
importance of civil liberties 396
legislative sovereignty 51, 53
role of politics 46–7
Royal Prerogative 174
rule of law
discretionary powers 104–5
equality 106–11
importance 104–5
legality 129
Discretionary powers
illegality 512–14
judicial review 337
rule of law 104–5
Discrimination
rule of law 106–11
Dougan, M. 99–101
Duffy, P. 466–7
Dworkin, R. 114–16

Early day motions 258–60
Elections
democratic legitimacy 20–1
fixed-term Parliaments 180
'Elective dictatorship' 3, 15, 36

Elliot, Mark 563–6, 567
Elster, J. 25–6
English Votes for English Laws *x*, *xi*,
311–14, 344
Equality
rule of law 106–11
EU law
judicial review 325
law-making 282
European Convention on Human Rights
application in UK prior to HRA 1998 409–15
incorporation by HRA 1998 34, 416–24
interpretation 407–9
margin of appreciation 408–9
overview 399–409
protected rights 401–6
ratification by UK 399, 406
European Union
legislative sovereignty
European Union Act 2011 95–101
membership 68–84
referendums 95–101
supremacy of EU law 68–71
UK courts 72–84
supremacy of EU law 68–71
UK's decision to leave *x*, 95
Miller v *Secretary of State for Exiting the
European Union* 192–5, 212–13
Ewing, K. D. 39, 84, 117
Exclusivity principle 581–9

Fair trial 469, 527–40
Finer, S. E. 11, 19–20, 39–40
Fixed-term Parliaments 180–3
Flinders, M. 38–9
Franks Report on Tribunals 649–50,
652–3, 669–72
Freedom of expression 518–20
Freedom of information 265–6
Friedrich, C. J. 10, 24–5
Fuller, Lon L. 113
Fundamental rights
see also **Human rights**
exercise of administrative decisions 398–9
legitimate expectations 560–1

Genn, H. 672–3, 675–6, 686
Gordon, M. 58, 67, 99–101
Gordon, R. 636–7
Gordon Review *xi*
Government
see also **Law-making; Select committees**
antecedent constitutions 1–2
correspondence with MPs 261–3
House of Commons
adjournment debates 257–8
debates on the floor of the House 246–52
distribution of time spent on
business 245–5, 292–3
early day motions 258–60
questions on the floor of the house 253–7
questions for written answer 253–7

reform 269–77
urgent questions 257
ministerial responsibility
    accountability 230–9
    collective 222–5
    individual responsibility 225–30
    limited government 35–9
    meaning 221–2
royal prerogative *see* **Prerogative powers**
rule of law 124–40
Westminster Hall 263
Gray, L. 675–6
Griffith, J. A. G. 26–7, 87
Gulland, J. 673–5

Hadfield, B. 342–3, 344
Hailsham, Lord 36
Hart, H. L. A. 56
Hendry, K. H. 650–2
Heuston, R. F. V. 56
    Dicey and the rule of law 106–7
    sovereignty 57
Houghton, J. 282, 333
House of Commons
    adjournment debates 257–8
    debates on the floor of the House 246–52
    distribution of time spent on
        business 245–6, 292–3
    early day motions 258–60
    questions for written answer 264–9
    questions on the floor of the house 253–7
    reform 269–77, 294–305
    urgent questions 257
House of Lords Select Committee on the
    Constitution 6–7
Human rights
    see also **Fundamental rights**
    Brazier, R. 4–5
    European Convention
        application in UK prior to HRA 1998 409–15
        incorporation by HRA 1998 34, 416–24
        interpretation 407–9
        margin of appreciation 408–9
        overview 399–409
        protected rights 401–6
        ratification by UK 399, 406
    implications of HRA 1998 424–6
    importance 396–9
    judicial independence 144, 145
    legislative sovereignty 84–7
    operation of HRA 1998
        declarations of incompatibility 456–63
        interpretation of legislation 444–56
        private litigants 432–44
        proportionality 407, 426, 476, 485, 489
        public authorities 427–32
        role of judiciary 463–91
Hunt, M. 434–6

Illegality
    discretionary powers 512–14
    exceeding jurisdiction 500–3

excessive interference with freedom of
    speech 518–20
grounds for judicial review 499–500
improper purposes 503–6
irrelevant considerations 506–12
mistake of fact 514–17
Improper purposes 503–6
    see also **Maladministration**
Independent judiciary
    accountability to Parliament 161–3, 165–6
    appointments 152–9, 167
    Constitutional Reform Act 2005 142–6
    discipline 160–1
    effects of statutory reform 142–6
    expanded constitutional role 141–2
    Lord Chancellor 147–9
    media and public perceptions 164–72
    parliamentary privilege 168–72
    rule of law as political doctrine 113,
        114–17, 123
    Supreme Court 150–2
Injunctions
    prerogative orders 498
Irrationality 540–7
    proportionality and 562–7
Irvine, Lord
    constitutional reform 33–4
    operation of HRA 1998 444–5
    role of judiciary 463–6

Jaconelli, J. 201
Jennings, Sir Ivor 56, 57, 61, 65, 105, 107, 200
Johnson, N. 36
Judge, D. 49
Judicial review
    appeals distinguished 495–7
    claim procedure 568–80
    constitutional role 492–5
    control over legislative powers 326–41
    devolution 377–81
    discretionary nature
        availability of alternative remedies 600–4
        needs of good administration 604–6
    exclusions 337, 606–8
        discretionary powers 337
        partial invalidity 338–41
    exclusivity principle 581–90
    illegality
        discretionary powers 512–14
        exceeding jurisdiction 500–3
        excessive interference with freedom of
            speech 518–20
        grounds for judicial review 499–500
        improper purposes 503–6
        irrelevant considerations 506–12
        mistake of fact 514–17
    irrationality 540–7
    proportionality and 562–7
    jurisdiction 594–7
    justiciability 597–600
    'leap-frogging' orders 571
    legitimate expectations 538–9, 547–61

Judicial review (*cont.*)
  pre-action protocol 575–8
  prerogative orders 498–9
  procedural improprieties
    fair trial 527–40
    meaning 520–2
    rule against bias 522–7
  proportionality 562–7
  reforms 571
  remedies 497–8
  role 492–5
  rule of law and 136–7
  standing 590–3
  sufficient interest 569, 590
  time limits 572, 578
  Upper Tribunal 663–6
  uses 497
  venue 578–80
Judiciary
  see also **Courts**
  independence
    accountability to Parliament 161–3, 165–6
    appointments 152–9, 167
    Constitutional Reform Act 2005 142–6
    discipline 160–1
    effects of statutory reform 142–6
    expanded constitutional role 141–2
    legal constitutionalism 142
    Lord Chancellor 147–9
    media and public perceptions 164–8
    parliamentary privilege 168–72
    rule of law as political doctrine 113,
      114–17, 123
    Supreme Court 150–2
  leadership in tribunals 657–63
  legal constitutionalism 26
  operation of HRA 1998 463–91
  separation of powers 29–35
Jurisdiction
  illegally exceeding jurisdiction 500–3
  judicial review 591–5
  ombudsmen 617–20
Justiciability
  judicial review 597–600

Kavanagh, A. 84, 453
Kelso, A. 38–9
Kennon, A. 246, 253–4
Kentridge, S. 462
Kershaw Report 207
Kirkham, R. 643–4
Knight, C. J. S. 117

Law-making
  control
    consultation 283–9
    delegated legislation 314–26
    financial privilege 321, 322
    judicial review 326–41
    parliamentary oversight 292–310, 312
    publicity 289–92

    revising parliamentary procedure 310–14
    Strathclyde Review 320–5
  delegated legislation 280, 314–26
  EU legislation 282
  parliamentary scrutiny
    post-legislative 305–7
    pre-legislative 299–305
  prerogative 282
  quality of 308–10
  quasi-legislation 282
  statutes 278–80
  volume of legislation 293, 314
Laws
  contrasted with conventions 200–1
  rule of law
    Dicey, A. V. 104–5
    government according to the law 124–40
    history and meaning 102–4
    political doctrine 117–23
    principle of legality 129, 130, 132, 133, 134
Laws, Sir J. 85–7
Le Sueur, A. 165–6
Legal constitutionalism 23–6, 142
Legality 129, 130, 132, 133, 134
Leggatt Review 685, 687
Legislation
  control over legislative powers
    consultation 283–9
    delegated legislation 314–26
    financial privilege 321, 322
    judicial review 326–41
    parliamentary oversight 292–310, 312
    publicity 289–92
    revising parliamentary procedure 310–14
    Strathclyde Review 320–5
  delegated legislation 280, 314–26
  EU legislation 282
  human rights interpretation 444–56
  parliamentary scrutiny
  post-legislation 305–7
  pre-legislation 299–305
  prerogative 282
  quality of 308–10
  quasi-legislation 282
  statutes 278–80
  volume 293, 314
Legislative sovereignty
  Acts of Union 58–61
  Bill of Rights 48–9
  challenges to validity 51–6
  Commonwealth independence 61–5
  control by judicial review 326–41
  control over legislative powers
    consultation 283–9
    judicial review 326–41
    publicity 289–92
  definition 46–7
  emergence of supreme law-making
    authority 47–50
  European Union
    European Union Act 2011 95–101

membership 68–84
referendums 95–101
supremacy of EU law 68–71
UK courts 72–84
human rights 84–7
Jackson v *Attorney General* 88–95
limiting the powers of successor
    Parliaments 56–68
procedural conditions 65–8
referendums 95–101
unlimited powers 50–1
Legitimacy
constitutionalism 10–16
defined 10–11
democracy 16–19
elections 20–1
levels/dimensions 11–13
Ponting jury verdict 15–16
relations of power 16–17
role of Parliament 217–21
significance 13–14
theory and practice distinguished 14–16
Legitimate expectations 538–9, 547–61
Leigh, I. 432–3
Lever, B. 675–6
Leyland, P. 343–4
Limited government
accountability 35–9
Cabinet system 37
'elective dictatorship' 3, 15, 36
legal constitutionalism 24–5
separation of judiciary 40–1
Lively, J. 35–6
Local Government Ombudsman
Annual Report 2015–16 647
jurisdiction 619–20
Review of Complaints 2015–16 612–13,
    635, 641
Locke, J. 29
London Assembly 345
Lord Chancellor 147–9
Loughlin, M. 26, 28
Low, S. 7
Lustgarten, L. 432–3

McAuslan, P. 14–16
McEldowney, J. F. 14–16
McIlwain, C. H. 1–2
McKay Commission 346–7
Macpherson, C. B. 16–18
Maladministration 623–7
Malleson, K. 142–4
Margin of appreciation 408–9
Marshall, G. 31, 57–8, 198–9, 222–3, 461–2
Miliband, R. 40–1
Ministerial responsibility
accountability
    Public Administration Select Committee
        (3rd Report) 230–4
    Public Service Committee Report 234–5
    regulatory state 235–9

collective
    confidence 222–3
    confidentiality 225
    unanimity 223–5
individual responsibility 225–30
limited government 35–9
meaning 221–2
Mistake of fact 514–17
Montesquieu, Baron de 29
Moodie, G. C. 198–9
Munro, C. R. 7, 49, 58, 80, 200–1
Murphy, W. F. 9–10

Natural justice 113, 134, 136, 327, 492, 496, 499,
    511, 520–2, 528–38, 581, 597, 606, 607
Northern Ireland 333–7
devolution 351–3, 359–65, 369–70, 370–3
police and justice powers, devolution
    of 392–4
'Northern Powerhouse' *xi*, 345
Norton, P. 217–19, 247

Ombudsmen
access
    difficulties 613
    Local Government Act 1974 614–15
    Parliamentary Commissioner Act 1967 614
alternative remedies, overlap with 621–3
competition with MPs 263
compliance with reports 611–5
dissatisfied complainants 647–8
findings 645–6
Gordon Review *xi*
injustice in consequence of
    maladministration 623–7
jurisdiction
    assessment 620
    Local Government Act 1974 619–20
    Parliamentary Commissioner Act
        1967 617–18
Local Government Ombudsman
    Annual Report 2015–16 647
    Review of Complaints 2015–16 612–13,
        635, 641
outcome of investigations 638–41
Parliamentary and Health Service
    Ombudsman
    Annual Report 2015–16 611–12,
        634–5, 647
    JUSTICE recommendations 609–11
    Principles for Remedy 634
    Principles of Good Administration 632
    Principles of Good Complaint Handling 633
Parliamentary Commissioner Act 1967 617–18
prisons 238
procedure
    improvement 630–8
    investigation and resolution 627–9
recommendations 645–6
reform 616
remedies 621

Oral hearings 676, 685, 686
Osmotherly rules 242–4

Page, A. 264–5
Page, A. C. 262–3
Paine, T. 1–2
Parliament
    see also **Legislative sovereignty; Ministerial**
        responsibility
    Bill of Rights 49
    correspondence with MPs 261–3
    dissolution 181, 182
    House of Commons
        adjournment debates 257–8
        debates on the floor of the House 246–52
        distribution of time spent on
            business 243–6, 292–3
        early day motions 258–60
        questions on the floor of the house 253–7
        questions for written answer 264–9
        reform 269–77
        urgent questions 257
    House of Lords Select Committee on the
        Constitution 6–7
    legislative sovereignty
        Acts of Union 58–61
        Bill of Rights 48–9
        challenges to validity 51–6
        Commonwealth independence 61–5
        definition 46–7
        emergence of authority 47–50
        human rights 84–7
        limiting the powers of its
            successors 56–68
        supreme law-making authority 47–50
        unlimited power 50–1
    ministerial responsibility 221–39
    role 217–21
    royal prerogative see **Prerogative powers**
    scrutiny of new legislation
        post-legislation 305–7
        pre-legislation 299–305
    unlimited power 50–1
    Westminster Hall 260–1
Parliamentary and Health Service
        Ombudsman
    Annual Report 2015–16 611–12, 634–5, 647
    JUSTICE recommendations 609–11
    Principles for Remedy 634
    Principles of Good Administration 632
    Principles of Good Complaint Handling 633
Parliamentary privilege
    independent judiciary 168–72
Political constitutionalism 26–8, 142
Politics
    rule of law as political doctrine
        general principles 117–23
        independence of judiciary 113, 123
        laws should be clear 118–20
        laws should be prospective 120–3
Prerogative orders 498–9

Prerogative powers
    archaic powers 176
    Attorney General 176
    codification 186–91
    constitutional powers 176
    control over legislative powers 326–41
    Crown 176–7
    interaction with statute 191–5
    judicial review 326–41
    law-making 282
    meaning 173–4
    Miller v *Secretary for State for Exiting the*
        European Union 192–5
    ministerial powers 174–5
    orders 498–9
    procedural improprieties 539
    statutory basis 177–86
    war powers 183–4
Prisons 238
Procedural impropriety
    fair trial 527–40
    meaning 520–2
    rule against bias 522–7
Proportionality
    human rights 407, 426, 476, 485, 489
    judicial review 562–7
    legitimate expectations 547, 559–60, 561
Proportionate dispute resolution 678–9, 680–3
Public appointments 273–7
Public authorities
    operation of HRA 1998 427–32

Quasi-legislation 282

Rawlings, R. 261
Raz, J. 113–16, 117
Referendums
    European Union 95–101
    legislative sovereignty 95–101
Reform
    House of Commons 269–77
    judicial independence
        accountability to Parliament 161–3, 165–6
        appointments 152–9, 167
        discipline 160–1
        effects of statutory reform 142–6
        expanded constitutional role 141–2
        Lord Chancellor 147–9
        media and public perceptions 164–8
        Supreme Court 150–2
    reviewing the Constitution 6–7
    scrutiny of new legislation 299–307
    select committees 240
    tribunals
        alternative dispute resolution 676–80
        appeals and judicial review 663–6
        Franks Report 649–50, 652–3, 669–72
        reviewing the administrative justice
            system 687–90
        Transformation of Justice 684–6
        two-tier organization 654–7

Remedies
  see also Judicial review
  Ombudsmen 621
  prerogative orders 498–9
Restrospectivity 383, 384
Richardson, G. 672, 686
Ridley, F. F. 3–4, 18–19
Rose, R. 278–80
Rousseau, J. -J. 16
Royal prerogative *see* Prerogative powers
Rule of law
  accountability 114–17
  Dicey, A. V.
    discretionary powers 104–5
    equality 106–11
    importance 104–5
  formal vs. substantive approaches 111–17
  government according to the law 124–40
  history and meaning 102–4
  political doctrine
    general principles 117–23
    independence of judiciary 113, 123
    laws should be clear 118–20
    laws should be prospective 120–3
  principle of legality 129, 130, 132, 133, 134
Russell, M. 219–21

Scotland
  devolution 348–9, 353–6, 367–8,
    373–6, 386–9
  independence referendum 387–8
Scott, C. 235–9
Scrutiny
  post-legislative 305–7
  pre-legislative 299–305
  role of Parliament 218–19
  select committees
    Osmotherly rules 242–4
    overview 240–5
Sedley, Sir S. 20
Select committees
  history and meaning of rule of law 102–3
  House of Lords 6–7
  ministerial responsibility
    Public Administration Select Committee
      (3rd Report) 230–4
    Public Service Committee Report 234–5
  Modernisation of the House of Commons
    (First Report) 294–308
  Osmotherly rules 242–4
  overview 240–5
  scrutiny of new legislation 294–308
  Wright Committee 240, 269–73
'Self-embracing' theory of
  sovereignty 56, 58
Separation of powers
  see also Independent judiciary
  legal constitutionalism 24, 29–35
Sewel convention 212–13, 366
Sovereignty *see* Legislative sovereignty

Standing for judicial review 590–3
State 39–45
  capitalism 40–1
  interests of 42–3
Statutes 278–80
Strathclyde Review 320–5
Strong, C. F. 29–30, 39
Supreme Court 150–2
  reference protocol and devolved
    legislatures 381–5

Tamanaha, B. 117
Thomas, R. 681–2
Thompson, B. 643–4
Tomkins, A. 27–8, 80, 84
Tomlinson, J. 681–2
Tribunals
  appeals and judicial review 663–6
  caseload statistics 666–9
  Franks Report 649–50, 652–3, 69–72
  rationale 649–54
  reviewing the administrative justice
    system 687–90
  role as 'court substitutes'
    alternative dispute resolution 676–80
    choice between tribunals and courts of
      law 652–3
    particular characteristics 669–76
    proportionate dispute resolution 678–9,
      680–3
  structure
    judicial leadership and
      composition 657–63
    two-tier organization 654–7
  Transformation of Justice reforms 684–6
Turpin, C. 221–2

United Kingdom
  see also Devolution
  decision to leave the EU *x*, 95
    Miller v *Secretary of State for Exiting the
      European Union* 192–5, 212–13
  democracy 16–23
  introduction 1–10
  legitimacy 10–16
  limited government 35–9
  State, the 39–45
United States
  early constitution 1–2
  separation of powers 29–30
Unreasonableness 333, 379, 398, 478, 499,
  514, 541, 544, 545, 547, 551, 562, 563

Validity
  challenges to legislative sovereignty 51–6
Vile, M. J. C. 24

Wade, E. C. S. 196–8
Wade, H. W. R. 56–7, 76–7, 460–1
Waldron, J. 23

Index

    devolution 350, 356–9, 368–9, 381–5
    fiscal powers, devolution of 389–91
War powers 183–4
Webber, J. 150–1

Westminster Hall 260–1
Wheare, K. C. 3, 7–9, 198, 199
Wilson, G. 199–200
Wolf-Phillips, L. 37–8
Wright Committee 240, 269–73

Aim High!
Concentrate